Classics Series

HANBURY AND MARTIN

MODERN EQUITY

The
University of
Law

Birmingham I Bristol I Chester I Guildford I London I Manchester I York

Classics Series

HANBURY AND MARTIN

MODERN EQUITY

Twenty-First Edition

JAMIE GLISTER
Associate Professor
Faculty of Law, the University of Sydney

JAMES LEE
Reader in English Law
The Dickson Poon School of Law, King's College London;
Associate Academic Fellow of the Honourable Society of the Inner Temple

SWEET & MAXWELL

First Edition   1935
Twenty-First Edition 2018

Published in 2018 by Thomson Reuters, trading as Sweet & Maxwell. Thomson Reuters is
registered in England & Wales, Company No.1679046.
Registered Office and address for service: 5 Canada Square, Canary Wharf, London, E14
5AQ.

For further information on our products and services, visit *http://www.sweetandmaxwell.co.uk*

Typeset by Letterpart Limited, Caterham on the Hill, Surrey, CR3 5XL.

Printed and bound in Great Britain by CPI Group (UK) Ltd, Croydon, CR0 4YY.

No natural forests were destroyed to make this product; only farmed timber was used and
re-planted.

A CIP catalogue record of this book is available for the British Library.

ISBN: 978 0 414 06037 1

Preface

This edition of the book is the second on which we have worked together, following the 20th edition in 2015: we reiterate our admiration for our predecessors for the first 19 editions, Harold Hanbury, Ronald Maudsley and Jill Martin.

The book follows the revised structure of the previous edition, although there have been internal amendments to certain chapters. The text throughout has been comprehensively updated in the light of developments in the law, and we highlight some of the points of interest in this Preface.

We noted in the preface to the 20th edition that there had been numerous landmark decisions of the UK Supreme Court between 2013 and 2015: *Pitt v Holt* [2013] 2 A.C. 108; *Williams v Central Bank of Nigeria* [2014] A.C. 1189; *FHR European Ventures v Cedar Capital Partners* [2015] A.C. 250; *AIB Group (UK) Plc v Mark Redler & Co Solicitors* [2015] A.C. 1503. The implications of those decisions continue to be worked out in the lower courts and are addressed in the relevant chapters.

Since the last edition of the book, there has been a significant public and political debate about tax evasion and tax avoidance, not least in the wake of the leaks and media investigations known as the "Panama Papers" in 2016 and the "Paradise Papers" in 2017. Similar concerns have emerged over the potential for trusts to be used to facilitate criminal activities. As a result, there has been a range of measures introduced, both in the UK and in offshore tax havens relating to trusts and transparency, an example of which is Directive 2015/849 on the prevention of the use of the financial system for the purposes of money laundering or terrorist financing. These provisions are discussed in a new section in Ch.3; the wider relevance of tax avoidance in the context of trusts adjudication is considered in Chs 10 (on taxation) and 29 (on rescission).

At the Supreme Court level, there have not been as many seismic decisions as between 2012 and 2015, but there are several of note. *Akers v Samba* [2017] UKSC 6; [2017] A.C. 424 considered formalities (Ch.6) and the operation of trusts in private international law. *Angove's Pty Ltd v Bailey* [2016] UKSC 47; [2016] 1 W.L.R. 3179 marks the continuing rejection in English law of the remedial constructive trust (Ch.12). On rescission in the case of misrepresenta- tion (Ch.29), the paired cases of *Sharland v Sharland* [2015] UKSC 60; [2016] A.C. 871 and *Gohil v Gohil* [2015] UKSC 61; [2016] A.C. 849 recast the law relating to the setting aside of court orders for material non-disclosure. *Burnden Holdings (UK) Ltd v Fielding* [2018] UKSC 14; [2018] 2 W.L.R. 885 examines limitation periods. On remedies, there are important observations in *Morris-Garner v One Step (Support) Ltd* [2018] UKSC 20; [2018] 2 W.L.R. 1353 on damages and *PJS v News Group Newspapers Ltd* [2016] UKSC 26; [2016] A.C. 1081 on injunctions.

The defence of illegality in private law has been a matter of considerable dispute amongst the Justices in recent years, with a series of cases concluded by the adoption in *Patel v Mirza* [2016] UKSC 42; [2017] A.C. 467 of a test based on a structured discretion: the controversy is addressed in Ch.14, which has been renamed "Trusts, Legal Policy and Illegality".

The Supreme Court Justices have also been active in the Privy Council, developing points of principle in trusts and equity, in some cases in a way that could cause conflict with English authorities: examples will be seen in the cases of *Marr v Collie* [2017] UKPC 17; [2017] 3 W.L.R. 150 (on cohabitation); and *Federal Republic of Brazil v Durant International Corp* [2015] UKPC 35; [2016] A.C. 297 (on tracing).

The focus of the book is on the English law of trusts and equity, but for this edition we have also strengthened references to the case law of other jurisdictions where appropriate, engaging with decisions from Australia, Canada, Hong Kong, New Zealand and Singapore. The Supreme Court has repeatedly emphasised the value of referring to comparative case law: in *FHR European Ventures* (above), Lord Neuberger PSC speaking for the Court, said (at [45]) that it is "highly desirable for all [common law] jurisdictions to learn from each other, and at least to lean in favour of harmonising the development of the common law round the world". Nor is the value of comparative law limited to judicial decisions: as we write, the New Zealand Parliament has before it a Trusts Bill, drawing upon recommendations of that jurisdiction's Law Commission, designed "to make trust law more accessible to everyday users".

The Law Commission of England and Wales has again been active in the field of trusts and equity. The Charities (Protection and Social Investment) Act 2016 implemented changes in charity law, and that work has been followed by the Consultation Paper *Technical Issues in Charity Law* (2017). The proposals in *Making a will* (2017) would have consequences for various aspects of equity, including formalities, mutual wills and rectification. Further projects, though not directly focused on trusts and equity, nevertheless have had an impact, as in the area of insurance law which has implications for rescission. The Commission has included a project on "Modernising Trust Law for a Global Britain" in its Thirteenth Programme of Law Reform. There have been other legislative proposals raised in Parliament as Private Member's Bills, such as the Civil Partnerships, Marriages and Deaths (Registration Etc.) Bill 2017–19 and the Cohabitation Rights Bill [HL] 2017–19. Other statutes can have relevant consequences even if trusts are not the direct focus of the legislation: in Ch.20 we examine the effect of data protection legislation on the traditional approach to beneficiaries' access to trust documents, as tested in *Dawson-Damer v Taylor Wessing LLP (Information Commissioner intervening)* [2017] EWCA Civ 74; [2017] 1 W.L.R. 3255.

At the time of writing, the impact of Brexit on the law of trusts is unclear. There are potential implications relating to a number of areas covered in this book: particularly taxation and pensions (for example, Institutions for Occupational Retirement Provision (IORP) II Directive 2016/2341). These issues are highlighted where possible, but, given the uncertainties (notwithstanding the passage of the European Union (Withdrawal) Act 2018) their examination is necessarily limited.

The operation of much High Court business was reorganised with the establishment of the Business and Property Courts in 2017, but this is an umbrella term covering many—though not all—of the functions of the Queen's Bench and Chancery Divisions. The three Divisions of the High Court remain.

While working on the book, James benefited from a period as a Senior Visiting Fellow at the University of New South Wales in the first half of 2018 and as a Visiting Professor in Equity and Trusts at Hong Kong University. He would like to thank both institutions and also gratefully acknowledges the support of the PC Woo & Co Research Fellowship from The Dickson Poon School of Law.

We should like to record our sincere thanks to our Editors, Amanda Strange initially and then Nicola Thurlow, various others involved in the production process, especially Tejal Parmar, Rebecca Sams, and the referees who reviewed the previous edition.

The cover image is a painting, 'Nafea faa ipoipo', or 'When will you marry?', by Paul Gauguin. The painting was the subject of litigation in a recent case, *ACLBDD Holdings Ltd, De Pury v Staechelin* [2018] EWHC 44 (Ch), which is mentioned in Ch.18.

As with the previous edition, we take joint responsibility for the entire text. Although we were able to accommodate some later developments during the editorial process, our aim has been to state the law as of 31 March 2018.

Jamie Glister and James Lee

Acknowledgements

The authors wish to thank the following people, all of whom either contributed to our understanding of the law of equity and trusts or otherwise helped bring this book to fruition: Tanya Aplin, Gabrielle Appleby, Anthony Arnull, Pat Ashton, Rosemary Auchmuty, Adam Baker, Elise Bant, Katy Barnett, Emily Barritt, Alan Bogg, Jonathan Bonnitcha, Ben Bowling, Adrian Briggs, Michael Bryan, Richard Buckley, Andrew Burrows, Andrew Butler, Gavin Byrne, Joseph Campbell, Michael Cardwell, Robert Chambers, Peter Clarke, Niamh Cleary, Dominic de Cogan, the Copeman/King family, Matthew Conaglen, Elizabeth Cooke, Robert Cryer, Tatiana Cutts, Paul Davies, Nuncio D'Angelo, Simone Degeling, Eric Descheemaeker, Martin Dixon, Gillian Douglas, Simon Douglas, Neil Duxbury, Matthew Dyson, James Edelman, Douglas Edlin, Keith Ewing, David Foster, Neil Foster, David Fox, Jonathan Garton, Martin George, Joshua Getzler, Stephen Gilmore, Isobel Glister, Lucy Glister, Ben Golder, Sarah Green, Anthony Guest, Laura Guthrie, Matthew Harding, Lusina Ho, Martin Hogg, Nicholas Hopkins, Jessica Hudson, Alison Jones, Ann Kennedy, Michael Lee, the late Norman Lee, Patricia Lee, Rebecca Lee, Simon Lee, Mark Leeming, Patricia Leopold, Justin Lewis-Oakes, Madeleine Lewis-Oakes, Rebecca Lewis-Oakes, Ying Khai Liew, Edith Little, Eva Lomnicka, John Lowry, William Lucy, Mark Lunney, Andrew Lynch, Hector MacQueen, Paul Matthews, Aileen McColgan, Ben McFarlane, Claire McIvor, Stephen McNulty, John Mee, Charles Mitchell, Alastair Mullis, Emer Murphy, Aruna Nair, Mary Neal, Donal Nolan, Richard Nolan, Jane Norton, Tim Nott, Claire Palmer, Feena Patel, James Penner, John Phillips, Natalie Pratt, Pauline Ridge, Joellen Riley, Andrew Robertson, the late Alan Rodger, Justine Rogers, Francis Rose, Desmond Ryan, Irit Samet, Andrew Sanders, Eloise Scotford, Helen Scott, Duncan Sheehan, Natasha Simonsen, Judith Skillen, Brian Sloan, Peter Smith, Jenny Steele, Cameron Stewart, Lindsay Stirton, Ruth Stirton, William Swadling, Tang Hang Wu, Alexander Turk, Peter Turner, Janet Ulph, Rachael Walsh, Charlie Webb, Leif Wenar, Jeni Whalan, George Williams, Sarah Williams, Gordon Woodman, Sarah Worthington, Joshua Wright, Katie Wright, Stephen Wright, Graham Virgo, Goh Yihan, and Man Yip.

JAG and JSFL

Grateful acknowledgment is made to the following authors and publishers for permission to quote from their works:

- RELX (UK) Limited, trading as LexisNexis:
  — All England Law Reports
  — Heydon, J.D., and Leeming, M.J., *Cases and Materials on Equity and Trusts*, 8th edn (2011)
- The High Court of Australia
- The Incorporated Council of Law Reporting for England and Wales

While every care has been taken to establish and acknowledge copyright, and contact the copyright owners, the publishers tender their apologies for any accidental infringement. They would be pleased to come to a suitable arrangement with the rightful owners in each case.

TABLE OF CONTENTS

PART I
Introduction

1. HISTORY AND PRINCIPLES

16. NON-CHARITABLE PURPOSE TRUSTS

17. TRUSTS OF PENSION FUNDS

PART III
Trustees and Fiduciaries

18. GENERAL PRINCIPLES OF THE ADMINISTRATION OF TRUSTS

19. DUTIES OF TRUSTEES IN RELATION TO THE TRUST PROPERTY

20. DUTIES OF TRUSTEES IN RELATION TO THE BENEFICIARIES

21. POWERS OF TRUSTEES

22. TRUSTEESHIP AND FIDUCIARY DUTIES

23. VARIATION OF TRUSTS

26. TRACING

PART V
Miscellaneous Equitable Remedies and Doctrines

27. SPECIFIC PERFORMANCE

29. RESCISSION AND RECTIFICATION

30. LICENCES AND ESTOPPEL

TABLE OF CASES

TABLE OF CASES

cxv

Rochdale Canal Co v King, 51 E.R. 924; (1853) 16 Beav. 630 Ct of Chancery 30–025
Rochdale Canal Co v King, 61 E.R. 270; (1851) 2 Sim. N.S. 78 Ct of
Chancery 27–048, 28–017
Roche, Re (1842) 2 Dr. & War. 287 . . . . 18–019, 18–020
Rochefoucauld v Boustead (No.1); sub nom. Rochefoucauld v Boustead [1897] 1 Ch. 196
CA 6–005, 12–020
Rochford v Hackman (1852) 9 Hare 475 . . . . 8–002, 8–004
Rodway v Landy [2001] EWCA Civ 471; [2001] Ch. 703; [2001] 2 W.L.R.
1775 . . . . 13–024, 13–029
Roffey v Shallcross, 56 E.R. 690; (1819) 4 Madd. 227 Ct of Chancery 27–029
Roger's Question, Re [1948] 1 All E.R. 328 CA 13–012
Roocroft v Ball [2016] EWCA Civ 1009; [2017] 1 W.L.R. 1137; [2017] 2 F.L.R. 810;
[2016] 3 F.C.R. 546 29–006
Rooney v Cardona (No.1); Rooney v Black Horse Life Assurance Co Ltd; Rooney v Black
Horse Financial Services Group Ltd; Rooney v Lloyds Bank Plc [1999] 1 W.L.R. 1388;
[1999] 1 F.L.R. 1236 CA (Civ Div) 13–002
Roper Curzon v Roper Curzon (1870-71) L.R. 11 Eq. 452 Ct of Chancery 21–036
Roper's Trusts, Re (1879) L.R. 11 Ch. D. 272 Ch D 18–045, 18–046
Rose (Deceased), Re; sub nom. Rose v Inland Revenue Commissioners [1952] Ch. 499;
[1952] 1 All E.R. 1217 CA 5–010, 5–011
Rose, Re; sub nom. Midland Bank Executor & Trustee Co Ltd v Rose [1949] Ch. 78; [1948]
2 All E.R. 971 Ch D 5–011
Rosemary Simmons Memorial Housing Association Ltd v United Dominions Trust Ltd
[1986] 1 W.L.R. 1440; [1987] 1 All E.R. 281 Ch D 15–020
Rosenthal, Re; sub nom. Schwartz v Bernstein [1972] 1 W.L.R. 1273; [1972] 3 All E.R. 552
Ch D 18–003, 24–037
Rosher, Re; sub nom. Rosher v Rosher (1884) L.R. 26 Ch. D. 801 Ch D 14–011
Rothko, Re 43 N.Y. 2d 305 (1977) 25–015
Routier v Revenue and Customs Commissioners [2017] EWCA Civ 1584; [2018] S.T.C.
910; [2017] B.T.C. 28; [2017] W.T.L.R. 1119 15–006
Rowbotham v Dunnett (1878) L.R. 8 Ch. D. 430 Ch D 6–028
Rowe v Prance [1999] 2 F.L.R. 787; [2000] W.T.L.R. 249 Ch D 1–033, 5–018, 13–011
Rowland v Witherden, 42 E.R. 379; (1851) 3 Mac. & G. 568 Ct of Chancery 21–012
Royal Bank of Scotland Plc v Chandra [2011] EWCA Civ 192; [2011] N.P.C. 26; [2011] 2
P. & C.R. DG1 29–009
Royal Bank of Scotland Plc v Etridge (No.2); Kenyon-Brown v Desmond Banks & Co
(Undue Influence) (No.2); Bank of Scotland v Bennett; UCB Home Loans Corp Ltd v
Moore; National Westminster Bank Plc v Gill; Midland Bank Plc v Wallace; Barclays
Bank Plc v Harris; Barclays Bank Plc v Coleman [2001] UKHL 44; [2002] 2 A.C. 773;
[2001] 3 W.L.R. 102 . . . . 1–048, 29–010, 29–011,
29–012, 29–013
Royal Bank of Scotland Plc v Highland Financial Partners LP [2013] EWCA Civ 328;
[2013] 1 C.L.C. 596 28–047
Royal Bank of Scotland v O'Donnell [2014] CSIH 84; 2014 G.W.D. 33-641 29–014
Royal Bristol Permanent Building Society v Bomash (1887) L.R. 35 Ch. D. 390 Ch
D 12–008
Royal Brunei Airlines Sdn Bhd v Tan; sub nom. Royal Brunei Airlines Sdn Bhd v Philip Tan
Kok Ming [1995] 2 A.C. 378; [1995] 3 W.L.R. 64 PC (Bru) 25–018, 25–020, 25–021,
25–022, 25–035
Royal Choral Society v Inland Revenue Commissioners [1943] 2 All E.R. 101
CA 15–014, 15–016
Royal College of Nursing v St Marylebone BC [1959] 1 W.L.R. 1077; [1959] 3 All E.R. 663
CA 15–019
Royal College of Surgeons of England v National Provincial Bank Ltd; sub nom.
Bland-Sutton's Will Trusts, Re; Bland-Sutton (Deceased), Re; National Provincial Bank
Ltd v Middlesex Hospital [1952] A.C. 631; [1952] 1 All E.R. 984 HL 15–004, 15–014,
15–015,
15–019, 15–025, 15–059
Royal National Lifeboat Institution (RNLI) v Headley [2016] EWHC 1948 (Ch); [2016]
W.T.L.R. 1433; [2017] 1 P. & C.R. DG4 22–001

TABLE OF STATUTES

TABLE OF STATUTORY INSTRUMENTS

TABLE OF FOREIGN LEGISLATION

TABLE OF TREATIES AND CONVENTIONS

PART I

INTRODUCTION

HISTORY AND PRINCIPLES

1.   GENERAL

EQUITY is a word with many meanings. In a wide sense, it means that which is **1–001** fair and just, moral and ethical; but its legal meaning is much narrower. Equity is the branch of the law which, before the Judicature Act of 1873 came into force, was applied and administered by the Court of Chancery.[1] It is not synonymous with justice in a broad sense. A litigant asserting some equitable right or remedy must show that his or her claim has

---

[1] This is "but a poor thing to call a definition"; Maitland, p.1.

"an ancestry founded in history and in the practice and precedents of the court administering equity jurisdiction. It is not sufficient that because we may think that the 'justice' of the present case requires it, we should invent such a jurisdiction for the first time."[2]

Developed systems of law have often been assisted by the introduction of a discretionary power to do justice in particular cases where the strict rules of law cause hardship.[3] Rules formulated to deal with particular situations may subsequently work unfairly as society develops. Equity is the body of rules which evolved to mitigate the severity of the rules of the common law. Its origin was the exercise by the Chancellor of the residual discretionary power of the King to do justice among his subjects in circumstances in which, for one reason or another, justice could not be obtained in a common law court.

1–002 Principles of justice and conscience are the basis of equity jurisdiction, but it must not be thought that the contrast between law and equity is one between a system of strict rules and one of broad discretion. Equity has no monopoly of the pursuit of justice. As Harman LJ has said, equitable principles are

"rather too often bandied about in common law courts as though the Chancellor still had only the length of his own foot to measure when coming to a conclusion. Since the time of Lord Eldon, the system of equity for good or evil has been a very precise one, and equitable jurisdiction is exercised only on well-known principles."[4]

In similar vein Lord Radcliffe, speaking of common lawyers, said that equity lawyers were "both surprised and discomfited by the plenitude of jurisdiction and the imprecision of rules that are attributed to 'equity' by their more enthusiastic colleagues."[5] More recently, Neuberger LJ, who as Lord Neuberger of Abbotsbury was President of the UK Supreme Court from 2012 to 2017, said:

"The fact that a particular type of right or relief is equitable does not, *pace* some judicial observations to the contrary, operate as a green light to invent new general or specific rules in order to achieve what one judge might regard as a fair result in a particular case or, to put it another way, to achieve 'a form of palm-tree justice'".[6]

Returning to the theme, his Lordship added:

"equity is not a sort of moral US fifth cavalry riding to the rescue every time a claimant is left worse off than he anticipated as a result of the defendants behaving badly, and the common law affords him no remedy."[7]

Just as the common law has escaped from its early formalism, so over the years equity has established strict rules for the application of its principles. Indeed, at

---

[2] *Re Diplock* [1948] Ch. 465 at 481, 482. See also Jessel MR in *Re National Funds Assurance Co* (1878) 10 Ch.D. 118 at 128: "This court is not, as I have often said, a Court of Conscience, but a Court of Law."

[3] The Praetor performed such a function in Roman Law: W. Buckland and A. McNair, *Roman Law and Common Law*, 2nd edn (Cambridge: Cambridge University Press, 1965), pp.1–6.

[4] *Campbell Discount Co Ltd v Bridge* [1961] 1 Q.B. 445 at 459.

[5] *Bridge v Campbell Discount Co Ltd* [1962] A.C. 600 at 626.

[6] *Edlington Properties Ltd v JH Fenner & Co Ltd* [2006] 1 W.L.R. 1583 at 1595–1596, quoting from *Muscat v Smith* [2003] 1 W.L.R. 2853 at 2865.

[7] (2009) 68 C.L.J. 537 at 540.

one stage the rules became so fixed that a *"rigor aequitatis"*[8] developed; equity itself displayed the very defect which it was designed to remedy. We will see that today some aspects of equity are strict and technical, while others leave considerable discretion to the court.

The field of equity is delineated by a series of historical events, and not by a pre-conceived theory; an outline of these events will be given in the next section. We will then see that, until the Judicature Act 1873, the Court of Chancery had almost exclusive equity jurisdiction[9]; rules of equity were not enforced in the common law courts. If a defendant to a common law action had an equitable defence to it, he had to go to Chancery to obtain an injunction to stay the proceedings in the common law court and then start a new action in Chancery to establish his equitable rights. This complicated system led to a number of difficulties, as we shall see. The Judicature Acts of 1873 and 1875 created the Supreme Court of Judicature, all of whose branches exercise common law and equity jurisdiction. The division between law and equity is less marked, therefore, than it was prior to those Acts, but it is still necessary for various reasons to know whether a rule has its origins in law or in equity.[10]

2. HISTORICAL OUTLINE

The long history of the Court of Chancery is a fascinating story, the details of which must be sought elsewhere[11]; it is not possible here to do more than mention, in broad outline, those aspects which are essential to the understanding of modern equity.

1–003

A. The Medieval Chancellor

In the medieval period the Chancellor was the most important person in the country next to the King himself: Maitland described him as "the king's prime minister",[12] "the king's secretary of state for all departments".[13] One very important function of the Chancery was to issue the royal writs which began an action at law.[14] By varying existing writs or inventing new ones, the Chancellor

1–004

---

[8] C.K. Allen, *Law in the Making*, 7th edn (Oxford: Oxford Clarendon Press, 1966), p.417.

[9] For the equity jurisdiction of the Court of Exchequer, see *Halsbury's Laws of England*, 5th edn, Vol.24, para.699, fn.4; H. Woolf et al (eds), *De Smith's Judicial Review*, 7th edn (London: Sweet & Maxwell, 2013), para.15–050. The Common Law Procedure Act 1854 had given common law courts a limited power to issue injunctions.

[10] Below, paras 1–020–1–023.

[11] Maitland Lectures, *The Constitutional History of England*, 1908 I–IV; Holdsworth; *H.E.L.* i, Ch.5; iv, pp.407–480; v, pp.215–338; vi, pp.518–551, 640–671; ix, pp.335–408; xii, pp.178–330; xiii, pp.574–668; xvi, pp.5–135; Plucknett, *Concise History of the Common Law*, 5th edn, Pt 5; Milsom, *Historical Foundations of the Common Law*, 2nd edn (1981) Chs 4, 9; Jones, *The Elizabethan Court of Chancery* (1967); (1965) 81 L.Q.R. 562; J. Barton (1966) 82 L.Q.R. 215; Keeton and Sheridan's *Equity*, 3rd edn (1985) Ch.2; Klinck, *Conscience, Equity and the Court of Chancery in Early Modern England* (Ashgate, 2010).

[12] Maitland, p.3.

[13] Maitland, p.2.

[14] See Maitland, *Forms of Action at Common Law* (1909).

could have some influence on the development of the law; a limited influence, however, for the decision to issue a writ (now called a claim form in the Civil Procedure Rules 1998) did not create a new form of action. The litigant could not proceed without it; but the common law court could still decide that the writ disclosed no claim recognised by the law.

B. Petitions to the Chancellor[15]

1–005 A claimant could only sue at common law if his complaint came within the scope of an existing writ. In the 13th century the available writs covered very narrow ground. Even if the claim came within the scope of an existing writ, it may have been that for some reason, such as the power and influence of the defendant, his opponent could not get justice before a common law court. But the King in his Council still retained wide discretionary power to do justice among his subjects, and the claimant could petition to the King and Council praying for a remedy.

Petitions were addressed to the Chancellor in situations in which a petitioner complained that his case was beyond the ordinary mechanism, and he sought another way. Milsom points out that, in its origins, this would not be regarded as an application of a separate and superior body of rules to those applied by the common law courts.

> "Not only was there no equity as a nascent body of rules different from those of the common law. There was no common law, no body of substantive rules from which equity could be different."[16]

If the mechanism appeared to work unfairly, as where juries were misled, corrupted or intimidated, the petitioner would seek another way. The Chancery

> "was the head office of the organisation, and it was here that application was made when the ordinary mechanisms appeared to be incapable of working. The approach to the chancellor has no more mysterious origin than that."[17]

Later the petition was used to obtain relief in cases where the common law was inflexible and incapable of providing a remedy. The common law developed into a comprehensive system, but a litigant could only sue at common law if his complaint came within the scope of an existing writ. By the 16th century local jurisdictions, where many matters not covered by common law writs had been dealt with, played a much smaller part. The common law was taking on the aspect of a substantive as well as a comprehensive system, and the application to Chancery was ceasing to look like a request for the same justice, withheld below by some mechanical fault. There seemed to be two parallel systems, and the relationship between them had to be explained in theory and worked out in practice.

---

[15] Holdsworth, *H.E.L.* i, pp.402 and following; Milsom, p.82.
[16] Milsom, p.84.
[17] Milsom, p.84.

C.   The Chancellor's Discretion

Maitland points out that in the 13th and 14th centuries the Chancellor probably did not regard himself as administering a new body of law.[18] He was trying to give relief in hard cases, and the medieval Chancellor was peculiarly well fitted for this work. He was usually an ecclesiastic, generally a bishop, and learned in the civil and canon law.[19] The Chancellor would give or withhold relief, not according to any precedent, but according to the effect produced upon his own individual sense of right and wrong by the merits of the particular case before him. No wonder that Selden could say that:

1–006

> "Equity is a roguish thing. For law we have a measure … equity is according to the conscience of him that is Chancellor, and as that is longer or narrower, so is equity. 'Tis all one as if they should make the standard for the measure a Chancellor's foot."[20]

D.   Attendance of the Defendant

In exercising this jurisdiction, the Chancellor was faced with the problem of ensuring the attendance of the defendant without the issue of a royal writ.

1–007

> "The Chancellor, having considered the petition or bill as it is called, orders the (defendant) to come before him and answer the complaint. The writ whereby he does this is called a *subpoena*—because it orders the man to appear upon pain of forfeiting a sum of money—*e.g. subpoena centum librarum*."[21]

The examination was made under oath; it did not need to be restricted to specific questions raised in the complaint; and issues of fact as well as issues of law were decided by the Chancellor.

E.   Enforcement

A further question was that of enforcement. If the petition was successful, the Chancellor's conclusion would usually be different from that which the common law court would have reached; otherwise the matter would have been litigated at common law. If the Chancellor found that Blackacre was owned by A, but that, in conscience, it should be beneficially owned by B, he could order A to convey the land to B, or to hold the legal estate for the exclusive benefit of B. The Chancellor did not and could not in these circumstances hold that B was the owner. A's right at law was undoubted, and the Chancellor could not change the law. What the Chancellor did was to issue an order to A either to convey the land to B, or to refrain from action interfering with B's right. The Chancellor's jurisdiction was against the person—in personam[22]—and directed to the conscience of the

1–008

---

[18] Maitland, p.5.

[19] There were some lay Chancellors at this period; see Trevelyan, *England in the Age of Wycliffe* (1899).

[20] Pollock (ed.) *Table Talk of John Selden* (1927), p.43; quoted Holdsworth, *H.E.L.* i, pp.467–468.

[21] Maitland, p.5.

[22] Below, para.1–018.

individual in question. The Chancellor had the power to back up his orders with the threat of imprisonment for those in contempt. Although there was, theoretically, no interference with common law property rights, there was in substance an interference with common law jurisdiction. This was the subject of dispute later on.[23]

F.   The Use[24]

1–009
> "If we were asked what is the greatest and most distinctive achievement performed by Englishmen in the field of jurisprudence I cannot think that we should have any better answer to give than this, namely the development from century to century of the trust idea."[25]

Such was the view of Maitland. Let us now examine the origins of that concept.

In medieval times, the Chancellor's jurisdiction was vague and undefined; as wide as the subject-matter of the petitions which invoked it. The basis of intervention was that it was necessary on grounds of conscience. His authority was unquestioned in cases of fraud and breach of confidence. As stated above, the most significant and far-reaching sphere of his jurisdiction was the enforcement of the use of land.

If land was given to A on A's undertaking to hold the land to the use and benefit of B, it was unconscionable for A to keep it for his own benefit. B however had no legal claim or title to the land. The conveyance to A gave him whatever legal estate was conveyed, and, at common law, A could exercise all the rights which that estate gave him.

Land might be given to A to the use of B for various reasons. If B were going on a crusade, then there had to be someone to perform and receive the feudal services. If B were a community of Franciscan friars which, because of the rule of poverty, was incapable of holding property, it was necessary for someone to hold the land for its benefit.[26] Perhaps, however, B was trying to escape from his creditors, or feared that a conviction for felony would result in the loss of his lands.[27] For various reasons it may have been advisable or necessary to put the legal title to B's land in A. If B conveyed to A subject to an undertaking to hold to the use of B, B would have no protection at common law beyond that given in the 14th century to covenants under seal; and if a third party conveyed the land to A to hold to the use of B, no relationship recognised by the common law existed between A and B.

The Chancellor interfered to compel A to hold the land for the exclusive use and benefit of B. The Chancellor could not say that B was the owner; A was. But all the beneficial interest in the land could be given to B by compelling A to keep the legal title only, and to give all the benefit of the land to B. This is what happened when the use was enforced. And, although the jurisdiction against A

---

[23] Below, para.1–013.
[24] Holdsworth, *H.E.L.* iv, pp.407–480; Ames, *Lectures on Legal History* (1913), pp.233–247; Plucknett, *Concise History of the Common Law*, 5th edn (1956), p.575; Milsom, Ch.9; (1965) 81 L.Q.R. 562; J. Barton (1966) 82 L.Q.R. 215; N. Jones (1997) 56 C.L.J. 175; (2013) 72 C.L.J. 91.
[25] Selected Essays, p.129.
[26] Maitland, p.25; Holdsworth, *H.E.L.* iv, p.415; Milsom, p.203.
[27] *Davies v Otty (No.2)* (1865) 35 Beav. 208.

was a jurisdiction in personam, the Chancellor would enforce B's rights, not only against A, but against other persons who took the land from A.[28] It was not long before it was said that A was the owner at law, B the owner in equity. In the terminology of the time, A was the feoffee to uses, B the *cestui que use*. The use was the forerunner, as we will see, of the trust.

Gradually, the Chancellors established the circumstances in which uses would be enforced. They had to decide also what equitable estates they would recognise; for example, if land were conveyed to A to the use of B for life and then to the use of C, should this be enforced? Broadly, the answer was that, in accordance with the maxim that equity follows the law, the estates and interests which could be created in equity corresponded with those which existed at law.

G. The Advantages of the Use

The employment of the use made it possible to avoid some of the feudal incidents. Under feudal law, the lord was entitled to a payment when an heir succeeded to feudal land, and to other valuable rights arising when the land was held by an under-age heir, and the right of escheat where there was no heir. These burdens could be avoided if the land was vested in a number of feoffees to uses. They were unlikely to die together or without heirs. Those who died could be replaced, and the feoffees would never be children. Thus, the use, to feudal land owners, had something of the appeal of tax planning techniques at the present day. It was possible also, in spite of the rule that freehold land could not be devised, to create effective dispositions of equitable interests on death by vesting the land in feoffees and declaring the uses on which the land was to be held after the settlor's death. Further, uses made possible the creation of new types of interests in land which were not possible at common law.[29] For a time also, until prevented by statute, land held to uses could be enjoyed by religious houses in defiance of the Statutes of Mortmain,[30] or be placed beyond the reach of creditors.

1–010

H. The Statute of Uses 1535

Henry VIII found that his purse was being emptied by the avoidance of feudal incidents which the system of uses made possible. To small tenants who had no tenants of their own, the system of uses was entirely beneficial. To large landowners, it was beneficial in so far as they were tenants, and harmful in so far as they were lords. To the King, it was entirely harmful, because he was lord of all and tenant of none. The first part of Henry VIII's reign had been expensive, and he was determined to restore the revenues of the Crown by attacking uses.

1–011

---

[28] Except a bona fide purchaser of a legal estate for value without notice, below, para.1–039; Maitland, pp.113–115.

[29] e.g. springing and shifting interests; Cheshire and Burn, *Modern Law of Real Property*, 18th edn (Oxford: Oxford University Press, 2011), p.97.

[30] Which forbade the conveyance of land to religious houses without permission of the Crown. Milsom, p.204.

The Statute of Uses of 1535 was intended to reduce greatly the scope of the use. After a grandiloquent preamble it provided, according to Maitland's summary of the first clause[31]:

> "[W]here any person or persons shall be seised of any lands or other hereditaments to the use, confidence, or trust of any other person or persons, in every such case such person and persons that shall have any such use, confidence or trust in fee simple, fee tail, for term of life or for years or otherwise shall stand and be seised deemed and adjudged in lawful seisin estate and possession of and in the same lands and hereditaments in such like estates as they had or shall have in the use."

In other words, the feoffees to uses were to disappear. The *cestui que use* was to have the legal estate.

The Statute did not however suppress all uses.[32] It only applied where the feoffee was *seised* to the use of another. If the feoffee held only a lease, she would not be seised, and the Statute would not apply. Again it did not apply to situations where the feoffees had active duties to perform. The feoffees were then necessary participants, and the Chancellor held that a duty to sell the land, or to collect the rents and profits of the land and pay them to X, was a sufficiently active duty to exclude the Statute.[33]

I.   A Use upon a Use: The Trust

1–012   It was possible, after the Statute, to create equitable interests in land by imposing a use upon a leasehold, or by requiring the legal owners of freehold land to collect the rents and profits and to pay them over to the beneficiaries. Such uses were not executed; nor were they invalid.[34] Passive uses of freehold land were, however, executed by the Statute, so that the beneficiary held the legal estate. What would happen if a second use were imposed? If land were limited to A to the use of B to the use of C, is it possible to argue that the first use will be executed, and that B will hold the legal estate to the use of C? Such a solution was reached by about 1700[35]; the second use is called a trust. A shorter form, which became settled practice, was to omit A, and to make the disposition "unto and to the use of B in trust for C".

The story of this development is confused and uncertain.[36] Most accounts start with the proposition that through the 16th century, the second use was repugnant to the first, and void.[37] When the turning-point came is unsettled, but it is clear that after the Restoration in 1660, a number of factors combined to facilitate the

---

[31] Maitland, p.35.

[32] Holdsworth, *H.E.L.* iv, pp.467–473.

[33] Maitland, pp.38–41.

[34] A.W.B. Simpson, *A History of The Land Law*, 2nd edn (Oxford: Oxford University Press, 1986), p.195.

[35] A.W.B. Simpson, *A History of The Land Law*, 2nd edn (1986), p.203.

[36] Milsom, p.208 suggests that the origin is in a situation in which a settlor wishes to settle upon himself with remainders over; J. Baker (1977) 93 L.Q.R. 33.

[37] Maitland, p.42; Ames, *Lectures on Legal History* (1913), pp.243–247; Holdsworth, *H.E.L.* iv, pp.471–473; *Jane Tyrell's Case* (1557) Dyer 155a.

recognition of passive trusts of freeholds. The abolition of military tenures[38] and the consequent freedom to devise all freehold land,[39] the reduction in the value of money which followed the development of the New World, and the changes in the constitutional and financial structure of the country in the 17th century, all helped to make the collection of feudal dues a minor factor in the royal revenues. The Civil War determined once and for all that the Government was to be financed by Parliamentary vote. There was now no reason of policy why passive trusts of freeholds should not be enforced as were active trusts and trusts of leaseholds. The enforcement of the second use as a trust was so similar to that of the enforcement of the use against a feoffee to uses centuries before that Lord Hardwicke was able to say, in 1738, in a remark of greater dramatic power than legal or mathematical accuracy:

> "[B]y this means a statute made upon great consideration, introduced in a solemn and pompous manner, by this strict construction, has had no other effect than to add at most, three words to a conveyance."[40]

J.   The Struggle over Injunctions

The story of the use and of the trust has taken us away from the chronological sequence. For it was at the close of the 16th century that the quarrel over the power of the Chancery to issue injunctions came to a head. The use of the injunction had the effect of rendering the common law inoperative. That the clash did not come earlier was due partly to the statesmanlike qualities of men like Sir Thomas More; and no doubt also to the reluctance to challenge the powers of royal officers in Tudor times. Chief Justice Coke was not willing to see the common law treated in this way, and in a number of cases decided that imprisonment for disobedience to injunctions issued by Chancery was unlawful.[41] In one case it was said that "if any court of equity doth inter-meddle with any matters properly triable at the common law, or which concern freehold, they are to be prohibited."[42] Lord Chancellor Ellesmere, equally determined, claimed that he was in no sense interfering with the common law; he was merely acting in personam, directing the individual that, on equitable grounds, he must not proceed to sue at law or enforce a judgment already obtained at law.

James I stepped in and referred the matter to Bacon, then Attorney General, and others learned in the law. Acting on their recommendations, and no doubt in accordance with his own political views and interests, he decided in favour of the Chancery.[43] The victory did not remain long unchallenged. The success of the Parliament and of the common lawyers in the political struggles of the 17th century provided further impetus for the attack on the Chancery. As late as 1690, following the Revolution, a Bill was introduced in the House of Commons to

1–013

---

[38] Tenures Abolition Act 1660.

[39] Previously only two-thirds of land held by knight service could be devised.

[40] *Hopkins v Hopkins* (1739) 1 Atk. 581 at 591; see Holdsworth, *H.E.L.* iv, p.449.

[41] *Heath v Rydley* (1614) Cro.Jac. 335; *Bromage v Genning* (1617) 1 Rolle 368; *Throckmorton v Finch* (1598) 3 Coke Inst. 124.

[42] i.e. liable to be subject to the writ of Prohibition; *Heath v Rydley* (1614) Cro.Jac. 335.

[43] *Reports of Cases in Chancery*, App.1, p.49; 21 E.R. 588.

restrain the interference by Chancery in any suit for which the proper remedy was at common law.[44] The Bill was not passed, and from that time the Chancellor's jurisdiction was not seriously challenged. Thereafter, law and equity worked together, as parts of a consistent whole; and this enabled Maitland to say that equity had come, not to destroy the law, but to fulfil it.[45]

K. The Transformation of Equity into the Modern System[46]

1–014   From the beginning of the Chancellorship of Lord Nottingham in 1673 and to the end of that of Lord Eldon in 1827, equity was transformed from a jurisdiction based upon the personal interference of the Chancellor into a system of established rules and principles. We have seen that the early Chancellors were ecclesiastics. Lawyers and others were sometimes appointed during the Tudor and Stuart periods. The retirement of Lord Shaftesbury[47] in 1672 was the last occasion (until modern times[48]) on which a non-lawyer held the Great Seal. This factor influenced the development of the system into one based on rules and precedents rather than on individual conscience. The first reported Chancery cases are dated 1557[49] and these cases are treated as authorities and followed.[50]

Lord Nottingham did much to weld together and consolidate the whole system. To him we owe the doctrine that there can be no "clog on the equity of redemption",[51] a classification of trusts,[52] and the modern rule against perpetuities.[53] Throughout the 18th century, equity, in a period of legislative stagnation, became the great force that moulded the progress of the law right up to the beginning of the 19th century. In this period, the modern law of trusts developed and was shaped to meet entirely new conditions of social life; equity took in hand the administration of the estates of deceased persons, on which depended the doctrines of election,[54] satisfaction,[55] ademption,[56] marshalling of assets,[57] and performance,[58] and in many cases it is possible to point to the

---

[44] Holdsworth, *H.E.L.* i, pp.463–465.

[45] Maitland, p.19.

[46] Pollock, *Essays in Legal History* (1907), p.286.

[47] A member of the Cabal of Charles II; he had been educated as a lawyer, but never practised; Holdsworth, *H.E.L.* i, p.411; vi, pp.525–526.

[48] Since the Constitutional Reform Act 2005, the Lord Chancellor need not be a lawyer; below, para.1–017. The House of Lords Constitution Committee Report into *The office of Lord Chancellor* (6th Report of Session 2014–15) recommended that the advantages of appointing a Lord Chancellor with a legal or constitutional background be given due consideration (para.109).

[49] "Choyce Cases in Chancery"; Holdsworth, *H.E.L.* v, pp.274–278; Jones, *The Elizabethan Court of Chancery* (1967), p.3.

[50] In the preface to Nelson's reports, at pp.2–3, the author said that "Equity became artificial Reason, and hath ever since such a mixture of law in it, that it would be much easier now for a Lawyer to preach, than for a Prelate to be a Judge of that Court"; Holdsworth, *H.E.L.* vi, p.669.

[51] *Howard v Harris* (1681) 1 Vern. 33.

[52] *Cook v Fountain* (1676) 3 Swan. 585.

[53] *Duke of Norfolk's Case* (1683) 2 Swan. 454.

[54] Snell, para.6–012.

[55] Snell, para.6–056.

[56] Snell, para.35–005.

[57] Snell, para.32–045.

[58] Snell, para.6–040.

Chancellor who first applied them.[59] In this period there were many great Chancellors, culminating in Lord Eldon (who served from 1801–1806 and 1807–1827), one of the greatest equity lawyers. His decisions were painstaking, learned and clear. As Holdsworth said:

> "He had a thorough grasp of existing rules and principles; but he looked as anxiously into all the facts and circumstances of each case. ... as if there were no such rules and as if, therefore, he was under the necessity of determining each case as one of first impression."[60]

The judgments were masterly. But it is hardly surprising that the business of the court was scandalously in arrears. The pattern and principles of equity were now established. "Nothing would inflict on me greater pain in quitting this place," Lord Eldon said, "than the recollection that I had done anything to justify the reproach that the equity of this court varies like the Chancellor's foot."[61]

L. The 19th Century and the Judicature Acts 1873 and 1875

The 19th century was a period of great development of the equitable jurisdiction, based upon the principles established by the end of Lord Eldon's tenure. The enormous industrial, international and imperial expansion of Britain in this period necessitated developments in equity to deal with a host of new problems. The accumulation of business fortunes required rules for the administration of companies and partnerships; and the change in emphasis from landed wealth to stocks and shares necessitated the development of new concepts of property settlements. **1–015**

Clearly the old organisation of the Chancery Court, overloaded in Lord Eldon's time, could not hope to deal with the mass of business. "Remember this," said Maitland to his students at the beginning of the 20th century,

> "that until 1813 there were only two judges in the Court of Chancery. There was the Lord Chancellor, and there was the Master of the Rolls, and it was but by degrees that the latter had become an independent judge; for a long time he appears merely as the Chancellor's assistant. In 1813 a Vice-Chancellor was appointed. In 1841 two more Vice-Chancellors. In 1851 two Lords Justices of Appeal in Chancery. When the Court was abolished in 1875, it had seven judges. Cases in the first instance were taken before the Master of the Rolls, or one of the three Vice-Chancellors, and there was an Appeal Court constituted by the Chancellor and the two Lords Justices; but the Chancellor could sit as a judge of first instance if he pleased and sometimes did so."[62]

At least, however, the judges could deal with their work without the fear of opposition from the common law. The two courts had now become "not rivals but partners in the work of administering justice."[63] The time had come for the fusion of these jurisdictions into a single Supreme Court.

---

[59] *Re Hallett's Estate* (1880) 13 Ch.D. 696 at 710.

[60] Holdsworth, *H.E.L.* i, p.468.

[61] Holdsworth, *H.E.L.* i, pp.468–469; *Gee v Pritchard* (1818) 2 Swan. 402 at 414.

[62] Maitland, p.14. At the time of writing there are 16 High Court judges, headed by the Chancellor of the High Court, allocated to the Chancery Division.

[63] Holdsworth, *H.E.L.* v, p.668.

Some limited steps were taken towards this fusion in the middle of the 19th century. The Common Law Procedure Act 1854 gave to the common law courts a certain power to give equitable remedies, and the Chancery Amendment Act 1858, commonly known as Lord Cairns' Act, gave to the Court of Chancery power to award damages in addition to, or in substitution for, an injunction or an order for specific performance.[64] The major change however came with the Judicature Acts 1873 and 1875. These Acts abolished the old separate Courts of Queen's Bench, Exchequer, Common Pleas, Chancery, Probate, the Divorce Court, and the Court of Admiralty; creating the Supreme Court of Judicature with a High Court divided into Divisions known as the Queen's Bench Division, Chancery Division, and the Probate, Divorce and Admiralty Division. The last Division was re-named the Family Division in 1970.[65] Its Admiralty jurisdiction was assigned to the Queen's Bench Division, and Probate business, other than non-contentious and common form probate business, to the Chancery Division. Each division exercises both legal and equitable jurisdiction.[66] Thus any issue can be adjudicated in any division; and any point of law or equity can be raised and determined in any division; but, for the sake of administrative convenience, cases are allocated to the divisions according to their general subject-matter.[67] Thus the court "is now not a Court of Law or a Court of Equity, it is a Court of complete jurisdiction."[68]

1–016   It was foreseen that a court which applied the rules both of common law and of equity would face a conflict where the common law rules would produce one result, and equity another. Section 25 of the Supreme Court of Judicature Act 1873 therefore provided for the solution of many problems in which those rules would conflict.[69] Subsection 11 contained a general residual clause:

> "Generally, in all matters not hereinbefore particularly mentioned in which there is any conflict or variance between the rules of equity and the rules of common law with reference to the same matter, the rules of equity shall prevail."

---

[64] Below, paras 27–044, 28–050.

[65] Administration of Justice Act 1970 s.1.

[66] Judicature Act 1873 s.24; Judicature Act 1925 ss.36–44; Senior Courts Act 1981 s.49.

[67] See Senior Courts Act 1981 Sch.1, below, para.1–049. The Court of Protection was established as a court of record by the Mental Capacity Act 2005. The operation of much High Court business was reorganised with the establishment of the Business and Property Courts in 2017, but this is an umbrella term covering many – though not all – of the functions of the Queen's Bench and Chancery Divisions. The three Divisions of the High Court remain.

[68] *Pugh v Heath* (1882) 7 App.Cas. 235 at 237, per Lord Cairns. Thus the three-fold division of the content of equity into the exclusive, concurrent and auxiliary jurisdictions lost importance after the Judicature Acts.

[69] Now Senior Courts Act 1981 s.49. Examples are found in s.25(1) of the Act of 1873, dealing with the order of priority of payment of debts of a person dying insolvent; and the refusal of common law but not of equity to recognise the assignment of debts and choses in action (s.25(6)). These matters are now dealt with by the Administration of Estates Act 1925 s.34(1) and Law of Property Act 1925 s.136 respectively. See *Job v Job* (1877) 6 Ch.D. 562; *Lowe v Dixon* (1885) 16 Q.B.D. 455; *Berry v Berry* [1929] 2 K.B. 316. See also Law of Property Act 1925 s.41.

The effect of the Judicature Act is best shown by the leading case of *Walsh v Lonsdale*.[70]

> The landlord agreed in writing to grant to the tenant a lease of a mill for seven years. The agreement provided that the rent was payable in advance if demanded. No grant by deed of the lease—as required for a lease exceeding three years *at law*—was ever made.
>
> The tenant entered and paid rent quarterly, not in advance. He became in arrears and the landlord demanded a year's rent in advance. It was not paid, and the landlord distrained. The tenant brought this action for illegal distress.[71]
>
> The action failed. The distress would have been illegal at law, because no seven-year lease had been granted, and the yearly legal tenancy which arose because of the entering into possession and payment of rent did not include the provision for payment of rent in advance.[72] In equity, however, the agreement for the lease was as good as a lease. The tenant was liable to pay a year's rent in advance and the distress was lawful.

It will be seen that the effect of the Act is procedural only. The rights of the parties, whether dependent on the rules of law or of equity, were under the Act determined at a single trial. But the same result would ultimately have been reached if the case had arisen before 1875; the procedure only would have differed. The claim, being one for damages for illegal distress, would have been brought at common law. To the tenant's argument that he held only on a lease from year to year, of which the covenant to pay rent a year in advance was not a term, the landlord would have had no reply in a court of law. The claim to specific performance of the agreement to take a lease was one that could only have been made in equity. The landlord would have had to obtain an injunction to stop the tenant's action at law, and then to obtain specific performance of the agreement; and then to have returned to the common law court with the lease duly created by deed in conformity with the decree of Chancery. The landlord would then have had a good defence in the common law court. The effect of the Judicature Acts was to enable the court to treat as done that which ought to be done, and to allow the landlord to use his equitable defence (based on his right to specific performance) to the common law claim. The principle that equity treats as done that which ought to be done was not new. The significance of the case is the recognition of that principle in a case involving a legal claim. The principle is not limited to agreements for leases, but is applicable to all cases where there is a specifically enforceable contract by a legal owner to convey or create a legal estate, such as a contract to sell, to grant a lease or a mortgage. The principle has been applied "once removed"; as where A agreed to sell Blackacre to B who had agreed to grant a lease to C. C was treated as the lessee in equity of the land.[73] C would not become a lessee at law until the legal lease had been properly granted.

---

[70] (1882) 21 Ch.D. 9; *Warmington v Miller* [1973] Q.B. 877; *Tottenham Hotspur Football and Athletic Co Ltd v Princegrove Publishers Ltd* [1974] 1 W.L.R. 113.

[71] A landlord could distrain (i.e. issue a distress) upon a tenant who was in arrears, and in doing so could take and sell sufficient goods of the tenant (with exceptions) as were necessary to pay the arrears; Megarry & Wade, 8th edn, para.19–076. (This common law remedy was abolished by Tribunals, Courts and Enforcement Act 2007 s.71, which commenced in April 2014: SI 2014/768).

[72] A yearly tenancy which arises in these circumstances includes only such terms of any agreement as are consistent with a yearly tenancy: see Megarry & Wade, 8th edn, para.17–088.

[73] *Industrial Properties (Barton Hill) Ltd v Associated Electrical Industries Ltd* [1977] Q.B. 580.

Whether developments since the Judicature Acts have had the effect of fusing not only the jurisdictions but law and equity themselves is a disputed question which can best be considered after looking into the nature of equitable rights.

M.   Current Role of the Lord Chancellor

1–017   In 2004 the Constitutional Reform Bill was introduced, providing for the abolition of the office of Lord Chancellor and the transfer of its functions to the Secretary of State for Constitutional Affairs (now the Secretary of State for Justice), the Lord Chief Justice and others. The proposal to abolish the office of Lord Chancellor met with resistance, and the Constitutional Reform Act 2005 retained the office, although the Lord Chancellor's judicial functions passed to the Lord Chief Justice.[74] Today the Lord Chancellor need not be a lawyer but must only appear to the Prime Minister "to be qualified by experience".[75] In practice the office of Lord Chancellor is now appended to the political appointment of Secretary of State for Justice.

3.   THE NATURE OF EQUITABLE RIGHTS

1–018   There was for many years a learned and unsettled controversy on the question of the nature of equitable rights; and particularly of the nature of the interest of a beneficiary under a trust. In its simplest form, one view emphasises the fact that a beneficiary's remedy, historically and practically, is in the form of an action against the trustee; a right in personam. On the other hand, equitable interests under trusts are equitable proprietary interests, corresponding to legal estates, and the beneficiary can properly be regarded as the owner of the beneficial interest; and ownership is a right in rem. The controversy attracted many great scholars; with Langdell, Ames, Maitland and Holland on one side, and Austin, Salmond, Pomeroy and Scott on the other.[76]

Much of this controversy centred upon whether the beneficiary's right was a right in personam or a right in rem. This was because Austin, following the classifications of Roman law, laid down that rights must be of one type or the other. But, for the discussion to become meaningful, it is necessary to know what these terms mean. They mean different things in different contexts. It seems that the proper meaning of a right in rem in the present context is "a right enforceable against the world with respect to a particular thing".[77] It is assumed throughout that a legal owner does have rights in rem. Rights, that is, against all the world with respect to property. How, then, does a beneficiary under a trust measure up to this test?

The basis of equitable jurisdiction, historically and presently, is that, in accordance with the maxim, equity acts in personam, equitable rights grew up

---

[74] Constitutional Reform Act 2005 s.7.
[75] Constitutional Reform Act 2005 s.2. See generally Lord Bingham (2006) 122 L.Q.R. 211. G. Gee [2014] P.L.11.
[76] D. Waters (1967) 45 C.B.R. at 221; A. Scott (1917) 17 Col.L.R. 269; H. Stone (1917) 17 Col.L.R. 467.
[77] E. Mockler (1962) 40 C.B.R. 270 at 279.

where the Chancellor was willing to intervene. The use has its origin in the insistence of the Chancellor that the feoffees to uses should administer the property for the benefit of the *cestui que use*. Similarly with the trust:

"Equity did not say that the *cestui que trust* was the owner of the land, it said that the trustee was the owner of the land, but added that he was bound to hold the land for the benefit of the *cestui que trust*."[78]

This raised the question of the effect of the sale of the land by the trustee. The answer was that the beneficiary's interest was effective against everyone except a bona fide purchaser for valuable consideration without notice, actual or constructive, of the equitable interest.

Indeed equity could not have done differently. Its remedies of specific performance and injunction were orders in personam. They ordered the defendant to do something or to refrain from doing something; and behind them was the threat that a recalcitrant defendant would be put in prison for contempt.

There is no space here to run through every aspect of equity jurisdiction to establish the point that equity acts in personam. One practical application of this proposition is the fact that a court of equity will exercise jurisdiction to order specific performance of a contract for the sale of land abroad,[79] or to administer assets abroad if the executors are in England.[80] Where a father bought a flat in France in his son's name and sought a declaration that the son was a trustee and an order to vest the property in the father, his action was classified as in personam for the purposes of the 1968 Brussels Convention,[81] so that the son's claim that only the French courts had jurisdiction failed.[82] Where a wife sought a declaration in the English courts as to her beneficial interest in land in England, her claim was classified as in personam. Thus the English courts did not have exclusive jurisdiction and the action was stayed because her husband had already commenced divorce and ancillary relief proceedings in France.[83] In *Re Hayward*,[84] on the other hand, the claim by the trustee in bankruptcy of a deceased legal and beneficial co-owner of a villa in Spain to his share of the property was held to be in rem, so that the Spanish court had exclusive jurisdiction under the Convention. It has been noted that the fact that English law has been incapable of determining conclusively whether trust interests are in rem or in personam "is a deficiency only exacerbated when the concepts are carried into private international law".[85]

---

[78] Maitland, p.17.

[79] *Penn v Lord Baltimore* (1750) 1 Ves.Sen. 444; *Richard West and Partners (Inverness) Ltd v Dick* [1969] Ch. 424; below para.27–004.

[80] *Ewing v Orr-Ewing (No.1)* (1883) 9 App.Cas. 34.

[81] See now art.24 of the Regulation (EU) No.1215/2012.

[82] *Webb v Webb* [1994] Q.B. 696; A. Briggs (1994) 110 L.Q.R. 526; P. Rogerson (1994) 53 C.L.J. 462; P. Birks (1994) 8 T.L.I. 99; J. Collier All E.R. Rev. 1994 p.81; C. MacMillan [1996] Conv. 125. See also *Ashurst v Pollard* [2001] Ch. 595; J. Harris [2001] L.M.C.L.Q. 205; J. Wass (2014) 63 I.C.L.Q. 103.

[83] *Prazic v Prazic* [2006] 2 F.L.R. 1128.

[84] [1997] Ch. 45.

[85] J. Stevens [1998] Conv. 145 at 150.

1–019   This debate does not prevent us from treating a beneficiary under a trust as having equitable ownership. A beneficiary's interest behind a trust has long been treated as having the basic characteristics of a proprietary interest in that it can be bought, sold, mortgaged, and devised or bequeathed. Even though, historically, the protection of the beneficiary was based on the Chancellor's willingness to proceed in personam against the trustee, that protection has ended up by creating rights in the nature of ownership.[86] To argue that a beneficiary's rights are proprietary is not to say that legal rights are the same as equitable, or that equitable ownership is the same as legal. Rather, it is to accept the basic peculiarity of ownership under the English law of trusts. The trustee is the owner at law; and the beneficiary is the owner in equity.

In relation to some claims affecting the trust property, the trustee is able to sue and not the beneficiary. Thus, the trustee sues for rent,[87] or for possession; and, with personalty, the trustee, not the beneficiary, sues for conversion of the trust property.[88] The beneficiary's right is to compel the trustee to take action; though she may, in some cases, take action herself on behalf of the trust, joining the trustee as defendant.[89] This right may sometimes be inadequate; as where the trustee has sold the property to a bona fide purchaser of the legal estate for value without notice, who will defeat the equitable ownership of the beneficiary.[90] Does this require us to say that the beneficiary's rights are personal against the trustee, and are not properly regarded as proprietary? This was the deciding test for the supporters of the theory that equitable rights must be regarded as being in personam. But it shows the inadequacy of the test which is being applied as a means of distinguishing equitable ownership from legal ownership; which is accepted as being a right in rem. For legal rights of ownership are not good against all the world. There are many ways in which the legal owner of a chattel or chose in action may be involuntarily deprived of legal ownership.[91] The situation of the bona fide purchaser is not determinative of the question whether the beneficiary's interest is proprietary; or whether her rights are in rem or in personam. It demonstrates simply that legal and equitable ownership may have different effects. It has even been held that a duty of care may be owed to a

---

[86] *Sinclair v Brougham* [1914] A.C. 398 at 444; Lord Evershed MR (1954) 70 L.Q.R. 326 at 331; *Tinsley v Milligan* [1994] 1 A.C. 340 at 371; *Akers v Samba Financial Group* [2017] UKSC 6; [2017] A.C. 424 at [82].

[87] *Schalit v Nadler Ltd* [1933] 2 K.B. 79.

[88] *MCC Proceeds Inc v Lehman Brothers International (Europe)* [1998] 4 All E.R. 675. The beneficiary can sue if she has a right to immediate possession, but then she sues *qua* possessor; *Healey v Healey* [1915] 1 K.B. 938 (detinue).

[89] See *Les Affréteurs Réunis Société Anonyme v Leopold Walford (London) Ltd* [1919] A.C. 801; *Parker-Tweedale v Dunbar Bank Plc* [1991] Ch. 12; *Bradstock Trustee Services Ltd v Nabarro Nathanson (A Firm)* [1995] 1 W.L.R. 1405; *Barbados Trust Co v Bank of Zambia* [2007] 1 Lloyd's Rep. 495; G. Tolhurst [2007] L.M.C.L.Q. 278; M. Smith (2008) 22 T.L.I. 140; R. Goode (2009) L.M.C.L.Q. 300 at 313–315; *Roberts v Gill & Co* [2011] 1 A.C. 240.

[90] The beneficiary will have a personal right against the trustee for compensation and may be able to trace the proceeds; below, Chs 24, 26.

[91] Sale of Goods Act 1979 ss.21–26; Factors Act 1889 ss.2, 8, 9; Hire Purchase Act 1964 Pt.3. See A. Tettenborn (2018) 77 C.L.J. 151.

beneficial owner of property just as much as to a legal owner, although this has been criticised as blurring legal and equitable ownership in a manner contrary to principle and authority.[92]

From a practical point of view, it can be said that where the problem involves the working of the trust machinery, so that the beneficiary asserts his rights by an action against the trustees to enforce their duties, the theory that equity acts in personam is wholly acceptable. But, in other cases, usually tax cases,[93] the theoretical view is overtaken by a pragmatic approach; and the result determined by the language of the statute and a number of policy questions relating to the purposes of the particular statute. This is an area where Austin's theoretical analysis is the least helpful.

4. THE RELATIONSHIP BETWEEN LAW AND EQUITY: FUSION[94]

The Judicature Act clearly "fused" the administration of law and equity by the creation of the High Court of Judicature exercising both law and equity and gave supremacy to equity in cases of conflict. A disputed question is whether that Act, or the subsequent development of law and equity, should be regarded as having effected the fusion of law and equity themselves. **1–020**

The orthodox view is that only the jurisdictions have been fused. The changes made by the Judicature Act gave rise to no new cause of action, remedy, or defence which was not available before. In a famous metaphor, Ashburner said that "the two streams of jurisdiction, though they run in the same channel; run side by side, and do not mingle their waters."[95] Thus, legal rights remain legal rights, and equitable rights remain equitable rights, though administered in the same court. Other bills which were introduced prior to the Judicature Act would indeed have fused law and equity; but they failed, and the Judicature Act was a more cautious measure.[96]

There are, however, statements by great judges to the effect that law and equity are fused. Sir George Jessel MR said, as early as 1881:

> "[T]here are not two estates as there were formerly, one estate in common law by reason of the payment of rent from year to year, and an estate in equity under the agreement. There is only one court, and equity rules prevail in it."[97]

---

[92] *Shell UK Ltd v Total UK Ltd* [2011] Q.B. 86; N. Macklam [2010] Conv. 265; K. Low (2010) 126 L.Q.R. 507; A. Rushworth and A. Scott [2010] L.M.C.L.Q. 536; P. Turner (2010) 69 C.L.J. 445.

[93] See *Baker v Archer-Shee* [1927] A.C. 844.

[94] See generally S. Degeling and J. Edelman (eds), *Equity in Commercial Law* (Sydney: Lawbook Co, 2005).

[95] Ashburner, *Principles of Equity*, 2nd edn, p.18. See also Lord Evershed MR (1954) 70 L.Q.R. 326; V. Delaney (1961) 24 M.L.R. 116; T. Watkin (1977) 6 A.A.L.R. 119. For a historical study, see P. Polden (2002) 61 C.L.J. 575.

[96] P. Baker (1977) 93 L.Q.R. 529 at 530.

[97] *Walsh v Lonsdale* (1882) 21 Ch.D. 14. He had previously expressed the orthodox view of the effect of the Act, in *Salt v Cooper* (1880) 16 Ch.D. 544 at 549.

Subsequently Lord Diplock[98] discussed Ashburner's metaphor, and declared:

"By 1977, this metaphor has in my view become most mischievous and deceptive. The innate conservatism of English lawyers may have made them slow to recognise that by the Supreme Court of Judicature Act 1873, the two systems of substantive and adjectival law formerly administered by courts of law and Courts of Chancery (as well as those administered by Courts of Admiralty, Probate and Matrimonial Causes), were fused."

Others have expressed views to the effect that we ought to be addressing our minds to the *combined effect* of the systems of law and equity, and that to keep the systems always distinct is pedantic, and an impediment to the natural development of the law.[99]

It is important, in this discussion, to be clear as to what is meant by the claim that law and equity are fused. If it means that there is now no distinction or difference between legal rights and remedies and equitable rights and remedies, it cannot be supported. It is still clear that legal ownership is different from equitable ownership; all the provisions of the legislation of 1925, dealing with unregistered land, are based on that assumption.[100] Perhaps more importantly today, the whole law of trusts assumes a distinction between legal and equitable rights. Further, as discussed below,[101] it is still basically true to say that an equitable claim will provide only an equitable remedy. An equitable claim is required for the revived writ[102] *ne exeat regno*.[103] The common law and equitable rules for tracing property are different, as explained in Ch.26; likewise the rules concerning the transmission of the burden of a restrictive covenant.[104] The illustrations could be multiplied.

1–021   Nor is it true, at the other extreme, to say that rights exercisable in the High Court today are the same as those existing in 1875; nor that the application of equitable doctrines in the court has not had the effect of refining and developing the common law rules.[105] Both legal and equitable rules have developed since 1873; and the development of legal rules has sometimes been influenced by established equitable doctrine, with the effect that a situation which would at one time have been treated differently at law and in equity is now treated in the same manner. If

---

[98] *United Scientific Holdings Ltd v Burnley BC* [1978] A.C. 904 at 925. All the members of the House indicated their general acceptance of the principle of fusion. See also *Chief Constable of Kent v V* [1983] Q.B. 34 at 41.

[99] See Lord Evershed (1948) J.S.P.T.L. 180; Lord Denning (1952) C.L.P. 1; V. Delaney (1961) 24 M.L.R. 116; Lord Denning, *Landmarks in the Law*, p.86 ("the fusion is complete"). See also A. Burrows (2002) 22 O.J.L.S. 1; S. Worthington (2002) 55 C.L.P. 223.

[100] The distinction between legal and equitable ownership is of little significance in registered land. But that is due to the classification of interests for the purposes of the system, and is unconnected with any question of fusion.

[101] Below, para.1–022.

[102] Now called a claim form in the Civil Procedure Rules 1998.

[103] See *Felton v Callis* [1969] 1 Q.B. 200; *Bayer AG v Winter* [1986] 1 W.L.R. 497; *Young v Young* [2012] Fam. 198. See below, para.28–075.

[104] See *Rhone v Stephens* [1994] 2 A.C. 310, especially at 321.

[105] P. Baker (1977) 93 L.Q.R. 536; Sir Anthony Mason (1994) 110 L.Q.R. 238 and (1997–98) 8 K.C.L.J. 1; J. Martin [1994] Conv. 13; Sir Peter Millett (1995) 9 T.L.I. 35 at 37.

that is what is meant by fusion, there is evidence of it, as shown below. It is a healthy and welcome development; and there are other situations which might be candidates for future inclusion.

In *Boyer v Warbey*,[106] the question arose whether covenants in a lease bound assignees, not only where the lease was by deed, but also where the lease was a valid written lease (not exceeding three years). The Court of Appeal held that, whatever the position before 1875, this was not an area where distinctions based on formalities were now acceptable, and that the covenant should bind. It was further suggested that the same result would follow if there was merely a contract for a lease which was enforceable in equity. Whether it was law or equity that regarded the lease as effective, the rule as to the running of covenants should be the same. In a limited sense this is "fusion" in that the reasons why a particular lease is effective are ignored in favour of a uniform consequential rule.

In *Tinsley v Milligan*[107] the question was whether an equitable interest could be asserted in spite of an element of illegality in its acquisition. Lord Browne-Wilkinson explained that legal and equitable interests had different incidents for historical reasons, but that "fusion" resulted in the adoption of a single rule as to the circumstances in which the court would enforce interests acquired under an illegal transaction. Thus the rule was the same whether the claim is to a legal or equitable title, and could be fully stated without reference to its origins. The rule adopted in *Tinsley* itself was recently modified in *Patel v Mirza*,[108] but there was still no suggestion that any weight ought to be placed on whether the rights in question were legal or equitable in origin.

In *Napier and Ettrick (Lord) v Hunter*[109] the nature of an insurer's subrogation right was in issue. Lord Goff examined the origins of subrogation at law and in equity and concluded that: "No doubt our task nowadays is to see the two strands of authority, at law and in equity, moulded into a coherent whole."[110] Similarly, it has been held that set-off, whether legal or equitable, can be raised as a defence whether the relief sought by the claimant is legal or equitable.[111] The House of Lords has held that compound interest may be recovered at common law as well as in equity.[112] In the context of limitation periods, it has been held that there is no distinction between an action for fraud at common law and an action in equity for deliberate and dishonest breach of fiduciary duty based on the same facts, which is the equitable counterpart of the common law claim[113]:

---

[106] [1953] 1 Q.B. 234, especially at 245–247, per Denning and Romer LJJ. See also *Australian Blue Metal Ltd v Hughes* [1963] A.C. 74 at 101–102.

[107] [1994] 1 A.C. 340 at 371, 375, 376.

[108] [2016] UKSC 42; [2017] A.C. 467; below, para.14–014.

[109] [1993] A.C. 713.

[110] [1993] A.C. 713 at 743.

[111] *BICC Plc v Burndy Corp* [1985] Ch. 232; (1985) 101 L.Q.R. 145; *Eller v Grovecrest Investments Ltd* [1995] Q.B. 272. The rules for legal and equitable set-off remain distinct; *Muscat v Smith* [2003] 1 W.L.R. 2853; R. Derham (2006) 122 L.Q.R. 469.

[112] *Sempra Metals Ltd (formerly Metallgesellschaft Ltd) v IRC* [2008] 1 A.C. 561.

[113] *Coulthard v Disco Mix Club Ltd* [2001] 1 W.L.R. 707.

"It would have been a blot on our jurisprudence if those self-same facts gave rise to a time bar in the common law courts but none in the court of equity".[114]

1–022   One indication of fusion is a situation where the legal remedy of damages may be given for breach of an equitable right. The converse, an equitable remedy for breach of a legal right, such as an injunction to restrain a tort, or specific performance of a contract, is explicable as the exercise of equity's concurrent jurisdiction and is not an example of fusion. However, the House of Lords went further in *Attorney General v Blake*,[115] holding that the equitable remedy of account of profits (which is traditionally associated with a fiduciary relationship) could be awarded in exceptional cases for breach of contract. This remedy, like injunctions and specific performance, could be awarded at the court's discretion where the remedy of damages, based on loss, would be inadequate. Although no direct authority could be found, it was considered a modest step which did not contradict any recognised principle on the grant or withholding of the remedy of account. Lord Nicholls observed that remedies are the law's response to a wrong. The different remedial responses of the common law and equity arose as "an accident of history".[116]

Prior to the Judicature Act, Lord Cairns' Act authorised, in certain circumstances, courts of common law to grant specific performance or an injunction instead of damages, and courts of equity to award damages. As will be seen, this Act still has scope for operation.[117] Generally, however, the breach of an equitable right will provide an equitable remedy only.

Although it is tolerably clear that damages are not generally available in England in response to breaches of equitable duties,[118] two further points must be made. First, this is not the case in all common law jurisdictions. For example, in *Aquaculture Corp v New Zealand Green Mussel Co Ltd*,[119] a breach of confidence case, Cooke P held that "equity and common law are now mingled or merged. … a full range of remedies should be available as appropriate, no matter whether they originated in common law, equity or statute". Secondly, much of the importance of the point has been lost with the growth of the remedy of equitable compensation. Thus the debate is no longer about the availability of a compensatory remedy for equitable wrongs,[120] but has instead moved on to the

---

[114] *Coulthard v Disco Mix Club Ltd* [2001] 1 W.L.R. 707 at 730. See also *Cia de Seguros Imperio v Heath (REBX) Ltd* [2000] 1 W.L.R. 112 at 124.

[115] *Attorney General v Blake* [2001] 1 A.C. 268. George Blake is a traitor who escaped to Moscow and wrote a book about his life as a spy. This was in breach of an undertaking not to divulge any official information gained as a result of his employment with the security services. See K. Barnett, *Accounting for Profit for Breach of Contract* (Oxford: Hart Publishing, 2012).

[116] *Attorney General v Blake* [2001] 1 A.C. 268 at 280.

[117] Below, paras 27–044, 28–050.

[118] Although there are cases where damages have been awarded; e.g. *Seager v Copydex Ltd* [1967] 1 W.L.R. 923, and *(No.2)* [1969] 1 W.L.R. 809; *Fraser v Thames Television Ltd* [1984] Q.B. 44. These cases generally predate the growth of equitable compensation, discussed below.

[119] [1990] 3 N.Z.L.R. 299 at 301; J. Beatson (1991) 107 L.Q.R. 209. See also *Day v Mead* [1987] 2 N.Z.L.R. 443; *Lac Minerals Ltd v International Corona Resources Ltd* (1989) 61 D.L.R. (4th) 14; *Canson Enterprises Ltd v Boughton* (1991) 85 D.L.R. (4th) 129; *Stevens v Premium Real Estate* [2009] NZSC 15 at [111].

[120] Some commentators would disagree: see S. Worthington (2000) 116 L.Q.R. 638 at 664.

question of how closely linked are equitable compensation and damages. Lord Reed commented on this point in *AIB Group (UK) Plc v Mark Redler & Co Solicitors*[121]:

> "As the case law on equitable compensation develops, however, the reasoning supporting the assessment of compensation can be seen more clearly to reflect an analysis of the characteristics of the particular obligation breached. This increase in transparency permits greater scope for developing rules which are coherent with those adopted in the common law. To the extent that the same underlying principles apply, the rules should be consistent. To the extent that the underlying principles are different, the rules should be understandably different."

On the New Zealand approach, exemplary damages[122] or damages for mental **1–023** distress[123] could be awarded for breach of equitable duties, and equitable compensation could be reduced for contributory negligence.[124] English courts have rejected the defence in cases of deceit and dishonest assistance in a breach of trust, unless the claimant has been "the author of his own misfortune".[125] As contributory negligence is not a defence at common law to intentional torts,[126] it has been said that equity should be no less rigorous. Thus if the breach involves conscious disloyalty (as opposed to a breach of the non-fiduciary duty of care), the defendant is disabled from asserting that the claimant contributed to the loss by his own want of care, although there may come a point where the loss is too remote.[127] As one commentator put it: "It would be anathema to the nature and function of fiduciary liability for such pleas to be accepted."[128] Whether a wider view on the applicability of contributory negligence or the availability of heads of damage such as mental distress is acceptable depends on whether the policy of the common law on which such concepts are based is the same policy as that on

---

[121] [2014] UKSC 58; [2015] A.C. 1503 at [136]. To the same effect *Swindle v Harrison* [1997] 4 All E.R. 705 at 714, per Evans LJ.

[122] Differing views were expressed in *Aquaculture Corp v New Zealand Green Mussel Co Ltd* [1990] 3 N.Z.L.R. 299. See P. McDermott (1995) 69 A.L.J. 773; *X v Attorney General* [1997] 2 N.Z.L.R. 623. Lindsay J in *Douglas v Hello! Ltd (No.3)* [2003] 3 All E.R. 996 at 1073 assumed without deciding that exemplary damages were available for breach of confidence (not discussed on appeal). See further J. Edelman (2003) 119 L.Q.R. 375; S. Elliott and C. Mitchell (2004) 67 M.L.R. 16; J. Edelman and S. Elliott (2004) 18 T.L.I. 116; J. Getzler and A. Burrows in S. Degeling and J. Edelman (eds) *Equity in Commercial Law* (2005), Ch.10 and Ch.15 respectively.

[123] Accepted by Cooke P in *Mouat v Clark Boyce* [1992] 2 N.Z.L.R. 559 (not discussed on appeal at [1994] 1 A.C. 428). An award of damages for mental distress was upheld by the Court of Appeal in *Douglas v Hello! Ltd (No.3)* [2006] Q.B. 125. The House of Lords did not consider this issue on appeal at [2008] A.C. 1.

[124] Also accepted by Cooke P in *Mouat v Clark Boyce* [1992] 2 N.Z.L.R. 559, in *Day v Mead* [1987] 2 N.Z.L.R. 443, and in Sir Peter Millett (1995) 9 T.L.I. 35 at 38. Differing views were expressed in *Canson Enterprises Ltd v Boughton* (1991) 85 D.L.R. (4th) 129. The proposition was firmly rejected in *Pilmer v Duke Group Ltd (In Liquidation)* (2001) 207 C.L.R. 165.

[125] *Corporacion Nacional del Cobre de Chile v Sogemin Metals Ltd* [1997] 1 W.L.R. 1396; *Standard Chartered Bank v Pakistan National Shipping Corp (Nos 2 and 4)* [2003] 1 A.C. 959.

[126] *Co-operative Group (CWS) Ltd v Pritchard* [2011] EWCA Civ 329.

[127] *Nationwide Building Society v Balmer Radmore* [1999] Lloyd's Rep. P.N. 241. It was noted that the topic was highly contentious and academic opinion sharply divided.

[128] M. Conaglen (2010) 126 L.Q.R. 72 at 101.

which equitable compensation is founded. As Lord Reed noted in the *AIB Group* case,[129] there will be occasions when such convergence exists, but it ought not to be assumed in all cases.[130]

Sufficient examples have been given to show that law and equity are not fused in a wholly substantive sense. What can be said is that more than a century of fused jurisdiction has seen the two systems, whose relationship is "still-evolving",[131] working more closely together; each changing and developing and improving from contact with the other; and each willing to accept new ideas and developments, regardless of their origin. They are coming closer together. But they are not yet fused.

5. THE MAXIMS OF EQUITY

1–024   The "maxims" of equity embody the general principles which evolved in the Court of Chancery. They are not rules which must be rigorously applied in every case, but are more in the nature of general guidelines illustrating the way in which equitable jurisdiction is exercised. A few examples of their operation must suffice,[132] but they should be borne in mind when considering the various rules and doctrines of equity.

1–025   **i. Equity will not suffer a wrong to be without a remedy.**   The principle behind this maxim is that equity will intervene to protect a right which, perhaps because of some technical defect, is not enforceable at law. It is not sufficient that the defendant may be guilty of some moral wrong: the claimant's right must be suitable for enforcement by the court. The classic example is the enforcement of trusts. The beneficiary had no remedy at common law if the trustee claimed the property for himself, as the trustee was the legal owner, but the beneficiary could enforce her rights in equity. The maxim is also reflected in the area of equitable remedies, which may be granted where the defendant's wrong is one not recognised by the common law. In the field of injunctions, for example, the claimant may obtain a *quia timet* injunction to restrain a threatened wrong although she has no cause of action at law until the wrong is committed.[133]

1–026   **ii. Equity follows the law.**   Clearly equity may not depart from statute law, nor does it refuse to follow common law rules save in exceptional circumstances.[134] Thus equitable interests in land correspond with the legal estates and interests.[135] As Mummery LJ stated:

---

[129] *AIB Group (UK) Plc v Mark Redler & Co Solicitors* [2015] A.C. 1503 at [136]; above, para.1–022.

[130] J. Martin [1994] Conv. 13 at 21–22.

[131] *Sempra Metals Ltd (formerly Metallgesellschaft Ltd) v IRC* [2008] 1 A.C. 561 at 629.

[132] For a more detailed survey, see Snell, Ch.5; Meagher, Gummow and Lehane, 5th edn, Ch.3.

[133] Below, para.28–042.

[134] For the conflicts between the rules of law and equity, see above, para.1–016.

[135] Equity, however, recognised certain future interests which were not recognised at law. See Cheshire and Burn, 18th edn (2011), p.97 (and, in more detail, 17th edn, pp.514–516).

"[I]f an interest in land does not satisfy the basic legal requirements for its existence, then it will not, as a general rule, exist as an interest in land either at law or in equity."[136]

Nor will equity depart from the common law rule that a third party cannot be made to perform a contract.[137] Where the legal title to land is held jointly, the equitable interests follow the legal unless a contrary intention is proved.[138]

iii. He who seeks equity must do equity.   A claimant who seeks equitable   1–027
relief must be prepared to act fairly towards the defendant. A person seeking an injunction will not succeed if he is unable or unwilling to carry out his own future obligations.[139] This maxim is also the foundation of the doctrine of election.[140]

iv. He who comes to equity must come with clean hands.   This principle is   1–028
closely related to the last one, save that the latter looks to the claimant's future conduct, while the "clean hands" principle looks to his previous conduct. Thus equity will not grant relief against forfeiture for breach of covenant where the breach in question was flagrant.[141] Examples abound in the field of equitable remedies: a tenant cannot get specific performance of a contract for a lease if he is already in breach of his obligations[142]; nor could a purchaser if he had taken advantage of the illiteracy of the vendor who was not separately advised[143]; so also in the case of injunctions,[144] but equitable relief will only be debarred on this ground if the claimant's blameworthy conduct has some connection with the relief sought. The court is not concerned with the claimant's general conduct. Thus in *Argyll (Duchess) v Argyll (Duke)*,[145] the fact that the wife's adultery had led to the divorce proceedings was no ground for refusing her an injunction to restrain her husband from publishing confidential material.

v. Where the equities are equal the law prevails.   1–129

vi. Where the equities are equal the first in time prevails.   These two related   1–030
maxims, dealing with the priorities of competing interests, may be dealt with together. They provide the foundation for the doctrine of notice.[146] Thus a prior equitable interest can only be defeated by a bona fide purchaser of a legal estate without notice. If the purchaser is bona fide and without notice, then the equities are equal and his legal estate prevails. If he took with notice the position is otherwise, as the equities are not equal. If he does not acquire a legal estate then

---

[136] *Mexfield Housing Co-operative Ltd v Berrisford* [2011] Ch. 244 at 268; K. Low (2011) 127 L.Q.R. 31.

[137] *Rhone v Stephens* [1994] 2 A.C. 310 (positive covenant relating to land).

[138] *Stack v Dowden* [2007] 2 A.C. 432; below, para.13–005.

[139] See *Chappell v Times Newspapers Ltd* [1975] 1 W.L.R. 482, where employees failed to get an injunction to restrain their dismissal where they refused to undertake not to become involved in strikes.

[140] Snell, para.6–012.

[141] See *Shiloh Spinners Ltd v Harding* [1973] A.C. 691.

[142] *Coatsworth v Johnson* (1886) 54 L.T. 520.

[143] *Mountford v Scott* [1975] Ch. 258.

[144] See *Hubbard v Vosper* [1972] 2 Q.B. 84.

[145] [1967] Ch. 302. See also *Fiona Trust & Holding Corp v Privalov* [2008] EWHC 1748 (Comm).

[146] Below, para.1–039. See *Halifax Plc v Omar* (2002) 2 P. & C.R. 26.

the first in time, i.e. the prior equitable interest, prevails, as equitable interests rank in order of creation in the absence of postponing conduct. The two maxims lost some of their importance in respect of real property after the introduction in 1925 of the system of registration of certain interests in land and by the introduction of registered title.[147]

1–031 **vii. Equity imputes an intention to fulfil an obligation.** Where a person is obliged to do some act, and does some other act which could be regarded as a performance of it, then it will be so regarded in equity. This is the basis of the doctrines of performance and satisfaction. For example, if a debtor leaves a legacy to her creditor (of an amount at least as great as the debt), this is presumed to be a repayment of the debt so that, unless the presumption is rebutted, the creditor cannot take the legacy and sue to recover the debt.

1–032 **viii. Equity regards as done that which ought to be done.** Where there is a specifically enforceable obligation, equity regards the parties as already in the position which they would be in after performance of the obligation. Therefore in equity a specifically enforceable contract for a lease creates an equitable lease. This is the doctrine of *Walsh v Lonsdale*.[148] Similarly, a specifically enforceable contract for the sale of land transfers the equitable interest to the purchaser, the vendor holding the legal title on constructive trust until completion.[149] The maxim is also the basis of the doctrine of conversion, and the rule in *Howe v Dartmouth*,[150] concerning the duty to sell unauthorised investments. The maxim has been invoked in modern times by the Privy Council and House of Lords. In *Attorney General for Hong Kong v Reid*[151] the issue was whether a fiduciary who took a bribe became constructive trustee of it or was merely personally accountable. Because he was under a duty to hand over the bribe to his principal, it was held that the property belonged to the principal in equity.[152] Similarly, in *Napier and Ettrick (Lord) v Hunter*[153] it was considered that the duty of an insured person to hand over any damages from the wrongdoer to the insurer was specifically enforceable, so that the insurer had immediate proprietary rights in the form of a lien over the money.

1–033 **ix. Equity is equality.** Where two or more persons are entitled to an interest in the same property, then the principle of equity is equal division, if there is no

---

[147] Below, para.1–046.
[148] (1882) 21 Ch.D. 9, above, para.1–016. A contract relating to land must be in writing; Law of Property (Miscellaneous Provisions) Act 1989.
[149] Below, para.12–008. See also *Davis v Richards & Wallington Industries Ltd* [1990] 1 W.L.R. 1511 (obligation to execute pension trust deed).
[150] (1802) 7 Ves. 137. The rule was abolished for new trusts by the Trusts (Capital and Income) Act 2013; below, Ch.20.
[151] [1994] 1 A.C. 324 (PC); below, para.22–029.
[152] The Court of Appeal considered the decision unsound in *Sinclair Investments (UK) Ltd v Versailles Trade Finance Ltd (In Administrative Receivership)* [2011] EWCA Civ 347; [2012] Ch. 453; but now see the authoritative approval of *Reid* by the Supreme Court in *FHR European Ventures LLP v Cedar Capital Partners LLC* [2014] UKSC 45; [2015] A.C. 250; below, para.22–031.
[153] [1993] A.C. 713.

good reason for any other basis for division.[154] Equity, therefore, dislikes the joint tenancy where, by the doctrine of survivorship, the last survivor takes all. This may be contrasted with the tenancy in common, where the interest of each party devolves upon his personal representative on his death. In the absence of an express declaration to the effect that the equitable interest is held jointly, equity presumes a tenancy in common in certain cases where at law the parties are joint tenants: for example, in the case of partnership property.[155] Even where the equitable interest is held jointly, equity leans in favour of severance, meaning that equity is ready to regard an act or dealing as an act of severance, whereby the equitable interest is converted to a tenancy in common, thus excluding the possibility of survivorship.[156]

x. Equity looks to the intent rather than the form.   This principle does not mean that formalities may be ignored in equity, but rather that equity looks at the substance rather than the form. Thus equity will regard a transaction as a mortgage even though it is not so described, if in substance it appears that the property was transferred by way of security. Similarly a trust may be created although the word "trust" has not been used.[157] A covenant will be regarded as a restrictive covenant if negative in substance even if it is worded in a positive form.[158] Although a party to a covenant can enforce the contract at law even though no consideration has been given, equity regards such a party as a volunteer and will not order specific performance in his favour.[159]

1–034

xi. Delay defeats equities.   Equity aids the vigilant and not the indolent. This is the foundation of the doctrine of laches, whereby a party who has delayed cannot obtain equitable relief. This doctrine is superseded where the Limitation Act 1980 deals with the matter.[160] For example, actions against trustees for breach of trust must, by s.21, be brought within six years, and delay short of this will not bar relief. Where, however, the claimant has a legal right, for example, upon a contract, delay may prevent the grant of an equitable remedy such as specific performance even though the legal right is not statute-barred.[161] Interlocutory injunctions must always be sought promptly, but it seems that delay may not prevent the grant of a final injunction where the cause of action is not statute-barred.[162]

1–035

---

[154] For a modern example, see *Rowe v Prance* [1999] 2 F.L.R. 787 (yacht).

[155] *Lake v Craddock* (1732) 3 P Wms 158.

[156] See *Burgess v Rawnsley* [1975] Ch. 429.

[157] Below, para.4–003.

[158] *Tulk v Moxhay* (1848) 18 L.J.Ch. 83 (covenant "to keep uncovered by buildings" held negative).

[159] *Cannon v Hartley* [1949] Ch. 213.

[160] Either expressly or by analogy; below, paras 24–040 and following.

[161] Below, para.27–036. See Limitation Act 1980 s.36(1).

[162] *Fullwood v Fullwood* (1878) 9 Ch.D. 176; *HP Bulmer Ltd & Showerings Ltd v J Bollinger SA* [1977] 2 C.M.L.R. 625, below, para.28–044.

The doctrine of laches continues to apply to those equitable claims which are outside the Limitation Act 1980, for example a claim to set aside a purchase of trust property by a trustee.[163] Similarly, claims to rescission and rectification may be barred by delay.[164]

1–036   **xii. Equity acts in personam.**   Equity has jurisdiction over the defendant personally. The personal nature of the jurisdiction is illustrated by the fact that failure to comply with an order, such as specific performance or an injunction, is a contempt of court punishable by imprisonment. Provided that the defendant is within the jurisdiction (or can be served outside it), it is no objection that the property which is the subject-matter of the dispute is outside it. Thus in the leading case of *Penn v Lord Baltimore*,[165] specific performance was ordered of an agreement relating to land boundaries in Pennsylvania and Maryland, the defendant being in England.

6.   EQUITABLE REMEDIES

1–037   At common law, the normal form of relief is an award of damages, to which a claimant who has proved her case is entitled as of right. One of the greatest contributions of equity has been to supplement the limited range of legal remedies by introducing a wide range of equitable remedies,[166] which can be awarded both to enforce rights which are exclusively equitable and those which are legal. Their common features are that they are discretionary, their availability depends upon the inadequacy of common law remedies (which, in the case of exclusively equitable rights, will not be available at all) and they are governed by the doctrine that equity acts in personam.

The most significant of these remedies are specific performance, whereby the court orders a party to a contract to perform her contractual obligations, and an injunction, whereby the court orders a person to do, or, more commonly, to refrain from doing, some particular act. These, plus the remedies of rescission and rectification of contracts, will be examined in the later chapters of this book. Other equitable remedies include delivery up and cancellation of documents,[167] account[168] and receivers.[169]

The ancient prerogative writ *ne exeat regno*,[170] later adapted by equity, prevents the defendant from leaving the jurisdiction before final judgment, its purpose being to coerce him to give security for an equitable debt, on pain of

---

[163] Below, para.24–048.
[164] Below, paras 29–017, 29–020. See *Humphreys v Humphreys* [2004] W.T.L.R. 1425 (undue influence).
[165] (1750) 1 Ves.Sen. 444, below para.27–004; *Hamlin v Hamlin* [1986] Fam. 11; *Webb v Webb* [1994] Q.B. 696; above, para.1–018. See also Civil Jurisdiction and Judgments Act 1982 s.30(1).
[166] See generally Meagher, Gummow and Lehane, 5th edn; Spry, *Equitable Remedies*, 9th edn (2014) Ch.1.
[167] Snell, para.14–007.
[168] Snell, para.20–003. See *Attorney General v Blake* [2001] 1 A.C. 268; J. Edelman [2001] L.M.C.L.Q. 9.
[169] Snell, para.19–001.
[170] For its history, see *Allied Arab Bank Ltd v Hajjar* [1988] Q.B. 787.

arrest. The stringent conditions for its grant were laid down in *Felton v Callis*.[171] Writs are still issued today, although a more modern approach is to grant an interlocutory injunction against leaving the jurisdiction.[172]

The remedy of the declaration had some connection with equity in origin,[173] but the jurisdiction to grant it is now governed wholly by statute.[174] Finally, although not "remedies" in the traditional sense, the constructive trust and the doctrine of tracing are sometimes so described. These will be examined in later chapters.[175]

The differing character of equitable remedies must be appreciated. First, it is obvious that factors such as fraud, misrepresentation and mistake are relevant to the exercise of a discretionary jurisdiction to issue injunctions and orders of specific performance. Here, the question is ordinarily one of the manner in which an already existing legal or equitable right is enforced.[176] The right itself is not affected. Thus if equity refuses to order specific performance of a contract due to a defendant's mistake, the claimant's right to sue for damages still subsists[177]; it is merely that a supplementary method of enforcement is denied. But secondly, other equitable remedies are larger in their effect; if equity rescinds a deed or a contract, a right to sue on that contract or deed ceases to be available at law. Equity will exercise this jurisdiction on grounds on which law takes no similar action, for instance, in cases of constructive fraud or wholly innocent misrepresentations, so that the equitable remedy affects the substance of a claimant's rights, and not merely the manner of their enforcement. This is also true when the equitable remedy of rectification is called into operation, a remedy by which a term of a document is varied so as to make it accord with the parties' real intentions. Thirdly, it should be noted that an equitable remedy may fulfil a task intermediate between the situations so far considered, the task of enabling a claimant to take full advantage of a right at common law. A claimant may, for instance, have a right at common law to rescind a contract for fraud, but may be at common law unable to exercise that right[178] because a precise restitutio in integrum is not possible. Equity has a wider discretion to rescind in such a case by devising a fair, if not a precise, return of the parties to something approaching their original positions.[179]

1–038

As we shall see, it is in the field of remedies that equity has displayed perhaps the greatest inventiveness and capacity for development, providing relief in new situations as they arise.[180]

---

[171] [1969] 1 Q.B. 200.

[172] Below, para.28–075.

[173] See H. Woolf et al (eds), *De Smith's Judicial Review*, 7th edn (2013), para.15–061.

[174] *Tito v Waddell (No.2)* [1977] Ch. 106 at 259, per Megarry VC. See also *Chapman v Michaelson* [1909] 1 Ch. 238.

[175] Below, Chs 12 and 26.

[176] Below, paras 27–033, 28–043.

[177] *Wood v Scarth* (1855) 2 K. & J. 33 (in equity); (1858) 1 F. & F. 293 (at law); *Webster v Cecil* (1861) 30 Beav. 62; *Johnson v Agnew* [1980] A.C. 367, below, para.27–046.

[178] And would be confined to an action for damages.

[179] *Spence v Crawford* [1939] 3 All E.R. 271; a decision showing that equity may be more willing to do so in cases of actual fraud than in others.

[180] See particularly search orders and freezing injunctions, below, paras 28–072, 28–075.

7.   THE BONA FIDE PURCHASER OF THE LEGAL ESTATE[181]

1–039   As we have seen, the use was enforceable against the feoffee to uses because the feoffee's conscience was bound by the undertaking which he had given to hold the property to the use and benefit of the *cestui que use*. Similarly with a trustee and beneficiary. So long as the same person remains trustee, this theory works quite simply. But if the legal estate passes from the trustee to another person, how is the conscience of the transferee affected? The question is then one of determining, as a matter of policy, whether this new holder of the legal estates is to be bound by the trust.[182] Any way in which the equitable ownership of a beneficiary is destroyed is of course a serious weakening of the position of the beneficiary; and equity strives always to protect him.[183]

Thus, a trust is binding on a person to whom the trustee gave the property[184]; or a mere occupier,[185] and also on a purchaser who bought it if she knew or could by reasonable inquiries have found out about the existence of the trust.[186] In short, the trust is binding on everyone coming to the land except the bona fide purchaser of a legal estate for value without notice actual, constructive or imputed.[187]

The doctrine applies to land and personalty. However, as far as land is concerned, its importance has diminished now that the system of registration of title applies throughout England and Wales. Under this system the doctrine of notice has little scope for application.[188] But some unregistered land remains, because there is no duty to register the title until a transaction of a specified kind after the area has become one of compulsory registration of title.[189] Even with unregistered land, the doctrine of notice was largely replaced, as will be seen, by the Land Charges Act 1925 (now the Act of 1972). In the account which follows, it should thus be borne in mind that in the case of registered land, the traditional doctrine applies only to transactions occurring before the title was registered, although some aspects of the doctrine have wider application.[190]

When a recipient of trust property satisfies all the elements of the bona fide purchase doctrine, the effect is to extinguish the equitable interest that formerly encumbered the legal title. This does not mean that the beneficiary's interest is somehow transferred to the recipient. Rather, the doctrine illustrates the inherent

---

[181] See D. Fox in P. Davies, S. Douglas and J. Goudkamp (eds), *Defences in Equity* (Oxford: Hart Publishing, 2018).

[182] Maitland, p.111. See also J. Howell [1997] Conv. 431.

[183] Maitland, p.220.

[184] *Re Diplock* [1948] Ch. 465 at 544–545.

[185] *Mander v Falcke* [1891] 2 Ch. 554.

[186] *Pilcher v Rawlins* (1872) L.R. 7 Ch.App. 250.

[187] Such a purchaser can pass her good title to a purchaser with notice under the rule in *Wilkes v Spooner* [1911] 2 K.B. 473.

[188] Interests protected on the register and overriding interests (Land Registration Act 2002 s.29 and Sch.3) are binding on a purchaser of registered land, regardless of notice, and whether legal or equitable. Land Registration Act 2002 replaced Land Registration Act 1925 with effect from October 2003.

[189] Land Registration Act 2002 s.4. The occasions for registration include sales, gifts, assents on death and certain mortgages and leases.

[190] Below, para.1–046.

limits of that equitable interest. The point is shown by the recent Supreme Court decision in *Akers v Samba Financial Group*,[191] where a trustee wrongly sold shares that he held on trust for a company. The question was whether this wrongful sale involved a "disposition" of the beneficiary company's property within the meaning of the Insolvency Act 1986 s.127; if so, the transfer of the shares to the purchaser would have been void. The Supreme Court held it did not constitute a "disposition" because the trustee's wrongful transfer of legal title to the shares was not itself apt to "dispose" of the beneficiary's interest. Instead, that interest was extinguished because of the operation of the bona fide purchase doctrine.

A. Purchaser for Value

The purchaser must have given value in money, or money's worth,[192] or the consideration of marriage.[193] Otherwise he is a mere donee, and bound by the trust regardless of notice. A purchaser includes a mortgagee[194] or lessee. Indeed, in this context the word "purchaser" carries its ancient meaning and merely denotes someone who takes an interest in property otherwise than by descent. For this reason a separate criterion of value is also required; it is not implicit in the term "purchaser".

1–040

In *Independent Trustee Services Ltd v GP Noble Trustees Ltd*,[195] a divorced wife received £1.48 million from her former husband as part of a divorce settlement that had been approved by court order. Unknown to the wife, the payment came from money that the husband had misappropriated from a pension fund. It was therefore subject to a trust while in the husband's hands. The wife initially took the money as a bona fide purchaser for value because she "had given value in the form of agreeing not to pursue any further claims for ancillary relief in return for the lump sum and other orders contained in the [court] order".[196] However, the protection of the bona fide purchase defence was removed when, subsequently, the wife successfully applied for the initial court order to be set aside in an attempt to secure a more valuable settlement. The wife had no longer provided value for the transfer of the £1.48 million, so the claimants (representing the defrauded pension trusts) could then trace and reclaim the remaining[197] funds in her hands.

---

[191] [2017] UKSC 6; [2017] A.C. 424 at [51], [72], [88].

[192] *Thorndike v Hunt* (1859) 3 De G. & J. 563. Nominal consideration does not suffice; *Nurdin & Peacock Plc v DB Ramsden & Co Ltd* [1999] 1 E.G.L.R. 119. See generally K.W. Ryan (1964) 2 Adel. L.R. 189. For the argument that promising to hold received property on trust amounts to valuable consideration see J. Hudson [2017] Conv. 195.

[193] i.e. a future marriage. An ante-nuptial settlement is deemed to be made for value in respect of the spouses and the issue of the marriage, below, para.5–022.

[194] *Kingsnorth Finance Co v Tizard* [1986] 1 W.L.R. 783; see Law of Property Act 1925 s.205(xxi).

[195] [2012] EWCA Civ 195; [2013] Ch. 91; T. Cutts [2013] L.M.C.L.Q. 17.

[196] [2013] Ch. 91 at [26] (the wife's argument, but accepted by the claimants).

[197] See below, para.26–009.

B.   Legal Estate

1–041   This doctrine is based on the maxim that when the equities are equal the law prevails. In the case of a purchase of a legal estate for value without notice, the equities are equal between the purchaser and the beneficiaries; the purchaser's legal estate is allowed to prevail.

The position is different where the purchaser is a purchaser of an *equitable* interest only.[198] The competition then is between two equitable interests; and the general rule here is that the first in time prevails.[199] By way of exception, a purchaser of an equitable interest can defeat prior "mere equities", such as rights to rectification or to set aside a voidable contract.[200]

C.   Notice

1–042   **i.   Meaning of Notice.**   Apart from legislation[201] a purchaser is taken to have notice of an equitable interest unless he can show that "he took all reasonable care and made inquiries, and that, having taken that care and made inquiry, he received no notice of the trust which affected the property".[202] He must show that he had no notice actual, constructive or imputed.

Actual notice is the simple case where the purchaser subjectively knew of the equitable interest. Constructive notice exists where knowledge of the equitable interest would have come to him if he had made all such inquiries as a prudent purchaser would have made. Imputed notice covers actual or constructive notice to his agent who was acting as such in the transaction in question.[203]

1–043   **ii.   Duty to Make Inquiries.**   The inquiries which should be made will depend on the type of property in question. A purchaser, however, should always inspect the premises, and has notice of the interest of a person in occupation of the property.[204]

1–044   *(a)   Land.*   With the unregistered title system, a vendor satisfied a purchaser of his ownership of the land by producing title deeds which traced the history of the ownership of the land. The title had to start with a good root of title[205] at least 15

---

[198] *Pilcher v Rawlins* (1872) L.R. 7 Ch.App. 250 (but cf. A. Reilly (2016) 10 J. Eq. 89, arguing that *Pilcher* is not authority for the proposition that acquisition of a legal title is required).

[199] *Re Morgan* (1881) 18 Ch.D. 93; *McCarthy and Stone Ltd v Hodge & Co* [1971] 1 W.L.R. 1547.

[200] *Shiloh Spinners Ltd v Harding* [1973] A.C. at 721. See, however, *Collings v Lee* [2001] 2 All E.R. 332 (where non-consensual transfer procured by fraudulent misrepresentation transferor retains full equitable interest and not a "mere equity" to set aside). For the position of mere equities in registered land, see Land Registration Act 2002 s.116.

[201] Especially Land Charges Act 1972, below, para.1–046.

[202] *Re Morgan* (1881) 18 Ch.D. 93 at 102, per Fry J.

[203] Law of Property Act 1925 s.199.

[204] *Barnhart v Greenshields* (1853) 9 Moo.P.C. 18; *Hunt v Luck* [1902] 1 Ch. 428; *Kingsnorth Finance Co Ltd v Tizard* [1986] 1 W.L.R. 783; cf. *Bristol and West Building Society v Henning* [1985] 1 W.L.R. 778.

[205] i.e. "a document which describes the land sufficiently to identify it, which shows a disposition of the whole legal and equitable interest contracted to be sold, and which contains nothing to throw any doubt on the title"; Megarry & Wade, 8th edn, para.15–078.

years old.[206] A prudent purchaser would examine that document and every one subsequent to it; he would normally be held to have constructive notice of every equitable interest which appeared on the title,[207] but not of those disclosed by earlier deeds with which he was not concerned. If he agreed to accept a title which began later than the statutory period of 15 years, he did so at his own risk, and would be bound by equitable interests disclosed by documents which were within the statutory period but prior to the agreed date.[208] There was an exception where there were in fact deeds which disclosed an equitable interest, but the vendor was able to produce an apparently perfect title after suppressing some of them.[209]

(b)   Personalty.   The doctrine of notice in the strict conveyancing sense does not apply to personalty, because there is no duty on the purchaser to examine the seller's title; and usually there are no documents of title.[210] A purchaser of shares is not required to inquire about beneficial ownership, nor may notice of any trust affecting the shares be entered on the company's register of shareholders. However, where some equitable interest or charge is disclosed to a purchaser of personalty or presents itself to his notice, he will be bound by it if it is not satisfied out of the purchase money.[211] The doctrine of constructive notice applies even to commercial dealings with personalty, where the facts known to the purchaser make it imperative to seek an explanation, without which it is obvious that the transaction is probably improper.[212] It has been emphasised that the courts should not interpret or develop the law of notice in such a way as to interfere unacceptably with ordinary and honest commerce.[213]

1–045

iii.   Registration.   The Land Charges Act 1925 introduced a system of registration of various interests in unregistered land.[214] Local land charges are dealt with in the Local Land Charges Act 1975. Most of the registrable interests are equitable, but a legal mortgage where the mortgagee did not take possession of the title deeds is included,[215] and one is a statutory creation.[216] Registration is deemed to be actual notice to all persons so long as the registration remains in force[217] whereas failure to register makes the charge void against a purchaser.[218]

1–046

---

[206]   Law of Property Act 1969 s.23.

[207]   *Carter v Carter* (1857) 3 K. & J. 617.

[208]   *Re Nisbet and Potts' Contract* [1906] 1 Ch. 386; affirming [1905] 1 Ch. 391.

[209]   *Pilcher v Rawlins* (1872) L.R. 7 Ch.App. 259.

[210]   See Factors Act 1889 s.1(4). The registration book of a car is not a document of title: *Joblin v Watkins and Roseveare (Motors) Ltd* [1949] 1 All E.R. 47.

[211]   *Nelson v Larholt* [1948] 1 K.B. 339.

[212]   *Macmillan Inc v Bishopsgate Investment Trust Plc (No.3)* [1995] 1 W.L.R. 978 at 1014 (shares); affirmed [1996] 1 W.L.R. 387. See also the sequel, *MCC Proceeds Inc v Lehman Brothers International (Europe)* [1998] 4 All E.R. 675.

[213]   *Sinclair Investments (UK) Ltd v Versailles Trade Finance Ltd (In Administrative Receivership)* [2012] Ch. 453; *Crédit Agricole Corp and Investment Bank v Papadimitriou* [2015] UKPC 13.

[214]   Land Charges Act 1972 does not apply to registered land; but all the interests contained in it can be protected by the entry of a notice under Land Registration Act 2002 (replacing earlier legislation).

[215]   Land Charges Act 1972 s.2(4) Class C(i).

[216]   Class F. See Family Law Act 1996, re-enacting Matrimonial Homes Act 1983.

[217]   Law of Property Act 1925 s.198(1).

[218]   Land Charges Act 1972 s.4; Law of Property Act 1925 s.199(1)(i).

It will be seen that this enactment vitally affected the old doctrine of notice. A purchaser is deemed to have notice of a charge if it is registered. If the charge is not registered, it has been held that she takes free even if she actually knows about it,[219] or if the interest in question is that of a person who is in actual occupation of the land,[220] and the House of Lords has held that the court cannot enquire into the good faith of the purchaser, nor into the adequacy of the consideration paid by her.[221]

D. Overreaching[222]

1–047 More important for our present purposes than the registration provisions are the equitable interests enjoyed by beneficial owners under trusts of land. Under the Law of Property Act 1925 s.1(1), the only legal estates which can exist in land after 1925 are the fee simple absolute in possession and the term of years absolute. Thus, in every case in which the beneficial ownership of land is split into successive interests (other than leases), the interests are equitable.

The 1925 legislation provided that all successive beneficial interests in land must be held either behind a trust for sale or under a strict settlement under the Settled Land Act 1925. Under Pt I of the Trusts of Land and Appointment of Trustees Act 1996, this dual system was replaced by the single system of the "trust of land". Although existing strict settlements were unaffected,[223] no new ones may be created. The 1996 Act applies to other trusts of land, whenever created. The "trust of land" now embraces situations (primarily co-ownership and intestacy) where statutory trusts for sale were imposed before the 1996 Act, expressly created trusts for sale, and bare trusts of land (where the land is held for an adult beneficiary absolutely entitled).[224] The legal estate is vested in trustees, who have a power of sale. When the land is sold by the trustees (or by the tenant for life of an existing strict settlement, in whom the legal estate is vested), the purchaser takes free from the beneficial interests, which are transferred to the proceeds of sale.[225] Thus the beneficiaries have interests in the proceeds which are equivalent to those which they had in the land. This is so whether the title is registered or unregistered.

This process of transfer of beneficial interests from the land to the purchase money is called "overreaching". Provided that any capital money which is payable is paid to at least two trustees, the purchaser takes free of the beneficial interests even if she knew of them. There is no room for the application of the

---

[219] *Hollington Brothers v Rhodes* [1951] 2 All E.R. 578.

[220] *Smith v Jones* [1954] 1 W.L.R. 1089; *Lloyd's Bank Plc v Carrick* [1996] 4 All E.R. 630.

[221] *Midland Bank Trust Co Ltd v Green* [1981] A.C. 513; B. Green (1981) 97 L.Q.R. 518; C. Harpum (1981) 40 C.L.J. 213; H. Johnson [1981] Conv. 361 (son, holding unregistered option to purchase valuable land granted by father, not protected when father sold to mother for £500).

[222] See generally D. Fox in P. Birks and A. Pretto (eds), *Breach of Trust* (Oxford: Hart Publishing, 2002), Ch.4.

[223] Save that no land held on charitable trusts may be settled land, s.2(5).

[224] s.1(1), (2).

[225] Law of Property Act 1925 s.2(1), as amended by the 1996 Act. See G. Ferris and G. Battersby (2003) 119 L.Q.R. 94, comparing the operation of the doctrine in registered and unregistered land; cf. S. Pascoe [2005] Conv. 140 at 151.

doctrine that occupation by the beneficiaries gives constructive notice to the purchaser.[226] Nor, in unregistered land, is there any machinery for the registration of such interests. It has been held that overreaching applies also to interests arising under the doctrine of proprietary estoppel.[227]

Where, however, the purchase money is paid to a sole trustee (for example, a husband who is sole legal owner of a house in which his wife has a share in equity), the doctrine of overreaching cannot apply. In such a case the doctrine of notice remains applicable in unregistered land, so that occupation by the wife is likely to give constructive notice to a purchaser or mortgagee.[228] In the case of an acquisition mortgage, however, where the legal owner could not have bought the property without the mortgage loan, it has been held that a person claiming an equitable interest has no rights against the mortgagee but only against the legal owner, even if in occupation.[229]

E. Other Applications of the Doctrine of Notice

The traditional doctrine of notice is now restricted in its application. The doctrine in its wider form, however, remains significant. As discussed above, it can apply even to commercial dealings with personalty.[230] The defence of purchaser without notice operates in the context of personal claims arising from the receipt of trust property transferred in breach of trust, and of proprietary claims based on tracing, as will be explained in Chs 25 and 26 respectively.

1–048

The House of Lords applied the doctrine in its wider sense in *Barclays Bank Plc v O'Brien*,[231] where the question was whether a wife could set aside a mortgage or guarantee entered into with the bank as a result of her husband's misrepresentation or undue influence. This was not the traditional doctrine because there was only one transaction. The issue was not whether the bank could take free of a prior interest but whether enforcement of the transaction by the bank would be taking advantage of the husband's equitable fraud. The solution lay in the doctrine of constructive notice, whether the land had a registered or unregistered title. This was: "not the same 'doctrine of notice' so beloved of

---

[226] *City of London Building Society v Flegg* [1988] A.C. 54. Overreaching can occur even if no capital money is payable at the time of the conveyance; *State Bank of India v Sood* [1997] Ch. 276 (mortgage to secure existing and future debts); M. Thompson [1997] Conv. 134; M. Oldham (1997) 56 C.L.J. 494; G. Ferris and G. Battersby [1998] Conv. 168 at 182. See also *HSBC Bank Plc v Dyche* [2010] 2 P. & C.R. 4; N. Gravells [2010] Conv. 169.

[227] *Birmingham Midshires Mortgage Services Ltd v Sabherwal* (2000) 80 P. & C.R. 256.

[228] *Kingsnorth Finance Co Ltd v Tizard* [1986] 1 W.L.R. 783; cf. *Bristol and West Building Society v Henning* [1985] 1 W.L.R. 778; *Abbey National Building Society v Cann* [1991] 1 A.C. 56; *Equity & Law Home Loans Ltd v Prestidge* [1992] 1 W.L.R. 137. (Equitable owner who acquiesced in or impliedly authorised mortgage by legal owner deemed to intend to cede priority to mortgagee.)

[229] *Abbey National Building Society v Cann* [1991] 1 A.C. 56.

[230] Above, para.1–045.

[231] [1994] 1 A.C. 180; below, para.29–011.

property lawyers and now largely replaced by registration of title."[232] Thus the doctrine has a role to play beyond the confines of unregistered land. Indeed, it "lies at the heart of equity".[233]

8. THE SUBJECT-MATTER OF EQUITY

1–049 In this Introduction, it has only been possible to mention certain heads of equitable jurisdiction as they became relevant, and it may be helpful to the understanding of equity to list the subjects which should properly be included within it. No list can be exhaustive. Certain matters however are assigned to the Chancery Division by the Senior Courts Act 1981.[234] They are:

1. the sale, exchange or partition of land, or the raising of charges on land;
2. the redemption or foreclosure of mortgages;
3. the execution of trusts;
4. the administration of the estates of deceased persons;
5. bankruptcy;
6. the dissolution of partnerships or the taking of partnership or other accounts;
7. the rectification, setting aside or cancellation of deeds or other instruments in writing;
8. probate business, other than non-contentious or common form business;
9. patents, trade marks, registered designs, copyright or design right;
10. the appointment of a guardian of a minor's estate;
11. all causes and matters involving the exercise of the High Court's jurisdiction under the enactments relating to companies.

All divisions of the High Court, however, exercise co-ordinate jurisdiction. Where a matter arises which has not been assigned to one division, it should go to whichever division is the more appropriate and convenient; in many cases the claimant's counsel will be able to choose. If the action is brought in the wrong division, it may be retained or transferred at the discretion of the judge.[235]

9. THE CREATIVITY OF EQUITY

1–050 One question which has arisen is whether the category of equitable interests is closed, or whether new ones might be created.[236] A clear example is the restrictive covenant, which, since Lord Eldon's day, has evolved from a contractual right to an equitable interest enforceable against the covenantor's

---

[232] M. Dixon and C. Harpum [1994] Conv. 421 at 423.

[233] *Barclays Bank Plc v O'Brien* [1994] 1 A.C. 180 at 195, per Lord Browne-Wilkinson. See also *Royal Bank of Scotland v Etridge* [2002] 2 A.C. 773.

[234] s.61 and Sch.1. This is not affected by the establishment of the Business and Property Courts.

[235] Senior Courts Act 1981 ss.61(6), 65.

[236] Eveleigh LJ in *Pennine Raceway Ltd v Kirklees MBC* [1983] Q.B. 382 at 392, said, "there has been a considerable development in the law in relation to equitable interests and I do not think that it is right to regard the category as closed." But at 397, Stephenson LJ preferred to express no view.

successors in title. One view is that the modern machinery for law reform should be relied upon in preference to judicial creativity.[237] Lord Neuberger, former President of the Supreme Court, has expressed doubts over equity's continued ability to invent.[238]

Bagnall J, in a case concerning matrimonial property, warned against unwarranted extensions of equitable jurisdiction in the following words:

> "In any individual case the application of these propositions may produce a result which appears unfair. So be it; in my view that is not an injustice. I am convinced that in determining rights, particularly property rights, the only justice that can be obtained by mortals, who are fallible and are not omniscient, is justice according to law; the justice which flows from the application of sure and settled principles to proved or admitted facts. So in the field of equity, the length of the Chancellor's foot has been measured or is capable of measurement. This does not mean that equity is past childbearing; simply that its progeny must be legitimate—by precedent out of principle. It is well that this should be so; otherwise no lawyer could safely advise on his client's title and every quarrel would lead to a law suit."[239]

Throughout this book it will be seen that the principles of equity have constantly developed and found new fields of application.[240] The reader, when examining these developments, might consider whether the words of Bagnall J have been heeded. A few examples must suffice here.

Many new developments have been seen in the field of injunctions, notably the evolution of search orders and freezing injunctions, designed respectively to prevent removal or destruction of evidence and to prevent the assets of the defendant from being dissipated.[241] Equity's excursions into the criminal law, however, have been restricted.[242] Similarly, equity's "intrusion" into the common law rules on mistake in contract has been rejected.[243]

The constructive trust also proved to be a fertile field, assisting in the enforcement of contractual licences against third parties[244]; and allowing unprotected interests to be enforced against purchasers of registered land.[245] Constructive and resulting trusts may operate to give security to unsecured creditors[246]; and to determine the ownership of matrimonial and "quasi-matrimonial" property.[247]

---

[237] As in the case of the matrimonial homes legislation (now Family Law Act 1996), replacing Lord Denning's "deserted wife's equity".

[238] Lord Neuberger MR, 'Has Equity had its day?' Lecture at the University of Hong Kong, 12 October 2010; Lord Neuberger, "Equity— The soul and spirit of all law or a roguish thing?", Lehane Lecture 2014, Supreme Court of New South Wales, 4 August 2014.

[239] *Cowcher v Cowcher* [1972] 1 W.L.R. 425 at 430.

[240] In some fields, however, the role of equity has declined. The entitlement to the funds on dissolution of an unincorporated association, for example, is today treated as more a matter of contract than of trusts. See below, para.11–013.

[241] Below, paras 28–072, 28–075.

[242] *RCA Corp v Pollard* [1983] Ch. 135; below, para.28–012.

[243] *Great Peace Shipping Ltd v Tsavliris Salvage (International) Ltd* [2003] Q.B. 679; below, para.29–004.

[244] *Ashburn Anstalt v Arnold* [1989] Ch. 1; below, para.30–015.

[245] *Peffer v Rigg* [1977] 1 W.L.R. 285; *Lyus v Prowsa Ltd* [1982] 1 W.L.R. 1044. See E. Cooke and P. O'Connor (2004) 120 L.Q.R. 640.

[246] *Barclays Bank Ltd v Quistclose Investments Ltd* [1970] A.C. 567, below, para.2–009. See also *Re Kayford* [1975] 1 W.L.R. 279.

[247] Below, Ch.13.

Other areas where equity's creativity has shown itself in modern times include proprietary estoppel[248] and the restriction of the rights of a mortgagee.[249] This brief survey indicates the dynamism of equity. The developments discussed above, and others, will be examined in the relevant parts of the book.

10.   THE RECOGNITION OF TRUSTS ACT 1987[250]

1–051   The trust is an English concept which has spread to common law, but not civil law, jurisdictions.[251] The 1984 Hague Convention on the Law applicable to Trusts and their Recognition establishes common principles between states on the law governing trusts and provides guidelines for their recognition. The UK, by means of the Recognition of Trusts Act 1987, has ratified the Convention.

The ratification does not have the effect of changing the substantive law of trusts of the UK, nor of importing trusts into civil law jurisdictions. The Convention seeks to establish uniform conflict of laws principles and to assist civil law states to deal with trust issues arising within their jurisdiction. Recognition implies, for example, that the trustee may sue and be sued in his or her capacity as trustee, and that the trust property is a separate fund and is not part of the trustee's estate.[252] A trust is to be governed by the law chosen by the settlor, expressly or by implication. In the absence of any such choice, the trust is to be governed by the law with which it is most closely connected.[253] The applicable law governs the validity and construction of the trust, and its effects and administration.[254]

---

[248] Below, para.30–022 and following.

[249] *Quennell v Maltby* [1979] 1 W.L.R. 318 (right to possession must be exercised bona fide and to protect security).

[250] D. Hayton (1987) 36 I.C.L.Q. 260; Underhill and Hayton, 19th edn, Ch.25; M. Lupoi (1998) 4 T. & T. 15; D. Hayton (ed.) *Modern International Developments in Trust Law* (Kluwer Law International, 1999), Chs 2, 3. J. Harris, *The Hague Trusts Convention. Scope, Application and Preliminary Issues* (Oxford: Hart Publishing, 2002).

[251] On 7 February 2007 the French Parliament adopted a new law instituting "La Fiducie", a device similar to the trust but formed contractually. See P. Matthews (2007) 21 T.L.I. 17.

[252] Article 11, as set out in the Schedule to the 1987 Act.

[253] Articles 6 and 7. See *Gomez v Gomez-Monche Vives* [2009] Ch. 245; D. Hayton (2009) 23 T.L.I. 3; *Martin v Secretary of State for Work and Pensions* [2010] W.T.L.R. 671; *C v C* [2015] EWHC 2699 (Ch).

[254] Article 8.

CHAPTER 2

NATURE AND CLASSIFICATION OF TRUSTS

1.   DISTINCTIONS

MANY attempts have been made to define a trust, but none of them has been wholly successful.[1] It is more useful to describe than to define a trust, and then to distinguish it from related but distinguishable concepts.

    2–001

    A trust is a relationship recognised by equity which arises where property is vested in a person or persons called the trustees, which those trustees are obliged to hold for the benefit of other persons called beneficiaries.[2] The interests of the beneficiaries will usually be laid down in the instrument creating the trust, but may be implied or imposed by law. The beneficiary's interest is proprietary[3] in the sense that it can be sold, given away or disposed of by will; but it will not bind someone who acquires the legal estate as a bona fide purchaser for value without notice of the beneficial interest.[4] The subject-matter of the trust must be some form of property. Commonly, it is legal ownership of land or of invested funds; but it may be of any sort of property—land, money, chattels, equitable interests,[5] choses in action,[6] etc. There may also be trusts for charitable purposes; such trusts are enforced at the suit of the Attorney General.[7]

---

[1] Co.Litt. 272b; Underhill and Hayton, 19th edn, para.1.1; Snell, para.21–001; *Halsbury's Laws of England*, 5th edn, Vol.98, para.1; A. Scott (1955) 71 L.Q.R. 39; P. Parkinson (2002) 61 C.L.J. 657; M. Leeming (2009) 7 T.Q.R. 5.

[2] Or, in the old cases, cestuis que trust.

[3] Above, para.1–018. Discretionary trusts and trusts for persons for particular purposes need separate consideration: below, Chs.9 and 16.

[4] Above, para.1–039.

[5] For example, where a beneficiary under a settlement makes a settlement of his beneficial interest.

[6] For example, a trust of the benefit of a covenant, or of a debt, or of a bank balance.

[7] Below, Ch.15.

A trust must be distinguished from certain other legal phenomena which resemble the trust, but which must be kept separate from it. The point of such distinguishing is threefold: first, to compare the different legal consequences of a trust and the related concept; secondly, to identify the circumstances in which the one concept must exist to the exclusion of the other; and thirdly, to identify the circumstances in which a trust may co-exist with the related concept, as may be the case, for example, with certain contracts and debts.

A. Bailment

2–002 Bailment is a relationship recognised by the common law, and arises where a chattel owned by X is, with X's permission, in the possession of Y.[8] The rights of the parties may or may not be governed by a contract. X is entitled to a certain standard of care by Y in her stewardship of X's chattel. But this is very different from a trust. For there is no transfer of ownership from X to Y; Y's duties are dependent on the rules of common law and not upon equity; and these duties are entirely different from, and minimal in character as compared with, those which would exist if Y held the property as trustee for X. A trustee of shares is the legal owner of the shares and the certificates, and not a mere bailee of the latter.[9] A bailor, X, could lose his legal ownership only through one of the ways in which legal owners may be deprived.[10] But if the property was held by Y on trust for X, X's equitable title could be defeated by the transfer of the legal title in the property to a bona fide purchaser for value without notice of the trust.[11]

B. Agency

2–003 The function of an agent is to represent the principal in dealings with third parties, while a trustee does not bring the beneficiaries into any relationship with third parties.[12] There are, however, many similarities. The relationship of trustee and beneficiary is fiduciary; that of principal and agent is normally fiduciary, but not inevitably so.[13] Both trustees and agents must act personally and not delegate their duties[14]; neither may make unauthorised profits from their office.[15]

---

[8] *Halsbury's Laws of England*, 5th edn, Vol.4, para.101; *Aluminium Industrie Vaassen BV v Romalpa Aluminium Ltd* [1976] 1 W.L.R. 676; *Re Goldcorp Exchange Ltd* [1995] 1 A.C. 74 at 97. There is some debate over the independence of bailment within the law of obligations: see, e.g., G. McMeel [2003] L.M.C.L.Q. 169.

[9] *MCC Proceeds Inc v Lehman Bros International (Europe)* [1998] 4 All E.R. 675 (beneficiary could not sue third party for conversion of certificates).

[10] e.g. through estoppel, or the operation of the Factors Act 1889 ss.2, 8, 9; Sale of Goods Act 1979 ss.21–26, or the Hire Purchase Act 1964, Pt.3.

[11] Above, para.1–039. See *MCC Proceeds Inc v Lehman Bros International (Europe)* [1998] 4 All E.R. 675, above.

[12] This is not to say that a trustee cannot be the agent of her beneficiaries; she can. Rather, it is to say that the office of trustee does not itself involve the trustee bringing beneficiaries into relationships with third parties. See A. Televantos [2016] Conv. 181.

[13] Below, para.22–017.

[14] Below, para.21–012.

[15] Below, Ch.22.

A significant distinction arises from the fact that the relationship of principal and agent is primarily debtor/creditor, while a trust is proprietary: the trust property vests in the trustee and the beneficiaries are the equitable owners. The crucial point here is that a proprietary right (so long as the property or its proceeds can be identified) is not affected by the defendant's insolvency, whereas a personal claim will abate with the claims of other creditors if the defendant cannot pay in full.

An agent does not necessarily hold any property for the principal. Even if she does, she may merely have possession rather than title. The principal will have proprietary rights against the agent only if the agent has acquired title to property for the benefit of the principal.

> "That proposition is clear enough in the abstract, but it is often extremely difficult to gauge, especially where the subject matter is money… (i) whether the agent has acquired title or mere possession, and (ii) if he or she has acquired title, whether there is an intention to create a trust or to allow the agent to take an absolute title subject to a merely personal monetary obligation."[16]

The above discussion relates to assets lawfully received by the agent on behalf of the principal. Where property is received in breach of fiduciary duty, as in the case of a bribe or secret commission, the agent holds the property on trust for the principal.[17] The consequence is that the principal's position does not depend on the agent's solvency, the principal is entitled to any increase in value of the property, and there may be consequences for tracing into the value of substituted property.

C. Contract

Trust and contract are quite different concepts. A contract is a common law personal obligation resulting from agreement between the parties. A trust is an equitable proprietary relationship which can arise independently of agreement. However, there are various situations in which the distinction may be difficult to draw, or where the facts may give rise to both[18]; contracts and trusts are not mutually exclusive.[19] **2–004**

i. Settlements and Covenants to Settle. Property which is vested in the trustees of a settlement is held upon the trusts of the settlement, and the beneficiaries are the owners in equity of their interests under the settlement. But if the property has not yet been conveyed to the trustees, and is merely subject to a covenant to settle, then, until the Contracts (Rights of Third Parties) Act 1999, **2–005**

---

[16] Heydon and Leeming, *Cases and Materials on Equity and Trusts*, 8th edn (LexisNexis, 2011), pp.586–587. See *Paragon Finance Plc v DB Thakerar & Co (A Firm)* [1999] 1 All E.R. 400 at 416.
[17] *FHR European Ventures LLP v Cedar Capital Partners LLC* [2014] UKSC 45; [2015] A.C. 250; below, para.22–031.
[18] As, for example, in the case of a constructive trust arising out of a specifically enforceable contract for sale, below, para.12–008.
[19] *Baird v Baird* [1990] 2 A.C. 548 at 560; *Imperial Group Pension Trust Ltd v Imperial Tobacco Ltd* [1991] 1 W.L.R. 589 at 597. These employee pension fund cases are an important illustration of the co-existence of contractual and trust relationships; below, para.17–005.

the beneficiaries could only enforce the covenant if they had given consideration or were parties to the deed.[20] This area is now subject to the development mentioned below.

2–006   **ii. Third Party Rights under a Contract.**   There has been much discussion of the question whether the inability of a third party to sue upon a contract can be overcome by finding that one of the parties to the contract contracted as trustee for her. This is not really a question of distinguishing a trust from a contract. The question is whether there is a trust of the benefit of the contract. The answer to that question depends on whether there is an intention to create a trust of the benefit of the contract; this question is discussed elsewhere.[21] The question has become of less significance since third parties may now enforce contracts for their benefit in certain circumstances under the Contracts (Rights of Third Parties) Act 1999.

2–007   **iii. Unincorporated Associations.**   An unincorporated association is not a legal entity. Where there is a gift to an unincorporated association, there have been doubts as to whether the property is held on trust for the purposes of the association, or whether it belongs absolutely to the members, to be dealt with according to their contract.[22] On the dissolution of such an association the ownership of its funds has sometimes been determined by applying trust principles, but today the matter is more commonly treated as one of contract.[23]

2–008   **iv. Contractual Licences.**   A contractual licence, normally involving the occupation of land, is created by agreement of the parties, applying the normal principles of the law of contract. There is authority,[24] however, especially in the context of enforceability against third parties, that a contractual licence may give rise to a constructive trust, thus giving the licensee an equitable interest in the land in addition to her contractual rights. The development of this theory is discussed elsewhere.[25]

D.   Debt

2–009   A debt may or may not be contractual. Whether the obligation is contractual or not, the duty of the debtor is to pay money to the creditor; that of a trustee is to hold the trust property on trust for the beneficiary. The debtor's obligation is personal. The trust is proprietary. We have seen that the distinction becomes crucial on insolvency. Further, a trustee must invest the trust funds, and the beneficiaries are entitled to the income. With a debtor, or a stakeholder, this is a matter of agreement, express or implied.[26]

---

[20] Below, Ch.5.
[21] Below, para.5–025.
[22] Below, para.16–014 and following.
[23] Below, para.11–013.
[24] See *Ashburn Anstalt v Arnold* [1989] Ch. 1.
[25] Below, para.30–016.
[26] *Duggan v Governor of Full Sutton Prison* [2004] 1 W.L.R. 1010.

On the other hand, it may be to a person's own advantage to be a trustee rather than a person subject to a personal obligation. If money is borrowed and then stolen from the borrower, it must still be repaid; but a trustee may not be liable for a loss which is not due to his own lack of care.[27]

A debt may, of course, be the subject-matter of a trust,[28] but the question here considered is whether the making of a loan can create a trust in favour of the lender. Sometimes a form of words is construed as creating both forms of obligation. There is no reason why, in certain circumstances, a debt and a trust cannot co-exist. The classic example is *Barclays Bank Ltd v Quistclose Investments Ltd*[29]:

> Rolls Razor Ltd, very much indebted to Barclays Bank, was in need of £209,719 to pay dividends which had been declared on its shares. This sum was borrowed from Quistclose under an arrangement whereby the loan was to be used only for that purpose. The money was paid into a separate account at Barclays Bank, the Bank having notice of the nature of the arrangement.
>
> Before the dividend was paid, Rolls Razor went into liquidation. The question was whether the money in the account was owned beneficially by Rolls Razor, in which case Barclays Bank claimed to set it off against the overdraft,[30] or whether Rolls Razor had received the money as trustee and still held it on trust for Quistclose.
>
> The House of Lords unanimously decided that the money had been received upon trust to apply it for the payment of dividends; that purpose having failed, the money was held on trust for Quistclose. The fact that the transaction was a loan, recoverable by an action at law, did not exclude the implication of a trust. The legal and equitable rights and remedies could co-exist. The Bank, having notice of the trust, could not retain the money against Quistclose.

The principle is that:

> "[E]quity fastens on the conscience of the person who receives from another property transferred for a specific purpose only and not therefore for the recipient's own purposes, so that such person will not be permitted to treat the property as his own or to use it for other than the stated purpose."[31]

The principle applies also where only part of the money lent is used for the specific purpose: the part not so applied is held on trust for the lender.[32]

Lord Millett in *Twinsectra v Yardley*[33] analysed the position as follows: a resulting trust for the lender arises as soon as the money is transferred to the borrower, but is subject to the borrower's power (or duty) to apply it to the

---

[27] *Morley v Morley* (1678) 2 Ch. Cas. 2.

[28] For an unusual example, see *Barclays Bank Plc v Willowbrook International Ltd* [1987] 1 F.T.L.R. 386, holding that where A charges to B a debt owed to A by C, any money paid by C to A is held by A on constructive trust for B.

[29] [1970] A.C. 567; see generally W. Swadling (ed.), *The Quistclose Trust* (Oxford: Hart Publishing, 2004).

[30] See J. Glister (2018) 134 L.Q.R. 478.

[31] *Carreras Rothmans Ltd v Freeman Mathews Treasure Ltd* [1985] Ch. 207 at 222.

[32] *Re EVTR Ltd* [1987] B.C.L.C. 647 (loan for buying equipment, part of which was never delivered and money refunded to debtor by vendor). See also *Latimer v Commissioner of Inland Revenue* [2004] 1 W.L.R. 1466; *Re Margaretta Ltd (In Liquidation)* [2006] W.T.L.R. 1271 (money held by solicitors solely for payment of VAT if liability to pay should be established); *Templeton Insurance Ltd v Penningtons Solicitors LLP* [2007] W.T.L.R. 1103.

[33] [2002] 2 A.C. 164; C. Rickett [2002] 10 R.L.R. 112; M. Thompson [2002] Conv. 387; J. Penner and J. Glister respectively (2002) 16 T.L.I. 165 and 223; T. Yeo and H. Tjio (2003) 119 L.Q.R. 8.

specified purpose. It is not enough that the money has been lent for a specified purpose: the question is whether the money was intended to be at the free disposal of the lender. If it was not, the *Quistclose* principle applies.[34] This analysis was applied by the Court of Appeal in *Bellis v Challinor*,[35] where it was confirmed that in the *Quistclose* line of cases the crucial intention is that of the transferor,[36] as the person creating the trust. The transferee's intention remains important, however, because the transferee will not be liable for breaching a trust of which she is unaware.[37]

2–010   The court in *Re Kayford Ltd (In Liquidation)*[38] went one step further, holding that circumstances apparently giving rise to a debt in fact created a trust which did not co-exist with the debt but actually excluded it. In that case, customers of a mail-order company paid in advance when ordering goods. The company, being in financial difficulties, decided to protect its customers in the event of its insolvency by opening a separate bank account, called "Customers' Trust Deposit Account", into which the purchase money was paid. Unlike in the *Quistclose* line of cases, here it was the *transferee* who created the trust. In liquidation proceedings it was held that the money was held on trust for the customers and did not form part of the assets of the company. The customer could create a trust by using appropriate words or, as here, the company could do it by taking suitable steps on or before receiving the money, thus transforming the obligations from debt to trust. The customers never became creditors, so no question of a fraudulent preference[39] of creditors could arise.[40]

The payer will not normally have proprietary rights if the money has not yet been paid into the designated account, even though the failure to pay in was a breach of trust.[41] It is otherwise if a trust has been declared of the money awaiting

---

[34] His Lordship expanded on the views he expressed in (1985) 101 L.Q.R. 269 and rejected the analysis in R. Chambers, *Resulting Trusts* (1997) Ch.3 (beneficial interest in borrower, subject to lender's contractual right to restrain misapplication). See also C. Rickett (1991) 107 L.Q.R. 608; J. Glister (2004) 63 C.L.J. 632.

[35] [2015] EWCA Civ 59; [2016] W.T.L.R. 43.

[36] [2015] EWCA Civ 59 at [57]. See J. Glister (2012) 6 J.Eq. 221.

[37] [2015] EWCA Civ 59 at [62]. References in other cases to the "mutual intention" of the parties must be read in this way; e.g. *Bieber v Teathers Ltd* [2012] EWHC 190 (Ch) at [18] (affirmed without comment [2012] EWCA Civ 1466; [2013] 1 B.C.L.C. 248).

[38] [1975] 1 W.L.R. 279; distinguished in *Re Multi Guarantee Co Ltd* [1987] B.C.L.C. 257, where a separate account was designated but no trust of the money was established because the company contemplated having further resort to the money. Also see *Re Farepak Food and Gifts Ltd (In Administration)* [2007] W.T.L.R. 1407 (no trust of customer contributions to a Christmas savings scheme that failed).

[39] The preference rules are now found in Insolvency Act 1986 s.239.

[40] cf. W. Goodhart and G. Jones (1980) 43 M.L.R. 489 at 494. The point that the customers never became creditors seems unconvincing. For this to be so, the trust must already have existed when the company received the money. See also Heydon and Leeming, *Cases and Materials on Equity and Trusts*, 8th edn (2011), p.597, suggesting that *Re Kayford Ltd* and the *Quistclose* case "provide startling opportunities for well-advised lenders to obtain protection against the prospect of the borrower's insolvency." Interestingly, however, such trusts are excluded from the functional personal property security registration systems in Australia, Canada and New Zealand: see J. Glister (2011) 34 U.N.S.W.L.J. 628. For a wider discussion of the normative underpinnings of such trusts, see E. Hudson (2017) 80 M.L.R. 775.

[41] *Re BA Peters Plc (In Administration)* [2010] 1 B.C.L.C. 142 (money paid for purchase of yacht which had not been delivered).

transfer to the account,[42] or if a trust arises on receipt of client funds by an investment firm under a statutory regulatory regime.[43]

Re Kayford Ltd was not referred to in *Customs and Excise Commissioners v Richmond Theatre Management Ltd*,[44] where a different, and somewhat surprising, result was reached in the context not of insolvency but of liability to value added tax. The theatre sold tickets in advance on terms which expressly imposed a trust on the money for the purchasers until the performance took place. Dyson J held that no trust was created because the terms also provided that the theatre was "not accountable for interest or otherwise in respect of the use of the ticket money after its receipt". It was considered that the effect of this clause was that the purchasers accepted the risk of insolvency and that it would be inequitable to put them in a better position than unsecured creditors in that event. There was no reference to *R. v Clowes (No.2)*[45] where, in the context of theft, the Court of Appeal said that the requirement to keep money separately normally indicates a trust, and the absence of such a requirement normally negatives it *if there were no other indicators of a trust*; the fact that the transaction contemplates the mingling of money is not necessarily fatal to a trust. There the terms of an investment brochure were held to establish that investors' money was received on trust for them, to the exclusion of a debtor/creditor relationship. **2–011**

E.   Conditions and Charges

The distinction between a trust and a charge is that a trust preserves the beneficiary's ownership of property vested in the trustee, whereas a charge provides security over the chargor's own beneficial property. The usual role of a charge is to provide security for a commercial creditor, but a charge in favour of a beneficiary may be imposed by equity where a trustee has wrongly mixed trust assets with her own.[46] **2–012**

It is sometimes difficult to determine whether a gift of property is subject to a trust or whether it is conditional upon, or charged with, the duty of making certain payments. Thus a bequest to X "but she is to pay £50 to Y" could give rise to several possible constructions, each of them having different consequences.[47]

The bequest could be construed as a gift to X upon trust to pay Y £50.[48] In that situation, Y would immediately become entitled in equity to the £50, provided that the property bequeathed was of sufficient value; a trustee is not required to

---

[42] *Re Kaupthing Singer & Friedlander Ltd (In Administration)* [2010] W.T.L.R. 79.

[43] *Lehman Brothers International (Europe) (In Administration) v CRC Credit Fund Ltd* [2011] Bus. L.R. 277; H. McVea [2011] L.M.C.L.Q. 411.

[44] [1995] S.T.C. 257; criticised P. Matthews [1995] B.T.R. 332. Compare the Scots case of *Clark & Whitehouse (Joint Administrators of Rangers Football Club Plc), Re Directions* [2012] CSOH 55.

[45] [1994] 2 All E.R. 316. See also *Re Lewis's of Leicester Ltd* [1995] 1 B.C.L.C. 428; *Mills v Sportsdirect.com Retail Ltd* [2010] 2 B.C.L.C. 143.

[46] Below, para.26–016.

[47] T. Thomas (1952) 11 C.L.J. 240.

[48] *Re Frame* [1939] Ch. 700 (devise to housekeeper "on condition that she adopt my daughter Alma and also gives to my daughters Jessie and May the sum of £5 each, and a like sum to my son Alexander."); cf. *Re Brace* [1954] 1 W.L.R. 955.

produce money of her own to make up deficiencies in the trust property.[49] If there is a surplus, a trustee is not, on principle, entitled to obtain any benefit from the trust and the surplus will usually be held upon a resulting trust.[50] But a possible construction is that, even if there was a trust of the £50, X was intended to take the surplus beneficially, the trust being applicable only to the £50.[51]

The bequest might also be construed as a gift to X conditional upon her performing the obligation. In that situation, Y obtains no interest in the £50; X has the choice of keeping the property and paying £50 or of declining both.[52] It could also be construed so as to impose a charge on the property. Here again, X will only be obliged to make the payment if she receives the property. Her obligation will be limited to the value of the property,[53] and she will be entitled to retain any surplus.[54] Y will have an equitable right by virtue of the charge,[55] but this right is a different one from that of a beneficiary under a trust.

Note that equity will protect the right of an insurer to be subrogated to the insured person's rights against the wrongdoer by imposing an equitable lien or charge, although not a trust, in favour of the insurer on the damages payable by the wrongdoer.[56] The imposition of a trust would be onerous, commercially undesirable and unnecessary to the protection of the insurer.

F. Interest under a Will or Intestacy

2–013   The relationship between a personal representative and a legatee or devisee bears many similarities to that of trustee and beneficiary. The origins of the relationship, however, are quite distinct, the former originating in the Ecclesiastical Court and the latter in Chancery and their basic function is different. The trustee's duty is to manage the trust so long as it continues. The personal representative's duty is to liquidate the estate and distribute the assets; either to individual beneficiaries, or, if a trust is established by the will, to the trustees. Commonly, the executors and the trustees are the same persons, and, as we shall see,[57] in the case of personalty the transfer to themselves is notional; in the case of land an assent is required. Although the two relationships often coalesce or overlap, there are important distinctions between them.

2–014   **i. Whether a Personal Representative is a Trustee.**   The definition of trustee in the Trustee Act 1925 includes a personal representative[58] where the context so

---

[49] *Re Cowley* (1885) 53 L.T. 494.

[50] *King v Denison* (1813) 1 V. & B. 260 at 272; *Re West* [1900] 1 Ch. 84; *Re Rees' WT* [1950] Ch. 204; below, para.6–034.

[51] *Re Foord* [1922] 2 Ch. 519 ("To my sister, Margaret Juliet, absolutely on trust to pay my wife per annum" £300); distinguished in *Re Osoba* [1979] 1 W.L.R. 247.

[52] *Attorney General v The Cordwainers Co* (1833) 3 Myl. & K. 534.

[53] *Re Cowley* (1885) 53 L.T. 494.

[54] *Re Oliver* (1890) 62 L.T. 533.

[55] *Parker v Judkin* [1931] 1 Ch. 475.

[56] *Napier and Ettrick (Lord) v Hunter* [1993] A.C. 713.

[57] Below, para.2–016.

[58] Trustee Act 1925 s.68(17); Administration of Estates Act 1925 s.33; Trustee Act 2000 s.35; *contra*, Income Tax Act 2007 s.463.

admits; and the Act, except where otherwise expressly provided, applies to executorships and administratorships.[59] A personal representative is sometimes treated in the Administration of Estates Act 1925 as a trustee.[60] A personal representative is under fiduciary duties which are very similar to those of a trustee. There are, however, a number of ways in which a personal representative has been held not to be a trustee.

(a) Different Periods of Limitation Apply. Generally, an action for the **2–015** recovery of trust property or for a breach of trust must be brought against a trustee within six years.[61] An action against a personal representative in respect of a claim to personal estate must be brought within 12 years, and an action for the recovery of arrears of interest on legacies within six years.[62] Where a personal representative completes the administration and continues as trustee of a will trust, any later breaches of her duty as trustee are governed by the six-year rule.[63]

(b) Power of Disposition of Personalty. The power of personal representa- **2–016** tives to dispose of pure personalty is *several*; that of trustees is *joint*.[64] This means that one of several executors can pass title to a chattel; but in a sale by trustees, all must combine. It thus becomes important to ascertain when a personal representative becomes a trustee. Where, of course, a will appoints certain persons as executors and other persons as trustees, the executors, on the completion of the administration, must assent to the vesting of the property subject to the trust in the trustees. In the case of personalty the assent may be oral, or even implied,[65] in the case of a legal estate in land however an assent must be in writing, and it becomes an essential document of title in the case of unregistered land.[66]

When however, the executors are appointed trustees also, or where no provision is made for the appointment of trustees in a will which provides for property to be held in trust after the completion of administration, the question arises of the way in which, and of the time at which, the executors become trustees. The principle is that the transition from executors to trustees occurs automatically after completion of the administration, but as far as powers of disposition of property are concerned, there must also have been a sufficient assent by the executors in their own favour as trustees.

---

[59] Trustee Act 1925 s.69.
[60] Administration of Estates Act 1925 ss.33, 46, 49; Intestates' Estates Act 1952.
[61] Limitation Act 1980 s.21(3); for exceptions, see s.21(1) and (2).
[62] Limitation Act 1980 s.22.
[63] *Davies v Sharples* [2006] W.T.L.R. 839.
[64] *Attenborough v Solomon* [1913] A.C. 76.
[65] *Attenborough v Solomon* [1913] A.C. 76. See C. Stebbings [1990] Conv. 257.
[66] "An assent to the vesting of a legal estate shall be in writing, signed by the personal representative, and shall name the person in whose favour it is given and shall operate to vest in that person the legal estate to which it relates; and an assent not in writing or not in favour of a named person shall not be effectual to pass a legal estate." Administration of Estates Act 1925 s.36(4). This does not apply to the vesting of an equitable interest in land; *Re Edwards's WT* [1982] Ch. 30.

In *Attenborough v Solomon*,[67] the House of Lords held that a pledge of silver plate by one of two executors, which was made 13 years after the completion of the administration of the estate, passed no title to the pledgee. The executors had long since become trustees; an assent in their own favour could be inferred from their conduct; and trustees must act jointly.

A similar view was taken in the cases allowing a personal representative to act as a trustee in the exercise of the statutory power of appointing new trustees.[68]

There is no distinction with regard to the power of disposition of land, the power being joint in both cases.[69] Formerly one of two or more personal representatives could enter into a contract to sell land, but this is no longer possible.[70] Where there is only a single personal representative, she may give a receipt for capital money arising on the sale,[71] while at least two trustees or a trust corporation are required in the case of a conveyance by a tenant for life or trustees of land.[72] It is necessary for all personal representatives who are registered shareholders of a company to execute any transfer of the shares.[73]

2–017 *(c) Tenure of Office.*   Formerly a personal representative held office for life (unless the grant was for a limited period) and could not retire. Now, however, the court may discharge an executor or administrator and appoint a substitute.[74] A trustee, on the other hand, may retire without a court order.[75] Subject to the above, a personal representative's duties terminate with the completion of the administration of the estate, but her liabilities are limited only by the passage of time. Thus solicitors who were sureties of an administrator and who handed over the residue of the estate to the administrator (who then absconded) were held liable on their bond.[76]

2–018 *(d) Duty to Estate; Duty to Beneficiaries.*   Executors and trustees are both subject to fiduciary duties. A trustee's duty is to the beneficiaries, and she must "hold the balance evenly between the beneficiaries to whom the property belongs."[77] With an unadministered estate, no legatee, devisee or next of kin, has, as will be seen,[78] beneficial ownership of the assets. The executor's duty is to the estate as a whole.[79] In *Re Hayes' Will Trusts*,[80] a testator appointed four persons, including his son, executors and trustees of his will, and gave power to

---

[67] [1913] A.C. 76.
[68] *Re Ponder* [1921] 2 Ch. 59; *Re Cockburn* [1957] Ch. 438. See also C. Stebbings [1984] Conv. 423.
[69] Administration of Estates Act 1925 s.2(2).
[70] Law of Property (Miscellaneous Provisions) Act 1994 s.16.
[71] Law of Property Act 1925 s.27(2).
[72] Trustee Act 1925 s.14; below, para.21–007.
[73] Companies Act 2006 s.773 (re-enacting earlier legislation). For electronic transfer, see below, para.5–014.
[74] Administration of Justice Act 1985 s.50. See *Re Steel* [2010] W.T.L.R. 531.
[75] Trustee Act 1925 ss.36, 39; below, paras 18–036—18–037.
[76] *Harvell v Foster* [1954] 2 Q.B. 367.
[77] *Re Hayes' WT* [1971] 1 W.L.R. 758 at 764.
[78] Below, para.2–020.
[79] *Re Charteris* [1917] 2 Ch. 379, where a postponement of sale of some assets acted to the disadvantage of the life tenant, although it was in the interest of the estate.
[80] [1971] 1 W.L.R. 758; J. Mummery (1971) 36 Conv.(N.S.) 136.

"my trustees… to sell… to any person… including my son despite his being a trustee and in his case at the value placed upon the same for purposes of estate duty."

In agreeing the estate duty valuation of the farm, it was held that the executors were not obliged to consider the implications of the fact that a low valuation benefited the son, while a high one benefited the other beneficiaries. They negotiated in the usual way with the District Valuer and agreed as low a valuation for tax purposes as they could obtain. This was the usual correct procedure, and they were right to sell to the son at that price.

(e) Vesting of a Legal Estate.   A further question arises, however, with a legal **2–019** estate in land. Where trustees under an existing trust make an appointment of a new trustee under a statutory power given to them by Trustee Act 1925 s.36,[81] the legal estate in the trust property vests in the new trustee under s.40.[82] Although personal representatives cannot appoint successors to their offices, they may, after they have become trustees following the completion of the administration of the estate, appoint additional or successor trustees. But in *Re King's Will Trusts*,[83] Pennycuick J held that the Trustee Act 1925 s.40 did not apply to an appointment of a new trustee by the surviving executor and trustee of a will, who had not previously assented in writing to the vesting of the legal estate in himself in his capacity as trustee. We have seen that an assent in writing is necessary for the vesting of a legal estate in land, and that it constitutes an essential document of title.[84] The executor could have assented to the vesting of the legal estate in himself and the new trustee after the appointment; or he could have assented, before the appointment, to the vesting in himself as trustee; in which case s.40 would have applied.

ii. The Nature of the Interest of a Legatee or Devisee.   A legatee or devisee **2–020** does not, on the testator's death, become equitable owner of any part of the estate. The executor takes full title to the testator's property, not merely a bare legal estate.[85] He is, by virtue of his office, subjected to various fiduciary duties, which can be enforced against him by persons interested; and these duties are inconsistent with his holding the property on trust for the legatee or devisee.[86] The equitable ownership is "in suspense".[87]

The fiduciary duties of the personal representatives are:

---

[81] Below, para.18–020.

[82] Registration is necessary in the case of registered land.

[83] [1964] Ch. 542; A.R. Mellows, *The Law of Succession*, 5th edn (Butterworths, 1993), pp.326–327.

[84] Above, para.2–016.

[85] *Commissioner of Stamp Duties (Queensland) v Livingston* [1965] A.C. 694 at 707–708, 712. But, for the purposes of inheritance tax, a person who would become entitled to a residuary estate (or part thereof) on the completion of the administration is treated as having become entitled at the death of the deceased: Inheritance Tax Act 1984 s.91.

[86] *Sudeley (Lord) v Attorney General* [1897] A.C. 11; *Corbett v Commissioners of Inland Revenue* [1938] 1 K.B. 567 at 575–577; *Passant v Jackson (Inspector of Taxes)* [1986] S.T.C. 164; see also *Skinner v Attorney General* [1940] A.C. 350. For a full discussion of Commonwealth cases, see D. Waters (1967) 45 C.B.R. 219.

[87] *J Sainsbury Plc v O'Connor (Inspector of Taxes)* [1991] S.T.C. 318 at 326.

"[T]o preserve the assets, to deal properly with them, and to apply them in a due course of administration for the benefit of those interested according to that course, the creditors, the death duty authorities, legatees of various sorts, and the residuary beneficiaries. They might just as well have been termed 'duties in respect of the assets' as trusts. What equity did *not* do was to recognise or create for residuary legatees a beneficial interest in the assets in the executor's hand during the course of administration."[88]

It may be, as with an insolvent estate, that nothing is left which can be applied for the beneficiaries. Even if the estate is solvent, the devisee or legatee is not the owner in equity of any asset in the estate. He has a chose in action, a right to compel the administration of the estate. In *Commissioner of Stamp Duties (Queensland) v Livingston*,[89] the question was whether succession duty was payable under a Queensland statute which applied to property situated in Queensland. A widow died domiciled in New South Wales, and was the residuary legatee under her husband's will. The estate of the husband, which was not administered at the date of the widow's death, contained land in Queensland. The Privy Council held that succession duty was not payable on that property. The widow was not the owner of it. She was the owner of a chose in action, and that was situated in New South Wales, the state of her domicile.

In *Eastbourne Mutual Building Society v Hastings Corp*,[90] a husband occupied a house on his wife's intestacy. He was unable to claim compensation for the value of the house on compulsory purchase, because the estate was not administered, and he had no interest in the house. Similarly, in *Lall v Lall*,[91] a widow wished to defend an action for possession of the matrimonial home, which had been owned by her deceased husband. No grant of administration of his estate had yet been made, and so she had no standing to defend the action. In *Re K (Deceased)*[92] residuary beneficiaries under an unadministered estate had not acquired an "interest in property" within s.2(7) of the Forfeiture Act 1982 so as to preclude the court from giving relief under the Act from the forfeiture rule in favour of an applicant who had killed the testator. On the other hand, in *Re Leigh's Will Trust*,[93] a bequest by a widow of "all the shares which I hold and any other interest or assets which I may have" in a particular company was held to be wide enough to include a claim to her husband's unadministered estate which contained such shares; and her claim passed under her will. Following on from this, a beneficiary of an unadministered estate who has taken possession of the land is a person "entitled to a beneficial interest in the land or in the proceeds of sale" within the Limitation Act 1980[94] (with the result that he cannot acquire title against the other beneficiaries).[95] Similarly, where a person entitled under an unadministered estate is bankrupt, the chose in action and its fruits are property of

---

[88] per Lord Radcliffe [1965] A.C. 694 at 707; *Re Hayes' Will Trusts* [1971] 1 W.L.R. 758; C. Davis (2002) 61 C.L.J. 423 at 424.

[89] [1965] A.C. 694. See also *Crowden v Aldridge* [1993] 1 W.L.R. 433; J. Ross Martyn [1994] Conv. 446; *Marshall (Inspector of Taxes) v Kerr* [1995] 1 A.C. 148; *Re Maye* [2008] 1 W.L.R. 315.

[90] [1965] 1 W.L.R. 861.

[91] [1965] 1 W.L.R. 1249; S. Bailey (1965) 23 C.L.J. 144.

[92] [1986] Ch. 180.

[93] [1970] Ch. 277; P.V. Baker (1970) 86 L.Q.R. 20.

[94] Limitation Act 1980 Sch.1 para.9.

[95] *Earnshaw v Hartley* [2000] Ch. 155.

the bankrupt capable of passing to his trustee in bankruptcy.[96] Property held by the personal representatives of an estate which has not been fully administered is property "held on trusts" for the purposes of s.1(1) of the Variation of Trusts Act 1958.[97]

While it is settled that a residuary legatee or devisee or an intestate successor has no equitable interest in any particular assets of an unadministered estate, the position of a specific legatee or devisee is less clear. While there is some authority that such a legatee or devisee does have an equitable interest in the property in question as from the testator's death,[98] some statements in the *Livingston* case cast doubt on this.[99] The better view is that a specific legatee or devisee has no equitable interest during the period of administration.[100] After all, the assets in question may need to be used for the discharge of debts even if the estate is solvent.

A devisee or legatee may be said to become the equitable owner of specific property once property has been allocated by the executor for the purpose.[101] In the case of a residuary gift or a claim on intestacy, the allocation cannot occur until the residuary accounts are prepared.[102] That is the time at which the executors are turning into trustees. The interest of the person entitled then becomes that of a beneficiary under a trust.

G. Powers[103]

i. Trusts Imperative; Powers Discretionary.   The distinction between trusts   **2–021**
and powers is fundamental. Trusts are imperative; powers are discretionary. Trustees must perform the duties connected with their trusts. A donee of a power (the person to whom the power is given) may exercise it, or not, at his choice. If the donee of a power created by will predeceases the testator then the power lapses, but it is otherwise in the case of a trust, which does not fail for lack of a trustee.[104]

Trustees are under a duty to hold the trust property for the beneficiaries in accordance with the terms of the trust. The beneficiaries under a trust are the owners in equity of the trust property. Objects of a power own nothing, unless

---

[96] *Official Receiver in Bankruptcy v Schultz* (1990) 170 C.L.R. 306; *Re Hemming (Deceased)* [2009] Ch. 313. See also *Re Robson* [2014] Ch. 470 (right of residuary legatee is property for the purposes of s.50 of the Political Parties, Elections and Referendums Act 2000, so a legacy given to the British National Party by a donor resident in Spain was void).

[97] *Re Bernstein* [2010] W.T.L.R. 559. See Ch.23 below.

[98] See *IRC v Hawley* [1928] 1 K.B. 578 at 583; *Re Neeld* [1962] Ch. 643 at 688.

[99] [1965] A.C. 694 at 707, 708. See also *Official Receiver in Bankruptcy v Schultz* (1990) 170 C.L.R. 306 at 312.

[100] Pending administration a specific devisee may make a valid contract to sell the land, which becomes specifically enforceable when his interest becomes proprietary: *Wu Koon Tai v Wu Yau Loi* [1997] A.C. 179.

[101] *Phillipo v Munnings* (1837) 2 Myl. & Cr. 309.

[102] *Re Claremont* [1923] 2 K.B. 718.

[103] G. Thomas, *Powers*, 2nd edn (2012); *Halsbury's Laws of England*, 5th edn, Vol.98; J. Hopkins (1971) C.L.J. 68; J. Harris (1971) 87 L.Q.R. 31; below, Ch.7.

[104] *Brown v Higgs* (1803) 8 Ves. 561.

and until the donee of the power makes an appointment in their favour.[105] Prior to any such exercise, they merely have a hope that the power will be exercised in their favour. Until the power is exercised, equitable ownership in such a case is in those who will take in default of an appointment, their interest being defeated by its exercise. Thus, if a testator by his will leaves property to his widow for life and after her death to his children in equal shares, the widow and the children obtain vested interests in the property. Compare this with a gift to the widow for life and after her death as she shall appoint among the children, and, in default of appointment, to charity. Then the children obtain nothing unless and until an appointment is made in their favour.

Whether a trust or a power has been created depends on the construction of the language of the instrument. A properly drafted instrument will leave no room for doubt.

The distinction is however complicated by the fact that a trust may give to the trustees considerable discretion. A trustee may be given a discretion to select beneficiaries from a specified class, or to determine the proportions in which specified beneficiaries are to take. This is the basis of a discretionary trust. Under such a trust no member of a class of the discretionary beneficiaries has an interest in a specific part of the trust property until the discretion of the trustees has been exercised in her favour. The beneficiaries *as a whole*, however, are the owners of the trust property. If all are adult and under no disability — and all are ascertainable — they may combine together to terminate the trust and demand a distribution of the property.[106] The trustees throughout are under an obligation to perform the trust; that is to say, in the context of a discretionary trust, to exercise their discretion; and so to make a selection after proper consideration. "If the trustees fail to exercise their discretion, the court can compel them to exercise the trust."[107] Thus a beneficiary under a discretionary trust cannot demand payment. She has, however, the right to demand that the trustees exercise their discretion in accordance with the trust. What happens if the trustees refuse to do so is one of the matters discussed in *McPhail v Doulton*.[108] The court could replace obstructive trustees with willing ones; and, if no suitable trustees would act, the court ultimately would need to make a selection. The point is that a discretionary trust puts the trustees under an obligation. Their duty is to make a selection. This is very different from a mere power to appoint; for in that case there is no duty to make a selection. It has been held, however, that the court has similar powers of intervention in the case of a fiduciary power where there is nobody to exercise it.[109]

2–022 Although the donee of a mere power of appointment is not obliged to exercise it, she does have certain duties. Thus she must consider periodically whether to exercise it, consider the range of objects, and the appropriateness of individual appointments. If she does decide to exercise the power, she must do so in a

---

[105] *Vestey v IRC* [1980] A.C. 1148.

[106] *Re Smith* [1928] Ch. 915; *Re Nelson* [1928] Ch. 920.

[107] per Lord Guest in *McPhail v Doulton* [1971] A.C. 424 at 444; *Re Locker's ST* [1977] 1 W.L.R. 1323.

[108] [1971] A.C. 424; below, para.4–010.

[109] *Mettoy Pension Trustees Ltd v Evans* [1990] 1 W.L.R. 1587; below, para.7–007.

responsible manner according to its purpose and, of course, refrain from making any appointment which is not within the terms of the power.[110] This is the case where the power is given to a trustee as such; the duties described above are necessary to the performance of her fiduciary role. Where, however, the donee of the power is not a fiduciary, she is not subjected to these fiduciary duties, although she must, of course, keep within the terms of the power.

But it is difficult in borderline cases to draw a dividing line between discretionary trusts and powers,[111] and between fiduciary and personal powers. The decision turns on the proper construction of the language of the instrument.[112]

The matter is made more difficult by reason of the fact that a discretionary trust may be "exhaustive" or "non-exhaustive". An exhaustive discretionary trust is one where the trustees' duty to exercise their discretion can only be satisfied by making a distribution. A non-exhaustive discretionary trust, on the other hand, is one where the settlor has given the trustees power to decide not to distribute all of the income, for example by giving them power to accumulate it for a certain period.[113] It must be admitted that the identification of the precise duty in the case of a non-exhaustive discretionary trust is a difficult task. The distinction from a power of appointment is a fine one, and the matter will be further discussed in Ch.9. For present purposes the position may be summarised as follows: whereas the donee of a fiduciary power of appointment need only consider exercising the power, the trustee of a discretionary trust must actually exercise it, although in the case of a non-exhaustive discretionary trust this duty may be satisfied by deciding to accumulate rather than to distribute.

ii. Terminology.   Nor is the matter helped by the terminology. Discretionary   2–023
trusts have been referred to as a "power in the nature of a trust", or "a power coupled with a duty", or even as a "trust power". Terminology of this type adds to confusion. The situation is that if the words, on their proper construction, are held to impose a duty, then the words create a trust—though one in which the trustees have a power of selection.

iii. Significance of the Distinction.   The question may be material in a number   2–024
of circumstances.

(a)   Whether the Class Takes if the Discretion is not Exercised.   If there is a   2–025
gift in favour of such members of a class as X shall select, and X fails to make a selection, will the gift take effect in favour of the class, or will it fail? If the power is construed as a mere power, the non-exercise of the power will cause it to

---

[110] *Re Hay's ST* [1982] 1 W.L.R. 202; A. Grubb [1982] Conv. 432; *Turner v Turner* [1984] Ch. 100.
[111] *Re Leek* [1969] 1 Ch. 563; *Re Gulbenkian's Settlements* [1970] A.C. 508 at 525; *McPhail v Doulton* [1971] A.C. 424 at 448; *Vestey v IRC* [1980] A.C. 1148. See also, in the context of charity, *Re Cohen* [1973] 1 W.L.R. 415.
[112] *Re Scarisbrick's WT* [1951] Ch. 622 at 635, per Lord Evershed MR; *Mettoy Pension Trustees Ltd v Evans* [1990] 1 W.L.R. 1587; *Gomez v Gomez-Monche Vives* [2009] Ch. 245.
[113] This led some commentators to take the view that there is no longer any analytical distinction between trusts and powers. See J. Davies [1970] A.S.C.L. 187; Y. Grbich (1974) 37 M.L.R. 643; M. Cullity (1976) 54 C.B.R. 229.

fail,[114] and the property will then pass on default of appointment, or go on resulting trust for the grantor. But if the gift is construed as a gift to the class subject to X's power of selection, the trust in favour of the class will take effect.

In *Burrough v Philcox*[115] a testator provided that the survivor of his children should have power, by will,

> "to dispose of all my real and personal estates amongst my nephews and nieces, or their children, either all to one of them or to as many of them as my surviving child shall think proper."

No appointments were made and the members of the class were held to take equally as a trust had been created. On the other hand in *Re Weekes' Settlement*,[116] a testatrix gave her husband a life interest and a power "to dispose of all such property by will amongst our children." He died intestate. There was held to be no trust, and so the children took nothing. In neither case was there a gift over in default.

The question is whether, on the proper construction of the words, it is possible to show an intention to benefit the objects in the event of no appointment being made.[117] It has been said that the courts are more inclined to such a construction when the objects are small in number, such as children under a marriage settlement.[118] But in *McPhail v Doulton*[119] a deed was held to create a trust which provided that the trustees "shall apply the net income in making at their absolute discretion" grants to employees, past and present, and their relatives and dependants. The principle to be applied was laid down by Lord Cottenham in *Burrough v Philcox*.[120]

> "When there appears a general intention in favour of a class, and a particular intention in favour of individuals of a class to be selected by another person, and the particular intention fails, from that selection not being made, the Court will carry into effect the general intention in favour of the class."

The presence of a gift over in default of appointment destroys any such implication; the gift over shows that the settlor is providing for a situation where the donee does not appoint to the class; and this is inconsistent with a trust in favour of the class.[121] But there is no hard and fast rule that a trust is intended if there is no gift over.[122]

---

[114] Subject to *Mettoy Pension Trustees Ltd v Evans* [1990] 1 W.L.R. 1587; below, para.7–007.

[115] (1840) 5 Myl. & Cr. 72. Such a trust, it is submitted, should be regarded as a fixed trust subject to defeasance by exercise of the power of selection, and thus unaffected by *McPhail v Doulton* [1971] A.C. 424. See below, para.4–021.

[116] [1897] 1 Ch. 289.

[117] *Re Llewellyn's Settlement* [1921] 2 Ch. 281; *Re Arnold* [1947] Ch. 131.

[118] *Re Perowne* [1951] Ch. 785 at 790.

[119] [1971] A.C. 424.

[120] (1840) 5 Myl. & Cr. 72 at 92.

[121] This is so even if the gift over is void; *Re Sprague* (1880) 43 L.T. 236. But it would not be so because of a residuary gift, or a gift over in default of there being any objects of the power; *Re Leek* [1969] 1 Ch. 563.

[122] *Re Weekes* [1879] 1 Ch. 289; *Re Combe* [1925] Ch. 210; *Re Perowne* [1951] Ch. 785; *McPhail v Doulton* [1971] A.C. 424.

Where the court finds that there is a trust, the question arises of the share which each of the beneficiaries will take. In the 19th century cases, where the question usually arose in the context of division among a family group, the rule of equal division was applied, on the principle that equality was equity.[123] Today the preferred approach would be to appoint a new trustee who is prepared to make a selection. But the House of Lords accepted, in *McPhail v Doulton*,[124] that there may be occasions when the court itself must make a decision on division.

(b) The Test of Certainty. With both trusts and powers, it is necessary for the beneficiaries, or the objects, to be defined with sufficient certainty to enable the trustees or the donees to exercise their functions, and for the court to supervise them. Before the decision in *McPhail v Doulton*, it was necessary to draw a distinction between the requirement of certainty in the case of trusts (fixed and discretionary) and that required for mere powers. *McPhail v Doulton*, however, decided that the test was the same for discretionary trusts and mere powers. The test came from *Re Gulbenkian's Settlements*,[125] a case on a power, and is whether "it can be said with certainty that any given individual is or is not a member of the class".[126]

2–026

This test will be discussed in detail in Ch.4. But it may be said here that the assimilation of the test of certainty for discretionary trusts and mere powers has greatly reduced the practical significance of the distinction between them. Prior to *McPhail v Doulton*,[127] most of the litigation on the distinction between discretionary trusts and mere powers concerned the question whether a class description had to comply only with the above test; or whether it was void for failure to comply with a stricter test which had earlier been applicable to all trusts.[128] That test was whether the description of the beneficiaries enabled the trustee to draw up a full list of the beneficiaries. That test still remains applicable to "fixed" as opposed to discretionary trusts; that is to say trusts which give a specific share to each beneficiary. Unless the court could make a complete list of all the beneficiaries, it would be impossible to make a division, or to supervise the trustees if they failed to distribute.

(c) Terminating the Trust. Where all the beneficiaries of a discretionary trust are adult and under no disability they may determine the trust and require the trust property to be shared out.[129] On the other hand, objects of a power can never claim any proprietary interest in the property unless and until the power has been exercised in their favour.

2–027

---

[123] This will still be the result if such was the settlor's intention; below, para.4–021.

[124] [1971] A.C. 424. Equal division would not be possible if the total membership of the class was not known. As will be seen, the certainty test propounded in *McPhail v Doulton* does not require all the objects to be ascertained.

[125] [1970] A.C. 508.

[126] per Lord Wilberforce in *McPhail v Doulton* [1971] A.C. 424 at 456; *Re Baden's Deed Trusts (No.2)* [1973] Ch. 9, below, para.4–012.

[127] [1971] A.C. 424.

[128] *IRC v Broadway Cottages Trust Ltd* [1955] Ch. 20.

[129] *Re Smith* [1928] 1 Ch. 915. This assumes that all the beneficiaries can be listed (which is not necessary for the valid creation of the trust, but which would be necessary for its collapse).

2.   CLASSIFICATION OF TRUSTS

2–028   Trusts have been variously classified and subdivided. The categories are not exclusive; some trusts could appear in more than one category. The basic division is between private trusts, and public or charitable trusts.[130] Charitable trusts, which are dealt with in Ch.15, are trusts for certain purposes which are so beneficial to the community that the Attorney General undertakes responsibility for their enforcement. They are accorded special privileges in terms of non-liability to tax, and in terms of perpetual duration. Private trusts, on the other hand, are trusts for persons, the beneficiaries; and the beneficiaries can enforce the trust. It may also be noted here that there are a few anomalous cases in which trusts for non-charitable purposes, usually for the building of monuments or the upkeep of particular animals, have been upheld. Such trusts are usually called non-charitable purpose trusts, or trusts of imperfect obligation. The latter name indicates one of their main anomalies; who will enforce such a trust? These trusts are dealt with in Ch.16.

Private trusts are divided into express, constructive and resulting trusts; and express trusts may be divided into executed and executory, and into completely constituted and incompletely constituted trusts. Sometimes implied trusts are included as a further category of private trusts.[131] This extra category of "implied trusts" serves little purpose, and the examples commonly given might preferably be regarded as express, resulting or constructive trusts, as the case may be. Trusts have often been established although express words to that effect have not been used,[132] yet such trusts are "express" because the settlors intended to create them. Trusts based on the presumed intention of the settlor as, for example, in the case of a voluntary conveyance, are sometimes described as implied trusts, but will here be treated as resulting trusts. Mutual wills are also sometimes described as implied trusts, but will here be treated as constructive trusts.

A.   Express Trusts

2–029   An express trust is one intentionally declared by the creator of the trust, who is known as the settlor, or, if the trust is created by will, the testator. A trust is created by a manifestation of an intention to create a trust; though certain formalities, as will be seen, are required in the case of lifetime trusts of land and of all testamentary trusts.

Two subdivisions of express trusts should be mentioned.

2–030   **i.   Executed and Executory.**   An executed trust is one in which the testator or settlor has marked out in appropriate technical expressions what interests are to be taken by all the beneficiaries. On the other hand, in an executory trust, the execution of some further instrument is required, in order to define the beneficial

---

[130] Historically "public trusts" were not synonymous with charitable trusts. The term referred to the protection of public money from unlawful application. See J. Barratt (2006) 69 M.L.R. 514.

[131] Such a classification at times appears in statutes, for example, Law of Property Act 1925 s.53(2).

[132] See *Paul v Constance* [1977] 1 W.L.R. 527, and the cases discussed under the heading "Certainty of Intention", below, para.4–003.

interests with precision. The property is immediately subject to a valid trust, but it remains executory until the further instrument is duly executed.

The practical significance of the distinction is that while the language of executed trusts is governed by strict rules of construction, executory trusts are construed more liberally. Where, in the case of an executed trust, the settlor has made use of technical expressions, as to the interpretation of which the law has laid down rules, equity will follow the law and give effect to such interpretation.[133] In the case of an executory trust, however, equity will attach less importance to the use or omission of technical words, but will seek to discover the settlor's true intention, and order the preparation of a final deed which gives effect to such intention. It is necessary, however, for the court to be able to ascertain, from the language of the instrument, the trusts which are intended to be imposed on the property.[134]

Executory trusts appeared most commonly in marriage articles, which often provided that certain property belonging to one of the parties should be settled upon them and their children, and in wills. They are rarely met today; due no doubt to the fact that many modern trusts have tax-saving implications, and it is necessary, for such purposes, to be precise and specific in drafting the trust. A rare example from modern times is *Pengelly v Pengelly*,[135] where a testator left property by will on a discretionary trust for a class of beneficiaries as his trustees should decide, to include some or all of his children, grandchildren and their spouses, widows and widowers. The will stated that the settlement was to be established by a deed executed by the trustees no later than two years after his death, and was to contain such powers and provisions as the trustees should decide. As it stood this was not a valid executory trust, as it failed sufficiently to define the class of beneficiaries. However, the court was able to rectify the will[136] by inserting the word "only" before "to include". As the class was thus confined to the specified relatives, the will created a valid immediate executory discretionary trust.

A pension fund trust provides another modern example. In *Davis v Richards & Wallington Industries Ltd*[137] the question arose as to entitlement to surplus funds. A pension scheme had been established by an interim trust deed, which provided for the execution of a definitive trust deed. This deed was later executed, and contained rules as to the entitlement to any surplus, but there was doubt as to its validity. In fact the definitive deed was upheld, but if it had not been, the court would have held the interim deed to be a valid executory trust. This could have been executed by a court order bringing into effect rules corresponding to those in the definitive deed, thereby resolving the issue as to the surplus.

---

[133] *Re Bostock's Settlement* [1921] 2 Ch. 469; see also Law of Property Act 1925 s.60(1); cf. *Re Arden* [1935] Ch. 326.
[134] *Re Flavel's Will Trusts* [1969] 1 W.L.R. 444 at 447 ("for formation of a superannuation and bonus fund for the employees").
[135] [2008] Ch. 375.
[136] Below, Ch.29.
[137] [1990] 1 W.L.R. 1511; disapproved on another point in *Air Jamaica Ltd v Charlton* [1999] 1 W.L.R. 1399.

2–031　　**ii.　Completely and Incompletely Constituted Trusts.**　　There cannot be a trust unless the trust is completely constituted. This heading is therefore irrational; it is dealing, not with two different types of trust, but with a rule for distinguishing what is a trust from something that is void. Nevertheless, it is convenient to make the point here, and to deal in more detail with the matter below.[138]

A trust is only valid if the title to the property is in the trustee and if the trusts have been validly declared. A declaration that A holds on trust for B is ineffective if the property is not vested in A. The trust becomes constituted and valid when the property is vested in A. The form of transfer to A depends on the nature of the property—land, chattel, money, shares in a company, copyrights, patents, debts or other choses in action—and the appropriate method must of course be used.[139] In the case of a trust of land there must also be written evidence of the declaration of trust; otherwise the trust will be unenforceable.[140] The settlor may of course declare herself trustee, and there is then an automatic constitution, because title was in the settlor throughout. Testamentary trusts are always completely constituted; for the executors, if not the trustees themselves, are under a duty to transfer the trust property to the nominated trustees.

Although no trust is created unless the trust is completely constituted, there are situations where intended beneficiaries under an incompletely constituted trust may compel the transfer of the property to the trustees. In general, they can do so if they have given consideration, but not if they are volunteers, for there is yet no trust and "equity will not assist a volunteer".[141]

B.　Resulting Trusts[142]

2–032　　A resulting trust exists where property has been conveyed to another, but the beneficial interest returns, or "results" to the transferor. This may happen in various situations; the simplest one is where the property is conveyed to trustees upon certain trusts which fail or which do not exhaust the whole beneficial interest. The part undisposed of results to the settlor. For example, if there is a gift on trust for X for life and then on trust for Y if Y attains the age of 21, but Y dies under 21 in X's lifetime, the property will result on X's death to the settlor. Such a resulting trust has been described as "automatic",[143] meaning that it arises by operation of law, without depending on the intention of the settlor.

Another category is the "presumed" resulting trust in favour of the transferor where property is conveyed to a volunteer.[144] This presumption of resulting trust is rebuttable by evidence of an intention to make a gift, or, where the volunteer is the transferor's wife or child, by the presumption of advancement.[145]

---

[138]　Below, Ch.5.

[139]　Below, para.5–014 and following.

[140]　Law of Property Act 1925 s.53(1)(b); below, para.6–003.

[141]　Below, Ch.5.

[142]　Below, Ch.11.

[143]　per Megarry J in *Re Vandervell's Trust (No.2)* [1974] Ch. 269 at 291.

[144]　Or in favour of the purchaser, as when X buys property but directs the vendor to transfer the property to Y.

[145]　Below, para.11–026.

C. Constructive Trusts[146]

While express trusts arise from the act of the parties, constructive trusts arise by operation of law. Equity says that in certain circumstances the legal owner of property must hold it on trust for others. The absence of the need for formalities in such circumstances is obvious. There is, however, much dispute and uncertainty as to the occasions on which constructive trusts arise, and also as to their nature.

2–033

The term has indeed been used in different senses. It can cover the duty of a trustee who has obtained benefits by fraud; the obligation of a transferee from an express trustee, unless she proves she was a bona fide purchaser for value without notice, to hold the transferred property on the trusts previously applicable; the obligation of a trustee who has made a profit, however innocently, through his office, to hold such profit for the benefit of his beneficiaries[147]; the position of a stranger to the trust who has dishonestly assisted in a breach of trust[148]; the relationship of vendor and purchaser between the contract and the execution of the conveyance[149]; and other relationships, such as licensees, and claimants to a matrimonial home, where the introduction of a constructive trust was considered to be necessary to enable the court to reach a just solution.[150] A controversial question is whether the "remedial" constructive trust, favoured in some commonwealth jurisdictions, is available to prevent unjust enrichment whenever the personal remedy is inadequate.[151]

D. Bare Trusts[152]

A distinction is sometimes made between bare or simple trusts, on the one hand, and "special" trusts on the other. There is said to be a bare trust when the trustee holds trust property in trust for an adult beneficiary absolutely. In such a situation the beneficiary may call for a conveyance of the legal estate at any time, and the

2–034

---

[146] Below, Ch.12. D. Waters, *The Constructive Trust* (London: Athlone Press, 1964); A. Oakley, *Constructive Trusts*, 3rd edn (London: Sweet and Maxwell, 1996); Y.K. Liew, *Rationalising Constructive Trusts* (Oxford: Hart Publishing, 2017).

[147] *Keech v Sandford* (1726) Sel.Cas. Ch. 61; *Boardman v Phipps* [1967] 2 A.C. 46.

[148] Below, Ch.25.

[149] Below, para.12–008.

[150] *Binions v Evans* [1972] Ch. 359 (licensee); *Eves v Eves* [1975] 1 W.L.R. 1338 (cohabitant); *Re Densham* [1975] 1 W.L.R. 1519 (wife).

[151] The latest view from the Supreme Court is that the remedial constructive trust is not, and should not be, recognised in English law: *FHR European Ventures LLP v Cedar Capital Partners LLC* [2015] A.C. 250 at [47], per Lord Neuberger.

[152] See P. Matthews [2005] P.C.B. 266 & 271.

trustee must comply.[153] In the meantime the trustee has no duties to perform and must deal with the trust property in accordance with the instructions of the beneficiary.[154]

It is said that all other trusts are "special" trusts. The description however, is not generally used except as a mode of contrast with a bare or simple trust.

A bare trust may arise at the outset, as where an absolute owner puts shares or other property into the name of trustees[155] or some other third party[156] to hold for himself. This may arise in a commercial context, as where a solicitor holds money for a client.[157] A trust which was not originally a bare trust may become one when an adult beneficiary becomes absolutely entitled, as on the death of X in a trust for X for life, remainder to Y. A bare trust need not be express, but can take the form of a resulting or constructive trust, as where the settlor fails to declare the beneficial interests[158] or did not intend any beneficial interest to pass to the fraudulent transferee.[159]

A bare trustee into whose name an absolute owner transfers property is sometimes called a "nominee".[160] This must be distinguished from the situation where the trustees vest securities in a nominee in order to facilitate share dealings. Such a person is in effect an agent of the trustees.[161]

E. Trusts in the Higher Sense and Trusts in the Lower Sense

2–035   The word "trust" is used in various contexts which have no relationship to the legal meaning of the term.[162] The Crown may entrust ministers or officials with property, perhaps providing that they shall hold it "in trust" for the benefit of some person or body of persons. While such a situation is capable of creating a trust in the legal or "lower" sense[163]:

> "'[T]rust' is not a term of art in public law and when used in relation to matters which lie within the field of public law, the words 'in trust' may do no more than indicate the existence of a duty owed to the Crown by the officer of state as servant of the Crown, to deal with the

---

[153] As, indeed, could a multiplicity of beneficiaries, all adult and under no disability; *Saunders v Vautier* (1841) 4 Beav. 115; below, para.23–001. See also *Clarence House Ltd v National Westminster Bank Plc* [2010] 1 W.L.R. 1216 ("virtual assignment" of lease whereby "virtual assignor" retained legal title did not create a bare trust for the "virtual assignee", who could not have called for a transfer of the legal estate as this was not permitted by the lease. It was an agency relationship).

[154] *Re Cunningham and Fray* [1891] 2 Ch. 567; D. Hayton (1992) 1 J.I.P. 3.

[155] *Grey v IRC* [1960] A.C. 1.

[156] *Hardoon v Belilios* [1901] A.C. 119; *Ingram v IRC* [2000] 1 A.C. 293.

[157] *Target Holdings Ltd v Redferns (A Firm)* [1996] 1 A.C. 421; *AIB Group (UK) Plc v Mark Redler & Co Solicitors* [2014] UKSC 58; [2015] A.C. 1503.

[158] *Vandervell v IRC* [1967] 2 A.C. 291.

[159] *Hodgson v Marks* [1971] Ch. 892.

[160] See *Ingram v IRC* [2000] 1 A.C. 293 (land conveyed by owner to solicitor as nominee as a step in a tax avoidance scheme).

[161] Below, para.21–012 (delegation of powers). See also custodian trustees at para.21–016, below.

[162] See R. Bartlett [1996] Conv. 186, discussing National Health Service Trusts.

[163] *Town Investments Ltd v Department of the Environment* [1978] A.C. 359 at 382, per Lord Diplock. But the Crown can be a trustee in the "lower sense"; *Civilian War Claimants Association Ltd v R.* [1932] A.C. 14; *Lonrho Exports Ltd v Export Credits Guarantee Department* [1999] Ch. 158.

property for the benefit of the subject for whom it is expressed to be held in trust, such duty being enforced administratively or by disciplinary sanctions and not otherwise; *Kinlock v Secretary of State for India*."[164]

Similarly, it may be alleged that the Crown is trustee for members of the public. In *Tito v Waddell (No.2)*[165] phosphate had been mined on Ocean Island by a British company until 1920, when the mining rights were acquired by the governments of the UK, Australia and New Zealand. The Ocean Islanders claimed that the Crown stood in a fiduciary position to them and was liable for various breaches of trust. The claim failed. Although the relevant documents used the word "trust", their wording was, as a matter of construction, consonant with the creation of a governmental obligation, for the breach of which the court was powerless to give relief. This governmental obligation, or "trust in the higher sense",[166] was not a true trust in the conventional sense. It created no fiduciary obligation, and was not justiciable in the courts.

---

[164] (1882) 7 App.Cas. 619.

[165] [1977] Ch. 106.

[166] The phrase is taken from *Kinlock v Secretary of State for India* (1882) 7 App.Cas. 619 at 625, per Lord Selborne LC. See further *High Commissioner for Pakistan in the United Kingdom v Jah* [2016] EWHC 1465 (Ch) per Henderson J at [46]–[74].

CHAPTER 3

EQUITY AND THE MODERN COMMERCIAL WORLD

1. GENERAL[1]

"In the modern world the trust has become a valuable device in commercial and financial dealings."[2]

3–001

"Trusts are now commonly part of the machinery used in many commercial transactions, for example across the spectrum of wholesale financial markets, where they serve a useful bridging role between the parties involved."[3]

It is important to understand the urgent commercial relevance of trusts: in this chapter, we shall identify some examples of the applications of trusts, and equitable doctrines and remedies more broadly, in commercial contexts.

We shall see these themes arise throughout subsequent chapters but it is appropriate to raise some of the considerations at the outset of our study. We shall particularly address some of the many cases that have come before the courts in the wake of the global financial crisis, and that have required the courts to engage with fundamental principles in complex economic situations.[4] We shall also consider the implications for the law of trusts of legislation responding to concerns about tax evasion and tax avoidance.

The Law Commission noted that:

---

[1] See generally S. Degeling and J. Edelman (eds), *Equity in Commercial Law* (Sydney: Lawbook Co, 2005); D. Hayton (1990) 106 L.Q.R. 87; Sir Anthony Mason (1994) 110 L.Q.R. 238; W. Goodhart (1996) 10 T.L.I. 38; M. Yip and J. Lee (2017) 37 L.S. 647. For an empirical study of "trust proliferation", see A. Hofri-Winogradow (2017) 31 T.L.I. 152.
[2] *Target Holdings v Redferns* [1996] A.C. 421 per Lord Browne-Wilkinson at 435; below, para.3–009.
[3] *AIB Group v Mark Redler & Co Solicitors* [2014] UKSC 58; [2015] A.C. 1503; below, para.3–009.
[4] Below, paras 3–005—3–007. See Lord Hope "A light at the end of the tunnel?—BNY in the UK Supreme Court", Banking and Financial Services Law Association, Gold Coast, Australia, 29 August 2013 (referring to *BNY Ltd v Eurosail Plc* [2013] UKSC 28; [2013] 1 W.L.R. 1408).

> "Trusts are the invention of the English courts and have spread throughout the common law world on account of their potential for flexible management of a wide range of financial relationships. Their history goes back centuries, and the modern world of finance and real property is pervaded by them to the extent that many individuals are trustees, or are the beneficiaries of trusts, without having the slightest ideas that this is the case."[5]

Indeed, the Commission has identified the trust as "an important global legal export bringing a range of business to the UK for lawyers, accountants, banks and trust companies",[6] and at the timing of writing, had proposed a project as part of its Thirteenth Programme of Law Reform called "Modernising Trust Law for a Global Britain", with the aim of "modernising trust law to enhance the competitiveness of this jurisdiction['s] trust services in a global market".[7]

Trusts are primarily about money and the preservation of wealth. The idea of the trust developed as a means for providing for the family. Although the trust still plays a significant role in establishing ownership of property on family breakdown,[8] it cannot "be doubted that equity has moved out of the family home and the settled estate and into the market-place".[9] The challenge for the courts is as to how principles developed in respect of traditional trusts can and should be applied to commercial situations.

A.   The Utility of Trusts

3–002   A major area of activity is in the holding of the property of charities and other non-profit organisations. A modern and significant role has also emerged for the trust in the constitution of pension funds,[10] although such trusts differ from traditional trusts in so far as there is a contractual relationship of employment and the beneficiaries have given consideration.[11] Unit trusts and investment trusts[12] are designed to spread investment risks. Another role is the safeguarding of property belonging to minors and those who lack mental capacity.[13] Thus the trust continues to be a form of property-holding of ever-increasing importance because of its adaptability and convenience in effecting complicated forms of settlement. The words of one judge, writing in the middle of the last century, remain accurate

---

[5] Law Com. No. 315, *Capital and Income in Trusts: Classification and Apportionment* (2009), para.1.1.

[6] Law Com. No. 377, *Thirteenth Programme of Law Reform* (2017), para.2.23.

[7] Law Com. No. 377, *Thirteenth Programme of Law Reform* (2017), para.2.24. It may be noted that the Commission asserts that the law of trusts is "outdated", apparently solely on the basis that some applicable legislation dates to 1925. A further companion project planned on Trust Law Arbitration was not taken forward as part of the 13th Programme: paras 4.55–8.

[8] Below, Ch.13.

[9] Sir Peter Millett (1995) 9 T.L.I. 35 at 36; Sir Anthony Mason (1997–98) 8 K.C.L.J. 1 at 4. H.G. Hanbury (1929) 45 L.Q.R. 196 at 200.

[10] Below, Ch.17.

[11] Below, para.17–005.

[12] Below, para.19–009. For other commercial uses of trusts, see D. Hayton (ed.), *Modern International Developments in Trust Law* (Kluwer Law International, 1999), Ch.8.

[13] Law Com. No. 315, *Capital and Income in Trusts: Classification and Apportionment* (2009), para.1.2.

today: "as the principles of equity permeate the complications of modern life, the nature and variety of trusts ever grow."[14]

If a settlor wishes to give property to his wife for life and after her death to various other members of the family, it would be possible to arrange a system of law by which it could be done without using a trust. Indeed, the early common law did so, in an elementary form. Roman law did so[15]; as do those countries which have followed modernised systems of Roman law.[16]

In England, full use has been made of the convenience of the system whereby the legal estate is in the trustees and the equitable or beneficial ownership is kept separate. We have seen that this is insisted upon for the creation of successive or concurrent interests in land under the 1925 legislation.[17] The legal title can be kept clear of beneficial interests; the land can be sold free of them to a purchaser, who can overreach them. Thus a most elaborate system of beneficial interests can be created without complicating the title to the land.

The same advantages exist with personalty. Most modern settlements deal wholly or partly with personalty in the form of investments. No system of legal future interests in personalty ever developed; for settlements of personalty did not arise until the system of trusts was well advanced. In this sphere also, it is most convenient to separate legal and equitable ownership; by doing so, the trustees can buy and sell shares without the purchaser being concerned with the beneficial interests.[18] The beneficial interests attach to whatever is held by the trustees for the time being.

The role of the Chancery lawyer is to be able to advise on these matters and to create the most appropriate trusts to meet the wishes of the settlor. As Sir Richard Snowden has remarked extra-curially, many of the original ideas of the trust

"still hold good, albeit that in today's world, the tenant and medieval crusader has been replaced by the oligarch, the international businessman and the celebrity, and increasingly the trust is employed in jurisdictions with low rates of taxation or low standards of regulation to keep assets and income away from the attention of creditors and the authorities."[19]

B.   Tax and Transparency

It should never be forgotten that taxation is one factor which dominates all others in the context of the creation of trusts in the modern law. Although the law of equity and trusts can be understood without it, it will be appreciated that the popular forms of trust in recent years have been those which reduce to a minimum the liability to tax.[20] As we have seen above, the trust can offer an

3–003

---

[14] *Re a Solicitor* [1952] Ch. 328 per Roxburgh J at 332.
[15] W.W. Buckland and A.D. McNair: *Roman Law and Common Law*, 2nd edn (Cambridge: Cambridge University Press, 1965), p.173.
[16] See B. Beinart (1980) 1 J.L.H. 6; J. Merryman (1974) 48 Tulane L.Rev. 917.
[17] Above, para.1–047.
[18] No notice of any trust can be entered on the register of shareholders (Companies Act 2006 s.126, re-enacting earlier legislation).
[19] R. Snowden (2017) 31 T.L.I. 99 at 99.
[20] The Finance Act 2006, however, removed many inheritance tax advantages of trusts; below, Ch.10.

attractive flexibility with respect to the organisation of assets.[21] The applicable legislation is considered in Ch.10, but the tax context is relevant throughout this subject and this book.

Trusts and their susceptibility to tax, both within the UK and in off-shore jurisdictions, have come into sharp focus in the period since the last edition of this book, with the publication of investigations into leaks of two tranches of information about so-called "hidden wealth": the "Panama Papers"[22] in 2016 and the "Paradise Papers"[23] in 2017. The investigations also highlighted concerns not only about tax, but also the use of the financial system for organised crime, such as money laundering or the financing of terrorism.

There have been various legislative changes in the wake of concerns highlighted by (though not limited to) these investigations, and significant political pressure for greater transparency in respect of trusts. The Criminal Finances Act 2017 s.1 extends relevant provisions of the Proceeds of Crime Act 2002 to cover circumstances where property is held in trust.[24] At the European level, there is a specific Directive,[25] while off-shore jurisdictions have also responded.[26] While the importance of preventing the funding of criminal activity must be acknowledged, care should be taken to focus on criminal behaviour, including tax evasion, which is illegal. Tax avoidance, however, is not illegal in itself: it can include legitimate tax planning in order to reduce liability legally. The narratives around such controversies often conflate the two,[27] as Professor Lee noted:

> "The effect of the media coverage has left the public believing that those who try to avoid tax legally are no different from those who evade tax and, even more importantly, those who follow measures intended by Parliament to allow taxpayers to minimise their tax bill are somehow 'dodgy'."[28]

---

[21] See e.g. D. Hayton (2015) 29 T.L.I. 30.

[22] J. Garside, H. Watt and D. Pegg, "The Panama Papers: how the world's rich and famous hide their money offshore", *The Guardian*, 3 April 2016.

[23] J. Garside, "Paradise Papers leak reveals secrets of the world elite's hidden wealth", *The Guardian*, 6 November 2017 *https://www.theguardian.com/news/series/paradise-papers* [accessed 4 July 2018]. Numerous media organisations were involved in the investigations, co-ordinated by the International Consortium of Investigative Journalists: the Guardian reports are cited for ease of reference.

[24] By inserting s.326H into the 2002 Act; the Explanatory Notes to the 2017 Act expressly refer to "the former Prime Minister's [David Cameron's] commitment to legislate following the International Consortium of Investigative Journalists (ICIJ) publication of what are known as the 'Panama Papers'".

[25] Directive 2015/849 on the prevention of the use of the financial system for the purposes of money laundering or terrorist financing; the Panama papers were also noted by Wathelet A-G in *Berlioz Investment Fund SA v Directeur de l'administration des contributions directes* [2018] 1 C.M.L.R. 1 at AG2 and fn.3. In the UK, see the Money Laundering, Terrorist Financing and Transfer of Funds (Information on the Payer) Regulations 2017 (SI 2017/692). See S. Wong (2017) 31 T.L.I. 137.

[26] See J. Edmondson [2017] P.C.B. 150.

[27] J. Edmondson [2017] P.C.B. 150 at 150; S. Wong (2017) 31 T.L.I. 137; N. Goh (2017) 36 C.J.Q. 484 (on Singapore). On the position in New Zealand, see M. Littlewood (2017) 31 T.L.I. 113 and [2017] N.Z.L.Rev. 59.

[28] N. Lee [2016] P.C.B. 99 at 99.

The saga has provoked much soul-searching amongst politicians and Chancery lawyers[29]: Sir Richard Snowden has identified in the UK "an increased intolerance of individuals and companies who engage in aggressive tax planning to avoid paying tax, never mind those who engage in tax evasion".[30] The drive for transparency will have significant implications for the operation of the law of trusts in the future[31]: "even the most enthusiastic supporter of the legitimately used trust has to accept that its reputation has not been enhanced by recent events such as the disclosure of the Panama Papers."[32]

B.   Insolvency

We have already seen several examples of the deployment of equitable concepts in commercial contexts. In particular, it was noted that a major consequence of establishing an interest under a trust is that the claimant will take priority in insolvency.[33] If the insolvent company or bankrupt is holding the property on trust for someone else, it does not form part of the assets available to the company or individual's creditors. Of course, the claimant may not be particularly interested in the legal or equitable technicalities of their "interests"— their approach is instrumental: the focus is that the end result is that they have a claim to the money, rather than sharing pro rata with other creditors or falling further behind in the queue.

3–004

In *Barclays Bank Ltd v Quistclose Investments Ltd*,[34] we saw that the House of Lords held that the loan of money for a specific purpose, in circumstances in which it is understood that the money is not to be at the free disposal of the recipient, was capable of giving rise to a trust.[35] In so holding, Lord Wilberforce in part justified this conclusion on the basis of commercial considerations:

> "I can appreciate no reason why the flexible interplay of law and equity cannot let in these practical arrangements, and other variations if desired: it would be to the discredit of both systems if they could not ... I can find no reason why the law should not give effect to it."[36]

Thus in *Quistclose* the lender was able to assert an interest under a trust in its favour, even though the arrangement was not otherwise a secured loan. We shall see in subsequent chapters that the courts pay close attention to the relevance of the insolvency regime and the propriety of recognising proprietary rights in new contexts.[37]

---

[29] D. Russell QC and T. Graham (2016) 22 T. & T. 481; P. Baker [2016] B.T.R. 252; P.L. Cross and B.R.J. Urquhart (2017) 23 T. & T. 8; 9

[30] R. Snowden (2017) 31 T.L.I. 99 at 105.

[31] D. Hayton (2015) 29 T.L.I. 30 at 38, taking the view that the commercial "uses of trusts will continue to grow unaffected in the new age of transparency. It is dynastic family trusts that are most affected in this new age".

[32] T. Lyons [2017] B.T.R. 631 at 631.

[33] Above, para.2–003; see also below, para.4–005.

[34] [1970] A.C. 567.

[35] Above, para.2–009; see also below, para.11–002.

[36] [1970] A.C. 567 at 582.

[37] See, e.g., *Angove's Pty Ltd v Bailey* [2016] UKSC 47; [2016] 1 W.L.R. 3179 per Lord Sumption at [27]–[28]. Below, paras 12–028—12–031.

2. TRUSTS IN THE WAKE OF THE GLOBAL FINANCIAL CRISIS AND THE CREDIT CRUNCH

3–005   In what is a book on modern equity rather than modern equity trading, it is only possible to offer an outline of the situation which arose during the financial crisis of 2007–8 and the associated fall in property markets and the decline in available credit (the "credit crunch").[38] There were various causes of the crisis, and factors which exacerbated it. Of particular relevance is the account in the opening of Rix LJ's judgment in *Westlb AG v Nomura Bank International Plc*[39]:

> "On 15 September 2008 Lehman Brothers in New York went into bankruptcy and world financial markets, which had been in a fragile state for more than a year, went into free fall. In the liquidity crisis which quickly ensued, the so-called 'credit crunch', values became entirely distorted. The best of shares, because they could at least be freely traded, suffered egregious mark-downs in price as their holders strived for liquidity. The worst of shares suffered even more horrendously. Banks, whose transactions had become hugely leveraged and which were in the very crucible of the credit crunch, saw their share price cut to ribbons as they struggled for survival."[40]

The fall of Lehman Brothers specifically has led to a great deal of ongoing litigation, as parties try to salvage their finances from the consequences. There have been five Supreme Court decisions on the saga alone.[41] Those cases have explored various aspects of the interaction between insolvency law and trusts principles. *Belmont Park Investments PTY Ltd v BNY Corporate Trustee Services Ltd*[42] considered the operation of "the anti-deprivation rule", which prevents the withdrawal of assets from an insolvent estate, and the "pari passu rule", which prevents contracting out of the statutory framework for the proper distribution of assets amongst creditors. *BNY Corporate Trustee Services Ltd v Neuberger*

---

[38] A very helpful two-page summary is offered by A. Paolini [2015] J.B.L. 432 at 432–434. For a sophisticated approach to the related European sovereign debt crisis, see P. O'Callaghan (2012) 32 L.S. 642. For a judicial view on the causes of the financial crisis in Ireland, see the judgment of Hardiman J in *Dellway Investments v NAMA* [2011] IESC 14; see also Lord Neuberger MR in *McKillen v Maybourne Finance Ltd* [2012] EWCA Civ 864 at [1].

[39] [2012] EWCA Civ 495.

[40] [2012] EWCA Civ 495 at [1]. See further *UBS AG (London Branch) v Kommunale Wasserwerke Leipzig GmbH* [2014] EWHC 3615 (Comm) per Males J at [520]; *AP-Fonden v Bank of New York Mellon SA/NV* [2013] EWHC 3127 (Comm) per Blair J at [67]; *Horn v Commercial Acceptances Ltd* [2011] EWHC 1757 (Ch), per Peter Smith J at [1]: "The transactions that are the subject matter of the present claim for example took place in 2006 and apart from one or two people with Cassandra like doom laden forecasts of the collapse of the world economy most people would not have expected a property market to fall as much as it did after 2008." *LB Holdings Intermediate 2 Ltd (The Joint Administrators of) v Lomas* [2015] EWCA Civ 485 per Lewison LJ at [1] "The collapse of Lehman Brothers in September 2008 sent shock waves round the financial world." A broader account of the onset of the crisis is offered by Blair J in *Banco Santander Totta SA v Companhia De Carris De Ferro De Lisboa SA* [2016] EWHC 465 (Comm); [2016] 4 W.L.R. 49 at [578]–[592]; I.H.-Y. Chiu [2016] J.B.L. 465 at 467–9.

[41] *Belmont Park Investments PTY Ltd v BNY Corporate Trustee Services Ltd* [2011] UKSC 38; [2012] 1 A.C. 383; *Re Lehman Brothers International (Europe)* [2012] UKSC 6; [2012] W.T.L.R. 1355; *BNY Corporate Trustee Services Ltd v Neuberger Berman Europe Ltd* [2013] UKSC 28; [2013] 1 W.L.R. 1408; *Re Nortel Companies* [2013] UKSC 52; [2014] 1 A.C. 209; and *The Joint Administrators of LB Holdings Intermediate 2 Ltd v The Joint Administrators of Lehman Brothers International (Europe)* [2017] UKSC 38; [2017] 2 W.L.R. 1497.

[42] [2011] UKSC 38; [2012] 1 A.C. 383.

Berman Europe Ltd[43] construed the effect of the provisions s.123 of the Insolvency Act 1986, which were incorporated into loan notes issued by an entity set up by Lehman Brothers. *Re Nortel Companies*[44] concerned the circumstances in which the Pensions Regulator may pursue members of a group of companies in order to provide financial support to a pension scheme deficit. *The Joint Administrators of LB Holdings Intermediate 2 Ltd v The Joint Administrators of Lehman Brothers International (Europe)*[45] concerned a number of issues arising from the insolvency legislation as it applies to administrations. Most relevant for our purposes, however, is the second of the Lehman Brothers appeals to the Supreme Court, *Re Lehman Brothers International (Europe)*.[46] There, Lord Hope observed that the applicable financial services legislation adopted "elementary principles" of English trusts law, such as the requirement of segregation and a corresponding declaration of trust if someone other than the account holder is to establish a proprietary interest in funds held in an account.[47]

An example of the application of these basic equitable principles to a dispute in the wake of the financial crisis is *Mills v Sportsdirect.Com Retail Ltd*.[48]   **3–006**

> SD sought to establish an entitlement to a proprietary interest in shares before the Icelandic bank KSF entered administration in the afternoon of 8 October 2008. SD had previously entered into an arrangement for a complex "securitisation" of shares, which were bought outright by KSF but were held on trust by a nominee, SNL. The shares would be repurchased and resold regularly between the two. Prior to 8 October 2008, there were concerns as to the protection of the assets against the background of the financial crisis and fears that KSF may enter a form of insolvency process (which it subsequently did). In the course of the negotiations over a final repurchase by SD of the shares (for around £16million), SD was principally concerned with the security of the shares, as they did not want to be in a position where they advanced cash but did not immediately receive the shares, such that those shares might be available to KSF's creditors. At one stage in a series of rapid communications between the parties on 8 October 2008,[49] the following conversation took place between a representative of SD and one of KSF:
>
> KSF: "[E]ssentially, we will put all of the stock into your account in the investment management business which is segregated, you provide us with the cash and then we will send it free of payment…"
>
> SD: "And where is it held currently?"
>
> …
>
> KSF: "Currently, it's in Treasury, so that's our account effectively, with that investment management business. So we can transfer that almost immediately."
>
> SD: "How can we get comfort that that legal process is safe and that transaction of moving

---

[43] [2013] UKSC 28; [2013] 1 W.L.R. 1408.

[44] [2013] 1 W.L.R. 1408. The effect of the crisis on investment portfolios and the broader economy also had implications for pensions funds, as seen in cases such as *British Airways Plc v Airways Pension Scheme Trustee Ltd* [2017] EWHC 1191 (Ch); [2017] Pens. L.R. 16 and *IMB United Kingdom Holdings Ltd v Dalgleish* [2017] EWCA Civ 1212; [2018] Pens. L.R. 1. See generally Ch.17.

[45] [2017] UKSC 38; [2017] 2 W.L.R. 1497.

[46] [2012] UKSC 6.

[47] [2012] UKSC 6 at [2]–[3].

[48] *Mills (Administrators of Kaupthing Singer and Friedlander Ltd) v Sportsdirect.Com Retail Ltd* [2010] EWHC 1072 (Ch). Other examples might also be given: Sir Richard Snowden offered *In re Lehman Brothers International (Europe) (In Administration) (No.2)* [2010] Bus. L.R. 489 as his preferred illustration of "judicial attitudes to the trust in a business setting": R. Snowden (2017) 31 T.L.I. 99 at 100.

[49] "If a week is a long time in politics, a quarter of an hour was a long time against the turbulent background of the markets on 8 October" [2010] EWHC 1072 (Ch) at [69].

it into that segregated client account is safe?"
KSF: "That's the crux."
SD: "That is the crux of it yes?"
KSF: "Exactly. I need to send you a note to that effect to give you that comfort."
DF: "And I need legal people to sort of say that it is then ringfenced and secure?"
AL: "Sure."[50]

As an email at 12:51 then confirmed, the shares were then segregated into part of an account expressly designated as SD's client account with a separate entity. Considering these facts, Lewison J found a trust was established in favour of SD,[51] applying an orthodox trust analysis of the kind that we shall consider in Ch.4.[52] SD was the beneficiary of the trust, the property was segregated, and the necessary intention was established. Even in a fast-moving commercial environment, and without a Chancery lawyer's precision, it was clear that the intention of the parties was for SD to acquire what we can recognise as an interest under a trust.

3–007   It will be apparent that the commercial and international dimensions to trusts litigation are significant in understanding the context of current trusts cases. But it should also be appreciated that there is an historical dimension. That point was made by Lord Collins in *Rubin v Eurofinance SA*, an international insolvency law case[53]:

"It is not only in recent times that there have been large insolvency proceedings with significant cross-border implications. Even before then there were the Russian Bank cases in the 1930s (arising out of the nationalisation and dissolution of the banks by the Soviet Government) and the Barcelona Traction case in the 1940s and 1950s ... but there is no doubt that today international co-operation in cross-border insolvencies has become a pressing need. It is only necessary to recall the bankruptcies or liquidations of Bank of Credit and Commerce International, Maxwell Communications, or Lehman Brothers, each with international businesses, assets in many countries, and potentially competing creditors in different countries with different laws. There is not only a need to balance all these interests but also to provide swift and effective remedies to combat the use of cross-border transfers of assets to evade and to defraud creditors."[54]

The global financial crisis and credit crunch were undoubtedly dramatic, "they were, or were a reflection of, a once in a century financial shock",[55] and Blair J

---

[50] [2010] EWHC 1072 (Ch) at [34].
[51] [2010] EWHC 1072 (Ch) at [52]–[73].
[52] An example of these principles applying to a case within the Lehman Brothers saga is *Pearson v Lehman Brothers Finance SA* [2011] EWCA Civ 1544.
[53] [2012] UKSC 46; [2013] 1 A.C. 236.
[54] [2013] 1 A.C. 236 at [14]. See also Rix LJ in *Rubenstein v HSBC Bank Plc* [2012] EWCA Civ 1184 at [117]: "in truth, although the Lehman Brothers collapse was both a symptom and a contributory cause of market turmoil, the underlying causes of that turmoil went infinitely beyond Lehman Brothers' difficulties. It stretched to a failure of confidence in marketable securities in which there had previously been greater confidence. And what is new about that?".
[55] *Abdullah v Credit Suisse (UK) Ltd* [2017] EWHC 3016 (Comm) per Andrew Baker J at [11], describing "financial market conditions in October 2008 [as] extraordinary".

has held that the "only true comparator of the GFC is the stock market crash of 1929 and the ensuing Great Depression, and even that may not be fully apposite".[56]

That said, and fully recognising the magnitude of the financial crisis, fluctuations in the economy and the property markets have occurred previously, and have given rise to legal problems which reverberate today. As well as Lehman Brothers,[57] the examples of BCCI[58] and Maxwell Communications[59] mentioned by Lord Collins have seen important developments in both case law and legislation which we shall consider later in this book.

3.   COMMERCIAL CONTEXTS

A theme which we shall see at various stages in chapters below is the extent to which equitable principles should differ in their application in the commercial context as opposed to the more traditional trusts settled for the family. Here we may take three examples (all of which are explored more fully in the appropriate chapters): consequences of breach of trust, trusts of land in the "domestic consumer context" and the interpretation of documents.

3–008

A.   Consequences of Breach of Trust

It was emphasised in the previous section that the property market goes through periods of buoyancy and periods of stagnation or decline. In the 1996 case of *Bristol & West Building Society v Mothew*,[60] Millett LJ said early in his judgment:

3–009

> "The collapse in the property market which accompanied the recession at the beginning of the present decade caused mortgage lenders to suffer serious losses. Unable to recover their advances from the borrowers or by the enforcement of their security they have sought to recover them from the valuers or solicitors on whose valuations or advice they have relied. In some cases they have been the victims of a fraud to which the valuers and solicitors have been parties. In other cases, such as the present, they have been unable to accuse their solicitor of anything more serious than negligence. Believing that the common law rules of causation and remoteness of damage might not enable them to recover the whole amount of their loss they have turned to equity and alleged breach of trust or fiduciary duty. We have thus been concerned to decide just what is involved in these concepts."

---

[56] *Banco Santander Totta SA v Companhia De Carris De Ferro De Lisboa SA* [2016] EWHC 465 (Comm); [2016] 4 W.L.R. 49 at [592] (quoting Ben Bernanke, Chairman of the US Federal Reserve at the time of the crisis, who regarded the crisis as "was almost certainly the worst in human history").

[57] There is a body of literature on developments in duties and liabilities of directors in the wake of the financial crisis, which "further underscored the severe consequences arising from directors pandering to the short-term interests of shareholders given the alignment of the interests of the former with those of the latter" E. Lim [2018] J.B.L. 169 at 182. See T.N. Al-Tawil (2018) 39 Comp. Law. 165; A. Young and M. Ko (2018) 39 Comp. Law. 58; J. Loughrey (ed.), *Directors' Duties and Shareholder Litigation after the Crisis* (Cheltenham: Edward Elgar, 2012); V. Comino [2018] J.B.L. 15; J. Chown and D. Russell (2017) 23 T. & T. 209; I.H.-Y. Chiu [2016] J.B.L. 465; J. Braithwaite (2016) 132 L.Q.R. 120; B. Clarke (2016) 56 Irish Jurist 139; E. Lee [2017] J.B.L. 473.

[58] See, e.g., *BCCI v Akindele* [2001] Ch. 437; below, para.25–013.

[59] Below, para.17–001.

[60] [1998] Ch. 1.

Referring to that quotation in 2012, HH Judge David Cooke observed at first instance in *AIB Group (UK) Plc v Mark Redler & Co*, that "[t]he issues referred to by Millett LJ have resurfaced and lie behind the present claim".[61] Whereas *Mothew* concerned the fall in the property market in the early 1990s, *AIB* concerned the next major fall in the late 2000s.

The appeal then made its way to the Supreme Court in *AIB Group (UK) Plc v Mark Redler & Co Solicitors*.[62] The basic facts were as follows:

> The solicitors for a bank negligently failed to clear one of the existing charges on a property, which amounted to a breach of trust. As a result, when the borrowers defaulted some years later, and the bank reclaimed the property, the previous charge had to be paid off first, so the Bank lost around £300,000. It was not disputed that the solicitor was liable for that loss. But the Bank also argued that the solicitor should be liable for the Bank's full loss as part of the story overall—the property had dramatically fallen in value during the period of the loan. The argument then was whether the Bank could recover that difference of £2.4 million, even though the full extent of the loss was not causally connected to the breach. The Supreme Court followed the House of Lords authority in *Target Holdings v Referns*[63] and held that the solicitors were only liable for the loss which would not have been caused but for their default.

The case is fully addressed in the relevant chapter below,[64] but we may consider one particular aspect here. In *Target Holdings*, Lord Browne-Wilkinson had seemed to suggest that there may, or ought to, be a divergence in approach to the treatment of trusts which are part of a commercial transaction:

> "It is wrong to lift wholesale the detailed rules developed in the context of traditional trusts and then seek to apply them to trusts of quite a different kind. In the modern world the trust has become a valuable device in commercial and financial dealings. The fundamental principles of equity apply as much to such trusts as they do to the traditional trusts in relation to which those principles were originally formulated. But in my judgment it is important, if the trust is not to be rendered commercially useless, to distinguish between the basic principles of trust law and those specialist rules developed in relation to traditional trusts which are applicable only to such trusts and the rationale of which has no application to trusts of quite a different kind."[65]

In *AIB Group v Mark Redler*, the two opinions for the Supreme Court were delivered by Lord Toulson JSC and Lord Reed JSC. As noted, the general approach in *Target Holdings* was endorsed, on the basis that it would be a "backward step" to depart from it.[66] The Justices also endorsed Lord Browne-Wilkinson's observations on the operation of these principles in the context of commercial trusts. For Lord Toulson, the key difference between a commercial trust and a traditional trust is that the former "arises out of a contract rather than the transfer of property by way of gift".[67] Thus, the contract will closely define and perhaps limit the trustee's duties in a way that may not be the case for a traditional trust. In Lord Toulson's view, Lord Browne-Wilkinson did

---

[61] [2012] EWHC 35 (Ch); [2012] P.N.L.R. 16 at [9].
[62] [2014] UKSC 58; [2015] A.C. 1503.
[63] *Target Holdings Ltd v Redferns* [1996] A.C. 421; below, para.24–009.
[64] Below, paras 24–010—24–013.
[65] [1996] A.C. 421 at 435. See further at 434.
[66] [2015] A.C. 1503 per Lord Toulson at [63].
[67] [2015] A.C. 1503 per Lord Toulson at [70].

not therefore intend that the principles vary according to the nature of the trust, but rather one must take account of the scope and purpose of the trust[68]:

> "the fact that the trust was part of the machinery for the performance of a contract is relevant as a fact in looking at what loss the bank suffered by reason of the breach of trust, because it would be artificial and unreal to look at the trust in isolation from the obligations for which it was brought into being. I do not believe that this requires any departure from proper principles."[69]

As we saw above, the decision in *AIB* is also important from the perspective of the fusion debate.[70] Recognition of the relevance of the commercial context and the contractual relationship between the parties does not necessarily prevent the courts from accepting that "a trust imposes different obligations from a contractual or tortious relationship, in the setting of a different kind of relationship".[71] Nor is the law "clinging atavistically to differences which are explicable only in terms of the historical origin of the relevant rules".[72]

B.   The "Domestic Consumer Context" in the Context of Land[73]

> "In law, 'context is everything' and the domestic context is very different from the commercial world."[74]   **3–010**

A different debate over the appropriateness of commercial considerations has been seen in the area of trusts of the family home. The principles in this area are principally found in two key decisions, that of the House of Lords in *Stack v Dowden*[75] and of the Supreme Court in *Jones v Kernott*.[76] We shall consider them in detail below,[77] but for now we can note that in this area context has been identified as not only important but also as affecting the applicable principles. The cases concerned the consequences of relationship breakdown where an unmarried[78] couple have been cohabiting in a house which has been purchased by one or both of the parties. The majority of the House of Lords in *Stack* decided that the question of beneficial ownership is managed initially by a presumption that the equitable interests match the legal interests.[79] If the property is in the name of one party only, the starting point is that that party is solely entitled to the property. If however the house is in joint names, the presumption is of joint beneficial ownership (50% each). "In the domestic consumer context, a conveyance into joint names indicates both legal and beneficial joint tenancy,

---

[68] [2015] A.C. 1503 at [70].

[69] [2015] A.C. 1503 at [71].

[70] Above, para.1–022. See also See J. Getzler, Ch.10, and D. Hayton, Ch.11, in S. Degeling and J. Edelman (eds.), *Equity in Commercial Law* (2005).

[71] [2015] A.C. 1503 per Lord Reed at [137]. M. Yip and J. Lee (2017) 37 L.S. 647 at 652–657.

[72] [2015] A.C. 1503 per Lord Reed at [138].

[73] N. Hopkins (2011) 31 L.S. 175.

[74] *Stack v Dowden* [2007] 2 A.C. 432, per Lady Hale at [69].

[75] [2007] 2 A.C. 432.

[76] [2011] UKSC 53; [2012] 1 A.C. 776.

[77] Considered below, Ch.13.

[78] See paras 13–003—13–004.

[79] *Stack v Dowden* [2007] 2 A.C. 432 per Lord Hope at [4].

unless and until the contrary is proved".[80] The framework of the common intention constructive trust applies, and it may be possible for a party to establish that the common intention of the parties was that interests should be different, but the burden is on them to do so.[81] The alternative approach, of a resulting trust[82] based on contributions to the purchase price, was rejected for the domestic consumer context.

Lord Neuberger disagreed with the majority's analysis in *Stack v Dowden*,[83] particularly on the isolation of the domestic consumer context as an area for separate judicial treatment[84]:

> "In the absence of statutory provisions to the contrary, the same principles should apply to assess the apportionment of the beneficial interest as between legal co-owners, whether in a sexual, platonic, familial, amicable or commercial relationship. In each type of case, one is concerned with the issue of the ownership of the beneficial interest in property held in the names of two people, who have contributed to its acquisition, retention or value."[85]

However, in both *Stack v Dowden* and *Jones v Kernott*, it was recognised that there will still be scope for the resulting trust in some situations, as where for example the couple were business partners as well as domestic partners.[86] Where there is a commercial (or perhaps "not-domestic") element, the idea that beneficial interests in the property may be quantified in relation to one's financial contributions might be thought to be more justifiable.

But the limits of what counts as the "domestic consumer context" are not clear, and have resulted in a flood of litigation.[87] The cases have included unsuccessful claims by women who helped in the male partner's business[88]; but also a dispute between a mother and daughter buying the mother's council house,[89] and various cases involving complex business empires and familial[90] or intimate relationships.[91] The Supreme Court has yet to reconsider the point since *Kernott*, but in the Privy Council decision of *Marr v Collie*,[92] it was held that "to consign the

---

[80] *Stack v Dowden* [2007] 2 A.C. 432 per Lady Hale at [58]; see too Lord Walker at [33].

[81] *Jones v Kernott* [2011] UKSC 53; [2012] 1 A.C. 776 per Lord Walker and Lady Hale's summary of the law at [51]–[52].

[82] Above, para.2–032; below, para.11–025.

[83] Below, para.13–006.

[84] We shall see that legislative frameworks do provide for the consequences of breakdown in the case of married couples and civil partners: paras 13–003—13–004.

[85] *Stack v Dowden* [2007] 2 A.C. 432 at [107].

[86] *Stack v Dowden* [2007] 2 A.C. 432 per Lord Walker at [32] (citing the High Court of Australia decision in *Muschinski v Dodds* (1985) 160 C.L.R. 583); *Jones v Kernott* [2011] UKSC 53; [2012] 1 A.C. 776 per Lord Walker and Lady Hale at [31].

[87] See below paras 13–018—13–019.

[88] *James v Thomas* [2008] 1 F.L.R. 1598; *Geary v Rankine* [2012] EWCA Civ 555; *Smith v Bottomley* [2013] EWCA Civ 953; *Curran v Collins* [2015] EWCA Civ 404.

[89] *Laskar v Laskar* [2008] 1 W.L.R. 2695.

[90] *Bhura v Bhura* [2014] EWHC 727 (Fam); *Singh v Singh* [2014] EWHC 1060 (Ch).

[91] *Favor Easy Management Ltd v Wu* [2012] EWCA Civ 1464; M. Yip and J. Lee [2013] Conv. 431.

[92] [2017] UKPC 17; [2017] 3 W.L.R. 1507 at [49]; M. George and B. Sloan [2017] Conv. 303; below paras 11–025 and 13–019.

reasoning in *Stack* to the purely domestic setting would be wrong",[93] and the mere presence of a "commercial dimension" did not prevent the application of the principles in *Stack*.[94]

C. Interpretation

A final example of ongoing consideration of the appropriateness of a common approach is to be found in the interpretation of wills. In *Marley v Rawlings*,[95] Lord Neuberger PSC led the court in considering a case involving a mistakenly signed will. A married couple had prepared wills at the same time, but their solicitor mistakenly gave each of them the other's to sign. The result was that the wills were not by themselves valid.[96] The wife died first, and then her husband, and the dispute arose between the legatee under Mr Rawlings' will and the couple's two children. One issue was whether the wills could be interpreted in a way to salvage them. Discussing the proper approach, Lord Neuberger noted recent case law on interpretation in commercial contract cases,[97] which has emphasised the search for the intention of the parties. Turning to wills, his Lordship said

3–011

> "it seems to me that the approach should be the same. Whether the document in question is a commercial contract or a will, the aim is to identify the intention of the party or parties to the document by interpreting the words used in their documentary, factual and commercial context".[98]

Indeed, his Lordship quoted a dictum of Lord Hoffmann on the importance of context in interpretation: "No one has ever made an acontextual statement. There is always some context to any utterance, however meagre."[99] A major exception in the context of wills, however, is that s.21 of the Administration of Justice Act 1982 enables the court to have regard in certain circumstances to extrinsic evidence as to the subjective intention of the testator, which is not permitted in the case of contracts.[100]

---

[93] [2017] 3 W.L.R. 1507 at [39]

[94] [2017] 3 W.L.R. 1507 at [40].

[95] [2014] UKSC 2; [2015] A.C. 129.

[96] The case is discussed fully below, para.29–025.

[97] Most significantly in *Rainy Sky SA v Kookmin Bank* [2011] 1 W.L.R. 2900. See further G. McMeel, *The Construction of Contracts: Interpretation, Implication, and Rectification* (Oxford: Oxford University Press, 2017). For more recent developments, see *Arnold v Britton* [2015] UKSC 36; [2015] A.C. 1619 and *Wood v Capita Insurance Services Ltd* [2017] UKSC 24; [2017] 2 W.L.R. 1095.

[98] [2015] A.C. 129 at [20].

[99] *Kirin-Amgen Inc v Hoechst Marion Roussel Ltd* [2004] UKHL 46; [2005] 1 All E.R. 667 at [64].

[100] [2015] A.C. 129 at [19].

D.   Conclusions

3–012   As indicated in this chapter, the relevance of commercial considerations, and of the context of cases more generally, should be appreciated throughout the study of the law of trusts and equity. In 1997, the former Chief Justice of Australia, Sir Anthony Mason observed:

> "The rise of the modern commercial economy, however, has raised in an acute form important issues concerning the extension and application of equitable doctrines and principles. That is because trusts are created in commercial settings and commercial transactions are so structured that they provide scope for the creation of relationships recognised in equity, with consequences for proprietary remedies and for third parties."[101]

The contemporary importance of trusts in the commercial context is illustrated by three landmark Supreme Court decisions on exactly those points identified by Sir Anthony Mason: *Williams v Central Bank of Nigeria*[102] on the liability of third parties; *FHR European Ventures LLP v Cedar Capital Partners LLC*[103] on proprietary remedies for breach of fiduciary duty; and, as we have seen above, *AIB Group (UK) Plc v Mark Redler & Co Solicitors*[104] on liability for breach of trust. Each of those cases is addressed in the appropriate chapter below, but we may note, with Lord Neuberger, that "equity is alive in the UK Supreme Court".[105] It will also be seen that the relevance and prevalence of commercial reasoning can be argued to pose a challenge to the application of equitable principles in these contexts.[106]

---

[101] (1997–98) 8 K.C.L.J. 1 at 4.

[102] [2014] UKSC 10; [2014] A.C. 1189; below, paras 25–035—25–036.

[103] [2014] UKSC 45; [2015] A.C. 250; below, paras 22–031—22–033; R. Snowden (2017) 31 T.L.I. 99 at 110–112. In a subsequent bribery case applying *FHR, Medsted Associates Ltd v Canaccord Genuity Wealth (International) Ltd* [2017] EWHC 1815 (Comm); [2018] 1 W.L.R. 314, (below, para.22–033) Teare J noted (at [113]) that the Panama Papers had revealed the identities of the shareholders of one of the companies involved.

[104] [2014] UKSC 58; [2015] A.C. 1503; below, paras 24–010—24–013.

[105] Lord Neuberger, "Equity—The soul and spirit of all law or a roguish thing?" Lehane Lecture 2014, Supreme Court of New South Wales, Sydney, 4 August 2014.

[106] M. Yip and J. Lee (2017) 37 L.S. 647; cf. R. Snowden (2017) 31 T.L.I. 99 at 112.

PART II

TRUSTS AND POWERS

CHAPTER 4

CERTAINTY AND CAPACITY

1. CERTAINTY

A PRIVATE express trust can only be created if the three certainties[1] are present; **4–001** certainty of intention; certainty of subject-matter; and certainty of objects. In addition to the three certainties, a trust must be validly constituted (meaning that the trust property must be vested in those intended to be trustees of it), and any necessary formalities must be satisfied. Those matters will be considered in Chs 5 and 6. It should also be noted that an otherwise-valid trust may fail if it contravenes the law; this is discussed in Ch.14.

The three certainties will be considered in turn below. Different considerations **4–002** apply to each, but they are inter-related.

> "Uncertainty in the subject of the gift has a reflex action upon the previous words, and shows doubt upon the intention of the testator, and seems to show that he could not possibly have intended his words of confidence, hope, or whatever they may be—his appeal to the conscience of the first taker—to be imperative words."[2]

Similar, but distinct, questions about certainty may arise in relation to a conditional gift; whether a condition precedent to taking,[3] or a condition of defeasance.[4] Further, the requirement of certainty of beneficiaries operates differently with discretionary as opposed to fixed trusts, and with trusts for

---

[1] See Lord Langdale in *Knight v Knight* (1840) 3 Beav. 148 at 173. Extrinsic evidence is not generally admissible to aid the construction of a trust deed; *Rabin v Gerson Berger Association Ltd* [1986] 1 W.L.R. 526.

[2] *Mussoorie Bank v Raynor* (1882) 7 App.Cas. 321 at 331. See also *North v Wilkinson* [2018] EWCA Civ 161 at [21], [24] (difficulties with certainty of subject-matter, being an undivided percentage share of a sole trader's business, cast doubt on whether a trust was truly intended).

[3] *Re Allen* [1953] Ch. 810; *Re Barlow's WT* [1979] 1 W.L.R. 278.

[4] *Clayton v Ramsden* [1943] A.C. 320; *Blathwayt v Lord Cawley* [1976] A.C. 397.

purposes as opposed to trusts for people. A trust for a non-charitable purpose is normally invalid; but where such a trust has been upheld, the court has insisted that the purpose be described with sufficient certainty.[5] With charitable trusts, there is no need to specify in any way which charity is to be benefited; but the language of the gift must clearly establish that the gift is applicable for charitable purposes only.[6]

A.   Certainty of Intention

4–003   We have already seen that a trustee is under an obligation, but that the obligation may be inferred from the nature of the gift, considered as a whole.[7] Technical words are not required. The question is whether, on the proper construction of the words used, the settlor or testator has shown a serious intention to create a trust, in the sense of the legal relationship recognised as a trust. A trust may be created without using the word "trust", and, conversely, the use of the word "trust" does not conclusively indicate the existence of a trust.[8] The settlor's subjective intentions are irrelevant in this respect: if she enters into arrangements which have the effect of creating a trust, it is not necessary that she should appreciate that; it suffices that she intends to enter into them.[9] A "precatory" expression of hope or desire, or suggestion or request, is not sufficient. ("Precatory" comes from the Latin verb meaning "to pray"). The words in each case must be examined to see whether the intention was to impose a trust upon the donee.

The Court of Chancery at one time leaned in favour of construing expressions of desire as intended to create a binding trust.[10] This was because an executor who had administered an estate was entitled to keep for himself any surplus which was undisposed of by the will, and the court was ready to find that he took as trustee in order to prevent this. This approach then spread beyond executors. In 1830, however, the Executors Act provided that undisposed-of residue should be held on trust for the next-of-kin; and from about the middle of the 19th century, a stricter construction was placed upon these "precatory words". Where, however, an express trust is construed from precatory words, it is, of course, just as much a trust as any other.[11]

Very old cases are therefore unhelpful as guides to construction in this area. *Lambe v Eames*[12] is usually regarded as the case which marks the "turning of the tide". There the testator gave his estate to his widow, "to be at her disposal in any way she may think best, for the benefit of herself and her family." By her will she gave part of the estate outside the family; it was held that she had been absolutely

---

[5] *Re Astor's ST* [1952] Ch. 534; below, para.16–013.

[6] Below, para.15–003. Charities Act 2011 s.1(1)(a).

[7] Above, para.2–021. In the context of charity, see *Re Cohen* [1973] 1 W.L.R. 415.

[8] *Tito v Waddell (No.2)* [1977] Ch. 106, above, para.2–035; *Customs and Excise Commissioners v Richmond Theatre Management Ltd* [1995] S.T.C. 257, above, para.2–011; *Singha v Heer* [2016] EWCA Civ 424; [2016] W.T.L.R. 1189 at [62]; cf. *Byrnes v Kendle* (2011) 243 C.L.R. 253.

[9] *Twinsectra Ltd v Yardley* [2002] 2 A.C. 164; *Bellis v Challinor* [2015] EWCA Civ 59 at 59.

[10] See, however, *Cook v Fountain* (1676) 3 Swan. 585.

[11] In *Re Williams* [1897] 2 Ch. 12 at 27 Rigby LJ protested against the use of the term "precatory trust", calling it a "misleading nickname".

[12] (1871) L.R. 6 Ch. 597. See also *Re Hamilton* [1895] 2 Ch. 370 at 374.

entitled to the property and that the gift was valid. Similarly, in *Re Adams and the Kensington Vestry*,[13] where a testator gave his estate:

> "unto and to the absolute use of my dear wife, Harriet … in full confidence that she will do what is right as to the disposal thereof between my children, either in her lifetime or by will after her decease."

The Court of Appeal held that she took absolutely.

But a trust will be found from precatory words if on a proper construction of the language that was the intention of the testator.

In *Comiskey v Bowring-Hanbury*,[14] a testator gave to his wife: **4–004**

> "the whole of my real and personal estate… in full confidence that… at her death she will devise it to such one or more of my nieces as she may think fit and in default of any disposition by her thereof by her will… I hereby direct that all my estate and property acquired by her under this my will shall at her death be equally divided among the surviving said nieces."

A majority of the House of Lords held that the testator intended to make a gift to his wife, with a gift over of the whole property at her death to such of her nieces as should survive her, shared according to the wife's will, and otherwise equally.

Where a form of words has once been held to create a trust, the testator's intention may be held to be such as to reach the same result, at any rate where the words were used as a precedent, even though the words used, when subjected to the stricter modern construction, might be expected to produce a different result.[15] Such cases are unusual, but the testator's intention is demonstrated by the deliberate attempt to use a valid phrasing to establish the trust.

Where the words used are held not to create a trust, the donee of the property takes beneficially.[16] This must be distinguished from the situation where there is certainty of intention to create a trust, but uncertainty as to the beneficiaries or the shares they are to take. In such cases, as we shall see, there is a resulting trust.

Where a testator leaves to his or her spouse or civil partner an interest in property which is in terms absolute, but by the same instrument purports to give his or her issue an interest in the same property, s.22 of the Administration of Justice Act 1982 provides that the spouse takes absolutely, in the absence of a contrary intention. This presumption did not apply where a testator left a bungalow "in trust for my wife", and then provided that it should be sold on her death and the proceeds shared between his children. The gift to the wife was not in terms absolute, as it was clear on a fair reading of the will that she was intended to have a life interest only.[17]

---

[13] (1884) 27 Ch.D. 394; *Mussoorie Bank v Raynor* (1882) 7 App.Cas. 321 ("feeling confident that she will act justly to our children in distributing the same"); *Re Diggles* (1888) 39 Ch.D. 253 ("it is my desire that she allows … an annuity of £25"); *Re Johnson* [1939] 2 All E.R. 458 ("I request that my mother will on her death leave the property or what remains of it … to my four sisters").
[14] [1905] A.C. 84.
[15] *Re Steele's WT* [1948] Ch. 603; following *Shelley v Shelley* (1868) L.R. 6 Eq. 540.
[16] *Lassence v Tierney* (1849) 1 Mac. & Cr. 551; *Hancock v Watson* [1902] A.C. 14; *Watson v Holland* [1985] 1 All E.R. 290; cf. *Re Pugh's WT* [1967] 1 W.L.R. 1261.
[17] *Harrison v Gibson* [2006] 1 W.L.R. 1212.

The question of certainty of intention may also arise where there is no document to construe. The question then is whether the acts or words of the parties indicate an intention to create a trust; as where a man tells his cohabitant that she can share his bank account[18]; or where a mail order company puts money sent by customers into a separate bank account.[19] This aspect of the problem will be discussed in Ch.5, where the requirements of the declaration of trust are examined.

Finally, the intention to create a trust must be genuine, and not a sham, as where the "settlor" did not intend the trust to be acted upon, but entered into it for some ulterior motive, such as deceiving creditors or the tax authorities.

> In *Midland Bank Plc v Wyatt*[20] a declaration of trust was executed by a husband and wife in 1987 (when the husband was contemplating a new business) whereby the family home, their only real asset, was apparently settled on the wife and daughters. The document was kept in a safe and the couple continued to act as absolute owners of the property, in particular by mortgaging it. The husband's business failed and the bank obtained a charging order against the house. The husband then revealed the trust document. This was held to be a sham. The inference was that the husband had "kept it up his sleeve for a rainy day" in order to defeat future creditors and had not otherwise intended it to have any effect.

This principle does not require a finding of fraud, and can apply if the transaction is the result of merely mistaken advice. Where the settlor and trustees are different persons, there will be no sham unless the trustees shared the settlor's intentions,[21] or at least did not care what they were signing.[22] A trust which was not a sham when created cannot later become one.[23] However, a sham trust could become genuine at a later stage, for example if new trustees (not knowing of the intentions of the settlor and the original trustees) exercised their powers and duties in accordance with its terms. The trust would be genuine as from their appointment.[24]

---

[18] *Paul v Constance* [1977] 1 W.L.R. 527. See also *Re Vandervell's Trusts (No.2)* [1974] Ch. 269; *Swain v The Law Society* [1983] 1 A.C. 598.

[19] *Re Kayford Ltd (In Liquidation)* [1975] 1 W.L.R. 279, above, para.2–010; cf. *Re Challoner Club (In Liquidation), The Times*, 4 November 1997 (no trust where members' money paid into separate account as terms of intended trust uncertain). See also *R. v Clowes (No.2)* [1994] 2 All E.R. 316 (terms of investment brochures indicated a trust); *Re Lewis's of Leicester Ltd* [1995] 1 B.C.L.C. 428 (company created trust by paying takings of concessionaires into separate account, although its commission had not been deducted from the payments, thus the company was also a beneficiary).

[20] [1995] 1 F.L.R. 696. See also *Re Pfrimmer Estate* (1936) 2 D.L.R. 460; *Rahman v Chase Bank (CI) Trust Co Ltd* [1991] J.L.R. 103 (Jersey); *Official Assignee in Bankruptcy v Wilson* [2008] W.T.L.R. 1235 (NZCA).

[21] *Shalson v Russo* [2005] Ch. 281; *Re the Esteem Settlement* [2004] W.T.L.R. 1 (Jersey Royal Court); *A v A* [2007] 2 F.L.R. 467; *JSC Mezhdunarodniy Promyshlenniy Bank v Pugachev* [2017] EWHC 2426 (Ch) (where the trustees were companies, so a further question of attribution arose). See generally M. Conaglen (2008) 67 C.L.J. 176; S. Douglas and B. McFarlane in R. Hickey and H. Conway (eds), *Modern Studies in Property Law vol 9* (Oxford: Hart Publishing, 2017), Ch.13.

[22] *A v A* [2007] 2 F.L.R. 467.

[23] *Shalson v Russo* [2005] Ch. 281.

[24] *A v A* [2007] 2 F.L.R. 467.

B.   Certainty of Subject-matter

The subject-matter of the trust may be an interest in land; it may be chattels or   **4–005**
money; it may be a chose in action, such as a covenant[25] or a debt owed to the
settlor. Whatever form it takes, it must be specified with reasonable certainty.
Testamentary gifts have failed where they concerned "the bulk of my estate",[26] or
"such parts of my estate as she shall not have sold",[27] or "the remaining part of
what is left"[28] or "all my other houses",[29] i.e. those remaining after a choice had
been made by another beneficiary who died before choosing. Similarly a
direction that the testator's widow was to get "such minimal part of [the] estate as
she might be entitled to under English law for maintenance purposes" was void
for uncertainty, as no such entitlement could be identified.[30] These cases should
be contrasted with one where the subject-matter of the gift is to be determined in
the discretion of a trustee. In *Re Golay's Will Trusts*,[31] a gift directing the
executors to allow a beneficiary to "enjoy one of my flats during her lifetime and
to receive a reasonable income from my other properties" was upheld. The
executors could select the flat. The words "reasonable income" were not intended
to allow the trustees to make a subjective decision: but they provided a sufficient
objective determinant to enable the court, if necessary, to quantify the amount.
The problem, however, is that no objective determination of words such as
"reasonable" can be made unless the context is known. In *Re Golay's Will Trusts*
it was assumed that the criterion was the beneficiary's previous standard of
living. The word "reasonable" in isolation has little meaning. If a testator were to
give "a reasonable legacy" to X, then no doubt the gift would fail, unless it was
clear that the amount was to be fixed by the executors.

Where the subject-matter of the trust is uncertain, then no trust is created.
There is nothing to form the subject-matter of a resulting trust. If the purported
trust has been attached to an absolute gift, then the absolute gift takes effect. It
may be, however, that the property itself is certain, but the beneficial shares are
not. Unless the trustees have a discretion to determine the amounts, then the trust
will fail, and the property will be held on a resulting trust for the settlor. This was
the case in *Boyce v Boyce*,[32] where the determination was to be made by a
beneficiary who died before choosing. Sometimes the problem will be solved by
the principle that equity is equality,[33] or by the court determining what is the
proper division according to the circumstances.[34]

---

[25] *Fletcher v Fletcher* (1844) 4 Hare 67; below, para.5–025. See also *Swift v Dairywise Farms Ltd*
[2000] 1 W.L.R. 1177 (trust of milk quota).

[26] *Palmer v Simmonds* (1854) 2 Drew. 221. See also *Choithram (T) International SA v Pagarani*
[2000] 1 W.L.R. 1 (left open whether trust of "all my wealth" void for uncertainty).

[27] *Re Jones* [1898] 1 Ch. 438; cf. *In the Estate of Last* [1958] P. 137 ("anything that is left" created
valid remainder interest).

[28] *Sprange v Barnard* (1789) 2 Bro.C.C. 585.

[29] *Boyce v Boyce* (1849) 16 Sim. 476.

[30] *Anthony v Donges* [1998] 2 F.L.R. 775.

[31] [1965] 1 W.L.R. 969.

[32] (1849) 6 Sim. 476.

[33] *Burrough v Philcox* (1840) 5 Myl. & Cr. 72.

[34] *McPhail v Doulton* [1971] A.C. 424 (selection of beneficiaries); below, para.4–010.

Certainty of subject-matter has been an issue more recently not only in relation to express trusts but also in the commercial context of the sale of goods. Where purchasers have paid for goods but have not taken delivery prior to the seller's insolvency, they may seek to gain priority over general creditors by claiming a trust of the goods in their favour. Where the goods have not been segregated but form part of a bulk, these claims failed (prior to a legislative reform mentioned below) on the ground that there cannot be a trust of unidentified chattels. Thus in *Re London Wine Co*[35] the buyers of wine stored in a warehouse and not segregated from the general stock of similar wine could not establish a trust. It was otherwise where the wine had been segregated for a group of customers (even though not appropriated to each individual customer), as in *Re Stapylton Fletcher Ltd*,[36] although the judge warned that the court:

"must be very cautious in devising equitable interests and remedies which erode the statutory scheme for distribution on insolvency. It cannot do it because of some perceived injustice arising as a consequence only of the insolvency."[37]

In that case the legal title had passed to the customers and there was no need to consider the trust argument.

The leading authority is *Re Goldcorp Exchange Ltd*,[38] where purchasers of bullion, who had paid but had not taken delivery, asserted proprietary rights on the insolvency of the company. Save for a group of customers whose bullion had been segregated, these claims were rejected by the Privy Council. Legal title had not passed, nor was there any trust, as there was no identifiable property to which any trust could attach. Thus the customers were unsecured creditors.

4–006   Although no doubt some chattels can be regarded as identical to other chattels of the same description, the rationale of the rule that there cannot be a trust of chattels which have not been segregated from a mass of similar chattels is that they are not necessarily identical. Even bottles of wine of the same label may not be identical; some may be "corked" and undrinkable. Legislation provides that purchasers who have paid for unascertained goods forming part of an identified bulk (where the goods are interchangeable) acquire property rights as tenants in common of the bulk, subject to any contrary agreement.[39] Thus they will prevail over general creditors in an insolvency. This provision does not, however, apply to the creation of express trusts of chattels.

The chattels rule does not apply to money, shares and other choses in action because, in the nature of things, there is no difference between one pound and another pound, or one share and another share of the same class in the same company.[40] Difficult problems do, however, arise.

---

[35] (1986) Palmer's Company Cases 121.

[36] [1994] 1 W.L.R. 1181 (tenancy in common).

[37] [1994] 1 W.L.R. 1181 at 1203.

[38] [1995] 1 A.C. 74; L. Sealy (1994) 53 C.L.J. 443.

[39] Sale of Goods Act 1979 ss.20A, 20B; inserted by the Sale of Goods (Amendment) Act 1995.

[40] Although they are often distinguishable by serial number. See L. Smith, *The Law of Tracing* (1997), p.224.

In *Hunter v Moss*[41] the settlor owned 950 shares in M Co, which had an issued share capital of 1,000. He orally declared a trust of 5% of the share capital, i.e. 50 shares. The Court of Appeal upheld the trust. Provided the shares were of the same class and in the same company, there was no need to segregate 50 shares before declaring the trust. *Re London Wine Co*[42] was distinguished as involving chattels. Cases upholding bequests[43] of part of a larger shareholding showed that the chattels rule did not apply to choses in action. Thus a declaration of trust of part of a larger shareholding or £50 out of a designated bank account with a larger balance would be valid. In fact the settlor had subsequently sold the shares to B Co in exchange for shares in B Co and cash, and the judgment was for 5% of the consideration.

The decision has been criticised, but before considering the criticisms it is necessary to examine a different situation, where a settlor attempts to create a trust of money but (unlike in the bank account example above) does not designate the source of the money. In *MacJordan Construction Ltd v Brookmount Erostin Ltd*[44] a building contract provided that the employer would retain 3% of the contract price as trustee for the builder (pending confirmation that the work was satisfactory). The retention fund was never set up. On the employer's insolvency the builder claimed entitlement to the retention money in priority to a bank which had a floating charge over all the assets. This claim failed because no identifiable assets had been impressed with a trust for the builder. There was merely a contractual right, which did not "carry with it any equitable interest of a security character in the assets for the time being of the employer."[45] This is clearly correct, being in effect no different from an attempt by X to declare himself trustee of £100 for Y without identifying the source of the money. Thus in *Hemmens v Wilson Browne (A Firm)*[46] a document purporting to give A the right to call on B for payment of £110,000 at any time did not create a trust (or any other right) because there was no identifiable fund to form its subject-matter.

Criticisms of *Hunter v Moss* point to the difficulties which could arise on subsequent dealings with the shareholding or bank account of which an unsegregated part is subject to a trust. Before any such dealings, the beneficiary could call for a transfer of the money or shares. But what would happen if, after declaring a trust of 50 out of 950 shares, the settlor then sold 50 shares and invested the proceeds (disastrously or profitably)? Whose 50 shares were they? There seems no reason why the tracing rules relating to mixed assets should not apply.[47] Those rules normally deal with trust property which has subsequently become mixed with other property, but there seems no reason why they should be so confined. In any event, it could be said that a settlor who declares a trust of part of his shareholding or bank balance becomes under a duty to segregate the trust assets from his own. Tracing will not work, on the other hand, in a case like *MacJordan* because there is no identifiable mixed fund; the employer there had only one bank account in credit at the insolvency but had never assumed an

4–007

---

[41] [1994] 1 W.L.R. 452; J. Martin [1996] Conv. 223.

[42] (1986) Palmer's Company Cases 121.

[43] *Re Cheadle* [1900] 2 Ch. 620; *Re Clifford* [1912] 1 Ch. 29. These are considered distinguishable in M. Ockelton (1994) 53 C.L.J. 448.

[44] [1992] B.C.L.C. 350.

[45] *MacJordan Construction Ltd v Brookmount Erostin Ltd* [1992] B.C.L.C. 350.

[46] [1995] Ch. 223 (a professional negligence action).

[47] Below, para.26–015.

obligation to set up the retention fund out of that account.[48] It may be that the tracing rules will not always work in a case like *Hunter v Moss*, but inability to trace need not mean that there was no valid trust in the first place.

It has been said that the approval of *MacJordan* by the Privy Council in *Re Goldcorp Exchange Ltd*[49] shows by inference that *Hunter v Moss* is incorrect.[50] This would be so only if *Hunter v Moss* and *MacJordan* were indistinguishable, but the discussion above sought to establish that *Hunter v Moss* may be distinguished on the basis that the larger asset from which the trust was carved was identified. It is submitted that the *Hunter v Moss* solution is fair, sensible and workable.[51] Unlike the other cases, it did not involve a claim by unsecured creditors to gain priority in insolvency. It is an example of the court's policy of preventing a clearly intended trust from failing for uncertainty.[52]

The academic criticisms of *Hunter v Moss* were noted with some sympathy by the High Court in the context of insolvency in *Re Harvard Securities Ltd (In Liquidation)*,[53] but the decision was regarded as binding and not effectively overruled by *Re Goldcorp*. It was noted that, after the latter decision, the House of Lords had refused the defendant in *Hunter v Moss* leave to appeal.[54] *Hunter v Moss* was referred to without disapproval in the Court of Appeal in part of the Lehman Brothers litigation, where Arden LJ said that "the shareholding was in existence, the shares were fungible [interchangeable] and thus the trust property could be identified".[55] It was also applied in the High Court in a family dispute, where a declaration of trust of 4,000 shares out of a 12,500 holding was held to have been made. The decision was upheld on appeal, but this aspect was not in issue.[56] *Hunter v Moss* has been followed in New South Wales after a full review of the academic opinions and of decisions in various jurisdictions. A declaration of trust of shares which formed part of a larger holding was upheld:

> "Given the nature of shares in a company, it is perfectly sensible to talk about an individual having a beneficial interest in 220,000 shares out of a parcel of 1.5 million, even if it is not possible to identify individual shares that are held on trust."[57]

Of course, there is no difficulty in a trust of a co-owned share, but that solution was rejected in *Hunter v Moss*: the claimant was held to be equitable owner of 50

---

[48] Below, para.26–017.

[49] [1995] 1 A.C. 74.

[50] D. Hayton (1994) 110 L.Q.R. 335; P. Birks (1995) 9 T.L.I. 43 at 45.

[51] See A. Clarke (1995) 48 C.L.P. 117; P. Parkinson (2002) 61 C.L.J. 657 at 663–676.

[52] See *Re Golay's WT* [1965] 1 W.L.R. 969; above, para.4–005; *Re Tepper's WT* [1987] Ch. 358; below, para.4–014.

[53] [1997] 2 B.C.L.C. 369; T. Villiers (1998–9) 9 K.C.L.J. 112.

[54] [1994] 1 W.L.R. 614.

[55] *Lehman Brothers International (Europe) (In Administration) v CRC Credit Fund Ltd* [2010] EWCA Civ 917; [2011] Bus. L.R. 277 at [171]; see also *Pearson v Lehman Brothers Finance SA* [2011] EWCA Civ 1544 at [69]; *North v Wilkinson* [2018] EWCA Civ 161 at [21].

[56] *Shah v Shah* [2010] EWHC 313 (Ch); affirmed [2010] EWCA Civ 1408; [2011] W.T.L.R. 519.

[57] *White v Shortall* (2006) 68 N.S.W.L.R. 650 at [212]. Campbell J agreed with the outcome in *Hunter v Moss*, although he did not find the reasoning to be "sufficiently persuasive" at [191]. In *Pearson v Lehman Brothers Finance SA* [2010] EWHC 2914 (Ch) at [232], Briggs J approved Campbell J's alternative reasoning to the same result (point noted but not examined on appeal [2011] EWCA Civ 1544 at [71]).

shares, and not to have a tenancy in common interest in the whole holding. Professor Goode has cogently argued that intangible assets such as shares of the same issue or a bank deposit can only be held (if not by a sole owner) in co-ownership.[58] Shares of the same issue are no more than fractions of a single asset, the share capital. A bank deposit (a debt owed by the bank) is a single asset. Thus a declaration of trust (or transfer) of a number of shares of the same issue or part of a bank balance must create co-ownership of the single asset and cannot be attacked for uncertainty of subject-matter on grounds of failure to segregate. As there is a single asset, segregation is not necessary (or indeed possible) for the creation of a co-owned share.

Before leaving the question of certainty of subject-matter, it might be said that uncertainty as to the precise scope of property subjected to a secret trust,[59] a trust arising under mutual wills,[60] a constructive trust of a family home,[61] or a proprietary estoppel claim,[62] has not proved fatal to its validity. Insistence on strict rules in these contexts could facilitate fraud or unjust enrichment.

C. Certainty of Objects: The Beneficiaries[63]

"It is clear law that a trust (other than a charitable trust) must be for ascertainable beneficiaries."[64] The test to be applied to determine certainty of objects depends upon the nature of the trust. With a "fixed" trust, it is, and always has been, that a trust is void unless it is possible to ascertain every beneficiary. With a discretionary trust, the House of Lords decided in *McPhail v Doulton*[65] that the test was: can it be said with certainty that any individual is or is not a member of the class?[66] That is the same test as was established for certainty of objects of a mere power in *Re Gulbenkian's Settlements*.[67] This assimilation of the tests for powers and discretionary trusts destroyed what used to be one of the most important reasons for distinguishing between trusts and powers.[68]

4–008

i. Fixed Trusts. A fixed trust is one in which the share or interest of the beneficiaries is specified in the instrument. The beneficiary is the owner of the equitable interest allocated to him or her. This situation is contrasted with a discretionary trust; where the trustees hold the trust property on trust for such member or members of a class of beneficiaries as they shall in their absolute

4–009

---

[58] [2003] L.M.C.L.Q. 379. Co-ownership is the legislative solution for goods; above, para.4–006.

[59] *Ottaway v Norman* [1972] Ch. 698, below, para.6–025.

[60] *Re Cleaver* [1981] 1 W.L.R. 939, below, para.12–012.

[61] *Gissing v Gissing* [1971] A.C. 886 at 909; *Stokes v Anderson* [1991] 1 F.L.R. 391. Likewise remedial constructive trusts, where they are recognised; *Fortex Group Ltd v MacIntosh* [1998] 3 N.Z.L.R. 171.

[62] *Thorner v Major* [2009] 1 W.L.R. 776; below, para.30–023.

[63] H. Cohen (1971) 24 C.L.P. 133; J. Harris (1971) 87 L.Q.R. 31; J. Hopkins (1971) 29 C.L.J. 68; Y. Grbich (1974) 37 M.L.R. 643; L. McKay (1973) 7 V.U.W.L.R. 258; C. Emery (1982) 98 L.Q.R. 551; Law Com. No. 58 para.63. For the position in Australia, see P. Creighton (2000) 22 Syd.L.R. 93.

[64] *Re Vandervell's Trusts (No.2)* [1974] Ch. 269 at 319, per Lord Denning; *Re Wood* [1949] Ch. 498.

[65] [1971] A.C. 424.

[66] *McPhail v Doulton* [1971] A.C. 424 at 454, 456, per Lord Wilberforce.

[67] [1970] A.C. 508; below, para.4–010.

[68] *Re Gestetner Settlement* [1953] Ch. 672.

discretion determine. In that situation, no beneficiary owns any part of the trust fund unless and until the trustees have exercised their discretion in that beneficiary's favour.[69]

Commonly, but not necessarily, there is a fixed trust where there are successive interests in favour of individual beneficiaries; such as a trust for A for life and then for B absolutely. Where there is a gift for a class, it is necessary in the case of a fixed trust to lay down what share each beneficiary is to take; a discretionary trust will provide for the trustees to exercise a discretion in the selection of a beneficiary. The requirement of certainty in discretionary trusts is considered in (ii) below. The point here is that if trust property is to be divided among a class of beneficiaries in equal (or in any other fixed) shares, the trust cannot, in the nature of things, be administered unless the number and identify of beneficiaries are known. Some of the language in *McPhail v Doulton*[70] might suggest the decision applied to all trusts. But it concerned a discretionary trust and the cases which it examines are cases of discretionary trusts.[71] Although the rule of certainty should be the minimum necessary to make the trust workable, a stricter rule is needed for fixed trusts. How could the trustee or the court administer a trust for "my employees, ex-employees and their relatives and dependants in equal shares"?[72] It has since been confirmed that, in the case of a fixed trust, it must be possible to identify each member of the class of beneficiaries.[73]

To summarise the position, what is required of a fixed trust is that the description of beneficiaries should involve neither conceptual nor evidential uncertainty.[74] But the court will strive to uphold the trust and a common-sense approach will be taken.[75] Furthermore, provided that the identity of the beneficiaries is known, it is no objection that their whereabouts or continued existence is not discoverable, as their shares can be paid into court.[76] The requirement is that a list will be able to be drawn, which is on the balance of probabilities complete, as to the maximum number of shares, at the time for distribution.

4–010   **ii.   Discretionary Trusts.**   The rule of certainty should be no stricter than is necessary to permit trustees to perform their duties. We have seen that, where the trust property is to be divided into specific shares, it is necessary for the trustees to know exactly how many beneficiaries there are. Until 1971, the same rule

---

[69] Below, para.9–013.

[70] [1971] A.C. 424; below, para.4–010.

[71] *Re Ogden* [1933] Ch. 678; *IRC v Broadway Cottages Trust* [1955] Ch. 20.

[72] *McPhail v Doulton* [1971] A.C. 424. See P. Matthews [1984] Conv. 22 and (2006) 122 L.Q.R. 268 at 276, suggesting that complete ascertainment is not necessary in the case of fixed trusts. This is doubted in J. Martin [1984] Conv. 304 and D. Hayton [1984] Conv. 307.

[73] *OT Computers Ltd v First National Tricity Finance Ltd* [2007] W.T.L.R. 165 at 174 (decided 2003) (a trust for "urgent suppliers" of a company in financial difficulty was insufficiently certain, whereas another trust for "customers" was allowed).

[74] Below, para.4–012.

[75] See *Gold v Hill* [1999] 1 F.L.R. 54 (oral direction to recipient to "look after Carol and the kids" sufficiently certain although it could be interpreted in various ways).

[76] C. Emery (1982) 98 L.Q.R. 551; cf. P. Matthews [1984] Conv. 22.

applied to discretionary trusts[77] (sometimes confusingly called "trust powers"[78]). If the trustees should fail or refuse to carry out their duty to select the beneficiaries and distribute, the court must be able to do so; and, it was argued, the court would necessarily distribute equally on the basis that equality is equity and, for that purpose, the beneficiaries must be identifiable.[79] The fallacy of this argument was shown in *McPhail v Doulton*.[80]

> Bertram Baden executed a deed establishing a fund to provide benefits for the staff of a company and their relatives and dependants. Clause 9(a) provided as follows:
>
> > "The trustees shall apply the net income of the fund in making at their absolute discretion grants to or for the benefit of any of the officers and employees or ex-officers or ex-employees of the company or to any relatives or dependants of any such persons in such amounts at such times and on such conditions (if any) as they think fit."
>
> The trustees were not obliged to exhaust the income of any year. Capital could be realised for the purpose of making grants if the income was insufficient.

The deed created a discretionary trust not a mere power. It was not possible to make a list of all the members of the class of beneficiaries. The House of Lords, however, held that the test for certainty in discretionary trusts was that applied to fiduciary powers in *Re Gulbenkian's Settlements*.[81] "Can it be said with certainty that any given individual is or is not a member of the class?"[82] The case was referred to the Chancery Division to determine whether the test was satisfied by the wording of clause 9(a). The Court of Appeal held that it was.[83]

In reaching a decision on the question of the test to be applied, it was necessary to deal with two main arguments in favour of the stricter test. First, that a trustee's duty to distribute could only be performed if the trustee was able to consider every possible claimant; and secondly, that the court could only execute the trust, on failure of the trustees to do so, by equal division of the fund. If these arguments could be answered, there was much to be said for assimilating the test with that for powers; for, although the distinction between trust and power is, in some contexts, basic to a lawyer, it is often difficult to ascertain which exists in any particular case. Thus a relaxation of the test was needed to save many trusts from failure.

A trustee's duty to distribute requires a consideration of the claims of possible recipients.   **4–011**

> "If [a trustee] has to distribute the whole of a fund's income, he must necessarily make a wider and more systematic survey than if his duty is expressed in terms of a power to make grants"[84];

---

[77] *IRC v Broadway Cottages Trust* [1955] Ch. 20.
[78] For a possible distinction between these two terms, see below, para.4–021.
[79] *McPhail v Doulton* [1971] A.C. 424 at 442, per Lord Hodson.
[80] [1971] A.C. 424; F. Crane (1970) 34 Conv.(N.S.) 287.
[81] [1970] A.C. 508.
[82] per Lord Wilberforce [1971] A.C. 424 at 454, 456.
[83] [1973] Ch. 9; below, para.4–012.
[84] [1971] A.C. 424 at 449, 457; (1971) 87 L.Q.R. 31 at 61–62.

and

> "a wider and more comprehensive range of inquiry is called for in the case of a trust power than in the case of a power."[85]

But the difference is only one of degree; there is no need for a trustee of a discretionary trust to "require the preparation of a complete list of names".[86] The difference does not justify a stricter rule for certainty in discretionary trusts.

The main question is whether the court can execute the trust upon the failure of the trustees to do so. This is primarily a theoretical problem. In the reported cases there have been no examples of trustees refusing to execute a discretionary trust; if a trustee did so, he or she could be removed and replaced. Secondly, "it does not follow that execution is impossible unless there can be equal division."[87] There are a number of cases, prior to 1801,[88] in which the court exercised a discretion in relation to distribution, deciding in accordance with guidance given by the circumstances of the case.[89] In many of these situations equal division would have been inappropriate. As indeed it would be in modern forms of discretionary trusts for the benefit of employees and their dependants. It would have been paradoxical if the trust in *McPhail v Doulton* had failed because of the court's inability to divide equally; for equal division would have been a nonsensical solution. Thus, the court, if called upon to execute a discretionary trust, will do so in the manner best calculated to give effect to the testator's intentions.

> "It may do so by appointing new trustees, or by authorising or directing representative persons of the classes of beneficiaries to prepare a scheme of distribution, or even, should the proper basis for distribution appear, by itself directing the trustees so to distribute."[90]

In cases where the trustees have failed to exercise their discretion within a reasonable time, the court may direct them to do so, provided there is no evidence of bias or obstinacy.[91] There is therefore no need to require a stricter rule for discretionary trusts than that which is applicable to powers.

It is thought that this less stringent test will also apply to purpose trusts upheld on the principle of *Re Denley's Trust Deed*[92] as being for the benefit of ascertainable individuals. It has been held that the strict test does not apply to

---

[85] [1973] Ch. 9 at 27.

[86] [1971] A.C. 424 at 449.

[87] [1971] A.C. 424 at 451.

[88] *Kemp v Kemp* (1801) 5 Ves.Jr. 849.

[89] *Mosely v Mosely* (1673) Fin. 53; *Clarke v Turner* (1694) Free Ch. 198; *Warburton v Warburton* (1702) 4 Bro.P.C. 1; *Richardson v Chapman* (1760) 7 Bro.P.C. 318.

[90] [1971] A.C. 424 at 457, per Lord Wilberforce. See also *Mettoy Pension Trustees Ltd v Evans* [1990] 1 W.L.R. 1587, holding that the court has similar powers of intervention in the case of fiduciary powers.

[91] *Re Locker's Settlement* [1977] 1 W.L.R. 1323; (1978) 94 L.Q.R. 177. The distribution must be in favour of those who were objects at the time the discretion should have been exercised. It is otherwise in the case of a mere power, where the default gift will operate if the power is not exercised within the proper time limits.

[92] [1969] 1 Ch. 373, below, para.16–002. See *R. v District Auditor Ex p. West Yorkshire Metropolitan CC* (1986) 26 R.V.R. 24, holding that "administrative unworkability" (below) was fatal to a *Re Denley* type of purpose trust.

Quistclose trusts.[93] Lord Millett has analysed such a trust as a resulting trust for the lender, subject to a power or mandate to apply the property for a specified purpose. Provided the power is sufficiently certain to enable the court to determine whether it is capable of being carried out or if the money has been misapplied, it is valid. If the power is uncertain, there is simply a resulting trust for the lender.[94]

iii.   Conceptual Uncertainty[95] and Evidential Difficulties.   In *Re Baden's Deed Trusts (No.2)*, Brightman J,[96] and then the Court of Appeal,[97] had to apply the test laid down by the House of Lords, and consider in particular whether the words "dependants" and "relatives" were too uncertain. In applying the test, "it is essential to bear in mind the difference between conceptual uncertainty and evidential difficulties."[98] The test is concerned with the former; "the court is never defeated by evidential uncertainty."[99] The illustration given of a conceptual question is that of the contrasting cases "someone under a moral obligation", which is conceptually uncertain and "first cousins", which is conceptually certain.[100] It would be possible in the latter case, but not in the former, to say with certainty "that any given individual is or is not a member of the class".[101] It is no objection that it may be difficult to establish whether or not any given person satisfies the description, so long as the description is conceptually clear.[102] In each case the precise words must of course be examined to see whether the test is satisfied. Once the class is determined as being conceptually certain the question of inclusion is an issue of fact. "Relatives" and "dependants" were both sufficiently certain.

4–012

Provided the class is certain in the above sense, it does not matter that the whereabouts or continued existence of an object is not known.[103]

iv.   Problems with the Test.   The test is not without its difficulties, theoretical and practical.

4–013

(a)   What is Conceptually Certain?   Different minds may take different views on the question of whether a particular description is conceptually certain or not. Indeed, the illustrations referred to above,[104] which were selected to make the point, are not wholly persuasive. The problem is that few descriptions of the kind likely to be encountered in trusts and powers are so clear as to admit of no

4–014

---

[93] Above, para.2–009.

[94] *Twinsectra Ltd v Yardley* [2002] 2 A.C. 164 (power to apply in acquisition of property).

[95] Sometimes called linguistic or semantic uncertainty.

[96] [1972] Ch. 607.

[97] [1973] Ch. 9; D. Hayton (1973) 36 Conv.(N.S.) 351.

[98] per Sachs LJ [1973] Ch. 9 at 19; see also, per Lord Wilberforce [1971] A.C. 424 at 457.

[99] [1973] Ch. 9 at 20; in *Re Tuck's ST* [1978] Ch. 49 at 59, Lord Denning MR in the context of a condition precedent, confessed that he found "the dichotomy most unfortunate".

[100] [1973] Ch. 9.

[101] Above, para.4–010.

[102] This is discussed further below. Such evidential difficulties would, however, invalidate a fixed trust; above, para.4–009.

[103] *Re Gulbenkian's Settlement Trusts* [1970] A.C. 508; C. Emery (1982) 98 L.Q.R. 551.

[104] Above, para.4–012.

borderline cases. Most fall between those which are indisputably certain, for example "Nobel prize winners", and those which are conceptually unclear, for example "friends". To insist on complete certainty would be to defeat most gifts. Dispositions ought if possible to be upheld and "should not be held void on a peradventure".[105] Words such as "relatives" may cause difficulties, but trustees can be expected to act sensibly and not to select a remote kinsman.[106] The best solution, it is submitted, is to regard such words as conceptually certain, leaving it to the claimant to establish his or her case, as discussed below. Words such as "friends", on the other hand, must fall on the wrong side of the line. Although "old friends" was upheld in *Re Gibbard*,[107] this was the result of applying a test which has not survived later decisions,[108] namely that it was sufficient that there was some person who could be shown to be within the class. Browne-Wilkinson J, in *Re Barlow's Will Trusts*,[109] attempted to clarify who a "friend" was. But that was in the context of a gift subject to a condition precedent, which, as we shall see,[110] is governed by a less strict test.

Conceptual uncertainty may in some cases be cured by a provision that the opinion of a third party (the trustees or another person) is to settle the matter. The provision is more likely to be upheld where the settlor (or testator) leaves the definition of a term to the third party as opposed to leaving it to the third party to determine the meaning the settlor himself intended it to have. In the former case, the settlor in effect adopts the meaning ascribed by the third party.[111] In *Re Coxen*,[112] it was held that the testator could validly make the trustees' opinion the criterion provided he had sufficiently defined the state of affairs on which they were to form their opinion. The question whether the testator's wife had "ceased permanently to reside" at a property passed this test, whereas in *Re Jones*[113] the question whether X should at any time have a "social or other relationship" with Y in the "uncontrolled opinion" of the trustees was insufficiently defined to enable the trustees to come to a proper decision. A gift to persons "having a moral claim" on the donor would be conceptually uncertain, but a gift to "such persons as the company may consider to have a moral claim" on the donor would satisfy the test.[114] Similarly, any uncertainty in the requirement of being of the Jewish faith and married to an "approved wife" could potentially be cured by a provision that disputes were to be decided by a Chief Rabbi.[115] The settlor or testator

---

[105] *Re Hay's Settlement Trusts* [1982] 1 W.L.R. 202 at 212.

[106] *Re Baden's Deed Trusts (No.2)* [1973] Ch. 9.

[107] [1967] 1 W.L.R. 42. See also *Re Byron's Settlement* [1891] 3 Ch. 474 (bare power).

[108] See *Re Gulbenkian's Settlement Trusts* [1970] A.C. 508.

[109] [1979] 1 W.L.R. 278. It was said that a trust or power in favour of "friends" would probably fail. See also *Re Byron's Settlement* [1891] 3 Ch. 474.

[110] Below, para.4–022.

[111] Thomas, *Powers*, 2nd edn (2012), paras 4.29–4.40.

[112] [1948] Ch. 747 at 761–762 (condition subsequent).

[113] [1953] Ch. 125 (condition subsequent).

[114] *Re Leek* [1969] 1 Ch. 563; cf. *Re Wright's WT* (1981) 78 L.S.Gaz. 841 (Gift to trustees "for such people and institutions as they think have helped me or my late husband" uncertain. There was an appeal on the issue of severance; below, para.4–019). See also *Re Coates* [1955] Ch. 495 (for any friends the testator's wife might feel he had forgotten). In the case of a discretionary trust, difficulties might arise if the court is called upon to execute it.

[115] *Re Tuck's Settlement Trusts* [1978] Ch. 49 (Lord Denning viewed the provision as being cured by the reference to the Chief Rabbi; in fact the majority held that the condition was in any event certain).

cannot, however, purport to oust the jurisdiction of the court by giving the trustees conclusive power to construe the words used.[116] Such a clause will be void as contrary to public policy. Assuming the power to resolve an uncertainty has been validly given to trustees, the court may intervene if it is exercised in bad faith, and possibly on other grounds.[117]

(b) Proof of Inclusion and Exclusion; Proving Negatives. Read strictly, the **4–015** test means that it must be possible to show either that any person is within the class or that she is not within it. But, how could you show that a person is, for example, not your relative? In *Re Baden's Deed Trusts (No.2)*,[118] Sachs LJ said that the claimant needs to show that she is within the class; if she cannot do that, she is not within it. His Lordship was here referring to evidential uncertainty. Clearly, conceptual uncertainty cannot be cured by casting the onus of proof on to the claimant, because the matter would not be susceptible of proof.[119]

Megaw LJ said that the test was satisfied[120]:

> "if, as regards at least a substantial number of objects, it can be said with certainty that they fall within the trust; even though, as regards a substantial number of other persons ... the answer would have to be, not 'they are outside the trust,' but 'it is not proven whether they are in or out'."

His Lordship recognised that the test could not be satisfied by mere proof that a single person fell within the class; that would be to return to the *Gibbard*[121] test which was rejected in *Gulbenkian*.[122] On the other hand, to require proof that any given person was or was not within the class would be to in substance return to the old rule necessitating a complete list. Hence the "substantial number of objects" standard.

Both Sachs LJ and Megaw LJ preferred a more liberal interpretation of the test than Stamp LJ. Stamp LJ considered that the test did indeed require trustees to be able to say affirmatively whether any given person is within or outside the class. His Lordship considered that the validity or invalidity of a discretionary trust depended on[123]:

> "whether you can say of any individual—and the accent must be on that word 'any' for it is not simply the individual whose claim you are considering who is spoken of—[that she] 'is or is not a member of the class,' for only thus can you make a survey of the range of objects or possible beneficiaries."

See also *Re Tepper's Will Trusts* [1987] Ch. 358, holding that the meaning of "Jewish faith" could be elucidated by extrinsic evidence of the faith as practised by the testator; cf. Administration of Justice Act 1982 s.21.

[116] *Re Wynn* [1952] Ch. 271; *Re Raven* [1915] 1 Ch. 673.

[117] Below, para.18–045.

[118] [1973] Ch. 9; and see J. Hopkins (1973) 31 C.L.J. 36.

[119] cf. *Re Barlow's Will Trusts* [1979] 1 W.L.R. 278; below, para.4–022.

[120] [1973] Ch. 9 at 24.

[121] [1967] 1 W.L.R. 42.

[122] [1970] A.C. 508.

[123] [1973] Ch. 9 at 28.

Stamp LJ agreed with the majority that the particular clause in question was valid; however, this was only because he felt able to construe "relatives" as meaning "next-of-kin" or "nearest blood relations".[124] Otherwise, he would have held the trust void for uncertainty.[125]

4–016   *(c)   Width of the Class; Administrative Unworkability.*[126]   Lord Wilberforce in *McPhail v Doulton*[127] indicated that there might be a difference in one situation between the test to be applied to discretionary trusts and that for mere powers. A description of beneficiaries which might comply with the certainty test laid down might be "so hopelessly wide as not to form 'anything like a class', so that the trust is administratively unworkable,"[128] and he hesitatingly gave as an example a class consisting of "all the residents of Greater London". This was said in the context of a discretionary trust. The question has arisen whether this concept applies also to mere powers. Buckley LJ assumed obiter that it did in *Blausten v IRC*.[129] This was doubted in *Re Manisty's Settlement*,[130] where Templeman J held that a mere power could not be invalid on the ground of width of numbers, preferring the view that its validity should depend on whether or not it was capricious. This point is discussed below. *Manisty* was preferred to *Blausten* by Megarry VC in *Re Hay's Settlement Trusts*.[131] A mere power, whether or not fiduciary, was not invalid on the ground of the size of the class. Mere numbers could not prevent the trustee from considering whether to exercise the power, nor from performing his other duties,[132] nor prevent the court from controlling him. But it was suggested that a discretionary trust in favour of the same wide class[133] as the mere power would have been void as administratively unworkable, as the duties of a discretionary trustee were more stringent, and the objects of a discretionary trust had rights of enforcement which objects of a mere power lacked. A similar view was taken in *R. v District Auditor Ex p. West Yorkshire Metropolitan CC*,[134] where a local authority, purporting to act under statutory powers, resolved to set up a trust "for the benefit of any or all or some of the

---

[124] The view of the majority was that it meant "descendants from a common ancestor", and was conceptually certain.

[125] It has long been established that "relatives" should be confined to next of kin only if this is necessary to save the gift, e.g. where the "list test" applies. See *Re Shield's WT* [1974] 2 W.L.R. 885; *Re Barlow's WT* [1979] 1 W.L.R. 278; *Re Poulton's WT* [1987] 1 W.L.R. 795.

[126] See S. Gardner (1991) 107 L.Q.R. 214 at 218: "it is not easy to see just what difficulty it is aimed at pre-empting".

[127] [1971] A.C. 424; criticised on this point in L. McKay (1974) 38 Conv.(N.S.) 269; Y. Grbich (1974) 37 M.L.R. 643.

[128] *McPhail v Doulton* [1971] A.C. 424 at 427.

[129] [1972] Ch. 256. The power was upheld because the trustees' power to include any other person as an object was subject to the settlor's consent. The settlor had, therefore, put "metes and bounds" on the otherwise unrestricted class.

[130] [1974] Ch. 17. In *Re Beatty's WT* [1990] 1 W.L.R. 1503; J. Martin [1991] Conv. 138, a fiduciary power given to trustees in favour of "such person or persons as they think fit" was upheld without mention of the concept of administrative unworkability.

[131] [1982] 1 W.L.R. 202.

[132] i.e. to make no unauthorised appointment; to consider the range of objects; to consider the appropriateness of any individual appointment.

[133] Any person except the settlor, settlor's spouse or trustees.

[134] (1986) 26 R.V.R. 24 (QBD); C. Harpum (1986) 45 C.L.J. 391.

inhabitants of the County of West Yorkshire".[135] There were 2,500,000 potential beneficiaries. The court was prepared to assume that "inhabitant" was sufficiently certain, but held the trust void for administrative unworkability as the class was far too large, applying Lord Wilberforce's dictum in *McPhail v Doulton*. *Re Manisty's Settlement* was distinguished as concerning a power, where the function of the court was more restricted. The weight of authority, therefore, supports the view that "administrative unworkability" can invalidate discretionary trusts but not mere powers.

(d) Capriciousness. There is no general principle of English law that a capricious disposition is invalid. Wigram VC in *Bird v Luckie*[136] said:

4–017

> "No man is bound to make a will in such a manner as to deserve approbation from the prudent, the wise, or the good. A testator is permitted to be capricious and improvident, and moreover is at liberty to conceal the circumstances and the motives by which he has been actuated in his dispositions."

But while a capricious legacy may be valid, the position may be otherwise in a discretionary trust or power. Unlike an outright gift, discretionary trusts and powers involve fiduciary obligations, the performance of which may be rendered impossible if their terms are capricious. In upholding a power of great width in *Re Manisty's Settlement*,[137] Templeman J held that the terms of the power need not provide guidance to the trustees; an absolute discretion did not preclude a sensible consideration of whether and how to exercise the power. The example of a class comprising "residents of Greater London" would be capricious and void, not on the basis of numbers, but on the ground that the terms of the power negatived any sensible intention on the settlor's part and any sensible consideration by the trustees. The objects must either be unlimited, in which case the trustees can perform their obligations sensibly, or limited to a "sensible" class. The disposition would be void if membership of the class of objects was accidental and irrelevant to any purpose or to any method of limiting or selecting beneficiaries.[138]

Is "capriciousness" the same notion as "administrative unworkability"? The latter, as we have seen, has been held inapplicable to mere powers, while the former has been held applicable to both mere powers and discretionary trusts.[139] In *R. v District Auditor Ex p. West Yorkshire Metropolitan CC*,[140] a trust for the benefit of 2,500,000 inhabitants of West Yorkshire was held void for administrative unworkability (as being too large a class), even though it was not

---

[135] The details of the trust, which was not charitable, are given below, para.16–003.

[136] (1850) 8 Hare 301. See also *Re James's Will Trusts* [1962] Ch. 226; *Nathan v Leonard* [2003] 1 W.L.R. 827 at 831: "a testator may dispose of his property as he wishes, however capriciously".

[137] [1974] Ch. 17.

[138] [1974] Ch. 17 at 26. See A. Grubb [1982] Conv. 432 at 435 explaining that the "appointment criteria", necessary to avoid invalidity on the ground of capriciousness, need not be apparent from the power itself.

[139] See *Re Manisty's Settlement* [1974] Ch. 17; *Re Hay's Settlement Trusts* [1982] 1 W.L.R. 202.

[140] (1986) 26 R.V.R. 24; C. Harpum (1986) 45 C.L.J. 391; above, para.4–016. See also *Re Harding* [2007] EWHC 3 (Ch); [2008] Ch. 235 at [15], where a trust for so large a class as the Black community in four London boroughs would have been void as unworkable had it not been held charitable.

capricious because the local authority (the settlor) had every reason to wish to benefit the inhabitants in the ways specified. Thus it appears that the two concepts are distinct, although the same example may give rise to invalidity on both grounds. Capriciousness has no necessary connection with width of numbers, which is the characteristic of administrative unworkability.

It might also be mentioned that the capricious exercise of a fiduciary power or trust, as where objects are chosen by height or complexion, will be invalid even though the power or trust is valid.[141]

4–018   *(e) Duty to Survey the Field.*   Clearly the trustees of a discretionary trust are not obliged to consider every object, as the trust may be valid although the identity of all the objects is not known. But as we have seen, Lord Wilberforce in *McPhail v Doulton*[142] considered that the trustees ought to make such a survey of the range of objects as would enable them to carry out their fiduciary duty, and that a wider or more comprehensive range of enquiry was called for in the case of discretionary trusts than in the case of powers. In the case of a wide-ranging discretionary trust, where the number of objects may run to hundreds of thousands, the trustees' duty is to assess, in a business-like way, "the size of the problem".[143] Megarry VC in *Re Hay's Settlement Trusts*[144] said:

> "The trustee must not simply proceed to exercise the power in favour of such of the objects as happen to be at hand or claim his attention. He must first consider what persons or classes of persons are objects of the power... there is no need to compile a complete list of the objects, or even to make an accurate assessment of the number of them: what is needed is an appreciation of the width of the field, and thus whether a selection is to be made merely from a dozen or, instead, from thousands or millions... Only when the trustee has applied his mind to the 'size of the problem' should he then consider in individual cases whether, in relation to other possible claimants, a particular grant is appropriate. In doing this, no doubt he should not prefer the undeserving to the deserving; but he is not required to make an exact calculation whether, as between deserving claimants, A is more deserving than B."

This was the duty which had emerged from cases concerning discretionary trusts, but "plainly the requirements for a mere power cannot be more stringent than those for a discretionary trust."[145] The duties of a trustee of a discretionary trust are more stringent than those of the donee of a fiduciary power because of the obligation to distribute. The precise scope of the less onerous duty to survey in the case of a power awaits clarification.[146]

---

[141] *Re Manisty's Settlement* [1974] Ch. 17; *Re Hay's Settlement Trusts* [1982] 1 W.L.R. 202.

[142] [1971] A.C. 424.

[143] *Re Baden's Deed Trusts (No.2)* [1973] Ch. 9 at 20 (per Sachs LJ).

[144] [1982] 1 W.L.R. 202 at 209–210.

[145] [1982] 1 W.L.R. 202 at 209–210. This may be contrasted with the view of Harman J in *Re Gestetner* [1953] Ch. 672 at 688: "there is no obligation on the trustees to do more than consider from time to time the merits of such persons of the specified class as are known to them." See also Templeman J in *Re Manisty's Settlement* [1974] Ch. 17 at 25.

[146] See A. Grubb [1982] Conv. 432 at 437, suggesting that the duty is merely to consider those who press claims and present themselves for inspection; there is no need to "go forth and search out worthy candidates". Presumably this duty arises only if the donee has decided to exercise the power. Also see Thomas, *Powers*, 2nd edn (2012), paras 10.05–10.20.

(f) Many Certain Categories; One Uncertain. Further difficulties could arise **4–019** with a definition of a class of beneficiaries which contained a long series of categories which complied with the *McPhail v Doulton* test, but to which there was added one category which did not. What, for example, would the court say to a trust in the same language as that in *McPhail v Doulton* but to which there was added "and any of my old friends", which is, let it be assumed, conceptually uncertain? The same problem could arise in a case of power.

In this situation, the class as the whole does not satisfy the test. It would however be unfortunate to declare the whole trust void because of the final addition. After all, the trust is workable as it is. Such a trust, however, may be held void unless it is possible to excise the offending phrase by severance: this suggestion has sometimes been made,[147] but the severance principle has yet to be established. Thus in *Re Wright's Will Trusts*,[148] where the class consisted of identifiable named charities and other bodies which could not be identified, the Court of Appeal refused to give effect to the gift in favour of the named charities only.

v. Effect of Certainty Test on Rights of Objects. When, prior to *McPhail v* **4–020** *Doulton*,[149] complete ascertainment of objects was required in the case of a discretionary trust, it was thought that each object had a right to be considered, and to share in the fund if the trustees failed in their duty to exercise their discretion. Clearly this is no longer accurate, now that the trust may be valid without the necessity of ascertaining the full membership of the class. The question of equal division in default of exercise has already been dealt with.[150] Any right to be considered must be confined to the situation where the claim is brought to the attention of the trustees. The right of the object is simply to require that the trustees perform their obligation to allocate the fund after surveying the range of objects, as described above.[151] If the unknown or unascertainable object is not considered by the trustees, at any rate he is no worse off than he would have been prior to *McPhail v Doulton*, when the possibility of his existence would have caused the discretionary trust to fail.

vi. Trust Powers in the Old Sense; Trusts with a Power of Selection. If, as **4–021** a matter of construction, it can be inferred that the settlor's intention was that the entire class should take if the trustee failed to make a selection, then no doubt equal division is still appropriate, in which case the "complete ascertainment" test must still be satisfied. This is more likely to be the case in a family trust, where the objects are not large in number, as in *Burrough v Philcox*.[152] It may be that the

---

[147] per Sachs LJ in *Re Leek* [1969] 1 Ch. 563 at 586 (assuming, however, that legislation would be required); and in the case of a power (Winn LJ) in *Re Gulbenkian's Settlements* [1968] Ch. 126 at 138 (CA). cf. decisions on trusts which are not exclusively charitable; below, para.15–063.

[148] (1999) 13 T.L.I. 48 (decided 1982); above, para.4–014.

[149] [1971] A.C. 424.

[150] Above, para.4–011.

[151] See generally *Re Hay's Settlement Trusts* [1982] 1 W.L.R. 202; *Turner v Turner* [1984] Ch. 100; *Murphy v Murphy* [1999] 1 W.L.R. 282 (undesirable for trustees to be "badgered" with claims by many beneficiaries).

[152] (1840) 5 Myl. & Cr. 72; above, para.2–025.

minority and the majority in *McPhail v Doulton* were talking at cross-purposes, the former having in mind the more old-fashioned "trust power" as described above, while the latter analysed the modern discretionary trust in favour of a large class, where the settlor could not have contemplated equal division.[153]

4–022   **vii. Gifts Subject to a Condition Precedent.**   A less strict test applies where there is a gift subject to a condition precedent as opposed to a discretionary trust or power. A degree of conceptual uncertainty does not invalidate such a gift.[154] The test, as laid down in *Re Allen*,[155] is that the gift is valid if it is possible to say that one or more persons qualify, even though there may be difficulty as to others.

This test was considered by Browne-Wilkinson J in *Re Barlow's Will Trust*,[156] where the testatrix left a valuable collection of paintings, directing her executor to sell those not specifically bequeathed, subject to a proviso that "any friends of mine who may wish to do so" be allowed to purchase any of them at a price below the market value. This disposition was held sufficiently certain. Total ascertainment of the testatrix's friends was not required. A "friend" was a person who had a relationship of long standing with the testatrix, which was a social as opposed to a business or professional relationship; and who had met her frequently when circumstances permitted.[157] The effect of the gift was to confer on her friends a series of options to purchase. There was no legal necessity to inform them of their rights, although this would be desirable. Any claimant must prove "by any reasonable test" that he or she qualified.[158] In case of doubt, the executors could apply to the court for directions. The justification for this less strict test was that in the case of individual gifts, unlike trusts and powers, uncertainty as to some beneficiaries did not affect the quantum of the gift in respect of those who clearly qualified. To uphold the gift in the case of the latter gave effect, at least in part, to the donor's intention.[159]

Although the "condition precedent" test is now settled, this decision illustrates the difficulties inherent in it. The trustees could be in real difficulty in giving effect to such a disposition. The solution that trustees could apply to court in cases of doubt is unsatisfactory. How can the court be in any better position than the trustees to pronounce on the question whether X is a "friend" of Y?[160]

---

[153] See Y. Grbich (1974) 37 M.L.R. 643; C. Emery (1982) 98 L.Q.R. 551. For the proper meaning of "trust power", see R. Bartlett and C. Stebbings [1984] Conv. 227.

[154] A stricter test applies to a condition subsequent. The distinction, though criticised by Lord Denning MR in *Re Tuck's Settlement Trusts* [1978] Ch. 49, was acknowledged by the House of Lords in *Blaithwayt v Lord Cawley* [1976] A.C. 397 at 425; below, para.14–005 and following. See also *Re Tepper's Will Trusts* [1987] Ch. 358; *Ellis v Chief Adjudication Officer* [1998] 1 F.L.R. 184.

[155] [1953] Ch. 810.

[156] [1979] 1 W.L.R. 278; criticised by L. McKay [1980] Conv. 263. C. Emery (1982) 98 L.Q.R. 551. See also Underhill and Hayton, 19th edn, paras 8.92–8.93.

[157] [1979] 1 W.L.R. 278 at 282.

[158] cf. *Re Baden's Deed Trusts (No.2)* [1973] Ch. 9, where the onus of proof on the claimant concerns evidential, and not conceptual, uncertainty.

[159] This has not been regarded as sufficient to justify a less strict test in the case of trusts and powers.

[160] See, however, s.58 of the Safeguarding Vulnerable Groups Act 2006, which refers to "friends" without attempting any definition.

2.   CAPACITY TO CREATE A TRUST

A putative settlor must, of course, possess the legal capacity to create a trust. The capacity to create a trust is, generally speaking, co-extensive with the ability to hold and dispose of a legal or equitable interest in property, but there are two special situations to consider.

4–023

A.   Children

A settlement made by a child is voidable; the child may repudiate it before or within a reasonable time after attaining the age of 18.[161]

4–024

B.   Persons who Lack Mental Capacity

A person is presumed to have mental capacity unless the contrary is established.[162] Capacity issues may affect the ability of a person to make a will or a gift or to create a trust. In the case of a lifetime gift, it seems that the test varies according to the size of the gift and its relationship to the sum of the assets owned by the donor. In *Re Beaney*,[163] a mother who was suffering from senile dementia made a gift of her house, the only substantial asset of her estate, to one daughter, Valerie, who had stayed at home to look after her mother for many years; but this had the effect of virtually disinheriting the other two (married) children. The position was summarised as follows[164]:

4–025

> "The degree or extent of understanding required in respect of any instrument is relative to the particular transaction which it is to effect. In the case of a will the degree required is always high. In the case of a contract, a deed made for consideration or a gift *inter vivos*, whether by deed or otherwise, the degree required varies with the circumstances of the transaction. Thus, at one extreme, if the subject-matter and value of a gift are trivial in relation to the donor's other assets a low degree of understanding will suffice. But, at the other, if its effect is to dispose of the donor's only assets of value and thus for practical purposes to pre-empt the devolution of his estate under his will or on his intestacy, then the degree of understanding required is as high as that required for a will, and the donor must understand the claims of all potential donees and the extent of the property to be disposed of."

It was held that Mrs Beaney's gift to Valerie was void, because she was not capable of understanding the conflicting claims of her other children. More recently, the question whether such a gift is void or voidable has been reconsidered and the position said to be "quite obscure".[165] The point remains unresolved.

---

[161] *Edwards v Carter* [1893] A.C. 360.

[162] Mental Capacity Act 2005 s.1(2).

[163] [1978] 1 W.L.R. 770; F. Crane [1978] Conv. 387. See also *Simpson v Simpson* [1992] 1 F.L.R. 601 (lifetime gift which upset the balance of the will held void for want of mental capacity; transferee of bank deposits held them on resulting trust); *Re Morris* [2001] W.T.L.R. 1137; *Pesticcio v Huet* [2003] W.T.L.R. 1327; *Williams v Williams* [2003] W.T.L.R. 1371; *Cattermole v Prisk* [2006] 1 F.L.R. 693.

[164] [1978] 1 W.L.R. 770 at 774.

[165] *Sutton v Sutton* [2009] EWHC 2576 (Ch); [2010] W.T.L.R. 115 at [50]. The point was not fully argued and did not affect the outcome.

In the case of wills, the capacity requirements are found in *Banks v Goodfellow*[166]:

> "It is essential to the exercise of [testamentary] power that a testator shall understand the nature of the act and its effects; shall understand the extent of the property of which he is disposing; shall be able to comprehend and appreciate the claims to which he ought to give effect; and, with a view to the latter object, that no disorder of the mind shall poison his affections, pervert his sense of right, or prevent the exercise of his natural faculties."

Provided the testator had capacity when he gave instructions for the will to be drawn up, the will is valid even though he had lost testamentary capacity by the date he signed it, so long as he then understood that he was executing a will for which he had given instructions.[167] This principle was held to apply to lifetime dispositions in *Re Singellos*.[168] Mrs Singellos gave instruction for a complex gift of assets worth £4.5 million aimed at avoiding inheritance tax, which required her to sign 21 documents. She had capacity when giving the instructions and when signing the first 12 documents, but was losing capacity when she signed the last nine at a later date shortly before her death. As she was still capable of understanding, and did understand, that the nine documents gave effect to her earlier instructions, the gift was valid.

4–026   Where a person lacks capacity to make a disposition, an application may be made to the Court of Protection. Under the Mental Capacity Act 2005 (replacing earlier legislation), the Court of Protection has wide powers of dealing with the property and affairs of a person who lacks capacity to make the decision in question: for example, the court may order the making of a will for the person lacking capacity, or may authorise lifetime gifts or settlements of their property.[169] The guiding principle for the court is the best interests of the person who lacks capacity.[170]

Applications to the court for the approval of schemes affecting the property of a person who lacks capacity have commonly been brought in circumstances in which it was desirable in the interests of the family to reduce the tax liability of a rich person. The applicant must show that the scheme is for the benefit of the person who lacks capacity. It is sufficient that it is the sort of settlement which that person would be likely to make in favour of other members of the family if he or she had not lacked capacity to do so.[171]

---

[166] (1869–70) L.R. 5 Q.B. 549 at 565; for a recent application see *Burns v Burns* [2016] EWCA Civ 37. In addition to capacity, the testator must know and approve the contents of the will: see *Fuller v Strum* [2002] 1 W.L.R. 1097; *Gill v Woodall* [2011] Ch. 380; *McCabe v McCabe* [2015] EWHC 1591 (Ch); B. Sloan [2017] Conv. 440. The Law Commission is currently reviewing the law of wills, including the question of capacity: see Law Com. CP No. 231, *Making a Will* (2017).

[167] *Parker v Felgate* (1883) L.R. 8P.D. 171; applied in *Perrins v Holland* [2011] Ch. 270.

[168] [2010] EWHC 2353 (Ch); [2011] Ch. 324.

[169] Mental Capacity Act 2005 ss.16, 18.

[170] Mental Capacity Act 2005 s.1(5). This may not always tally with the wishes of the person lacking capacity, although of course such wishes are important: *Re P* [2010] Ch. 33. See also *Re M* [2009] W.T.L.R. 1791.

[171] See *Re CWM* [1951] 2 K.B. 714; *Re C* [1960] 1 W.L.R. 92; *Re CEFD* [1963] 1 W.L.R. 329. For the variation of existing trusts, see Ch.23.

CHAPTER 5

CONSTITUTION OF TRUSTS

1. THE GENERAL PROBLEM

A. Requirements of Conveyance and Declaration

5–001 WE HAVE seen that the interest of the beneficiary under a trust is a proprietary interest. The legal title is in the trustee; the equitable and beneficial title is in the beneficiary. The trust may be of any form of property—land, chattels, money, choses in action—and for any interest known to the law, whether legal or equitable, in possession, remainder[1] or reversion. A manifested intention to create a trust is, as we have seen, one of the requirements for the creation of an express trust,[2] but it is not sufficient in itself. To declare that A is to hold Blackacre on trust for B does not create a trust unless Blackacre is conveyed to A. Similarly, a conveyance to A does not create a trust of Blackacre for B unless the trust is properly declared. In short, it is necessary both to declare the trust *and* to convey the property to the trustee.

Many difficulties have been caused by failure to observe these basic propositions. Even where they are observed, complications can arise, and a number of questions are left open. Is it necessary that the conveyance and the declaration be contemporaneous? If X conveys Blackacre to A to hold upon trust for B, a trust is created in favour of B; also if X conveys to A upon trust and later declares the trusts.[3] If X conveys Blackacre to A, X cannot then tell A to hold on trust for B, because after the conveyance A became the absolute owner. May the declaration precede the conveyance? May X create a trust for B by declaring that A is to hold on trust for B; and later convey Blackacre to A? This issue raises a number of difficulties as we will see; they will be discussed in this chapter and also in Ch.6.

B. Methods of Benefiting an Intended Donee

5–002 If X is the legal and beneficial owner, X can make B the beneficial owner in any one of three ways:

5–003 **i. Outright Transfer.** X can simply transfer legal ownership to B. In the case of land, this transaction is called a conveyance. With a chattel, it is called a sale or gift; with a chose in action, it is called an assignment; with shares it is usually called a transfer. Whatever the type of transaction, X can, by following the correct procedure appropriate to the type of property,[4] transfer his or her entire interest to B.

5–004 **ii. Transfer to Trustee.** X may transfer the property to A to hold on trust for B. Provided that the legal title is correctly transferred to A, according to the type of property concerned, A will become legal owner; and provided that an intention

---

[1] *Re Ralli's WT* [1964] Ch. 288.
[2] Above, para.4–003.
[3] *Re Tyler* [1967] 1 W.L.R. 1269; *Grey v IRC* [1960] A.C. 1; below, para.6–011.
[4] See below, para.5–014.

to create a trust in favour of B is sufficiently manifested, B will become equitable and beneficial owner. A will hold on trust for B.

iii. **Declaration of Self as Trustee.**   X may declare that he or she holds the property on trust for B. In this situation all that is necessary is a declaration of trust in favour of B. There is no problem of the legal estate being vested in the trustee. It was, and remains, in X, who is the trustee, holding on trust for B.   **5–005**

C.   Invalid Transfers Not Construed as Declarations of Trust

In *Milroy v Lord*,[5] after mentioning the three methods of benefiting a donee that are outlined above, Turner LJ said[6]:   **5–006**

> "[I]f the settlement is intended to be effectuated by one of the modes to which I have referred, the Court will not give effect to it by applying another of those modes. If it is intended to take effect by transfer, the court will not hold the intended transfer to operate as a declaration of trust, for then every imperfect instrument would be made effectual by being converted into a perfect trust."

The principle that an invalid transfer will not be construed as a declaration of trust is seen in the sad case of *Jones v Lock*.[7] A father, being chided for failing to bring a present from Birmingham for his baby son, produced a £900 cheque payable to himself, saying: "Look you here, I give this to baby; it is for himself." He gave it to the child, who was about to tear it up, and the father took it away and put it in a safe. The father died soon afterwards and the cheque was found among his effects.

The question was whether the son was entitled to the cheque or whether it formed part of the father's estate. If part of the estate, the proceeds would be divided among the father's children by his first wife and the baby son would receive no provision from his father.[8] It would belong to the father's estate unless he had given it to the child, or had declared himself trustee of it. Clearly, he had not given it to the child, because a gift of a non-bearer cheque requires endorsement.[9] Had he declared himself trustee? Stuart VC held that there had been a valid declaration of trust, but Lord Cranworth LC allowed an appeal. Quite simply, the case concerned a failed gift: there was no evidence that the father intended to declare himself trustee of the cheque, and to burden himself with a trustee's duties, including that of investing it and being personally liable for failure to do so. There was no gift, and no declaration of trust. Although a regrettable result, the child took nothing.

---

[5] (1862) 4 De G.F. & J. 264; 45 E.R. 1185.

[6] (1862) 4 De G.F. & J. 264 at 274–75.

[7] (1865) L.R. 1 Ch.App. 25. See also *Deslauriers v Guardian Asset Management Ltd* [2017] UKPC 34 at [34]–[45] (intended transfer on trust not to be seen as immediate self-declaration of trust).

[8] The father had not changed his will since the birth of the new baby. On the day he died, he met his solicitor and told him that he would come to the solicitor's office the following Monday "to alter my will, that I may take care of my son".

[9] Under the Cheques Act 1992 s.1, cheques are no longer transferable if they are crossed and the words "account payee" appear.

5–007   Although failed legal transfers will not be saved by being construed as valid declarations of trust, there are other ways in which equity may intervene and give effect to the transfer. These are considered immediately below. As will be seen, when equity does give effect to failed legal transfers, it is sometimes said that the transferor holds the property on constructive trust for the transferee. However, it is important to realise that a finding that a transferor holds property on constructive trust is not inconsistent with the principle that an invalid transfer will not be construed as a declaration of trust. Equity does not in these cases construe failed transfers as valid declarations; it simply gives effect to failed transfers. The mechanism that equity uses to give effect to the failed transfers can be called a constructive trust, but that trust does not respond to any declaration made by the transferor.

D.   Purchasers and Volunteers

5–008   Returning to the three methods of X benefiting B outlined above, it can be seen that there is no question of a transfer of legal property when X intends to make a self-declaration of trust. The legal title is already in X and will remain there. But the first two methods do require a valid transfer of legal property: method (i) concerns an outright transfer of property from X to B; method (ii) concerns a transfer of property from X to A on trust for B. What is B's position if the legal transfer (either directly to B or to A on trust for B) is not completed? In short, what is equity's response to a failed legal transfer? The answer depends on whether or not consideration is present.

5–009   **i.   Purchasers.**   If B has provided consideration for a promised outright transfer of property (in effect, if B has *bought* the property), then B can sue X for damages for breach of contract if X does not transfer it. If damages would be inadequate, B can seek specific performance of the contract.[10] When specific performance is available it is said that X holds the legal title on "constructive trust" for B, who may then compel X to complete the legal transfer. The details of this vendor-purchaser constructive trust are given in Ch.12 below,[11] but it can be noted here that the language should be used with caution. The trust label does not necessarily help in determining matters such as which party is entitled to interim rents or dividends, or what duties are owed by the "trustee" to the "beneficiary". Indeed, the true position is simply that equity will intervene in cases where consideration is present and where damages would be an inadequate remedy.[12] That intervention may take the form of ordering X (or X's representatives) to complete the legal transfer to B.

What if, instead of an outright transfer to B, X had promised to transfer property to A on trust for B? If B provided consideration for that promise then, as above, B could sue X for damages or seek specific performance. If the contract was instead between X and A alone, then B could only sue X directly under the

---

[10] Below, Ch.27.
[11] Below, para.12–008.
[12] See *Scott v Southern Pacific Mortgages Ltd* [2014] UKSC 52; [2015] 1 A.C. 385 at [60]–[64]; *Chang v Registrar of Titles* (1976) 137 C.L.R. 177 at 190; P.G. Turner (2012) 128 L.Q.R. 582.

Contracts (Rights of Third Parties) Act 1999.[13] However, as will be seen below, various mechanisms within the general law may also allow for the enforcement of X's promise by B.[14]

ii. Volunteers. If X gratuitously promises to transfer property to B, or to A on trust for B, it would seem that little could be done if X breaks that promise. There is no contract to enforce at law, and equity will not assist a volunteer. But the position is not so straightforward: while equity will not assist a volunteer, neither will it "strive officiously to defeat a gift".[15] This means that a purported legal transfer will be complete in equity if the donor has done all that he or she can do to complete the transfer according to the legal requirements. For example, in the case of a gift of shares, the donor may have executed a share transfer form and sent it to the company so that the donee may be registered as the new owner.[16] The Articles of private companies usually provide that the directors may refuse to register transfers of shares, so the legal transfer will not be completed immediately, and may not be completed at all. Nonetheless, in such a case the transfer will be treated as complete in equity when the donor sends the properly-executed transfer form to the company, even though the transfer is ineffective (or is not yet effective) at law.

Again, while it may be simpler to say that the gift is "complete in equity",[17] it is often said in these cases that X holds the legal title on constructive trust for the donee.[18] The use of the word "trust" is not as potentially misleading in the volunteer context because here equity will only intervene at all if the position is such that, for example, the donor ought to hold interim dividends for the donee.[19] But there is still little to be gained by using the term.

5–010

Many of the leading cases involve purported transfers into settlements; that is, they involve transfers on trust. The transfer from X to A is regarded as complete in equity, with A holding those equitable rights on trust for B. However, the principles apply equally to cases of outright transfers from X to B as they do to transfers from X to A on trust for B. Indeed, the leading case, *Re Rose*, involved both an outright transfer and a transfer on trust.

5–011

> In *Re Rose*,[20] a settlor by voluntary deed transferred two tranches of shares in a private company. The first tranche was to his wife absolutely; the second was to trustees to be held on certain trusts. The directors, who had power to refuse to register transfers, registered the transfers some two months later. The settlor later died at a time at which the shares would be treated as part of his estate for tax purposes if the date of the transfer were the date of

---

[13] Below, para.5–021.

[14] Below, paras 5–023–5–027.

[15] *Choithram (T) International SA v Pagarani* [2001] 1 W.L.R. 1 at 11, per Lord Browne-Wilkinson.

[16] For the legal requirements of transfers of shares, see Companies Act 2006 ss.770–772; Stock Transfer Act 1963 s.1.

[17] See *Mascall v Mascall* (1985) 50 P. & C.R. 119 at 126–128, per Browne-Wilkinson LJ.

[18] See *Re Rose* [1952] Ch. 499 at 501; Oakley, *Constructive Trusts*, 3rd edn (1996), p.318; J. Garton [2003] Conv. 364.

[19] See *Re Rose* [1952] Ch. 499 at 518.

[20] [1952] Ch. 499 (judgment given ex tempore); *Re Fry* [1946] Ch. 312; *Re Rose* [1949] Ch. 78 (this case is unconnected with the later Court of Appeal decision from 1952, but shares a name, features the same judge—Jenkins J, later Jenkins LJ—and stands for the same principle); *Re Paradise Motor Co Ltd* [1968] 1 W.L.R. 1125; *Vandervell v IRC* [1967] 2 A.C. 291 at 330.

registration; but would not be so treated if the date was the date of the deed. The Court of Appeal held that the relevant date was that of the deed; for the settlor had at that time done everything possible to divest himself of the property by executing the instrument and delivering it to the transferees. All that was needed in addition was the formal act of registration by the third party.[21]

The *Re Rose* principle was applied to a transfer of registered land in *Mascall v Mascall*,[22] where a father executed a transfer of a house to his son, a volunteer, and handed over the land certificate. After the transfer had been sent to the Inland Revenue for stamping, and returned, the father (having fallen out with the son), sought a declaration that the transfer was ineffective. The son had not yet sent the documents to the Land Registry in order to become registered proprietor and had, therefore, not acquired legal title.[23] It was held that the gift was complete. The father had done all that he could, as the application to the Land Registry could be made by the son, from whom the father had no right to recover the transfer and land certificate.

In the case of the assignment of a lease which has not been completed by registration, the *Re Rose* principle would apply as between assignor and assignee, but has been held not to affect the legal position as between the assignor and the landlord.[24] Thus the assignor retained the right to exercise an option to terminate conferred by the lease. The issue was not the ownership of the equitable interest, which would be resolved by *Re Rose*, but the location of the legal estate, from which derived the legal rights and duties of the landlord and tenant.

5–012   *(a) Unconscionability as the underlying principle?*   The Court of Appeal reviewed the authorities in *Pennington v Waine*,[25] where the donor had executed a share transfer form concerning shares in a private company in favour of her nephew, with the intention that he should become director of the company (which position required him to own shares). The share transfer form was not delivered to the nephew, nor had he been registered as shareholder by the date of her death a few weeks later. The donor had sent the transfer form to her agent, the company auditor, who told the nephew that he need take no further steps with regard to the shares. The nephew signed a form of consent to act as director and was duly appointed. It was held that the shares did not form part of the donor's estate on her death, as there had been an equitable assignment in favour of the nephew.

The Court of Appeal did not seek to detract from the principle that equity will not assist a volunteer to perfect an imperfect gift. The execution of the share transfer form took effect as an equitable assignment in circumstances where it was clear that the donor intended it to have immediate effect. Clarke LJ reached his decision primarily by relying on s.1(1) of the Stock Transfer Act 1963, which

---

[21] Compare *Re Fry* [1946] Ch. 312, where the donor was domiciled abroad and had not, at the critical time, done everything that was needed of him, as he had not obtained Treasury consent to the transfer (although he had applied for it); *Re Transatlantic Life Assurance Co Ltd* [1980] 1 W.L.R. 79.

[22] (1985) 50 P. & C.R. 119. cf. *Corin v Patton* (1990) 169 C.L.R. 540 (gift incomplete where transferor had not requested mortgagee to produce land certificate, without which transferee could not be registered). The extension of the *Re Rose* principle to registered land has been criticised: see A. Ollikainen-Read [2018] Conv. 63.

[23] The current provision is Land Registration Act 2002 s.6.

[24] *Brown & Root Technology Ltd v Sun Alliance and London Assurance Co Ltd* [2001] Ch. 733.

[25] [2002] 1 W.L.R. 2075.

provides that shares may be transferred by an instrument in writing, with no reference to any requirement of delivery of the instrument to the transferee. Arden LJ, with whom Schiemann LJ agreed, placed more emphasis on the principle that a gift is complete in equity if the stage has been reached where it would be unconscionable to retract.[26] In the present case, it would have been unconscionable as the donor had told the donee of the transfer and he had been appointed director on the strength of it. In these circumstances, delivery of the form to the transferee was not prerequisite to the validity of the transfer as an equitable assignment.

This decision may be viewed as a hard case making bad law. It has been rightly criticised as leading to uncertainty as to whether a failed absolute gift will be treated as a perfect gift of the beneficial interest. The "unconscionable" test creates uncertainty as to whether and when (essential for tax and other purposes) the beneficial interest passes.[27] It is difficult to disagree with the view that the court conferred upon itself an unfettered discretion to give effect to ineffective transactions if it would be unconscionable not to do so.[28] Given that the donor's agent represented that the donee need take no further action, and that the donee then accepted appointment as a director, it may have been better treated as an instance of estoppel rather than as a case about imperfect gifts.

However, although the academic criticism highlighted the potential for uncertainty, *Pennington v Waine* has not been widely applied in the years since the decision. The case was distinguished in *Zeital v Kaye*,[29] where the Court of Appeal took a more orthodox approach. A held a share in a company on trust for B, and the question was whether B had transferred his equitable interest to C, a woman with whom he had a relationship after separating from his wife some 20 years previously. B had given her a stock transfer form (which A had signed, leaving the date and transferee blank), but without adding her name as transferee. This was not effective to transfer B's equitable interest, as it was neither an assignment nor a declaration of trust. C relied on the *Re Rose* principle, but it did not apply because B had not done all he could. Although C could have completed the blank transfer form, B had not given her the share certificate, which was necessary for registration as a shareholder. (It was lost, but B had not asked A to obtain a replacement.) The share certificate had not been handed over in *Pennington*, but in that case the certificates were held by the company, and so no question arose as to the donor's failure to deliver the certificate to the donee. Thus B's widow and daughters were entitled to the share on B's death intestate. The case may be contrasted with *Shah v Shah*,[30] where X sent a letter to Y, stating that: "I am as from today holding 4,000 shares in the above company for you". X

---

[26] [2002] 1 W.L.R. 2075 at 2090.
[27] H. Tjio and T. Yeo [2002] L.M.C.L.Q. 296; D. Ladds (2003) 17 T.L.I. 35. See also P. Clarke [2002] All E.R. Rev., p.229; A. Doggett (2003) 62 C.L.J. 263; H. Delany and D. Ryan [2008] Conv. 401 at 430. The decision is given a cautious welcome in J. Garton [2003] Conv. 364. See also C. Tham [2006] Conv. 411 suggesting a contractual analysis.
[28] M. Halliwell [2003] Conv. 192.
[29] [2010] EWCA Civ 159; [2010] W.T.L.R. 913; G. Griffiths [2010] Conv. 321.
[30] [2010] EWHC 313 (Ch); affirmed [2010] EWCA Civ 1408; [2011] W.T.L.R. 519; *ND v SD* [2017] EWHC 1507 (Fam) at [229]–[238].

enclosed a signed undated stock transfer form but no share certificate. The letter was held to be a declaration of trust, so it was not necessary to consider the other aspects.

E. Dealings with Equitable Property

5–013   Although the focus of this discussion is on transfers and declarations of trust made in respect of *legal* property, it should be noted that similar principles apply to dealings with equitable property. X may be a beneficiary of a trust who is seeking to assign his or her equitable interest to B; or who is seeking to assign the equitable interest to A on trust for B; or who is seeking to declare a sub-trust of X's equitable interest for B. X may also be seeking to benefit B by directing the trustee to hold on trust for B. Different formal rules apply to dealings with equitable interests than apply to dealings with legal interests,[31] but the general principle remains that those formalities must be completed before any interest will be validly transferred (and, therefore, before any trust of that interest will be constituted). As in the case of legal property, exceptions exist in the cases of transfers for value.[32] As for volunteers, it appears that the formal requirements in the Law of Property Act 1925 s.53(1)(c) are not susceptible to a "do all you can do" analysis: the formalities are either completed, or ipso facto the assignor has not done all they can do. But, following *Pennington v Waine*,[33] it would presumably be possible for an incomplete equitable assignment to be given effect on the grounds that it would be unconscionable to retract it.

2.   TRANSFER OF THE PROPERTY TO TRUSTEES UPON TRUST

A.   Legal Interests

5–014   The transfer to the trustees must accord with the rules applicable to the property concerned.[34] Legal estates in land must be transferred by deed,[35] equitable interests[36] and copyright[37] by writing (which may include an electronic document[38]), chattels by deed of gift[39] or by an intention to give coupled with a

---

[31] The formal rules, chiefly contained in Law of Property Act 1925 s.53(1)(c), are discussed below, para.6–008.

[32] See *Oughtred v IRC* [1960] A.C. 206; *Neville v Wilson* [1997] Ch. 144, discussed below, paras 6–016—6–017.

[33] [2002] 1 W.L.R. 2075.

[34] For the position where the trustee disclaims, see *Mallott v Wilson* [1903] 2 Ch. 494; P. Matthews [1981] Conv. 141.

[35] Law of Property Act 1925 s.52(1). Registration of freeholds and leases of over seven years is necessary under the registered title system; Land Registration Act 2002.

[36] Law of Property Act 1925 s.53(1)(c).

[37] Copyright Designs and Patents Act 1988 s.90(3).

[38] Below, para.6–008.

[39] Thus it has been held that a trust of a painting was validly constituted without physical delivery to the trustees (one of whom was in Ireland) on the ground that the formal declaration of trust transferred the property in the painting to the trustees, each of whom had a copy of the document and agreed to act; *Jaffa v Taylor Gallery Ltd*, *The Times*, 21 March 1990.

delivery of possession,[40] a bill of exchange by endorsement,[41] and shares by the appropriate form of transfer followed by registration.[42] Since the establishment of the CREST system in 1996, it has been possible to transfer shares in most quoted companies electronically, thereby avoiding the need for transfer forms and share certificates, but this does not detract from the principle that legal title passes only on registration.

In *Milroy v Lord*,[43] a settlor executed a voluntary deed purporting to transfer shares in the Bank of Louisiana to Samuel Lord to be held on trust for the claimant. The shares, however, could only be transferred by the appropriate transfer form followed by registration of the name of the transferee in the books of the Bank. Lord held a power of attorney to act on behalf of the settlor, and it would have enabled him to take all necessary further steps to obtain registration. But this was not actually done, and the settlor could have revoked the power before it had been done.[44] The Court of Appeal in Chancery held that no trust for the claimant had been constituted.

On the other hand, once the property has been vested in the trustees, and the trusts declared, the trust is constituted, and the settlor is unable to reclaim the property, even though the beneficiaries may be volunteers.[45] It has been held that the trust may be constituted where the property is vested in the trustees, even though it reached them in a capacity distinct from their office as trustees of the trust in question.

5–015

In *Re Ralli's Will Trusts*,[46] a testator left his residuary estate on trust for his widow for life and then for his two daughters Irene and Helen. Helen's marriage settlement included a covenant to settle existing and after-acquired property in favour of (in the events which happened) volunteers. Helen predeceased her mother and so never transferred her remainder interest pursuant to her covenant. The claimant was the trustee both of the testator's will and also of Helen's marriage settlement. Buckley J had to decide on what trusts the residue was held. He concluded, as one ground for his decision, that the vesting of the property in the trustee was sufficient to constitute the trusts of the remainder interest even though the property came to him in his other capacity as trustee of the will.

"The circumstance that the [claimant] holds the fund because he was appointed a trustee of the will is irrelevant. He is at law the owner of the fund, and the means by which he became so have no effect upon the quality of his legal ownership."[47]

This may be contrasted with *Re Brooks' Settlement Trusts*,[48] where a settlor made a voluntary settlement under which he purported to assign after-acquired property to the trustee, Lloyds Bank. Subsequently a power of appointment under

[40] *Kilpin v Raltey* [1892] 1 Q.B. 582; *Re Cole* [1964] Ch. 175; *Thomas v Times Book Co Ltd* [1966] 1 W.L.R. 911; J. Thornely (1953) 11 C.L.J. 355; A. Diamond (1964) 27 M.L.R. 357.
[41] Bills of Exchange Act 1882 s.31; see, however, Cheques Act 1957 ss.1, 2.
[42] See Companies Act 2006 ss.770–772.
[43] (1862) 4 De G.F. & J. 264; 45 E.R. 1185.
[44] See *Mascall v Mascall* (1984) 50 P. & C.R. 119 at 127, per Browne-Wilkinson LJ.
[45] *Paul v Paul* (1882) 20 Ch.D. 742; *Jefferys v Jefferys* (1841) Cr. & Ph. 138; *Re Ellenborough* [1903] 1 Ch. 697 (the assets received under her sister's will); *Re Bowden* [1936] Ch. 71; similarly for voluntary covenants to settle: *Re Adlard* [1954] Ch. 29. For the current position with regard to the enforcement of the covenant, see Contracts (Rights of Third Parties) Act 1999, below, para.5–021.
[46] [1964] Ch. 288.
[47] [1964] Ch. 288 at 301.
[48] [1939] 1 Ch. 993, not cited in *Re Ralli's WT*.

another settlement of which Lloyds Bank was also trustee was exercised in the settlor's favour. It was held that the settlor was entitled to be paid the appointed sum by the Bank because the assignment of a mere expectancy was ineffective. Thus, the beneficiaries had no claim.

B. Equitable Interests

5–016 The same general principle applies where the settlor's interest is equitable. A correct transfer of the equitable interest to a trustee upon properly declared trusts is necessary to create a trust of that equitable interest. A disposition of an equitable interest must be in writing.[49] In *Kekewich v Manning*,[50] shares were held on trust for A for life and then for B. B assigned his equitable interest in remainder to trustees to hold on certain trusts, and this was held to create a trust of the equitable interest in remainder.

3. DECLARATION OF SELF AS A TRUSTEE

5–017 There is no difficulty if a settlor wishes to declare himself trustee of some or all of his property. All that is needed is a manifestation of an intention to declare a trust; and, if the property is land or an interest in land, evidence in writing of such intent. The settlor:

> "need not use the words, 'I declare myself a trustee,' but he must do something which is equivalent to it, and use expressions which have that meaning; for, however anxious the Court may be to carry out a man's intention, it is not at liberty to construe words otherwise than according to their proper meaning."[51]

The issues which arise in this section are quite different from those that have been discussed in this chapter so far. Earlier, the question was whether the property was vested in the trustee. Here, there is no such problem; if there is a trust the settlor is trustee (or may be one of co-trustees, as mentioned below[52]). The question here is whether a trust has properly been declared. The problems usually arise in cases where the settlor's intention was to make a gift to a donee but the gift failed, and the question is whether the intent to benefit the donee can be construed as a declaration of trust in his favour.

As we have seen, the rule is that equity will not construe a void gift as a declaration of trust. What is needed is a manifestation of an intention to declare a trust. *Jones v Lock* has already been considered.[53] Similarly, in *Richards v*

---

[49] Law of Property Act s.53(1)(c); below, para.6–008.
[50] (1851) 1 De G.M. & G. 176; *Gilbert v Overton* (1864) 2 H. & M. 110.
[51] *Richards v Delbridge* (1874) L.R. 18 Eq. 11 at 14, per Jessel MR.
[52] *Choithram (T) International SA v Pagarani* [2001] 1 W.L.R. 1 (PC); below, para.5–018. See also *Wallbank and Wallbank v Price* [2008] 2 F.L.R. 501; *Stablewood Properties Ltd v Amrit Virdi* [2010] EWCA Civ 865; [2011] W.T.L.R. 723 (declaration of trust subject to security interest).
[53] (1865) L.R. 1 Ch.App. 25; above, para.5–006.

Delbridge,[54] a grandfather who was entitled to leasehold premises endorsed on the lease a memorandum as follows: "This deed and all thereto belonging I give to [my grandson] from this time forth, with all the stock-in-trade." He delivered the document to the grandson's mother, and then died, making no mention of the property in his will. Jessel MR held that no interest passed; not at law, because the endorsement was ineffective to assign a lease; and not in equity, for the words were inappropriate for the declaration of a trust.

These cases may be contrasted with the situation where the legal owner has not attempted to transfer the property to the third party, but has shown that he considers himself to hold the property as trustee for the third party. Whether or not, in any case, the evidence is sufficient will depend on the facts; it has been held that the intent can be implied from conduct where the evidence is clear.[55]

So in *Paul v Constance*,[56] an intention to declare a trust could be inferred from the conduct and words of the parties. Mr Constance was separated from his wife, and lived with the claimant, Mrs Paul. He received, as damages for an injury suffered at work, a cheque for £950, and he and Mrs Paul decided to put it into a deposit account at Lloyds Bank. The account was opened in the name of Mr Constance only, because he and Mrs Paul felt an embarrassment in opening a joint account in different names. Mr Constance indicated on many occasions that the money was as much Mrs Paul's as his. On his death, the widow claimed the money in the account as part of her husband's estate. The question was whether the account was owned beneficially by Mr Constance, or whether, on the particular facts, he had shown an intention to hold the property as trustee for Mrs Paul, or as trustee for the two of them in equal shares. The Court of Appeal found that the evidence was sufficient to support an intention in Mr Constance to declare himself a trustee for them both in equal shares, although it was not easy to pinpoint a specific moment of declaration. Mrs Paul was thus able to recover half of the proceeds of the account.

5–018

This decision was applied in *Rowe v Prance*,[57] where the defendant, a wealthy man who was conducting an extra-marital relationship with the claimant, Mrs Rowe, acquired an ocean-going boat which was registered in his sole name. After the relationship broke down, Mrs Rowe succeeded in her claim to a half share. The defendant had repeatedly referred to the boat as "our boat", had assured Mrs Rowe that her interest in the boat was her security, and had felt bound to give an explanation (although absurd[58]) as to why he alone could be registered as owner. As no formalities were required in the case of personalty, the trust had been sufficiently declared. On the other hand, where a house in the joint names of a

---

[54] (1874) L.R. 18 Eq. 11. See also *Pappadakis v Pappadakis* [2000] W.T.L.R. 719 (invalid assignment failing to identify assignee who would hold on trust could not operate as declaration of trust).

[55] *New, Prance and Garrard's Trustee v Hunting* [1897] 2 Q.B. 19. See also *Re Kayford Ltd* [1975] 1 W.L.R. 279; *Re Chelsea Cloisters Ltd* (1981) 41 P. & C.R. 98; *Ong v Ping* [2017] EWCA Civ 2069.

[56] [1977] 1 W.L.R. 527; criticised in Heydon and Leeming, *Cases and Materials on Equity and Trusts*, 8th edn (2011), p.174: "The law of express trusts normally requires an intention to benefit the *cestui que trust* specifically by way of trust—a mere intention to benefit him in some way is insufficient."

[57] [1999] 2 F.L.R. 787.

[58] He stated that the claimant could not be registered as she did not possess a master's certificate.

mother and father was transferred, pursuant to a consent order, to the mother "for the benefit of the child", no trust was created for the child, who had since fallen out with her mother and left home.[59]

An unusual situation arose in *Choithram (T) International SA v Pagarani*,[60] where a wealthy man who had just executed a trust deed establishing a charitable foundation made an oral statement along the lines of "I now give all my wealth to the foundation". He instructed his accountant to transfer his assets to the trustees, of whom he was one, but he died before this was done. The Privy Council held that, as the settlor was one of the co-trustees, the trust was constituted by his declaration of trust of property vested in him, even though the property had not yet been vested in the co-trustees. In such a case, the settlor was obliged to give effect to the trust by transferring the property into the names of all the trustees. While the words used in the present case were normally appropriate to an outright gift, in the context they could only mean that the settlor was giving his wealth to the trustees of the foundation, to be held on the trusts set out in the trust deed. His words, therefore, amounted to a declaration of trust.

5–019 A lenient view of the requirements of a declaration of trust was taken by the Court of Appeal in *Re Vandervell's Trusts (No.2)*.[61] An option to purchase certain shares was held by trustees on a resulting trust for Mr Vandervell. The trustees exercised the option, using money from Vandervell's children's settlement. It was held that the shares were henceforth held on trust for the children's settlement. There was no declaration of trust by Vandervell,[62] but such a declaration could be inferred from certain acts of the trustees[63]: first, the use of the money from the children's settlement; secondly, the subsequent payment of the dividends to that settlement; and thirdly, the trustees' notification to the Revenue that they now held the shares on trust for that settlement. Arguably the second and third acts merely indicate what the trustees thought the position to be, so only the first could operate as the declaration of trust. Even then, it may be a stretch to interpret the use of money from the children's settlement as a declaration of trust.[64]

It should be noted that it is not necessary that the beneficiary should be aware of the declaration of trust.[65] The beneficiary becomes equitable owner just as he would become legal owner if the property had been conveyed to him.

---

[59] *Re B (Child: Property Transfer)* [1999] 2 F.L.R. 418.

[60] [2001] 1 W.L.R. 1; J. Hopkins (2001) 60 C.L.J. 483; C. Rickett [2001] Conv. 515; P. Clarke [2001] All E.R. Rev. 265. See also *Shah v Shah* [2011] W.T.L.R. 519; above para.5–012. cf. *Deslauriers v Guardian Asset Management Ltd* [2017] UKPC 34 at [34]–[45] (settlor to be the beneficiary of an intended transfer on trust, but not the trustee).

[61] [1974] Ch. 269.

[62] Which would have been a "disposition" within the meaning of Law of Property Act 1925 s.53(1)(c): see below, paras 6–012—6–013.

[63] The option was held on such trusts as might thereafter be declared by Vandervell or the trustees: see *Re Vandervell's Trusts (No.2)* [1974] Ch. 269 at 323, per Stephenson LJ and Lawton LJ; *Vandervell v IRC* [1967] 2 A.C. 291 at 315–317, per Lord Upjohn. Pending any such declaration, it was held on resulting trust for Vandervell.

[64] Megarry J thought such a proposition "monstrous": *Re Vandervell's Trusts (No.2)* [1974] Ch. 269 at 299.

[65] *Middleton v Pollock* (1876) 2 Ch.D. 104; *Standing v Bowring* (1885) 31 Ch.D. 282.

4. COVENANTS TO SETTLE

If a settlor has neither conveyed the property to trustees nor declared himself a trustee, no trust is created. If he has covenanted by deed to settle the property, the crucial question is whether or not the intended beneficiary can compel him to carry out the covenant and settle it.

5–020

A. Contracts (Rights of Third Parties) Act 1999

Formerly the general rule was that a third party could not enforce a contract purporting to benefit him. The position was changed by the Contracts (Rights of Third Parties) Act 1999. Section 1 of the Act, which does not affect any right or remedy of a third party that exists apart from the Act,[66] provides that a third party may in his own right enforce a term of the contract if the contract expressly provides that he may, or if the term purports to confer a benefit on him, unless on a proper construction of the contract it appears that the parties did not intend the term to be enforceable by the third party. The section further provides that the third party must be expressly identified by name, as a member of a class, or as answering a particular description, but need not be in existence when the contract is entered into.[67] Thus a third party could enforce a covenant to convey property to trustees for his benefit.

5–021

Clearly s.1 enables a third party who falls within it to enforce the contract by an action for damages. So far as specific performance is concerned, s.1(5) provides:

> "[T]here shall be available to the third party any remedy that would have been available to him in an action for breach of contract if he had been a party to the contract (and the rules relating to damages, injunctions, specific performance and other relief shall apply accordingly)."

This might be interpreted as meaning that the third party may obtain specific performance if the subject-matter is such that the remedy of damages would be inadequate.[68] On the other hand, it is established that a volunteer may not obtain specific performance.[69] In *Cannon v Hartley*,[70] a volunteer beneficiary who was a party to a deed was able to sue upon it for damages, but would not have been able to obtain specific performance. It is difficult to see why a third party, who has not given consideration, should be in a better position under the 1999 Act.

---

[66] Contracts (Rights of Third Parties) Act 1999 s.7.

[67] See *Avraamides v Colwill* [2006] EWCA Civ 1533.

[68] Consider the Explanatory Notes to s.1, to the effect that subs.(5) "makes it clear that the courts may award all the remedies which are available to a person bringing a claim for breach of contract to a third party seeking to enforce his rights under subs(1). The normal rules of law applicable to those remedies... apply to the third party's claim."

[69] Below, para.27–019. See N. Andrews (2001) 60 C.L.J. 353 at 361 for the view that s.1(5) is an exception to the volunteer rule.

[70] [1949] Ch. 213; below, para.5–022. On the distinction between a deed poll and a deed inter partes, and the question whether a non-executing party may enforce, see *Moody v Condor Insurance Ltd* [2006] 1 W.L.R. 1847.

The law relating to covenants to settle which were entered into prior to the 1999 Act will be considered in the remainder of this part and in Part 5 of this chapter.

B. Covenants to Settle prior to the Contracts (Rights of Third Parties) Act 1999

5–022   A beneficiary who has given consideration can enforce the covenant by obtaining specific performance; one who has not given consideration cannot do so. Again, equity will not assist a volunteer.

For this purpose, "consideration" has a wider meaning than at common law, in that equity also treats as having given consideration, in the case of a covenant in a marriage settlement, the husband and wife and issue of the marriage.[71] Illegitimate children, children by a former marriage, and children to whom one of the parties stands in loco parentis, cannot normally be included.[72]

> In *Pullan v Koe*,[73] a marriage settlement of 1859 settled property on the husband and wife and prospective children, and also contained a covenant by the wife to settle on the same trusts any property she later acquired of the value of £100 and upwards. In 1879 the wife received £285, part of which was invested in bearer bonds, which remained at the bank in the husband's name until his death in 1909. The question was whether the trustees could then take steps to obtain the bonds from his executors and hold them on the trusts of the settlement. It was held that it was their duty to do so.
>
> Indeed, the beneficiaries could have taken action themselves if the trustees had refused to do so. Here, however, the common law action on the covenant was barred by the lapse of time; but the court held that the £285 was impressed with the trust at the moment the wife received it, and that the trust could be enforced against the bonds.

Such a covenant would not however be enforceable in favour of next-of-kin, for they are volunteers.[74] Thus, if there had been no children of the marriage, the next-of-kin would not have been able to enforce the covenant.

Where the covenant is enforced by persons within the marriage consideration, the court may order the covenantor to settle the property in accordance with the covenant[75]; or, as in *Pullan v Koe*, declare that the property is subject to the trusts of the settlement. However where one of the intended beneficiaries is a party[76] to the covenant, even though a volunteer, he may sue for damages, although the equitable remedy of specific performance would not lie.

---

[71] *Attorney General v Jacobs-Smith* [1895] 2 Q.B. 341. "Issue" includes remoter issue; *MacDonald v Scott* [1893] A.C. 642.

[72] See *Attorney General v Jacobs-Smith* [1895] 2 Q.B. 341; *Rennell v IRC* [1962] Ch. 329 at 341, affirmed [1964] A.C. 173; *Re Cook's ST* [1965] Ch. 902 at 914.

[73] [1913] 1 Ch. 9. See C. Rickett (1979) 32 C.L.P. 1 at 4–5.

[74] *Re D'Angibau* (1880) 15 Ch.D. 228; *Re Plumptre's Marriage Settlement* [1901] 1 Ch. 609; *Re Cook's ST* [1965] Ch. 902.

[75] This may have the effect of benefiting volunteers, as in *Davenport v Bishopp* (1843) 2 Y. & C.C.C. 451 (life interest to husband, remainder to volunteers).

[76] For the meaning of which, see *Beswick v Beswick* [1968] A.C. 58 at 102.

In *Cannon v Hartley*,[77] a settlement upon a separation, to which the spouses and a daughter were parties, provided that the father should pay to the daughter any sum exceeding £1,000 which he might inherit from his parents. Having inherited, he failed to make the payment. The daughter was a volunteer. She could however sue upon her father's covenant, and recover damages for breach of covenant at common law.

5. ACTION FOR DAMAGES BY THE TRUSTEES. TRUSTS OF CHOSES IN ACTION

There is no difficulty in enforcing a completely constituted trust of a chose in action.[78] Where a contractual right is held by A on trust for B, A may sue and obtain damages or specific performance on behalf of B[79]; or B may obtain such relief on his own account if A refuses to act, joining A as a co-defendant in the action.[80]

5–023

The question is whether this principle can assist a volunteer in the case of a covenant to settle existing or after-acquired property.[81] Such a volunteer may now be able to enforce the covenant directly under the Contracts (Rights of Third Parties) Act 1999.[82] The remainder of this section deals with the position where the covenant was entered into prior to that Act and is unaffected by it. In such a case could not the trustees sue, recover damages, and hold them on trust for the volunteer? Or could not the volunteer argue that there is already a completely constituted trust of the benefit of the covenant, a trust of a chose in action for which they are the beneficiaries, and thus entitled to enforce?

The courts have given volunteers little comfort in this respect. In *Re Pryce*,[83] Eve J held that the trustees should not be compelled to pursue whatever remedy they may have at law on the covenant, and in *Re Kay's Settlement*,[84] Simonds J decided that they should be instructed not to do so. In *Re Cook's Settlement Trusts*,[85] Buckley J refused to allow volunteers to enforce a covenant even though another person had given consideration. These, however, are all decisions of courts of first instance, and the matter should be analysed more closely.

---

[77] [1949] Ch. 213. See generally M. Macnair (1988) 8 L.S. 172, suggesting that there is some historical support for allowing specific performance of covenants in favour of volunteers.

[78] Below, para.5–025.

[79] *Lloyd's v Harper* (1880) 16 Ch.D. 290.

[80] *Les Affréteurs Réunis Société Anonyme v Leopold Walford Ltd* [1919] A.C. 801; *Parker-Tweedale v Dunbar Bank Plc* [1991] Ch. 12. This exception to the privity rule is less important after the Contracts (Rights of Third Parties) Act 1999. For problems where a trust is declared of a non-assignable contract, see *Barbados Trust Co v Bank of Zambia* [2007] 1 Lloyd's Rep 495; A. Trukhtanov (2007) 70 M.L.R. 848; P. Turner (2008) 67 C.L.J. 23; M. Smith (2008) 124 LQR. 517 and [2008] 22 T.L.I. 140; R. Goode [2009] L.M.C.L.Q. 300 at 313–315.

[81] i.e. property which might come subsequently to the settlor. It was common in a marriage settlement for the spouses to covenant to add to the settlement any such property.

[82] Above, para.5–021.

[83] [1917] 1 Ch. 234. For criticism of this line of cases see J.D. Heydon & M.J. Leeming, *Jacobs' Law of Trusts in Australia*, 8th edn (2016), paras 6.11–6.14.

[84] [1939] Ch. 329.

[85] [1965] Ch. 902.

A. Action by the Trustees

5–024   There are certain difficulties which lie in the way of the proposition that the trustees, as parties to the covenant, can sue to recover damages with a view to holding the money received on trust for the (volunteer) beneficiaries. One question is whether the trustee would recover substantial damages in an action at law on the covenant. If the trustee can recover only nominal damages, the action will be of no help to the beneficiary. The general rule is that the claimant may recover in an action for breach of contract damages sufficient to compensate him for his loss. Damages suffered by third parties are not recoverable by the claimant unless, as explained below, the claimant contracted as trustee for the third parties.

The real question, however, is this: what does the common law regard as the claimant's own loss? In the context of a voluntary covenant to settle, it has been said:

> "[F]or breach of a covenant to pay a certain sum the measure of damages (if that is the appropriate expression) is the certain sum; and for breach of a covenant to transfer property worth a certain sum, it is the value of the property".[86]

There is no doubt that this is the usual rule, as shown by the cases where the volunteer beneficiary is a party to the covenant.[87] Applying this rule, substantial damages should be recoverable at law by A where X covenants to pay a certain sum (or to transfer Blackacre) to A to be held on trust for B. It is no answer at common law to say that A suffers no loss by the breach of such a covenant. At law the position is no different from that of a trustee of a completely constituted trust, who may recover substantial damages for the breach of any contract he may make as trustee even though he personally suffers no loss.

> In *Re Cavendish-Browne's Settlement Trusts*,[88] the covenantor was absolutely entitled under two wills to land in Canada, which he entered into a voluntary covenant to settle. The trustees sued for damages and were awarded a sum equivalent to the value of the property which would have come into their hands if the covenant had been performed, to be held on the trusts of the settlement.

This, then, supports the view that a covenantee may recover substantial damages at law for breach of a covenant to settle, although he has suffered no loss personally. We saw, however, that it was held in *Re Kay's Settlement*[89] that the covenantee should not sue.

---

[86]   D. Elliott (1960) 76 L.Q.R. 100 at 112; J. Barton (1975) 91 L.Q.R. 236 at 238; D. Goddard [1988] Conv. 19 at 21. See also M. Friend [1982] Conv. 280 at 281, agreeing that substantial damages are available on the basis of debt in the case of a voluntary covenant to pay money, but suggesting that this is less clear in the case of specific property other than money.

[87]   *Cannon v Hartley* [1949] Ch. 213.

[88]   [1916] W.N. 341; (1916) 61 S.J. 27. See Underhill and Hayton, 19th edn, para.9.118 for the view that any damages should be held on resulting trust for the covenantor.

[89]   [1939] Ch. 329.

B.   Trust of the Benefit of the Covenant

If there is a completely constituted trust of the benefit of the covenant, there is no **5–025** difficulty, as has been seen,[90] in enforcing it, either by the trustees on behalf of the beneficiaries, or by the beneficiaries themselves. It was said, however, in *Re Cook's Settlement Trusts*,[91] that a covenant to settle future property cannot be the subject-matter of a trust, because it does not "create a debt enforceable at law … that is to say, a property right."[92] It is submitted that this restriction is not supportable. Of course, future property itself, or unascertained property, or a mere hope of acquisition, cannot be the subject-matter of a trust.[93] But a covenant to pay a sum to be ascertained in the future is just as good a chose in action as a covenant to pay a specified sum, and it creates legal property of value. The subject-matter of the trust is the benefit of the covenant, the chose in action; not the property which will be obtained by its performance.[94] There is no difficulty in a trust of a bank account, which is a chose in action, its value varying with the state of the account from day to day; nor in a trust of an insurance policy under which the obligation is to pay an undetermined sum on a future event which may not happen. The decision in *Re Cook's Settlement Trusts* is justifiable, however, on the basis that there was no manifestation of an intention to create a trust of the benefit of the covenant.

While there is no difficulty in the concept of a trust of the benefit of a covenant, there is considerable difficulty in deciding when such a trust will arise.[95] The critical case is *Fletcher v Fletcher*,[96] a decision which presents certain difficulties.

> Ellis Fletcher entered into a voluntary covenant with trustees to pay to them £60,000 to be held on trust, in the events which happened, for his illegitimate son Jacob. The trustees did not wish to accept the trust or to receive the money unless they were required to do so. Wigram VC held that Jacob was able to claim the money, saying that equity would either allow Jacob to use the name of the trustees to sue at law, or to recover in his own name in a court of equity. Wigram VC explained the matter thus:
>
>> "I cannot, I admit, do anything to perfect the liability of the author of the trust, if it is not already perfect. This covenant, however, is already perfect. The covenantor is liable at law, and the Court is not called upon to do any act to perfect it. One question made in argument has been whether there can be a trust of a covenant the benefit of which shall belong to a third party; but I cannot think that there is any difficulty in that… the real question is whether the relation of trustee and *cestui que trust* is established in the present case."[97]

There was, then, a trust of the benefit of the covenant, and the beneficiary could enforce it. The crucial question in such a case is whether or not there has been a manifestation of an intention to declare a trust of a chose in action, and this is a

---

[90]   Above, para.5–023.
[91]   [1965] Ch. 902.
[92]   [1965] Ch. 902 at 913.
[93]   Below, para.5–028.
[94]   *Williamson v Codrington* (1750) 1 Ves.Sen. 511; *Lloyd's v Harper* (1880) 16 Ch.D. 290.
[95]   *Vandepitte v Preferred Accident Insurance Corp of New York* [1933] A.C. 70; *Re Schebsman* [1944] Ch. 83; *Scruttons Ltd v Midland Silicones Ltd* [1962] A.C. 446.
[96]   (1844) 4 Hare 67.
[97]   (1844) 4 Hare 67 at 74.

matter in which the courts have not, over the years, maintained a consistent approach. There are some difficulties in holding that there was a trust of the chose in action on the facts of *Fletcher v Fletcher*. In the first place, positive evidence of intention is lacking. Ellis Fletcher covenanted that he would pay the £60,000 to trustees "to be held on the following trusts". There is clearly a trust which will affect the money once it is received by the trustee, but no evidence of an intention by either party to create a trust of a chose in action. It cannot be assumed from the fact that the property itself is to be subjected to a trust that an immediate trust of the benefit of the covenant was also intended.[98]

Another question is whether the relevant intention is that of the covenantor (settlor) or the covenantee (trustee). Certainly there was no intention to create a trust of the chose in action on the part of the trustees, if that is the requirement, in *Fletcher v Fletcher*: they did not know about the arrangement, and wished to decline the trust upon hearing of it. A trust of tangible property is declared by the owner of the property, whether he declares himself trustee or transfers it to another on trust. As a general rule, a trust of a debt is declared by the creditor. Thus, in *Paul v Constance*,[99] the question whether a trust of a bank account had been created was determined by examining the intention of the account-holder (creditor), Mr Constance. It is submitted, however, that a distinction must be drawn between covenants supported by valuable consideration and those which are not. Where there is consideration, the relevant intention to create a trust of the chose in action is that of the covenantee.[100] This will usually be proved by showing that the latter covenanted as trustee for the persons nominated by the covenantor. Where, on the other hand, the covenant is voluntary, as in *Fletcher v Fletcher*, the covenantor is the creator of the trust, and if he manifests an intention that the covenantee's rights under the promise shall be held in trust, the covenantee immediately becomes trustee of his rights under the covenant.

C. Specific Performance at the Suit of the Contracting Party

5–026 *Beswick v Beswick*[101] suggests the possibility of another approach to this problem. If the administratrix of old Mr Beswick could in that case obtain specific performance against young Mr Beswick and compel him to perform his promise to make payments to the widow Beswick (a volunteer), can it not be argued that the trustee-covenantees should be able to obtain specific performance of the promise to settle property in favour of volunteers?

---

[98] This is the position taken by the courts, and by the majority of commentators: see, e.g., Rickett (1979) 32 C.L.P. 1 at 10–11; J.D. Feltham (1982) 98 L.Q.R. 17 (arguing that intention to declare a trust is required, but would normally be assumed); B. McFarlane and C. Mitchell, *Hayton & Mitchell: Commentary & Cases on the Law of Trusts & Equitable Remedies*, 14th edn (2015) para.2–088; but cf. J.D. Heydon & M.J. Leeming, *Jacobs' Law of Trusts in Australia*, 8th edn (2016) para.6.09, arguing that a trust of the benefit of a covenant must on principle always exist, since the covenantee will not hold his or her rights against the covenantor beneficially.

[99] [1977] 1 W.L.R. 527; above, para.5–018.

[100] See the insurance cases: *Vandepitte v Preferred Accident Insurance Corp of New York* [1933] A.C. 70; *Swain v The Law Society* [1983] 1 A.C. 598. The question in these cases is whether the policy-holder intended to hold the company's obligation on trust.

[101] [1968] A.C. 58; below, paras 27–047—27–050.

It is submitted however that the principle of *Beswick v Beswick* does not apply to the case of voluntary covenants. In that case, old Mr Beswick gave consideration for the promise of young Mr Beswick and had a right of action for damages against him. When the loss was shown to be nil, and the damages therefore nominal, specific performance became available instead. That remedy is available where the legal remedy of damages is inadequate.[102] Where valuable consideration has been given, the remedy of nominal damages is inadequate, although there is no loss to the contracting party, because the result is the unjust enrichment of the defendant. In the case of a voluntary covenant to pay to trustees, the situation (assuming that damages would be nominal[103]) is different. There is no unjust enrichment of the covenantor; nominal damages are therefore adequate. Specific performance in any event is not available to a volunteer, and most trustees are volunteers. Furthermore, the availability of specific performance in *Beswick v Beswick* was not hampered by the principle that trustees are not allowed to sue,[104] because the claimant there was not a trustee.[105]

We have seen that it made no difference in *Re Cook's Settlement Trusts*[106] that one of the parties had given consideration.

    5–027

> In *Re Cook's Settlement Trusts*, property including a Rembrandt was settled on H for life, remainder to his son, F. Under the terms of a resettlement the property became F's absolutely and he covenanted to pay to the trustees the proceeds of sale of the Rembrandt (and other pictures) if sold in H's lifetime, to be held on trust for F's children (volunteers). F gave the Rembrandt to his wife, who wished to sell it. Buckley J held that the trustees could not enforce the covenant if the Rembrandt were sold.

The decision preceded *Beswick v Beswick*, in which *Re Cook's* was apparently not cited. A similarity between the two cases appears on close analysis. H entered into a contract for consideration with F, one of the terms of which was that F would confer a benefit on X. If H had sued F, could he succeed, as in *Beswick v Beswick*, by saying that the damages awardable for the breach were inadequate, and that specific performance of the covenant to pay should be decreed in favour of X? The covenant was not in terms to pay to the volunteers, but to the trustees, who would hold the money in trust for them; but this seems immaterial. It is H who, on this reasoning, could sue (although he would not be obliged to) and not the trustees; but the action should not be dependent upon H's physical survival, for his estate, on the reasoning of *Beswick v Beswick*,[107] should be able to do so. It is submitted, however, that *Beswick v Beswick* will not enable trustees to enforce voluntary covenants to settle.

That line of reasoning is wholly separate from the question of the enforcement of a covenant in the *Fletcher v Fletcher* type of situation. There, no consideration was given. The covenant was voluntary. It would be enforceable by, or on behalf

---

[102] Ch.27.

[103] Which may not be correct; above, para.5–024. See, however, *Staden v Jones* [2008] 2 F.L.R. 1931 at 1938.

[104] Above, para.5–023.

[105] She was a personal representative, but the position was exactly the same as if Mr Beswick senior had been in a position to bring the action himself. There was no trust.

[106] [1965] Ch. 902; above, para.5–023.

[107] See also *Coulls v Bagot's Trustee* (1967) 119 C.L.R. 460.

of the beneficiaries if, and only if, there was found to be a trust of the chose in action. That brings us back to the most basic question of all in relation to the creation of trusts: whether the settlor has manifested an intention to create a trust.

All this has been of reduced importance since the Contracts (Rights of Third Parties) Act 1999.[108] That Act permits third parties in certain cases to enforce contracts in their own right. The old learning, however, remains relevant in relation to covenants entered into before the Act.

6.   TRUSTS OF FUTURE PROPERTY

5–028   A contract for consideration to convey future property to trustees upon trust is valid[109] and, in most cases, specifically enforceable.[110] A voluntary covenant to convey future property to trustees is actionable at law by a beneficiary who is a party to the covenant.[111] If the beneficiary is not a party he or she may have rights of enforcement under the Contracts (Rights of Third Parties) Act 1999. A purported assignment of an expectancy[112] cannot be a conveyance because there is nothing to convey. Nor can there be a valid declaration of trust of property not yet existing.[113] If consideration is given for a purported conveyance, it will be construed as a contract to assign and enforceable as such.[114] But if it is made gratuitously it is a nullity.[115]

> In *Re Ellenborough*,[116] the sister of Lord Ellenborough purported to convey by voluntary settlement the property which she would receive under her brother's will. On his death she declined to transfer the property to the trustees, and Buckley J held that the trustees could not compel her to do so.

A further question is whether such a gratuitous covenant, assignment or declaration in respect of future property can subsequently be treated as an effective declaration of trust if the property does later vest in the trustee. The situation can arise if the property, on materialising, is transferred to trustees

---

[108] Above, para.5–021. The ambiguous drafting of s.1(5) in relation to the availability of specific performance to the third party has been noted.

[109] *Re Lind* [1915] 2 Ch. 345; *Re Gillott's Settlements* [1934] Ch. 97; *Re Haynes' WT* [1949] Ch. 5.

[110] *Pullan v Koe* [1913] 1 Ch. 9.

[111] *Cannon v Hartley* [1949] Ch. 213; above, para.5–022.

[112] *Williams v CIR* [1965] N.Z.L.R. 345; ("the first £500 of the net income which shall accrue to the assignor ... from the Trust."). An assignment of the assignor's life interest under the trust would, of course, have been valid.

[113] cf. *Re Ralli's WT* [1964] Ch. 288 (valid declaration of trust of remainder interest, which is not future property). See also *Simpson v Simpson* [1992] 1 F.L.R. 601 (share of proceeds of sale of cottage which was not yet sold).

[114] *Re Burton's Settlement* [1955] Ch. 82. See also *Don King Productions Inc v Warren* [2000] Ch. 291 (agreement for value to assign non-assignable contracts took effect as declaration of trust of benefit of contracts).

[115] *Meek v Kettlewell* (1842) 1 Hare 464; *Re Brooks' ST* [1939] Ch. 993; *Williams v CIR* [1965] N.Z.L.R. 345.

[116] [1903] 1 Ch. 697; cf. *Re Bowden* [1936] Ch. 71; *Re Adlard* [1954] Ch. 29. A purported disclaimer of rights under the will or intestacy of a living person for no consideration is a nullity: *Re Smith* [2001] 1 W.L.R. 1937; criticised J. Glister [2014] Conv. 11 at 14–15.

without a further declaration of the trusts, or where the property vests in the settlor after he has declared the trusts on which he is to hold it.

We have seen that, prior to the Contracts (Rights of Third Parties) Act 1999, a covenant in a marriage settlement to settle after-acquired property was not enforceable at the suit of the next-of-kin because they were volunteers[117]; and that a deed purporting to convey future property upon trust is ineffective.[118] But if, in either of these cases, the property found its way into the hands of the trustees, it would presumably be held upon the trusts declared in the relevant documents.[119] If the settlor, in either case, conveyed the property to the trustees, that action could be construed as a further declaration of the trusts; but if the property reached the trustees by another route, being conveyed perhaps by the executors of the testator from whom the property came,[120] or coming into the hands of the trustee in a different capacity,[121] the possibility of finding that there was a further declaration of trust is less strong. There appear to be three possible solutions to such a case: that the trustees take beneficially, that they hold on trust for the settlor, or that they hold on the trusts declared in the previous document. The first is obviously untenable. The second involves the proposition that the settlor could claim back in equity property which he had covenanted or purported to settle.[122] The third avoids the necessity of making the ultimate destination of the property depend upon the route by which it reached the trustees; it is consistent with the expressed intention of the parties and appears to be the most satisfactory solution.[123]

Where the property comes to the settlor himself, it is possible for the court to hold that a previous declaration of trust,[124] followed by the vesting of the property in him, constitutes the trust. It is clear that a previous declaration is not of itself sufficient[125]; subsequent confirmation of a previous declaration is sufficient.[126] In less obvious cases, it is no doubt a question of construction to determine whether or not the settlor is to be taken to have made a subsequent declaration or to have affirmed a previous one. If he made the declaration every day, the last declaration being made the moment before he received the property, this would no doubt be sufficient. But, in the absence of authority, it is unsafe to predict to what extent an argument on these lines might be acceptable. What is clear in these cases is that the beneficiaries must show that the trust was properly

---

[117] *Re D'Angibau* (1880) 15 Ch.D. 228; *Re Plumptre's Settlement* [1910] 1 Ch. 609.

[118] *Re Ellenborough* [1903] 1 Ch. 697; *Re Brooks' ST* [1939] Ch. 993.

[119] *Re Ellenborough* [1903] 1 Ch. 697. Miss Emily Towry Law had already handed over to the trustees the property which she received under her sister's will; and no attempt was made to recover it.

[120] *Re Adlard* [1954] Ch. 29.

[121] *Re Ralli's WT* [1964] Ch. 288.

[122] Dicta in *Re Ralli's WT* [1964] Ch. 288, indicate that this could be regarded as unconscionable. cf. *Re Brooks' ST* [1939] Ch. 993.

[123] So held in *Re Ralli's WT*, discussed above, para.5–015.

[124] As opposed to a mere covenant to settle or purported assignment; *Re Ellenborough* [1903] 1 Ch. 697.

[125] *Brennan v Morphett* (1908) 6 C.L.R. 22; *Williams v CIR* [1965] N.Z.L.R. 345.

[126] *Re Northcliffe* [1925] Ch. 651.

declared and properly constituted. There appears to be nothing intrinsically wrong in holding that the declaration of a trust may precede its constitution, as in the secret trusts cases.[127]

7. EXCEPTIONS TO THE RULE THAT EQUITY WILL NOT ASSIST A VOLUNTEER

A. The Rule in *Strong v Bird*

5–029
Where an incomplete gift is made during the donor's lifetime, and the donor appointed the donee as executor,[128] or, in the case of an intestacy, the donee is appointed administrator,[129] the vesting of the property in the donee in his capacity as executor or administrator may be treated as the completion of the gift, overriding the claims of the beneficiaries under the will or intestacy. Similarly with the release of a debt owed to the donor. At common law, the appointment of the debtor as executor released the debt. In equity such a debtor had to account to the estate unless the testator intended in his lifetime to release the debt, such intention continuing until death.

> In *Strong v Bird*,[130] B borrowed £1,100 from A, his stepmother, who lived in his house, paying £212 10s. a quarter for board, and it was agreed that the debt should be paid off by a deduction of £100 from each quarter's payment. Deductions of this amount were made for two quarters; but on the third quarter-day and thereafter, A paid the full amount. Thus on her death, some four years later, £900 remained owing. B was appointed her sole executor, and proved the will. Later A's next-of-kin claimed for the balance of the debt. It was held that the appointment of B as executor released the debt.

It is necessary to show that the donor intended to make an immediate lifetime gift[131] (or to release a debt, as the case may be), and also that he or she had a continuing intention until the date of death. Thus, an intention to make a testamentary gift is not sufficient.[132] The intention must relate to a specific item of property. It is not sufficient that there was a vague desire to provide something for the donee. In *Re Gonin*,[133] a mother wished to leave her house to her daughter, who had given up a career to look after her parents, but thought for some reason that she could not do so because the daughter was illegitimate. Instead, she wrote a cheque for £33,000 in the daughter's favour, which was found after her death. (The cheque could not be cashed, as the bank's mandate to pay is terminated by

---

[127] Ch.6.

[128] (1874) L.R. 18 Eq. 315. It is sufficient if he is appointed one of the executors; *Re Stewart* [1908] 2 Ch. 251. See also *Blackett v Darcy* [2006] W.T.L.R. 581 (New South Wales Supreme Court held that the rule applied where an imperfect gift was made to joint donees, only one of whom was appointed executor).

[129] *Re James* [1935] Ch. 449; *Re Gonin* [1979] Ch. 16 (where, however, doubts were expressed by Walton J). In *Strong v Bird* itself, the rule was said only to apply to an executor.

[130] (1874) L.R. 18 Eq. 315; *Re James* [1935] Ch. 449 (a gift of realty).

[131] cf. *Re Ralli's WT* [1964] Ch. 288, above, para.5–015 (covenant to settle in the future). See also *Simpson v Simpson* [1992] 1 F.L.R. 601 (future gift of proceeds of sale of cottage which was not yet sold).

[132] *Re Stewart* [1908] 2 Ch. 251; *Re Innes* [1910] Ch. 188.

[133] [1979] Ch. 16; (1977) 93 L.Q.R. 488.

notice of death.)[134] The daughter became administratrix, but failed in her claim to the house. There was no evidence of a continuing intention that the daughter should have an immediate gift of the house. The drawing of the cheque, as a substitute, pointed the other way. Nor will the rule apply if the testator, subsequently to the act on which the executor relies as establishing the intention to give a chattel, acted inconsistently with that intention by giving or lending the chattel to someone else,[135] nor if the testator, having once had an intention to give, forgot the gift, and treated the property as his own.[136]

B.   Donatio Mortis Causa[137]

i.   The Principle.   A *donatio mortis causa* is a lifetime gift which is conditional upon, and which takes effect upon, death. It must be distinguished on the one hand from a normal lifetime gift, under which title passes immediately to the transferee; and, on the other hand, from a testamentary gift which takes effect under the provisions of a will. It may therefore be regarded as an exception either to the rules governing lifetime gifts, or to the rules governing testamentary gifts. In the present context, we are concerned with the former aspect. But the assistance of equity will not be required by the donee in all cases. Where the subject-matter is a chattel which has been delivered to the donee, the donee's title is complete on the donor's death, no further act being necessary. In the case of a chose in action or land, on the other hand, the donee's title is not complete on the donor's death as the legal title vests in the donor's personal representatives. The donee can seek the assistance of equity to compel the personal representatives to do whatever is necessary to perfect the donee's title.[138] It is in this latter situation that the doctrine of *donatio mortis causa* can be seen as an exception to the rule that equity will not assist a volunteer to perfect an imperfect gift.

    The three essentials for a valid *donatio mortis causa* were laid down by Lord Russell CJ in *Cain v Moon*.[139]

(a)   The gift must have been in contemplation, though not necessarily in the expectation, of death[140];

(b)   the subject-matter of the gift must have been delivered to the donee[141];

(c)   the gift must have been made under such circumstances as to show that the property is to revert to the donor if he should recover.[142]

5–030

---

[134] Bills of Exchange Act 1882 s.75.

[135] *Re Freeland* [1952] Ch. 110.

[136] *Re Wale* [1956] 1 W.L.R. 1346.

[137] See Borkowski, *Deathbed Gifts—The Law of Donatio Mortis Causa* (1999); Law Com. CP No. 231, *Making a Will* (2017), Ch.13.

[138] *Duffield v Elwes* (1827) 1 Bli.(N.S.) 497; *Re Lillingston* [1952] 2 All E.R. 184.

[139] [1896] 2 Q.B. 283; *Wilkes v Allington* [1931] 2 Ch. 104 at 109; *Re Craven's Estate* [1937] Ch. 423 at 426; *King v Dubrey* [2015] EWCA Civ 851; [2016] Ch. 221 at [50].

[140] *Wilkes v Allington* [1931] 2 Ch. 104.

[141] *Cain v Moon* [1896] 2 Q.B. 283.

[142] *Re Lillingston* [1952] 2 All E.R. 184.

In addition, the obvious risk of fraudulent claims means that courts will require clear evidence of the purported gift and will subject that evidence to strict scrutiny.[143]

5–031 **ii. Contemplation of Death.**   Commonly, *donationes mortis causa* are made in reference to a particular illness, but the principle applies equally to other causes such as a hazardous journey,[144] or possibly even to the contemplation of active service in war.[145] However, the donor must have been contemplating death more particularly than by merely reflecting that we must all die someday. In *King v Dubrey*, Jackson LJ reviewed the authorities and concluded that the donor "should be contemplating his impending death. That means [he] should be contemplating death in the near future for a specific reason".[146] The donor in *King v Dubrey* was a woman who was 81 years old at the relevant time, but she was in reasonable health and had no particular reason to contemplate death in the near future. The Court of Appeal held that she had not been contemplating her impending death in the appropriate sense, and so overturned the trial judge's finding that she had made a valid *donatio* of her house to her nephew.[147]

If death occurs, the *donatio* may still be valid even though it comes from a cause different from that contemplated. In *Wilkes v Allington*[148] the donor was suffering from an incurable disease, and made a gift in the knowledge that he had not long to live; as things turned out, he had an even shorter time than he imagined, for he died two months later of pneumonia. It was held that the gift remained valid. On the other hand, if the donor recovers from the particular circumstance that caused death to be feared, then the *donatio* fails and is revoked. It does not "run on" until death finally occurs by some other cause.[149]

5–032 **iii. Delivery of Subject-matter.**   A *donatio mortis causa* will not be valid without a delivery of the property to the donee[150] with the intention of parting with the "dominion" over it. It will not suffice if the property is handed over merely for safe custody.[151]

---

[143] *Cosnahan v Grice* (1862) 15 Moo. P.C. 215 at 223; *King v Dubrey* [2016] Ch. 221 at [52], [64], [91].

[144] According to *Thompson v Mechan* [1958] O.R. 357, the ordinary risks of air travel do not suffice.

[145] *Agnew v Belfast Banking Co* [1896] 2 I.R. 204 at 221.

[146] *King v Dubrey* [2016] Ch. 221 at [55]; H. Cumber [2016] Conv. 56.

[147] [2016] Ch. 221 at [68], overturning *King v Dubrey* [2014] EWHC 2083 (Ch); [2014] W.T.L.R. 1411. The Court also held that *Vallee v Birchwood* [2014] Ch. 271 had been wrongly decided on the point.

[148] [1931] 2 Ch. 104 (the case was approved by the Court of Appeal in *King v Dubrey* [2016] Ch. 221 at [55], but without direct comment on the point of death occurring from a different cause). *Re Dudman* [1925] 1 Ch. 553 provides that a valid *donatio mortis causa* cannot be made in contemplation of suicide, although that decision predated the abolition of suicide as a crime by the Suicide Act 1961 s.1.

[149] *King v Dubrey* [2016] Ch. 221 at [57].

[150] *Ward v Turner* (1752) 2 Ves.Sen. 431.

[151] *Hawkins v Blewitt* (1798) 2 Esp. 663.

(a) Chattels. The donor must hand over either the chattel itself or the means of getting control over it such as, for example, a key to the box or place where the subject-matter is located.[152] In the case of a car, it is not necessary that the log book be handed over.[153]

5–033

(b) Choses in Action. The position is more difficult if the title to the chose in action does not pass by mere delivery of any document. The donor must hand over such documents as constitute "the essential indicia or evidence of title, possession or production of which entitles the possessor to the money or property purported to be given".[154] Thus the delivery of a bank deposit pass-book,[155] a Post Office Savings Bank-book,[156] national savings certificates[157] or a cheque or promissory note payable to the donor[158] have been held to create a *donatio mortis causa* of the chose in action represented by the document in question, so that, on the death of the donor, the donee can compel the personal representatives to perfect the transfer of legal title.

5–034

(c) Land. It had long been considered that land could not be the subject-matter of a *donatio mortis causa*. Although there was no English authority directly in point, Lord Eldon had doubted the possibility.[159] The reason may have been the supposed difficulty of parting with the "dominion" over land. The matter was reviewed by the Court of Appeal in *Sen v Headley*.[160]

5–035

> The claimant and the deceased, who was separated from his wife, had lived together for 10 years until 1964, after which they remained on close terms. When the deceased was terminally ill in hospital he said to the claimant, "The house is yours, Margaret. You have the keys. They are in your bag. The deeds are in the steel box." The claimant had always had a set of keys to the house. After the deceased died (intestate), the claimant found the box in a cupboard, used the key (which the deceased had slipped into her bag) and took possession of the deeds.

The Court of Appeal upheld the claimant's entitlement to the house. The title deeds were essential indicia of title to the house (which had an unregistered

---

[152] *Re Lillingston* [1952] 2 All E.R. 184; *Re Cole* [1964] Ch. 175. It may not suffice if the donor retains a duplicate key; *Re Craven's Estate* [1937] Ch. 423 at 428. cf. *Woodard v Woodard* [1995] 3 All E.R. 980 (possible retention of second set of car keys by donor who was too ill to use them held insignificant).

[153] *Woodard v Woodard* [1995] 3 All E.R. 980; J. Martin [1992] Conv. 53.

[154] *Birch v Treasury Solicitor* [1951] Ch. 298 at 311. cf. *Re Weston* [1902] 1 Ch. 680; *Delgoffe v Fader* [1939] Ch. 922.

[155] *Birch v Treasury Solicitor* [1951] Ch. 298; *Hobbes v NSW Trustee & Guardian* [2014] NSWSC 570.

[156] *Re Weston* [1902] 1 Ch. 680. It is otherwise if withdrawals may be made without producing the book; *Delgoffe v Fader* [1939] Ch. 922.

[157] *Darlow v Sparks* [1938] 2 All E.R. 235.

[158] Even though unendorsed and therefore not transferable by delivery. See *Re Mead* (1880) 15 Ch.D. 651; *Wilson v Paniani* [1996] 3 N.Z.L.R. 378 (where the claim failed because there was no delivery).

[159] *Duffield v Elwes* (1827) 1 Bli.(N.S.) 497 (where a *donatio mortis causa* of a mortgage of land was upheld).

[160] [1991] Ch. 425; M. Halliwell [1991] Conv. 307; J. Thornely (1991) 50 C.L.J. 404; P. Baker (1993) 109 L.Q.R. 19. In *King v Dubrey* [2016] Ch. 221 no *donatio* was found because the donor did not contemplate her impending death and because her intention was more consistent with a testamentary intention than with a conditional, revocable gift. However, handing over the deeds of the house did satisfy the requirement of delivery of subject-matter: at [73].

title[161]), and had been constructively delivered to her. As in the case of a chose in action, parting with dominion over the essential indicia of title sufficed. The donor's continuing theoretical ability to deal with the property, and his retention of keys to the house to which he knew he would not return, did not amount to a retention of dominion. Every *donatio mortis causa*, whether or not of land, circumvented the Wills Act. The additional statutory formalities for lifetime transfers of land provided no greater obstacle than the Wills Act, as the trust on the donor's death was implied or constructive. The exception to the formality rule now contained in s.53(2) of the Law of Property Act 1925 was not as well developed in Lord Eldon's day as now. The policy of the law that formalities were required for the transfer of land should be upheld, but it should be acknowledged that that policy had been substantially modified by the developments in estoppel and constructive trusts. The doctrine of *donatio mortis causa* was anomalous, but to except land from it would be a further anomaly.

5–036   **iv. The Intention of the Donor.**   The donor's intention must be to make a gift which is conditional upon death, and which will therefore be revoked upon recovery by the donor. Thus, there is no *donatio mortis causa* if the intention is to make an immediate unconditional gift, even though the gift may fail,[162] nor where the intention is to make a future gift.[163] The conditional nature of the gift need not be expressed, but may be implied from the circumstances.[164]

If it is inevitable that the donor will die from the contemplated cause, then the courts will relax the requirement that the donor specifically make the gift revocable on survival.[165]

5–037   **v. Revocation.**   In addition to automatic revocation upon the donor's recovery,[166] the donor may revoke expressly, or by recovering dominion over the subject-matter,[167] but the donor cannot revoke by will, the reason being that the donee's title is complete before the will takes effect.[168] It might be added that the gift fails if the donee predeceases the donor.[169]

5–038   **vi. Exceptions.**   It has been held that a *donatio mortis causa* cannot be made of the donor's own cheque[170] or promissory note.[171] The former is merely a

---

[161] The result would be the same if the land certificate of registered land had been delivered. However, there is no role for a land certificate under the Land Registration Act 2002. There are no indicia of title outside the register, and it is doubtful whether handing over the keys to the property would suffice.

[162] *Edwards v Jones* (1836) 1 My. & Cr. 226.

[163] *Solicitor to the Treasury v Lewis* [1900] 2 Ch. 812.

[164] *Re Lillingston* [1952] 2 All E.R. 184.

[165] *Wilkes v Allington* [1931] 2 Ch. 104 at 111; *King v Dubrey* [2016] Ch. 221 at [58].

[166] *Staniland v Willott* (1852) 3 Mac. & G. 664.

[167] *Bunn v Markham* (1816) 7 Taunt. 224.

[168] *Jones v Selby* (1710) Prec.Ch. 300 at 303; *Hudson v Spencer* [1910] 2 Ch. 285 (criticised H. Cumber [2016] Conv. 56, 60–61).

[169] *Tate v Hilbert* (1793) 2 Ves. 111 at 120.

[170] *Re Beaumont* [1902] 1 Ch. 886.

[171] *Re Leaper* [1916] 1 Ch. 579.

revocable mandate to the bank,[172] while a gift of the latter is merely a gratuitous promise, thus they are not the "property" of the donor at all. It may be otherwise if the cheque is actually paid in the donor's lifetime, or before the bank has been informed of his death, or if it has been negotiated for value.[173]

There is some authority that stocks and shares cannot form the subject-matter of a *donatio mortis causa*. It was held in *Ward v Turner*[174] that South Sea annuities could not be the subject-matter of such a gift. The decision may have been based on the inadequacy of the transfer on the facts, but it has been applied in cases concerning railway stock[175] and building society shares.[176] On the other hand, it has been held that shares in a public company can be the subject-matter of a *donatio mortis causa*.[177] This exception is, therefore, a doubtful one.

C. Statutory Exception: Conveyance to Child

For the sake of completeness, the position concerning a conveyance to a child is mentioned, although the exception arises from statute and not from the rules of equity.

5–039

A conveyance (whether it is for value or not) which purports to convey a legal estate to a child[178] operates as a declaration that the land is held in trust for the child.[179]

---

[172] Only a holder for value can sue.
[173] *Tate v Hilbert* (1793) 2 Ves. 111. See also *Blackett v Darcy* [2006] W.T.L.R. 581.
[174] (1752) 2 Ves.Sen. 431.
[175] *Moore v Moore* (1874) L.R. 18 Eq. 474.
[176] *Re Weston* [1902] 1 Ch. 680.
[177] *Staniland v Willott* (1852) 3 Mac. & G. 664.
[178] Who is incapable of holding a legal estate; LPA 1925 s.1(6).
[179] Trusts of Land and Appointment of Trustees Act 1996 Sch.1 para.1 (replacing earlier legislation).

CHAPTER 6

FORMALITIES AND SECRET TRUSTS

1. GENERAL

WE SAW in Ch.4 that the creation of a private express trust requires the three **6–001** certainties, and in Ch.5 that the trust must be validly constituted. This chapter will address the further requirement of compliance with any necessary formalities.

The word "formalities" is not a legal term of art. It is perfectly proper, for example, to speak of the "formalities" involved in effecting an outright transfer of legal property. There, the term is used without any reference to trusts or equitable interests at all. In the area of equity and trusts, however, "formalities" usually refers to certain legislative writing requirements that must be satisfied when a person seeks to declare a trust of property, or when a person seeks to transfer an existing equitable interest to another person. Those two occasions will be considered in turn in Parts 2 and 3 of this chapter. Part 4 examines the doctrine of secret trusts, whereby testamentary dispositions may be enforced even though they do not comply with the formality requirements of the Wills Act 1837.

2.   DECLARATIONS OF TRUST

6–002   The basic rule is that a settlor may create a trust by manifesting an intention to create it.[1] No formalities are required for the creation or enforcement of a lifetime trust of personalty.[2] A lifetime trust of land may also be created informally,[3] although such a trust will only be enforceable by the courts if it is evidenced in writing under the Law of Property Act 1925 s.53(1)(b). All testamentary trusts of whatever property must be in writing, signed by the testator and attested by two witnesses as required by the Wills Act 1837 s.9.[4]

Although no formalities are required for their creation, in practice lifetime trusts of all property are created in writing and usually by deed. This is because such trusts usually have as one of their objects the saving of tax, and this can only be achieved where there is clear documentary proof of the date and terms of the trust.

A.   Land

6–003   With regard to trusts of land, the Law of Property Act 1925 s.53(1)(b), provides:

> "A declaration of trust respecting any land or any interest therein must be manifested and proved by some writing signed by some person who is able to declare such trust or by his will."[5]

These requirements apply to express trusts only, and "do not affect the creation or operation of resulting, implied or constructive trusts".[6] The requirements apply to both lifetime and testamentary trusts of land, but the cases usually involve lifetime trusts. This is because a testamentary trust of land must also satisfy the

---

[1] The manifestation may be oral, written, or inferred from conduct; but "the mere existence of some unexpressed intention in the breast of the owner of the property does nothing": *Re Vandervell's Trusts (No.2)* [1974] Ch. 269 at 294. cf. the resulting trust arising on rebuttal of a presumption of advancement; below, para.11–034.

[2] *M'Fadden v Jenkyns* (1842) 1 Ph. 153; *Paul v Constance* [1977] 1 W.L.R. 527; *Re Kayford* [1975] 1 W.L.R. 279. These cases deal with declarations of trusts of personalty made by legal owners. Lifetime declarations of trusts of personalty by existing beneficiaries, i.e. declarations of sub-trust, are considered below, para.6–015.

[3] For a recent example, see *Ong v Ping* [2017] EWCA Civ 2069.

[4] As amended by the Administration of Justice Act 1982 s.17. The Law Commission is currently reviewing the law of wills, including the formalities required: see Law Com. CP No. 231, *Making a Will* (2017).

[5] Replacing Statute of Frauds 1677 s.7. Note that Law of Property Act 1925 s.53(1)(a) provides that "no interest in land can be created or disposed of except by writing signed by the person creating or conveying the same, or by his agent thereunto lawfully authorised in writing, or by will, or by operation of law". This provision does not apply to declarations of trust: see *Secretary, Dept of Social Security v James* (1990) 95 A.L.R. 615 at 622, per Lee J, referring to equivalent legislation in Western Australia, "Section 34(1)(b) would be either an odd exception, or otiose, if s.34(1)(a) were to be construed as including the declarations of trust in respect of land specifically provided for in s.34(1)(b)".

[6] Law of Property Act 1925 s.53(2). Dispositions of interests arising under such trusts are subject to the formality requirements: below, para.6–014.

formalities prescribed in the Wills Act, and these are more stringent than those in s.53(1)(b). Compliance with the Wills Act will, therefore, automatically involve compliance with s.53(1)(b).[7]

The declaration of trust need not itself be in writing, and failure to comply with the requirements of s.53(1)(b) renders the trust unenforceable rather than void.[8] The writing may also be created after the declaration of trust is made,[9] although courts will naturally be sceptical of written evidence that a landowner declared a trust of her property years earlier; especially so if the effect of that declaration would mean the property no longer being available to the landowner's creditors. Of course, even though an oral trust of land will be enforceable when accompanied by appropriate signed writing, it is still advisable actually to declare the trust in signed writing in the first place.[10] Doing so may avoid the problem that will now be discussed.

i. Signed by whom? Under s.53(1)(b) the writing must be "signed by some person who is able to declare such trust". This must be the settlor in self-declaration cases[11] and it would seem also to be the settlor in cases of transfer on trust where the declaration of trust itself is made in writing. However, the position is trickier in cases of transfers on oral trusts. Clearly, the best evidence will be written evidence of the oral declaration of trust made contemporaneously with the conveyance and signed by the settlor. Evidence created prior to the conveyance and signed by the settlor should also be acceptable, as long as it can properly be seen as evidencing the trust that was later declared. But what about evidence created after the conveyance: should the signed writing be created by the settlor or by the trustee?

6–004

The cases do not provide a clear answer,[12] and academic views are divided. The argument for the trustee being the "person who is able to declare such trust" is that the trustee is the apparent beneficial owner, notwithstanding the as-yet unenforceable trust.[13] On this analysis the settlor cannot be the relevant person because a transferor is not able to declare a trust once a conveyance has already occurred. On the other hand, it is the *prior* declaration of trust that is being

---

[7] On secret trusts of land, i.e. those that do *not* comply with Wills Act 1837 s.9, see below, para.6–039.

[8] *Gardner v Rowe* (1828) 5 Russ. 258.

[9] *Ong v Ping* [2017] EWCA Civ 2069 at [62].

[10] Trusts of land in New Zealand must be declared in writing and not merely proved by writing: Property Law Act 2007 s.25(2).

[11] *Wright v Wright* [2011] 1 F.L.R. 387 involved a self-declaration of trust by a father, who then attempted to avoid the trust by raising s.53(1)(b) and saying that there was no relevant writing. The judge held that an affidavit signed by the father in other litigation, when he stated that he held the house on trust, supplied the required writing.

[12] There are several cases where the trustee signed the writing but where the point was not crucial: *Gardner v Rowe* (1828) 5 Russ. 258; *Perpetual Executors & Trustees Association of Australia Ltd v Wright* (1917) 23 C.L.R. 185. In *Mountain v Styak* [1922] N.Z.L.R. 131, the New Zealand Court of Appeal allowed an appeal on the grounds that the trustee could create the signed writing, but with respect the reasoning is not easy to follow and there is certainly nothing in the case that suggests the settlor could *not* create the required writing. The settlor signed the writing in *Tierney v Wood* (1854) 19 Beav. 330, but again the point was not crucial.

[13] See T.G. Youdan (1984) 43 C.L.J. 306 at 316; cf. Underhill and Hayton, *Law of Trusts and Trustees*, 19th edn (2016), para.12.11.

evidenced and enforced. It seems logical that evidence of an earlier declaration of trust ought to be signed by someone who was able to declare that earlier trust, not by someone who would be able to declare it now.[14] There is admittedly some risk of self-serving claims if A is able, post-transfer, to create the evidence that B holds on trust for A. But it should be remembered that the existence of the trust still needs to be proved on the balance of probabilities. The evidence being in signed writing is an extra requirement that a claimant must satisfy, but it does not follow from the mere fact that evidence satisfies s.53(1)(b) that a trust will automatically be found.

Quite simply, the point is not settled. It may be that both the settlor and the trustee are competent to create post-transfer evidence that will satisfy s.53(1)(b). This is not easy to square with the words of the statute, but it may be the most appropriate solution, bearing in mind again that mere admissibility of evidence does not determine whether or not a trust is found to exist.

In the recent case of *Taylor v Taylor*,[15] a father and son bought land to hold on trust for themselves as joint tenants. A dispute later arose as to whether that trust was enforceable. The vendors of the land had promised to declare the trusts on completion of the sale and they had signed a transfer form that referred to the land being transferred on trust to the purchasers. The purchasers themselves had not signed that form, but it was still held to evidence the trust for the purposes of s.53(1)(b) because it was the vendors, prior to completion, who were the people "able to declare such trusts".[16] Clearly, pre-transfer evidence is properly created by those settling the trusts, who in this case were the vendors. However, Judge Matthews went on to say that a later notice of severance of the joint tenancy, which both purchasers had signed after the land had been conveyed to them, would also have sufficed to evidence the initial trust. This indicates that the trustees are competent to create post-transfer evidence that satisfies s.53(1)(b) because by that time they are the people able to declare the trusts.[17] However, there was no occasion to consider whether the vendors could also have created post-transfer evidence that would have satisfied s.53(1)(b).

6–005   **ii.   The Instrument of Fraud Principle.**   The question which next arises concerns the effect, if any, of an oral declaration of a trust of land that is not accompanied by written evidence. What should be done if a transferee procures a conveyance of land on the strength of an oral agreement to hold on trust for the transferor or a third party and then seeks to shelter behind the s.53(1)(b) requirements and keep the property beneficially? Equity, where possible, will not permit a statute to be used as an instrument of fraud. However, as will be seen, it

---

[14] Indeed, it may be that no-one could declare it now. If A conveyed land to B on oral trust for C, and C later died before any written evidence was created, no-one would now be able to declare a trust for C.

[15] [2017] EWHC 1080 (Ch).

[16] This position was not affected by the vendors at that time holding on constructive trust for the purchasers: see [2017] EWHC 1080 (Ch) at [44]–[47]; discussing *Oughtred v IRC* [1960] A.C. 206; below, para.6–016. It seems that the transfer form was viewed as evidence of the trust that would later be declared on completion (perhaps by the vendors' conduct in conveying the land when they had promised to declare trusts on that conveyance), rather than as a document through which the trusts were actually declared.

[17] [2017] EWHC 1080 (Ch) at [44].

is arguable that the cases now go further than is necessary to prevent the transferee keeping the property beneficially. Instead, it seems that s.53(1)(b) has lost much of its force.

> In *Rochefoucauld v Boustead*,[18] the claimant was the mortgagor of some land. It was sold by the mortgagee to the defendant, who had orally agreed to hold the land on trust for the mortgagor subject to the repayment to the defendant of the purchase price, and expenses. The defendant sold the land at a profit, but did not account to the mortgagor. The defendant became bankrupt.
>
> The mortgagor obtained an order for an account. The Court of Appeal refused to allow the Statute of Frauds to prevent the proof of fraud:
>
>> "[I]t is a fraud on the part of a person to whom land is conveyed as a trustee, and who knows it was so conveyed, to deny the trust and claim the land himself. Consequently, notwithstanding the statute, it is competent for a person claiming land conveyed to another to prove by parol evidence that it was so conveyed upon trust for the claimant, and that the grantee, knowing the facts, is denying the trust and relying upon the form of conveyance and the statute, in order to keep the land himself."[19]

The principle of this decision is that, in the case of fraud, oral evidence is admissible to establish the trust in spite of the statute. The trust enforced should therefore be the orally-declared express trust,[20] with the fraud justifying disapplication of the s.53(1)(b) requirements. However, the modern approach is to treat trusts established in this way as constructive[21]; such trusts would then fall outside the s.53(1)(b) requirements by virtue of s.53(2). In *Bannister v Bannister*,[22] A sold two cottages to B at below market rate, with B agreeing to hold one of the cottages on trust for A.[23] There was no relevant writing. The Court of Appeal, although apparently following *Rochefoucauld*, treated it as a case of constructive trust. The analysis has been applied and extended in later decisions.[24]

Where the conveyance is by A to B on an oral trust for A, the effect of this doctrine is clearly that B holds on trust (whether properly characterised as express, resulting or constructive) for A. The more difficult case is where the conveyance is by A to B on an oral trust for C. Should the beneficial interest be enjoyed by C, or be held on trust for A?[25] The latter is all that is necessary to

6–006

---

[18] [1897] 1 Ch. 196. See Y.K. Liew in C. Mitchell & P. Mitchell (eds), *Landmark Cases in Equity* (2012), Ch.14; *Rationalising Constructive Trusts* (Oxford: Hart Publishing, 2017), Ch.4.

[19] [1897] 1 Ch. 196 at 206, per Lindley LJ.

[20] See W. Swadling in C. Mitchell (ed.), *Constructive and Resulting Trusts* (Oxford: Hart Publishing, 2010), Ch.3; (2016) 10 J. Eq. 1.

[21] But cf. *Hodgson v Marks* [1971] Ch. 892; below, para.11–021, where a resulting trust was enforced.

[22] [1948] 2 All E.R. 133.

[23] The arrangement was characterised as a life interest in the property for A determinable if A moved out.

[24] See *Binions v Evans* [1972] Ch. 359; *Lyus v Prowsa Ltd* [1982] 1 W.L.R. 1044; *Anstalt v Arnold* [1989] Ch. 1; *Staden v Jones* [2008] EWCA Civ 936; [2008] 2 F.L.R. 1931; *De Bruyne v De Bruyne* [2010] EWCA Civ 519; [2010] 2 F.C.R. 251; *Chaudhary v Yavuz* [2011] EWCA Civ 1314; [2013] Ch. 249; B. McFarlane (2004) 120 L.Q.R. 667; S. Gardner in C. Mitchell (ed.), *Constructive and Resulting Trusts* (2010), Ch.2.

[25] See G. Costigan (1915) 28 H.L.R. 237 at 366; T.G. Youdan (1984) 43 C.L.J. 306 and [1988] Conv. 267; J.D. Feltham [1987] Conv. 246.

prevent B from benefitting, whereas to give the benefit to C may look like outright disregard of the statute. Nonetheless, it now seems that C may also rely on the fraud principle against B. In *Staden v Jones*,[26] following a review of the authorities, Arden LJ explained the decision in *Bannister v Bannister* as follows:

> "[T]he ratio of the decision turns on the fact that there has been an arrangement on the basis of which an interest in the property has been conveyed, and that the party, against whom the constructive trust is sought to be enforced, has relied on the absolute nature of the conveyance and denied the arrangement into which the parties have come."[27]

On the point of whether only A could enforce the trust and not C, Arden LJ held that such a "restriction on the principle would not be consistent with the principle itself".[28] C could enforce the trust against B.

6–007   The final area where s.53(1)(b) still has some force concerns an oral self-declaration of trust where A declares that he or she holds land on trust for C. The fraud doctrine cannot be invoked here,[29] and it has been held that C cannot assert a constructive trust and thereby avoid s.53(1)(b) unless he or she has detrimentally relied on the declaration of trust.[30]

3.   Transfers of Equitable Interests

6–008   The Law of Property Act 1925 s.53(1)(c) provides[31]:

> "A disposition of an equitable interest or trust subsisting at the time of the disposition must be in writing signed by the person disposing of the same, or by his agent thereunto lawfully authorised in writing or by will."

The subsection applies to equitable interests in both land and personalty.[32] It also applies to both lifetime and testamentary dispositions; however, as with the s.53(1)(b) requirements discussed above,[33] the cases invariably concern lifetime dealings because compliance with the Wills Act formalities will automatically involve compliance with s.53(1)(c).[34]

---

[26] [2008] 2 F.L.R. 1931.

[27] [2008] 2 F.L.R. 1931 at [31].

[28] [2008] 2 F.L.R. 1931 at [32].

[29] *Smith v Matthews* (1861) 3 De G.F.& J. 139. See T.G. Youdan (1984) 43 C.L.J. 306 at 325; J.D. Feltham [1987] Conv. 246 at 247.

[30] *Midland Bank Ltd v Dobson* [1986] 1 F.L.R. 171; cf. *Re Densham* [1975] 1 W.L.R. 1519.

[31] Re-enacting Statute of Frauds 1677 s.9, with some alterations, the most significant one being that s.9 applied to "all grants and assignments of any trust or confidence" while s.53(1)(c) applies to a "disposition of an equitable interest or trust".

[32] Some jurisdictions have amended this; e.g. New Zealand only requires writing if the equitable interest is in land or in a mixed fund that includes land: Property Law Act 2007 s.25(2). Some jurisdictions, e.g. Hong Kong, have abolished their equivalents of s.53(1)(c) altogether. For a review of common law jurisdictions see L. Bennett Moses in L. Bennett Moses et al (eds), *Property and Security: Selected Essays* (2010), Ch.2.

[33] Above, para.6–003.

[34] The term (testamentary) "disposition" in Wills Act 1837 s.1 is, in respect of its application to dealings with equitable interests, at least as wide as "disposition" in s.53(1)(c).

Lord Wilberforce noted in *Vandervell v IRC* that s.53(1)(c) "is certainly not easy to apply to the various transactions in equitable interests which now occur."[35] Such transactions have included attempts to avoid stamp duty on share transfers, and the practice of putting shareholdings in nominees. A question which has more recently arisen is whether and how far the subsection applies to securities held in trust which are traded electronically.[36] A more general question is whether the subsection may be satisfied by electronic writing and signature. Statutes requiring transfers to be in signed writing may be modified by secondary legislation so as to permit electronic documents,[37] but it seems that requirements of writing and signing may in any event already be capable of being satisfied by an electronic document.[38] A signed email may, therefore, suffice.[39]

A. Disposition[40]

The crucial words in the subsection are "disposition" and "subsisting". As will be seen, it has proved very difficult to identify those dealings that are properly classified as dispositions for the purposes of s.53(1)(c) and which therefore must be carried out in writing. "Subsisting" is also important as it indicates that the subsection only applies where an equitable interest has already been separated from the legal estate.[41] This means that an initial declaration of trust over legal property is not caught by s.53(1)(c),[42] although we have already seen that a declaration of trust over land will only be enforceable if it satisfies s.53(1)(b).

6–009

i. Assignment of Equitable Interest. The simple case is where a beneficiary under a trust assigns his or her interest to another. This is a disposition of an equitable interest, and is void unless in writing. This is so whether the beneficial interest is a limited interest, such as a life interest, or an absolute interest which is held on a bare trust by a nominee. The disposition must actually be in writing, and not merely evidenced in writing,[43] but a number of connected documents can provide the necessary writing.[44]

6–010

---

[35] *Vandervell v IRC* [1967] 2 A.C. 291 at 329.

[36] Some statutory disapplication of s.53(1)(c) has been effected: see Stock Transfer Act 1982 s.1(2); Uncertificated Securities Regulations 2001 (SI 2001/3755) r.38(5); Unit Trusts (Electronic Communications) Order 2009 (SI 2009/555); *Mills v Sportsdirect.com Retail Ltd* [2010] EWHC 1072 (Ch); [2010] 2 B.C.L.C. 143.

[37] Electronic Communications Act 2000 s.8. See Open-Ended Investment Companies (Amendment) Regulations 2009 (SI 2009/553) r.2(4) (modifying the writing requirements of Law of Property Act 1925 s.136).

[38] See Pt 3 of the Advice from the Law Commission, *Electronic Commerce: Formal Requirements in Commercial Transactions* (2001).

[39] *J Pereira Fernandes SA v Mehta* [2006] 1 W.L.R. 1543 (but the inclusion of the sender's email address is not a signature).

[40] G. Jones (1966) 24 C.L.J. 19; S. Spencer (1967) 31 Conv.(N.S.) 175; G. Battersby [1975] Ottawa L.R. 483 and [1979] Conv. 17; D. Sugarman and F. Webb (1978) 94 L.Q.R. 170. There is no disposition where a condition remains unfulfilled; *Chandler v Clark* (2003) 1 P. & C.R. 15.

[41] See *Westdeutsche Landesbank Girozentrale v Islington LBC* [1996] A.C. 669 at 706; *Kinane v Mackie-Conteh* [2005] W.T.L.R. 345.

[42] For declarations of trust over equitable property, see below, para.6–015.

[43] cf. Law of Property Act 1925 s.53(1)(b).

[44] *Re Danish Bacon Co Staff Pension Fund Trusts* [1971] 1 W.L.R. 248 at 255.

6–011   **ii.   Direction to Trustees to Hold on Trust for Another.**   Where a beneficiary directs the trustee to hold his or her interest upon other trusts, there is a disposition of the beneficiary's interest. This is the basis of *Grey v IRC*,[45] which was concerned with an attempt by the settlor to save stamp duty on shares being put into a settlement. At that time ad valorem stamp duty (i.e. varying with the value of the interest transferred) was payable on deeds of gift, although this is no longer the position.[46] The duty was payable upon the instruments through which property was transferred, not on the transaction itself.[47] So, if the valuable interest could be moved independently of a document, tax liability could be minimised.

> In *Grey v IRC*,[48] the settlor made six settlements of nominal sums in favour of his grandchildren. Later, he transferred shares of substantial value to the trustees, as his nominees, on trust for himself. That transfer attracted only nominal stamp duty. Then he orally instructed the trustees to hold that property upon the trusts of the six settlements. Finally, the trustees executed documents confirming that they held the shares upon the trusts of the settlements. The settlor, though not expressed to be a party, executed the documents.
>
> It was accepted that the trusts were validly declared. The question was whether they were declared by the settlor's oral declaration, in which case the subsequent documents were truly confirmatory, and passed no beneficial interest; or whether, as the Revenue argued, the documents themselves effected a disposition of an existing equitable interest within s.53(1)(c), in which case they were subject to ad valorem duty.[49]
>
> In argument, Pennycuick QC posed the question thus:
>
>> "If X holds property in trust for A as absolute owner and A then directs X to hold the property on the settlement trusts for the benefit of B, C, and D, and X accepts the trust, is that direction a 'disposition of a subsisting equitable interest within the meaning of section 53?'"[50]

The House of Lords answered affirmatively. While the trustees held the shares as nominees for the settlor, the settlor owned the entire beneficial interest. When the trustees held them upon the trusts of the settlements, the beneficial interest passed from the settlor to the beneficiaries under the settlements. That, according to the natural meaning of the word, was a disposition. Ad valorem stamp duty was payable on the documents.

It seems that the settlor's objectives would have been achieved if he had orally declared himself trustee of the shares for the grandchildren while still the legal owner; following the declaration with a confirmatory document; and retiring, when he wished, in favour of other trustees. Since *declarations* of trust are not caught by s.53(1)(c), the grandchildren would have received the valuable interest without the need for any document. A confirmatory document would not itself

---

[45] [1960] A.C. 1; J. Thornley (1960) 18 C.L.J. 31; G. Battersby [1979] Conv. 17; B. Green (1984) 47 M.L.R. 385. See also *Crowden v Aldridge* [1993] 1 W.L.R. 433.

[46] Finance Act 1985 s.82. Stamp duty was abolished (subject to certain exceptions) by the Finanace Act 2003, which introduced stamp duty land tax in relation to land.

[47] *IRC v Angus* (1889) 23 Q.B.D. 579; *Oughtred v IRC* [1960] A.C. 206 at 227.

[48] [1960] A.C. 1. See also *Halley v The Law Society* [2003] W.T.L.R. 845 (money held on trust in solicitor's client account).

[49] It was conceded that the documents should be regarded as dispositive in the event of the oral directions being held ineffective. See B. Green (1984) 47 M.L.R. 385 at 391.

[50] [1960] A.C. 1 at 4.

transfer any interest. Any later change in the legal ownership on the appointment of new trustees would have only attracted nominal duty.

Finally, it appears that s.53(1)(c) is satisfied if the equitable owner writes to the trustee in terms which refer to prior oral instructions to hold on new trusts, even though the writing does not include the particulars of the new trusts.[51]

iii. Conveyance of Legal Estate by Trustee. The subsection does not apply where the trustee conveys the legal estate to a third party who is intended to receive both legal and beneficial title. **6–012**

> In *Vandervell v IRC*,[52] Mr Vandervell wished to give sufficient money to the Royal College of Surgeons to found a Chair of Pharmacology. He decided to do so by arranging for the transfer to the College of shares in Vandervell Products Ltd, subject to an option exercisable by Vandervell Trustees Ltd, a company which acted as trustee for various Vandervell family trusts, to repurchase the shares for £5,000. The shares were initially held by the National Provincial Bank Ltd as nominee for Mr Vandervell.
>
> The Bank transferred the shares to the College subject to the option. Dividends amounting to £250,000 were declared on the shares and paid to the College, and that income in the hands of the College, being a charity, was not subject to income tax. But the Revenue claimed surtax from Mr Vandervell on the ground that he had not completely divested himself of the beneficial interest in the property.[53] The Revenue succeeded on the ground that there had been no declaration of the trusts on which the option to repurchase was held by Vandervell Trustees Ltd, and accordingly they held the option on a resulting trust for Mr Vandervell.[54]

A second argument of the Revenue, which was unsuccessful, concerned s.53(1)(c). The Revenue argued that, since the Bank had held the shares on trust for Mr Vandervell, the transfer by the Bank to the College transferred only the bare legal estate. On this analysis, the equitable interest in the shares could not leave Mr Vandervell except by a disposition in writing signed by him, of which there was none. If A holds property on trust for B, and A transfers the legal title to X, a volunteer, the ordinary rule is that X takes subject to B's equitable interest. This suggests that, if the volunteer X is *not* to take subject to B's subsisting equitable interest, then B must indeed effect a "disposition" of it. Nonetheless, the House of Lords held that s.53(1)(c) was not applicable to a case where the trustee transfers legal title to a third party who is intended to receive the property both legally and beneficially.

Although the decision must be regarded as settling the point, with respect the reasoning is not entirely clear. It seems fair to say that the s.53(1)(c) point was considered to be weak and their Lordships spent little time dealing with it. Lord Upjohn could "see no relevant difference"[55] between, first, an outright transfer of

---

[51] *Re Tyler* [1967] 1 W.L.R. 1269. *Grey* was cited in argument but not referred to in the judgment.

[52] [1967] 2 A.C. 291; G. Jones (1966) 24 C.L.J. 19; S. Spencer (1967) 31 Conv.(N.S.) 175; N. Strauss (1967) 30 M.L.R. 461; J. Harris (1975) 38 M.L.R. 557; R. Nolan (2002) 61 C.L.J. 169, explaining the decision as an application of the doctrine of overreaching, above, para.1–047.

[53] The current legislation is Income Tax (Trading and Other Income) Act 2005 s.624.

[54] That option was later exercised using money from one of the family trusts: see *Re Vandervell's Trusts (No.2)* [1974] Ch. 269; below para.6–014.

[55] [1967] 2 A.C. 291 at 311; cf. the similar views of Lord Donovan at 317–318. Lord Reid simply agreed that the s.53(1)(c) argument failed (at 307), and Lord Pearce agreed with Lord Upjohn (at 309). Lord Wilberforce's views on the point are somewhat different and seem to depend on a particular view of how Vandervell caused the shares to be transferred to the College; viz., that Vandervell did not actually direct the Bank (at 329–330).

legal title by a "full" legal and beneficial owner, and, secondly, a beneficiary directing the trustee to transfer legal title to a recipient with the intention that the recipient take as a full legal owner. Yet although both situations involve the recipient taking as a full legal owner, that does not mean they are the same. The first never concerns any equitable interests and simply involves a transfer of legal title. Section 53(1)(c) is not engaged because there is no subsisting equitable interest. On the other hand, the second example does involve a subsisting equitable interest because the property is initially held on trust. The recipient may not receive that equitable interest, since he cannot hold the legal title on trust for himself; but it would still appear that the beneficiary "disposes" of it.

It seems that the House of Lords decided that s.53(1)(c) does not apply to cases where the recipient is intended to take full legal title on the grounds that the rationale for the subsection has no application to such cases. Lord Upjohn said:

> "[T]he object of the section, as was the object of the old Statute of Frauds, is to prevent hidden oral transactions in equitable interests in fraud of those truly entitled, and making it difficult, if not impossible, for the trustees to ascertain who are in truth his beneficiaries. But when the beneficial owner owns the whole beneficial estate and is in a position to give directions to his bare trustee with regard to the legal as well as the equitable estate there can be no possible ground for invoking the section where the beneficial owner wants to deal with the legal estate as well as the equitable estate."[56]

Presumably, however, the subsection would apply if the beneficial owner were to direct that the legal title should be transferred to X, who should hold on trust for Y. In such a case the equitable interest, although passing at the same time as the legal title, would remain separated from it and the policy rationale for the writing requirements in s.53(1)(c) would still obtain. Such a result also appears to be required by *Grey v IRC*.[57]

6–013 The situations just described involve an authorised conveyance of legal title by the trustee. A trustee might alternatively transfer legal title in breach of trust. If the conveyance is made to a volunteer then there is no disposition of the beneficiary's equitable interest because it still binds the property in the recipient's hands.[58] The same is true if the recipient gives value but has notice of the beneficiary's interest. If, on the other hand, the recipient is a bona fide purchaser for value without notice then the beneficiary's interest in the property is extinguished.[59] But this does not involve a "disposition" of that interest for the purposes of s.53(1)(c); if it did, the bona fide purchase doctrine could not operate because such "dispositions" would invariably be void for lack of writing. More fundamentally, the bona fide purchase example does not involve any form of transfer of the beneficiary's equitable interest to the recipient, but instead shows the inherent limits of that equitable interest (as susceptible to extinguishment on sale to an innocent recipient).[60]

---

[56] [1967] 2 A.C. 291 at 311.
[57] [1960] A.C. 1. See the discussion of this point in R.C. Nolan (2002) 61 C.L.J. 169 at 186–187.
[58] *Re Diplock* [1948] Ch. 465.
[59] Above, para.1–039.
[60] See *Akers v Samba Financial Group* [2017] UKSC 6; [2017] A.C. 424 at [51], [72], [88]; above, para.1–039. The case involved the word "disposition", but in the context of the Insolvency Act 1986

iv. Declaration of Trust by Trustees. The decision in *Vandervell v IRC* did **6–014** not exhaust the subtleties of s.53(1)(c) in its application to Mr Vandervell's affairs. Faced with the surtax claim in 1961 in respect of the dividends paid to the Royal College of Surgeons, he instructed Vandervell Trustees Ltd to exercise the option. They did so, in the same year, using £5,000 from the Vandervell children's settlement. The College duly transferred the shares to Vandervell Trustees Ltd, who informed the Revenue that the shares were held on the trusts of the children's settlement. Dividends were declared on the shares and were collected by the trustee company. In 1965, Mr Vandervell executed a deed formally assigning to Vandervell Trustees Ltd any right or interest he might still have in the option or the shares, to be held on the trusts of the children's settlement.

The Revenue assessed Mr Vandervell to surtax in respect of the years 1961–65. Up to 1961, there was a resulting trust in his favour of the option; that had been decided in *Vandervell v IRC*. But the Revenue argued that Mr Vandervell had not disposed of that interest in writing until 1965. The option had been converted into the shares in 1961, but the Revenue argued that the beneficial interest remained in Mr Vandervell until the 1965 deed.

The executors of Mr Vandervell's estate stepped in before the Revenue's claim was litigated, and claimed from Vandervell Trustees Ltd the dividends paid during 1961–1965.[61] This claim to the dividends succeeded before Megarry J on the ground that the resulting trust which applied to the option applied also to the shares, and there had been no valid declaration of trust in favour of the children's settlement. This was reversed by the Court of Appeal, which held that the trustee company held the dividends on the trusts of the children's settlement.

The point of difference between the Court of Appeal and Megarry J concerned whether or not new trusts of the option had been validly declared. Megarry J took the view that no new trusts had been declared,[62] so the option and its fruits (the shares) were held beneficially for Mr Vandervell until 1965. Mr Vandervell was therefore entitled to the dividends from 1961–1965. In contrast, the Court of Appeal held that new trusts had been declared in favour of the children's settlement when the trustees used money from that settlement to exercise the option.[63] We have already seen that this involves a very lenient approach to the requirements for a valid declaration of trust[64]; nonetheless, that is what the Court of Appeal decided.

---

s.127 rather than Law of Property Act 1925 s.53(1)(c). The relevant point is the analysis of equitable rights and the operation of the bona fide purchase doctrine.

[61] *Re Vandervell's Trusts (No.2)* [1974] Ch. 269. The executors applied to join the Revenue as second defendants, but Vandervell Trustees Ltd successfully objected: *Vandervell Trustees Ltd v White* [1971] A.C. 912.

[62] See *Re Vandervell's Trusts (No.2)* [1974] Ch. 269 at 299–300.

[63] In fact, Stephenson and Lawton LJJ appeared to think that the resulting trust of the option was extinguished and new trusts were declared of the shares. But the legal rights conferred by the option were not extinguished simply because money had been paid. If, as must be the case, it was the payment of money from the children's settlement to the College that amounted to the declaration of trust in favour of the children's settlement, then at least for some short period until the completed transfer of the shares it would have been the rights in the option that were held on those trusts.

[64] Above, para.5–019.

Accepting that there was a declaration of trust in favour of the children's settlement in 1961, why did this not amount to a disposition of Mr Vandervell's subsisting equitable interest in the option? Although characterised as a "declaration" of trusts in favour of the children's settlement, it had the effect of shifting the equitable interest from Mr Vandervell to the children. Of course, if the device was caught by s.53(1)(c) it would have failed for lack of writing and Mr Vandervell may have succeeded in claiming the 1961–65 dividends.[65] On this point the key lies in recognising that the terms of the trust on which the trustee company held the option included the power for *either* the trustees *or* Mr Vandervell to declare new trusts. In 1961, by using money from the children's settlement, the trustee company declared that the option and its fruits would henceforth be held on the trusts of the children's settlement. It appears that Mr Vandervell's consent to this declaration was also required[66]; however, this just goes to the circumstances under which the *trustees* may validly declare the new trusts. As long as the *act* of declaration was not Mr Vandervell's, it would not involve a disposition by him, and s.53(1)(c) would not be engaged.[67] The distinction may be a fine one, but it is necessary to distinguish between activities that are properly seen as authorised acts of trustees and those that are properly seen as dispositions by beneficiaries.[68]

6–015   **v. Declaration of Sub-Trust by Equitable Owner.**   A beneficiary may declare that he or she holds an existing equitable interest on trust for another. Is this a "disposition of an equitable interest subsisting at the time of the disposition" within the meaning of s.53(1)(c), such that the declaration must be in writing? First, the definition of "disposition" in the Law of Property Act 1925 s.205 does not include a declaration of trust.[69] As a matter of principle, it can also be argued that a declaration of trust does not involve dealing with an interest that was "subsisting at the time of the disposition", since the new trust interest only arises on declaration. On the other hand, it was said in *Grainge v Wilberforce*[70] that, "where A was trustee for B, who was trustee for C, A holds in trust for C, and must convey as C directed." Thus, B "disappears from the picture",[71] and C becomes the beneficiary. If it is true that B "drops out", it may amount to a disposition of B's interest to C.

---

[65] Such a claim may still have failed on other grounds, such as estoppel.
[66] *Re Vandervell's Trusts (No.2)* [1974] Ch. 269 at 324, 325.
[67] See D. Hayton and C. Mitchell, *Hayton & Marshall Commentary and Cases on The Law of Trusts and Equitable Remedies*, 12th edn (2005), para.2–46. See also *Drakeford v Cotton* [2012] EWHC 1414 (Ch); [2012] 3 All E.R. 1138; discussed on this point below, para.11–024.
[68] See R.C. Nolan (2002) 61 C.L.J. 169 at 186–187.
[69] Contrast Conveyancing Act 1919 (N.S.W.) s.7 (although declarations of sub-trust are still not caught by Conveyancing Act 1919 s.23C(1)(c), the equivalent of Law of Property Act 1925 s.53(1)(c), for the reasons given in the following paragraphs).
[70] (1889) 5 T.L.R. 436 at 437; see also *Re Tout & Finch* [1954] 1 W.L.R. 178; *DHN Food Distributors Ltd v Tower Hamlets LBC* [1976] 1 W.L.R. 852; *Corin v Patton* (1990) 169 C.L.R. 540 at 579.
[71] *Grey v IRC* [1958] Ch. 375 at 382, per Upjohn J.

Clearly B will not "drop out" if he retains active duties under the sub-trust, as where he declares a trust of his interest for such of a class as he shall select.[72] These cases are not caught by s.53(1)(c) because the interest held on sub-trust was not one that subsisted at the time the sub-trust was created. The more difficult question is whether "bare" sub-trusts, where B declares himself trustee of his entire interest for C, and might therefore "drop out", are caught by s.53(1)(c). Even here, however, the better view is that these declarations of trust do not fall within the subsection.[73]

The point was considered by the Court of Appeal in *Nelson v Greening & Sykes (Builders) Ltd*.[74] The case did not involve s.53(1)(c), nor was there any express declaration of trust by B. A was trustee of land for B under a constructive trust of land arising out of A's contract to sell the land to B.[75] B held his interest on resulting trust for C because C had provided the purchase money.[76] Following "regrettably pointless" litigation between the parties, a charging order was made against B's interest in the land "as trustee"[77] prior to the date on which the legal title was transferred to C. It was held that the charging order was valid because it was made at a time when A held on trust for B, who held on trust for C, and B had not "dropped out". The authorities[78] on "dropping out" were saying that the trustee (A) might decide as a matter of practicality that it was more convenient to deal directly with the beneficiary of the sub-trust (C), but this did not mean that, as a matter of law, the intermediate trustee (B) ceased to be a trustee.[79] Since B remains a trustee as a matter of law even in the case of a "bare" sub-trust, then, like other sub-trusts, C's interest is not one that subsisted at the time the sub-trust was created. For this reason the declaration falls outside the requirements of s.53(1)(c).

vi. Specifically Enforceable Oral Contracts for Sale.   *Oughtred v IRC*,[80]   **6–016**
like *Grey v IRC*, concerned an attempt to avoid stamp duty on a share transfer.

> Mrs Oughtred was the owner of 72,700 shares in a company and was also tenant for life under a settlement which contained 100,000 preference shares and 100,000 ordinary shares. Her son, Peter, was entitled in remainder. In order to reduce the estate duty which would be payable on Mrs Oughtred's death, an oral agreement was made in 1956 under which Peter would surrender his remainder interest in the settled shares in consideration for the transfer to him of his mother's 72,700 shares.
>
> A deed was executed by Mrs Oughtred and Peter which recited that the settled shares were then held in trust for Mrs Oughtred absolutely. The trustees then transferred the settled shares to Mrs Oughtred; and she transferred the 72,700 shares to Peter. The question was whether ad

---

[72] *Re Lashmar* [1891] 1 Ch. 258 at 268; see Law Com. No. 260, *Trustees' Powers and Duties* (1999), p.61.

[73] See C.H. Tham (2017) 31 T.L.I. 76.

[74] [2008] 1 E.G.L.R. 59; *The Times*, 22 January 2008. See *Sheffield v Sheffield* [2013] EWHC 3927 (Ch) at [82]–[85].

[75] Below, para.12–008.

[76] Below, para.11–025.

[77] Under s.2(1)(b)(ii) of the Charging Orders Act 1979.

[78] In particular *Grey v IRC* [1960] A.C. 1.

[79] Nor did they apply to a case where the trust property was a purchaser's interest under a contract for sale.

[80] [1960] A.C. 206. See P.G. Turner [2006] Conv. 390, discussing Australian decisions on equivalent legislation.

valorem stamp duty was payable on the transfers. The document selected for the purpose of the claim was the transfer of the shares from the trustees to Mrs Oughtred.

The question depended on whether or not Mrs Oughtred was owner in equity of the shares before the legal transfer. Provided a contract is specifically enforceable, a constructive trust is said to arise as soon as the contract is entered into, whereby the equitable interest passes to the purchaser by virtue of his right to specific performance.[81] Contracts for the sale of land are normally specifically enforceable, provided they are in writing, as required by s.2 of the Law of Property (Miscellaneous Provisions) Act 1989. Contracts for the sale of personalty are specifically enforceable only if the remedy of damages would be inadequate. Thus contracts to sell shares in a public company are not normally specifically enforceable, but the position is otherwise in the case of shares in a private company, which are not available for purchase on the market. Mrs Oughtred was accordingly able to claim that the equitable interest had passed to her by virtue of her right to specific performance of the contract; or, putting the same point another way, that Peter, after the agreement, held his interest as constructive trustee for her (constructive trusts being exempted from the writing requirement by s.53(2)). The later document would then be only a transfer of the bare legal estate.

The House of Lords, however, by three to two, held to the contrary. For the majority, Lord Jenkins, with whose speech Lord Keith agreed,[82] accepted that Mrs Oughtred's interest, after the agreement, was similar to that of a purchaser of land between contract and conveyance. The purchaser's interest:

> "is no doubt a proprietary interest of a sort, which arises, so to speak, in anticipation of the execution of the transfer for which the purchaser is entitled to call. But its existence has never (so far as I know) been held to prevent a subsequent transfer, in performance of the contract, of the property contracted to be sold from constituting for stamp duty purposes a transfer on sale of the property in question."[83]

So here, the transfer of the legal estate was an instrument attracting duty.

Lord Radcliffe, dissenting along with Lord Cohen, took the view that Mrs Oughtred became equitable owner of the reversionary interest in the settled shares by virtue of the specifically enforceable agreement to exchange. She became the absolute owner in equity.

> "There was... no equity to the shares that could be asserted against her, and it was open to her, if she so wished, to let the matter rest without calling for a written assignment, from her son... It follows that, in my view, this transfer cannot be treated as a conveyance of the son's equitable reversion at all."[84]

---

[81] Below, para.12–008.

[82] The third member of the majority, Lord Denning, gave similar reasons to Lord Jenkins although without examining in detail the constructive trust point.

[83] [1960] A.C. 206 at 240. See also *Henty and Constable (Brewers) Ltd v IRC* [1961] 1 W.L.R. 1504 at 1510; *Taylor v Taylor* [2017] 4 W.L.R. 83 at [47]. *Oughtred* was applied in *Parinv (Hatfield) Ltd v IRC* [1998] S.T.C. 305 (sub nom. *Bishop Square Ltd v IRC* (1999) 78 P. & C.R. 169) involving an unsuccessful attempt to avoid stamp duty by executing a declaration of trust for the purchaser prior to the transfer ("The appeal is as hopeless as any that I have heard").

[84] [1960] A.C. 206 at 228.

This argument points out a number of questions relating to the nature of the interest which Mrs Oughtred held before the legal transfer from the trustees; the majority speeches leave these questions unanswered. It had always been held that stamp duty[85] was payable on a conveyance of land, even though the beneficial interest in the property passed on the signing of the contract; similarly with a purchase of shares. This factor may have influenced the court's approach to the application of s.53. *Oughtred* may thus be viewed as a policy decision.

Later decisions in varying contexts have tended to support the view that an equitable interest can pass under a contract without engaging s.53(1)(c), although the point is rarely fully argued. In *Re Holt's Settlement*,[86] concerning the Variation of Trusts Act 1958, Megarry J, relying on the minority judgments in *Oughtred*, accepted the proposition that where there is a specifically enforceable agreement, the beneficial interest passes to the purchaser under a constructive trust without writing. Similarly in *DHN Food Distributors Ltd v Tower Hamlets LBC*,[87] concerning compulsory purchase, the Court of Appeal assumed that an equitable interest in land could pass without writing where the transaction was contractual.[88] In *Chinn v Collins*,[89] concerning a capital gains tax avoidance scheme, Lord Wilberforce said that:

6–017

> "The legal title to the shares was at all times vested in a nominee... and dealings related to the equitable interest in these required no formality. As soon as there was an agreement for their sale accompanied or followed by payment of the price, the equitable title passed at once to the purchaser... and all that was needed to perfect his title was notice to the trustees or the nominee... ".

The shares were in a public company, but Lord Wilberforce did not appear to consider a specifically enforceable contract to be essential to this proposition which, it should be noted, led to the establishment of capital gains tax liability. Neither *Oughtred* nor even s.53 itself was cited.

Tax liability was not involved in *Neville v Wilson*,[90] where nominees held shares in U Ltd on trust for J Ltd, a family company. The shareholders of J Ltd agreed informally to liquidate the company and to divide its equitable interest in the U Ltd shares amongst themselves in proportion to their existing shareholdings. The question was whether s.53(1)(c) invalidated this agreement (in which case the equitable interest would have passed to the Crown when J Ltd was struck off the register). The Court of Appeal held that each shareholder's agreement gave rise to an implied or constructive trust so that s.53(2)[91] applied. Thus the

---

[85] Stamp duty was replaced by stamp duty land tax in relation to land transactions by the Finance Act 2003.

[86] [1969] 1 Ch. 100 at 116.

[87] [1976] 1 W.L.R. 852 at 865, 867.

[88] This argument is no longer tenable in the case of land because the contract must be in writing; Law of Property (Miscellaneous Provisions) Act 1989 s.2. See *United Bank of Kuwait Plc v Sahib* [1997] Ch. 107.

[89] [1981] A.C. 533 at 548.

[90] [1997] Ch. 144; R. Nolan (1996) 55 C.L.J. 436; M. Thompson [1996] Conv. 368; P. Milne (1997) 113 L.Q.R 213; cf. *United Bank of Kuwait Plc v Sahib* [1997] Ch. 107, where Chadwick J held that a contract to assign an equitable interest by way of mortgage required writing to satisfy s.53(1)(c) and doubted whether s.53(2) could apply. The point was not argued on appeal.

[91] "This section does not affect the creation or operation of resulting, implied or constructive trusts."

agreement was effective to vest the equitable interest in the shareholders without writing. The analysis of Lord Radcliffe in his dissent in *Oughtred* that a specifically enforceable agreement to assign passed the equitable interest to the assignee was correct. It was noted that Lords Jenkins and Keith had left the point open and that Lord Denning had rejected the application of s.53(2) without giving reasons.

The difficulties of this area are discussed more fully in Ch.12 below.[92]

6–018   **vii.   Variation of Trusts Act 1958.**   We shall see in Ch.23 that the Variation of Trusts Act 1958 gave power to the court to approve, on behalf of categories of persons unable to make the decision for themselves, variations of the existing beneficial interests under trusts where it is for the benefit of the beneficiaries to do so. Many variations had been approved by the courts when suddenly, in *Re Holt's Settlement*,[93] Megarry J asked whether it was not necessary for the disposition of each existing beneficial interest to be in writing under s.53(1)(c). Megarry J was able to satisfy himself that writing was not necessary, and the threat of invalidity to most of the variations previously approved was removed. The details of the matter are best postponed until the Act is explained.[94]

6–019   **viii.   Right of Nomination under Staff Pension Fund.**   The rules of the pension fund of the Danish Bacon Co Ltd provided—as is common—that employees could nominate a person to receive moneys due in the case of death in service. Such a nomination might arguably be regarded as a lifetime disposition of an equitable interest under the pension fund trust; or as a testamentary disposition in that it took effect only in the event of the employee's death. In *Re Danish Bacon Co Staff Pension Fund Trusts*,[95] Megarry J held that it was not a testamentary disposition. He very much doubted "whether the nomination falls within section 53(1)(c)"[96]; but held that, even if it did, the necessary writing was supplied by two connecting documents.

6–020   **ix.   Disclaimer.**   In *Re Paradise Motor Co Ltd*,[97] a stepfather made a gift of shares to his stepson. The transfer, though technically defective, was sufficient to make the stepson equitable owner of the shares. The stepson knew nothing of the transfer. When he became aware of the circumstances, he stated in unmistakable language that he wished to make no claim to the shares. But when the company was in liquidation, he changed his mind and claimed his share of the proceeds. On the question whether there could be a disclaimer of an equitable interest without compliance with s.53(1)(c), it was held that "a disclaimer operates by

---

[92] Below, para.12–008.
[93] [1969] 1 Ch. 100.
[94] Below, para.23–018.
[95] [1971] 1 W.L.R. 248. Followed by the Privy Council in *Baird v Baird* [1990] 2 A.C. 548 (application of Wills Act depends on each scheme); *Gold v Hill* [1999] 1 F.L.R. 54 (nomination did not dispose of any equitable interest).
[96] [1971] 1 W.L.R. 248 at 256.
[97] [1968] 1 W.L.R. 1125.

way of avoidance and not by way of disposition."[98] The disclaimer was not a disposition within the meaning of s.53(1)(c),[99] so did not need to be made in writing. The stepson's disclaimer was effective and his claim failed.

Although it is said that disclaimers operate by way of avoidance, it does not follow that the initial transfer of property is void ab initio for all purposes. For example, in some circumstances tax may be charged on the value of the disclaimed property.[100] The Inheritance Tax Act 1984 s.142 provides for a special form of statutory disclaimer that does immunise the disclaiming party from liability for inheritance tax; however, this form of disclaimer must be made in writing.

x. Surrender. While it is clear that disclaimers are not "dispositions" within the meaning of s.53(1)(c), the position of surrenders is more complicated. Two situations can be distinguished: first, a surrender by a beneficiary that has the effect of passing an equitable interest to a new beneficiary or of enlarging the interests of other existing beneficiaries; secondly, a surrender by a beneficiary to the trustee so that the trustee becomes beneficially entitled.[101] As to the former, in *Re Schar (dec'd)*,[102] one of three joint tenants executed a "deed of disclaimer". Despite its name, the deed was held not to operate by way of disclaimer but instead to release the beneficiary's interest to the remaining two beneficiaries. It was not necessary to examine whether the writing was necessary. In *IRC v Buchanan*,[103] a surrender by a mother so that her children became entitled instead was found to be a "disposition" within the meaning of income tax legislation.

6–021

As to the latter situation, the House of Lords in *Newlon Housing Trust v Alsulaimen*[104] considered that the surrender of a lease would be a "disposition" within s.37 of the Matrimonial Causes Act 1973. On the other hand, and more directly on the point, Dixon J held in *Crichton v Crichton*[105] that a release to a trustee would not require writing under the (Victorian) Trusts Act 1915 s.73. However, that legislation used the original Statute of Frauds wording that

---

[98] *Re Paradise Motor Co Ltd* [1968] 1 W.L.R. 1125 at 1143 (the report refers to s.53(2) but this must be a slip for s.53(1)(c)); *Dewar v Dewar* [1975] 1 W.L.R. 1532; *Allied Dunbar Assurance Plc v Fowle* [1994] 1 E.G.L.R. 122; *Lohia v Lohia* [2001] W.T.L.R. 101 (affirmed on appeal unreported 25 October 2001).

[99] But see Law of Property Act 1925 s.205(1)(ii).

[100] See *Re Stratton's Disclaimer* [1958] Ch. 42. Also, while a trustee's disclaimer operates to revest legal title in the transferor, it does not undo the trust that was constituted on the initial transfer: *Mallott v Wilson* [1903] 2 Ch. 494.

[101] The object of a discretionary trust or power can renounce his or her position in the class: *Re Gulbenkian's Settlement (No.2)* [1970] Ch. 408 at 418; but cf. Y.K. Liew and C. Mitchell (2017) 11 J.Eq. 133 at 154. In any case, s.53(1)(c) is not engaged as such an object does not relevantly have an equitable interest.

[102] [1951] Ch. 280.

[103] [1958] Ch. 289. The legislation was Finance Act 1936 s.21. The modern equivalent is the Income Tax (Trading and Other Income) Act 2005 s.629.

[104] [1999] 1 A.C. 313.

[105] (1930) 43 C.L.R. 536.

required "grants and assignments" of equitable interests to be made in writing, and Dixon J noted that the modern term "disposition" may have a more general meaning.[106]

It may be noted that the reason given for s.53(1)(c) not applying to the transfer of shares to the College in *Vandervell v IRC*[107]—viz., that the Statute of Frauds could have no operation when a recipient of legal title was intended to receive that title beneficially—suggests that a surrender to a trustee would not fall within s.53(1)(c).

4. SECRET TRUSTS

A. Introduction[108]

6–022   We have seen that all testamentary dispositions, of whatever type of property, must be in writing and signed by the testator, in the presence of two or more attesting witnesses present at the same time.[109] We now turn to consider the effect of intended testamentary dispositions that fail to comply with these formalities.

The problem over the enforcement of secret trusts is the fact that the terms of the trusts are not expressed in a form which complies with the Wills Act; though, in cases in which the testator's intention is clear and there is no possibility of doubt or fraud, there is a real compulsion to enforce the secret trust. The question is whether the enforcement of the secret trust infringes the Wills Act; or whether there is recognised doctrine which allows secret trusts to be enforced in spite of the Wills Act. What should be done, for example, where a legatee or devisee persuades the testator to make a will in the legatee's favour in reliance on an oral promise to hold on trust for a third party? Or where an intestate successor similarly persuades the intending testator not to make a will at all? The point is particularly difficult because merely returning the property to the testator through the mechanism of a resulting trust is not satisfactory: a deceased testator cannot think again about how to effect his wishes, and a resulting trust for the residuary estate is often what he most wanted to avoid.

There may be many reasons why a testator wishes to be secret about his testamentary dispositions. In many of the older cases, the reason was that he wished to make a gift to support an illegitimate child and its mother. To include the gift in the will would give unwanted publicity; either among members of the family when its provisions are disclosed, or to any person who makes official application to examine the will. Nowadays, the usual reason is that the testator

---

[106] (1930) 43 C.L.R. 536 at 562. The original "grants and assignments" language still applies in Northern Ireland: Statute of Frauds 1695 (Ir) s.6.

[107] [1967] 2 A.C. 291; above, para.6–012.

[108] L. Sheridan (1951) 67 L.Q.R. 314; J. Andrews (1963) 27 Conv.(N.S.) 92; R. Burgess (1972) 36 Conv.(N.S.) 113; P. Critchley (1999) 115 L.Q.R. 631; D. Kincaid [2000] Conv. 420; Y.K. Liew, *Rationalising Constructive Trusts* (2017), Ch.5.

[109] Wills Act 1837 s.9. The Law Commission is currently reviewing the law of wills, including the formalities required: see Law Com. CP No. 231, *Making a Will* (2017).

cannot make up his mind upon all the details of the disposition of his estate.[110] By using a secret trust, he is able to escape from the policy of the Wills Act, and to retain for himself a power to make future gifts which do not comply with the Act. (It may be noted that it is also common to make a lifetime settlement and then, by will, to add further property to the settlement. The details of the disposition—the terms of the settlement—do not in that case appear in the will; but this is not a proper case of a secret trust, but of incorporating the other document into the will by reference.)

To create a secret trust the testator will usually arrange to leave a legacy to a trusted friend—often his solicitor—who undertakes to hold it upon certain trusts. Alternatively, the will may give it to him "to be held upon such trusts as I have declared to him." The question in the former case is whether the friend could keep the legacy for himself; if not, and clearly in the latter case he cannot, who can claim it: the intended beneficiaries, or the estate?

Different considerations apply to these two situations, as will be seen. The former case is known as a fully secret trust; the latter a half-secret trust. Before attempting to answer these questions in the context of secret trusts, it is necessary to mention other ways in which a trust or gift may be created by will although the will does not spell out the precise terms. First, the details may be supplied by extrinsic evidence, the admissibility of which is governed by the principles relating to the construction of wills. Thus if the testator creates a trust in favour of "my grandchildren" or "my partners" their identity can be established by extrinsic evidence. The trust is an ordinary testamentary trust, not a secret trust. What the testator cannot do is to make a gift in favour of persons named in an unattested document, unless that document is incorporated into the will. This leads us to the second way of creating a trust, the details of which do not appear in the will itself. This is the doctrine of incorporation by reference, which bears superficial similarity to the doctrine of half-secret trusts, but which must be distinguished from it.

B. Incorporation by Reference

"[I]f a testator, in a testamentary paper duly executed, refers to an existing unattested testamentary paper, the instrument so referred to becomes part of his will; in other words it is incorporated into it; but it is clear that, in order that the informal document should be incorporated in the validly executed document, the latter must refer to the former as a written instrument then existing—that is at the time of execution—in such terms that it may be ascertained."[111]

6–023

It is not sufficient that the document was in existence; it must be *referred to as an existing document.* Where the doctrine of incorporation applies, the incorporated document is admitted to probate, and the advantage of secrecy is lost. We will see that this doctrine appears to be in the minds of some judges when they are dealing

---

[110] This has been described as an abuse of the doctrine, as secrecy is irrelevant; T. Watkin [1981] Conv. 335. See *Re Snowden* [1979] Ch. 528. A survey of modern levels of usage is discussed in R. Meager [2003] Conv. 203.

[111] *In bonis Smart* [1902] P. 238 at 240, per Gorell-Barnes J. For an unusual example, see *Re Berger (Deceased)* [1990] Ch. 118.

with cases of secret trusts, and that the rules applicable to this doctrine have sometimes been applied to secret trust cases.[112]

It is common practice to make a bequest to trustees of an existing settlement to be held by them upon the trusts of that settlement. There is no difficulty in doing so if the existing settlement is incorporated by reference in the will. However, the requirement that only an existing document may be incorporated causes difficulty where a settlement is amended after the date of the will. In *Re Jones*,[113] a testamentary gift which attempted to include future alterations of the settlement was held void even though no alterations were made. The testator was there attempting to reserve for himself a power to dispose of his property by future unattested document.[114] Is this so whenever there is a testamentary addition to a settlement which includes a power of revocation or amendment? A strict application of the rules of incorporation by reference would suggest that it is; but the courts have been willing, where possible, to find a construction which will allow the testamentary gift to be upheld.[115]

> In *Re Schintz's Will Trusts*,[116] a settlor made a settlement in which he expressly reserved a power to amend or to revoke. His will provided that the residuary estate should be held on the trusts of the settlement and those which might be created by future deeds executed under the power of amendment or revocation, "or as near thereto as the situation will admit." No new trusts were declared. Wynn-Parry J upheld the gift, finding as a matter of construction that the words referring to the future deeds were "otiose and ... really no more than descriptive of the terms of the settlement."[117] *Re Jones* was distinguished on that ground.

It is not common for a settlor to reserve a power of revocation and amendment, for tax reasons. But the point is important because it is common to include in settlements a provision for the trustees to have power to amend the trusts, or to appoint upon new trusts, or to terminate the settlement; and it is necessary to know the effect of these factors upon a testamentary addition to the settlement.

If the settlement has not been changed at the date of the testator's death, the question is whether the testamentary addition is valid or not. Where the settlement has been altered, there are three possible solutions; first, that the testamentary addition is void; secondly, that it takes effect upon the settlement in its original form; thirdly, that it takes effect upon the settlement as amended. The testator's intention would in most cases be the third choice. He will know of the amendment of the trust made before his death, and which may have been made for tax or for family reasons. But clearly the doctrine of incorporation by reference is incapable of incorporating an amendment made after the date of the will. We have seen that the courts can sometimes escape the necessity of holding the gift void. But the second solution is not satisfactory on any argument.

---

[112] For differing views as to whether this doctrine is the basis of half-secret trusts, see P. Matthews [1979] Conv. 360; D. Hodge [1980] Conv. 341; T. Watkin [1981] Conv. 335; P. Critchley (1999) 115 L.Q.R. 631.

[113] [1942] Ch. 328.

[114] The gift was to the trustees of the settlement, "or any substitution thereof or modification thereof or addition thereto which I may hereafter execute."

[115] *Re Edwards' WT* [1948] Ch. 440.

[116] [1951] Ch. 870.

[117] [1951] Ch. 870 at 877.

The third solution could be achieved by legislation, such as exists in the United States,[118] which enables the testamentary gift to be held on the trusts of the settlement in accordance with any amendments made to those trusts prior to the testator's death. In England the matter must be resolved by applying the doctrine of incorporation by reference, with all its limitations.[119]

C. Fully Secret Trusts

Turning to secret trusts proper, there are three requirements that must be satisfied for the valid creation of a fully secret trust. First, the testator must intend that the legatee receive the property subject to a legal obligation. Most commonly the testator will intend the legatee to hold the legacy on trust for a secret beneficiary,[120] but the doctrine also applies if the legatee is to hold the property subject to certain secret conditions or charges. Secondly, that obligation must be communicated to the legatee. Thirdly, the legatee must accept the obligation. These requirements will be considered in turn. The difficulties generally arise in relation to the second and third: what exactly must be communicated, to whom, when, and by what means? What constitutes acceptance on the part of the legatee, and what is the position if he or she later refuses to perform the trust?

6–024

The simple case involves a testator making a will in a certain way because a prospective legatee has agreed to take the property subject to a secret obligation. However, the doctrine also applies where a testator fails to revoke a gift made in an existing will,[121] or where an intestate, in reliance on the undertaking of those entitled on intestacy, fails to make a will at all.[122]

i. Intention and Obligation.   The testator must intend the legatee to take subject to a legal obligation. In *McCormick v Grogan*,[123] the testator by will left all of his property to his friend Mr Grogan. In a letter kept with the will, the testator had listed several people along with the amounts of money that he wished them to receive. This included a £10 annuity for Mr McCormick that had not been paid. But the letter ended by saying that Mr Grogan was not "to act strictly to the foregoing instructions", and that it was left to his good judgment to do as he thought the testator would wish. The House of Lords held that the letter could not therefore operate to place Mr Grogan under a legal obligation. Instead, the testator had intended to give Mr Grogan "full and complete control over the property, and to leave the instructions simply as a guide which might assist him in the discretion which he would himself exercise".[124] There was no secret trust for Mr McCormick.

6–025

---

[118] See Uniform Testamentary Additions to Trusts Act 1991, authorising what are known as "pour-over" bequests.

[119] For other possibilities, see *Re Playfair* [1951] Ch. 4.

[120] In which case the subject-matter and objects of the trust must also be certain.

[121] *Moss v Cooper* (1861) 1 J. & H. 352.

[122] *Stickland v Aldridge* (1804) 9 Ves.Jr. 516 at 519; J. Fleming (1948) 12 Conv.(N.S.) 28.

[123] (1869) L.R. 4 H.L. 82. See also *Margulies v Margulies* [2008] W.T.L.R. 1853.

[124] *McCormick v Grogan* (1869) L.R. 4 H.L. 82 at 95. Also, even if it had been construed as a legal obligation, Mr Grogan had not accepted it.

The straightforward case involves a legatee agreeing to hold property on trust for a secret beneficiary. However, a secret trust may impose an obligation not only to hold on trust for a beneficiary on the testator's death, but also an obligation to make provision for an intended beneficiary after the legatee's death.

In *Re Gardner (No.1)*,[125] a wife left her estate to her husband for life, and there was an agreement that the property should be divided among certain beneficiaries on his death. The husband died intestate, and the Court of Appeal decided that he held the property, after his life interest, on trust for the beneficiaries.

Ottaway v Norman[126] took the matter a stage further. The testator agreed with his housekeeper that she should have a bungalow after his death, and she agreed to leave it to the testator's son by her will. The testator left the bungalow (plus its contents and some money) to her absolutely. She first made a will in favour of the testator's son; but she then changed that will, and left the bungalow to the defendant. Brightman J held that the son was entitled to the bungalow and its contents, although not to the money.

The enforcement of a secret trust in this situation creates a number of problems concerning the status of the trust during the housekeeper's lifetime, and the theoretical basis on which secret trusts are enforced. This question is discussed below, but some of the questions arising from *Ottaway v Norman* are more conveniently considered in Ch.12.

6–026   **ii. Communication.**   The obligation must be communicated to the legatee before the testator's death.[127] Where an absolute gift has taken effect in favour of the donee, it is too late to impose a trust. This is so whether the disposition is a lifetime transfer or a gift by will, which takes effect on the testator's death. Thus in *Wallgrave v Tebbs*[128] no secret trust was established where the testator's instructions were not communicated to the legatees, who took absolutely on the face of the will, but were found among his papers after his death.

If the testator discloses to the legatee the fact that he is to hold the legacy on trust, but does not disclose the terms of the trust before his death, the legatee will hold on resulting trust for the estate.[129] The intended trust, not being declared before the death, cannot be enforced. The imposition of the resulting trust will prevent the unjust enrichment of the legatee.

In *Re Boyes*,[130] a legacy was given to the testator's solicitor, who had undertaken to hold the property according to directions which he would receive by letter. The letter was found only after the death. The solicitor accepted that he held as trustee, and wished to carry out the trust. Kay J held that there was a resulting trust in favour of the next-of-kin, and explained the rule by saying:

---

[125] [1920] 2 Ch. 523; *Re Young* [1951] Ch. 344; below, para.6–037.

[126] [1972] Ch. 698; D. Hayton (1972) 36 Conv.(N.S.) 129.

[127] Regardless of the date of execution of the will: *Moss v Cooper* (1861) 1 J. & H. 352 at 367.

[128] (1855) 2 K. & J. 313; *McCormick v Grogan* (1869) L.R. 4 H.L. 82; *Re Boyes* (1884) 26 Ch.D. 531; *Re Hawkesley's Settlement* [1934] Ch. 384.

[129] Similarly if the terms, although disclosed, are unlawful or uncertain. See *Re Pugh's WT* [1967] 1 W.L.R. 1262; *Brown v Pourau* [1995] 1 N.Z.L.R. 352; *Gold v Hill* [1999] 1 F.L.R. 54 ("Look after Carol and the kids" sufficiently certain).

[130] (1884) 26 Ch.D. 531; *Re Hawkesley's Settlement* [1934] Ch. 384.

"The essence of all these decisions is that the devisee or legatee accepts a particular trust which thereupon becomes binding upon him, and which it would be a fraud in him not to carry into effect."[131]

This situation is similar to that of half-secret trusts in that the legatee takes as a trustee. But there is an important difference. In *Re Boyes*, the gift was absolute on its face; the trust could have been enforced if the terms had been declared before death. Where the existence of a trust is disclosed on the face of the will (a half-secret trust), the communication, as we shall see, must be prior to or contemporaneous with the execution of the will.[132]

The communication may be made orally or in writing, but must be sufficiently imperative.[133] It appears that, just as "a ship which sails under sealed orders, is sailing under orders though the exact terms are not ascertained by the captain till later,"[134] a testator may, during his lifetime, give to the legatee a sealed envelope which is not to be opened until the testator's death. This is sufficient provided the legatee knows that it contains details of the trust.

6–027

Finally, the testator must communicate not only the trust and the terms, but also the identity of the property to be held on trust.

In *Re Colin Cooper*,[135] the testator left £5,000 to two persons as trustees, and informally communicated to them the terms of the trust. By a later codicil he purported to increase the sum to be devoted to the secret trust to £10,000, they "knowing my wishes regarding that sum." This addition was not communicated to the trustees. It was held that the first instalment could be devoted to the secret trusts; but the later instalment went on a resulting trust.[136]

(a)   Tenants in Common and Joint Tenants.   Where a testamentary gift is made to two or more persons as tenants in common, and secret trusts are communicated to some but not all of the tenants in common, those to whom the communication was made are bound, the others taking beneficially.[137] "To hold otherwise would enable one beneficiary to deprive the rest of their benefits by setting up a secret trust."[138]

6–028

But where a gift is made to them as joint tenants, a distinction is made between the case where the trust is communicated before the making of the will, and where the communication is between the will and the death. In the former case, all joint tenants are bound.[139] In the latter, only those who have accepted the trust are bound by it,[140] "the reason being that the gift is not tainted with any fraud in procuring the execution of the will."[141]

---

[131] *Re Boyes* (1884) 26 Ch.D. 531 at 536.
[132] Below, para.6–033.
[133] *Margulies v Margulies* [2008] W.T.L.R. 1853.
[134] *Re Keen* [1937] Ch. 236 at 242, per Lord Wright; *Re Boyes* (1884) 26 Ch.D. 531 at 536.
[135] [1939] Ch. 811; criticised in D. Kincaid [2000] Conv. 420 at 428–430.
[136] Had it been a fully secret trust, the legatees would have been beneficially entitled to the addition.
[137] *Tee v Ferri* (1856) 2 K. & J. 357.
[138] *Re Stead* [1900] 1 Ch. 237 at 241.
[139] *Jones v Badley* (1868) L.R. 3 Ch.App. 362; *Re Gardom* [1914] 1 Ch. 662; *Re Young* [1951] Ch. 344.
[140] *Moss v Cooper* (1861) 1 J. & H. 352.
[141] *Re Stead* [1900] 1 Ch. 237 at 241, per Farwell J.

Farwell J was dissatisfied with his own explanation. He confessed that he was "unable to see any difference between a gift made on the faith of an antecedent promise and a gift left unrevoked on the faith of a subsequent promise."[142] It has been suggested that gifts upon secret trusts to joint tenants and tenants in common should be decided on the principle of *Huguenin v Baseley*,[143] that "no man may profit by the fraud of another".[144] Thus if A induces B to make or leave unrevoked a will leaving property to A and C whether as joint tenants or tenants in common, C will be bound if the testator would not have made any gift to C unless A had promised. If the testator would still have left property to C even if A had not promised, C is not bound. Whether A and C are joint tenants or tenants in common, and whether A's promise was before or after the making of the will are matters of evidence that may help to determine whether or not there was such an inducement, but of themselves both matters are inconclusive. The argument is persuasive; but the cases say otherwise. The wrong turning was taken in *Rowbotham v Dunnett*.[145]

The principles discussed above have emerged from cases concerning fully secret trusts. Of course, in the case of half-secret trusts there could be no question of the legatees taking beneficially. The issue would be whether a valid half-secret trust could be created by communication to fewer than the whole number of trustees. It seems that the principles applicable to fully secret trusts would be applied by analogy, bearing in mind that half-secret trustees will invariably be joint tenants, and that communication after the will is ineffective in the case of half-secret trusts, as explained below. Hence communication to one of the trustees prior to the making of the will is effective.[146]

6–029   **iii.   Acceptance.**   The legatee must also accept the obligation before the death of the testator. This acceptance can be implied through silence: as Wood VC put it in *Moss v Cooper*, the requirement is "acquiescence either by words of consent or by silence".[147]

A difficulty arises if the legatee seeks to revoke his or her acceptance of the obligation. Clearly, any revocation must be communicated to the testator. It is suggested in Underhill and Hayton that if the revocation was communicated such that the testator had a reasonable opportunity to make another will, and chose not to do so, then the legatee should take beneficially. However, if the revocation was communicated as the testator was on his deathbed, it would seem wrong to allow the legatee to take beneficially.[148]

Another point arises in relation to fully secret trusts: can the secret trustee defeat the secret beneficiary's interest by disclaiming the property?[149] In *Re*

---

[142] *Re Stead* [1900] 1 Ch. 237 at 241.

[143] (1807) 14 Ves. 273.

[144] B. Perrins (1972) 88 L.Q.R. 225 at 226.

[145] (1878) 8 Ch.D. 430.

[146] See *Re Gardom* [1914] 1 Ch. 662.

[147] (1861) 1 J. & H. 352 at 366.

[148] Underhill and Hayton, 19th edn, para.12.112.

[149] See J. Glister [2014] Conv. 11, arguing that the legacy cannot be disclaimed so as to defeat the interest.

Maddock,[150] Cozens-Hardy LJ said obiter that renunciation by a fully secret trustee would defeat the trust. By contrast, Lord Buckmaster in *Blackwell v Blackwell*[151] said:

> "in the case [of a fully secret trust] the legatee might defeat the whole purpose by renouncing the legacy and the breach of trust would not in that case enure to his own benefit, but I entertain no doubt that the Court, having once admitted the evidence of the trust, would interfere to protect its defeat."

iv. Proof. As we will see, the historical justification for the enforcement of secret trusts was that the legatee would otherwise be permitted to commit fraud. A high standard of proof is required to prove fraud, and there are dicta in many cases indicating that a secret trust can only be proved where there is "clear evidence",[152] and suggesting that the standard is the same as that required to support the rectification of a written instrument.[153] In *Re Snowden*,[154] however, Megarry VC disregarded the historical connection of the doctrine of secret trusts and the requirement of fraud, and laid down that the standard required to prove communication and acceptance is the ordinary civil standard of proof required to establish an ordinary trust. The evidence may, of course, establish an intention to create a trust, and its acceptance by the legatee, without establishing who the beneficiaries were. The legatee would then hold on resulting trust.[155] If questions of fraud or other special factors arose, the standard required would rise. The onus is on the person contending that the trust exists.[156]

6–030

D. Half-secret Trusts

Where the will gives property to a legatee *upon trust*, without, however, saying what the intended trusts are, the question of the enforcement of a secret trust communicated to the legatee has been treated very differently from the case where the property was given to the legatee *absolutely* in the will.[157] The courts have found it more difficult to enforce a secret trust in the former case—where the legatee takes expressly as trustee—than in the latter case. It is difficult to see any sense, however, in a rule which allows a secret trust to be enforced if the trust is nowhere mentioned in the will but holds it void if the testamentary gift discloses the fact that the legatee takes as trustee. If it is right that secret trusts are

6–031

---

[150] [1902] 2 Ch. 220 at 231.

[151] [1929] A.C. 318 at 328.

[152] See *McCormick v Grogan* (1869) L.R. 4 H.L. 82 at 87, per Lord Westbury; *Ottaway v Norman* [1972] Ch. 698 at 699.

[153] *Fowler v Fowler* (1859) 4 De G. & J. 250 at 264; *Crane v Hegeman-Harris Co Inc* [1939] 4 All E.R. 68 at 71; *Joscelyne v Nissen* [1970] 2 Q.B. 86 at 98; *Ottaway v Norman* [1972] Ch. 698.

[154] [1979] Ch. 528 at 537; C. Rickett (1979) 38 C.L.J. 260; B. Robertson (1991) 107 L.Q.R. 194.

[155] *Re Boyes* (1884) 26 Ch.D. 531.

[156] *Jones v Badley* (1868) L.R. 3 Ch.App. 362.

[157] Difficult questions can arise if the legacy simply says "to X" and does not add either "absolutely" or "on trust": see *Rawstron (Executrices of the Estate of Lucian Freud) v Freud* [2014] EWHC 2577 (Ch).

express trusts operating wholly outside the scope of the Wills Act (a point which is further discussed below),[158] it is difficult to see why the two situations should not be treated alike.

There is a historical explanation. 19th century judges said that secret trusts were enforced to prevent fraud. The element of fraud, however, was not present in the case of the gift to a legatee as trustee. As he took in a fiduciary capacity, he could in no circumstances take the property for himself. There was no possibility of fraud, and no justification, so the argument ran, for not applying the Wills Act. And it was at one time held that the mention of the existence of a trust did prevent the operation of the doctrine of secret trusts.[159] The validity of half-secret trusts was not finally established until the House of Lords decision in *Blackwell v Blackwell*[160] in 1929.

> The testator by a codicil gave a legacy of £12,000 to legatees upon trust to apply the income "for the purposes indicated by me to them." The trust had been accepted prior to the execution of the codicil. The House of Lords enforced the trust. They were assisted by *Re Fleetwood*[161] and *Re Huxtable*[162] where it was held that the secret trust doctrine applied although the gift was in terms a gift upon trust, and where therefore there was no question of fraud in the legatee. Lord Sumner concluded that:
>
>> "it is communication of the purpose to the legatee, coupled with acquiescence or promise on his part, that removes the matter from the provision of the Wills Act and brings it within the law of trusts, as applied in this instance to trustees, who happen also to be legatees."[163]
>
> The effect of the bequest "remains to be decided by the law as laid down by the Courts before and since the [Wills] Act, and does not depend on the Act itself."[164] Thus the trust operated outside the Act and could be enforced without proof of fraud.

6–032 **i. Timing of Communication.** In *Blackwell v Blackwell*, the trusts were communicated before the will and were stated to have been so communicated. Will the same rule apply where the trusts are or may be declared in the future? On the one hand, there is logically no difference between declarations of trusts before and after the will; for the will is ambulatory and of no effect until the death. The distinction is not made, as we have seen, with fully secret trusts.[165] If the trust operates independently of the Wills Act, the date of the will should be immaterial. On the other hand, it is more difficult to *assume* acquiescence where the communication is after the will; in the absence of proof of express agreement, the fact of non-revocation may be the only basis on which to presume acquiescence. More importantly:

---

[158] Below, paras 6–037–6–039.

[159] *Moss v Cooper* (1861) 1 J. & H. 352 at 367; *Le Page v Gardom* (1915) 84 L.J.Ch. 749 at 752; W. Holdsworth (1937) 53 L.Q.R. 501.

[160] [1929] A.C. 318. If the words in the will are insufficient to impose a trust, any secret trust will be fully secret: *Jankowski v Petek Estate* (1995) 131 D.L.R. (4th) 717 (gift to executor "to deal with as he may in his discretion decide upon").

[161] (1880) 15 Ch.D. 594.

[162] [1902] 2 Ch. 793.

[163] [1929] A.C. 318 at 339–340; *Ottaway v Norman* [1972] Ch. 698 at 711.

[164] [1929] A.C. 318 at 339.

[165] Above, para.6–026; *Re Gardner (No.1)* [1920] 2 Ch. 523.

"[A] testator cannot reserve to himself a power of making future unwitnessed dispositions by merely naming a trustee and leaving the purposes of the trust to be supplied afterwards."[166]

To allow that to be done by half-secret trust would be to give a wider rule for secret trusts (which might be oral) than that which as we have seen is applied in the case of incorporation of documents by reference.[167] It would be surprising if the law of wills permitted this; but, if the proper explanation of the enforcement of secret trusts is that they operate outside the will and independently of the Wills Act, then the rules relating to incorporation by reference are quite irrelevant.[168] And what Lord Sumner feared can always be achieved by a fully secret trust.

With half-secret trusts, however, the distinction appears to be made. In *Re Keen*[169] the testator gave a sum of money to trustees:

6–033

"to be held upon trust and disposed of by them among such person, persons or charities as may be notified by me to them or either of them during my lifetime."

Previously, one of the trustees had been given a sealed envelope containing the name of the beneficiary of the intended trust. In deciding in favour of the residuary legatees, the Court of Appeal held that the handing over of the sealed envelope was a communication of the trust, but that this, being *prior* to the date of the will,[170] was inconsistent with the terms of the will which provided for "a future definition ... of the trust subsequent to the date of the will," while "the sealed letter relied on as notifying the trust was communicated ... before the date of the will."[171]

The trust would, however, have failed independently of the question of inconsistency. The disposition contained a power to declare trusts in the future. This was void, for it "would involve a power to change a testamentary disposition by an unexecuted codicil and would violate section 9 of the Wills Act."[172]

The criticisms of this rule have been discussed. The contrary rule exists in Ireland,[173] New South Wales,[174] and in most of the American jurisdictions.[175] The matter is still open to the Supreme Court; it may be that the true ratio of *Re Keen* is the narrow point of inconsistency; but it was followed in *Re Bateman's Will Trusts*,[176] where, it seems, the rule was not challenged. The present position is unsatisfactory; there is no sense in a rule which (in the case of communication

---

[166] *Blackwell v Blackwell* [1929] A.C. 318 at 339, per Lord Sumner.

[167] *In bonis Smart* [1902] P. 238; P. Matthews [1979] Conv. 360.

[168] W. Holdsworth (1937) 53 L.Q.R. 501; *Moss v Cooper* (1861) 1 J. & K. 352 at 367.

[169] [1937] Ch. 236; *Johnson v Ball* (1851) 5 De G. & Sm. 85; R Burgess (1972) 23 N.I.L.Q. 263.

[170] *Re Huxtable* [1902] 2 Ch. 793.

[171] *Re Keen* [1937] Ch. 236 at 248; *Re Rees' WT* [1950] Ch. 204.

[172] *Re Keen* [1937] Ch. 236 at 247; *Johnson v Ball* (1851) 5 De G. & Sm. 85; *Re Hetley* [1902] 2 Ch. 866.

[173] *Riordan v Banon* (1876) 10 Ir.R.Eq. 469; contra *Balfe v Halfpenny* [1904] 1 Ir.R. 486; *Re Browne* [1944] Ir.R. 90; L. Sheridan (1951) 67 L.Q.R. 413; J. Mee [1992] Conv. 202; P. Coughlan (1991) 5 T.L.I. 69.

[174] *Ledgerwood v Perpetual Trustee Co Ltd* (1997) 41 N.S.W.L.R. 532, following *Re Browne* [1944] Ir.R. 90.

[175] American Law Institute, *Restatement of Trusts*, §18, 3rd edn, 2003, comment (c).

[176] [1970] 1 W.L.R. 1463.

between the will and the death) enforces a trust in a bequest "to X" but disregards the trust in a bequest "to X upon trust".[177]

Other views are that the distinction is justified because wills creating half-secret trusts are invariably drawn up by solicitors, and so stricter rules are appropriate[178]; or that consistency should be achieved by requiring the communication to be before the will even in the case of a fully secret trust. If the trusteeship was accepted after the will, the legatee would hold on trust for the residuary legatee or next-of-kin. This would have the advantage of preventing reliance on the doctrine of secret trusts by testators who are merely indecisive[179] and thus not within the rationale of the doctrine.[180]

We have seen that the doubts concerning the effectiveness of a communication after the will in the case of a half-secret trust derive from the testamentary formality rules. These rules do not apply to the analogous situation of a trust of a life policy nomination. In *Gold v Hill*[181] the insured nominated X and referred to him (erroneously) as executor on the nomination form. Later he informed X of the nomination and asked him to use the proceeds to "look after" his partner and children and to make sure that his widow got nothing. It was held that a trust analogous to a half-secret trust was validly created even though the communication was after the nomination.

E.   Can the Secret Trustee Benefit?

6–034   The legatee may claim that the testator intended him to take some benefit from the gift, perhaps, for example, a specific sum, or possibly any surplus after performing the trust. Two separate questions arise here. First, was this the testator's intention? Secondly, how far is evidence of such an intention admissible in favour of the trustee?

To consider first the question of intention, it is necessary to construe the language of the will to determine whether the testator's intention was to make the legatee a trustee of the whole of the property given, or to make a beneficial gift to him subject to his performing certain obligations.[182] In the former case, any surplus left after carrying out the trusts is held upon resulting trusts; in the latter,

---

[177] But see B. Perrins [1985] Conv. 248, supporting the communication rules as being based on the extrinsic evidence rule.

[178] D. Wilde [1995] Conv. 366. S. Evans [2014] Conv. 229 questions whether solicitor-drafted half-secret trusts remain a useful way of maintaining secrecy, since their existence is disclosed on the will and in a dispute the solicitor may be forced to give evidence of the circumstances surrounding the making of the will.

[179] As in *Re Snowden* [1979] Ch. 528.

[180] T. Watkin [1981] Conv. 335. See also the discussion of how the suggested reform would operate in the case of a person who refrains from making a will in reliance upon the acceptance of a trust by the next-of-kin.

[181] [1999] 1 F.L.R. 54. It was doubted in *Kasperbauer v Griffith* [2000] W.T.L.R. 333, whether a secret trust or any trust could be made of a pension scheme death benefit, as it was not owned by the testator: at most he could require it to be paid to his estate rather than to his widow under the rules of the pension scheme.

[182] Above, para.2–012. This construction is more likely where the legatee is a relative for whom the testator may be supposed to have been intending to provide. See *Irvine v Sullivan* (1869) L.R. 8 Eq. 673 (fiancée).

the legatee may keep it. There is thus no difficulty in a case where the will itself makes it clear that the trust does not extend to the whole of the legacy, but the will may be silent on the matter, and the only evidence extrinsic. This leads us to the second question, namely whether the trustee may be permitted to prove his claim to benefit by relying on documentary or even oral evidence.

The difficulty, whether the trust be fully or half-secret, is the danger of fraud by the secret trustee. A further problem in the case of a half-secret trust is that the evidence would contradict the terms of the will, which impose a trust on the entire legacy.[183]

> In *Re Rees' WT*[184] the testator by will appointed a friend and his solicitor (thereinafter called his trustees) to be executors and trustees. He left the whole estate "unto my trustees absolutely they well knowing my wishes concerning the same."
>
> The testator had told the trustees that he wished them to make certain payments and to retain any surplus for themselves. A substantial surplus remained. It was held that the trustees were not entitled to the surplus, which passed as on intestacy. The will, on its true construction, imposed a trust on the whole, and evidence was not admissible to show that the trustees were to take a benefit. It was not without significance that the trustee was the testator's solicitor. As Evershed MR said:
>
>> "In the general public interest it seems to me desirable that, if a testator wishes his property to go to his solicitor and the solicitor prepares the will, that intention on the part of the testator should appear plainly in the will and should not be arrived at by the more oblique method of what is sometimes called a secret trust."[185]

In *Re Tyler*,[186] however, there are suggestions that evidence is admissible as to all the terms of a trust, including any in favour of the trustee himself, although such evidence will not lightly be admitted. Pennycuick J found difficulty in the reasoning of *Re Rees*. But evidence contained in the (now deceased) trustee's own written memorandum did not suffice.[187]

Finally, we have seen that if a secret trust fails for non-compliance with the communication rules, or for uncertainty, the secret trustee holds on trust for the residuary legatee or next-of-kin. She could not claim the legacy for herself if the trust was half-secret, or, although fully secret, if she had accepted trusteeship. A question might arise as to whether the secret trustee could take the property if she herself was the residuary legatee or next-of-kin. There is no reason in principle why she should not, as she would be claiming in a different capacity.

---

[183] We have seen, in the context of communication, that evidence inconsistent with the will is not admissible; *Re Keen* [1937] Ch. 236, above, para.6–033.

[184] [1950] Ch. 204. See also *Re Pugh's WT* [1967] 1 W.L.R. 1262, suggesting that it is easier to infer an intention that a sole trustee should take beneficially than that two or more trustees should do so.

[185] [1950] Ch. 204 at 211.

[186] [1967] 1 W.L.R. 1269 (concerning a lifetime trust). See also *Ottaway v Norman* [1972] Ch. 698 where the secret trustee took a benefit in the form of a life interest. This was clearly the testator's intention and the point was not discussed. In any event, the interest had already been enjoyed.

[187] Although generally such a memorandum is *admissible* under the Civil Evidence Act 1995 to prove the terms of the trust.

F. Theoretical Basis of Secret Trusts

6–035   The formal requirements for a will, contained in the Wills Act 1837, are based upon a sound policy. It is important to avoid doubt, fraud and uncertainty in connection with testamentary dispositions; and it is essential to rely upon written formalities as there is no other way of ascertaining the intention of the testator. If secret trusts, which effectively create dispositions of property on death, are to be allowed, it is important to justify the failure to apply the provisions of the Wills Act. In terms of policy, it is easy to favour an exception in cases in which the intention of the testator is clear, and is opposed only by the formalities which were set up in the hope of establishing it. But further justification is needed. The Wills Act is a statute, and not merely an expression of policy. The question is whether some theory can be found to justify the enforcement of secret trusts.

6–036   **i. Fraud.**   In the early cases (which, as we have seen, concerned fully secret trusts)[188] it was said that secret trusts were enforced to prevent the fraud that the legatee would perpetrate if he kept the property for himself. In *McCormick v Grogan*,[189] Lord Westbury said:

> "My Lords, the jurisdiction which is invoked here by the Appellant is founded altogether on personal fraud. It is a jurisdiction by which a Court of Equity, proceeding on the ground of fraud, converts the party who has committed it into a trustee for the party who is injured by that fraud ... The Court of Equity has, from a very early period, decided that even an Act of Parliament shall not be used as an instrument of fraud; and if in the machinery of perpetrating a fraud an Act of Parliament intervenes, the Court of Equity, it is true, does not set aside the Act of Parliament, but it fastens on the individual who gets a title under that Act, and imposes upon him a personal obligation, because he applies the Act as an instrument for accomplishing a fraud. In this way the Court of Equity has dealt with the Statute of Frauds, and in this manner, also, it deals with the Statute of Wills."[190]

To base the court's intervention on the ground of fraud could well be a sufficient justification for not applying the Wills Act; but the next step was not so obvious. It would be wrong for the legatee to keep the property, but it was difficult to see how the prevention of fraud would justify the projection forward of the beneficial interest to the intended beneficiary.[191] This matter became all the more clear once the courts were dealing with the question of half-secret trusts. As the legatee was expressed to take as trustee, there was no possibility of fraud in the sense of the legatee being personally enriched. On what basis, then, could the intended beneficiary claim the property? It may be said that a secret trustee who relies on the Wills Act to defeat the testator's expectation commits a fraud against the testator and the secret beneficiary even in the absence of personal benefit,[192] and authority on mutual wills confirms that fraud can be perpetrated without gain.[193] This wider concept of fraud could then explain the enforcement of both

---

[188] Above, para.6–031.
[189] (1869) L.R. 4 H.L. 82; above, para.6–025. See also *Thynn v Thynn* (1684) 1 Vern. 296.
[190] *McCormick v Grogan* (1869) L.R. 4 H.L. 82 at 97.
[191] cf. the fraud principle in the context of oral trusts of land; above, para.6–006.
[192] See *Riordan v Banon* (1876) 10 Ir.R.Eq. 469; D. Hodge [1980] Conv. 341 at 345.
[193] *Re Dale (Deceased)* [1994] Ch. 31.

fully and half-secret trusts. But the reasoning here is circular[194]: we can only recognise a fraud being perpetrated against the "beneficiary" if we have already decided to identify that person as such, and so have already decided to suspend the Wills Act.

ii. Lifetime Trust Outside the Will. The modern view is that secret trusts **6–037** can be enforced because they are not trusts created by will; but are trusts arising outside and independently of the will[195]; that they arise by reason of the personal obligation accepted by the legatee.[196]

> In *Re Young*,[197] the testator made a bequest to his wife with a direction that on her death she should leave the property for the purposes which he had communicated to her. One of the purposes was that she would leave a legacy of £2,000 to the chauffeur. The chauffeur had witnessed the will. A witness may not normally take a legacy, and the question was whether he had thereby forfeited his interest.[198] Danckwerts J held that he had not; the trust in his favour was not a trust contained in the will but one created separately and imposed upon the legatee.[199]

It is one thing to say that the trust operates outside the will, but it is another to say just how and when the trust takes effect. If some of the propositions discussed in Ch.5 are sound, the most natural way for this to occur is to treat the communication to the trustee as the declaration of trust, and the vesting of the property in the trustee by the will as the constitution of the trust.[200] If this is so, it is a lifetime declaration, and the Wills Act has no effect upon it; the only statutory formalities that are relevant are Law of Property Act 1925 s.53(1)(b),[201] which requires that declarations of trusts of land should be evidenced in writing. There would be no awkward distinction between declarations prior to and subsequent to the will in half-secret trusts[202]; the sole question would be whether or not a trust

---

[194] As pointed out in A. Oakley, *Constructive Trusts*, 3rd edn (1996), p.248.

[195] *Cullen v Attorney General for Northern Ireland* (1866) L.R. 1 H.L. 190 at 198; *Blackwell v Blackwell* [1929] A.C. 318 at 340. The theory is rejected in P. Critchley (1999) 115 L.Q.R. 631. See also B. McFarlane (2004) 120 L.Q.R. 667.

[196] "I think the solution is to be found by bearing in mind that what is enforced is not a trust imposed by the will, but one arising from the acceptance by the legatee of a trust communicated to him by the testator, on the faith of which acceptance the will was made or left revoked, as the case might be": *Blackwell v Blackwell* [1929] A.C. 318 at 342.

[197] [1951] Ch. 344; *Cullen v Attorney General for Northern Ireland* (1866) L.R. 1 H.L. 190.

[198] Wills Act 1837 s.15. cf. *Re Fleetwood* (1880) 15 Ch.D. 594; *O'Brien v Condon* [1905] Ir.R. 51. If it is the secret trustee who attests there should be no difficulty if it is a half-secret trust, as he or she takes no beneficial interest on the face of the will. The position is more difficult if it is fully secret, but *Re Armstrong* (1969) 7 D.L.R. (3d.) 36 suggests that the legacy and secret trust survive.

[199] To the contrary is *Re Maddock* [1902] 2 Ch. 220, where the property subject to a fully secret trust was treated as being subject to a specific bequest for the purpose of the payment of debts out of the estate. No doubt the legacy would be treated as part of the estate for tax purposes and for the purposes of the Inheritance (Provision for Family and Dependants) Act 1975, rather than as property disposed of prior to the death.

[200] R.H. Maudsley in R. Pound et al (eds), *Perspectives of Law* (1964), Ch.11 (where much of the material in this section first appeared).

[201] Above, para.6–003. *Re Baillie* (1886) 2 T.L.R. 660 at 661; but there was no writing in *Ottaway v Norman* [1972] Ch. 698; below, para.6–039.

[202] *Re Keen* [1937] Ch. 236; above, para.6–033.

was declared of the property before the death, and whether that trust became properly constituted by the vesting of the property in the trustee.

6–038   We have seen that the usual rule in the case of property coming to a person who had previously declared herself trustee of it was that the trust did not become constituted without a further manifestation of intention.[203] It was submitted that where a third person accepted an instruction to hold the property on certain trusts and the settlor subsequently transferred the property to her without further declaration, the trust would be constituted. It should make no difference whether the property passed to the trustee by a conveyance or by a will.[204] It will probably fail however if the trustee predeceases the testator, at any rate in the case of a fully secret trust.[205] Assuming its terms were known, it may be that a half-secret trust could be saved by the maxim "a trust does not fail for want of a trustee".[206]

Ottaway v Norman[207] raises a further complication. There the secret trust was upheld as to the bungalow (and its contents). Assuming that it is correct to say that the testator made a lifetime declaration that the bungalow was to be held on trust for his son after the housekeeper's death, and that the trust was constituted by the vesting of the property in the housekeeper as trustee, then the trust of the bungalow arose on the testator's death, the housekeeper's interest effectively being a life interest. But the son also claimed entitlement to so much of the money left to the housekeeper as remained at her death. This claim failed. The testator had not intended to impose an obligation on the housekeeper as to *all* her money, nor had he intended to impose an obligation as to the money derived from his will, because this would be unworkable unless this money was to be kept separately, which was not envisaged. But Brightman J was content to assume, without deciding, that if property was given on the understanding that the primary donee would dispose of such assets, if any, as he may still have at his death in favour of a secondary donee, there would be a valid trust, "in suspense"[208] during the lifetime of the primary donee but attaching to the estate of the primary donee on the latter's death. This would be a "floating trust",[209] such as was recognised by the High Court of Australia in *Birmingham v Renfrew*[210] but which can hardly be said to be a recognised legal concept. The situation during the primary donee's lifetime would be similar to that existing during the lifetime of the survivor of makers of mutual wills. But the origin of the trust is of course quite different. In the former case it is based upon the declaration of the trust, followed by communication and acceptance and the vesting of the property in the trustee; in

---

[203] Above, para.5–028.

[204] As with the property received by Miss Towry Law from her sister and conveyed to the trustees: *Re Ellenborough* [1903] 1 Ch. 697; *Re Adlard* [1954] Ch. 29; *Re Ralli's WT* [1964] Ch. 288.

[205] *Re Maddock* [1902] 2 Ch. 220 at 251; A. Oakley, *Constructive Trusts*, 3rd edn (1996), p.250; cf. D. Kincaid [2000] Conv. 420 at 439.

[206] Unless the particular trustee is regarded as essential to the trust. For the view that a half-secret trust would also fail, see D. Wilde [1995] Conv. 366 at 373; cf. A. Oakley, *Constructive Trusts*, 3rd edn (1996), p.250. The question of disclaimer by the secret trustee has already been considered; above, para.6–029.

[207] [1972] Ch. 698; D. Hayton (1972) 36 Conv.(N.S.) 129; R. Burgess (1972) 36 Conv.(N.S.) at 115; J. Hackney [1971] A.S.C.L. 375 at 384.

[208] [1972] Ch. 698 at 713.

[209] D. Hayton (1972) 36 Conv.(N.S.) at 132.

[210] (1937) 57 C.L.R. 666. Applied in *Re Cleaver* [1981] 1 W.L.R. 939.

the case of mutual wills, it is based on the contract between the parties followed by the death of the first testator in reliance upon non-revocation by the survivor. Once the trust has attached, however, the problems are similar, and will be discussed in Ch.12.

Until the property has so vested, there is no completely constituted trust; the declaration can have no effect, and cannot create property rights. The will can be revoked or altered, or the property may be disposed of during the testator's lifetime. The testator can revoke his instructions to the secret trustee at any time,[211] and if he acts as if he had forgotten the declaration or assumed it to be no longer existent, no doubt it will be treated as having expired. It is therefore difficult to explain the legal basis of the decision in *Re Gardner (No.2)*.[212] We have seen that a wife left her estate to her husband for life,[213] and that after his death it was to be held on secret trust for three named beneficiaries. One of the beneficiaries predeceased the wife. The representatives of the deceased beneficiary successfully claimed the share.

A gift by will normally lapses if the donee predeceases the testator,[214] and the estate of the donee can only claim if the donee acquired some interest in the property before he died. No such interest could exist in this case; and the theory which suggests that a secret trust can be treated as a lifetime declaration of trust does not suggest that any interest is obtained by any beneficiary prior to the constitution of the trust by vesting of the legal estate in the trustee.

iii.   Express or Constructive Trust.
Closely connected with the theoretical basis of secret trusts is the question whether a secret trust is properly categorised as an express or constructive trust.[215] The question is not merely academic, for, as we have seen,[216] constructive trusts of land are excepted from the requirement of written evidence. Is an oral secret trust of land enforceable?

6–039

An express trust is one declared by the settlor; a constructive trust is one imposed by the law. The analysis of secret trusts as being declarations outside the will categorises them as express trusts, whether they are fully or half-secret.[217] In the case of a half-secret trust the will itself expressly declares a trust. While this element is absent with a fully secret trust, such a trust may claim to be express on the basis of the testator's express declaration to the secret trustee. There is

---

[211] But any substituted instructions given after the will is executed will be invalid in the case of a half-secret trust. See also M. Pawlowski and J. Brown [2000] Conv. 388.

[212] [1923] 2 Ch. 230. The decision is, in fact, easy to explain in practical terms: the surviving two beneficiaries each only asked for a one-third share, so the only parties left to claim the dead beneficiary's share were the heirs of that beneficiary and the heirs of the trustee. If the surviving two beneficiaries had asked for half each they would have received it: see J. Glister [2014] Conv. 11 at 16–18.

[213] *Re Gardner (No.1)* [1920] 2 Ch. 523; above, para.6–025.

[214] A special exception is made in the case of children of the testator who predecease him, leaving issue: Wills Act 1837 s.33. Such a gift takes effect in favour of the issue.

[215] One view is that the attempt to classify as express or constructive is misguided because the secret trust doctrine is concerned with the procedural question of admitting evidence of a trust and not with the nature of the trust itself; B. Perrins [1985] Conv. 248 at 253.

[216] Above, para.6–005.

[217] cf. Y.K. Liew, *Rationalising Constructive Trusts* (2017), at p.80: "Such a tightly-drawn link is unjustified … the nature of the trusts does not necessarily correlate to the justificatory theories in this way".

authority that a half-secret trust of land is not enforceable without written evidence.[218] In *Ottaway v Norman*,[219] a fully secret trust of land was upheld without written evidence; however, the point was not discussed.

Fully secret trusts however have, as it were, another string to their bow. They were enforced long before secret trusts were thought of as taking effect outside the will. We have seen that they have been said on high authority to be enforceable on the ground of fraud,[220] and they can claim also to be constructive trusts.[221] Indeed, fully secret trusts are often given as examples of constructive trusts, albeit in cases where the point is not in issue.[222] It is submitted that fully secret trusts can be enforced under either head.

6–040   **iv. Conclusion.**   Ultimately, the enforcement of secret trusts is a matter of policy relating to testamentary dispositions. The rules of the Wills Act 1837 are intended to achieve a reasonable degree of certainty in respect of testamentary dispositions. Secret trusts have, in effect, created a wide gap in the law relating to testamentary formalities. It is possible to take the view that secret trusts should not be enforced beyond preventing the unjust enrichment of the fraudulent legatee; or, on the other hand, to hold that the testator's intention should be upheld in every case. This is really a matter for the legislature, and it is submitted that it would be more satisfactory to review the whole matter and to incorporate into the statutory scheme as much of the secret trust doctrine as it is desired to retain.[223] At the time of writing, the Law Commission is reviewing the law of wills in general but not the law of secret trusts.[224] Excluding secret trusts from consideration may be thought peculiar, especially since the law of *donationes mortis causa* is included.[225]

---

[218] *Re Baillie* (1886) 2 T.L.R. 660 at 661.

[219] [1972] Ch. 698. See also *Stickland v Aldridge* (1804) 9 Ves.Jr. 516; *Brown v Pourau* [1995] 1 N.Z.L.R. 352; C. Rickett [1996] Conv. 302.

[220] *McCormick v Grogan* (1869) L.R. 4 H.L. 82; above, para.6–036.

[221] This is assumed obiter in *Re Cleaver* [1981] 1 W.L.R. 939 at 947.

[222] See, e.g., *Paragon Finance Plc v Thakerar & Co* [1999] 1 All E.R. 400 at 408–409; *De Bruyne v De Bruyne* [2010] 2 F.L.R. 1240 at [51]; *Crossco No.4 UnLtd v Jolan Ltd* [2011] EWCA Civ 1619 at [94].

[223] See E. Challinor [2005] Conv. 492; J. Griffin (2017) 23 T. & T. 373, both favouring abolition.

[224] Law Com. CP No. 231, *Making a Will* (2017) para.1.26.

[225] Above, para.5–030.

CHAPTER 7

POWERS

1. POWERS[1] AND TRUSTS

A POWER is an authorisation to do certain things which affect property to which   **7–001**
the appointor is not solely entitled, and in which he or she may have no beneficial
interest at all. A person may hold a power in a personal or an official capacity, a
distinction relevant to whether that person has fiduciary obligations. The source
of the power may be express grant or a statute. Thus trustees have by statute
powers of investment, sale, and so on.[2] They may also be given other powers by
the terms of the trust instrument, such as a power of appointment which enables

---

[1] See *Farwell on Powers*, 3rd edn (1916); G. Thomas, *Powers*, 2nd edn (2012); *Halsbury's Laws of England Vol 98: Trusts and Powers*, 5th edn (2013), Parts 4 & 5; Nolan (2009) 68 C.L.J. 293.
[2] See below, Ch.21.

those holding the power to effect the disposal of the settlor's property by "appointing" it to other people. It is with "powers" in the latter sense that this chapter is concerned.

It has been seen that there are important points of distinction between powers and trusts.[3] Essentially a trust is imperative and a power discretionary. The dividing line is not always clear; for many trusts contain discretionary elements; and many powers are given to trustees who are governed by fiduciary duties in the exercise of their powers.

The practical importance of the distinction lies in the extent of the obligations imposed on a trustee as compared with the donee of a power, for example, the question how far he or she is obliged to consider the claims of possible recipients,[4] also the extent of the rights of objects of a trust as compared with a mere power, including the question of entitlement to the property in default of exercise and the question whether the beneficiaries, all being adult and under no disability, can terminate the trust and either divide the trust property[5] or dispose of it.[6]

Whether a particular disposition creates a mere power or a discretionary trust is a question of construction. This has already been discussed.[7]

2. BARE POWERS AND FIDUCIARY POWERS

7–002   A distinction must also be made between a bare power (sometimes called a personal power) and a power to which some fiduciary obligation is attached, such as a power given to trustees of property exercisable in relation to that property.[8] Several aspects of this distinction will be explained in connection with powers of appointment. Of general application however is the rule that a bare power given to an individual can only be exercised by that individual,[9] and a bare power given to two or more by name cannot (subject to any contrary intent in the instrument creating it) be executed by the survivor.[10] But a power given to trustees is prima facie given to them by virtue of their office, and may be exercised by the survivor,[11] or by their successors in office,[12] and powers given to two or more

---

[3] Above, paras 2–021—2–027.

[4] *McPhail v Doulton* [1971] A.C. 424; especially at 456; above, para.4–011.

[5] *Saunders v Vautier* (1841) 4 Beav. 115; *Re Brockbank* [1948] Ch. 206; above, para.2–027, below, para.23–001.

[6] *Re Smith* [1928] Ch. 915; *Re Nelson* (1918) [1928] Ch. 920n.

[7] See above, para.2–025.

[8] On whether the powers of trust protectors are bare or fiduciary, see Underhill and Hayton, 19th edn, paras 1.77–1.94; *Re Piedmont & Riviera Trusts; Jasmine Trustees Ltd v L* [2015] JRC 196; (2015) 19 I.T.E.L.R. 210; *JSC Mezhdunarodniy Promyshlenniy Bank v Pugachev* [2017] EWHC 2426 (Ch) at [181]–[203].

[9] *Re Harding* [1923] 1 Ch. 182; *Re Lysaght* [1966] Ch. 191.

[10] Thomas, *Powers* (2012), para.1.53; *Re Beesty's WT* [1966] Ch. 223 (contrary intention).

[11] *Re Bacon* [1907] 1 Ch. 475; *Bersel Manufacturing Co Ltd v Berry* [1968] 2 All E.R. 552; Trustee Act 1925 s.18(1).

[12] *Re Smith* [1904] 1 Ch. 139; *Re De Sommery* [1912] 2 Ch. 622.

trustees jointly may be exercised by the survivor or survivors of them, or by the personal representatives of the last of them, pending the appointment of new trustees.[13]

3. POWERS OF APPOINTMENT

A power of appointment is one given by the donor of the power to the donee of the power (the appointor) to appoint property to some person (the appointee). Such powers are useful in that they make it possible for the donee of the power to take into consideration circumstances existing at the date of the appointment which the settlor or testator could not have foreseen. Thus, a husband may give his estate to his widow for her life, and after her death to their children. He may leave his widow to decide upon the shares which each child is to receive by giving to her a power to appoint among the children in such shares as she shall in her absolute discretion select, with a gift in default of appointment to the children in equal shares. Powers feature in trusts of all sorts, and modern trusts commonly give various powers of appointment to the trustees in addition to imposing the obligation to hold the property upon trust. In such situations, the property is owned by the beneficiaries who are entitled in default of appointment, subject to defeasance upon the exercise of the power.[14]

7–003

A. General, Special and Intermediate (or Hybrid) Powers

A gift to A for life with remainder to whomsoever he shall appoint is a general power; A may appoint to himself and become absolute owner. A general power is for many purposes equivalent to ownership.[15] If, however, in the illustration given above, the power were exercisable only by will, it would still be a general power even though A would then be unable to appoint to himself. A special power is one in which the choice of appointees is restricted by the terms of the power: for example a power to appoint in favour of one's own children, or of the employees of a company and their families and dependants.[16] The power is special even though the appointor is himself a member of the restricted group.[17] A power which does not fit neatly into these categories is one where the donee is given power to appoint to anyone except certain people or groups of people, for instance himself,[18] or all persons except the settlor and his wife,[19] or to all

7–004

---

[13] Trustee Act 1925 s.18, and see also s.36(7); *Re Wills' Trust Deeds* [1964] Ch. 219, below, para.7–029.

[14] *Re Brooks' ST* [1939] Ch. 993 at 997; Thomas, *Powers* (2012), para.1.41.

[15] See, for example, Inheritance Tax Act 1984 s.5(2); *Melville v IRC* [2002] 1 W.L.R. 407 (effect reversed by Finance Act 2002 s.119); Inheritance (Provision for Family and Dependants) Act 1975 s.25(1).

[16] *Re Gestetner* [1953] Ch. 672; *Re Sayer* [1957] Ch. 423.

[17] *Re Penrose* [1933] Ch. 793. See, however, Perpetuities and Accumulations Act 2009 s.11.

[18] *Re Park* [1932] 1 Ch. 580; *Re Byron's Settlement* [1891] 3 Ch. 475 (except "her husband or any friend or relative of his.") *Re Abraham's WT* [1969] 1 Ch. 463 at 474; *Re Lawrence's WT* [1972] Ch. 418 (except his "wife's relatives").

persons living at the death of the donee[20]; such powers are called intermediate or hybrid powers,[21] and they may be treated as general powers for some purposes, and special for others.[22] Intermediate powers are classified as special powers for the purpose of the Wills Act 1837 s.27.[23] For the purposes of the rule against perpetuities[24] a power is special unless it is exercisable by one person only and he could at all times transfer the interest to himself or his personal representatives.

A power may be exercisable in the donee's lifetime, or by will, or by either method. A power which is exercisable by will only is called a testamentary power; and may be general or special.

B. The Requirement of Certainty; Wide Powers; Capricious Powers

7–005   These matters have been dealt with in Ch.4, where the requirements of trusts and powers are compared.

C. Duties of Donee of Power; Rights of Objects

7–006   A donee of a power is not, as such, under any fiduciary duties. In the example given above of the power given to the wife to determine the shares in which the children shall receive the property from their father's estate, the widow is under no obligation to exercise the power or even to consider its exercise, although if she does exercise it, then she owes a duty to the default beneficiaries to keep within the terms of the power.[25] This is a bare, or personal, power of appointment. This must be contrasted with a fiduciary power held by a trustee by virtue of her office, which in turn must be distinguished from the obligation of a trustee of a discretionary trust.

A discretionary trust is a trust in which the property is held by the trustees on trust, not for named beneficiaries in fixed proportions, but on trust for such members of a class of beneficiaries as the trustees shall in their absolute discretion select. That situation has many points of similarity with a power of appointment held by trustees to appoint among a group of objects, although the distinction remains that a trust is obligatory; a power permissive.

Although a power is discretionary and permissive, a trustee who is the donee of a power must act in accordance with his fiduciary duty. The duties in the case of a fiduciary power arise, as it were, not from the power, but those inherent in the office of trustee. Thus, a trustee may not disregard a power, or forget about it,

---

[19] To avoid aggregation of the income of the trust with that of the settlor; Income Tax (Trading and Other Income) Act 2005 ss.619–648 (replacing earlier provisions). Also to avoid "reservation of benefit" under the inheritance tax system. See Ch.10.

[20] *Re Jones* [1945] Ch. 105.

[21] *Re Lawrence's WT* [1972] Ch. 418; *Re Manisty's Settlement* [1974] Ch. 17; *Re Hay's ST* [1982] 1 W.L.R. 202; *Re Beatty's WT* [1990] 1 W.L.R. 1503.

[22] See *Halsbury's Laws of England Vol 98: Trusts and Powers*, 5th edn (2013) at [42].

[23] Below, para.7–010.

[24] Perpetuities and Accumulations Act 2009 s.11.

[25] *Re Hay's ST* [1982] 1 W.L.R. 202.

or release it. His fiduciary duty requires him to give consideration to the exercise of the power, and particularly to any application made to him by an object of the power requesting an exercise in his favour.[26] "Trustees of a power must consider from time to time whether and how to exercise the power."[27]

> "A settlor or testator who entrusts a power to his trustees must be relying on them in their fiduciary capacity so they cannot simply push aside the power and refuse to consider whether it ought in their judgment to be exercised."[28]

The duties of the donee of a fiduciary power were analysed by Megarry VC in *Re Hay's Settlement Trusts*.[29] The donee must make no unauthorised appointment; must consider periodically whether to exercise the power; must consider the range of objects; and must consider the appropriateness of individual appointments. These duties, which were not intended to be exhaustive,[30] were further explained as follows: the donee, if exercising the power, must do so:

> "in a responsible manner according to its purpose. It is not enough for him to refrain from acting capriciously; he must do more. He must 'make such survey of the range of objects or possible beneficiaries' as will enable him to carry out his fiduciary duties."[31]

The donee must not simply exercise the power in favour of those objects who happen to be at hand or to claim his attention. He must first consider who the objects are. He need not compile a list or assess the number:

> "[W]hat is needed is an appreciation of the width of the field, and thus whether a selection is to be made merely from a dozen or, instead, from thousands or millions... Only when the trustee has applied his mind to 'the size of the problem' should he then consider in individual cases whether, in relation to other possible claimants, a particular grant is appropriate. In doing this, no doubt he should not prefer the undeserving to the deserving; but he is not required to make an exact calculation whether, as between deserving claimants, A is more deserving than B."[32]

The question arises of what the court will do if the trustees fail in their duty to consider the exercise of the power. **7–007**

> "Normally the trustee is not bound to exercise it, and the court will not compel him to do so. That, however, does not mean that he can simply fold his hands and ignore it, for normally he must from time to time consider whether or not to exercise the power, and the court may direct him to do this."[33]

A recalcitrant trustee may be removed. Where the power has been exercised, the court "will intervene if the trustees exceed their power, and possibly if they are

---

[26] *Re Gestetner* [1953] Ch. 672 at 688; *Re Manisty's Settlement* [1974] Ch. 17 at 25.

[27] *Re Manisty's Settlement* [1974] Ch. 17 at 22; *Re Gestetner* [1953] Ch. 672 at 688; *Re Abraham's WT* [1969] 1 Ch. 463 at 474; *Re Gulbenkian's Settlements* [1970] A.C. 508 at 518; *McPhail v Doulton* [1972] A.C. 424 at 456.

[28] *Re Gulbenkian's Settlements* [1970] A.C. 508 at 518.

[29] [1982] 1 W.L.R. 202.

[30] For the duty not to delegate, and to appoint in good faith, see below, paras 7–017—7–018.

[31] [1982] 1 W.L.R. 202 at 209, quoting from *McPhail v Doulton* [1971] A.C. 424 at 449.

[32] [1982] 1 W.L.R. 202 at 210.

[33] [1982] 1 W.L.R. 202 at 209.

proved to have exercised it capriciously."[34] The court will also intervene if the trustees have failed in any other respect to discharge the duties described above. Thus, in *Turner v Turner*,[35] the exercise of a power of appointment was invalid when the trustees, who were not professional trustees, failed to appreciate their powers and duties and left all the decision-making to the settlor (who was not a trustee). They executed documents of appointment on his direction without reading them, and without understanding that they had a discretion. The settlor "held the reins", and the trustees acted as a "rubber-stamp". This was a breach of their duty to consider the exercise of the power and the appropriateness of the appointments made. There was no effective exercise at all,[36] and the appointments accordingly were null and void, save to the extent that one appointment concerned land and was effective to transfer the legal title, which was held on trust by the appointee for the trustees of the settlement.

The principles on which the court will declare the exercise (or purported exercise) of a fiduciary power such as a power of appointment to be either void or voidable are more fully discussed below.[37]

A further question is whether the court may intervene in a more positive way than merely removing a trustee or setting aside an appointment made in breach of duty. It was held in *Mettoy Pension Trustees Ltd v Evans*[38] that where the court was called upon to intervene (because of breach of duty or where there was nobody left to exercise a fiduciary power),[39] it could adopt any of the methods suggested by Lord Wilberforce in *McPhail v Doulton*[40] in the context of discretionary trusts. Thus it could appoint new trustees, authorise the beneficiaries to prepare a scheme of distribution, or itself order a distribution.[41]

Whatever the form of the court's intervention, it is based upon the breach by the trustee of his fiduciary duty, and not upon any property right or entitlement among the objects of the power to compel a payment to them. Thus, in appropriate cases, an object of a power may seek the intervention of the court to compel disclosure of documents by the trustees.[42] The right of an object is not to compel an exercise of the power, in his own favour or at all, but merely to insist that the trustees consider the exercise of the power, to restrain any invalid exercise of the power, and, of course, to retain any property duly appointed to him.[43]

---

[34] *McPhail v Doulton* [1971] A.C. 424 at 456, per Lord Wilberforce.

[35] [1984] Ch. 100. See also *Re Hastings-Bass* [1975] Ch. 25.

[36] Described as "equitable non est factum" in *Pitt v Holt* [2013] UKSC 26; [2013] 2 A.C. 108 at [43], per Lord Walker.

[37] See discussion of *Pitt v Holt* [2013] 2 A.C. 108; below, paras 18–046—18–048.

[38] [1990] 1 W.L.R. 1587; S. Gardner (1991) 107 L.Q.R. 214; J. Martin [1991] Conv. 364; Vinelott J (1994) 8 T.L.I. 35.

[39] See now Pensions Act 1995 s.25(2) (fiduciary powers exercisable by independent trustee of pension fund on employer's insolvency).

[40] [1972] A.C. 424.

[41] Reliance was placed on *Klug v Klug* [1918] 2 Ch. 67, below, para.18–046, which was not cited in *Re Manisty's Settlement* [1974] Ch. 17, where the appointment of new trustees is said to be the only remedy. The *Mettoy* approach was followed in *Thrells Ltd v Lomas* [1993] 1 W.L.R. 456 and *Re William Makin & Sons Ltd* [1993] O.P.L.R. 171 (pension trust cases).

[42] *Schmidt v Rosewood Trust Ltd* [2003] 2 A.C. 709.

[43] *Vestey v IRC (No.2)* [1979] Ch. 198; affirmed [1980] A.C. 1148.

D. Power to Apply for Purposes

There is no reason why a power should not permit the application of money for specific purposes, as opposed to being paid to persons. The purposes must be sufficiently certain to enable a court to determine whether any particular application is within the terms of the power or not.[44] Such a power may be useful as a means of permitting the application of money to non-charitable purposes; a trust for non-charitable purposes lacks a means of enforcement and is void. That is a problem which is not faced by a power. The matter is discussed in Ch.16.

7–008

4. EXERCISE OF POWERS OF APPOINTMENT

A. General Rule

i. Lifetime. No technical words are required for the exercise of a power. All that is required is an intention on the part of the donee that the fund shall pass to someone who is an object of the power.[45] If the appointment relates to land, it must comply with Law of Property Act 1925 s.53(1)(b), and be evidenced in writing, signed by the donee of the power. An appointment of personalty may be made orally.[46] The terms of the power may require certain further formalities[47] for its exercise, or specific reference to the power or to the property subject to it,[48] and such requirements must be strictly complied with. Thus, if a power is to be executed by deed, it cannot be validly exercised by will,[49] and a power to be executed by will cannot be validly exercised by any instrument to take effect in the lifetime of the donee of the power.[50]

7–009

ii. By Will. The Wills Act 1837 s.27, provides, in relation to both realty and personalty, and subject to a contrary intention, that, where a testator has a "power to appoint in any manner he may think proper", a general devise[51] or bequest shall operate as an execution of the power. This clearly excludes special powers,

7–010

---

[44] See *Twinsectra Ltd v Yardley* [2002] 2 A.C. 164 at 169, per Lord Hoffmann: "The charge of uncertainty is levelled against the terms of the power to apply the funds. 'The acquisition of property' was said to be too vague. But a power is sufficiently certain to be valid if the court can say that a given application of the money does or does not fall within its terms."

[45] *Re Ackerley* [1913] 1 Ch. 510; *Re Lawrence's WT* [1972] Ch. 418.

[46] *Halsbury's Laws of England Vol 98: Trusts and Powers*, 5th edn (2013) at [532], giving the reason that the execution of the power is a declaration of trust in favour of the appointee (rather than a disposition of a subsisting equitable interest). cf. Thomas, *Powers* (2012), para.7.102

[47] *Hawkins v Kemp* (1803) 3 East 410; subject to Law of Property Act 1925 s.159, below, para.7–014.

[48] *Re Lane* [1908] 2 Ch. 581; *Re Priestley's WT* [1971] Ch. 562 (Pennycuick VC); *Re Priestley's WT* [1971] Ch. 858 (CA); *Re Lawrence's WT* [1972] Ch. 418; these latter three cases discussed by C. Sherrin (1971) 121 N.L.J. 41, 597, 808.

[49] *Re Phillips* (1889) 41 Ch.D. 417 at 419; Thomas, *Powers* (2012), para.7.104.

[50] *Reid v Shergold* (1805) 10 Ves.Jr. 370; *Re Evered* [1910] 2 Ch. 147 at 156.

[51] e.g. a devise which refers generally to realty and not specifically to separate pieces; e.g. "all my realty".

and also intermediate or hybrid powers, which in any way restrict the donee's freedom of choice.[52] The section applies even though the will was executed before the power was created.[53]

Any power to which the section does not apply is only exercised by will if "there is an indication of intention to exercise the power", a sufficient indication being "either a reference to the power or a sufficient reference to the property subject to the power."[54] Whether or not this is so in any particular case is often a question of great difficulty.[55]

B. Excessive Execution[56]

7-011   The donee has only the power which is given to her by the instrument. Thus she may not exercise it in favour of non-objects; nor in breach of the perpetuity rule; nor impose unauthorised conditions.[57] Any such purported exercise will be void. Difficult questions can arise when an appointment is partly good and partly bad, as where there is an appointment of a sum greater than that authorised; or where some of the appointees are objects and some are not. The rule is that the court will sever the good from the bad where possible:

> "If there is a complete execution of the power with the addition of something improper, the execution is good and the excess bad, whereas if there is no complete execution, or if the boundaries between the excess and the execution are not distinguishable, the whole appointment fails. In order to be valid, the appointment must be distinct and absolute."[58]

It is believed that this rule will apply where the exercise of a power makes an appointment and contains a release; if the release is invalid, the rest of the appointment may stand.[59]

C. Defective Execution

7-012   The donee of a power should exercise it in accordance with the provisions of the instrument creating it. Thus the necessary formalities should be observed, and the required consents obtained. Failure to comply will usually render the exercise void, but there is a jurisdiction in equity[60] and under statute to validate certain cases of defective execution.

---

[52] *Re Ackerley* [1913] 1 Ch. 510; *Re Byron's Settlement* [1891] 3 Ch. 474 (death of excluded persons would make the power general).

[53] *Boyes v Cook* (1880) 14 Ch.D. 53.

[54] *Re Ackerley* [1913] 1 Ch. 510 at 513.

[55] See *Re Ackerley* [1913] 1 Ch. 510, and the references in fn.48 above.

[56] See *Halsbury's Laws of England Vol 98: Trusts and Powers*, 5th edn (2013), Part 5; Thomas, *Powers* (2012), Ch.8.

[57] See *Re Hay's ST* [1982] 1 W.L.R. 202, below, para.7–017.

[58] *Halsbury's Laws of England Vol 98: Trusts and Powers*, 5th edn (2013) at [620]; *Re Holland* [1914] 2 Ch. 595; see also *Halsbury* at [621]–[625] for illustrations. The rule applies also where part of the appointment is void under the doctrine of "fraud on a power", below, para.7–018.

[59] Below, para.7–027.

[60] There are very few modern cases on defective execution in equity. The second edition of the leading modern work, Thomas, *Powers* (2012), omits discussion of the area because it has "little, if

i. In Equity. Where the donee shows an intention to execute the power "in discharge of moral or natural obligations"[61] equity will act upon the conscience of those entitled in default to compel them to make good the defect in the execution. Relief may be obtained in favour of purchasers for value, creditors, charities, and persons to whom the donee is under a moral or natural obligation to provide.[62]

7–013

The essential features of the intended execution must be proved; these are the intention to dispose of the property to the persons to be benefited and the amount of the benefit. Also, the defects must not go to the essence of the power.[63] There will not normally be relief against the non-execution of a power,[64] except perhaps in the case of fraud by the person entitled in default.[65] The doctrine applies to defects in the form of the execution of the power, but not to the situation where the trustees have purported to exercise the power after it has expired.[66]

In *Re Shinorvic Trust*,[67] the settlor of a discretionary trust purported to exercise a power to add his long-term partner to the class of beneficiaries. The execution of the power was formally defective because the required deed was not witnessed. The Jersey Royal Court held that the settlor's partner was someone to whom he owed a moral obligation to provide, and the court therefore declared that the settlor's partner had been properly added as a beneficiary from the date of the defective deed.[68]

The equitable jurisdiction applies to the execution of express powers generally, but not to defective execution of statutory powers; for:

> "it is difficult to see how the court can give validity to any such act if done otherwise than in accordance with the statutory requirements; to give relief in such a case would be to legislate afresh."[69]

ii. By Statute.

(a) Lifetime Appointment. Law of Property Act 1925 s.159, provides that the execution of a deed of appointment will be valid if executed in the presence of and attested by two or more witnesses, even though it does not comply with additional formalities stipulated in the instrument. This provision does not

7–014

---

any, application in modern circumstances": para.8.37. However, the book was published before *Re Shinorvic Trust* [2012] JRC 081 and *English v Keats* [2018] EWHC 673 (Ch), discussed below.

[61] *Chapman v Gibson* (1791) 3 Bro.C.C. 229 at 230, 29 E.R. 505 at 505–6.

[62] *Halsbury's Laws of England Vol 98: Trusts and Powers*, 5th edn (2013) at [629]. See *Re Shinorvic Trust* [2012] JRC 081.

[63] *Kennard v Kennard* (1872) L.R. 8 Ch.App. 227.

[64] *Holmes v Coghill* (1806) 12 Ves.Jr. 206. cf. *Mettoy Pension Trustees v Evans* [1990] 1 W.L.R. 1587; above, para.7–007. In *English v Keats* [2018] EWHC 673 (Ch), only three of four trustees signed a deed of appointment. This could still be characterised as a defective execution, rather than no execution at all: at [61]–[62].

[65] *Vane v Fletcher* (1717) 1 P.Wms. 352 at 355.

[66] *Breadner v Granville-Grossman* [2001] Ch. 523 (where trustees executed the power of appointment one day too late).

[67] [2012] JRC 081.

[68] [2012] JRC 081 at [58].

[69] *Farwell on Powers*, 3rd edn (1916), p.394. cf. Thomas, *Powers*, 1st edn (1998), pp.500–501, where it is suggested that relief might be given if the defective execution was procured by fraud, accident or mistake, or where the statutory provision was ambiguous.

however dispense with any necessary consents, nor does it apply to any acts required to be performed which have no relation to the mode of executing and attesting the document. Nor does it require a power to be exercised by deed where another method of exercise complies with the terms of the power.

7–015   *(b)   Appointment by Will.*   Similarly, an appointment by will is valid as regards execution and attestation if the provisions of the Wills Acts relating to the formalities of wills are complied with.[70]

D.   Contract to Exercise

7–016   A valid contract to exercise a general power, if capable of specific performance, operates as a valid exercise of the power in equity; but there can never be specific performance of a contract to exercise a testamentary power, and the only remedy for breach is an action for damages against the estate.[71] A contract to exercise a special testamentary power is not enforceable[72]; but a release, in appropriate circumstances,[73] can be effective, as can a contract not to exercise the power[74]; the property will then go in default of appointment.

5.   DELEGATION OF POWERS

7–017   In general, a person to whom a discretion has been given, whether personally or by virtue of his being in a fiduciary relationship, may not delegate his discretion to others. *Delegatus non potest delegare.*[75] A donee may delegate the performance of merely ministerial acts[76]; and the donee of a general power equivalent to absolute ownership may appoint to a class in such proportions as another shall select.[77] But many powers involve a personal discretion and this prevents delegation.[78] There is no objection however to a testator or settlor giving a power of appointment to a trustee.[79] Such a power given by a testator is not to be impugned as a delegation of testamentary disposition. In *Re Beatty's Will Trusts*[80] the testatrix gave her personal estate and £1.5 million to trustees to

---

[70] Wills Act 1837 s.10; Wills Act 1963 s.2; *Taylor v Meads* (1865) 4 De G.J. & S. 597 at 601.

[71] *Re Parkin* [1892] 3 Ch. 510.

[72] *Re Bradshaw* [1902] 1 Ch. 436; *Re Cooke* [1922] 1 Ch. 292.

[73] Below, para.7–025.

[74] *Re Evered* [1910] 2 Ch. 147.

[75] Below, para.21–012.

[76] *Re Hetling and Merton's Contract* [1893] 3 Ch. 269; *Farwell on Powers,* 3rd edn (1916), pp.503–504; Thomas, *Powers* (2012), para.6.09.

[77] Thomas, *Powers* (2012), para.6.06; *Re Triffitt's Settlement* [1958] Ch. 852 (explained in *Re Hay's ST* [1982] 1 W.L.R. 202 as showing that the rule does not apply to bare powers). See also *Fonu v Merrill Lynch Bank and Trust Co (Cayman) Ltd* [2011] W.T.L.R. 1249 (non-fiduciary power to revoke settlement could be delegated).

[78] *De Bussche v Alt* (1878) 8 Ch.D. 286; *Re Morris' Settlement* [1951] 2 All E.R. 528; *Re Hunter's WT* [1963] Ch. 372.

[79] *Houston v Burns* [1918] A.C. 337; *Attorney General v National Provincial & Union Bank* [1924] A.C. 262; *Re Park* [1932] 1 Ch. 580; *Re Abraham's WT* [1969] 1 Ch. 463 at 475; *Re Manisty's Settlement* [1974] Ch. 17 at 26.

[80] [1990] 1 W.L.R. 1503; J. Davies (1991) 107 L.Q.R. 211; J. Martin [1991] Conv. 138.

allocate "to or among such person or persons as they think fit." Hoffmann J upheld the power, rejecting the supposed "anti-delegation" rule: there was no doubt as to the validity of testamentary powers, whether special, general or intermediate.

In the absence of express provision in the instrument creating a special power, the donee may not appoint on discretionary trust.[81] This question arose in *Re Hay's Settlement Trusts.*[82]

> Trustees had a power to appoint to "such persons or purposes" as they should in their discretion select, except the settlor, her husband, or the trustees. Prior to the appointment, the income was to be applied, at the trustees' discretion, for the settlor's nephews and nieces or for charity. The trustees exercised the power of appointment by appointing the property to themselves on a discretionary trust for similar purposes. Prior to the distribution, the income was to be applied to any person or charity. Megarry VC held that the exercise of the power was void, so that the property vested in the persons entitled in default of appointment (the period during which the power was exercisable having expired). The appointment did not designate the persons appointed, as the settlement required. It merely provided a mechanism whereby the appointees might be ascertained. The power was to appoint persons, and not to nominate persons to make an appointment. Intermediate powers were subject to the rule against unauthorised delegation, and it was immaterial that the donees of the power were the same persons as the trustees of the discretionary trust.

If the donee appoints on protective trusts,[83] the determinable life interests will be valid, but the discretionary trusts due to take effect on forfeiture of the life interest are void and the trusts in default take effect.[84] There is no objection, however, to the inclusion in an appointment of a power of advancement.[85] Generally, where it is desired that the donee should be able to make an appointment which itself includes a power of appointment or involves any other delegation of discretion, express provision should be made in the instrument creating the power.

6. FRAUD ON A POWER

An appointor, in the typical case of a special power of appointment with a gift over in default, is under no duty to exercise the power; but if he chooses to exercise the power, he must exercise it honestly.[86] Unless he is a fiduciary,[87] he need not weigh the merits of the possible beneficiaries; he may appoint all the available assets to any one beneficiary, who may indeed be himself.[88] But he must exercise it within the limits imposed by the donor or testator who created

7–018

---

[81] *Re Morris' Settlement* [1951] 2 All E.R. 528.

[82] [1982] 1 W.L.R. 202.

[83] Below, Ch.8.

[84] *Re Boulton's ST* [1928] Ch. 703; *Re Morris' Settlement* [1951] 2 All E.R. 528; *Re Hunter* [1963] Ch. 372.

[85] *Re Mewburn's Settlement* [1934] Ch. 112; *Re Morris' Settlement* [1951] 2 All E.R. 528; *Re Wills' WT* [1959] Ch. 1; *Pilkington v IRC* [1964] A.C. 612; below, para.21–042.

[86] *Cloutte v Storey* [1911] 1 Ch. 18.

[87] In which case, see *Re Hay's ST* [1982] 1 W.L.R. 202, above, para.7–017. See also *A v B* [2016] EWHC 340 (Ch), below, para.23-015.

[88] *Re Penrose* [1933] Ch. 793.

it.[89] If, of course, he expressly exceeds those limits the exercise of the power will be void unless it can be cut down by severing the invalid excess.[90] But the doctrine of fraudulent exercise of a power goes further than this, for it extends to the intent with which a power is exercised. The theory is that, in the case of a special power, the property is vested in those entitled in default of its exercise subject to its being divested by a proper exercise of the power,[91] and that an exercise of the power for any "sinister object" is not proper, is a fraud on those entitled in default, and void.[92] It should be appreciated that the term "fraud" is used here in a special sense: "The equitable doctrine of 'fraud on a power' has little, if anything, to do with fraud".[93] It involves "an appointment ostensibly within the scope of a power, but made for an improper purpose".[94]

A.   Prior Agreement

7–019   The first type of case in which an apparently valid exercise of a power will be void for what in this context is termed fraud[95] is where the appointment is made as the result of a prior agreement with the appointee as to what he will do with the proceeds. Such an exercise of a power will be wholly void save when the appointor is the person entitled in default, or where the person entitled in default is a party to it.[96]

B.   Benefit to Appointor

7–020   A second type of case is where the power is exercised so as to benefit the appointor. The benefit is usually financial in character, as where an appointment is made to an ailing child by its father, who will benefit on the child's death,[97] but it is not restricted to financial benefit.[98] For the exercise of the power to be void, there must be more than a hope of benefit. Thus an appointment to a healthy child by a father will be valid.[99] For fraud to operate, the appointment must have been made with intent to benefit the appointor. An appointment is sometimes made, however, which in fact benefits the appointor, but which is clearly intended to,

---

[89] Y. Grbich (1977) 3 Monash L.R. 210, describing the doctrine of fraud on a power as an "ultra vires appointments" doctrine. See also R. Nolan (2009) 68 C.L.J. 293 at 297–304.

[90] *Churchill v Churchill* (1867) L.R. 5 Eq. 44; *Re Oliphant* (1917) 86 L.J.Ch. 452.

[91] *Re Brook's ST* [1939] Ch. 993.

[92] *Vatcher v Paull* [1915] A.C. 372. The void (rather than voidable) result of a fraudulently-exercised power was accepted, although without enthusiasm, in *Pitt v Holt* [2011] EWCA Civ 197; [2012] Ch. 132 at [101]; approved on this point [2013] 2 A.C. 108 at [93].

[93] *Medforth v Blake* [2000] Ch. 86 at 103; *Dalriada Trustees Ltd v Faulds* [2011] EWHC 3391 (Ch); [2012] 2 All E.R. 734 at [66]–[72]; *Eclairs Group Ltd and Glengary Overseas Ltd v JKX Oil & Gas Plc* [2015] UKSC 71; [2015] Bus.L.R. 1395 at [15] ("The principle has nothing to do with fraud.").

[94] *Pitt v Holt* [2013] 2 A.C. 108 at [61]. See also *Hillsdown Holdings Plc v Pensions Ombudsman* [1997] 1 All E.R. 862 at 883; *Eclairs Group Ltd and Glengary Overseas Ltd v JKX Oil & Gas Plc* [2015] Bus.L.R. 1395 at [14]–[24].

[95] See the classification in Thomas, *Powers*, para.9.13.

[96] See generally *Vatcher v Paull* [1915] A.C. 372.

[97] *Lady Wellesley v Earl Mornington* (1855) 2 K. & J. 143.

[98] *Cochrane v Cochrane* [1922] 2 Ch. 230.

[99] *Henty v Wrey* (1882) 21 Ch.D. 332.

and does, benefit the appointees; this is true of many an appointment that forms part of the variation of a trust, for the tax savings achieved will often be a benefit to the appointor. Thus in *Re Merton*,[100] Wynn-Parry J decided that there was no inflexible rule that forced him to declare such an exercise of a power to be void. The intent that renders an appointment void is a matter "of fact or of inference rather than of law",[101] and must be ascertained as a single fact after consideration of all the relevant evidence.[102] Such a benevolent view has not always been taken, however.[103]

Pension trusts provide further scope for the application of the doctrine, as in *Hillsdown Holdings Plc v Pensions Ombudsman*.[104] In that case the pension scheme had a substantial actuarial surplus. Its rules did not permit payment of surplus to the employer, but did permit the transfer of funds to another scheme provided the transfer did not seriously prejudice the members. The trustees transferred the entire fund to another pension scheme, of which the rules could be amended to permit the payment of surplus to the employer. This was done pursuant to an agreement with the employer whereby the benefit to the members would be increased and the surplus (over £11 million) paid to the employer. Although the trustees acted under legal advice and considered the arrangement to be beneficial to the members, it was a breach of trust in the nature of a fraud on a power. The power to transfer the funds had been exercised improperly for the collateral purpose of paying the surplus to the employer.

C.   Non-objects

An appointment is sometimes drafted so that the intent appears to be to benefit objects of the power, but the real intent is to benefit non-objects. It will then be void, even though the appointee was in no sense a party, and might not even have known of the appointment or its intent.[105] Thus, in *Re Dick*[106]:

> A widow had a power to appoint amongst her brothers and sisters and their issue, but she wished to provide for a family who were looking after her. She had inadequate free capital to do so. She appointed by will to her favourite sister, but coupling the appointment with a request "without imposing any trust or legal obligation" that the sister should provide an annuity for the family concerned. The Court of Appeal held that the absence of obligation on the appointee was not crucial; but rather that the whole intent in making the appointment was to secure a benefit to non-objects by subjecting the appointee to "strong moral suasion to

7–021

---

[100] [1953] 1 W.L.R. 1096 at 1100; *Re Robertson's WT* [1960] 1 W.L.R. 1050.

[101] *Re Holland* [1914] 2 Ch. 595 at 601, per Sargant J.

[102] *Re Crawshay* [1948] Ch. 123.

[103] *Re Wallace's Settlements* [1968] 1 W.L.R. 711; *Re Brook's Settlement* [1968] 1 W.L.R. 1661.

[104] [1997] 1 All E.R. 862. See Thomas, *Powers*, paras 9.06, 9.35–9.36.

[105] *Re Nicholson's Settlement* [1939] Ch. 11. This case decided that the doctrine as to the real intent behind an appointment did not apply to a power exercisable only in favour of one person and so exercised. But see the criticism in Sheridan, *Fraud in Equity* (1957) p.122.

[106] [1953] Ch. 343; *Re Kirwan* (1884) 25 Ch.D. 373 cf. *Re Marsden's Trusts* (1859) 4 Drew. 594.

benefit a non-object, which suasion the [appointee] would in the appointor's opinion, be unable to resist."[107] This intent was enough to constitute the exercise of the power as fraudulent.

Difficulties arise from this rule as to real intent, for it is not easy to distinguish cases such as *Re Dick* from cases where there was a real intent to benefit the appointee but coupled with a hope that the appointee would benefit a non-object, which cases are of course not within the doctrine of fraud on a power. But the intent in many cases is simply dual—genuinely to benefit the appointee but also to subject him to strong moral persuasion as to part of the benefit appointed. It may therefore be relevant in *Re Dick* that a substantial proportion of the sum appointed would have been absorbed by the annuity and that a great deal of planning and discussion had gone into the making of the appointment coupled with the expression of the request in formal memoranda. For the danger inherent in extending the doctrine too far is that, if the appointment is void, the appointee loses all benefit unless the appointor is alive to reappoint,[108] a loss to the appointee which is not justified if intent to benefit him was a substantial element in the exercise of the power.

D.   Excessive Exercise; Severance

7–022   If there is a genuine intent to benefit the appointee, something expressly superadded so as to benefit a non-object can be severed, leaving the appointment valid.[109] But severance will not occur in the absence of such a genuine intent.[110] Again if, in a will by which he exercises a power, a testator makes a gift of *his own* property conditional on the appointee resetting the *appointed* property, this is a valid condition on his own gift and the exercise of the power also is valid, provided there was a genuine intent to benefit the appointee.[111] This would be difficult to reconcile with strict emphasis on the intent with which a power was exercised as being "entire and single".[112]

---

[107] The matter was put in this way by Cohen LJ in *Re Crawshay* [1948] Ch. 123 at 135, a case which contained the additional vitiating factor of a covenant by the appointee assigning to non-objects any benefits received by the exercise of the power; H. Hanbury (1948) 64 L.Q.R. 221.

[108] There can be no severance in these cases as there is nothing to sever. But *Re Chadwick's Trusts* [1939] 1 All E.R. 850 shows that a fresh appointment is valid if free from the element that vitiated a prior one.

[109] *Re Kerr's WT* (1878) 4 Ch.D. 600; *Re Holland* [1914] 2 Ch. 595; *Re Burton's Settlements* [1955] Ch. 82; *Price v Williams-Wynn* [2006] W.T.L.R. 1633.

[110] *Re Cohen* [1911] 1 Ch. 37. Severance will not of course occur when there has been a prior agreement with the appointee.

[111] *Re Burton's Settlements* [1955] Ch. 82.

[112] In *Re Simpson* [1952] Ch. 412, Vaisey J had held that *Re Crawshay* and *Re Dick* impelled him to take this strict view on facts analogous to those in *Re Burton's Settlements* in which case, however, Upjohn J refused to follow the lead.

E. Releases

The doctrine of fraud on a power does not apply to releases, for releases simply benefit those entitled in default. It is irrelevant that the appointor, in releasing his power, is intended to benefit thereby, as he has no duty in respect of the disappointed objects.[113] Nor does the doctrine apply to the revocation of the exercise of a power.[114] An appointment may only be revoked where such right of revocation has been reserved. Where such right exists, it seems that the appointor is under no duty to the appointees. It has even been said that, in revoking, he may stipulate for a benefit, but it would be strange if, by first exercising a power and then revoking it, an appointor could obtain a benefit rightly denied him on an appointment, and it is significant that, in the leading case,[115] the revocation was followed by a release.[116]

7–023

F. Position of Third Parties

Those entitled in default of appointment who can challenge the exercise of the power as fraudulent have an equitable interest in the property appointed. A voluntary appointee who receives legal title to property will therefore take subject to that equitable interest. However, the purchaser of a legal estate from that appointee will take free of the equitable interest (and therefore not be affected by the fraudulent exercise of the power) as long as he or she acts bona fide and without notice of the fraud.[117]

7–024

If no legal title passes, the position is complicated. The equitable interest of those entitled in default of appointment in principle prevails over the third party who purchases from the appointee, since the appointee had no legal title to give.[118] The Law of Property Act 1925 s.157 protects such third party purchasers, but only if the vendor-appointee was at least 25 years of age at the time of sale, and only to the extent to which he was presumptively entitled in default of appointment.[119]

---

[113] *Re Somes* [1896] 1 Ch. 250. Releases may be an important element in the variation of a trust; *Re Ball's Settlement Trusts* [1968] 1 W.L.R. 899, below, para.23–019; *A v B* [2016] EWHC 340 (Ch), below, para.23–015

[114] *Re Greaves* [1954] Ch. 434.

[115] [1954] Ch. 434.

[116] cf. Evershed MR in *Re Greaves* [1954] Ch. 434 at 448.

[117] *Halsbury's Laws of England Vol 98: Trusts and Powers*, 5th edn (2013) at [637].

[118] *Cloutte v Storey* [1911] 1 Ch. 18. See also *Turner v Turner* [1984] Ch. 100, above, para.7–007, on the effect of appointments made in breach of the duty to consider; and *Re Hay's ST* [1982] 1 W.L.R. 202, above, para.7–017, on the effect of an appointment in breach of the duty not to delegate.

[119] For analysis of this provision see Thomas, *Powers* (2012), para.9.123.

7.   RELEASE OF POWERS

A.   Why Release?

7–025   As a power is discretionary, it may be asked why it becomes advantageous to release it as opposed merely to not exercising it. This may be for various reasons; for example, to create indefeasible interests in those entitled in default,[120] to make a gift charitable by releasing a power to appoint to anyone else,[121] to avoid the "reservation of benefit" rules under the inheritance tax system by excluding the settlor from the class of objects,[122] to avoid the effect of income tax legislation which provides in certain circumstances for the income of a settlement to be treated as that of the settlor,[123] and to exclude a settlor from a class of objects so that the trust assets will not be subject to a freezing order.[124]

B.   How to Effect a Release

7–026   Trustees may in effect surrender their trusts and powers by paying the money into court under the Trustee Act 1925 s.63[125]; or they may apply to the court for an administration order; or they may ask the court for directions as to the way in which they should act on questions arising in the administration of the trust. Usually, however, the court will not give general directions concerning the exercise of discretionary powers in the future.[126]

Trustees may also effect a release of a power, in appropriate circumstances, by executing a deed of release, or by a contract not to exercise the power.[127] A power may also be extinguished by implication by any dealing with the property by the donee which is inconsistent with its further exercise[128]; or by obtaining the approval of the court to an arrangement which is so inconsistent.

Another way of releasing a power is, somewhat counterintuitively, to exercise it. It is common for trust deeds to include a power for trustees to appoint on new trusts; this can be used to appoint the trust assets on new trusts which are identical to the old ones except that, for example, the settlor and/or the settlor's spouse are omitted. This is in effect a partial release of the earlier power.[129]

---

[120] *Re Mills* [1930] 1 Ch. 654; *Mettoy Pension Trustees Ltd v Evans* [1990] 1 W.L.R. 1587 (where default beneficiary insolvent).

[121] *Re Wills* [1964] Ch. 219.

[122] Below, para.10–011.

[123] Income Tax (Trading and Other Income) Act 2005 ss.624, 625 (previously Finance Act 1958 s.22); *Blausten v IRC* [1972] Ch. 256; D. Hayton (1972) 36 Conv.(N.S.) 127.

[124] *Re the New Huerto Trust* (2015) 18 I.T.E.L.R. 447; R. Davern (2016) 22 T. & T. 753.

[125] Below, para.19–026; this is now rare. See also *Thrells Ltd v Lomas* [1993] 1 W.L.R. 456 (exercise of fiduciary power properly surrendered to court to avoid conflict of duties).

[126] *Re Allen-Meyrick's WT* [1966] 1 W.L.R. 499; below, para.19–025.

[127] Law of Property Act 1925 ss.155, 160.

[128] *Re Christie-Miller's Settlement* [1961] 1 W.L.R. 462; *Re Wills* [1964] Ch. 219; *Muir v IRC* [1966] 1 W.L.R. 251, 1269; *Re Courtauld's Settlement* [1965] 2 All E.R. 544; *Blausten v IRC* [1972] Ch. 256.

[129] *Re Wills* [1964] Ch. 219; *Muir v IRC* [1966] 1 W.L.R. 251, 1269; *Blausten v IRC* [1972] Ch. 256.

C. Validity of Release

It is not possible to lay down with confidence what are the circumstances in which, in the absence of express provision,[130] a release will be valid. The Law of Property Act 1925 s.155, provides that: "A person to whom any power, whether coupled with an interest or not, is given may by deed release, or contract not to exercise, the power."

The question arose whether this provision applied to a situation where the donees of the power were trustees who held the power in a fiduciary capacity. Admittedly they cannot be compelled to exercise it; but can they be allowed to release it? The courts answered this question in the negative[131]; the problem is how to determine which are the cases to which the statute does not apply.

i. Trusts. It may be that the situation does not really involve a power but instead a discretionary trust. Here the trustees are under a duty to appoint; if they fail to do so, the court will declare the property to be held on trust for the possible appointees.[132] There is no question of release here.

ii. Fiduciary Powers. Where a power is conferred upon a person by virtue of his office, he may not release it "*In the absence of words in the trust deed authorising [him] so to do.*"[133] Here there may be a gift over in default, either to the class of appointees or to a different class. This is a power proper, and not a trust. But the power is one given to the trustees to be exercised in a fiduciary capacity. They cannot discard it; they are, as has been seen,[134] under a duty to consider from time to time whether and how to exercise the power. This is so whether it is given to them as trustees, or whether it is given to persons by name if on the true view of the facts, they were selected as donee of the power because they were trustees.[135] Conversely, persons selected as individuals may be described as trustees. In *Re Wills' Trust Deeds*[136] a power of appointment in respect of property which was the subject of a *settlement* was given to the trustees of the settlor's *will*; this was not given by virtue of their office. Modern pension fund cases provide illustrations of the rules as to the release of powers. In *Re Courage Group's Pension Schemes*[137] fiduciary powers were vested in a committee set up to manage a pension scheme. It was held that even if existing members of the committee could release, fetter, or agree not to exercise their powers (which was not decided),[138] they could not deprive their successors of the

7–027

7–028

7–029

---

[130] Cases where the power is released by the property being appointed on new trusts necessarily involve express provision for release; otherwise there would be no power to appoint on the new trusts.

[131] *Re Eyre* (1883) 49 L.T. 259; *Saul v Pattinson* (1886) 55 L.J.Ch. 831.

[132] Equal division is not necessary in the case of the modern discretionary trust; above, para.4–011.

[133] *Muir v IRC* [1966] 1 W.L.R. 1269 at 1283, per Harman LJ (original emphasis); *Blausten v IRC* [1972] Ch. 256.

[134] Above, para.7–006.

[135] *Re Cookes' Contract* (1877) 4 Ch.D. 454.

[136] [1964] Ch. 219 (the actual decision probably does not survive that of the Court of Appeal in *Muir v IRC* [1966] 1 W.L.R. 1269).

[137] [1987] 1 W.L.R. 495.

[138] See H. Arthur (1993) 7 T.L.I. 69.

right to exercise their powers. In *Mettoy Pension Trustees Ltd v Evans*[139] there was a power in favour of the pension fund beneficiaries, with the employer company taking in default. On the company's insolvency, the liquidator sought to release the power in the interests of the creditors. This could not be done because the power was fiduciary.[140] The liquidator could not exercise the power because of a conflict of duties,[141] and so the court could intervene to protect the objects.[142]

7–030   **iii. Bare Powers.**   Where the power is given to a person in his private capacity, the donee is prima facie able to release it, even if the release operates in favour of the donee, as where a father releases a power so that the shares of his sons (who are entitled in default) become absolute, and that of a deceased son passes to the donee.[143] A release, or a covenant not to exercise it, (which will be equivalent to a release)[144] may be effective if it refers only to part of the property,[145] or if it relates only to one or more of several objects.[146]

7–031   **iv. Variation of Trusts Act 1958.**   Section 1 of the Variation of Trusts Act 1958 makes no express reference to powers. Many powers are vested in trustees, as in the case of discretionary or protective trusts; and a variation of such powers will no doubt be covered by the provisions of the Act. It appears that an arrangement under the Act which recites the release of a power,[147] or one which is inconsistent with the future exercise of the power,[148] will effectively release it.

---

[139] [1990] 1 W.L.R. 1587.

[140] The power was held to be fiduciary, but subsequent cases suggest that the case was wrongly decided on this point: see *Imperial Group Pension Trust Ltd v Imperial Tobacco Ltd* [1991] 1 W.L.R. 589 at 596.

[141] See now Pensions Act 1995 s.25(2).

[142] Above, para.7–007.

[143] *Re Radcliffe* [1892] 1 Ch. 227; an appointment in favour of the estate of the deceased son would have been a fraud on the power. See also *Re Somes* [1896] 1 Ch. 250.

[144] per Buckley LJ in *Re Evered* [1910] 2 Ch. 147 at 161.

[145] *Re Evered* [1910] 2 Ch. 147.

[146] *Re Brown's Settlement* [1939] Ch. 944.

[147] *Re Christie-Miller's Settlement* [1961] 1 W.L.R. 462.

[148] *Re Courtauld's Settlement* [1965] 2 All E.R. 544; *Re Ball's ST* [1968] 1 W.L.R. 899.

CHAPTER 8

PROTECTIVE TRUSTS

1. THE GENERAL PROBLEM

A DEBTOR'S property is in principle available for the satisfaction of his   **8–001**
creditors and, if he becomes bankrupt, it will pass to his trustee in bankruptcy; but
it is possible, by making use of a protective trust, to obtain a measure of
protection against such an event.

In the development of protective trusts, the courts have been torn between two
conflicting pressures. On the one hand, nobody should have the power of
defeating his creditors by putting his property beyond their grasp; on the other, a
settlor should be able to create a trust in any form, so long as it is not unlawful;
and there is much to be said for allowing some means of protecting a person's
dependants from the ill-effects of his extravagance. The technique of protective
trusts involves the giving of a determinable life interest with a gift over upon the
happening of certain events. Originally, the gift over was usually in favour of
other members of the family[1]; but the modern practice is to provide for a gift over
to trustees to hold on discretionary trusts in favour of a class which includes the
life tenant and members of his family; and this pattern is provided for by the
Trustee Act 1925 s.33.[2]

---

[1] e.g. *Re Detmold* (1889) 40 Ch.D. 585.

[2] Below, para.8–005.

2. DETERMINABLE AND CONDITIONAL INTERESTS

8–002 A distinction is made in law between an interest subject to a condition subsequent and a determinable interest.[3] The former exists where there is a gift of an absolute interest which is then cut down by the application of a condition; such as a gift to X absolutely, but if he should change his nationality, then over to Y. A determinable interest exists where something less than an absolute interest is given in the first place; as a gift to X until he changes (or so long as he retains) his nationality. The distinction is subtle[4]; it depends entirely upon the language of the gift[5]; but it is a distinction that has importance in several contexts. The relevance in the present context is twofold: first, that a condition against alienation is void[6]; secondly, that a condition subsequent, being one which effects a forfeiture of an existing interest, is strictly construed[7]; if the condition is held void, the interest becomes absolute.[8] The determining event, however, in the case of a determinable interest is less strictly construed; and if it should be held invalid, the whole interest fails.[9]

Thus it is clear that a *condition* so drafted as to terminate an interest upon alienation[10] or bankruptcy[11] is void and the prior interest is absolute. But an interest *determinable* on alienation or bankruptcy is valid.[12] The basis of protective trusts is therefore a determinable life interest.

In *Belmont Park Investments Ltd v BNY Corporate Trustee Services Ltd*,[13] the Supreme Court held that an interest which is (genuinely) determinable on bankruptcy may still offend the anti-deprivation rule. The property would then be available for distribution among the bankrupt's creditors. However, the decision expressly does not affect the operation of protective trusts.[14]

---

[3] *Brandon v Robinson* (1811) 18 Ves.Jr. 429 at 433 (Lord Eldon); Megarry & Wade, 8th edn, para.3–058; Cheshire and Burn, 18th edn, Ch.17. The clue to the existence of a determinable limitation is the use of words such as "until", "so long as", "whilst", as distinct from phraseology such as "but if" and "when, if ever".

[4] "Little short of disgraceful to our jurisprudence," per Porter MR in *Re King's Trusts* (1892) 29 L.R.Ir. 401 at 410; "The distinction is not a particularly attractive one, being based on form rather than substance", per Rattee J in *Re Scientific Investment Pension Plan Trusts* [1999] Ch. 53 at 59. See R. Goode (2011) 127 L.Q.R. 1 at 8.

[5] Confirmed in *Belmont Park Investments Ltd v BNY Corporate Trustee Services Ltd* [2011] UKSC 38; [2012] 1 A.C. 383 at [88].

[6] *Re Brown* [1954] Ch. 39.

[7] *Clavering v Ellison* (1859) 7 H.L.Cas. 707; *Sifton v Sifton* [1938] A.C. 656.

[8] *Re Greenwood* [1903] 1 Ch. 749.

[9] *Re Moore* (1888) 39 Ch.D. 116. (Gift of a weekly sum to T's sister "whilst … living apart from her husband" construed as a gift determinable upon returning to her husband, and held void); *Re Tuck's ST* [1978] Ch. 49.

[10] *Brandon v Robinson* (1811) 18 Ves.Jr. 429; *Re Dugdale* (1888) 38 Ch.D. 176; *Re Brown* [1954] Ch. 39; Glanville Williams (1943) 59 L.Q.R. 343.

[11] *Re Sanderson's Trust* (1857) 3 K. & J. 497; *Re Scientific Investment Pension Plan Trusts* [1999] Ch. 53.

[12] Below, para.8–004; see also the earlier authorities relied on by Turner VC in *Rochford v Hackman* (1852) 9 Hare 475.

[13] [2012] 1 A.C. 383 at [89], [105]–[108].

[14] [2012] 1 A.C. 383 at [124].

3. SELF-PROTECTION

A settlor cannot make a settlement which will protect himself against his own bankruptcy.[15]

8–003

> In *Re Burroughs-Fowler*,[16] the settlor, by ante-nuptial settlement, settled property upon trust to pay the income to himself for life or until one of certain events should occur, including his bankruptcy, after which event the income was to be paid to his wife. The settlor was adjudicated bankrupt during the wife's lifetime. It was held that the life interest vested indefeasibly in his trustee in bankruptcy, who could validly dispose of it.

A settlor may however protect himself against other forms of alienation, voluntary or involuntary. And if the limitation, as is usual, provides for the termination of his interest upon any one of such events *or* upon his bankruptcy, the gift over, as we have seen, is void in the event of bankruptcy, but valid in all other cases.[17] If the gift over has already taken effect upon, for example, an attempt to charge the life interest, the subsequent bankruptcy of the settlor has no effect upon it.

> In *Re Detmold*,[18] a marriage settlement of the settlor's own property provided for the payment of the income to the settlor for life or "till he shall become bankrupt or shall ... suffer something whereby the same ... would ... by operation of law ... become ... payable to some other person ..." and, after such determination, on trust to pay the income to his wife. In July 1888, an order was made appointing a judgment creditor to be receiver of the income; and in September 1888, the settlor was adjudicated bankrupt. It was held that the forfeiture took place upon the involuntary alienation of the income by process of law. The wife then became entitled to the income, and she did not lose the right on the subsequent bankruptcy.

4. PROTECTED LIFE INTERESTS IN PERSONS OTHER THAN THE SETTLOR

A person cannot make a settlement of his own property upon himself until bankruptcy, and then over. However, a trust created by A to pay the income to B until B dies or becomes bankrupt alienates or charges his life interest, and then over to C, is good in the event of the occurrence of any of those events, including B's bankruptcy.[19] The essence of the device of protected life interests[20] is that, on the occurrence of a determining event, such as alienation or bankruptcy, the interest of the life tenant determines, and the trustees then hold the property on discretionary trusts for the benefit of the life tenant and his family.

8–004

---

[15] *Mackintosh v Pogose* [1895] 1 Ch. 505. This rule is preserved by Trustee Act 1925 s.33(3). Nor may he settle his property on a third party to prejudice his own creditors; below, para.14–019 and following.

[16] [1916] 2 Ch. 251; *Official Assignee v NZI Life Superannuation Nominees Ltd* [1995] 1 N.Z.L.R. 684.

[17] *Re Detmold* (1889) 40 Ch.D. 585; *Re Brewer's Settlement* [1896] 2 Ch. 503; *Re Johnson* [1904] 1 K.B. 134.

[18] (1889) 40 Ch.D. 585.

[19] *Re Ashby* [1892] 1 Q.B. 872; *Re Scientific Investment Pension Plan Trusts* [1999] Ch. 53.

[20] L. Sheridan (1957) 21 Conv.(N.S.) 110.

Some early attempts to reach this result failed, owing to the absence of any clear gift over of the income.[21] Eventually, however, discretionary trusts became accepted.[22]

The court may exercise its jurisdiction to vary trusts so as to convert a beneficial interest into a protected life interest where it is feared that the beneficiary cannot manage his affairs in a responsible manner.[23]

5. TRUSTEE ACT 1925 SECTION 33

8–005 Before 1926 it was necessary to set out expressly the terms of the protective trusts; and a settlor may still do so if he wishes.[24] In relation, however, to trusts coming into operation after 1925, the Trustee Act 1925 s.33, "provides a shorthand arrangement whereby a settlor may establish a trust without setting forth in detail all the terms upon which the property is to be held."[25] The section applies even if the statutory formula "on protective trusts" is not used, so long as the intention is clear.[26] The section then applies subject to any modification contained in the instrument creating the trust.[27]

Subsection 33(1)[28] provides:

> "Where any income, including an annuity or other periodical income payment, is directed to be held on protective trusts for the benefit of any person (in this section called 'the principal beneficiary') for the period of his life or for any less period, then, during that period (in this section called the 'trust period') the said income shall, without prejudice to any prior interest, be held on the following trusts, namely—
>
> (i)   Upon trust for the principal beneficiary during the trust period or until he… does or attempts to do or suffers any act or thing, or until any event happens, other than an advance under any statutory or express power,[29] whereby, if the said income were payable during the trust period to the principal beneficiary absolutely during that period, he would be deprived of the right to receive the same or any part thereof,[30] in any of which cases… this trust of the said income shall fail or determine;
>
> (ii)   [and during the remainder of the trust period]… the said income shall be held upon trust for the application thereof for the maintenance or support, or otherwise for the benefit, of all or any one or more exclusively of the other or others of the following persons[31] (that is to say)—

---

[21] The point is discussed in *Rochford v Hackman* (1852) 9 Hare 475.

[22] And may take effect where the forfeiture precedes the settlement; as where the bankruptcy began before the testator died: *Metcalfe v Metcalfe* [1891] 3 Ch. 1. See also *Re Forder* [1927] 2 Ch. 291; *Re Walker* [1939] Ch. 974.

[23] *Hambro v Duke of Marlborough* [1994] Ch. 158; below, para.23–008 (unsuitability of Marquess of Blandford to manage Blenheim). See also *Re Abram (Deceased)* [1996] 2 F.L.R. 379 (protected life interest ordered under Inheritance (Provision for Family and Dependants) Act 1975, where any capital sum would have gone to applicant's creditors).

[24] *Re Shaw's Settlement* [1951] Ch. 833; *Re Rees (Deceased)* [1954] Ch. 202; *Re Munro's ST* [1963] 1 W.L.R. 145.

[25] E.N. Griswold, *Spendthrift Trusts* (1936), p.375.

[26] *Re Wittke* [1944] Ch. 166 ("under protective trusts for the benefit of my sister").

[27] Trustee Act 1925 s.33(2).

[28] As amended by the Civil Partnership Act 2004.

[29] Below, para.8–010.

[30] See *Re Smith's Will Trusts* (1981) 131 N.L.J. 292.

[31] Relationships are to be construed in accordance with s.1 of the Family Law Reform Act 1987 (i.e. without regard to legitimacy): Trustee Act 1925 s.33(4).

(a)   the principal beneficiary and his or her spouse or civil partner, if any, and his or her children or more remote issue, if any; or

(b)   if there is no spouse or civil partner or issue of the principal beneficiary in existence, the principal beneficiary and the persons who would, if he were actually dead, be entitled to the trust property or the income thereof or the annuity fund, if any, or arrears of the annuity, as the case may be;

   as the trustees in their absolute discretion, without being liable to account for the exercise of such discretion, think fit."

6.   FORFEITURE OF THE LIFE TENANTS INTEREST

It is necessary in each case to decide whether or not the event which has occurred is sufficient to determine the interest of the life tenant, and thus to bring the discretionary trusts into operation.[32] The question usually arises under trusts governed by the Trustee Act 1925 s.33. Where the question arises in respect of an express protective trust, the question will depend on the construction of the particular trust under consideration.[33] The principles applicable will however be the same.

8–006

   It will be appreciated that a forfeiture is not in the bankruptcy cases a disaster. The forfeiture deprives the life tenant of his life interest, which would otherwise have become available to his creditors. The effect of the forfeiture is to allow the protective provisions to come into effect, and to keep the principal beneficiary's interest from his trustee in bankruptcy.[34]

A.   Determining Events

If the principal beneficiary alienates his interest, or goes bankrupt, a forfeiture obviously occurs. In other circumstances, it is often difficult to draw a clear dividing line between those which will and those which will not effect a forfeiture. The matter is best explained by illustrations. The first three are cases of express protective trusts in which the instrument provided that the life interest should be determinable upon the happening of some event whereby some or all of the income became payable to another person.

8–007

   In *Re Balfour's Settlement Trusts*,[35] the trustees had, at the life tenant's request, and in breach of trust, advanced parts of the capital to him. They then asserted their right to retain the income of the fund in order to make good the breach. Subsequently, the life tenant became bankrupt. Farwell J held that the life tenant's interest had determined because the trustees became entitled to the income.[36] The life interest was thus saved from the bankruptcy.

---

[32] *Re Brewer's Settlement* [1896] 2 Ch. 503.

[33] *Re Brewer's Settlement* [1896] 2 Ch. 503 at 507; *Re Dennis' ST* [1942] Ch. 283 at 286; *Re Hall* [1944] Ch. 46.

[34] See *Re Scientific Investment Pension Plan Trusts* [1999] Ch. 53; *Belmont Park Investments Ltd v BNY Corporate Trustee Services Ltd* [2012] 1 A.C. 383.

[35] [1938] Ch. 928; *Re Gordon* [1978] Ch. 145.

[36] Distinguishing *Re Brewer's Settlement* [1896] 2 Ch. 503, where bankruptcy took place before the trustees exercised their right.

In *Re Baring's Settlement Trusts*,[37] a sequestration order was made against the property of a mother who failed to obey a court order to return her children to the jurisdiction. Morton J held that the order effected a forfeiture, although the mother's loss of income was only temporary.

In *Re Dennis' Settlement Trusts*,[38] the settlor's son was entitled to a protective life interest under a family settlement. A rearrangement took place on his attaining the age of 21, and provided that for the next six years the trustees should pay to him only part of the income and should accumulate the rest for him. The rearrangement caused a forfeiture.

In *Re Gourju's Will Trusts*,[39] the protective trust was one governed by the Trustee Act 1925 s.33. The life tenant ceased to be entitled to receive the income of the trust because she lived in Nice, which became enemy occupied country during the Second World War. This caused a forfeiture. The Custodian of Enemy Property had no claim; nor could the trustees treat the tenant for life as still entitled, and retain income for her until the end of the war. The discretionary trusts came into effect, and the income was payable to one or more members of the class of beneficiaries.

On the other hand, residence in enemy occupied territory did not cause a forfeiture in *Re Hall*,[40] where forfeiture was to take place if the annuitant should "do or suffer any act" whereby the annuity should be payable elsewhere. The annuity could no longer be paid to the annuitant; but this was not due to anything that she had done or permitted; the Custodian of Enemy Property was entitled. Nor was there a forfeiture where a life tenant under a protective trust (terminable if the income became "payable to… some other person") assigned his interest to the trustees of his marriage settlement (of which he was tenant for life), authorised the trustees to charge their expenses to the fund and appointed them his attorneys to receive the income.[41] Again there was no forfeiture where the life tenant lacked mental capacity and a receiver was appointed.[42] Nor does the fact that a receiver's (or now a deputy's) fees become payable out of the estate of such a person effect a forfeiture.[43] An authority to pay to creditors the dividends due from a company for a period of time during which the company declared no dividend did not cause a forfeiture.[44]

B.   Order of the Court under the Trustee Act 1925 Section 57[45]

8–008   The court may make an order under the Trustee Act 1925 s.57, which may affect the operation of a trust. If an order is made authorising the trustees to raise money to pay the debts of a life tenant under a protective trust, there is no forfeiture; for

---

[37] [1940] Ch. 737.

[38] [1942] Ch. 283.

[39] [1943] Ch. 24; *Re Wittke* [1944] Ch. 166; *Re Allen-Meyrick's Will Trusts* [1966] 1 W.L.R. 499. See also Trading with the Enemy (Custodian) (No.2) Order 1945 (S.R. & O. 1945 No.887) providing that vesting in the Custodian should not take place if it would cause a forfeiture.

[40] [1944] Ch. 46; *Re Harris* [1945] Ch. 316; *Re Pozot's ST* [1952] Ch. 427.

[41] *Re Tancred's Settlement* [1903] 1 Ch. 715. Similarly an assignment of income already accrued; *Re Greenwood* [1901] 1 Ch. 887.

[42] *Re Oppenheimer's WT* [1950] Ch. 633; *Re Marshall* [1920] 1 Ch. 284. Receivers are replaced by deputies under the Mental Capacity Act 2005.

[43] *Re Westby's Settlement* [1950] Ch. 296; Mental Capacity Act 2005 s.56(2), re-enacting earlier legislation.

[44] *Re Longman* [1955] 1 W.L.R. 197.

[45] Below, para.23–007.

the power must be treated as if it had been "inserted in the trust instrument as an over-riding power."[46] If the order provides that the life tenant effects an insurance policy to secure a like amount of money at his death, and that the trustees shall pay the premiums out of the income if the life tenant fails to do so, there is no forfeiture so long as the life tenant makes the payments; but if the life tenant fails to pay and they become payable by the trustees from the income, there would be a forfeiture.[47]

C. Order of the Court under the Matrimonial Causes Acts 1859–1973

It is not clear whether a forfeiture is effected when a court order is made which alters a protected life interest under a marriage settlement.[48] In *Re Richardson's Will Trusts*,[49] the court ordered that the principal beneficiary should charge his interest with an annual payment of £50 in favour of his divorced wife. The charge was held to create a forfeiture. On the other hand, in *General Accident Fire and Life Assurance Corp Ltd v IRC*[50] an order diverting part of the income from the life tenant in favour of a former wife was held not to effect a forfeiture.

8–009

These cases are distinguishable on a narrow ground of construction of s.33.[51] But the broader ground of the decision, that this situation has no relevance to the real purpose of protective trusts, would seem to apply to the charge in *Re Richardson's Will Trusts* as much as to the diversion of part of the income in the *General Accident* case. It is submitted that the principle of the *General Accident* case is sound. As Donovan LJ said[52]:

> "[T]he section is intended as a protection to spendthrift or improvident or weak life tenants. But it can give... no protection against the effect of a court order such as was made here. Furthermore, if such an order involves a forfeiture much injustice could be done."

Perhaps the problem can be rationalised with the cases on s.57 by saying with Russell LJ, who made clear, however, that he did not rest his decision on this approach: "the settlement throughout was potentially subject in all its trusts to such an order as was made."[53] *Re Richardson's Will Trusts* was not mentioned; but an earlier case on the Matrimonial Causes Act 1859 in favour of forfeiture, *Re Carew*,[54] was overruled. It is tempting to say that *Re Richardson's Will Trusts* is wrong; but it should be noted that in that case, as in *Re Carew*, the decision in

---

[46] *Re Mair* [1935] Ch. 562 at 565, per Farwell J.

[47] *Re Salting* [1932] 2 Ch. 57 at 65.

[48] Which the court has power to do under Matrimonial Causes Act 1973 s.24(1).

[49] [1958] Ch. 504, illustrating the advantage of establishing a series of protective trusts, "one set until the beneficiary is twenty-five, another from twenty-five to thirty-five, a third from thirty-five to forty-five, and another for the rest of his life." A forfeiture of, or a charge upon, the principal beneficiary's interest in one of the trusts would not affect his interest in subsequent trusts. He would get a fresh start. R. Megarry (1958) 74 L.Q.R. 182.

[50] [1963] 1 W.L.R. 1207.

[51] [1963] 1 W.L.R. 1207. See Donovan LJ at 1217 and Russell LJ at 1221.

[52] [1963] 1 W.L.R. 1207 per Donovan LJ at 1218.

[53] [1963] 1 W.L.R. 1207 at 1222.

[54] (1910) 103 L.T. 658.

favour of forfeiture advanced the broad policy of s.33; for the forfeiture in those cases allowed the discretionary trusts to operate when otherwise the trustee in bankruptcy would have claimed the interest.

7. ADVANCEMENTS

8–010   Section 33(1) expressly exempts, as a cause of forfeiture, an advancement under any statutory[55] or express power. Thus the fact that the life tenant no longer receives the income of the part of the capital which has been advanced does not effect a forfeiture.[56] It appears that the same rule applies in the case of an express protective trust.[57]

8. EFFECT OF FORFEITURE

8–011   When a forfeiture has taken place, the life interest of the principal beneficiary is terminated, and the trusts in s.33(1)(ii), or those expressly contained in the instrument, as the case may be, come into play.[58] The termination is not usually, however, an occasion of charge to inheritance tax,[59] although this rule is subject to certain restrictions where the protective trust arises on or after 22 March 2006.[60] Under s.33, there are discretionary trusts in favour of the principal beneficiary and other persons, depending on whether or not a spouse or civil partner or issue of the principal beneficiary is in existence. The trustees may apply the income for the remainder of the trust period for any member of the discretionary class. The principal beneficiary is not entitled to any income; but the trustees may, if they wish, pay it to him. They must pay the income to one or more of the members.[61] If the trustees decide to pay some income to the principal beneficiary, they face the problem that the money may be claimed by the trustee in bankruptcy as the assignee of his "interest" under the discretionary trust,[62] or perhaps only the surplus above that needed for his "mere support".[63] They may, however, in their absolute discretion, apply the money for his use and benefit.[64] Thus:

---

[55] The statutory power of advancement is contained in Trustee Act 1925 s.32, as amended by Inheritance and Trustees' Powers Act 2014 s.9; below, para.21–038.

[56] See however *General Accident Fire and Life Assurance Corp Ltd v IRC* [1963] 1 W.L.R. 1207 which suggests that an advancement does not effect a forfeiture and that the proviso to s.33 is for the avoidance of doubt.

[57] *Re Hodgson* [1913] 1 Ch. 34; *Re Shaw's Settlement* [1951] Ch. 833; *Re Rees (Deceased)* [1954] Ch. 202. *Re Stimpson's Trusts* [1931] 2 Ch. 77 is to the contrary, but was doubted in the latter two cases.

[58] See also the forfeiture clause in *Re Scientific Investment Pension Plan Trusts* [1999] Ch. 53 (interest passed to pension scheme trustees with power to apply to member's dependants).

[59] Inheritance Tax Act 1984 s.88; below, para.10–027.

[60] Inheritance Tax Act 1984 s.88(3)–(6) as amended by Finance Act 2006 Sch.20 para.24.

[61] *Re Gourju's WT* [1943] Ch. 24.

[62] *Re Coleman* (1888) 39 Ch.D. 443; *Re Bullock* (1891) 64 L.T. 736 at 738.

[63] *Re Ashby* [1892] 1 Q.B. 872 at 877.

[64] *Re Bullock* (1891) 64 L.T. 736; *Re Coleman* (1888) 39 Ch.D. 443; *Re Smith* [1928] Ch. 915 at 919; *Public Trustee v Ferguson* [1947] N.Z.L.R. 746.

> "[I]f the trustees were to pay an hotel-keeper to give him a dinner he would get nothing but the right to eat a dinner, and that is not property which could pass by assignment or bankruptcy."[65]

It is safer to pay the money to third persons in satisfaction of services provided for the bankrupt.

---

[65] *Re Coleman* (1888) 39 Ch.D. 443 at 451.

CHAPTER 9

DISCRETIONARY TRUSTS

1.   GENERAL

IT HAS been seen that discretionary trusts were used as a means of dealing with   **9–001**
the income of a protective trust after the interest of the principal beneficiary had
ended. Other advantages which discretionary trusts could offer came to be
appreciated, especially in the context of estate duty saving, and they developed
into one of the principal tools of estate and tax planners. Estate duty was replaced
by capital transfer tax (now inheritance tax) in the Finance Act 1975. An
explanation of the current tax position will be delayed until the next chapter, so
that the fiscal situation of different types of trusts may be considered together. It
will then be seen that discretionary trusts suffered substantially upon the
introduction of capital transfer tax, and became at a disadvantage in relation to

other trusts.[1] The disadvantage was increased when the discretionary trust became the only form of trust to be initially chargeable to inheritance tax upon its lifetime creation. However, as we shall see in the next chapter, the Finance Act 2006 withdrew many inheritance tax advantages from non-discretionary trusts. Outright gifts and some non-discretionary trusts are potentially exempt (i.e. chargeable only if the transferor dies within seven years).[2] The importance of discretionary trusts has been to some extent reduced because of their current inheritance tax treatment, but they need to be examined because they retain many advantages outside the fiscal field; also because they raise a number of interesting and important theoretical questions in the law of trusts.

2.   USES OF DISCRETIONARY TRUSTS

9–002   There are various reasons why a settlor may prefer to establish discretionary trusts rather than fixed trusts. As previously indicated, the most important reason used to be the saving of estate duty, and this will be referred to in the following chapter. The emphasis is now on the other advantages.

A.   To Protect the Beneficiary Against Creditors

9–003   If one member of a class of beneficiaries under a discretionary trust goes bankrupt, the trustee in bankruptcy is not entitled to claim any part of the fund.[3] The trustee in bankruptcy is however entitled to goods and money paid over by the trustees to the beneficiary in the exercise of their discretion[4]; or perhaps only to the amount in excess of that needed for the maintenance of the beneficiary.[5] The trustee in bankruptcy is however excluded if the trustees make the maintenance payments to third parties, such as a hotel keeper[6] or tradesman.[7]

We saw in the previous chapter that discretionary trusts are employed under protective trusts as a means whereby a protected life tenant may continue to receive some benefit from settled funds after his or her bankruptcy. Indeed, this was their earliest use.

---

[1] Although the rules applicable to discretionary trusts were substantially amended and rationalised by the Finance Act 1982.

[2] Below, para.10–008 and following.

[3] *Re Ashby* [1892] 1 Q.B. 872 at 877; *Re Bullock* (1891) 64 L.T. 736. If the bankrupt is the sole member of the discretionary class, the interest passes to the trustee in bankruptcy: *Green v Spicer* (1830) 1 Russ. & M. 395. See also *Re Trafford's Settlement* [1985] Ch. 32, below, para.9–015.

[4] *Re Coleman* (1888) 39 Ch.D. 443.

[5] *Re Ashby* [1892] 1 Q.B. 872 at 877; *Page v Way* (1840) 3 Beav. 20, above, para.8–011.

[6] *Re Coleman* (1888) 39 Ch.D. 443 at 451; above, para.8–011.

[7] *Godden v Crowhurst* (1842) 10 Sim. 642 at 656.

B. To Continue to Exercise Control over Young or Improvident Beneficiaries

Many take the view that it is unwise to put large sums of money at the disposal of beneficiaries if they are young or extravagant. This is due not only to the fear of the loss of family capital in case of insolvency; but also because a rich young beneficiary may be encouraged to develop habits of idleness and extravagance, and waste the inheritance; older beneficiaries may already have done so. While the discretionary trust is in operation, each member of the class of beneficiaries is entitled only to the money which the trustees see fit to allocate to him or her in the exercise of their discretion. The settlor may, whether or not he or she is a trustee, be able to influence the selection so as to exercise some element of control over the beneficiaries.[8]

9–004

C. To React to Changes in Circumstances

The trustees can exercise their discretion in relation to distribution of income and capital according to the circumstances existing at the time. When the trust is set up, there is no way of knowing how the beneficiaries will fare in the future; which of them will be most in need; which will be deserving, which spendthrift, which inebriate; which will marry millionaires, and which missionaries. The trustees can take all these factors into consideration in making their decisions; and will be much influenced by the wishes of the settlor. In making these decisions, they will also take tax factors into consideration; it is more economical to give income to those with smaller incomes; and capital given to rich beneficiaries may bear inheritance tax not only on the distribution but also when disposed of by them. Decisions by trustees which favour one beneficiary over another may of course give rise to criticism and resentment by disappointed beneficiaries.[9] All these factors need to be taken into consideration. It might be added that a discretionary trust may be used where the settlor wishes to provide for a beneficiary without making him or her ineligible for means-tested state benefits, as the beneficiary has no entitlement to capital or income.

9–005

3. USUAL FORM OF DISCRETIONARY TRUSTS

A. Trustees' Discretion

The essential feature of a discretionary trust is that the property is conveyed to trustees to be held by them on trust to apply the income or the capital or both for the benefit of the members of a class of beneficiaries in such proportions as the trustees shall, in their absolute discretion, think fit. Most discretionary trusts are concerned with distribution of income; the distribution of capital is commonly

9–006

---

[8] But if the settlor influences the trustees to such an extent that they fail to exercise their discretion independently, the appointment will be void; *Turner v Turner* [1984] Ch. 100, below, para.9–021.
[9] The trustees need not disclose the reasons for their decisions; *Re Beloved Wilkes's Charity* (1851) 3 Mac. & G. 440, below, para.18–042.

effected under a power to appoint. It used to be common to include a wider class of beneficiaries as objects of the power of appointment, and a narrower, more specific class of beneficiaries of the discretionary trusts.[10] But, since *McPhail v Doulton*,[11] the test of certainty of beneficiaries of a discretionary trust has been assimilated to that of objects of a mere power, and the wider class can now be employed for both purposes. During the period of the trust, no individual beneficiary is entitled to any share of the property, income or capital; she receives what the trustees see fit to give her and no more.

B. The Trust Period

9–007　Provision will be made for the discretionary trust to continue for the trust period; which can be any desired period which is not in excess of the perpetuity period. Discretionary trusts provide a special situation for the application of the perpetuity rule. Since no individual beneficiary has any interest under the trust, property only vests in a beneficiary upon the exercise of the trustees' discretion in his or her favour; and such a vesting is void unless it takes place within the perpetuity period.[12] A discretionary trust can only exist, therefore, for the duration of the perpetuity period.

A discretionary trust will therefore be designed to terminate before the end of the period. This is normally done by postulating the "trust period" at the conclusion of which the discretionary trust will terminate, and providing for a gift over on fixed trusts which will themselves vest within the perpetuity period. Since 1964, a period of years not exceeding 80 years could be specified.[13] For instruments made on or after 6 April 2010 the perpetuity period is 125 years.[14]

C. Power to Accumulate

9–008　In many cases the income beneficiaries will not need the trust income each year. Until quite recently, it was possible to save tax by retaining income in the trust because the rate applicable to the trust was lower than that of a beneficiary who paid higher rate income tax, but this is no longer the case.[15] The trustees are commonly given a power to accumulate. Without such a power, they will be obliged to distribute the income[16]; not to any particular beneficiary, but among the beneficiaries. It was noted above[17] that such a power makes the distinction between exhaustive and non-exhaustive discretionary trusts. The trust is non-exhaustive as to the income if the income is not required to be distributed

---

[10] *Re Gestetner* [1953] Ch. 672.
[11] [1971] A.C. 424; above, para.4–010.
[12] *Re Coleman* [1936] Ch. 528.
[13] Perpetuities and Accumulations Act 1964 s.1.
[14] Perpetuities and Accumulations Act 2009 s.5. No other perpetuity period may be specified.
[15] This is because the tax rate applicable to trusts has been increased to 45%. See below, para.10–002.
[16] *Re Gourju's WT* [1943] Ch. 24; *Re Locker's ST* [1977] 1 W.L.R. 1323; subject to Trustee Act 1925 s.31, below, para.21–023.
[17] Above, para.2–022.

each year; and non-exhaustive as to the capital if the trustees are not obliged to distribute all the capital during the currency of the trust.

For instruments made before 6 April 2010[18] there are statutory restrictions upon powers of accumulation. The permitted periods are (by the Law of Property Act 1925 s.164 as amended by the Perpetuities and Accumulations Act 1964 s.13):

(a)   the life of the grantor or settlor; or

(b)   a term of 21 years from the death of the grantor, settlor or testator; or

(c)   the duration of the minority or respective minorities of any person or persons living or en ventre sa mère[19] at the death of the grantor, settlor or testator; or

(d)   the duration of the minority or respective minorities only of any person or persons who under the limitations of the instrument directing the accumulations would, for the time being, if of full age be entitled to the income directed to be accumulated; or

(e)   a term of 21 years from the date of the making of the disposition; or

(f)   the duration of the minority or respective minorities of any person or persons in being at that date.

The settlor could select whichever period he or she wished. If the settlor chose a period in excess of those permitted, the accumulation would be invalid only as to the excess. At the conclusion of the period of accumulation, the income must be distributed.

The rule against excessive accumulations was abolished by the Perpetuities and Accumulations Act 2009 in relation to instruments made on or after 6 April 2010,[20] with the exception of charitable trusts.[21] The former restrictions still apply to a will made before that date even though the testator dies after the commencement of the Act of 2009, and they also apply to an instrument made in the exercise of a special power of appointment if the instrument creating the power took effect before that date.[22] Thus, in the case of instruments to which the Act of 2009 applies, the income may be accumulated for the whole of the perpetuity period of 125 years,[23] although of course this is subject to any contrary provision in the instrument.

---

[18] The date on which Perpetuities and Accumulations Act 2009 came into operation. The Act implemented the proposals in Law Com. No. 251, *The Rules Against Perpetuities and Excessive Accumulations* (1998).

[19] In his or her mother's womb.

[20] s.13.

[21] s.14.

[22] s.15.

[23] This is the period laid down by s.5.

D. Power to Add to, or to Exclude from, the Class of Beneficiaries

9–009   The trustees may be given a power to add new members to the class of beneficiaries, or to exclude existing members.[24] The power to exclude members became important when the Finance Act 1958[25] provided that a settlor should be liable to income tax upon the income of a settlement if the settlor or the spouse of the settlor might benefit from the income or property of the settlement. Many settlements in existence at that date included the spouse of the settlor as a member of the class of beneficiaries, and the Act provided that the settlor should not be so liable if, amongst other conditions, the power to make the payments was not exercisable after 9 April 1959.

A difficulty could arise if the trustees decided to exclude a member of the class for no good reason. Arbitrary exclusion will be inconsistent with the trustees' fiduciary duties.[26] It might also be construed as an improper release of a power held in a fiduciary capacity.[27] Yet it is difficult to see how the excluded member could establish loss; because, as a member of a class of beneficiaries under a discretionary trust, he or she was not entitled to any interest under the trust, and would be deprived of nothing except the hope or expectation of favourable consideration by the trustees.

It may be useful also to give power to the trustees to add new members to the class. Care has to be taken to ensure that the trustees cannot include persons, such as the settlor or the settlor's spouse, whose inclusion would have damaging tax consequences.[28] The power to add new members to the class is usually done by defining a class of excepted persons, and giving to the trustees a power to include in the class of beneficiaries any person who was not a member of the excepted class. Such a provision was upheld in *Re Manisty's Settlement*,[29] concerning a power of appointment; the settlor's mother, and any person who should become his widow, were added to the class of beneficiaries. The validity of trusts and powers in favour of very large classes was discussed in Ch.4.

---

[24] *Re Manisty's Settlement* [1974] Ch. 17; *Blausten v IRC* [1972] 1 Ch. 256; *Re the New Huerto Trust* (2015) 18 I.T.E.L.R. 447.

[25] s.22; now Income Tax (Trading and Other Income) Act 2005 ss.624, 625; *Watson v Holland* [1985] 1 All E.R. 290.

[26] Below, paras 9–020—9–021.

[27] Above, para.7–027.

[28] Inclusion of the settlor (but probably not the settlor's spouse) would, for example, attract the "reservation of benefit" rules of inheritance tax; below, para.10–011. Moreover, following the Supreme Court's decision in *Pitt v Holt* [2013] UKSC 26; [2013] 2 A.C. 108, the scope for undoing such arrangements once the tax consequences are appreciated has been dramatically reduced.

[29] [1974] Ch. 17; the power was described as an "intermediate" power (also known as a "hybrid" power); above, para.7–004: *Re Park* [1932] 1 Ch. 580; *Re Abraham's WT* [1969] 1 Ch. 463. See also *Re Hay's ST* [1982] 1 W.L.R. 202.

E. Power to Appoint Upon New Trusts

It is common to give to trustees power to appoint on further trusts, including discretionary and protective trusts, and also in favour of trustees of a foreign settlement[30] and to give them full power of delegation. This makes possible a resettlement on new trusts at the end of any specified accumulation period, or at any time at which it becomes advantageous for fiscal or other reasons,[31] to do so. Such an appointment must keep within the perpetuity period as measured from the date of the original settlement,[32] and it may not provide for accumulation for any period beyond that which was available to the original settlor.[33] Time starts to run afresh only if appointments are made to a beneficiary who resettles; but such a course would result in a double transfer of the capital, which may have damaging inheritance tax consequences.

9–010

F. Miscellaneous Administrative Provisions

Trustees of every trust need to be given the powers necessary to enable them to perform their duties. Obvious powers which they need are the power to sell, to invest, to apply income for the maintenance of child beneficiaries, to make advancements, to make payments to, and accept receipts from, guardians of children, etc. It was at one time necessary to include all such powers in the settlement. But now the basic necessary powers are given to trustees by the Trustee Acts 1925 and 2000, discussed in detail below.[34] The statutory powers can be added to, or restricted, by the terms of the trust instrument. It is usual, in the case of a discretionary trust, to give to the trustees the widest and most extensive powers. They may also be given a power to amend the trust. In terms of bulk, these administrative provisions will form the greater part of the trust instrument.

9–011

4. THE SELECTION OF TRUSTEES

The selection of the right trustees is important in the case of any trust; but particularly so in the case of a discretionary trust, where the trustees are given such extensive discretionary powers. The technical aspects of the matter are postponed to Ch.18; but it may be useful here to anticipate some of that discussion. The settlor, in conferring such broad discretion, will wish to select individuals whose judgment and co-operation she respects. She can select her most trusted friends, but they may have no expertise in investment, accounting,

9–012

---

[30] Below, para.18–032.

[31] *Re the New Huerto Trust* (2015) 18 I.T.E.L.R. 447 (trustees wished to appoint on new trusts that excluded the settlor from the class so the trust assets would not be subject to a freezing order); R. Davern (2016) 22 T. & T. 753.

[32] *Pilkington v IRC* [1964] A.C. 612.

[33] Because the appointors cannot be given powers in excess of those available to the settlor. For the available accumulation period, see above, para.9–008.

[34] Below, Ch.21.

law or taxes.[35] She may thus favour the inclusion of some professionals; who should do the job more efficiently; but they will need to be paid for their work. In a case of executorships or trusts generally, it is common to appoint a corporate trustee, usually the Executor and Trustee Company of a bank, but there may be reluctance to appoint a corporate trustee in a case of a discretionary trust, because it may be felt that the trust officer will not be in as good a position as a personal friend to exercise the broad discretions contained in a discretionary trust. It is common to select a mixture of professionals and non-professionals; and there is no legal reason why a corporation and an individual should not be trustees.[36]

As the disposition of the property is dependent upon the discretion of the trustees, the settlor may wish to be appointed trustee in order to be able to participate in decisions on distribution. The settlor remaining in the picture as a trustee will probably not have the same potential tax consequences as the settlor being a member of the class of beneficiaries, but the appointment of the settlor as trustee is still best avoided.[37] Even if she is not a trustee, it is possible for the settlor to exert some influence upon the trustees in the way in which they exercise their discretion.[38] However, if the settlor effectively dictates the distribution of the property in such a way that the trustees exercise no independent discretion, any appointments so made will be void.[39]

5.   THE NATURE OF THE INTEREST OF THE BENEFICIARIES UNDER A DISCRETIONARY TRUST

9–013   The nature of the interest of beneficiaries under a discretionary trust raises some important theoretical and practical questions. The discussion will tie in with some of the points made earlier in the distinction between trusts and powers.[40] In that context, the present discussion will justify the recognition of the basic difference between trusts and powers as being one of obligation or discretion. But it will be clear that the "duty" concept in the case of discretionary trusts is a very different duty from that recognised in the case of fixed trusts.

A.   Exhaustive and Non-Exhaustive Discretionary Trusts

9–014   If the trustees are required to distribute the whole of the income, the discretionary trust is exhaustive. Where, as in the case of most modern discretionary trusts, the trustees may apply the income for some purposes other than distribution among the beneficiaries, as where there is a power to accumulate income not so applied,

---

[35] For an illustration of the dangers of appointing such persons without the inclusion of professionals, see *Turner v Turner* [1984] Ch. 100, below, para.9–021.

[36] Although there may be some differences between such trustees when it comes to the application of statutory provisions, such as those relating to remuneration: Trustee Act 2000 s.29, below, para.22–003.

[37] If she can derive a benefit from her trusteeship, the settlor may still fall foul of the "reservation of benefit" tax rules that would bite on her being a member of the class of beneficiaries; below, para.10–008.

[38] For example, by a "letter of wishes".

[39] *Turner v Turner* [1984] Ch. 100.

[40] Above, para.2–021.

there is a non-exhaustive discretionary trust. The rights of the beneficiaries are more complex in the case of a non-exhaustive discretionary trust. For the income beneficiaries cannot argue that they are, as a group, *entitled* to the income. The income may be accumulated in whole or in part and added to the capital.

B.   The Nature of the Interest of the Beneficiaries

i.   Individual Beneficiaries.   In the case of a fixed trust, we saw that the   **9–015** beneficiary's interest is regarded as proprietary. She is the owner of an equitable interest under the trust. This is not so in the case of a beneficiary under a discretionary trust.[41] She is dependent upon the exercise by the trustees of their power of selection in her favour.[42] This point was crucial to the success of discretionary trusts in the estate duty days; because estate duty was payable when property "passed" on a death,[43] as on the death of a life tenant.[44] A discretionary beneficiary could not be said to be entitled to any quantifiable share. She therefore owned no part of the property and no property passed on her death. The position is similar under the current inheritance tax system. As we will see in the next chapter, the death of a discretionary beneficiary is not an event upon which the trust fund is taxable. Inheritance tax is, however, payable on a payment to a beneficiary and on certain other occasions. A sole member of a class of discretionary beneficiaries cannot claim entitlement to the income so long as there is a possibility that another member could come into existence.[45]

The trust fund may be regarded as financial resources of a sole beneficiary for the purpose of an order for financial provision (in favour of or against the beneficiary) under s.25 of the Matrimonial Causes Act 1973,[46] provided the order would not put improper pressure on the trustees in the exercise of their discretion.[47] This does not undermine the principle that a discretionary trust object does not have a proprietary interest: "under s.25 the court looks at resources; not just at ownership".[48]

---

[41] *JSC Mezhdunarodniy Promyshlenniy Bank v Pugachev* [2015] EWCA Civ 139; [2016] 1 W.L.R. 160 at [13].

[42] She can renounce her position as class member: *Re Gulbenkian's Settlement (No.2)* [1970] Ch. 408 at 418 (release for value; status of a voluntary release not decided). See also Y.K. Liew and C. Mitchell (2017) 11 J.Eq. 133 at 154.

[43] Finance Act 1894 s.2.

[44] *Earl Cowley v IRC* [1899] A.C. 198.

[45] *Re Trafford's Settlement* [1985] Ch. 32 (capital transfer tax). See also *Figg v Clarke (Inspector of Taxes)* [1997] 1 W.L.R. 603 (capital gains tax).

[46] See *Charman v Charman* [2007] W.T.L.R. 1151 (discretionary trust founded by husband treated as his resources); G. Kleiner and P. Munro (2007) 21 T.L.I. 117; cf. *A v A* [2007] 2 F.L.R. 467. See also *SR v CR (Ancillary Relief: Family Trusts)* [2009] 2 F.L.R. 1083; *B v B (Ancillary Relief)* [2010] 2 F.L.R. 887; *M v W (Ancillary Relief)* [2010] 2 F.L.R. 1484; *Whaley v Whaley* [2011] EWCA Civ 617; [2011] W.T.L.R. 1267.

[47] *Browne v Browne* [1989] 1 F.L.R. 291 (order against wife who was sole beneficiary); *J v J (C Intervening) (Minors: Financial Provision)* [1989] Fam. 29 (maintenance of two children, the only beneficiaries, who would become absolutely entitled at majority).

[48] *Whaley v Whaley* [2011] W.T.L.R. 1267 at [113] per Lewison J. Compare the Australian approach to the same issue: see *Kennon v Spry* [2008] HCA 56; (2008) 238 C.L.R. 366; L. Aitken (2009) 32 Aust. Bar Rev. 173.

9–016   **ii.   The Class.**   Whether or not the *class* of beneficiaries is properly regarded as the owner is a different matter. We have seen that a sole beneficiary of a discretionary trust and the beneficiaries entitled upon the determination of the trust on his death, may, if all are adult and under no disability, call for the capital to be paid over to them, or may validly assign to a third party who will become the beneficiary.[49]

Cases on estate duty have indicated that a class of beneficiaries may not hold a proprietary interest which "passes" for estate duty purposes. "Two or more persons," said Lord Reid:

> "cannot have a single right unless they hold it jointly or in common. But clearly objects of a discretionary trust do not have that: they have individual rights, they are in competition with each other and what the trustees give to one is his alone."

This was said in *Gartside v IRC*,[50] which was a case of a non-exhaustive discretionary trust, but in *Re Weir's Settlement*[51] and *Sainsbury v IRC*[52] the same analysis was applied to exhaustive discretionary trusts. Lord Reid's rejection of the "group or class" interest concept "seems equally applicable, whether the trust is exhaustive or not exhaustive."[53] The question has ceased to be of significance in relation to estate duty, but is relevant to determine where the beneficial interest is in a discretionary trust; and whether the class of beneficiaries, all being adult and under no disability, is able to call for a transfer of the legal title and to terminate the trust. It is submitted that the beneficial ownership should be in all those persons in whose favour the discretion may be exercised, including the beneficiaries of an accumulation provision under a non-exhaustive trust; and that, on the principle of *Re Smith*,[54] they should be able to terminate the trust in appropriate circumstances, if all adult and under no disability.[55]

C.   Powers and Duties

9–017   It may be useful at this stage to recapitulate some of the points, discussed above,[56] in connection with the nature of rights, duties and discretions in the context of trusts and powers. It will be seen that the basic distinction between trusts and powers continues to be that between obligations and discretions; but it is important to be able to identify what the trustees' duty is in the case of a discretionary trust. There are various contexts in which the question of the distinction between trusts and powers arises.

---

[49] *Green v Spicer* (1830) 1 Russ. & My. 395; *Re Smith* [1928] Ch. 915.
[50] [1968] A.C. 553 at 605–606.
[51] [1969] 1 Ch. 657, reversed on a different point [1971] Ch. 145.
[52] [1970] Ch. 712.
[53] [1970] Ch. 712 at 724, per Ungoed-Thomas J.
[54] [1928] Ch. 915; *Saunders v Vautier* (1841) 4 Beav. 115, affirmed Cr. & Ph. 240.
[55] This will not be possible unless all members are ascertainable, which may not be the case since *McPhail v Doulton* [1971] A.C. 424.
[56] Above, para.2–021.

i. Fixed Trust. At one end of the spectrum is the case of trustees of a fixed trust. This is clearly an obligation upon the trustees. Having once accepted the trusteeship, they have no choice of whether or not to perform the trust. They are obliged to do so; they can be required by the court to perform, and are personally liable for breach. Some of the trustees' duties will require the exercise of a discretion in their performance. Thus, trustees are under a duty to invest[57]; but, they will of course exercise a discretion in the selection of investments. The trustees' duty may be seen as a correlative of the beneficiaries' rights. The position is wholly different from that at the other end of the spectrum; that of the donee of a power held in a non-fiduciary capacity. As will be seen, the question whether to exercise such a power is wholly a matter of the donee's discretion.

9–018

ii. Trust with a Power of Selection. We have seen that there are cases in which the trustees hold property upon trust for a specified group of persons, subject to a power to select the shares and proportions in which those persons shall take. Thus in *Burrough v Philcox*[58] the disposition was "among my nephews and nieces, or their children, either all to one or to as many of them as my surviving child shall think proper." We saw that, in the absence of an appointment being made, the nieces and nephews took in equal shares. The nieces and nephews thus held a vested interest under the trust, subject to divestment upon an appointment being made. Their situation is exactly the same as it would have been if the testamentary provisions had given to a donee a power to appoint, and in default of appointment to my nephews and nieces in equal shares. Those entitled in default are treated as owners in equity subject to divestment on the exercise of the power.[59] The trust in their favour is a fixed trust.[60] The division into equal shares makes it necessary to identify each member, and to know how many there are. This case is the same as that of a fixed trust; but the beneficiaries' interests are subject to defeasance. The trustee's duty to the beneficiaries is clear. It is a question of construction whether the instrument creates such a trust or creates a discretionary trust, discussed below.

9–019

iii. Discretionary Trusts: Exhaustive and Non-exhaustive. A discretionary trust may require the trustees to distribute all the income; or it may give to the trustees a power to accumulate it.[61] Similarly, it may require the trustees to dispose of the capital during the trust period, or it may provide for a gift over of the assets of the trust at the end of the trust period. Whether the trust is exhaustive or non-exhaustive, an individual beneficiary is not regarded as having any proprietary interest in the trust property.[62] If the trust is exhaustive, there is authority to say the class as a whole, if adult and under no disability, can terminate the trust.[63]

9–020

---

[57] Below, para.19–005.

[58] (1840) 5 My. & Cr. 72.

[59] *Re Brooks' ST* [1939] Ch. 993 at 997.

[60] And thus not affected by the decision in *McPhail v Doulton* [1971] A.C. 424, above, para.4–009. See C. Emery (1982) 98 L.Q.R. 551.

[61] Above, para.9–008.

[62] Above, para.9–015.

[63] *Re Smith* [1928] Ch. 915; *Re Nelson* [1928] Ch. 920; above, para.9–016.

This raises the question: what is the trustee's duty? Clearly, it is different from the case of a fixed trust. Where are the beneficiary's correlative rights? This situation does not fit neatly into the right-duty correlation. The beneficiary has no proprietary rights. Is it correct to describe the situation as a trust; which, by definition, involves a duty? The answer, it is submitted, is: yes; this is a trust, and it involves a duty, although different from that in the case of a fixed trust.

The duty here is to exercise the discretion. In the case of an exhaustive discretionary trust, a selection must be made; whereas if the discretionary trust is non-exhaustive, the discretion may be exercised by deciding to accumulate. As Harris argued persuasively, "the discretionary trust in fact depends on a rule-concept of duty, with no such necessity for correlative rights."[64] Herein is the trustee's duty in a discretionary trust; and here is the point of distinction between a discretionary trust and a mere power. Each member of the class of beneficiaries under a discretionary trust has standing to sue in order to have the trustees' duty performed.[65] Not that such a beneficiary will necessarily benefit by the performance of the trustees' duty; as it is a duty, not to pay to that beneficiary, but to exercise their discretion as described above.

In *Re Locker's Settlement*,[66] the terms of an exhaustive discretionary trust required the trustees to pay, divide and apply the income for charitable purposes or among the class of beneficiaries as the trustees "shall in their absolute discretion determine". Because of subsequent expressions of wishes by the settlor, the trustees failed to make distributions of income from 1965 to 1968. The question arose in 1975 what should be done with that income, and particularly whether the trustees' discretion had expired.

Goulding J held that the discretion still continued, and that the trustees should apply their discretion in the distribution of the money among those who were members of the class of beneficiaries in the relevant years. In discussing the question of the trustees' duty and the court's power to enforce the exercise of the discretion, he said:

> "[I]t is common ground that it was the duty of the trustees to distribute the trust income within a reasonable time ... A court of equity, where the trustees have failed to discharge their duty of prompt discretionary distribution of income, is concerned to make them, as owners of the trust assets at law, dispose of them in accordance with the requirements of conscience."[67]

If the trustees refuse to perform their duty, the court can itself execute the trust:

> "by appointing new trustees, or by authorising or directing representative persons of the classes of beneficiaries to prepare a scheme for distribution, or even, should the proper basis for distribution appear, by itself directing the trustees so to distribute."[68]

The trustees in *Locker* were ready and willing to perform, and did so.

---

[64] (1971) 87 L.Q.R. 231.

[65] *Tempest v Lord Camoys* (1882) 21 Ch.D. 571; *Whaley v Whaley* [2011] W.T.L.R. 1267 at [112].

[66] [1977] 1 W.L.R. 1323; *Re Gourju's WT* [1943] Ch. 24; *McPhail v Doulton* [1971] A.C. 424.

[67] [1977] 1 W.L.R. 1323 at 1325.

[68] [1977] 1 W.L.R. 1323 at 1325, quoting Lord Wilberforce in *McPhail v Doulton* [1971] A.C. 424 at 457.

The point is that the trustees under these circumstances are under a duty to distribute. That is an obligation which is subject to enforcement by the court in one of the ways stated. *Locker* was a case of an exhaustive discretionary trust; though the individuals in the class of beneficiaries were not, as a class, entitled to the whole of the income, because the trustees could make payments to charity. The duty and obligation of the trustees, however, is the same in the case of a non-exhaustive discretionary trust as in *McPhail v Doulton*[69] itself. The difference is that in a non-exhaustive trust the duty to exercise the discretion can be satisfied by deciding to accumulate.

iv. Powers Held as Trustee; Fiduciary Powers.[70]   The situation is quite   **9–021**
different where the trustees, as one of the terms of the trust instrument, are given a power of appointment. Here there is no duty to exercise; and the court will not order the trustee to exercise the discretion. Typical is *Re Allen Meyrick's Trust*[71] where the will gave property to trustees to hold:

> "upon trust that they may apply the income thereof in their absolute discretion for the maintenance of my said husband and subject to the exercise of their discretion on trust for my two godchildren... in equal shares absolutely."

Various difficulties arose. The husband was an undischarged bankrupt. Some of the money was applied in paying the rent and certain debts. The trustees could not agree on the disposal of other income, and attempted to surrender their discretion to the court. The court refused to accept this surrender of discretion, and was willing only to hear applications for directions in particular circumstances as they arose. Nor were the trustees ordered to exercise their discretion. The trust here was in favour of the godchildren, subject to the overriding power. If the trustees could not reach unanimity as to the exercise of the power, the godchildren became entitled.

This is not, of course, to say that the trustees in this situation are not subject to duties in relation to the exercise of the power. They hold the power in a fiduciary capacity, and are subject to fiduciary duties in the way in which they make their decision. They must do more than refrain from acting capriciously. Their duty is to consider periodically whether to exercise the power, and to consider the range of objects in such manner as will enable them to discharge their fiduciary duties. If they decide to exercise the power they must, of course, keep within its terms; they must exercise it in a responsible manner according to its purpose and consider the appropriateness of individual appointments.[72] The court will intervene if they exceed their powers or act capriciously.[73] Furthermore, they must not release the power, nor delegate it without authority.[74] They must

---

[69] [1971] A.C. 424

[70] See Ch.7.

[71] [1966] 1 W.L.R. 499.

[72] *Re Hay's ST* [1982] 1 W.L.R. 202; A. Grubb [1982] Conv. 432. These duties, which were laid down in *McPhail v Doulton* [1971] A.C. 424, *Re Gestetner* [1953] Ch. 672, and *Re Gulbenkian's ST* [1970] A.C. 508, are not necessarily exhaustive.

[73] *McPhail v Doulton* [1971] A.C. 424 at 456–457. See also *Pitt v Holt* [2013] 2 A.C. 108; below, para.18–046.

[74] *Re Hay's ST* [1982] 1 W.L.R. 202.

appreciate that the discretion is theirs and not that of the settlor. If they merely obey the settlor's instructions without any independent consideration, they will be in breach of the duties described above, and any appointment made in such circumstances will be void.[75] These duties stem from the fact that the power is fiduciary; not from any duty to exercise the power. If they decide not to do so, the court will not interfere. It has been held, however, that the court must step in where a fiduciary power is left with no-one to exercise it.[76] In such a case, the court can adopt any of the methods indicated by Lord Wilberforce in *McPhail v Doulton* in the context of discretionary trusts, i.e. it may appoint new trustees, direct the beneficiaries to prepare a scheme of distribution, or itself direct a distribution.[77]

9–022   **v. Powers Held in a Non-Fiduciary Capacity.**   As is seen in Ch.7, no duty is imposed upon a donee who holds a power in a non-fiduciary capacity. If a grandparent leaves property on trust for his grandchildren, and gives his son a power to appoint in favour of charity, the son is under no duty to appoint or even to consider the rival claims of charity or the grandchildren. He is, of course, if he makes an appointment, required to keep within the terms of the power, and to avoid exercising the power for an improper purpose.

9–023   **vi. The Rule of Certainty in Ascertaining Beneficiaries or Objects.**   This aspect of discretionary trusts is fully discussed in Ch.4.

9–024   **vii. Discretionary Trusts and Inheritance Tax.**   Since the introduction of inheritance tax, discretionary trusts have suffered in popularity by reason of their exclusion from the "potentially exempt transfer" regime.[78] The lifetime creation of such trusts is, therefore, taxable even if the settlor survives a further seven years. For this reason few discretionary trusts of substantial size (other than "offshore" trusts) are likely to be created under the present tax system, although more modest discretionary trusts falling within the settlor's inheritance tax "nil rate band"[79] are still attractive. However, as we will see in the following chapter, the inheritance tax disadvantages of discretionary trusts were extended to most other kinds of trusts by the Finance Act 2006.

---

[75] *Turner v Turner* [1984] Ch. 100.

[76] *Mettoy Pension Trustees Ltd v Evans* [1990] 1 W.L.R. 1587 (fiduciary powers of company directors ceased on appointment of liquidator, but could not be exercised by liquidator or receiver because of conflict of duties); S. Gardner (1991) 107 L.Q.R. 214; J. Martin [1991] Conv. 364.

[77] *Mettoy Pension Trustees Ltd v Evans* [1990] 1 W.L.R. 1587 at 1616–1618.

[78] Below, para.10–008.

[79] Below, para.10–019 and following.

CHAPTER 10

TAXATION AND TRUSTS

1. ESTATE AND TAX PLANNING

THE most significant factor in the lifetime creation of trusts has been the avoidance of taxation: "in our society, a great deal of intellectual effort is devoted to tax avoidance".[1] A wealthy person may benefit the family by making gifts to them, and then leave property to them by will. But tax legislation imposes higher rates on larger accumulations of property, and this wealthy person will seek ways of conferring benefits on the family and at the same time reducing tax liability. The tax payable by 10 people on incomes of £10,000 each is less in total than that payable by one person with an income of £100,000. Similarly, tax on capital is at its highest in large concentrations. More details of the income, and especially of the capital tax system, will be given below. The point here is that a wealthy person can best preserve the family fortune by sharing it out, and that this has commonly been done by creating lifetime trusts. This tax planning of an estate is one of the most important and sophisticated functions of trust lawyers.

10–001

In earlier times, the courts in determining the effectiveness of any scheme of tax avoidance applied the principle laid down by Lord Tomlin in *IRC v Duke of Westminster*: "every man is entitled if he can to order his affairs so that the tax

---

[1] *UBS AG v Revenue and Customs Commissioners* [2016] UKSC 13; [2016] 1 W.L.R. 1005 per Lord Reed JSC at [1].

attaching under the appropriate Acts is less than it otherwise would be."[2] But starting in *WT Ramsay v IRC*,[3] the House of Lords began to elaborate a new and much more restrictive principle to apply in dealing with questions of the effectiveness of complex tax avoidance schemes. Where there occurs a pre-ordained series of transactions (or a single composite transaction) designed to reduce tax payable by a particular taxpayer the court is free to disregard any of those transactions if they are inserted for no good commercial purposes other than the reduction of tax. The transactions will be treated as a single composite whole and taxed accordingly. There has been a "definitive move from a generally literalist interpretation to a more purposive approach."[4] It is, however, "no more than a useful aid",[5] and judges should be conscious of "the need to apply the *Ramsay* approach with sensitivity to the particular fiscal context which is relevant".[6] In the most recent Supreme Court decision to consider the approach, Lord Hodge JSC summarised three relevant aspects[7]:

> "First, the tax code is not a seamless garment. As a result[,] provisions imposing specific tax charges do not necessarily militate against the existence of a more general charge to tax which may have priority over and supersede or qualify the specific charge... Secondly, it is necessary to pay close attention to the statutory wording and not be distracted by judicial glosses which have enabled the courts properly to apply the statutory words in other factual contexts. Thirdly, the courts must now adopt a purposive approach to the interpretation of the taxing provisions and identify and analyse the relevant facts accordingly."

The approach applies to the creation and manipulation of trusts as well as to commercial and corporate dealings.[8]

As the circumstances of each individual differ, so each situation needs individual treatment. The estate- or tax-planner, with the assistance of accountants and other specialists, will present to the client various possible solutions, indicating the tax implications of each. The client must then decide how much to give away immediately and irrevocably, and to whom; and how much to keep. What is kept will be disposed of by will, and a testamentary trust

---

[2] [1936] A.C. 1 at 19.

[3] [1982] A.C. 300. See also *IRC v Burmah Oil Co Ltd* (1981) 54 T.C. 200; *Furness v Dawson* [1984] A.C. 474; *Craven (Inspector of Taxes) v White* [1989] A.C. 398 (where the House of Lords refused to extend this principle); *Ensign Tankers (Leasing) Ltd v Stokes* [1992] 1 A.C. 655; *Moodie v IRC* [1993] 1 W.L.R. 266; *IRC v McGuckian* [1997] 1 W.L.R. 991; *The Collector of Stamp Revenue v Arrowtown Assets Ltd* [2003] HKCFA 52; *Barclays Mercantile Business Finance Ltd v Mawson (Inspector of Taxes)* [2005] 1 A.C. 684.

[4] *RFC 2012 Plc (In Liquidation) (formerly The Rangers Football Club Plc) v Advocate General for Scotland* [2017] UKSC 45; [2017] 1 W.L.R. 2767 per Lord Hodge at [12].

[5] *MacNiven (HM Inspector of Taxes) v Westmoreland Investments Ltd* [2003] 1 A.C. 311 at 320; *Barclays Mercantile Business Finance Ltd v Mawson (Inspector of Taxes)* [2005] 1 A.C. 684. See Lord Templeman (2001) 117 L.Q.R. 575; Lord Walker (2004) 120 L.Q.R. 412; J. Freedman (2007) 123 L.Q.R. 53; *UBS AG v Revenue and Customs Commissioners* [2016] 1 W.L.R. 1005 per Lord Reed JSC at [61]–[72]; D. de Cogan (2016) 75 C.L.J. 474; H.L. McCarthy and S. Black [2016] B.T.R. 257; Lord Reed [2016] B.T.R. 288; S. Daly (2017) 1366 Tax Journal 8; J. Lee (2017) 31 T.L.I. 219.

[6] *UBS AG v Revenue and Customs Commissioners* [2016] 1 W.L.R. 1005 per Lord Reed JSC at [95].

[7] *RFC 2012 Plc (In Liquidation) (formerly The Rangers Football Club Plc) v Advocate General for Scotland* [2017] 1 W.L.R. 2767 at [15]; G. Mulley (2017) 76 C.L.J. 502.

[8] *IRC v Fitzwilliam* [1993] 1 W.L.R. 1189 (but *Ramsay* principle did not apply on facts, Lord Templeman dissenting); J. Kirkbride [1994] Conv. 67. See also the general anti-abuse rule in Finance Act 2013 Pt.5.

may be created. Those whose fortunes are insufficient to create tax problems will not be concerned with lifetime tax planning; but may, again, create testamentary trusts on their deaths.

Three forms of taxation are particularly relevant to the financial affairs of trusts: income tax, capital gains tax, and inheritance tax. They will be dealt with in turn.

2. INCOME TAX

Tax is chargeable upon an individual's taxable income at the rates laid down annually in the Finance Act. For the 2017/18 tax year, the first £33,500 of taxable income is subject to the basic rate of 20%, after which the higher rate of 40% is payable. An additional rate of 45% applies to income above £150,000. Special rates are payable on UK dividends: 7.5% in the case of basic-rate taxpayers; 32.5% in the case of higher-rate taxpayers; and 38.1% for those who pay income tax at the additional rate. There are a number of allowances and reliefs to which individuals are entitled, most notably the tax-free personal allowance of £11,500 available to people with incomes below £100,000, and the dividend allowance of £5,000.

10–002

We are concerned, however, with the taxation of trusts. Trustees are not individuals for income tax purposes. Trusts as such therefore enjoy no personal allowances. The income of a trust (other than a discretionary trust) is chargeable at the basic rate, and the trustees are assessable.[9] In a wide range of circumstances the income arising under a trust may be treated as the settlor's income.[10] The trustees need take no action in respect of dividend income from most stock exchange investments, which is normally paid net of the ordinary rate payable on UK dividends. The beneficiary who is entitled to the income is responsible for the payment of any dividend upper rate tax which may be due; and it is often convenient to arrange for the dividends to be paid direct to him. The trustees will, however, need to deduct and account for income tax which is due on any income of the trust which has been received without deduction of tax, such as income from land or profits if they carry on a trade.

Trustees must also deduct and account for the rate applicable to trusts (currently 45%), which becomes due in the case of the income of a trust where there is no person currently entitled to the income.[11] With such a trust, the income may either be paid out at the discretion of the trustees or, if the trust contains such a power, it may be accumulated. If it is accumulated, it is taxed at the rate applicable to trusts (45%). Where the income is paid to or for the benefit of a

---

[9] There is no specific statutory provision. The higher rates do not apply to trustees because they are not "individuals".

[10] Income Tax (Trading and Other Income) Act 2005 ss.619–648, replacing earlier provisions. These provisions are intended to prevent and penalise tax avoidance.

[11] Income Tax Act 2007 s.9 as amended by Finance Act 2012 s.1(3). The trust rate on dividends is 38.1%. This includes income of a discretionary trust or an accumulation and maintenance trust; below, paras 10–019, 10–024. The tax is charged on the whole income of the trust, after deducting expenses properly chargeable to income under the general law; *Carver v Duncan (Inspector of Taxes)* [1985] A.C. 1082; *Revenue and Customs Commissioners v Trustees of the Peter Clay Discretionary Trust* [2009] Ch. 296.

beneficiary, the ultimate tax liability is dependent upon the beneficiary's tax situation.[12] He is treated as having received the value of the payment grossed up to reflect the rate applicable to trusts.[13] If the beneficiary's taxable income is already in excess of £150,000, he will have no further liability as the tax already paid (45%) and the tax due at his personal rate on income above £150,000 (45%) are the same. On the other hand, if his other income does not exhaust his allowances and reliefs and the basic or higher rate, he may claim a repayment of an appropriate amount on producing to the Revenue the trustees' certificate of deduction of tax. It will thus be seen that income tax may be saved if the trustees have a discretion as to the distribution of income, and use it to make payments to those on low incomes whose tax rate is lower than the trust's. There is, of course, no choice where the beneficiaries are entitled to the income or a specified share. Moreover none of the above consequences apply if the sum as received by the beneficiary is capital (rather than income) in his hands, for example where it is paid pursuant to a power of appointment restricted to capital or out of accumulated income.[14]

10–003   Reforms were introduced by the Finance Act 2005 to reduce the tax payable by discretionary trusts and to reduce compliance burdens on small trusts of this kind. Where a trust is subject to the rate applicable to trusts (45%) or the dividend trust rate (38.1%), the first £1,000 of annual income is charged at the basic rate (20%) instead of the rate applicable to trusts. Dividends within this first slice of income are taxed at the ordinary rate of 7.5%.[15]

The Finance Act 2005 also introduced reforms to reduce the income tax and capital gains tax burdens on trusts with "vulnerable beneficiaries".[16] "Vulnerable beneficiaries" are of two kinds. The first kind is disabled beneficiaries, which (broadly) means those who lack mental capacity to manage their affairs and those who are eligible to receive certain disability-related benefits. The second is minors where at least one of their parents has died. In these cases the trustees and the "vulnerable beneficiary" (or person acting on his behalf) may jointly elect to adopt a special tax treatment, whereby the trustees' liability will be what the beneficiary's liability would have been if he had received the income directly. This will normally result in a lower tax bill because the trustees can use the beneficiary's personal allowances and the basic rate band. The trust must be a "qualifying trust", and various other restrictions also apply.

Income tax on "pre-owned" assets, introduced by the Finance Act 2004, is discussed below.[17]

---

[12] But where the payment is in favour of the unmarried child under 18 of the settlor, the income is treated as that of the settlor: Income Tax (Trading and Other Income) Act 2005 s.629 (similarly where the income is retained in a bare trust for the settlor's child: s.631).

[13] Income Tax Act 2007 s.494.

[14] See *Stevenson (Inspector of Taxes) v Wishart* [1987] 1 W.L.R. 1204.

[15] Now see Income Tax Act 2007 s.491. Section 491(4) sets out the way in which types of income are to be allocated to the first £1,000 slice.

[16] See Finance Act 2005 Pt.2 Ch.4.

[17] Below, para.10–013.

3.   CAPITAL GAINS TAX

Capital gains tax was introduced by the Finance Act 1965, and originally imposed   **10–004**
at a rate of 30% upon the gains accruing upon the disposal of an asset. The
position is now governed by the consolidating Taxation of Chargeable Gains Act
1992.

Capital gains tax is payable upon a sale, exchange or gift.[18] The tax is not
payable on death, though the deceased's property is deemed to be acquired by his
personal representatives on his death at a consideration equal to its then market
value.[19] This generally involves a "tax-free uplift" in the notional acquisition cost
of the assets in question, since their market value at death is usually greater than
their acquisition cost to the deceased. When the personal representatives pass the
assets to the legatee[20] no disposal is deemed to occur and the legatee acquires the
assets with an acquisition cost equal to that of the personal representatives.

The capital gains tax rate paid by individuals depends on their income tax
position and on the type of property from which they made the capital gain. Basic
rate income tax payers pay capital gains tax at 18% on gains made from
residential property, and 10% on other gains, up to the basic rate income tax band
limit. Beyond that limit, and for individuals who already pay income tax at the
higher or additional rate, the rate of capital gains tax is 28% on residential
property and 20% on other chargeable assets. The latter rates also apply to
trustees.

There are many exemptions from liability to capital gains tax, the most
important being an annual exempt amount of (in 2017/18) £11,300 for individuals
and £5,650 for a trust,[21] the taxpayer's main or only residence,[22] a chattel worth
less than £6,000,[23] and gilt-edged securities.[24]

The settlor of a new trust will be liable to capital gains tax on creating the trust
since this is a disposal even where the settlor declares himself trustee.[25] Once a
trust is established, the trustees will be affected by capital gains tax in two quite
different ways. First, in relation to the disposition of assets of the trust. On a
disposal, the trustees are liable to tax on gains, as individuals would be. This
situation normally arises where trustees sell investments in the ordinary course of
administration of the trust. Secondly, there are certain occasions on which a
disposal is deemed to have been made. Disposals are deemed to be made on
various occasions, but the only one in this context on which tax may be
chargeable is that on which a person becomes absolutely entitled against the

---

[18]   Also when a disposal is deemed to occur, as where a capital sum is derived from an asset: Taxation
of Chargeable Gains Act 1992 ss.22–24.

[19]   Taxation of Chargeable Gains Act 1992 s.62.

[20]   Taxation of Chargeable Gains Act 1992 s.62. Defined in s.64(2) to include "any person taking
under a testamentary disposition or on an intestacy or partial intestacy, whether he takes beneficially
or as trustee…".

[21]   Taxation of Chargeable Gains Act 1992 s.3(2), Sch.1. Trusts with "vulnerable beneficiaries" may
use the higher sum.

[22]   Taxation of Chargeable Gains Act 1992 s.222.

[23]   Taxation of Chargeable Gains Act 1992 s.262.

[24]   Taxation of Chargeable Gains Act 1992 s.115.

[25]   Taxation of Chargeable Gains Act 1992 s.70. The rules relating to offshore trusts cannot be dealt
with here.

trustee[26] as, for example, where the beneficiary becomes absolutely entitled upon fulfilling a condition, such as majority, or where an advancement is made to a beneficiary.

4. INHERITANCE TAX

10–005   Inheritance tax is a modified version of its predecessor, capital transfer tax, which itself replaced estate duty. Capital transfer tax replaced estate duty by the Finance Act 1975,[27] with effect from 26 March 1974. This was part of a complete reorganisation of the structure of the taxation of capital, which was extended to lifetime gifts. A wealth tax, in the form of an annual tax on ownership of assets, was planned in 1974, but was never introduced. The application of capital transfer tax to lifetime gifts was largely removed by the Finance Act 1986, in which the tax was renamed as inheritance tax.[28]

A.   Estate Duty

10–006   Before 26 March 1974, estate duty was the only tax on private capital. It was a death tax only, and payable upon property passing on a death.[29] It could therefore be avoided by disposing of property before death; save that transfers made within seven years before death were subject to the tax.[30]

The disposal would often be by the lifetime creation of a trust. The settlor would wish to avoid estate duty, not only on his death, but also upon the deaths of the beneficiaries. It was held that estate duty was payable upon the whole capital of a trust upon the death of a life tenant, or of the holder of some other limited interest.[31] The members of a class of beneficiaries of a discretionary trust owned no interest, however, in the fund[32]; they had no more than a hope that the trustees' discretion would be exercised in their favour. This meant it was possible, until 1969, to avoid liability to estate duty on the death of the settlor and of any of the beneficiaries by creating a discretionary trust at least seven years before the death of the settlor.[33] No wonder that the tax was called a "voluntary tax". The Finance Act 1969 imposed a charge upon the death of any beneficiary who had received payments of income in the past seven years.[34] The charge was on a portion of the

---

[26] Taxation of Chargeable Gains Act 1992 s.71. See *Jenkins (Inspector of Taxes) v Brown* [1989] 1 W.L.R. 1163; *Swires (Inspector of Taxes) v Renton* [1991] S.T.C. 490; *Figg v Clarke (Inspector of Taxes)* [1997] 1 W.L.R. 603 (beneficiaries not absolutely entitled if birth of further class member possible, however unlikely). A deemed disposal, whether or not tax is charged, has the effect of establishing the acquisition value in the hands of the recipient.

[27] The provisions are now consolidated by the Inheritance Tax Act 1984.

[28] Finance Act 1986 s.100. The chronology seems confusing because the Finance Act 1986 s.100 effected a renaming of what had been the Capital Transfer Tax Act 1984. That Act was renamed the Inheritance Tax Act 1984.

[29] Finance Act 1894 ss.1, 2.

[30] Finance Act 1968 s.35.

[31] *Cowley (Earl) v IRC* [1899] A.C. 198.

[32] Eventually so decided in *Gartside v IRC* [1968] A.C. 553; above, para.9–016.

[33] See *Pearson v IRC* [1980] Ch. 1 at 25, per Templeman LJ.

[34] Finance Act 1969 ss.36, 37.

capital equivalent to the share of the income received by the deceased during the "relevant" period. This system had little time to work, and would not in any case have been very effective because the trustees of a discretionary trust could pay the income to those whom they judged least likely to die in the near future; and so long as the income was thus disposed of, there was no objection to making capital payments to the old and sick beneficiaries.[35]

B. Capital Transfer Tax

In a White Paper on Capital Transfer Tax[36] and a Green Paper on Wealth Tax,[37] **10–007** the Labour Government in 1974 announced its intention of imposing both taxes. The policy was to effect a levelling of wealth[38]; estate duty, with all its loopholes, had conspicuously failed to do so. Capital transfer tax was a tax on capital transfers, whether during life or on death, and was planned to tax family capital, whether or not settled, at least once a generation. The Wealth Tax would go further, and impose a tax annually on capital. The imposition of a wealth tax would take some time, and the Government appreciated that it needed to be preceded by capital transfer tax.

Capital transfer tax in its original form was a cumulative tax applying to all transfers of value made by an individual after 26 March 1974 until the final transfer on death. Rates were progressive, and those chargeable on death (or on transfers within three years of death) were double those chargeable on lifetime transfers. The tax was modified by subsequent Conservative Governments, in particular by altering the cumulation principle. Instead of cumulating all transfers (made after 26 March 1974), only those made within the previous 10 years had to be cumulated, the figure finally being reduced to seven years.[39] The rates of tax being progressive, these amendments were beneficial to the transferor. Further substantial modifications were made by the Finance Act 1986, which renamed the tax as inheritance tax, to which we now turn.

C. Inheritance Tax

The most significant changes brought about by the 1986 Act were the **10–008** introduction of the "potentially exempt transfer" and the reintroduction of the estate duty principle of "reservation of benefit". These are explained in the outline of inheritance tax which follows. As we will see, the rules on the taxation of trusts were significantly changed by the Finance Act 2006.

The central concept of inheritance tax is the transfer of value, which may be chargeable, exempt or potentially exempt.[40] There is a transfer of value where a person makes a disposition as a result of which the value of his estate

---

[35] See Finance Act 1969 s.37(3)(b).
[36] Cmnd. No. 5705 of 1974.
[37] Cmnd. No. 5705 of 1974.
[38] "The Government is committed to use the taxation system to promote greater social and economic equality. This requires a redistribution of wealth as well as income." Preface to Green Paper.
[39] Finance Act 1986 s.101.
[40] Inheritance Tax Act 1984 ss.1, 2, 3A.

immediately after the disposition is less than it would have been but for the transfer, and the value transferred is the amount by which the estate is the less.[41] On a death, the deceased is treated as making a transfer of value of the whole of his estate immediately before the death.[42] There are special rules relating to settled property,[43] which will be examined below, and a number of exemptions and reliefs. The most important exemptions relate to transfers of any amount between spouses or civil partners, whether in the lifetime or on death,[44] and certain personal exemptions.[45] Other reliefs and exemptions relate to situations which were familiar with estate duty, and include gifts to charities, works of art, agricultural or business property, and woodlands. They cannot be examined here.

Aside from exemptions and reliefs, there is also a "nil-rate band" within which inheritance tax is not payable. The standard nil-rate band in 2017/18 is £325,000, although that figure can be increased by a further £100,000 by the additional "residence" nil-rate band.[46] This new provision applies where a person dies on or after 6 April 2017; where that person owned a "qualifying residential interest" in property; and where that interest is inherited by a lineal descendant of the deceased, or the spouse or civil partner of a lineal descendant. Any unused part of a deceased's nil-rate band (including any unused residence nil-rate band) can be carried over to a surviving spouse or civil partner of the deceased, to be utilised on the death of the survivor.[47]

The exemptions referred to above may be described as substantive exemptions, to distinguish them from the potentially exempt transfer, introduced by the Finance Act 1986.[48] A lifetime transfer by an individual made on or after 18 March 1986 is potentially exempt. As in the days of estate duty, it becomes chargeable if the transferor does not survive for seven years. If he dies within three years, the rates are those chargeable on a death. If he dies between three and seven years from the transfer, there is a taper relief on a sliding scale.[49] In certain exceptional cases, in particular the creation of certain types of trust, a lifetime disposition is *immediately* chargeable,[50] although at half the rates applicable on death.[51] If the settlor dies within seven years, the rates are increased as described above.

In the case of a lifetime transfer which is either initially chargeable or which becomes so by reason of death within seven years, and in the case of a transfer on death, the rates of tax are affected by any chargeable transfers within the previous

---

[41] Inheritance Tax Act 1984 s.3. It may include an omission to claim an entitlement: s.3(3).

[42] Inheritance Tax Act 1984 s.4.

[43] Inheritance Tax Act 1984 Pt III.

[44] Inheritance Tax Act 1984 s.18; the reference to civil partners was inserted by The Tax and Civil Partnership Regulations 2005 (SI 2005/3229). There was famously no exemption applicable to two sisters who had lived together their whole lives: *Burden v UK* [2008] All E.R. (D) 391 (Apr).

[45] Inheritance Tax Act 1984 ss.19–28. These include £3,000 per donor per year; £250 per donee per year; normal expenditure out of income; gifts in consideration of marriage or civil partnership of various permitted amounts up to £5,000; and payments for the maintenance of dependants. (s.11).

[46] Inheritance Tax Act 1984 ss.8D–8M, introduced by Finance (No.2) Act 2015 s.9. The figure of £100,000 applies to the tax year 2017/18.

[47] Inheritance Tax Act 1984 ss.8A, 8B and 8C, introduced by Finance Act 2008 s.10 and Sch.4.

[48] Inheritance Tax Act 1984 s.3A, introduced by Finance Act 1986 s.101 and Sch.19.

[49] Inheritance Tax Act 1984 s.7.

[50] Inheritance Tax Act 1984 s.3A.

[51] Inheritance Tax Act 1984 s.2.

seven years, which must be cumulated.[52] No tax will be payable if the transfer falls within the nil-rate band (including, if appropriate, the additional "residence" nil-rate band). Thereafter the rate is 40% if the transfer was on death or within three years of death, and 20% in the case of an initially chargeable lifetime transfer. As mentioned above, there is a sliding scale applicable to a potentially exempt transfer which becomes chargeable.[53] To encourage charitable giving, the 40% rate is reduced to 36% for deaths on or after 6 April 2012 where at least 10% of the net estate is left to charity.[54]

In the case of an initially chargeable lifetime transfer, the tax may be paid by the transferor or the transferee. If it is paid by the transferor, the value of the chargeable transfer is the amount by which his estate is reduced, therefore the amount of the transfer for tax purposes must include the tax. It will be necessary to "gross up" the sum transferred. The amount of tax payable on any sum varies, not only with the size of the sum, but also with the total of prior chargeable transfers within the previous seven years. The calculations in any particular case can be formidable, and will be worked out in each case from grossing up tables. On the other hand, if the transferee pays the tax, the actual amount of the transfer is treated as the gross gift, and added to the transferor's total gifts. The amount of tax payable will be less; but the amount received by the transferee will also be less.

10–009

The last transfer which a person makes is that of the estate on death. The rates applicable are those which begin at the total value of any taxable lifetime gifts within the previous seven years, grossed up as necessary. There is no question of grossing up the estate at death. Any tax is deducted prior to distribution. The incidence of tax as between specific and residuary beneficiaries is another problem.[55]

It is thus necessary to keep a "score" of taxable lifetime gifts, pay tax on them if due, and apply the seven-year cumulation rule when calculating the tax liability on subsequent chargeable gifts, and ultimately on death. The tax planner's job is to enable the client to make the best use of available exemptions and reliefs, and of the potentially exempt transfer. The adviser's dilemma is that the calculations have to be made on a number of assumptions about future events and tax liabilities.

i. Reservation of benefit. Before examining the special rules relating to trusts, mention must be made of the principle of reservation of benefit. Although familiar under the estate duty regime, this concept was not relevant to capital transfer tax. It was reintroduced by the Finance Act 1986 and is a fundamental feature of inheritance tax. The object of this principle is that the donor should not be permitted to take advantage of the potentially exempt transfer rule by making gifts where he effectively retains an interest. As Lord Hoffmann has put it:

10–010

---

[52] Inheritance Tax Act 1984 s.7.
[53] Inheritance Tax Act 1984 s.7(4).
[54] Inheritance Tax Act 1984 Sch.1A, introduced by Finance Act 2012 Sch.33.
[55] Inheritance Tax Act 1984 ss.38, 39.

"Not only may you not have your cake and eat it, but if you eat more than a few *de minimis* crumbs of what was given, you are deemed for tax purposes to have eaten the lot".[56]

Where an individual makes a gift on or after 18 March 1986 the property is treated as subject to a reservation in two cases (amendments added by the Finance Acts 1999 and 2003 are dealt with below). First, where possession and enjoyment of the property is not bona fide assumed by the donee prior to the seven-year period ending with the donor's death (or, if the donor died within seven years of the gift, at the date of the gift). Secondly, where the property is not enjoyed "to the entire exclusion, or virtually to the entire exclusion, of the donor and of any benefit to him by contract or otherwise" at any time during the seven years ending with his death (or, if the donor died within seven years of the gift, at any time after the gift[57]). There are certain exceptions, for example where the donor occupies the property for full consideration in money or money's worth.[58] Nor does the principle apply where the gift falls within certain of the substantive exemptions, for example (subject to exceptions) the spousal exemption.[59]

A transfer into a joint account may involve a gift with reservation if the transferor and the second accountholder hold as joint tenants rather than as tenants in common. In *Matthews v Revenue & Customs*,[60] the deceased Mrs Matthews opened a joint account with her son. No withdrawals or deposits were made apart from interest accrual. Mrs Matthews died eight years later and the Revenue Commissioners determined that the whole of the monies in the account were liable to inheritance tax. An appeal by the son was dismissed. The Tribunal Judge held that the mother had made a gift of a joint interest in the whole of the bank account, but that gift involved a reservation of benefit because either party could properly withdraw all of the funds for his or her own benefit. The result would have been different if the account had been held by the mother and son as tenants in common: the initial gift of a half-share would be a potentially exempt transfer, but in *Matthews* the mother survived for seven years.

The effect of a gift with reservation of benefit is that the property is treated as remaining in the estate of the donor. Hence the making of a gift with reservation normally has no immediate inheritance tax consequence, but the property will be treated as part of the donor's estate on death (at its value at that time) and taxed accordingly.[61] If during his lifetime there is a change of circumstances so that there is no longer a reservation of benefit, for example where the donor renounces any benefit retained, a potentially exempt transfer is treated as made at that time, so that the donor must survive a further seven years if tax is to be avoided.[62] If he dies within seven years, the property is taxed on its value at the date of the release

---

[56] *Ingram v IRC* [2000] 1 A.C. 293 at 304.

[57] Finance Act 1986 s.102. For a recent analysis of "entire exclusion" see *Buzzoni v Revenue and Customs Commissioners* [2013] EWCA Civ 1684 at [30]–[57]; C. Whitehouse [2014] P.C.B. 129. Note also s.102ZA, introduced by Finance Act 2006 Sch.20 para.33 (beneficiary who continues to occupy after termination of interest in possession deemed to have made gift with reservation of benefit).

[58] Finance Act 1986 Sch.20 para.6.

[59] Finance Act 1986 s.102(5). The exceptions are discussed below, para.10–012.

[60] [2012] UKFTT 658 (TC). See also *Sillars v IRC* [2004] W.T.L.R. 591.

[61] Finance Act 1986 s.102(3).

[62] Finance Act 1986 s.102(4).

of benefit, not of the prior gift. In the case where the lifetime gift is initially chargeable, as in the case of the creation of certain trusts, the property subject to a reservation will be treated as part of the settlor's estate on his death and taxed again, but relief is given against this double charge.[63]

Cases on estate duty and comparable Commonwealth legislation afford guidance as to what is a reservation of benefit.[64] In the context of trusts, the settlor will be treated as reserving a benefit if he is among the class of objects of a discretionary trust,[65] even though he receives nothing. They will be treated similarly if the settlor is a remunerated trustee of the settlement.[66] The settlor does not, however, reserve a benefit by reason of being an unpaid trustee,[67] nor if he has a reversionary interest in the settled property, because the subject-matter of the gift does not include the reversion.[68]

10–011

The reservation of benefit principle does not apply to gifts between spouses.[69] This gave rise to a loophole whereby a gift by a married person could be routed through a trust for his or her spouse, as illustrated by *IRC v Eversden*.[70] In that case a settlement was created in 1988 in which the settlor's spouse had a life interest, followed by a discretionary trust which included the settlor as a beneficiary. The spouse died in 1992. It was held that no inheritance tax was payable on the settlor's death in 1998 because the reservation of benefit rule (which would otherwise have applied because the settlor was a beneficiary of the discretionary trust) was excluded by the spouse exemption. The effect was that the spouse exemption applied once and for all when the settlement was created, and was not confined to the period during which the spouse's life interest continued. This avoidance scheme was, however, closed by the Finance Act 2003.[71] The general spousal exemption still exists, but the effect of the 2003 amendment is that it no longer excludes the application of the reservation of benefit principle where the settlor has an interest in the settled property during the period following the termination of the spouse's interest.

10–012

ii. "Pre-owned" assets. Concerns as to the scale of inheritance tax avoidance by the use of schemes which were not caught by the reservation of benefit rule led the Government to levy income tax on "pre-owned" assets from 2005.[72] Income tax is payable by a person who has disposed of assets of any kind after 18

10–013

---

[63] Finance Act 1986 s.104; Inheritance Tax (Double Charges Relief) Regulations 1987 (SI 1987/1130).

[64] See *Chick v Commissioner of Stamp Duties of New South Wales* [1958] A.C. 435; *Nichols v IRC* [1975] 1 W.L.R. 534; *Munro v Commissioner of Stamp Duties of New South Wales* [1934] A.C. 61; *St Aubyn v Attorney General* [1952] A.C. 15. See also (1986) 83 L.S.Gaz 3728.

[65] *Attorney General v Heywood* (1887) 19 Q.B.D. 326; *IRC v Eversden* [2003] W.T.L.R. 893. It does not seem that the inclusion of his spouse would have this effect; (1986) 83 L.S.Gaz. 3728.

[66] *Oakes v Commissioner of Stamp Duties of New South Wales* [1954] A.C. 57.

[67] *Commissioner of Stamp Duties of New South Wales v Perpetual Trustee Co Ltd* [1943] A.C. 425; (1986) 83 L.S.Gaz. 3728.

[68] *Commissioner of Stamp Duties of New South Wales v Perpetual Trustee Co Ltd* [1943] A.C. 425.

[69] Finance Act 1986 s.102(5).

[70] [2003] W.T.L.R. 893.

[71] Finance Act 1986 s.102(5A) and (5B), inserted by Finance Act 2003 s.185.

[72] Finance Act 2004 s.84 and Sch.15. The rules have limited application to intangible property: Sch.15 para.8(1).

March 1986 but retained some benefit in circumstances where the reservation of benefit rule does not apply. The income tax charge applies also if the taxpayer provided the funds to enable another person to buy property in which the taxpayer enjoys some benefit.[73] Only an outline can be given here.

Where income tax is chargeable under this rule, the former owner is treated as receiving the market rent in the case of land (less any lower rent actually received) or a prescribed percentage of the capital value of property other than land.

As mentioned above, income tax is not chargeable where the asset is treated as part of the donor's estate for inheritance tax purposes under the reservation of benefit rule (or otherwise). Nor is it chargeable where the reservation of benefit rule would have applied but for the spouse exemption. Thus in these cases inheritance tax and income tax will be avoided.

The main exemptions from this income tax rule (most of which apply only to chattels and land) are as follows:

- a transfer to a spouse, or to a former spouse pursuant to a court order;
- a transfer whereby the asset became settled property in which the settlor's spouse (or former spouse pursuant to a court order) has an interest in possession;
- where the transferor disposed of his whole interest except for an expressly reserved right over the property and the transaction was at arm's length with an unconnected person or was such as might be expected to be made at arm's length with an unconnected person;
- where the transferor disposed of part of his interest and the transaction was at arm's length with an unconnected person or was such as might be expected to be made at arm's length with an unconnected person[74];
- the value of the benefit enjoyed by the transferor does not exceed £5,000 in the tax year in question;
- the disposal was exempt for inheritance tax purposes as being for the maintenance of the family;
- the disposal was exempt for inheritance tax purposes under the annual £3,000 or small gifts exemptions;
- where the transferor became owner by inheriting the property but it was later diverted to another beneficiary by a deed of variation.[75]

The person who would otherwise be subject to the income tax charge for pre-owned assets may elect to have the asset treated as part of his estate for inheritance tax purposes.[76] If such an election is made, the taxpayer avoids

---

[73] This rule is excluded where a gift of money was made at least seven years before the taxpayer enjoyed a benefit in the property bought with the money.

[74] This exemption was introduced by the Charge to Income Tax by Reference to Enjoyment of Formerly Owned Property Regulations 2005 (SI 2005/724) in order to exempt commercial equity release schemes.

[75] Below, para.23–002. This exemption and that in the fifth bullet point above extend to intangible property.

[76] Finance Act 2004 Sch.15 paras 21–23. The election must be made no later by 31 January in the year following the first year that the income tax charge is payable: HMRC Guidance Note IHT501.

income tax, but in effect his inheritance tax planning is reversed: property which he no longer owns and which escaped the reservation of benefit rule is treated as part of his estate for inheritance tax purposes.

5. INHERITANCE TAX AND SETTLEMENTS[77]

Family trusts have been used for many years as ways of avoiding tax. Not surprisingly, trusts in general, and discretionary trusts in particular, were treated harshly by the capital transfer and inheritance tax legislation. There were originally, for inheritance tax purposes, two broad categories of settlements; those in which there was an interest in possession and those in which there was not, these being primarily discretionary trusts. The rules relating to reservation of benefit, discussed above,[78] must be borne in mind in relation to both categories.

10–014

When the Finance Act 1986 introduced the potentially exempt transfer, the only type of trust to benefit from it was the accumulation and maintenance trust.[79] The lifetime creation of other settlements was initially chargeable irrespective of seven-year survival. This position was subsequently modified so that the lifetime creation of an interest in possession settlement became potentially exempt.[80] The lifetime creation of a discretionary trust (other than an accumulation and maintenance trust) remained initially chargeable.

However, the Finance Act 2006 introduced new rules which severely restrict the inheritance tax advantages of interest in possession and accumulation and maintenance settlements. In effect the discretionary trust regime now applies to other kinds of settlement, subject to certain narrow exceptions. This means that the creation of most trusts is initially chargeable and also subject to the charging regime (called the "relevant property" regime) applicable to discretionary trusts after their creation. Thus the current classification is based on whether or not the trust is of "relevant property".

In the account which follows it will be necessary to consider the treatment of interest in possession settlements both before and after the Finance Act 2006.

A. Settlements in which there is an Interest in Possession

This category deals with the standard form situation of a fixed trust for successive beneficiaries, whose interests are specified in the trust instrument; as a trust for Mrs X for her life, and after her death for her children in equal shares. A beneficiary has an interest in possession if he is entitled to the income as it arises.

10–015

---

[77] Inheritance Tax Act 1984 Pt III. "Settlement" is defined in s.43(2). A bare trust is not included. The rules relating to foreign elements cannot be dealt with here.

[78] Above, para.10–010.

[79] Below, para.10–024.

[80] Finance (No.2) Act 1987 s.96 and Sch.7.

He is so entitled even though the trustees have a power to revoke or to appoint elsewhere, but not if they have a power to accumulate the income, even if unexercised.[81]

10–016   **i.   Before the Finance Act 2006.**   The following account deals with interest in possession trusts created before 22 March 2006. These trusts are unaffected by the Finance Act 2006 while the interest in possession continues. If the interest in possession terminates on or after 22 March 2006, the tax treatment depends on whether the settlement then ends, as will be further explained below.

A person entitled to an interest in possession is treated for the purposes of inheritance tax as being beneficially entitled to the property in which his interest subsists.[82] Mrs X would thus be regarded, for purposes of inheritance tax, not merely as the owner of a life interest in the trust property, but as the owner of the property itself. There are special provisions to deal with cases where there is a shared entitlement to the income,[83] or where the beneficiary is entitled to a fixed amount,[84] and also for the beneficiary who is entitled to the use and enjoyment of property which does not produce income.[85]

10–017   When an interest in possession comes to an end, the person entitled to the interest is treated as having at that time made a transfer of value of his interest. His interest is regarded as coming to an end on his disposing of or surrendering his interest, or on its termination in whole or in part by an appointment being made of the property in which his interest subsisted.[86] Where the interest in possession terminates during the lifetime of the person entitled to it, the transfer is potentially exempt.[87] If the disposal is for a consideration in money or money's worth, the value of the property is treated as reduced by the amount of the consideration,[88] but in determining that amount, the value of a reversionary interest in the property (which the tenant for life may acquire on a partition) must be left out of account.[89] Additionally, depreciatory transactions between the trustees and the persons interested under the settlement (as where the value of the trust property is reduced by granting a long lease of the property at a low rent) are treated as transfers of value.[90] Where a person dies entitled to an interest in

---

[81] See *Pearson v IRC* [1981] A.C. 753; W. Murphy (1980) 43 M.L.R. 712; J. Tiley (1980) 39 C.L.J. 246; (1981) 97 L.Q.R. 1; *Re Trafford's Settlement* [1985] Ch. 32; *Swales v IRC* [1984] 3 All E.R. 16; *Miller v IRC* [1987] S.T.C. 108.

[82] Inheritance Tax Act 1984 s.49. Accordingly, reversionary interests are "excluded property" (s.48); but there are exceptions.

[83] Inheritance Tax Act 1984 s.50(1).

[84] Inheritance Tax Act 1984 s.50(2).

[85] Inheritance Tax Act 1984 s.50(5).

[86] Inheritance Tax Act 1984 ss.51, 52.

[87] Finance (No.2) Act 1987 s.96. A different rule applies if the interest terminates on or after 22 March 2006 and the settlement does not then end; below, para.10–018.

[88] Which will be less than the value of the property in which the interest subsisted. See Inheritance Tax Act 1984 s.49(2), dealing with the case where more than the actuarial value is paid.

[89] Inheritance Tax Act 1984 s.52(2).

[90] Inheritance Tax Act 1984 s.52(3).

possession, he is treated as having made a transfer of value immediately before his death of the property in which the interest subsisted.[91]

As the coming to an end of an interest in possession is treated as a transfer of value by the person beneficially entitled to that interest, the *rate* of any tax chargeable is determined by his personal scorecard.[92] There is, however, no question of grossing up; for the value of the transfer is not the loss to the transferor, but the value of the property in which the interest subsisted.[93]

There are certain reliefs and exemptions.[94] No tax is payable where an interest in possession comes to an end and (subject to certain qualifications) it reverts to the settlor,[95] or to the spouse, civil partner, widow or widower of the settlor.[96]

There is total or partial relief where the person whose interest comes to an end becomes on the same occasion entitled either to the property or to another interest in possession in the property; there is a potentially exempt transfer only to the extent that the value of the property to which he becomes entitled is less than the value of the property in which his interest subsisted.[97] If, however, the life tenant becomes absolutely entitled by purchasing the reversion, he makes a potentially exempt transfer of the amount of the purchase price.[98] The result of these rules in the case of partition is that there is a potentially exempt transfer of that part of the fund to which the remainderman becomes absolutely entitled.

Some of the general exemptions which apply to transfers of non-settled property apply also to termination of interests in possession, for example, transfers to a spouse or to charity, the annual exemption (£3,000) and marriage consideration[99]; and also transfers for family maintenance.[100] Finally, quick succession relief reduces the rate of tax where tax is payable on the termination of an interest in possession in settled property within five years of a previous chargeable transfer.[101]

ii. After the Finance Act 2006.[102] The general position is that the creation of a lifetime trust with an interest in possession is immediately chargeable at the rate of 20% so far as the assets exceed the settlor's nil-rate band. The trust is subject

10–018

---

[91] Inheritance Tax Act 1984 s.4. See *IRC v Lloyds Private Banking Ltd* [1998] S.T.C. 559 (right to reside for life gave interest in possession so that capital value taxed on death).

[92] Inheritance Tax Act 1984 s.52(1). But the tax is payable out of the settled property, and the trustees are responsible for it, concurrently with the beneficiary; s.201.

[93] Inheritance Tax Act 1984 s.52(1).

[94] Terminations under protective trusts are dealt with below, para.10–027. See also Inheritance Tax Act 1984 s.90 (trustees' annuities).

[95] Inheritance Tax Act 1984 s.54(1).

[96] Inheritance Tax Act 1984 s.54(2). Or the civil partner or surviving civil partner.

[97] Inheritance Tax Act 1984 s.53(2). This relief is restricted by s.53(2A), as substituted by Finance Act 2008 s.140, where the person becomes entitled to another interest in possession on or after 12 March 2008.

[98] Otherwise the life tenant could reduce the value of his taxable estate, as his free estate is reduced by the payment, while the value of the trust property in his estate is unaffected. See Inheritance Tax Act 1984 ss.10, 55.

[99] Inheritance Tax Act 1984 s.57. But the small gifts exemption (£250) does not apply. Valuation reliefs on business and agricultural property are also available to settlements.

[100] Inheritance Tax Act 1984 s.11.

[101] Inheritance Tax Act 1984 s.141.

[102] The provisions are found in Finance Act 2006 s.156 and Sch.20.

to the "relevant property" regime applicable to discretionary trusts.[103] This means that a "periodic charge" of up to 6% of the value of the trust assets will be levied on every tenth anniversary, and that an "exit charge" will be payable on capital leaving the trust, as where the trustees advance or appoint capital. The life tenant is no longer treated as owning the property for inheritance tax purposes, which means that the spouse exemption does not apply where a settlor gives an interest in possession to his spouse. It also means that the value of the trust property is no longer aggregated with the life tenant's free estate on his death. The only situation in which the lifetime creation of an interest in possession trust is favourably treated is in the case of a trust for a disabled person, which is subject to the rules applying to the creation of an interest in possession trust before the Finance Act 2006.[104]

Where an interest in possession trust arises on or after 22 March 2006 under a will or intestacy, the old rules apply.[105] The spouse exemption will, therefore, apply where the interest in possession is in favour of the spouse of the deceased. However, the old rules do not apply indefinitely. When the interest in possession ends (either in the lifetime or on the death of the life tenant), the discretionary trusts "relevant property" regime takes over if the settlement continues.[106]

We saw that an interest in possession created before 22 March 2006 was not affected by the Finance Act 2006 while the interest continued, or if it terminated before that date.[107] Where such an interest in possession terminates (in the lifetime or on the death of the life tenant) on or after 22 March 2006, the transitional provisions of the Finance Act 2006 apply. Where the settlement itself comes to an end on the termination of the life interest (as where there is a partition or the remainder beneficiary becomes absolutely entitled on the life tenant's death), the old rules apply. This means that a lifetime termination is a potentially exempt transfer, and that, where the interest in possession ends on death, the value of the settled property is aggregated for inheritance tax purposes with the life tenant's free estate.[108]

Where the settlement continues after the termination of the interest in possession, the general rule is that the settlement then becomes subject to the "relevant property" regime applicable to discretionary trusts.[109]

---

[103] Below, para.10–019.

[104] Inheritance Tax Act 1984 ss.49(1A), 89A and 89B, inserted by Finance Act 2006 Sch.20 paras 4 and 6. This is in addition to the preferential rules for disabled trusts which previously existed; below, para.10–027. Preferential treatment is also given to interest in possession trusts arising under life policies created before 22 March 2006; Finance Act 2006 Sch.20 para.11.

[105] Inheritance Tax Act 1984 ss.49(1A) and 49A, inserted by Finance Act 2006 Sch.20 paras 4 and 5.

[106] Unless it continues in favour of a disabled beneficiary, a bereaved minor (below, para.10–025) or an "age 18 to 25 trust" (below, para.10–026).

[107] Above, para.10–016.

[108] Inheritance Tax Act 1984 s.3A(1A), introduced by Finance Act 2006 Sch.20 para.9. The old rules also apply if the property passes into a disabled trust on termination of the interest in possession.

[109] Similarly where property is added to a pre-existing interest in possession trust on or after 22 March 2006: the addition is subject to the "relevant property" regime. But there is a distinction between the addition of *property* to a pre-existing settlement and the addition of *value* to a pre-existing settlement. The latter does not become subject to the new regime: see HMRC, *Inheritance Tax Manual*, IHTM16074 and following; C. Whitehouse [2013] P.C.B. 304.

B. Settlements in which there is No Interest in Possession

i. Discretionary Trusts. In the context of inheritance tax, a discretionary **10–019** trust means a settlement in which there is no interest in possession. The taxation regime depends on the concept of "relevant property".[110] This used to mean settled property in which there was no interest in possession, other than certain types of settlements which were preferentially treated.[111] As explained above, the Finance Act 2006 has brought most interest in possession trusts into the "relevant property" regime. The lifetime creation of a trust of "relevant property" is initially chargeable so far as the assets exceed the settlor's nil-rate band, although at half the rate applicable on death (20% as opposed to 40%).[112]

(a) *The "Exit" Charge.* Tax is chargeable on any part of the funds which **10–020** ceases to be "relevant property".[113] This covers not only the simple case of a payment of capital to a beneficiary, including the winding-up of the trust, but also (before the changes made by the Finance Act 2006) the situation where the trustees converted the trust into an accumulation and maintenance settlement.[114] There are certain exceptions to this rule; for example, no tax is payable in respect of a payment of costs or expenses, nor where the payment is income for income tax purposes in the hands of the recipient.[115] Only a limited number of the general exemptions, such as distributions to charity, are available.[116]

(b) *The 10-Year Charge.* The "exit" charge alone is not sufficient, for the **10–021** capital may not be distributed until the end of the trust period, which, as has been seen, may not occur until just before the end of the perpetuity period.[117] It is provided, therefore, that tax is payable on the whole of the settled funds every 10 years, although only at 30% of the "effective rate", as described below.[118] Thus the capital is fully taxed broadly once a generation, whether the capital is distributed or retained, or the trust is converted into another form.

(c) *Rates of Tax.* Different rules apply to the "exit" charge and the 10-year **10–022** charge, although in both cases the rates applicable to lifetime transfers are used. Only an outline can be given here.

---

[110] Inheritance Tax Act 1984 s.58, as amended by Finance Act 2006.

[111] Inheritance Tax Act 1984. The exceptions include accumulation and maintenance trusts (as amended by Finance Act 2006), discussed below, para.10–024, and the special trusts mentioned in para.10–027.

[112] Above, para.10–008.

[113] Inheritance Tax Act 1984 s.65(1)(a). Tax is also chargeable where the trustees make a disposition resulting in the reduction in the value of the property; s.65(1)(b). See *IRC v Macpherson* [1989] A.C. 159.

[114] Below, para.10–024; *Inglewood (Lord) v IRC* [1983] 1 W.L.R. 366.

[115] Inheritance Tax Act 1984 s.65(5); *Stevenson (Inspector of Taxes) v Wishart* [1987] 1 W.L.R. 1204. See also s.65(4), (6)–(8).

[116] The annual exemption (£3,000) is not available. The valuation reliefs available for business and agricultural property do apply.

[117] Above, para.9–007.

[118] Inheritance Tax Act 1984 ss.64, 66.

In the case of the "exit" charge, the rate depends on whether the charge is payable before or after the first 10-year anniversary. In both cases the amount on which tax is payable is the amount by which the value of the "relevant property" is diminished by the event in question.[119] The rate before the first 10-year anniversary is the "appropriate fraction" of the rate payable on an assumed chargeable transfer made at the time of the "exit" charge, where the amount is the value of the settled property at the date of the settlement, and the hypothetical cumulative total is the settlor's chargeable transfers during the seven years prior to the creation of the settlement. The "appropriate fraction" is 3/10 multiplied by N/40, where N is the number of completed quarters (i.e. three-month periods) between the creation of the settlement and the chargeable event.[120]

Where an "exit" charge arises after a 10-year anniversary, tax is charged at the "appropriate fraction" of the rate at which it was charged on the last 10-year anniversary. The "appropriate fraction" is N/40, where N is the number of completed quarters between the last 10-year anniversary and the chargeable event.[121]

In the case of the 10-year charge, tax is charged on the value of the "relevant property" on the day before the 10-year anniversary, at 30% of the "effective rate" which would have been charged on a hypothetical transfer at that time. At current rates the maximum 10-year charge is therefore 6%.[122] It is assumed that the hypothetical transferor's cumulative total to be taken into account includes the settlor's chargeable transfers during the seven years preceding the creation of the settlement, plus the amounts, if any, subjected to an "exit charge" in the 10 years before the 10-year anniversary in question.[123]

10–023 *(d) "Same-day additions".* Until recently, well-advised settlors could achieve certain tax advantages by creating "pilot trusts". These trusts would be established by the settlement of a nominal amount with a view to the settlor adding significant funds later, often through bequests made in his or her will. As long as the pilot trusts were created on different days, each would be entitled to its own nil-rate band. In 2014 the Government introduced a proposal to introduce a single "settlement nil-rate band" that could be allocated among several settlements.[124] That proposal was soon dropped, but changes introduced in the Finance (No.2) Act 2015 seek to achieve much the same policy goal by introducing the concept of a "same-day addition".[125] A "same-day addition"

---

[119] "Grossing-up" occurs; Inheritance Tax Act 1984 s.65(2).
[120] Inheritance Tax Act 1984 s.68. Different rules apply to settlements made before 27 March 1974: s.68(6).
[121] Inheritance Tax Act 1984 s.69. This rule applies also to settlements made before 27 March 1974.
[122] Being 30% of the effective rate of 20% applicable to lifetime transfers.
[123] Inheritance Tax Act 1984 s.66.
[124] See HMRC Consultation document, *Inheritance tax: A fairer way of calculating trust charges* (6 June 2014); but the proposal was dropped within six months: *Autumn Statement 2014* (December 2014) para.2.73.
[125] Finance (No.2) Act 2015 Sch.1, introducing Inheritance Tax Act 1984 ss.62A–C, and making certain other amendments to Inheritance Tax Act 1984 Pt.3 Ch.3. See generally C. Whitehouse [2015] P.C.B. 47 and [2015] P.C.B. 209.

happens when a settlor transfers value into one or more existing settlements,[126] or creates a new settlement, on the same day. When this occurs, the tax position of any one of those settlements—for the purposes of the exit charge or the 10-Year charge—will be calculated to include transfers of value that were made to other settlements on the same day.[127] The advantages associated with creating several individual settlements are thereby lost.

ii. Accumulation and Maintenance Settlements. An accumulation and   **10–024**
maintenance settlement is one in which no interest in possession exists, but one or more beneficiaries will, on attaining a specified age not exceeding 25 years, become entitled to an interest in possession.[128]

It has long been common practice to create accumulation and maintenance settlements in favour of children in the family, and to give to the trustees power to apply the income at their discretion for the maintenance and education of the children, and to accumulate any income not so applied; and power to advance some or all of the capital for the advancement or benefit of the beneficiaries. The powers are now statutory,[129] subject to the expression of a contrary intention, and are discussed in more detail in Ch.21.

The income of the trust will be taxed at the rate applicable to trusts (currently 45%).[130] Where income is paid to or applied for the maintenance or education of a beneficiary, the income is taxed according to the tax status of the beneficiary. But there is one important limitation. If the beneficiary is a child of the settlor who is under 18 and not married or in a civil partnership,[131] any income paid to or applied for the beneficiary's maintenance or education is aggregated for tax purposes with the income of the settlor.[132] There is no aggregation, however, if such income is accumulated.

Before the Finance Act 2006, accumulation and maintenance trusts were very favourably treated. However, that Act withdrew the inheritance tax advantages for the future. Where such a trust is created on or after 22 March 2006 it is subject to the "relevant property" regime applicable to discretionary trusts in general.[133] This means that the lifetime creation of such a trust is not potentially exempt—as it previously was—but attracts an immediate charge at the rate of 20% (so far as the nil-rate band is exceeded). It is also subject to the 10-year charge and to exit charges on distributions of capital.

---

[126] The transfer of value need not take the form of a transfer of property: Inheritance Tax Act 1984 s.62A(5); cf. fn.109 above.

[127] Settlements existing before 10 December 2014 are exempt as "protected settlements", as long as no further transfers of value are made to them: Inheritance Tax Act 1984 s.62C. A narrow exception, allowing protected status to be maintained, exists for settlors who made testamentary transfers into the settlement and died before 6 April 2017.

[128] Inheritance Tax Act 1984 s.71. There are other conditions. See *Inglewood (Lord) v IRC* [1983] 1 W.L.R. 366.

[129] Trustee Act 1925 s.31; below, para.21–023.

[130] Above, para.10–003.

[131] cf. grandchildren of the settlor.

[132] Income Tax (Trading and Other Income) Act 2005 ss.629 (similarly where the income is retained in a bare trust for the settlor's child: s.631).

[133] Inheritance Tax Act 1984 s.71, as amended by Finance Act 2006 Sch.20 para.2.

The favourable rules applying to accumulation and maintenance trusts created before 22 March 2006 were as follows. Lifetime creation was a potentially exempt transfer.[134] The usual rules governing discretionary trusts did not apply,[135] so that there was no 10-year charge nor any exit charge on a distribution of capital to the beneficiary (on an advancement or when his interest vested), nor on the death of a beneficiary before becoming entitled to the capital.[136] The advantages just described continue to apply after 22 March 2006 to a trust created before that date only if the beneficiaries become entitled to capital at the age of 18. Few such trusts meet this condition, as the usual age of vesting is 21 or 25.

The effect of the Finance Act 2006 is that it is no longer possible to create favourably treated trusts for children or grandchildren by lifetime disposition. However, the Act provides two situations where a trust for children (but not grandchildren) may be created on death without attracting the "relevant property" rules.

10–025   **iii. Trusts for Bereaved Minors.**   Such a trust is one created by the will (or intestacy) of a parent for the benefit of a minor, at least one of whose parents has died.[137] The minor must become absolutely entitled to the capital no later than the age of 18. It must not be possible for the trustees to apply income or capital other than for the minor's benefit. Although inheritance tax may be payable on the parent's death, none will be payable while the trust exists or when the capital vests (nor if the minor dies under the age of 18).

10–026   **iv. Age 18 to 25 Trusts.**   These are similar to trusts for bereaved minors save that a later vesting age is permitted. However, exit charges are payable if the capital vests after the age of 18. The 18 to 25 trust is one arising under the will of a parent for the benefit of a minor who will become entitled to the capital at an age no greater than 25.[138] Inheritance tax may be payable on the parent's death, but none is payable before the minor reaches 18. The trustees must not have power to apply capital or income elsewhere. An exit charge will be payable when capital is paid to the beneficiary (by advancement or when the interest vests) at an age from 18 to 25. The maximum exit charge rate is 4.2% and the 10-year charge does not apply.

These exceptions from the full "relevant property" regime are narrow, in that they can only arise on the death of a parent of the minor. Other relatives may create life interests, bare trusts or absolute gifts in favour of minors in their wills, but other trusts for minors attract no favourable treatment.

---

[134] Inheritance Tax Act 1984 s.3A.

[135] Inheritance Tax Act 1984 s.58(1)(b).

[136] Inheritance Tax Act 1984 s.71(4). The beneficiary would normally be entitled to income from the age of 18; Trustee Act 1925 s.31(1)(ii).

[137] Inheritance Tax Act 1984 s.71A, inserted by Finance Act 2006 Sch.20 para.1. "Parent" includes step-parent. The provisions apply also to trusts created under the Criminal Injuries Compensation Scheme.

[138] Inheritance Tax Act 1984 s.71D. "Parent" includes step-parent, and trusts created by the Criminal Injuries Compensation Scheme are included.

C.   Protective and Other Trusts

Other forms of trusts which are entitled to special treatment are protective trusts,[139] superannuation schemes,[140] trusts for the benefit of employees[141] and for disabled persons,[142] charitable trusts,[143] newspaper trusts,[144] maintenance funds for historic buildings,[145] and various special compensation funds, such as those maintained by Lloyd's and the Law Society.[146]

10–027

A protective trust does not fit neatly into the two categories into which trusts are divided for inheritance tax purposes; for there is an interest in possession during the currency of the interest of the principal beneficiary, but a discretionary trust after the forfeiture. There is a charge to inheritance tax upon the death of the principal beneficiary; but not usually on the forfeiture of his interest, which, for the purpose of inheritance tax, is deemed to continue during the currency of the discretionary trusts which then arise.[147]

---

[139] Inheritance Tax Act 1984 s.88; above, Ch.8.

[140] Inheritance Tax Act 1984 ss.58(1)(d), 151.

[141] Inheritance Tax Act 1984 s.86.

[142] Inheritance Tax Act 1984 s.89; *Barclays Bank Trust Co Ltd v Commissioners for HM Revenue and Customs* [2011] W.T.L.R. 1489. The lifetime creation of a trust for a disabled person is favourably treated by Finance Act 2006; above, para.10–018.

[143] Inheritance Tax Act 1984 s.58(1)(a). As to temporary charitable trusts, see s.70.

[144] Inheritance Tax Act 1984 s.87.

[145] Inheritance Tax Act 1984 s.58(1)(c) and Sch.4.

[146] Inheritance Tax Act 1984 s.58(1)(e).

[147] Inheritance Tax Act 1984 s.88, as amended by Finance Act 2006 Sch.20 para.24. The rule is modified where the protective trust arises on or after 22 March 2006.

CHAPTER 11

RESULTING TRUSTS

1. GENERAL

A RESULTING trust is a situation in which a transferee is required by equity to hold property on trust for the transferor; or for the person who provided the purchase money for the transfer. The beneficial interest results, or comes back, to the transferor or to the party who makes the payment. In effect the resulting trust is the basis of a claim to recover one's own property.[1] This situation can arise in a wide variety of circumstances, and it has been seen that resulting trusts overlap with other categories.[2]

Resulting trusts are not subject to all the rules of express trusts. Their creation is not dependent on compliance with formalities[3]; and a child may be a resulting trustee.[4] Resulting trustees are not subject to all the duties and liabilities of express trustees, and often will not owe fiduciary obligations to their beneficiaries.[5]

The true nature of the resulting trust has been much scrutinised in recent years. The main points for debate have been the role of intention, the question of whether the beneficial interest remains in the transferor or is returned to him, and

11–001

---

[1] See *MacMillan Inc v Bishopsgate Investments Trust Plc (No.3)* [1995] 1 W.L.R. 978 at 989.

[2] Above, para.2–028.

[3] Law of Property Act 1925 s.53(2).

[4] *Re Vinogradoff* [1936] W.N. 68.

[5] See *Lonrho Plc v Fayed (No.2)* [1992] 1 W.L.R. 1 at 12; R. Chambers, *Resulting Trusts* (Oxford: Oxford University Press, 1997), Ch.9; P. Millett (1998) 114 L.Q.R. 399.

the linked question of whether the trust comes into effect only when the conscience of the transferee is affected by notice.

It used to be said that resulting trusts fell into two categories: presumed and automatic.[6] Under this classification the presumed resulting trust, arising in the case of transfers to volunteers, depended on the presumed intent of the transferor, whereas automatic resulting trusts, arising on failure to dispose of the beneficial interest, were imposed by operation of law without regard to intention. This classification is no longer favoured by the judiciary,[7] although it retains some academic support.[8] The most widely held view is that all resulting trusts are based on the absence of any intention by the transferor to pass a beneficial interest to the transferee.[9] In the case of transfers on trust, the fact of the transfer being made on trust establishes the absence of intention to benefit the recipient. In the case of apparently-absolute transfers to volunteers, the absence of intention is rebuttably presumed[10]:

> "Like a constructive trust, a resulting trust arises by operation of law, though unlike a constructive trust it gives effect to intention. But it arises whether or not the transferor intended to retain a beneficial interest—he almost always does not—since it responds to the absence of any intention on his part to pass a beneficial interest to the recipient."

11–002 On one view it might be supposed that where a transferor fails to dispose of the beneficial interest, he must still have it. In other words, the effect of the resulting trust is that the beneficial interest remains in the transferor throughout. Lord Reid put it thus:

> "[T]he beneficial interest must belong to or be held for somebody: so if it was not to belong to the donee or to be held by him in trust for somebody it must remain with the donor".[11]

This view has a firm historical foundation.[12] The modern analysis, however, is that the transferor's absolute beneficial interest is not to be regarded as comprising separate legal and equitable interests, so that only the legal interest passes to the transferee in situations where resulting trusts arise. In such cases the

---

[6] *Re Vandervell's Trusts (No.2)* [1974] Ch. 269 (Megarry J).

[7] *Westdeutsche Landesbank Girozentrale v Islington LBC* [1996] A.C. 669 at 708 (Lord Browne-Wilkinson). See generally P. Birks [1996] R.L.R. 3.

[8] W. Swadling (2008) 124 L.Q.R. 72 at 98.

[9] See *Twinsectra Ltd v Yardley* [2002] 2 A.C. 164 at 190; *Chan Yuen Lan v See Fong Mun* [2014] 3 S.L.R. 1048; P. Birks in S. Goldstein (ed.), *Equity and Contemporary Legal Developments* (Jerusalem, 1992), p.335; Chambers, *Resulting Trusts* (1997); P. Millett (1998) 114 L.Q.R. 399; R. Chambers (2001) 15 T.L.I. 2; R. Chambers in C. Mitchell (ed.), *Constructive and Resulting Trusts* (Oxford: Hart Publishing, 2010), Ch.9. Contra W. Swadling (1996) 16 L.S. 110; (2008) 124 L.Q.R. 72; J. Mee (2014) 73 C.L.J. 86; (2017) 70 C.L.P. 189. As will be seen, it remains a separate question whether every situation in which there is an absence of intention to benefit the recipient ought to give rise to a resulting trust.

[10] *Air Jamaica Ltd v Charlton* [1999] 1 W.L.R. 1399 at 1412, Lord Millett giving the advice of the Privy Council. See also Lord Millett's judgment in *Twinsectra Ltd v Yardley* [2002] 2 A.C. 164 (dissenting on another issue).

[11] *Vandervell v IRC* [1967] 2 A.C. 291 at 308 (see also 313, 329). See further W. Swadling (2008) 124 L.Q.R. 72 at 100, criticising the reasoning but supporting the result.

[12] J. Mee in C. Mitchell (ed.), *Constructive and Resulting Trusts* (2010), Ch.7. See also J. Penner in Ch.8 of the same work, favouring the "retention" analysis.

transferee takes the absolute title but holds on trust for the transferor, who acquires for the first time a separate equitable interest.[13]

Building on this point, Lord Browne-Wilkinson has sought to establish that the resulting trust (or indeed any other trust) will take effect only when the conscience of the transferee is affected by her becoming aware that she has received property which was not intended for her benefit.[14] His Lordship regarded this theory as "uncontroversial", but it appears problematic and unsupported by authority. It has been much criticised.[15] Who would be entitled to the beneficial interest, for example dividends on shares, pending the acquisition of knowledge by the trustee? To link the creation of a resulting trust with the conscience of the trustee "would be a difficult and dangerous departure from existing law. There is little to be gained by such a move and much to be lost".[16] A preferable view is that the resulting trust arises as soon as the property is transferred, but the transferee does not become subject to liability for breach of trust until she is aware of the position.[17] Lloyd LJ took this view in *Independent Trustee Services Ltd v GP Noble Trustees Ltd*:

> "Despite what Lord Browne-Wilkinson said, it seems to me that it is appropriate to speak of [the transferee] holding on trust for [the transferor] in this situation, provided that one is not misled into thinking that to call the relationship one of trustee and beneficiary tells you, of itself, what the duties and liabilities of the trustee are."[18]

The situations in which resulting trusts arise will now be examined. The main examples, discussed below, involve incomplete disposal of the beneficial interest and transfers of property to volunteers. There are other cases where resulting trusts have been held to arise in circumstances where the transferor intended the property to revert to him unless used for a particular purpose. Such trusts might be regarded as express. An example is *Barclays Bank Ltd v Quistclose Investments Ltd*,[19] where the lender (Quistclose Investments) and the borrower (Rolls Razor) intended that the borrower should hold the funds on trust for the lender if they could not be used to pay the dividend; but there was no formal declaration. Lord Millett's analysis is that the money is held on resulting trust for

---

[13] *Westdeutsche Landesbank Girozentrale v Islington LBC* [1996] A.C. 669 at 706 (Lord Browne-Wilkinson); *DKLR Holding Co (No.2) Pty Ltd v Commissioner of Stamp Duties (NSW)* (1982) 149 C.L.R. 431; J. Mee (2017) 70 C.L.P. 189.

[14] *Westdeutsche Landesbank Girozentrale v Islington LBC* [1996] A.C. 669.

[15] P. Birks [1996] 4 R.L.R. 3 at 20; G. Jones (1996) 55 C.L.J. 432; P. Millett (1998) 114 L.Q.R. 399 and [1998] 6 R.L.R. 283; W. Swadling (1998) 12 T.L.I. 228; P. Oliver (1997–98) 8 K.C.L.J. 147; N. McBride (1998) 57 C.L.J. 33 at 35–36; B. Häcker (2009) 68 C.L.J. 324.

[16] Chambers, *Resulting Trusts* (1997), p.208, highlighting problems with taxation, insurance, priorities and so forth. See also R. Chambers (2010) 63 C.L.P. 631 at 648.

[17] Chambers, *Resulting Trusts* (1997); P. Millett (1998) 114 L.Q.R. 399 at 404; N. McBride (1998) 57 C.L.J. 33 at 35–36; J. Glister (2012) 6 J. Eq. 221 at 225–227; cf. C. Harpum in P. Birks and F. Rose (eds) *Restitution and Equity—Volume 1: Resulting Trusts and Equitable Compensation* (London: LLP, 2000), Ch.9 at p.166.

[18] [2012] EWCA Civ 195; [2013] Ch. 91 at [80] (with the agreement of Tomlinson LJ).

[19] [1970] A.C. 567.

the lender as soon as it is transferred, but subject to the borrower's power or duty to apply it to the specified purpose.[20] This situation has already been considered.[21]

A.   Transfers on Trust

11–003   Where property is conveyed to a person in the capacity of a trustee, there will be a resulting trust for the grantor of any part of the beneficial interest which is not disposed of. This result arises by operation of law. It will be discussed in more detail in Part 2.

B.   Apparent Gifts

11–004   If A voluntarily transfers property to B there will be a presumption that B holds the property on resulting trust for A. This presumption may of course be rebutted. In the case of a transfer to the transferor's wife or child, or to a person to whom the transferor stands in loco parentis, the presumption is reversed by the countervailing presumption of advancement.[22] These matters are discussed in Part 3.

11–005   Closely related to the previous category are transfers to people who provide none or only part of the purchase price. This category includes cases where the transfer is made to B, but some or all of the purchase price is provided by A, or where the conveyance is to A and B jointly, but the purchase price is provided unequally. Again, a resulting trust will be presumed in favour of those who paid the purchase price unless the parties' relationship means that a presumption of advancement applies instead. These purchase-money resulting trusts are also discussed in Part 3. However, special rules apply in the context of shared homes. The complex questions of the division of property ownership between spouses or cohabitants, where the contribution to the family may be in ways other than the payment of money, will be dealt with in Ch.13.

2.   TRANSFERS ON TRUST

A.   Where a Trust Fails

11–006   A resulting trust may arise on the failure, for a variety of reasons, of an express trust. In *Morice v Bishop of Durham*,[23] a legacy was given to the Bishop of Durham on trust "for such objects of benevolence and liberality" as he should select. That trust was void as a non-charitable purpose trust, and the testator's

---

[20] *Twinsectra Ltd v Yardley* [2002] 2 A.C. 164.

[21] Above, para.2–009.

[22] The presumption of advancement will be abolished by the Equality Act 2010 s.199, but at the time of writing the section has not been brought into force and has lain dormant for eight years. If and when the section is brought into force, the presumption of advancement will still apply in relation to property dealings that occur before that date. See below, para.11–028.

[23] (1804) 8 Ves. 399; (1805) 10 Ves. 522; below, para.16–005.

next-of-kin were entitled under a resulting trust. In *Essery v Cowlard*,[24] an intending wife executed a pre-nuptial settlement in which she conveyed the trust property to trustees upon trust for herself, the intended husband and the issue of the marriage. The marriage never took place, but the parties cohabited and children were born. Six years later, the woman successfully reclaimed the property. The trusts failed as the "contract to marry had been definitely and absolutely put an end to".

In *Re Ames' Settlement*,[25] property had been settled by the husband's father upon the trusts of a marriage settlement, and the marriage took place. Eighteen years later, the wife obtained a decree of nullity (which then had the effect of declaring the marriage void from the outset).[26] Vaisey J decided, after the husband's death, that the property was held on a resulting trust for the executors of the settlor.

Difficult questions arise as to the effect of void transactions. In the rare case where the vitiating factor prevents legal title passing in the first place, there is no need for a resulting trust.[27] Where, however, the legal title passes and, notwithstanding the vitiating factor, the transferor intended the transferee to become absolute owner, there is no resulting trust but merely personal liability. Thus in *Westdeutsche Landesbank Girozentrale v Islington LBC*,[28] where the bank paid money to the local authority under a transaction which was ultra vires the local authority, the latter was subject only to personal liability as the bank had intended the authority to become absolute owner in spite of its mistaken belief as to the validity of the transaction. Where a transaction is merely voidable, as in the case of misrepresentation or undue influence, legal title passes to the transferee. There is at that point no resulting trust for the transferor,[29] who has only a mere equity to set aside the transaction. An equitable interest will vest in the transferor on rescission,[30] but the transferee is the absolute owner until then.[31] On rescission

---

[24] (1884) 26 Ch.D. 191; *Burgess v Rawnsley* [1975] Ch. 429 (if conveyance taken jointly for a purpose which fails, resulting trust to each party of his share).

[25] [1946] Ch. 217.

[26] A decree of nullity in respect of a voidable marriage now operates to annul the marriage only from the date of the decree absolute: Matrimonial Causes Act 1973 s.16. See also the court's power to make property adjustments under s.24.

[27] See P. Millett (1998) 114 L.Q.R. 399 at 415–416.

[28] [1996] A.C. 669.

[29] The argument for a resulting trust was made in Chambers, *Resulting Trusts* (1997), Ch.7; but now see R. Chambers (2001) 15 T.L.I. 2 at 7. See also R. Nolan in P. Birks and F. Rose (eds) *Restitution and Equity—Volume 1: Resulting Trusts and Equitable Compensation* (2000), Ch.7.

[30] This may be called a resulting trust, although it is rarely necessary to use the label. See *El Ajou v Dollar Land Holdings Plc* [1993] 3 All E.R. 717 at 734 (reversed on other grounds [1994] 2 All E.R. 685); *Twinsectra Ltd v Yardley* [1999] Lloyd's Rep. Bank. 436 at 462 (reversed on other grounds [2002] 2 A.C. 164). One reason to call it a resulting trust is to distinguish it from the type of (constructive) trust that responds to the conscience of the recipient: see below, paras 26–011–26–013.

[31] See *Bristol & West Building Society v Mothew* [1998] Ch. 1 at 22; *Shalson v Russo* [2005] Ch. 281 at [111], [122]–[127]; *Independent Trustee Services Ltd v GP Noble Trustees Ltd* [2013] Ch. 91 at [103]–[104]; P. Millett (1998) 114 L.Q.R. 399 at 416 and [1998] 6 R.L.R. 283; S. Worthington [2002] 10 R.L.R. 28.

the transferor's equitable interest vests retrospectively for the purpose of allowing him to trace in equity, although not for all purposes.[32]

B. Incomplete Disposal of Beneficial Interest

11–007   Unskilful drafting and the failure to foresee and provide for future contingencies may leave the beneficial ownership incomplete.[33] A resulting trust will then arise, although, as will be seen, some sets of circumstances can render this result so inconvenient that other solutions are sought.

The fact that an equitable interest is not fully disposed of may not become apparent until some time has elapsed since the constitution of the trust.

In *Re Trusts of the Abbott Fund*,[34] a sum of money was collected, to be used for the maintenance of two deaf and dumb ladies. It was held by Stirling J that the ladies had no enforceable interests in the capital sum and that, on their death, the sum remaining went on resulting trust to the subscribers.

The consequent problem of distribution on resulting trust among subscribers becomes acute when the number of subscribers is great, and the gifts are mostly anonymous, as in *Re Gillingham Bus Disaster Fund*.[35]

A number of marine cadets were injured or killed when a bus was driven into the rear of a marching column. The mayors of three towns appealed for subscriptions to a fund that would initially care for the disabled and thereafter be available for "worthy causes" in memory of those killed. More money was contributed than could be used for the object (liability at common law for the accident having been accepted) and the second object failed as it had not been confined within the limit of legal charity.[36] Harman J held that, despite the manifest inconvenience of such a decision, a resulting trust arose. All subscribers, large or small, intended to contribute to a specific purpose; on that purpose being attained or no longer attainable, each donor had an interest by way of resulting trust. There was no evidence on which to arrive at any other conclusion. The suggestion that the money should be treated as bona vacantia was regarded by Harman J as taking the line of least resistance in a manner unauthorised by law.

> "The resulting trust arises where [the donor's] expectation is for some unforeseen reason cheated of fruition and is an inference of law based on after-knowledge of the event."[37]

---

[32] *Bristol & West Building Society v Mothew* [1998] Ch. 1 at 23; *Shalson v Russo* [2005] Ch. 281 at [125]–[127]; *Independent Trustee Services Ltd v GP Noble Trustees Ltd* [2013] Ch. 91 at [53].

[33] See *Re Cochrane* [1955] Ch. 309; *John v George* [1995] 1 E.G.L.R. 9 (conveyance to trustees on trust for daughter at 18 gave rise to resulting trust until she reached 18).

[34] [1900] 2 Ch. 326, below, para.16–002.

[35] [1958] Ch. 300, below, para.16–002.

[36] Charities Act 2011 s.63 (below, para.15–079) provides the most convenient solution to this type of case, but it applies only when the gift is charitable. The fund was finally wound up in 1965, when the remainder of the money was paid into court. It was announced on 5 April 1993, that the money (£7,300) was to be paid out and used for a memorial to the victims. For a different solution, see *Re West Sussex Constabulary's Widows, Children and Benevolent Fund Trust* [1971] Ch.1, below para.11–013.

[37] [1958] Ch. 300 at 310.

C. Methods of Disposal of Surplus Funds

A resulting trust is not, however, the most appropriate solution in many situations; and, although something of a digression, it will be convenient here to examine other solutions. The question arises particularly in two contexts: first, that of gifts to persons for stated purposes, without specifying what is to be done when the purposes are completed; and, secondly, in the context of the dissolution of unincorporated associations.

11–008

In determining the correct solution in each of these contexts, two points will be of particular significance. First, did the transferor intend to dispose of his whole interest; or did he intend to transfer for a particular purpose only? Secondly, was the transfer made to a person in a capacity of trustee? If so, a resulting trust may be expected of the surplus.

i. Transfer to Persons for Particular Purposes. If property is given for the care and maintenance of certain persons, what is to happen to the property when the period of maintenance comes to an end? Do the intended beneficiaries (or their estates) keep the property, or does it return on a resulting trust to the donor? The answer will depend on the intention of the donor, which has to be ascertained from all the surrounding circumstances. The construction of the gift in *Re Trusts of the Abbott Fund*[38] may be regarded as unusual. It will be noted that the beneficiaries in that case had died. More commonly, the gift is regarded as absolute. The principle of construction was laid down in *Re Sanderson's Trust*[39] as follows:

11–009

> "If a gross sum be given, or if the whole income of the property be given, and a special purpose be assigned for that gift, the court always regards the gift as absolute, and the purpose merely as the motive of the gift, and therefore holds that the gift takes effect as to the whole sum or the whole income, as the case may be."

This principle is illustrated by the decisions below.

> In *Re Andrew's Trust*,[40] a fund was subscribed for the children of a deceased clergyman. An accompanying letter showed that the contributions were made "for or towards their education;... as being necessary to defray the expenses of all, and that solely in the matter of education." After their formal education was completed, the question arose of the disposal of the surplus. Kekewich J decided that the children were entitled in equal shares.
>
> In *Re Osoba*[41] there was a gift by will of a residuary estate, consisting, for present purposes, of a freehold house in London, to the testator's widow on trust to be used "for her maintenance and for the training of my daughter up to University grade and for the maintenance of my aged mother ... ". The mother predeceased the testator; the widow died in 1970, and the daughter's education up to university grade was completed in 1975. The children under an earlier marriage claimed the residue on intestacy.
>
> The Court of Appeal found that the testator's intention was to provide absolute gifts for the beneficiaries, the references to maintenance and to education being rather expressions of motive. In the absence of words of severance, the beneficiaries took as joint tenants, with the daughter becoming entitled, on her mother's death, to the whole. The result would have been the same if the daughter had not gone to university.

---

[38] [1900] 2 Ch. 326.

[39] (1857) 3 K. & J. 497 at 503 (Page Wood VC); *Barlow v Grant* (1684) 1 Vern. 255.

[40] [1905] 2 Ch. 48.

[41] [1979] 1 W.L.R. 247.

ii.   Surplus Funds on Dissolution of Unincorporated Association.[42]

11–010   *(a)   Trust or Contract.*   As will be seen in Ch.16, funds and other assets of such an association will sometimes be held by trustees on an express trust for the members and sometimes by the treasurer or committee on a bare trust; in either case the property rights in the assets of the society are likely to be governed by the rules of the society which operate as a contract between the members. The question whether the property is held upon the terms of any trust created by the donor, or whether it is held by the members absolutely according to their contractual rights is relevant here also. The question commonly arises on a dissolution. It will be seen in the analysis which follows that the distinction between rights governed by a trust and those governed by a contract has not always been kept clear. In the case of a failure of a trust, the most appropriate solution is by way of resulting trust. In a case of dissolution of a society where the rights of the members are governed by a contract (i.e. by the rules of the society) the likely solution is in accordance with the terms of the contract; and if the contract is silent; by equal division among the remaining members. The Crown might claim the fund as bona vacantia. It may also have to be considered whether any third party contributors may have a claim to participate in the distribution along with the members. Whether the matter is regarded as one of trust or contract affects the question of who is entitled and the calculation of the share. All these solutions will be demonstrated here, although the analysis in the earlier cases was subject to criticism by Walton J in *Re Bucks Constabulary Fund (No.2)*.[43]

11–011   *(b)   Meaning of Dissolution.*   An association may be wound up in a formal manner, but in the absence of a formal dissolution, the question arises as to the circumstances which will justify a finding that the body has ceased to exist. In *Re GKN Bolts and Nuts Ltd (Automotive Division) Birmingham Works, Sports and Social Club*,[44] the trustees of a social club had purchased a sports ground for £2,200 in 1946. In 1975, membership cards ceased to be issued and the last annual general meeting was held. No further accounts were taken, the stock of drinks was sold and the steward dismissed. A special meeting was convened on 18 December 1975 to deal with an offer to buy the land. Resolutions were passed that the land be sold, but no sale then took place. In 1978, the trustees sold the land for £253,000. One question which arose was the date the club ceased to exist.[45] It was held that mere inactivity did not suffice, unless it was so prolonged or so circumstanced that the only reasonable inference was spontaneous dissolution, in which case the court must select a date. On the facts, it ceased to

---

[42] See generally J. Warburton, *Unincorporated Associations: Law & Practice*, 2nd edn (London: Sweet & Maxwell, 1992); S. Gardner [1992] Conv. 41. For the meaning of "unincorporated association" see *Conservative and Unionist Central Office v Burrell* [1982] 1 W.L.R. 522, below, para.16–020.

[43] [1979] 1 W.L.R. 936; below, para.11–014.

[44] [1982] 1 W.L.R. 774. See also *Re William Denby & Sons Ltd Sick and Benevolent Fund* [1971] 1 W.L.R. 973; *Re Bucks Constabulary Widows' and Orphans' Fund Friendly Society (No.2)* [1979] 1 W.L.R. 936.

[45] The question of entitlement to the money is dealt with below, para.11–016.

exist on 18 December 1975, on the basis of inactivity coupled with positive acts to wind it up. This would be so even if the resolution to sell the land was invalid, as by that date the club's activities had ceased and it had become incapable of carrying out its objects.

The court can order that an unincorporated association be dissolved under its inherent jurisdiction. In *Keene (Trustees of the Graphic Reproduction Federation) v Wellcom London Ltd*,[46] Peter Smith J refused to make a declaration that the dormant Graphic Reproduction Federation had spontaneously dissolved,[47] but he did order that the association be dissolved as at the date of his judgment. The net assets were distributed amongst the members as at the date of dissolution.

(c)   Resulting Trust for Members.   In *Re Printers' and Transferrers' Society*,[48]   **11–012**
a society was founded to raise funds by weekly contributions to defend and support its members in maintaining reasonable remuneration for their labour, and to provide strike and lock-out benefits for members. The scale of payments varied according to the length of time a claimant had been a member of the society, and different conditions applied to printers and transferrers respectively. No provision was made by the rules for the distribution of the funds of the society on a dissolution. At the time of its dissolution the society consisted of 201 members, and its funds amounted to £1,000. The question arose as to how the sum was to be distributed. The Attorney General made no claim to the fund as bona vacantia. It was held that there was a resulting trust in favour of those who had subscribed to the fund, and that the money was divisible amongst the existing members at the time of the dissolution, in proportion to the amount contributed by each member to the funds of the society irrespective of fines, or payments made to members in accordance with the rules.

In *Re Hobourn Aero Components Air Raid Distress Fund*,[49] a fund was established during the Second World War for employees of a company who were on war service or who sustained loss in air raids. The fund was financed by voluntary subscriptions among the employees, but it was not charitable. The Crown made no claim to the fund as bona vacantia. After the war, the fund was found to have a surplus. It was held that each contributor, past or present, had an interest in the surplus by way of resulting trust in proportion to the amount he had contributed, but subject to adjustment in relation to any benefit he had received from the fund.

This conclusion, although logically consistent with the resulting trust analysis, is less convenient than the decision in *Re Printers' and Transferrers' Society*,[50] in that it concentrates attention on all the contributors to a society, however remote in time past, and not on those who have retained a connection with it. There is much to be said for the simpler solution of the earlier case, which, however, Cohen J in the present case thought defensible only in cases where the ascertainment of the true entitlements would be too difficult. A more recent

---

[46] [2014] EWHC 134 (Ch).
[47] [2014] EWHC 134 (Ch) at [20]: "Whilst it sleeps it is not dead".
[48] [1899] 2 Ch. 184.
[49] [1946] Ch. 86 (affirmed at 194), see especially 97–98; following *Re British Red Cross Balkan Fund* [1914] 2 Ch. 419.
[50] [1899] 2 Ch. 184.

example is provided by *Air Jamaica Ltd v Charlton*,[51] where, however, the surplus arose in the context of a pension trust rather than an association. That part of the surplus which derived from the members' contributions resulted to them and was divided pro rata between the members and the estates of deceased members in proportion to their contributions, irrespective of benefits received and the dates of the contributions.

11–013　*(d)　Contractual Basis.*　In *Cunnack v Edwards*,[52] a society governed by the Friendly Societies Act 1829[53] had been established in 1810 to raise a fund, by the subscriptions of its members, to provide annuities for the widows of its deceased members. By 1879 all the members had died. The last widow-annuitant died in 1892, the society then having a surplus of £1,250. A claim to the assets was made by the personal representatives of the last surviving members. It was held that there was no resulting trust in favour of the personal representatives of the members of the society. Each member had paid away his money in return for the protection given to his widow, if he left one. "Except as to this he abandoned and gave up the money for ever."[54] The assets went to the Crown as bona vacantia.

In *Re West Sussex Constabulary's Widows, Children and Benevolent (1930) Fund Trust*,[55] a fund had been established to provide benefits to widows and certain dependants of members who died. The income of the fund came from members' subscriptions, the proceeds of entertainments, sweepstakes, raffles and collecting boxes and various donations and legacies. On the amalgamation of the West Sussex Constabulary with other police forces in 1968, the question arose of the distribution of the fund.

Goff J held that the surviving members had no claim because first, the members had received all that they had contracted for, and secondly, the money was paid on the basis of contract, and not of trust. The funds went as bona vacantia to the Crown. The possibility that living members may have a contractual claim on the basis of frustration of the contract or failure of consideration was met by the Crown giving an indemnity to the trustees.

Contributions from outside sources were divided into three categories. The first two, proceeds of entertainments, etc. and collecting boxes, could not be the subject of a resulting trust,[56] they were out-and-out payments.[57] Identifiable donations, however, and legacies were in a different position. The object of the gift had failed, and the property was held on resulting trust. On the latter point, it is difficult to see why third party contributors, even if identifiable, should have any claim in such circumstances. The validity of the initial gift is usually

---

[51] [1999] 1 W.L.R. 1399, PC; C. Harpum [2000] Conv. 170; C. Rickett and R. Grantham (2000) 116 L.Q.R. 15. The bona vacantia solution of *Davis v Richards & Wallington Industries Ltd* [1990] 1 W.L.R. 1511, below, para.11–015, was considered wrong.

[52] [1896] 2 Ch. 679. The decision was distinguished in *Re Bucks Constabulary Fund (No.2)* [1979] 1 W.L.R. 936 as turning upon the combined effect of the rules and the 1829 Act.

[53] For the special position of Friendly Societies, see J. Warburton, *Unincorporated Associations: Law & Practice*, 2nd edn (1992), pp.5–6.

[54] [1896] 2 Ch. 679 at 683.

[55] [1971] Ch. 1; M. Albery (1971) 87 L.Q.R. 464.

[56] Not following *Re Gillingham Bus Disaster Fund* [1958] Ch. 300, above, para.11–007.

[57] *Re Welsh Hospital (Netley) Fund* [1921] 1 Ch. 655; *Re Hillier's Trusts* [1954] 1 W.L.R. 9; *Re Ulverston and District New Hospital Building Trust* [1956] Ch. 622.

explained on the basis that it is an absolute gift to the members of the association.[58] If that is so, such contributions should be dealt with on the same basis as the rest of the funds. It is submitted that there is no room here for a resulting trust for third parties.

The more acceptable modern solution to the distribution of assets of an **11–014** unincorporated society is among the members. The matter is regarded as one of contract between the members, express or implied. On this analysis, the resulting trust solution is no longer appropriate. This is so, even though the assets of the society may be vested in trustees; as is indeed required in the case of unincorporated Friendly Societies.[59] The trustees then hold the assets on trust for the members according to the rules of the society. The rules may provide for the distribution upon dissolution. Otherwise, the assets will be divided among the members at the time of the dissolution.

Re Bucks Constabulary Fund (No.2)[60] was another case of the distribution of a fund established to provide benefits for the widows and orphans of deceased police officers and the provision of payments on the death of a member or during sickness. The Bucks Constabulary amalgamated with other constabularies and in 1968 the fund was wound up.

The question of the proper method of distribution came before Walton J, who held that the assets should be divided equally among members alive at the date of dissolution. He emphasised the distinction between property held under the terms of the trust, and that governed by contract. In such a case, quoting Brightman J,[61]

"The right of the member of the fund to receive benefits is a contractual right and the member ceases to have any interest in the fund if and when he has received the totality of the benefits to which he was contractually entitled. In other words, there is no possible claim by any member founded on a resulting trust... If it has been dissolved or terminated, the members entitled to participate would *prima facie* be those persons who were members at the date of dissolution or termination."[62]

The *West Sussex* decision, although distinguishable on the ground that it did not involve a Friendly Society, was criticised by Walton J on the basis that the principle of law applicable to the members' club cases should have governed the distribution. It made no difference whether or not the association was for the benefit of the members themselves. They controlled the assets, which were theirs all along. Thus bona vacantia was not an appropriate solution in that case.

Walton J suggested that, if there was only one member left, the property would be ownerless and would pass to the Crown. Lewison J subsequently disagreed, holding that the sole surviving member of a non-charitable unincorporated association was entitled to the assets on the basis that the members were the joint

---

[58] Below, para.16–019.

[59] Friendly Societies Act 1974 s.54. The Friendly Societies Act 1992 provides for the incorporation of Friendly Societies carrying on mutual insurance business for the members and their families.

[60] [1979] 1 W.L.R. 936; C. Rickett (1980) 39 C.L.J. 88; B. Green (1980) 43 M.L.R. 626.

[61] *Re William Denby and Sons Ltd Sick and Benevolent Fund* [1971] 1 W.L.R. 973 at 978.

[62] [1979] 1 W.L.R. 936 at 948.

tenants in equity, subject to any contractual restrictions.[63] The property accrued to the last member by the doctrine of survivorship, and neither the Crown nor any former members or their estates had any entitlement. This, it is submitted, is the correct analysis. As Lewison J pointed out, diverting the property from the last surviving member to the Crown would be a breach of art.1 of the First Protocol to the European Convention on Human Rights (right to peaceful enjoyment of possessions).

11–015   Similar problems may arise in the context of surplus pension funds. As this situation involves a trust rather than an unincorporated association, it may be expected (in the absence of rules in the pension scheme to deal with it) that the surplus would be held on resulting trust for the contributors. In *Davis v Richards & Wallington Industries Ltd*,[64] however, Scott J considered that any resulting trust to the members would be excluded by implication, partly because of the difficulty of calculating their shares in view of the different benefits received, and partly because tax relief would be lost if the members received under a resulting trust any sums in excess of the maximum benefits permitted by the relevant legislation. Thus the bona vacantia solution was preferred. This analysis was considered to be wrong by the Privy Council in *Air Jamaica Ltd v Charlton*[65] on the basis that a resulting trust arising on a conveyance to trustees cannot be avoided simply because the transferor does not intend to retain the beneficial interest. It may arise even where the transferor positively wished to part with the beneficial interest: "a resulting trust is not defeated by evidence that the transferor intended to part with the beneficial interest if he has not in fact succeeded in doing so".[66] The two reasons given by Scott J should not have excluded a resulting trust, which arose by operation of the general law and outside the scope of the tax legislation. The alleged difficulty of calculating the shares rested on the erroneous assumption that the benefits received by each member had to be taken into account. In the present case, the proper solution was a resulting trust for the employer[67] and the members. The members' share was divided pro rata between the members and the estates of deceased members in proportion to their contributions, irrespective of benefits received and the dates of the contributions.

11–016   *(e) Methods of Distribution Among the Members.*   If entitlement is on the basis of a resulting trust, the distribution will be made amongst all members, past and present, including personal representatives of deceased members, in shares proportionate to their contributions. Past members may be excluded if the

---

[63] *Hanchett-Stamford v Attorney General* [2009] Ch. 173. *Cunnack v Edwards* [1896] 2 Ch. 679, above, para.11–013, was distinguished as all members there had disappeared or their claims had been satisfied. The grounds for distinguishing *Cunnack* are criticised by S. Baughen [2010] Conv. 216 at 228.

[64] [1990] 1 W.L.R. 1511.

[65] [1999] 1 W.L.R. 1399.

[66] [1999] 1 W.L.R. 1399 at 1412, citing *Vandervell v IRC* [1967] 2 A.C. 291, below, para.11–018, a case where the transferor certainly wished to part with the beneficial interest.

[67] A clause in the deed excluding any repayment to the employer was to preclude any amendment to the scheme allowing such repayment and did not prevent a resulting trust arising outside the scheme.

calculation would prove too difficult.[68] We have seen, however, that the resulting trust analysis is not usually favoured today in cases of unincorporated associations. It is also unlikely, in view of *Re Bucks Constabulary Fund (No.2)*,[69] that the Crown will establish a claim to the assets as bona vacantia in many cases, or, as submitted above,[70] that outside contributors will have any claim.

Assuming that the contractual basis is adopted, only those members existing at the date of dissolution will normally be entitled. And unless the rules provide otherwise, the distribution will be on a per capita basis, prima facie in equal shares, and ignoring actual contributions. However, in *Re North Harrow Tennis Club*,[71] the club's rules provided that in the event of dissolution any surplus assets would be divided between past and present members in proportion to their years of membership. Edward Pepperall QC, sitting as a Deputy High Court Judge, ordered the club's remaining assets to be distributed in that fashion.

In *Re Sick and Funeral Society of St John's Sunday School, Golcar*,[72] a society was formed in 1866 to provide sickness and death benefits for its members. Those under 13 paid 1/2d per week, and the others paid 1d. The benefits for those paying the whole subscription were twice those of the smaller subscribers. Upon the winding up of the society, the surplus funds were held distributable among the members as at that date on a per capita basis, but as the benefits and burdens differed among the two classes of members, the proper basis for distribution was full shares for full members and half shares for the children. The per capita basis did not favour new members at the expense of older ones, as each got what he paid for: the newer members had had the benefits of membership for a short time and the older members for a longer time. The latter could not complain if they did not receive more in the winding up.

In *Re Bucks Constabulary Fund (No.2)*,[73] Walton J held that the prima facie rule of equal division applied also to Friendly Society cases, although in the past some of those cases had favoured a distribution in proportion to contributions.[74] This approach was also adopted in *Re GKN Bolts & Nuts Ltd (Automotive Division) Birmingham Works, Sports and Social Club*,[75] where those entitled to share the assets on a per capita basis were the full members and the ordinary members. Honorary, temporary and associate members, who neither paid subscriptions nor had voting rights, were excluded.

iii. Trust and Charge. Here also the distinction between a trust and a charge is important.[76] A distinction was drawn by Lord Eldon in *King v Denison*[77] between devises *charged with payment* of debts, and devises *on trust to pay*   **11–017**

---

[68] *Re Hobourn Aero Components Air Raid Distress Fund* [1946] Ch. 86 at 97.
[69] [1979] 1 W.L.R. 936.
[70] Above, para.11–013.
[71] [2017] EWHC 2476 (Ch). Giving past members an entitlement to the surplus on dissolution creates obvious problems if the club wishes to alter that part of its rules.
[72] [1973] Ch. 51.
[73] [1979] 1 W.L.R. 936. See also *Elvidge v Coulson*, *The Times*, 27 August 2003.
[74] *Re Printers' and Transferrers' Society* [1899] 2 Ch. 184; *Re Lead Workmens Fund Society* [1904] 2 Ch. 196.
[75] [1982] 1 W.L.R. 774. The facts have been given, above, para.11–011. See also *Re St Andrew's Allotment Association* [1969] 1 W.L.R. 229; *Re Horley Town Football Club* [2006] W.T.L.R. 1817.
[76] Above, para.2–012.

debts. In the former case it is assumed that the testator intended a beneficial interest for the devisee, subject to the payment of debts; in the latter case it is assumed that he intended merely to use the devisee as a vehicle for payment of the debts, and not to confer any benefit upon him. In the latter case there will, therefore, be a resulting trust of any surplus for the residuary devisee, or those entitled on intestacy; but there will be no resulting trust in the former case. In construing the language of a gift, it must be remembered that equity will not allow trustees themselves to give evidence that what was intended was a conditional gift.[78]

D. No Beneficial Interests Declared

11–018   Where property is conveyed to persons in circumstances in which they are intended to take as trustees, then, if no beneficial interests are declared, they will hold on resulting trust for the grantor; as where a transfer is made to a nominee.[79]

The *Vandervell* litigation serves as a warning of the crucial importance of attention to detail in tax planning. There were two visits to the House of Lords and three to the Court of Appeal. The problem was caused by the fact that Mr Vandervell's advisers overlooked the possibility of the existence of a resulting trust, when all that Mr Vandervell was doing was trying to give away a large sum of money to charity.

In 1958 Vandervell decided to found a Chair of Pharmacology at the Royal College of Surgeons with a gift of £250,000. This was to be effected by a scheme under which a block of shares in Vandervell Products Ltd would be transferred to the College, and the necessary dividends subsequently declared on them. As the College is a charity, such dividends would be free of liability to income tax and surtax. The shares were to be transferred subject to an option to repurchase for £5,000 in favour of Vandervell Trustees Ltd, a private company whose only function was to act as trustee for various trusts connected with the Vandervell family and business. It was trustee of the Vandervell children's trust.

The transfer of the shares was made in 1958, and between then and 1961 the necessary dividends were paid to the College. The Revenue assessed Vandervell for surtax on the dividends on the ground that he had not entirely disposed of all his interest in the property,[80] because, in the absence of a declaration of trust of the option, it was held on resulting trust for Vandervell. The Revenue succeeded. That was *Vandervell v IRC*.[81] Before discussing the reasoning, it will be best to complete the story.

On receiving the Revenue's claim in 1961, Vandervell arranged for Vandervell Trustees Ltd to exercise the option, and they did so, taking £5,000 from the

---

[77] (1813) 1 Ves. & Bea. 260; *Smith v Cooke* [1891] A.C. 297; *Re West* [1900] 1 Ch. 84; *Re Foord* [1922] 2 Ch. 519, distinguished in *Re Osoba* [1979] 1 W.L.R. 247, above, para.11–009.

[78] *Re Rees* [1950] Ch. 204; *Re Pugh* [1967] 1 W.L.R. 1262; *Re Tyler* [1967] 1 W.L.R. 1269; cf. *Smith v Cooke* [1891] A.C. 297.

[79] *Hodgson v Marks* [1971] Ch. 892; *Vandervell v IRC* [1967] 2 A.C. 291.

[80] Income Tax Act 1952 s.415(2). Now Income Tax (Trading and Other Income) Act 2005 s.624.

[81] [1967] 2 A.C. 291; G. Jones (1966) 24 C.L.J. 19; S. Spencer (1967) 31 Conv.(N.S.) 175; N. Strauss (1967) 30 M.L.R. 461; R. Nolan (2002) 61 C.L.J. 169.

children's settlement to finance it. All the dividends since that date were paid to Vandervell Trustees Ltd, who applied them to the children's settlement. They so informed the Revenue.

The Revenue then assessed Vandervell to surtax in respect of the years 1961–65, on the footing that the shares were held on trust for him during that period. In 1965 he at last executed a deed which transferred all or any interest which he may have in the shares in favour of the children's settlement. In 1967 he died.

Before this claim of the Revenue was litigated, Vandervell's estate stepped in and claimed the dividends from Vandervell Trustees Ltd. If the estate succeeded, the Revenue's claim was clearly good; and the Revenue attempted to join the litigation in support. The defendants successfully excluded them.[82] In *Re Vandervell's Trusts (No.2)*[83] the estate succeeded before Megarry J, but failed before the Court of Appeal.

In the first case, *Vandervell v IRC*,[84] the Revenue succeeded by a majority of three to two. The option was held on trust for Vandervell. He was effectively the grantor of the option, although it was in form granted by the Royal College. It was taken by Vandervell Trustees Ltd upon trust, but no effective trusts of the option were declared, "and so the defendant company held the option on an automatic trust for Mr Vandervell."[85] In this situation, there was, as Lord Wilberforce said:

11–019

> "no need, or room to invoke a presumption. The conclusion, on the facts found, is simply that the option was vested in the trustee company as a trustee on trusts, not defined at the time, possibly to be defined later. But the equitable, or beneficial interest, cannot remain in the air: the consequence in law must be that it remains in the settlor."[86]

An indication of the parties' intention, as opposed to what they might be supposed to have desired, would of course have changed the whole situation. But the donor's mere intention not to have the beneficial interest cannot prevent an "automatic" resulting trust.[87]

In *Re Vandervell's Trusts (No.2)*,[88] the Court of Appeal, reversing Megarry J, found that the resulting trust of the option in favour of Vandervell terminated with the exercise of the option; and that a trust of the shares had been declared in favour of the children's settlements.[89] At this point there was no longer a "gap in the beneficial ownership"[90] such that Mr Vandervell would be entitled under a resulting trust. Importantly, the declaration of new trusts for the children's

---

[82] *Re Vandervell's Trusts (No.1)* [1971] A.C. 912.

[83] [1974] Ch. 269.

[84] [1967] 2 A.C. 291.

[85] As described in *Re Vandervell's Trusts (No.2)* [1974] Ch. 269 at 296 (Megarry J).

[86] [1967] 2 A.C. 291 at 329.

[87] [1974] Ch. 269 at 298 (Megarry J); *Air Jamaica Ltd v Charlton* [1999] 1 W.L.R. 1399.

[88] [1974] Ch. 269; P. Clarke (1974) 38 Conv.(N.S.) 405; J. Harris (1975) 38 M.L.R. 557; G. Battersby (1975) 7 D.L.R. 483.

[89] The finding of a declaration of trust can be criticised: see above, para.5–019.

[90] [1974] Ch. 269 at 320, per Lord Denning MR.

settlement was effective because it did not amount to a disposition of Mr Vandervell's subsisting equitable interest.[91]

3. APPARENT GIFTS

A. Presumption of Resulting Trust

11–020 Where property is transferred from A to B, or purchased by A in the name of B, then B will normally be presumed to hold the property on a resulting trust for A. There are three exceptions to this general rule. First, no presumption of resulting trust applies if A is B's husband or parent. In these situations a presumption of advancement applies instead.[92] Secondly, it may be that no presumption of resulting trust exists in the case of a voluntary conveyance of land (although it does apply to purchases of land in another's name). Thirdly, special rules apply to the ownership of family homes.[93]

The presumption of resulting trust is rebuttable, as is the presumption an advancement. When a presumption of resulting trust is rebutted the recipient usually takes the property absolutely.[94] When a presumption of advancement is rebutted the recipient usually holds on resulting trust for the transferor or purchaser.[95]

i. Voluntary Transfers.

11–021 *(a) Land.* There may be a distinction between land and personalty in the context of voluntary transfers of property. In the case of land, the Law of Property Act 1925 s.60(3) provides:

> "In a voluntary conveyance a resulting trust for the grantor shall not be implied merely by reason that the property is not expressed to be conveyed for the use or benefit of the grantee."

The question is whether this section prevents a presumption of resulting trust from arising on a voluntary conveyance of land. That issue will be discussed further below. But regardless of whether s.60(3) prevents a presumption of resulting trust from arising, the section does not preclude the finding of a resulting trust on general equitable principles.[96] So, where the transferor establishes by evidence that no gift was intended, a resulting trust will be found notwithstanding s.60(3).

In *Hodgson v Marks*,[97] Mrs Hodgson was an old lady who was the registered owner of a house. A lodger, Evans, lived there. Mrs Hodgson developed an

---

[91] Above, para.6–014.
[92] See below, para.11–026.
[93] These will be considered in Ch.13.
[94] Although, e.g., the recipient may take on trust for a third party.
[95] See below, para.11–034. Again, the recipient may also take on trust for a third party.
[96] Note that a resulting trust analysis will no longer be employed in a domestic context, even where there is a voluntary conveyance rather than the purchase of property, as considered in Ch.13. See, for example, *Aspden v Elvy* [2012] EWHC 1387 (Ch).
[97] [1971] Ch. 892.

affection for Evans, and trusted him to look after all her affairs. Her nephew disapproved of Evans, and tried to persuade Mrs Hodgson to turn him out. To protect Evans, she transferred the house to him, under an oral agreement that she would continue to be beneficial owner. Evans, as registered owner, sold it to a bona fide purchaser, Marks, and the question was whether Mrs Hodgson was protected against Marks.

The Court of Appeal held that she remained beneficial owner in equity, and that this was an overriding interest.[98] The express oral agreement in her favour was unenforceable under the Law of Property Act 1925 s.53(1)(b).[99] Evidence of her intention was however admissible, and this gave rise to a resulting trust of the beneficial interest, which was not affected by s.53(1). Since the case was decided by reference to Mrs Hodgson's *actual* intention, there was no need to decide whether a presumption of resulting trust (that is, a *presumption* as to her intention) existed. Russell LJ specifically commented that "we are not concerned with the debatable question whether on a voluntary transfer of land by A to stranger B there is a presumption of a resulting trust".[100]

Whether or not a presumption of resulting trust does apply to voluntary conveyances of land, given the words of s.60(3), is a difficult question to answer. Several cases indicate that the section prevents a presumption from arising,[101] but the point cannot be regarded as settled and another recent case goes the other way.[102] In the Supreme Court case of *Prest v Petrodel Resources Ltd*,[103] a presumption of resulting trust was applied to conveyances of land that were expressed to be for £1 but that Lord Sumption treated as "gratuitous". Section 60(3) was not mentioned.

The argument that s.60(3) prevents a presumption of resulting trust arising is based simply on the plain words of the legislation. The argument that it does not prevent a presumption arising is more subtle. The section was enacted because of a wish to simplify voluntary conveyances. Under the Statute of Uses 1535, it was necessary to insert a use for the benefit of the grantee into a voluntary conveyance. If this was not done, a use would result to the grantor; that use would be executed by the Statute; and the conveyance would be ineffective. The reforms of 1925, which included the repeal of the Statute of Uses, were intended to simplify conveyancing and it has been said that, without the enactment of s.60(3), practitioners may have believed that the inclusion of an expression such as "to the use of" or "for the benefit of" was still necessary in order to render a voluntary

---

[98] Because she was in actual occupation. The provision is now found in LRA 2002 s.29 and Sch.3, para.2.

[99] cf. W. Swadling in P. Birks and F. Rose (eds), *Restitution and Equity—Volume 1: Resulting Trusts and Equitable Compensation* (2000), Ch.4, and in C. Mitchell (ed.), *Constructive and Resulting Trusts* (2010), Ch.3, and in (2016) 10 J. Eq. 1, arguing that the trust enforced was express, with the formality rules of s.53(1)(b) being disapplied on the grounds that a statute intended to prevent fraud may not itself be used as an engine of fraud. For further discussion, see above, para.6–005.

[100] [1971] Ch. 892 at 933.

[101] See *Lohia v Lohia* [2001] W.T.L.R. 101; *Ali v Khan* [2002] EWCA Civ 974; [2009] W.T.L.R. 197 at [24]; *CPS v Malik* [2003] EWHC 660 (Admin); Chambers, *Resulting Trusts* (1997), p.18

[102] *National Crime Agency v Dong* [2017] EWHC 3116 (Ch); J. Mee [2018] Conv. 184.

[103] [2013] UKSC 34; [2013] 2 A.C. 415 at [49].

conveyance effective.[104] For this reason it can be argued that s.60(3) is a purely technical provision, and does not speak to the question of whether a presumption of resulting trust arises.[105]

11–022   *(b) Personalty.*   In relation to personality, the initial presumption is that a voluntary transfer to a recipient gives rise to a resulting trust in favour of the transferor. The presumption applies to transfers into the recipient's sole name and into the joint names of the transferor and the recipient. The application of the presumption can yield surprising results.

In *Re Vinogradoff*,[106] the testatrix had transferred a sum of £800 War Loan, then standing in her name, into the joint names of herself and her granddaughter, then four years old. The testatrix continued to receive the dividends until her death. Farwell J held that, even though a child may not be appointed a trustee, the presumption of resulting trust applied, and the granddaughter held that property on resulting trust for the estate of the testatrix.

11–023   One common example of a voluntary transfer of property occurs when A deposits money into a joint bank account held in the names of A and B.[107] In many cases there will be no room for a presumption of resulting trust (or a presumption will be immediately rebutted) because the documentation involved in opening the joint account will contain "a binding declaration as to beneficial interests" that will decide the question of beneficial title.[108] However, in the absence of such a declaration, B will be presumed to hold his share on resulting trust for A.

If A's true intention is that A should keep the property while alive, but that B should acquire a beneficial interest when A dies, this may appear to be a testamentary disposition that would require compliance with the Wills Act formalities. But this is not so. In *Russell v Scott*, a case from the High Court of Australia involving a joint account held by an aunt and her nephew, Dixon and Evatt JJ explained why[109]:

> "Succession *post mortem* is not the same as testamentary succession … In equity, the deceased was entitled in her lifetime so to deal with the contractual rights conferred by the chose in action as to destroy all its value, namely, by withdrawing all the money at credit. But the elastic or flexible conceptions of equitable proprietary rights or interests do not require that, because this is so, the joint owner of the chose in action should in respect of the legal right vested in him be treated as a trustee to the entire extent of every possible kind of beneficial interest or enjoyment … In respect of his *jus accrescendi* his conscience could not be bound."

---

[104] Cheshire and Burn, 18th edn, p.158. Of course, with the repeal of the Statute of Uses, the consequences on the finding of a resulting use would have been different: the conveyance of the legal estate would still have been effective.

[105] *National Crime Agency v Dong* [2017] EWHC 3116 (Ch) at [25]–[26], [34].

[106] [1935] W.N. 68; *Thavorn v Bank of Credit & Commerce International SA* [1985] 1 Lloyd's Rep. 259 (resulting trust where aunt opened bank account in name of 15-year-old nephew).

[107] *Standing v Bowring* (1885) 16 Ch.D. 282; *Russell v Scott* (1936) 55 CLR 440; *Young v Sealey* [1949] Ch. 278; *Re Figgis* [1969] Ch. 123; *Aroso v Coutts & Co* [2001] W.T.L.R. 797; *Drakeford v Cotton* [2012] 3 All E.R. 1138; *Whitlock v Moree (Bahamas)* [2017] UKPC 44.

[108] *Whitlock v Moree (Bahamas)* [2017] UKPC 44 at [27] (where the majority of the Privy Council considered that the account document in that case did contain such a declaration, while the minority thought it did not).

[109] *Russell v Scott* (1936) 55 C.L.R. 440 at 454–455; applied in *Drakeford v Cotton* [2012] 3 All E.R. 1138 at [63], [73].

An extra twist on this analysis can be seen in *Drakeford v Cotton*.[110] There, the transferor's intention changed after the transfer into joint names had occurred. At first, the joint account was held by a mother and her daughter on trust for the mother.[111] A few months later, the mother decided that the daughter should take the account beneficially when the mother died. As we have seen, this second arrangement would not amount to a testamentary disposition and would in theory be valid. However, Morgan J asked whether effecting the *change* in the mother's intention would involve the disposition of a subsisting equitable interest under the Law of Property Act 1925 s.53(1)(c). If so, it would be void for lack of writing.

11–024

Morgan J held that s.53(1)(c) was not infringed because, on true construction of the facts, the mother and daughter as legal owners had declared new trusts for themselves. "That declaration of trust meant that [the mother] was not able to set up an outstanding beneficial interest in herself as that would be incompatible with the intended new beneficial interests."[112]

It must be noted that Morgan J did not have the benefit of argument on the point. Nonetheless, the reasoning is not easy to interpret. A legal owner can always declare new trusts, although as a matter of priority such new trusts will normally rank behind earlier interests that conflict with the later interest. The earlier interest may be postponed in appropriate cases, of course, but it would appear to be inconsistent with *Grey v IRC*[113] to say that a new interest declared by trustees would take priority over a beneficiary's earlier interest on the grounds that the beneficiary asking the trustees to declare the new interest amounted to postponing conduct. If that analysis is not inconsistent with *Grey* then its legal viability would certainly emasculate *Grey*.

It could alternatively be argued that the beneficiary gave the trustees the power to appoint on new trusts. If and when the trustees exercised that power, the beneficiary's initial interest would be overreached.[114] No question of a disposition would arise because the beneficiary would simply create a power in the trustee to create a new interest that would overreach the previous one. This analysis may undermine *Grey* too,[115] although it might be argued that it is the combined result of *Vandervell v IRC* and *Re Vandervell's Trusts (No.2)*. Either way, the correct explanation of this aspect of *Drakeford v Cotton* will be important unless (as may prove to be the case) it is confined only to instances of survivorship and the beneficial interest in joint accounts.

---

[110] [2012] EWHC 1414 (Ch); [2012] 3 All E.R. 1138.

[111] This was a positive finding; i.e., it did not depend on a presumption of resulting trust or advancement: see [2012] 3 All E.R. 1138 at [47]. Query whether the mother was therefore entitled under an *express* trust, in which case the correct analysis on the s.53(1)(c) point becomes even more important.

[112] [2012] 3 All E.R. 1138 at [80].

[113] [1960] A.C. 1.

[114] This is the preferable explanation of why s.53(1)(c) did not apply in *Re Vandervell's Trusts (No.2)* [1974] Ch. 269: see D. Hayton and C. Mitchell, *Hayton & Marshall Commentary and Cases on The Law of Trusts and Equitable Remedies*, 12th edn (2005), para.2–46.

[115] See R. Nolan (2002) 61 C.L.J. 169 at 186, considering a similar example and concluding that it would engage s.53(1)(c).

11–025   **ii.   Purchases in the Name of Another.**   Where A purchases real or personal property but tells the seller to transfer the property to B instead, a resulting trust in favour of A will be presumed. In the words of Eyre CB[116]:

> "The trust of a legal estate, whether freehold, copyhold or leasehold; whether taken in the names of the purchaser and others, jointly, or in the names of others without that of the purchaser; whether in one name or several, whether jointly or successive, results to the man who advances the purchase-money."

The presumption arises when A funds a purchase made in the joint names of A and B,[117] and where A funds a purchase made in the name of B alone.[118] It also arises where property purchased with the contributions of both A and B is conveyed into B's name only,[119] or where A and B contribute unequal funds but become joint legal owners.

Following *Stack v Dowden*,[120] the presumption no longer applies in the context of ownership of the family home. The position in respect of commercial or investment property bought by family members is unclear. In *Laskar v Laskar*,[121] Lord Neuberger thought it would not be right to apply the principles from *Stack* to such cases and instead he applied a resulting trust analysis.[122] In the subsequent case of *Marr v Collie*,[123] a case that concerned property bought by a cohabiting couple, but not their family home, Lord Kerr said for the Privy Council:

> "The Board does not consider … that *Laskar* is authority for the proposition that the principle in *Stack v Dowden* (that a conveyance into joint names indicates legal and beneficial joint tenancy unless the contrary is proved) applies only in "the domestic consumer context". Where a property is bought in the joint names of a cohabiting couple, even if that is as an investment, it does not follow inexorably that the "resulting trust solution" must provide the inevitable answer as to how its beneficial ownership is to be determined. Lord Neuberger did not intend to draw a strict line of demarcation between, on the one hand, the purchase of a family home and, on the other, the acquisition of a so-called investment property in whatever circumstances that took place. It is entirely conceivable that partners in a relationship would buy, as an investment, property which is conveyed into their joint names with the intention that the beneficial ownership should be shared equally between them, even though they contributed in different shares to the purchase. Where there is evidence to support such a conclusion, it would be both illogical and wrong to impose the resulting trust solution on the subsequent distribution of the property."

The essential point made in *Marr v Collie* for present purposes is that a resulting trust outcome that precisely reflects contributions to the purchase price

---

[116] *Dyer v Dyer* (1788) 2 Cox 92 at 93; 30 E.R. 42 at 43. The principle is not limited to legal estates of land: see *In Re A Policy No 6402 Of The Scottish Equitable Life Assurance Society* [1902] 1 Ch. 282 at 284–285 (purchase of insurance policy); *The Venture* [1908] P. 218 at 229–230 (purchase of yacht); *Parrott v Parkin* [2007] 2 F.L.R. 444 at [50] (another yacht, called "Up Yaws").

[117] *Benger v Drew* (1721) 1 P. Wms. 781; 24 E.R. 613; *Fowkes v Pascoe* (1875) L.R. 10 Ch.App. 343.

[118] *In Re A Policy No 6402 Of The Scottish Equitable Life Assurance Society* [1902] 1 Ch. 282.

[119] *Wray v Steele* (1814) 2 Ves. & Bea. 388; 35 E.R. 366; *The Venture* [1908] P. 218 at 229–230.

[120] [2007] 2 A.C. 432; see Ch.13 below.

[121] *Laskar v Laskar* [2008] 1 W.L.R. 2695 (house bought by mother and daughter, but as investment property and not family home). N. Piska [2008] Conv. 441.

[122] Although his Lordship did not think it appropriate to apply a presumption of advancement: [2008] 1 W.L.R. 2695 at [20]; below, para.11–030.

[123] [2017] UKPC 17 at [49]; M. George and B. Sloan [2017] Conv. 303; J. Roche [2017] C.L.J. 303.

will very rarely be appropriate in family situations, even as regards property other than a family home. It will rarely be appropriate because it will rarely be what the parties intended.[124] Put like this, there is no problem with continuing to apply an initial presumption of resulting trust in this context, while also recognising that it is more likely to be rebutted because family members will not normally intend such property to be held strictly according to the value of their respective contributions.

B. Presumption of Advancement

The presumption of advancement is a presumption working in the opposite direction to the presumption of resulting trust. It arises where the donor or purchaser is the husband or parent (including people in loco parentis) of the person to whom property is transferred. In such cases the property is presumed to have been given absolutely, as a gift, rather than on trust. Like the presumption of resulting trust, however, the presumption of advancement can be rebutted.[125]   **11–026**

Various rationales have been given for the existence of the presumption of advancement and for the particular relationships to which it applies.[126] Some older cases make reference to the "natural love and affection" between the parties, with such affection meaning that an outright gift was probably intended.[127] Yet this rationale cannot explain why the presumption does not apply to transfers from wives to husbands, from grandparents (unless they are in loco parentis)[128] to grandchildren, from siblings to each other, or why a mother–child presumption of advancement has taken so long to be recognised.[129]   **11–027**

A more popular modern justification is that the presumption of advancement recognises statutory duties that the transferor owes to maintain and support the recipient. The fact that these obligations are normally owed equally by husbands and wives to each other, and by both parents to their children, justifies the equalisation of the presumption relationships.[130] However, while the older cases do refer to equity presuming the fulfilment of some kind of obligation,[131] it is

---

[124] [2017] UKPC 17 at [53]–[55]. See Lord Neuberger, "The Plight of the Unmarried" (speech delivered 21 June 2017), expressing the view that the special principles from *Stack v Dowden* do not apply to assets other than the family home, even following *Marr v Collie*. Lord Neuberger was a member of the Board in *Marr v Collie*.

[125] Below, para.11–033.

[126] See generally J. Glister in C. Mitchell (ed.), *Constructive and Resulting Trusts* (2010), Ch.10; Tey T.H. [2007] Sing.J.L.S. 240.

[127] *Grey v Grey* (1677) 2 Swans. 594; 36 E.R. 742; *Dyer v Dyer* (1788) 2 Cox 92; 30 E.R. 42; *Garrett v Wilkinson* (1848) 2 De G. & Sm. 244; 64 E.R. 110; *Sayre v Hughes* (1868) L.R. 5 Eq. 376.

[128] See *Ebrand v Dancer* (1680) 2 Chan. Cas. 25; 22 E.R. 829.

[129] Natural love and affection was good consideration in the law of uses, in that a conveyance for natural love and affection would raise a use in the feoffee (and therefore not a resulting use to the feoffor): see W. Holdsworth, *A History of English Law vol iv,* 3rd edn (1945, repr 1966), p.425.

[130] *Nelson v Nelson* (1995) 184 C.L.R. 538 at 574–575, 586; *Pecore v Pecore* [2007] 1 S.C.R. 795 at [32]; *Lau Siew Kim v Yeo Guan Chye Terence* [2008] 2 S.L.R. 108 at [63]; *Lee Tso Fong v Kwok Wai Sun* [2008] 4 HKC 36 at [14]. It also justified limiting the presumption of advancement to transfers made to minor children in *Pecore v Pecore* [2007] 1 S.C.R. 795.

[131] *Grey v Grey* (1677) 2 Swans. 594; 36 E.R. 742; *Murless v Franklin* (1818) 1 Swans. 13; 36 E.R. 278; *Bennet v Bennet* (1879) 10 Ch.D. 474; *McCabe v Ulster Bank Ltd* [1939] I.R. 1.

doubtful that this was a duty to maintain and support the recipient. First, the Poor Law duties on men to maintain family members applied to a wider range of relationships than the presumption of advancement ever has: sons were required to support their parents, and grandfathers to support their grandchildren.[132] In time those duties also applied to women.[133] Secondly, duties to maintain and support have always applied to infant children.[134] Recent cases have used this as a reason to limit the presumption of advancement to transfers to infant children.[135] However, in the early cases a transfer to an infant child was actually seen as evidence that a gift was *not* intended.[136] The reason was that the child was too young to make use of the transferred property. Advancement continued to be presumed in the case of minor children because it was even more unlikely that a father intended his infant child to be his trustee,[137] but the point remains that equity did not view the father as discharging a maintenance obligation in respect of an infant child.

Instead the more persuasive historical explanation is that, in applying a presumption of advancement, equity was presuming the fulfilment of a duty on the transferor to establish the recipient in life. It was, quite genuinely, a presumption of *advancement*. The duty was not legally enforceable: a son could not bring an action against his father to claim proper provision. But equity could still presume fulfilment of the duty if that father actually made a relevant transfer or purchase. The best explanation of this is to be found in Meredith J's judgment in the Irish case of *McCabe v Ulster Bank Ltd*[138]:

> "Courts of Equity have recognised the obligation of a father to make provision for his child. It is a duty of nature, recognised by Courts of Equity. A gift in discharge of that obligation is an advancement ... Advancement is different from maintenance and support, and the provision which advancement has in contemplation goes far beyond anything resting on legal obligation."

11–028 The Law Commission has called the presumption of advancement "archaic and discriminatory".[139] The gender bias of the presumption was thought likely to contravene the European Convention on Human Rights,[140] which led to the abolition of the presumption in s.199(1) of the Equality Act 2010. However, at

---

[132] See, e.g., the Poor Relief Act 1601.

[133] See the Married Women's Property Act 1882 s.21; the Poor Law Act 1927 s.41. See generally N. Wikeley, *Child Support: Law and Policy* (2006), Chs.2 and 3.

[134] The statutory duty applied to adult children as well as infants until the National Assistance Act 1948, but the common law duty has only ever applied to infants: see N. Lowe and G. Douglas, *Bromley's Family Law*, 10th edn (2007), p.916.

[135] *Pecore v Pecore* [2007] 1 S.C.R. 795 at [36]; followed in *Musson v Bonner* [2010] W.T.L.R. 1369 at [28]. In *Laskar v Laskar* [2008] 1 W.L.R. 2695 at [20]. Lord Neuberger noted that the presumption is "weaker where, as here, the child was over 18 years of age and managed her own affairs at the time of the transaction".

[136] See, e.g., *Binion v Stone* (1663) 2 Freem. 169; 22 E.R. 1135.

[137] As Freeman wrote in his report of *Binion v Stone* (1663) 2 Freem. 169 at 169; 22 E.R. 1135 at 1136.

[138] [1939] I.R. 1 at 17–18.

[139] Law Com. No. 320, *The Illegality Defence* (2010), para.1.26. See also A. Blackham (2015) 21 T. & T. 786.

[140] Article 5 of the Seventh Protocol. In fact it is highly doubtful this is the case: see J. Glister (2010) 73 M.L.R. 807. The UK has not yet ratified the Seventh Protocol.

the time of writing, the relevant section still has not been brought into force. Even assuming that s.199 is brought into force at some point, the presumption of advancement will remain relevant for some considerable time because by s.199(2) the abolition of the presumption has no effect in relation to:

(a)   anything done before the commencement of this section, or
(b)   anything done pursuant to any obligation incurred before the commencement of this section.

If s.199 is brought into force, a presumption of resulting trust will apply to transfers and purchases that were formerly subject to a presumption of advancement.[141]

i.   Husband and Wife.   The presumption of advancement applies where a husband makes a transfer to his wife. In *Re Eykyn's Trusts*[142] in 1877, Malins VC said:

> "The law of this court is perfectly settled that where a husband transfers money or other property into the name of his wife only, then the presumption is, that it is intended as a gift or advancement to the wife absolutely at once… ".

11–029

Special considerations apply to the ownership of the marital home, which will be discussed in Ch.13. However, transfers of chattels to a wife are within the presumption. The presumption also applies where the gift is made before marriage, but with a specific marriage (which in fact takes place) in mind.[143] There is no presumption of advancement where a man puts property into the name of his unmarried partner,[144] nor is there such a presumption where a wife puts property into the name of her husband.[145] There is probably no presumption of advancement between parties to a civil partnership.[146] The position of same-sex married couples remains to be seen.

ii.   Parent and Child.   The traditional position is that a presumption of advancement applies to transfers made by fathers to their children, but not to transfers made by mothers to their children. In *Bennet v Bennet*,[147] Sir George Jessel MR said:

11–030

---

[141] See the Explanatory Notes to the Equality Act 2010; cf. W. Swadling in A. Burrows et al (eds), *Judge and Jurist: Essays in Memory of Lord Rodger of Earlsferry* (2013), Ch.47. In New Zealand, both presumptions have been abolished as between spouses: Property (Relationships) Act 1976 s.4(3).
[142] (1877) 6 Ch.D. 115 at 118; quoted in *Pettitt v Pettitt* [1970] A.C. 777 at 815.
[143] *Moate v Moate* [1948] 2 All E.R. 486; *Ulrich v Ulrich* [1968] 1 W.L.R. 180; E. Ellis (1975) 119 S.J. 108. A void marriage is not included. As to engaged couples, see Law Reform (Miscellaneous Provisions) Act 1970 s.2(1). One effect of s.2(1) is that the presumption of advancement applies to resolve disputes between couples whose engagement has ended; *Mossop v Mossop* [1989] Fam. 77; cf. *Bernard v Josephs* [1982] Ch. 391 at 400.
[144] *Diwell v Farnes* [1959] 1 W.L.R. 624.
[145] *Mercier v Mercier* [1903] 2 Ch. 98; *Heseltine v Heseltine* [1971] 1 W.L.R. 342.
[146] There does not seem to be a case on the point. The Law Commission took the view that the presumption probably did not apply to civil partners in a short paper, *The Presumption of Advancement: Does it Have Any Effect in Practice?* (2006).
[147] (1879) 10 Ch.D. 474 at 478.

> "But in our law there is no moral legal obligation—I do not know how to express it more shortly—no obligation according to the rules of equity—on a mother to provide for her child: there is no such obligation as a Court of Equity recognises as such."

This was one of the discriminatory aspects of the presumption that led to s.199 of the Equality Act 2010. However, it can now be stated with reasonable confidence that English courts will apply a presumption of advancement to transfers from a mother to her child. In *Laskar v Laskar*,[148] Lord Neuberger referred, in a case involving a mother and daughter, to the "presumption of advancement as between parent and child". In *Close Invoice Finance Ltd v Abaowa*,[149] counsel for the mother conceded that a presumption of advancement applied on the facts because the mother stood in loco parentis to her daughter. But Simon Picken QC, sitting as a Deputy High Court Judge, made it clear that he would have found it to apply anyway, on the straightforward ground that the presumption of advancement now applied to mothers. In *Patel v Mirza*,[150] Lord Toulson assumed that a presumption of advancement would apply between mother and daughter.

The parental presumption has already been equalised in many other common-law jurisdictions: mothers and fathers are treated the same in respect of property transfers to their children in Australia,[151] Canada,[152] Hong Kong,[153] New Zealand,[154] and probably in Singapore.[155] In the analogous sphere of the presumption against "double portions" (whereby substantial lifetime provision for a child may be taken to adeem, or cancel, a legacy to that child), it has also been held that the presumption should apply to gifts made by mothers. Traditionally, only a father or person in loco parentis could make a portion, but nowadays "it suffices for a gift to be capable of being a portion that it is made by either parent for the benefit of a child".[156]

Unlike the spousal presumption, which does not apply to "de facto" spouses, the parental presumption of advancement was always applied to persons in loco parentis.

C.   Rebutting the Presumptions

11–031   **i.   Initial Application.**   The presumption of advancement applies to transfers of property between people who stand in the *general* relationships of husband–wife and parent–child. The presumption of resulting trust applies to

---

[148] [2008] 1 W.L.R. 2695 at [20] (although his Lordship did not purport to state a new extension of the presumption, and did not in fact apply the presumption). See also *Hounga v Allen* [2014] UKSC 47; [2014] 1 W.L.R. 2889 at [30].

[149] [2010] EWHC 1920 (QB).

[150] [2016] UKSC 42, [2017] A.C. 467 at [18] (Lord Toulson was making the point that *Tinsley v Milligan* [1994] 1 A.C. 340 would have been decided differently if the parties were mother and daughter; below, para.11–036).

[151] *Brown v Brown* (1993) 31 N.S.W.L.R. 582; *Nelson v Nelson* (1995) 184 C.L.R. 538.

[152] *Pecore v Pecore* [2007] 1 S.C.R. 795.

[153] *Suen Shu Tai v Tam Fung Tai* [2014] HKCA 327.

[154] *Re Brownlee* [1990] 3 N.Z.L.R. 243.

[155] *Lau Siew Kim v Yeo Guan Chye Terence* [2008] 2 S.L.R. 108 at [62]–[68]; *Chia Hang Kiu v Chia Kwok Yeo* [2016] SGHC 198 at [59].

[156] *Re Cameron (Deceased)* [1999] Ch. 386 at 405.

transfers of property outside those relationships.[157] However, with the exception of establishing whether a non-parent truly stands in loco parentis to a child, the specifics of a particular relationship are not relevant to the point of which initial presumption applies. Evidence of the particularly close personal and financial relationship between two siblings ought not to mean that a presumption of advancement applies to a transfer of property between them. Obviously the specifics of that relationship will be relevant to whether or not a gift was actually intended; nonetheless, it is important to keep separate the questions of (i) which initial presumption to apply, and (ii) whether that presumption has been rebutted.

ii. Strength of the Presumptions.   It is easy to find judicial comments to the **11–032** effect that the presumptions may vary in strength. In *Fowkes v Pascoe*,[158] Mellish LJ suggested that the presumption of resulting trust "must, beyond all question, be of very different weight in different cases". In *Shephard v Cartwright*,[159] Viscount Simonds said that the presumption of advancement between parent and child "should not give way to slight circumstances". In *Pettitt v Pettitt*,[160] Lord Upjohn commented that both the presumptions of advancement and resulting trust could be rebutted by "comparatively slight" evidence. In *McGrath v Wallis*,[161] the Court of Appeal thought that the observations in *Pettitt v Pettitt* as to the weakness of the presumption of advancement between husband and wife applied equally to father and child.

Despite the frequency of these comments, they should not be given too much weight. Comments on the weakness or strength of a presumption would only have meaning if they meant that, when deciding what a transferor actually intended, judges applied a standard of proof different to the balance of probabilities. Yet the modern approach is to treat both presumptions as "long stops" that supply the answer only when a finding cannot be made on the evidence before the court.[162] References to the strength of presumptions should be seen in this light: the particular circumstances of a case may mean that a gift was very likely or very unlikely to have been intended, but that does not mean the presumption itself is strong or weak. Those circumstances are simply part of the evidence that the court may take into account.

iii. Facts Needed to Rebut.   The rebuttal of either presumption will normally **11–033** be achieved by introducing evidence of whatever arrangement was positively intended. Most obviously, the presumption of resulting trust can be rebutted by evidence of the transferor's intention to make a gift. Evidence of an intended loan will rebut both a presumption of advancement and a presumption of resulting

---

[157] Voluntary conveyances of land aside: above, para.11–021.

[158] (1875) L.R. 10 Ch. App. 343 at 352.

[159] [1955] A.C. 431 at 445, citing *Finch v Finch* (1808) 15 Ves. 43. See also *Chettiar v Chettiar* [1962] A.C. 294.

[160] [1970] A.C. 777 at 814, citing *Fowkes v Pascoe* (1875) L.R. 10 Ch. App. 343 and *Re Gooch* (1890) 62 L.T. 384. See also *Murless v Franklin* (1818) 1 Swans. 13; 36 E.R. 278.

[161] [1995] 2 F.L.R. 114. See also *Laskar v Laskar* [2008] 1 W.L.R 2695 at [20].

[162] See *Lohia v Lohia* [2001] EWCA Civ 1691 at [19]–[21]; *Kyriakides v Pippas* [2004] 2 F.C.R. 434 at [76]; *Pecore v Pecore* [2007] 1 S.C.R. 795 at [42]–[44]; *M v M* [2013] EWHC 2534 (Fam) at [176]. The presumption of resulting trust was described as a "long stop" by Lord Upjohn in *Vandervell v IRC* [1967] 2 A.C. 291 at 313.

trust,[163] and evidence of a declared trust for a third party will also rebut either presumption. The outcomes in these cases will reflect what was intended: evidence of a gift will mean that the transferee receives the property as a gift; evidence of a loan will mean that the transferee receives property beneficially but subject to a debt; evidence of a declared trust for a third party will mean that the transferee holds the property on that trust.[164]

Nonetheless, it is important to appreciate that the presumptions of advancement and resulting trust respond to the transferor's *intention*, and that a successful rebuttal does not require the transferor's intention to be *effected*. A presumption of resulting trust will be rebutted by evidence that the transferor intended to part with beneficial ownership.[165] To rebut a presumption of advancement, a transferor (or those claiming through him) must prove only that he did not intend a gift. The transferor does not need to prove that he transferred the property on declared and enforceable[166] trusts for himself.

In *McGrath v Wallis*,[167] a house was acquired for the occupation of a family (parents, son and daughter) but was put in the adult son's name to enable a mortgage loan to be obtained (the father being unemployed). The father contributed £34,500 towards the price of £42,995, the balance being raised by the mortgage. The father's solicitors drew up a declaration of trust whereby the beneficial interest was to be held as to 80% for the father and 20% for the son, but, for reasons which were not established, it was never executed. After the death of the parents, the son claimed absolute entitlement, but the Court of Appeal held that the presumption of advancement was rebutted. The parties' intentions were to hold in shares proportionate to their contributions. The decisive features were that the son alone was acceptable as mortgagor (which alone was probably enough to rebut the presumption); there was no evidence that the father had instructed the solicitors not to proceed with the declaration; and there was no reason why the father, who was only 63 at the time and not ill, should wish to give the house to the son.

In *Warren v Gurney*,[168] a father bought a house for his daughter, who was shortly to get married, to live in. The conveyance was taken in the name of the daughter, but the father retained the title deeds. On his death 15 years later, the daughter claimed to be the beneficial owner of the house. The Court of Appeal held that there was a presumption of advancement in her favour, but that it had been rebutted by the fact of the retention of the title deeds, accompanied by evidence contemporaneous with the purchase in 1929.

---

[163] *Bennet v Bennet* (1879) 10 Ch.D. 474; cf. J. Mee (2014) 73 C.L.J. 86 at 98.

[164] Assuming that trust can be enforced. The analysis when an intended trust for a third party cannot be enforced is complicated: see above, para.6–006.

[165] *Westdeutsche Landesbank Girozentrale v Islington LBC* [1996] A.C. 669 at 708; *Aroso v Coutts & Co* [2001] W.T.L.R. 797; W. Swadling (1996) 16 L.S. 133; P. Millett (1998) 114 L.Q.R. 399 at 402.

[166] Note the Law of Property Act 1925 s.53(1)(b); above, para.6–003. Interestingly, Lord Nottingham apparently thought that trusts of land arising on the rebuttal of a presumption of advancement *would* require writing under the Statute of Frauds: see *Elliot v Elliot* (1677), reported in D.E.C. Yale (ed.), *Lord Nottingham's Chancery Cases* (1957 & 1961), case 751.

[167] [1995] 2 F.L.R. 114; criticised in J. Dewar (1995) 25 Fam. Law 552.

[168] [1944] 2 All E.R. 472; see also *Pettitt v Pettitt* [1970] A.C. 777.

It will be noted that, in both *McGrath v Wallis* and *Warren v Gurney*, presumptions of advancement were rebutted by evidence that would not satisfy s.53(1)(b) of the Law of Property Act 1925.[169] The presumptions were not rebutted by evidence of declared, enforceable trusts for the fathers; they were rebutted by evidence that the fathers did not intend gifts. The outcomes were not express trusts for the fathers; they were resulting trusts for them. This is interesting as a matter of principle because, in advancement cases, equity has no reason to second-guess the legal outcome. As Ashburner put it, "there is, strictly speaking, no presumption of advancement. The child or wife has the legal title. The fact of his being a child or wife of the purchaser prevents any equitable presumption from arising".[170] Or, in the words of the High Court of Australia, it is "called a presumption of advancement but it is rather the absence of any reason for assuming that a trust arose or in other words that the equitable right is not at home with the legal title".[171] Be that as it may, it is clear that rebuttal of the presumption of advancement depends on a proved lack of a positive intention to make a gift. It may be said that an underlying presumption of resulting trust springs back up on rebuttal of the presumption of advancement,[172] or it may be said that the proved lack of intention to benefit itself grounds a resulting trust.[173] Either way, rebuttal of the presumption of advancement does not require the successful establishment of another intended outcome (although that will, a fortiori, rebut the presumption too).

11–034

iv. Admissibility of Transferor's Statements. In *Shephard v Cartwright*,[174] C caused shares in companies he was promoting to be allotted to himself, his wife and his three children in 1929. The companies made considerable profits and in 1934 a public company was formed; the original shareholders received partly new shares and partly cash for their old shares. C, in fact, controlled the whole family wealth, and the shares and money were divided between his wife and children for tax reasons. The wife and children at all times acquiesced in C's activities, and signed powers of attorney and powers to withdraw money at his wish.

11–035

By 1936, the cash had all been withdrawn by C and spent. Dividends on the shares allotted to the children were, however, treated as the income of the children, not the income of C. The House of Lords upheld a claim by the children

---

[169] See also *Chaudhary v Chaudhary* [2013] EWCA Civ 758 at [35] (presumption of advancement in respect of a contribution to the purchase of land rebutted because the transferor "must have subjectively intended that the £5,000 would be for their benefit").

[170] W. Ashburner, *Principles of Equity* (London: Butterworth & Co, 1902), pp.148–149. See also W. Swadling (2008) 124 L.Q.R. 72; J. Glister (2011) 33 Syd. L.R. 39.

[171] *Martin v Martin* (1959) 110 C.L.R. 297 at 303.

[172] See *Brown v Brown* (1993) 31 N.S.W.L.R. 582 at 589: "[if] there is no presumption of advancement or the presumption of advancement is rebutted in evidence, then the exception does not apply and the basic presumption operates".

[173] Which seems a simpler explanation: see Chambers, *Resulting Trusts* (1997), pp.32–33; R. Chambers in C. Mitchell (ed.), *Constructive and Resulting Trusts* (2010) Ch.9, pp.285–286; note *Hodgson v Marks* [1971] Ch. 892, discussed above, para.11–021; and see Lord Sumption's explanation of *Tinsley v Milligan* [1994] 1 A.C. 340 in *Patel v Mirza* [2016] UKSC 42; [2017] A.C. 467 at [238] (albeit that Lord Sumption's is a minority opinion).

[174] [1955] A.C. 431.

against C's estate to recover the cash drawn by him on their bank accounts. The onus of rebutting the presumption of advancement lay on C's executors, and there was nothing in C's conduct that was truly inconsistent with the presumption. The House of Lords also applied the rule that evidence of declarations and conduct subsequent to the original transaction is admissible only against the party making them, though those made at the time of the original transaction are admissible for or against him. This has become known as the "rule in *Shephard v Cartwright*".

It has been doubted whether this principle, which was based on the law of evidence at that time, has any further role.[175] In *Lavelle v Lavelle*,[176] Lord Phillips MR said:

> "it is not satisfactory to apply rigid rules of law to the evidence that is admissible to rebut the presumption of advancement. Plainly, self-serving statements or conduct of a transferor, who may long after the transaction be regretting earlier generosity, carry little or no weight. But words or conduct more proximate to the transaction itself should be given the significance that they naturally bear as part of the overall picture."

Since *Lavelle v Lavelle*, courts have occasionally applied the strict rule in *Shephard v Cartwright* without criticism.[177] However, it appears that *Lavelle* was not cited in those cases. When *Lavelle* has been cited, it has been followed on the point.[178]

11–036   **v. Transfers for Unlawful Purposes.**   A further question is whether a transferor who has put property in the name of the transferee to achieve an unlawful purpose may rebut the presumption of advancement by proving his real intention. If the relevant presumption is that of resulting trust, the question is whether he may rely on it in spite of the illegality.

Until recently, the position was that a transferor could not rely on evidence of an illegal purpose to establish his or her claim. However, the presence of an illegal purpose would not frustrate a claim that could be established without reference to that illegal purpose. The point was shown by *Tinsley v Milligan*.[179]

> Two women purchased a house together but agreed to put it only into the name of one of them (the claimant) in order to facilitate fraudulent claims to housing benefit by the other (the defendant). Both were parties to the fraud, which was perpetrated over several years, but had now ceased. Eventually the claimant sought to evict the defendant.

The House of Lords held that the defendant could assert ownership of her equitable interest. The operative presumption was that of a resulting trust. The defendant merely had to found her claim on that presumption and not on any illegality. In the words of Lord Browne-Wilkinson, a claimant "is entitled to

---

[175] See E. Fung (2006) 122 L.Q.R. 651.

[176] [2004] 2 F.C.R. 418 at [19].

[177] *Antoni v Antoni* [2007] W.T.L.R. 1335 (P.C.); *Ben Hashem v Ali Shayif* [2009] 1 F.L.R. 115.

[178] *Close Invoice Finance Ltd v Abaowa* [2010] EWHC 1920 (QB); *M v M* [2013] EWHC 2534 (Fam). See also M. Yip and J. Lee [2013] Conv. 431 at 437.

[179] [1994] 1 A.C. 340.

recover if he is not forced to plead or rely on the illegality, even if it emerges that the title on which he relied was acquired in the course of carrying through an illegal transaction".[180]

The reasoning in *Tinsley v Milligan* meant that the presumptions of resulting trust and advancement operated in rather sharp fashion. This was because a transfer from a husband to wife, or parent to child, would attract a presumption of advancement. If that transfer had been made for some illegal purpose, the transferor could not raise that illegal purpose in order to rebut the presumption of advancement.[181] However, if the parties stood in a relationship that attracted a presumption of resulting trust, as did the women in *Tinsley v Milligan*, then the transferor could recover because he or she would not need to rely on the illegal purpose; simply establishing a relevant transfer or purchase in the other's name would suffice to raise a presumption of resulting trust. The outcome therefore depended on the formal[182] relationship between the parties, rather than on their relative blameworthiness or the objective seriousness of their wrongdoing. For these reasons, the decision of the House of Lords was much criticised.[183]

Following a review by the Law Commission,[184] and several instances where the Supreme Court made plain that it wanted to revisit *Tinsley v Milligan*,[185] the opportunity arose in *Patel v Mirza*.[186]   **11–037**

> Mr Mirza proposed a scheme with Mr Patel to place bets on the movement of shares in the Royal Bank of Scotland (RBS). The plan was to rely upon insider information from a contact at the bank who was aware of discussions with the government. Mirza received £620,000 from Patel for placing the bets ahead of an expected statement from the Chancellor of the Exchequer which would have an effect on the price of RBS shares. This agreement was an offence under Criminal Justice Act 1993, s.52, as a conspiracy to commit insider trading. In the event, the bets were never placed and the Chancellor's statement was never made. Patel brought a claim to recover the substantial sum which he had paid to Mirza. Mirza argued that he could rely on the defence of illegality.

---

[180] [1994] 1 A.C. 340 at 376.
[181] See *Re Emery's Investment Trusts* [1959] Ch. 410; *Gascoigne v Gascoigne* [1918] 1 K.B. 223 (transfers from husband to wife); *Chettiar v Chettiar* [1962] A.C. 294; *Collier v Collier* [2003] W.T.L.R. 617 (transfers from father to child). Note the "repentance" exception; below, para.11–038; and also Lord Sumption's explanation that the lack of an intention to make a gift, regardless of the reason, would properly rebut the presumption of advancement: *Patel v Mirza* [2017] A.C. 467 at [238]; see above, para.11–034.
[182] See above, para.11.031.
[183] R. Thornton (1993) 52 C.L.J. 394; M. Lunney (1993) 7 T.L.I. 114; M. Halliwell [1994] Conv. 62 and [2004] Conv. 439; H. Stowe (1994) 57 M.L.R. 441; R. Buckley (1994) 110 L.Q.R. 3. For a different analysis, see N. Enonchong (1995) 111 L.Q.R. 135. Later cases followed *Tinsley*, but without enthusiasm: see e.g. *Silverwood (Geoffrey) (Executor of the Estate of Daisy Silverwood) v Silverwood (Arnold)* (1997) 74 P. & C.R. 453 at 458; *Lowson v Coombes* [1999] Ch. 373 at 385; *Collier v Collier* [2003] W.T.L.R. 617.
[184] Law Com. No. 320, *The Illegality Defence* (2010); P. Davies [2010] Conv. 282; D. Sheehan [2010] L.M.C.L.Q. 543.
[185] See *Hounga v Allen* [2014] 1 W.L.R. 2889; *Les Laboratoires Servier v Apotex Inc* [2014] UKSC 55; [2015] 1 A.C. 430 at [64]; *Jetivia SA v Bilta (UK) Ltd (In Liquidation)* [2015] UKSC 23; [2016] A.C. 1 at [15].
[186] [2017] A.C. 467. The broader ramifications of the case are considered in Ch.14 below.

The Supreme Court unanimously held that Mr Patel could recover the money. The majority disapproved of the "reliance" test in *Tinsley v Milligan*[187]; that test was thought to be arbitrary because its application depended upon what the claimant had to prove, rather than the illegality in question. Instead, the Supreme Court embraced a three stage "range of factors" approach. Lord Toulson, giving the leading judgment for the majority,[188] said:

> "The essential rationale of the illegality doctrine is that it would be contrary to the public interest to enforce a claim if to do so would be harmful to the integrity of the legal system ... In assessing whether the public interest would be harmed in that way, it is necessary a) to consider the underlying purpose of the prohibition which has been transgressed and whether that purpose will be enhanced by denial of the claim, b) to consider any other relevant public policy on which the denial of the claim may have an impact and c) to consider whether denial of the claim would be a proportionate response to the illegality, bearing in mind that punishment is a matter for the criminal courts."[189]

On the facts of the case, Mr Patel had satisfied the usual requirements of a claim for unjust enrichment. Taking into account the range of factors that Lord Toulson identified, the majority concluded that it would not harm the integrity of the justice system to allow Mr Patel to enforce that claim. Lord Kerr put the point thus:

> "[W]hy should Mr Mirza's wrongful retention of Mr Patel's money not be weighed against the undoubted illegality on the part of Mr Patel in entering an agreement to wrongly benefit from Mr Mirza's claimed ability to obtain access to insider information? If one concentrates on the illegal nature of the contract to the exclusion of other considerations, an incongruous result in legal and moral terms may be produced. This can be avoided by taking into account and giving due weight to the second and third of Lord Toulson JSC's considerations *viz* countervailing public policies which would be wrongly discounted by denial of the claim and the proportionality of refusing to acknowledge its legitimacy."[190]

11–038   Prior to *Patel v Mirza*, there was a well-established exception whereby a transferor could rely on evidence of an illegal purpose if he or she had suitably "repented".[191] While genuine repentance was once required,[192] eventually the doctrine depended simply on the illegal purpose not having been carried out.[193] In

---

[187] Above, para.11–036.

[188] The majority consisted of Lord Toulson, Lady Hale, Lord Kerr (who gave a short concurring opinion), Lord Wilson, Lord Hodge and Lord Neuberger (who gave a concurring opinion with some further reflections). Even those Justices who were not attracted to Lord Toulson's "range of factors" approach—Lords Mance, Clarke and Sumption—and who favoured the retention of some form of reliance test, considered that the operation of the test in cases such as *Collier v Collier* [2003] W.T.L.R. 617 was inappropriate.

[189] [2017] A.C. 467 at [120].

[190] [2017] A.C. 467 at [127].

[191] See generally I. Samet in C. Mitchell (ed.), *Constructive and Resulting Trusts* (2010), Ch.12.

[192] See, e.g., *Groves v Groves* (1829) 3 Y. & J. 163; *Parkinson v College of Ambulance Ltd* [1925] 2 K.B. 1 at 16. This was rejected by Millett LJ in *Tribe v Tribe* [1996] Ch. 107 at 135: "I would hold that genuine repentance is not required. Justice is not a reward for merit; restitution should not be confined to the penitent". But the position may be different in Singapore: see *Ochroid Trading Ltd v Chua Siok Lui (trading as VIE Import & Export)* [2018] SGCA 5 at [171]–[176]: "[a]s presently advised, we are of the view that there must be genuine and voluntary withdrawal".

[193] Including not carried out in part: see *Q v Q* [2009] 1 F.L.R. 935; M. Pawlowski [2009] Conv. 145 (purpose partly carried out by making false statements in tax returns).

Sekhon v Alissa,[194] for example, a mother who had a house conveyed into her daughter's name was able to establish beneficial ownership where her alleged purpose of capital gains tax evasion had not been carried out simply because the house had not yet been sold. In *Tribe v Tribe*,[195] a father expected to be made liable for damage caused to property of which he was tenant. The man transferred shares to his son in order to deceive the landlord as to his assets and thereby safeguard them. In fact the matter of the repairs was resolved without resort to deception. When the son claimed to be entitled to the shares, the Court of Appeal held that the presumption of advancement was rebutted by evidence of the father's intentions, which were not consistent with a gift to the son. Although his purpose was illegal, the illegality had not been carried out.[196] This was the result even though there was no true "repentance" and the father had not sought to recover the shares until the danger had passed.

The position of the "repentance" exception following *Patel v Mirza* is not clear.[197] Lord Toulson said in his leading judgment that the issue did not need to be discussed,[198] and it may be that any factors relevant to the exception will now fall to be considered under the heads of his Lordship's general schema for assessing claims involving an illegal purpose.[199] Lord Sumption, who disagreed with Lord Toulson's "range of factors" approach, preferred to analyse the repentance exception as identifying circumstances when restitution would be awarded to prevent the recipient's unjust enrichment. If the purpose of a payment is illegal, it will not be enforceable; therefore, to the extent the payment has not actually been used in satisfaction of that purpose, the basis for the payment must fail.[200]

---

[194] [1989] 2 F.L.R. 94. The presumption was of resulting trust but the case predated *Tinsley v Milligan* [1994] 1 A.C. 340.

[195] [1996] Ch. 107; criticised S. Cretney (1996) 26 Fam. Law 30; G. Virgo (1996) 55 C.L.J. 23; F. Rose (1996) 112 L.Q.R. 386; P. Pettit (1996) 10 T.L.I. 51; N. Enonchong [1996] R.L.R. 78.

[196] *Perpetual Executors and Trustees Association of Australia Ltd v Wright* (1917) 23 C.L.R. 185 was applied.

[197] The Court of Appeal had applied the exception in allowing the claimant to recover: see *Patel v Mirza* [2014] EWCA Civ 1047; [2015] Ch. 271. The Supreme Court agreed with the result but for different reasons.

[198] [2017] A.C. 467 at [116].

[199] Compare G. Virgo (2016) 22 T. & T. 1090 at 1097; A. Burrows (2017) 70 C.L.P. 55 at 60. See generally S. Green and A. Bogg (eds.) *Illegality After Patel v Mirza* (Oxford: Hart Publishing, 2018).

[200] [2017] A.C. 467 at [246]–[250].

CHAPTER 12

CONSTRUCTIVE TRUSTS

1. GENERAL

A CONSTRUCTIVE trust is one which arises by operation of law, and not by reason of the intention of the parties, express or implied.[1]   **12–001**

> It is impossible to prescribe exhaustively the circumstances sufficient to create a constructive trust but it is possible to recognise particular factual circumstances that will do so and also to recognise other factual circumstances that will not.[2]

---

[1] For a different view, see C. Rickett (1999) 18 N.Z.U.L.R. 305.

[2] *Yeoman's Row Management Ltd v Cobbe* [2008] 1 W.L.R. 1752 at 1769 (Lord Scott).

"there are few areas in which the law has been so completely obscured by confused categorisation and terminology as the law relating to constructive trustees."[3]

The constructive trust has been "a ready means of developing our property law in modern times."[4] Broadly, the principle provides that, if a person holds a property in circumstances where in equity and good conscience it should be held or enjoyed by someone else, he will be compelled to hold the property on trust for that other person.[5] Such a statement can be criticised as being too general to be helpful. The historical development of this area of equity can be viewed as having developed pragmatically, relying on the precedents and paying too little attention to general principle: "constructive trusts are often regarded as the workhorses of equity".[6] In the middle of the 20th century, a constructive trust was used as a means of reaching a desired result over a wide variety of cases; constructive trusts of a "new model",[7] "wherever justice and good conscience require it"[8]: that "new model" is now consigned to history.[9] Modern developments have caused Lord Millett to say that "the language of constructive trust has become such a fertile source of confusion that it would be better if it were abandoned".[10] The confusion could be avoided if the term were to be confined to "a situation in which it would be unconscionable for one party to deny the other's beneficial proprietary interest in a particular and identified property".[11] Finally, the court will not impose a constructive trust if it would be inconsistent with an express trust whose terms cover the situation.[12]

As will be seen, the Supreme Court has endeavoured to clarify the terminology in this area.[13] The liability of "strangers to the trust"—third parties—has historically been described as being that of a "constructive trustee", but it is now properly categorised as a personal liability in equity. Those claims are dealt with separately in Ch.25.

---

[3] *Williams v Central Bank of Nigeria* [2014] UKSC 10; [2014] A.C. 1189 at [7] (Lord Sumption JSC).

[4] *Sen v Headley* [1991] Ch. 425 at 440 (Nourse LJ).

[5] *Soar v Ashwell* [1893] 2 Q.B. 390; Lord Millett [1999] 14 *Amicus Curiae* 4; Waters, *The Constructive Trust* (London: Athlone Press, 1964); Oakley, *Constructive Trusts*, 3rd edn, (London: Sweet & Maxwell, 1996); Elias, *Explaining Constructive Trusts* (The Lawbook Exchange Ltd, 2002); Mitchell (ed.), *Constructive and Resulting Trusts* (London: Hart Publishing, 2010); Liew, *Rationalising Constructive Trusts* (London: Hart Publishing, 2017).

[6] M. Dixon [2017] Conv. 89 at 92.

[7] *Eves v Eves* [1975] 1 W.L.R. 1338 at 1341.

[8] *Hussey v Palmer* [1972] 1 W.L.R. 1286 at 1290, per Lord Denning MR.

[9] Below, paras 12–026—12–031.

[10] (1995) 9 T.L.I. 35 at 38.

[11] (1995) 9 T.L.I. 35 at 39. See also *Paragon Finance Plc v DB Thakerar & Co (A Firm)* [1999] 1 All E.R. 401 at 409.

[12] *Pankhania v Chandegra* [2012] EWCA Civ 1438; *Whitlock v Moree* [2017] UKPC 44 per Lord Briggs at [24].

[13] In *Williams v Central Bank of Nigeria* [2014] UKSC 10; [2014] A.C. 1189 and *Angove's Pty Ltd v Bailey* [2016] UKSC 47; [2016] 1 W.L.R. 3179. See also D. Jensen in E. Bant and M. Bryan (eds), *Principles of Proprietary Remedies* (Sydney: Thomson Reuters, 2013).

A.   Overlap in Classification

We saw, in discussing the classification of trusts,[14] that there is an overlap **12–002** between resulting and constructive trusts. Normally it makes little practical difference whether a trust is described as constructive or resulting. The formality rules, for example, apply to neither type.[15] But the tendency to merge the two categories makes any definition of a constructive trust even harder to formulate.

> "It has been suggested that nomenclature in this context is unimportant. There is, however, some risk that confusion of terminology may lead to confusion of thought".[16]

Distinctions have been emphasised in the context of the conflict of laws, where it has been said that a resulting trust involves the claim of an equitable owner to assert a continuing proprietary interest in his own property, while a constructive trust may be imposed in appropriate circumstances where a breach of fiduciary obligation has given rise to an equity between the parties.[17] Similarly in the context of family property, where a distinctive species of the "common intention" constructive trust has been developed which is quantified differently from the proportionate shares arising under a resulting trust, the latter now being viewed as inappropriate in the domestic consumer context and possibly further afield.[18]

The constructive trust is usually regarded as a residual category; one which is called into play where the court desires to impose a trust and no other suitable category is available.[19]

B.   Establishing the Existence or the Terms of the Trust

The imposition of a constructive trust is often a determination that previously **12–003** declared trusts are enforceable against someone other than the original trustee, or extend to additional property.[20] Thus, a recipient of trust property, not being a

---

[14] Above, para.2–028.

[15] Law of Property Act 1925 s.53, above, para.6–003.

[16] The Child & Co Oxford Lecture (1984) "The Informal Creation of Interests in Land," at p.4 (Sir Christopher Slade); cf. F. Bates [1982] Conv. 424 at 431.

[17] *Macmillan Inc v Bishopsgate Investment Trust Plc (No.3)* [1995] 1 W.L.R. 978; affirmed on other grounds (to which the distinction was not relevant) at [1996] 1 W.L.R. 387. See also *Westdeutsche Landesbank Girozentrale v Islington LBC* [1996] A.C. 669 at 707 and *Akers v Samba Financial Group* [2017] UKSC 6; [2017] A.C. 424.

[18] *Drake v Whipp* [1996] 1 F.L.R. 826 (lax terminology a "potent source of confusion"); *Stack v Dowden* [2007] 2 A.C. 432; *Jones v Kernott* [2011] UKSC 53; [2012] 1 A.C. 776; *Chan Yuen Lan v See Fong Mun* [2014] 3 S.L.R. 104; H.W. Tang [2015] Conv. 169; *Marr v Collie* [2017] UKPC 17; [2017] 3 W.L.R. 150. See above, para.11–025 and Ch.13, below.

[19] Examples include *James v Williams* [2000] Ch. 1 (intestacy beneficiary who took possession of land was constructive trustee for co-beneficiaries so that no limitation period applied); cf. *Nolan v Nolan* [2004] W.T.L.R. 1261; *Ord v Upton* [2000] Ch. 352; *De Bruyne v De Bruyne* [2010] W.T.L.R. 1525. See generally E. Bant and M. Bryan (eds), *Principles of Proprietary Remedies* (Sydney: Thomson Reuters, 2013).

[20] Bowen LJ in *Soar v Ashwell* [1893] 2 Q.B. 390 at 396. This point remains valid, but Bowen LJ's dicta were clarified insofar as they relate to limitation by the majority of the Supreme Court in *Williams v Central Bank of Nigeria* [2014] UKSC 10; [2014] A.C. 1189, see e.g. Lord Neuberger PSC at [74]–[89].

bona fide purchaser without notice from a trustee, takes the property subject to the existing trusts. A trustee who makes an improper profit holds the profit on the trusts which had previously been declared of the property out of which the profit was made.[21] It may be, however, that the constructive trust doctrine will determine the trusts on which a person, admittedly a trustee, will hold the property. Thus, in a case of mutual wills, the executor of the second party to die needs to know whether he holds on the trusts of that party's will, or under the agreement which was the basis of the mutual wills.[22] Thus the constructive trust covers situations in which either the existence of the trusteeship or the terms of the trust or both are determined by operation of law.

C. The Duties of a Constructive Trustee

12–004   The duties and liabilities of a constructive trustee are not necessarily the same as those of an express trustee. A decision that X holds as constructive trustee does not necessarily subject him to the usual trustees' duties in respect of investments, etc.[23] If a person purchases property with constructive but not actual notice of a trust, the beneficiaries may enforce the trust against him; but if he is not informed of their claims for some time, it seems that he will not be subjected also to liability for failure to invest in trustee investments and to the usual standard of care which is required of express trustees in the performance of their duties.[24] The duties of a constructive trustee have not been firmly established; they probably vary with the circumstances and will be greater for a fraudulent trustee than for others.

D. Distinction Between Constructive Trusts, Accountability and Proprietary Remedies

12–005   Circumstances giving rise to a constructive trust may also give rise to other remedies. Strictly speaking, a person can only be a trustee, express or constructive, if there is vested in her certain property which she holds upon trust.[25] Constructive trusteeship should be distinguished from an equitable proprietary remedy after tracing, and personal actions in equity, whether against a fiduciary for an account or against strangers to the trust. They are considered in more detail in subsequent chapters.[26]

---

[21] Below, para.12–007.

[22] Below, paras 12–012—12–018.

[23] See *Lonrho Plc v Fayed (No.2)* [1992] 1 W.L.R. 1 at 12. See also *Jasmine Trustees Ltd v Wells & Hind (A Firm)* [2007] 1 All E.R. 1142, discussing the liabilities of a "trustee de son tort." Below, paras 25–029—25–031.

[24] For examples of where the duty to invest arises, see C. Mitchell and S. Watterson in C. Mitchell (ed.), *Constructive and Resulting Trusts* (Oxford: Hart Publishing, 2010), pp.138–140.

[25] *Re Barney* [1892] 2 Ch. 265 at 272; *Westdeutsche Landesbank Girozentrale v Islington LBC* [1996] A.C. 669. "Possession is the hallmark of a trustee's role and shapes a trustee's duties" per Lord Mance in *Williams v Central Bank of Nigeria* [2014] UKSC 10 at [161] (dissenting); *Angove's Pty Ltd v Bailey* [2016] UKSC 47; [2016] 1 W.L.R. 3179 at [29].

[26] Below, Chs 22, 25 and 26.

Where a trustee (express or constructive) has had trust property vested in him but has wrongfully disposed of it, he will commonly be regarded as retaining his status as trustee. Subject to what is said below concerning tracing, the absence of trust property means that the remedy against him is personal only. Where, however, no trust property has ever been vested in the defendant (as where liability arises from dishonestly assisting the trustees in a breach of trust),[27] he cannot properly be called a trustee, constructive or otherwise. The remedy against him is personal only. The defendant is *accountable*; he is not a constructive trustee of any property. After some period of doubt, chiefly in the context of applicable limitation periods,[28] it has now been confirmed at the highest level that dishonest assistants and knowing recipients are not constructive trustees.[29] If the defendant has insufficient assets, the claimant will be unable to obtain compensation in full.

Separately, it may be possible to show that the property, wrongly obtained and disposed of, is now represented by money or by some other property in the trustee's or a third party's hands. This process of identification is called "tracing", and it may allow the beneficiary to go on to make a proprietary claim in respect of the substitute property.[30]

The advantages of tracing the money (or other property) in this way are twofold.[31] First, if the defendant should become insolvent, the claimant takes in priority to the general creditors, for the money traced is trust money, and is kept out of the defendant's insolvency.[32] Secondly, if the money has been invested successfully by the defendant, the claimant is entitled to a share of the investments which is proportionate to the share which the trust money contributed to the invested fund.[33]

A distinction between constructive trusteeship and susceptibility to the tracing process is that the latter may be available against a person who is not liable as constructive trustee. For example, where trust property is transferred to an innocent volunteer, i.e. a person who is not a purchaser and who thus takes subject to the trust but who has neither actual nor constructive knowledge of it, the volunteer is apparently not liable as constructive trustee, but the tracing process for an equitable claim lies against him while he still has the property or its identifiable proceeds.[34]

There are thus three separate matters to consider in such situations: constructive trusts, proprietary remedies, and personal actions. They are all inter-related, but each is distinct. Many decisions have failed to make these distinctions, or to make clear whether the issue is one of accountability or one of trust,[35] although the matter has recently been clarified at the appellate level.[36]

---

[27] Below, para.25–017.

[28] e.g. *Soar v Ashwell* [1893] 2 Q.B. 390 and *Paragon Finance Plc v DB Thakerar & Co (A Firm)* [1999] 1 All E.R. 401.

[29] *Williams v Central Bank of Nigeria* [2014] UKSC 10; [2014] A.C. 1189; J. Lee (2015) 131 L.Q.R. 39.

[30] Below, Ch.26.

[31] See Lewison LJ in *FHR European Ventures LLP v Mankarious* [2014] 1 Ch. 1 at [14].

[32] e.g. *Re Hallett's Estate* (1880) 13 Ch.D. 696.

[33] e.g. *Re Tilley's WT* [1967] Ch. 1179.

[34] *Re Diplock* [1948] Ch. 465. See discussion below, para.25–004.

[35] *Reading v Attorney General* [1951] A.C. 507; *Boardman v Phipps* [1967] 2 A.C. 46.

This chapter will only examine constructive trusts properly so called. Personal liability, which was traditionally but inappropriately treated as "constructive trusteeship" is addressed in Ch.25. Accountability for profits and the question of liability to proprietary remedies are considered in Chs 22 and 26.

2.   WHEN A CONSTRUCTIVE TRUST ARISES

12–006   Constructive trusts can arise over a wide variety of situations. This section serves to illustrate that variety, with extensive reference to other chapters. Importantly, the analysis of the Supreme Court in three key decisions, *Williams v Central Bank of Nigeria*,[37] *FHR European Ventures LLP v Cedar Capital Partners LLC*,[38] and *Angove's Pty Ltd v Bailey*[39] has resolved and addressed (and in some circumstances resolved) some of the uncertainties as to the scope and availability of the constructive trust.

A.   Unauthorised Profit by a Trustee or Fiduciary

12–007   A fiduciary may not make use of his position to gain a benefit for himself. Trustees, personal representatives and agents[40] are by their position "debarred from keeping a personal advantage derived directly or indirectly out of his fiduciary or quasi-fiduciary position."[41] With other fiduciaries, such as company directors[42] and partners,[43] the question is one of fact whether the benefit was obtained by reason or independently of, the fiduciary relationship. The category of fiduciaries is not closed.[44] These matters are dealt with in Ch.22. We shall there see that a trustee must not renew in his own favour any lease held on trust;[45] nor may he purchase the reversion on any such lease; nor may he purchase the trust property. He must not make any incidental profits out of his trusteeship. In the present context, one example will suffice:

> In *Boardman v Phipps*,[46] the trustees held a minority shareholding in a private company which was not being efficiently managed. Boardman had acted as solicitor to the trust, and was therefore a fiduciary. He decided that the beneficiaries would be in a better position if the trustees had control of the company, but no trust money was available to buy the extra shares. Boardman and one of the beneficiaries therefore bought the necessary shares themselves and reorganised the company. All this was done in good faith and with the object of enhancing the trust holding. Both the personal and the trust holdings increased in value. A majority of the

---

[36] *Sinclair Investments (UK) Ltd v Versailles Trade Finance Ltd (In Administrative Receivership)* [2012] Ch. 453; *Sinclair* has been overruled in key respects by the Supreme Court (below, Ch.22, Part 3), but is not affected on this point; *FHR European Ventures LLP v Cedar Capital Partners LLC* [2014] UKSC 45; [2015] A.C. 250.

[37] [2014] UKSC 10; [2014] A.C. 1189.

[38] [2014] UKSC 45; [2015] A.C. 250.

[39] [2016] UKSC 47; [2016] 1 W.L.R. 3179.

[40] *De Bussche v Alt* (1878) 8 Ch.D. 286 at 310; *Boardman v Phipps* [1967] 2 A.C. 46.

[41] *Re Biss* [1903] 2 Ch. 40 at 56.

[42] Below, para.22–019.

[43] *Clegg v Fishwick* (1849) 1 Mac. & G. 294.

[44] *English v Dedham Vale Properties Ltd* [1978] 1 W.L.R. 93.

[45] *Keech v Sandford* (1726) Sel. Cas. t. King 61.

[46] [1967] 2 A.C. 46, below, paras 22–022—22–024.

House of Lords held that Boardman was constructive trustee of the profit made on his personal shareholding. The opportunity to make the profit arose out of his fiduciary relationship with the trust and certain confidential information had been used in the process. However, compensation was ordered from the trust in recognition of the work and skill involved.

B. The Vendor under a Specifically Enforceable Contract for Sale

A contract for sale is specifically enforceable where the remedy of damages would be inadequate.[47] Contracts relating to personalty are rarely specifically enforceable,[48] as the property may be purchased elsewhere. If this is not so, as in the case of shares in a private company, then the contract will be specifically enforceable.[49] In the present context, however, we are mainly concerned with contracts relating to land. The availability of specific performance means that, in equity, the purchaser is regarded as already the owner. Thus it has many times been said by high authority that a vendor of land, on the conclusion of the contract of sale, becomes a trustee of the land for the purchaser.[50] He must take reasonable care to preserve the property pending completion.[51] Any changes in the nature of the property between contract and completion, for example by fire or flooding, if they occur without the fault of the vendor, are at the purchaser's risk.[52] If the vendor sells to another, he holds the purchase money on trust for the purchaser.[53] Beyond that, however, there is little agreement.[54] It is clear at least that this is not an ordinary trusteeship: the vendor has been described variously as trustee only in a qualified sense[55]; "a quasi-trustee",[56] and "constructive trustee or a trustee *sub modo*".[57] Lord Cairns[58] explained that the trustee was entitled to protect his own interest in the property. Similarly, the vendor is entitled to keep for himself the rents and profits of the land (or dividends in the case of shares[59]) until the date of the completion of the sale,[60] and to retain possession against the purchaser until the purchase price has been paid; and he retains a lien on the land

12–008

---

[47] Below, Ch.27.

[48] P.G. Turner (2012) 128 L.Q.R. 582 at 604.

[49] See *Oughtred v IRC* [1960] A.C. 206; *Neville v Wilson* [1997] Ch. 144; *Michaels v Harley House (Marylebone) Ltd* [2000] Ch. 104; *Hniazdzilau v Vajgel* [2016] EWHC 15 (Ch) at [177].

[50] *Lysaght v Edwards* (1876) 2 Ch.D. 499 at 507; Waters, *The Constructive Trust* (1964), Ch.2; Oakley, *Constructive Trusts* (1996), Ch.6. See further *Nelson v Greening & Sykes (Builders) Ltd* [2008] 1 E.G.L.R. 59.

[51] *Englewood Properties Ltd v Patel* [2005] 1 W.L.R. 1961.

[52] *Paine v Meller* (1801) 6 Ves.Jr. 349. As to insurance, see Law of Property Act 1925 s.47. For the view that the risk does not pass to the purchaser see M. Thompson [1984] Conv. 43.

[53] *Lake v Bayliss* [1974] 1 W.L.R. 1073; *Shaw v Foster* (1872) 5 H.L. 321 at 327; F. Crane (1974) 38 Conv.(N.S.) 357.

[54] Cotton, Brett and James LJJ in *Rayner v Preston* (1881) 18 Ch.D. 1 expressed different views on the situation.

[55] Cotton LJ in *Rayner v Preston* (1881) 18 Ch.D. 1 at 6; *Lysaght v Edwards* (1876) 2 Ch.D. 499 at 506; *Royal Bristol Permanent Building Society v Bomash* (1887) 35 Ch.D. 390 at 397 ("a modified sense"); *Re Hamilton-Snowball's Conveyance* [1959] Ch. 308.

[56] *Cumberland Consolidated Holdings Ltd v Ireland* [1946] K.B. 264 per Lord Greene MR at 269.

[57] *Berkley v Poulett* (1977) 242 E.G. 39 per Stamp LJ at 43.

[58] *Shaw v Foster* (1872) L.R. 5 H.L. 321 at 338.

[59] *J. Sainsbury Plc v O'Connor (Inspector of Taxes)* [1991] S.T.C. 318.

[60] *Cuddon v Tite* (1858) 1 Giff 395.

for the price if the land is conveyed before the price is paid,[61] and time runs under the Limitation Act 1980 against the vendor in respect of possession of the land.[62] The relationship between the parties contains a number of aspects in which they are hostile and the vendor self-interested. The relationship is, therefore, "not a full trust in the classic sense".[63]

The view in the Privy Council has similarly been that the situation is something of a hybrid. In *Jerome v Kelly*,[64] Lord Walker of Gestingthorpe was of the view that it would be[65]

> "wrong to treat an uncompleted contract for the sale of land as equivalent to an immediate, irrevocable declaration of trust (or assignment of beneficial interest) in the land. Neither the seller nor the buyer has unqualified beneficial ownership. Beneficial ownership of the land is in a sense split between the seller and buyer on the provisional assumptions that specific performance is available and that the contract will in due course be completed, if necessary by the court ordering specific performance."

Lord Wilson has since endorsed this dictum, in the case of *Maharaj v Johnson*, noting that "following execution of a contract for sale of land a vendor retains certain temporary rights in relation to it and the better view is that they are proprietary rather than contractual".[66]

Once the date for completion has arrived and the price is paid in full, the vendor must immediately convey. This is an example of a trusteeship arising because the bare legal estate is in one person, and the entire beneficial ownership in another.[67] Until that situation has arisen, it does not seem that any useful purpose is served by stating that the relationship between the parties is one of trustee and beneficiary. The position at law is that they are parties to a contract and no more. In equity additional rights arise by reason of the fact that specific performance is available as a remedy in favour of an innocent party. Equity then treats as done that which ought to be done, and considers the purchaser as being the owner in equity. Hence, where a receiver was appointed upon the vendor company's insolvency before completion, the contract remained specifically enforceable against the receiver as opposed to merely sounding in damages.[68] This is not attributable to any trust, but to the characteristics of a specifically enforceable contract for sale, whereby the equitable interest passes to the purchaser and is not destroyed by the subsequent insolvency of the vendor. The trust cannot be enforced against a purchaser if the contract, being unregistered,

---

[61] *Mackreth v Symmons* (1808) 15 Ves.Jr. 329. See further S. Worthington (1994) 53 C.L.J. 263.

[62] *Bridges v Mees* [1957] Ch. 475; cf. *Hyde v Pearce* [1982] 1 All E.R. 1029.

[63] Roth J in *Luxe Holding Ltd v Midland Resources Holding Ltd* [2010] EWHC 1908 (Ch) at [31], seemingly endorsed on this point by Lord Mance in *Akers* [2017] A.C. 424 at [31].

[64] [2004] UKHL 25; [2004] 1 W.L.R. 1409.

[65] [2004] 1 W.L.R. 1409 at [32].

[66] *Maharaj v Johnson (Trinidad and Tobago)* [2015] UKPC 28 at [17].

[67] *Lloyds Bank Plc v Carrick* [1996] 4 All E.R. 630; M. Thompson [1996] Conv. 295; S. Cretney (1997) 27 Fam. Law 95; N. Hopkins (1998) 61 M.L.R. 486. cf. *Baker v Craggs* [2016] EWHC 3250 (Ch).

[68] *Freevale Ltd v Metrostore (Holdings) Ltd* [1984] 1 All E.R. 495 (a receiver, unlike a liquidator, has no statutory right to disclaim contracts); D. Milman and S. Coneys [1984] Conv. 446; *Re Coregrange Ltd* [1984] B.C.L.C. 453.

does not bind him.[69] In many other respects the contractual nature of the relationship is apparent; each party is continuing to guard his own interests against the other in a way which is quite inconsistent with the existence of the relationship of trustee and beneficiary.

A further question is whether the vendor becomes trustee for a sub-purchaser, if the purchaser has entered into a contract to sell to the sub-purchaser. In such a case, the sub-purchaser, by virtue of his contract with the purchaser, is entitled to specific performance and is treated as the owner in equity. In *Berkley v Earl Poulett*[70] the vendor, with the concurrence of the purchaser, had allegedly allowed certain fixtures to be taken away. The sub-purchaser claimed that the vendor was in breach of the trustee's duty to take proper care of the property. A majority of the Court of Appeal considered that no fiduciary duty was owed to the sub-purchaser. It was not that the vendor was a trustee and therefore had fiduciary duties; rather that the vendor owed duties to the purchaser and was labelled a trustee. A sub-purchaser's right is to have the purchaser enforce the contract against the vendor.

No doubt it is too late now to say that the relationship between vendor and purchaser is not that of trustee and beneficiary,[71] even after the Supreme Court's recent willingness to analyse other traditional constructive trustee areas for the validity of their credentials.[72] For the Justices did consider an attempt to establish a vendor-purchaser constructive trust in *Southern Pacific Mortgages Ltd v Scott*.[73] **12–009**

> The vendor had agreed to sell the interest in her home to a purchaser, who in turn promised that the vendor would be entitled to stay in occupation at a discounted rate, in return for the vendor paying back some of the completion money.[74] This arrangement was not in the contract of sale, however. The purchaser obtained a buy to let mortgage which was inconsistent with the terms of the agreement and with the subsequent grant of tenancy to the vendor. The purchaser then disappeared, defaulting on the loan, and the lender sought possession of the property. The vendor claimed that she had an equitable interest from the moment when the contracts were exchanged, which amounted to an unregistered interest overriding the lender's interests.[75] The Supreme Court held that the order for possession had been correctly made. Lord Collins held:
>
> > "the vendors acquired no more than personal rights against the purchasers when they agreed to sell their properties on the basis of the purchasers promises that they would be entitled to remain in occupation."[76]

---

[69] *Lloyds Bank Plc v Carrick* [1996] 4 All E.R. 630.

[70] (1977) 242 E.G. 39.

[71] cf. Hopkins, *The Informal Acquisition of Rights in Land* (2000), p.64, relying on *Westdeutsche Landesbank Girozentrale v Islington LBC* [1996] A.C. 669.

[72] As in *Williams v Central Bank of Nigeria* [2014] UKSC 10; [2014] 2 W.L.R. 355.

[73] The appeal was a test case and is also known as *Re North East Property Buyers Litigation* [2014] UKSC 52; [2015] A.C. 385; A. Televantos and L. Maniscalco (2015) 74 C.L.J. 27; N. Hopkins [2015] Conv. 245; P. Sparkes [2015] Conv. 301; S. Lee [2015] P.C.B. 77.

[74] These sale and rent back transactions later became a regulated activity under s.19 of the Financial Services and Markets Act 2000 and the then Financial Services Authority in 2012 reported that such transactions, viewed as unsuitable and potentially exploitative, are now very rare: [2014] UKSC 52, Lord Collins at [3].

[75] By virtue of s.29(2)(a)(ii) of and para.2 of Sch.3 to the Land Registration Act 2002.

[76] [2015] A.C. 385 at [79].

The answer to the question (as framed by Lady Hale DPSC) "Can a prospective purchaser grant proprietary rights before completion?"[77] was "no".[78] In any event, the court expressed some doubt as to the applicability of the trust to the question "whether a contract of sale can have a proprietary effect on parties other than the parties to the contract".[79]

Thus, in *Scott*, there was no scope for a trust to arise on the facts, and the court did not engage with the broader questions about the nature of the interest.

Yet there will remain considerable controversy over this issue and the terminology must still be treated carefully.[80] Unlike other cases of constructive trusts, the element of improper conduct is absent and the situation must, at best, be treated as anomalous.[81] Indeed, Mr. Swadling has argued that the trust is a fiction which "has no rational basis".[82]

The vendor-purchaser trust is well-entrenched in English law, however, and does have its defenders. As Justice McLure has succinctly put it in response to Swadling, "the vendor-purchaser constructive trust is not the (non) functional equivalent of a human appendix".[83] A thorough reconsideration has been offered by Dr Turner,[84] who seeks to defend the vendor-purchaser trust, arguing that the rationale is "to protect the interest that the vendor and purchaser each have in the contract being performed".[85] Turner argues that the vendor-purchaser trust "comprises several equities that can be seen as plural 'responses' to plural 'events'". His approach is thus to conceive of the "trust" as a process throughout which various equities may arise. While not necessarily on all fours with the "single event" focus given the facts in the *Scott* (in which his article was cited),[86] it is submitted that Turner's analysis has much to commend it as resolving some of the uncertainties in this field.

C. Common Intention Constructive Trust

12–010   Constructive trusts are capable of arising in response to the "common intention" of the parties. As we shall see in Ch.13, this species of the trust has been adopted and developed extensively and distinctively in the context of trusts of the family

---

[77] [2015] A.C. 385 at [104].

[78] "To put it another way: you cannot give an interest in land if you have no interest to give, or to carve one out of (nemo dat quod non habet)": M. Dixon [2014] Conv. 461 at 462.

[79] [2015] A.C. 385 at [65].

[80] P.G. Turner (2012) 128 L.Q.R. 582 "Subject to the proviso that any answer to the question of whether a 'trust' exists depends on the purpose for which the question is asked, and subject likewise to linguistic propriety, a reader of those judicial statements owes a duty to give them sense."

[81] See W. Swadling in Degeling and Edelman (eds), *Equity in Commercial Law* (Sydney: Lawbook Co, 2005), Ch.18.

[82] W. Swadling [2011] C.L.P. 399; see also *Taylor v Taylor* [2017] EWHC 1080 (Ch); [2017] 4 W.L.R. 83 per Judge Paul Matthews at [46]: "To the extent that it is properly to be regarded as a trust at all, the constructive trust arising on a contract to purchase land is simply a form of equitable protection for the purchaser".

[83] C. McClure in E. Bant and M. Bryan (eds), *Principles of Proprietary Remedies* (2013) Ch.8.

[84] P.G. Turner (2012) 128 L.Q.R. 582. See also P.G. Turner [2012] L.M.C.L.Q. 549.

[85] (2012) 128 L.Q.R. 582 at 584.

[86] *Southern Pacific Mortgages Ltd v Scott* [2015] A.C. 385 by Lord Collins at [60].

home. The potential for such a trust being found in other contexts has been confirmed by the Court of Appeal in *Matchmove Ltd v Dowding*[87]:

> Matchmove was a company operated by a Mr Francis, who was formerly a friend of the claimants. Matchmove planned to buy a property containing a plot of land and an adjacent meadow, and to divide the plot of land into two separate plots. The parties made an oral agreement for the purchase of a property that comprised a building plot and a meadow. A written contract was agreed for the building plot, but not for the meadow. The claimants paid one third of the total purchase price, and also made various payments in respect of a legal dispute over a right of way over the meadow with a third party. It was argued that in the absence of a written contract, the Law of Property (Miscellaneous Provisions) Act 1989, s.2 was an obstacle to the claim in respect of the meadow. The Court of Appeal held that the meadow was held on constructive trust for the claimants, as the judge had found that the parties intended their oral agreement to be "binding immediately".[88] Drawing upon previous authority,[89] it was agreed that a common intention constructive trust could arise:
>
> > "where (i) there was an express agreement between parties as to the ownership of property (ii) which was relied upon by the claimant (iii) to his or her detriment such that (iv) it would be unconscionable for the defendant to deny the claimant's ownership of the property.[90]"

The effect of recognising a constructive trust on these facts is that the lack of writing is not an obstacle (by virtue of s.2(5) of the 1989 Act). Dixon has criticised the approach in *Matchmove* as looking "very much like a remedial response to bad behaviour that is conveniently called a constructive trust to be exempt from s.2(1) of the 1989 Act".[91] We shall see further examples of constructive trusts which are said to arise in response to "common intention" in the remainder of this chapter.

D.   *Pallant v Morgan*

A constructive trust has been recognised as arising in order to give effect to what is called the "*Pallant v Morgan* equity"[92]: the basic circumstances involve A and B informally agreeing that A shall acquire specific property for joint benefit and B in reliance thereon refraining from attempting to acquire it. A cannot thus retain the whole benefit and is constructive trustee of a share for B. The exact juridical nature of this "equity" and the reasons for the trust arising have been matters of considerable recent controversy both in the Court of Appeal and in the academic literature.[93] It seems tolerably clear, however, that it is a constructive trust, on the

12–011

---

[87] [2016] EWCA Civ 1233; [2017] 1 W.L.R. 749 at [32].

[88] [2017] 1 W.L.R. 749 at [35]–[36],

[89] e.g. *Kinane v Mackie-Conteh* [2005] EWCA Civ 45, [2005] 1 W.T.L.R. 345; *Herbert v Doyle* [2010] EWCA Civ 1095.

[90] [2017] 1 W.L.R. 749 at [29].

[91] M. Dixon [2017] Conv. 89 at 92.

[92] *Pallant v Morgan* [1953] Ch. 43,

[93] M. Thompson [2001] Conv. 265; S. Gardner in C. Mitchell (ed), *Constructive and Resulting Trusts* (Oxford: Hart Publishing, 2010); B. McFarlane (2004) 120 L.Q.R. 667; M. Yip (2013) 22 L.S. 549 at 550; J. Grower [2016] Conv. 434.

basis either that it responds to the parties' common intention[94] (along the lines seen in the previous section) or a breach of fiduciary duty by the purchaser.[95]

Chadwick LJ, in explaining *Pallant v Morgan* in *Banner Homes Group PLC v Luff Developments Ltd*[96] took the view that the trust was one of common intention. For the equity to arise, it is necessary for the parties to have agreed to embark on an arrangement which precedes the purchase of property by one of the parties, envisaging that the other party will acquire an interest in the property upon the purchase. Any reservations of options (or the opportunity to reserve one's position) will be taken into account.[97] The claimant must have either acted to their detriment[98] or conferred an advantage on the other defendant.[99] The doctrine was considered in *Generator Developments Ltd v Lidl UK GmbH*.[100]

> The claimant was a property development company and the defendant is a company which operates supermarkets: the parties had been in discussions over the acquisition of an industrial estate in Essex. The founder of Generator was friends with the vendor of the estate. Lidl was described as the "Buyer" of the property, Generator was to be the "Delivery Partner" and seek planning permission. Lidl would then sell the freehold of the property to Generator, who would build flats and a store and lease the store to Lidl. The proposed arrangement was expressed to require Board approval and to be "subject to contract". Generator spent about £30,000 on architects, mechanical and engineering consultants and structural engineers. Generator and Lidl were still negotiating over their agreement when Lidl purchased the property and no longer wished to proceed with the joint venture. It was held that Lidl owned the property outright.

In *Generator*, Lewison LJ noted the "general point that equity will not intervene in a case in which parties are consciously relying on honour alone"[101]: a key question in a *Pallant v Morgan* context is whether the parties intended their agreement to be binding. Although the doctrine may be of commercial utility, it is recognised that it is has the potential to disrupt certainty in commercial contexts, where, as Etherton LJ noted, parties "do not expect their rights to be determined in an 'ambulatory' manner by retrospective examination of their conduct and words over the entire period of their relationship."[102] The negotiations between Generator and Lidl throughout proceeded on the basis that the parties' rights would be finalised by written contracts and that they bore the attendant risks until such contracts were agreed. To recognise a trust in such a context would

---

[94] *Crossco No.4 Unlimited v Jolan Ltd* [2011] EWCA Civ 1619; [2012] 2 All E.R. 754 per Arden LJ at [95].

[95] As Etherton LJ would have analysed it in *Crossco* [2011] EWCA Civ 1619 at [88] (viewing the common intention analysis as "untenable" at [87]); supported by Lewison LJ in *Generator Developments Ltd v Lidl UK GmbH* [2018] EWCA Civ 396 at [71]. However, the majority *in Crossco* (Arden LJ and McFarlane LJ) held that the Court of Appeal was bound by the analysis in *Banner Homes* [2000] Ch. 372.

[96] [2000] Ch. 372 at 398–9; P. Clarke [2000] All E.R. Rev. 245; N. Hopkins [2002] Conv. 35.

[97] *Michael v Phillips* [2017] EWHC 614 (QB).

[98] *Michael v Phillips* [2017] EWHC 614 (QB).

[99] *Kiwak v Reiner* [2017] EWHC 3018 (Ch) at [116]. It is not necessary for there to be a correlation between advantage to the defendant and disadvantage to the claimant: [2000] Ch. 372 at 399.

[100] [2018] EWCA Civ 396.

[101] [2018] EWCA Civ 396 at [63].

[102] *Crossco* [2011] EWCA Civ 1619 per Etheton LJ at [87]; *Cobbe v Yeoman's Row Management Ltd* [2008] 1 W.L.R. 1752 at [68] and [81]; *Generator* [2018] EWCA Civ 396 at [46].

potentially disrupt the proper allocation of risk: "it cannot be unconscionable to exercise a right which has been expressly reserved to both parties by means of the 'subject to contract' formula".[103]

In *Farrar v Miller*,[104] another panel of the Court of Appeal seemed more sanguine about the flexibility of the *Pallant v Morgan* doctrine. At present, the analysis in *Banner Homes* remains authoritative, and *Pallant v Morgan* should be regarded as responding to the common intention of the parties where the criteria are met. However, the fiduciary analysis has weighty judicial support behind it. It is even arguable that *Pallant v Morgan* should not be understood as a distinct doctrine.[105] It is clear that the controversy merits consideration by the Supreme Court.

E.   Mutual Wills[106]

Two persons (often spouses) may agree that, on the death of the first to die, all their property shall be enjoyed by the survivor, and after his or her death by nominated beneficiaries (for example, children of a previous marriage); and may make mutual wills to that effect.[107] The survivor may be given a life interest,[108] an absolute interest[109] or no interest at all.[110] The question is whether, and to what extent, such an agreement controls the devolution of their property.

i.   Agreement Necessary.   Before any remedy can be obtained, an agreement **12–012** to make wills and not to revoke them[111] between the parties must be proved. The agreement must indicate that the wills are to be mutually binding, whether or not expressed in the language of revocation.[112] The standard of proof is the ordinary civil standard (i.e. on balance of probabilities); the evidence must be "clear and satisfactory" and may be extrinsic, as where the agreement is substantiated by

---

[103] [2018] EWCA Civ 396 at [85].

[104] [2018] EWCA Civ 172 per Patten LJ at [88] (also rejecting characterisation of the *Pallant v Morgan* equity as a "remedial constructive trust"; see Part 3 below).

[105] M. Yip (2013) 22 L.S. 549 at 550 "there is no proper jurisprudential basis for this independent doctrine".

[106] C. Rickett (1989) 105 L.Q.R. 534; Oakley, *Constructive Trusts* (1996), 3rd edn, pp.263–274; Cassidy, *Mutual Wills* (Sydney: Federation Press, 2000). *De Bruyne v De Bruyne* [2010] EWCA Civ 519; [2010] 2 F.L.R. 1240 per Patten LJ at [51], endorsed by Coleridge J in *AM v SS v WS* [2014] EWHC 2887 (Fam) at [25]. G.Ll.H. Griffiths [2011] Conv. 511; S. Hudson and B. Sloan in W. Barr (ed.), *Modern Studies in Property Law* (Oxford: Hart Publishing, 2015), Ch.9; Y.K. Liew (2016) 133 L.Q.R. 664; and Y.K. Liew in C. Mitchell and B. Häcker (eds.), *Current Issues in Succession Law* (Oxford: Hart Publishing, 2016); Law Com. CP No. 231, *Making a Will* (2017), Ch.12.

[107] This arrangement should be distinguished from the making of wills which mirror each other's provisions, as considered in the rectification case of *Marley v Rawlings* [2014] UKSC 2; [2015] A.C. 129.

[108] *Dufour v Pereira* (1769) Dick. 419.

[109] *Re Green* [1951] Ch. 148.

[110] *Re Dale (Deceased)* [1994] Ch. 31.

[111] *In the Goods of Heys* [1914] P. 192.

[112] *Re Goodchild (Deceased)* [1997] 1 W.L.R. 1216 (mistaken belief of first testator that wills mutually binding may enable intended beneficiary to claim under the Inheritance (Provision for Family and Dependants) Act 1975 on death of survivor). See also *Re Walters* [2009] Ch. 212.

family conversations.[113] The mere fact that the wills were made simultaneously and in the same form is not, of itself, proof of an agreement although it is a relevant circumstance to be taken into account.[114] The agreement must amount to a clear contract at law, not a mere common understanding.[115] But the court may infer an agreement from the conduct of the parties, the circumstances and the terms of the wills.[116] Preferably the agreement, if there was one, should be recited in the will. The mere making of wills in similar form is not sufficient, as in *Re Oldham*,[117] where Astbury J said[118]:

> "[Each may] have thought it quite safe to trust the other... But that is a very different thing from saying that they bound themselves by a trust that should be operative in all circumstances and in all cases... The fact that the two wills were made in identical terms does not necessarily connote any agreement beyond that of so making them... there is no evidence... that there was an agreement that the trust in the mutual will should in all circumstances be irrevocable by the survivor who took the benefit."

On the other hand, in *Re Cleaver*,[119] the evidence of mutual wills was found in the simultaneity and similarity of the parties' original wills; a pattern of successive wills made together; the faithful terms of the first will made after the husband's death; and the fact that, in family conversations, the wife had regarded herself as under an obligation to leave her estate to the children. A valuable recent consideration of the mutual wills doctrine is the decision of Judge Paul Matthews (sitting as a High Court judge) in *Legg v Burton*[120]:

> A husband and wife made mirror wills, with their estates to pass "absolutely and beneficially and without any sort of trust obligation" to the other and thereafter equally to their two daughters, the claimants. After her husband died, the wife changed her will several times, with her final will leaving small amounts to the claimants but the majority to the defendants (her grandchildren and their partners). At her death, the main asset was the house which she and her husband had owned. The question was whether the terms in the original wills stating "without any trust obligation" prevented a constructive trust arising. It was held that the mutual wills doctrine had given rise to a constructive trust, and that it was capable of arising from a proprietary estoppel rather than a contract alone.[121]

---

[113] *Re Cleaver* [1981] 1 W.L.R. 939; *Re Newey* [1994] 2 N.Z.L.R. 590; C. Rickett [1996] Conv. 136; *Charles v Fraser* [2010] W.T.L.R. 1489; *Fry v Densham-Smith* [2011] W.T.L.R. 387.

[114] [1981] 1 W.L.R. 939. Where mirror wills are not intended to be mutual wills, it is desirable for the will to include such a statement, though see now *Legg v Burton* [2017] 4 W.L.R. 186

[115] *Re Goodchild (Deceased)* [1997] 1 W.L.R. 1216; *Birch v Curtis* [2002] 2 F.L.R. 1158; D. Rowell (2003) 43 *Trusts and Estates* 14.

[116] *Dufour v Pereira* (1769) Dick. 419; *Stone v Hoskins* [1905] P. 194; *Re Hagger* [1930] 2 Ch. 190; *Re Green* [1951] Ch. 148. Y.K. Liew (2016) 133 L.Q.R. 664 "Given the centrality of the relevant agreement to the mutual wills doctrine, as well as the extensive legal consequences which flow from the imposition of a constructive trust, courts have been rightly circumspect in inferring agreements."

[117] [1925] Ch. 75.

[118] [1925] Ch. 75 at 88–89; *Gray v Perpetual Trustee Co* [1928] A.C. 391.

[119] [1981] 1 W.L.R. 939.

[120] [2017] EWHC 2088 (Ch); [2017] 4 W.L.R. 186.

[121] [2017] EWHC 2088 (Ch); [2017] 4 W.L.R. 186 at [24]. This approach is consistent with the analysis of Y.K. Liew (2016) 133 L.Q.R. 664 at 674–5 but compare the Law Commission, Law Com. CP No. 231, *Making a Will* (2017), paras 12.6–12.8. For a similar view outwith the mutual wills context, see *Ghazaani v Rowshan* [2015] EWHC 1922 (Ch) at [192]–[193].

This approach makes clear that there is no difficulty in the application of the mutual wills doctrine with s.2 of the Law of Property (Miscellaneous Provisions) Act 1989, which requires a contract for the disposition of an interest in land to be in writing if it is to be binding. Any contract is not binding, but the agreement can still be, not least because the section (by s.2(5)) does not affect constructive trusts.

ii. Remedies on the Contract.   The agreement is binding between the parties. If it is broken by the first party to die, his estate will be liable in damages to the survivor.[122] If the breach is by the second party to die, as by revocation or alteration of his will, it has always been assumed that no remedy could be obtained against him or his estate under the contract. The law which has developed on the subject is based upon a trust which arises in appropriate cases in favour of the beneficiaries. **12–013**

It is arguable that the principle of *Beswick v Beswick*[123] could apply in this situation. The estate of the first to die is in a similar position to Mrs Beswick, the administratrix. It seems that an action for specific performance of the contract would lie by the estate against the survivor or his estate. An examination of the problems which have arisen in treating the interests of the beneficiaries as trusts, as will be seen, makes a contractual solution attractive.[124] The court in *Re Dale (Deceased)*[125] rejected the argument that the second testator could be ordered to make a will in accordance with the contract, or restrained from revoking it. It may remain arguable that specific performance could be obtained to enforce a conveyance of the property.[126]

Until quite recently there could have been no question of the beneficiary suing in contract because of the privity doctrine. It may now be possible for the beneficiary to enforce the contract in his own right under the Contracts (Rights of Third Parties) Act 1999, in the case of contracts between testators made after the Act.[127] The Act does not affect rights or remedies of third parties which are otherwise available, thus the trust solution remains.[128]

iii. Trusts Created by Mutual Wills.   A will is always revocable; an agreement not to revoke it does not make it irrevocable.[129] Thus, if the survivor of an agreement to make mutual wills revokes his will, he will die intestate: and if he makes a new will, that later one will be admitted to probate.[130] But the disposition of his property on his death will be affected by the agreement. For the principle is established that the agreement between the parties, followed by the **12–014**

---

[122] *Robinson v Ommanney* (1883) 23 Ch.D. 285; but not where the revocation of the first will is by the subsequent marriage of the covenantor. See further C. Rickett (1991) 54 M.L.R. 581.
[123] [1968] A.C. 58.
[124] See T. Youdan (1979) 29 U. of Toronto L.J. 390. The executor must be willing to sue. See K. Hodkinson [1982] Conv. 228, suggesting that the ultimate beneficiary should be the executor; C. Rickett (1989) 105 L.Q.R. 534.
[125] [1994] Ch. 31; A. Brierley (1995) 58 M.L.R. 95. *Beswick v Beswick* was not discussed.
[126] Below, para.27–026.
[127] See s.10; C. Davis (2002) 61 C.L.J. 423 at 430. The Act is outlined at para.5–021, above.
[128] s.7(1).
[129] *Vynior's Case* (1609) 8 Co.Rep. 81b.
[130] *Charles v Fraser* [2010] W.T.L.R. 1489 (all non-dispositive parts of the new will are valid).

death of the first party, who has relied on the undertaking of the other party to observe the agreement, creates trusts in favour of the intended beneficiaries, which are enforceable against the property of the survivor.[131] In *Legg v Burton*, Judge Paul Matthews stated[132]: "if there is a mutual will trust, it arises outside the will, and so words such as this in the will would not affect it. In any event, the clause referred to is a standard form clause, regularly included in wills of this kind."

However, a number of difficulties arise concerning the operation of such trusts, as we shall now see.[133]

12–015   *(a) When Does the Trust Arise?*   It has been said that there are three possibilities.[134] When the agreement was made; when the first testator dies; or when the survivor dies. It is clear that no trust exists from the date of the agreement. For either party can revoke or alter his will[135] before either dies, on giving notice to the other[136]; and even notice is not necessary in the case of the first to die, for the survivor has notice on the first death and will not be prejudiced.[137] The survivor in such circumstances is unable to establish any trust in his favour against the estate of the first to die.[138] Nor can the death of the survivor be the correct time. For where a beneficiary died between the date of the death of the first to die and the survivor, the estate of that beneficiary was able to claim its share on the ground that the interest was vested and there was no lapse.[139] Of these three possibilities, it seems therefore that the trust arises on the death (without having revoked his will) of the first to die.[140]

Previously, a fourth possibility was arguable: that the trust arises when the survivor receives a benefit under the first will. On this question there were dicta both ways. Most of the dicta favoured the view that the trust is imposed only where the survivor takes a benefit.[141] Clauson J, however, in *Re Hagger*[142] said obiter that the trust would arise "even though the survivor did not signify his election to give effect to the will by taking benefits under it".

It was held by Morritt J in *Re Dale (Deceased)*,[143] after a full review of all the authorities, that the doctrine of mutual wills applies even where the survivor does not benefit from the will of the first testator. A husband and wife agreed that each

---

[131] *In the Goods of Heys* [1914] P.192; *Stone v Hoskins* [1905] P. 194 (later will of first to die).

[132] [2017] 4 W.L.R. 186 at [33].

[133] These difficulties are discussed in T. Youdan (1979) 29 U. of Toronto L.J. 390 at 411–419.

[134] J. Mitchell (1951) 14 M.L.R. 137.

[135] See *Re Hobley (Deceased)*, *The Times*, 16 June 1997 (effect of mutual wills destroyed where first to die had altered his will in a minor but not insignificant way).

[136] *Dufour v Pereira* (1769) Dick. 419 at 420.

[137] (1769) Dick. 419. See also *Re Hobley* [2006] W.T.L.R. 467.

[138] *Stone v Hoskins* [1905] P. 194.

[139] *Re Hagger* [1930] 2 Ch. 190; cf. *Re Gardner (No.2)* [1923] Ch. 230.

[140] *Thomas and Agnes Carvel Foundation v Carvel* [2008] Ch. 395; R. Kerridge (assisted by A.H.R. Brierley) *Parry and Kerridge: The Law of Succession*, 13th edn (London: Sweet and Maxwell, 2016), p.131.

[141] *Dufour v Pereira* (1769) Dick. 419 at 421; *Stone v Hoskins* [1905] P. 194 at 197; *Re Oldham* [1925] Ch. 75 at 87. See also *Re Cleaver* [1981] 1 W.L.R. 939.

[142] [1930] 2 Ch. 190 at 195. See R. Burgess (1970) 34 Conv.(N.S.) 230; K. Hodkinson [1982] Conv. 228 at 230.

[143] [1994] Ch. 31; D. Brown (1993) 7 T.L.I. 18; C. Sherrin All E.R. Rev. 1993, 415.

would leave his or her whole estate to their son and daughter equally. The husband died first, leaving his estate of £18,500 in this way. The wife later made a new will leaving her daughter £300 and the rest of her estate of £19,000 to her son. It was held that the son, as executor, held the estate on trust for himself and the daughter equally. Benefit by the survivor was a sufficient but not a necessary requirement for the operation of the doctrine. The survivor committed a fraud on the first testator who died in reliance upon their bargain even if he or she did not benefit from the will. That this was the true basis of the doctrine appeared from *Dufour v Pereira*[144]:

"[H]e, that dies first, does by his death carry the agreement on his part into execution. If the other then refuses, he is guilty of a fraud, can never unbind himself, and becomes a trustee of course. For no man shall deceive another to his prejudice."[145]

Morritt J considered that the imposition of the trust was consistent with all the authorities, supported by some of them and was in furtherance of equity's original jurisdiction to intervene in cases of fraud.

(b) To what Property Does the Trust Attach?[146]   This may be clear from the **12–016** express terms of the will.[147] Failing that, and subject always to a contrary intention, there are four possibilities; that the trust attaches to the property, if any, which the survivor receives from the estate of the first to die; or to all the property that the survivor owned at that time; or to all the property which the survivor owned at his death; or to all property which the survivor owned at any time since the first death.

Clearly, the trust must include any property received from the first to die. If the will gave only a life interest, there is no scope for the trust in respect of that property. If the gift is absolute, the imposition of a trust in favour of ultimate beneficiaries will in effect reduce the survivor's interest to a life interest.

The position is more complex in relation to the property of the survivor. *Re Hagger*[148] suggests that the trust attaches at least to all the property which the survivor had at the time of the first death. Morritt J held that the trust embraced the survivor's whole estate at his or her death.[149] This means that a lifetime disposition by the survivor would be a breach of trust; indeed it would make nonsense of the trust if he could so dispose of the property.[150] This raises the question of acquisitions by the survivor by his own efforts after the first death. After all, the property acquired after the date of the wills by the first to die was

---

[144] As more fully reported in *Hargrave's Juridical Arguments*, Vol.2 (1797), p.304.

[145] *Hargrave's Juridical Arguments*, Vol.2, 1797, p.304 at 310 (Lord Camden).

[146] See L. Sheridan (1977) 15 Alberta L.Rev. 211. *Legg v Burton* [2017] 4 W.L.R. 186 at [68]–[70].

[147] As in *Re Green* [1951] Ch. 148, where the wills provided that if the other spouse predeceased, the residue was to be divided into halves, one half being considered as the testator's personal property and the other as the benefit received from the other spouse. It was held that the trust attached only to the latter.

[148] [1930] 2 Ch. 190. (Interest of beneficiary vested before death of survivor.)

[149] *Re Dale (Deceased)* [1994] Ch. 31; cf. *Re Walters* [2009] Ch. 212 at 222, where the claim related only to the property of the deceased (the survivor was alive).

[150] See however Astbury J in *Re Oldham* [1925] Ch. 75 at 87, 88; suggesting that the trust attaches only to property held by the survivor at death.

included in his estate; and the agreement, in the absence of a contrary provision, would apply to all property. The agreement thus acts like a covenant to settle after-acquired property, and the property becomes subject to the trust on its becoming vested in the trustee.[151] If this is correct, the effect of mutual wills is to reduce the survivor to the position of a life tenant in respect of all his property. He may use the income, but the capital is held on trust for the ultimate beneficiaries.

In *Re Cleaver*,[152] Nourse J, relying on the Australian decision *Birmingham v Renfrew*,[153] adopted the view there expressed that the survivor could enjoy the property as an absolute owner in his lifetime, "subject to a fiduciary duty which, so to speak, crystallised on his death and disabled him only from voluntary dispositions *inter vivos*".[154] This meant dispositions calculated to defeat the agreement. There was no objection to ordinary gifts of small value. The difficulty however, is that any such duty not to dissipate the assets in the survivor's lifetime will be unenforceable if the beneficiary does not discover his rights until the survivor's death. Although Nourse J affirmed the requirement of certainty of subject-matter, this is not fully consistent with his formulation of the rights and duties of the parties.[155] If, on the other hand, the survivor's obligation is merely not to dispose of the property *by will* inconsistently with the agreement,[156] then the difficulties are all the greater; for the trust property would be indefinite until his death. These problems were not examined in *Re Dale (Deceased)*.[157]

12–017   *(c)   The Survivor as Trustee.*   If it is correct that the survivor becomes a trustee of all the property he owns or acquires before his death, the consequences of the doctrine could be draconian for the survivor, for example if he acquires new dependants after the death of the first testator, or wins the lottery; similarly if the agreed beneficiary acquires a fortune elsewhere or is guilty of misconduct.[158] As far as the beneficiaries are concerned, there is very little opportunity to ensure that proper control over the survivor is maintained. Purchasers have no notice of the trusts, and the trust property may be lost on alienation to them.[159] Also, the survivor may have no idea that he is a trustee. If land is included in the trusts the lack of knowledge of all parties concerned may result in disputes and uncertainties as to title if it is alienated without observing the proper procedures. And, as noted above, further problems arise if the trust is treated as attaching only on the death of the survivor; and as "floating"[160] or as being "in suspense"[161] in the meantime. This is the problem, it should be noted, created in the field of

---

[151] *Paul v Paul* (1882) 20 Ch.D. 742; *Re Ralli's WT* [1964] Ch. 288.
[152] [1981] 1 W.L.R. 939. Similarly, in *Goodchild v Goodchild* [1997] 1 W.L.R. 1216.
[153] (1936) 57 C.L.R. 666.
[154] (1936) 57 C.L.R. 666 at 690. cf. *Palmer v Bank of NSW* (1975) 7 A.L.R. 671. See also *Healey v Brown* [2002] W.T.L.R. 849 (duty "crystallises" at moment of lifetime disposition in breach).
[155] See K. Hodkinson [1982] Conv. 228.
[156] See *Palmer v Bank of NSW* (1975) 7 A.L.R. 671.
[157] [1994] Ch. 31.
[158] See P. O'Hagan (1994) 144 N.L.J. 1272.
[159] *Pilcher v Rawlins* (1872) L.R. 7 Ch.App. 259.
[160] D. Hayton (1972) 36 Conv.(N.S.) 129 at 132; C. Davis (2002) 61 C.L.J. 423 at 427.
[161] per Brightman J [1972] Ch. 698 at 713; *Re Cleaver* [1981] 1 W.L.R. 939.

secret trusts by dicta in *Ottaway v Norman*.[162] The possibilities of trouble are unlimited; they have not yet been finally worked out.

iv. Conclusion.   It is clear that the imposition by law of a trust in cases of   **12–018**
mutual wills is a clumsy way of dealing with a complicated problem. A contractual solution under the *Beswick* principle would be much more satisfactory; but this has not been accepted.[163] The impact of the Contracts (Rights of Third Parties) Act 1999 in this area remains to be seen.[164] A solution based on the idea of a floating charge has also been suggested.[165] For the present, persons who wish to leave property by way of mutual wills should be advised to consider most carefully the trusts on which they wish the property to be held; what property is to be included; the position during the survivor's lifetime; whom they wish to be trustees; what administrative powers the trustees should have; and how best the scheme desired can be carried out from an inheritance tax point of view. It is the duty of a solicitor acting for testators making mirror wills to ascertain the intentions of both as to revocation, to advise on the effect of mutual wills, and to ensure that any agreement is clearly and accurately recorded.[166]

The Law Commission has found that mutual wills are rarely used in practice.[167] And yet the case law is a useful example of the operation of constructive trusts. The law in this context, as in most other areas of constructive trusts, imposes a trust in an attempt to prevent one party from committing a fraud on the other.[168] It is a kind of salvage operation; a salvage of a wreck which competent legal advice would have avoided in the first place.[169] The recently expressed view of the Court of Appeal is that the mutual wills doctrine:

> "[C]ontinues to be a source of contention for the families of those who have invoked it. The likelihood is that in future even fewer people will opt for such an arrangement and even more will be warned against the risks involved."[170]

Nevertheless, the Law Commission in its current Wills Consultation has declined to recommend the abolition of the doctrine, viewing its infelicities as "counterbalanced by the practical consideration that, however inflexible or inconvenient, they can provide a method of protecting a person's assets."[171] This approach has also received support from Judge Paul Matthews:

---

[162] [1972] Ch. 698 at 713 ("suspended trust" where donee obliged to bequeath to X whatever remains at the donee's death), above, para.6–025. J. Glister [2014] Conv. 11 at 23-4.

[163] *Re Dale (Deceased)* [1994] Ch. 31.

[164] M. Pawlowski and J. Brown [2012] Conv. 467 at 474. *Birch v Curtis* [2002] EWHC 1158 (Ch) per Rimer J at [61].

[165] K. Hodkinson [1982] Conv. 228, at 231. This does not solve the problem that the "beneficiaries" are often unaware of the situation.

[166] *Charles v Fraser* [2010] W.T.L.R. 1489; G. Griffiths [2011] Conv. 511.

[167] Law Com. CP No. 231, *Making a Will* (2017), para.12.3. See also M. Pawlowski and J. Brown [2012] Conv. 467; G.Ll.H. Griffiths [2011] Conv. 511, 514.

[168] *De Bruyne v De Bruyne* [2010] W.T.L.R. 1525 per Patten LJ at [51].

[169] For a different view, see F. Sunnucks (1988) 138 N.L.J. 351.

[170] *Re Walters* [2009] Ch. 212 at 215; P. Luxton [2009] Conv. 498.

[171] Law Com. CP No. 231, *Making a Will* (2017), para.12.31. The Commission did not believe that there was a case for placing the doctrine on a statutory footing (at para.12.32): "the disadvantages of mutual wills, and their comparative rarity, mean that we view negatively any attempt to increase their

> "It is wrong to treat every testator as if he or she were a private client lawyer or textbook writer, seeing the whole range of possible cases. Each testator, however, sees only his or her own case... there may be more to be said for entering into a mutual wills agreement than the textbooks give credit for. To elderly people, extra security is particularly valuable."[172]

More generally, it may be thought that abolition of the mutual wills doctrine, being an example of the incidence of constructive trusts, would be difficult, especially given its interconnections with other doctrines.[173]

F.   Secret Trusts

12–019   It is unsettled whether secret trusts, and more particularly half-secret trusts, are to be regarded as express or constructive. The practical significance of the distinction is that, in the case of land, s.53 of the Law of Property Act 1925 requires written evidence in the case of express trusts, but not in the case of constructive trusts. We have considered this matter in detail in Ch.6.[174]

G.   Conveyance by Fraud

12–020   Where property has been obtained by the fraud of the defendant, she may be compelled to hold it as a constructive trustee. The trust is not imposed in every case.[175] While it is difficult to define the circumstances in which the trust will be imposed, some broad principles are in practice clear. In the case of a conveyance of land, the transferee may be prevented, by the imposition of a constructive trust, from setting up the apparently absolute nature of the conveyance in order to defeat a beneficial interest which, by oral agreement, was intended to remain in the transferor,[176] or in some third party.[177] The scope of this principle when

---

popularity, which we fear might be the result of codification". The Commission also conceded that mutual wills was one of the areas which "assumed less importance" during the development of the paper: para.1.24.

[172] [2017] 4 W.L.R. 186 at [62]–[63].

[173] Law Com. CP No. 231, *Making a Will* (2017), para.12.30. See also the *Consultation Response on Behalf of the Society of Legal Scholars Property & Trusts Law Section* (available at *http://www. legalscholars.ac.uk/wp-content/uploads/2016/03/Making-A-Will-SLS-Response.pdf* [accessed 4 July 2018]); Y.K. Liew (2016) 133 L.Q.R. 664 at 676–7 and Y.K. Liew in C. Mitchell and B. Häcker (eds), *Current Issues in Succession Law* (Oxford: Hart Publishing, 2016). New Zealand has adopted a legislative solution: see, New Zealand Wills Act 2007, applying only where both testators have died; N. Richardson (2010) 24 T.L.I. 99.

[174] Above, para.6–039.

[175] For example, if the claimant had acquiesced in the fraud; *Lonrho Plc v Fayed (No.2)* [1992] 1 W.L.R. 1. See *Halifax Building Society v Thomas* [1996] Ch. 217. See also below paras 26–011—26–013.

[176] *Rochefoucauld v Boustead* [1897] 1 Ch. 196; *Bannister v Bannister* [1948] 2 All E.R. 133; *Hodgson v Marks* [1971] Ch. 892. "[It] is far too late to complain that informal agreements are being given effect to. Despite the Statute of Frauds 1677, the courts have been giving effect to informal agreements governing property since the late 17th century, when equity regarded it as unconscionable for the legal owner not to give effect to his promise. The doctrines of common intention constructive trust and proprietary estoppel are simply modern manifestations of that practice." *Culliford v Thorpe* [2018] EWHC 426 (Ch), per HHJ Paul Matthews at [57].

[177] *Binions v Evans* [1972] Ch. 359; *Peffer v Rigg* [1977] 1 W.L.R. 285; *Lyus v Prowsa Developments Ltd* [1982] 1 W.L.R. 1044; *Staden v Jones* [2008] 2 F.L.R. 1931. See also J. Feltham [1987] Conv.

applied to third parties has recently been described as "narrowly confined", because of its potential to "cut across the underlying premise of the land registration system".[178] Lloyd LJ has said that it will be only in exceptional circumstances that such a claim would and should succeed.[179] It should never be enough to establish such a trust "in any case where the third party right is only identified by way of general words in the contract", as the focus is on the purchaser's conscience being bound.[180]

Where owners of land appointed an agent to sell their property, but the agent instead procured a transfer into his own name by fraudulent misrepresentation, for no consideration and in breach of fiduciary duty, he held the property on trust for the transferors. The Court of Appeal considered it to be immaterial whether the trust was labelled implied, resulting or constructive.[181]

Similarly, situations in which a will is fraudulently revoked, or where the testator is fraudulently prevented from making a will, or fraudulently induced to leave property to a legatee or devisee, are all appropriate for the imposition of a constructive trust. These situations are discussed under the heading of secret trusts.[182]

H. Acquisition of Property by Killing[183]

Where a beneficiary kills the testator, or next of kin kills an intestate, there is good reason to prevent him from benefiting from his crime.[184] The English courts have established a rule to this effect, but they:

12–021

> "[H]ave worked out no rational theory for their actions in depriving killers[185]... there has been little discussion of the theoretical basis for a deprivation... and generally they have considered that the killer does not gain legal title".[186]

Such a result is contrary to the enactments relating to succession, testate or intestate, but clearly a rule of public policy can override statutory provisions.[187] If the killer does not acquire any title to the property in question, as in the pension and insurance cases, then there is no need for the imposition of a constructive

---

246; E. Cooke and P. O'Connor (2004) 120 L.Q.R. 640, discussing these cases in the context of the Land Registration Act 2002. P. Clark [2013] Conv. 169.

[178] *Groveholt v Hughes* [2012] EWHC 3351 (Ch) per David Richards J at [14].

[179] *Chaudhary v Yavuz* [2011] EWCA Civ 1314; [2013] Ch. 249 at [64]. See also *Cosmichome Ltd v Southampton City Council* [2013] EWHC 1378 (Ch); [2013] 1 W.L.R. 2436 per Sir William Blackburne at [68].

[180] *Chaudhary v Yavuz* [2011] EWCA Civ 1314; [2013] Ch. 249 at [65]. In *Lyus v Prowsa Developments Ltd* [1982] 1 W.L.R. 1044, for example, the relevant third-party rights in question were specifically identified, and the claimants' right was not registrable.

[181] *Collings v Lee* [2001] 2 All E.R. 332.

[182] For a fuller discussion, see Ch.6.

[183] T. Youdan (1973) 89 L.Q.R. 235, which has been used as the basis of this account; American Law Institute, *Third Restatement of the Law of Restitution and Unjust Enrichment* (2011), para.45; G. Virgo [1998] 6 R.L.R. 34 at 46–61; P. Smith (2004) 18 T.L.I. 194.

[184] *In the Estate of Crippen* [1911] P. 108.

[185] (1973) 89 L.Q.R. 235.

[186] (1973) 89 L.Q.R. 235 at 251.

[187] See, for example, *R. v Chief National Insurance Commissioner, Ex p. Connor* [1981] Q.B. 758.

trust. If, on the other hand, the killer acquires legal title, for example if it has been vested in him before the killing was discovered,[188] then he will be subjected to a constructive trust which is imposed to prevent unjust enrichment. A bona fide purchaser from the wrongdoer would then be protected.[189]

Whichever solution is reached, a number of problems remain.

12–022 **i. Type of Killing.**   Killing may be effected by any means from murder to accident. The deprivation principle only applies to criminal killing. The rule has not in the past been applied to all cases of manslaughter.[190] However, formulations based on whether the act was deliberate or violent have not proved satisfactory, and the position now appears to be that the rule applies to all types of manslaughter.[191] In *Dunbar v Plant*,[192] the public policy rule was applied to the survivor of a suicide pact, who had aided and abetted the other's suicide, but full relief was granted under the Forfeiture Act 1982 (discussed below).

12–023 **ii. Means of Acquisition.**   The principle applies when the killer benefits by testamentary gift,[193] or under the victim's intestacy,[194] and also under a life insurance policy on the victim's life[195]; and, in the days when suicide was a crime, the estate of a suicide was held to be unable to claim the benefits of an insurance policy.[196] Similarly, a woman who kills her husband cannot at common law claim a widow's pension.[197] More complicated questions arise where one joint tenant kills another, or a remainderman kills the life tenant. In the case of a joint tenancy, the killing effects a severance, so that the joint tenant does not profit under the doctrine of survivorship. Thus he holds the legal estate on trust for himself and the victim's estate in equal shares.[198] In the case of the remainderman killing the life tenant, the best course would be to postpone the killer's enjoyment until the time at which the victim's life expectation would terminate.[199]

The principle does not apply where the claimant has rights which had already crystallised prior the death of the deceased. In *Henderson v Wilcox*,[200] the claimant was convicted of the manslaughter of his mother. There were Family Protection Trusts of which the claimant was a discretionary beneficiary: his

---

[188] Law Com. No. 295, *The Forfeiture Rule and the Law of Succession* (2005), para.3.23.

[189] *Re Cash* (1911) 30 N.Z.L.R. 571; *Beresford v Royal Insurance Ltd* [1938] A.C. 586 at 600.

[190] *Gray v Barr* [1971] 2 Q.B. 554; *Re K (Deceased)* [1986] Ch. 180; cf. *Re Hall* [1914] P. 1; *Re Giles* [1972] Ch. 544; *Jones v Roberts* [1995] 2 F.L.R. 422; R. Buckley (1995) 111 L.Q.R. 196; *Re S (Deceased)* [1996] 1 W.L.R. 235.

[191] *Re Land* [2007] 1 W.L.R. 1009 (manslaughter by gross negligence).

[192] [1998] Ch. 412; M. Thompson [1998] Conv. 45; S. Bridge (1998) 57 C.L.J. 31.

[193] *Re Pollock* [1941] Ch. 219.

[194] *Re Sigsworth* [1935] Ch. 89.

[195] *Cleaver v Mutual Reserve Fund Life Association Ltd* [1892] 1 Q.B. 147; *Davitt v Titcumb* [1990] Ch. 110; J. Martin [1991] Conv. 50 (mortgage protection policy).

[196] *Beresford v Royal Insurance Ltd* [1938] A.C. 586.

[197] *R. v Chief National Commissioner, Ex p. Connor* [1981] 1 Q.B. 758 (manslaughter). As submitted above, this is not a case of constructive trust, as the claimant acquires no title to any property. Though see Forfeiture Act 1982 s.4.

[198] *Dunbar v Plant* [1998] Ch. 412.

[199] (1973) 89 L.Q.R. 235 at 250.

[200] [2015] EWHC 3469 (Ch).

interest under those trusts were "neither created nor enlarged" by his mother's death.[201] He was, however, prevented from benefiting under her will.

iii. Destination of Property.   To deprive the wrongdoer does not solve all the   **12–024** problems. One question is whether persons claiming through the wrongdoer should benefit from the crime. In *Re DWS (Deceased)*,[202] X murdered his parents, who died intestate, leaving no other children. X's only child, Y, claimed his grandparents' estates under s.47 of the Administration of Estates Act 1925, which provides that a grandchild is entitled to the share of a child who has predeceased the intestate. Y's claim failed on the basis that the public policy rule did not require the court to treat the murderer as having predeceased the victim. Thus the property devolved on the class of next-of-kin ranking after the issue of the intestate. However, this result was generally considered unfair, and it was reversed by the Estates of Deceased Persons (Forfeiture Rule and Law of Succession) Act 2011.[203] In other cases, the proper solution will be for the property to go to the victim's residuary legatee, or as on his intestacy,[204] or to the other members of a class of which the wrongdoer was one[205]; or, where there are special circumstances to show what the victim's intention was, as where it was shown that the killing took place in order to prevent the victim from changing his will in favour of another, then the flexibility introduced by the concept of the constructive trust should allow the property to be claimed by "the person who, in the eyes of equity, has the best right to it."[206]

iv. Statutory Relief.   It is provided by the Forfeiture Act 1982[207] that the   **12–025** court may grant relief from the forfeiture of inheritance and other rights to persons guilty of unlawful killing[208] other than where the killer has been convicted of murder,[209] where the court is satisfied that the justice of the case so requires.[210] A convicted person must bring proceedings for this purpose within three months of any conviction.[211] The Act applies to benefits under a will or upon intestacy; nominations; a *donatio mortis causa*; and property held on trust

---

[201] [2015] EWHC 3469 (Ch) at [17]–[18].

[202] [2001] Ch. 568.

[203] s.1 (intestacy) and s.2 (wills).

[204] See *Re Jones (Deceased)* [1998] 1 F.L.R. 246 (court cannot rewrite contingencies attached to residuary gift).

[205] *Re Peacock* [1957] Ch. 310.

[206] (1973) 89 L.Q.R. 235 at 257. See *Macmillan Cancer Support v Hayes* [2017] EWHC 3110 (Ch) below, para.12–025.

[207] P. Kenny (1983) 46 M.L.R. 66; A. Mithani and A. Wilton (1983) 80 L.S.Gaz. 910. The operation of the Act insofar as it applies in Scotland was modified by the Succession (Scotland) Act 2016 s.15.

[208] Including aiding, abetting, counselling or procuring the death; s.1(2). The survivor of a suicide pact will usually obtain relief; *Dunbar v Plant* [1998] Ch. 412.

[209] s.5.

[210] s.2(2). Degree of moral blame is significant; *Re K (Deceased)* [1986] Ch. 180; *Re Murphy* [2003] W.T.L.R. 687. The requirements of justice are not the same as sympathy for the applicant: *Henderson v Wilcox* [2015] EWHC 3469 (Ch) at [60]; *Chadwick v Collinson* [2014] EWHC 3055 (Ch).

[211] s.2(3); *Re Land* [2007] 1 W.L.R. 1009. But the Act and the doctrine may apply even in the case of acquittal, because the civil standard of proof is lower; *Gray v Barr* [1971] 2 Q.B. 554.

before the death which would devolve on the offender as a result of the death.[212] Speaking of the jurisdiction under the Act, Mummery LJ stated in *Dunbar v Plant*[213]:

> "The court is entitled to take into account a whole range of circumstances relevant to the discretion, quite apart from the conduct of the offender and deceased: the relationship between them; the degree of moral culpability for what has happened; the nature and gravity of the offence; the intentions of the deceased; the size of the estate and the value of the property in dispute; the financial position of the offender, and the moral claims and wishes of those who would be entitled to take the property on the application of the forfeiture rule."

An example of total relief from forfeiture can be found in the tragic case of *Macmillan Cancer Support v Hayes*[214]:

> *Macmillan Cancer Support v Hayes*[215] concerned the deaths of a devoted husband and wife. The husband had been diagnosed with terminal cancer and his wife, who suffered from dementia, was to be admitted permanently to a care home. He smothered her with a pillow and then committed suicide.[216] They had made similar wills with the property to go to various charities. However, if the husband was prevented from inheriting under his wife's will, the property would go to her distant relatives (as the couple had no children). HHJ Mark Raeside QC held that justice and the public interest in the case required modification of the forfeiture rule to afford total relief. The charities were therefore entitled to the relevant donations, notwithstanding that this would take effect through the husband's will. Relevant factors were that the beneficiaries of each will were largely identical and so there was no advantage to the husband or those claiming through him, and the gifts would comply with the wife's intentions.[217]

The court may grant relief as to all or part of the property.[218] In the case of social security benefits, such as a widow's pension, the Act confers the discretion not on the court but on the Upper Tribunal.[219] Finally, it is provided that the forfeiture principle does not preclude an application under the Family Provision legislation.[220]

I. Constructive Trusts of a 'New Model': Justice and Good Conscience

12–026   Any account of the law of constructive trusts would be incomplete without mention of the wide purported extension of the operation of constructive trusts Lord Denning MR attempted by the introduction of what his Lordship called "a constructive trust of a new model".[221] The broad principle was that a constructive

---

[212] s.2(4). See *Re S (Deceased)* [1996] 1 W.L.R. 235 (joint life insurance).

[213] [1998] Ch. 412 at 427H.

[214] [2017] EWHC 3110 (Ch).

[215] [2017] EWHC 3110 (Ch).

[216] Therefore, the husband was found to have unlawfully killed his wife but had not been convicted of her murder (so s.5 of the 1982 did not apply): [2017] EWHC 3110 (Ch) at [28].

[217] [2017] EWHC 3110 (Ch) at [32],

[218] s.2(1) and (5); *Re K (Deceased)* [1986] Ch. 180.

[219] s.4, as amended. See (1984) 81 L.S.Gaz. 288; (1988) 85 L.S.Gaz. 37 (sequel to *Re K (Deceased)*).

[220] s.3. See *Re Land* [2007] 1 W.L.R. 1009.

[221] *Eves v Eves* [1975] 1 W.L.R. 1338 at 1341. Lord Denning MR credited Lord Diplock with the midwifery of the new model trust, pointing to *Gissing v Gissing* [1971] A.C. 886, at 905.

trust may be imposed, regardless of established legal rules, in order to reach the result required by equity, justice and good conscience. The principle was thus articulated in *Hussey v Palmer*[222]:

> "It is a trust imposed by law wherever justice and good conscience require it. It is a liberal process, founded on large principles of equity… It is an equitable remedy by which the court can enable an aggrieved party to obtain restitution."

Such a principle, if it survived, would have effected a complete swing on the pendulum so far as the principles of English law concerning constructive trusts are concerned. The law in this field was once criticised as being too restricted[223]; in that the older cases would find a constructive trust only where the facts brought the case within one of the limited and established categories of constructive trust, usually requiring a fiduciary relationship. The new model opened up the possibility of finding a constructive trust in any situation in which the established rules lead to a result which would appear to be inconsistent with equity, justice and good conscience.[224]

Not surprisingly, this doctrine was applied in cases where satisfactory solutions under established doctrines proved particularly difficult to find. Illustrations came from the plight of the deserted wife or cohabitant and the problem of the licensee of land whose expectations had been disappointed. We shall see in the next chapter that, in the context of claims to an interest in the family home, the traditional property approach has been to the effect that the interests of the parties must be determined according to the principles of property law and not to what the court thinks would be "fair", as established by the House of Lords in *Pettitt v Pettitt*[225] and *Gissing v Gissing*.[226] In *Eves v Eves*,[227] involving an unmarried couple, the man bought a house as a joint home. He had it conveyed into his sole name, giving as an excuse the fact that the woman was under 21 years old. She did a great deal of heavy work in the house and garden, beyond ordinary housework. After they separated, the court held that she was entitled to a quarter share of the house.

> "In strict law she has no claim upon him whatever. She is not his wife. He is not bound to provide a roof over her head. He can turn her into the street… And a few years ago even equity would not have helped her. But things are altered now…"

It would be:

> "[M]ost inequitable for him to deny her any share in the house. The law will impute or impose a constructive trust by which he was to hold it in trust for both of them."[228]

---

[222] [1972] 1 W.L.R. 1286 at 1289.
[223] D.W.M. Waters, *The Constructive Trust* (London: Athlone Press, 1964).
[224] R. Maudsley (1977) 28 N.I.L.Q. 123.
[225] [1970] A.C. 777.
[226] [1971] A.C. 886.
[227] [1975] 1 W.L.R. 1338.
[228] [1975] 1 W.L.R. 1338 at 1341.

12–027   The courts were thus "invoking the constructive trust as an equitable remedy to do justice inter partes."[229] While a liberalisation of the application of equitable remedies is generally to be welcomed, it is important to appreciate that the "new model" constructive trust left a number of problems in its wake. The concept of "justice" alone is too vague to be used as the basis for determining property rights, and, inevitably, the imposition of the constructive trust on this basis would be impossible to forecast. The constructive trust does not represent "a medium for the indulgence of idiosyncratic notions of fairness and justice".[230]

Further, a trust creates equitable proprietary rights, and these can operate more widely than the dispute between the parties. The question of the rights of third parties arises: whether, in particular, a purchaser or mortgagee is bound by a licensee's right of occupation, or by a cohabitant's claim to share in the home.

It is important also to appreciate that the "new model" constructive trust went far beyond the principle of the remedial constructive trust to prevent unjust enrichment,[231] although some examples of the remedial constructive trust differ little from Lord Denning's formulation.[232] The provision of a remedy for unjust enrichment does not require an unlimited free-wheeling discretion as to the imposition of a constructive trust. There must at least be general guidelines for the exercise of the discretion. The law of unjust enrichment lays down with reasonable clarity when an action will lie. Some of the English cases seemed to treat a constructive trust as a magic formula to reach a just result between the parties, regardless of existing proprietary rights in them, or of the interests of persons who were not parties to the dispute.

Present indications, however, are that the "new model" constructive trust, which declined after the retirement of Lord Denning MR, will not revive. Although we shall see that the House of Lords and Supreme Court now favour a broad approach to ascertaining the parties' intentions concerning their shares in the family home, this does not go as far as deciding a case on the basis of what the court itself considers a fair result.[233]

3.   THE POSSIBILITY OF A REMEDIAL CONSTRUCTIVE TRUST

12–028   We saw that the duties of a constructive trustee differ from those of an ordinary trustee, although the extent of the difference is unclear.[234] If the claimant merely wishes to have the property returned, the question is whether a constructive trust

---

[229] A. Oakley (1973) 26 C.L.P. 17 at 35.

[230] *Muschinski v Dodds* (1985) 160 C.L.R. 583 per Deane J at 615.

[231] Below, paras 12–028—12–031.

[232] See M. Bryan (1994) 8 T.L.I. 74 at 79, discussing Australian decisions.

[233] *Stack v Dowden* [2007] 2 A.C. 432 at 456; *Jones v Kernott* [2012] 1 A.C. 776; below, para.13–007. See generally T. Etherton (2008) 67 C.L.J. 265. See also Commonwealth authority: *Allen v Snyder* [1977] 2 N.S.W.L.R. 685 at 701: "the legitimacy of the new model is at least suspect; at best it is a mutant from which further breeding should be discouraged". *Carly v Farrelly* [1975] 1 N.Z.L.R. 356; G. Samuels (1978) 94 L.Q.R. 347; *Muschinski v Dodds* (1985) 160 C.L.R. 583. W. Gummow (1978) 94 L.Q.R. 351.

[234] See generally, E. Bant and M. Bryan (eds), *Principles of Proprietary Remedies* (2013).

need be considered as anything beyond a means of demanding the return of the property to which he is entitled in equity.[235]

Such a constructive trust is regarded as a "remedial rather than substantive" institution.[236] The constructive trust is imposed under this doctrine whenever it is needed to prevent unjust enrichment. Like other equitable remedies, it is available where the legal remedy is inadequate. Thus, in a case of unjust enrichment the claimant will bring a common law personal action; but if the defendant still has the property, and either the claimant wants specific recovery, or the defendant is insolvent, or the property has increased in value, the claimant will be able to assert a constructive trust.[237] The English cases have however, traditionally regarded the constructive trust as a substantive institution,[238] or an "institutional" trust, vindicating a pre-existing proprietary right.

The remedial constructive trust has been accepted in Australia,[239] Canada,[240] New Zealand[241] and Singapore.[242] The position in Hong Kong is not yet settled.[243] In the jurisdictions where it has been recognised, the remedial constructive trust has not replaced the traditional institutional constructive trust, but exists alongside it.[244]

One distinction between institutional and remedial constructive trusts may lie in the date from which the claimant may assert proprietary rights. This question

---

[235] See A. Scott (1955) 71 L.Q.R. 71; *Carl Zeiss Stiftung v Herbert Smith & Co* [1969] 2 Ch. 276 at 300.

[236] R. Pound (1920) 33 Harv.L.R. 420. See also R. Goode (1983) 3 L.S. 283 at 292; D. Hayton [1988] Conv. 259; C. Rickett (1991) 107 L.Q.R. 608; Elias, *Explaining Constructive Trusts* (2002), 159–163; D. Wright, *The Remedial Constructive Trust* (Sydney: Butterworths, 1998); Liew, *Rationalising Constructive Trusts* (2017), Ch.11.

[237] See *Lac Minerals Ltd v International Corona Resources Ltd* (1989) 61 D.L.R. (4th) 14.

[238] See *Re Sharpe* [1980] 1 W.L.R. 219, where the notion of imposing a constructive trust as a remedy was described as a novel concept in English law.

[239] *Muschinski v Dodds* (1985) 160 C.L.R. 583; K. Mason [2007] 15 R.L.R. 1.

[240] *Pettkus v Becker* (1980) 117 D.L.R. (3d) 257; *Lac Minerals Ltd v International Corona Resources Ltd* (1989) 61 D.L.R. (4th) 14; G. Hammond (1990) 106 L.Q.R. 207; *Rawluk v Rawluk* (1990) 65 D.L.R. (4th) 161; *Soulos v Korkontzilas* [1997] 2 S.C.R. 217; *Sun Indalex Finance, LLC v United Steelworkers* [2013] 1 S.C.R. 271. In Canada, the remedial constructive trust has been described as having "become the pre-eminent vehicle for addressing the financial consequences of the breakdown of domestic relationships": *Kerr v Baranow* [2011] 1 S.C.R. 269 per Cromwell J at [3]. The exact scope of the remedial constructive trust's operation and availability in Canada remains somewhat debated: see e.g. *Moore v Sweet* [2017] ONCA 182.

[241] *Powell v Thompson* [1991] 1 N.Z.L.R. 579 at 615 ("a broad equitable remedy for reversing that which is inequitable or unconscionable"); *Equiticorp Industries Group Ltd v Hawkins* [1991] 3 N.Z.L.R. 700. But caution is needed in insolvency cases; *Fortex Group Ltd v MacIntosh* [1998] 3 N.Z.L.R. 171.

[242] *Wee Chiaw Sek Anna v Ng Li-Ann Genevieve* [2013] 3 S.L.R. 801; M. Yip (2014) 20 T. & T. 373; M. Yip (2014) 8 J. Eq. 77; *Zhou Weidong v Liew Kai Lung* [2017] SGHC 326 at [79]–[82]; though see *CPIT Investments Ltd v Qilin World Capital Ltd* [2017] SGHC(I) 5 Vivian Ramsey IJ at [199] "a remedial constructive trust in Singapore law, as in other legal systems, is only to be imposed sparingly".

[243] *Ip Tin Chee v Ching Hing Construction Co Ltd* [2003] HKCFI 1214 at [90]; and *Cheung Hon Hung v Siu Wai Chun* [2014] HKDC 979 at [76].

[244] *Muschinski v Dodds* (1985) 160 C.L.R. 583 at 613–615. It should also be noted that in some jurisdictions the phrase "remedial constructive trust" is used in the sense of as a formula for equitable relief rather than as involving the imposition of a trust: see e.g. *Secretary of Justice v Hon Kam Wing* [2003] HKCFI 1005; [2003] 1 HKLRD 524; and *McNab v Graham* [2017] VSCA 352 per Tate JA. See below, para.25–035.

has significance for third parties acquiring interests in the property before the court makes its order. It seems clear that the traditional institutional constructive trust vindicates a pre-existing proprietary interest which is operative before the date of the court order.[245] The effect of a remedial constructive trust, on the other hand, may be to confer a new proprietary interest on the claimant.[246] In such a case it will have prospective effect only, operating from the date of the court order which creates it.[247]

It has been frequently debated whether the doctrine does, or should, exist as a matter of English law. Although the normative question of its desirability may remain open, the UK Supreme Court has repeatedly rejected the remedial constructive trust. Millett J warned that, while equity must be flexible, "its intervention must be based on principle; there must be some relationship between the relief granted and the circumstances which give rise to it".[248] To which his Lordship has added:

> "[T]here is neither room nor need for the remedial constructive trust. In my view it is a counsel of despair which too readily concedes the impossibility of propounding a general rationale for the availability of proprietary remedies. We need to be more ready to categorise wrongdoers as fiduciaries and to extend the situations in which proprietary remedies are made available, but we can do all this while adhering to established principles".[249]

Similarly, "the remedial constructive trust is a judicial discretion to vary property rights and, as such, an object of suspicion".[250] Lord Browne-Wilkinson, on the other hand, suggested in *Westdeutsche Landesbank Girozentrale v Islington LBC*[251] that the introduction of the remedial constructive trust might in the future provide a satisfactory basis for developing proprietary restitutionary remedies.[252] Lord Scott also expressed a preference for the ability of the courts to decide cases on "principles of remedial constructive trusts", but this was a minority view.[253]

12–029 The Court of Appeal considered the putative remedial doctrine in *Re Polly Peck International Plc (In Administration) (No.2)*,[254] where it was said that there was

---

[245] This is assumed in the English cases such as *Lloyds Bank Plc v Rosset* [1991] 1 A.C. 107; below, para.13–011. See *Westdeutsche Landesbank Girozentrale v Islington LBC* [1996] A.C. 669 at 716.

[246] *Lac Minerals Ltd v International Corona Resources Ltd* (1989) 61 D.L.R. (4th) 14 at 50. The term "imposed proprietary remedy" is preferred in C. Rickett (1999) 18 N.Z.U.L.R. 305 at 331.

[247] *Muschinski v Dodds* (1985) 160 C.L.R. 583 at 615; cf. *Rawluk v Rawluk* (1990) 65 D.L.R. (4th) 161. The argument of the applicants in *Polly Peck* [1998] 3 All E.R. 812 was that the remedial constructive trust should be imposed retrospectively.

[248] *Lonrho Plc v Fayed (No.2)* [1992] 1 W.L.R. 1 at 9 (no constructive trust where claim had no proprietary base). See also Sir Peter Millett (1991) 107 L.Q.R. 71 at 85.

[249] (1995) 9 T.L.I. 35 at 40. See also *Paragon Finance Plc v DB Thakerar & Co (A Firm)* [1999] 1 All E.R. 401 at 413: the distinction between institutional trusts and the remedial formula is the distinction "between a trust and a catch-phrase".

[250] *The Frontiers of Liability*, Vol.2, p.24, P. Birks; cf. at 165, D. Waters and 186, S. Gardner. See also P. Birks [1996] R.L.R. 3; Oakley, *Constructive Trusts*, 3rd edn (1996), p.26; Goff and Jones, 9th edn, Chs 37 and 38. U.L.R. 509. The remedial constructive trust is considered unavailable in Jersey; *Re the Esteem Settlement* [2004] W.T.L.R. 1.

[251] [1996] A.C. 669.

[252] *Westdeutsche Landesbank Girozentrale v Islington LBC* [1996] A.C. 669 at 716.

[253] *Thorner v Major* [2009] UKHL 18 at 20.

[254] [1998] 3 All E.R. 812. See also *Fortex Group Ltd v MacIntosh* [1998] 3 N.Z.L.R. 171.

no prospect of the imposition of a remedial constructive trust[255] on the assets of an insolvent company so as to give the claimants a proprietary interest, to the detriment of creditors. To do so would confer a priority not accorded by the insolvency legislation. Although the law moves, it[256]:

> "[C]annot be legitimately moved by judicial decision down a road signed 'No Entry' by Parliament. The insolvency road is blocked off to remedial constructive trusts, at least when judge-driven in a vehicle of discretion".

Nourse LJ emphasised that his conclusions were not confined to insolvency, because property rights could only be varied by statute.[257] The decision was at the time said to be "the end of the remedial constructive trust"[258]; similarly, "It bangs the door shut on the 'remedial constructive trust' in this jurisdiction".[259] Other recent decisions appear to have left the door closed.[260]

On the other hand, Lord Scott in *Thorner v Major*[261] suggested that cases involving representations about inheritance prospects should be treated as giving rise to a remedial constructive trust rather than proprietary estoppel, but the other members of the House of Lords based their decision firmly on proprietary estoppel.[262] It may also be noted that Sir Terence Etherton (now MR) has argued extra-curially that the constructive trust deployed in *Stack v Dowden*[263] was a radical departure from the institutional constructive trust giving rise to an identifiable property right before judgment, and was in fact a discretionary remedial constructive trust giving proprietary restitutionary relief for unjust enrichment, although the decision of the House of Lords was not couched in those terms.[264] And it is arguable that the flexibility introduced by the recognition of the ability to impute a common intention as to beneficial shares the domestic consumer context may point towards a more discretionary approach. This argument in respect of the *Stack* common intention constructive trust is considered in Ch.13.

However, the recent views of Justices of the Supreme Court have been firmly   **12–030**
against the remedial constructive trust. The Court was led in this adopting this

---

[255] Defined by Nourse LJ at 830 as the grant of a proprietary right, as a remedy, to someone who, beforehand, had no such right.

[256] [1998] 3 All E.R. 812 at 827, per Mummery LJ. See also *Halifax Building Society v Thomas* [1996] Ch. 217 at 229; P. Birks (1996) 10 T.L.I. 2; P. Watts (1996) 112 L.Q.R. 219; P. Jaffey [1996] R.L.R. 92. See further *Glasgow v ELS Law Ltd* [2017] EWHC 3004 (Ch) at [65] and R. Snowden (2017) 31 T.L.I. 99.

[257] [1998] 3 All E.R. 812 at 831.

[258] P. Birks (1998) 12 T.L.I. 202. See also Sir Peter Millett (1998) 114 L.Q.R. 399; P. Matthews (1998) 4 *Trusts & Trustees* 14; C. Rickett and R. Grantham [1999] L.M.C.L.Q. 111.

[259] P. Birks and W. Swadling All E.R. Rev. 1998 at 415; cf. D. Wright [1999] R.L.R. 128. See also Law Com. Discussion Paper, *Sharing Homes* (2002), p.25, fn.92: "there has been a relatively steadfast refusal to develop constructive trusts as a purely remedial device."

[260] *Ultraframe (UK) Ltd v Fielding* [2007] W.T.L.R. 835 at 881; *Turner v Jacob* [2008] W.T.L.R. 307 at 332; *De Bruyne v De Bruyne* [2010] W.T.L.R. 1525 at 1541.

[261] [2009] 1 W.L.R. 776.

[262] For this reason, any reliance on the dictum, as in *Seward v Seward* unreported 20 June 2014 Ch D, should be viewed with circumspection.

[263] [2007] 2 A.C. 432; above, para.13–005.

[264] T. Etherton (2008) 67 C.L.J. 265 and [2009] Conv. 104.

stance by Lord Neuberger, its recently retired President. In *FHR European Ventures LLP v Cedar Capital Partners LLC*,[265] Lord Neuberger on behalf of the Supreme Court repeated that[266]

> "[the] remedial constructive trust... is a concept which has authoritatively been said not to be part of English law."

The latest reiteration of the English position is to be found in the important case of *Angove's Pty Ltd v Bailey*[267]:

> The applicant was an Australian winemaker which contracted with an English company to act as its sales agent in the UK. The terms of the agency agreement provided that it was terminable on six months' notice by either side or immediately upon administration or going into liquidation. When the agent went into administration, the applicant sought to terminate the agreement and the agent's authority to collect further sums due on outstanding invoices from customers and then separately account for commission. Voluntary liquidation then followed and the liquidators of the agent argued that it was still entitled to collect the balances from customers and then deduct its commission. There were two points before the Supreme Court: whether the applicant was entitled to revoke the agent's authority; if not, whether the moneys collected by the agent on its behalf were held on constructive trust. The Supreme Court held that the applicant had been entitled to revoke the authority of the agent,[268] and the applicant's appeal was allowed. The constructive trust point was therefore strictly obiter, but Lord Sumption went on to hold that the moneys were not held on trust for the principal, disapproving earlier cases.[269] He observed:
>
>> "Property rights are fixed and ascertainable rights. Whether they exist in a given case depends on settled principles, even in equity. Good conscience therefore involves more than a judgment of the relative moral merits of the parties... It cannot be a sufficient answer to that question to say that it would be "contrary to any ordinary notion of fairness" for the general creditors to benefit by the payment. Reasoning of this kind might be relevant to the existence of a remedial constructive trust, but not an institutional one."[270]

The Court therefore disapproved the reasoning in *Neste Oy* of Bingham J who had taken the view that the "true question" was "not whether money has been received by a party of which he could not have compelled the payment, but whether he can now, with a safe conscience, ex aequo et bono, retain it"[271] Bingham J's analysis was regarded by Lord Sumption as productive of uncertainty, being inconsistent with the statutory regime for insolvency and thus

---

[265] [2014] UKSC 45; [2015] A.C. 250.
[266] [2015] A.C. 250 at [47]. See also Lord Neuberger MR (as he then was) in *Sinclair Investments (UK) Ltd v Versailles Group* [2011] EWCA Civ 347 at [37]. S. Worthington (2013) 72 C.L.J. 720. Below, paras 22–028—22–033.
[267] [2016] UKSC 47; [2016] 1 W.L.R. 3179; P. Watts (2017) 133 L.Q.R. 11; H. Wong [2016] Conv. 481; J. Grower (2018) 81 M.L.R. 141.
[268] [2016] 1 W.L.R. 3179 at [6]–[7]; [16]–[17].
[269] [2016] 1 W.L.R. 3179 at [25]–[31]; the title "unconscionable assertion of title to money payments by agents" cited by Lord Sumption at [20] was quoting from Lewin, 19th edn (2015), para.7.040, then relying on the now-disapproved *Neste Oy v Lloyd's Bank Plc* [1983] 2 Lloyd's Rep. 658 and *In re Japan Leasing Europe Plc* [1999] B.P.I.R. 911.
[270] [2016] 1 W.L.R. 3179 at [28].
[271] [1983] 2 Lloyd's Rep. 658 at 666.

elevating the rights of the principal over other creditors in circumstances which did not justify it.[272] Instead the availability for a constructive trust was much more limited:

> "where money is paid with the intention of transferring the entire beneficial interest to the payee, the least that must be shown in order to establish a constructive trust is (i) that that intention was vitiated, for example because the money was paid as a result of a fundamental mistake or pursuant to a contract which has been rescinded, or (ii) that irrespective of the intentions of the payer, in the eyes of equity the money has come into the wrong hands, as where it represents the fruits of a fraud, theft or breach of trust or fiduciary duty against a third party. One or other of these is a necessary condition, although it may not be a sufficient one."[273]

Finally, it may be noted that, having disapproved the approach in *Neste Oy*, Lord Sumption floated the possibility that the outcome in *Neste Oy* could be justified on the alternative analysis of mistake, but held that it was unnecessary to decide it on the appeal.[274] Given that the discussion of the constructive trust was itself unnecessary to resolve the appeal, it is regrettable that the opportunity was not taken to offer greater clarity in the law.[275]

To conclude, we may note that Lord Sumption's starting point for his approach in *Angove's v Bailey* was a broad and definitive rejection of the remedial constructive trust[276]:   **12–031**

> "English law is generally averse to the discretionary adjustment of property rights, and has not recognised the remedial constructive trust favoured in some other jurisdictions, notably the United States and Canada. It has recognised only the institutional constructive trust."

But the debate will continue, in cases[277] as well as in the literature.[278] Professor Conaglen, in commenting on *FHR European Ventures*, said:

> "It remains to be seen to what degree England finds itself able to hold to its approach in future, and whether its lack of flexibility in this regard might generate injustice, although that question in turn re-opens to a significant degree the very debate the Supreme Court has sought to quiet."[279]

---

[272] [2016] 1 W.L.R. 3179 at [27]–[28].

[273] [2016] 1 W.L.R. 3179 at [30].

[274] [2016] 1 W.L.R. 3179 at [32].

[275] M. Yip and J. Lee (2017) 37 L.S. 647 at 663-4.

[276] [2016] 1 W.L.R. 3179 at [27]. Sir Richard Snowden, extra-curially, has described Lord Sumption's view as a "clear and obviously correct statement of the policy that must apply in the event of insolvency and of the limitations of the principles of trust law in this context" (2017) 31 T.L.I. 99 at 111.

[277] There are still occasions to be found where the remedial constructive trust can be raised unchallenged as a matter of principle: for example, *Walden v Atkins* [2013] EWHC 1387 (Ch) (though no such trust was found); *Apollo Ventures Co Ltd v Manchanda* [2018] EWHC 58 (Comm) at [59]; and, in Ireland, *Finnegan v Hand* [2016] IEHC 255 per Michael White J at [67] (with respect, based on a misreading of the majority view of *Thorner v Major*).

[278] C. Rotherham (2012) 65 C.L.P. 529. Y.K. Liew (2016) C.L.J. 528. On the merits of discretion in equity generally, see M. Harding (2016) 132 L.Q.R. 278.

[279] M. Conaglen (2014) 73 C.L.J 490 at 493; W. Gummow (2015) 131 L.Q.R. 21 at 26.

As a matter of principle and authority, however, it can still be stated that the remedial constructive trust is not formally recognised in English law. As Lord Neuberger has said extra-curially,

> "the remedial constructive trust represents an unnecessary weapon in the judiciary's armoury, a book too many in equity's library, and a discretion too many in a Chancery judge's locker."[280]

---

[280] "The Remedial Constructive Trust—Fact or Fiction" Banking Services and Finance Law Association Conference, Queenstown, New Zealand, 10 August 2014.

CHAPTER 13

TRUSTS OF THE FAMILY HOME

1. INTRODUCTION

IN THE last two chapters, we saw the part played by the doctrines of resulting **13–001** and constructive trusts in the acquisition of property interests. In this chapter, we will examine the special considerations which apply to the matrimonial or family home.[1] The law in this area has been developed significantly by the courts over the past decade, particularly in the wake of the 2007 decision of the House of Lords in *Stack v Dowden*[2] and the 2011 decision of the Supreme Court in *Jones v Kernott*.[3] The first part of the chapter will deal with the establishment of a

---

[1] We use here "family home" as a term of convenience, although, as will be seen, the principles properly apply at least "in the domestic consumer context": *Stack v Dowden* [2007] 2 A.C. 432, per Baroness Hale at [58]. Professor Mee has also pointed out that "there is an imperfect match between the area of the law of equity conveniently described as 'trusts of the family home' and the issue of the property consequences of relationship breakdown", not least because many cohabiting couples will be renting rather than owning their homes: J. Mee (2016) 56 Irish Jurist 161 at 161.

[2] [2007] 2 A.C. 432.

[3] [2011] UKSC 53; [2012] 1 A.C. 776. In *Seagrove v Sullivan* [2014] EWHC 4110 (Fam), Holman J at [37] expressed his frustration that, in the light of the recent consideration by the House of Lords and Supreme Court in *Stack v Dowden* and *Jones v Kernott* respectively, "it would be surprising, frankly, if it was necessary to look beyond those two authorities; but most certainly, when the Supreme Court

proprietary interest in the home. Where the purchase of the property is in the "domestic consumer context",[4] there is no presumption of a resulting trust: instead the presumption is that the parties intended the beneficial shares to reflect those at law.[5] The second part will examine some of the problems of co-ownership of land. To complete the picture, reference should also be made to Ch.30, where it will be seen that those who cannot establish an interest under a trust of the family home might nevertheless acquire rights as licensees or under the doctrine of estoppel.

2. ACQUISITION OF INTERESTS IN THE HOME

A. Background to the Problem: Marriage, Civil Partnership and Unmarried Cohabitation[6]

13–002 In the case of a married couple, one problem which arises is that the older rules of property law, which became established at a time when the wife was less likely to be earning her living than is the case today, do not properly recognise her contribution to the relationship. Speaking in 1999, Robert Walker LJ observed:

> "Until little more than a century ago the common law did not permit married women to own any property whatsoever. It became the property of her husband. When a measure of reform was proposed in 1856 one Member of Parliament protested, 'If a woman had not full confidence in a man, let her refrain from marrying him.'"[7]

The modern view is that marriage is a partnership between equals, in which both partners has an economic contribution to make.[8] But a wife does not always insist on the matrimonial home being conveyed to the spouses jointly; or on a declaration of trust of a share of the house in favour of herself. Nor is justice done to her by the presumption of a resulting trust, based on payment of the purchase money; first, because childcare and housework are not money-producing, and secondly, because if she has a job, her earnings may be spent on household expenses and not in contributing to the purchase price of the house. "The cock can feather the nest because he does not have to spend most of his time sitting on it."[9] The question then is how to ensure that the ownership of the home is appropriately shared.

---

has, on more than one recent occasion, traversed all the historic law in relation to this topic, it is quite ridiculous and completely disproportionate to produce bundles of no less than 32 authorities."

[4] Though see *Marr v Collie* [2017] UKPC 17; [2017] 3 W.L.R. 1507 considered below, para.13–019.

[5] [2011] UKSC 53, per Lord Walker and Lady Hale at [25].

[6] R. Probert, *The Changing Legal Regulation of Cohabitation: From Fornication to Family, 1600–2010* (2012); C. Lind (2014) 77 M.L.R. 641; S. Gardner (2013) 72 C.L.J. 301; A. Sanders (2013) 62 I.C.L.Q. 629.

[7] *Rooney v Cardona* [1999] 1 F.L.R. 1236 per Robert Walker LJ at 1240.

[8] Speaking in the context of a case involving surety for debts, David Richards LJ has recently remarked that "the clear trend in the law has been to provide financial emancipation to women and to enable couples to keep their property and financial affairs separate to such extent as they desire": *Armstrong v Onyearu* [2017] EWCA Civ 268 at [80].

[9] per Sir Jocelyn Simon, extra-judicially, quoted by Lord Hodson in *Pettitt v Pettitt* [1970] A.C. 777 at 811.

Married couples who reach the end of their relationship, whether on divorce[10] or on death,[11] can invoke the court's discretionary powers to order a distribution of the property of the spouses. Since the enactment of the Marriage (Same Sex Couples) Act 2013, marriage of same sex couples has been lawful, and the same provisions apply whatever the gender of the spouses.[12] Same sex couples also retain the choice of registering their relationship under the Civil Partnership Act 2004.[13] If that is done, their property and financial rights are broadly similar to those of married couples, and their tax position corresponds to that of spouses.[14] One partner may acquire a share or enhanced share by making a substantial improvement to property in which either or both have an interest.[15] Either party may refer to court any question relating to the title to or possession of property (whether or not it is still in the possession or control of the other party), and the court may make such order as it thinks fit.[16] The registered partners are put in the same position as married couples in relation to wills, intestacy and the administration of estates.[17] If the partnership is terminated by breakdown, the court may make the same kind of orders for financial relief as in the case of married couples, for example property adjustment orders and orders for sale or pension-sharing.[18]

13–003

The Civil Partnership legislation is presently limited to same sex couples. Other couples only have the option of marriage. Section 15 of the 2013 Act provided for a review of "the operation and future of the Civil Partnership Act 2004 in England and Wales". That review was conducted through consultation and reported in 2014[19]: no change was proposed because of a lack of consensus. During a debate on a Private Member's Bill (the Civil Partnerships, Marriages and Deaths (Registration Etc.) Bill 2017–19), the Westminster Government committed in February 2018 to review the position again.[20]

In June 2018, as this edition was going to press, the UK Supreme Court gave judgment in the case of *R. (on the application of Steinfeld and Keiden) v*

---

[10] Matrimonial Causes Act 1973, as amended by Family Law Act 1996; *Wachtel v Wachtel* [1973] Fam. 72. Property disputes between spouses are best settled under this jurisdiction; *Williams v Williams* [1976] Ch. 278 at 286; *Suttill v Graham* [1977] 1 W.L.R. 819 at 824. The statutory jurisdiction does not apply to engaged couples by reason of Law Reform (Miscellaneous Provisions) Act 1970 s.2(1); *Mossop v Mossop* [1989] Fam. 77; JEM [1988] Conv. 286.

[11] Inheritance (Provision for Family and Dependants) Act 1975.

[12] Marriage (Same Sex Couples) Act 2013 s.1(1). The first marriages under the legislation took place on 29 March 2014.

[13] The 2013 Act s.9 also provides for the conversion of a civil partnership into marriage: this procedure was provided for by the Marriage of Same Sex Couples (Conversion of Civil Partnership) Regulations 2014 (SI 2014/3181).

[14] As a result of regulations made under FA 2005 s.103.

[15] s.65. For the provisions relating to married couples, see below, para.13–016.

[16] ss.66, 67. Such applications may be made within three years of the termination of the civil partnership; s.68.

[17] s.71 and Sch.4. This includes applications under the Inheritance (Provision for Family and Dependants) Act 1975.

[18] s.72 and Schs 5–7.

[19] Department for Culture, Media and Sport, *Civil Partnership Review (England And Wales)—Report on Conclusions*.

[20] The Parliamentary Under-Secretary of State for the Home Department (Victoria Atkins), HC Deb 2 February 2018, vol 635, Col 1120

Secretary of State for Education.[21] The litigation had involved a series of public law and human rights challenges to the lack of availability of civil partnerships for couples of opposite sexes. The Supreme Court unanimously held that the Secretary of State's position of "wait and evaluate" for an indefinite period with regard to the operation of civil partnerships was unjustifiable, and issued a declaration of incompatibility.[22] It remains to be seen whether legislative reform will now follow.

13–004   The rest of the chapter deals only with the general law, which applies, subject to legislative exceptions, equally to married and unmarried couples. A difficulty frequently encountered, as will be seen, is that the parties do not formulate their intention at the time the property is acquired, but consider the matter only when their relationship breaks down.[23] As Lord Briggs has put in a Privy Council decision on joint bank accounts[24]:

> "Persons acquiring property, in particular residential property in joint names, at least in England, have a notoriously poor track-record in making an express declaration as to their beneficial interests in relation to the property."

And, as Lord Neuberger has remarked, "when cohabitants fall out, the law has to deal with the fall-out from the falling out."[25] The result is a situation where "the unattainable precision of property law collides with the casual inarticulacy of home sharing".[26] The challenge for the law is increased by the fact that a significant and increasing proportion of couples cohabit outside marriage or civil partnership. The 2011 Census recorded that cohabiting couples accounted for 12% of the adult household population in England and Wales.[27] Should their relationship break down, the court has no statutory power to adjust their property interests. Where the parties are neither married nor registered civil partners (or where parties remain in a marriage or civil partnership, for the legislation only applies at the *end* of the relationship), their rights are determined according to the principles of property law, making whatever use is appropriate of evidence of agreement, declarations of trust (which comply with the necessary formalities applicable to trusts of land) and of inferences and presumptions. As Lord Hope of Craighead put it in *Stack v Dowden*,

> "The situation is complicated by the fact that there is no single, or paradigm, set of circumstances. The only feature which these cases have in common is that the problem has not been solved by legislation. The legislation which enables the court to reallocate beneficial

---

[21] [2018] UKSC 32.

[22] See e.g. [2018] UKSC 32, per Lord Kerr at [50]: "I should make it unequivocally clear that the government had to eliminate the inequality of treatment immediately... taking time to evaluate whether to abolish or extend could never amount to a legitimate aim for the continuance of the discrimination".

[23] See *Carlton v Goodman* [2002] 2 F.L.R. 259 per Ward LJ at 273: "I WILL TRY ONE MORE TIME: ALWAYS TRY TO AGREE ON AND THEN RECORD HOW THE BENEFICIAL INTEREST IS TO BE HELD. It is not very difficult to do." (Ward LJ's own emphatic capital letters).

[24] *Whitlock v Moree (Bahamas)* [2017] UKPC 44 at [25].

[25] See Lord Neuberger, "The Plight of the Unmarried" (speech delivered 21 June 2017).

[26] A. Briggs (2012) 128 L.Q.R. 183, 183.

[27] 2011 Census: General Report for England and Wales (Office for National Statistics, 2015) para.9.33: the percentage had increased from 9.8% in 2001.

interests in the home and other assets following a divorce does not apply to cohabiting couples. Otherwise the circumstances which define relationships between cohabiting couples and their property interests are infinitely various."[28]

The possibility of giving the court, in the case of married couples, a wide discretionary power to declare what are the appropriate shares to be held by disputing spouses in any particular case has been rejected[29]; likewise the concept of community of property.[30] The most recent Law Commission proposals are considered below.[31]

The first question to determine is whether each party owns an interest in the property. If so, there is co-ownership, and the house is held upon trust, even though legal title may be vested only in one.[32] The next question is to determine what the share of each party is, which is a question of quantification.[33]

A number of other problems can arise, such as a decision on sale if one party wishes to sell and the other to retain; questions as to the right to possession and the payment of rent; and the protection of an occupying co-owner if the sole legal owner sells to a third party.

B.   Legal Title in Both Parties

i.   *Stack v Dowden.*   Where the legal title is in both parties, the beneficial **13–005** interest will prima facie also be shared.[34] Any express declaration of the beneficial interests in the title documents will be conclusive.[35] Since April 1998, the Land Registry form which applies to the 'Transfer of whole of registered title' (the TR1 form) has provided the opportunity in box 10 for the parties to choose between:

> The transferee is more than one person and they are to hold the property on trust for themselves as joint tenants, or
> > they are to hold the property on trust for themselves as tenants in common in equal shares, or
> > they are to hold the property on trust (with the opportunity to specify shares).

---

[28] [2007] 2 A.C. 432 at [2].

[29] *Gissing v Gissing* [1971] A.C. 886.

[30] Law Com. No. 52, para.59. See also Law Com. No. 90, para.5.20.

[31] Below, para.13–021.

[32] Below, para.13–010.

[33] Snowden J has recently suggested that it is not necessary to conduct the two stage analysis (so as to quantify the exact extent of a party's beneficial interest) in the specific context of being able to make a charging order under the Charging Orders Act 1979: *Walton v Allman* [2015] EWHC 3325 (Ch); [2016] 1 W.L.R. 2053, distinguishing (at [52]) the line of cases discussed here, on the basis that (at [57]) "it is sufficient for the purposes of giving the court jurisdiction to make a charging order under the 1979 Act that the court is satisfied that the judgment debtor has some beneficial interest in relevant property, even though the precise extent of that interest cannot be quantified at the time the charging order is made".

[34] *Pettit v Pettit* [1970] A.C. 777 at 813–814. See also *Crossley v Crossley* [2006] 2 F.L.R. 813.

[35] See *Goodman v Gallant* [1986] Fam. 106; S. Juss (1986) 45 C.L.J. 205; J. Martin [1986] Conv. 355. (Severance of beneficial joint tenancy must result in equal shares even though unequal contributions.) *Pankhania v Chandegra* [2012] EWCA Civ 1438, below, para.13–009.

Nevertheless, parties are not obliged to avail themselves of the opportunity provided by the form because the transfer is valid even if the boxes are not completed.[36] It remains possible, therefore, to have a transfer into joint names but with no express declaration of the beneficial interests, either where the title was unregistered, or where a transfer of registered land occurred before 1998, or where the current form was used but the boxes were not completed.

The principles which apply to ascertain the beneficial interests of parties who are co-owners of the legal title were examined by the House of Lords in *Stack v Dowden*[37]:

> An unmarried couple, Mr S and Ms D, purchased a house in joint names as a family home. D paid 65% of the purchase price from an account in her name and funded by her. The balance was provided by a loan secured by a joint mortgage and two endowment policies, one in joint names and one in D's name. S paid the mortgage interest and the premiums on the joint policy. The loan was repaid by lump sums, to which S contributed about 60%. S and D had four children and lived together for nearly 20 years, but had separate bank accounts and investments. After they separated, it was held that S was entitled to 65% of the net proceeds of sale.

The House of Lords, led by Baroness Hale, set out to simplify the law by identifying "the correct starting point" and laying out "the right framework".[38] Their Lordships confirmed that the normal assumption was that, as equity followed the law, the beneficial interests of legal joint owners would also be joint. Similarly, in the case of sole legal ownership, the starting point was an assumption of sole beneficial ownership. In both cases, the burden of establishing otherwise was on the person claiming that the beneficial ownership did not follow the legal ownership.[39] In order to succeed in such a claim, the facts would have to be "very unusual",[40] and the mere fact that the contributions were unequal would not suffice.[41]

In the case of a domestic property, the strict resulting trust approach based on financial contributions to the purchase was no longer appropriate.[42] "In law, 'context is everything' and the domestic context is very different from the commercial world."[43] To rebut the presumption of equal shares, the search was for shared intentions in the light of the whole course of conduct. Relevant factors would include any advice or discussions at the time of the purchase, why the

---

[36] *Stack v Dowden* [2007] 2 A.C. 432 per Baroness Hale of Richmond at [52], noting that "if this [were] invariably complied with, the problem confronting us here [would] eventually disappear"; cf. A. Moran [2007] Conv. 364. A proposal for mandatory completion was not implemented; E. Cooke (2011) 41 Fam. Law 1142.

[37] [2007] 2 A.C. 432.

[38] [2007] 2 A.C. 432, per Lord Hope at [3].

[39] [2007] 2 A.C. 432, per Baroness Hale at [56].

[40] [2007] 2 A.C. 432, per Baroness Hale at [92].

[41] See e.g. *Barnes v Phillips* [2015] EWCA Civ 1056; [2016] H.L.R. 3; and *R. v Taylor* unreported, 9 February 2017, per Turner J at [47] "In the context of an enduring and loving relationship many couples would regard a predominately monetary assessment of their respective contributions as being invidious even in circumstances of quite significant financial disparity."

[42] Cases such as *Springette v Defoe* [1992] 2 F.L.R. 388 and *Huntingford v Hobbs* [1993] 1 F.L.R. 736 were disapproved. The position was confirmed by the Supreme Court in *Jones v Kernott* [2011] UKSC 53; [2012] 1 A.C. 776 at [25].

[43] [2007] 2 A.C. 432, per Baroness Hale at [69].

property was in joint names, the nature of the relationship, whether they had any children for whom both were responsible for providing a home, how the purchase was financed, how the parties arranged their finances, and how they discharged the outgoings and expenses. An arithmetical calculation would be unlikely to be important, as it would be easier to infer that the parties intended that each should contribute as much to the household as they reasonably could and that they would share the eventual benefit or burden equally. In the present case, Ms Dowden had contributed more, and they did not pool their resources. Everything apart from the house itself was kept strictly separate. This was considered very unusual,[44] as they had lived together for a long time and had children. Ms Dowden had, therefore, discharged the burden of establishing that she was entitled to more than half, and her share was 65%.

Lord Neuberger agreed with the result, but not the reasoning.[45] He favoured the resulting trust approach, which on the facts led to the same result,[46] and considered that the majority had crossed the line between inferring the parties' intentions and imputing them.[47] An inferred intention is one which is objectively deduced to be the subjective actual intention of the parties, while an imputed intention is attributed to the parties even though they had no such intention. His Lordship considered the "whole course of dealing" concept to be too vague. In his view, beneficial ownership is normally judged at the time of acquisition. There is much force in Lord Neuberger's comment that the rejection of the resulting trust solution where the contributions were unequal amounted to

13–006

> "a resurrection of the 'family assets' hypothesis disposed of in *Pettit v Pettit.*[48] It involves invoking a presumption of advancement between unmarried cohabitants, where such a presumption has never applied, and at a time when, as I have mentioned, the court is increasingly unenthusiastic about the presumption, even in relationships where it does apply."[49]

Applying the principles as stated by the majority in *Stack*, the Court of Appeal held in *Fowler v Barron*[50] that a man who had paid the deposit, all the mortgage repayments and all direct outgoings was unable to rebut the presumption that the beneficial interest was held jointly with his unmarried partner:

---

[44] Research indicates that such arrangements are more common than their Lordships thought; R. Probert (2007) 37 Fam. Law 924; N. Piska (2008) 71 M.L.R. 120; G. Douglas, J. Pearce and H. Woodward (2009) 72 M.L.R. 24.

[45] Professor Paterson reported fascinating insights about the judicial deliberations amongst the panel in *Stack v Dowden*: A. Paterson, *Final Judgment* (Oxford: Hart Publishing, 2013), pp.99, 129 and 154.

[46] The two approaches will not necessarily lead to the same result, as the common intention approach will not be dependent upon contributions alone. However, in her appeal, Ms Dowden only sought 65%, which corresponded to her contribution to the property on Lord Neuberger's analysis: [2007] 2 A.C. 432, per Baroness Hale at [84] and Lord Neuberger at [122]. This point has become important in the light of *Marr v Collie (Bahamas)* [2017] UKPC 17; [2017] 3 W.L.R. 1507, considered below para.13–019.

[47] See now *Jones v Kernott* [2011] UKSC 53; [2012] 1 A.C. 776; below, para.11–006. See also *Abbott v Abbott* [2008] 1 F.L.R. 1451.

[48] [1970] A.C. 777 at 795, 809–810, 816–817.

[49] [2007] 2 A.C. 432 at [112]. See also Lord Neuberger's complementary "The conspirators, the tax man, the Bill of Rights and a bit about the lovers" 2008 Chancery Bar Association Annual Lecture.

[50] [2008] W.T.L.R. 819; N. Piska [2008] Conv. 451; *Gibson v Revenue and Customs Prosecutions Office* [2009] Q.B. 348.

"the parties intended that it should make no difference to their interests in the property which party paid for what expense ... There was no prior agreement as to who would pay what. The inference from this ... was that the parties simply did not care about the respective size of each other's contributions."[51]

The fact that his intention had been that she should only inherit the property in the event on his death was irrelevant, since that had not been communicated to his partner. It could not thus be a "common" intention.

Stack v Dowden was subject to intense academic scrutiny.[52] Some commentators welcomed the majority decision, regarding it as a legitimate extension of the law to satisfy social justice.[53] However, it was perceived by many as having created uncertainty as to the circumstances necessary to establish unequal shares, and thus to have done little to reduce litigation.[54] The rejection of resulting trusts was "an act of abolition... with the benefit of almost no reasoning, and even a mistaken view of their nature".[55] In the wake of *Stack*, there were many decisions seeking to explore the relevant principles (some of which are considered below).[56]

13–007   **ii. *Jones v Kernott.*** The academic and judicial response to *Stack v Dowden* made it inevitable that the principles would be reconsidered at the highest level again, and so it was that the Supreme Court decided *Jones v Kernott*[57] in 2011. The latter decision has since been described as providing "the starting point for the road map through this area of the law".[58] The question before the court was whether the shares of beneficial joint tenants of a property had changed over time since their separation.

A property was bought in the joint names of an unmarried couple in 1985. Both contributed financially (she was a mobile hairdresser and he drove an ice-cream van) and it was common

---

[51] [2008] W.T.L.R. 819 per Arden LJ at [41].

[52] S. Gardner (2016) 132 L.Q.R. 373 at 377: "It is a feature of this area of the law that, however much commentators may try to rationalise it, the authorities themselves are highly indeterminate, and thus leave a striking degree of scope for improvisation in succeeding decisions."

[53] T. Etherton (2008) 67 C.L.J. 265 at 279; cf. T. Etherton [2009] Conv. 104. See also M. Pawlowski [2007] Conv. 352; M. Harding [2009] Conv. 309. For a full analysis see S. Gardner (2008) 124 L.Q.R. 422.

[54] A. Cloherty and D. Fox (2007) 66 C.L.J. 517; M. Dixon [2007] Conv. 352; G. Douglas (2008) 38 Fam. Law 639; G. Lightman (2008) 22 T.L.I. 11; R. Lee (2008) 124 L.Q.R. 209; P. Wee [2007] L.M.C.L.Q. 455.

[55] W. Swadling (2007) 123 L.Q.R. 511 at 518; P. Sparkes [2011] Conv. 156.

[56] Including *Holman v Howes* [2007] EWCA Civ 877; *James v Thomas* [2007] EWCA Civ 1212; *Morris v Morris* [2008] EWCA Civ 257; *Laskar v Laskar* [2008] EWCA Civ 347; [2008] W.L.R. 2695; *Fowler v Barron* [2008] EWCA Civ 377; *Gibson v Revenue & Customs Prosecution Office* [2008] EWCA Civ 645; [2009] 2 W.L.R. 471; *Williamson v Sheikh* [2008] EWCA Civ 990; *Qayyum v Hameed* [2009] EWCA Civ 352; [2009] 2 F.L.R. 962; *Kernott v Jones* [2010] EWCA Civ 578; [2010] W.L.R. 2401. See E. Cooke, "Taking Women's Property Seriously: Mrs Boland, the House of Lords, the Law Commission and the Role of Consensus" in J. Lee (ed.), *From House of Lords to Supreme Court: Judges, Jurists and the Process of Judging* (Oxford: Hart Publishing, 2011).

[57] [2011] UKSC 53; [2012] 1 A.C. 776; S. Gardner (2012) 128 L.Q.R. 178; A. Briggs (2012) 128 L.Q.R. 183; J. Mee (2012) 128 L.Q.R. 500; M. Dixon [2012] Conv. 83; M. Pawlowski [2012] Conv. 149; M. Yip [2012] Conv. 159; J. Mee [2012] Conv. 167; R.H. George (2012) 71 C.L.J. 39.

[58] *S v J (Beneficial Ownership)* [2016] EWHC 586 (Fam); [2016] Fam. Law 811 per Roberts J at [58].

ground that they originally held in equal shares. When the man left in 1993 he stopped contributing to the mortgage and outgoings. Around 1995 they agreed to cash in a joint life insurance policy and to divide the proceeds. The man then bought another property for himself. The county court ruled (on the woman's application) that her share had increased to 90% because she had paid over 80% of the mortgage interest. This ruling was upheld by the High Court, but on the man's appeal to the Court of Appeal it was held (by a majority) that an intention to vary their shares could not be spelled out from the fact that one party alone lived there, paying the outgoings and supporting their children, and so their shares remained equal. The Supreme Court allowed the woman's appeal and restored the original ruling, so that her share was 90%.

The starting point was that they were joint tenants at law and in equity, but this could be displaced by showing that they later formed a common intention that their shares should change. Their common intention (if not express) was to be deduced objectively from their conduct. If it was clear that the parties had changed their original intention but it was not possible to ascertain, either by direct evidence or inference, what shares they intended to have, each was entitled to such share as the court considered fair, having regard to their conduct and whole course of dealing in relation to the property.

Although the decision of the Supreme Court was unanimous, there were differences in the reasoning. Lord Walker and Lady Hale delivered a joint leading judgment. They noted that *Stack v Dowden* had attracted much comment, some of it adverse, and sought to clarify that decision[59] by reiterating its principles and confirming that the presumption of a resulting trust no longer applied to a purchase in joint names for joint occupation by a married or unmarried couple whose contributions were unequal.[60] The Supreme Court did not, however, refer to any of the Court of Appeal decisions which had followed *Stack v Dowden*, with the exception of the case under appeal.[61]

The Justices discussed the difference between inference and imputation, accepting that the search was primarily to ascertain the parties' actual intentions, whether expressed or inferred from conduct. If the parties' actual intentions could be discovered, whether expressly or by inference, it was not open to the court to impose a different solution on them just because the court considered it fair. Crucially, the Justices established that it was possible to impute an intention— that is, to ascribe an intention to the parties which they did not actually have:

> "if [the court] cannot deduce exactly what shares were intended, it may have no alternative but to ask what their intentions as reasonable and just people would have been had they thought about it at the time. This is a fallback position which some courts may not welcome, but the court has a duty to come to a conclusion on the dispute put before it."[62]

Lord Walker and Lady Hale considered that the conceptual difference between inferring and imputing was clear, but "the difference in practice may not be so great".[63]

---

[59] [2011] UKSC 53; [2012] 1 A.C. 776 per Lord Walker of Gestingthorpe and Baroness Hale of Richmond JJSC at [46] "It is always salutary to be confronted with the ambiguities which later emerge in what seemed at the time to be comparatively clear language". A. Paterson, *Final Judgment* (2013), 217.

[60] [2011] UKSC 53; [2012] 1 A.C. 776 at [25].

[61] *Kernott v Jones* [2010] EWCA Civ 578; [2010] W.L.R. 2401. One first instance decision *Adekunle v Ritchie* [2007] W.T.L.R. 1505 was cited by the joint judgment: [2012] 1 A.C. 776 at [16].

[62] [2011] UKSC 53; [2012] 1 A.C. 776 at [47].

[63] [2012] 1 A.C. 776 per Lord Walker of Gestingthorpe and Baroness Hale of Richmond JJSC at [34].

In the present case, there was, in the majority's view, no need to impute an intention that the parties' shares would change because the county court judge had made a finding that their intentions had in fact changed. When the parties cashed in the life policy and the man purchased a home, the "logical inference" was that they intended that the man's interest in the property should crystallise then. He would have the sole benefit of any capital gain in his own home and the woman would have the sole benefit of any capital gain in the other property. This intention could be inferred from their conduct. Lord Walker and Lady Hale concluded that the "whole course of dealing", which the court would take into account, should be given a broad meaning and that each case would turn on its own facts. Financial contributions would be relevant but so would many other factors.[64] As Floyd LJ has subsequently noted, "the exercise is not a rigidly arithmetical one".[65]

They added that, if the shares had remained the same, it would have been necessary to consider matters such as equitable accounting[66] in relation to the man's share of the mortgage interest and whether he could claim an occupation rent (though this was unlikely while the house was needed for the children).

Lord Collins agreed with the joint judgment that, if it was impossible to ascertain or infer what shares were intended, each would be entitled to a fair share in the light of the whole course of dealing. He considered that "the difference between inference and imputation will hardly ever matter" and that "what is one person's inference will be another person's imputation".[67]

13–008   Lord Kerr agreed that the appeal should be allowed but highlighted the differences in the reasoning of the members of the court, principally over the role of imputation. Unlike Lord Walker and Lady Hale, Lord Kerr found it difficult to infer that the man intended his interest in the property to crystallise when he bought his own home:

> "[The] conscientious quest to discover the parties' actual intention should cease when it becomes clear either that this is simply not deducible from the evidence or that no common intention exists. It would be unfortunate if the concept of inferring were to be strained so as to avoid the less immediately attractive option of imputation."[68]

Lord Wilson welcomed[69] the development that a common intention as to the size of their shares could be imputed to the parties, though he left open the question (which did not arise) whether the court could impute an intention that one party should have a share at all if it was not otherwise identifiable. However, he considered that Lord Walker and Lady Hale might have gone too far in suggesting that the difference between inferring and imputing a common

---

[64] The overall principles which are to be applied are summarised by Lord Walker of Gestingthorpe and Baroness Hale of Richmond JJSC [2011] UKSC 53; [2012] 1 A.C. 776 at [51].
[65] *Sandhu v Sandhu* [2016] EWCA Civ 1050 at [12].
[66] Below, para.13–017.
[67] [2011] UKSC 53; [2012] 1 A.C. 776 at [65].
[68] [2011] UKSC 53; [2012] 1 A.C. 776 at [72].
[69] [2011] UKSC 53; [2012] 1 A.C. 776 at [78].

intention may not be great. He found it impossible to infer that the parties intended their shares to be 90% and 10%, but was prepared to impute such an intention.

Opinions will differ as to whether the shares allocated to the parties were in fact "fair",[70] and whether it is right for the court to impute intentions to the parties which they never had.[71] The alternative would be that, if the parties have not expressed their intentions, and they cannot be inferred, their shares must remain as they were. What seems clear is that a fact-sensitive principle requiring the court to examine the "whole course of dealing" over many years in order to decide on their fair shares is a recipe for litigation.[72]

iii. Express Agreement or Declaration in Joint Names Cases. It remains **13–009** possible[73] that there may be evidence that the parties did express their common intention, both to share the beneficial interest in the property and as to their respective shares. Where there is a valid declaration of trust, there is no prospect of using the principles in *Stack* and *Kernott* to go behind that trust.[74] This position was confirmed in *Pankhania v Chandegra*[75]:

> A house was purchased in the names of a woman and her nephew as joint tenants in equal shares, with a declaration of trust to that effect. The nephew never lived at the property, which was intended as the aunt's matrimonial home. The aunt had insufficient income to obtain a mortgage and so the nephew was included as joint tenant in order to facilitate a mortgage by the taking into account of his salary. The Court of Appeal considered whether the interests were as declared in the trust instrument, or whether there was a common intention for the house to be held in the name of the aunt alone. The Court of Appeal held that the shares were as expressed in the declaration, which was valid. Mummery LJ noted:
>
> > "reliance on *Stack v Dowden* and *Jones v Kernott* for inferring or imputing a different trust in this and other similar cases which have recently been before this court is misplaced where there is an express declaration of trust of the beneficial title and no valid legal grounds for going behind it."[76]

---

[70] See S. Gardner (2016) 132 L.Q.R. 373.

[71] A. Hayward [2016] Conv. 233.

[72] The concern is partly born out of the apparent "drive for exceptionalism" which has existed since *Stack*: A. Hayward [2016] Conv. 233, 240. As Brian Sloan has put it in another context, [2017] Conv. 440 at 458: "but surely some of the core advantages of presumptions and precision on the circumstances in which they are both raised and rebutted is that they shape legal advice and might avoid a trial altogether".

[73] Although not necessarily usual: above, para.13–005.

[74] "Once the beneficial ownership of the land is determined by the documents, it is conclusive in the absence of fraud, mistake or some other vitiating factor" per Judge Paul Matthews sitting as judge of a High Court in *Taylor v Taylor* [2017] EWHC 1080 (Ch) at [49]. Similarly, Judge Elizabeth Cooke, sitting as a Deputy High Court Judge in the Chancery Division, in *Gaspar v Zaleski* [2017] EWHC 1770 (Ch) stated (at [77]) that "The argument that the constructive trust takes effect simultaneously with the express trust seems to me to drive a heavy goods vehicle through the law set out in *Goodman v Gallant* [1986] Fam 106, which is that the express trust is determinative unless changed later. Not surprisingly there is no authority in support of that argument, and I reject it."

[75] [2012] EWCA Civ 1438; M. Dixon [2013] Conv. 1. *Artist Court Collective Ltd v Khan* [2016] EWHC 2453 (Ch), per Henderson J at [43].

[76] [2012] EWCA Civ 1438 at [28].

There may also be evidence of express agreement short of a valid declaration of trust, as demonstrated by *Gallarotti v Sebastianelli*.[77]

> Two business associates and friends had bought a flat together on a mortgage, each making a cash contribution but with S making the larger contribution. There was an express agreement between the parties that their shares would be 50:50, but only on the basis that G would make larger payments towards the mortgage, which he never did. After the parties fell out, G sought a declaration of his interest in the property, claiming 50%. The Court of Appeal held that the parties' agreement was contingent on G paying more towards the mortgage: when that did not occur, "The logical result of the agreement, therefore, was that the agreement for 50/50 sharing was at an end ... It was wholly implausible that Mr Sebastianelli should make a substantial gift to Mr Gallarotti."[78] The court declared that S had a 75% share in the flat and G had a 25% share.

C.   Conveyance to One Party Only

13–010   We turn now to the cases where the property is in the name of one party only.[79] One question which had been raised after *Stack v Dowden* was whether the general principles applied to both single and joint names cases.[80] The joint judgment addressed this point in *Jones v Kernott*:

> "At a high level of generality, there is of course a single regime: the law of trusts ... We recognise that a 'common intention' trust is of central importance to 'joint names' as well as 'single names' cases ... Nevertheless it is important to point out that the starting point for analysis is different in the two situations. That is so even though it may be necessary to enquire into the varied circumstances and reasons why a house or flat has been acquired in a single name or in joint names."[81]

It will be seen that the application to single names cases has left some points uncertain.

If the house is conveyed to one party only, to the man, let us assume, for that has historically been the usual case, then he will prima facie be the owner of the whole beneficial interest as well.[82] If the documents of title expressly declare the beneficial interests, that, in the absence of fraud or mistake, is conclusive,[83] although those who were not parties to the deed cannot be prejudiced by such a declaration if they have contributed.[84] Failing that, the woman may claim a share of the beneficial interest in various ways. First, there may be an express contract in writing,[85] or a trust in her favour which is evidenced in writing.[86] Subject to estoppel arguments, an oral contract for the disposition of an interest in land is void. An oral declaration of a trust of land which is not evidenced in writing is

---

[77] [2012] EWCA Civ 865.

[78] [2012] EWCA Civ 865 per Arden LJ at [26].

[79] B. Sloan (2015) 35 L.S. 226.

[80] See, for example, S. Gardner and K. Davidson (2011) 127 L.Q.R. 13.

[81] [2011] UKSC 53; [2012] 1 A.C. 776 at [16].

[82] *Stack v Dowden* [2007] 2 A.C. 432, per Baroness Hale at [56].

[83] *Pettitt v Pettitt* [1970] A.C. 777 at 813; *Goodman v Gallant* [1986] Fam. 106. See also para.13–009 above.

[84] See *City of London Building Society v Flegg* [1988] A.C. 54.

[85] Law of Property (Miscellaneous Provisions) Act 1989 s.2. See L. Bently and P. Coughlan (1990) 10 L.S. 325.

[86] Law of Property Act 1925 s.53(1)(b); above, para.6–003.

unenforceable unless it has been acted upon so as to give rise to a constructive trust.[87] This is discussed below. If there is no express agreement or declaration, direct contributions in money or money's worth have traditionally been regarded as giving rise to a resulting trust, but the House of Lords and Supreme Court no longer favour this approach, as we have seen. Finally, a trust has been imposed in some cases simply in the interests of justice.[88]

i. Express Agreement or Declaration.   If the declaration is contained in the   **13–011**
documents of title, then it will be conclusive, as stated above.[89] If it is not contained in the documents of title but is nevertheless evidenced in writing, it is enforceable under s.53(1)(b) of the Law of Property Act 1925.[90] These formality requirements do not apply to resulting or constructive trusts.[91] In the present context, the question arises as to the circumstances necessary for the imposition of a constructive trust where there is an express oral declaration or agreement.

The first point to consider is what constitutes an express oral declaration or agreement. The question is whether prior to the acquisition, or exceptionally at some later date,[92] the parties had an agreement to share (whether or not it dealt with the size of the shares), based on evidence of express discussions,[93] however imperfectly remembered and however imprecise the terms.[94] A common intention to renovate a house as a joint venture or to share it as a family home does not of itself amount to a common intention to share the beneficial ownership.[95] An excuse as to why the property is in the man's name can, however, be treated as an express declaration of an intention to share the beneficial ownership.[96] In *Williamson v Sheikh*,[97] a young woman had provided the equity in the property bought with her older male partner, into whose sole name the house had been conveyed. The parties had been to see a solicitor and a draft declaration of trust

---

[87] *Midland Bank Ltd v Dobson* [1986] 1 F.L.R. 171; *Grant v Edwards* [1986] Ch. 638.

[88] *Cooke v Head* [1972] 1 W.L.R. 518; A. Oakley (1973) C.L.P. 17 at 25; *Eves v Eves* [1975] 1 W.L.R. 1338.

[89] Above, para.13–009.

[90] For a recent case on this subsection, see *Taylor v Taylor* [2017] EWHC 1080 (Ch).

[91] Law of Property Act 1925 s.53(2); Law of Property (Miscellaneous Provisions) Act 1989 s.2(5); *Yaxley v Gotts* [2000] Ch. 162.

[92] *Bernard v Josephs* [1982] Ch. 391; *Burns v Burns* [1984] Ch. 317; *Austin v Keele* (1987) 61 A.L.J.R. 605; *Lloyds Bank Plc v Rosset* [1991] 1 A.C. 107; *Stokes v Anderson* [1991] 1 F.L.R. 391; *Edwards v Edwards* (2015) 18 I.T.E.L.R. 691, below para.13–016.

[93] See the example of *Cutting v McGough*, unreported, 17 December 2017, in which District Judge DG Morgan MBE found that such an express agreement had been made "after a series of discussions about the [relevant] works" on the property in question.

[94] *Lloyds Bank Plc v Rosset* [1991] 1 A.C. 107. But see N. Glover and P. Todd (1996) 16 L.S. 325.

[95] *Lloyds Bank Plc v Rosset* [1991] 1 A.C. 107. See also *Otway v Gibbs* [2001] W.T.L.R. 467 (using words such as "our home" does not suffice); *Mollo v Mollo* [2000] W.T.L.R. 227 (accommodation "for the boys" gave them no interest).

[96] *Eves v Eves* [1975] 1 W.L.R. 1338 (excuse that woman under 21); *Grant v Edwards* [1986] Ch. 638 (excuse that joint names might prejudice her divorce proceedings); criticised B. Sufrin (1987) 50 M.L.R. 94; S. Gardner (1993) 109 L.Q.R. 263 at 265 and 282; cf. R. Smith (1993) 3 Carib.L.R. 96; P. Milne (1995) 145 N.L.J. 423, 456. See also *Rowe v Prance* [1999] 2 F.L.R. 787 (woman entitled to half share of boat registered in man's name; "absurd" excuse that she did not possess a master's certificate); S. Baughen [2000] Conv. 58; *Van Laethem v Brooker* [2006] 2 F.L.R. 495 (excuse about capital gains tax). Such cases may be better understood as cases of estoppel: see Ch.30.

[97] [2008] EWCA Civ 990.

had been drawn up with the beneficial interests 60:40 in favour of the woman. This declaration had not been executed, but was taken, with the contribution to the purchase price, as evidence of express common intention to share the beneficial interest sufficient to rebut the presumption of sole beneficial ownership.[98] Where, however, the circumstances do not otherwise justify the recognition of a constructive trust, the fact that a supposed "excuse" was given will not suffice to establish a common intention to share beneficial ownership.[99]

Assuming that an express common intention is established, the claimant must also show that she has acted upon it to her detriment if a constructive trust (or estoppel) is to arise.[100] An oral agreement alone cannot suffice, as this would infringe the formality rules and could prejudice the legal owner's creditors.[101] It is clear that significant contributions in money or money's worth, even though indirect, will satisfy the requirements of detrimental reliance. Thus in *Grant v Edwards*,[102] a woman was entitled to a half share where, pursuant to an express oral declaration, she had made substantial indirect contributions to the mortgage by applying her earnings to the joint household expenses in addition to keeping house and bringing up the children. The Court of Appeal considered that any detrimental act relating to the joint lives of the parties would have sufficed. Such a view provides an opportunity for a sympathetic treatment of a woman who has made no financial contribution.[103] In a similar vein, the Privy Council has said that once a common intention has been established it may not be difficult to find conduct on the part of the woman which is referable to the creation of her beneficial interest.[104]

The House of Lords reviewed these principles in *Lloyds Bank Plc v Rosset*.[105] In that case there was no express common intention. If there had been, the wife's acts of decorating and supervising renovation works would not have constituted detrimental reliance, as they were acts which any wife would do.[106] Acts which have been considered sufficient include refraining from seeking repayment of a loan or interest upon it,[107] and a payment of £12,000 to the man so that he could

---

[98] And the draft declaration was also used when calculating the shares. cf. *Arif v Anwar* [2015] EWHC 124 (Fam); [2015] Fam. Law 381.

[99] *Curran v Collins* [2015] EWCA Civ 404, per Lewison LJ at [75] "[*Eves v Eves* [1975] 1 W.L.R. 1338 and *Grant v Edwards* [1986] Ch. 638] do not establish the proposition that the mere giving of a 'specious excuse' necessarily or even usually leads to an inference that the person to whom the excuse is given can reasonably regard herself as having an immediate entitlement to an interest in the property in question".

[100] The onus is on the legal owner to prove that any detrimental act was not done in reliance upon the common intention; *Greasley v Cooke* [1980] 1 W.L.R. 1306; *Maharaj v Chand* [1986] A.C. 898.

[101] *Midland Bank Ltd v Dobson* [1986] 1 F.L.R. 171; cf. *Re Densham* [1975] 1 W.L.R. 1519. See also *Supperstone v Hurst* [2006] 1 F.L.R. 1245.

[102] [1986] Ch. 638. See also *Eves v Eves* [1975] 1 W.L.R. 1338; *Chan Pui Chun v Leung Kam Ho* [2003] 1 F.L.R. 23.

[103] B. Sufrin (1987) 50 M.L.R. 94; J. Montgomery [1987] Conv. 16; A. Lawson (1996) 16 L.S. 218; cf. *Coombes v Smith* [1986] 1 W.L.R. 808, below, para.30–013.

[104] *Austin v Keele* (1987) 61 A.L.J.R. 605 at 610.

[105] [1991] 1 A.C. 107; J. Davies (1990) 106 L.Q.R. 539; M. Thompson [1990] Conv. 314; S. Cretney All E.R. Rev. 1990, p.138; M. Dixon (1991) 50 C.L.J. 38; S. Gardner (1991) 54 M.L.R. 126.

[106] cf. *Ungurian v Lesnoff* [1990] Ch. 206; M. Oldham (1990) 49 C.L.J. 25 (common intention to create life interest sufficiently acted upon by decorating and refurbishment).

[107] *Risch v McFee* (1991) 61 P. & C.R. 42.

buy out his estranged wife's share and pay the mortgage on her new house.[108] In *Smith v Bottomley*,[109] the Court of Appeal declined to determine whether in principle a promise to marry could constitute sufficient detrimental reliance.[110] *Curran v Collins*[111] confirmed that the "need for detrimental reliance on the part of the claimant is an essential feature of this kind of case",[112] rejecting the suggestion that *Stack v Dowden* and *Jones v Kernott* had abolished the requirement.[113] Judge Paul Matthews has made the recent obiter observation that there are implications for formality rules if the reliance requirement were to be relaxed:

> "if there really were no need for detrimental reliance, and intention were everything, the room for the operation of the statutory requirement section 53(1)(b) of the Law of Property Act 1925 for signed writing as evidence would become very small indeed."[114]

ii. Direct Contributions.   The traditional approach used to be that there would be a purchase money resulting trust in favour of a person who contributed to the purchase price. Beneficial ownership would then be enjoyed in the proportion in which the purchase money was provided.[115] If the purchase money was provided equally, the parties would be beneficial joint tenants. If the contributions were unequal, they would be tenants in common. Payment of, or substantial contributions to the mortgage instalments, would usually suffice[116]; however, such payments did not give rise to a resulting trust unless the payer had assumed liability to make them when the property was purchased (although they could found a constructive trust).[117] For a resulting trust to arise, any payments had to be in money or money's worth.[118] Where property was put into a person's name (solely or jointly) in order to facilitate a mortgage advance, he or she would not normally acquire an interest where the understanding was that another person would make all the repayments.[119]

13–012

The presumption of advancement once arose in a case where a husband has transferred or arranged for the transfer of the legal estate to his wife; but, as has

---

[108] *Stokes v Anderson* [1991] 1 F.L.R. 391.

[109] [2013] EWCA Civ 953.

[110] [2013] EWCA Civ 953 per Sales J at [62]. See also *Walsh v Singh* [2010] 1 F.L.R. 1658 (no claim where woman gave up Bar career and helped in man's business, expecting marriage).

[111] [2015] EWCA Civ 404.

[112] [2015] EWCA Civ 404 per Lewison LJ at [77]. At [78] Lewison LJ described the absence of detrimental reliance as "fatal" to the claimant's case.

[113] [2015] EWCA Civ 404 at [78]. See further B. Sloan (2015) 35 L.S. 226 at 228.

[114] *Taylor v Taylor* [2017] EWHC 1080 (Ch); [2017] 4 W.L.R. 83 at [61].

[115] *Re Roger's Question* [1948] 1 All E.R. 328; *Bull v Bull* [1955] 1 Q.B. 234. A strict view was taken in *Winkworth v Edward Baron Development Co Ltd* [1986] 1 W.L.R. 1512, where, however, the protection of creditors was a significant factor. See J. Warburton [1987] Conv. 217.

[116] *Springette v Defoe* (1993) 65 P. & C.R. 1. The share of a party who contributed capital via a mortgage will be debited with any outstanding principal; *Savill v Goodall* [1993] 1 F.L.R. 755.

[117] P. Matthews (1994) 8 T.L.I. 43; Law Com. No. 307, *Cohabitation: The Financial Consequences of Relationship Breakdown* (2007), A.28, A.29; *Barrett v Barrett* [2008] 2 P. & C.R. 17.

[118] *Muetzel v Muetzel* [1970] 1 W.L.R. 188; *Wachtel v Wachtel* [1973] Fam. 72. A council tenant's discount in exercising a right to buy is usually treated as a financial contribution; *Ashe v Mumford* (2001) 33 H.L.R. 67.

[119] *Re Share (Lorraine)* [2002] 2 F.L.R. 88; *Carlton v Goodman* [2002] 2 F.L.R. 259.

been seen, statements in *Pettitt v Pettitt*[120] show that the influence of the presumptions has been much reduced. The presumption of advancement was abolished by the Equality Act 2010, although the relevant provisions are still not in force at the time of writing.[121] There was no presumption of advancement where a wife was transferred shares to her husband[122]; nor in the case of an unmarried couple.[123]

Doubt was cast on the resulting trust approach by the House of Lords in *Lloyds Bank Plc v Rosset*, where direct contributions were regarded as giving rise to a constructive trust rather than a resulting trust. Many subsequent cases adopted the constructive trust approach, although there was some confusion. As we have seen,[124] the House of Lords and Supreme Court firmly rejected the resulting trust analysis in *Stack v Dowden*[125] and *Jones v Kernott* in the context of the family home. Both cases involved a property in joint names, but the rejection of the resulting trust was not intended to be confined to that situation. The presumption of a resulting trust may still apply, however, in the context of commercial property or property bought as an investment, even where the purchasers are family members, although as will be seen below, the scope for its application may have been reduced by the recent Privy Council decision in *Marr v Collie*.[126]

13–013   The remainder of this section deals with interests arising under a constructive trust where the person claiming a share of the property held in the name of the other party has made a direct contribution. Cases in the 1990s prior to *Stack v Dowden* displayed a broad approach.[127] In the light of subsequent developments, we may however begin with *Oxley v Hiscock*,[128] where the Court of Appeal reviewed the relevant authorities (and it is still important to understand the background to the more recent authority). In that case an unmarried couple both made direct contributions to the acquisition of a house which was in the man's

---

[120] [1970] A.C. 777. See also *Simpson v Simpson* [1992] 1 F.L.R. 601.

[121] Above, para.11–028.

[122] *Heseltine v Heseltine* [1971] 1 W.L.R. 342 (personalty); see more generally on presumptions in the case of bank accounts *Whitlock v Moree (Bahamas)* [2017] UKPC 44.

[123] Unless they had agreed to marry; Law Reform (Miscellaneous Provisions) Act 1970 s.2(1); *Mossop v Mossop* [1989] Fam. 77. As to "agreement to marry", see *Shaw v Fitzgerald* [1992] 1 F.L.R. 357.

[124] Above, paras 13–005—13–008.

[125] Lord Neuberger's minority view favoured the resulting trust approach. See Law Com. No. 307, *Cohabitation: The Financial Consequences of Relationship Breakdown* (2007), A.25.

[126] [2017] UKPC 17; [2017] 3 W.L.R. 1507; M. George and B. Sloan [2017] Conv. 303. cf. *Laskar v Laskar* [2008] 1 W.L.R. 2695 (property bought by mother and daughter for letting).

[127] *McHardy and Sons (A Firm) v Warren* [1994] 2 F.L.R. 338, questioned in J. Dewar (1994) 24 Fam. Law 567. See also *Halifax Building Society v Brown* [1996] 1 F.L.R. 103 (loan from mother-in-law for deposit). *Midland Bank Plc v Cooke* [1995] 4 All E.R. 562. See S. Cretney and P. Clarke All E.R. Rev. 1995, pp.286 and 312 respectively; S. Gardner (1996) 112 L.Q.R. 378; M. Oldham (1996) 55 C.L.J. 194; G. Battersby [1996] 8 C.F.L.Q. 261; N. Glover and P. Todd (1996) 16 L.S. 325 at 340; M. Dixon [1997] Conv. 66. *Drake v Whipp* [1996] 1 F.L.R. 826; A. Dunn [1997] Conv. 467. See also *Le Foe v Le Foe* [2001] 2 F.L.R. 970 (direct contributions of about 10% combined with indirect contributions gave wife a half share); *Mollo v Mollo* [2000] W.T.L.R. 227.

[128] [2005] Fam. 211; P. Clarke All E.R. Rev. 2004, p.274; R. Bailey-Harris (2004) 34 Fam. Law 571; S. Gardner [2004] 120 L.Q.R. 541; M. Thompson [2004] Conv. 496. See also *Cox v Jones* [2004] 2 F.L.R. 1010; R. Probert [2005] Conv. 168.

name. There was evidence of an express common intention to share, but no evidence of intention as to the size of their respective shares. Chadwick LJ, with whom the other members of the court agreed, considered that the law had moved on from the mathematical resulting trust approach of cases like *Springette v Defoe*.[129] In cases involving the family home, where the parties had an express common intention to share but had not discussed the size of their shares, or where their common intention was inferred from their direct contributions, there is no necessary inference that their shares should be proportionate to their contributions. Thus in effect the constructive trust overrides the resulting trust in this type of case. The court will "supply or impute" a common intention as to what their shares should be, on the basis of what is fair in the circumstances, including later acts and conduct (such as paying outgoings or housekeeping). On that basis the woman was held entitled to 40%, which modestly exceeded her financial contributions. His Lordship considered that, in cases of this kind, proprietary estoppel principles would lead to the same outcome.

The *Oxley v Hiscock* line of cases was discussed by the House of Lords in *Stack v Dowden*, and the majority of their Lordships confirmed that a wide view should be taken of what counts as a contribution in cases of this kind. The *Oxley* approach, requiring the court to have regard to the "whole course of dealing" between the parties, was endorsed, but not insofar as it suggested that "fairness" was the determinant factor above other considerations. The same view was taken in *Jones v Kernott*, where Lord Collins described the judgment of Chadwick LJ in *Oxley* as "magisterial".[130] Although *Jones v Kernott* involved a property in joint names, the Supreme Court indicated that the court should apply the same principles in a case where the property was in one name only when deciding on the extent of the parties' shares, once it had been established that they had a common intention to share the beneficial interest.[131]

The difficulty with this approach is that the width of discretion leads to uncertainty and litigation. Indeed, the Law Commission[132] considered this "broad brush" approach to be an arbitrary method of quantifying shares.

The approach to quantification in a single names case was considered by HHJ Behrens in *Aspden v Elvy*.[133] The case is significant as the first in which the court imputed intention as to shares under *Jones v Kernott*. The facts were "on any view ... unusual"[134]:

> The claimant had owned a farm, which included a barn. He lived at the property with the defendant and their children. The couple separated and the defendant and the children moved nearby. The claimant subsequently transferred the barn to the defendant. The barn was converted in order to make it suitable for the defendant and the children to live there, although the claimant never lived there with them (living in a caravan next door). The question was whether the claimant had any beneficial interest in the barn.

---

[129] (1992) 65 P. & C.R. 1. The House of Lords in *Stack v Dowden* [2007] 2 A.C. 432 confirmed that *Springette* should not be followed.

[130] [2012] 1 A.C. 776 at [61].

[131] [2012] 1 A.C. 776 at [52].

[132] Law Com. Discussion Paper, *Sharing Homes* (2002), paras 2.87, 2.109.

[133] [2012] EWHC 1387 (Ch); J. Lee [2012] Conv. 421.

[134] [2012] EWHC 1387 (Ch) at [2].

The judge inferred a common intention to share from the parties' course of dealing,[135] but found that the parties had not considered the shares which each should have. It was therefore necessary to impute an intention. Counsel's submissions as to extent of the claimant's interest "suggested wildly differing results, ranging from 10% on behalf of the defendant to 75% on behalf of the claimant.[136] HHJ Behrens expressly anchored the quantification by imputation to the claimants' contribution to the property:

> "In the end I have decided that the appropriate fair assessment of the interest is 25%. To my mind that represents a fair return for the investment of £65,000 to £70,000 and the work carried out by Mr Aspden in a property now worth £400,000. The figure is somewhat arbitrary but it is the best I can do with the available material."[137]

It is notable that the judge's approach focused on the financial considerations as the way in which to work out the appropriate quantification of the claimant's interest via imputation.

The next question is whether, in the absence of a direct contribution or express agreement, a common intention to share may be inferred solely from indirect contributions or other conduct.

13–014   **iii. Indirect Contributions.**   In *Gissing v Gissing*,[138] the House of Lords rejected the claim of a wife who had paid £220 for furnishings and for laying a lawn, plus some household expenses, because she had made no contribution to the purchase price. It was, however, accepted that a wife who contributed indirectly by relieving her husband of household expenses and thereby enabling him to pay the mortgage would be entitled to an interest.[139]

Subsequent decisions in the Court of Appeal, primarily in Lord Denning's time as Master of the Rolls, supported the view that substantial financial contributions, even though indirect, would suffice for the acquisition of a share.[140] Thus interests were acquired by the contribution of physical labour on the property,[141] or by unpaid work in the family business which enabled the husband to put the money saved towards the purchase of property.[142] Domestic duties in the home, on the other hand, have never sufficed. In *Burns v Burns*,[143] the woman's housework, childcare, decorating and the purchase of chattels for the home over a period of 17 years gave her no share. If this was unjust, it was suggested that the remedy lay with Parliament.

13–015   In English law it appears that, in the absence of an express common intention, indirect contributions alone may not suffice. In *Lloyds Bank Plc v Rosset*, where the wife had made no substantial contribution, direct or indirect, Lord Bridge

---

[135] [2012] EWHC 1387 (Ch) at [124]–[125].

[136] [2012] EWHC 1387 (Ch) at [127].

[137] [2012] EWHC 1387 (Ch) at [128]. His Honour went on to note that he would have reached the same result on the basis of estoppel.

[138] [1971] A.C. 886.

[139] [1971] A.C. 886 at 903, 907–908.

[140] *Falconer v Falconer* [1970] 1 W.L.R. 1333; *Hargrave v Newton* [1971] 1 W.L.R. 1611; *Wachtel v Wachtel* [1973] Fam. 72.

[141] *Cooke v Head* [1972] 1 W.L.R. 518. For improvements, see below, para.13–016.

[142] *Nixon v Nixon* [1969] 1 W.L.R. 1676.

[143] [1984] Ch. 317 (unmarried couple). See also *Richards v Dove* [1974] 1 All E.R. 888; *Layton v Martin* (1986) 16 Fam. Law 212; *Windeler v Whitehall* [1990] 2 F.L.R. 505 (housework and business entertaining insufficient).

took the opportunity to state that direct contributions (whether initially or by payment of the mortgage) were necessary, and that "it is at least extremely doubtful whether anything less will do."[144] The earlier cases of *Eves v Eves*[145] (extensive decorative work and heavy gardening) and *Grant v Edwards*[146] (substantial indirect contributions to the mortgage by applying earnings to household expenses, plus running the home) were held to have been correctly decided because both involved an express common intention. In the absence of the latter, neither claimant would have succeeded, because the conduct in each case "fell far short" of conduct which would by itself have supported a claim to a share.[147] However, Lord Bridge's view in *Rosset* was for a long time considered too restrictive, and the House of Lords in *Stack v Dowden* subsequently expressed the view (obiter, as the case involved direct contributions and a property in joint names) that Lord Bridge's well-known comment that it was "extremely doubtful if anything less will do" (i.e. anything less than direct contributions in the absence of an express common intention) failed to take full account of the views expressed in *Gissing v Gissing*. Baroness Hale, giving judgment for the Privy Council in *Abbott v Abbott*,[148] again doubted the need for direct contributions, saying that the law had "moved on" since *Rosset*.[149] *Abbott v Abbott* was a single names case in which the property was in the sole name of the husband[150] and the wife claimed a share under the principles in *Stack v Dowden*. However, on the facts, the husband had accepted that his wife had an interest, though he disputed the amount.[151] The first question of whether she had an interest at all was therefore conceded rather than decided. This view on the law having "moved on" since *Rosset* cannot yet be said to be firmly established,[152] and it remains unclear how a party who has made only domestic contributions will fare.[153] Indeed, Baroness Hale DPSC did not comment on the status of *Rosset* in this respect when considering its relevance on another point in the more recent decision of *Southern Pacific Mortgages Ltd v Scott*.[154]

While the claim of a party who cannot establish an express common intention and whose only contributions are indirect remains in doubt (although greatly

---

[144] [1991] 1 A.C. 107 at 133. An example of "anything less" that might "do", even on the restrictive *Rosset* approach could be *Nixon v Nixon* [1969] 1 W.L.R. 1676, where one party's expenditure on bills and other costs enables the other party to pay the mortgage.

[145] [1975] 1 W.L.R. 1338.

[146] [1986] Ch. 638.

[147] For a recent example of just such a failure to establish an interest, see *Curran v Collins* [2015] EWCA Civ 404.

[148] [2007] UKPC 53; [2008] 1 F.L.R. 1451; criticised M. Dixon [2007] Conv. 456; R. Lee (2008) 124 L.Q.R. 209. The Privy Council repeated that the constructive trust has replaced the resulting trust in cases on the family home.

[149] [2007] UKPC 53; [2008] 1 F.L.R. 1451 at [6] and [19].

[150] The appeal to the Privy Council was from Antigua and Barbuda, which did not have equivalent matrimonial legislation to that in England.

[151] [2007] UKPC 53; [2008] 1 F.L.R. 1451 at [19].

[152] *Rosset* was still cited by Anthony Elleray QC sitting as a Deputy High Court Judge in *AIB Group (UK) Plc v Turner* [2015] EWHC 3994 (Ch).

[153] Law Com. No. 307, *Cohabitation: The Financial Consequences of Relationship Breakdown* (2007), para.2.13.

[154] [2014] UKSC 52; [2015] A.C. 385 at [105]–[111]. *Rosset* was not mentioned in the most recent key Privy Council authority of *Marr v Collie* [2017] UKPC 17; [2017] 3 W.L.R. 1507.

strengthened by the comments in *Stack v Dowden* and *Abbott v Abbott*), where a party has made direct contributions, any indirect contributions may also be taken into account in assessing the shares the parties are assumed to have intended.[155] In *Le Foe v Le Foe*,[156] the wife contributed indirectly in the early years by paying for general outgoings while her husband made the mortgage payments. After inheriting some money she made direct contributions of about 10% of the value of the house, primarily by way of mortgage payments. The husband claimed that her direct contributions led to the inference of a common intention that she should have a 10% share. The judge referred to *Gissing v Gissing* and *Burns v Burns* and held that her indirect contributions justified the inference of a common intention to share, and that her share should be quantified at 50%. This approach reduces any remaining impact of *Lloyds Bank Plc v Rosset*. Finally, we saw that the Supreme Court in *Jones v Kernott* did not shrink from imputing intentions to the parties in order to arrive at their "fair shares". However, Lord Wilson left open the question whether the court could impute the common intention to share at the first stage, which in a single names case is that one party should have a share at all if no such common intention had been expressed or could be inferred. "That question will merit careful thought."[157]

In subsequent cases, the courts have vigorously policed the distinction between the two stages, and rejected the possibility of imputation at the first stage.[158] For example, in *Barnes v Phillips*, Lloyd Jones LJ (as he then was) said[159]:

> "Throughout their joint judgment [in *Kernott*] Lord Walker and Baroness Hale make clear that imputation is not permissible at the stage of determining whether there has been a common change of intention, but only at the second stage of determining the share of each in circumstances where inference is not possible."

A final point to note is that the Court of Appeal has also been cautious with respect to interfering with apportionments carried out by judges at first instance.[160]

13–016   **v. Substantial Improvements.**   Some of the problems of indirect contributions arose where one of the parties had made a substantial contribution in time or money to the improvement of the property subsequent to the purchase. The Matrimonial Proceedings and Property Act 1970 s.37, which applies only to married couples[161] (with a similar provision for civil partners),[162] provides that:

---

[155] *Midland Bank Plc v Cooke* [1995] 4 All E.R. 562; *Oxley v Hiscock* [2005] Fam. 211.

[156] [2001] 2 F.L.R. 970 (High Court); M. Pawlowski (2002) 32 Fam. Law 190; M. Thompson [2002] Conv. 273.

[157] [2012] 1 A.C. 776 at [84].

[158] *Capehorn v Harris* [2015] EWCA Civ 955; [2016] H.L.R. 1, per Sales LJ at [21] and [23]; A Dymond (2016) 19 J.H.L. 57 at 58–9.

[159] *Barnes v Phillips* [2015] EWCA Civ 1056; [2016] H.L.R. 3 at [25]. A Dymond (2016) 19 J.H.L. 57 at 60.

[160] See e.g. *Curran v Collins* [2015] EWCA Civ 404, per Arden LJ at [29]–[33] (on the importance of fact finding) and [41]–[43] (on evaluation); *Barnes v Phillips* [2015] EWCA Civ 1056; [2016] H.L.R. 3; A. Dymond (2016) 19 J.H.L. 57 at 60.

[161] And to engaged couples by reason of Law Reform (Miscellaneous Provisions) Act 1970 s.2(1); *Dibble v Pfluger* [2011] 1 F.L.R. 659.

> "[W]here a husband or wife contributes in money or money's worth to the improvement of real or personal property in which... either or both of them has or have a beneficial interest, the husband or wife so contributing shall, if the contribution is of a substantial nature and subject to any agreement between them to the contrary express or implied, be treated as having then acquired by virtue of his or her contribution a share or an enlarged share, as the case may be, in that beneficial interest of such an extent as may have been then agreed or, in default of such agreement, as may seem in all the circumstances just ... ".[163]

Lord Denning said that this provision was declaratory of the previous law,[164] and indeed the language of the statute is declaratory. As far as unmarried couples are concerned, substantial improvements may give rise to an interest on the basis of common intention or estoppel, even though s.37 does not apply.[165]

Examples can be found of an interest being established in cases of substantial improvement outside of the legislative framework: in *Edwards v Edwards*,[166] it was held by the Eastern Caribbean Supreme Court that a wife had established a common intention to share the beneficial interest in a property, which was solely in her husband's name, by paying substantial renovation costs and the purchase of furniture and appliances for the home.[167]

vi. Date for Valuation of the Share. If it is established that a person is entitled to a share of the home under a trust (express or constructive), and in the absence of any intention of the parties to change their respective shares,[168] it follows that he or she is entitled to share proportionately in any increase (or decrease) in its value, although occurring after separation, until such time as the property is sold.[169] This principle has been firmly upheld by the Court of Appeal.[170] Credit will be given by way of "equitable accounting" for expenditure such as mortgage payments and repairs incurred by the occupying co-owner after separation.[171]

13–017

---

[162] Above, paras 13–002–13–003.

[163] *Griffiths v Griffiths* [1973] 1 W.L.R. 1454; *Re Nicholson (Deceased)* [1974] 1 W.L.R. 476.

[164] *Davis v Vale* [1971] 1 W.L.R. 1021; *Jansen v Jansen* [1965] P. 478.

[165] *Thomas v Fuller-Brown* [1988] 1 F.L.R. 237 (where the claim failed because the inference was that the expenditure was in return for rent-free accommodation); *Passee v Passee* [1988] 1 F.L.R. 263; J. Warburton [1988] Conv. 361. It is otherwise if the money was advanced as a loan; *Spence v Brown* (1988) 18 Fam. Law 291; cf. *Hussey v Palmer* [1972] 1 W.L.R. 1286. See generally M. Pawlowski (2009) 39 Fam. Law 680.

[166] (2015) 18 I.T.E.L.R. 691.

[167] (2015) 18 I.T.E.L.R. 691 per Thom JA at [41]–[43]. Amongst other things, Mrs. Edwards paid $10,000 for the installation of kitchen fixtures, covered the costs of a Jacuzzi, shower and toilet, and she borrowed $55,000 for further furniture and appliances.

[168] *Jones v Kernott* [2011] UKSC 53; [2012] 1 A.C. 776.

[169] Or the co-ownership ends in another way, e.g. if one buys the other out. See *Young v Lauretani* [2007] 2 F.L.R. 1211.

[170] *Turton v Turton* [1988] Ch. 542; J. Warburton [1987] Conv. 378; (1987) 103 L.Q.R. 500; J. Montgomery (1988) 18 Fam. Law 72; I. Hardcastle (1989) 86/31 L.S.Gaz. 31; *Gordon v Douce* [1983] 1 W.L.R. 563; *Passee v Passee* [1988] 1 F.L.R. 263. See also *Cousins v Dzosens* (1984) 81 L.S.Gaz. 2855; *Bernard v Josephs* [1982] Ch. 391.

[171] *Wilcox v Tait* [2007] 2 F.L.R. 871; G. Lightman (2008) 22 T.L.I. 11.

D. The Relevance of Contexts and the "Commercial Dimension" in the Purchase of Property[172]

13–018   It was noted above that the framework under *Stack v Dowden* and *Jones v Kernott* applies in the domestic consumer context.[173] Outside of that context, the courts were initially reluctant to apply the framework. Where the purchase is part domestic and part commercial, it was held that the question should be what the primary purpose of the purchase was, in *Laskar v Laskar*.[174]

> In *Laskar v Laskar*, Lord Neuberger, who had of course disagreed with the analysis in *Stack*, led the Court of Appeal in concluding that the principles did not apply in a case where a mother and daughter had together purchased the mother's council house at a discount, His Lordship said:
>
> > "the primary purpose of the purchase of the property was as an investment, not as a home. In other words this was a purchase which, at least primarily, was not in 'the domestic consumer context but in a commercial context. To my mind it would not be right to apply the reasoning in *Stack v Dowden* to such a case as this, where the parties primarily purchased the property as an investment for rental income and capital appreciation, even where their relationship is a familial one."
>
> It was thus appropriate to apply a resulting trust approach instead, with the shares 2:1 in favour of the mother, to reflect their respective contributions and taking into account the mother's discount for buying her own council house.

It was noted above that no comment was made on this decision in *Jones v Kernott*,[175] although Lord Walker and Lady Hale did recognise that an exception to the search for the parties' common intention was "where the classic resulting trust presumption applies. Indeed, this would be rare in a domestic context, but might perhaps arise where domestic partners were also business partners."[176]

It should also be noted that there was a further observation from the Justices in *Jones v Kernott* that whether the resulting trust presumptions remained appropriate in contexts outside the family home was not the issue in that case.[177] Etherton LJ (as he then was) has since said that the common intention constructive trust is a "specific jurisprudential response"[178] to the problems of cohabitation and that the "special features, in terms of policy, facts and law [in such cases], do not apply in a commercial context."[179] Similarly Chief Master Marsh in *Erlam v Rahman*,[180] a case concerning the beneficial ownership of rental properties by a husband and wife, held that the *Stack* approach "has no

---

[172] N. Hopkins (2011) 31 L.S. 175; M. Yip [2016] Conv. 347.

[173] *Stack v Dowden* [2007] 2 A.C. 432 per Baroness Hale at [58].

[174] [2008] 1 W.L.R. 2695 at [17]; N. Piska [2008] Conv. 441; *Uddin v Bashir* [2012] EWHC 1673 (Ch), Judge Simon Barker QC at [70]. See also (pre-dating *Stack v Dowden*) *Hammond v Mitchell* [1991] 1 W.L.R. 1127; L. Clarke and R. Edmunds (1992) 22 Fam. Law 523.

[175] Indeed, in 2016 Chief Master Marsh described *Laskar* as "[appearing] to be a somewhat neglected decision": *Erlam v Rahman* [2016] EWHC 111 (Ch) at [41].

[176] [2011] UKSC 53; [2012] 1 A.C. 776 at [31]. The Court of Appeal considered "just such a case" in *Graham-York v York* [2015] EWCA Civ 72, per Tomlinson LJ at [22].

[177] [2011] UKSC 53; [2012] 1 A.C. 776 per Lord Walker and Lady Hale JJSC at [53].

[178] *Crossco No.4 Unlimited v Jolan Ltd* [2011] EWCA Civ 1619 at [85]; M. Yip (2013) 33 L.S. 549.

[179] [2011] EWCA Civ 1619 at [86].

[180] [2016] EWHC 111 (Ch).

application to a property bought by a married couple for investment rather than as a home. It was not a purchase in the 'domestic consumer context'".

This position has however been thrown into doubt by the decision of the Privy Council in *Marr v Collie*.[181] The Judgment of the Board was given by Lord Kerr, and the panel included Lord Neuberger, Lady Hale and Lord Wilson, all of whom, as we have seen, made important contributions in *Stack* and *Kernott*. The appeal in *Marr* came to the Privy Council from the Bahamas:

13–019

> Mr Marr, a Canadian banker, and Mr Collie, a Bahamian building contractor, were in a relationship for 17 years. During the course of their relationship, they bought several properties, along with a boat, a truck and works of art. The general arrangement appeared to be that Mr Marr would finance the purchase of the properties, and Mr Collie would carry out construction and maintenance. After their relationship ended, there was a dispute over the ownership of the various items of real and personal property. Mr Marr claimed that, having paid virtually all of the payment costs for the real properties in joint names, he was entitled to sole beneficial ownership of them. In respect of one of the properties, Mr Marr had at one stage e-mailed a bank indicating that they would have a 50% each in it. One property in South Westridge was conveyed in Mr Marr's name only, with a view to Mr Marr claiming permanent residency in the Bahamas: it was intended that this property would be their joint home. The judge at first instance, relying on *Laskar*, held that the *Stack v Dowden* presumption of joint beneficial ownership did not apply outside the domestic consumer context.
>
> The Privy Council remitted the case to be determined by the Supreme Court of the Bahamas in the light of the Board's decision. Although the shares were yet to be determined, the decision is of major interest because of its implications for the law in this area. In particular, the Board held that "to consign the reasoning in *Stack* to the purely domestic setting would be wrong"[182]:

> > "In this, as in so many areas of law, context counts for, if not everything, a lot. Context here is set by the parties common intention – or by the lack of it."[183]

Lord Kerr continued that when Lady Hale had said that the *Stack* approach applied "at least in the domestic consumer context", it was "clear that she did not intend that the principle should be confined exclusively to the domestic setting".[184] The mere "commercial dimension" to a purchase does not prevent the *Stack* approach applying: "the intention of the parties will still be a crucial factor".[185]

Furthermore, Lord Kerr went on to say, *Laskar* was not authority for the proposition that the principle in *Stack v Dowden* (that a conveyance into joint names indicates legal and beneficial joint tenancy unless the contrary is proved) applies only in 'the domestic consumer context'"[186]:

> "Lord Neuberger did not intend to draw a strict line of demarcation between, on the one hand, the purchase of a family home and, on the other, the acquisition of a so-called investment property in whatever circumstances that took place. It is entirely conceivable that partners in a

---

[181] [2017] UKPC 17; [2017] 3 W.L.R. 1507; M. George and B. Sloan [2017] Conv. 303. See also J. Roche, (2017) 76 C.L.J. 493, with the caveat that the suggestion therein at 495–6 that the different approaches of the majority and Lord Neuberger "all point in the same direction" should be understood in light of how the case was argued, as explained above, fn.47.

[182] [2017] 3 W.L.R. 1507 at [39].

[183] [2017] 3 W.L.R. 1507 at [54].

[184] [2017] 3 W.L.R. 1507 at [40].

[185] [2017] 3 W.L.R. 1507 at [40].

[186] [2017] 3 W.L.R. 1507 at [49].

relationship would buy, as an investment, property which is conveyed into their joint names with the intention that the beneficial ownership should be shared equally between them, even though they contributed in different shares to the purchase."[187]

The decision has been criticised by George and Sloan as rendering the law in this area "even more needlessly complex and uncertain".[188] Although its implications are yet to be worked out, several brief observations may be made about the decision in *Marr*. First, it is not clear what the status of *Laskar* is: the Privy Council does not state that it was wrongly decided and was not purporting to exercise its power to depart from English authorities recognised by the Supreme Court in *Willers v Joyce*.[189] What exactly a first instance judge in England and Wales is to make of *Marr* is difficult, as they would still be formally bound by the Court of Appeal in *Laskar*. It must be said that the *Marr* reading of *Laskar* is far from the most obvious one: indeed, it seems incompatible with Lord Neuberger's avowed attempt to confine the scope of *Stack*.[190] Second, the uncertainty has arisen in part from the apparent reluctance of the Supreme Court or Privy Council to engage with intervening Court of Appeal decisions on the *Stack* framework in *Kernott* and the *Stack/Kernott* framework in *Marr v Collie*. If the *Marr* interpretation of *Laskar* is correct and has always been the view of their Lordships, it is surprising that it did not merit a mention in *Kernott* itself. It is regrettable that their Lordships did not otherwise avail themselves of the opportunity more generally to clarify the points of uncertainty which had been raised in the wake of *Stack*. The tensions as to when the common intention constructive trust can apply have been shown with properties operated as a business in which a couple both worked (which is distinct from the purchase of investment properties such as in *Marr*). An example is *Geary v Rankine*,[191] where a woman who helped to run her partner's guesthouse failed to establish an interest under a common intention constructive trust. Lewison LJ said that the burden of establishing an interest under a trust is "all the more difficult to discharge where, as here, the property was bought as an investment rather than as a home". *Laskar* was not cited in the decision, but the emphasis on context is clear:

> "it is an impermissible leap to go from a common intention that the parties would run a business together to a conclusion that it was their common intention that the property in which the business was run, and which was bought entirely with money provided by one of them, would belong to both of them."[192]

---

[187] [2017] 3 W.L.R. 1507 at [49].

[188] George and Sloan [2017] Conv. 303 at 312.

[189] *Willers v Joyce (No.2)* [2016] 3 W.L.R. 534; George and Sloan [2017] Conv. 303 at 310–311. On the authority of Privy Council decisions after *Willers* more generally, see P. Mirfield, (2017) 133 L.Q.R. 1.

[190] See Lord Neuberger, "The conspirators, the tax man, the Bill of Rights and a bit about the lovers" 2008 Chancery Bar Association Annual Lecture, in which his Lordship describes himself (at para.3) as having "made a nuisance of myself in the Court of Appeal" and "sounding off" on *Stack* in *Laskar*, and saying that he remained "defiant" on the topic. See also Lord Neuberger, "The Plight of the Unmarried" (speech delivered 21 June 2017).

[191] [2012] EWCA Civ 555; K. Lees [2012] Conv. 412.

[192] [2012] EWCA Civ 555 at [22]. *James v Thomas* [2008] 1 F.L.R. 1598; criticised R. Probert (2009) 62 C.L.P. 316 at 334–6. See also *Morris v Morris* [2008] Fam. Law 521; and *Curran v Collins* [2015] EWCA Civ 404 per Lewison LJ at [80].

This significance of context more broadly has been emphasised in other cases,[193] and may take into account cultural factors.[194] It is clear that the approach in *Kernott* can apply beyond cohabiting couples: we have seen several examples of purchases between family members or friends. However, there may still be limits: in *Wodzicki v Wodzicki*,[195] a woman had been permitted to live in a property bought in the joint names of her father and step-mother. After her father's death, she claimed to be entitled to the property as sole beneficial owner. David Richards LJ accepted that "approach may be applied outside the precise confines of a co-habiting couple",[196] but thought it inappropriate to apply it on the facts of the case: "there was nothing close about the relationship between the appellant and the respondent. There is no evidence that they even saw each other once the appellant had settled at the property."[197]

Although these cases were decided before the Privy Council's judgment in *Marr*, and so the framing of the approach would need to be revised, it cannot be said that they would all be decided differently now,[198] not least because of the lack of detailed guidance from the Board. What is clear that the scope for the resulting trust to operate seems too have been reduced yet further.[199] It is regrettable if final appellate courts broaden the applicable framework in such cases without offering specific guidance as to the circumstances as to the relevant limits. As Gardner has written more generally of this area, after over a decade of case law following the questions posed in *Stack*, "has the time not come for a properly conducted effort to settle [the] answers?"[200]

E. Alternative Solutions

Another solution might be to base such claims on the doctrine of proprietary estoppel, where the act of detrimental reliance need not take the form of financial contributions, and which does not require a search for an artificial common

13–020

---

[193] For an excellent survey see M. Yip [2016] Conv. 347.

[194] *Favor Easy Management Ltd v Wu* [2012] EWCA Civ 1464 (businessman transferring property into the name of his mistress held to have made a gift, raising considerations of Chinese culture and its implications for context); M. Yip and J. Lee [2013] Conv. 431. See also *Bhura v Bhura* [2014] EWHC 727; S. Gardner [2015] Conv. 332. cf. *Singh v Singh* [2014] EWHC 1060 (Ch), in which Sir William Blackburne was content to assume, at [117], in the context of a family-controlled business empire, that the principles in *Stack v Dowden* and *Jones v Kernott* did properly apply (although the point was not argued). *Haque v Raja* [2016] EWHC 1950 (Ch), per Henderson J at [29].

[195] [2017] EWCA Civ 95.

[196] [2017] EWCA Civ 95 at [25], noting the example of *Gallarotti v Sebastianelli* [2012] EWCA Civ 865.

[197] [2017] EWCA Civ 95 at [25].

[198] For example, in *Gaspar v Zaleski* [2017] EWHC 1770 (Ch), Judge Elizabeth Cooke, sitting as a Deputy High Court Judge in the Chancery Division, said at [30] that "since this was an investment purchase and not a family home the starting point is not – as it was in *Stack v Dowden* [2007] UKHL 17—that equity follows the law and the parties are beneficial joint tenants unless that presumption can be displaced." However, in that case it was common ground that the parties had agreed to share the beneficial interest, the dispute was about which party was telling the truth as to what the agreement was (also at [30]).

[199] Indeed, Lord Briggs has said that "Generally speaking, the resulting trust is the solution of last resort": *Whitlock v Moree (Bahamas)* [2017] UKPC 44 at [25].

[200] S. Gardner (2016) 132 L.Q.R. 373, 377. See also B. Sloan (2015) 35 L.S. 226, 251.

intention,[201] although estoppel itself has elements of artificiality.[202] Modern cases tended to assimilate the doctrines of constructive trusts and proprietary estoppel,[203] although this view is not conclusive.[204] It appears that interests under constructive trusts crystallise as soon as a sufficient act of detrimental reliance has occurred, prior to their vindication by the court, so that they can affect third parties.[205] It is now established that proprietary estoppel interests may take effect before the court order.[206] The Court of Appeal expressed the view not only that constructive trusts in the context of the family home are "almost interchangeable" with proprietary estoppel, but also that estoppel interests of a family nature are overreachable in the same way as interests under trusts by payment to two trustees.[207]

However, Lord Walker in *Stack v Dowden* retreated from his previous support of the "assimilation" approach, saying:

> "I am now rather less enthusiastic about the notion that proprietary estoppel and 'common intention' constructive trusts can or should be completely assimilated. Proprietary estoppel typically consists of asserting an equitable claim against the conscience of the 'true' owner. The claim is a 'mere equity'. It is to be satisfied by the minimum award necessary to do justice... A 'common intention' constructive trust, by contrast, is identifying the true beneficial owner or owners, and the size of their beneficial interests."[208]

Other solutions have been found in Commonwealth jurisdictions.[209] In Australia the property rights of unmarried couples, including same-sex couples, have been recognised by legislation,[210] and a similar approach has been adopted in New

---

[201] *Gillies v Keogh* [1989] 2 N.Z.L.R. 327; M. Bryan (1990) 106 L.Q.R. 213. See also J. Eekelaar [1987] Conv. 93; M. Thompson and D. Hayton [1990] Conv. 314 and 370 respectively; cf. P. Ferguson (1993) 109 L.Q.R. 114; D. Hayton (1993) 109 L.Q.R. 485; Law Com. Discussion Paper, *Sharing Homes* (2002), para.2.104.

[202] *Phillips v Phillips* [1993] 3 N.Z.L.R. 159, doubting estoppel as the way forward.

[203] *Grant v Edwards* [1986] Ch. 638; *Austin v Keele* (1987) 61 A.L.J.R 605; *Lloyds Bank Plc v Rosset* [1991] 1 A.C. 107 (but see S. Gardner (1991) 54 M.L.R. 126 and (1993) 109 L.Q.R. 263); *Hammond v Mitchell* [1991] 1 W.L.R. 1127; *Lloyds Bank Plc v Carrick* [1996] 4 All E.R. 630; P. Ferguson (1996) 112 L.Q.R. 549; *Yaxley v Gotts* [2000] Ch. 162 at 176–177; *Chan Pui Chun v Leung Kam Ho* [2003] 1 F.L.R. 23; *Oxley v Hiscock* [2005] Fam. 211; *Supperstone v Hurst* [2006] 1 F.L.R. 1245; *Van Laethem v Brooker* [2006] 2 F.L.R. 495.

[204] *Stokes v Anderson* [1991] 1 F.L.R. 391; *Hyett v Stanley* [2004] 1 F.L.R. 394.

[205] Implicit in *Lloyds Bank Plc v Rosset* [1991] 1 A.C. 107. See D. Hayton [1990] Conv. 370; J. Warburton (1991) 5 T.L.I. 9; P. Evans [1991] Conv. 155; Sir Nicolas Browne-Wilkinson (1996) 10 T.L.I. 98 (Presidential Address to the Holdsworth Club, University of Birmingham, 1991); P. Matthews in Mitchell (ed.), *Constructive and Resulting Trusts* (Oxford: Hart Publishing, 2010), 50–60.

[206] Below, para.30–036.

[207] *Birmingham Midshires Mortgage Services Ltd v Sabherwal* (2000) 80 P. & C.R. 256; below, para.30–037. For the distinction between trusts and estoppel concerning onus of proof, see P. Ferguson (1993) 109 L.Q.R. 114.

[208] [2007] 2 A.C. 432 at 448 (retreating from his view in *Yaxley v Gotts* [2000] Ch. 162 at 177).

[209] See S. Wong (1998) 18 L.S. 369; Law Com. Discussion Paper, *Sharing Homes* (2002), Pt IV. For the position in Ireland, see J. Mee (2016) 56 Irish Jurist 161. See also Lloyd Jones LJ in *Barnes v Phillips* [2015] EWCA Civ 1056; [2016] H.L.R. 3 at [35].

[210] Family Law Amendment (De Facto Financial Matters and Other Measures) Act 2008, amending the Family Law Act 1975; H. Baker (2009) 39 Fam. Law 1201; S. Leigh and D. Barry (2011) 41 Fam. Law 404; Law Com. Discussion Paper, *Sharing Homes* (2002), paras 5.20–5.22; M. Pawlowski (2003) 33 Fam. Law 336; K. Kiernan, A. Barlow and R. Merlo [2006] 36 Fam. Law 1074.

Zealand.[211] In 2006, a statutory scheme dealing with the property rights of cohabiting couples was introduced in Scotland.[212] More recently, Ireland has legislated to offer a variety of options[213] in a similar fashion to that proposed by the Law Commission of England and Wales.[214] At common law,[215] the principles of unconscionability and unjust enrichment have been utilised in Australia, New Zealand and Canada,[216] although "unconscionability is not a notion which makes hard cases easier to decide".[217]

F.   Potential Reform

The Law Commission has considered that this area is in need of reform. In 2002, the Commission was unable to propose any scheme based on property law principles which could apply satisfactorily to the diverse kinds of relationships it would need to cover.[218] The law at the time was considered complicated, difficult to apply and unsuited to the informality of home sharers. The Commission therefore refocused its efforts on those who cohabit without entering into marriage, civil partnership or other express arrangement (such as a declaration of trust). In 2007, shortly after the decision in *Stack v Dowden*, the Commission published its Report.[219] It considered that the need for statutory intervention remained.[220]

13–021

The proposed statutory scheme would apply only to cohabitants who are neither married to each other nor civil partners. Unless they had a child together, they would be eligible only if they lived as a couple in a joint household for a

---

[211] New Zealand Property (Relationships) Amendment Act 2001.

[212] Family Law (Scotland) Act 2006; E. Hess (2009) 39 Fam. Law 405.

[213] Civil Partnership and Certain Rights and Obligations of Cohabitants Act 2010 (Ireland) Pt 15; J. Mee (2016) 56 Irish Jurist 161, 173–179.

[214] Below, para.13–021.

[215] For the position in Hong Kong, see M. Lower [2016] Conv. 453, commenting on *Ying v Brillex Development Ltd* CACV 120/2014 (the Court of Final Appeal dismissed an application for leave to appeal [2016] HKCFA 36; [2017] 4 HKC 1).

[216] *Baumgartner v Baumgartner* (1988) 62 A.L.J. 29; *Gillies v Keogh* [1989] 2 N.Z.L.R. 327; *Peter v Beblow* (1993) 101 D.L.R. (4th) 621. See generally R. Chambers [2006] 14 R.L.R. 146; M. McInnes (2011) 127 L.Q.R. 339; M. Lower [2011] Conv. 515.

[217] M. Bryan (1990) 106 L.Q.R. 25 at 28; M. Bryan (1994) 8 T.L.I. 74; M. Halliwell, *Equity and Good Conscience in a Contemporary Context* (London: Old Bailey Press, 1997) Ch.4. See also S. Gardner (1993) 109 L.Q.R. 263, advocating the "communality" approach based on the relationship itself, with less emphasis on intention or contribution. M. Lower [2016] Conv. 453, commenting on *Ying v Brillex Development Ltd* 17 I.T.E.L.R. 950.

[218] Law Commission Discussion Paper: *Sharing Homes* (July 2002), para.3.100; criticised R. Probert (2002) 32 Fam. Law 834; C. Rotherham [2004] Conv. 268. See also S. Bridge and Lord Justice Thorpe (2002) 32 Fam. Law 743 and 891 respectively; Baroness Hale (2004) 34 Fam. Law 419; A. Barlow and G. James (2004) 67 M.L.R. 143.

[219] Law Com. No. 307, *Cohabitation: The Financial Consequences of Relationship Breakdown* (2007). The report contained no draft Bill. See generally S. Bridge (2007) 37 Fam. Law 998 and 1076 and (2008) *Trusts and Estates Law & Tax Journal* 26. The proposals are criticised by D. Hughes, M. Davis and L. Jacklin [2008] Conv. 197, where an opt-in system or the extension of civil partnerships to heterosexual couples are preferred. See also G. Douglas, J. Pearce and H. Woodward [2008] Conv. 365 and (2009) 72 M.L.R. 24; S. Singer (2009) 39 Fam. Law 234; R. Probert (2009) 62 C.L.P. 316; Baroness Hale of Richmond (2011) 41 Fam. Law 1341 at 1342.

[220] Law Com. No. 307 (2007), para.2.12. See also S. Bridge (2007) 37 Fam. Law 911 at 915.

continuous minimum period before separation. The Law Commission did not select the minimum period, but recommended that it should be between two and five years.

The next condition would be that the applicant must have made a "qualifying contribution", which means any contribution, whether or not financial, to the shared lives of the parties or to the welfare of members of their families. Financial relief will be available where, as a result of this contribution, the respondent has retained a benefit or the applicant has an economic disadvantage. A retained benefit could be either capital (for example from the other party's contribution to the acquisition of the home), income, or related to earning capacity. An economic disadvantage means a present or future loss, for example by reduced earning capacity through childcare. Claims would have to be brought within two years of the separation.

Where these conditions were satisfied, the court could direct the payment of capital (by way of a lump sum or instalments), pension sharing, or a transfer of property. It would not order maintenance by way of periodical payments. Discretionary factors, in particular the welfare of minor children, could be taken into account in deciding the form of relief.

Cohabitants would be free to opt out of the statutory scheme by written agreement signed by both parties. Where they had not opted out, claims would be regulated by the statutory scheme, to the exclusion of the general law of trusts, estoppel and contract.

Where separation occurred on death, the proposal was to enhance existing rights under the Inheritance (Provision for Family and Dependants) Act 1975 if the survivor would have been eligible under the statutory scheme.

Overall, the Commission determined that the rights of unmarried cohabitees were not a matter for the general law. Rather,

> "A coherent set of statutory remedies providing financial relief between cohabitants would provide a way of doing better justice between the parties on separation, while respecting the interests of affected third parties."[221]

It was announced on 6 March 2008 that the Government proposed to take no action pending the outcome of research by the Scottish Executive into the cost and efficacy of provisions in the Family Law (Scotland) Act 2006, which were similar in many ways to the proposals of the Law Commission. A Private Members' Bill, the Cohabitation Bill, was introduced in the House of Lords in 2008 but was not enacted. In September 2011, the Government announced that it did not plan to implement the Law Commission's proposals during the 2010–2015 Parliament. That decision drew a response from the Law Commission:

> "We hope that implementation will not be delayed beyond the early days of the next Parliament, in view of the hardship and injustice caused by the current law. The prevalence of

---

[221] Law Com. No. 307 (2007), para.2.16.

cohabitation, and of the birth of children to couples who live together, means that the need for reform of the law can only become more pressing over time."[222]

The Justices of the Supreme Court have also commented upon the possibility of legislative reform, both judicially[223] and extra-judicially.[224] In *Jones v Kernott*, Lord Wilson lamented "the continued failure of Parliament to confer upon the courts limited redistributive powers in relation to the property of each party upon the breakdown of a non-marital relationship".[225] In *Gow v Grant*,[226] concerning the Family Law (Scotland) Act 2006, Lady Hale reaffirmed her belief in the desirability of a legislative scheme. Such a scheme would, in her Ladyship's view, be "less costly and more productive of settlements as well as achieving fairer results than the present law".[227] The "'sufficient basis for changing the law' [has] already been amply provided by the long-standing judicial calls for reform".[228] At the time of writing, a Cohabitation Rights Bill 2017–19, intended to implement the Law Commission's proposals,[229] has been introduced by Lord Marks of Henley-on-Thames.[230]

3. CONSEQUENCES OF CO-OWNERSHIP

A. The Trust of Land

The two forms of co-ownership existing under the modern law are the joint **13–022** tenancy and the tenancy in common. Here only a brief outline will be given, as the details may be found in the land law books.[231] Under the Law of Property Act 1925, a trust for sale was imposed on both forms of co-ownership, while successive interests came within the Settled Land Act 1925. This system operated for many years, but was subject to criticism partly because the dual system was perceived as unnecessary and partly because the duty to sell which arose under the trust for sale was not readily understood by co-owners. Furthermore, this duty to sell brought into play the doctrine of conversion, often with inconvenient and artificial results. The effect of this doctrine was that the interests of the co-owners

---

[222] Professor Elizabeth Cooke, Law Commissioner, "Statement on the Government's response to the Law Commission report 'Cohabitation: The Financial Consequences of Relationship Breakdown'", 6 September 2011.

[223] See e.g. the late Lord Toulson's remarks (as Toulson LJ) in granting permission to appeal in *Curran v Collins* [2013] EWCA Civ 382 at [13]: "As I have already indicated, the law is regarded by many in this area as profoundly unsatisfactory but it has to be applied as it is".

[224] See Lord Neuberger, "The Plight of the Unmarried" (speech delivered 21 June 2017).

[225] [2011] UKSC 53; [2012] 1 A.C. 776 at [78].

[226] [2012] UKSC 29.

[227] [2012] UKSC 29 at [47].

[228] [2012] UKSC 29 at [50]. A Cohabitation Bill 2014–15 failed to make progress before the 2015 General Election.

[229] See e.g. Speech by Lord Marks QC to Liberal Democrat Party Conference, 16th September 2013 *http://www.resolution.org.uk/site_content_files/files/lord_marks_speech_on_cohabitation___16_ sept_2013.pdf* [accessed 4 July 2018].

[230] His Lordship introduced a similar Bill in 2016, but it made no progress before the proroguing of Parliament for the 2017 General Election.

[231] For example, M. Thompson and M. George, *Thompson's Modern Land Law* (Oxford: Oxford University Press, 2017), Chs 9 and 10.

were treated as personalty, which gave rise to difficulties, particularly in the interpretation of many legislative provisions.

Following Law Commission proposals,[232] the dual system of the trust for sale and the strict settlement was replaced by the "trust of land" under the Trusts of Land and Appointment of Trustees Act 1996, which applies to both concurrent and successive interests. While pre-existing settlements under the Settled Land Act 1925 (other than those relating to charity land) are preserved, no new settlements may be created.[233] The definition of "trust of land"[234] is "any trust of property which consists of or includes land", whether the trust is express, implied, resulting or constructive, including a trust for sale and a bare trust. With the exception of pre-existing strict settlements, the 1996 Act applies to trusts of land created before and after its commencement (1 January 1997).

Under the trust of land, the trustees have a power of sale, but no duty to sell. (Other powers and duties will be mentioned where relevant in the following sections). The interests of the beneficiaries are overreached on sale (provided there are at least two trustees), as under the previous legislation.[235] Trusts for sale may still be expressly created,[236] but, as already mentioned, fall within the definition of a "trust of land". All express trusts for sale of land, whenever created, include (despite any provision to the contrary) a power to postpone the sale, and the trustees are not liable in any way for postponing sale for an indefinite period in the exercise of their discretion.[237] Although the duty to sell remains in such a case, the doctrine of conversion was abolished in respect of all trusts for sale of land whenever created, save for those created by the will of a testator dying before the commencement of the 1996 Act.[238] Thus the interests of the beneficiaries are no longer interests in personalty, but are recognised as interests in the land itself.

As already mentioned, the 1925 legislation imposed a trust for sale on co-owned land (and in various other circumstances, such as intestacy). Under the current regime the statutory trust for sale is replaced by the trust of land. While the legal estate, if vested in more than one person, must be held jointly, the beneficial interest may be held either on a joint tenancy or on a tenancy in common. The relevant legislation is Law of Property Act 1925 s.34 (tenancies in common) and s.36 (joint tenancies), as amended by the 1996 Act to reflect the replacement of the trust for sale by the trust of land.[239] To facilitate conveyancing, the legal joint tenancy cannot be severed, but severance of any equitable joint tenancy can be effected by any of the means applicable before

---

[232] No.181 (1989) *Trusts of Land*. On the 1996 Act see N. Hopkins [1996] Conv. 411; Smith, *Plural Ownership* (2005), Part III.

[233] Trusts of Land and Appointment of Trustees Act 1996 s.2. Entailed interests may no longer be created; Sch.1 para.5. See, however, E. Bennett Histed (2000) 116 L.Q.R. 445; S. Pascoe [2001] Conv. 396.

[234] Trusts of Land and Appointment of Trustees Act 1996 s.1.

[235] Above, para.1–047.

[236] See P. Pettit (1997) 113 L.Q.R. 207; R. Mitchell [1999] Conv. 84.

[237] Trusts of Land and Appointment of Trustees Act 1996 s.4.

[238] Trusts of Land and Appointment of Trustees Act 1996 s.3.

[239] Trusts of Land and Appointment of Trustees Act 1996 Sch.2.

1926; and also by notice in writing to the other joint tenants.[240] The purpose of severance is to convert the joint tenancy into a tenancy in common and thereby to prevent the application of the doctrine of survivorship (whereby the survivor of joint tenants takes the whole).

B. Occupation Rights

Historically, difficulties arose concerning the occupation rights of beneficiaries **13–023** under a trust for sale, whether imposed expressly or, more commonly, by statute, as in the case of co-ownership. The difficulty stemmed from the old doctrine of conversion, whereby the interests of the beneficiaries were regarded as in the proceeds of sale, not the land. Although the situation was somewhat obscure, decisions in the 1980s upheld the occupation rights of the beneficiaries, regarding the doctrine of conversion as artificial.[241] Thus it was held in *Bull v Bull*[242] that a son, who held the legal estate on trust for sale for himself and his mother as equitable tenants in common, was not entitled to evict his mother.

The occupation rights of beneficiaries are now governed by the Trusts of Land and Appointment of Trustees Act 1996, whenever the trust of land arose. The Act abolished the doctrine of conversion.[243] Section 12 provides that a beneficiary beneficially entitled to an interest in possession is entitled to occupy at any time if at that time (a) the purposes of the trust include making the land available for his occupation (or for the occupation of beneficiaries of a class of which he is a member or of beneficiaries in general) or (b) the land is held by the trustees so as to be so available.[244] The section does not confer a right to occupy land if it is either unavailable or unsuitable for occupation by him,[245] and is subject to s.13, discussed below. When considering whether the property is suitable for occupation, the court looks at the nature of the property and the characteristics, circumstances and requirements of the particular beneficiary. If it is suitable for occupation by a couple, it will not be considered unsuitable for the sole occupation of the partner remaining after the relationship breaks down.[246] Thus a beneficiary will normally be entitled to occupy unless, for example, the land has been let, or it is clear that the purpose of the trust is the sale of the property and division of the proceeds among the beneficiaries.[247]

---

[240] Law of Property Act 1925 s.36(2); *Re Draper's Conveyance* [1969] 1 Ch. 486; *Harris v Goddard* [1983] 1 W.L.R. 1203; *Quigley v Masterson* [2011] EWHC 2529 (Ch) (one joint tenant's application to be joined to proceedings involving the other joint tenant qualified as notice of severance); N.P. Gravells (2012) 71 C.L.J. 42.

[241] *Williams & Glyn's Bank Ltd v Boland* [1981] A.C. 487; *City of London Building Society v Flegg* [1988] A.C. 54.

[242] [1955] 1 Q.B. 234; cf. *Barclay v Barclay* [1970] 2 Q.B. 677 (express testamentary trust for sale).

[243] s.3.

[244] See *Creasy v Sole* [2013] EWHC 1410 (Ch); *Davis v Jackson* [2017] EWHC 698 (Ch).

[245] s.12(2). See J. Ross Martyn [1997] Conv. 254 at 260. In *Davis v Jackson* [2017] EWHC 698 (Ch), Snowden J held (at [48]–[49]) that it was "difficult to envisage any circumstance in which it would be 'suitable' for a trustee in bankruptcy to take up occupation of a domestic house with the bankrupt and/or their co-habitee... I therefore do not accept that I am bound to apply the statutory regime under TOLATA to this case".

[246] *Chan Pui Chun v Leung Kam Ho* [2003] 1 F.L.R. 23.

[247] As in the testamentary trust for sale in *Barclay v Barclay* [1970] 2 Q.B. 677.

13–024   Section 13(1) of the 1996 Act provides that where two or more beneficiaries are entitled to occupy under s.12, the trustees may, provided they do not act unreasonably, exclude or restrict the entitlement of any one or more (but not all) of them. If a building lends itself to physical partition, the trustees may restrict one beneficiary to a particular part and the other to the other part.[248] They may also impose reasonable conditions from time to time on any beneficiary in relation to his occupation.[249] The matters to which the trustees must have regard in exercising these powers include (a) the intention of the person or persons (if any) who created the trust, (b) the purposes for which the land is held, and (c) the circumstances and wishes of each of the beneficiaries who is (or apart from any previous exercise by the trustees of those powers would be) entitled to occupy the land under s.12.[250] The conditions which they may impose include the payment of outgoings or expenses in respect of the land, or the assumption of any other obligation in relation to the land or to any activity which is or is proposed to be conducted there.[251] If the entitlement of any beneficiary has been excluded or restricted under the section, conditions may be imposed on any other beneficiary requiring her to compensate the beneficiary whose rights have been excluded or restricted, or to forgo a benefit under the trust so as to benefit the other beneficiary.[252] The trustees may not exercise their powers so as to prevent any person in occupation (whether or not by reason of any entitlement under s.12) from continuing to occupy, or in a manner likely to have that result, unless he consents or the court gives approval.[253] Disputes concerning the exercise of the trustees' powers under s.13 may be resolved by an application to court under s.14, where the circumstances and wishes of each beneficiary with occupation rights will be considered.[254]

Prior to the 1996 Act, occupying co-owners were in certain cases obliged to pay rent to non-occupying co-owners, as where the latter had been "ousted" by the occupier,[255] or where the occupier had presented a divorce petition against the non-occupier,[256] or as a condition of postponing a sale.[257] As a general principle, however, no rent was payable to a beneficiary who chose not to occupy.[258] The position was somewhat uncertain, but the matter now falls within s.13 which, as mentioned above, permits the imposition of conditions by the trustees including the compensation of a non-occupying beneficiary by an occupier.[259] The court may direct the payment of rent in any case where it is necessary in order to do broad justice between co-owners, and "ouster" is not required.[260] It has been held

---

[248] *Rodway v Landy* [2001] Ch. 703 (doctor's surgery).
[249] s.13(3). See *Rodway v Landy* [2001] Ch. 703 (contribution to costs of adapting building).
[250] s.13(4).
[251] s.13(5).
[252] s.13(6).
[253] s.13(7). The court will have regard to the matters set out in s.13(4).
[254] See s.15(2); below, para.13–028.
[255] See *Dennis v McDonald* [1982] Fam. 63.
[256] *Re Pavlou (A Bankrupt)* [1993] 1 W.L.R. 1046 (Millett J, discussing also the question of set-off against mortgage interest paid by the occupier).
[257] *Harvey v Harvey* [1982] Fam. 83.
[258] *Jones (AE) v Jones (FW)* [1977] 1 W.L.R. 438.
[259] See also Family Law Act 1996 s.40(1)(b) (periodical payments while occupation order in force).
[260] *Murphy v Gooch* [2007] 2 F.L.R. 934.

that ss.12 to 15 of the 1996 Act do not provide an exhaustive regime for compensation for exclusion of a beneficiary from occupation. In cases not expressly covered by the Act, the old principles of equitable accounting may still apply. Thus a co-owner in sole occupation may be ordered to pay rent to the trustee in bankruptcy of the other co-owner on the basis of equitable accounting.[261]

One problem with ss.12 and 13 is that they are ill-suited to trusts arising out of co-ownership, where the trustees and beneficiaries are frequently the same persons. Indeed, it has been said that these sections contain a "cross-fertilisation of ideas implemented without concrete policy considerations",[262] and that the Act has unintentionally curtailed the occupation rights of co-owners by eroding the concept of unity of possession, and that beneficiaries should be able to resort to their general law rights where these are superior to those conferred by the Act.[263]

Finally, a spouse or civil partner who is not a legal owner may assert occupation rights under the Family Law Act 1996 (replacing Matrimonial Homes Act 1983) whether or not he or she has an equitable interest in the home.[264] This right is registrable, but failure to register will not affect enforcement against the other spouse, or enforcement of any rights arising independently by reason of an equitable interest in the home.

C.   Sale by Sole Trustee

Under the trust of land and its predecessor, the trust for sale, at least two trustees **13–025** are necessary if the overreaching machinery is to operate.[265] While there are likely to be at least two trustees in the case of an expressly created trust of land, the difficulty which arises in many cases of co-ownership is that the land is vested in one person only. That person holds on trust for all those who are beneficially entitled, but the overreaching machinery will not operate. As we saw in the earlier parts of this chapter, the question whether a person other than the legal owner has acquired an interest is often difficult, so that the existence of the trust may not be appreciated, either by the parties or the purchaser (or mortgagee).

Where there are two trustees, the interests of the beneficiaries will be overreached whether or not they are occupying[266] and whether the title is registered or unregistered. Where there is a sole trustee, the principles applicable to registered and unregistered titles must be considered separately.

---

[261] *French v Barcham* [2009] 1 W.L.R. 1124; B. McFarlane All E.R. Rev. 2009, 318. See also *Re Byford* (2004) 1 P. & C.R. 12; H. Conway [2003] Conv. 533; N. Berry (2005) 155 N.L.J. 486. See *Davis v Jackson* [2017] EWHC 698 (Ch).

[262] S. Pascoe [2006] Conv. 54. See also S. Bright [2009] Conv. 378.

[263] D. Barnsley (1998) 57 C.L.J. 123; cf. S. Pascoe [2006] Conv. 54.

[264] Former spouses, cohabitants and former cohabitants may in certain cases obtain occupation orders whether or not they have an equitable interest. These are not registrable.

[265] Law of Property Act 1925 s.2.

[266] *City of London Building Society v Flegg* [1988] A.C. 54; cf. Law Com. No. 188, *Transfer of Land; Overreaching; Beneficiaries in Occupation*. This Report has not been implemented; [1998] Conv. 349.

If the title is unregistered,[267] the question whether the transferee, typically a mortgagee, is bound by the equitable interests depends on whether the mortgagee had notice, actual or constructive, of the interest of the beneficiary. The equitable co-ownership usually arises by virtue of one party having contributed to the purchase price, or to the mortgage payments; and there will be nothing in the documents of title to indicate this. The question is whether the beneficiary's occupation gives constructive notice. It was at one time held that a bank mortgagee dealing with the husband as sole legal owner did not have constructive notice of the wife's equitable interest by contribution, even though the bank knew that the parties lived together in the house.[268] This view soon became untenable.[269] So many wives have a share in the home that a reasonable mortgagee should consider the possibility. If it made insufficient inquiries, the fact of the wife's (or other beneficiary's) occupation gives constructive notice of her rights. The question whether sufficient inquiries had been made arose in *Kingsnorth Finance Co v Tizard*,[270] where a wife had a half share in a house which was vested in her husband alone. When the marriage broke down, she slept elsewhere but came to the house every day to look after the children and kept her possessions there. The husband mortgaged the property, falsely stating that he was single. The mortgagee's surveyor inspected the house at a time when the husband had arranged for the wife to be out. He saw evidence of the children's occupation and was told that the wife had left. The husband later emigrated, leaving the loan of £66,000 unpaid. It was held that the wife was in occupation for the purpose of constructive notice. In order for physical presence to amount to occupation, it did not need to be exclusive, continuous or uninterrupted, nor was it negatived by regular absences. When the surveyor discovered that the mortgagor was married, he was put on enquiry as to the wife's rights. As no further enquiries were made, the mortgagee had constructive notice of her rights.

13–026   It should be added that where spouses or civil partners occupy a matrimonial home, a spouse who has no legal title may protect his or her statutory rights of occupation under the Family Law Act 1996 (replacing Matrimonial Homes Act 1983) by registration, whether or not that spouse has any equitable interest in the home. But there is no possibility of protecting a substantive equitable interest by registration in cases of unregistered title.

In the case of registered land, the doctrine of notice does not apply. Equitable interests are binding on a purchaser only if proper steps have been taken to protect them by entering a notice or a restriction; or if the interest is an

---

[267] i.e. not subject to the provisions of the Land Registration Act (now the Act of 2002) at the time of the transaction. Many titles remain unregistered even though the registration system applies in all areas. Sale is a transaction which triggers a duty to register. Likewise, various other transactions including the grant of a first legal mortgage; Land Registration Act 2002 s.4. Priority disputes, however, commonly arise some years after the mortgage and may still be governed by unregistered land principles.

[268] *Caunce v Caunce* [1969] 1 W.L.R. 286.

[269] *Williams & Glyn's Bank Ltd v Boland* [1981] A.C. 487.

[270] [1986] 1 W.L.R. 783.

"overriding interest"; which is binding although not protected by entry on the register. The issue came to a head in *Williams & Glyn's Bank Ltd v Boland*.[271]

> Mr and Mrs Boland each contributed towards the purchase of, and to the mortgage payments due upon, a matrimonial home. Title was taken in the sole name of Mr Boland, and he was registered as sole proprietor. Later, Mr Boland mortgaged the house to the Bank. On default being made in the mortgage payments, the Bank started proceedings for possession. The wife resisted this claim on the ground that she was entitled to an equitable interest in the house which the Bank could not override. It was accepted that the wife had, by virtue of her financial contribution, an equitable interest in the house. The question whether this interest was valid against the Bank depended on whether it was an overriding interest under the provision then in force: Land Registration Act 1925 s.70(1)(g)[272]; it could not otherwise be binding, because the wife had taken no steps to protect it by entry on the register. Nor could it be overreached by the payment to a sole trustee. The House of Lords unanimously held that the wife's interest was an overriding interest as she was "in actual occupation" at the execution of the mortgage.[273] Lord Scarman emphasised the importance of construing the legislation in the light of current social policy, and of protecting the "beneficial interest which English law now recognizes that a married woman has in the matrimonial home."[274]

It is thus necessary to make inquiries of all persons in occupation, whether spouse, cohabitant, or other persons; for their interests are capable of being binding as overriding interests on the purchaser or mortgagee. It should be appreciated however, that a wife (or other person) with an overriding interest cannot necessarily prevent a sale by the mortgagee, although she will still have a prior claim to her share of the proceeds.[275]

The provisions on overriding interests were modified by the Land Registration **13–027** Act 2002. Although the interest of a person "in actual occupation" may still override a registered disposition, an exception is made in the case of:

> "[A]n interest
> (i)   which belongs to a person whose occupation would not have been obvious on a reasonably careful inspection of the land at the time of the disposition; and
> (ii)   of which the person to whom the disposition is made does not have actual knowledge at that time.[276]"

The principles discussed above are subject to an important proviso. An equitable co-owner in occupation can rely neither on constructive notice (in unregistered

---

[271] [1981] A.C. 487; J. Martin [1980] Conv. 361; S. Freeman (1980) 43 M.L.R. 692; M. Prichard (1980) 39 C.L.J. 243; R. Smith (1981) 97 L.Q.R. 12. See also D. Wilde [1999] Conv. 382; P. Omar [2006] Conv. 509; M. Conaglen (2006) 69 M.L.R. 582; N. Jackson (2006) 69 M.L.R. 214 and [2007] Conv. 120.

[272] s.70(1)(g) protected "The rights of every person in actual occupation of the land or in receipt of the rents and profits thereof, save where enquiry is made of such person and the rights are not disclosed…".

[273] This is the relevant date, rather than the later date of registration of the legal charge; *Abbey National BS v Cann* [1991] 1 A.C. 56.

[274] [1981] A.C. 487 at 510.

[275] *Bank of Baroda v Dhillon* [1998] 1 F.L.R. 524; R. Wells (1998) 28 Fam. Law 208; S. Pascoe [1998] Conv. 415; *Halifax Mortgage Services Ltd v Muirhead* (1998) 76 P. & C.R. 418.

[276] Land Registration Act 2002 ss.29, 30 and Sch.3 para.2; N. Jackson (2003) 119 L.Q.R. 660; B. Bogusz [2011] Conv. 268. This modification would not have affected the decision in *Boland*. The Act of 2002 preserves the exception in the previous legislation to the effect that the interest of an occupier of whom enquiry was made and who failed to disclose his rights is not overriding.

land) nor on an overriding interest by reason of occupation (in registered land) where he or she was aware of the mortgage transaction and did not bring the equitable interest to the attention of the mortgagee.[277] This seems to be a version of the doctrine of estoppel. The principle is that in such circumstances it is impossible to infer any common intention other than that the equitable owner authorised the legal owner to raise money by mortgage which would have priority to any beneficial interest. Apparently, it is not relevant that the mortgagee failed to make the inquiries which might have revealed the interest. As has been said, this seems to be a reversal of the doctrine of notice; the onus has shifted to the occupier to declare his rights to a purchaser (mortgagee) of whom he has notice, or be deemed to concede priority.[278] In the case of an acquisition mortgage, the House of Lords has taken the principle further by holding that a purchaser who depends on a mortgage in order to buy the property acquires on completion only an equity of redemption, (i.e. the property already subject to the mortgage). Thus, a third party claiming a beneficial interest as against the purchaser can assert no rights against the mortgagee, whether or not the third party was aware of the mortgage, as decided by *Abbey National BS v Cann*.[279] The effect of these principles is to restrict the application of *Williams & Glyn's Bank Ltd v Boland* and *Kingsnorth Finance Co v Tizard* to subsequent mortgages of which the co-owner was unaware.

The approach in *Abbey National BS v Cann* has been endorsed by the Supreme Court in recent years.[280]

> In *Southern Pacific Mortgages Ltd v Scott*,[281] the vendor had agreed to sell the interest in her home to a purchaser, who in turn promised that the vendor would be entitled to stay in occupation at a discounted rate, in return for the vendor paying back some of the completion money.[282] This arrangement was not in the contract of sale, however. The purchaser obtained a buy to let mortgage which was inconsistent with the terms of the agreement and with the subsequent grant of tenancy to the vendor. The purchaser then disappeared, defaulting on the loan, and the lender sought possession of the property. The vendor claimed that she had an equitable interest from the moment when the contracts were exchanged, which amounted to an unregistered interest overriding the lender's interests.[283] The Supreme Court held that the order for possession had been correctly made, and that no equitable interest had arisen,

---

[277] *Bristol and West Building Society v Henning* [1985] 1 W.L.R. 778; *Paddington Building Society v Mendelsohn* (1985) 50 P. & C.R. 244; criticised P. Todd [1985] Conv. 361; [1986] Conv. 57; M. Thompson (1986) 49 M.L.R. 255 and (1986) 6 L.S. 140.

[278] M. Welstead (1985) 44 C.L.J. 354.

[279] [1991] 1 A.C. 56; S. Baughen and P. Evans [1991] Conv. 116 and 155 respectively. As to remortgages, see *Equity & Law Home Loans Ltd v Prestidge* [1992] 1 W.L.R. 137; R. Smith (1992) 108 L.Q.R. 372; M. Lunney (1993) 56 M.L.R. 87; J. Dewar (1993) 23 Fam. Law 231.

[280] *R. v Waya* [2012] UKSC 51; [2013] 1 A.C. 294 per Lord Walker of Gestingthorpe JSC and Hughes LJ at [50].

[281] The appeal was a test case and is also known as *Re North East Property Buyers Litigation* [2014] UKSC 52; [2015] A.C. 385; the issues relating to the vendor purchaser constructive trust have been considered in the previous chapter: paras 12–016—12–017.

[282] These sale and rent back transactions later became a regulated activity under s.19 of the Financial Services and Markets Act 2000 and the then Financial Services Authority in 2012 reported that such transactions, viewed as unsuitable and potentially exploitative, are now very rare: [2014] UKSC 52 per Lord Collins at [3].

[283] By virtue of s.29(2)(a)(ii) of and para.2 of Sch.3 to the Land Registration Act 2002.

because the purchaser had no interest in the land before the contract was executed. Even if it had, *Cann* would have applied so that there was one single transaction.[284]

The essential outcome has been endorsed by commentators.[285] However, although the basic principles have been confirmed, other obiter dicta in *Scott* on the applicability of *Cann* have been criticised as leading to uncertainty.[286] Baroness Hale welcomed[287] the fact that the Law Commission announced that, as part of its Twelfth Programme of Reform, it would review the land registration regime, with particular emphasis on a number of areas, including fraud.[288]

D.   Disputes over Sale[289]

Disputes commonly arise, primarily on the breakdown of a relationship, as to whether the property should be sold or not. The question may also arise on the death of a co-owner, if his or her share devolves on a third party. Where the legal estate is vested in all the co-owners, they (being trustees) must act unanimously in the exercise of any power.[290] Since the commencement of the Trusts of Land and Appointment of Trustees Act 1996, trustees of land have a power of sale instead of the duty to sell which formerly existed under the statutory trust for sale imposed in cases of co-ownership. Thus the power of sale cannot be exercised unless all agree. In cases of dispute, as explained below, they can apply to court under s.14 of the 1996 Act, replacing s.30 of the Law of Property Act 1925.

    13–028

It may be that the legal estate is vested in one co-owner only, as where a husband holds the legal estate on trust for himself and his wife as co-owners in equity. In the last section we saw the effect of a sale or mortgage by a sole trustee. Here we shall consider the position prior to any such disposition. The question of unanimity does not arise, because there is only one trustee. In the event of a dispute, the wife (or other equitable co-owner) may apply to court under s.14 if she has the opportunity to act in time. In any event, sale will be hampered if she has registered her statutory right of occupation[291] or (in the case of registered land) has protected her equitable interest by the entry of a restriction or a notice. Even if she has not done so, her interest is likely to prevail against the purchaser or mortgagee if she is in occupation.[292] She may also seek an injunction to prevent sale without the appointment of a second trustee to safeguard the proceeds of sale, or to restrain the husband from disregarding his statutory duty to

---

[284] [2015] A.C. 385 at [114].

[285] M. Dixon [2014] Conv. 461.

[286] M. Dixon [2014] Conv. 461; A. Televantos and L. Maniscalco (2015) 74 C.L.J. 27.

[287] [2015] A.C. 385 at [122].

[288] The Law Commission published a consultation in 2016: *Updating the Land registration Act 2002: A Consultation Paper* (Consultation Paper No. 227). At the time of writing, the Commission planned to publish its final report and draft Bill in the summer of 2018.

[289] Illuminatingly considered by M. Dixon (2011) 70 C.L.J 579.

[290] *Re Mayo* [1943] Ch. 302; below, para.17–007. The parties may have made express provisions for sale or for one to buy the other out; *Miller v Lakefield Estates Ltd* (1989) 57 P. & C.R. 104.

[291] Family Law Act 1996, re-enacting Matrimonial Homes Act 1983; *Wroth v Tyler* [1974] Ch. 30.

[292] As an overriding interest (registered land) or under the doctrine of notice (unregistered land); above, para.13–026.

consult the beneficiaries.[293] Section 11 of the Trusts of Land and Appointment of Trustees Act 1996 (re-enacting the previous legislation) provides that the trustees, in the exercise of any function relating to the land, shall (so far as practicable) consult the beneficiaries of full age and beneficially entitled to an interest in possession, and, so far as consistent with the general interest of the trust, give effect to the wishes of those beneficiaries or of the majority of them, according to the value of their combined interests.[294] Clearly this section is of limited assistance to a beneficiary with a minority interest, and will result in a stalemate if there are two disputing co-owners who are equally entitled. In certain cases, however, it will resolve the situation. A purchaser (or mortgagee) is not concerned to see that the trustees' duties to consult the beneficiaries and to have regard to their rights have been complied with, whether the title to the land is unregistered[295] or registered.[296]

13–029   Assuming that the dispute cannot otherwise be resolved, application may be made to court under s.14 of the 1996 Act. The application may be made by a trustee or any person having an interest in the property.[297] Thus the trustee in bankruptcy of a beneficiary (whose position is discussed below) or chargee of a beneficial interest may apply, as under the previous law. The court may make such order as it thinks fit (a) relating to the exercise by the trustees of any of their functions (including an order relieving them of any obligation to obtain the consent of, or to consult, any person in connection with the exercise of any of their functions),[298] or (b) declaring the nature or extent of a person's interest in the property[299]; but may not appoint or remove trustees under this section.[300]

The matters to which the court is to have regard include (a) the intentions of the person or persons (if any) who created the trust,[301] (b) the purposes for which the property subject to the trust is held,[302] (c) the welfare of any child who occupies or might reasonably be expected to occupy any land subject to the trust

---

[293] *Waller v Waller* [1967] 1 W.L.R. 451. See also *Lee v Lee* [1952] 2 Q.B. 489n (jurisdiction under Married Women's Property Act 1882 s.17).

[294] This duty may be excluded in an express trust. Also, the trustees must have regard to the rights of the beneficiaries when exercising the powers of an absolute owner conferred by s.6 of the 1996 Act s.6(5); G. Ferris and G. Battersby [2009] Conv. 39. Section 11 does not apply to one of joint lessees who serves a notice to quit; *Notting Hill Housing Trust v Brackley* [2001] EWCA Civ 601; [2002] H.L.R. 10.

[295] Trusts of Land and Appointment of Trustees Act 1996 s.16(1).

[296] Land Registration Act 2002 s.26; E. Cooke [2002] Conv. 11 at 23–25; G. Ferris and G. Battersby (2003) 119 L.Q.R. 94; S. Pascoe [2005] Conv. 140; G. Owen [2013] Conv. 377.

[297] s.14(1). See generally N. Hopkins (2009) 125 L.Q.R. 310.

[298] See *Page v West* [2010] W.T.L.R. 1811.

[299] See *Lowson v Coombes* [1999] Ch. 373.

[300] Trusts of Land and Appointment of Trustees Act 1996 s.14(2), (3).

[301] This refers to intentions at the time the trust was created; *W v W (Joinder of Trusts of Land Act and Children Act Applications)* [2004] 2 F.L.R. 321 (holding also that related applications under the Children Act 1989 should be heard with the application under the 1996 Act). In contested divorce cases ancillary relief proceedings are preferable to proceedings under the 1996 Act; *Smith v Smith* [2010] W.T.L.R. 519.

[302] This means the purposes at the time the court deals with the matter; *Rodway v Landy* [2001] Ch. 703; *Holman v Howes* [2006] 1 F.L.R. 1003.

as his home, and (d) the interests of any secured creditor of any beneficiary.[303] So far as applications relating to the exercise of the trustees' powers under s.13 to exclude or restrict occupation rights are concerned, the court will also consider the circumstances and wishes of each of the beneficiaries who is (or apart from any previous exercise by the trustees of those powers would be) entitled to occupy the land under s.12.[304] In the case of any other application, the court will also consider the circumstances and wishes of any beneficiaries of full age and entitled to an interest in possession or (in case of dispute) of the majority (according to the value of their combined interests).[305] Different considerations apply to applications by a trustee in bankruptcy, which are discussed below.

In *Finch v Hall*,[306] David Donaldson QC, sitting as a Deputy Judge of the High Court, considered an application for an order of sale of a house in Winchester. The four parties were siblings who were the registered owners of their late parents' property, holding the property as tenants in common with a 25% share each. They agreed in writing that a sale of the property could only be permitted if the positive consent of all four of them had been obtained, a provision described in the agreement as "of fundamental importance". One sibling refused to agree to a particular sale because he was convinced that it would be possible to obtain a higher price for the property. The court concluded that it would not be appropriate to override the clear terms of the agreement: "The role of the court is to act with rather than against the parties' agreement."[307]

In *Bagum v Hafiz*,[308] the Court of Appeal considered for the first time[309] aspects of the discretionary powers under s.14. The house in question was owned by Mrs Bagum and her two sons in equal shares as tenants in common. There was a dispute between the three of them and Mrs Bagum, the claimant, sought an order that one son (Mr Hafiz) buy the interest of the other son (Mr Hai). At first instance HHJ May QC held that she had no jurisdiction to make such an order, but instead ordered that the trustees should sell the property on terms that Mr Hafiz should "first have the opportunity to buy it for a price determined upon valuation evidence by the court, failing which (within six weeks of that determination) the Property should be sold on the open market, with liberty for all the beneficial owners to bid". The Court of Appeal confirmed that the judge was correct as to jurisdiction and that the exercise of her discretion could not be challenged. First, the trustees of land cannot directly "deal with or dispose of beneficial interests under the trust".[310] Second, however, the order made the judge, although "an unusual form of order",[311] was nevertheless within the powers conferred by the 1996. In the words of Briggs LJ:

> "the clear object and effect of sections 14 and 15 is to confer upon the court a substantially wider discretion, exercised upon the basis of wider considerations, than might be enjoyed by the trustees themselves, acting without either the consent of their beneficiaries or an order of the court."[312]

---

[303] Trusts of Land and Appointment of Trustees Act 1996 s.15(1). See *The Mortgage Corp v Shaire* [2001] Ch. 743.

[304] Trusts of Land and Appointment of Trustees Act 1996 s.15(2). For ss.12 and 13, see above, para.13–024.

[305] Trusts of Land and Appointment of Trustees Act 1996 s.15(3). This does not apply to applications relating to s.6(2) (power to convey to adult beneficiaries absolutely entitled without request).

[306] [2013] EWHC 4360 (Ch).

[307] [2013] EWHC 4360 (Ch) at [24].

[308] [2015] EWCA Civ 801.

[309] [2015] EWCA Civ 801 per Briggs LJ at [1].

[310] [2015] EWCA Civ 801 per Briggs LJ at [17].

[311] [2015] EWCA Civ 801 per Briggs LJ at [29].

[312] [2015] EWCA Civ 801 per Briggs LJ at [23]. See further *Parkes v Wilkes* [2017] EWHC 1556 (Ch); [2017] 4 W.L.R. 123.

Decisions on the predecessor legislation (s.30 of the Law of Property Act 1925) may afford some guidance, bearing in mind, however, that those decisions were influenced by the primacy of the duty to sell which then arose under the statutory trust for sale in cases of co-ownership. Another distinction is that s.30, unlike s.15 of the 1996 Act, did not spell out the factors to be taken into account by the court. As under the previous law, the provision of a home for the parties' children will continue to be a significant, although not paramount, consideration in family cases.[313] The width of s.15, however, makes it unlikely that much resort will need to be made to the previous authorities, which must be treated with caution. It has been held that s.15 gives the court a wider discretion than under the previous law to refuse an order for sale of the family home, and that it is no longer the position that applications by chargees and trustees in bankruptcy are to be similarly treated.[314] Thus a chargee may be less likely to secure an order for sale than under the previous law, although whether the creditor is receiving proper recompense for being kept out of his money is still a powerful consideration.[315]

The court must exercise its discretion compatibly with the European Convention on Human Rights, but a due consideration of the factors set out in s.15 ordinarily enables the court to balance the respective rights of the creditor and of the debtor's family.[316]

> In *Fred Perry (Holdings) Ltd v Genis*,[317] Master Price considered an application for an order for possession and sale of a house, brought by a firm who had secured judgments against the first defendant. The first defendant lived there with his wife and two children, the children attending specialist Jewish schools nearby. The wife and children's rights were invoked, relying on art.8 (right to respect for his private and family life, his home and his correspondence) and art.1 of the First Protocol (on the right to the peaceful enjoyment of his possessions). Master Price recognised that "there may be cases in which the question arises as to whether an order for sale is a disproportionate interference with the rights of family members".[318] However, on the facts he was satisfied that an order for sale was proportionate given the balancing exercise provided for by the framework in ss.14 and 15. The operation of the sale was deferred for a year to enable relocation and for the children's education to be rearranged.

13–030   Where, however, the sale is requested by the trustee in bankruptcy of one party, different considerations arise: "Bankruptcy has, in relation to the matrimonial

---

[313] See *Williams v Williams* [1976] Ch. 278; *Re Evers' Trust* [1980] 1 W.L.R. 1327 (unmarried couple); *Harris v Harris* (1996) 72 P. & C.R. 408 (no sale on father's death where deed of family arrangement had provided for retention as family home for father and son, who still occupied). For property other than the family home, see *Re Buchanan-Wollaston's Conveyance* [1939] Ch. 738.

[314] *The Mortgage Corp v Shaire* [2001] Ch. 743; S. Pascoe and M. Thompson [2000] Conv. 315 and 329 respectively; M. Oldham (2001) 60 C.L.J. 43; P. Clarke All E.R. Rev. 2001, p.258. See generally M. Dixon (2011) 70 C.L.J. 579.

[315] *Bank of Ireland Home Mortgages Ltd v Bell* [2001] 2 F.L.R. 809; R. Probert [2002] Conv. 61. For the position where both co-owners are the debtors, see *Close Invoice Finance Ltd v Pile* [2009] 1 F.L.R. 873.

[316] *National Westminster Bank Plc v Rushmer* [2010] 2 F.L.R. 362.

[317] [2015] 1 P. & C.R. DG5.

[318] [2015] 1 P. & C.R. DG5 at DG11. There was also a challenge based on the wife's home rights in respect of the Family Law Act 1996, but Master Price held that it would create "an unjustifiable anomaly" to treat the wife differently from the legislative scheme under the Trusts of Land and Appointment of Trustees Act 1996.

home, its own claim to protection".[319] The rights of the creditors are in competition with the interests of all the beneficiaries. They do not automatically defeat the interests of the family; but the reported cases indicate that it is only in exceptional circumstances that the trustee in bankruptcy will not succeed,[320] although sale may be deferred for a short time if the spouse has some prospect of buying the bankrupt's share.[321] The fact that the bankrupt's family will be unable to buy a comparable home and that his children's schooling may be disrupted are not exceptional circumstances justifying refusal of an order for sale; they are the "melancholy consequences of debt and improvidence".[322]

The law in this area was amended by the Insolvency Act 1986, following an examination by the Review Committee on Insolvency Law and Practice.[323] The 1986 provisions have in turn been amended by the Trusts of Land and Appointment of Trustees Act 1996. Where an application for sale is made under s.14 of the 1996 Act by the trustee in bankruptcy of a co-owner, the position is governed by s.335A of the Insolvency Act 1986. On such an application the court shall make such order as it thinks just and reasonable, having regard to:

(a)   the interests of the bankrupt's creditors;

(b)   where the application is made in respect of land which includes a dwelling-house which is or has been the home of the bankrupt or the bankrupt's spouse[324] or former spouse,

    (i)   the conduct of the spouse or former spouse, so far as contributing to the bankruptcy,

    (ii)   the needs and financial resources of the spouse or former spouse, and

    (iii)   the needs of any children; and

(c)   all the circumstances of the case other than the needs of the bankrupt.[325]

Where, however, the application is made after a year from the vesting in the trustee in bankruptcy, the court must assume that the interests of the creditors outweigh all other considerations save in exceptional circumstances. These do not include the needs of the bankrupt.[326] It has been said that "exceptional circumstances" reflects the same test as had been applied in the case law prior to

13–031

---

[319] *Re Bailey* [1977] 1 W.L.R. 278 at 279, per Megarry VC.

[320] *Re Solomon* [1967] Ch. 573; *Re Turner* [1974] 1 W.L.R. 1556; *Re McCarthy* [1975] 1 W.L.R. 807; *Re Lowrie* [1981] 3 All E.R. 353; *Re Densham* [1975] 1 W.L.R. 1519, cf. *Re Holliday* [1981] Ch. 405 (no order until 1985, where no creditors pressing, more assets than debts, and debtor bankrupt on his own petition); C. Hand (1981) 97 L.Q.R. 200; A. Sydenham [1982] Conv. 74; C. Hand [1983] Conv. 219; I. Goldrein (2011) 41 Fam. Law 1227. For the equity of exoneration, see *Re Pittortou* [1985] 1 W.L.R. 58.

[321] *Re Gorman* [1990] 1 W.L.R. 616.

[322] *Re Citro* [1991] Ch. 142 at 157 (bankruptcy prior to Insolvency Act 1986). See also *Barclays Bank Plc v Hendricks* [1996] 1 F.L.R. 258.

[323] 1982, Cmnd. 8558. Some jurisdictions offer greater protection by "homestead legislation". See Joint Family Homes Act 1964 (New Zealand); Gray, *Elements of Land Law*, 5th edn (Oxford: Oxford University Press, 2009), p.1016; P. Omar [2006] Conv. 157.

[324] "Spouse" now includes a registered civil partner; s.335A as amended by the Civil Partnership Act 2004.

[325] The "needs" of the bankrupt include his financial, medical, emotional and mental needs; *Everitt v Budhram (A Bankrupt)* [2010] Ch. 170.

[326] *Everitt v Budhram (A Bankrupt)* [2010] Ch. 170.

the 1986 Act.[327] This provision, therefore, gives some protection to the family by delaying the sale, but the trustee will normally succeed after a year. Some decisions, however, reveal a more "humanitarian" approach.[328] There are similar provisions relating to occupation orders under s.33 of the Family Law Act 1996 in cases of bankruptcy.[329]

The trustee in bankruptcy may apply under s.14 of the 1996 Act for the sale of a jointly owned home even where the bankrupt's spouse is entitled to occupy under an order of the divorce court postponing sale until her remarriage or some other future event.[330] Such an order does not give the spouse an absolute right to occupy until one of the specified events happens. Whether the trustee will succeed depends on the application of s.335A of the 1986 Act.

A question which has been aired in recent cases is whether s.335A is compatible with art.8 of the European Convention on Human Rights, which protects the right to respect for one's private and family life and home.[331] In *Barca v Mears*,[332] it was suggested that the interpretation of the section might need to be reconsidered in the light of art.8, but the point was left open. The question was further debated in *Nicholls v Lan*,[333] where the wife's schizophrenia was an "exceptional" circumstance, but she co-owned another house. It was held that s.335A was not inconsistent with the qualified rights protected by art.8. It was added that the interests of creditors should not be dismissed just because there was no specific evidence of their identities or concerns. It appears, therefore, that the right to respect for the home is a consideration to be weighed in the balance, but that arguments based on art.8 are unlikely to prevail.[334] Indeed,

---

[327] *Re Citro* [1991] Ch. 142 (in the context of s.336); J. Hall (1991) 50 C.L.J. 45; S. Cretney (1991) 107 L.Q.R. 177; A. Lawson [1991] Conv. 302; D. Brown (1992) 55 M.L.R. 284.

[328] *Judd v Brown, Bankrupts* [1998] 2 F.L.R. 360 (no order for sale where bankrupt's wife being treated for cancer); *Re Raval (A Bankrupt)* [1998] 2 F.L.R. 718 (order suspended for a year where bankrupt's wife mentally ill); *Claughton v Charalamabous* [1999] 1 F.L.R. 740 (order suspended until bankrupt's wife, who was chronically ill and had reduced life expectancy, vacated the house or died); *Re Haghighat (A Bankrupt)* [2009] 1 F.L.R. 1271 (order suspended for three years as wife cared for vulnerable adult child at home). The appeal was dismissed at [2010] EWCA Civ 1521. See also *Re Bremner (A Bankrupt)* [1999] 1 F.L.R. 912 (where bankrupt husband terminally ill, elderly wife's need to care for him at home was an "exceptional circumstance").

[329] Insolvency Act 1986 ss.336, 337, as amended. See *Re Bremner (A Bankrupt)*, above, fn.237. These provisions now apply to civil partners; Civil Partnership Act 2004 s.82 and Sch.9.

[330] *Avis v Turner* [2008] Ch. 218. An order for sale was granted; *Turner v Avis* [2009] 1 F.L.R. 74.

[331] S. Nield and N. Hopkins (2013) 33 L.S. 431. Article 8 is set out in Sch.1 of the Human Rights Act 1998:

"8(1) Everyone has the right to respect for his private and family life, his home and his correspondence.

8(2) There shall be no interference by a public authority with the exercise of this right except such as is in accordance with the law and is necessary in a democratic society in the interests of national security, public safety or the economic well-being of the country, for the prevention of disorder or crime, for the protection of health or morals, or for the protection of the rights and freedoms of others."

[332] [2005] 2 F.L.R. 1; M. Dixon [2005] Conv. 161; A. Baker [2010] Conv. 352. See also *Donohoe v Ingram* [2006] 2 F.L.R. 1084; *Holtham v Kelmanson* [2007] W.T.L.R. 285.

[333] [2007] 1 F.L.R. 744; M. Pawlowski [2007] Conv. 78. Sale was ordered but postponed for 18 months. See also *National Westminster Bank Plc v Rushmer* [2010] 2 F.L.R. 362.

[334] Although art.8 was held to be relevant in allowing the defendants to continue in possession of the property in question pending an appeal in *Hawk Recovery Ltd v Hall* [2016] EWHC 1307 (Ch) per Master Matthews at [32].

"it is difficult to escape the conclusion that little more than a nod has been accorded to the effect of the [Human Rights] Act upon the meaning of 'exceptional circumstances'."[335]

In *Ford v Alexander*,[336] Peter Smith J considered the potential impact of art.8 on s.335A, in the light of an argument based on a recent Supreme Court decision concerning art.8 and local authority landlords.[337] The Supreme Court had, however, expressly stated that those decisions were not concerned with private landowners,[338] and so Peter Smith J concluded that the previous authorities on s.335A were unaffected. It was held that the relevant provisions of s.335A

"do not infringe Article 8 (2). They provide a necessary balance as between the rights of creditors and the respect for privacy and the home of the debtor. That balance serves the legitimate aim of protecting the rights and freedoms of others."[339]

The Enterprise Act 2002[340] affords some relief to the bankrupt in relation to property which was the residence of the bankrupt or his spouse or former spouse at the date of the bankruptcy. If the trustee in bankruptcy has not sold the property or applied for an order for possession or sale within three years of that date, the property revests in the bankrupt and ceases to be available to creditors.

---

[335] *Official Receiver for Northern Ireland v Rooney* [2009] 2 F.L.R. 1437 at 1449 (on the equivalent legislation in Northern Ireland).
[336] [2012] EWHC 266 (Ch).
[337] *Manchester City Council v Pinnock* [2010] UKSC 45.
[338] [2010] UKSC 45 at [50].
[339] [2012] EWHC 266 (Ch) at [49]. D. Cowan and C. Hunter (2012) 15 J.H.L. 58.
[340] s.261, inserting s.283A into the Insolvency Act 1986, with effect from 1 April 2004. *Hunt v Conwy County BC* [2014] 1 W.L.R. 254.

TRUSTS, LEGAL POLICY AND ILLEGALITY

A TRUST, though otherwise valid, may fail because it contains an element of unlawfulness or immorality, or is contrary to public policy. It is impossible to categorise all the possible grounds of unlawfulness, and only some of the more important ones can be mentioned here. Particular consideration is given to the decision of the Supreme Court in *Patel v Mirza*,[1] which attempted to address controversies concerning the defence of illegality in private law.   **14–001**

1. TRUSTS CONTRARY TO THE GENERAL POLICY OF THE LAW

A. Purposes Contrary to Law, Public Policy or Morality

Such trusts are likely to fail in any event, apart from any question of unlawfulness, on the ground that they are non-charitable purpose trusts, as we shall see below.[2] There are, perhaps for this reason, few examples of cases   **14–002**

---

[1] [2016] UKSC 42; [2017] A.C. 467, below para.14–014.
[2] Below, Ch.16. See, for example, *Brown v Burdett* (1882) 21 Ch.D. 667, where a "useless" trust to seal up a house for 20 years failed. M. Pawlowski (2016) 179 T.E.L.&.T.J. 4.

decided on the basis of illegality, but one such is *Thrupp v Collett*,[3] where a testator attempted to provide for paying the fines of convicted poachers. Sir John Romilly MR held the trust void on the ground that it was against public policy. It was held in *Bowman v Secular Society*[4] that the denial of Christianity was not of itself an illegal purpose, but it was suggested in *Thornton v Howe*[5] that a trust whose purpose was adverse to all religion or subversive of morality would be void.[6] Trusts for the furtherance of illegal or immoral activities, such as, for example, terrorism or prostitution,[7] would also fail. Likewise a trust for a fraudulent purpose, such as placing money with a company in order to give it the false appearance of a credit balance.[8] The Law Commission[9] regarded an "illegal trust" as comprising the following: a trust which it would be legally wrongful to create or impose; a trust which is created to facilitate fraud or some other legal wrong or which arises as a result of a transaction or arrangement with that objective; a trust which is created in return for the commission of a legal wrong or the promise to commit a legal wrong; a trust which expressly or necessarily requires a trustee or beneficiary to commit a legal wrong or which tends or is intended to do so; and a trust which is otherwise contrary to public policy at common law. However, this aspect was not included in the final report, which was confined to a different aspect of illegality in the law of trusts.[10]

It was at one time established that gifts by deed or will for future illegitimate children were void on the ground that they would tend to encourage immorality.[11] The position was changed by s.15(7) of the Family Law Reform Act 1969 (now replaced by the Family Law Reform Act 1987 s.19).[12]

B. Statutory Provisions Against Discrimination

14–003 **i. Background.** It is unlawful to discriminate against persons with particular characteristics in areas such as employment, the provisions of goods and services and the disposal of property. Thus the Sex Discrimination Act 1975 made discrimination on grounds of sex unlawful in these areas, and the Race Relations Act 1976 (replacing earlier legislation) did likewise in the case of racial discrimination. Discrimination on the grounds of religion or belief was prohibited in the employment field by regulations, and the prohibition was extended to other

---

[3] (1858) 26 Beav. 125.
[4] [1917] A.C. 406 (Lord Finlay LC dissenting).
[5] (1862) 31 Beav. 14.
[6] This is a high threshold: *Buckley v Barlow* [2016] EWHC 3017 (Ch); M. Herbert [2017] P.C.B. 71.
[7] See Harman LJ's example of a "school for prostitutes or pickpockets" in *Re Pinion* [1965] Ch. 85 at 105. See also *Sutton v Mishcon de Reya (A Firm)* [2004] 1 F.L.R. 837 (contract for cohabitation).
[8] *Re Great Berlin Steamboat Co* (1884) 26 Ch.D. 616.
[9] Law Com. CP No. 154, *Illegal Transactions: The Effect of Illegality on Contracts and Trusts* (1999), para.8.22; below, para.14–011. See also *Re the Esteem Settlement* [2004] W.T.L.R. 1 at 45 (Jersey Royal Court), accepting that, in exceptional circumstances, an initially valid trust could become void as being contrary to public policy.
[10] Law Com. No. 320, *The Illegality Defence* (2010), above, paras 11–036—11–038.
[11] *Occleston v Fullalove* (1873-74) L.R. 9 Ch.App. 147; cf. *Re Hyde* [1932] 1 Ch. 95. The claim of an illegitimate beneficiary might have failed in any event on the ground that gifts were generally construed as confined to legitimate relatives.
[12] This Act replaces the concept of the illegitimate child with that of the unmarried parent.

areas by the Equality Act 2006. That Act also enabled regulations to be made to prohibit discrimination on the ground of sexual orientation. Age discrimination was also prohibited by regulations in the field of employment and training.

ii. Equality Act 2010. The statutory provisions mentioned above were replaced and in some respects extended by the Equality Act 2010. The Act prohibits discrimination against persons who share "protected characteristics", which are: age, disability, gender reassignment, marriage and civil partnership, pregnancy and maternity, race, religion or belief, sex and sexual orientation.[13] "Race" is defined as including colour, nationality, ethnic or national origins.[14] "Religion" means any religion or lack of religion (for example atheism), and "belief" means any religious or philosophical belief or a lack of belief.[15]

    14–004

The areas in which discrimination is made unlawful by the 2010 Act include employment, public sector services, education, occupational pension schemes and the disposal of property. Subject to what is said below about charitable trusts, the legislation does not extend to discrimination in the making of a gift or trust. But trustees, just as any other individuals, are bound by the provisions relating to employment, disposal of property and so on. As will be seen, these provisions are especially significant in the administration of charitable trusts.

iii. Charitable Trusts. The Equality Act 2010 contains special provisions relating to charitable trusts, which replace and harmonise the separate exceptions in the previous legislation. There is no breach of the Act if benefits are conferred on persons who share a "protected characteristic" (for example race, age or sex), provided this is a proportionate means of achieving a legitimate aim or is to prevent or compensate for a disadvantage linked to the characteristic.[16] In other words, it is lawful to discriminate in favour of such groups of persons, but not against them.[17] Thus there is nothing unlawful in single sex charities, such as the YMCA, as long as the provisions of the Act are satisfied. In the case of educational charities, however, the single sex restriction may be removed or modified by ministerial order.[18] So far as religion and belief are concerned, it is not of itself unlawful for a charity to require members and persons wishing to become members to accept a particular religion or belief, and to restrict the benefits and facilities accordingly.[19]

    14–005

Special rules apply to discrimination on the basis of colour. While the general position is that the Equality Act 2010 does not affect a provision in a charitable

---

[13] Equality Act 2010 s.4.

[14] Equality Act 2010 s.9. The UK Government has consulted on whether to include "caste" under race. At the time of writing, the relevant consultation has closed but the government is yet to respond: *Caste in Great Britain and Equality Law: A Public Consultation* (closed 18 September 2017). See further *Chandhok v Tirkey* [2015] I.C.R. 527.

[15] Equality Act 2010 s.10.

[16] s.193(1), (2).

[17] Thus the provisions contained in *Re Dominion Students' Hall Trust* [1947] Ch. 183, which contained a restriction among the users of a hostel to "members of the [British] Empire of European origin" would be unlawful (as was also the case under previous legislation). See also *Re Gwyon* [1930] 1 Ch. 255.

[18] Equality Act 2010 Sch.14.

[19] Equality Act 2010 s.193(5).

instrument which provides for conferring benefits on persons who share "protected characteristics", including race, it is not permissible to discriminate even in favour of a class defined by reference to colour.[20] Any such provision is to take effect as if it provided for conferring the benefits in question on persons of the class which results if the colour qualification is disregarded.

Finally, it should be noted that even where discrimination in a charitable trust is not made unlawful by the legislation, the removal of discriminatory provisions is possible under the cy-près doctrine.[21]

C. Conditions Precedent and Subsequent; Determinable Interests

14–006   Questions involving illegality often arise in connection with the validity of conditions imposed upon otherwise valid gifts.[22] A condition precedent is one which must be satisfied before the gift can vest, whereas a condition subsequent operates to defeat an already vested gift by forfeiture. A determinable interest, on the other hand, is one which will automatically determine on the occurrence of the determining event, no question of forfeiture being involved.[23] It is not always easy, as a matter of construction, to decide whether a condition is intended to operate as a condition precedent or subsequent, or to distinguish conditional and determinable interests.[24] It seems that the latter are less susceptible to, although not immune from, attack on the ground of public policy.[25]

Apart from any question of illegality, conditions have frequently failed on the ground of uncertainty. A distinction has been drawn between conditions precedent and subsequent. A stricter test of certainty applies to a condition subsequent, which must be so framed that at the outset the beneficiary knows the exact event which will divest his interest.[26] Lord Denning MR described this distinction as a "deplorable dichotomy", serving only to defeat the settlor's intention.[27] Even in the case of a condition subsequent, however, the court is reluctant to pronounce the condition void for uncertainty. So in *Re Tepper's Will Trusts*,[28] where a

---

[20] s.193(4). See *Re Harding* [2008] Ch. 235 (gift to "black community" of four London boroughs was charitable but took effect without the colour qualification).

[21] Below, para.15–066. See *Re Lysaght* [1966] Ch. 191; *Re Dominion Students' Hall Trust* [1947] Ch. 183; *Canada Trust Company v Ontario Human Rights Commission* (1990) 69 D.L.R. (4th) 321; *Re Peach Estate* 2009 NSSC 383. The promotion of racial harmony is now a charitable purpose; Charities Act 2011 s.3(1)(h), replacing previous legislation.

[22] Where several conditions are attached to one gift, the valid conditions may be severed from any which are invalid: *Re Hepplewhite Will Trusts*, *The Times*, 21 January 1977.

[23] Above, para.8–002.

[24] See, for example, *Re Tuck's Settlement Trusts* [1978] Ch. 49; *Re Johnson's Will Trusts* [1967] Ch. 387; *Re Tepper's Will Trusts* [1987] Ch. 358.

[25] See *Re Johnson's Will Trusts* [1967] Ch. 387 at 396; *Re Moore* (1888) 39 Ch.D. 116; Megarry and Wade, *The Law of Real Property*, 8th edn, para.3–066.

[26] *Re Tepper's Will Trusts* [1987] Ch. 358. The test applying to conditions precedent is that laid down in *Re Allen* [1953] Ch. 810: conceptual uncertainty may not defeat such conditions, see *Re Barlow's Will Trusts* [1979] 1 W.L.R. 278, above, para.4–022. See generally Underhill and Hayton, 19th edn, paras 8.91–8.99; L. McKay [1980] Conv. 263.

[27] *Re Tuck's Settlement Trusts* [1978] Ch. 49 at 60. But the distinction was acknowledged by the House of Lords in *Blathwayt v Lord Cawley* [1976] A.C. 397 at 425.

[28] [1987] Ch. 358. See also *Ellis v Chief Adjudication Officer* [1998] 1 F.L.R. 184 (gift of house to daughter subject to condition subsequent that she should care for her mother in the house upheld). A

condition subsequent required the beneficiaries to remain within the Jewish faith and not to marry outside it, the court regarded as admissible extrinsic evidence of the Jewish faith as practised by the testator, to elucidate the meaning of his words.[29]

Assuming that the condition does not fail for uncertainty, the next question is whether it will be void as being illegal or otherwise contrary to public policy. The matter was discussed in *Nathan v Leonard*,[30] where a condition subsequent to the effect that if any beneficiary challenged the will, all dispositions would be forfeited and the estate would devolve to others was not contrary to public policy on the ground that it might deter an application under the Inheritance (Provision for Family and Dependants) Act 1975, nor because of its arbitrary nature. The categories discussed below involve the types of condition which have been most frequently encountered. The validity of conditions relating to bankruptcy has already been discussed.[31]

i. **Marriage, Separation and Divorce.** Where property is given by way of a determinable gift until marriage, and then to other beneficiaries, the limitation is unobjectionable.[32] Conditions, on the other hand, will be void if they are designed to prevent marriage or to encourage divorce or separation.

14–007

As far as conditions restraining marriage are concerned, a distinction is drawn between total and partial restraints. A condition subsequent, operating to divest the property on marriage, is void if its object is to restrain marriage altogether.[33] But conditions operating only in the event of a second or subsequent marriage, or merely requiring consent to marriage,[34] are not void.[35] Nor is there any objection to a condition in restraint of marriage with certain persons, or a certain class.[36] The rules relating to partial restraints on marriage differ according to whether the gift is of realty or personalty, the reason being that the personalty rules evolved in the ecclesiastical courts, whereas the realty rules were developed by the common law. The result of this historical distinction is as follows: in the case of personalty a condition imposing a partial restraint on marriage is invalid as being merely "*in*

---

condition which is impossible to fulfil is spent and the gift absolute; *Re Chambers* [2001] W.T.L.R. 1375 (condition relating to pet animals which had died).

[29] Relying on Lord Denning's view in *Re Tuck's Settlement Trusts* [1978] Ch. 49, where, however, the will expressly provided that the Chief Rabbi could determine the meaning of "Jewish faith" and "approved wife". cf. Administration of Justice Act 1982 s.21.

[30] [2003] 1 W.L.R. 827. The condition failed for uncertainty, however.

[31] Above, para.8–003.

[32] *Re Lovell* [1920] 1 Ch. 122.

[33] *Lloyd v Lloyd* (1852) 2 Sim.(N.S.) 255. This includes a condition which in practice amounts to a general restraint: *Re Lanyon* [1927] 2 Ch. 264 (condition against marriage with any blood relation). It seems that similar rules would apply to a condition precedent. See *Re Wallace* [1920] 2 Ch. 274.

[34] *Re Whiting's Settlement* [1905] 1 Ch. 96.

[35] *Allen v Jackson* (1875) 1 Ch.D. 399.

[36] *Jenner v Turner* (1880) 16 Ch.D. 188; *Perrin v Lyon* (1807) 9 East. 170 (condition against marrying a person born in Scotland or of Scottish parents upheld). See also the cases on religion, discussed below.

terrorem" if there is no express gift over on the occurrence of the marriage[37] whereas in the case of realty, a partial restraint is never invalid, whether or not there is a gift over.[38]

Conditions designed to induce the separation or divorce of a husband and wife are void as being contrary to public policy.[39] But if the parties have already decided upon a separation, the trusts in any deed of separation are not invalid,[40] nor is a post-nuptial agreement providing for the consequences of a future separation.[41] Thus there is no objection where the true object of a disposition is merely to make provision for a party during the separation.[42]

It will be seen that most of these cases were decided at a time when the sanctity of marriage was perhaps regarded more highly than it is today. A stricter view was taken of relationships outside marriage than is now the case. Thus, in the past, trusts or covenants to create trusts were held void if created in consideration of a future immoral association.[43] The modern tendency might be to discover some other form of consideration from the beneficiary.[44]

14–008   **ii. Parental Duties.**   A condition calculated to bring about the separation of parent and child is void as being contrary to public policy,[45] even where the parents are divorced.[46] Similarly, a condition designed to interfere with the exercise of parental duties.[47] In *Blathwayt v Lord Cawley*,[48] a settlement provided for the forfeiture of the interest of any child who became a Roman Catholic. It was argued that the condition was void on the ground that it would hamper parental duties in religious instruction. The House of Lords rejected this argument:

---

[37] *Leong v Lim Beng Chye* [1955] A.C. 648 (a residuary gift is not a gift over).

[38] Another possible distinction is that in the case of realty, but not personalty, even a general restraint is valid if intended merely to provide for the beneficiary while unmarried, rather than to promote celibacy: *Jones v Jones* (1876) 1 Q.B.D. 279.

[39] *Re Johnson's Will Trusts* [1967] Ch. 387; *Re Caborne* [1943] Ch. 224. See also *Re Hepplewhite Will Trusts, The Times*, 21 January 1977.

[40] *Wilson v Wilson* (1848) 1 H.L.C. 538. It is otherwise if the provision is designed to discourage reconciliation.

[41] *MacLeod v MacLeod* [2010] 1 A.C. 298. See also *Egerton v Egerton* [1949] 2 All E.R. 238 at 242 and (on pre-marital agreements) *Radmacher v Granatino* [2010] UKSC 42; [2011] 1 A.C. 534.

[42] *Re Lovell* [1920] 1 Ch. 122. As to the admissibility of any evidence of the settlor's motive, see *Re Johnson's Will Trusts* [1967] Ch. 387.

[43] See *Re Vallance* (1884) 26 Ch.D. 353; *Ayerst v Jenkins* (1873) L.R. 16 Eq. 275. See also *Re Jones* [1953] Ch. 125, where a condition prohibiting a "social or other relationship" with X failed for uncertainty.

[44] See, for example, *Tanner v Tanner* [1975] 1 W.L.R. 1346, (contract was inferred between a man and his mistress in consideration of her looking after the house and family); cf. *Coombes v Smith* [1986] 1 W.L.R. 808.

[45] *Re Boulter (No.2)* [1922] 1 Ch. 75.

[46] *Re Piper* [1946] 2 All E.R. 503.

[47] *Re Borwick* [1933] Ch. 657; *Re Sandbrook* [1912] 2 Ch. 471. These two decisions must be read in the light of the comments made in *Blathwayt v Lord Cawley* [1976] A.C. 397, discussed below.

[48] [1976] A.C. 397.

"To say that any condition which in any way might affect or influence the way in which a child is brought up, or in which parental duties are exercised, [is invalid] seems to me to state far too wide a rule."[49]

iii. Religion.   It has already been noted that prohibitions on discrimination on grounds of religion or belief do not apply to private trusts.[50] Conditions restricting freedom of religion have long been popular with settlors and testators. While such conditions have sometimes failed for uncertainty, especially in the case of conditions subsequent,[51] it has never been held that such provisions are contrary to public policy, even in the case of charitable trusts.[52] In *Blathwayt v Lord Cawley*,[53] the facts of which have already been given, Lord Cross said that while it may be wrong for the Government to discriminate on religion, it does not follow that it is against public policy for an adherent of one religion to distinguish in disposing of his property; any other view amounts to saying that:

14–009

"[I]t is disreputable for him to be convinced of the importance of holding true religious beliefs and of the fact that his religious beliefs are the true ones."[54]

It had been argued that the Race Relations Acts and the European Convention on Human Rights showed that the law was against discrimination. Lord Wilberforce said:

"I do not doubt that conceptions of public policy should move with the times and that widely accepted treaties and statutes may point the direction in which such conceptions, as applied by the courts, ought to move. It may well be that conditions such as this are, or at least are becoming, inconsistent with standards now widely accepted."[55]

But this did not justify the introduction of a new rule, for to do so would reduce another freedom, that of testamentary disposition.

"Discrimination is not the same thing as choice: it operates over a larger and less personal area, and neither by express provision nor by implication has private selection yet become a matter of public policy."[56]

iv. Race.   We have already seen that discrimination on the grounds of race or colour is made unlawful by the Equality Act 2010 (replacing earlier legislation),

14–010

---

[49] [1976] A.C. 397 at 426 (per Lord Wilberforce).

[50] Above, para.14–004.

[51] *Clayton v Ramsden* [1943] A.C. 320 (forfeiture on marriage to person not of Jewish parentage and faith); *Re Abraham's Will Trusts* [1969] 1 Ch. 463; *Re Tepper's Will Trusts* [1987] Ch. 358. A condition precedent is less likely to fail on this ground: see e.g. *Re Tuck's Settlement Trusts* [1978] Ch. 49 (marriage to "approved wife" of Jewish blood and faith not uncertain); D. Cooper and D. Herman (1999) 19 L.S. 339. See also *Re Evans* [1940] Ch. 629.

[52] See *Re Lysaght* [1966] Ch. 191; cf. *Canada Trust Company v Ontario Human Rights Commission* (1990) 69 D.L.R. (4th) 321. See also Equality Act 2010 s.193(5); above, para.14–005.

[53] [1976] A.C. 397. See also *Re Remnant's Settlement Trusts* [1970] 1 Ch. 560; *Clayton v Ramsden* [1943] A.C. 320. The heir to the throne may not be a Roman Catholic by virtue of the Act of Settlement 1701. However, the Succession to the Crown Act 2013 s.2 removed the previous bar on those married to a Catholic succeeding to the Crown.

[54] [1976] A.C. 397 at 429.

[55] [1976] A.C. 397 at 426.

[56] [1976] A.C. 397 at 426.

and that, apart from special provisions relating to charities, the Act has no application to private trusts. It seems that it is not contrary to public policy for a settlor to discriminate on these grounds, although the point is not unarguable. There is little authority on the point, which has arisen mainly in connection with charitable trusts.[57] Many of the comments made by the House of Lords in *Blathwayt v Lord Cawley* in the context of religion would apply equally to racial discrimination, save that the dictum of Lord Cross[58] loses all conviction if race is substituted for religious beliefs.

14–011   **v. Alienation.**   Conditions operating as a complete restraint on the alienation of property are void as being contrary to public policy.

> In *Re Brown*,[59] a testator devised land among his four sons subject to a condition which would have produced forfeiture of his interest by any son who mortgaged or sold his interest other than among his brothers. The condition was held to be equivalent to a general restraint on alienation, and therefore void, since the class of permitted alienees was small and bound to get smaller.

A partial restraint on alienation is valid.[60] Discrimination in the disposal of property is unlawful, subject to exceptions, under the Equality Act 2010 (replacing earlier legislation).[61]

Restraints even of a general nature may be valid if they take the form of a determinable interest.[62] Section 33 of the Trustee Act 1925 itself provides such an example.[63]

14–012   **vi. The Future of the Freedom to Discriminate.**   The persistence of this common law position has been staunchly criticised by Professor Harding,[64] particularly since Lord Wilberforce's dicta in *Blathwayt v Lord Cawley*[65] pre-date the incorporation of the European Convention on Human Rights into English Law via the Human Rights Act 1998.[66] In his article, Harding cited *Pla v Andorra*,[67] which has since been relied upon by Mark Herbert QC, sitting as a deputy High Court judge, in *In Re Erskine 1948 Trust*.[68] That case concerned the use by a settlor of "statutory next of kin", which applying the statutory definition

---

[57] See *Re Gwyon* [1930] 1 Ch. 255; *Re Dominion Students' Hall Trust* [1947] Ch. 183. In neither case was public policy discussed.

[58] [1976] A.C. 397 at 429; above para.14–009.

[59] [1954] Ch. 39; cf. *Caldy Manor Estate Ltd v Farrell* [1974] 1 W.L.R. 1303 (covenant against alienation not unlawful).

[60] See *Re MacLeay* (1875) L.R. 20 Eq. 186; doubted in *Re Rosher* [1884] 25 Ch. 801. It is arguable that even partial restraints should be invalid as repugnant to ownership.

[61] Part 4.

[62] *Re Dugdale* (1883) 38 Ch.D. 176 at 178–181, per Kay J; *Re Leach* [1912] 2 Ch. 422.

[63] Above, para.8–005 (the protective trust).

[64] M. Harding (2011) 31 O.J.L.S. 303.

[65] [1976] A.C. 397. See also *Re Remnant's Settlement Trusts* [1970] 1 Ch. 560; *Clayton v Ramsden* [1943] A.C. 320. The heir to the throne may not be a Roman Catholic by virtue of the Act of Settlement 1701. However, the Succession to the Crown Act 2013 s.2 removed the previous bar on those married to a Catholic succeeding to the Crown.

[66] M. Harding (2011) 31 O.J.L.S. 303 at 312–6.

[67] (2004) 42 E.H.R.R. 522.

[68] [2013] Ch. 135.

applicable at the time of the settlement, excluded adopted children in the absence of a contrary intention.[69] The judge determined that the settlement must be construed in such a way as to avoid discrimination against adopted children.[70] Although *In Re Erskine* is not directly on the point of the general freedom to discriminate,[71] concerning as it does the role of a legislative definition of statutory next of kin, the case may point to a judicial willingness to consider the importance of the principle of non-discrimination when weighed against testamentary autonomy.[72] Indeed, as Lord Wilberforce noted in *Blathwayt*, public policy can "move with the times".[73]

2.   CONSEQUENCES OF ILLEGALITY AND ILLEGALITY AS A DEFENCE

Historically, the general position appears to have been that if an express trust fails **14–013** on the ground of unlawfulness, a resulting trust to the settlor or his estate ensues.[74] This is so even if the trust was designed to encourage an offence prohibited by statute.[75] Where the trust is only partly unlawful, the whole fails if the proportion to be devoted to the unlawful purpose is unascertainable,[76] whereas if that proportion is ascertainable, only that part fails.[77] Where a condition subsequent is unlawful, the gift takes effect as an absolute interest: the condition alone is void.[78] In the case of a condition precedent, a distinction is drawn between realty and personality. As far as realty is concerned, the gift itself fails if the condition is bad.[79] Where the gift is of personality, however, it takes effect free of the condition where the illegality is only a *malum prohibitum*.[80] But where the illegality is a *malum in se*, the gift fails. In the case of a determinable interest, the gift fails if the determining event is unlawful.[81] Where property has been transferred to a volunteer for an unlawful purpose, the question arises whether the court will assist the transferor to recover the property. There are thus several ways in which illegality may affect the law of trusts or equity: illegality may prevent a trust arising in the first place, prevent a condition operating, or it may be raised as a defence to a claim.

---

[69] Administration Act 1925 s.50 and Adoption of Children Act 1926 s.5.

[70] [2013] Ch. 135 at [54]–[56].

[71] Indeed, *Blathwayt* was cited in argument but not in the judgment.

[72] See also *Re the Y Trust and the Z Trust* [2017] JRC 100 at [35]; below, para.23–027.

[73] [1976] A.C. 397 at 426.

[74] Above, para.11–006. cf. *Ayerst v Jenkins* (1873) L.R. 16 Eq. 275 (described as a "difficult case" in Law Com. CP No. 154, *Illegal Transactions: The Effect of Illegality on Contracts and Trusts* (1999) at p.69).

[75] *Thrupp v Collett* (1858) 26 Beav. 125.

[76] *Chapman v Brown* (1801) 6 Ves. 404.

[77] *Mitford v Reynolds* (1842) 1 Ph. 185. There is some authority that in such a case the whole can go to the lawful part: *Fisk v Attorney General* (1867) L.R. 4 Eq. 521.

[78] *Re Beard* [1908] 1 Ch. 383. This is so whether the gift is realty or personality.

[79] *Re Elliott* [1952] Ch. 217.

[80] i.e. something made unlawful only by statute. See *Re Piper* [1946] 2 All E.R. 503. The distinction was apparently not discussed in *Re Hepplewhite Will Trusts*, *The Times*, 21 January 1977.

[81] *Re Moore* (1888) 39 Ch.D. 116. For the application of the perpetuity rule to conditional and determinable interests, see Perpetuities and Accumulations Act 1964 s.12: the interest becomes absolute if the determining event or breach of condition does not occur within the perpetuity period.

This area was reviewed by the Law Commission in a project which was completed in 2010.[82] The Commission considered that the present law is unclear as to what happens when an express trust fails for illegality. While the appropriate response will normally be that the property results to the settlor, there may be cases where the settlor's illegal motivation has been so grave that a resulting trust in his favour should be excluded. The Commission proposed that the court should have a discretion to decide who should be entitled to the property, for example to declare that the trustee is the legal and beneficial owner. This statutory discretion should be based on factors such as the gravity of the illegal conduct, deterrence and proportionality. The Law Commission had also previously proposed the abolition of the distinction in consequence between *malum pohibitum* and *malum in se*,[83] but this aspect of illegality was not included in the final report.[84] The Government indicated that it had no plans to implement the proposals on illegality.[85] The approach has since been developed by the courts.

14–014 The illegality defence in private law has been the subject of extensive consideration by the Supreme Court, with four cases between 2014 and 2016:[86] as Lord Sumption put it, there had been a "longstanding schism between those judges and writers who regard the law of illegality as calling for the application of clear rules, and those who would wish to address the equities of each case as it arises."[87] It is the former approach which has prevailed, drawing inspiration from the Law Commission's work. The controversies culminated in *Patel v Mirza*.[88]

> Mr Mirza proposed a scheme with Mr Patel to place bets on the movement of shares in the Royal Bank of Scotland (RBS). The plan was to rely upon insider information from a contact at the bank who was aware of discussions with the government. Mirza received £620,000 from Patel for placing the bets ahead of an expected statement from the Chancellor of the Exchequer which would have an effect on the price of RBS shares. This agreement was an offence under Criminal Justice Act 1993, s.52, as a conspiracy to commit insider trading. In the event, the bets were never placed and the Chancellor's statement was never made. Patel brought a claim to recover the substantial sum which he had paid to Mirza. Mirza argued that he could rely on the defence of illegality.

---

[82] Law Com. No. 320, *The Illegality Defence* (2010), see paras 2.87–2.102. Lord Sumption described the Law Commission as having "struggled valiantly with the issue": *Jetivia SA v Bilta (UK) Ltd (In Liquidation)* [2015] UKSC 23 at [62].

[83] Law Com. CP No. 154, *Illegal Transactions: The Effect of Illegality on Contracts and Trusts* (1999), p.170.

[84] Law Com. No. 320, *The Illegality Defence* (2010), para.2.114.

[85] Ministry of Justice, HC1900, *Report on the implementation of Law Commission proposals* (March 2012) para.52: "The application of the draft Bill is … very wide and there is some concern about the risk of unintended consequences and of a new statutory scheme introducing new uncertainties in the law. Therefore, on balance, and given that reform of this area of the law cannot be considered a pressing priority for the Government at present, we are minded not to implement the Commission's proposals."

[86] *Hounga v Allen* [2014] 1 W.L.R. 2889; *Les Laboratoires Servier v Apotex Inc* [2014] UKSC 55; [2015] 1 A.C. 430; *Jetivia SA v Bilta (UK) Ltd (In Liquidation)* [2015] UKSC 23; *Patel v Mirza* [2017] A.C. 467.

[87] [2017] A.C. 467 at [226].

[88] [2016] UKSC 42; [2017] A.C. 467; J. Goudkamp (2017) 133 L.Q.R. 14; J. Fisher [2016] L.M.C.L.Q. 483; A. Grabiner (2017) 76 C.L.J. 19,

The Supreme Court unanimously held that Patel was entitled to recover the money, but there was a divergence of opinion among the Justices as to the reasons why. The majority, led by Lord Toulson,[89] disapproved of the previous "reliance" test in *Tinsley v Milligan*,[90] The rule, which was discussed in Ch.11, was that the transferor may recover if she did not have to rely on her own illegality,[91] or if the illegality had not been carried out.[92] This test had produced arbitrary results because application of the defence depended upon what the claimant had to prove, rather than the illegality in question. The Supreme Court instead embraced a three stage "range of factors" approach:

> "The essential rationale of the illegality doctrine is that it would be contrary to the public interest to enforce a claim if to do so would be harmful to the integrity of the legal system ... In assessing whether the public interest would be harmed in that way, it is necessary a) to consider the underlying purpose of the prohibition which has been transgressed and whether that purpose will be enhanced by denial of the claim, b) to consider any other relevant public policy on which the denial of the claim may have an impact and c) to consider whether denial of the claim would be a proportionate response to the illegality, bearing in mind that punishment is a matter for the criminal courts."[93]

This approach involves what is "clearly a fact-sensitive enquiry".[94] The minority, Lords Sumption, Mance and Clarke, thought it inappropriate that "the law of illegality should be generally rewritten",[95] and would have preserved the reliance test in some form, as it "accords with principle".[96] For Lord Sumption, every "alternative test which has been proposed would widen the application of the defence as well as render its application more uncertain".[97]

There is some uncertainty as to the exact scope of *Patel* as clarifying the operation of the illegality defence across private law.[98] The full implications will need to be worked out in the cases and the literature, but the approach in *Patel* certainly indicates that the Justices were seeking to address the defence generally.[99] However, in a tort case considering *Patel*, Jay J said his provisional view that he did not "read *Patel* as intending to supply a complete answer to all illegality cases".[100] On the other hand, Martin Spencer J has endorsed *Patel* as being "intended to cover all cases where the common law doctrine of illegality is

14–015

---

[89] Joining Lord Toulson in the majority were Lady Hale, Lord Kerr (who gave a short concurring opinion), Lord Wilson, Lord Hodge and Lord Neuberger (who gave a concurring opinion with some further reflections); the minority comprised Lords Mance, Clarke and Sumption.

[90] Above, paras 11–036—11–038.

[91] *Tinsley v Milligan* [1994] 1 A.C. 340.

[92] *Tribe v Tribe* [1996] Ch. 107.

[93] [2017] A.C. 467 per Lord Toulson at [120].

[94] *Hague Plant Ltd v Hague* [2016] EWHC 2663 (Ch) per Norris J at [221].

[95] [2017] A.C. 467 per Lord Mance at [204].

[96] [2017] A.C. 467 per Lord Sumption at [239].

[97] [2017] A.C. 467 per Lord Sumption at [239].

[98] See generally the chapters in S. Green and A. Bogg, *Illegality After Patel v Mirza* (Oxford: Hart Publishing, 2018).

[99] See e.g. [2017] A.C. 467 per Lord Toulson at [2]: "Illegality has the potential to provide a defence to civil claims of all sorts, whether relating to contract, property, tort or unjust enrichment, and in a wide variety of circumstances."

[100] *Henderson v Dorset Healthcare University NHS Foundation Trust* [2016] EWHC 3275 (QB) at [84].

pleaded as a defence to a civil claim".[101] The Singapore Court of Appeal has already declined to adopt *Patel* in that jurisdiction.[102] The role, if any, of the *locus poenitentiae* exception under the *Patel* framework is not clear.[103] At the very least for present purposes, the Privy Council has confirmed that *Patel* departs from *Tinsley v Milligan*.[104]

An example of the remaining uncertainty over the scope of *Patel* is in the more technical issues of legal policy as outlined in this chapter, such as the position regarding conditions precedent mentioned above[105]: these points of uncertainty remain because the reform to the defence of illegality was effected by the courts and not by the legislature.

3.   PERPETUITY, DURATION AND INALIENABILITY

A.   General

14–016   One of the most common causes over the years of invalidity of interests under a trust has been the failure to comply with the rule against perpetuities. The law was simplified by the Perpetuities and Accumulations Act 1964, which applies to dispositions coming into effect after 15 July 1964. Following recommendations of the Law Commission,[106] further simplifications were introduced by the Perpetuities and Accumulations Act 2009. As the newer legislation applies only to instruments taking effect after its commencement date (6 April 2010),[107] the Act of 1964 will continue in operation for many years to come.[108] It will therefore be necessary below to consider both the scheme prior to the 2009 Act and the current framework under it. But the key point is, as Lord Walker JSC observed, that "the rule against perpetuities has lost its terrors"[109] with the introduction of the Perpetuities and Accumulations Acts.

The rule grew up in connection with settlements of land, but now applies mainly to trusts of personalty. The subject is one which has caused much confusion, not least in connection with the Act of 1964; and a few general comments may be helpful.

B.   Tying Up Land

14–017   The perpetuity rule is based on a policy against the tying up of lands for an undue length of time. The struggle began in the earliest years of common law. Conditions against alienation were held void. Entails were by statute inalienable,

---

[101] *Gujra v Roath* [2018] EWHC 854 (QB); [2018] W.L.R.(D) 235, per Martin Spencer J at [25].
[102] *Ochroid Trading Ltd v Chua Siok Lui* [2018] SGCA 5 at [176].
[103] Above, para.11–038.
[104] *Cenac v Schafer (Saint Lucia)* [2016] UKPC 25 per Sir Kim Lewison at [20].
[105] Above, para.14–013.
[106] Law Com. No. 251, *The Rules against Perpetuities and Excessive Accumulations* (1998).
[107] Perpetuities and Accumulations Act 2009 s.15. The new rules do not apply to wills made before the commencement date if the testator died on or after that date.
[108] As recognised by Newey J in *Souglides v Tweedie* [2012] EWHC 561 (Ch) at [26] (the point stands though Newey J's decision was reversed on appeal: [2012] EWCA Civ 1546; [2013] Ch. 373).
[109] *Pitt v Holt* [2013] UKSC 26; [2013] 2 A.C. 108 at [15].

but by 1472 it was recognised that an entail could be barred, turned into a fee simple and alienated.[110] The old rule against perpetuities prevented a series of contingent life estates. Alienability was successfully being maintained. But once it was decided that executory interests were valid and indestructible,[111] it was possible to create interests limited to vest at an indefinite time in the future. The rule against perpetuities was designed to restrict the extent to which future vesting could be postponed.

C.   Remote Vesting. Life in Being Plus 21 Years

The permitted period at common law was a life in being plus 21 years; permitting, in effect, a grant to the first son of A to attain the age of 21 years. For A's son must attain the age of 21 years, if he ever does, within 21 years of A's death.[112] A period of gestation was also allowed in the case of posthumous children.   **14–018**

One could not wait and see whether the gift vested in time or not. The common law rule was that the interest was void if it *might* vest outside the period; even if in fact it vested the next day.

Thus, a gift to the first son of A to attain the age of 22 years was void at common law if A was still alive; even if A had a son of 21 years and 11 months at the time. For that son might die, another son be born, and A die; and A's first son to attain the age of 22 might do so more than 21 years after the death of any persons alive at the date of the gift. This one simple example illustrates the ruthless operation of the rule.

D.   Wait and See

i.   Perpetuities and Accumulations Act 1964.   The Perpetuities and Accumulations Act 1964 dealt with this situation in three ways; first, by permitting a settlor to specify as the perpetuity period for the purpose of the disposition a period of years not exceeding 80[113]; secondly, by a number of specific reforms on individual points which had caused difficulty, and thirdly, by introducing a system of wait and see.[114] If the law was unrealistic because it made void an interest which vested in fact within the period merely because it might have vested outside it, an obvious solution would be to make its validity depend on whether or not it does in fact vest within it. That is the theory of "wait and see".   **14–019**

---

[110] *Taltarum's Case YB* 12 Edw. 4, 19.

[111] *Pells v Brown* (1620) Cro. Jac. 590.

[112] Scientific advances in reproduction have made this statement untrue, but if sperm or embryos are used after a man's death, he is in some circumstances treated as the father; Human Fertilisation and Embryology Act 1990 s.28, as amended by the Human Fertilisation and Embryology (Deceased Fathers) Act 2003. See also in related contexts H. Legge (2001) 27 Tru. & E.L.J. 10 and N. Maddox [2017] Conv. 408.

[113] s.1.

[114] s.3.

There was much disagreement as to the identity of the lives in being at common law.[115] The 1964 Act, however, laid down, in s.3, its own list of statutory lives in being, to be used where the wait and see rule is invoked. Although certain common law lives in being, such as "royal lives", are not included, the statutory class is generally wider than the class of common law lives in being.

One would have thought it obvious that, on enacting wait and see, the common law rule should be abolished. It no longer has any part to play. If a disposition must vest, if at all, within the period, then it will vest, if at all, within the period. Thus, the common law test is contained within the wait and see test. There is no advantage in knowing that an interest complies with the common law test. The interest remains contingent, and its value is dependent, not on compliance with the common law rule, but upon its likelihood of vesting. Compliance with the common law rule is irrelevant in a system of wait and see.[116]

Nevertheless, the Act of 1964 retained the common law rule. Wait and see only applies to "void" limitations.[117] So it is necessary to apply the common law rule to test validity, and to apply wait and see if it fails to comply with the common law rule. It is tempting to ignore the common law rule. Every limitation which was valid at common law would also be valid under wait and see: unless, however, there could be some situation in which a gift was validated by a common law life who is not in the statutory list, and the interest does not in fact vest within 21 years of the death of the survivor of the statutory lives. Because the class of statutory lives does not coincide exactly with the common law lives, that is theoretically possible.[118] But it was absurd to retain all the common law learning in order to save such a rare gift. The common law rule should have been abolished.[119]

If it had been, the application of the wait and see rule would have been simple. In the case of any gift, all that would be necessary would be the writing down of the measuring lives, the recording of their deaths, and the addition of 21 years. The interests which had then vested would be valid; those which had not vested would be void.

14–020   **ii. Perpetuities and Accumulations Act 2009.**   The Perpetuities and Accumulations Act 2009 introduced a simpler rule in relation to instruments taking effect on or after its commencement, primarily by imposing a mandatory perpetuity period of 125 years.[120] If a settlor or testator specifies any other perpetuity period, it will be overridden by the statutory period. A further

---

[115] J. Morris and H. Wade (1964) 80 L.Q.R. 486 at 495–508; D. Allan (1965) 81 L.Q.R. 106 at 108; R. Maudsley (1970) 86 L.Q.R. 357 and (1975) 60 Cornell L.R. 355; Maudsley, *The Modern Law of Perpetuities* (1979); R. Deech (1981) 97 L.Q.R. 593; J. Dukeminier (1986) 102 L.Q.R. 251.

[116] R. Maudsley (1970) 86 L.Q.R. 357 at 372 and (1975) 60 Cornell L.R. 355; Maudsley, *The Modern Law of Perpetuities* (1979).

[117] Perpetuities and Accumulations Act 1964 s.3.

[118] As in the case of dispositions governed by a royal lives clause.

[119] R. Maudsley (1975) 60 Cornell L.R. 355 at 370.

[120] Perpetuities and Accumulations Act 2009 s.5.

consequence of this provision is that the old common law rule has no relevance to instruments governed by the 2009 Act. The "wait and see" rule applies, just as under the Act of 1964.[121]

Although the Act of 2009 does not in general apply to trusts created before its commencement, trustees of such trusts may by deed "opt in" to a perpetuity period of 100 years if it would be difficult or not reasonably practicable to ascertain whether the lives in being had ended.[122] It is also possible for trustees of existing trusts to apply to the court for approval of a variation to extend the trust period to reflect the 125-year period now available under the 2009 Act.[123]

E.   Duration and Inalienability

Separate from the perpetuity rule governing remoteness of vesting, but a further manifestation of the same policy, is the rule which declares void trusts which might continue for too long a period; longer, that is, than the perpetuity period. The rule is not affected by the Perpetuities and Accumulations Act 2009.[124]   **14–021**

The matter will be discussed in connection with non-charitable purpose trusts.[125] In so far as they are permitted, they must be limited to the perpetuity period. The restriction upon duration does not apply to charitable trusts, nor to most pension trusts.[126]

It should be added that this rule is not in any way inconsistent with the ownership of property in fee simple by a person or a corporation. Those owners may alienate at any time. They may of course keep the property forever; but the property is not tied up in any way. Thus in *Bowman v Secular Society*,[127] a gift to the "Secular Society", a society devoted to furthering anti-Christian beliefs, having survived an attack on the grounds of public policy, had nothing to fear on the score of perpetuity, as the Society was a limited company, and able to deal freely with its property.

4.   ATTEMPTS TO KEEP PROPERTY FROM CREDITORS

A.   General

A creditor can demand payment from his debtor out of the debtor's property. If the debtor's property is insufficient to pay his debts, he is insolvent, and it will not be possible to pay all the creditors in full. Generally speaking, before   **14–022**

---

[121] Perpetuities and Accumulations Act 2009 s.7.

[122] s.12.

[123] *A v B* [2016] EWHC 340 (Ch); [2016] 2 P. & C.R. DG8 (Warren J) and *Allfrey v Allfrey* [2015] EWHC 1717 (Ch); [2015] 2 P. & C.R. DG17 (Deputy Judge Cousins QC) on variation generally, see below, Ch.23.

[124] Perpetuities and Accumulations Act 2009 s.18.

[125] Below, para.16–022; cf. *Re Dean* (1889) 41 Ch.D. 552 and *Re Hooper* [1932] 1 Ch 38, recently doubted in the South Australian case of *Phillips v McCabe* [2016] SASC 27. For difficulties arising with unincorporated associations, see *Re Grant's Will Trusts* [1980] 1 W.L.R. 360, below, para.16–018.

[126] Below, paras 15–004, 17–028.

[127] [1917] A.C. 406.

bankruptcy the debtor may choose which creditors he pays first[128]; but after bankruptcy the bankruptcy law provides for a fair sharing out of his property.

When a person foresees the danger of his own[129] future insolvency—as where he is entering upon a business venture—there is the temptation to put property out of the reach of creditors, by, for example, creating a settlement in favour of the family, in this or other jurisdictions.[130] If the business venture succeeds the profits will flow in; if it fails, the creditors will be unpaid; but the family will be cared for.[131] It may also be that a settlement is made for other reasons, such as the reduction of tax liability,[132] but insolvency subsequently occurs. The question for consideration here is the extent to which a creditor can upset dispositions made by debtors of property which would otherwise be available for the creditors, whether or not there is a bankruptcy.[133]

B.   Insolvency Act 1986

14–023   **i.   Transactions Defrauding Creditors.**   Section 423[134] of the Insolvency Act 1986, replacing s.172 of the Law of Property Act 1925, provides that a transaction at an undervalue may be set aside if the court is satisfied that the person entering into the transaction (the debtor) did so for the purpose:

(a)   of putting assets beyond the reach of a person who is making, or may at some time make, a claim against him; or

(b)   of otherwise prejudicing the interests of such a person in relation to the claim which he is making or may make.

The court may make such order as it thinks fit for

(a)   restoring the position to what it would have been if the transaction had not been entered into; and

(b)   protecting the interests of persons who are victims of the transaction (defined as a person who is, or is capable of being, prejudiced by the transaction).[135]

---

[128]   *Middleton v Pollock* (1876) 2 Ch.D. 104.

[129]   Where he foresees his beneficiary's insolvency, the protective trust may be employed; above, Ch.8.

[130]   For offshore asset protection trusts, see B. Marrache and G. Davis (1993) 143 N.L.J. 721; P. Matthews (1995–96) 6 K.C.L.J. 62. T. Pagone (2014) 20 T. & T. 1081.

[131]   "If I succeed in business, I make a fortune for myself. If I fail, I leave my creditors unpaid. They will pay the loss", per Jessel MR in *Re Butterworth, Ex p. Russell* (1882) 19 Ch.D. 588 at 598. See also *Midland Bank Plc v Wyatt* [1995] 1 F.L.R. 697. T. Molloy (2011) 17 T. & T. 784,

[132]   Above, para.10–001.

[133]   Although this chapter necessarily focuses on the main legislative frameworks, other statutes provide for anti-avoidance provisions: see e.g. the valuable survey in the context of the Care Act 2014 in B. Sloan [2015] Conv. 489.

[134]   See generally G. Miller [1998] Conv. 362. For the application of the Limitation Act 1980, see *Giles v Rhind* [2008] 3 W.L.R. 1233. A brief recent illustration of a successful challenge under s.423 is *Ali v Bashir* [2014] EWHC 3853 (Ch).

[135]   See *Hill v Spread Trustee Co Ltd* [2007] 1 W.L.R. 2404 (intention to deceive Inland Revenue).

The section applies equally to transactions entered into by individuals and by corporate bodies.[136]

(a) Transactions at an Undervalue.   By s.423(1), a person enters into a   **14–024**
transaction with another person at an undervalue if:

(a) he makes a gift to the other person or he otherwise enters into a transaction with the other on terms that provide for him to receive no consideration; or
(b) he enters into a transaction with the other in consideration of marriage; or
(c) he enters into a transaction with the other for a consideration the value of which, in money or money's worth, is significantly less than the value, in money or money's worth, of the consideration provided by himself.

Thus the section applies where a husband makes a gift of money to his wife, transfers his interest in the matrimonial home to her,[137] or purchases property in the joint names of himself and his wife without any contribution from her.[138] Similarly where a married couple declare a trust of the family home for the wife and children.[139] The position is the same concerning civil partners.[140] When assessing "undervalue" the court will view the transaction as a whole.[141] In *Agricultural Mortgage Corp Plc v Woodward*,[142] an insolvent farmer, whose land was mortgaged for £700,000, granted a tenancy at the full market rent of £37,250 to his wife, to ensure that the mortgagee could not get vacant possession. It was argued that the full rent prevented the application of s.423. The Court of Appeal set aside the tenancy on the ground that the wife received benefits beyond those granted by the tenancy agreement, namely the safeguarding of her home, the ability to carry on the family business freed from the claims of creditors, and the surrender value of the tenancy, which gave her a "ransom" position against the mortgagee.

(b) Intention.   As stated above, the court must be satisfied that the person   **14–025**
entering into the transaction did so for the purpose of putting assets beyond the reach of, or of otherwise prejudicing, an existing or potential claimant. In this context, "purpose is not the same as result" and "a by-product [of the transaction] is not enough".[143] The court was satisfied that the requisite purpose existed where a husband who was threatened with legal actions, and who knew there was doubt as to his insurance cover, made substantial gifts to his wife upon receiving a large

---

[136] See also Insolvency Act 1986 s.207.
[137] *Re Kumar (A Bankrupt)* [1993] 1 W.L.R. 224 (assumption of sole liability for the mortgage by the wife was worth significantly less than value of share transferred).
[138] *Moon v Franklin, The Independent*, 22 June 1990.
[139] *Midland Bank Plc v Wyatt* [1995] 1 F.L.R. 697 (the trust was in any event a sham; above, para.4–004). See also *Zarbafi v Zarbafi* [2014] EWCA Civ 1267.
[140] s.423(1)(b) was amended by the Civil Partnership Act 2004 Sch.27 para.121.
[141] *Tailby v HSBC Bank Plc* [2015] B.P.I.R. 143 (personal guarantee by bankrupt in respect of overdraft facility for an associated company not a transaction under value).
[142] (1995) 70 P. & C.R. 53. See also *Delaney v Chen* [2012] 2 E.G.L.R. 15.
[143] *JSC Mezhdunarodniy Promyshlenniy Bank v Pugachev* [2017] EWHC 2426 (Ch) per Birss J at [443].

sum from the sale of his practice.[144] Indeed, where a debtor transfers assets to his family at an undervalue when an action by creditors is expected, the retained assets being insufficient, there is a strong prima facie case of intention to prejudice the creditor.[145] It is not necessary, however, to establish dishonesty. Thus the section may apply even where the transfer was considered proper by legal advisers.[146] Putting the assets beyond the reach of creditors must be a substantial purpose of the transaction but need not be the sole or dominant motive.[147]

As under the previous law, it is not necessary that there should be existing creditors at the time of the transaction. It makes no difference whether the anticipated creditors are those of the settlor himself or of a company he plans to set up.[148] Nor is it necessary that the person seeking to set aside the transaction should be technically a "creditor".[149]

14–026   *(c)   Persons who may Apply to Court.*   Where the debtor, being an individual, is now bankrupt, or, being a body corporate, is being wound up or is the subject of an administration order under the 1986 Act, the application may only be made by the official receiver, the trustee of the bankrupt's estate or the liquidator or administrator of the body corporate. The victim of the transaction, as defined above,[150] may apply with the leave of the court, but this is in effect a class action, giving no priority to the applicant.[151] However, the section has been held to require that "the victim has to be a victim of both the improper purpose and the undervalue. He/she must suffer an adverse consequence from the undervalue".[152] Where a voluntary arrangement has been approved under the 1986 Act, the application may be made by the supervisor of the voluntary arrangement or the victim of the transaction. In any other case, for example where there is no insolvency, the application may be made by the victim of the transaction. These provisions are found in s.424 of the 1986 Act, which further provides that any application made under the section is treated as made on behalf of every victim of the transaction.

14–027   *(d)   Orders to be made.*   Sections 423(2) and 425 of the 1986 Act set out the orders which may be made by the court.[153] These include orders:

---

[144] *Moon v Franklin, The Independent,* 22 June 1990.

[145] *Barclays Bank Plc v Eustice* [1995] 1 W.L.R. 1238.

[146] *Arbuthnot Leasing International Ltd v Havalet Leasing (No.2)* [1990] B.C.C. 636. It should be added that legal professional privilege will be overridden on the ground of "iniquity" if a client seeks legal advice as to how to structure a transaction to defeat creditors; *Barclays Bank Plc v Eustice* [1995] 1 W.L.R. 1238; see also the discussion in *Kerman v Akhmedova* [2018] EWCA Civ 307.

[147] *Moon v Franklin, The Independent,* 22 June 1990; *Midland Bank Plc v Wyatt* [1995] 1 F.L.R. 696; *IRC v Hashmi* [2002] W.T.L.R. 1027; A. Keay [2003] Conv. 272.

[148] *Midland Bank Plc v Wyatt* [1995] 1 F.L.R. 696.

[149] See *Cadogan v Cadogan* [1977] 1 W.L.R. 1041.

[150] Above, para.14–023.

[151] *Dora v Simper* [2000] 2 B.C.L.C. 561.

[152] *Westbrook Dolphin Square Ltd v Friends Life Ltd (No.2)* [2014] EWHC 2433 (Ch); [2015] 1 W.L.R. 1713, per Mann J at [406].

[153] See *Moon v Franklin, The Independent,* 22 June 1990 (order compelling return of unspent portion of gift and restraining dealing with land).

(a)   requiring any property transferred by the impugned transaction to be vested in any person, either absolutely or for the benefit of all the persons on whose behalf the application is treated as made; or

(b)   requiring any property representing the application of the proceeds of sale of property transferred by the impugned transaction or of money transferred by it to be so vested; or

(c)   requiring any person to pay to any other person in respect of benefits received from the debtor such sums as the court may direct.

(e)   Third Parties.   Section 425(2) provides that any order made may affect the property of, or impose an obligation on, any person whether or not he was a party to the transaction, but the order shall not prejudice any interest in property[154] acquired from a person other than the debtor which was acquired in good faith, for value and without notice of the circumstances making s.423 applicable, or prejudice any interest deriving from such an interest. Nor shall the order require a person who received a benefit from the transaction in good faith, for value and without notice of the circumstances to pay any sum unless he was a party to the transaction. "Value" here bears its ordinary meaning.   **14–028**

ii. Bankruptcy Provisions.   The Insolvency Act 1986 deals with transactions at an undervalue and preferences by individuals or corporate bodies[155] within a certain time limit prior to insolvency.   **14–029**

(a)   Transactions at an Undervalue.   In the case of the insolvency of an individual, s.339 permits the trustee of the bankrupt's estate to apply to court for an order where the individual entered into a transaction at an undervalue within certain time limits discussed below. The court may make such order as it thinks fit for restoring the position to what it would have been but for the transaction. "Undervalue" here bears the same meaning as under s.423.[156] Thus, as under the previous law, the trustee may obtain the wife's share in the matrimonial home to the extent that she has not contributed to its acquisition.[157] The case law has addressed the question whether a property adjustment order on divorce may be set aside under these provisions.[158] The Court of Appeal has held that such an order, whether made at a contested hearing or by consent, is not made without consideration and cannot normally be set aside under s.339 on the subsequent bankruptcy of the transferor spouse. It was noted that the court had jurisdiction to set aside a property adjustment order under the bankruptcy provisions,[159] but as Thorpe LJ observed: **14–030**

---

[154] See *Chohan v Saggar* [1994] B.C.L.C. 706 (mortgage); *BTI 2014 LLC v Sequana SA (No.2)* [2017] EWHC 211 (Ch).

[155] The provisions relating to companies will not be dealt with here.

[156] Above, para.14–023.

[157] *Re Densham* [1975] 1 W.L.R. 1519; *Claughton v Charalamabous* [1999] 1 F.L.R. 740. See also *Re Windle* [1975] 1 W.L.R. 1628.

[158] *Hill v Haines* [2008] Ch. 412; D. Capper (2008) 124 L.Q.R. 361; *Re Jones (A Bankrupt)* [2008] 2 F.L.R. 1969.

[159] Matrimonial Causes Act 1973 s.39; *Wright v Wright* [2011] 1 F.L.R. 387.

"Between the two systems of law [that is, insolvency and ancillary relief] there needs to be a fair balance which on the one hand protects the creditors against collusive orders in ancillary relief and on the other protects orders justly made at arms [sic] length for the protection of the applicant and the children of the family."[160]

Such orders would thus be set aside only in rare cases, as where the order had been obtained by collusion, fraud, mistake or misrepresentation.[161] The transfer by one spouse to the other is not regarded as a transaction at an undervalue because the spouse's ability to seek an ancillary relief order is a right recognised by the law.[162] The value of the right may be quantified by reference to the value of the property ordered to be transferred. Thus a fair balance is maintained between protecting creditors against collusive orders and protecting the bankrupt's spouse and children.[163]

14–031 *(b) Preference of Creditors.* Where an individual is adjudged bankrupt and has given a preference to any person within time limits discussed below, the trustee of the bankrupt's estate may apply to court for an order under s.340. The court may make such order as it thinks fit for restoring the position to what it would have been if that individual had not given that preference. An individual gives a preference to a person if that person is a creditor,[164] surety or guarantor, and the effect is to put that person into a better position than he would otherwise have been in in the event of the individual's bankruptcy. An order may only be made if the individual was influenced by a desire to produce the effect mentioned above, but this is presumed where the other person was an associate.[165]

14–032 *(c) Time Limits.* Section 341 provides a five-year time limit, ending with the day of the making of the bankruptcy application or presentation of the bankruptcy petition,[166] in the case of a transaction at an undervalue. In the case of a

---

[160] [2008] Ch. 412 at [60].

[161] See *Sands v Singh* [2016] EWHC 636 (Ch) at [73](v).

[162] *Independent Trustee Services Ltd v GP Noble Trustees Ltd* [2012] EWCA Civ 195; [2013] Ch. 91; cf. *Claridge's Trustee in Bankruptcy v Claridge* [2011] EWHC 2047 (Ch); *Gendrot v Chadwick* [2018] EWHC 48 (Ch) (purported declaration of trust by husband in favour of his wife of three properties, including the family home). *Green v Austin* [2014] B.P.I.R. 1176 (court unaware that husband had been insolvent at the time of consent order in relevant proceedings); cf. *Robert v Woodall* [2016] EWHC 2987; [2017] 4 W.L.R. 11 (trustee in bankruptcy not entitled to seek a lump sum or property adjustment order under the Matrimonial Causes Act 1973).

[163] Under Insolvency Act 1986 s.335A, the court may also postpone an order of sale of the bankrupt's house where family members are in occupation and exceptional circumstances obtain, but only in "truly exceptional" circumstances should that extend beyond a period of months: *Grant v Baker* [2016] EWHC 1782 (Ch); [2017] 2 F.L.R. 646 (Henderson J); *Pickard v Constable* [2017] EWHC 2475 (Ch) (Warren J).

[164] This result could be avoided if the apparent "creditor" was in reality a beneficiary under a trust who never became a creditor. See *Re Kayford* [1975] 1 W.L.R. 279, above, para.2–010. As noted, the position with respect to companies is not covered here, but see the Law Commission's proposals on Law Com. No. 368, *Consumer Prepayments on Retailer Insolvency* (2016); K. Akintola [2018] J.B.L. 1.

[165] As defined by s.435. The definition includes relatives of the individual or of his spouse, registered civil partner, partners, employers, employees and related companies.

[166] As amended by Enterprise and Regulatory Reform Act 2013 Sch.19 para.33 (SI 2016/191).

preference which is not an undervalue, the period is six months save in the case of an associate, where the period is two years.

Except in the case of a transaction at an undervalue made within two years[167] before the bankruptcy, no order may be made with respect to a transaction entered into within the above time limits unless the individual was insolvent at the time or became insolvent in consequence of the transaction or preference. In the case of a transaction at an undervalue entered into with an associate, there is a rebuttable presumption that the individual was or became insolvent at the time of the transaction. A person is insolvent for this purpose if he cannot pay his debts as they fall due, or if the value of his assets is less than his liabilities.

(d)   Orders to be made.   Section 342 sets out the orders which the court may make for the benefit of the bankrupt's estate. These are similar to the orders which may be made under s.425.[168] Exceptionally, the court may decide to make no order, where justice so requires.[169]   **14–033**

(e)   Third Parties.   No order may prejudice any interest in property acquired from a person other than the bankrupt and acquired in good faith and for value. A purchaser is rebuttably presumed not to be in good faith in two situations.[170] The first is where he had notice at the time he acquired his interest of the fact that the earlier transaction was at an undervalue (or was a preference) and of the fact that the earlier transferor had been adjudged bankrupt or that the petition on which he was later adjudged bankrupt had been presented. The second situation is where the purchaser was an associate of, or was connected with, the bankrupt or the person with whom the bankrupt entered into the transaction at an undervalue (or to whom preference was given). Thus mere notice of the fact that the previous transaction was at an undervalue does not suffice. Similar rules apply to a person who has received a benefit from the transaction or preference in good faith and for value. Such a person shall not be required to pay any sum to the trustee unless he was a party to the transaction or was given a preference at a time when he was a creditor of the bankrupt.   **14–034**

C.   Protection of the Spouse and Family

The previous sections dealt with attempts by a debtor to deprive his creditors of satisfaction by transferring property by way of voluntary settlement to other persons, usually members of his family, whom the debtor wishes to protect. We now deal with what is in effect the converse of that problem; cases where the defendant is trying to deprive his spouse or family of assets which should   **14–035**

---

[167] The exercise of a power of appointment within this period is not caught by the rule if the settlement was made outside the period; *Clarkson v Clarkson* [1994] BCC 921, although see the judgment of Lord Collins of Mapesbury for the Board of the Privy Council in *Tasarruf Mevduati Sigorta Fonu v Merrill Lynch Bank and Trust Co (Cayman) Ltd* [2011] UKPC 17; [2012] 1 W.L.R. 1721.

[168] Above, para.14–028.

[169] *Singla v Brown* [2008] Ch. 357 (no order made to disturb transaction whereby bankrupt's half share reduced to 1% as the parties had never intended him to have more than a nominal interest).

[170] s.342.

properly be available to them. This occurs in matrimonial proceedings, and also in relation to the rights of dependants upon a death.

14–036　　**i. Matrimonial Causes Act 1973 Section 37.**　　Section 37 protects a spouse[171] from activities of the other spouse which may diminish the assets available for the purposes of financial relief under the Act. If the court is satisfied that one spouse is about to make a disposition[172] or transfer with the intention of depriving the applicant of financial relief, it may make such order as it thinks fit for the purpose of protecting the applicant's claim.[173] Where the defendant spouse has made a disposition of property, other than one made for valuable consideration to a bona fide purchaser without notice of any intention to defeat the applicant's claim,[174] the disposition may be set aside.[175]

The intention to defeat the applicant's claim must be affirmatively proved, except in cases where the disposition was made within three years before the date of the application, in which case there is a rebuttable statutory presumption[176] that the intention is to defeat the applicant's claim for financial relief.

Outwith the insolvency context, in *Prest v Petrodel Resources Ltd*,[177] the Supreme Court had to consider a case where the husband had allegedly hidden his assets by transferring them into the names of companies which he controlled. The argument on behalf of the wife was that the 1973 Act (specifically ss.24 and 25) empowered the courts to "pierce the corporate veil" in appropriate cases where the spouse had sought to frustrate the process. Lord Sumption emphatically rejected this suggestion[178]:

> "Courts exercising family jurisdiction do not occupy a desert island in which general legal concepts are suspended or mean something different. If a right of property exists, it exists in every division of the High Court and in every jurisdiction of the county courts. If it does not exist, it does not exist anywhere."[179]

However, on the facts in *Prest*, the Supreme Court determined that the properties, having been transferred for only nominal consideration, were held on resulting trust for the husband. Although it will always be a fact-sensitive enquiry, the courts will be alive to sham attempts to conceal the proper beneficial ownership of property.[180] Following *Prest*, it has been held that the jurisdiction under s.37 of

---

[171] Similar provisions relating to civil partners are found in the Civil Partnership Act 2004 Sch.5 para.74.
[172] The wide definition in s.37(6) includes a trust, but not any provision made in a will.
[173] s.37(2)(a).
[174] Called a "reviewable disposition" and defined in s.37(4).
[175] See also *Lowson v Coombes* [1999] Ch. 373.
[176] s.37(5).
[177] [2013] UKSC 34; [2013] 2 A.C. 415. T. Cheng-Han [2015] J.B.L. 20; C. Hare (2013) 72 C.L.J. 511.
[178] Even though recognising the husband's "persistent obstruction and mendacity": [2013] UKSC 34; [2013] 2 A.C. 415 at [43].
[179] [2013] UKSC 34; [2013] 2 A.C. 415 at [37]; C.K.Y. Wong (2017) 38 Co. Lawyer 158; M. Hsiao [2017] Conv. 101.
[180] [2013] UKSC 34; [2013] 2 A.C. 415 at [52]; A.W.L. See [2018] Conv 31.

the 1973 Act only relates to "property" and the assets of a family business do not fall within the jurisdiction unless the structure is a sham and where either spouse has total authority over the company.[181]

ii. Inheritance (Provision for Family and Dependants) Act 1975.[182] A **14–037** similar problem arises in connection with statutory schemes which restrict a person's powers of free disposal of his property by will, in order to provide for the surviving spouse and children and other dependants. This is an old problem; originally answered by the surviving spouse's right to dower or curtesy, and now governed by a wide variety of provisions (such as "forced heirship") in various parts of the world. A common solution is to give to the surviving spouse, and sometimes to children, a fractional share of the estate. The system in England and Wales is to give to the court a discretionary power to make an award to a surviving spouse and other dependants on the ground that the disposition of the deceased's estate (whether by will or intestacy) is not such as to make reasonable financial provision for the applicant.[183] But these schemes could be thwarted if a person who wished to deprive a widow and dependants could give away all his property before death.[184]

Provisions to deal with this problem are contained in ss.10–13 of the Act. In short, the court is given power to require a donee from the deceased to provide sums of money,[185] up to, but not in excess of, the value of the gift,[186] if the gift was made within six years before the death of the donor, and was made "with the intention of defeating an application for financial provision under this Act."[187] Protection is given to persons who gave full valuable consideration for a transfer. The intention is to be determined on a balance of probabilities,[188] and need not be the sole intention of the donor in making the gift. Similar provisions in s.11 deal with contracts to leave property by will; and transfers to trustees in s.13.[189]

---

[181] *C v C* [2015] EWHC 2795 (Fam); [2016] Fam. Law 20.

[182] As amended by the Inheritance and Trustees' Powers Act 2014 s.6, which applied the detailed amendments in Sch.2, and somewhat broadened the court's powers. The amendments did not affect the gist of the existing regime.

[183] s.2; the leading case on the making of such provision under the Act is now *Ilott v Mitson* [2017] UKSC 17; [2017] 2 W.L.R. 979, but it need not be considered here.

[184] See *Schaefer v Schuhmann* [1972] A.C. 572. It is possible that such transfers could be set aside independently of any statutory provisions in a case of fraud. See *Cadogan v Cadogan* [1977] 1 W.L.R. 1041.

[185] s.10(2); see also s.10(6), giving the factors which the court shall take into consideration.

[186] Valued, in the case of gifts other than cash, at the date of death of the deceased, or, if the property was disposed of by the donee, the value at the date of disposal.

[187] s.10(2).

[188] s.12.

[189] A recent example is *Dellal v Dellal* [2015] EWHC 907 (Fam).

CHAPTER 15

CHARITABLE TRUSTS

1.   INTRODUCTION[1]

15–001   CHARITABLE purposes are those which are considered to be of such value and importance to the community that they receive especially favourable treatment. Charity law was modernised by the Charities Act 2006, since consolidated with other charity legislation by the Charities Act 2011. However, much of the old law on charitable purposes is preserved in the current legislation. As Lloyd LJ noted, the "law as to the purposes that are charitable is notoriously difficult and unsatisfactory, partly because of its historical development."[2] In 2016–17, charities regulated by the Charity Commission had an income of nearly £75 billion.[3]

Prior to the Act of 2006, the definition of charity derived from the old Preamble to the Charitable Uses Act of 1601, an Act which was passed for the purpose of remedying abuses which had grown up in the administration of charitable trusts. The Preamble contained a general catalogue of the purposes then regarded as charitable. Since that time, purposes which were regarded as

---

[1] See generally *Tudor on Charities*, 10th edn (2015); Picarda, *The Law and Practice Relating to Charities*, 4th edn and Supplement (2014).
[2] *Helena Partnerships Ltd v Revenue and Customs Commissioners (Attorney General intervening)* [2012] EWCA Civ 569 at [22].
[3] Charity Commission, *Annual Report and Accounts 2016–17*, p.2.

being within the "spirit and intendment"[4] or "within the equity"[5] of the statute were accepted as being charitable. In 1891, Lord Macnaghten summarised these purposes into four categories. These were the relief of poverty, the advancement of education, the advancement of religion, and other purposes beneficial to the community.[6] The Preamble was repealed by the Charities Act 1960.[7] As no definition replaced it, Lord Macnaghten's classification continued until replaced by a new statutory definition in the Act of 2006, which was based on existing case law and decisions of the Charity Commissioners on the registration of charities.[8]

The Charities Act 2006 updated the list of charitable purposes, with clearer emphasis on delivering a public benefit; facilitated the more efficient administration of charities; introduced a new legal form of charitable body (the charitable incorporated organisation); increased accountability for charities which are not required to be registered; improved the regulation of charity fundraising; and replaced the Charity Commissioners with the modernised Charity Commission, with modernised functions. This framework has been preserved by the Charities Act 2011, with additional reforms introduced by the Charities (Protection and Social Investment) Act 2016. In 2017, the Law Commission completed its project on *Technical Issues in Charity Law*, which may lead to further reform in this area[9]: those proposals are noted below where applicable.

We shall see that charitable trusts are accorded a number of concessions over other trusts in terms of enforcement, perpetuity, certainty and taxation.[10] To earn these concessions, especially in relation to taxation,[11] a trust must be of benefit to the public, and not merely to private individuals. The policy in question behind most litigation concerning charitable trusts is an examination of whether the purposes are so useful to the public as to earn the concessions. This has to be carried out against a background of cases decided in earlier times when the condition of society was very different. In the days when the State made little or no provision for the poor and uneducated or for other general welfare purposes, and at a time when religious observance was unchallenged,[12] trusts for these categories were clearly for the public benefit. At the present time, however, many of the welfare and educational needs of society are provided from public sources, and purposes reflecting other needs have been recognised and are now included in the new statutory categories. Judicial attitudes to gifts for charitable purposes have varied. From the 1940s onwards, when taxation became higher, the courts became more astute to restrict the scope of charity especially by emphasising the requirement of public benefit. However, Lord Hailsham of St. Marylebone said:

---

[4] *Morice v Bishop of Durham* (1805) 9 Ves. 399 at 405.

[5] See *Incorporated Council of Law Reporting v Attorney General* [1972] Ch. 73 at 87–88.

[6] *Commissioners for Special Purposes of Income Tax v Pemsel* [1891] A.C. 531.

[7] s.38. See Charities Act 2011 Sch.7 para.1.

[8] Such decisions are published in the Charity Commission's Annual Reports and on its website.

[9] Law Com. No. 375, *Technical Issues in Charity Law* (2017); at the time of writing, the Government has yet to respond to the Law Commission's Report.

[10] *Dingle v Turner* [1972] A.C. 601 per Lord Cross at 624.

[11] J. Jaconelli [2013] Conv. 96 at 112.

[12] In *In Re St Andrew's (Cheam) Lawn Tennis Club Trust* [2012] EWHC 1040 (Ch) at [1], Arnold J noted "the secularisation of English society".

> "In construing trust deeds the intention of which is to set up a charitable trust, and in others too, where it can be claimed that there is an ambiguity, a benignant construction should be given if possible."[13]

In similar vein, the intention of the Legislature is to encourage charitable giving (by tax incentives), and the development of the voluntary sector as a whole.

As mentioned above, one of the reforms of the Charities Act 2006 was the introduction of a new legal entity, the charitable incorporated organisation (CIO).[14] This offered a new corporate vehicle for charities, designed to reduce the administrative burdens on corporate charities.[15] It is not obligatory for charities to operate in this way, but conversion to the modern form is likely to be considered advantageous, and it is proving popular.[16] Further details need not be given here.

2.   ADVANTAGES ENJOYED BY CHARITABLE TRUSTS

A.   Purpose Trusts

15–002   Charitable trusts are purpose trusts. But there is no need for human beneficiaries to enforce them, as there is in the case of non-charitable purpose trusts.[17] Individuals who may benefit from a charitable trust have no standing to enforce them.[18] Charitable trusts are enforced by the Attorney General in the name of the Crown,[19] although the general administration of charitable trusts is overseen by the Charity Commission.[20] There must of course be an obligation upon the trustees; a mere power to apply to charitable purposes cannot be a trust.[21] It should be emphasised that this chapter deals with charitable *trusts*. The legal position differs in many ways where the charity is incorporated.[22]

---

[13] *IRC v McMullen* [1981] A.C. 1 at 14; *Re Koeppler's WT* [1986] Ch. 423; *Re Hetherington (Deceased)* [1990] Ch. 1; *Guild v IRC* [1992] 2 A.C. 310. The "benignant" approach applies only where a disposition would otherwise be void; *IRC v Oldham Training and Enterprise Council* [1996] S.T.C. 1218.

[14] Now Charities Act 2011 Pt 11.

[15] In *Children's Investment Fund Foundation (UK) v Attorney General* [2017] EWHC 1379 (Ch); [2018] 2 W.L.R. 259 Sir Geoffrey Vos C considered the duties owed to a charity company by its members, holding (at [145]) that "it would be contrary to the whole regime established by the increasingly prescriptive legislative regime reflected in the Charities Act 2011 if the member of a company such as [in that case] could vote in his own interests or in a manner detrimental to the charitable objects of the company". That decision was based on specific facts: the Chancellor noted that he had "looked at numerous charities' cases over three centuries and the present position has not arisen before. It may never arise again" (at [155]).

[16] There were just under 5,000 applications for registrations for CIOS in 2016–17, an increase of 9% on the previous year: *Annual Report and Accounts 2016–17*, p.22.

[17] Below, Ch.16.

[18] *Hauxwell v Barton-on-Humber UDC* [1974] Ch. 432; Charities Act 2011 s.115.

[19] See *Attorney General v Wright* [1988] 1 W.L.R. 164; *Attorney General v Cocke* [1988] Ch. 414. The Commission may exercise these powers with the consent of the Attorney-General; Charities Act 2011 s.114.

[20] Charities Act 2011 ss.13–20.

[21] *Re Cohen* [1973] 1 W.L.R. 415, where a gift to trustees to apply to a charitable purpose "the whole or any part" of the fund "in such manner and at such time or times as my trustees shall in their absolute and uncontrolled discretion think fit", was held to create a trust.

[22] For the distinctions, see J. Hill (1993–94) 2 *Charity Law and Practice Review* 133.

B. Objects Need Not be Certain

There is no requirement that the objects of the trust must be certain in the same **15–003** sense as with other trusts. Rather, the only requirement is that the court can be certain that the purposes are exclusively charitable.[23] So there must be no doubt that the objects of the trust are exclusively charitable, and the purpose expressed must not be so vague and uncertain that the court could not control the application of the assets.[24] But a trust for "charitable purposes" will be valid, even though it may seem vague. The court and the Charity Commission[25] have jurisdiction to establish a scheme for the application of the funds for specific charitable purposes. The relaxation of the certainty rule is only in respect of the particular form of charitable purpose intended.[26]

Where no trust has been created, but only a general intention expressed that the property should go to charity, the court has no jurisdiction. In such a case the Crown disposes of the gifts by sign manual.[27] But the Crown acts on principles very similar to those by which the court is governed.

C. May be Perpetual

Statements have often been made by judges to the effect that the Rule against **15–004** Perpetuities does not apply to charities.[28] That is not so. With the exception of the rule in *Christ's Hospital v Grainger*,[29] explained below, the rule governs the remoteness of vesting in the case of gifts to charities in the same way that it governs remoteness in the case of other gifts.[30]

Charitable trusts, however, may be perpetual in duration. Indeed, the purpose of many charitable trusts could be said never to be capable of final achievement.[31] Many charitable trusts have existed for centuries. If a perpetual gift of income only is made to a charity, the charity cannot claim the capital, as an individual could do in such circumstances.[32] But where property is given

---

[23] This was the common law rule, now contained in Charities Act 2011 s.1(1), albeit that it is not framed as a test of certainty.

[24] *Re Koeppler's Will Trusts* [1986] Ch. 423, where the formation of an informed international public opinion and the promotion of greater co-operation in Europe and the West were held too vague and uncertain to be charitable in themselves, but these aims did not destroy the charitable nature of the gift, which was to further the work of an educational project.

[25] Charities Act 2011 s.69; below, para.15–089.

[26] See *Moggridge v Thackwell* (1792) 1 Ves.Jr. 464; (1803) 7 Ves.Jr. 36; (1807) 13 Ves.Jr. 416.

[27] *Moggridge v Thackwell* (1792) 1 Ves.Jr. 464; *Re Smith* [1932] 1 Ch. 153; *Re Bennett* [1960] Ch. 18; *Re Hetherington* [1990] Ch. 1.

[28] *Goodman v Mayor of Saltash* (1882) 7 App.Cas. 633 at 642; *Commissioners for Special Purposes of Income Tax v Pemsel* [1891] A.C. 531 at 580–581; *Attorney General v National Provincial and Union Bank Ltd* [1924] A.C. 262 at 266.

[29] (1849) 1 Mac. & G. 460; *Re Tyler* [1891] 3 Ch. 252; *Royal College of Surgeons v National Provincial Bank Ltd* [1952] A.C. 631.

[30] *Re Wightwick's WT* [1950] Ch. 260; *Re Green's WT* [1985] 3 All E.R. 455.

[31] *Re Delius* [1957] Ch. 299.

[32] *Re Levy* [1960] Ch. 346.

absolutely to a charity with a direction to accumulate the income for a period of time, a charity may terminate the accumulation, and claim the principal forthwith.[33]

The exception to the rule regulating remoteness of vesting is that a gift over from one charity to *another charity* is not subject to the rule.[34] The gift over to the second charity is valid even if it takes effect outside the perpetuity period.[35]

The reason for the exception is that "there is no more perpetuity created by giving to two charities rather than by giving to one."[36] The explanation looks to the vesting for charitable purposes, rather than vesting in one specific charity. Once vested in charity, then, subject to express provision to the contrary, a trust will continue, even if the purposes become impossible of fulfilment; the property will be applied cy-près.[37] All that is done by the provision for vesting in another charity is to make express the selection of the charity to be benefited when the first gift terminates.

This rule therefore seems logical; and also reasonable when the gift over is to take effect upon the happening of some event related to the carrying out of the purposes of the charity, as was the case in *Christ's Hospital v Grainger*,[38] and *Royal College of Surgeons v National Provincial Bank*.[39] In the hands of conveyancers,[40] it can be used to produce, in effect, a perpetual non-charitable trust by making a gift to one charity conditional upon carrying out a non-charitable purpose, and terminable in favour of another charity upon its failure to do so. This is not a satisfactory use of charity privilege: but this loophole was not questioned in the *Royal College of Surgeons* case. The rule is confirmed by the Perpetuities and Accumulations Act 2009 in spite of these opportunities for exploitation.[41]

The Law Commission recommended that the rule against excessive accumulations of income should in general be abolished, but should still apply to charitable trusts.[42] Otherwise income could be tied up for many years, during which there would be no public benefit. The Perpetuities and Accumulations Act 2009 now provides that any power or duty to accumulate charitable income must cease after 21 years.[43]

---

[33] *Wharton v Masterman* [1895] A.C. 186; *Re Knapp* [1929] 1 Ch. 341.

[34] A gift from non-charity to a charity is caught: *Re Bowen* [1892] 2 Ch. 291. So also a gift from a charity to a non-charity; *Re Bowen* (above); *Re Peel's Release* [1921] 2 Ch. 218; *Re Engels* [1943] 1 All E.R. 506.

[35] *Christ's Hospital v Grainger* (1849) 1 Mac. & G. 460.

[36] per Shadwell VC in the court below (1848) 16 Sim. 83 at 100. See also *Royal College of Surgeons v National Provincial Bank Ltd* [1952] A.C. 631 at 650.

[37] Below, Part 8.

[38] (1849) 1 Mac. & G. 460.

[39] [1952] A.C. 631.

[40] *Re Tyler* [1891] 3 Ch. 252.

[41] s.2(2).

[42] Law Com. No. 251, *The Rules against Perpetuities and Excessive Accumulations* (1998), para.10.21.

[43] s.14. The new rule relates only to instruments taking effect after commencement.

D.   Fiscal Advantages

As explained below, charities enjoy tax advantages of two broad kinds. First, the **15–005** organisation itself may be exempt from paying a particular tax on its capital or income. Secondly, a person who makes a charitable gift may be eligible for tax relief on their own capital or income. Until recently, there was no relief if the gift was to a charity in another jurisdiction. This was changed by the Finance Act 2010, so that gifts made by a donor in this jurisdiction to charities in the EU[44] may attract tax relief. However, the Act went further by imposing new requirements on domestic charitable bodies for the purposes of eligibility for tax relief. The four conditions to be satisfied for this purpose by charities in this jurisdiction and in the EU are as follows.[45] First, the body must be established for charitable purposes only within the meaning of s.2 of the Charities Act 2011.[46] In other words, it must be carrying out activities which English law would recognise as exclusively charitable. Secondly, the body must be subject to the control of a court in the UK in the exercise of its charity jurisdiction, or of a court in the EU[47] exercising a corresponding jurisdiction. Thirdly, the body must have complied with registration requirements in England and Wales[48] or any corresponding requirement in the European jurisdiction. Fourthly, its managers must be fit and proper persons. While the first three conditions are not controversial, the fourth one is, as the arbiter of whether this condition is met is HMRC, not the Charity Commission. We will now examine the reliefs available to charitable bodies and donors where these conditions are satisfied.

Charities are exempt from income tax, provided that the income is applied for **15–006** charitable purposes only.[49] They may recover from the Revenue income tax paid or credited prior to the payment of interest. Relief is also available with respect to "Gift Aid" donations.[50] Alternatively, donors who are employees may utilise the payroll deduction scheme.[51] Further, no income tax is chargeable in respect of profits of any trade carried on by the charity, if the profits are applied solely to the purposes of the charity and either the trade is exercised in the course of the carrying out of a primary purpose of the charity, or the work in connection with the trade is mainly carried out by beneficiaries of the charity.[52] Again the profits

---

[44] The Taxes (Definition of Charity) (Relevant Territories) Regulations 2010 (SI 2010/1904). The Regulations apply also to charities in Iceland, Norway and Liechtenstein.

[45] Finance Act 2010 s.30 and Sch.6. The conditions have applied to all charity tax reliefs and exemptions since April 2012. The rules apply also to Community Amateur Sports Clubs.

[46] Below, para.15–008. The definition applies for this purpose regardless of where the body is established.

[47] Or Iceland, Norway or Liechtenstein.

[48] Below, paras 15–086—15–087.

[49] Currently Income Tax Act 2007 s.527. See *IRC v Educational Grants Association Ltd* [1967] Ch. 993; *IRC v Helen Slater Charitable Trust Ltd* [1982] Ch. 49.

[50] Income Tax Act 2007 ss.413–430 and 520–522 (Finance Act 2015 s.20 extended Gift Aid eligibility of payments by an intermediary, with effect from 6 April 2017); Finance Act 2007 s.60.

[51] Income Tax (Earnings and Pensions) Act 2003 Pt 12 (replacing earlier legislation); D. Morris [1989] Conv. 175.

[52] Income Tax Act 2007 ss.524–526; J. Hill and J. de Souza (1989) 3 *Trust Law & Practice* 98.

must be applied solely to the purposes of the charity. Similarly, charitable corporations are exempt from paying corporation tax.[53]

Gifts of any amount in favour of charity are exempt from inheritance tax if made by way of payment from a discretionary trust,[54] or by way of gift by an individual during his lifetime or on death.[55] Similarly, transfers from a charitable trust are exempt from inheritance tax.[56] To encourage charitable giving, the 40% rate was recently reduced to 36% for deaths on or after 6 April 2012 where at least 10% of the net estate is left to charity.[57]

No capital gains tax arises where a gain accrues to a charity and the gain is applicable and is applied for charitable purposes.[58] Nor will a donor be under any such liability in respect of a disposal to charity.[59] Charities may also claim relief from stamp duty and tax on conveyances.[60]

Charities, however, do have to bear Value Added Tax on goods and services which they purchase.[61] This liability will be particularly burdensome for many charities in respect of the maintenance and repair of buildings. Also, VAT may be chargeable in respect of goods and services provided, on payment, by some charities.[62] The Finance Act 2015 provides for certain classes of charities to claim refunds of VAT for supplies of medical and scientific equipment.[63]

All charities are entitled to exemption in respect of a significant percentage of the non-domestic rates of the properties which they occupy,[64] wholly or mainly used for charitable purposes.[65] This includes premises used wholly or mainly for the sale of goods donated to a charity and applied for the purposes of a charity.[66] Relief can also be granted at the discretion of the rating authority up to the whole amount of the rates.[67] Churches, church halls and similar premises used for

---

[53] Corporation Tax Act 2010 s.481.

[54] Inheritance Tax Act 1984 s.76.

[55] Inheritance Tax Act 1984 s.23. See also ss.25, 26.

[56] Inheritance Tax Act 1984 s.58(1)(a).

[57] Finance Act 2012 s.209 and Sch.33, inserting Sch.1A into the Inheritance Tax Act.

[58] Taxation of Chargeable Gains Act 1992 s.256.

[59] Taxation of Chargeable Gains Act 1992 s.257.

[60] Finance Act 2003 s.68.

[61] For specific exemptions, see the consolidating Value Added Tax Act 1994 Sch.9.

[62] See *Customs and Excise Commissioners v Automobile Association* [1974] 1 W.L.R. 1447; Annual Report 1974 paras 17–21; J. Warburton (1995/96) 3 *Charity Law and Practice Review* 37. However, some goods supplied to or by charities are zero-rated under Sch.8 of the 1994 Act; on the scope of these provisions see e.g. *Eynsham Cricket Club v Revenue and Customs Commissioners* [2017] S.T.I. 1901.

[63] Finance Act 2015 s.66(1) inserting ss.33C–D in the Value Added Tax Act 1994. The qualifying charities are "Palliative care charities", "Air ambulance charities", "Search and rescue charities" and "Medical courier charities" (all as defined in s.33D).

[64] Local Government Finance Act 1988 s.43(5), (6) (as amended by the Localism Act 2011).

[65] *South Kesteven DC v Digital Pipeline Ltd* [2016] EWHC 101 (Admin); [2016] 1 W.L.R. 2971 per Elias LJ at [13]: "the test is not whether the activity being conducted on the premises is wholly or mainly charitable; it is whether the premises are being used wholly or mainly for charitable activity".

[66] Local Government Finance Act 1988 s.64(10); Hansard, HL, Vol.499, col.874, 13 July 1988.

[67] Local Government Finance Act 1988 s.47.

religious purposes are entitled to relief in respect of the whole of the rates,[68] as are those providing facilities for the disabled.[69]

In view of the extent of income and other assets thus exempted, this is a formidable list of fiscal advantages, and explains the prominence of Revenue cases in charity litigation.

Measures have been taken to prevent abuse of these tax advantages, for example by requiring charities to take reasonable steps to ensure that payments made to overseas bodies will be applied to genuine charitable purposes and requiring them to justify certain loans or investments as being for the benefit of charity and not for tax avoidance.[70] These provisions restrict tax relief where funds are applied for non-charitable purposes and prevent manipulation of charity tax advantages by individuals.

3. THE DEFINITION OF CHARITY: BASICS

A. Position Before the Charities Act 2006

Prior to the 2006 Act, a claim to charitable status was determined by considering whether the purpose came within Lord Macnaghten's classification as exemplified by the cases decided in accordance with it. Lord Macnaghten said: **15–007**

> "Charity in its legal sense comprises four principal divisions: trusts for the relief of poverty; trusts for the advancement of education; trusts for the advancement of religion; and trusts for other purposes beneficial to the community."[71]

It is obvious that these heads provided no precise definition. Charity law has always adapted to social changes, and, as has been explained, the significance of tax exemption, and also the development of State agencies to provide education, relief from poverty, and other purposes needed by society transformed the concept of charity. It should be appreciated that the Charity Commissioners had a major role in the development of this concept, and their successor the Charity Commission continues to do so.[72]

Over the years, more purposes were recognised by the courts and the Commissioners. They could not have been contemplated by the Charitable Uses Act 1601, nor by Lord Macnaghten. They were accepted by applying the principle that purposes analogous to, or within the spirit of, purposes already recognised as charitable should also be recognised as charitable. As we shall see, this approach was preserved by the Charities Act 2006 (now Charities Act 2011).

---

[68] Local Government Finance Act 1988 Sch.5 para.11. In *Gallagher (Valuation Officer) v Church of Jesus Christ of Latter-Day Saints* [2008] 1 W.L.R. 1852, a Mormon Temple failed to obtain exemption in respect of premises to which only approved members of the faith were admitted. Similarly, the Exclusive Brethren in *Broxtowe BC v Birch* [1983] 1 W.L.R. 314.

[69] Local Government Finance Act 1988 Sch.5 para.16.

[70] See Income Tax Act 2007 s.547; Corporation Tax Act 2010 s.500. On measures to restrict abuse, see *Routier v Revenue and Customs Commissioners* [2017] EWCA Civ 1584; [2017] B.T.C. 28.

[71] *Commissioners for Special Purposes of Income Tax v Pemsel* [1891] A.C. 531 at 583.

[72] Below, para.15–083.

B. The Charities Acts 2006 and 2011

15–008 The Act of 2006 took the radical step of defining a charitable purpose, but did so by reference to purposes already recognised by the courts and the (then) Commissioners. Lord Macnaghten's first three categories were retained,[73] but the fourth ("other purposes beneficial to the community") was replaced by a list of specific purposes which reflect those which had been recognised under the old fourth category (with some clarifications, as will be seen below). Reference will, therefore, continue to be made to much of the previous case law. In 2011, the Charities Act was passed to consolidate the Charities Act 2006 with other charity legislation. The Act of 2011 provides that "charity" means an institution which is established for charitable purposes only, and is subject to the control of the High Court in the exercise of its jurisdiction with respect to charities.[74] Section 2 of the Act of 2011 defines a "charitable purpose" as one which is for the public benefit[75] and which falls within any of the following descriptions,[76] which are set out in s.3(1):

(a) the prevention or relief of poverty;

(b) the advancement of education;

(c) the advancement of religion;

(d) the advancement of health or the saving of lives;

(e) the advancement of citizenship or community development;

(f) the advancement of the arts, culture, heritage or science;

(g) the advancement of amateur sport;

(h) the advancement of human rights, conflict resolution or reconciliation or the promotion of religious or racial harmony or equality and diversity;

(i) the advancement of environmental protection or improvement;

(j) the relief of those in need by reason of youth, age, ill-health, disability; financial hardship or other disadvantage;

(k) the advancement of animal welfare;

(l) the promotion of the efficiency of the armed forces of the Crown, or of the efficiency of the police, fire and rescue services or ambulance services;

(m) any other purposes—

    (i) that are not within paragraphs (a) to (l) but are recognised as charitable purposes by virtue of section 5 (recreational and similar trusts, etc.) or under the old law,[77]

    (ii) that may reasonably be regarded as analogous to, or within the spirit of, any purposes falling within any of paragraphs (a) to (l) or sub-paragraph (i), or

---

[73] Subject to the clarification that the "poverty" purpose includes the prevention as well as the relief of poverty: now Charities Act 2011 s.3(1)(a): below, para.15–012.

[74] Charities Act 2011 s.1. "Institution" includes incorporated bodies, trusts and undertakings: s.9(3).

[75] Below, para.15–040.

[76] For an overview of the scope of each description, see the Charity Commission's *Charitable Purposes* Guidance, 16 September 2013.

[77] Below, para.15–036. The "old law" means that in force immediately before 1 April 2008; s.3(4).

(iii)   that may reasonably be regarded as analogous to, or within the spirit of, any purposes which have been recognised, under the law relating to charities in England and Wales, as falling within sub-paragraph (ii) or this sub-paragraph.

This, therefore, preserved the charitable status of purposes already recognised as charitable, whether or not included in the statutory list, and retains the flexibility of the previous law by allowing further development to meet changing social need. It should be noted that the purposes listed in s.3 are not properly described as "charitable purposes" by themselves, since they may *only* be recognised as charitable if they are *also* for the public benefit.

C.   Public Benefit

It should also be noted at this stage that each purpose involves two elements; the purpose must be beneficial, such as the advancement of education, and there must be an element of *public* benefit, that is to say, education being advanced in a way that will benefit the whole community, or a sufficiently substantial part of it.[78]

15–009

Before the Charities Act 2006, there was (or was understood to be) a presumption that the relief of poverty and the advancement of religion and education were for the public benefit,[79] whereas this had to be established in the case of purposes within the old fourth category ("other purposes beneficial to the community"). One of the most significant features of the Act of 2006 was that it removed any presumption. The relevant subsection is now found in s.4(2) of the Charities Act 2011, which provides that, in determining whether the public benefit requirement is satisfied, "it is not to be presumed that a purpose of a particular description is for the public benefit". It must, therefore, be demonstrated in all cases.

This change was most likely to affect independent fee-paying schools, whose charitable status had long been the subject of debate.[80] It could also affect religious sects with few adherents. The requirement applies to all charities, including those registered before the implementation of the Charities Act 2006.

Before the Act of 2006, it was established that the requirement of benefit to a sufficient section of the community varied according to the category of charity in question. The Act does not expressly deal with this point, and it appears that this principle continues.

The Charity Commission must issue guidance as to the operation of the public benefit requirement, to promote awareness and understanding of it.[81] It must carry out checks on organisations which have already been registered, as well as

---

[78] See generally J. Hackney (2008) 124 L.Q.R. 347.
[79] Subject to the analysis of the Upper Tribunal in *R. (on the application of Independent Schools Council v Charity Commission for England and Wales* [2012] Ch. 214, at [89]–[93]: below, para.15–052. B. Sloan (2012) 71 C.L.J. 45.
[80] See below, para.15–052.
[81] Charities Act 2011 s.17.

assess whether any organisation applying for registration satisfies the require-ment. The public benefit requirement is examined in detail below.[82]

D. Exclusively Charitable

15-010 A trust will not fail to be charitable because it may in its operation incidentally benefit the rich, or other non-objects of charity.[83] But if a non-charitable purpose is an object, the trust cannot be charitable, for it is not wholly and exclusively "for charitable purposes only".[84] A statement of objects which includes non-charitable purposes is not saved by adding, "in so far as they are of a charitable nature".[85]

E. Charitable Purposes Overseas

15-011 Many charities will carry out activities in other jurisdictions: in 2016–17, over 16,500 charities declared at least some aspect of operation outside of England and Wales.[86] Special problems arise where the benefits arising from charitable trusts are to be enjoyed abroad. There is no rule requiring the benefits to be retained in this country.[87] But, how can the court or the (English) trustees control the application of the funds? Should tax privileges be given by HMRC for the benefit of communities abroad?[88] We have seen that tax privileges may now be available to charities established in other (primarily European Union) jurisdictions,[89] but the point under discussion here is whether organisations established in England and Wales to provide benefits abroad may be charitable.

The test of public benefit is the same whether the activity is at home or abroad,[90] as our courts cannot judge what is for the benefit of the public in a

---

[82] Below, Part 5.

[83] *Verge v Somerville* [1924] A.C. 496; *Re Resch's WT* [1969] 1 A.C. 514. But a trust for the relief of poverty will fail if it may benefit persons who are not poor: *Re Gwyon* [1930] 1 Ch. 255.

[84] Charities Act 2011 s.1(1)(a), restating the previous law. For an example of a charity failing for not being exclusively charitable, see *Bishop (on behalf of Crocels Community Media Group) v The Charity Commission for England and Wales* UT/2016/0149 (purposes including "Improving fraternity between nations", "Advancing the understanding and promoting the cause of peace", and "Innovating for the abolition or reduction of standing armies")

[85] *McGovern v Attorney General* [1982] Ch. 321. See also *Helena Partnerships Ltd v Revenue and Customs Commissioners* [2012] EWCA Civ 569 per Lloyd LJ at [105] in respect of "for the benefit of the community". Compare *Charity Commission for Northern Ireland v Bangor Provident Trust* [2015] NICA 21; [2017] N.I. 59 where the trust was found still to be charitable where trustees were empowered "to do all other things as are incidental or conducive to the attainment of [the charitable] objects".

[86] *Annual Report and Accounts 2016–17*, p.12.

[87] *Re Robinson* [1931] 2 Ch. 122 at 126 (gift to German Government for the benefit of its soldiers disabled in the First World War held charitable). *Public benefit: the public benefit requirement* (PB1) (September 2013) 9.

[88] Annual Report 1963, paras 69–76.

[89] Finance Act 2010 s.30 and Sch.6; above, paras 15–005–15–006.

[90] *Camille and Henry Dreyfus Foundation Inc v IRC* [1954] Ch. 672 at 684; *Re Niyazi's Will Trusts* [1978] 1 W.L.R. 910 (trust for construction of working men's hostel in Cyprus charitable). See now *The Human Dignity Trust v The Charity Commission for England and Wales* CA/2013/0013 at [77]–[78].

foreign country. This does not mean that there must be a benefit to the public in this country. The courts should first consider if the activity would be charitable if it operated at home. If so, it is charitable even though operated abroad unless it would be contrary to public policy to recognise it.[91] For example, our courts would not consider an institution operating abroad whose object was contrary to the law of the state in question to be charitable. As we have seen,[92] the jurisdiction of the court and the Charity Commission over charities may be exercised only in respect of charities established in England and Wales according to English law, and not over bodies established and administered abroad.[93]

It has been said that the court would be bound to take account of the probable results of the execution of the trust on the inhabitants of the country concerned, which would doubtless have a history and social structure quite different from that of the UK. So in *McGovern v Attorney General*,[94] a trust to procure the abolition of torture or inhuman or degrading treatment or punishment[95] in all parts of the world was not charitable, one reason being that the court would have no satisfactory means of judging the probable effects of, say, legislation to abolish the death penalty on the local community. In *The Human Dignity Trust* case,[96] the First-Tier Tribunal concluded that it was "for the public benefit of the community in England and Wales (and, indeed, the UK), as well as in the country where such a contravention [of human rights standards] occurs, for this situation to be addressed and for the human rights standards recognised by the international community to be promoted and protected",[97] but this was limited to countries where the relevant human rights standards had been incorporated into the constitution of the relevant state.

4. THE DEFINITION OF CHARITY: PURPOSES UNDER CHARITIES ACT 2011 SECTION 3(1)

A. The Prevention or Relief of Poverty

i. Meaning of Poverty. The relief of poverty has always been one of the main categories of charity. The Charities Act 2006 clarified that the category included the "prevention" of poverty as well as its "relief".[98] There is no definition of poverty. Its meaning can only be understood by examining the cases on the subject. **15–012**

---

[91] See *Re Carapiet's Trusts* [2002] W.T.L.R. 989 (advancement in life of Armenian children charitable).

[92] Charities Act 2011 s.1; above, para.15–008.

[93] *Gaudiya Mission v Brahmachary* [1998] Ch. 341.

[94] [1982] Ch. 321, below, para.15–038.

[95] Including punishment inflicted by process of law.

[96] *The Human Dignity Trust v The Charity Commission for England and Wales* CA/2013/0013.

[97] CA/2013/0013 at [78].

[98] Now Charities Act 2011 s.3(1)(a). See also s.3(1)(j), dealing with the relief of those in need by reason of (amongst other things) financial hardship.

"It is quite clearly established that poverty does not mean destitution;... it may not unfairly be paraphrased as meaning persons who have to 'go short' in the ordinary acceptance of that term ..."[99]

It is thus a matter of degree. Most of the cases come from a time before welfare payments were available from public funds. Such payments are intended to relieve poverty and hardship, and it could be argued that eligibility for such payments should be the test of poverty. But, if that were so, charity in this area would duplicate the work of a good welfare programme. If relief of poverty is the duty of the State, what scope is there for private charity? This is a problem which is met in many of the areas of charity today, especially in connection with trusts for the relief of poverty and for education and health. Private charity is useful to fill the gaps which the welfare state programme leaves uncovered.

15–013   **ii.   Illustrations.**   Gifts for the benefit of the poor are clearly charitable.[100] Also "needy" persons,[101] or "indigent"[102] persons. Often a group of poor is confined to a particular location,[103] or religion,[104] or to a group which is assumed to be in need of help,[105] or victims of a disaster.[106] Persons of "limited means"[107] are included, and trusts for gentlewomen and distressed gentlefolk.[108] On the other hand, in *Re Sanders' Will Trusts*,[109] a gift for the provision of housing for the working classes was not charitable. A gift which includes persons who are not in need will be excluded. In *Re Gwyon*,[110] a fund providing for a gift of clothing to boys in Farnham and district failed on the ground that the conditions for qualification, precise though they were in many ways, failed to exclude affluent children.[111] It is no objection, however, that the scheme operates by way of bargain rather than bounty, i.e. that the beneficiaries are required to contribute to the cost of the benefits they receive.[112]

---

[99] *Re Coulthurst* [1951] Ch. 661 at 665–666. See generally A. Dunn (2000) 20 L.S. 222.

[100] *Re Darling* [1896] 1 Ch. 50: "to the poor and the service of God."

[101] *Re Scarisbrick* [1951] Ch. 622; *Re Cohen* [1973] 1 W.L.R. 415.

[102] *Weir v Crum-Brown* [1908] A.C. 162: "indigent bachelors and widowers who have shown sympathy with science."

[103] *Re Lucas* [1922] 2 Ch. 52 (oldest respectable inhabitants in Gunville).

[104] *Re Wall* (1889) 42 Ch.D. 510.

[105] *Attorney General v Ironmongers Co* (1834) 2 My. & K. 576 (debtors); *Biscoe v Jackson* (1887) 35 Ch.D. 460 (soup kitchen for the parish of Shoreditch); *Re Coulthurst* [1951] Ch. 661 (widows and orphaned children of employees); *Cawdron v Merchant Taylors' School* [2010] W.T.L.R. 775 (sons or dependants of "old boys" killed or disabled in the Great War).

[106] *Re North Devon and West Somerset Relief Fund Trust* [1953] 1 W.L.R. 1260 (flood disaster).

[107] *Re Gardom* [1914] 1 Ch. 664; *Re De Carteret* [1933] Ch. 103.

[108] *Mary Clark Home Trustees v Anderson* [1904] 2 K.B. 645; *Re Gardom* [1914] 1 Ch. 664; *Re Young* [1951] Ch. 344.

[109] [1954] Ch. 265. cf. *Re Niyazi's WT* [1978] 1 W.L.R. 910 (gift for "the construction of a working men's hostel" in Famagusta, Cyprus held charitable by Megarry VC "although it was desperately near the border-line", at 915).

[110] [1930] 1 Ch. 255.

[111] They also excluded "black boys". This would not be permitted today, below, para.15–047. See further T. Watkin [1981] Conv. 131.

[112] *Re Cottam's WT* [1955] 1 W.L.R. 1299; *Re Resch's WT* [1969] 1 A.C. 514; *Joseph Rowntree Memorial Trust Housing Association Ltd v Attorney General* [1983] Ch. 159 (dwellings for sale to elderly at 70% cost).

There is no need for the trust to be an endowment. A trust may be charitable although the trustees may distribute the capital. A trust was upheld in *Re Scarisbrick*[113]:

> "[F]or such relations of my… son and daughters as in the opinion of the survivor of my… son and daughters shall be in needy circumstances… as the survivor… shall by deed or will appoint."

This was a trust for "poor relations", and such trusts are excepted from the general rule that the beneficiaries must not be defined by a personal connection.[114] But there can be no charitable trust, even in the poverty category, where the persons to be benefited are specified individuals.

B.   The Advancement of Education[115]

i.   Meaning of Education.   This purpose had its origin in the phrases in the   **15–014**
Preamble which spoke of "the maintenance of schools of learning, free schools and scholars in universities" and "the education and preferment of orphans". The endowments, some very ancient, of many schools and colleges and universities are based on this provision. Education in school and university is now however accepted as being within the responsibility of the State; and it is not surprising that modern cases have substantially widened the concept of educational charity. It can now cover almost any form of worthwhile instruction or cultural advancement, except for purely professional or career courses.

The following trusts have been held charitable under this purpose: education in the art of government,[116] the production of a dictionary,[117] the support of London Zoological Society,[118] the establishment and maintenance of museums,[119] the support of learned literary, scientific and cultural societies,[120] a search for the Shakespeare manuscript,[121] choral singing in London,[122] the promotion of the music of Delius,[123] classical drama and acting,[124] the publication of the Law Reports,[125] the study and dissemination of ethical principles and cultivation of a

---

[113] [1951] Ch. 622; *Re Cohen* [1973] 1 W.L.R. 415.

[114] *Dingle v Turner* [1972] A.C. 601; below, para.15–049.

[115] This was one of the main categories of charity before the Charities Act 2006 and is now found in s.3(1)(b) of the Charities Act 2011.

[116] *Re McDougall* [1957] 1 W.L.R. 81. But not for the promotion of political causes; below, para.15–038. The holding of conferences with a "political flavour" but not of a party-political nature was upheld in *Re Koeppler's WT* [1986] Ch. 423.

[117] *Re Stanford* [1924] 1 Ch. 73.

[118] *Re Lopes* [1931] 2 Ch. 130.

[119] *British Museum Trustees v White* (1826) 2 Sm. & St. 594; *Re Pinion* [1965] Ch. 85 at 105.

[120] *Royal College of Surgeons v National Provincial Bank Ltd* [1952] A.C. 631; *Re Shakespeare Memorial Trust* [1923] 2 Ch. 398; *Re British School of Egyptian Archaeology* [1954] 1 W.L.R. 546.

[121] *Re Hopkins' WT* [1965] Ch. 669.

[122] *Royal Choral Society v IRC* [1943] 2 All E.R. 101.

[123] *Re Delius* [1957] Ch. 299.

[124] *Re Shakespeare Memorial Trust* [1923] 2 Ch. 398.

[125] *Incorporated Council of Law Reporting for England and Wales v Attorney General* [1972] Ch. 73.

rational religious sentiment[126] and even a "sort of finishing school for the Irish people" where "self-control, oratory, deportment and the art of personal contact" were to be taught.[127]

Charities Act 2011 s.3(1)(f) recognises as a separate purpose "the advancement of the arts, culture, heritage or science". Some of the examples just given could be regarded as involving either or both the advancement of education and the advancement of the arts, culture, heritage or science. Clearly there is a potential for overlap in the list of purposes set out in s.3 in the Act of 2011, just as in the case of the four heads of charity recognised prior to the Act of 2006. However, as will be seen below, it matters which purpose is chosen when it comes to the assessment of public benefit, as public benefit can only be judged in the context of the specific purpose.

15–015   **ii.   Research.**   Education requires something more than the mere accumulation of knowledge. There must be some sharing, or teaching or dissemination, some way of showing that the public will benefit. This is all the more so since there is no longer any presumption of public benefit applicable to education.[128] There is no difficulty in the case of research which is likely to produce material benefit to the community, such as medical or scientific research.[129] Such purposes would in any case come under other purposes. On literary, cultural and scholarly subjects, Wilberforce J considered in *Re Hopkins*[130]:

> "[T]hat the word 'education'... must be used in a wide sense, certainly extending beyond teaching, and that the requirement is that, in order to be charitable, research must either be of educational value to the researcher or must be so directed as to lead to something which will pass into the store of educational material, or so as to improve the sum of communicable knowledge in an area which education may cover—education in this last context extending to the formation of literary taste and appreciation."

In *Re Hopkins*,[131] there was a testamentary gift to the Francis Bacon Society, "to be earmarked and applied towards finding the Bacon-Shakespeare manuscripts."[132] Wilberforce J concluded that a:

---

[126] *Re South Place Ethical Society* [1980] 1 W.L.R. 1565. The Society was also charitable under the old fourth heading.

[127] *Re Shaw's WT* [1952] Ch. 163.

[128] Now Charities Act 2011 s.4(2). See *Independent Schools Council v Charity Commission* [2012] Ch. 214, below, para.15–052.

[129] *Royal College of Surgeons v National Provincial Bank Ltd* [1952] A.C. 631; Trusts for the funding of research into cryonics have recently been held to be charitable in New Zealand: *Re The Foundation For Anti-Aging Research And The Foundation For Reversal Of Solid State Hypothermia* [2016] NZHC 2328.

[130] [1965] Ch. 669 at 680.

[131] [1965] Ch. 669. See also *McGovern v Attorney General* [1982] Ch. 321, where research into human rights and dissemination of the results would have been charitable. The trust failed for other reasons.

[132] There is a long-standing theory that Sir Francis Bacon was the author of some of the plays attributed to Shakespeare.

> "[S]earch, or research, for the original manuscripts of England's greatest dramatist (whoever he was) would be well within the law's conception of charitable purposes. The discovery would be of the highest value to history and to literature."[133]

The gift was held to be a valid charitable trust under this head and under what was then the fourth head ("other purposes beneficial to the community"). *Re Shaw*[134] was distinguished.

> George Bernard Shaw, by his will, directed that his residuary estate should be devoted to researching the advantages of a proposed British alphabet of 40 letters, in which each letter would indicate a single sound; and to translate his play "Androcles and the Lion" into the new alphabet. Harman J held that the gift was not charitable "if the object be merely the increase of knowledge, that is not in itself a charitable object unless it be combined with teaching or education."[135]

Whether the trust in this case would be held charitable under Wilberforce J's test depends on the usefulness of the research, and that is a matter of judgment. Not every type of knowledge, whether researched, disseminated or taught is capable of being education: not schools for pickpockets,[136] nor guides to bomb-making or to effective money-laundering, for example, as the public benefit requirement would not be met.

iii. Artistic and Aesthetic Education. In *Royal Choral Society v IRC*,[137] the Court of Appeal upheld as charitable a trust to promote the practice and performance of choral works. Lord Greene MR said of the view that education meant a master teaching a class[138]:   **15–016**

> "I protest against that narrow conception of education when one is dealing with aesthetic education. In my opinion, a body of persons established for the purpose of raising the artistic state of the country … is established for educational purposes."

In *Re British School of Egyptian Archaeology*,[139] a trust to excavate and discover Egyptian antiquities, to hold exhibitions and to promote the training and assistance of students in the field of Egyptian history was held charitable. In *Re Delius*,[140] a gift to increase the general appreciation of the musical work of the composer was for the advancement of education. The last three examples would now also likely fall within the separate purpose "the advancement of the arts, culture, heritage or science".[141]

iv. Subjective Evaluation. The question whether a purpose is educational or not will depend in many cases upon the evaluation of its quality and usefulness for that purpose. Music, drama, literature, archaeology, museums; these and many   **15–017**

---

[133] [1965] Ch. 669 at 679.
[134] [1957] 1 W.L.R. 729.
[135] [1957] 1 W.L.R. 729 at 737, referring to Rigby LJ in *Re Macduff* [1896] 2 Ch. 451.
[136] per Harman J [1957] 1 W.L.R. 729 at 737; and in *Re Pinion* [1965] Ch. 85 at 105.
[137] [1943] 2 All E.R. 101.
[138] [1943] 2 All E.R. 101 at 104.
[139] [1954] 1 W.L.R. 546.
[140] [1957] Ch. 299.
[141] Charities Act 2011 s.3(1)(f).

more are included. But not bad music, ham acting, pornography, useless digging or collections of rubbish, as the public benefit requirement would not be satisfied. In *Re Delius*,[142] Roxburgh J recognised that there would be difficulty if a manifestly inadequate composer had been chosen. A judge may be assisted by expert evidence. But that may not be conclusive, and artistic evaluation changes with the times. It is clear that the court will require to be satisfied of the merit of artistic work. The mere opinion of the donor that the relevant work is meritorious, or that the gift is for the public benefit, does not make it so.

In *Re Pinion*,[143] a testator gave his studio and its contents to trustees to enable it to be used as a museum for the display of his collection of furniture and objets d'art, and paintings, some of which were by the testator himself. Expert opinion was unanimous that the collection had no artistic merit. One expert expressed his surprise that "so voracious a collector should not by hazard have picked up even one meritorious object."[144] The Court of Appeal held the trust void. "I can conceive," said Harman LJ, "of no useful object to be served in foisting upon the public this mass of junk. It has neither public utility nor educational value."[145]

15–018   **v. Youth. Sports at School and University.**   Education has historically been specially concerned with the young. In many situations a provision for the young will be held charitable although the same provision for older people might fail.

In *Re Mariette*,[146] there was a gift to provide Eton fives courts and squash rackets courts at Aldenham School. Eve J upheld this, on the principle that learning to play games at a boarding school was as important as learning from the books.

The sporting facilities need not be limited to a particular school or institution. In *IRC v McMullen*,[147] a trust to provide facilities for pupils at schools and universities in the UK to play association football or other games or sports was held valid by the House of Lords. Lord Hailsham said[148]:

> "The picture of education when applied to the young... is complex and varied... It is the picture of a balanced and systematic process of instruction, training and practice containing both spiritual, moral, mental and physical elements... I reject any idea which would cramp the education of the young within the school or university campus, limit it to formal instruction, or render it devoid of pleasure in the exercise of skill."

But this wide definition of education was not without its limits. Lord Hailsham stated that the mere playing of games or enjoyment or amusement or competition was not per se charitable nor necessarily educational; and that a trust for physical education per se and not associated with persons of school age or just above was not necessarily a good charitable gift. Trusts for sport outside educational facilities and the services were formerly considered not charitable[149] unless they

---

[142] [1957] Ch. 299.
[143] [1965] Ch. 85.
[144] [1965] Ch. 85 at 107.
[145] [1965] Ch. 85 at 107.
[146] [1915] 2 Ch. 284. For sport outside universities and schools, see below, para.15–028.
[147] [1981] A.C. 1; J. Warburton [1980] Conv. 173, 225.
[148] [1981] A.C. 1 at 18.
[149] *Re Nottage* [1895] 2 Ch. 649 (a prize for a yacht race).

came within the scope of the Recreational Charities Act 1958.[150] That position has since changed with the recognition of other purposes. The Charities Act 2006, following decisions of the Charity Commissioners, recognised the advancement of amateur sport as a charitable purpose.[151] This is discussed below.[152] Intelligent games like chess are educational for young people,[153] and the definition of sport now found in the Charities Act 2011 includes games which promote health by involving mental skill.[154] We can say that purposeful activities for the young receive favourable treatment. The Boy Scout Movement[155] and the National Association of Toy Libraries[156] are charities, and a gift for an annual treat or field day for school children at Turton was upheld as encouraging a study of natural history.[157]

vi. Professional Bodies. Professional bodies may be charitable if their object   **15–019**
is the advancement of education. The object of the Royal College of Surgeons[158] was stated in the royal charter of 1800 to be "the due promotion and encouragement of the study and practice of the... art and science of surgery".

The fact that the College gives assistance and protection to its members is ancillary only; and the College was held to be a charity. Similarly, the Royal College of Nursing,[159] as the advance of nursing as a profession in all or any of its branches was a charitable purpose. The Construction Industry Training Board was held to be charitable,[160] and subsequently most of the Industrial Training Boards were registered as charities.[161]

But if the object or one of the objects of the society is to promote the status of the profession or the welfare of its members, it will not be charitable. The General Medical Council was formerly held not to be charitable for this reason, but changes in its constitution led the Charity Commissioners to recognise it as

---

[150] Below, para.15–036.
[151] Now Charities Act 2011 s.3(1)(g).
[152] Below, para.15–028.
[153] *Re Dupree's Deed Trusts* [1945] Ch. 16.
[154] s.3(2)(d). Bridge has also been accepted as a sport on this basis by the Charity Commission: *English Bridge Union Ltd v Revenue and Customs Commissioners* [2015] UKUT 401 (TCC). The campaign for bridge's recognition as a sport in other areas continues, however: the Fourth Chamber of the European Court of Justice held that bridge was not a sport for tax purposes, in a reference from the same litigation: [2017] S.T.C. 2317. Dove J dismissed a challenge to the English Sports Council's exclusion of bridge as a sport: *R. (on the application of English Bridge Union) v The English Sports Council* [2015] EWHC 2875 (Admin) .
[155] *Re Webber* [1954] 1 W.L.R. 1500.
[156] Annual Report 1973, para.41. Now the National Association of Toy and Leisure Libraries, which extends the concept to adults with special needs.
[157] *Re Mellody* [1918] 1 Ch. 228.
[158] *Royal College of Surgeons v National Provincial Bank Ltd* [1952] A.C. 631.
[159] *Royal College of Nursing v St Marylebone BC* [1959] 1 W.L.R. 1077; *Institute of Civil Engineers v IRC* [1932] 1 K.B. 149.
[160] *Construction Industry Training Board v Attorney General* [1973] Ch. 173.
[161] Annual Report 1973 para.39; cf. *IRC v Oldham Training and Enterprise Council* [1996] S.T.C. 1218 (not exclusively charitable because promotion of commerce conferred private benefits).

charitable as promoting public health, the benefit to doctors being incidental.[162] Such a purpose now also falls within the separate head of the advancement of health.[163]

15–020   **vii.   Political Propaganda Masquerading as Education.**   Political purposes are not charitable. They might be for the public benefit, but they are partisan. The court cannot determine whether any particular programme is for the public benefit.[164] Nor can such a trust be charitable even where the testator's project has subsequently been endorsed by Parliament.[165] A trust for political purposes will fail. Attempts have been made to foster the doctrines of a political party under the guise of a trust for education by providing for the advancement of adult education on the lines of the principles of that party.[166] In *Re Hopkinson*,[167] Vaisey J explained the principle as follows:

> "Political propaganda masquerading... I do not use the word in any sinister sense... as education is not education within the statute of Elizabeth... In other words it is not charitable."[168]

But there is no doubt that, historically, the prospects of success have been greater if purposes are presented in the form of education. In *Re Scowcroft*,[169] the gift was of income to be applied "for the furtherance of Conservative principles and religious and mental improvement", and this succeeded. Similarly in *Re Koeppler's Will Trusts*[170] a gift to further the work of an educational project was held charitable even though the testator's express aspirations (the formation of informed international public opinion and the promotion of greater co-operation in Europe and the West) were not regarded as charitable. The project involved conferences with a "political flavour", but did not further the interests of a particular political party, nor seek to change the law or government policies. On the other hand, The Countryside Alliance's purpose to educate the public about a variety of countryside practices and to conduct research into them did not lead to the production of balanced material and so the purpose was not furthered in a way which was exclusively charitable.[171]

---

[162] Annual Report 2001/02 p.19.

[163] Now Charities Act 2011 s.3(1)(d); below, para.15–025.

[164] *Bowman v Secular Society* [1917] A.C. 406 at 421.

[165] *Re Bushnell* [1975] 1 W.L.R. 1596 (national health system introduced after testator's death but before the litigation); R. Cotterrell (1975) 38 M.L.R. 471.

[166] *Bonar Law Memorial Trust v IRC* (1933) 49 T.L.R. 220 (Conservative); *Re Hopkinson* [1949] 1 All E.R. 346 (Socialist); cf. *McDougall* [1957] 1 W.L.R. 81. See also *Re Ogden* [1933] Ch. 678, where, however, a trust for Liberal institutions was upheld on other grounds.

[167] [1949] 1 All E.R. 346. See also *McGovern v Attorney General* [1982] Ch. 321 and *Southwood v Attorney General* [2000] W.T.L.R. 1199, below, para.15–038, where essentially political trusts were not saved by educational elements.

[168] [1949] 1 All E.R. 346 at 350.

[169] [1898] 2 Ch. 638; cf. in the field of religion, *Re Hood* [1931] 1 Ch. 240 (spreading Christian principles by extinguishing "the drink traffic").

[170] [1986] Ch. 423; T. Watkin [1985] Conv. 412.

[171] Charity Commission Decision, The Countryside Alliance—Application for Registration, 23 March 2017, paras 41–42. The Commission did recognise (at para.41) that such material "does not have to absolutely neutral its view", but must not be one-sided.

While a students' union may be a charitable body,[172] as being ancillary to the educational purposes of the college or university,[173] the donation of union funds for political, or indeed for charitable purposes which are not educational, is not permitted. So, in *Baldry v Feintuck*,[174] the use of union funds to campaign for the restoration of free school milk was restrained as political, although the fact that a students' union has political clubs is not inconsistent with its charitable status.[175]

viii.   Private and Independent Schools.[176]   An educational institution cannot be charitable if it is operated for profit.[177] The modern practice is to operate fee-paying schools as non-profit-making bodies which can then obtain the fiscal benefits available to educational charities.[178] The Charities Act 2006 removed the presumption of public benefit, which must now be actively demonstrated by private schools. The change raised issues relating to the establishment of public benefit, and the situation is considered in detail below.[179]   **15–021**

C.   The Advancement of Religion

i.   Meaning of Religion.   The advancement of religion was one of the four heads of charity prior to the Charities Act 2006, and is now part of the statutory definition.[180] The promotion of religious harmony is a separate purpose.[181] Under the previous law it was presumed that the advancement of religion was for the public benefit, but the presumption has now been removed, so that public benefit must in principle be demonstrated in every case.[182]   **15–022**

---

[172]   See the Charity Commission's Written evidence to the *Joint Committee On Human Rights Inquiry Into Freedom Of Speech In Universities* (January 2018) and further evidence (February 2018). In its February evidence, the Commission noted (at para.1.7.11) that "it is not the place of the Commission as independent regulator to take a view on whether or not certain categories of organisation should or should not be charities. The test for whether or not an institution is a charity is a legal test set by Parliament".

[173]   *London Hospital Medical College v IRC* [1976] 1 W.L.R. 613. The National Union of Students is not a charity (see *Attorney General v Ross* [1986] 1 W.L.R. 252), but it has set up a separate charity, NUS Charitable Services.

[174]   [1972] 1 W.L.R. 552. In *Webb v O'Doherty* (1991) 3 Admin. L.R. 731, expenditure on a campaign to end the 1990–91 Gulf War was restrained.

[175]   *Attorney General v Ross* [1986] 1 W.L.R. 252; P. Clarke All E.R. Rev. 1985 at 320. (Preliminary issue as to whether Attorney General had standing to seek injunction to restrain donation of union funds to striking miners and famine aid in Ethiopia). By similar reasoning, a charity cannot guarantee the liabilities of a non-charity; *Rosemary Simmons Memorial Housing Association Ltd v United Dominions Trust Ltd* [1986] 1 W.L.R. 1440. See further J. Warburton [1988] Conv. 275. At the time of writing, the Commission is considering guidance on charities that are connected with non-charitable organisations: see   *https://www.gov.uk/government/consultations/charities-that-are-connected-with-non-charitable-organisations-maintaining-your-charitys-separation-and-independence*   [accessed   4 July 2018].

[176]   M. Synge (2011) 70 C.L.J. 649.

[177]   *Re Girls' Public Day School Trust* [1951] Ch. 400.

[178]   *Abbey, Malvern Wells Ltd v Minister of Local Government and Housing* [1951] Ch. 728.

[179]   *Independent Schools Council v Charity Commission* [2012] Ch. 214. Below, para.15–052.

[180]   Now Charities Act 2011 s.3(1)(c).

[181]   Now Charities Act 2011 s.3(1)(h).

[182]   Charities Act 2011 s.4(2).

It was at one time considered that, for the purposes of charity law, a religion had to be "monotheistic".[183] The emphasis was on belief in one god, or a god.[184] However, a more pluralist approach is now taken, as befits a multicultural society: "the immigrations of the 20th century have diversified the religious landscape of the United Kingdom".[185] Charities Act 2011 s.3(2)(a) provides that "religion" includes a religion which involves belief in more than one god, and a religion which does not involve belief in a god. However, the legislation provides no guidance as to whether a system of belief constitutes a religion. The Charity Commission had stated that belief in a "Supreme Being" rather than a god was required,[186] but this was subsequently modified in supplementary guidance.[187] That guidance lists the characteristics of a religious belief as:

- "Belief in a god (or gods) or goddess (or goddesses), or supreme being, or divine or transcendental being or entity or spiritual principle ('supreme being or entity') which is the object or focus of the religion;
- a relationship between the believer and the supreme being or entity by showing worship of, reverence for or veneration of the supreme being or entity;
- a degree of cogency, cohesion, seriousness and importance;
- an identifiable positive, beneficial, moral or ethical framework."

Some of the decisions preceding the Act of 2006 are still of assistance on this point. They laid down that religion involves a spiritual belief going beyond morality or a recommended way of life. In *Re South Place Ethical Society*,[188] one question was whether the Society's objects, which were the "study and dissemination of ethical principles and the cultivation of a rational religious sentiment", were charitable under this heading. Dillon J held that they were not. Similarly, the objects of a body such as the Freemasons, whose rules demand the highest personal, social and domestic standards, do not constitute a religion, even though they insist upon a belief in a divine spirit.[189] In any event, to be charitable, a trust must be for the *advancement* of religion; and this means:

> "[T]he promotion of spiritual teaching in a wide sense and the maintenance of the doctrines on which this rests, and the observances that serve to promote and manifest it—not merely a foundation or cause to which it can be related."[190]

---

[183] *Bowman v Secular Society* [1917] A.C. 406.
[184] *Re South Place Ethical Society* [1980] 1 W.L.R. 1565. The position of Buddhism was left open, but this was resolved by the Act of 2006.
[185] *Shergill v Khaira* [2014] UKSC 33; [2015] A.C. 359 per Lord Neuberger PSC, Lord Sumption and Lord Hodge JJSC at [55].
[186] *Charitable Purposes* Guidance, 16 September 2013, section 5.
[187] *The Advancement of Religion for the Public Benefit*, December 2008.
[188] [1980] 1 W.L.R. 1565. The Society was charitable under other headings; above, para.15–022.
[189] *United Grand Lodge of Ancient Free and Accepted Masons of England and Wales v Holborn BC* [1957] 1 W.L.R. 1080. The promotion of spiritualism was held to advance religion in *Re Sacred Hands Spiritual Centre* [2006] W.T.L.R. 873. The Druid Foundation has been accepted by the Charity Commission; P. Luxton [2011] Conv. 144.
[190] *Keren Kayemeth le Jisroel v IRC* [1932] A.C. 650.

More recently, however, the Charity Commission has considered that developments in the law justified a revised approach to the question of whether the Theosophical Society was entitled to be registered as a charity: relying on *South Place Ethical Society*, it was held that the charity was exclusively charitable.[191]

So far as Christianity is concerned, no distinction is drawn between the various denominations.[192] Thus, trusts for Roman Catholics,[193] Quakers,[194] Baptists,[195] Methodists,[196] and the Exclusive Brethren,[197] have been upheld. So also small groups, promoting minority religions. In *Thornton v Howe*,[198] Romilly MR went so far as to hold as charitable a trust for the publication of the sacred writings of Joanna Southcott, who claimed that she was with child by the Holy Ghost and would give birth to a new Messiah. In *Re Watson*,[199] Plowman J upheld a trust for "the continuation of the work of God... in propagating the truth as given in the Holy Bible" by financing the continued publication of the books and tracts of one Hobbs who, with the testator, was the leading member of a very small group of undenominational Christians. Expert evidence regarded the intrinsic value of the work as nil; but it confirmed the genuineness of the belief of the adherents of that small group. Now that public benefit must be demonstrated, the result may be different in these two cases.[200] It has recently been reaffirmed that the court will not pass value judgements on particular sects.[201]

15–023

Non-Christian religions were recognised before the advent of the Charities Act 2006, as: "the law of charity does not now favour one religion to another."[202] A gift for the promotion of the Jewish religion has been upheld.[203] Likewise the promotion of the faith of a Hindu sect,[204] and trusts for the use of properties as

---

[191] *Annual Report and Accounts 2016–17*, pp.8 and 41–2. Earlier authority prior to the 2006/11 Acts had decided otherwise: *Berry v St Marylebone BC* [1958] Ch. 406.

[192] *Dunne v Byrne* [1912] A.C. 407; *Re Flynn* [1948] Ch. 24.

[193] *Dunn v Byrne* [1912] A.C. 407.

[194] *Re Manser* [1905] 1 Ch. 68.

[195] *Re Strickland's WT* [1936] 3 All E.R. 1027.

[196] "The Voice of Methodism" was registered in 1965; Annual Report App.C, para.1.

[197] *Holmes v Attorney General*, *The Times*, 12 February 1981. The Charity Commission revisited the position on the Plymouth Brethren in January 2014, holding that *Holmes* was no longer a binding precedent as having been influenced by the former presumption of public benefit prior to the Charities Act 2006. But the Commission did, subject to some required amendments confirm the charity registration for the Preston Down Trust: *Annual Report and Accounts 2013–14: Legal Annex*, p.45.

[198] (1862) 31 Beav. 14. As this gift was to take effect out of land, it was void as infringing the Statutes of Mortmain, now repealed. See C. Stebbings (1997) 18 *Legal History* 1; P. Ridge (2010) J.L.H. 177.

[199] [1973] 1 W.L.R. 1472. See also *Funnell v Stewart* [1996] 1 W.L.R. 288 (faith healing upheld); R. Fletcher (1996) 112 L.Q.R. 557.

[200] Charities Act 2011 s.4(2). See M. Harding (2008) 71 M.L.R. 159.

[201] *Buckley v Barlow* [2016] EWHC 3017 (Ch).

[202] *Varsani v Jesani* [1999] Ch. 219 at 235. See also *Neville Estates Ltd v Madden* [1962] Ch. 832; *Gilmour v Coats* [1949] A.C. 426 at 457–458.

[203] *Neville Estates Ltd v Madden* [1962] Ch. 832.

[204] *Varsani v Jesani* [1999] Ch. 219.

Sikh Gurdwaras.[205] There seems little doubt that all non-Christian religions will be treated equally, although there can be difficult questions if charitable status is claimed for some sects or cults.[206]

The Supreme Court decision in *R. (Hodkin) v Registrar General of Births, Deaths and Marriages*[207] is of significance here, although it is not a case on charity law and it must be recognised, as Lord Toulson noted, that there "has never been a universal legal definition of religion in English law".[208]

> The case concerned s.2 of the Places of Worship Registration Act 1855. The claimant was a Scientologist who wished to marry her fiancé at a Church of Scientology chapel. There was a certification in writing to the Registrar General, seeking the registration of the chapel for solemnisation of marriages under s.41 of the Marriage Act 1949. To be so registered, the chapel had to be a "place of meeting for religious worship" under s.2 of the 1855 Act. The Registrar refused on the basis that the Court of Appeal decision in *R. v Registrar General, Ex p. Segerdal*[209] bound her to record that Scientology services were not acts of religious worship. The claimant sought judicial review and appealed to the Supreme Court. The Supreme Court unanimously held that the chapel could be registered as a place of religious worship: the phrase "place of meeting for religious worship" was

> > "to be interpreted in accordance with contemporary understanding of religion and not by reference to the culture of 1855."[210]

> Lord Toulson noted that the approach to religion under the Charities Act 2011 had no direct application to the 1855 Act, but "it is a further indication that the understanding of religion in today's society is broad."[211] His Lordship then described religion, for the purposes of the 1855 Act:

> > "in summary as a spiritual or non-secular belief system, held by a group of adherents, which claims to explain mankind's place in the universe and relationship with the infinite, and to teach its adherents how they are to live their lives in conformity with the spiritual understanding associated with the belief system. By spiritual or non-secular I mean a belief system which goes beyond that which can be perceived by the senses or ascertained by the application of science ... Such a belief system may or may not involve belief in a supreme being, but it does involve a belief that there is more to be understood about mankind's nature and relationship to the universe than can be gained from the senses or from science. I emphasise that this is intended to be a description and not a definitive formula."[212]

The Supreme Court took this stance in *Hodkin* in part because of concerns about the courts being drawn into "difficult theological territory... because Ideas about the nature of God are the stuff of theological debate".[213]

---

[205] An example of such trusts was the background to the Supreme Court decision in *Shergill v Khaira* [2014] UKSC 33; [2015] A.C. 359; P. Smith (2016) 18 Ecc. L.J. 36; S.S. Juss [2016] P.L. 198.

[206] On "fringe" religious organisations, see Annual Report 1976 paras 103–108; and on exorcism, paras 65–67. The Unification Church (the "Moonies") has also been registered; Annual Report 1982 paras 36–38, App.C. On Rastafarianism, see D. O'Brien (2001) 151 N.L.J. 509.

[207] [2013] UKSC 77; [2014] 1 A.C. 610; R. Sandberg (2014) 16 Ecc.LJ. 198.

[208] [2013] UKSC 77; [2014] 1 A.C. 610 at [34].

[209] [1970] 2 Q.B. 697 (now overruled by the Supreme Court).

[210] [2013] UKSC 77; [2014] 1 A.C. 610 per Lord Toulson at [34]. His Lordship continued: "It is no good considering whether the members of the legislature over 150 years ago would have considered Scientology to be a religion because it did not exist".

[211] [2013] UKSC 77; [2014] 1 A.C. 610 at [55].

[212] [2013] UKSC 77; [2014] 1 A.C. 610 at [58].

[213] [2013] UKSC 77; [2014] 1 A.C. 610 at [52]; see also [54].

The question is what impact, if any, the decision may have on the position in charity law, both specifically for the Church of Scientology and more broadly for the approach to other religions. The Charity Commissioners (as they then were) decided that the Church of Scientology was not a religion for the purposes of charity law in 1999.[214] In part, the Commissioners relied upon the *Segerdal* case as persuasive,[215] but that case has now been overruled. The Charity Commission provisionally commented on the *Hodkin* decision in its 2013–14 Annual Report.[216] It conceded that the approach to belief system and religious worship under charity law's definition of religion may need to be modified in the light of *Hodkin*. However, the Commission reiterated that the charity must still be for the public benefit, and (although the Commission does not refer to this in the Annual Report) the Commissioners in 1999 did raise concerns, albeit obiter, about whether Church of Scientology could be said to be established for the public benefit.[217] And a case can be made that *Hodkin* may be limited: the "collective understanding of religious freedom [in *Hodkin*] may be appropriate for the purposes of registration law but should not have wider application".[218]

At the very least, it seems clear that the position on the advancement of religion calls for reconsideration in the light of the reasoning in *Hodkin*, and the decision illustrates the challenges facing the courts and the Commission over analysing the "fine theological or liturgical niceties as to how precisely [adherents] see and express their relationship with the infinite".[219]

In December 2016, the Charity Commission considered an application[220] by the Temple of the Jedi Order for registration as a Charitable Incorporated Organisation under the purposes of the advancement of religion and/or the promotion of moral and ethical improvement for the benefit of the public. Jediism purported to source "its terminology in the books, films and video games comprising the Star Wars [movie franchise]". Applying *Hodkin*, the Commission noted that it was "not satisfied that the observance of the Force within Jediism is characterised by a belief in one or more gods or spiritual or non-secular principles or things which is an essential requirement for a religion in charity law".[221] It further concluded that[222]:

> "There is scope for individuals, consistent with Jediism and the Jedi Doctrine promoted by [the Order], to pursue a spiritual path, a philosophy or way of life outside of the scope of a religion, as that term is defined in charity law. Any cogency and cohesion that is present is eroded by

---

[214] *Decision of the Charity Commissioners for England and Wales on the Application for Registration as a Charity by The Church of Scientology (England and Wales)*, 17 November 1999.

[215] *Decision on the Charity Commissioners on The Church of Scientology*, 16.

[216] *Annual Report and Accounts 2013–14: Legal Annex*, p.46.

[217] *Decision of the Charity Commissioners*, 37–49 (whether in terms of rebutting the presumption of public benefit for the advancement of religion or under the old fourth head of other purposes for the public benefit).

[218] R. Sandberg (2014) 16 Ecc.LJ. 198 at 202.

[219] [2013] UKSC 77; [2014] 1 A.C. 610 per Lord Toulson at [64]. cf. e.g., J. Rivers (2012) Ecc.L.J. 371, at 398, speaking generally of religion and the law, fearing that "Religion [is acquiring] all the moral weight of stamp-collecting or train-spotting".

[220] Charity Commission Decision, *The Temple of the Jedi Order – Application for Registration*, 16 December 2016.

[221] *The Temple of the Jedi Order – Application for Registration*, [18].

[222] *The Temple of the Jedi Order – Application for Registration*, [30].

the individual's ability to develop themselves within a loose framework and follow an individual experiential philosophy or way of life as a secular belief system."

The Commission emphasised that it "is not concerned with the truth or otherwise of [the Order's] teachings".[223] Rejected the application was.

15–024   **ii.   Related Purposes.**   A large number of purposes have been accepted as charitable, although indirectly connected with the advancement of religion. Again, only a few illustrations need be selected. Many of these relate to the erection of churches or the maintenance of the fabric of religious buildings; which includes a window,[224] a tomb in the church,[225] and bells.[226] A trust for a graveyard, even though restricted to one denomination, is charitable,[227] but not a trust for individual tombs in the churchyard.[228]

A similar approach has been applied to trusts for the benefit of the clergy,[229] or for the church choir,[230] and also for retired missionaries.[231] Where the testator uses phrases like "for God's work",[232] or "for his work in the parish",[233] the court will often find circumstances to indicate that the purposes are intended to be limited to charitable religious purposes.[234]

D.   The Advancement of Health; Saving Lives[235]

15–025   This purpose originates from the old Preamble to the Charitable Uses Act of 1601, which included in the list of charitable purposes "the relief of aged, impotent and poor people". "Impotent" meant sick or disabled. The new statutory head of "the advancement of health and the saving of lives" overlaps to some extent with other purposes, such as education and the relief of those in need by reason of (amongst other things) ill-health.[236] It is notable also that the advancement of amateur sport has a link to health, as "sport" is defined as meaning sports or games which promote health by involving physical or mental skill or exertion.[237]

The advancement of health includes "the prevention or relief of sickness, disease or human suffering".[238] We have seen that the advancement of education

---

[223] *The Temple of the Jedi Order – Application for Registration*, [8].
[224] *Re King* [1923] 1 Ch. 243; *Re Raine* [1956] Ch. 417.
[225] *Hoare v Osborne* (1866) L.R. 1 Eq. 585.
[226] *Re Pardoe* [1906] 2 Ch. 184; an extreme case, as the purpose was to commemorate the restoration of the Monarchy.
[227] *Re Manser* [1905] 1 Ch. 68; *Re Eighmie* [1935] Ch. 524.
[228] *Lloyd v Lloyd* (1852) 2 Sim.(N.S.) 225.
[229] *Middleton v Clitherow* (1798) 3 Ves.Jr. 734 (stipends); *Re Williams* [1927] 2 Ch. 283 (education of candidates for Ministry); *Re Forster* [1939] Ch. 22.
[230] *Re Royce* [1940] Ch. 514.
[231] *Re Mylne* [1941] Ch. 204; *Re Moon's WT* [1948] 1 All E.R. 300.
[232] *Re Barker's WT* (1948) 64 T.L.R. 273. See also *Re Darling* [1896] 1 Ch. 50.
[233] *Re Simson* [1946] Ch. 299; below, para.15–057.
[234] *Re Moon's WT* [1948] 1 All E.R. 300.
[235] Charities Act 2011 s.3(1)(d).
[236] Charities Act 2011 s.3(1)(b) and (j).
[237] Charities Act 2011 s.3(1)(g) and 3(2)(d).
[238] Charities Act 2011 s.3(2)(b).

has been held to include medical research,[239] and that bodies such as the Royal College of Nursing and the General Medical Council have been held charitable under that purpose. Those examples may now be regarded as falling under both purposes.

The advancement of health category will now include examples previously upheld under the old fourth category ("other purposes beneficial to the community"). Trusts for the support of hospitals have long been recognised.[240] Indeed, prior to the introduction of the National Health Service in 1946, hospitals were amongst the greatest beneficiaries of charitable gifts. Ancillary purposes are included if their object is to improve the quality of the service.[241] A private hospital run for profit is not a charity.[242]

The saving of lives was already recognised as charitable, and the charitable status of bodies such as the Royal National Lifeboat Institution is long established. Disaster funds may be charitable, and the special issues affecting disaster appeals are discussed below.[243]

E.   The Advancement of Citizenship

This purpose, which incorporates the advancement of community develop-   **15–026**
ment,[244] had been recognised in the decisions of the Charity Commissioners prior to the 2006 Act.[245] It includes rural or urban regeneration, and the promotion of civic responsibility, volunteering, the voluntary sector or the effectiveness or efficiency of charities.[246]

The Charity Commissioners considered that an appeal to fund a public memorial to a respected national figure of historical importance, such as Earl Mountbatten of Burma, could be charitable as being likely to foster patriotism and good citizenship.[247] Scout and Guide groups would be included as promoting good citizenship.

F.   The Advancement of the Arts, Culture, Heritage or Science[248]

We have seen that, prior to the Charities Act 2006, this purpose was accepted as   **15–027**
an aspect of the advancement of education.[249] The examples given under that head may now be regarded as falling within either of these overlapping categories.

---

[239] *Royal College of Surgeons v National Provincial Bank Ltd* [1952] A.C. 631; above, para.15–015.

[240] *Re Smith's WT* [1962] 2 All E.R. 563.

[241] *Re White's WT* [1951] 1 All E.R. 528 (benefits for nurses); *Re Dean's WT* [1950] 1 All E.R. 882 (accommodation for relatives).

[242] *Re Resch's WT* [1969] 1 A.C. 514 at 540.

[243] Below, para.15–065.

[244] Charities Act 2011 s.3(1)(e).

[245] e.g. Annual Report 2003/2004, 8.

[246] Charities Act 2011 s.3(2)(c).

[247] Annual Report 1981, paras 68–70. A purpose trust for the establishment of a memorial to an individual may otherwise be valid as a non-charitable purpose trust: below, para.16–010.

[248] Charities Act 2011 s.3(1)(f).

[249] Above, paras 15–015—15–017.

G.   The Advancement of Amateur Sport

15–028   In *Re Nottage*,[250] it was held that a trust to fund a prize for a yacht race was not charitable, because the promotion of sport was not a charitable purpose. However, we saw that the provision of sporting facilities for children and young people has long been accepted as charitable as being for the advancement of education.[251] Sporting and other recreational activities could be charitable under the Recreational Charities Act 1958 (which has been consolidated in the Charities Act 2011).[252] Before the Charities Act 2006, the Commissioners had accepted that the promotion of community participation in healthy sport was a charitable purpose, as opposed to the promotion of a particular sport for its own sake.[253]

The Charities Act 2006 provided that the advancement of amateur sport is a charitable purpose.[254] "Sport" means sports or games which promote health by involving physical or mental skill or exertion.[255] This overlaps to some extent with the advancement of health.[256] We saw that the promotion of chess for young people was upheld as a charitable purpose as being educational.[257] This would now be charitable without any restriction to young people as promoting health by involving mental skill.

H.   The Advancement of Human Rights; Conflict Resolution; Promotion of Religious or Racial Harmony; Equality and Diversity

15–029   This purpose gathers together various related purposes which had been recognised by the Charity Commissioners. Research into human rights is charitable as being for the advancement of education,[258] and the promotion of human rights was subsequently recognised as charitable, along with the promotion of equality and diversity and the promotion of religious harmony.[259]

The Charities Act 2006 incorporated into one heading "the advancement of human rights, conflict resolution or reconciliation or the promotion of religious or racial harmony or equality and diversity".[260]

The promotion of peace had been recognised some 70 years before the Act of 2006,[261] provided the purpose was not political.[262]

---

[250] [1895] 2 Ch. 649.

[251] Above, para.15–018.

[252] Below, para.15–036.

[253] Annual Report 2003/2004, 8.

[254] Now Charities Act 2011 s.3(1)(g). A registered sports club is not charitable; below, para.15–036.

[255] Charities Act 2011 s.3(2)(d).

[256] Charities Act 2011 s.3(1)(d).

[257] *Re Dupree's Deed Trusts* [1945] Ch. 16; above, para.15–018.

[258] *McGovern v Attorney General* [1982] Ch. 321 (the Amnesty International Trust, which was not charitable because other objects were political).

[259] Annual Report 2003/2004, 8.

[260] Now Charities Act 2011 s.3(1)(h).

[261] *Re Harwood* [1936] Ch. 285; below, para.15–072.

[262] Below, para.15–038.

The meaning of this purpose was considered for the first time by the First Tier Tribunal in the case of *The Human Dignity Trust v Charity Commission*[263]:

> The Trust appealed against the Charity Commission refusal to register the Trust as a charity, which had been established to "support people whose human rights are violated by the criminalisation of private, adult, consensual homosexual conduct".[264] It pursued its aims in a number of ways, including strategic constitutional litigation in foreign countries. The Commission had taken the view that the objects were too vague and uncertain, with the result that it could not be concluded that the purposes were exclusively charitable, and also the concern that the trust had a political purpose. The Tribunal allowed the appeal, concluding that "the term 'human rights' in s. 3 (1) (h) of the [2011] Act has no 'particular meaning under the law relating to charities in England and Wales' for the purposes of s. 3 (3) of the Act",[265] and that
>
> > "Parliament must have had the 'living instrument' approach in mind in leaving the term 'human rights' undefined in the Act. It follows that the scope of the rights falling within the description of charitable purposes in the Act may evolve and change from time to time."[266]

Taking this approach, the relevant rights purported to be protected by the Trust's objects—"the right to human dignity, to be free from cruel, inhuman or degrading treatment or punishment, the right to privacy and to personal and social development" all fell within the scope of s.3(1)(h).[267]

I. The Advancement of Environmental Protection or Improvement

Protection of the environment, both within and outside the UK, has been recognised as a charitable purpose for many years, but it is now a separate purpose within the statutory definition.[268] Gifts for the preservation of natural amenities have been held charitable,[269] and the charitable status of the National Trust long established. In 2017, the Commission rejected an application by The Countryside Alliance, which had argued that one of its purposes—"to preserve, protect and promote the heritage and practice of activities relating to wildlife, the countryside, wildlife management together with the management of the natural environment"—fell within this statutory purpose. The Commission held that the

15–030

---

[263] *The Human Dignity Trust v The Charity Commission for England and Wales* CA/2013/0013 at [33]ff.

[264] CA/2013/0013, [8].

[265] CA/2013/0013, [43].

[266] CA/2013/0013, [44].

[267] The exact status of all these rights was not interrogated by the Tribunal.

[268] Charities Act 2011 s.3(1)(i).

[269] *Re Granstown* [1932] 1 Ch. 537; *Re Corelli* [1943] Ch. 332. Though cf. *Baddeley v Sparrow* [2015] UKUT 420 (TCC) at [66]: "The fact that the [Bath] Recreation Ground is an area of green open space in the heart of an historic and culturally important city is not, in our view, a sufficient basis for a conclusion that a trust for its preservation as open space is a charitable public purpose."

purpose lacked certainty and clarity and was too broadly phrased:[270] in particular "management" may not be the same as preservation, protection or improvement of the environment.[271]

J.   Youth, Age, Ill-health, Disability, Financial Hardship

15–031   The Charities Act 2006 included in its list of charitable purposes "the relief of those in need by reason of youth, age, ill-health, disability, financial hardship or other disadvantage".[272] This includes relief given by the provision of accommodation or care to the persons just mentioned.[273] Parts of this broad category originate from the old Preamble to the Charitable Uses Act of 1601, which included as charitable "the relief of aged, impotent and poor people". We have seen that the prevention or relief of poverty is a separate purpose under what is now the Charities Act 2011,[274] but it overlaps with those in need by reason of financial hardship. There is also some overlap between the advancement of health category[275] and the relief of those in need by reason of ill-health or disability.

Charities such as Barnardo's (children) and Age UK are well known. An example of the relief of the disabled is *Re Lewis*,[276] where a gift of £100 each to 10 blind girls and 10 blind boys in Tottenham was charitable. A gift to found a children's home is charitable,[277] and this may be viewed as for the relief of those in need by reason of youth. Examples of relief of the aged abound. In *Re Robinson*,[278] a gift for old people over 60 years of age was upheld. Trusts for the provision of housing for the aged are charitable.[279] While there is no requirement that the aged (or sick or disabled) persons who are being relieved should be poor, the word "relief" implies a need attributable to their condition as aged (or sick or disabled) persons which they may be unable to alleviate from their own resources. It is not synonymous with "benefit". Thus "a gift of money to the aged millionaires of Mayfair would not relieve a need of theirs as aged persons".[280]

---

[270] Charity Commission Decision, The Countryside Alliance – Application for Registration, 23 March 2017, paras 29–38. See further *Annual Report and Accounts 2016–17*, pp.7 and 42–3.

[271] Charity Commission Decision, The Countryside Alliance – Application for Registration, 23 March 2017, para.33.

[272] Now Charities Act 2011 s.3(1)(j). On financial hardship, see *Re AITC Foundation* [2005] W.T.L.R. 1265 (hardship through investment losses).

[273] Charities Act 2011 s.3(2)(e).

[274] Above, para.15–012.

[275] Above, para.15–025.

[276] [1955] Ch. 104.

[277] *Re Sahal's WT* [1958] 1 W.L.R. 1243.

[278] [1951] Ch. 198; *Re Gosling* (1900) W.R. 300 ("old and worn-out clerks" of the bank).

[279] *Joseph Rowntree Memorial Trust Housing Association Ltd v Attorney General* [1983] Ch. 159; *Re Cottam* [1955] 1 W.L.R. 1299.

[280] [1983] Ch. 159 at 171.

K. The Advancement of Animal Welfare

While gifts for specified animals are not charitable,[281] it has long been accepted   **15–032**
that trusts for the welfare of animals generally are charitable, and this was
recognised in the Charities Act 2006.[282] Originally charitable status was limited
to the welfare of animals useful to humans,[283] but this utilitarian approach was
replaced by the principle that kindness to animals tends to "promote feelings of
humanity and morality generally, repress brutality, and thus elevate the human
race".[284] Thus a home for lost dogs,[285] a trust for cats needing care and
attention,[286] and animal hospitals[287] have been held charitable.

However, not all purposes broadly for the benefit of animals are charitable. In
National Anti-Vivisection Society v IRC,[288] the Society, whose purpose was the
total suppression of vivisection, was not charitable, because vivisection was
considered a necessary part of medical research. The court had to weigh
conflicting moral and material benefits, and held that, on balance, the purpose of
the Society was not beneficial to the public, but was in fact detrimental. In *Re
Grove-Grady*,[289] a trust to set up an animal refuge where the animals would be
safe from molestation by humans was held not charitable on the ground that a
sanctuary which deprived humans of all involvement was not for the public
benefit. However, animal sanctuaries generally are charitable, and some purposes
connected with animals may be charitable as being for the advancement of
education,[290] or for environmental preservation.[291]

L. The Promotion of the Efficiency of the Armed Forces, Police and Rescue Services

These purposes were recognised in the miscellaneous fourth head before the   **15–033**
Charities Act 2006. So, for example, the promotion of sport in the Army is
charitable as encouraging efficiency,[292] and a gift to a voluntary fire brigade has
been held charitable.[293] The legislation now provides that "the promotion of the
efficiency of the armed forces of the Crown, or of the efficiency of the police, fire
and rescue services or ambulance services" is a charitable purpose.[294]

While the promotion of the efficiency of the police is a charitable purpose, the
provision of mere recreational facilities will not suffice. In *IRC v Glasgow Police*

---

[281] Below, para.16–011.
[282] Now Charities Act 2011 s.3(1)(k).
[283] *London University v Yarrow* (1857) 1 De G. & J. 72.
[284] *Re Wedgwood* [1915] 1 Ch. 113 at 122. See also *Re Green's WT* [1985] 3 All E.R. 455.
[285] *Re Douglas* (1887) 35 Ch.D. 472.
[286] *Re Moss* [1949] 1 All E.R. 495.
[287] *London University v Yarrow* (1857) 1 De G. & J. 72.
[288] [1948] A.C. 31.
[289] [1929] 1 Ch. 557 (compromised on appeal; *Attorney General v Plowden* [1931] W.N. 89).
[290] *Re Lopes* [1931] 2 Ch. 130.
[291] Above, para.15–030.
[292] *Re Gray* [1925] Ch. 362. See also *Re Good* [1905] 2 Ch. 60 (gift to officers' mess held charitable).
[293] *Re Wokingham Fire Brigade Trusts* [1951] Ch. 373.
[294] Charities Act 2011 s.3(1)(l). Fire and rescue services are defined in s.3(2)(f) as meaning services
provided by fire and rescue authorities under Pt 2 of the Fire and Rescue Services Act 2004.

Athletic Association,[295] the Association, whose object was to promote "all forms of athletic sport and general pastimes" was held not charitable. While the improvement of the efficiency of the police and the encouragement of recruiting were charitable purposes, the provision of mere recreation for the police was not. As the provision of recreation was not merely incidental, the Association's purposes were not exclusively charitable.

M. Other Purposes

15–034   We have seen that s.3 of the Charities Act 2011 sets out a list of specific purposes which are charitable. This is followed by the residual category of other purposes.[296] These are any other purposes in s.3(1)(m):

> (i)   that are not within paragraphs (a) to (l) but are recognised as charitable purposes by virtue of section 5 (recreational and similar trusts, etc.) or under the old law,[297]
>
> (ii)   that may reasonably be regarded as analogous to, or within the spirit of, any purposes falling within any of paragraphs (a) to (l) or sub-paragraph (i) or,
>
> (iii)   that may reasonably be regarded as analogous to, or within the spirit of, any purposes which have been recognised, under the law relating to charities in England and Wales, as falling within sub-paragraph (ii) or this sub-paragraph.

This provision ensures that purposes already recognised as capable of being charitable continue to have that status (subject to the public benefit requirement) even though not expressly mentioned in the statutory list, and also provides the flexibility to allow further development by preserving the "analogy" approach adopted by the courts and the Commissioners before the 2006 Act.

15–035   **i. Purposes Recognised under the Previous Law.**   Most of the purposes which previously fell within the old fourth category of "other purposes beneficial to the community" are now expressly mentioned in the statutory definition. Examples of charitable purposes not expressly mentioned and consequently falling within this residual category include the protection of the country against enemy attack,[298] the promotion of agriculture,[299] and a gift "unto my country England".[300] The publication of the law reports had been found to be charitable in the *Incorporated Council of Law Reporting* case[301] and it was recognised in the *Human Dignity Trust* case that this charitable purpose of "promoting the sound administration of the law" properly includes "the conduct of strategic litigation [to enforce existing rights] before a competent constitutional court".[302]

---

[295] [1953] A.C. 380. See also Annual Report 1984, para.17 (Police Memorial Trust to commemorate officers killed on duty held charitable).

[296] Charities Act 2011 s.3(1)(m).

[297] Below, para.15–036.

[298] *Re Driffill* [1950] Ch. 92.

[299] *IRC v Yorkshire Agricultural Society* [1928] 1 K.B. 611; *Brisbane CC v Attorney General for Queensland* [1979] A.C. 411. The limits of this purpose were considered in the Charity Commission Decision, The Countryside Alliance – Application for Registration, 23 March 2017.

[300] *Re Smith* [1932] 1 Ch. 153.

[301] *Incorporated Council of Law Reporting for England and Wales v Attorney General* [1972] Ch. 73; (1972) 88 L.Q.R. 171 (also held to be for the advancement of education).

[302] *The Human Dignity Trust v The Charity Commission for England and Wales* CA/2013/0013 [64].

Also falling under this heading are the old "locality cases". A principle developed whereby the conferring of benefits which were restricted to a precise locality was regarded as charitable, as a way of saving a gift which would otherwise fail.[303] These cases are treated as anomalous and are not to be extended,[304] but they will be followed in cases that are directly similar.[305]

ii. Recreational Charities. Although gifts for the provision of recreation grounds for the general public have held charitable,[306] recreation as such was not regarded as charitable prior to the Recreational Charities Act 1958. Thus in *Williams' Trustees v IRC*[307] a trust for promoting the interests of the Welsh community in London by various means, most of which were charitable, failed because they involved a social and recreational element. In *IRC v Baddeley*,[308] land was conveyed to a Methodist Mission:

15–036

> "[F]or the promotion of the religious, social and physical well-being of persons resident in…
> West Ham and Leyton… by the provision of facilities for religious services and instruction;
> and for the social and physical training and recreation."

of persons likely to become members of the church. The House of Lords held that these purposes were not exclusively charitable because of the inclusion of purely social purposes.

The Recreational Charities Act 1958 was repealed and replaced, and the relevant provision is now s.5 of the Charities Act 2011,[309] which provides as follows:

(1) It is charitable (and is to be treated as always having been charitable) to provide, or assist in the provision of, facilities for—
    (a)   recreation, or
    (b)   other leisure-time occupation,
    if the facilities are provided in the interests of social welfare.
(2) The requirement that the facilities are provided in the interests of social welfare cannot be satisfied if the basic conditions are not met.
(3) The basic conditions are—
    (a)   that the facilities are provided with the object of improving the conditions of life for the persons for whom the facilities are primarily intended,[310] and
    (b)   that—
        (i)   those persons have need of the facilities because of their youth, age, infirmity or disability, poverty, or social and economic circumstances, or
        (ii)   the facilities are to be available to members of the public at large or to male, or to female, members of the public at large.
(4) Subsection (1) applies in particular to—

---

[303] The leading case is *Goodman v Saltash Corp* (1882) 7 App. Cas. 633.

[304] *Houston v Burns* [1918] A.C. 337.

[305] See *Peggs v Lamb* [1994] Ch. 172; *Re Harding* [2008] Ch. 235.

[306] *Re Hadden* [1932] 1 Ch. 133; *Oldham BC v Attorney General* [1993] Ch. 210.

[307] [1947] A.C. 447. The trust was later validated under the Charitable Trusts (Validation) Act 1954, para.15–064, below; Annual Report 1977, paras 71–80.

[308] [1955] A.C. 572.

[309] Consolidating the amendments in Charities Act 2006. See also Charities Act 2011 s.6: a registered sports club, as defined in s.6(2), is not charitable: for analysis of s.6, see *Eynsham Cricket Club v Revenue and Customs Commissioners* [2017] S.T.I. 1901 at [60]–[71].

[310] See *Cuppage v Lawson* [2011] W.T.L.R. 975 (working men's club).

(a)   the provision of facilities at village halls, community centres and women's institutes, and

(b)   the provision and maintenance of grounds and buildings to be used for purposes of recreation or leisure-time occupation,

and extends to the provision of facilities for those purposes by the organising of any activity.

But this is subject to the requirement that the facilities are provided in the interests of social welfare.

(5)   Nothing in this section is to be treated as derogating from the public benefit requirement.

The 1958 Act would not have affected the outcome of the cases previously discussed,[311] as the facilities in those cases were for the benefit of restricted classes who would not appear to have been in need of them in the way required by the Act.

The provision now found in s.5(3)(a) of the Charities Act 2011 refers to the object of "improving the conditions of life" of the intended users, and the question previously arose as to whether this impliedly confined the operation of the Act to facilities for "the deprived". The House of Lords in *Guild v IRC*[312] held that this was not so: the Act applied where the object was to improve the conditions of life of the community generally.

The social welfare element requires something more than a group of individuals combining together, as a club or society, to benefit themselves. The Charity Commissioners considered that there were two characteristics: an ethical element (meeting needs which ought to be met by society, otherwise the conditions of life of the class concerned would be inadequate), and altruism (seeking to improve the conditions of life of others).[313] Facilities for entertainment alone are unlikely to qualify.

15–037   **iii. Analogous Purposes.**   No list, however long, can capture all the purposes which may be considered charitable as society changes. Before the Charities Act 2006, it had long been established that purposes which were "within the spirit" of, or analogous to, purposes already established as charitable were themselves charitable. The legislation retained this principle, thereby ensuring adequate flexibility to meet future developments.

When a new purpose arises, it is not sufficient to show that it is beneficial. It must be beneficial in the same sense as established charitable purposes. Cases decided before the Act of 2006 illustrate this principle. In *Scottish Burial Reform and Cremation Society v Glasgow City Corp*[314] a non-profit-making cremation society was held charitable by analogy with cases holding burial grounds to be so, although neither facility was mentioned in the old Preamble to the Charitable Uses Act of 1601 which was then the source of charitable purposes.[315] On the

---

[311] *Williams v IRC* [1947] A.C. 447 (Welsh people in London); *IRC v Baddeley* [1955] A.C. 572 (Methodists in West Ham and Leyton): *IRC v Glasgow Police Athletic Association* [1953] A.C. 380.

[312] [1992] 2 A.C. 310 (public sports centre held charitable); H. Norman [1992] Conv. 361; J. Hopkins (1992) 51 C.L.J. 429.

[313] Decisions, Vol.5 (1997), p.7. The provision of internet facilities in a deprived area has been recognised; Annual Report 2003/2004, 27.

[314] [1968] A.C. 138.

[315] J. Jaconelli [2013] Conv. 96 at 102.

other hand, we have seen from the cases decided before the Recreational Charities Act 1958[316] that the provision of recreational facilities, although beneficial to the community, was nevertheless not beneficial in the way which the law regarded as charitable.

The scope of the Preamble was considered by the Court of Appeal in *Helena Partnerships Ltd v Revenue and Customs Commissioners*.[317]

> The company was incorporated and, by its memorandum and articles of association, had defined its objects as the provision of "housing, accommodation, assistance to help house people, associated facilities and amenities and any other object which can be carried out by a social landlord for the benefit of the community".[318] It was not to trade for profit. The company was not registered as a charity, but it was argued that it would have qualified as one during the relevant period.[319] The Court of Appeal held that not all of the purposes were charitable, as "the provision of housing without regard to a relevant charitable need is not in itself charitable".[320] Nor could they be brought within the spirit of the preamble or extended by analogy:
>
>> "It is not sufficient to assert, or even for the relevant constituent document to stipulate, that the activities or operations of the body in question are to be undertaken for the benefit of the community. More is required. The purpose or purposes must be of the right kind, falling within the spirit and intendment of the preamble, directly or by analogy."[321]
>
> If the *Helena* objects were to be charitable, they could only be charitable if justified in respect of the direct benefit provided[322] (as for example under what would now be s.3(1)(j) of the 2011 Act).

5. POLITICAL TRUSTS ARE NOT CHARITABLE[323]

Trusts whose object, direct or indirect, is the support of one political party are clearly not charitable.[324] The borderline between such trusts and trusts where political propaganda was "masquerading as education" has been discussed.[325]

15–038

The general principle is that political trusts are not charitable. This position generally includes purposes which would require a change in the law. This principle is not affected by the Charities Acts 2006 and 2011. In *Re Bushnell*,[326] the testator left money for "the advancement and propagation of the teaching of socialised medicine." The trust was neither an educational charity nor charitable under any other heading. The testator had died in 1941, and at that time

---

[316] Above, para.15–036.

[317] [2012] EWCA Civ 569.

[318] [2012] EWCA Civ 569 at [12].

[319] The case concerned a tax accounting period between July 2002 and March 2004, and so predates the 2006 and 2011 Acts, but the principles are relevant for the extension of charitable purposes under what is now s.3(1)(m) of the 2011 Act.

[320] [2012] EWCA Civ 569 at [107].

[321] [2012] EWCA Civ 569 per Lloyd LJ at [63].

[322] [2012] EWCA Civ 569 per Lloyd LJ at [110].

[323] C. Walton [2014] Conv. 317; D. Jensen (2015/16) 18 C.L. & P.R. 57.

[324] *Bonar Law Memorial Trust v IRC* (1933) 49 T.L.R. 220 (Conservative); *Re Ogden* [1933] Ch. 678 (Liberal); *Re Hopkinson* [1949] 1 All E.R. 346 (Socialist: the whole tenor of the gift was to mask political propaganda as education).

[325] Above, para.15–020.

[326] [1975] 1 W.L.R. 1596.

legislation would have been required to achieve the purpose. The desirability of such legislation was a political matter. It made no difference that a national health service had subsequently been introduced, as the relevant time for judging the matter was the testator's death.

A second reason for the failure of the Anti-Vivisection trust[327] was that the objects of the Society required a change in the law. The majority treated this as necessarily being a political purpose. Lord Normand stressed that this should only be so where, as here, the change in the law was a *predominant object*,[328] while Lord Porter, who dissented, would have excluded only trusts which were purely political,[329] that is to say, where the object is to be attained *only* by a change in the law. Ultimately "it is a question of degree of a sort well known to the courts."[330]

The treatment as political of any trust whose object is to change the law has been criticised,[331] and the Supreme Court of New Zealand has held that a more modern approach is not to regard "charitable" and "political" purposes as mutually exclusive.[332] But whether the proposed change is for the public benefit "is not for the court to judge, and the court has no means of judging."[333] The Legislature decides on changes in the law. The judges' duty is to apply it. The judges should not be put in a position of being asked to hold that a controversial object, often a minority view, is so obviously for the public good that it should be pursued perpetually and tax-free.

The matter arose in *McGovern v Attorney General*,[334] where a non-charitable body, Amnesty International, sought to obtain charitable status for part of its activities by setting up the Amnesty International Trust, to which were transferred those aspects of its work which were thought to be charitable. The objects were: (i) the relief of needy persons who were, or were likely to become, prisoners of conscience, and their relatives; (ii) attempting to secure the release of prisoners of conscience; (iii) the abolition of torture or inhuman or degrading treatment or punishment; and (iv) research into human rights and disseminating the results of the research.[335] These objects were to be carried out in all parts of the world. Purposes (i) and (iv), if standing alone, would have been charitable, but the inclusion of the other objects caused the trust to fail on the ground that it was

---

[327] *National Anti-Vivisection Society v IRC* [1948] A.C. 31; above, para.15–032.

[328] [1948] A.C. 31 at 77–78. See *Re Collier* [1998] 1 N.Z.L.R. 81 (promotion of euthanasia); *Hanchett-Stamford v Attorney General* [2009] Ch. 173 ("Performing and Captive Animals Defence League"); G. Griffiths [2009] Conv. 428.

[329] [1948] A.C. 31 at 56.

[330] *National Anti-Vivisection Society v IRC* [1948] A.C. 31 at 77.

[331] e.g. H. Biehler (2015) 29 T.L.I. 97.

[332] *Re Greenpeace Of New Zealand Inc* [2014] NZSC 105 at [115].

[333] per Lord Simonds [1948] A.C. 31 at 62.

[334] [1982] Ch. 321; T. Watkin [1982] Conv. 387; R. Nobles (1982) 45 M.L.R. 704; F. Weiss (1983) 46 M.L.R. 385; C. Forder [1984] Conv. 263; G. Santow (1999) 52 C.L.P. 255. See also *Re Koeppler's WT* [1986] Ch. 423; where the formation of an informed international public opinion and the promotion of greater co-operation in Europe and the West were not regarded as charitable, although the gift was upheld as being for the furtherance of the work of a charitable educational project.

[335] The promotion of human rights is charitable; above, para.15–029. See, however, *R. v Radio Authority Ex p. Bull* [1998] Q.B. 294 (promotion of awareness of human rights with object of bringing pressure to bear on a government is political); J. Stevens and D. Feldman [1997] P.L. 615.

political.[336] A trust could not be charitable if its direct and main object was to secure a change in the law of the UK or of foreign countries, for example by repealing legislation authorising capital or corporal punishment. The court could not judge whether this would be for the public benefit, locally or internationally. Nor could a trust be charitable if a direct and principal purpose was to procure the reversal of government policy or of governmental decisions at home or abroad.[337] Object (ii) was not simply for the "relief or redemption of prisoners or captives",[338] but involved putting pressure on foreign governments and authorities. To ascribe charitable status to such a trust could prejudice the relations of this country with the foreign country concerned. This public policy consideration could not be ignored. On the other hand, in the *Human Dignity Trust* case, the Tribunal distinguished *McGovern*: the HDT pursued strategic litigation to promote human rights "by establishing whether particular laws are valid, through a process of constitutional interpretation".[339] Unlike in *McGovern*, the HDT

> "is not concerned with procuring the reversal of lawful government policies and decisions. It is concerned only with reversing decisions and policies which are unlawful by virtue of binding, justiciable, superior constitutional law or applicable human rights law".[340]

The Tribunal was careful to stress, however, that its decision turned on its own facts, given the particular type of litigation undertaken by the charity.[341]

Trusts for the promotion of peace have run into difficulties.[342] While the desirability of peace as an objective is not a matter of political controversy, and indeed the advancement of conflict resolution or reconciliation is a charitable purpose,[343] the promotion of peace will be political if designed to challenge government policies. So in *Southwood v Attorney General*,[344] the "advancement of the education of the public in the subject of militarism and disarmament" was not charitable as the dominant purpose was to promote pacifism and to challenge the policies of Western governments. Likewise, in *Re Collier*,[345] a trust to promote world peace was political and indeed unlawful where the testator was encouraging soldiers to "down arms". More recently, in *Bishop (on behalf of Crocels Community Media Group) v The Charity Commission for England and*

15–039

---

[336] It was not saved by a proviso restricting it to charitable purposes.

[337] The decision was distinguished in *Re Koeppler's WT* [1986] Ch. 423, where an educational project involving conferences with a "political flavour" was held charitable. The project was not concerned with party politics nor did it seek to change laws or government policies.

[338] Preamble to the Charitable Uses Act 1601.

[339] *The Human Dignity Trust v The Charity Commission for England and Wales* CA/2013/0013 at [95].

[340] CA/2013/0013 at [89].

[341] CA/2013/0013 at [113].

[342] "Even if an end in itself may be seen as of general public benefit (such as the promotion of peace) the means of promotion may entail a particular point of view which cannot be said to be of public benefit" per Elias CJ, McGrath and Glazebrook JJ in *Re Greenpeace Of New Zealand Inc* [2014] NZSC 105 at [116].

[343] Charities Act 2011 s.3(1)(h).

[344] [2000] W.T.L.R. 1199; J. Garton (2000) 14 T.L.I. 233.

[345] [1998] 1 N.Z.L.R. 81.

Wales,[346] Rose J considered the specified purposes which included "advancing the understanding and promoting the cause of peace, [innovating] for the abolition or reduction of standing armies" and held them not to be exclusively charitable: "even though Crocels may be right in assuming that all Governments want to reduce the cost of war in financial and human terms, the achievement of that goal depends on persuading Governments to take different decisions giving this priority".[347]

The question arises whether an existing charity may become involved in pursuing "causes" relating to the work with which it is concerned. It was suggested in *McGovern v Attorney General*[348] that if the objects had been charitable, it would not have mattered that the trustees had incidental powers to employ political means to further these objects. The Charity Commission publishes guidance to charity trustees, including the following points (with the emphasis on what charities can properly do)[349]:

(i)   While political activity must not be the sole activity, charities may undertake it provided it is done only in the context of supporting the delivery of their charitable purposes.

(ii)   Campaigning, advocacy and political activity are all legitimate and valuable activities for charities.

(iii)   While charities cannot exist for a political purpose (any purpose directed at furthering the interests of a political party, or securing or opposing a change in the law, policy or decisions in this country or abroad), charities can campaign for a change in the law, policy or decisions if this would support their charitable purpose.

(iv)   Although charities may not support a political party, they may support specific policies advocated by political parties if the policy would help to achieve their charitable purpose.

(v)   Charities may respond to legislative initiatives, support or oppose Bills during their passage through Parliament, lobby Members of Parliament, and so forth.

(vi)   When considering campaigning, charities must weigh up the possible benefits against the costs and risks in deciding whether it is likely to be effective for the achievement of their charitable purposes. They may use emotive or controversial material if it is lawful and justifiable.

(vii)   The above principles apply equally to campaigning and political activity overseas.

Charities may not thus act in a politically partisan way under charity law, but there may also be restrictions under electoral law. The existing Charity Commission guidance has been supplemented by further guidance from the

---

[346] UT/2016/0149.

[347] UT/2016/0149 at [14].

[348] [1982] Ch. 321.

[349] *Guidance on Campaigning and Political Activity by Charities* (CC9, March 2008 version); the Charity Commission confirmed that this guidance remains current on 19 November 2014 ("Commission clarification on campaigning guidance" *https://www.gov.uk/government/news/ commission-clarification-on-campaigning-guidance* [accessed 4 July 2018]).

Electoral Commission,[350] following the passage of the Transparency of Lobbying, Non Party Campaigning and Trade Union Administration Act 2014. This legislation imposes rules on "non-party campaigners" that may campaign in the run up to elections: there are restrictions on spending in relation to "regulated campaign activity".

6.   PUBLIC BENEFIT[351]

A.   Preliminary Points

"Public benefit runs through every aspect of the legal definition of charity".[352] A **15–040** gift can only be charitable if it is for the public benefit. There are two aspects to the public benefit requirement. First, the purpose in question must be for the public benefit; secondly, the benefit must be available to the public at large or a sufficient section of the community. On the first point, we saw that the Charities Act 2006 removed the presumption that the relief of poverty and the advancement of religion and education were for the public benefit, so that it must be demonstrated in all cases.[353] On the second point, it was established before the Act of 2006 that the requirement of benefit to a sufficient section of the community varied according to the charitable purpose in question.

The legislation requires the Charity Commission to issue guidance on the operation of the public benefit requirement, in order to promote awareness and understanding of it.[354] The Commission's first Guidance, under the 2006 Act, was published in January 2008, along with the Commission's legal analysis of existing case law.[355] However, it has since been replaced by a trio of guides,[356] following the Upper Tribunal's decision in the *Independent Schools Council* case.[357]

Supplementary guidance will be published from time to time, relating to particular types of charity. The guidance does not create new public benefit law, nor does it create a new legal definition of public benefit. It sets out a framework of factors to consider when assessing public benefit in the light of modern conditions,[358] based on the principles contained in the existing case law. It applies

---

[350] Electoral Commission, *Charities and Campaigning* (2014) (the guidance was produced in collaboration with the Charity Commission).

[351] The leading texts are J. Garton, *Public Benefit in Charity Law* (Oxford: Oxford University Press, 2013) and M. Synge, *The 'New' Public Benefit Requirement: Making Sense of Charity Law?* (Oxford: Hart Publishing, 2015). See also J. Jaconelli [2013] Conv. 96.

[352] J. Garton, *Public Benefit in Charity Law* (2013) vii.

[353] Charities Act 2011 s.4(2); above, para.15–009.

[354] Charities Act 2011 s.17.

[355] *Analysis of the Law underpinning Charities and Public Benefit*. Supplementary guidance on poverty, religion, education and fee-charging was published in December 2008. The guidance has been replaced by *Public Benefit: Analysis of the law relating to public benefit* (September 2013).

[356] *Public benefit: the public benefit requirement* (PB1) (September 2013); Further guides are *Public benefit: running a charity* (PB2); and *Public benefit: reporting* (PB3).

[357] *Independent Schools Council v Charity Commission* [2012] Ch. 214. Further directions were given at [2011] UKUT B27 (TCC).

[358] "The concept of 'public benefit' is not... fixed; as society changes, so too perceptions of what is for the public benefit can change in the future just as much as they have changed in the past. The

to existing registered charities (whose trustees must take steps to address the position if the principles are not satisfied[359]), and to applications to register. The decisions of the Commission may be challenged by an appeal to the First-tier and the Upper Tribunal and then to court.[360]

Charity trustees are under a duty to carry out their charity's aims for the public benefit, to have regard to the Commission's guidance, and to report on their charity's public benefit in their Annual Reports.[361]

The 2013 guidance sets out two aspects of Public Benefit, which each contains two legal requirements, as follows[362]:

"The 'benefit aspect'"

"The 'benefit aspect' of public benefit is about whether the purpose is beneficial."

"Legal requirement: to satisfy the 'benefit aspect' of public benefit:
- a purpose must be beneficial[363]
- any detriment or harm that results from the purpose must not outweigh the benefit[364]"

"The 'public aspect'"

"The 'public aspect' of public benefit is about whom the purpose benefits."

"Legal requirement: to satisfy the 'public aspect' of public benefit the purpose must:
- benefit the public in general, or a sufficient section of the public
- not give rise to more than incidental personal benefit."

B. The Benefit Aspect

15–041   **i. Purpose must be Identifiably Beneficial.**   Different charitable aims involve different kinds of benefit. It must be possible to recognise and identify the benefit, even though it may not be quantifiable.[365] For example, the benefit of viewing works of art can be identified although it cannot be measured.[366] In some cases, the benefit will be obvious, for example aiding the victims of a hurricane, while in other cases evidence may be needed, for example as to the merits of a collection of paintings.[367] Even where the benefit to the public of an organisation's purpose is clear, for example, conducting cancer research, it would

---

incremental development of the concept of 'public benefit' can continue." *Attorney General v The Charity Commission for England and Wales* FTC/84/2011 at [77].

[359] They cannot simply "opt out" of charitable status. The assets of an organisation which ceases to be charitable must be applied under the cy-près doctrine; below, para.15–078.

[360] See Charities Act 2011 Part 17. The Law Commission has recommended the review of rights of challenge to the Tribunal: *Technical Issues in Charity Law* (2017) para.9.40.

[361] Below, para.15–092.

[362] *Public benefit: the public benefit requirement* (PB1) (September 2013) 5.

[363] PB1, Part 3.

[364] PB1, Part 4.

[365] PB1, Part 3.

[366] The Guidance offers further examples of the architectural merit of a building under the advancement of heritage, the healing benefits of a therapy under advancement of health and the educational merit of a training programme under the advancement of education: PB1, Part 3.

[367] *Re Pinion* [1965] Ch. 85; above, para.15–017.

have to show that its research was properly conducted. The Commission has added that the view that a purpose is beneficial should not be based only on personal views.[368]

If the benefit is not capable of proof, it will not be recognised. For example, we have seen that the courts have held that they cannot assess the benefit of a "political" purpose.[369] Nor can they assess the value of intercessory prayers of a religious order:

> In *Gilmour v Coats*,[370] a gift of £500 was made to a Carmelite Priory "if the purposes of [the Priory] are charitable". The Priory consisted of a community of about 20 cloistered nuns, who devoted their lives to prayer, contemplation and self-sanctification, and engaged in no external work.
>
> The House of Lords held that the purposes were not charitable because they lacked public benefit. This could not be found in the benefits conferred upon the public by the prayers of the nuns according to Roman Catholic doctrine, because such benefit was "manifestly not susceptible of proof"[371] in a court of law. Nor could it be found in the edification of the public by the example of the spiritual life followed by the nuns, as that was too vague and intangible; nor by the availability of the religious life being open to all women of the Roman Catholic faith.

This decision cast doubt on the charitable status of gifts for the saying of masses (although such gifts had been held charitable in *Re Caus*).[372] The charitable nature of such a gift has since been upheld in *Re Hetherington (Deceased)*,[373] where the testatrix left £2,000 to the Roman Catholic Bishop of Westminster[374] for masses for the souls of her husband, parents, sisters and herself. One reason was that the celebration of a religious rite in public conferred a sufficient public benefit in the edifying effect it had on those attending. Celebration of the rite in private would not suffice because the benefit conferred by prayer was incapable of proof and the edification of the private class attending was not a public benefit.[375] There was no express term that the masses should be said in public, but in practice they would be and the gift was so construed.

ii. Detriment must not Outweigh Benefit. The public benefit requirement **15–042** will not be satisfied where the achievement of the aim, although of some benefit, is outweighed by significant harmful effects. We saw that in *National*

---

[368] PB1, Part 3. In the Charity Commission's Decision on *The Temple of the Jedi Order – Application for Registration*, 16 December 2016, above para.15–023, the Commission noted (at [46]) that "although [the Order] is web-based and accessible to the public, it is not evident what positive beneficial impact [the Order] has on society in general". The Commission did however not find any issues of harm or detriment from the Order purposes (at [55]); below, para.15–042.

[369] *McGovern v Attorney General* [1982] Ch. 321; above, para.15–038.

[370] [1949] A.C. 426. Sufficient public benefit was found in *Holmes v Attorney General, The Times*, 12 February 1981 (Exclusive Brethren). The Charity Commission published guidance on public benefit and the advancement of religion in December 2008.

[371] [1949] A.C. 426 at 446. See C. Rickett [1990] Conv. 35. The problem can be overcome if the convent does external work. See Decisions, Vol.3 (1995), 11 (Society of the Precious Blood).

[372] [1934] Ch. 162.

[373] [1990] Ch. 1. The second reason for upholding the gift was that it provided stipends for the priests saying the masses, and thereby assisted in the endowment of the priesthood.

[374] It was held that the testatrix plainly meant the Archbishop of Westminster [1990] Ch. 1 at 13.

[375] *Gilmour v Coats* [1949] A.C. 426; *Hoare v Hoare* (1886) 56 L.T. 147. Trusts for the saying of private masses may be valid as anomalous non-charitable purpose trusts; below, para.16–012.

Anti-Vivisection Society v Inland Revenue Commissioners[376] the moral benefit to mankind in suppressing vivisection was outweighed by the material benefit of the medical research it assisted, and so the Society was not charitable. An inconsequential detriment would not tilt the balance. For example, the benefits of providing motorised transport for the disabled would not be outweighed by the possible harm to the environment. The Commission has stressed that "where the benefit of a purpose is obvious and commonly recognised, there is an even greater need for evidence of detriment or harm to be clear and substantial, if it is to outweigh that benefit."[377]

C.   The Public Aspect

15–043   **i.   Public in General or Sufficient Section of the Public.**   "For a purpose to be charitable it must benefit either: the public in general or a sufficient section of the public".[378] The "public in general" means that all of the public can benefit from the purpose, and is not limited by any particular characteristic. Unless specified to be limited, the starting point is that the purpose will benefit the public in general. The example given by the Charity Commission is the conservation of an endangered species[379]; the advancement of citizenship under s.1(3)(e) may be another.

As we shall see below, various legal requirements apply, but generally a purpose will be deemed to benefit a sufficient section of the public, such as by locality, charitable need or a "protected characteristic".[380] So long as the numbers are not negligible, it does not matter that the class is small, so long as it is a "public class". These principles are explained in more detail in the following sections.

ii.   Sufficient Section of the Public.

15–044   *(a)   Defining who can benefit on the basis of where people live*   Where the benefit is not to the public generally, any restrictions must be legitimate, proportionate, rational and justifiable. Where the restrictions are reasonable, it is accepted that society as a whole benefits indirectly by the help given to the sections of the community who benefit directly. There is no difficulty in providing benefits in a particular geographical area (at home or overseas), so long as there are no inappropriate restrictions on the persons in the area who may benefit. For example, it could be charitable to provide public gardens in a particular area, but not if they were restricted to use by persons of a particular faith. As Lord Simonds said in *IRC v Baddeley*[381]:

---

[376] [1948] A.C. 31; above, para.15–032.
[377] PB1, Part 4.
[378] PB1, Part 5.
[379] PB1, Part 5.
[380] PB1, Part 5, p.11.
[381] [1955] A.C. 572 at 592.

"A bridge which is available for all the public may undoubtedly be a charity and it is indifferent how many people use it. But confine its use to a selected number of persons, however numerous and important, it is then clearly not a charity. It is not of general public utility: for it does not serve the public purpose which its nature qualifies it to serve."

It is necessary to distinguish between:

"[R]elief extended to the whole community yet by its very nature advantageous only to the few and a form of relief accorded to a selected few out of a larger number equally willing to take advantage of it... Who has ever heard of a bridge to be crossed only by impecunious Methodists?"[382]

The Charity Commission also notes that the geographical restriction should not be so narrow as to render the section of the public insufficient (as in the case of a few named houses).[383]

(b) Defining who can benefit by reference to people of communities with a particular charitable need.   In other cases, the restrictions may lie in beneficiaries being confined to those who have a need, such as ill-health, which it is charitable to relieve. It may be that the class in need is a sufficient section of the public but, in any event, it is for the benefit of society as a whole that assistance is given to those in need of it. **15–045**

(c) Defining who can benefit by reference to protected characteristics.   Trusts for the advancement of religion provide further examples. We saw that charity law does not distinguish between one religion and another.[384] Advancing a particular religion provides sufficient public benefit even though adherents may be a small minority. However, if their number is negligible, the public benefit test is unlikely to be satisfied.[385] Subject to that point, a gift to a church will be charitable even though the congregation is small. A trust is charitable if it makes a religious activity available to the public if they wish to take advantage of it. Another aspect is that it may be a sufficient benefit to society to have amongst it persons who have enjoyed the benefit of religious experience. *Gilmour v Coats*,[386] where a closed order was not charitable, may be contrasted with *Neville Estates Ltd v Madden*,[387] where a trust for the advancement of religion among the members of a particular synagogue was held charitable because the court was: **15–046**

"[E]ntitled to assume that some benefit accrues to the public from the attendance at places of worship of persons who live in this world and mix with their fellow citizens."[388]

Section 193 of the Equality Act 2010 permits some restrictions on benefits in the case of protected characteristics with regard to charities as where funds are

---

[382] [1955] A.C. 572 at 592.
[383] PB1, Part 5.
[384] Above, para.15–023.
[385] See *Re Watson* [1973] 1 W.L.R. 1472; above, para.15–023.
[386] Above, para.15–041.
[387] [1962] Ch. 832.
[388] [1962] Ch. 832 at 853.

devoted to those of a particular faith, sexuality, gender, race and other characteristics.[389] The test under s.193 of the Act permits for provision of the benefits to be restricted if it is:

(a)   a proportionate means of achieving a legitimate aim, or
(b)   for the purpose of preventing or compensating for a disadvantage linked to the protected characteristic.[390]

15–047   *(d) Defining who can benefit by reference to a person's skin colour.*   The exception for charities to restrict the provision of benefits does not apply to restrictions on the basis of a person's skin colour. In such a case, s.193(4) provides:

If a charitable instrument enables the provision of benefits to persons of a class defined by reference to colour, it has effect for all purposes as if it enabled the provision of such benefits—
(a)   to persons of the class which results if the reference to colour is ignored, or
(b)   if the original class is defined by reference only to colour, to persons generally.

15–048   *(e) Defining who can benefit by reference to a person's occupation or profession.*   Where benefits are confined to members of an organisation, restrictions on membership must be reasonable and justifiable. However, in some cases, such as learned societies, the public at large benefits from the work of the society.[391] The Charity Commission gives the further example of a charity to "relieve the sickness and disability of serving, former and retired teachers and their [dependants]".[392]

15–049   *(f) Defining who can benefit by reference to a person's family relationship, contractual relationship (e.g. employment by an employer) or membership of an unincorporated association.*   The general rule is that the beneficiaries must not be defined by a personal connection (called a "personal nexus" in some of the cases), such as a family relationship or being employees of a common employer.[393] There is an exception relating to charities for the relief of poverty, where gifts to the "poor relations" of X or the "poor employees" of X have been upheld.

It is necessary, however, to distinguish between a gift to a class or group of poor persons, and a gift to specified poor individuals. The former will be charitable, even if the group is small, and personally connected with the donor; gifts to poor relations have been upheld since the middle of the 18th century,[394]

---

[389]   Above, paras 14–003—14–005. See also recreational charities; above, para.15–036.
[390]   Equality Act 2010 s.193(1).
[391]   See *Re South Place Ethical Society* [1980] 1 W.L.R. 1565; *Re Koeppler's WT* [1986] Ch. 423.
[392]   PB1, Part 5 (the Commission guidance refers to "dependents").
[393]   PB1, Part 5 (the "common employer" provision refers to a single organisation or company and therefore is distinct from one's occupation or profession as considered above).
[394]   *Isaac v Defriez* (1754) Amb. 595. They are discussed at length in *Re Compton* [1945] Ch. 123, and in *Re Scarisbrick* [1951] Ch. 622. See also *Dingle v Turner* [1972] A.C. 601.

although the Charity Commission at once stage expressed doubts as to their survival.[395] Jenkins LJ explained them as follows:

> "I think that the true question in each case has really been whether the gift was for the relief of poverty amongst a class of persons… or was merely a gift to individuals, albeit with relief of poverty amongst those individuals as the motive of the gift… ."[396]

Thus, a gift to such of the testator's relatives as shall be poor or "in special need"[397] or "in needy circumstances"[398] is charitable. Similarly a gift to "poor and needy" members of a class of six named relatives of the testator and their issue, there being 26 members at the testator's death and a likelihood of a substantial increase in future.[399] It does not matter that the distribution of capital can be made so as to exhaust the principal.[400] This relaxation in favour of poverty trusts applies also in connection with trusts for the relief of poverty among members of a friendly society,[401] or a professional association,[402] or employees of a company.

In *Dingle v Turner*,[403] a testator created a trust for paying pensions to:

> "[P]oor employees of E. Dingle and Co Ltd who are of the age of 60 years at least or who being of the age of 45 years at least are incapacitated from earning their living by reason of some physical or mental infirmity."

At the date of the testator's death, the company employed over 600 persons, and there was a substantial number of ex-employees. The House of Lords upheld the gift as a charitable trust. The poor relations cases had been recognised for 200 years, and, even if anomalous, should not be overruled. It would be illogical to draw a distinction between poor relations, and poor employees or poor members. All forms of trusts for the relief of poverty should be treated the same, and there was no need to introduce into the poverty cases the stricter requirements of public benefit applicable to other forms of charitable trusts. Lord Cross suggested that one reason for the different treatment of poverty trusts—a practical justification but not the historical explanation—is that there is for a settlor a "temptation to enlist the assistance of the law of charity in private endeavours"[404] in order to gain the tax benefits, though the danger is not so great in the field of relief of

---

[395] *Analysis of the Law underpinning the Prevention or Relief of Poverty for the Public Benefit*, December 2008, paras 48, 58, 59; cf. A. Rahmatian [2009] Conv. 12. See further below in this paragraph, Attorney General's reference, FTC/84/2011.

[396] In *Re Scarisbrick* [1951] Ch. 622 at 655; see also at 650–651; *Re Cohen* [1973] 1 W.L.R. 415 at 426; *Dingle v Turner* [1972] A.C. 601 at 617.

[397] *Re Cohen* [1973] 1 W.L.R. 415.

[398] *Re Scarisbrick* [1951] Ch. 622.

[399] *Re Segelman* [1996] Ch. 171; E. Histed [1996] Conv. 379. The inclusion of named persons as objects of charity may be an extension of the rule.

[400] *Re Scarisbrick* [1951] Ch. 622; *Dingle v Turner* [1972] A.C. 601.

[401] *Re Buck* [1896] 2 Ch. 727.

[402] *Spiller v Maude* (1886) 32 Ch.D. 158n. (aged and decayed actors).

[403] [1972] A.C. 601; *Re Gosling* (1900) 48 W.R. 300 (old and worn-out clerks in a banking firm); *Gibson v South American Stores (Gath & Chaves) Ltd* [1950] Ch. 177 ("necessitous and deserving employees, ex-employees and their dependants").

[404] *Dingle v Turner* [1972] A.C. 601 at 625.

poverty. Three Law Lords[405] doubted whether the fiscal considerations should be given any relevance in deciding whether a gift was charitable. There seems little doubt, however, that they often have been given such relevance.[406]

The Attorney General, at the request of the Charity Commission, made a reference for a Tribunal determination as to the continuing validity of the poor relations cases. The Tribunal strongly reaffirmed that trusts for the relief or prevention of poverty satisfy the public benefit requirement even where limited by a personal nexus.[407]

The Charity Commission has since reiterated that the exception remains valid for charities for the prevention or relief of poverty in its revised guidance on public benefit.[408]

15–050   A trust which is not for the relief of poverty cannot be charitable if the beneficiaries are selected on the basis of a personal connection, either with the donor or between themselves. Thus, a trust for the education of named persons or for descendants of named persons[409] is not charitable. But a trust for the education of children of members of a particular profession[410] is charitable, as are trusts for specified schools and colleges, and even "closed" scholarships from a specified school to a college at Oxford or Cambridge[411]; unless, of course, the number of possible beneficiaries was derisory.

In *Oppenheim v Tobacco Securities Trust Co*,[412] income was to be applied in "providing for… the education of children of employees or former employees of the British-American Tobacco Company Ltd… or any of its subsidiary or allied companies" and there was power also to apply capital. The number of employees of the company and the subsidiary and allied companies exceeded 100,000. The House of Lords held that there was a personal connection between the members of the class of beneficiaries and they did not constitute a section of the public. The trust failed.

In the leading majority speech, Lord Simonds said that to constitute a section of the community for these purposes, the:

---

[405] Lords Dilhorne, McDermott and Hodson.

[406] Above, para.15–001.

[407] To the First-tier Tribunal (Charity), but transferred to the Upper Tribunal (Tax and Chancery Chamber) FTC/84/2011: the case considered a variety of charities including the Professional Footballers' Association Benevolent Fund and Stock Exchange Benevolent Fund. Warren J noted at [17] the "evident concern that the making of the Reference caused to the 1500 or so benevolent charities which the Charity Commission estimated were affected by it", thus emphasising the significance of the exception. The Tribunal invoked Evershed MR in *Re Scarisbrick* [1951] Ch. 622 at 640: "If there must be an anomaly, let it be itself logical and coherent". See also H. Biehler (2014) 28 T.L.I. 145 (also considering the situation under the Irish Charities Act 2009).

[408] *Public benefit: the public benefit requirement* (PB1) (September 2013), Annex A.

[409] *Re Compton* [1945] Ch. 123. "A trust established by a father for the education of his sons is not a charity"; per Lord Simonds in *Oppenheim v Tobacco Securities Trust Ltd* [1951] A.C. 297 at 306.

[410] *Hall v Derby Sanitary Authority* (1885) 16 Q.B.D. 163.

[411] It is difficult to see how some of these trusts satisfy the *Oppenheim* rule; see Lord McDermott in *Oppenheim* [1951] A.C. 297 at 318. See also the anomalous "founder's kin" cases; *Re Christ's Hospital* (1889) 15 App. Cas. 172, which are now doubtful.

[412] [1951] A.C. 297.

"[P]ossible (I emphasize the word 'possible') beneficiaries must be not numerically negligible, and, secondly, that the quality which distinguishes them from members of the community... must be a quality which does not depend on their relationship to a particular individual... A group of persons may be numerous but, if the nexus between them is their personal relationship to a single propositus or to several propositi, they are neither the community nor a section of the community for charitable purposes."[413]

Lord McDermott, dissenting, pointed out the difficulties which arise in trying to lay down a positive rule in such a situation[414]:

"[I]f the bond between those employed by a particular railway is purely personal, why should the bond between those who are employed as railwaymen be so essentially different? Is a distinction to be drawn in this respect between those who are employed in a particular industry before it is nationalised and those who are employed therein after that process has been completed and one employer has taken the place of many?... Is the relationship between those in the service of the Crown to be distinguished from that obtaining between those in the service of some other employer? Or, if not, are the children of, say, soldiers or civil servants to be regarded as not constituting a sufficient section of the public to make a trust for their education charitable?"[415]

The question, he thought, should be one of degree, depending upon the facts of each particular case. All five Law Lords sitting in *Dingle v Turner*[416] supported this view. This does not necessarily mean that *Oppenheim* would be decided differently. Taking all factors into account, these educational trusts for employees are attempts to use charity's fiscal privileges for the benefit of the company by providing a tax-free fringe benefit for the employees.[417] Such trusts should fail, not on the ground that the employees, however numerous, can never constitute a class of the public, but because the *purpose* of the trust, being a company purpose, is not charitable.[418] A trust for the advancement of religion among employees might be different[419]; as might an "entirely altruistic educational trust... if the size of the company is sufficiently large."[420] It is obvious that it is easier to criticise the personal connection test than it is to improve upon it; and "it may well be that Lord Cross's half-way house creates more problems than it solves."[421]

A related question arises as to whether a donor can effectively obtain benefits for a group of private individuals by means of a charitable trust. He cannot do so by setting up a charitable trust in favour of the public and relying on the trustees to make grants in favour of a narrow group.   **15–051**

---

[413] [1951] A.C. 297 at 306. On this numerical negligibility test, see M. Synge (2016) 132 L.Q.R. 303.

[414] See also Cross J in *Re Mead's Trust Deed* [1961] 1 W.L.R. 1244 at 1249; and Lord Denning MR in *IRC v Educational Grants Association Ltd* [1967] Ch. 993 at 1009; "There is no logic in it."

[415] [1951] A.C. 297 at 317–318.

[416] [1972] A.C. 601.

[417] "It is an admirable thing that the children of employees should have a higher education, but I do not see why that should be at the expense of the taxpayer", per Harman LJ in *IRC v Educational Grants Association Ltd* [1967] Ch. 993, at 1013.

[418] *Dingle v Turner* [1972] A.C. 601.

[419] G. Jones (1974) 33 C.L.J. 63 at 66.

[420] Annual Report 1971 para.21.

[421] G. Jones (1974) 33 C.L.J. 63.

It is impossible to say what percentage of a trust for charity could properly be spent in favour of a private group.[422] In *Re Koettgen's Will Trusts*,[423] there was a trust for the promotion of commercial education among members of the public unable to acquire it at their own expense; and a direction that preference be given to the families of employees of a named company in respect of a maximum of 75% of the income. This was charitable. Lord Radcliffe in *Caffoor v Income Tax Commissioner, Colombo*,[424] thought that *Re Koettgen* "edged very near to being inconsistent with" *Oppenheim*.[425] If a preference in favour of a private group is desired, it is essential to make it subsidiary to the trust in favour of the public; and the 75% which succeeded in *Koettgen* should be regarded as the maximum.[426] If, however, there is an absolute right in favour of a private group, and not merely a preference, then the trust cannot be charitable. It is a matter of construction into which category the gift falls.[427] In *Re Duffy*,[428] Roth J held that a gift for the benefit of residents at a particular old people's care home, which had 33 single rooms (and therefore never more than 33 residents) could not be regarded as for the benefit of sufficient section of the community. The gift was not therefore charitable.[429]

15–052 *(g) Fee-Charging by Charities After The Independent Schools Council Case.* It is not unusual for charities to charge for their services, whether they be museums, independent schools, private hospitals, universities, sports centres or other organisations.[430] An organisation cannot be charitable if operated for private profit. Assuming that this is not the case, if the practical effect of charging is that those who cannot afford to pay are excluded, the public benefit test will not be satisfied.

The organisation may be able to establish sufficient public benefit if it makes provision for exemption from charges or if it offers other benefits to those who cannot afford them. It may also be argued that an organisation (such as a fee-paying school or private hospital) which provides services which the State would otherwise have to provide benefits the public at large by relieving public funds. It appears that this remoter benefit does not suffice if it is the only benefit available to those who cannot afford the fees. In *Re Resch's WT*,[431] a case involving a private hospital for paying patients which was held to be charitable, nobody was expressly excluded, but in practice many could not afford to pay. The

---

[422] The current legislation is Income Tax Act 2007 s.527 and Corporation Tax Act 2010 s.481 which permit exemption for a charitable body *so far as the income is applied to charitable purposes only*: above, para.15–006. In *IRC v Educational Grants Association Ltd* [1967] Ch. 993, non-charitable payments were ultra vires. If the objects permit such payments, the body is not charitable (subject to *Re Koettgen*) and there will be no tax exemption.

[423] [1954] Ch. 252.

[424] [1961] A.C. 584.

[425] [1961] A.C. 584 at 604.

[426] See Annual Report 1978, paras 86–89.

[427] *Re Martin, The Times*, 17 November 1977.

[428] [2013] EWHC 2395 (Ch); M. Synge (2016) 132 L.Q.R. 303.

[429] [2013] EWHC 2395 (Ch) at [16].

[430] See *Joseph Rowntree Memorial Trust Housing Association Ltd v Attorney General* [1983] Ch. 159; above, para.15–013 (housing for the elderly).

[431] *Re Resch's WT* [1969] 1 A.C. 514 (Privy Council).

decision appears to hold that both direct and indirect benefits (relief of pressure on beds and staff at the public general hospital) may be taken into account, but that the indirect benefits alone would not be sufficient, as in practice this would make the public benefit requirement ineffectual.[432]

It has long been the case that fee-paying independent schools have offered free or subsidised places, or have made their facilities available to state school pupils. It was mentioned above that the Charity Commission issued revised Public Benefit Guidance in 2013. That revision was necessary following the decision of the Upper Tribunal on the Commission's approach to public benefit in the context of independent schools in *Independent Schools Council v Charity Commission*.[433]

> The Independent Schools Council, which is a council representing over 1,000 independent schools of which the majority were charities, sought a judicial review in order to quash parts of the Charity Commission's public benefit guidance in relation to independent charitable schools. The Attorney General also made a reference in relation to the guidance on fee-charging charities. The Upper Tribunal held that it was up to the charity trustees of the school to assess how their obligations might best be fulfilled in the context of their school's own circumstances and that there were no objective benchmarks applicable to every case. However, the ruling has otherwise done little to clarify the law in this area. The Tribunal distinguished between two senses of public benefit:
> "The first aspect is that the nature of the purpose itself must be such as to be a benefit to the community: this is public benefit in the first sense. In that sense, the advancement of education, referred to in the Preamble under the guise of "schools of learning, free schools and scholars in universities", has the necessary element of benefit to the community... The second aspect is that those who may benefit from the carrying out of the purpose must be sufficiently numerous, and identified in such manner as, to constitute what is described in the authorities as "a section of the public": this is public benefit in the second sense."[434]
> When considering public benefit in the first sense, the starting point (though not a presumption) was that education in schools was capable of being for the public benefit in the first sense, and any alleged "disbenefits" were political matters. For public benefit in the second sense, the Tribunal found that mere token provision for the poor would not suffice, and that a school which only admitted those whose families could afford fees would not be charitable. Crucially, the Tribunal held that the focus should be on the establishment of the institution for charitable purposes only (under then s.1 of the 2006 Act). That meant that the inquiry was not to focus on the activities by which the school went about achieving its purpose. Both direct and indirect benefits could be taken into account, and these could be assessed broadly.[435]

As a result, the Tribunal required some corrections to the Charity Commission guidance, which it held had focused unduly on a reasonable provision for the poor. The decision, in the words of one commentator, appeared "to empower trustees at the expense of the Charity Commission".[436]

As a result of the decision in the *Independent Schools Council* case, the Commission withdrew its guidance in 2011 and then, following consultation, issued the current guidance, which has been addressed throughout this part of the

---

[432] The Upper Tribunal did "not find it easy to derive clear principles from *Re Resch's WT*" in *Independent Schools Council v Charity Commission* [2012] Ch. 214 at [162].

[433] *Independent Schools Council v Charity Commission* [2012] Ch. 214. Further directions were given at [2011] UKUT B27 (TCC).

[434] [2012] Ch. 214 at [44].

[435] [2012] Ch. 214 at [196]–[207]. The approach in the Independent Schools Case was reiterated by members of the panel in *Attorney General v The Charity Commission for England and Wales* FTC/84/2011.

[436] B. Sloan (2012) 71 C.L.J. 45 at 47. See also J. Garton (2014) 67 C.L.P. 373.

chapter. Further guidance on ensuring that the poor can benefit is now contained in the Commission's guidance on "Public benefit: running a charity".[437] The revised guidance distinguishes between the level at which charges may be set[438] and the provision to be made to ensure that the poor[439] can benefit from the charity.[440]

15–053   This is related to the principle that the opportunity to benefit must not be unduly restricted by ability to pay any fees charged. If a charity which charged high fees, for example an independent school, made only a small reduction for those who could not afford the fees, people in poverty would be excluded and so the public benefit requirement would not be satisfied unless other benefits were provided for those who could not afford even the reduced fees.

As Lindley LJ said:

> "I am quite aware that a trust may be charitable though not confined to the poor, but I doubt very much whether a trust would be declared charitable which excluded the poor."[441]

15–054   **iii. Incidental benefit.**[442]   A "personal benefit" or "private benefits" must only be incidental to the carrying out of the charity's aims. It is "incidental" where it is "a necessary result or by-product" of carrying out the purpose.[443] For example, the publication of the law reports is for the benefit of the community but incidentally benefits members of the legal profession by assisting them in their practice.[444] If the private benefits go beyond the incidental, it is doubtful whether the aims would be exclusively charitable[445]: for example, the Commission rejected one of the Countryside Alliance's purposes as not being charitable (the promotion of game production). It had as its primary result "private benefit accruing to those commercially involved in the production of game for eating", and so such private benefit was more than incidental.[446]

7.   THE INTERPRETATION OF CHARITABLE GIFTS AND PURPOSES

15–055   A number of special questions arise in connection with the construction of instruments which are claimed to create charitable trusts. The problems here discussed provide a further reminder of the importance of proper draftsmanship when setting up a charitable trust. The Charity Commission will help with

---

[437] PB2: Part 5 and Annex C.

[438] PB2: Annex C, 16.

[439] PB2: Annex C, 16: charges which the poor cannot afford "will usually mean charges that someone of modest means will not find readily affordable".

[440] PB2: Annex C, 17–8.

[441] *Re Macduff* [1896] 2 Ch. 451 at 464.

[442] PB1, Part 6.

[443] PB1, Part 6.

[444] *Incorporated Council of Law Reporting for England and Wales v Attorney General* [1972] Ch. 73.

[445] Below, para.15–059. See also para.15–019 (professional bodies); para.15–099 (payments to trustees).

[446] Charity Commission Decision, The Countryside Alliance – Application for Registration, 23 March 2017, para.27.

advice,[447] and they will give reasons for any refusal to register, and make it possible for the trusts to be redrafted. The Commission provides detailed guidance to draftsmen on drafting object clauses, for this may allow non-charitable purposes to be included.[448] In *McGovern v Attorney General*,[449] a trust included political objects, but the deed provided that the objects were "restricted to those which are charitable according to the law of the UK but subject thereto they may be carried out in all parts of the world." This proviso did not have the "blue-pencil" effect of cancelling out the non-charitable parts, and hence the trust was not charitable. The restriction was merely intended to make it clear that the trustees, when operating outside the UK, should be restricted to purposes charitable by UK law. In so far as the purposes of the trust included political and thus non-charitable objects, the proviso could not save it.

A. The Motive of the Donor

The charitable motive of the donor, even if expressed, is not of major significance. In *Re King*,[450] a will provided for the erection of a stained-glass window in a church in memory of her parents, her sister and the testatrix herself. This was held to be a valid charitable gift. The fact that the intention was "not to beautify the church or benefit the parishioners, but to perpetuate the memory of the testatrix and her relations"[451] was immaterial. Conversely, a non-charitable gift, such as a gift for the suppression of vivisection, cannot be made charitable by the donor's charitable motive.[452] But a clear charitable intent may help to turn an ambiguity in favour of charity; especially, as has been seen, where it is possible to find an intention to benefit the poor.[453]

15–056

B. The Charitable Status of the Trustee[454]

The charitable nature of a trust is determined by the terms of the trust and not by the status of the trustee. Non-charitable trustees may hold property on charitable trusts, and charity trustees may, subject, in the case of a corporation, to the terms of their incorporation, hold property on non-charitable trusts. But the charitable status of the trustee can in some cases, where the terms of the trust are not spelled out, lead the court to construe the terms of the trust as charitable. A gift to a bishop or vicar, without the purposes being specified, may be charitable. In *Re Flinn*,[455] a gift to:

15–057

---

[447] Now Charities Act 2011 s.110.
[448] Charity Commission, *How to write charitable purposes* (September 2013).
[449] [1982] Ch. 321, above, para.15–038.
[450] [1923] 1 Ch. 243, following *Hoare v Osborne* (1865-66) L.R. 1 Eq. 585.
[451] [1923] 1 Ch. 243 at 245.
[452] *National Anti-Vivisection Society v IRC* [1948] A.C. 31.
[453] *Biscoe v Jackson* (1887) 35 Ch.D. 460; *Re Coulthurst's WT* [1951] Ch. 193; *Re Cottam* [1955] 1 W.L.R. 1299; above, para.15–013.
[454] V. Delaney (1960) 25 Conv. (N.S.) 306.
[455] [1948] Ch. 241.

> "His Eminence the Archbishop of Westminster Cathedral for the time being to be used by him for such purposes as he shall in his absolute discretion think fit"

was upheld. So, also, gifts to such officers for their work, for this is treated as being wholly charitable. In *Re Rumball*,[456] a gift "to the bishop for the time being of the diocese of the Windward Islands to be used by him as he thinks fit in his diocese" was upheld.

But there is a danger in saying too much; where the terms of the gift specify the purposes and allow any part of the fund to be used for non-charitable purposes, the gift is void. The cases turn on the finest points of construction. In *Farley v Westminster Bank*,[457] a gift to a vicar "for parish work" was held invalid, as it includes some non-charitable activities. But in *Re Simson*,[458] a gift to a vicar "for his work in the parish" was held valid. The former phrase is held to be dispositive, thus enlarging the ambit of the gift and producing the result that a charitable trustee holds on non-charitable trusts, while the latter phrase is held to be merely descriptive of the vicar's responsibilities. The many pages in the reports dealing with these refinements bring no credit to our jurisprudence.

C. The Objects Must be Exclusively Charitable

15–058 To be charitable, the funds of a trust must be applicable for charitable purposes only: as we have seen, this principle is now found in Charities Act 2011 s.1(1)(a).

15–059 **i. Main and Subsidiary Objects.** A trust may be charitable, however, even if some expenditure is permitted on non-charitable purposes, but only if those non-charitable purposes are entirely subsidiary to the main charitable purposes. The question is whether:

> "The main purpose of the body... is charitable and the only elements in its constitution and operation which are non-charitable are merely incidental to that purpose."[459]

Failure of a trust for this reason is fairly obvious in cases such as *Morice v Bishop of Durham*[460] and *IRC v Baddeley*[461] where the purposes are patently too widely expressed but it is less obvious in cases where the non-charitable element is latent. In *Ellis v IRC*,[462] land was conveyed to trustees for use:

> "[G]enerally in such manner for the promotion and aiding of the work of the Roman Catholic Church in the district as the Trustees with the consent of the Bishop may prescribe."

---

[456] [1956] Ch. 105.

[457] [1939] A.C. 430.

[458] [1946] Ch. 299.

[459] *IRC v City of Glasgow Police Athletic Association* [1953] A.C. 380 per Lord Cohen at 405. See N. Gravells [1978] Conv. 92.

[460] (1804) 9 Ves.Jr. 399; (1805) 10 Ves.Jr. 522 ("objects of benevolence and liberality").

[461] [1955] A.C. 572; above, para.15–036.

[462] (1949) 31 T.C. 178, following *Dunne v Byrne* [1912] A.C. 407. See also *IRC v Educational Grants Association Ltd* [1967] Ch. 993 at 1010 and 1015; *Oxford Group v IRC* [1949] 2 All E.R. 537, at 539–540.

The Court of Appeal held that assets could be spent on subsidiary objects which were not necessarily conducive to the main (and undoubtedly charitable) object; such subsidiary objects existed in their own right and prevented the gift from being "for charitable purposes *only*".

An acute form of this problem occurs where the furtherance of a charitable purpose also benefits particular groups of persons. For instance in *IRC v City of Glasgow Police Athletic Association*,[463] the House of Lords held that a police athletic association, intended to benefit policemen in Glasgow, was not wholly ancillary to increasing the efficiency of the Glasgow police force and therefore not charitable. On the other hand, the benefits to the medical profession in the constitution of the General Medical Council are ancillary to the promotion of public health[464]; similarly in the case of surgeons in relation to the advancement of surgery in the constitution of the Royal College of Surgeons.[465] In *Re Coxen*,[466] a substantial gift to a charity included provision for an annual dinner for the trustees; and this was held charitable as being ancillary to the better administration of the charity. And in *London Hospital Medical College v IRC*,[467] a students' union was held to be a charitable trust where its predominant object was to further the purposes of the college, even though one of its objects was to confer private and personal benefits on union members.[468]

ii. And/Or Cases.   Nowhere is the draftsman's error more obvious than in this group of cases. If a purpose is described as "charitable and benevolent"— philanthropic, useful, or any other such adjective—the purposes are wholly charitable. For the purposes, to qualify, must be, amongst other things, charitable; and that is enough. But if the draftsman says charitable *or* benevolent, there is prima facie an alternative; and the funds could be applied for purposes which are benevolent, but not charitable. But the question is one of construction in each case: is the word conjunctive or disjunctive?

15–060

(a)   Cases of "or".   In *Blair v Duncan*[469] the words were: "such charitable or public purposes as my trustee thinks proper"; in *Houston v Burns*,[470] "public, benevolent, or charitable purposes"; in *Chichester Diocesan Fund and Board of Finance v Simpson*[471] "charitable or benevolent"; in each of these cases the gift

15–061

---

[463] [1953] A.C. 380.

[464] Above, para.15–019.

[465] *Royal College of Surgeons v National Provincial Bank Ltd* [1952] A.C. 631; see also *Incorporated Council of Law Reporting v Attorney General* [1972] Ch. 73.

[466] [1948] Ch. 747.

[467] [1976] 1 W.L.R. 613. See also *Re South Place Ethical Society* [1980] 1 W.L.R. 1565 (social activities held to be ancillary to the objects of ethical humanist society); *Funnell v Stewart* [1996] 1 W.L.R. 288.

[468] See generally on this point J. Chevalier-Watts (2015) 21 T. & T. 371.

[469] [1902] A.C. 37. See also the Privy Council decision in *Attorney General of the Cayman Islands v Wahr-Hansen* [2001] 1 A.C. 75 (trust for "religious, charitable or educational institutions or organisations or institutions operating for the public good" invalid).

[470] [1918] A.C. 337.

[471] [1944] A.C. 341; the trustees of the will paid the sums over to various charities, not anticipating the litigation by the next-of-kin which, in the event, occurred and the sequel was *Ministry of Health v Simpson* [1951] A.C. 251. The litigation also included *Re Diplock* [1948] Ch. 465: below, paras 26–027—26–028.

was held not to be charitable, in that the words were wide enough to justify the trustees in disposing of the fund, or an unascertainable part of it, to non-charitable objects.

In *Re Macduff*,[472] a bequest of money "for some one or more purposes, charitable, philanthropic or—" was held to be bad, not by reason of the blank, but because there may be philanthropic purposes that are not charitable.

But in *Re Bennett*[473] the words were: "for the benefit of the schools, and charitable institutions, and poor, and other objects of charity, or *any other* public objects," and Eve J held that the addition of the word "other" entitled him to apply the ejusdem generis rule of interpretation and dispensed him from the necessity of reading the word "or" disjunctively; the gift was, therefore, upheld as a charitable gift of the whole.

15–062   *(b)   Cases of "and".*   Lord Davey in *Blair v Duncan*[474] said that if the words had been "charitable *and* public" effect might be given to them, because they could be construed to mean charitable purposes of a public character. Some cases support this view, the word "and" being regarded as having the power to draw the other word into the orbit of the charitable. This view is borne out by *Re Sutton*[475] and *Re Best*,[476] where gifts to "charitable and deserving objects" and "charitable and benevolent" objects respectively were upheld. In *Attorney General of the Bahamas v Royal Trust Co*,[477] on the other hand, a gift for the "education and welfare" of Bahamian children and young people was held void on a disjunctive construction. To construe the words conjunctively would result in a single purpose of educational welfare, but the word "welfare" was regarded as too wide to permit such a construction. The addition of a third word, "without any conjunction, copulative or disjunctive,"[478] was in *Williams v Kershaw*[479] held fatal to a gift to "benevolent, charitable and religious" purposes, and in *Re Eades*[480] Sargant J refused to uphold a gift for "such religious, charitable and philanthropic objects" as three named persons should jointly appoint.

In *Attorney General v National Provincial and Union Bank of England*,[481] there was a gift "for such patriotic purposes or objects and such charitable institution or institutions or charitable object or objects in the British Empire" as the trustees should select. The House of Lords interpreted this as a gift for any or all of four categories, two of which might not be charitable, and so held the whole gift void.

---

[472] [1896] 2 Ch. 451.

[473] [1920] 1 Ch. 305. See also *Guild v IRC* [1992] 2 A.C. 310 (gift to specified recreational charitable purpose "or some similar purpose in connection with sport" upheld).

[474] [1902] A.C. 37 at 44.

[475] (1885) 28 Ch.D. 464.

[476] [1904] 2 Ch. 354.

[477] [1986] 1 W.L.R. 1001; cf. *Re Carapiet's Trusts* [2002] W.T.L.R. 989 (education and advancement in life of Armenian children).

[478] *Re Sutton* (1885) 28 Ch.D. 464 per Pearson J at 466.

[479] (1835) 5 Cl. & F. 111 per Sir Charles Pepys MR at 113: the testator "intended to restrain the discretion of the trustees, only within the limits of what was benevolent, or charitable, or religious".

[480] [1920] 2 Ch. 353.

[481] [1924] A.C. 262.

So we cannot say more than that prima facie the word "or" causes the words to be read disjunctively; the word "and" causes them to be read conjunctively.

iii. Severance. Where the language permits funds to be applied partly for charitable and partly for non-charitable purposes, the court will, in some cases, apply a doctrine of severance, separating the charitable from the non-charitable, and allow the former to stand although the latter may fail. $\qquad$ **15–063**

In *Salusbury v Denton*,[482] a testator bequeathed a fund to his widow to be applied by her in her will, in part towards the foundation of a charity school, and as to the rest towards the benefit of the testator's relatives. The widow died without making any apportionment, but it was held, relying on the maxim "Equality is Equity", that the court would divide the fund into halves.

The distinction between this and the "charitable or benevolent" cases is well brought out by Page-Wood VC[483]:

> "It is one thing to direct a trustee to give *a part* of a fund to one set of objects, and the *remainder* to another, and it is a distinct thing to direct him to give 'either' to one set of objects 'or' to another… This is a case of the former description. Here the trustee was bound to give a part to each."

The crux of the matter is that the whole of a fund cannot be devoted to non-charity; once this is established, the court will endeavour to quantify what proportion of the capital assets is needed to support the non-charitable part,[484] and then hold the remaining part to be validly devoted to charity. In the absence of factors requiring a different division, the court will divide equally.[485] But there may be good reasons for making an unequal division.

iv. Charitable Trusts (Validation) Act 1954. If the terms of a trust coming into operation before 16 December 1952[486] are such that the property could be applied exclusively for charitable purposes, but could also be applied for non-charitable purposes (called in the Act an "imperfect trust provision") then as from 30 July 1954, the terms shall be treated as if they permitted application for charitable purposes only.[487] Actions under the Act have been said to be "a comparative rarity".[488] $\qquad$ **15–064**

The simple case covered by this provision would be a gift, prior to 16 December 1952, for "charitable or benevolent purposes". It would have saved the trusts of the *Diplock* will,[489] and was applied in the case of a trust deed some of whose purposes were charitable and others not.[490] The difficulty arises where

---

[482] (1857) 3 K. & J. 529.

[483] (1857) 3 K. & J. 529 at 539; the italics are the Vice-Chancellor's.

[484] In most cases this will produce partial invalidity.

[485] *Hoare v Osborne* (1865-66) L.R. 1 Eq. 585.

[486] The date of publication of the Committee on the Law and Practice relating to Charitable Trusts (1952) Cmnd. 8710 (the Nathan Report).

[487] s.1(2); *Re Chitty's WT* [1970] Ch. 254. The Act does not apply to assets already distributed; s.2.

[488] M. Herbert [2017] P.C.B. 71, commenting on *Buckley v Barlow* [2016] EWHC 3017 (Ch).

[489] *Chichester Diocesan Fund and Board of Finance v Simpson* [1944] A.C. 341; above, para.15–061.

[490] *Re Mead's Trust Deed* [1961] 1 W.L.R. 1244; *Re South Place Ethical Society* [1980] 1 W.L.R. 1565 ("purposes either religious or civil"). The trust in *Williams Trustees v IRC* [1947] A.C. 447, para.15–036, above, was eventually saved by the Act; Annual Report 1977, paras 71–80.

there is no express mention of any charitable purposes, but where the purposes are capable of including charitable purposes.[491] It was said in *Re Gillingham Bus Disaster Fund*[492] that a trust for "worthy causes" was covered, and in *Re Wykes' Will Trust*, a trust for welfare purposes was upheld as those purposes are akin to the relief of poverty. The Act was recently held to apply to a trust for the "benefit" of employees of a company and their widows and children which was intended as a hardship fund, although no charitable purpose was expressly stated.[493] On the other hand, a trust for division among institutions and associations, some of which were not charitable, was not validated[494]; nor was a trust providing various benefits for employees which was not intended as a hardship fund, because it was essentially a private discretionary trust and contained no indication of an intention to benefit the public.[495] The principle seems to be that where there is a clear flavour of charity present, "a quasi-charitable trust" as Cross J put it,[496] the donor of such a gift would not feel that his intentions were being distorted by the whole of his gift being made available to charity. Or, to put it another way, the test is whether anyone could have complained if the whole fund had been applied to charity from the start.[497] It would thus cover "worthy causes," but not a case involving the mere possibility of charitable benefit.[498] In a more modern case it has been said that the Act contains "beneficial and salutary provisions, despite the denigration of the legislation, soon after the passage of the Act, by an earlier generation of Chancery judges".[499]

Legislation in Commonwealth jurisdictions[500] has gone much further, and gives the courts a "blue pencil" power. Where non-charitable purposes are, or are deemed to be, within the ambit of a trust obviously intended to be charitable,[501] the trust is carried out as if the non-charitable elements were not present.

---

[491] *Re Gillingham Bus Disaster Fund* [1959] Ch. 62; *Re Wykes* [1961] Ch. 229; *Re Mead's Trust Deed* [1961] 1 W.L.R. 1244.

[492] [1959] Ch. 62 at 80.

[493] *Ulrich v Treasury Solicitor* [2006] 1 W.L.R. 33, where a fund worth £3,000 in 1927 was now worth £600,000. See also *Cawdron v Merchant Taylors' School* [2010] W.T.L.R. 775.

[494] *Re Harpur's WT* [1962] Ch. 78.

[495] *Re Saxone Shoe Co Ltd's Trust Deed* [1962] 1 W.L.R. 943.

[496] [1962] 1 W.L.R. 943 at 957–958.

[497] *Ulrich v Treasury Solicitor* [2006] 1 W.L.R. 33; *Buckley v Barlow* [2016] EWHC 3017 (Ch).

[498] cf. *Re Mead's Trust Deed* [1961] 1 W.L.R. 1244 which goes rather far in restricting a trust to "poor" members of a union. The decision was doubted in *Ulrich v Treasury Solicitor*.

[499] *Cuppage v Lawson* [2010] EWHC 3785 (Ch); [2011] W.T.L.R. 975 HH Judge Hodge QC, sitting as a Judge of the High Court, at [71] (Act applied to trusts for working men's club and for welfare of the working population of East Grinstead).

[500] e.g. (New South Wales) Charitable Trusts Act 1993 s.23; (New Zealand) Charitable Trusts Act 1957 s.61B; (Victoria) Charities Act 1978 s.7M. See also Charities Act (Northern Ireland) 2008 s.29A (added by the Charities Act (Northern Ireland) 2013 s.2)).

[501] *Leahy v Attorney General for New South Wales* [1959] A.C. 457.

D.   Disaster Appeals

Problems can arise when public appeals for donations are made after some **15–065** accident or disaster, if insufficient thought has been given to the question whether the fund is to be charitable or not. Such was the case with the loss of Penlee Lifeboat in Cornwall in 1982, when over £2 million was donated by the public to the dependants of the lost crew, numbering eight families. If charitable, the fund would attract tax relief but, contrary to the expectations of some donors, it could not be simply divided amongst the families, as charitable funds, being essentially public in nature, cannot be used to give benefits to individuals exceeding those appropriate to their needs. Any surplus would, as we shall see under the cy-près doctrine below, be applied to related charities.[502] If, on the other hand, the fund was not charitable, it would not attract tax relief, but could be distributed entirely among the dependants if, upon construing the terms of the appeal, that was the intention of the donors. If that was not their intention, the surplus would not be applicable cy-près, but would result to the subscribers or perhaps devolve upon the Crown as bona vacantia.[503] Similar problems can arise if the appeal is on behalf of one specific person, such as a sick child. In the *Penlee* case[504] it was decided, after negotiations with the Attorney General and the Charity Commissioners, to forgo tax relief and to treat the fund as private, so that the money could be divided among the families.[505]

The terms of an appeal are all-important in determining the status of the fund, and the consequences flowing from that status. The Charity Commission now has issued guidance for both established charities and individuals seeking to set up appeals in such situations,[506] and encourages individuals to think carefully before starting a new charity, as opposed to giving to an existing organisation, such as the Disasters Emergency Committee.[507]

8.   CY-PRÈS

A.   The Cy-Près Doctrine Prior to 1960

Where property is given for charitable purposes and the purposes cannot be **15–066** carried out in the precise manner intended by the donor, the question is whether the trust should fail, or whether the property should be applied for other

---

[502] Below, para.15–066.

[503] *Re Gillingham Bus Disaster Fund* [1959] Ch. 62; *Re West Sussex Constabulary's Widows, Children and Benevolent (1930) Fund Trust* [1971] Ch. 1; above, para.11–013.

[504] Which was not litigated. See Annual Report 1981, paras 4–8; H. Picarda (1982) 132 N.L.J. 223.

[505] The Charity Commissioners stated that the fund was not charitable; Annual Report 1981 para.6. If it had been charitable, as being for the relief of victims of a disaster (*Re North Devon and West Somerset Relief Fund Trusts* [1953] 1 W.L.R. 1260), presumably it would not be possible to forgo that status.

[506] *Disaster appeals: Charity Commission guidance on starting, running and supporting charitable disaster appeals*, CC40 (1 August 2012). The 2012 guidance updated and expanded the previous guidance issued in 2002. See I. McLean and M. Johnes (1999) 19 L.S. 380.

[507] *Annual Report and Accounts* 2016–17, 19.

charitable purposes. The cy-près[508] doctrine, where it applies, enables the court (or the Commission) to make a scheme for the application of the property for other charitable purposes as near as possible to those intended by the donor, and thus to increase the resources available to the charity sector.[509] This is judicial cy-près. If a gift is to charity but not upon trust, it is disposed of by the Crown under prerogative cy-près.[510] The distinction is not however always observed.

The cy-près jurisdiction was very narrow until the reforms of the Charities Act 1960, and was available only where it was "impossible" or "impracticable" to carry out the purposes of the trust.[511] Thus, trusts for the distribution of loaves of bread to the poor or of stockings for poor maidservants continued until modern times. Performance of such trusts was cumbersome, uneconomical, inconvenient, but not impossible nor impracticable. But it had at least, by the turn of the 19th century, become impracticable to apply money for the advancement and propagation of the Christian religion among the infidels of Virginia,[512] or for "the redemption of British slaves in Turkey or Barbary."[513]

Re Dominion Students' Hall Trust[514] showed the furthest development of the doctrine by the courts. One of the objects of a charity was to promote community of citizenship, culture and tradition among all members of the British Community of Nations; and it maintained a hostel for students in Bloomsbury. But the benefits of the charity were restricted to students of European origin. The cy-près power was used to remove the "colour bar". It could not be said that it was "absolutely impracticable" to carry on the charity in its present state; but, by 1947:

> "[T]o retain the condition, so far from furthering the charity's main object, might defeat it and would be liable to antagonize those students, both white and coloured, whose support and goodwill it is the purpose of the charity to sustain. The case, therefore, can be said to fall within the broad description of impossibility… ".[515]

Later, in *Re J W Laing Trust*,[516] concerning a settlement of shares worth £15,000 in 1922, the question was whether the court could delete a term imposed by the settlor that the capital and income should be distributed no later than 10 years after his death. The investment was now worth £24 million. The trust was for Christian evangelical causes, and the individuals and bodies who would be the

[508] "cy-près" means "as near" or "so near" in French.
[509] See J. Garton (2007) 21 T.L.I. 134 and J. Picton [2015] Conv. 480. Above, para.15–003.
[510] Above, para.15–003. But even if there is no trust, the court has jurisdiction if there is an analogous legally binding restriction; *Liverpool and District Hospital for Diseases of the Heart v Attorney General* [1981] Ch. 193 (charitable corporation); J. Warburton [1984] Conv. 112. J. Picton [2014] Conv. 473.
[511] See *Re Weir Hospital* [1910] 2 Ch. 124.
[512] *Attorney General v City of London* (1790) 3 Bro.C.C. 121. Annual Report 1971, paras 65–69; see also *Re Robinson* [1923] 2 Ch. 332. (The wearing of a black gown by the preacher was impracticable because it was likely to offend the congregation and defeat the main object.)
[513] *Ironmongers' Co v Attorney General* (1844) 10 Cl. & F. 908.
[514] [1947] Ch. 183; see Equality Act 2010 s.193 (replacing earlier legislation); above, para.14–004; *Public benefit: the public benefit requirement* (PB1) (September 2013) 10; D. Morris (2012) 65 C.L.P. 295.
[515] [1947] Ch. 183 at 186, per Evershed J.
[516] [1984] Ch. 143; P. Luxton [1985] Conv. 313. Section 13 of the Charities Act 1960 (now the 2011 Act s.62) did not apply; below, para.15–077.

[416]

recipients were unsuited to receive large capital sums. The deletion of this term was approved under the court's inherent jurisdiction, as it had become inexpedient in the very altered circumstances of the charity.

It is convenient also at this stage to note that a distinction is made between the initial failure of a charitable trust, and a failure after the time when the trust has been in operation. Application cy-près is much easier in the latter case; for, after application to charity, there is no resulting trust for the donor.[517] If the donor wants the property to pass to a third party, or to return to himself or his estate, he must expressly so provide by a gift over to take effect within the perpetuity period.[518] In the case of initial failure, the gift will lapse unless there is, on the proper construction of the instrument, a paramount intention to benefit charity. These situations will now be examined.

B. Initial Failure. Paramount Charitable Intent

i. Width of Charitable Intent. Where a charitable trust fails as being   15–067
ineffective at the date of the gift, the gift will either lapse and fall into residue, or the property will be applied cy-près. The decision depends on the width of charitable intent shown by the donor. If the intention was that the property should be applied for a specified purpose, which cannot be carried out, or for one specific charitable institution which no longer exists, the gift will lapse. But if the court finds a wider intent, a paramount or general charitable intention, the property may be applied cy-près.

In *Re Rymer*,[519] there was a legacy of £5,000 "to the rector for the time being of St Thomas's Seminary for the education of priests for the diocese of Westminster." At the time of the testator's death, the Seminary had ceased to exist, and the students had been transferred to another Seminary in Birmingham. The Court of Appeal held that the gift failed. It was a gift "to a particular seminary for the purposes thereof." There was no wider intent.

This may be contrasted with *Re Lysaght*,[520] where the testatrix gave funds to the Royal College of Surgeons to found medical studentships. The gift was subject to restrictions, in that the students were to be male, the sons of qualified British-born medical men, themselves British-born, and not of the Jewish or Roman Catholic faith. The Royal College of Surgeons declined to accept the gift on these terms. As it was held that the particular trustee was essential to the gift, the refusal of the College would cause the gift to fail. Buckley J held that there was a paramount charitable intention. The particularity of the testatrix's directions was not fatal to such a construction, as the directions were not an essential part of her true intention. A scheme was ordered whereby the money was payable to the College on the trusts of the will, but omitting the religious disqualification.

---

[517] *Re Wright* [1954] Ch. 347 at 362–363. But see P. Luxton [1983] Conv. 107.
[518] Below, para.15–075.
[519] [1895] 1 Ch. 19; *Re Spence* [1979] Ch. 483; *Kings v Bultitude* [2010] W.T.L.R. 1571; J. Picton [2011] Conv. 69 and [2015] Conv. 480.
[520] [1966] Ch. 191, particularly at 201–202.

This liberal approach was followed in *Re Woodhams (Deceased)*,[521] where the testator left money to two music colleges to found annual scholarships for:

> "[T]he complete musical education of a promising boy who is an absolute orphan and only of British Nationality and Birth from any one of Dr. Barnardo's Homes or the Church of England Children's Society Homes."

The two colleges declined the gifts because it would be impractical to restrict the scholarships as required by the testator, but were prepared to accept them if available for boys of British nationality and birth generally. The gift failed for impracticability, but a paramount charitable intention to further musical education was found. The restriction to orphans from the named homes was not essential to the testator's purpose. Thus the gift was applicable cy-près under a scheme whereby the restriction was deleted.

Where the testatrix has provided in her will for an alternative residuary gift in the event of the initial bequest to a charity failing, that may negate a general charitable intention.[522]

15–068   **ii.   Has the Gift Failed? Continuation in Another Form.**   A gift to a defunct charity may be regarded as not having failed at all, on the basis that it is continuing in another form. It may have been amalgamated with a similar charity by scheme, or have been reconstituted under more effective trusts. In such a case the gift may take effect in favour of the body now administering the assets of the old charity.[523] Or the court may construe the gift as being for the purposes of the named charity, so that the nomination of a defunct charity does not cause the gift to fail. Provided the purposes still exist the gift takes effect in favour of a body furthering those purposes. It will be appreciated that the significance of holding that such a gift has not failed is that it is not necessary to find a general charitable intention. A scheme will be ordered to give effect to the gift, but it will not be a cy-près scheme.

15–069   *(a)   Gift in Augmentation of Funds of Defunct Charity.*   In *Re Faraker*,[524] there was a gift to "Mrs Bayley's Charity, Rotherhithe". A charity had been founded by a Mrs Hannah Bayly in 1756 for the benefit of poor widows in Rotherhithe. This, with a number of other local charities, had been consolidated under a scheme by the Charity Commissioners in 1905, and the funds were held in various trusts for the benefit of the poor in Rotherhithe. The Court of Appeal held that the Bayly

---

[521] [1981] 1 W.L.R. 493.

[522] *Games v Attorney General* (2012) 14 I.T.E.L.R. 792 (Isle of Man), although if the alternative gift is also to a charity, as in *Games*, the point may be moot.

[523] A gift to a charity which has merged with another will usually be effective under what is now Charities Act 2011 s.311; (though the application of this section will depend upon the terms of the will or gift: see *Berry v IBS-STL (UK) Ltd* [2012] EWHC 666 (Ch); [2012] P.T.S.R. 1619).

[524] [1912] 2 Ch. 488; *Re Lucas* [1948] Ch. 424; *Re Broadbent* [2001] W.T.L.R. 967; cf. *Re Slatter's WT* [1964] Ch. 512; J. Farrand (1964) 28 Conv.(N.S.) 313.

trusts had not been destroyed by the scheme, and that the consolidated charities were entitled to the legacy. The gift had not failed, because a perpetual charity cannot die.[525]

(b)   *Gifts for Purposes. Unincorporated Associations and Charitable Corpora-*   **15–070**
tions.   In considering whether a gift is effectively for the purposes of the named institution, a distinction is drawn between gifts to unincorporated societies and to corporations.

> "Every bequest to an unincorporated charity by name without more must take effect as a gift for a charitable purpose... a bequest which is in terms made for a charitable purpose will not fail for lack of a trustee but will be carried into effect either under the Sign Manual or by means of a scheme"[526];

unless the testator's intention was to the contrary. On the other hand:

> "[A] bequest to a corporate body... takes effect simply as a gift to that body beneficially, unless there are circumstances which show that the recipient is to take the gift as a trustee. There is no need in such a case to infer a trust for any particular purpose."[527]

Thus a gift to a defunct charitable corporation lapses and fails,[528] and cy-près application is possible only if there was a general charitable intention. In *Re Finger's Will Trusts*,[529] there was a gift to the National Radium Commission (unincorporated) and to the National Council for Maternity and Child Welfare (incorporated). Both had ceased to exist by the testatrix's death. The gift to the unincorporated charity was construed as a gift to charitable purposes. As those purposes still existed there was no failure, as a trust does not fail for lack of a trustee. A scheme was ordered to settle the destination of the gift, but this was not a cy-près scheme and no general charitable intention was necessary.[530] In the case of the incorporated charity, on the other hand, it was a gift to a legal person which had ceased to exist, and was not a purpose trust.[531] The gift therefore failed, but was saved from lapse by the finding of a general charitable intention, and was accordingly applied cy-près. The incorporation of a charity may have wider

---

[525] Distinguished in *Re Stemson's WT* [1970] Ch. 16 (involving a terminable corporate charity), and *Re Roberts* [1963] 1 W.L.R. 406.

[526] *Re Vernon's WT* [1972] Ch. 300 per Buckley J at 303; *Re Finger's WT* [1972] Ch. 286; R. Cotterell (1972) 36 Conv.(N.S.) 198; J. Martin (1974) 38 Conv.(N.S.) 187. See also *Liverpool and District Hospital for Diseases of the Heart v Attorney General* [1981] Ch. 193 (charitable corporation does not hold as trustee, but court has cy-près jurisdiction on winding-up). See Charities Act 2011 ss.197, 198, for the position where a charitable corporation ceases to be charitable or otherwise alters its objects.

[527] *Re Vernon's WT* [1972] Ch. 300n. See also *Re ARMS (Multiple Sclerosis Research) Ltd* [1997] 1 W.L.R. 877 (no failure where incorporated charity existed at testator's death although insolvent, thus legacy available to its creditors).

[528] Unless the testator has indicated that the corporation was to take as trustee for its purposes.

[529] [1972] Ch. 286; applied by the Court of Appeal in *Re Koeppler's WT* [1986] Ch. 423. If the purposes had ceased to exist, the gift to the unincorporated charity would fail, but could be applied cy-près if there was a general charitable intention.

[530] It would be otherwise if the donor intended the particular institution and no other, as in *Re Rymer* [1895] 1 Ch. 19.

[531] See also *Phillips v The Royal Society for the Protection of Birds* [2012] EWHC 618 (Ch).

consequences, as in a case involving the insolvent Wedgwood Museum Trust (although it is not a cy-près decision).[532] In that case, an entire collection of rare pottery and art was held by the museum company which was part of the Wedgwood group of companies. The intention was to protect the collection in the event of the group encountering financial difficulties, but there had been no separate trust created for the collection to be held for charitable purposes. The result was that the entire collection was available to meet the costs and liabilities of the entire group of companies when the Wedgwood group became insolvent, including a £134.7 million pension deficit.

The approach above involves a technical distinction which might not be appreciated by the testator, but it has a certain logic. One difficulty which remains is that the same facts may allow either the *Re Faraker* construction or that adopted in *Re Finger's Will Trusts* in the case of the unincorporated charity, although the results are different. While both constructions avoid the finding of a failure and the need for a general charitable intention, the result of the *Re Faraker* construction is that the gift goes to the body now administering the funds of the defunct charity, even if its purposes are different. In *Re Faraker* itself, the defunct charity was specifically for widows, while the new consolidated charity was for the poor generally, so that it "was not bound to give one penny to a widow,"[533] thus defeating the testator's intention to some extent. The result in *Re Finger's Will Trusts* is that the gift is devoted, by means of a scheme, to the testator's purpose. It may be that the court would decline to apply *Re Faraker* where the purposes of the new body were widely different. Thus in *Re Roberts*,[534] a gift was made to the Sheffield Boys' Working Home, which had wound up and transferred most of its assets to the Sheffield Town Trust. The claim of the latter body was rejected as an undesirable extension of the *Re Faraker* principle, as it purposes were different. The money was applied, by means of an ordinary scheme, to the purposes to which the defunct Home had been dedicated.

Both constructions, however, were rejected in *Re Spence*,[535] where money was left to a specified Old Folks Home "for the benefit of the patients." The home was no longer in use at the testatrix's death. Megarry VC held that the gift failed and could not be applied cy-près. It was not a general gift to the old people of the district. Following *Re Harwood*,[536] it was said that if a particular institution is correctly identified, then it is that institution and no other which is intended:

> "It is difficult to envisage a testator as being suffused with a general glow of broad charity when he is labouring, and labouring successfully, to identify some particular specified institution or purpose as the object of his bounty."[537]

---

[532] *Re Wedgwood Museum Trust Ltd (In Administration) (also known as Young v Attorney General)* [2011] EWHC 3782 (Ch); [2013] B.C.C. 281 (HH Judge Purle QC).
[533] [1912] 2 Ch. 488 at 496.
[534] [1963] 1 W.L.R. 406. See J. Martin (1974) 38 Conv.(N.S.) 187.
[535] [1979] Ch. 483.
[536] [1936] Ch. 285.
[537] [1979] Ch. 483 at 493.

This decision clearly offers a very narrow view of the cy-près doctrine. A testator should always be careful to identify his beneficiary correctly. It is difficult to see why this should automatically negative a general charitable intention.

iii. Projects. The cases so far discussed have dealt with gifts to institutions, corporate or unincorporated. The same rules apply in principle also to cases where there is a gift for a purpose or project such as, for example, the payment of a schoolmaster at a school to be built,[538] or the establishment of a soup kitchen and cottage hospital.[539] In such cases, the question is whether the project is on the balance of probabilities capable or incapable of being implemented. If it is incapable, then, in the absence of wider intent, the gift will fail and will fall into residue. There is no "wait and see" provision.[540]

15–071

iv. Non-existent Charity. In *Re Harwood*,[541] it was said that, where there was a gift for a non-existent charity, it was easier to find a general charitable intent in a case where the institution had never existed than it was in the case where an identifiable institution had ceased to exist.

15–072

In that case, a testatrix, who died in 1934, left £200 to the Wisbech Peace Society and £300 to the Peace Society in Belfast. The Wisbech Society had existed prior to 1934, but had ceased by that date to exist. There was no evidence that the Peace Society of Belfast had ever existed. The former failed, but in respect of the latter Farwell J was able to find an intention to "benefit societies whose object was the promotion of peace",[542] and the £300 was applied cy-près.

Similarly, in *Re Satterthwaite's Will Trusts*,[543] where a testatrix, who hated the whole human race, left her residuary estate to a number of institutions concerned with animal welfare. Most of them were charitable, but a dispute arose over the share left to the London Animal Hospital. There was no charity of that name, but the claimant, a veterinary surgeon, carried on a practice under that trade name at a time prior to the date of the will and death. The Court of Appeal considered the gift as being to a non-existent charitable institution, and not to the claimant. A sufficiently wide charitable intent was discerned from the nature of the other shares (notwithstanding that one share was to a non-charity), and thus cy-près application was ordered.

v. A Group of Donees; Mostly Charitable. It may be that the testator has made a number of gifts, all of which are charitable except one. It can be argued that the intention clearly was to apply all the money for charitable purposes. On

15–073

---

[538] *Re Wilson* [1913] 1 Ch. 314.

[539] *Biscoe v Jackson* (1887) 35 Ch.D. 460.

[540] *Re White's WT* [1955] Ch. 188; *Re Tacon* [1958] Ch. 447 at 453–455.

[541] [1936] Ch. 285; cf. *Re Goldschmidt* [1957] 1 W.L.R. 524, where a gift to a non-existent charity was not applied cy-près, but fell into residue, which was also given to charity.

[542] [1936] Ch. 285 at 288. But the decision was doubted by the High Court in *Re Koeppler's Will Trusts* [1984] Ch. 243, on the basis that the purpose was political and not charitable. It was not cited in the Court of Appeal [1986] Ch. 423.

[543] [1966] 1 W.L.R. 277.

the other hand, as Buckley J said in *Re Jenkins' Will Trusts*,[544] "if you meet seven men with black hair and one with red hair, you are not entitled to say that here are eight men with black hair."[545] A gift for a non-charitable purpose is not made charitable by being included in a list of other gifts which are charitable. So held Buckley J when determining that a gift for the abolition of vivisection failed and could not be applied cy-près. This may be contrasted with *Re Satterthwaite's Will Trusts*, where the gift in question was construed as charitable, and hence the cy-près doctrine could apply.

C. Subsequent Failure

15–074 Once assets are effectively dedicated to charity, there can be no question of a lapse or a resulting trust save where the gift effectively provides for it. Width of charitable intent is irrelevant. All that is necessary is that the property has been given "out and out" to charity, in the sense that the donor did not envisage its return in any circumstances.

In *Re Wright*,[546] a testatrix who died in 1933 provided for the foundation, on the death of a tenant for life, of a convalescent home for impecunious gentlewomen. The scheme was practicable in 1933, but not in 1942 when the tenant for life died. The Court of Appeal held that 1933 was the crucial date; at that date the scheme was practicable, dedication to charity occurred, and the possibility of a lapse or resulting trust was excluded. Cy-près was available in 1942 irrespective of width of charitable intent.

This rule is now firmly established,[547] but it was not always so, and it is not possible to reconcile some earlier cases on the subject, in particular the "surplus" cases. In *Re King*,[548] £1,500 was bequeathed for one stained-glass window in a church. The cost of the window could not exceed £800. Romer J held that the whole of £1,500 had been dedicated to charity with the necessary consequences that any surplus would be applied cy-près (in fact for a second window) irrespective of width of intent.[549] But in *Re Stanford*,[550] where £5,000 was bequeathed for the purpose of completing and publishing an etymological dictionary and over £1,500 remained unspent when the task was complete, Eve J. held that the surplus fell into residue.

Such a result is only justifiable if the surplus can be regarded as a case of initial impossibility pro tanto.[551] Similar confusion can be seen in the cases where the surplus has arisen in the circumstances of a public appeal. In *Re Welsh*

---

[544] *Re Jenkins' WT* [1966] Ch. 249.

[545] [1966] Ch. 249 at 256.

[546] [1954] Ch. 347; *Re Slevin* [1891] 2 Ch. 236, where an orphanage was in existence at the testator's death, but came to an end before the money was paid over. Cy-près application was ordered; *Re Moon's WT* [1948] 1 All E.R. 300.

[547] *Re Tacon* [1958] Ch. 447, a case of a contingent gift; cf. *Re JW Laing Trust* [1984] Ch. 143, J. Warburton [1984] Conv. 319.

[548] [1923] 1 Ch. 243.

[549] J. Picton (2014) 28 T.L.I. 78.

[550] [1924] 1 Ch. 73.

[551] See *Tudor on Charities*, 10th edn, Ch.10.

Hospital (Netley) Fund[552] and *Re North Devon and West Somerset Relief Fund Trusts*[553] money was collected for purposes which were fulfilled, leaving surplus. The surplus was held applicable cy-près on the basis that there was a general charitable intention. If these cases are to be regarded as involving subsequent failure, it is difficult to see why such an intention is necessary. All that is required is an "out and out" gift to charity. Thus, in *Re Wokingham Fire Brigade Trusts*,[554] a surplus was applicable cy-près without the need to discover a general charitable intention. It is submitted that this approach, which was approved obiter by the Court of Appeal in *Re Ulverston and District New Hospital Building Trusts*[555] (involving initial failure as insufficient funds were collected) is to be preferred. A further instance of its application is the case of *Phillips v The Royal Society for the Protection of Birds*.[556] In that case the testatrix left money in her will to a bird sanctuary which was a corporate body. The corporate body ceased to exist shortly after the testatrix's death: the funds were applied cy-près to a cognate charity which had largely taken over the collection of the former charity's birds.

D. Termination in Favour of Non-charity

It was seen that a donor could, if he wished, make express provision for a gift over to a third party or to himself or to his estate upon the failure of a charitable gift within the period of perpetuity.[557] Before the Perpetuities and Accumulations Act 1964, a resulting trust after a determinable interest was immune from the perpetuity rule, although any express gift over was subject to it. Thus a determinable charitable gift could terminate at a remote time and result to the settlor. It could not be applied cy-près because, although a subsequent failure, there was no "out and out" gift to charity.[558] However, in the case of a charitable gift subject to a condition subsequent, the gift took effect as absolute if the gift over was void for perpetuity. The cy-près doctrine would then apply in the usual way on any subsequent failure, to the exclusion of a resulting trust.[559]

15–075

Under s.12 of the 1964 Act, the perpetuity rule became applicable to resulting trusts, but the Act also introduced the "wait and see" rule.[560] Similar provisions apply under the Perpetuities and Accumulations Act 2009.[561] Thus in the case of a determinable charitable gift, a gift over or resulting trust will operate to the exclusion of the cy-près doctrine if the determining event occurs within the perpetuity period. If it does not, the gift becomes absolute, so that cy-près will

---

[552] [1921] 1 Ch. 655; cf. *Re British Red Cross Balkan Fund* [1914] 2 Ch. 419.

[553] [1953] 1 W.L.R. 1260.

[554] [1951] Ch. 373.

[555] [1956] Ch. 622. The case illustrates the difficulties since resolved by provisions now found in Charities Act 2011 s.63, below, para.15–079. Section 63 does not apply to the surplus cases unless it becomes established that a general charitable intention is necessary, contrary to the view expressed in the text.

[556] [2012] EWHC 618 (Ch) (HH Judge Cooke).

[557] Above, para.15–066.

[558] *Re Randell* (1888) 39 Ch.D. 213.

[559] *Re Peel's Release* [1921] 2 Ch. 218; *Bath and Wells Diocesan Board of Finance v Jenkinson* [2001] W.T.L.R. 353.

[560] s.3(1).

[561] ss.1(4), 7, 10.

apply on any subsequent failure. Likewise if the charitable gift is subject to a condition subsequent. On breach of condition within the perpetuity period, the gift over (or resulting trust in default) will take effect. If, however, the condition is not broken within that period, the charitable gift becomes absolute. Thus the cy-près doctrine is available because, whatever the donor's intention, the gift is by statute an "out and out" gift to charity.

E. The Widening of Cy-Près Jurisdiction. Charities Act 2011 Section 62

15–076   **i. General.**   As part of the policy of modernising charitable trusts, the Charities Act 2011[562] offered reforms in the application of the cy-près doctrine.[563] Before examining these reforms it must be emphasised that it is the trustees' duty, where some or all of the property may be applied cy-près, to take steps to have the property so applied.[564] This situation will arise where there is an existing trust for outdated objects; for purposes which were once useful, but are now unnecessary, or overtaken by statutory services; or where the income of the trust has during the years become inadequate for the purpose, or, perhaps so large that there is a surplus. In short, the policy is to enable the trustees, with the help of the Charity Commission, to make the best use, in modern conditions, of funds dedicated to charity.

15–077   **ii. Section 62.**[565]   Section 62 provides for application cy-près in five situations:

(1)   Subject to subsection (3), the circumstances in which the original purposes of a charitable gift can be altered to allow the property given or part of it to be applied cy-près are—

(a)   where the original purposes, in whole or in part,—

(i)   have been as far as may be fulfilled, or

(ii)   cannot be carried out, or not according to the directions given and to the spirit of the gift,

(b)   where the original purposes provide a use for part only of the property available by virtue of the gift,

(c)   where—

(i)   the property available by virtue of the gift, and

(ii)   other property applicable for similar purposes, can be more effectively used in conjunction, and to that end can suitably, regard being had to the appropriate considerations, be made applicable to common purposes,

(d)   where the original purposes were laid down by reference to—

(i)   an area which then was but has since ceased to be a unit for some other purpose, or

(ii)   a class of persons or an area which has for any reason since ceased to be suitable, regard being had to the appropriate considerations, or to be practical in administering the gift, or

(e)   where the original purposes, in whole or in part, have, since they were laid down—

(i)   been adequately provided by other means,

---

[562]   The reforms were first introduced by the Charities Act 1960.

[563]   E. Neale [2012] P.C.B. 226.

[564]   Charities Act 2011 s.61.

[565]   Re-enacting previous legislation.

     (ii)   ceased, as being useless or harmful to the community or for other reasons, to be in law charitable, or

     (iii)   ceased in any other way to provide a suitable and effective method of using the property available by virtue of the gift, regard being had to the appropriate considerations.

(2)   In subsection (1) "the appropriate considerations" means—

     (a)   (on the one hand) the spirit of the gift concerned, and

     (b)   (on the other) the social and economic circumstances prevailing at the time of the proposed alteration of the original purposes.

(3)   Subsection (1) does not affect the conditions which must be satisfied in order that property given for charitable purposes may be applied cy-près, except in so far as those conditions require a failure of the original purposes.

In the case of subsequent failure, width of charitable intent is of no significance, but the Commission endeavours to follow the spirit of the original gift, so far as this is consistent with proper application of the funds. Before the Charities Act 2006, the legislation provided that regard must be had to the spirit of the gift. The Act of 2006 added that that regard must also be had to the social and economic circumstances prevailing at the time of the proposed alteration. Most of the case law illustrations below predate the Act of 2006, but it appears that they would be decided the same way now. Nothing in the legislation requires a cy-près scheme where such a scheme was not required before the 1960 Act.[566]

15–078   The first occasion on which the original provision was litigated was *Re Lepton's Charity*.[567] A will dating from 1715 instructed trustees to pay £3 per annum to the Minister, and the "overplus of the profits" to the poor. At that time, the income was £5 per annum, and in 1970 the income from the proceeds of sale of the land was nearly £800. Pennycuick VC raised the payment to £100 per annum. This was consistent with the spirit of the gift. Subsection (1)(a) applied because "the original purposes" covered the purposes as a whole; it was not necessary to consider separately the gift of the annuity and that of the surplus. In any case subs.(1)(e)(iii) would have applied.

    In *Re JW Laing Trust*,[568] the question which arose was whether what is now s.62 could be utilised in order to dispense with the donor's requirement that the capital and income be distributed no later than 10 years after his death. It was held that the provision could not be deleted under subs.(1), as the "original purposes"[569] which the court could there review meant the objects of the trust, whereas the settlor's direction was merely administrative. The provision was, however, deleted under the court's inherent jurisdiction. In *Peggs v Lamb*,[570] a trust was created in the Middle Ages for the freemen of Huntingdon and their widows. It was charitable on the basis of the anomalous "locality" cases.[571] In the past the freemen were a substantial section of the public and a suitable class of charitable objects. At present there were only 15 members, and they claimed equal division of the annual income, irrespective of need, which would give them over £30,000 each. A cy-près scheme was ordered to enable the money to be

---

[566] *Oldham BC v Attorney General* [1993] Ch. 210.

[567] [1972] Ch. 276.

[568] [1984] Ch. 143. The facts were given at para.15–066, above.

[569] See further *Oldham BC v Attorney General* [1993] Ch. 210.

[570] [1994] Ch. 172.

[571] Above, para.15–035.

distributed amongst the inhabitants of the borough as a whole, in accordance with the spirit of the gift. The case fell within what is now s.62(1)(d), on the basis that the class had ceased to be suitable recipients of charitable funds. It was not necessary to decide whether what is now s.62(1)(e)(ii) also applied, on the basis that they were no longer a section of the public. What is now s.62(1)(e)(iii) was satisfied in *Varsani v Jesani*,[572] where a Hindu sect split into two groups. The groups could not resolve their differences, as each thought that it alone professed the faith. To give the sect's assets to one group would have been contrary to the spirit of the gift, which was the desire to provide facilities for followers of the sect. The solution was to divide the assets between the two groups.

Subsection (1)(e)(ii) will apply to the endowments of any bodies which were once charitable but lose that status as a result of the stricter "public benefit" requirement of the Charities Acts 2006 and 2011. Perhaps also the section would, if then available, have applied to anti-vivisection trusts, for these had been held charitable in *Re Foveaux*,[573] but non-charitable in *National Anti-Vivisection Society v IRC*[574] in 1948. The same would seem to apply to charities which have been removed from the Register on the ground that they have ceased to be charitable.

15–079   **iii.   Section 63.**[575] **Charity Collections.**   Finally, it is necessary to refer to s.63. This provides:

> Property given for specific charitable purposes which fail is applicable cy-près as if given for charitable purposes generally, where it belongs—
> (a)   to a donor who after—
>   (i)   the prescribed advertisements and inquiries have been published and made, and
>   (ii)   the prescribed period beginning with the publication of those advertisements has ended,[576]
>   cannot be identified or cannot be found,[577] or
> (b)   to a donor who has executed a disclaimer in the prescribed form of the right to have the property returned.

In the case of the proceeds of cash collections by means of collecting boxes or other means not adapted for distinguishing one gift from another, or the proceeds of lotteries and similar money-raising activities, the property is conclusively presumed to belong to unidentifiable donors, without any advertisement or inquiry. In other cases, the court or the Commission may direct the property to be treated as belonging to unidentifiable donors, without any advertisement or

---

[572] [1999] Ch. 219. See also *White v Williams* [2010] W.T.L.R. 1083 (schism in Bibleway Church UK).

[573] [1895] 2 Ch. 501.

[574] [1948] A.C. 31. Lord Simonds suggested at 64–65 that application cy-près would have been possible before the 1960 Act.

[575] Re-enacting previous legislation.

[576] The trustees are not liable to any person in respect of the property if no claim is received before expiry of this period; s.63(2).

[577] Such donors may claim from the cy-près recipient within six months of the scheme; s.63(5). For an example of the operation of these provisions see *Re Henry Wood Memorial Trust* [1966] 1 W.L.R. 1601 (failure of Mile End Memorial Hall Fund through lack of financial support).

inquiry, if it appears that it would not be reasonable, having regard to the amounts[578] or the lapse of time since the gifts, to return it.[579]

Section 63 applies only to cases of initial failure. Section 66 provides that charitable purposes are deemed to fail, for the purposes of the section, where any difficulty in applying the property to those purposes makes it available for return to the donors.[580] In the case of subsequent failure, the property is not so available.

This solution is much more sensible than any attempt to solve the problem by applying the usual cy-près doctrine, involving either the imputation of an artificial general charitable intent, or, failing that, a search for the many donors of tiny gifts, with the possibility of a claim by the Crown to the property as bona vacantia.

Section 65 assists further by providing that a solicitation for charitable gifts (such as an appeal) may include a statement to the effect that unless, at the time of the gift, the donor makes a declaration giving him the opportunity to reclaim his gift if the charitable purpose should fail, it will be applied cy-près. Where the donor makes such a declaration and the purpose does fail, the section sets out a process to be followed to return the donation or to apply it cy-près if the donor cannot be traced. The Law Commission has proposed simplification of the statutory regime under ss.63 to 66 of the 2011 Act.[581]

F. The Cy-Près Scheme

Section 67 of the Charities Act 2011[582] sets out how the power of the court or the Commission to make a cy-près scheme is to be exercised. The court or the Commission must have regard to three matters (under s.67(3)): (a) the spirit of the original gift; (b) the desirability of securing that the property is applied for charitable purposes which are close to the original purposes; and (c) the need for the charity which will apply the property under the scheme to have purposes which are suitable and effective in the light of current social and economic circumstances. If the scheme provides for the property to be transferred to another charity, the scheme may require the trustees of that charity to ensure that the property is applied for purposes which are, so far as is reasonably practicable, similar in character to the original purposes.

15–080

The section applies to cy-près schemes generally, whether or not involving charity collections.

---

[578] The Law Commission has suggested that donations not exceeding £120 should be applicable cy-près without the need to contact donors (unless the donor has specifically stated that donation should be returned if the purpose fails): *Technical Issues in Charity Law* (2017) para.6.46, Recommendation 11.

[579] Charities Act 2011 s.64.

[580] See D. Wilson [1983] Conv. 40, arguing that this is never the case where the gift is anonymous and indistinguishable, because the property either goes cy-près by the imputation of a general charitable intent (see *Re Hillier* [1954] 1 W.L.R. 700) or to the Crown as bona vacantia.

[581] Law Com. No. 375, *Technical Issues in Charity Law* (2017) para.6.65, Recommendation 12.

[582] Re-enacting previous legislation.

G.   Small Charities; Spending Capital; Mergers

15–081   Under s.267[583] of the 2011 Act, trustees of an unincorporated charity may resolve (if at least two-thirds of them agree) to pass all of its property to another charity if its gross income in the last financial year did not exceed £10,000 and it does not hold any land on trusts which stipulate that it is to be used for the purposes of the charity. The trustees must be satisfied that this would further the purposes of their charity and that the purposes of the charity receiving the property are substantially similar. There are various safeguards, including a duty to notify the Commission, which may direct the trustees to give a public notice, so that representations may be made.

Alternatively, the trustees of an unincorporated charity may resolve (if at least two-thirds of them agree) to replace the purposes of the charity. This may be done under s.275[584] of the 2011 Act, which sets out the same conditions as mentioned above in relation to annual income and land. The trusts may be modified by replacing all or any of the purposes of the charity with other charitable purposes, provided the trustees are satisfied that it is expedient in the interests of the charity to do so and that the new purposes are similar in character so far as is reasonably possible. Similar safeguards apply as in the case of transfer of property mentioned above. The Law Commission has recommended the replacement of s.275 with a new broader statutory power for unincorporated charities to make changes to their governing documents, with the new power not to depend upon an income threshold.[585]

Sections 281 to 314 of the 2011 Act[586] make further provision for the optimum use of charity funds by permitting the expenditure of capital (which would not otherwise be allowed) and facilitating the merger of charities. Broadly, trustees of an unincorporated charity may resolve that all or part of the permanent endowment may be spent if this would enable the purposes of the charity to be carried out more effectively than if only the income could be spent.[587] Where the capital was given by a particular individual or institution and the endowment fund exceeds £10,000 and the income in the last financial year exceeded £1,000, the Commission must be notified of the trustees' resolution and concur with it.[588]

Provision is made for the merger of two or more charities in circumstances where, for example, one charity transfers its property to another and ceases to

---

[583] Some of the conditions are set out in s.268. See also s.271, dealing with objections to the resolution by the Commission. Section 273 modifies the provisions where the charity has a permanent endowment. The Law Commission has recommended repeal of s.280: *Technical Issues in Charity Law* (2017) para.11.48.

[584] See also s.280, which enables the trusts of an unincorporated charity to be modified in relation to administrative powers and procedures; F. Quint [2013] P.C.B. 334. The Law Commission has proposed replacement of s.280: Law Com. No. 375, *Technical Issues in Charity Law* (2017), para.4.121.

[585] Law Com. No. 375, *Technical Issues in Charity Law* (2017), para.4.28ff.

[586] Re-enacting previous legislation.

[587] s.281.

[588] s.282. The Secretary of State may amend the relevant sums by order: s.285.

exist, or where two charities transfer their property to a new charity and then cease to exist. The Commission must maintain a register of such mergers.[589]

The Law Commission has proposed various reforms to facilitate mergers in appropriate cases, to review thresholds and to vary the restrictions on the use of permanent endowment.[590]

9.   THE ADMINISTRATION OF CHARITIES

A.   Legislative position

It will be seen below that the current law, consolidating various incremental reforms, is contained in the Charities Act 2011, supplemented by further legislation. As noted above,[591] the Law Commission has proposed further reform in its Technical Issues in Charity Law, and these proposals are noted where relevant below.

15–082

B.   The Authorities

i.   The Charity Commission.   The Charities Act 2006 established the Charity Commission for England and Wales as a corporate body, with statutory objectives, functions, powers and duties.[592] The aim of this reform was to improve accountability and transparency.

15–083

The objectives of the Commission are: (i) the public confidence objective, to increase public trust and confidence in charities, (ii) the public benefit objective, to promote awareness and understanding of the operation of the public benefit requirement of charities, (iii) the compliance objective, to promote compliance by charity trustees with their legal obligations,[593] (iv) the charitable resources objective, to promote the effective use of charitable resources, and (v) the accountability objective, to enhance the accountability of charities to donors, beneficiaries and the public.[594]

The general functions of the Commission include, in particular, to determine whether institutions are charities or not; to encourage and facilitate the better administration of charities; and to identify, investigate and deal with mismanagement of charities or misconduct.[595]

The Commission must also publish an Annual Report.[596] In recent years, the Commission has had to address various high-profile instances of charity failings

---

[589] s.305. A gift to a charity which has ceased to exist under a merger will normally take effect as a gift to the charity which still exists; s.311.

[590] Law Com. No. 375, *Technical Issues in Charity Law* (2017).

[591] Above, para.15–001.

[592] Now Charities Act 2011 s.13.

[593] The Commission used its compliance powers 1,099 times in 2016–17: *Annual Report and Accounts 2016–17*, p.15.

[594] Charities Act 2011 s.14. See also Lord Mance JSC in *Kennedy v Charity Commission* [2014] UKSC 20 at [45].

[595] Charities Act 2011 s.15. See also s.16 (general duties) and s.20 (incidental powers). The Commission may charge fees in some cases; s.19.

[596] Charities Act 2011 Sch.1 para.11.

and failures:[597] in its 2016–17 Annual Report, the Commission observed that "Public scrutiny of unacceptable fundraising practices, data protection violations and poor governance resulted in trust and confidence in charities falling to unprecedented levels in 2016."[598]

15–084   ii. The Official Custodian for Charities.   The Commission is required to appoint an Official Custodian for Charities,[599] a corporation sole. The original object was that charity trustees could vest trust property in the custodian and thereby avoid "the necessity for periodical transfers of land and securities upon the appointment of new trustees",[600] and the necessity to reclaim income tax on investments, as dividends are remitted without deduction. The role of the Official Custodian has been reduced, in order to increase the responsibility of the trustees. The Official Custodian now rarely holds property other than land.[601]

15–085   iii. The Visitor.   Ecclesiastical[602] and eleemosynary[603] corporations are subject to the jurisdiction of the visitor in relation to their internal affairs. The visitor once had an important role to play in the universities, but the Education Reform Act 1988 abolished the visitor's jurisdiction in relation to the appointment, employment and dismissal of university staff, and most student complaints are now dealt with by the Office of the Independent Adjudicator for Higher Education.[604] Ecclesiastical corporations are visitable by the ordinary. In the case of eleemosynary corporations, the founder may appoint a visitor. If none is appointed, the founder (or his heirs) is the visitor by operation of law.[605] A similar principle applies where the Crown is the founder.

The visitor's jurisdiction stems from the power recognised by the common law in the founder of an eleemosynary corporation to provide the law under which it was to be governed and to be sole judge of the interpretation and application of those laws, either himself or via the person appointed as visitor.

---

[597] Such as the collapse of the Keeping Kids Company Charity, which led to an inquiry by the Public Administration and Accounts Committee: *Annual Report and Accounts 2016–17*, 3 and *Annual Report 2015–16*, p.11.

[598] *Annual Report and Accounts 2016–17*, p.2.

[599] Charities Act 2011 s.21, re-enacting previous legislation. The Custodian has no management powers; *Muman v Nagasena* [2000] 1 W.L.R. 299.

[600] Annual Report 1970, para.75.

[601] For the provisions as to land, see Charities Act 2011 ss.90–95.

[602] Corporations existing for the furtherance of religion and the perpetuation of the rites of the Church.

[603] The original meaning was corporations whose object was the distribution of free alms, or the relief of individual distress; *Re Armitage's WT* [1972] Ch. 438. But for the purpose of visitatorial powers, corporate schools and most universities became included. Similarly the Inns of Court; see *R. v Visitors to the Inns of Court, Ex Calder* [1994] Q.B. 1 and *O'Connor v Bar Standards Board* [2017] UKSC 78.

[604] The complaints scheme is governed by the Higher Education Act 2004, as amended by the Consumer Rights Act 2015 and the Higher Education and Research Act 2017.

[605] *Phillips v Bury* (1694) Skinn. 447. If the heirs die out or cannot act, the Crown is the visitor.

C.   The Register

Section 29[606] of the 2011 Act requires the Commission to maintain a public   **15–086**
register on which all charities are to be included except for (a) exempt
charities,[607] (b) any charity excepted by order and whose gross income does not
exceed £100,000 a year, (c) any charity excepted by regulation and whose gross
income does not exceed £100,000 a year and (d) any charity whose gross income
does not exceed £5,000. As of 31 March 2017, there were over 167,000 charities
on the register.[608] The purpose of the register, which is online, is allow people to
obtain information about charities: charities' details on the register were viewed
13.1 million times during 2016–17.[609] Those which are excepted are those which
are national institutions (exempt charities), small ones, and others such as
ecclesiastical charities and some armed forces charities where provision for
obtaining the necessary information already exists.

D.   Decisions on Registration

It is the duty of trustees of charities to register,[610] enforceable by order of the   **15–087**
Commission.[611] Registration is much to the advantage of the trustees, for it raises
a conclusive presumption of being a charity,[612] and of being entitled therefore to
the privileges accorded to charity. However, this is subject to an important
exception. In order to be eligible for tax relief, the organisation must also satisfy
the further requirements imposed by the Finance Act 2010.[613]

The decision to register an applicant is that of the Charity Commission, and an
account of recent decisions is given in the Annual Reports. In this way, the
development of charity law is greatly influenced by the Commission.[614] Any
person who may be affected by registration may object to registration, or apply
for removal.[615] Nearly all these matters are finally disposed of by the
Commission, but there is an appeal system, with appeals lying in the main to the
First Tier Tribunal.[616] An appeal from the Tribunal's decision lies to the High

---

[606] Re-enacting previous legislation.
[607] s.30. Exempt charities are regulated by other bodies, such as the Higher Education Funding
Council.
[608] *Annual Report and Accounts 2016–17*, p.4. There were also 16,455 subsidiaries.
[609] *Annual Report and Accounts 2016–17*, p.22. This was an increase of 5 million on the previous
year.
[610] Charities Act 2011 s.35.
[611] s.335.
[612] s.37.
[613] s.30 and Sch.6; above, para.15–005.
[614] "Where the law is dated, unclear or imprecise and, unless strict precedent binds us, we approach
the cases in a way we think the courts would." *Annual Report and Accounts 2016–17*, p.4.
[615] Charities Act 2011 s.36; on standing, see *Nicholson v Charity Commission for England and Wales*
[2016] UKUT 198 (TCC) (UT (Tax)).
[616] See now Charities Act 2011 Pt 17. In *Watch Tower Bible & Tract Society of Britain v The Charity
Commission* [2016] EWCA Civ 154, it was held that the Tribunal does not have jurisdiction to
entertain a challenge to an order for the production of documents under s.52 of the Charities Act 2011:
such an order must be challenged by judicial review.

Court. The Attorney General may appeal to the Tribunal from a decision of the Commission, and may intervene in proceedings before the Tribunal or High Court.

In making its decision, the Commission is aware of the need for flexibility, and for keeping the law of charities in tune with changing circumstances. The number of applications for registration has been rising in recent years: in 2016–17, the Commission approved 6,045 charity registration applications.[617]

E. Advice

15–088 The Commission may also give to any charity trustee an opinion or advice on any matter affecting the performance of his duties or the proper administration of the charity, and a trustee acting upon it is deemed to have acted in accordance with the trust.[618] The Commission's advice is also available where an application is made to register a new charity. If the application is refused, the reason will be given so that the language may be amended. It is not of course possible to alter the terms of established trusts which fail to be registered.

F. Other Powers of the Charity Commission

15–089 **i. Schemes.** The Charity Commission has concurrent jurisdiction with the High Court in establishing schemes for the administration of a charity.[619] This helps the trustees of charities to administer them more efficiently and to make better use of their funds and property. Schemes may cover the appointment of new bodies of trustees, the vesting of property in new trustees, the provision of new cy-près objects in place of objects which have become impracticable, the extension of the trustees' investment powers, and the grouping or amalgamation of charities. Schemes are usually made by the Commission on the application of a charity, or where the court, on directing a scheme, orders that the Commission shall settle the scheme.[620] It is the duty of charity trustees to secure the effective use of charity property.[621] If they unreasonably refuse or neglect to apply for a scheme in circumstances in which they ought, in the interest of the charity, to do so, the Commission may proceed as if an application for a scheme had been made in the case of a charity at least 40 years old.[622]

15–090 **ii. Consent to Proceedings.** By s.115 of the Charities Act 2011, no court proceedings relating to the administration of a charity (other than an exempt

---

[617] *Annual Report and Accounts 2016–17*, p.22.

[618] Charities Act 2011 s.110.

[619] Charities Act 2011 s.69; The exercise of the Commission's power to make cy-près schemes was discussed above, para.15–066.

[620] Charities Act 2011 s.69. As to the right of appeal, see *Childs v Attorney General* [1973] 1 W.L.R. 497.

[621] Charities Act 2011 s.61.

[622] Charities Act 2011 s.70(5). The restriction to charities 40 years old was introduced in order to protect donors against official intervention to alter the terms of trusts within the donor's lifetime.

charity) shall be entertained unless authorised by the Commission.[623] This is to prevent the dissipation of charitable funds in legal proceedings over matters which the Commission could resolve, or, as it was recently put in *Abdelmamoud v The Egyptian Association In Great Britain Ltd*,[624] "to avoid the funds of a charity being squandered in internal disputes that are not in the best interest of the charity."[625] The Law Commission has recommended that it be possible to obtain authorisation from the court where the Charity Commission would face a conflict of interest in considering whether to authorise charity proceedings.[626]

iii. Dealings with Charity Property. Charity trustees are subject to various statutory restrictions on dealings in charity property. Of particular importance is s.117 of the Charities Act 2011,[627] restricting the trustees' powers[628] to sell, lease or otherwise dispose of charity land.[629] The trustees require an order of the court or of the Commission unless the following conditions are satisfied: (a) the trustees have obtained and considered a written report on the proposed disposition from a qualified surveyor; (b) they have advertised the proposed disposition as advised by the surveyor; and (c) they are satisfied that the terms are the best reasonably obtainable.[630] Where the trustees hold land on trusts which stipulate that it is to be used for the purposes (or any particular purpose) of the charity, they must also give public notice and invite and consider representations.[631] Such land could be sold in certain circumstances under the previous law.[632]   **15–091**

Under s.105 of the Act of 2011, the Commission has a general power to authorise dealings with charity property which the trustees would otherwise have no power to do. The Law Commission has proposed reform in respect of trustees' powers in relation to land and its acquisition.[633]

iv. Accounts; Inquiries. The Commission oversees the trustees' duty to provide accounts,[634] and, if dissatisfied in any way, may institute inquiries.[635]   **15–092**

---

[623] This provision may also apply to steps within existing proceedings: *Park v Cho* [2014] EWHC 55 (Ch).
[624] [2015] EWHC 1013 (Ch).
[625] [2015] EWHC 1013 (Ch) per Edward Murray (sitting as a Deputy Judge of the Chancery Division) at [73]. See also Birss J in *Choudhury v Stepney Shahjalal Mosque & Cultural Centre Ltd* [2015] EWHC 743 (Ch) at [21].
[626] *Technical Issues in Charity Law* (2017), para.15.18 and Recommendation 40.
[627] See also s.124 (mortgages).
[628] Deriving from the Trusts of Land and Appointment of Trustees Act 1996 s.6 (which cannot be excluded by the settlor; s.8(3)), or under the founding instrument or statute.
[629] Such land is no longer settled land but is held on a trust of land; Trusts of Land and Appointment of Trustees Act 1996 s.2(5).
[630] s.119. Neither s.117 nor s.124 (mortgages) applies to exempt charities. A disposition not complying with s.117 is valid in favour of a purchaser in good faith; s.122(6). See *Bayoumi v Women's Total Abstinence Educational Union Ltd* [2004] Ch. 46; D. Dennis [2006] Conv. 219.
[631] s.121.
[632] See *Oldham BC v Attorney General* [1993] Ch. 210; and more recently *Baddeley v Sparrow* [2015] UKUT 420 (TCC) (concerning the Bath Recreation Ground).
[633] *Technical Issues in Charity Law* (2017) Ch.7, and Recommendations 16 to 21.
[634] Charities Act 2011 Pt 8.

Ultimately, they may remove trustees from office.[636] The Commission may be alerted by HMRC and other public authorities to the possible misapplication of charity funds.[637]

It was in the area of accounts and audit that much disquiet was felt over the possibility of abuse and maladministration by charity trustees. Provisions now found in the Charities Act 2011 impose more rigorous duties on trustees of unincorporated charities[638] to keep accounting records and to prepare annual accounts, which must be audited.[639] The trustees must prepare and (in some case) send annual reports to the Commission of their activities, with a statement of accounts and the auditor's report.[640] The Commission may grant a unifying order enabling two or more charities with the same trustees to file consolidated accounts.[641] By Charities Act 2011 s.177, "Charity trustees" means "persons having the general control and management of the administration of a charity", and the court's jurisdiction over them extends to those whose role in the affairs of a charity falls within this definition even if not a "trustee in the strict sense".[642]

G. Investment

15–093   **i.   Investment Powers.**   The wide powers of investment conferred by the Trustee Act 2000 (discussed in Ch.18) apply to charity trustees. As mentioned below, this legislation also permits them to delegate their investment powers. The Charities (Protection and Social Investment) Act 2016 has implemented the recommendations of the Law Commission[643] by introducing reforms in respect of social investment by charities: these changes are more fully addressed in Ch.19,[644] but broadly they aim to clarify the extent to which charity trustees can take into account considerations beyond the maximisation of financial returns when considering and making investments. By s.4 of the Trusts (Capital and Income) Act 2013,[645] charitable trustees have the power to invest the endowment

---

[635] Charities Act 2011 s.46. Examples may be found in most of the Annual Reports. On appeals in respect of decisions under s.46 (and also s.52 on production of documents), see *Watch Tower Bible & Tract Society of Britain v The Charity Commission* [2016] EWCA Civ 154.

[636] Charities Act 2011 s.79, below, para.15–098. See also *Attorney General v Schonfeld* [1980] 1 W.L.R. 1182.

[637] Charities Act 2011 ss.54, 55. Disclosure of information by the Commission to other public authorities is dealt with by s.56.

[638] Companies Act 2006 Pt 15, applies to corporate charities. Charities Act 2011 Pt 11, governs Charitable Incorporated Organisations. The rules do not apply to exempt charities, but s.136 of the 2011 Act imposes a duty to keep accounts on them.

[639] ss.130–132, 144.

[640] ss.162–164. The reports are subject to public inspection; s.170. The trustees must also send annual returns in prescribed form to the Commission; s.169. Persistent default in these duties is an offence; s.173.

[641] s.12(2). The order may apply to all or any of the purposes of the Act.

[642] *Trustees of the Celestial Church of Christ, Edward Street Parish v Lawson* [2017] EWHC 97 (Ch); [2017] P.T.S.R. 790 per Judge Hodge QC at [39].

[643] Law Commission, *Social Investment by Charities: The Law Commission's Recommendations* (September 2014); see Charity Commission guidance CC14 (2011) and also *Harries v Church Commissioners for England* [1992] 1 W.L.R. 1241.

[644] Below, para.19–021.

[645] Inserting ss.104A and B into the Charities Act 2011. Below, para.19–005.

fund, or a portion of it, on a "total return" basis, which affords more flexibility. The trustees must be satisfied that it is in the interests of the charity to invest in accordance with special Commission regulations.

ii. Pooling. COIF Common Deposit Scheme. Without statutory authority, **15–094** different bodies of trustees could not pool their funds for investment purposes, for this would involve a delegation of the trustees' investment powers, which was not permitted prior to the Trustee Act 2000. Section 96 of the 2011 Act (re-enacting earlier provisions) gives power to the court or the Commission to create common investment schemes under which the investment of property transferred to the fund is invested by trustees appointed to manage the fund, and the participating charities are entitled to shares related to their contributions.[646] The predecessor legislation established the Charities Official Investment Fund, which is open to all charities.

The Charities Act 2011 also authorises the creation of common deposit schemes,[647] whereby money can be deposited at interest.

H. Delegation

The Trustee Act 2000 widened trustees' delegation powers, as discussed in Ch.21. **15–095** Special rules, however, apply to delegation by charity trustees. They may delegate:

(a) any function consisting of carrying out a decision that the trustees have taken;
(b) any function relating to the investment of trust assets (including the management of land held as an investment); and
(c) any function relating to the raising of funds otherwise than by means of profits of a trade which is an integral part of carrying out the trust's charitable purpose.[648]

Charity trustees may exercise the statutory powers of appointing nominees and custodians,[649] save in relation to assets vested in the official custodian for charities.[650]

---

[646] Annual Report 1970 paras 68–74; 1971 para.90; *Re London University's Charitable Trust* [1964] Ch. 282.

[647] s.100. See also Trustee Act 2000 s.38.

[648] Trustee Act 2000 s.11(3). Other functions may be added by statutory instrument.

[649] Trustee Act 2000 ss.16, 17. The Charity Commission has provided guidance: Appointing nominees and custodians (CC42, 2011).

[650] Above, para.15–084.

I.   Trustees

15–096   **i.   Capacity.**   One of the means by which the Charities Act 2011 aims to prevent fraud and maladministration is by the disqualification[651] of certain persons from holding the office of trustee of a charity.[652] Those disqualified include persons convicted of an offence involving dishonesty or deception, undischarged bankrupts and persons previously removed from charity trusteeship on the grounds of misconduct or mismanagement:[653] the grounds for disqualification were revised and expanded by the Charities (Protection and Social Investment) Act 2016, which also provides that those disqualified from charity trusteeship are disqualified from positions with senior management functions in a charity.[654] Also a Local Authority may not be trustee of an eleemosynary charity.[655] We have seen that the appointment of a charity as trustee may colour the construction which a court will place upon the language of the trust, but does not ensure that a trust is charitable.[656]

15–097   **ii.   Number. Majority Vote.**   There is no limit upon the number of persons who may be trustees of a charity.[657] Too great a number of trustees is an obvious inconvenience. But decisions of trustees of a charity may be taken by majority vote and need not be unanimous.[658]

15–098   **iii.   Retirement, Removal and Suspension.**   Charity trustees may retire in the same way as trustees of private trusts.[659] The Commission may suspend a trustee on being satisfied as a result of inquiries[660] that (a) there has been a failure to comply with an order or direction of the Commission, or other misconduct or mismanagement or (b) that it is necessary or desirable for the purpose of protecting the property of the charity,[661] or it may appoint additional trustees or make orders for the protection of the property, such as the appointment of a receiver and manager. Where it is satisfied that both conditions (a) and (b) are fulfilled, it may order the removal of a trustee or other officer who has been responsible for or privy to the misconduct or mismanagement or has contributed to or facilitated it.[662] It may also (or instead) order a scheme for the administration of the charity. The Commission may also, by order made of its

---

[651] The Commission has produced guidance on automatic disqualification for individuals (*https://www.gov.uk/guidance/automatic-disqualification-rules-for-charity-trustees-and-charity-senior-positions* [accessed 4 July 2018]) and charities (*https://www.gov.uk/guidance/automatic-disqualification-rule-changes-guidance-for-charities* [accessed 4 July 2018]).

[652] s.178. By s.183, it is an offence to act while disqualified. The disqualification may be waived by the Commission; Charities Act 2011 s.181.

[653] There is a public register of persons so removed.

[654] Now s.178(2) and (4–3),

[655] *Re Armitage* [1972] Ch. 438.

[656] Above, para.15–057.

[657] Trustee Act 1925 s.34.

[658] *Re Whiteley* [1910] 1 Ch. 600 at 608.

[659] Below, Ch.18, Part 11.

[660] Under Charities Act 2011 s.46. *Jones v Attorney General* [1974] Ch. 148 and *Mountstar (PTC) Ltd v The Charity Commission for England and Wales* [2013] CA/2013/0001 (FTT(C)).

[661] s.76.

[662] See *Weth v Attorney General* [1999] 1 W.L.R. 686.

own motion, remove a charity trustee who has been discharged from bankruptcy within the last five years, who is a corporation in liquidation, lacks mental capacity to act, has failed to act, or is abroad or cannot be found.[663] In such cases, it may appoint a replacement or additional trustee. These provisions do not apply to exempt charities. It can thus be seen that extensive powers have been given to the Commission for the protection of charities in the circumstances described above.[664]

iv. Remuneration. The Trustee Act 2000 extends trustees' powers to charge **15–099** for their services, as discussed in Ch.21. The Law Commission recommended that charity trustees should be excluded, on the ground that public confidence in the sector might otherwise be undermined.[665] The provisions of the Act of 2000 whereby trust corporations may receive remuneration although the trust instrument confers no such entitlement do not apply to charity trustees, but the Secretary of State may by regulations make provision for the remuneration of charity trustees who are trust corporations or who act in a professional capacity.[666] The Charities Act 2011[667] permits a charity trustee (or a person connected with the trustee, such as a spouse) to be remunerated from charity funds by a written agreement made with the charity or its trustees (as the case may be). Various conditions apply, including that the remuneration must not exceed a reasonable amount, and it is in the best interests of the charity for the services to be provided by the trustee (or connected person).

A related question is whether charity trustees should be prohibited from supplying goods and services to a charity on the ground that this might create a conflict of interest and duty.[668] This is permitted in certain circumstances.[669] The Law Commission has proposed some extension of powers for trustee remuneration for the supply of goods.[670]

v. Misapplication or other Breach. An application by the trustee for **15–100** purposes not covered by the terms of the trust is a misapplication of charity funds, which may give rise to personal liability on the trustee, and may be restrained by injunction,[671] or may be the subject of an inquiry by the Charity Commission.[672] A charity trustee (or auditor) may be relieved from liability (wholly or partly) by order of the Charity Commission if it considers that he is or may be personally liable for breach of duty but has acted honestly and reasonably

---

[663] Charities Act 2011 s.80.

[664] Charities Act 2011 ss.76–85.

[665] Law Com. No. 260, *Trustees' Powers and Duties* (1999), para.7.22.

[666] Trustee Act 2000 ss.29, 30.

[667] s.185. The Law Commission has proposed that this power should extend to allowing the supply of goods by a trustee: *Technical Issues in Charity Law* (2017) para.6.65, Recommendation 25.

[668] Below, Ch.21.

[669] Annual Report 1971 para.93.

[670] *Technical Issues in Charity Law* (2017) para.6.65, Ch.9.

[671] *Baldry v Feintuck* [1972] 1 W.L.R. 552 (resolution to apply Students' Union funds for political purposes).

[672] Above, para.15–092.

and ought fairly to be excused.[673] This is in addition to the similar powers of the court to grant relief under s.61 of the Trustee Act 1925.[674]

---

[673] Charities Act 2011 s.191.
[674] Below, para.24–037.

CHAPTER 16

NON-CHARITABLE PURPOSE TRUSTS

1. THE GENERAL PROBLEM

A. Private Trusts, Purpose Trusts, Charitable Trusts

16–001   A PRIVATE trust is essentially a trust in favour of ascertainable individuals. A charitable trust is a trust for purposes which are treated in law as charitable. The question for consideration in this chapter is whether or not it is possible to establish a trust for non-charitable purposes.

We have considered in earlier chapters questions relating to the setting up of trusts for individuals, and the previous chapter considered charitable trusts. The purpose trusts now under consideration are those which do not come within these categories. What of a trust, for example, to feed the testator's horses and hounds,[1] to set up a monument,[2] or to be applied for useful or benevolent purposes?[3] There is no question of any such trusts having any privilege in relation to taxation or to perpetuity, such as is allowed in the case of charitable trusts. The question is whether they are valid or void.[4]

B. Trusts for Persons and Purposes

16–002   With any particular trust, there may be a question of construction to determine whether the trust is for persons or for purposes. Most purposes affect persons, and there is no reason why a trust should not be treated as a trust for persons where the beneficiaries are to be benefited in some way other than by payment of money. Thus, a trust for the education of the children of X can be construed as a trust of which the children of X are the beneficiaries.[5] A trust for the promotion of fox-hunting (before hunting with hounds became illegal) would be treated as a trust for a purpose, although it might be said that the individual sportsman might benefit from it.[6]

There are various examples of trusts in which the beneficiaries enjoy only a limited proprietary interest. Where, for example, a debtor assigns an asset to trustees for the payment of his debts, his creditors do not, unless there has been an absolute assignment, take any surplus.[7] In *Re the Trusts of Abbott Fund*,[8] it was accepted that a trust for the maintenance of two old ladies was valid although it seems that they did not become owners of any proprietary interest. In *Re*

---

[1] *Re Dean* (1889) 41 Ch.D. 554.

[2] *Mussett v Bingle* [1876] W.N. 170; *Re Endacott* [1960] Ch. 232.

[3] *Morice v Bishop of Durham* (1804) 9 Ves.Jr. 399.

[4] See generally L. Sheridan (1953) 17 Conv.(N.S.) 46; O. Marshall (1953) 6 C.L.P. 151; Morris and Leach, Ch.12; Maudsley, *The Modern Law of Perpetuities* (1979), pp.166–178; P. Lovell (1970) 34 Conv.(N.S.) 77; J. Harris (1971) 87 L.Q.R. 31; L. McKay (1973) 37 Conv.(N.S.) 420; N. Gravells (1977) 40 M.L.R. 397; K. Widdows (1977) 41 Conv.(N.S.) 179; P. Matthews in A. Oakley (ed.), *Trends in Contemporary Trust Law* (Oxford: Oxford University Press, 1996) Ch.1.

[5] See J. Davies [1968] A.S.C.L. at 439. See also *Re Osoba* [1979] 1 W.L.R. 247, above para.11–009.

[6] *Re Thompson* [1934] Ch. 342, below, para.16–012.

[7] *Re Rissik* [1936] Ch. 68.

[8] [1900] 2 Ch. 326, above, para.11–007; contrast *Re Andrew's Trust* [1905] 2 Ch. 48; *Re Foord* [1922] 2 Ch. 519; above, paras 2–012, 11–007.

Gillingham Bus Disaster Fund,[9] a fund collected for the benefit of injured cadets was not invalid, although there was no suggestion that the cadets could ever have claimed the assets of the fund. It may be possible to support these latter decisions as examples of discretionary trusts for the benefit of individuals; but they were not so drafted, and it may be preferable to regard them as examples of trusts for persons to be benefited in a particular way. The proper analysis of trusts of this kind was little discussed until the decision of Goff J in *Re Denley's Trust Deed* in 1969.[10]

In that case, a plot of land was conveyed to trustees to hold, for a period determined by lives

> "for the purpose of a recreation or sports ground primarily for the benefit of the employees of the company and secondarily for the benefit of such other person or persons (if any) as the trustees may allow."

Goff J upheld the trust as one for the benefit of the employees. They were ascertainable, and the trust was one which the court could control. If it had been construed as a trust for non-charitable purposes, it would have been void.

> "The objection [to non-charitable purpose trusts] is not that the trust is for a purpose or an object per se, but that there is no beneficiary or cestui que trust."[11]

Here, however, "the trust deed expressly states that... the employees of the company shall be entitled to the use and enjoyment of the land."[12] It was therefore "outside the mischief of the beneficiary principle".[13] He contrasted this situation with

> "a purpose... trust, the carrying out of which would benefit an individual or individuals, where that benefit is so indirect or intangible or which is otherwise so framed as not to give those persons any *locus standi* to apply to the court to enforce the trust"[14]

in which case the trust would have been a non-charitable purpose trust, and void.

The same line of reasoning was applied in *Re Lipinski's Will Trusts*,[15] a case of a gift to an unincorporated association. There, the testator bequeathed his residuary estate to trustees in trust as to one-half for the Hull Judeans (Maccabi) Association: **16–003**

> "[I]n memory of my late wife to be used solely in the work of constructing the new buildings for the association and/or improvements to the said buildings."

---

[9] [1959] Ch. 62, above, para.11–007. The residue for "worthy causes" was void for uncertainty.

[10] [1969] 1 Ch. 373. See also *Wicks v Firth* [1983] A.C. 214 (non-charitable trust to award scholarships assumed valid).

[11] [1969] 1 Ch. 373 at 383.

[12] *Re Denley's Trust Deed* [1969] 1 Ch. 373 at 383.

[13] *Re Denley's Trust Deed* [1969] 1 Ch. 373 at 383.

[14] *Re Denley's Trust Deed* [1969] 1 Ch. 373 at 382. For discussion of locus standi to enforce the *Re Denley* type of trust, see A. Everton [1982] Conv. 118 at 124.

[15] [1976] Ch. 235; (1977) 93 L.Q.R. 167; K. Widdows (1977) 41 Conv.(N.S.) 179; N. Gravells (1977) 40 M.L.R. 231; *Re Turkington* [1937] 4 All E.R. 501. See further below, para.16–029.

At first sight, this would appear to be a gift to an unincorporated association to be applied for its (non-charitable) purposes.[16] We shall see,[17] however, that gifts to unincorporated associations are normally upheld as gifts to the members rather than invalidated as purpose trusts. To the extent that the testator's superadded purpose hindered this construction, *Re Denley's Trust Deed*[18] came to the rescue.

The beneficiaries, the members of the association, were ascertainable; there was no problem of perpetuity,[19] because they could, according to the rules of the association, terminate the trust for their own benefit.[20] The implication of these factors will be discussed later in the chapter.

Such cases show a more liberal judicial tendency in connection with the construction of gifts of this type.[21] *Re Denley*, however, could not save the trust in *R. v District Auditor, Ex p. West Yorkshire MCC*,[22] where a local authority, purporting to act under statutory powers, resolved to create a trust "for the benefit of any or all or some of the inhabitants of the County of West Yorkshire" in any of four ways: (i) to assist economic development in the county in order to relieve unemployment and poverty; (ii) to assist bodies concerned with youth and community problems in West Yorkshire; (iii) to assist and encourage ethnic and minority groups in West Yorkshire; and (iv) to inform all interested and influential persons of the consequences of the abolition (proposed by the Government) of the Council and other metropolitan county councils and of other proposals affecting local government in the county. The capital and income were to be applied within a short period, avoiding any perpetuity problems, but the trust was void as a non-charitable purpose trust. It was not within the purpose trust exceptions illustrated by *Re Denley* and *Re Lipinski* because there were no "ascertained or ascertainable beneficiaries". Even if "inhabitant" was sufficiently certain, the class of 2,500,000 potential beneficiaries was so large that the trust was unworkable. It has never been established what certainty test applies to a *Re Denley* trust,[23] but this decision suggests that the class of beneficiaries, even if conceptually certain and not capricious, must not be too wide. A private trust which fails for "administrative unworkability"[24] cannot be rescued by the *Re Denley* principle.

It is necessary now to consider the objections to non-charitable purpose trusts.

---

[16] In favour of this construction, counsel relied on the reference to the testator's late wife's memory as indicating an intention to create an endowment; and on a requirement that the money was to be used "solely" for the stated purposes.

[17] Below, Part 5.

[18] [1969] 1 Ch. 373.

[19] Below, para.16–022. cf. *Re Grant's WT* [1980] 1 W.L.R. 360, below, para.16–018.

[20] By altering the constitution of the association. The beneficiaries in *Re Denley*, on the other hand, would seem to have no right to divide up the assets under the *Saunders v Vautier* principle (below, para.23–001), but no perpetuity problem arose because the trust was expressly confined to the perpetuity period.

[21] P. Lovell (1970) 34 Conv.(N.S.) 77; J. Harris (1972) 87 L.Q.R. 31.

[22] [1986] R.V.R. 24; C. Harpum (1986) 45 C.L.J. 391. The certainty aspects are discussed above, para.4–016.

[23] Although it is clear that the test for certainty of anomalous non-charitable trusts is a strict one: see *Re Endacott* [1960] Ch. 232.

[24] Above, para.4–016.

2. Objections to Purpose Trusts

If a disposition is construed as a trust for non-charitable purposes, there are **16–004** various objections which may be made to it. The first of these objections denies the possibility of existence of non-charitable purpose trusts. It has not however been consistently applied; and purpose trusts for the building of graves and monuments and the care of specific animals, which succeeded in the 19th century[25] are now regarded as anomalous, but still tolerated, exceptions to the rule.[26] The other objections accept the possibility of the existence of non-charitable purpose trusts, but impose restrictions upon them.

Before examining the objections, it should be said that a case may be made out that English law does not prohibit non-charitable purpose trusts.[27] Such trusts were regularly permitted before the 20th century, but, on this view, a wrong turning was taken in cases such as *Re Endacott*,[28] where the supposed rule was "invented". Many of the cases commonly cited as supporting the invalidity of purpose trusts were in fact based on uncertainty, perpetuity or some other defect. Indeed, the trust in *Morice v Bishop of Durham*[29] failed for uncertainty. Trusts for beneficiaries do not fail if there is no current beneficiary (for example, where they are unborn); the real point is that the trustees are accountable not to the beneficiaries but to the court. Nevertheless, the rule against non-charitable purpose trusts has become so entrenched that it is unlikely that the contrary view could prevail unless legislation intervenes.[30] Thus, the basic position remains as observed by Arnold J in *In Re St Andrew's (Cheam) Lawn Tennis Club Trust*[31]:

> "It is, regrettably, fairly plain that the trust deed is an attempt to achieve the legally impossible: a perpetual trust for a non-charitable purpose, namely to enable the members of the club to play tennis."

A. The Beneficiary Principle; Enforceability

The first objection may be seen in a celebrated dictum of Sir William Grant MR **16–005** in *Morice v Bishop of Durham*.[32] "Every other [i.e. non-charitable] trust must have a definite object. There must be somebody in whose favour the court can decree performance."[33] A trust, as we have seen, is an obligation. The objection is that there cannot be an obligation upon the trustees unless there is a correlative right in someone else to enforce it. With charitable trusts, as we have seen, the Attorney General and the Charity Commission are charged with the duty of

---

[25] Below, para.16–009.

[26] per Roxburgh J in *Re Astor's ST* [1952] Ch. 534 at 547.

[27] P. Baxendale-Walker, *Purpose Trusts*, 2nd edn (Bloomsbury, 2009).

[28] [1960] Ch. 232; below, para.16–010.

[29] Below, para.16–005.

[30] Equally, the existing exceptions may be sufficiently entrenched as to await legislation to remove them.

[31] [2012] 1 W.L.R. 3487 per Arnold J at [62]. See also *Gillan v HEC Enterprises Ltd* [2016] EWHC 3179 (Ch) per Morgan J at [56] noting that "a non-charitable purpose trust… would not seem to be legally possible".

[32] (1804) 9 Ves.Jr. 399.

[33] (1804) 9 Ves.Jr. 399 at 404.

enforcement.[34] With private trusts, no public official is involved. The trust is void unless there are human beneficiaries capable of enforcing the trust. In effect, the objection is that there is no beneficial owner of the property. Acceptance of this principle renders non-charitable purpose trusts totally void.

B.   Uncertainty

16–006   It was seen in the previous chapter that charitable trusts benefit from a more generous approach to certainty than other trusts: a trust "for charitable purposes" is vague but sufficiently certain.[35] Non-charitable purpose trusts do not benefit from such tolerance. If non-charitable purpose trusts are recognised at all by the law, they are only valid if the purposes are expressed with sufficient certainty to enable the court to control the performance of the trust. The point commonly arises in the cases where incompetent draftsmanship has failed to create a charitable trust; where, for example, the property is to be applied for charitable or benevolent purposes,[36] or, as in *Morice v Bishop of Durham*, for "such objects of benevolence and liberality as the Bishop of Durham in his own discretion shall most approve of." "Benevolence" and "liberality" are wider concepts than "charity", and the trust was not therefore applicable for charitable purposes only. The purposes were uncertain and the trust void. Indeed, this reason was more clearly emphasised by Sir William Grant MR than was the earlier objection. Having established that the trust was not for charitable purposes, and that the Bishop did not claim any personal benefit for himself, he said[37]:

> "That it is a trust, unless it be of a charitable nature, too indefinite to be executed by this Court, has not been, and cannot be denied. There can be no trust, over the exercise of which this Court will not assume a control; for an uncontrollable power of disposition would be ownership and not trust. If there be a clear trust, but for uncertain objects, the property, that is the subject of the trust, is indisposed of; and the benefit of such trust must result to those, to whom the law gives the ownership in default of disposition by the former owner. But this doctrine does not hold good with regard to trusts for charity. Every other trust must have a definite object. There must be somebody, in whose favour the Court can decree performance."

This objection could be met by specifying in sufficient detail the purposes to which the property is to be applied. Trusts for specific purposes like feeding the testator's animals, or maintaining a tomb or monument, usually pass this test. But

---

[34] There is evidence that historically charitable trusts were enforced by individuals; Baxendale-Walker, *Purpose Trusts*, 2nd edn (2009).

[35] Above, para.15–003.

[36] For such a purpose would not be exclusively charitable. Above, paras 15–058—15–064. *Blair v Duncan* [1902] A.C. 37; *Houston v Burns* [1918] A.C. 337; *Chichester Diocesan Fund and Board of Finance v Simpson* [1944] A.C. 341; *Re Atkinson's Will Trusts* [1978] 1 W.L.R. 586. It may be noted that in Ireland, s.49(1) of the Charities Act 1961 provides that "where any of the purposes of a gift includes or could be deemed to include both charitable and non-charitable objects, its terms shall be so construed and given effect to as to exclude the non-charitable objects and the purpose shall, accordingly, be treated as charitable". This provision was recently utilised by Gilligan J in *Daly v Murphy* [2017] IEHC 650 to apply a gift of the residue of an estate to "my Executor to apply same for such purposes as my executor in his absolute discretion shall think fit" to charitable purposes only.

[37] (1804) 9 Ves.Jr. 399 at 404–405.

general projects, even carefully drafted, are likely to be held void. The point only becomes significant, of course, if the problem of the beneficiary principle has been surmounted.

C. Excessive Delegation of Testamentary Power

There have been judicial statements to the effect that purpose trusts created by will are void because, in the absence of anyone to enforce the trust, the trustees are left to determine the application of the property; thus "the testator has imperfectly exercised his testamentary power; he has delegated it, for the disposal of his property lies with them, not with him."[38] The objection is not relevant to non-testamentary trusts. Of the trust in *Re Denley's Trust Deed*, Goff J said[39]:

> "If this were a will, a question might arise whether this provision might be open to attack as a delegation of the testamentary power. I do not say that would be so, but in any case it cannot be said of a settlement inter vivos."

The status of the objection was, however, not established, even with wills. Special, general and intermediate powers are permitted in wills[40]; and, "an anti-delegation rule is really an anti-power rule."[41]

In *Re Beatty's Will Trusts*[42] Hoffmann J, upholding a testamentary disposition to trustees to allocate, "to or among such person or persons as they think fit", rejected the supposed "anti-delegation" rule. Thus there is no objection on this basis to the validity of purpose trusts. Moreover, the acceptance of the validity of testamentary powers is significant. For, as will be seen,[43] one way of effecting a non-charitable purpose where there are willing trustees, may be to give them *power* to apply money to a particular purpose, and not to attempt to require them to do so.

D. Perpetuity

A charitable trust may last for ever; a non-charitable trust is void if it is to continue beyond the perpetuity period.[44] The reason is that perpetual non-charitable purpose trusts would conflict with the *policy* of the perpetuity rule, which is the prevention of the tying up of property for too long a period.

In its more usual context, the rule against perpetuities deals with the limit of time to which the vesting of future interests may be postponed. An outline of this

16–007

16–008

---

[38] *Leahy v Attorney General for New South Wales* [1959] A.C. 457 at 484; *Re Wood* [1949] Ch. 498 at 501.

[39] [1969] 1 Ch. 373 at 387.

[40] *Re Park* [1932] 1 Ch. 580; *Re Abraham's WT* [1969] 1 Ch. 463; *Re Gulbenkian's Settlements* [1970] A.C. 508; *Re Manisty's Settlement* [1974] Ch. 17; *Re Hay's Settlement Trusts* [1982] 1 W.L.R. 202. Above, para.7–004.

[41] D. Gordon (1953) 69 L.Q.R. 334 at 342.

[42] [1990] 1 W.L.R. 1503; J. Martin [1991] Conv. 138.

[43] Below, para.16–031.

[44] Most pension trusts are exempted.

has already been given.[45] In the present context, however, we are not concerned with future vesting. We are concerned with a situation in which the property is vested in the trustees to be applied by them for certain non-charitable purposes for a period which may exceed that of perpetuity. This situation will arise if either the capital or the income of the fund is to be so applied. If the trust relates to income, then the capital must be maintained in order to produce the income. It is no answer to say that, since the trustees may sell the present investments and purchase others, the capital is not inalienable. The objection relates, not only to alienability, but to duration. Whatever happens to individual investments, an obligation to retain the capital as a fund for an excessive period violates the rule. Accordingly, a non-charitable purpose trust is valid, if at all, only if it is confined to the perpetuity period. The matter is examined below.[46]

3.   EXCEPTIONAL CASES UPHOLDING PURPOSE TRUSTS[47]

16–009   Until *Re Astor's Settlement Trusts*[48] in 1952, it was arguably possible to establish a trust for a non-charitable purpose for the period of perpetuity. The old authorities cover a narrow field, being nearly all concerned with trusts for building or maintaining monuments or tombs, or for caring for the testator's animals.[49] But the language of the judgments is general, and there are occasional cases outside those fields. As will be seen, *Re Astor's Settlement Trusts* underlined the beneficiary principle; and it is clear that trusts for non-charitable purposes will fail unless they are kept strictly within the narrow confines of these exceptional cases.

A.   Tombs and Monuments

16–010   Reasonable provision for the building of a tomb or a gravestone for a testator may be regarded as a funeral expense, and valid independently of any doctrine relating to purpose trusts.[50] But bequests for family burial enclosures have been upheld as purpose trusts[51]; as have bequests for monuments to other people, such as the testator's wife's first husband.[52] Such a gift may be for the building of the monument which, it seems, may be assumed to be done within the period of perpetuity[53]; or for the care or the maintenance of the graves for a period limited to the period of perpetuity. An example is *Re Hooper*.[54]

---

[45] Above, Ch.14, Part 3.
[46] Below, para.16–022.
[47] Morris and Leach, pp.310–319; Maudsley, *The Modern Law of Perpetuities* (1979), pp.168–176.
[48] [1952] Ch. 534; below, para.16–013.
[49] A survey of practitioners in 2006 concluded that such trusts are still in use, mainly for animals; J. Brown [2007] Conv. 148.
[50] *Trimmer v Danby* (1856) 25 L.J.Ch. 424. Gray thought that it was the only justification for upholding such trusts: *The Rule Against Perpetuities*, 4th edn (1942) pp.310–311.
[51] *Pirbright v Salwey* [1896] W.N. 86; *Re Hooper* [1932] 1 Ch. 38.
[52] *Mussett v Bingle* [1876] W.N. 170.
[53] Below, para.16–022.
[54] [1932] 1 Ch. 38.

A testator gave a sum of money to trustees for the care and upkeep of certain family graves and monuments, and a tablet in a window in a church so far as the trustees could legally do so. Maugham J upheld the gift for a period of 21 years.[55]

Similarly, in *Mussett v Bingle*,[56] Hall VC held that since the executors were ready to carry out a bequest of £300 to erect a monument to the testator's wife's first husband, "it must be performed accordingly." But he held void for perpetuity a further gift for its upkeep.

Such trusts must of course comply with the requirement of certainty. In *Re Endacott*,[57] the Court of Appeal held void a residuary gift amounting to some £20,000 "to the North Tawton Devon Parish Council for the purpose of providing some useful memorial to myself." Such a trust, though specific in the sense that it indicated a purpose capable of expression, was "of far too wide and uncertain a nature to qualify within the class of cases cited."[58] No doubt was cast upon *Re Hooper* and the early cases. Yet *Re Endacott* may illustrate the stricter modern approach to purpose trusts.[59] Alternatively, perhaps it indicates the willingness of the court to allow reasonable sums to be spent upon these purposes, and a reluctance to uphold such grandiose schemes. This policy, as will be seen, is articulated in *Re Astor*. The Parish Councils and Burial Authorities (Miscellaneous Provisions) Act 1970 s.1 provides that a burial authority or a local authority may agree by contract to maintain a grave, or memorial or monument for a period not exceeding 99 years.

B.   Animals

Gifts for the care of specific animals, though not charitable, have also been upheld. There was no argument on the point in *Pettingall v Pettingall*[60] where an annuity of £50 to be applied in maintaining the testator's favourite black mare was held valid. In *Re Dean*,[61] the leading case, North J, relying on *Mitford v Reynolds*[62] and the monument cases, upheld a gift of £750 per annum for the period of 50 years for the maintenance of the testator's horses and hounds if they should so long live. He met head-on the argument that the court will not recognise a trust unless it is capable of being enforced by someone, by pronouncing: "I do not assent to that view."[63] There was no objection to such a provision, "provided, of course, that it is not to last for too long a period."[64] It is difficult to see how the gift could be upheld for a 50-year period; for the horses and hounds could not be the measuring lives for the period of perpetuity. This aspect of the matter is discussed below.[65] The case has been accepted as authority for the proposition that trusts for the upkeep of specific animals are valid for the

16–011

---

[55] Relying on *Pirbright v Salwey* [1896] W.N. 86.
[56] [1876] W.N. 170. See also *Trimmer v Danby* (1856) 25 L.J.Ch. 424.
[57] [1960] Ch. 232.
[58] [1960] Ch. 232 at 247.
[59] See below, para.16–013.
[60] (1842) 11 L.J.Ch. 176.
[61] (1889) 41 Ch.D. 552.
[62] (1848) 16 Sim. 105.
[63] (1889) 41 Ch.D. 552 at 556.
[64] (1889) 41 Ch.D. 552 at 557.
[65] Below, para.16–023.

perpetuity period. A possible difficulty, it has been suggested,[66] is that the fund might be claimed by the person who now owns the animal (e.g. as specific or residuary legatee). A fund to maintain another's property can be claimed by that other without applying it to the purpose.[67] Another solution might be to give the fund to the person acquiring the animal on the testator's death, determinable on the death of the animal or on the trustee's decision that it is improperly maintained.[68]

C.   Other Anomalous Purposes

16–012   Trusts for other purposes have on occasion been upheld; and others which have failed have been refused on the ground of perpetuity, without any indication that they would not have been valid if confined to the permitted period.

Trusts for the saying of masses for the benefit of private individuals have been considered to come into this category. Until the House of Lords decision in *Bourne v Keane* in 1919,[69] such trusts were regarded as being trusts for superstitious uses and void. *Bourne v Keane* held them valid. Such trusts have since been upheld as charitable in *Re Hetherington*[70] where the masses are said in public. Even where the masses are said in private, the trust is arguably charitable on the basis that public benefit can be found in the endowment of the priesthood. The acceptance of such trusts as charitable makes it unnecessary to consider them in the category of private purpose trusts.

One possible member of this category of miscellaneous purpose trusts is a trust for non-Christian private ceremonies. In *Re Khoo Cheng Teow*,[71] the Supreme Court of the Straits Settlements held valid a gift to be applied for the period of perpetuity in the performance of ceremonies called Sin Chew to perpetuate the testator's memory. The gift was not charitable; but the court held that it was valid for a period measured by royal lives plus 21 years.

A decision which has perhaps been elevated to a position of importance which it does not merit is *Re Thompson*[72]:

> An alumnus of Trinity Hall, Cambridge, bequeathed a legacy to one Lloyd, an old friend, to be applied in such manner as he should think fit towards the promotion and furtherance of fox-hunting, and gave the residuary estate to Trinity Hall. Lloyd made no claim to any beneficial interest, but desired to carry out the testator's wishes if he should be permitted to do so. Trinity Hall also was anxious that the trust should be performed; but felt it its duty, as a charity, to submit that the trust was void for lack of a beneficiary. There was no problem of perpetuity, and Clauson J held that the purpose was sufficiently certain. He upheld the gift by ordering the money to be paid to Lloyd upon his giving an undertaking to apply it for these stated objects, and gave to Trinity Hall liberty to apply if the money should be used for other purposes.

---

[66] P. Matthews (1983) 80 L.S.Gaz. 2451.

[67] *Re Bowes* [1896] 1 Ch. 507 (money directed to be laid out in planting trees on an estate belonged to the owners of the estate absolutely.) See also *Re Lipinski's Will Trusts* [1976] Ch. 235.

[68] See P. Matthews (1983) 80 L.S.Gaz. 2451, discussing other possibilities.

[69] [1919] A.C. 815.

[70] [1990] Ch. 1; N. Parry [1989] Conv. 453; above, para.15–041. See also *Re Caus* [1934] Ch. 162.

[71] [1932] Straits Settlements L.R. 226.

[72] [1934] Ch. 342. Fox-hunting with hounds has been illegal in England and Wales since the Hunting Act 2004. However, the gift in *Re Thompson* did not refer specifically to hunting with hounds.

The case is one of very limited significance. It does not, as has sometimes been claimed,[73] provide a solution to the beneficiary problem, by holding that the party entitled in default can enforce a purpose trust. Enforcement is contrary to the interest of the party entitled in default; he is interested to restrain misapplication, which is a very different matter. In *Re Thompson*, there was no contest, as all parties desired enforcement. The case was only litigated because Trinity Hall, as a charity, could not, without the court's approval, forgo its strict legal claim to the property.

4. THE FAILURE OF THE ASTOR TRUST[74]

Subsequent decisions have made clear that this line of anomalous cases will not be extended.[75] Indeed, the requirement of certainty may be understood as being that one must be certain that the given trust falls squarely within an existing exception. They are regarded as "concessions to human weakness or sentiment",[76] "troublesome, anomalous and aberrant,"[77] and as "occasions when Homer has nodded."[78] Purpose trusts generally have failed under the beneficiary principle, and on the ground of uncertainty. In these circumstances, compliance with the perpetuity rule is no escape. Two examples illustrate the general point:

16–013

> In *Re Astor's Settlement Trusts*,[79] a lifetime settlement was made in 1945, expressly limited to a period of lives in being plus 21 years, under which the trustees were to hold a fund upon various trusts for non-charitable purposes, including "the maintenance of good relations between nations... the preservation of the independence of the newspapers", and other similar purposes in favour of independent newspapers. Roxburgh J held the trust void; both because there was no one who could enforce the trust, and also on the ground of uncertainty.
>
> *Re Shaw*[80] concerned the will of George Bernard Shaw, which provided that the residue of the estate should be applied to research the utility of the development of a 40-letter British alphabet in the place of the present one, and for the translation of his play "Androcles and the Lion" into the new alphabet. Harman J held that the trust was not charitable, and that it failed on the beneficiary principle. The trustees were willing to carry out the testator's wishes if they were permitted to do so. But the judge concluded: "I am not at liberty to validate this trust by treating it as a power. A valid power is not to be spelled out of an invalid trust."[81]

These cases show the current trend in situations where the gift is construed as a gift for purposes. The insistence upon an ascertained beneficiary reflects the analysis of the law of trusts before the days when discretionary trusts became common. We have seen that a beneficiary under a discretionary trust is not entitled to specific property; only to a limited right to be considered. In the wake

---

[73] See Roxburgh J in *Re Astor's ST* [1952] Ch. 534 at 543.
[74] O. Marshall (1953) 6 C.L.P. 151; L. Sheridan (1953) 17 Conv.(N.S.) 46; L. Leigh (1955) 18 M.L.R. 120.
[75] *Re Endacott* [1960] 2 Ch. 232 at 246.
[76] *Re Astor's ST* [1952] Ch. 534 at 547.
[77] *Re Endacott* [1960] 2 Ch. 232 at 251.
[78] [1960] 2 Ch. 232 at 250.
[79] [1952] Ch. 534.
[80] [1957] 1 W.L.R. 729. Considered above, para.15–015.
[81] [1957] 1 W.L.R. 729 at 731, relying on *IRC v Broadway Cottages Trust* [1955] Ch. 20 at 36.

of *McPhail v Doulton*,[82] it was argued that the decision manifested a basic change in the conceptual development of the law of trusts:

> "It has broken the stranglehold imposed on the development of trusts ... by a rigid conception of a framework of fixed equitable interests and correlatively narrow obligations... it does not take much crystal-ball gazing to see the impact this extension will have on all the old sterile purpose trust and unincorporated association debates."[83]

5. UNINCORPORATED ASSOCIATIONS[84]

16–014   An unincorporated association exists where two or more persons are bound together for one or more common purposes by mutual undertakings, each having mutual duties and obligations, in an organisation which has rules identifying in whom control of the organisation and its funds is vested, and which can be joined or left at will.[85] The assessment of whether or not a body constitutes such an association is "necessarily high[ly] fact specific"[86] and caution should be applied in reading between different statutory contexts.[87]

Special problems arise in connection with the holding of property by unincorporated associations.[88] An unincorporated association is not a legal person, and, with the exception of trade unions,[89] cannot be the owner of property or the subject of legal rights and duties.[90] The question which we shall consider here is the effect of gifts to such associations, and the various ways in which their property is held. The latter is determined by the terms of the gift or by the constitution or rules of the association. The question of entitlement to the funds on the dissolution of the association has been dealt with already in Ch.11.[91]

---

[82] [1971] A.C. 424; above, para.4–010.

[83] Y. Grbich (1974) 37 M.L.R. 643 at 655–656; J. Harris (1972) 89 L.Q.R. 31; J. Davies [1970] A.S.C.L. 189.

[84] See generally on this topic, N. Stewart QC, N. Campbell and S. Baughen, *The Law of Unincorporated Associations* (Oxford: Oxford University Press, 2011).

[85] *Conservative and Unionist Central Office v Burrell (Inspector of Taxes)* [1982] 1 W.L.R. 522. (The definition was for tax purposes, but seems to be of general application). See P. Creighton [1983] Conv. 150, doubting the last requirements; R. Rideout (1996) 49 C.L.P. 187. *Norbrook Laboratories Ltd v Carr* [2013] EWHC 476 (QB), per HHJ Anthony Thornton QC at [95]. There is some controversy over the extent of liability of unincorporated associations in tort (*Petrou v Bertoncello* [2012] EWHC 2286 (QB)), although it is clear that such associations may be vicariously liable: *The Catholic Child Welfare Society v Various Claimants & The Institute of the Brothers of the Christian Schools* [2012] UKSC 56; [2013] 2 A.C. 1 and compare *Hickey v McGowan* [2017] IESC 6.

[86] *Williams (The Sustainable Totnes Action Group) v Devon CC* [2015] EWHC 568 (Admin), per HHJ Cotter QC at [47].

[87] See, for example, *Mendoza Ltd v London Borough Of Camden (Localism Act 2011)* [2016] UKFTT CR-2015-0015 (GRC) on the meaning of "unincorporated body" in the context of the Localism Act 2011, and *The National Federation of Occupational Pensioners v Revenue and Customs* [2018] UKFTT 26 (TC) per Judge Sarah Falk at [105]–[110].

[88] See Warburton, *Unincorporated Associations: Law and Practice*, 2nd edn (London: Sweet & Maxwell, 1992), Ch.5.

[89] Trade Union and Labour Relations (Consolidation) Act 1992 s.10.

[90] It is otherwise in the context of tax; *Worthing Rugby Football Club Trustees v IRC* [1987] 1 W.L.R. 1057.

[91] Above, paras 11–010—11–016.

A. Charitable Purposes

The assets of an unincorporated association may be held upon charitable trusts (for example, a society for the relief of the poor). As seen in Ch.15, a charitable trust is valid even though it is a purpose trust; the usual rules of certainty of objects do not apply; it may continue forever; and it enjoys a number of tax privileges.

16–015

B. Non-Charitable Purposes

We have seen that, generally speaking, trusts for the promotion of non-charitable purposes are void. Hence gifts to non-charitable unincorporated associations will fail if construed as purpose trusts. But such a result may be avoided if it is possible to regard the gift as in favour of the members, as described below. Such a construction may be adopted even where the donor has expressly stated that his gift is for particular non-charitable purposes.[92]

16–016

C. Property Held on Trust for the Members

The property of an unincorporated association may be held on trust for the members of the association, and not for its purposes. Such a trust must comply with the usual rules for the creation of a trust. There must be an intention to create a trust, and there must be ascertainable beneficiaries. This will often be made clear by the terms of the constitution of the society; or, in the case of societies governed by statute, such as friendly societies, by the terms of the statute governing them. The Friendly Societies Act 1974 s.54(1) provides that the property of an unincorporated friendly society shall vest in the trustees for the time being of the society, for the use and benefit of the society and its members.[93] It was at one time thought that there was no need to identify the beneficiaries of property held by unincorporated associations; and that a gift to persons holding the property as trustees was good so long as the trustees had power to spend the capital. A society could then dispose of any of its assets at any time; there would be no more tendency to inalienability than in the case of an individual holding property, and, it was argued, no reason for invalidating it. Thus, in *Re Drummond*,[94] a gift was made to the Old Bradfordians Club, London, to be utilised as the committee should think best in the interests of the club or school. Eve J upheld the gift. It was not, he said, a gift to the members, but the committee was free to spend the money as it thought fit on the specified objects. It did not tend to a perpetuity, and was valid.

16–017

---

[92] *Re Lipinski's Will Trusts* [1976] Ch. 235, above, para.16–003; *Re Horley Town Football Club* [2006] W.T.L.R. 1817 (land settled on trust "for the primary purpose of securing a permanent ground for the Horley Football Club").

[93] See *Re Bucks Constabulary Fund (No.2)* [1979] 1 W.L.R. 937. The Friendly Societies Act 1992 provides for the incorporation of such societies carrying on mutual insurance business.

[94] [1914] 2 Ch. 90; *Re Price* [1943] Ch. 422 ("To the Anthroposophical Society of Great Britain to be used at the discretion of the Chairman and Executive Council of the Society for carrying out the teaching of the founder Dr. Rudolf Steiner."); W. Hart (1937) 53 L.Q.R. 24 at 46.

If the trustees could spend only the income however—if, in other words, the capital was tied up as an endowment—the trusts on which the assets were held would be perpetual and void. This view, which appeared to have been approved by the House of Lords,[95] dealt, however, only with the perpetuity aspect of the problem. It ignored the necessity to analyse the property interests which were created.

> In *Leahy v Attorney General for New South Wales*,[96] a testator provided that Elmslea, a sheep station of some 730 acres, should be held upon trust for "such order of nuns of the Catholic Church or the Christian Brothers as my executors and trustees shall select". The gift was not valid as a charitable trust because some of the orders were purely contemplative orders which are not charitable in law.[97]
>
> Nor was it valid as a private trust. In view of the nature of the property and the fact that the members of the selected orders might be very numerous and spread across the world, there was no intention to create a trust in favour of the individual members of selected orders.[98] The testator's intention clearly was to establish an endowment. The gift would have failed if it had not been rescued by a statute of New South Wales which permitted partly charitable trusts to be applied wholly in favour of those parts which were charitable. The trustees' power of selection did not therefore extend to contemplative orders.

16–018   Later cases, however, showed a "retreat from *Leahy*"[99] and have found a different construction, enabling the gift to be held valid as being a trust for the members of the association.[100] This even proved possible, applying the principle of *Re Denley's Trust Deed*,[101] where the donor has stated that his gift is to be applied for specific non-charitable purposes.[102] The position was analysed in *Neville Estates v Madden*,[103] where Cross J held that the property interests of the members of an association would fall into one of three categories. There might be a gift to the members at the relevant date as joint tenants, giving each a right of severance of his part; or a gift subject to the contractual rights and liabilities of the members towards each other, which prevent severance and cause a member's interest, on his death or resignation, to accrue to the remaining members; or a gift to present and future members, in which case the gift, unless confined to the perpetuity period, would be void.[104] A fourth possibility is that this situation creates a specialised form of co-ownership, whose rules should be worked out separately,

---

[95] *Macaulay v O'Donnell*, 10 July 1933; reported at [1943] Ch. 435n; *Carne v Long* (1860) 2 De G.F. & J. 75.

[96] [1959] A.C. 457.

[97] *Gilmour v Coats* [1949] A.C. 426; above, para.15–041.

[98] [1959] A.C. 457 at 486; cf. *Re Smith* [1914] 1 Ch. 937, where a bequest to the Society of Franciscan Friars of Clevedon County, Somerset was construed as a gift to the members of the community at the date of the testator's death; *Cocks v Manners* (1871) L.R. 12 Eq. 574 (a share of residue to the "Dominican Convent of Carisbrooke payable to the Superior for the time being").

[99] F. Crane (1977) 41 Conv.(N.S.) 139.

[100] K. Widdows (1977) 41 Conv.(N.S.) 179; C. Rickett (1980) 39 C.L.J. 88; J. Warburton [1985] Conv. 318. See generally P. Kohler (2000) 53 C.L.P. 236 at 259–266.

[101] [1969] 1 Ch. 373, above, para.16–002. This did not involve an unincorporated association, but the reasoning is applicable to gifts to such associations.

[102] *Re Lipinski's Will Trusts* [1976] Ch. 235.

[103] [1962] Ch. 832 at 849; *Re Recher's WT* [1972] Ch. 526 at 538, below, para.16–019.

[104] A relatively recent example of a gift in that third category failing is *In re St Andrew's (Cheam) Lawn Tennis Club Trust* [2012] 1 W.L.R. 3487.

and independently of the law of trusts,[105] but this has been rejected by the High Court.[106] All these possible solutions fail to explain how the equitable interest of a member passes on his resignation without compliance with Law of Property Act 1925 s.53(1)(c).[107]

Gifts to unincorporated associations can involve perpetuity problems of two distinct kinds, relating to remoteness of vesting and perpetual duration. To avoid both problems, the trust must be for the benefit of members who are both ascertainable during the perpetuity period and also able to claim a division of the funds before that period expires. If the members are not so ascertainable, the trust will fail, subject to what is said below, for remoteness of vesting. If the capital is to be retained as an endowment, the trust will be void as a perpetual trust.[108]

Cross J in *Neville Estates v Madden*[109] referred to the problem of remoteness of vesting in his third category (gift to present and future members). This problem was resolved by the Perpetuities and Accumulations Act 1964, which excluded from the gift any members not ascertainable within the perpetuity period.[110] The 1964 Act did not remove the problem of perpetual duration (inalienability), and this rule is also unaffected by the Perpetuities and Accumulations Act 2009.[111] The gift will fail if:

> "[T]here is something in its terms or circumstances or in the rules of the association which precludes the members at any time from dividing the subject of the gift between them on the footing that they are solely entitled in equity".[112]

This aspect of the perpetuity rule caused the gift to fail in *Re Grant's Will Trusts*.[113] The trust was for the purposes of the Chertsey Labour Party Headquarters, which were not charitable. The members of this local association did not control the property, nor could they change the rules of the association and thereby gain control, because the rules were subject to the approval of, and capable of alteration by, an outside body (the National Executive Committee). Although it seems that a way around this problem could have been found,[114] the

---

[105] Ford, *Unincorporated Non-Profit Associations* (1959) Pt 1, especially at pp.5–8, 21–23.

[106] *Hanchett-Stamford v Attorney General* [2009] Ch. 173; below, para.16–019.

[107] Morris and Leach, pp.313–318; J. Hackney [1971] A.S.C.L. at 379. The *Re Denley* approach (above, para.16–002), whereby the beneficiary has no proprietary interest, does not encounter these difficulties. See further S. Baughen [2010] Conv. 216 at 225.

[108] *Carne v Long* (1860) 2 De G.F. & J. 75.

[109] [1962] Ch. 832.

[110] s.4(4). This provision is repeated in s.8 of the Perpetuities and Accumulations Act 2009 in relation to instruments taking effect after its commencement.

[111] Perpetuities and Accumulations Act 2009 s.18: "This Act does not affect the rule of law which limits the duration of non-charitable purpose trusts".

[112] *Re Lipinski's Will Trusts* [1976] Ch. 235 at 244, quoting the summary of Cross J's categories in *Tudor on Charities*, 6th edn (1967) p.150.

[113] [1980] 1 W.L.R. 360; B. Green (1980) 43 M.L.R. 459; G. Shindler [1980] Conv. 80; cf. *Re Horley Town Football Club* [2006] W.T.L.R. 1817 (fact that rules conferred voting rights on non-member did not bring the *Re Grant* principle into play).

[114] See Heydon and Leeming, *Cases and Materials on Equity and Trusts*, 8th edn (LexisNexis Butterworths, 2011), p.727, suggesting that control by the outside body was not as significant as the case suggests. The beneficiaries could be treated as including the members of that body also. Another possibility is that the members could disaffiliate from the national body. See also *News Group*

trust was held void for perpetuity, even though the restriction on disposing of the capital was not one imposed by the testator.[115]

D.   Ownership by Members on Contractual Basis[116]

16–019   The contractual analysis provides a method by which unincorporated associations can validly hold property without the necessity of discovering an intention to create a trust, and by which gifts to the association, in order to escape invalidity as purpose trusts, need not be regarded as taking effect as immediate distributive shares in favour of the members, which is unlikely to have been the donor's intention. Members of an association can:

> "[B]and themselves together as an association or society, pay subscriptions and validly devote their funds in pursuit of some lawful non-charitable purpose. An obvious example is a members' social club"[117]

where it would in most cases be difficult to find an intention to create a trust. Their assets, whether donations or members' subscriptions, are held by the trustees or by the committee or officers of the club on the terms of the constitution or rules of the club, which are themselves a contract by the members with each other. A trust is interposed simply because it is normally inconvenient (and impossible in the case of land)[118] for the assets to be vested in all the members. This is a bare trust and does not detract from the contractual analysis.

This solution avoids some of the difficulties which arise from an analysis which regards the members as beneficiaries under a private trust. The members' rights are contractual, and of course they depend upon the rules of the association. A member will not usually be able to claim his share at any time; but the members as a whole control the committee's activities in accordance with the rules, and can usually take the decision to wind up the association and share out the proceeds. A member's rights terminate on death or resignation, and a new member obtains rights in relation to the assets during his period of membership. As the members are joint tenants, the last surviving member is entitled to the

---

Newspapers Ltd v SOGAT 82 [1986] I.C.R. 716, where *Re Grant* was distinguished because the members of a local branch of a trade union had control over the branch assets and could in theory secede from the union and divide the assets.

[115] For criticism, see P. Luxton [2007] Conv. 274 at 280.

[116] See for a recent example *Re North Harrow Tennis Club* [2017] EWHC 2476 (Ch). It should also be noted that it is also possible for a club to be a proprietary club, in that though, having members, the ownership may remain in a proprietor, and the analysis in this section would not apply. The point was considered (in the context of a mosque) by HHJ Purle QC, sitting as a Deputy Judge of the High Court in *Rehman v Ali* [2015] EWHC 4056 (Ch) at [55] "Proprietary clubs may run appeals from time to time to raise funds. That would be for the benefit of the members indirectly because, as members of the club, they would enjoy the product of the funds so raised. If, however, the club is not a charity, then any donor takes the risk that the money will eventually simply ensure for the benefit of the proprietor. That is relatively commonplace, though not always fully understood."

[117] *Re Recher's WT* [1972] Ch. 526 at 538, per Brightman J.

[118] Law of Property Act 1925 s.34(2).

property under the doctrine of survivorship.[119] Questions concerning the contractual rights of members usually arise on the termination of an association, as we have seen.[120]

The fact that the assets are held by the members on a contractual basis does not prejudge the construction of a gift by a third party to the association. But the court will lean in favour of validity, and is likely to regard such a gift as an accretion to the funds of the association. In *Re Recher's Will Trust*,[121] there was a gift in trust for "The London and Provincial Anti-Vivisection Society". Brightman J held that the assets of the society were owned by the members in accordance with the rules. "There is no private trust or trust for charitable purposes or other trust to hinder the process."[122] If it was correct that a gift to such an association must be construed as a (void) purpose trust or as distributive shares in favour of the members, then it would be difficult to make a donation in favour of the body, which would be contrary to common sense. The solution was that the gift could be construed as a beneficial gift in favour of the members, not so as to entitle them to an immediate distributive share, but as an accretion to the funds of the society subject to the contract of the members as set out in the rules. Such a construction was equally available whether the society existed to promote the interest of its members ("inward-looking") or, as in the present case, to promote some outside purpose ("outward-looking"). If the society had remained in existence, the gift would have been good. In fact, however, it had been dissolved before the date of the gift.

As has been pointed out,[123] the question whether a gift to an association is subject to any restriction on its use depends on the intention of the members as expressed in their contract with each other. Thus, whether the gift is one to the members in severable shares or subject to the purposes of the association normally depends not on the donor's intention but on the rules of the association. To be valid, any restrictions imposed by the donor must infringe neither the beneficiary principle nor the perpetuity rule.[124]

6.   MANDATE OR AGENCY

The principles described above apply to unincorporated associations, which have already been defined.[125] It may be that an organisation (which is not incorporated) fails to satisfy the requirements of an unincorporated association. This was the case in *Conservative and Unionist Central Office v Burrell*

16–020

---

[119] *Hanchett-Stamford v Attorney General* [2009] Ch. 173; G. Griffiths [2009] Conv. 428; S. Baughen [2010] Conv 216.

[120] Above, para.11–013. S. Baughen [2010] Conv 216. See recently *Re North Harrow Tennis Club* [2017] EWHC 2476 (Ch).

[121] [1972] Ch. 526; J. Mummery (1972) 35 Conv.(N.S.) 381; P. Hogg (1971) 8 M.U.L.R. 1; R. Baxt (1973) 47 A.L.J. 305. The "accretion to funds" solution is adopted by the New South Wales Succession Act 2006 s.43. See also *Artistic Upholstery Ltd v Art Forma (Furniture) Ltd* [1999] 4 All E.R. 277; *Re Horley Town Football Club* [2006] W.T.L.R. 1817; P. Luxton [2007] Conv. 274.

[122] [1972] Ch. 526 at 539; *Re Bucks Constabulary Fund (No.2)* [1979] 1 W.L.R. 937.

[123] P. Matthews [1995] Conv. 302. See also S. Gardner [1998] Conv. 8.

[124] See *Re Lipinski's Will Trusts* [1976] Ch. 235.

[125] Above, para.16–014.

(Inspector of Taxes),[126] where the Crown claimed that the Conservative Party was an unincorporated association. If this were so, Central Office would be assessable to corporation tax, as opposed to income tax, on certain income. The Court of Appeal rejected the Crown's claim. The Party was an amorphous combination of various elements, but not an unincorporated association, because the members had no mutual rights and obligations, there were no rules governing control (which lay in the party leader), and no event in history could be identified as marking the creation of the party as an association.[127]

Of interest in the present context was the analysis of the legal effect of a contribution to such a body. Where the body was not an unincorporated association, the *Re Recher*[128] analysis could not apply. The legal basis was mandate or agency. The contributor gives the recipient (e.g. the treasurer) a mandate to use the gift in a particular way. He can demand its return unless the mandate becomes irrevocable, as when the gift is added to a mixed fund with the authority of the contributor. There is no trust, only the fiduciary element inherent in the relationship of principal and agent. Once the mandate has become irrevocable, the contributor's rights are to an account of expenditure, and to restrain a misapplication. Difficulties might arise where there was a change of the office-holder to whom the mandate was given. More seriously, the mandate theory could not explain the validity of bequests to such organisations, as agency cannot be set up at death. No solution to this problem was offered, the Court of Appeal being content to suggest that the answer was "not difficult to find".[129]

16–021   It remains possible that the mandate theory could be applied in other situations.[130] In view of its limitations, especially with regard to testamentary gifts, this is perhaps doubtful.

Another possibility, which is related to the mandate idea, is to utilise the type of trust upheld by the House of Lords in *Barclays Bank Ltd v Quistclose Investments Ltd*[131] as a means of achieving an abstract purpose trust.[132] In that case money was lent for a specific purpose (the payment of dividends), on the basis that it would be held for the lender if not applied to the purpose. It was held that the debtor took the money on trust to apply it for the purpose. As the purpose could no longer be carried out (because of the debtor's insolvency), the money was held on trust for the lender. Lord Millett's analysis is that the borrower holds on resulting trust for the lender but with a power (or, in some cases, a duty) to carry out the lender's revocable mandate. It is not a purpose trust, but simply a

---

[126] [1982] 1 W.L.R. 522. See generally P. Smart [1987] Conv. 415.

[127] Criticised in P. Creighton [1983] Conv. 150; "It may be as misleading to deny the organisation its status as an unincorporated association because its origins are obscure as it would be to deny the existence of a living human being on the ground that his birth certificate could not be found."

[128] Above, para.16–019.

[129] [1982] 1 W.L.R. 522, per Brightman LJ at 530 (perhaps referring to the principle of *Re Denley's Deed Trust* [1969] 1 Ch. 373, above, para.16–002, or to the fact that the testator may authorise his executors to give a mandate).

[130] It was referred to in connection with members' subscriptions in *Re Recher's Will Trusts* [1972] Ch. 526 at 539. The reasoning might apply to cases such as *Re Gillingham Bus Disaster Fund* [1959] Ch. 62, above, para.16–002, involving public donations to non-charitable purposes.

[131] [1970] A.C. 567; above, para.2–009.

[132] Chambers, *Resulting Trusts* (1997), p.90. See also C. Rickett (1991) 107 L.Q.R. 608; cf. *Re Australian Elizabethan Theatre Trust* (1991) 102 A.L.R. 681.

trust subject to a power to apply the money for a purpose.[133] It seems that the same reasoning would apply if the money was not a loan. So long as the mandate or power is not uncertain or contrary to public policy, this is a means of achieving the application of money to an abstract purpose.[134]

7. PERPETUITY

A. Excessive Duration[135]

A non-charitable purpose trust, even though otherwise valid, is void if it may last beyond the period of perpetuity; this being a rule designed to produce an effect analogous to the rule controlling remoteness of vesting, and applying the same general policy. If, therefore, a purpose trust survives an attack under the beneficiary principle, it must be restricted to the period of perpetuity: "The rule against inalienability is, in reality, just one of the devices that is employed to keep the development of such trusts in check."[136]

16–022

In applying the rule against excessive duration, the courts have been more generous than in other aspects of perpetuity law. First, they have assumed that a monument will be erected within the period.

> In *Mussett v Bingle*,[137] a testator gave £300 to be applied in the erection of a monument to his wife's first husband, and £200, the interest on which was to be applied in maintaining it. The latter gift was perpetual and void. The former was upheld. In the absence of any objection on the ground of perpetuity, the court must have assumed that the monument would be erected within the period.

Secondly, a trust will be upheld if the instrument provides that it is to continue "so long as the law allows" or some similar period. The gift is good for 21 years.[138] If no such saving phrase is included, the trust is wholly void.[139] The court will not supply the necessary words to meet the testator's obvious intention. The "wait and see" principle has never applied to purpose trusts.[140] If it did, it would at least have solved this problem.

Thirdly, the courts have on various occasions taken judicial notice of the fact that an animal's lifespan is limited to 21 years. If the animal could not live that long, the trust could not endure beyond the period. Danckwerts J in *Re Haines*[141] took judicial notice of the fact that a cat could not live for more than 21 years.

---

[133] *Twinsectra v Yardley* [2002] 2 A.C. 164.

[134] See recently R. Hedlund and A.L. Rhodes [2017] Conv. 254 and E. Hudson (2017) 80 M.L.R. 775.

[135] Morris and Leach, pp.321–327; Maudsley, *The Modern Law of Perpetuities*, pp.166–178.

[136] Law Com. No. 251, *The Rules Against Perpetuities and Excessive Accumulations* (1998), para.1.14.

[137] [1876] W.N. 170 mentioned above, para.16–010.

[138] *Pirbright v Salwey* [1896] W.N. 86; *Re Hooper* [1932] 1 Ch. 38.

[139] Contra, *Re Budge* [1942] N.Z.L.R. 356, where a trust to apply the income in keeping a grave neat and tidy was held valid for 21 years. Morris and Leach, p.322.

[140] Perpetuities and Accumulations Act 1964 s.15(4); Perpetuities and Accumulations Act 2009 s.18; below, para.16–024; cf. New Zealand Perpetuities Act 1964; Maudsley, *The Modern Law of Perpetuities*, App. D.

[141] *The Times*, 7 November 1952.

Biologists have corrected him, showing that a cat may live for 25 years.[142] It seems that, if the courts are willing to take judicial notice of longevity, it should be permissible to take evidence of the age of the cats in question; for if the youngest cat is over four, the particular trust would not last for more than 21 years.

B.   Human Lives Only

16–023   North J in *Re Dean*[143] may be taken to have applied some such doctrine. He upheld a gift of an annual sum for the period of 50 years if any of the testator's horses and hounds should so long live. The perpetuity point was not dealt with, and it seems almost as if the learned judge assumed that the life of an animal could be used as a measuring life for the purposes of the rule (which should not be correct). The better doctrine however was provided by Meredith J in *Re Kelly*[144]:

> "If the lives of dogs or other animals could be taken into account in reckoning the maximum period of 'lives in being and twenty-one years afterwards' any contingent or executory interest might be properly limited, so as only to vest within the lives of specified carp, or tortoises, or other animals that might live for over a hundred years, and for twenty-one years afterwards, which, of course, is absurd. 'Lives' means human lives. It was suggested that the last of the dogs could in fact not outlive the testator by more than twenty-one years. I know nothing of that. The court does not enter into the question of a dog's expectation of life. In point of fact neighbours' dogs and cats are unpleasantly long-lived; but I have no knowledge of their precise expectation of life. Anyway the maximum period is exceeded by the lives of specified butterflies and twenty-one years afterwards. And even, according to my decision—and, I confess, it displays this weakness on being pressed to a logical conclusion—the expiration of the life of a single butterfly, even without the twenty-one years, would be too remote, despite all the world of poetry that may be thereby destroyed … there can be no doubt that 'lives' means lives of human beings, not of animals or trees in California."

Re Dean is unsupportable on this point. All other purpose trusts which may last beyond the period of perpetuity have been held void.

C.   A Fixed Number of Years

16–024   As we are dealing here with a question of duration and not one of remoteness of vesting of beneficial interests, it would be much more convenient to have a perpetuity period which was gauged by a number of years, rather than one measured by lives. It is possible to argue that a court should hold that purpose trusts can last for 21 years only; for no purpose trust, with the exception of *Re Howard*,[145] when a parrot was to be fed during the lives of the survivor of two servants, has been upheld for any other or longer period. Yet a royal lives clause was not challenged in *Re Astor's Trusts*.[146] In *Re Moore*,[147] the objection was to

---

[142] Morris and Leach, p.323; Maudsley, p.170.
[143] (1889) 41 Ch.D. 552. Above, para.16–011.
[144] [1932] I.R. 255 at 260–261.
[145] *The Times*, 30 October 1908. Law Com. No. 251, *The Rules Against Perpetuities and Excessive Accumulations* (1998), para.8.35, confirms that the period is lives (if any) plus 21 years.
[146] [1952] Ch. 534 (although of course the trust failed on other grounds).

the excessive number of lives chosen and not to the fact that lives were chosen, and in *Re Khoo Cheng Teow*,[148] the Supreme Court of the Straits Settlements upheld a non-charitable purpose trust for the period of royal lives plus 21 years.

The matter is therefore to be addressed, if at all, by legislation, but it has been preserved rather than modified. The Perpetuities and Accumulations Act 1964 left the period at lives plus 21 years.[149]

More recent Law Commission proposals on the reform of the perpetuity rule did not affect the rule against excessive duration. This was expressly excluded from the scope of the Report on the ground that it belonged more properly in a review of non-charitable purpose trusts and unincorporated associations.[150] The Law Commission proposals were implemented by the Perpetuities and Accumulations Act 2009, the general effect of which is to replace the common law perpetuity period with a fixed period of 125 years. However, this does not apply to purpose trusts, as s.18 provides:

> This Act does not affect the rule of law which limits the duration of non-charitable purpose trusts.

Thus the period for purpose trusts remains lives in being plus 21 years, or 21 years if there are no relevant lives in being.

8. USELESS OR CAPRICIOUS PURPOSES

One question which has to be faced when considering whether, as a matter of policy, purpose trusts should be enforced is that of excluding trusts which are useless, wasteful, capricious, or even harmful or illegal.[151] This aspect of the matter was in the mind of Roxburgh J in *Re Astor's Trusts* when he said[152]: **16–025**

> "[I]t is not possible to contemplate with equanimity the creation of large funds directed to non-charitable purposes which no court and no department of state can control, or in the case of maladministration reform."

The question ultimately is that of the extent to which one person, usually deceased, should be allowed to deprive the community or individuals within it, of the beneficial use of capital. The larger the amount, and the longer the period of application, the greater the problem of alienation. We have seen that the greatest difficulty has been experienced in trying to draw a line between charitable and

---

[147] [1901] 1 Ch. 936.

[148] [1932] Straits Settlements Report 226.

[149] Perpetuities and Accumulations Act 1964 s.15(4): "Nothing in this Act shall affect the operation of the rule of law rendering void for remoteness certain dispositions under which property is limited to be applied for purposes other than the benefit of any person or class of persons in cases where the property may be so applied after the end of the perpetuity period." Reform has occurred elsewhere: See Trusts (Guernsey) Law 2007 (unlimited duration, replacing previous limit of 100 years); F. Noseda (2008) 22 T.L.I. 117; Belize Trusts Act 1992 (120 years). For the position in the US, see L. Waggoner (2011) 127 L.Q.R. 423.

[150] Law Com. No. 251 para.1.14.

[151] M. Pawlowski and J. Brown (2012) 26 T.L.I. 109. See also Ch.14.

[152] [1952] Ch. 534 at 542.

other trusts.[153] This does not augur well for the creation of a precise and recognisable line between acceptable and non-acceptable non-charitable purpose trusts; but it is no reason for insisting on holding all non-charitable purpose trusts void. "The answer, of course, is that the courts will have to strike down the silly purposes and uphold the sensible ones."[154]

> In *Brown v Burdett*,[155] the testator devised a freehold house to trustees upon trust to block up almost all the rooms of the house for a period of 20 years, and, subject thereto, to a devisee. Bacon VC decided that he must "'unseal' this useless, undisposed of property",[156] and declared that there was an intestacy as to the period of 20 years.

There are forthright comments from Scottish judges in their disapproval of the waste of money on useless projects:

> "I consider that, if it is not unlawful, it ought to be unlawful, to dedicate by testamentary disposition, for all time, or for a length of time, the whole income of a large estate… to objects of no utility, private or public, objects which benefit nobody, and which have no other purpose or use than that of perpetuating at great cost, and in an absurd manner, the idiosyncrasies of an eccentric testator.[157]
>
> "The prospect of Scotland being dotted with monuments to obscure persons cumbered with trusts for the purpose of maintaining these monuments in all time coming, appears to me to be little less than appalling."[158]

9. ALTERNATIVE SOLUTIONS

16–026 The present position in English law may be explained as follows: non-charitable purpose trusts are void under the beneficiary principle; there are recognised exceptions in trusts for animals and monuments, which, to be valid, must be certain, not useless or capricious, and confined to the period of perpetuity; and a trust may be upheld if, although expressed as a purpose trust, it is directly for the benefit of ascertainable individuals. Some take the view that this is too restricted a position. We now consider, in the light of the above survey, ways in which the effecting of a non-charitable purpose can be achieved.

A. By the Draftsman

16–027 **i. Incorporation.** A society may be incorporated to advance such purposes. The matter then leaves the law of trusts, and the problem here discussed disappears. This is the simplest practical solution (although there may be other consequences following incorporation).

---

[153] Above, Ch.15.
[154] L. Sheridan (1959) 4 U. of W.A.L.R. at 239. M. Pawlowski and J. Brown (2012) 26 T.L.I. 109 at 111.
[155] (1882) 21 Ch.D. 667; see also *McCaig v University of Glasgow*, 1907 S.C. 231; *McCaig's Trustees v Kirk-Session of United Free Church of Lismore*, 1915 S.C. 426 (bronze statues at £1,000 each); *Aitken v Aitken*, 1927 S.C. 374 (massive bronze equestrian statue); *Mackintosh's Judicial Factor v Lord Advocate*, 1935 S.C. 406 (erection of vault).
[156] (1882) 21 Ch.D. 667 at 673.
[157] *McCaig v University of Glasgow* 1907 S.C. 231 at 242.
[158] *McCaig's Trustees v Kirk-Session of United Free Church of Lismore* 1915 S.C. 426 at 434.

ii. Mandate or Agency. Consideration should also be given to the possibility **16–028** of utilising the mandate or agency theory expounded in *Conservative and Unionist Central Office v Burrell*.[159] The principle could also be invoked in the case of gifts to unincorporated associations, although it is doubtful whether it has much to offer here, not least because it cannot be the basis of a testamentary gift.[160] Where this principle can be utilised, the matter then leaves the law of trusts, as in the case of incorporation. The problem of purpose trusts disappears, but other problems, as we have seen, take its place.

iii. Gift to Members of an Association and Not for Purposes Only. In *Re* **16–029** *Lipinski's Will Trusts*,[161] Oliver J emphasised the distinction between:

> "[T]he case where a purpose is prescribed which is clearly intended for the benefit of ascertained or ascertainable beneficiaries ... and the case where no beneficiary at all is intended... or where the beneficiaries are unascertainable."

This distinction is crucial. A gift to provide recreational facilities may be a gift for beneficiaries if those persons are intended to be benefited[162]; and similarly a gift to an association where it is construed as a gift for the members as an accretion to their funds.[163] The problem of construction was substantial in the cases discussed; but there is no need for any difficulty to arise if the draftsman is aware of the possibilities and frames the gift accordingly.

iv. Conveyancing Devices. A gift over from one charity to another may **16–030** validly take place at any time in the future; the rule against perpetuities does not apply.[164] Advantage was taken of this rule in *Re Tyler*,[165] to achieve a non-charitable purpose.

> A gift was made to the London Missionary Society, committing to their care the family vault, and if they failed to comply with the request the money was to go to the Bluecoat School. The gift was upheld. It could last perpetually if the value of the gift was sufficient to encourage the London Missionary Society to perform the task. If the task became unprofitable, as no doubt it would do by the progress of inflation, the gift over would take effect. The Bluecoat School would be under no obligation to perform the task. Indeed, if an attempt was made to impose an obligation on either donee by requiring any part of the income to be applied for the non-charitable purpose, the gift would have been void as not exclusively charitable.[166]

The Law Commission recommended no change to the exception from the perpetuity rule of gifts over from one charity to another, although noted that the

---

[159] Discussed in Part 6, above. See also the *Quistclose* trust, above, para.2–009.
[160] Above, Part 5.
[161] [1976] Ch. 235 at 246.
[162] *Re Denley's Trust Deed* [1969] 1 Ch. 373.
[163] *Re Recher's WT* [1972] Ch. 526; *Re Lipinski's WT* [1976] Ch. 235.
[164] *Christ's Hospital (Governors) v Grainger* (1849) 1 Mac & G. 460.
[165] [1891] 3 Ch. 252.
[166] *Re Dalziel* [1943] Ch. 277. See further P. Smart [1987] Conv. 415.

exception has been employed as a means of enforcing non-charitable purpose trusts in perpetuity.[167] The exception is confirmed in the Perpetuities and Accumulations Act 2009.[168]

16–031　**v.　Draft as a Power; not as a Trust.**　The beneficiary principle applies to trusts. There must be someone who can enforce the trust. With a power, there is no question of enforcement; although questions of certainty and perpetuity arise. Assuming however that these are overcome, could not the purpose be achieved by giving the property, not to a trustee upon trust, but to the ultimate beneficiary subject to a power in a third party to apply the property for the stated purpose for the perpetuity period?

There is little authority on the validity of such a power. Clearly, a power can be something other than a general or special power to appoint to persons.[169] Lord Millett has analysed the "*Quistclose* trust"[170] as involving a resulting trust for the lender, subject to a power or mandate to apply the money to the designated purpose (in that case the acquisition of property). The power was valid provided it was sufficiently certain to allow the court to determine if it was capable of being carried out or if the money had been misapplied.[171] It may be, then, that a power to apply the income for the improvement of land,[172] or for research into the advantages of the 40-letter alphabet,[173] could, if limited to the period of perpetuity, be valid. It seems that the same rule should apply to repairing monuments or feeding animals. The person entitled in default could restrain misapplication.

There seems to be nothing contrary to policy in allowing the purpose to be effected in this way. Policy questions will arise, as has been seen, where an eccentric testator provides for large sums to be applied for useless, capricious or harmful purposes for a substantial period.[174]

Arguments have been put forward to the effect that an instrument which purports to create a purpose trust should be construed as a power so as to allow the purpose to be carried out.[175] Supporters of this view argued that this is a way of achieving the testator's or settlor's intention without conflicting with any rules of policy. In *Re Shaw*,[176] Harman J appeared to find some attraction in the argument; but he rejected it, following what Jenkins LJ had said in

---

[167] Law Com. No. 251, *The Rules against Perpetuities and Excessive Accumulations* (1998), paras 7.34, 7.37.

[168] s.2(2).

[169] See *Re Douglas* (1887) 35 Ch.D. 472; J. Gray (1902) 15 H.L.R. 67; L. Sheridan (1959) 4 U. of W.A.L.R. at 260. See also *Re Clarke* [1923] 2 Ch. 407, where a power to appoint to *uncertain* non-charitable objects failed.

[170] Above, para.2–009. cf. J. Penner in W. Swadling (ed.), *The Quistclose Trust: Critical Essays* (Oxford: Hart Publishing, 2004), Ch.3.

[171] *Twinsectra v Yardley* [2002] 2 A.C. 164.

[172] *Re Aberconway's ST* [1953] Ch. 647.

[173] *Re Shaw* [1957] 1 W.L.R. 729.

[174] See Morris and Leach, 2nd edn, p.320. M. Pawlowski and J. Brown (2012) 26 T.L.I. 109.

[175] D. Potter (1949) 13 Conv.(N.S.) 418 at 424; A. Kiralfy (1950) 14 Conv.(N.S.) 374; L. Sheridan (1959) 4 U. of W.A.L.R. at 240–244 and (1953) 17 Conv.(N.S.) 46 at 59.

[176] [1957] 1 W.L.R. 729 at 746.

Commissioners of Inland Revenue v Broadway Cottages Trust[177]; "We do not think that a valid power is to be spelt out of an invalid trust."[178]

B. By the Legislature

If reform is to come, it will come best from the Legislature. The basic question is **16–032** whether gifts for non-charitable purposes should be upheld. If so, it is necessary to find a means of addressing the beneficiary principle, and this would most conveniently be done by enacting that trusts for non-charitable purposes (if sufficiently certain) should be construed as powers.[179] The purpose could then be carried out by the trustees if they elected to do so. If they did not, the purpose would fail and the property would go to those entitled in default. The power would be valid only if it was sufficiently certain. It may be thought appropriate to limit such trusts to a period of 21 years.[180] The danger of maladministration would be no greater than that already encountered in the case of the permitted purpose trusts discussed in Part 3 above. But it is clear that no extension of the categories will be offered at common law.

To any statutory solution, it may be objected that it does not answer the anxiety expressed by Roxburgh J in *Re Astor's Settlement Trusts*[181] that it was not in the general interest that large sums of money should be applied for non-charitable purposes for long periods of time. The period of perpetuity can be about 100 years, and non-charitable purposes include all those which at one end are nearly charitable and those which are so useless as to be capricious. In validating gifts for purposes, it is important to ensure that funds are made available for purposes which are useful to the public rather than for the satisfaction of the private interests of a settlor or testator. Resources are scarce, and need to be put to good use. The problem is one which exists also in the case of gifts which are drafted in the form of powers. No doubt, the amount of money involved and the duration of the trust will be factors which will be relevant to a decision. But capricious trusts are the rare ones: the fact that settlors may attempt to create them is no reason for failing to establish a rational method of validating the useful trusts.

---

[177] [1955] Ch. 20 at 36.

[178] This view may also be thought to be consistent with the principle that Equity will not perfect an imperfect gift: above Ch.5.

[179] See Ontario Perpetuities Act 1990 s.16. Alternatively, legislation could validate a purpose trust where the trust deed requires the appointment of an "enforcer"; D. Hayton (ed.), *Modern International Developments in Trust Law* (Kluwer Law International, 1999), p.282. Indeed, a purpose trust with an "enforcer" appointed under the terms of the trust may be valid without legislation; D. Hayton (2001) 117 L.Q.R. 96. See also J. Langbein (2001) 15 T.L.I. 66, discussing the US Uniform Trust Code, which permits purpose trusts for 21 years.

[180] New Zealand Perpetuities Act 1964 s.20, though see New Zealand Law Commission, *Review of the Law of Trusts: Preferred Approach* (Issues Paper 31, 2012), Ch.14. At the time of writing, the New Zealand Government has introduced a Trusts Bill 2017, designed to implement the Commission's proposals (see *http://www.legislation.govt.nz/bill/government/2017/0290/latest/d56e2.html* [accessed 4 July 2018]. By cl.16 it would import a "maximum duration" of 125 years, and the rule against perpetuities would be abolished. The 1964 Act would be repealed.

[181] [1952] Ch. 534.

Alternatively, it may be considered that, in the light of the reforms to the law of charities since 2006 seen in the previous chapter, any further revision to the law of purpose trusts may be viewed with some circumspection.

C.   Offshore Jurisdictions[182]

16–033   Purpose trusts are now permitted by statute in many jurisdictions to facilitate estate planning and asset protection schemes, by exploiting the point that neither the settlor nor any other person is the beneficial owner of the property.[183] This has been done in the interests of attracting lucrative trusts business to the jurisdiction in question. Typically such legislation permits non-charitable purpose trusts to last for long periods such as 120 years, and provides for enforcement by the "protector" of the settlement or by an "enforcer".[184] Of particular interest is the Cayman Islands Special Trusts (Alternative Regime) Law 1997.[185] This permits non-charitable purpose trusts (commonly known as STAR trusts) which are exempt from the perpetuity rule, which are enforceable by "enforcers" and which do not fail for uncertainty (any uncertainty may be resolved by the court settling a scheme). Such trusts may also include human beneficiaries, but they have no standing to enforce the trust. This has given rise to a debate as to whether a "STAR trust" is really a trust at all, because the fundamental obligations owed by trustees to beneficiaries are absent,[186] or, to put it more strongly, that the fiduciary obligations of trustees have become "nothing more than a farce."[187] The danger is that a resulting trust might then arise in favour of the settlor, thus defeating his objectives. A settlor may seek to take advantage of these offshore enactments by including a provision in the trust instrument that the trust is to be governed by the law of a specified jurisdiction.[188] The attraction is that the beneficial ownership appears to be in abeyance, which is useful for confidentiality and secrecy, with possible adverse effects on dependants, creditors and tax authorities. Thus, the suspicion is that "purpose trust legislation simply encourages hidden ownership by putting assets into a no-man's land".[189] The purpose trust vehicle can be used for "off balance sheet" transactions, as where a company is set up to acquire an asset from another company and thus take it off the latter's balance sheet, to be held on a purpose trust. There has been no appetite to introduce such legislation

---

[182] See above, para.3–003.

[183] See P. Matthews in A. Oakley (ed.), *Trends in Contemporary Trusts Law* (1996), Ch.1; Baxendale-Walker, *Purpose Trusts* (1999); (1999) 5 *Trusts & Trustees*, pp.5–92.

[184] See, for example, the Belize Trusts Act 1992; Trusts (Amendment No.4) (Jersey) Law 2006 (unlimited duration); Trustee Act 2001 (Mauritius); T. Tey (2009) 23 T.L.I. 151.

[185] Now substantially incorporated into Trusts Law (2011 Revision).

[186] P. Matthews (1997) 11 T.L.I. 67; A. Duckworth (1998) 12 T.L.I. 16; P. Matthews (1997) 11 T.L.I. 67, at 98; A. Duckworth (1999) 13 T.L.I. 158; J. Hilliard (2003) 17 T.L.I. 144.

[187] T. Tey (2009) 23 T.L.I. 183 at 193.

[188] See the Hague Convention art.6. Under art.18, effect will not be given to this if it would be manifestly incompatible with public policy. See also art.2, defining a trust, for the purpose of the Convention, as being "for the benefit of a beneficiary or for a specific purpose."

[189] D. Hayton (ed.), *Modern International Developments in Trust Law* (1999) at 12.

in the UK, because "there is a feeling that pure purpose trusts may be hijacked for shady dealings involving hiding beneficial ownership".[190]

---

[190] D. Hayton (ed.), *Modern International Developments in Trust Law* (1999) at 305. For a more positive view by the same author, see D. Hayton (2001) 117 L.Q.R. 96 and D. Hayton in Birks and Pretto (eds), *Breach of Trust* (Oxford: Hart Publishing, 2002), pp.382–383. Legislation is advocated in M. Pawlowski and J. Summers [2007] Conv. 440.

CHAPTER 17

TRUSTS OF PENSION FUNDS

1. INTRODUCTION

PENSION fund trusts are a special category of express trusts. The special **17–001** treatment of pension fund beneficiaries reflects the fact that their entitlements arise from their contracts of employment. Unlike traditional beneficiaries, they are not volunteers. As we shall see, dedicated legislation governs the operation of pension funds. In many ways, however, pension trusts are subject to the same principles as any other trusts, and the pension trust case law has contributed much to the development of the general law of trusts.[1] The purpose of this chapter is to examine pension funds as an important modern illustration of the law of trusts in operation and to consider the ways in which pension fund trusts are treated differently from traditional trusts. Before doing so it is necessary to appreciate the different types of pension schemes available and to understand the terminology.

A long-term European goal has been cross-border membership of pension schemes through the establishment of European pension funds covering workers in several member states, to reflect the principle of free movement of workers.[2] It remains to be seen what provision will be made in this respect after Brexit.

This area of the law was reviewed extensively in the 1990s, as a result of the misappropriation of about £453 million from the pension funds of the employees of Mirror Group Newspapers and the Maxwell Communications Corporation by

---

[1] See G. Moffat (1993) 56 M.L.R. 471, examining whether a separate pensions law is developing, or whether the developments in modern pensions cases are applicable generally. See also Vinelott J (1994) 8 T.L.I. 35; M. Milner [1997] Conv. 89; D. Hayton [2005] Conv. 229. For the "property" rights of pension beneficiaries, see R. Nobles (1994) 14 L.S. 345 and D. Pollard 27 (2013) T.L.I. 131. For a fuller treatment of the topic in this chapter, see D. Pollard, *The Law of Pension Trusts*, (Oxford: Oxford University Press, 2013).

[2] See Pensions Act 2004 Pt 7 (partially in force); see also most recently the Institutions for Occupational Retirement Provision (IORP) II Directive 2016/2341; below, para.17–015.

Robert Maxwell.[3] The focus of the ensuing debate was the question whether pension schemes should continue to be governed by the law of trusts, and how the scheme members (the beneficiaries) could be better safeguarded against fraud, mismanagement and insolvency. The matter was referred to the Pension Law Review Committee, chaired by Professor Roy Goode. The Goode Report[4] favoured retaining the law of trusts as the most suitable mechanism for dealing with pension funds, primarily because of the well-established principles concerning the fiduciary responsibilities of trustees and the proprietary rights of beneficiaries, conferring protection from the employer's insolvency. Of course, no legal mechanism can fully prevent deliberate wrongdoing.

The Committee recommended various ways in which the rights of pension beneficiaries might be enhanced and safeguarded by the enactment of special rules going beyond the protection afforded to beneficiaries of traditional trusts under the general law. In particular, they recommended the introduction of a regulatory body, a compensation scheme to apply in cases of misappropriation, a minimum funding requirement to prevent a shortfall of funds in the case of funded schemes, restrictions on employers' rights to surplus funds, and reforms relating to the appointment, removal and disqualification of trustees. Most of their recommendations, some in modified form, were implemented by the Pensions Act 1995. Since that Act, the pensions legislation has again been overhauled by the Pensions Act 2004. While parts of the 1995 Act remain in force, the Act of 2004 introduced new rules on pension scheme funding, the Pensions Regulator and the Pension Protection Fund.

More recently, there has been considerable development of the law on pensions in the wake of the global financial crisis[5] as well as further legislative reform. Thus, the Taxation of Pensions Act 2014[6] introduced changes with effect from 6 April 2015 enabling much greater flexibility for individuals over the age of 55 in respect of how and when they may access the funds held in a pension scheme by reducing the tax consequences of drawing down on the pension. The Hutton Report[7] in March 2011 recommended that public sector final salary schemes should be replaced by schemes based on the employee's average salary over the period of employment, to reduce costs to the taxpayer.[8] The Report also proposed wider reform of the approach to public sector pensions. These reforms were broadly given effect by the Public Service Pensions Act 2013.

---

[3] Most of the money was recovered; *The Times*, 20 February 1996.

[4] *Pension Law Reform: Pension Law Review Committee Report* (1993), Cmnd. 2342; D. Chatterton (1993) 7 T.L.I. 91. See also D. Hayton [1993] Conv. 283.

[5] For an example of the complexities of pensions legislation and its interactions with the insolvency framework, see one of many cases involving the aftermath of the collapse of Lehman Bros: *Bloom v Pensions Regulator* [2013] UKSC 52; [2014] A.C. 209.

[6] Some provisions were anticipated by transitional provisions in the Finance Act 2004: R. Ellison [2014] B.T.R. 381

[7] *Independent Public Service Pensions Commission: Final Report.*

[8] For example, in 2007 the civil service pension was changed for new entrants from a final salary scheme to one based on the member's average salary during service. The Universities Superannuation Scheme for employees of certain Higher Education and associated institutions changed from a final salary scheme for new entrants on 1 October 2011.

As will appear, the overall effect of the various reforms is that current pensions legislation amounts to something of a patchwork quilt of rules and principles.

A.   Types of Pension Scheme

Pension provision falls into three broad categories: the state pension, a personal pension (a form of investment made by an individual with an insurance company, to which the employer may contribute) and an occupational pension scheme, which is organised by an employer to provide pensions and other benefits for employees (and usually for their dependants) on leaving employment (by retirement or otherwise) or on death. The last category is the subject of this chapter. Occupational pension schemes themselves take various forms, but in essence trust law will apply where assets are segregated and invested to provide pension benefits. Many public sector schemes (such as those for teachers and the civil service) are established by legislation and are unfunded in the sense that there is no trust fund set aside to provide benefits. The employees' security is founded on the statute rather than on the segregation of assets. State pensions are also unfunded, benefits being paid from current contributions. A non-statutory scheme is unfunded where the employer does not set aside and accumulate assets in a separate trust fund in advance of the benefits commencing to be paid. Most private schemes, however, are funded.

17–002

We are concerned with funded schemes, where a fund is held on trust to make provision in advance for future liabilities to members by accumulating assets. The assets are invested and the investments held by the trustees. This may be contrasted with an insured scheme, where the trustees have effected an insurance contract for each member which guarantees benefits corresponding to those promised under the scheme rules. In other words, this is an investment through the medium of an insurance company, the trustees using the contributions to pay the premiums. The insurance is the only significant asset of the scheme. If the sums payable by the insurer are sufficient at all times to cover all benefits, the scheme is said to be fully insured. Most small schemes are run through insurers.

The benefits to which an employee is entitled depend on whether the scheme is earnings-related (a defined *benefit* scheme) or whether it is a "money purchase" scheme (a defined *contribution* scheme). An earnings-related scheme (sometimes called a final salary scheme) is where the benefit is calculated by reference to the member's pensionable earnings for a period of pensionable service ending at or before normal pension date or leaving service. There is normally a restriction on the number of years (e.g. 40) which qualify as pensionable service, and not all earnings (e.g. a bonus or allowance) are pensionable. The scheme may require contributions from employees (a contributory scheme) or may not (non-contributory). The benefits are usually based on a fraction of the final salary for each year of pensionable service. The cost of providing these defined benefits cannot be accurately predicted, so the employer in a contributory scheme undertakes to pay whatever sum is needed to top up employee contributions. If the fund is in surplus, the employer may be able to take a "contributions holiday",

17–003

by temporarily suspending its contributions.[9] It follows that the risk of poor investment performance falls on the employer in an earnings-related scheme.

A "money purchase" scheme is where the benefits of an individual member are determined by reference to the contributions paid into the scheme by or on behalf of that member, usually increased by an amount based on the investment return of those contributions.[10] The contributions are fixed (normally a percentage of salary) by the scheme, and the benefits vary according to investment performance. Thus the employee takes the risk of poor investments, but also takes the benefit of good performance.[11] The fund is either used to purchase an annuity to provide the pension, or a pension may be paid from the fund according to the size of the member's account in the fund.

Most new schemes are now money purchase schemes. Earnings-related schemes have become too onerous and expensive for employers as a result of poorly performing stock markets worldwide, increasing life expectancy and the burden of regulation. This has led to the closure of large numbers of earnings-related schemes, which have either been wound up and replaced by money purchase schemes or closed to new members.

The Pensions Act 2008 (as amended by the Pensions Act 2011) aimed to address the lack of pension provision by requiring employers to enrol eligible employees with low to moderate earnings into a personal or occupational pension scheme (money purchase or defined benefit) chosen by the employer, who must make contributions to it.[12] A trust-based pension scheme which can be chosen by employers was set up under the Act. It is called the National Employment Savings Trust ("NEST"), and is an occupational pension scheme for tax purposes.[13] The scheme is operated by the National Employment Savings Trust Corporation in consultation with panels of members and participating employers. The scheme started operation in October 2012, in respect of the largest employers. By 31 March 2017, the scheme had 4.5 million members, with 327,000 employers participating in the scheme and assets under management of £1.7 billion.[14] It now extends to all employers.

17–004 When a funded scheme is being set up, the trust deeds are lengthy and take time to prepare. It is, therefore, usual to have an interim trust deed with outline rules, which appoints the first trustees. This enables the scheme to be started without delay, and provisional tax relief to be secured.[15] In due course this is replaced by the final (or definitive) trust deed.

---

[9] A thirty-year "holiday" was a breach of trust by the trustees of the British Airways pension fund; (1996) 10 T.L.I. 26. See also *National Grid Co Plc v Mayes* [2001] 1 W.L.R. 864; M. Thomas and B. Dowrick [2002] J.B.L. 304.

[10] For the definition of a "money purchase" scheme and distinctions from defined benefit schemes, see *Bridge Trustees Ltd v Yates* [2011] 1 W.L.R. 1912.

[11] The trustees are subject to the usual standard of prudence with regard to the investments; see N. Moore (1999) 13 T.L.I. 2; below, paras 19–005—19–020.

[12] For a Scots perspective on auto-enrolment and its implications, see A. Wyper (2017) 21 Edin. L.R. 352.

[13] Pensions Act 2008 s.67 and Sch.1; National Employment Savings Trust Order (SI 2010/917), as amended by the National Employment Savings Trust (Amendment) Orders 2013/597, 2015/178 and 2018/368.

[14] NEST Pension Scheme Annual Report and Accounts for year ending 31 March 2017.

[15] For the fiscal benefits, see below, para.17–029.

Many cases deal with entitlement to surplus funds, the contest normally involving beneficiaries, employers, creditors of an insolvent employer, or companies which have taken over the employer company and wish to syphon off the surplus. At present, as the world economy continues to emerge from the global financial crisis, a deficit is much more likely than a surplus. Of course, a surplus cannot arise in the case of a money purchase scheme or an unfunded scheme. In the case of a funded earnings-related scheme, any surplus is notional if the scheme is ongoing, and calculations can be controversial: "A surplus or a deficit can be an evanescent thing depending on the fluctuations of volatile markets. The existence of a surplus or a deficit can depend upon the basis of the assessment which is used."[16] A surplus is said to exist whenever, according to actuarial calculations, the value of the assets exceeds the estimated liabilities. There will be an *actual* surplus only if the scheme is wound up, leaving an excess after discharge of liabilities. Where a pension scheme is terminated by winding-up, the assets will usually be applied to the purchase of annuities to provide pensions for members, or the assets and liabilities may be transferred to another pension scheme.

B.   Beneficiaries not Volunteers

The fact that pension trust beneficiaries are not volunteers puts them in certain respects in a different position from the beneficiaries of traditional family trusts. The consideration arises from the fact that the pension benefits are a form of deferred remuneration for their services[17] and from their contributions (if any) to the fund.

17–005

> In *Mettoy Pension Trustees Ltd v Evans*,[18] the scheme contained a power of appointment in favour of the members, any surplus not so appointed going to the employer, which was in liquidation. The fact that the members were not volunteers was influential in classifying the power as fiduciary rather than personal. Had it been only personal (i.e. a bare power), the unpalatable conclusion would have been that the entire surplus would have gone to the creditors, the power proving to be of illusory benefit to the members. The classification of the power as fiduciary meant that it could not be released[19] (in the interests of the creditors), and, further, that the court could intervene to secure the exercise of the power.[20]

---

[16] *British Airways Plc v Airways Pension Scheme Trustee Ltd* [2017] EWHC 1191 (Ch); [2017] Pens. L.R. 16 per Morgan J at [426].

[17] See *Brooks v Brooks* [1996] A.C. 375. This meant that the husband (the employee) and not the employer was regarded as settlor of the marriage settlement constituted by the pension scheme.

[18] [1990] 1 W.L.R. 1587. (This point is unaffected by the Supreme Court's disapproval of *Mettoy* in respect of Warner J's treatment of the *Re Hastings-Bass* principle in *Pitt v Holt* [2013] UKSC 26; [2013] 2 A.C. 108; below, paras 18–046—18–046.) See also *Thrells Ltd v Lomas* [1993] 1 W.L.R. 456; *In Re William (Makin) & Sons Ltd* [1993] B.C.C. 453; *Air Jamaica Ltd v Charlton* [1999] 1 W.L.R. 1399 at 1407. As to whether the employer is to be regarded as a beneficiary, see D. Pollard (2006) 20 T.L.I. 21; J. Hilliard (2009) 23 T.L.I. 119 at 122–124; D. Fox (2010) 69 C.L.J. 240.

[19] See also *Re Courage Group's Pension Schemes* [1987] 1 W.L.R. 495; P. Stear (2016) 30 T.L.I. 126; above, para.7–029.

[20] This controversial aspect of the decision was discussed at para.7–007, above. See now Pensions Act 1995 s.25 (fiduciary powers exercisable by independent trustee on insolvency, as amended by Pensions Act 2004); *JIB Group Ltd v The Commissioners for Her Majesty's Revenue & Customs* [2012] UKFTT 547 (TC); [2012] S.T.I. 2860. Below, para.17–010.

In *Davis v Richards & Wallington Industries Ltd*,[21] there were doubts whether the definitive (final) trust deed had been validly executed. This deed provided that any surplus should belong to the employers after increasing the pension benefits to the statutory maximum. If the deed was invalid the trust would be incompletely constituted. However, as the beneficiaries were not volunteers they could compel the execution of a valid deed and their rights (by applying the maxim that equity regards as done that which ought to be done) were as if such a deed had already been executed. In fact the deed was held valid.

In *Entrust Pension Ltd v Prospect Hospice Ltd*,[22] Henderson J observed:

"In the context of a pension scheme ... I think it would be wrong to equate the Trustee's discretionary and fiduciary power to award a share of surplus with a mere power in a family trust, where on a conventional analysis the relevant trust property is regarded as vested in the beneficiaries entitled in default of exercise of the power, subject only to any valid exercise of the power."[23]

In a pension trust, the trustee/beneficiary relationship exists in parallel with the contractual employer/employee relationship and the pension scheme must be interpreted against this background. This is illustrated by *Imperial Group Pension Trust Ltd v Imperial Tobacco Ltd*.[24]

The company had power under the scheme to consent to an increase in benefits. The issue was whether it was under a duty to consider the interests of the members and not just its own interests when granting or withholding consent. It was held that the implied contractual obligation of good faith between employer and employee (meaning that the employer would not act in a manner calculated or likely to destroy or damage the relationship of confidence and trust between employer and employee) applied to the exercise of the employer's rights and powers under the pension scheme just as it applied to its other rights and powers. The power to give or withhold consent was accordingly subject to a restriction that it could not be validly exercised in breach of the obligation of good faith. Thus the pension trust "lies at the interface between trust and employment law."[25]

The applicability of the *Imperial* duty was considered by the Court of Appeal in *IBM United Kingdom Holdings Ltd v Dalgleish*,[26] where it was alleged that IBM's approach to reorganising its pension scheme amounted to various breaches of the duty:

"in cases which do involve the exercise of an employer's discretionary powers, whether express ... implied, then, in our judgment, the effect of the recent case law is that, in order to decide whether the employer's act is or is not in breach of the implied duty, a rationality approach equivalent to the *Wednesbury* test (including both its limbs) should be adopted, taking into account the employment context of the given case. Such an approach is required because the court does not and must not substitute its own decision for that of the decision-maker, in these cases the employer. Correspondingly, such a rationality approach

---

[21] [1990] 1 W.L.R. 1511; above, para.11–015. The decision was disapproved on another point in *Air Jamaica Ltd v Charlton* [1999] 1 W.L.R. 1399.

[22] [2012] EWHC 1666 (Ch); [2012] Pens. L.R. 341.

[23] [2012] EWHC 1666 (Ch); [2012] Pens. L.R. 341 at [118].

[24] [1991] 1 W.L.R. 589. On the good faith requirement, see M. Thomas and B. Dowrick [2007] Conv. 495. See also T. Scaramuzza (2013) 27 T.L.I. 111. On the position in Australia, see S. Donald and C. Hodkinson (2015) 29 T.L.I. 39 at 45–6, commenting on the implications of *Commonwealth Bank of Australia v Barker* [2014] HCA 32; (2014) 253 C.L.R. 169.

[25] Vinelott J (1994) 8 T.L.I. 35.

[26] [2017] EWCA Civ 1212; [2018] Pens. L.R. 1. See also *UC Rusal Alumina Jamaica Ltd v Wynette Miller* [2014] UKPC 39; [2015] Pens. L.R. 15, e.g. at [55] (Lord Mance).

should be applied in deciding whether a person who has a non-fiduciary discretionary power under an occupational pension scheme, such as those vested in Holdings in the present case, has respected the constraints imposed by the Imperial duty in relation to the exercise of the power, in addition to asking the question whether the power has been exercised for a proper purpose."[27]

The Court went on to hold that the expectations of employees and members of a pension scheme "do not constitute more than a relevant factor" to be taken into account by the relevant decision-maker.[28]

The fact that pension trust beneficiaries are not volunteers may allow them to be more favourably treated than other beneficiaries in the matter of costs. In *McDonald v Horn*,[29] it was held that, contrary to the usual rule, pension beneficiaries may obtain a "pre-emptive costs order" where there are serious allegations of impropriety and breach of trust against the employers and trustees. Thus the beneficiaries would obtain their costs, and any costs which they might be ordered to pay to the defendants, out of the fund whether or not their action ultimately proved successful. The fact that the beneficiaries had given consideration made the action analogous to an action by a minority shareholder on behalf of a company, where such an order could be made.

The jurisdiction to award a protective costs order can extend to the situation in which the representative beneficiary may not represent the full range of beneficiaries, as held by Arnold J in *Re IMG Pension Plan*.[30] Similarly, the equitable jurisdiction to grant relief for a mistake in a voluntary disposition does not extend to a pension trust.[31]

As a general proposition, however, the ordinary principles of trust law apply to pension trusts as to other trusts. This was emphasised in *Wilson v Law Debenture Trust Corp Plc*,[32] where it was held that the principle of *Re Londonderry's Settlement*,[33] whereby trustees are not obliged to give reasons for the exercise of their discretions to the beneficiaries, applied equally to pension fund trusts.[34] Although the court must have regard to the fact that the beneficiaries are not volunteers when construing the trust deed, effect must be given to settled principles of trust law in determining the effect of the deed on its true construction. The Privy Council has counselled that:

---

[27] [2017] EWCA Civ 1212 per Sir Timothy Lloyd (delivering the judgment of the court) at [45]–[46]; see also [2017] EWCA Civ 1144; [2017] Pens. L.R. 20 per Gloster LJ at [56].

[28] [2017] EWCA Civ 1212 at [232]; see further [235]–[268] (disagreeing with the approach of Warren J at first instance: *IBM United Kingdom Holdings Ltd v Dalgleish* [2014] EWHC 980 (Ch); [2014] Pens. L.R. 335 and [2015] EWHC 1385 (Ch)).

[29] [1995] 1 All E.R. 961.

[30] [2010] EWHC 321 (Ch); [2010] Pens. L.R. 131. However a protective costs order is not appropriate where the member is bringing a personal claim alone: *Pell Frischmann Consultants Ltd v Prabhu* [2013] EWHC 2203 (Ch); [2014] I.C.R. 153.

[31] *Smithson v Hamilton* [2008] 1 All E.R. 1216.

[32] [1995] 2 All E.R. 337; P. O'Hagan (1995) 145 N.L.J. 1414. Member trustees will have access to reasons.

[33] [1965] Ch. 918; below, para.18–043.

[34] A contrary view has been taken by Lord Browne-Wilkinson (1992) 6 T.L.I. 119 at 125; D. Schaffer (1994) 8 T.L.I. 27 and 118; Sir Robert Walker [1996] P.L.R. 107 and D. Hayton [2005] Conv. 229 at 234–237. Pension scheme trustees must record their decisions but not the reasons for them. See D. Pollard (1997) 11 T.L.I. 11 and 42.

> "The provisions of a pension scheme should be construed to give reasonable and practical effect to the scheme, bearing in mind the practical consequences and the fact that it has to be operated against a changing commercial background."[35]

In interpreting the rules of a pension scheme the court should take the same approach as when interpreting any other written instrument, taking into account, as the Supreme Court has emphasised, the need to focus on "the relevant words... in their documentary, factual and commercial context".[36] Lewison LJ has noted in addition some features of special relevance to the interpretation of pension schemes:

> "First, all or almost all pension schemes are intended to be tax efficient and to comply with Inland Revenue requirements. So Inland Revenue requirements are relevant to their interpretation. Second, pension schemes should be interpreted to have reasonable and practical effect. Third, since the rules of a pension scheme affect all those who join it (in some cases many years after its inception) other background facts have a very limited role to play."[37]

2. SPECIAL RULES APPLICABLE TO PENSION TRUSTS

17–006 There are many statutory provisions which apply special rules to pension trusts. The reasons for the special legislative framework are the special nature of pension fund trusts in terms of the size of the funds, their quasi-public nature, the opportunities for misappropriation by the employer, the non-volunteer status of the beneficiaries, and the public interest in the encouragement of such trusts. Most of the provisions are contained in the Pensions Acts 1995 and 2004, but others, relating in particular to taxation and the application of the perpetuity rule, are found elsewhere.

A. Pensions Acts 1995 and 2004

17–007 As discussed at the beginning of this chapter, the main objective of the Act of 1995 was to protect the beneficiaries from the effects of maladministration, fraud and insolvency. Illustrations of this objective include the provision that the trustees must keep proper books and records and must keep any money received by them in a separate account at an institution authorised under the Financial Services and Markets Act 2000,[38] and that an employer who fails to pay over any contributions deducted from members within a certain period commits an offence.[39] The 1995 Act sought also to strike a fair balance between the interests of current employees, pensioners and employers. To the extent that any of the statutory provisions discussed below conflict with the terms of a pension scheme,

---

[35] *Scully v Coley* [2009] UKPC 29 per Lord Collins of Mapesbury at [30]; *Re BCA Pension Trustees Ltd* [2015] EWHC 3492 (Ch).

[36] *Arnold v Britton* [2015] UKSC 36; [2015] A.C. 1619 per Lord Neuberger PSC at [15].

[37] *Barnardo's v Buckinghamshire* [2016] EWCA Civ 1064; [2017] Pens. L.R. 2 at [10]; *Wedgwood Pension Plan Trustee Ltd v Salt* [2018] EWHC 79 (Ch).

[38] Pensions Act 1995 s.49, as amended by the Financial Services Act 2012.

[39] s.49(8).

such terms are overridden by the Act.[40] Provision is also made for modifying pension schemes in order to implement the requirements of the Act[41]: the amended provisions "are still aimed at preventing modifications that adversely affect subsisting rights."[42]

The provisions of the 1995 Act mentioned above (and others) remain in force. However, major changes to other aspects of pension fund regulation were introduced by the Pensions Act 2004, most of which came into force on or before 6 April 2005. The minimum funding rules of the 1995 Act were perceived to be unsatisfactory and were replaced. As noted, other major features of the Pensions Act 2004 were the introduction of the Pensions Regulator and the Pension Protection Fund. These are considered below.

i. Pensions Regulator. The Pensions Act 2004[43] introduced the Pensions **17–008** Regulator. The Regulator (a corporate body) has wide powers, designed to promote good administration (for example by issuing codes of practice[44]) and to reduce the risk of under-funding and fraud.

The Pensions Regulator may, by an order under s.3 of the 1995 Act,[45] prohibit a person from being a trustee of a particular pension scheme, a particular kind of pension scheme or pension schemes in general if satisfied that he is not a fit and proper person to be a trustee of the scheme or schemes in question. Such an order, which is revocable, operates to remove the trustee. A similar regime applies to corporate trustees under s.3A of the 1995 Act, which was added by the Pensions Act 2014.[46] Section 4[47] of the 1995 Act enables the Pensions Regulator to make an order suspending a trustee in various circumstances, as where a bankruptcy petition has been presented against him or proceedings commenced for an offence involving dishonesty or deception, and such proceedings have not been concluded. While the order is in force, the person is prohibited from exercising any functions as trustee of the scheme or schemes in question. A person who purports to act as trustee while prohibited or suspended is guilty of an offence, but things done by him while purporting to act are not invalid merely because of the prohibition or suspension.[48] The 1995 Act contains further provisions which

---

[40] s.117. *British Vita Unlimited v British Vita Pension Fund Trustees Ltd* [2007] EWHC 953 (Ch) and *Allied Domecq (Holdings) Ltd v Allied Domecq First Pension Trust Ltd* [2008] Pens. L.R. 425.

[41] s.68 as amended by Pensions Act 2004. Schemes often contain express modification powers, the exercise of which is restricted by s.67 (ss.67 and 67A-67I substituted for s.67 by Pensions Act 2004). See *BCA Pension Trustees Ltd* [2015] EWHC 3492 (Ch); [2016] Pens. L.R. 17 (correction of a drafting error); *Sterling Insurance Trustees Ltd v Sterling Insurance Group Ltd* [2015] EWHC 2665 (Ch). Section 69 of the Pensions Act 1995 was amended by Pensions Act 2014.

[42] *Danks v Qinetiq Holdings Ltd* [2012] EWHC 570 (Ch); [2012] Pens. L.R. 131 per Vos J at [39], endorsed by Newey J in *Arcadia Group Ltd v Arcadia Group Pension Trust Ltd* [2014] EWHC 2683 (Ch); [2014] I.C.R. D35. The approaches of both Vos and Newey JJ were approved by the Court of Appeal in *Barnardo's v Buckinghamshire* [2016] EWCA Civ 1064; [2017] Pens. L.R. 2.

[43] Part I and Schs 1–3. An appeal from the Pensions Regulator lies in the first instance to the First-tier Tribunal: Transfer of Tribunal Functions Order 2010/22, art.2.

[44] Pensions Act 2004 s.90.

[45] As substituted by Pensions Act 2004 s.33. The Regulator must keep a register of prohibited trustees for inspection; Pensions Act 2004 ss.66, 67.

[46] s.46(2).

[47] As amended by Pensions Act 2004 s.34.

[48] Pensions Act 1995 s.6.

disqualify certain persons from acting as trustee of any occupational pension scheme. This is dealt with below.[49] Section 7 of the 1995 Act permits the Pensions Regulator to appoint a new trustee in place of one who has been removed or disqualified, or where the appointment is necessary to secure that the number of trustees is sufficient or that the trustees as a whole have the necessary skills.[50]

In addition to the powers discussed above, the Pensions Regulator has jurisdiction under s.10 of the 1995 Act to impose financial penalties on trustees and other persons,[51] such as the director of a corporate trustee, in respect of various breaches of their statutory duties.[52] It may also seek injunctions to restrain misuse or misappropriation of assets,[53] and apply to court for the restitution of assets which have been misused or misappropriated.[54] The Pensions Act 1995 s.16 provides that:

> (1) If, on the application of the Regulator, the court is satisfied that there has been a misuse or misappropriation of any of the assets of an occupational or personal pension scheme, it may order any person involved to take such steps as the court may direct for restoring the parties to the position in which they were before the misuse or misappropriation occurred.
> (2) For this purpose a person is "involved" if he appears to the court to have been knowingly concerned in the misuse or misappropriation of the assets.

It has recently been held at first instance that the Pensions Regulator does not need to establish dishonesty when bringing claims for restitution under this section[55]: "knowingly concerned" merely requires that the defendant knew of the facts that made their actions amount to a misuse or misappropriation.[56]

The Pensions Regulator may order an occupational pension scheme to be wound up in order to protect the interests of the members or if the scheme is no longer required or should be replaced by a different scheme.[57] These winding-up powers enable the Pensions Regulator to make a freezing order to prevent an immediate risk to the interests of scheme members.[58] Other powers of the Pensions Regulator include the power to recover any unpaid employer's

---

[49] Below, para.17–011.

[50] The court also has an inherent jurisdiction to appoint a trustee, as in *Dalriada Trustees v Bluefin Trustees* [2017] EWHC 1085 (Ch), where the Regulator had appointed the claimant as trustee of eight occupational pensions schemes, but there were complications with respect to assets falling outside of the relevant schemes. The Regulator had no power to appoint trustees in respect of such assets, but the court approved their appointment.

[51] See e.g. *All Metal Services Ltd v Pensions Regulator* [2017] UKUT 323 (TCC); [2017] Pens. L.R. 21.

[52] Trustees may not be indemnified out of the trust assets for financial penalties; Pensions Act 2004 s.256.

[53] Pensions Act 2004 s.15. The Regulator's ability to seek an injunction was held not to be a free-standing right without an underlying claim in obiter dicta by Nugee J in *Re Bovey Cranbrook RBS; Pensions Regulator v Dalriada Trustees* [2013] EWHC 4346 (Ch).

[54] Pensions Act 2004 s.16 (restitution). For information gathering by the Regulator, see Pensions Act 2004 ss.72–79.

[55] *Pensions Regulator v Payae Ltd* [2018] EWHC 36 (Ch); [2018] I.C.R. D3.

[56] [2018] EWHC 36 (Ch) per HHJ Pelling at [12]–[13].

[57] Pensions Act 1995 s.11, as amended.

[58] Pensions Act 2004 ss.23–32.

contributions,[59] to issue an improvement notice to any person considered to be contravening the pensions legislation,[60] and to enter and inspect business premises.[61]

In addition to the Pensions Regulator, the Pensions Ombudsman has jurisdiction over occupational and personal pension schemes. He[62] may investigate and determine various complaints and disputes relating primarily to maladministration,[63] which is not given a statutory definition.[64] A breach of trust does not automatically constitute maladministration.[65] The Ombudsman may not direct steps to be taken (such as the repayment of money to the fund or the setting aside of a deed) unless the court could do so.[66] An example of a finding by the Pensions Ombudsman of maladministration is *NHS Business Services Authority v Leeks*.[67]

> An employee complained to the Ombudsman after working for two years after reaching the maximum possible accrual of pension entitlement at the age of 60, because neither her employer nor the defendant scheme administrator informed her of the relevant fact. As a result, she had paid contributions for the extra two years. The defendant argued that the maladministration should not cover limitations of an automated system. Sales J upheld the finding of maladministration, given the expertise and responsibility of the administrator.[68]

It appears that he may direct the payment of damages for distress.[69]

ii. Trustees. The supervisory powers of the Pensions Regulator over trustees, including the powers of removal, suspension and appointment, were noted above. The 1995 and 2004 Acts contain further important provisions concerning trustees, which are designed primarily to ensure good administration and to dilute the influence of the employer.

17–009

---

[59] Pensions Act 2004 s.17, as amended by the Public Service Pensions Act 2013.
[60] Pensions Act 2004 s.13, as amended by the Public Service Pensions Act 2013.
[61] Pensions Act 2004 ss.73–76.
[62] Anthony Arter was appointed the Pensions Ombudsman in May 2015 for a four-year term.
[63] Pension Schemes Act 1993 ss.145–151, as amended by Pensions Acts 1995 and 2004. On the resolution of pension disputes, see J. Clifford (1998) 12 T.L.I. 26. The Ombudsman does not have precedence over the courts in terms of jurisdiction: *Pell Frischmann Consultants Ltd v Prabhu* [2013] EWHC 2203 (Ch); [2014] I.C.R. 153 per Penelope Reed QC, sitting as a Deputy Judge of the Chancery Division, at [47]. Appeals from the Ombudsman lie to the court only on points of law: Pension Schemes Act 1993 s.151(4); *McShee v MMC UK Pension Fund Trustees Ltd* [2016] EWHC 1574 (Ch); [2016] Pens. L.R. 239.
[64] *Baugniet v Capita Employee Benefits Ltd* [2017] EWHC 501 (Ch); [2017] Pens. L.R. 13.
[65] *Law Debenture Trust Corp Plc v Pensions Ombudsman* [1998] 1 W.L.R. 1329.
[66] *Hillsdown Holdings Plc v Pensions Ombudsman* [1997] 1 All E.R. 862; *Edge v Pensions Ombudsman* [2000] Ch. 602; *Pensions Ombudsman v EMC Europe Ltd* [2012] EWHC 3508 (Ch); [2013] I.C.R. 567.
[67] [2014] EWHC 1446 (Ch); [2014] I.C.R. 948. For an example of a determination of the Ombudsman being varied, see *NHS Business Services Authority v Wheeler* [2014] EWHC 2155 (Ch); [2014] Pens. L.R. 639 (large payment paid to family of deceased on mistaken belief as to doctor's membership status of pension scheme recoverable).
[68] [2014] EWHC 1446 (Ch); [2014] I.C.R. 948 at [29].
[69] *Swansea City Council v Johnson* [1999] Ch 189. *East Sussex CC v Jacobs* [2003] EWHC 3323 (Ch), *The Times*, 23 January 2004, and by Warren J in *IBM United Kingdom Holdings Ltd v Dalgleish* [2014] EWHC 980 (Ch); [2014] Pens. L.R. 335 at [1469] (the point did not arise on appeal). The upper limit on "unexceptional cases" has been recommended to be raised from £1,000 to £1,600: *Baugniet v Capita Employee Benefits Ltd* [2017] EWHC 501 (Ch); [2017] Pens. L.R. 13.

17–010   *(a)   Constitution.*   The constitution of the trustee body must require that representatives of the scheme members be included, and that a trustee who is independent of the employer must be appointed on the employer's insolvency.

The trustees must make and implement arrangements for the selection of "member-nominated trustees".[70] They must constitute at least one-third of the total number of trustees. A greater number cannot be appointed without the employer's approval. Where the trustee is a company, the requirement is for "member-nominated directors".[71] Failure to comply may result in a civil penalty under s.10 of the 1995 Act. The Pensions Act 2004 removed this possibility of employers opting out of the member-nominated trustee provisions, and also permitted the proportion of one-third to be increased to half by regulations.[72]

Where a person is both a trustee and a beneficiary, as in the case of member-nominated trustees, difficult problems of conflict of interest and duty might arise.[73] Where, for example, trustees have a discretion to use a surplus to augment the benefits of the members, any balance going to the employer, the question arises whether they can validly exercise their discretion in such a way as to benefit themselves in their capacity as members.[74] This is resolved by s.39 of the 1995 Act, which provides that:

> [N]o rule of law that a trustee may not exercise the powers vested in him so as to give rise to a conflict between his personal interest and his duties to the beneficiaries shall apply to a trustee of a trust scheme, who is also a member of the scheme, exercising the powers vested in him in any manner, merely because their exercise in that manner benefits, or may benefit, him as a member of the scheme.[75]

An independent trustee must be appointed in circumstances connected with the insolvency of the employer, as where an insolvency practitioner begins to act in relation to the employer or if the official receiver becomes the liquidator of the employer company or the receiver and manager or trustee in bankruptcy of an individual employer.[76] The appointment is made by order of the Pensions Regulator.[77] Once appointed, and so long as the circumstances requiring the appointment continue, only the independent trustee may exercise any discretionary powers of the trustees under the scheme and any fiduciary powers of the employer.[78]

---

[70]   Pensions Act 2004 s.241.

[71]   Pensions Act 2004 s.242.

[72]   Pensions Act 2004 s.243.

[73]   An unsuccessful challenge to the voting by Member-Nominated Trustees can be found in the recent decision of *British Airways Plc v Airways Pension Scheme Trustee Ltd* [2017] EWHC 1191 (Ch); [2017] Pens. L.R. 16.

[74]   See *In Re William (Makin) & Sons Ltd* [1993] B.C.C. 453; M. Milner (1996) 10 T.L.I. 15; *Re Drexel Burnham Lambert UK Pension Plan* [1995] 1 W.L.R. 32; *Edge v Pensions Ombudsman* [2000] Ch. 602.

[75]   See generally M. Fitzsimons (2006) 20 T.L.I. 211.

[76]   Pensions Act 1995 s.22; (ss.22–25 amended by Pensions Act 2004 s.36). "Independent" is defined in s.23(3). He may be paid fees by the employer or from the trust fund; s.25(6). An independent trustee was already required in such circumstances under previous legislation.

[77]   s.23 (at the time of writing, some amendments to the section made by the Pension Schemes Act 2015 s.44(3) have not yet been brought into force).

[78]   s.25. The employer, if previously sole trustee, ceases to be trustee on the appointment of the independent trustee.

(b) *Disqualification.*   Certain categories of persons are disqualified by s.29 of the 1995 Act from being trustee of any occupational pension scheme. Broadly, the disqualification applies to a person convicted of any offence involving dishonesty or deception; an undischarged bankrupt; a company of which any director is disqualified under the section; a person who has made a composition with creditors and has not been discharged; and a person disqualified from acting as a company director.   **17–011**

A trustee who becomes disqualified ceases to be a trustee and commits an offence if he subsequently purports to act,[79] although things done by him while purporting to act as trustee are not invalid merely because of the disqualification.[80]

(c) *Majority Decisions.*   Under the general law, trustees (other than charity trustees) must act unanimously, unless the trust instrument provides otherwise.[81] Section 32 of the 1995 Act provides an exception for trustees of an occupational pension scheme, who may, unless the trust scheme provides otherwise, make decisions by majority. As a safeguard, the trustees must give each trustee notice of occasions at which decisions may be taken, so far as reasonably practicable.[82]   **17–012**

(d) *Knowledge and Understanding.*   The Pensions Act 2004 introduced a requirement for trustees to be more professional. They must be conversant with the trust deed and scheme rules, the scheme's statements of investment and funding principles, and any documents recording policy adopted by the trustees relating to the administration of the scheme. They must have knowledge and understanding of the law relating to pensions and trusts, and the principles of scheme funding and investment. The degree of knowledge and understanding required is that appropriate for enabling the trustee to exercise his functions as trustee of the scheme.[83] These provisions do not affect any rule of law requiring a trustee to have knowledge of, or expertise in, any matter.[84]   **17–013**

iii.   Professional Advisers.   The trustees or managers of every occupational pension scheme must appoint an individual or a firm as auditor and an individual as actuary.[85] Where the trust assets include investments, an individual or firm must be appointed as fund manager.[86] The trustees of the pension scheme (and any connected persons and associates) are ineligible to act as auditor or actuary of the scheme.[87]   **17–014**

---

[79] s.30(3).

[80] s.30(5).

[81] Below, para.18–007.

[82] s.32(2)(b).

[83] Pensions Act 2004 ss.247–248. Section 248A applies similar provisions to members of boards of public service pension schemes, as added by the Public Service Pensions Act 2013 Sch.4 para.19.

[84] Pensions Act 2004 s.249; ss.249A–B require internal controls to ensure compliance.

[85] Pensions Act 1995 s.47. The duty to obtain audited accounts is imposed by regulations, the present source of which is s.41.

[86] Pensions Act 1995 s.47. For delegation of investment powers to the fund manager, see below.

[87] Pensions Act 1995 s.27. Contravention is an offence under s.28.

17–015   **iv.   Investment.**   Under the general law, pension trusts have been governed by the same investment principles as traditional trusts,[88] although the courts, appreciating the need for the trustees of large pension funds to have wide investment powers, have been ready to exercise their jurisdiction to vary trusts by extending these powers.[89] It has been recognised since the Pensions Act 1995 that the special nature of pension trusts requires special treatment.

17–016   *(a)   General Principles.*   The trustees of an occupational pension scheme have, subject to the provisions of the 1995 Act on choosing investments[90] and to any restriction in the scheme, the same power to make an investment of any kind as if they were absolutely entitled to the assets.[91] They must ensure that a written statement in prescribed form of the principles governing investment decisions is prepared, maintained and revised from time to time.[92] Neither the trust scheme nor the statement may restrict the investment power by reference to the employer's consent.

The exercise of the power of investment by the trustees is governed by s.36 of the Pensions Act 1995 and regulations made under it.[93] Regulations may specify criteria to be applied in choosing investments and may require diversification. Before investing and at suitable intervals thereafter, the trustees must obtain and consider proper advice[94] on the question whether the investment is satisfactory having regard to the principles contained in their policy statement and the requirements of the regulations so far as they relate to the suitability of investments.[95] The trustees or fund manager must exercise their powers with a view to giving effect to the principles of their policy statement, so far as reasonably practicable.[96] Failure to comply with these investment duties may result in the imposition of a financial penalty under s.10 of the 1995 Act, but the statutory duty of care under the Trustee Act 2000 does not apply to investment powers under occupational pension schemes.[97] Finally, regulations may prohibit trustees from borrowing money or acting as guarantor.[98]

Building upon previous work,[99] the Law Commission has considered the extent to which pension funds may make social investments, and has agreed that, where the options for investment do not entail a sacrifice of competitive returns,

---

[88] See *Cowan v Scargill* [1985] Ch. 270; below, paras 19–019—19–020. On pension trusts, specifically, see S. Daykin (2014) 28 T.L.I. 165.
[89] See *Mason v Farbrother* [1983] 2 All E.R. 1078; below, para.19–023.
[90] Pensions Act 1995 s.36(1), below.
[91] Pensions Act 1995 s.34(1). "Investment" is not defined. The wide investment powers conferred by the Trustee Act 2000 do not apply as there is no need for them; Trustee Act 2000 s.36.
[92] s.35, as substituted by Pensions Act 2004 s.244.
[93] s.36 was amended by Pensions Act 2004 s.245, introducing the power to make regulations governing investment by trustees. Where investment discretions have been delegated to a fund manager, as discussed below, the fund manager must exercise his discretion in accordance with the regulations.
[94] Defined in s.36(6); For an example of a breach of this duty, see *Dalriada Trustees Ltd v Mcauley* [2017] EWHC 202 (Ch); [2017] Pens. L.R. 8.
[95] s.36(3), (4).
[96] s.36(5).
[97] Trustee Act 2000 s.36.
[98] Pensions Act 1995 s.36A, introduced by Pensions Act 2004 s.246.
[99] Law Com. No. 350, *Fiduciary Duties of Investment Intermediaries* (2014).

there is sufficient flexibility in the law for such investments to be made, but that perceptions and structural limitations are an obstacles.[100] The Commission therefore recommended a range of measures to bring about behavioural change in the consideration of social investments. The government has broadly accepted these proposals, and at the time of writing, was consulting upon their implementation.[101] The position will be complicated by the prospective incorporation of a new European pensions directive, the Institutions for Occupational Retirement Provision (IORP) II Directive,[102] which would require Member States to permit institutions "take into account potential long-term impact of investment decisions on environmental, social and governance factors".[103] The deadline for the transposition of the Directive would be 13 January 2019, before the anticipated departure (and subject to any transition period) of the UK from the EU on 29 March 2019.[104] The broader issue of ethical considerations with regard to investment by trustees is considered under the general principles in Ch.19.[105]

(b) Delegation to Fund Manager.   Under the general law, a trustee may not **17–017** delegate the exercise of his discretions without authority, and this led to inconvenient problems over the delegation of investment decisions to fund managers prior to the Trustee Act 2000.[106] The Pensions Act 1995 already provided that trustees of occupational pension funds could delegate investment decisions to a fund manager authorised to conduct investment business under financial services legislation.[107] The trustees are not responsible for the act or default of such a fund manager if they have taken all reasonable steps to satisfy themselves that the manager has appropriate knowledge and experience and is carrying out his work competently and in accordance with statutory duties.[108] Alternatively, the trustees may delegate investment decisions by power of attorney under s.25 of the Trustee Act 1925,[109] or, subject to any restriction in the trust scheme, to a fund manager not authorised to conduct investment business under the Financial Services and Markets Act 2000, or may authorise two or more of their number to make investment decisions on their behalf.[110] In these three cases, however, the trustees as a whole remain liable for any breaches resulting from any acts or defaults in the exercise of the discretion.[111]

---

[100] Law Com. No. 374, *Pension Funds and Social Investment* (2017).

[101] Department for Digital, Culture, Media & Sport and Department for Work & Pensions, *Pension funds and social investment: the Government's final response* (June 2018).

[102] Directive 2016/2341.

[103] IORP Directive, art.19(1)(b).

[104] Department for Work and Pensions: EU Law: Written Answer 59844: 17 January 2017. *https://www.parliament.uk/business/publications/written-questions-answers-statements/written-question/Commons/2017-01-12/59844* [accessed 4 July 2018].

[105] Below, paras 19–019—19–019.

[106] Below, paras 21–012—21–013.

[107] Pensions Act 1995 s.34(2): the relevant financial services legislation is the Financial Services and Markets Act 2000, as amended by the Financial Services Act 2012.

[108] s.34(4).

[109] Below, para.21–019.

[110] s.34(5).

[111] s.34(5); Trustee Act 1925 s.25(5).

As the Pensions Act 1995 provides for delegation of investment decisions by trustees of occupational pension schemes, the power to delegate such decisions under the Trustee Act 2000 is inapplicable, as is the power under that Act to appoint nominees and custodians.[112] Other powers of delegation under the Trustee Act 2000 do apply to pension scheme trustees, although subject to certain restrictions.[113] The statutory duty of care under the Act of 2000 does not apply to pension scheme trustees when delegating investment decisions or appointing nominees or custodians pursuant to their powers under the 1995 Act or under the pension scheme provisions.[114]

17–018   *(c)   Exclusion of Liability.*   Liability for failure to take care or to exercise skill in the performance of investment functions exercisable by the trustees or the fund manager cannot be excluded or restricted by an instrument or agreement.[115] On the question whether the trustees may be exempted from responsibility for the acts and defaults of fund managers, we have seen that the trustees are not liable for the acts of fund managers who are authorised to conduct investment business, and so the point does not arise in such a case. In the case of delegation to fund managers who are *not* authorised to conduct investment business, where such delegation is permitted by s.34(5) of the 1995 Act, the trustees are normally liable for the acts and defaults of such a person, as mentioned above. In this case, however, the liability may be validly excluded or restricted provided the trustees have taken all reasonable steps to satisfy themselves that the fund manager has appropriate knowledge and experience and is carrying out his work competently and in accordance with statutory duties.[116]

17–019   *(d)   Employer-related Investments.*   Investments of pension fund assets in the employer's business, such as the purchase of shares in the employer company or loans to the employer, are subject to restrictions[117] because of the danger they present on the employer's insolvency. If a substantial proportion of the fund could be invested in the employer company, the losses would be great if the employer went into liquidation. Section 40 of the Pensions Act 1995 obliges the trustees or managers of an occupational pension scheme to ensure that current restrictions on employer-related investments are complied with. Failure to do so may result in the imposition of a financial penalty under s.10, and a trustee or manager who agrees to invest in contravention of the restrictions commits an offence.

17–020   **v.   Scheme Funding.**   The scheme funding requirements are designed to ensure that any inadequacies of funding will be revealed by a regular monitoring process and remedied in various ways, usually by an increase in contributions by

---

[112] Trustee Act 2000 s.36.

[113] Trustee Act 2000 s.36.

[114] Trustee Act 2000 s.36.

[115] Pensions Act 1995 s.33; *Dalriada Trustees Ltd v Mcauley* [2017] EWHC 202 (Ch); [2017] Pens. L.R. 8. On trustee exemption clauses generally, see para.18–005, below.

[116] s.34(6).

[117] Pensions Act 1995 s.40. See I. Greenstreet (1994) 8 T.L.I. 56; D. Pollard and D. Heath (2010) 24 T.L.I. 13.

the members or by the employer. The provisions apply to occupational pension schemes other than money purchase schemes.

The present scheme funding rules are provided by the Pensions Act 2004. The new rules, although stricter than the former approach of a "minimum funding rule" under the 1995 Act, are more flexible in that they are "scheme specific". The statutory funding objective is that each scheme must have sufficient assets to cover its liabilities.[118] The trustees must prepare a statement of funding principles which sets out their policy for ensuring that the scheme meets its funding objectives.[119] They must obtain an actuary's valuation of the assets and liabilities at regular intervals.[120] They must also prepare and keep under review a schedule of employer's and members' contributions, to be certified by the actuary.[121]

The actuary must inform the Pensions Regulator if his valuation of the fund shows that the trustees are failing to meet their funding objectives, or if he is unable to certify the schedule of contributions.[122] A recovery plan must then be drawn up, setting out the steps to be taken to meet the statutory funding objective.[123] A copy must be sent to the Regulator. The plan must be agreed between the trustees and the employer. The trustees must report any failure to reach agreement to the Regulator, which will exercise various powers to remedy the situation, such as directing increased contributions.[124] If the situation cannot be remedied, the scheme will be wound up, as discussed below.[125]

Trustees or actuaries who fail to comply with the obligations described above may incur a financial penalty under s.10 of the Pensions Act 1995.

vi. Surplus. Much of the pension trust litigation has involved entitlement to surplus funds.[126] Surpluses arose primarily in the 1980s because of the huge growth in the value of investments at that time. The opposite is the case at the present time. Where the scheme is ongoing, any surplus is notional, and means that the actuarial estimation of the assets at a given time exceeds the actuarial estimation of the liabilities. Such a calculation involves many projections and assumptions. There will be an actual surplus only if the scheme is wound up and all liabilities discharged. Surplus on a winding up is dealt with in the following section. Where the scheme is ongoing, the question is one of rights and duties in the application of the surplus rather than ownership as such.   **17–021**

The application of a surplus (actual or notional) will be crucial where the employer is insolvent,[127] or where the employer company is taken over by a   **17–022**

---

[118] Pensions Act 2004 s.222. See R. Evans (2007) 21 T.L.I. 177. See *British Airways Plc v Airways Pension Scheme Trustee Ltd* [2017] EWHC 1191 (Ch); [2017] Pens. L.R. 16 per Morgan J at [77]–[82].
[119] Pensions Act 2004 s.223.
[120] Pensions Act 2004 s.224.
[121] Pensions Act 2004 s.227.
[122] Pensions Act 2004 ss.225, 227.
[123] Pensions Act 2004 s.226.
[124] Pensions Act 2004 ss.229, 231.
[125] Below, para.17–023.
[126] See generally D. Pollard (2003) T.L.I. 2.
[127] See *Mettoy Pension Trustees Ltd v Evans* [1990] 1 W.L.R. 1587; above, para.7–007; *Thrells Ltd v Lomas* [1993] 1 W.L.R. 456.

company which proposes to "raid" the surplus,[128] or where, on a partial sale of the employer company, the employees are transferred to the purchaser's pension scheme and dispute the decision of the trustees of the original scheme not to transfer any of the substantial surplus to the purchaser's scheme.[129]

As explained below, the tax regime requires the taxation of any payments to the employer from the surplus, to avoid exploitation of pension fund tax reliefs.[130]

The Pensions Act 1995 (as amended) imposes further restrictions on payments of surplus to the employer from a scheme which is ongoing.[131] Where the scheme confers power on any person (including the employer) other than the trustees to make payments to the employer, it can be exercised only by the trustees.[132] The power can be exercised only on complying with strict conditions, including that the trustees are satisfied that it is in the interest of members to exercise it in the manner proposed.[133]

17–023   **vii. Winding Up.**   On this event, which may occur on the employer's insolvency and in other circumstances specified in the scheme rules,[134] the members' rights crystallise. Liabilities to them must be discharged and any surplus assets distributed. The trustees may be able to rely on s.27 of the Trustee Act 1925 if they had no notice of a member's claim, but in practice it will be difficult for them to show that they had no notice.[135] It has already been noted that a pension scheme may be wound up by the order of the Pensions Regulator in certain circumstances.[136] The 1995 Act (as amended) contains other provisions dealing with the discharge of liabilities and distribution of surplus on the winding up of an earnings-related scheme. (The question of insufficient or excess assets will not arise with a money purchase scheme, where the level of benefits is not defined and depends on the performance of the investments). The assets must be applied to discharge liabilities to members and others in a specified order.[137] Liabilities may be discharged in various ways, such as by transferring credits to another scheme, by transfer to certain personal pension schemes, by the purchase of annuities or by cash payments.[138] If the assets are insufficient to discharge the liabilities, the deficit is treated as a debt from the employer to the trustees,

---

[128] See *Re Courage Group's Pension Scheme* [1987] 1 W.L.R. 495.

[129] *Wilson v Law Debenture Trust Corp Plc* [1995] 2 All E.R. 337; above, para.17–005.

[130] Below, para.17–032.

[131] See generally *National Grid Co Plc v Mayes* [2001] 1 W.L.R. 864.

[132] s.37(2), as amended by Pensions Act 2004 s.250. See also s.251, as amended by Pensions Act 2011 s.25.

[133] s.37(3), as amended.

[134] For example, a solvent employer may wish to wind up an earnings-related scheme in order to replace it with a money purchase scheme.

[135] Below, para.19–029; *MCP Pension Trustees Ltd v Aon Pension Trustees Ltd* [2011] 3 W.L.R. 455.

[136] s.11; above, para.17–008. See also Pensions Act 2004 s.154 (winding up of failing scheme where rescue not possible).

[137] s.73, as substituted by Pensions Act 2004 s.270 and amended by the Pension Schemes Act 2015.

[138] s.74, as amended by Pensions Act 2004 s.270. A. Slocombe (2012) 26 T.L.I. 120.

without prejudice to any other right or remedy of the trustees.[139] A debt owed to a pension scheme by an employee under s.75 is assignable by the trustee.[140]

Where there are surplus assets, the scheme will normally provide for their allocation, often by requiring payment to the employer after augmenting benefits. In the rare case where the scheme makes no effective provision for surplus, the general law applies. Such a case came before the Privy Council in *Air Jamaica Ltd v Charlton*.[141]

> A pension scheme had been discontinued. An amendment to the scheme purporting to permit the payment of surplus to the employer was invalid because the power to amend was void for perpetuity. The surplus was held on a resulting trust as to half for the employer and half for the members (including the estates of deceased members) in proportion to their contributions. The decision of Scott J in *Davis v Richards & Wallington Industries Ltd*,[142] to the effect that any share of the members would go to the Crown as bona vacantia on the basis (primarily for tax reasons) that the members must have intended to exclude a resulting trust, was wrong, having been based on an incorrect analysis of the role of intention. The fact that the extra benefits under a resulting trust would exceed the limits for tax relief was not a proper ground for rejecting a resulting trust for members.

As stated above, on insolvency of the employer, any fiduciary powers, including powers relating to the allocation of surplus, are exercisable only by the independent trustee.[143] The 1995 Act (as amended) makes further provisions for the allocation of surplus assets on the winding up of an approved scheme, of which the rules either permit or prohibit distribution to the employer. If the scheme confers power on the employer or trustees to distribute assets to the employer, the power can only be exercised where all liabilities have been fully discharged and notice has been given to the members.[144]

Sanctions for failure to comply with these provisions include the imposition of a financial penalty under s.10.

viii. Information to Members. As explained in Ch.19, trustees are under a general law duty to provide information and accounts to the beneficiaries. In addition, s.41 of the 1995 Act[145] provides for regulations requiring the trustees to make copies of various documents available to the members and prospective members and their spouses (and to certain other persons). The documents in question include the trustees' statement of funding principles, audited accounts,

17–024

---

[139] s.75, as variously amended. See *Re Merchant Navy Ratings Pension Fund* [2015] EWHC 448 (Ch) (Asplin J). See also *Re Rigid Containers Group Staff Pension Fund* [2013] EWCA Civ 1714; [2014] Pens. L.R. 143.

[140] *Trustee of the Singer & Friedlander Ltd Pension and Assurance Scheme v Corbett* [2014] EWHC 3038 (Ch); [2015] Pens. L.R. 31 (Birss J).

[141] [1999] 1 W.L.R. 1399; above, para.11–012.

[142] [1990] 1 W.L.R. 1511.

[143] Pensions Act 1995 s.25(2); above, para.17–010. The court retains an inherent power to appoint the independent trustee to exercise in certain other powers in exceptional circumstances: see *Bridge Trustees Ltd v Noel Penny (Turbines) Ltd* [2008] EWHC 2054 (Ch); [2008] Pens. L.R. 345.

[144] s.76, as amended.

[145] As amended by the Pensions Act 2004. See also s.203 of the Act of 2004 (information to members concerning involvement of the Board of the Pension Protection Fund).

actuarial valuations of assets and liabilities of the scheme, certificates relating to the scheme funding requirement and reports (required by the Act) concerning any failure to meet that requirement.

17–025   **ix.   Compensation.**   Although the aim of the pensions legislation is to prevent the misappropriation of pension funds, no statutory mechanism can provide totally effective safeguards. The legislation, therefore, provides a compensation scheme to diminish hardships suffered when the safeguards do not prevent losses as in the plight of employees who have lost their pensions on the employer's insolvency. The Pensions Compensation Board, set up by the Pensions Act 1995, was replaced in the Pensions Act 2004 by the Board of the Pension Protection Fund.[146]

The PPF Board intervenes where the insolvency of an employer (of which it must be notified) leaves a defined benefit (final salary) scheme in deficit, so that members will lose some or all of their benefits.[147] If the scheme cannot be rescued, the Board is responsible for ensuring that compensation is paid to the members, whereupon the scheme is wound up.[148] It may direct legal proceedings to be taken, for example to recover misappropriated assets.[149]

The Pension Protection Fund[150] does not provide a full guarantee of benefits, because payments are standardised and subject to capping.[151] It derives its funds from a levy (which is partly risk-based) payable by defined benefit occupational pension schemes.[152] This may further discourage employers from setting up or continuing with such schemes.

The statutory compensation scheme was not retrospective, and so provided no help to some 85,000 people who had lost their pensions through the employer's insolvency before the commencement of the scheme. In 2006, the Parliamentary Commissioner (Ombudsman) upheld a complaint against the then Government for misleading people over the safety of occupational pension schemes. The Government rejected the Ombudsman's findings but, following judicial review proceedings by the pensioners, finally agreed a compensation package.[153]

The prospective availability of compensation from the fund is not a relevant factor for the trustees to take into account when exercising any power under the pension scheme rules, as this would be contrary to public policy.[154]

---

[146] Pensions Act 2004 Pt 2.

[147] This would not have helped the Maxwell pensioners, as the employer companies did not go into liquidation.

[148] Pensions Act 2004 s.161.

[149] Pensions Act 2004 s.134.

[150] Pensions Act 2004 s.173. See also ss.182, 188 (the Fraud Compensation Fund).

[151] The detailed provisions are contained in Sch.7 as amended by Pensions Act 2008 Sch.8 and Pensions Act 2011 Sch.4. The amount is set by Statutory Instrument.

[152] Pensions Act 2004 s.174. See also s.189 (levy for the Fraud Compensation Fund). On eligible schemes, see *FSS Pension Trustees Ltd v The Board of the Pension Protection Fund* [2014] EWHC 1397 (Ch); [2014] Pens. L.R. 303.

[153] *R. (on the application of Bradley) v Secretary of State for Work and Pensions* [2009] Q.B. 114; J. Varuhas (2009) 72 M.L.R. 102.

[154] *Independent Trustee Services Ltd v Hope* [2010] I.C.R. 553; D. Fox (2010) 69 C.L.J. 240.

x. Alienability   Other provisions of the Pensions Act 1995 deal with the   **17–026**
alienability of pension rights and the position on the bankruptcy of a scheme
member. The purpose of a pension scheme is not to provide members with a
disposable asset but to ensure an income on retirement. s.91 of the 1995 Act
provides that accrued rights under an occupational pension scheme cannot be
assigned, surrendered, charged or subjected to any right of set-off.[155] Recent
decisions have clarified the scope of this provision: the Court of Appeal held in
Bradbury v British Broadcasting Corp[156] that the section protects the "actual,
accrued rights of employees"[157]; it does not prevent the variation of other terms
of the employment contract merely because those terms would have a bearing on
the future acquisition of rights to a pension.[158]

The general prohibition under s.91, which reflects the provisions normally
found in pension schemes,[159] does not apply to assignments to or surrenders for
the benefit of the member's widow, widower or dependant, and there are limited
exceptions permitting a charge or set-off by the employer.

xi. Bankruptcy.   Where a member of an approved occupational or personal   **17–027**
pension scheme is made bankrupt, pension rights are excluded from the
bankrupt's estate for the purposes of the Insolvency Act 1986 and are thus
unavailable to creditors.[160] The Court of Appeal in *Re Henry*[161] confirmed that
the effect of these provisions is that the trustee in bankruptcy cannot require a
bankrupt exercise a right to receive sums under a pension and thus convert
potentially payable sums into 'income': to hold that uncrystallised pension rights
were income would "drive a coach and horses through the protection afforded to
a bankrupt's pension rights by the 1986 Act and pension legislation".[162]

The provisions of the 1986 Act relating to the setting aside of certain
dispositions made prior to bankruptcy[163] are extended so that contributions to an
occupational or personal pension scheme may be ordered by the court to be
recovered by the trustee in bankruptcy to the extent that the contributions were
excessive and have unfairly prejudiced the creditors.[164] The court will consider in
particular whether the contributions were made for the purpose of putting assets
beyond the reach of creditors. The overall picture is, as Gloster LJ put it,[165]

---

[155] *Gleeds (Head Office) (A Firm) v Briggs* [2016] EWCA Civ 1284; [2017] Pens. L.R. 4 (court
approving compromise where certain partners gave up additional benefits in exchange for the sum of
£100). Forfeiture, meaning any manner of deprivation or suspension (e.g. for misconduct), is
prohibited by s.92.
[156] [2017] EWCA Civ 1144; [2017] Pens. L.R. 20.
[157] [2017] EWCA Civ 1144 per Gloster LJ at [45].
[158] [2017] EWCA Civ 1144 at [48].
[159] See *Re Scientific Investment Pension Plan Trusts* [1999] Ch. 53, above, para.8–001.
[160] Welfare Reform and Pensions Act 1999 s.11 (personal approved pensions) and Pensions Schemes
Act 1993 s.159(5) (occupational pensions).
[161] [2016] EWCA Civ 989; [2017] 1 W.L.R. 391.
[162] [2017] 1 W.L.R. 391 per Gloster LJ at [38], disapproving (at [55]) *Raithatha v Williamson* [2012]
EWHC 909 (Ch); [2012] 1 W.L.R. 3559.
[163] Above, Ch.14, Part 4.
[164] s.342 A, B and C of the Insolvency Act 1986, inserted by Pensions Act 1995, and amended by
Welfare Reform and Pensions Act 1999 s.15.
[165] *Re Henry* [2017] 1 W.L.R. 391 at [45].

"Parliament has decided to draw the balance between, on the one hand, the interests of the state in encouraging people to save through the medium of private pensions (so that in old age or infirmity they will not be a burden on the resources of the state), and, on the other, the interests of creditors in receiving payment of their debts, by the mechanism of sections 342A to 342C of the 1986 Act which enable a trustee to claw back excessive pension contributions made by the bankrupt where such contributions have unfairly prejudiced the bankrupt's creditors."

B. Other Statutory Provisions

17–028   **i. Rule Against Perpetuities.**   As explained in Ch.14, the perpetuity rule prevents the vesting of property at a remote date beyond the perpetuity period (lives in being plus 21 years, a specified period not exceeding 80 years under the Perpetuities and Accumulations Act 1964, or 125 years under the Perpetuities and Accumulations Act 2009)[166] and also invalidates non-charitable purpose trusts which are not confined in duration to the perpetuity period.[167] It will be appreciated that the perpetuity rule could prove troublesome if applied to occupational pension schemes.[168] The perpetuity rule is based on public policy, namely that it is undesirable for economic and other reasons to have property tied up for long periods of time save for charitable purposes (to which the rule does not apply). In the case of pension funds, there is a countervailing public interest in encouraging the provision of retirement pensions. The Perpetuities and Accumulations Act 2009[169] provides, therefore, that occupational, personal and public service pension schemes are exempted from the perpetuity rule. However, the rule applies to nominations of benefits by scheme members and instruments exercising powers of advancement under pension schemes.[170]

17–029   **ii. Tax Relief.**   The public interest in the provision of retirement benefits beyond the state pension results in significant tax relief for occupational pension schemes. Previously tax relief depended on the scheme being an "exempt approved scheme", but that regime was replaced by the Finance Act 2004 (with effect from 6 April 2006) by a registration requirement. In order to obtain tax relief, the pension scheme must be registered under s.153 of the Act.[171] Registration may be withdrawn by decision of HMRC on certain grounds, for example failure to pay a substantial amount of tax due, or where a false declaration was made to secure registration.[172] A scheme may be registered whether it is earnings-related or money purchase, and whether the investments are held by the trustees or through the medium of an insurer. The Act of 2004 sets out a framework of principles for the payment of pensions in the context of tax relief.[173] The details cannot be given here, but examples include the rule that a

---

[166] Above, Ch.14, Part 4.

[167] Above, para.14–018.

[168] See *Air Jamaica Ltd v Charlton* [1999] 1 W.L.R. 1399 (no exemption in Jamaica).

[169] s.2(4).

[170] Perpetuities and Accumulations Act 2009 s.2(5).

[171] Finance Act 2004 ss.186 to 203, as amended, most recently by Finance Act 2018.

[172] Finance Act 2004 ss.157, 158. The decision may be appealed; s.159. De-registration leads to a tax charge; below, para.17–032.

[173] Finance Act 2004 ss.165 to 168, as amended by the Taxation of Pensions Act 2014; *Danvers v Revenue and Customs Commissioners* [2016] UKUT 569 (TCC); [2017] Pens. L.R. 6.

pension may not be paid before the minimum pension age[174] save in cases of ill-health, and that death benefits may not be paid other than to a dependant of the member.

The court will not vary a pension trust in a manner which could put at risk its tax exempt status.[175] The effect of loss of eligibility for tax relief is severe, but this does not justify the exclusion of a resulting trust of surplus funds in favour of the members which would put their benefits above the statutory limits for tax exemption.[176]

(a) Tax Relief for Contributions. Provided the scheme is registered, tax relief is given to both employer and employee contributions. Contributions by the employer are treated as trading expenses and thus deductible from income and corporation tax liability.[177] Contributions by the employee are deductible from taxable income, subject to certain conditions.[178] A further benefit is that the employer's contributions are not taxable as remuneration of the employee.[179] Ultimately the pension itself will be subject to income tax whether or not the scheme is registered,[180] although lump sums payable on retirement are tax free. **17–030**

(b) Tax Relief for the Pension Fund. Provided the scheme is registered, the fund itself attracts significant relief. Neither income tax[181] nor capital gains tax[182] is payable on the investments. **17–031**

(c) Overfunding. In view of the above reliefs there might be a temptation to put more money than is required into the pension fund, which could either be used to pay excessive benefits or retrieved by the employer as surplus. The exploitation of tax relief is prevented in various ways. We have seen that the statutory framework for tax relief now contained in the Finance Act 2004 lays down conditions which must be satisfied in order for payments from pension funds to be authorised.[183] If unauthorised payments[184] are made to the members or the employer, a tax charge of 40% is levied.[185] Unauthorised payments can **17–032**

---

[174] This was 50 before 6 April 2010 and 55 on and after that date; Finance Act 2004 s.279.

[175] *Brooks v Brooks* [1996] 1 A.C. 375.

[176] *Air Jamaica Ltd v Charlton* [1999] 1 W.L.R. 1399, disapproving on this point *Davis v Richards & Wallingham Industries Ltd* [1990] 1 W.L.R. 1511; above, para.11–015.

[177] Finance Act 2004 s.196. Various restrictions on the available relief were added as ss.196A–L by the Finance Act 2012.

[178] Finance Act 2004 s.188, as amended by the Finance Act 2014; *Sippchoice Ltd v Revenue and Customs Commissioners* [2018] UKFTT 122 (TC).

[179] Income Tax (Earnings and Pensions) Act 2003 s.307.

[180] Income Tax (Earnings and Pensions) Act 2003 s.393 and Pt 9.

[181] Finance Act 2004 s.186.

[182] Taxation of Chargeable Gains Act 1992 s.271, as amended by Finance Act 2004 s.187. For inheritance tax relief, see Inheritance Tax Act 1984 s.86 (trusts for the benefit of employees).

[183] Above, para.17–029.

[184] In *Dalriada Trustees Ltd v Faulds* [2011] EWHC 3391 (Ch); [2012] I.C.R. 1106 held that reciprocal loans between pension schemes to enable each scheme to give immediate benefits to a member of the other scheme (an arrangement called a "pensions reciprocation plan") were unauthorised payments within Finance Act 2006 s.173.

[185] Finance Act 2004 s.208. See also s.209 (unauthorised payments surcharge—15%) and s.239 (scheme sanction surcharge).

lead to the scheme being de-registered, whereupon tax is charged at 40% on the assets of the scheme.[186] If a surplus (which has had the benefit of tax relief) has built up, it cannot be used as a tax shelter. An unauthorised payment of surplus to the employer will be taxed at 40%, as just mentioned. The first call on a surplus is the increase of benefits, after which contributions may be reduced or suspended. Where a payment of surplus to the employer is authorised by the scheme rules and the tax legislation, it is taxed at 35%.[187]

3. EQUAL TREATMENT[188]

17–033   Article 157 of the Treaty on the Functioning of the European Union (the Lisbon Treaty) embodies the principle that men and women should receive equal pay for equal work. Clearly this has no scope for application to traditional trusts conferring benefits by way of bounty, but it does apply to occupational pension schemes because, as we have seen, pension entitlements are a form of deferred remuneration for services. Thus it was held by the European Court of Justice in *Barber v Guardian Royal Exchange Assurance Group*[189] that pension rights fell within art.119, with the result that the common practice of conferring pension entitlements on women employees at an earlier age than their male counterparts was no longer permissible. There were doubts as to the precise scope of the *Barber* decision, and so the matter was tested again in the European Court of Justice in *Coloroll Pension Trustees Ltd v Russell*.[190] It was there held that trustees are bound to do everything within the scope of their powers to ensure compliance with the equal pay principle. Thus the trustees are bound, in the exercise of the powers and the performance of the duties laid down in the trust deed, to observe the principle of equal pay and treatment.[191] The decisions have led to various cases on the alteration of provisions in order to achieve the equalisation of benefits.[192] The Equality Act 2010, replacing a provision in the Pensions Act 1995, provides that an occupational pension scheme which does not contain a sex equality rule shall be treated as including one.[193]

---

[186] Finance Act 2004 s.242.

[187] Finance Act 2004 ss.177, 207. See also Pensions Act 1995 s.37, above (restrictions on exercise of power to make payments to employer).

[188] Outside the European context, the Privy Council held provisions of a Cook Islands pension scheme to be discriminatory against migrant workers in *Arorangi Timberland Ltd v Minister of the Cook Islands National Superannuation Fund (Cook Islands)* [2016] UKPC 32; [2017] 1 W.L.R. 99. The Supreme Court considered a further aspect of the interaction between equality legislation and pensions in *Walker v Innospec* Ltd [2017] UKSC 47; [2017] 4 All E.R. 1004, in holding that statutory provisions relating to the payment of occupational pension benefits to same-sex partners were discriminatory.

[189] [1991] 1 Q.B. 344.

[190] [1995] I.C.R. 179.

[191] In *Department of Constitutional Affairs v O'Brien* [2013] UKSC 6; [2013] 1 W.L.R. 522, the Supreme Court held, on a different aspect of EU Law, that judicial recorders were workers under the Part-time Workers (Prevention of Less Favourable Treatment) Regulations 2000 and thus entitled to a pension on the same terms as full-time judges; the litigation is ongoing, with a further reference having been made to the CJEU (*Ministry of Justice v O'Brien* [2017] UKSC 46; [2017] I.C.R. 1101).

[192] See, for example, *Vaitkus v Dresser-Rand UK Ltd* [2014] EWHC 170 (Ch); [2014] Pens. L.R. 153 (HH Judge Jarman QC) and *Safeway Ltd v Newton* [2017] EWCA Civ 1482; [2018] Pens. L.R. 2.

[193] s.67. See also Pensions Act 2004 s.171 ("Equal treatment").

4. PENSIONS ON DIVORCE OR DISSOLUTION OF A CIVIL PARTNERSHIP

Another matter of concern, which will be dealt with only in outline here, is the **17–034** extent to which the pension entitlement of one spouse must be shared with the other spouse on divorce. A wife who has brought up a family instead of working may have little or no pension provision of her own and may suffer serious financial difficulty if her former husband's pension (often the most valuable family asset after the matrimonial home) is not available to her. The question whether and how pension benefits should be shared is a matter of government policy. One way is to take the husband's pension into account by giving a greater share of other assets to the wife on divorce. Alternatively, the pension itself may be split or earmarked as a source of payments to the spouse, either on divorce or later, when it comes to be paid. Pension sharing on divorce may be ordered under the Matrimonial Causes Act 1973, as amended by the Welfare Reform and Pensions Act 1999 and the Pensions Act 2008. "Earmarking" enables an order made on divorce to take effect when the pension benefits under an occupational or personal pension scheme become payable to the scheme member. At that stage all or part of the benefits may be diverted to the former spouse.[194] The rules relating to spouses apply also to registered civil partners.[195] The details of pension sharing and earmarking are beyond the scope of this book.

---

[194] Matrimonial Causes Act 1973 ss.21A, 24B-G and 25B-E. See also Pensions Act 2004 s.220.
[195] Civil Partnership Act 2004, as amended by Pensions Act 2008. As seen above, para.13–003, marriage of same sex couples has been lawful since the Marriage (Same Sex Couples) Act 2013.

PART III

TRUSTEES AND FIDUCIARIES

CHAPTER 18

GENERAL PRINCIPLES OF THE ADMINISTRATION OF TRUSTS

1. ONEROUS NATURE OF OFFICE

18–001   THE office of trustee is an onerous one. We shall discuss in some detail a trustee's duties, powers and liability; there is little to be said as to her rights. In the performance of her office a trustee must act exclusively in the interest of the trust. She stands to gain nothing from her work in the absence of a clause authorising remuneration, although professional trustees now have charging powers under the Trustee Act 2000.[1] She is required to observe the highest standards of integrity,[2] and a reasonable standard of care and skill in the management of the affairs of the trust; and she is subjected to onerous personal liability if she fails to reach the standards set. Nor may she compete in business with the trust; or be in a position in which her personal interests conflict with those of the trust. She may thus be forced to forgo opportunities which would be available to her if she were not a trustee.[3]

It may well be asked why people consent to become trustees. To this there are two principal answers. First, professional trustees undertake the work only where they are entitled to be paid. Solicitors, banks (Executor and Trustee Departments) and insurance companies come into this category. Most trusts of any size will have a professional trustee. There may be non-professional trustees also; but in any case the bulk of the work of administration—investment, distribution, accounting, tax payments, etc.—will in fact be done by professionals, either the trustees or others employed by them. Secondly, members of the family of (or people otherwise connected to) the settlor or testator will often consent to be trustees out of feelings of duty to the settlor or testator. Where there is no professional trustee, the non-professionals will, as will be seen,[4] usually employ professional agents such as a solicitor, investment manager and accountant to perform the technical duties of the trust. It may well be better to have such experts appointed as trustees in the first place, so that technical matters will not be overlooked.[5] It is usual and common to appoint a mixture of professional trustees and non-professional. There is much to be said for appointing a corporation such as a bank which may be expected to have unrivalled facilities, dependability and permanence.

The settlor (typically in the case of an offshore trust) may also provide for the appointment of a "protector", an independent fiduciary to oversee the exercise of the trustees' powers.[6]

---

[1] Below, para.22–003. Charity trustees may be paid in certain cases; above, para.15–099.

[2] Below, para.18–002.

[3] *Boardman v Phipps* [1967] 2 A.C. 46; below, Ch.21.

[4] Below, Ch.21, Part 7.

[5] For the dangers inherent in appointing no professional trustees, see *Turner v Turner* [1984] Ch. 100, above, para.7–007. See generally C. Bell (1988) 2 *Trust Law & Practice* 86.

[6] See A. Penney [1995] 4 J.Int.P. 31; P. Matthews (1995) 9 T.L.I. 108; P. Hobson (1996) 2 *Trusts & Trustees* 6; D. Waters in A. Oakley (ed.) *Trends in Contemporary Trust Law* (Oxford: Oxford University Press, 1996), p.63; Underhill and Hayton, 18th edn, paras 1.78–1.92; J. Hilliard (2003) 17 T.L.I. 144; A. Duckworth (2006) 20 T.L.I. 180 and 235; T. Tey (2010) 24 T.L.I. 110. K.H. Lau (2012) 26 T.L.I. 39. For recent judicial consideration of the role of protector see *JSC Mezhdunarodniy Promyshlenniy Bank v Pugachev* [2017] EWHC 2426 (Ch) per Birss J (in which the protector was also the settlor and a beneficiary, who had retained for himself the power to remove trustees "with or without cause") at [222]–[278].

2.   Standards Applicable to Trustees

A.   Duties and Discretions

A distinction must be made between a trustee's duties on the one hand and her **18–002** powers or discretions on the other. A duty is an obligation which *must* be carried out. The rules of equity require strict and diligent performance of a trustee's duties. On the other hand, a power is discretionary; it may be exercised, or it may not. This is so whether the power is one given to trustees by statute, or is a power or discretion contained in the instrument creating the trust, or relates to the general management of the affairs of the trust. The distinction should be thought of as what the trustee must (or must not) do, in the case of duties, and what they may or may not do, in the case of powers.

Trustees must act honestly; and must take, in managing trust affairs, "all those precautions which an ordinary prudent man of business would take in managing similar affairs of his own."[7] This formula has now been largely overtaken by the statutory duty of care discussed in the next section. If the trustee properly performs her duties, powers and discretions, she is not liable for loss[8] to or depreciation[9] of the trust property arising from factors beyond his control.

We shall see that many of the rules relating to trustees' duties are more strict in their terms than in their practical application. Much of the work of administration of a trust is necessarily done by professionals. This development has led to great relaxation, first by the courts[10] and then by statute,[11] of the requirement that the trustee should act personally. Further, exemption clauses[12] which exclude the trustees' personal liability in certain circumstances have become widespread; and the Trustee Act 1925 s.61, gives the court a discretion to excuse a trustee who has acted honestly and reasonably and ought fairly to be excused.[13]

B.   The Statutory Duty of Care

The standard of conduct required of trustees was put on a statutory basis by the **18–003** Trustee Act 2000. It was previously laid down in *Speight v Gaunt*[14] that in the management of trust affairs the trustee must act as an ordinary prudent business person would act in managing similar affairs of her own. Section 1 of the Trustee Act 2000 provides that a trustee:

---

[7] per Lord Blackburn in *Speight v Gaunt* (1883) 9 App.Cas. 1 at 19; in similar terms, Lord Watson in *Learoyd v Whiteley* (1887) 12 App.Cas. 727 at 733. The common law was restated by Trustee Act 2000 s.1: para.18–003 below.

[8] *Morley v Morley* (1678) 2 Ch.Cas. 2.

[9] *Re Chapman* [1896] 2 Ch. 763.

[10] *Speight v Gaunt* (1883) 9 App.Cas. 1: below, para.21–012; *Learoyd v Whiteley* (1887) 12 App.Cas. 727; *Shaw v Cates* [1909] 1 Ch. 389. For the applications in the charity context, see *Re Cup Trust* [2016] EWHC 876 (Ch); [2016] 3 W.L.R. 218.

[11] TA 2000 Pt IV.

[12] Below, para.18–005.

[13] Below, para.24–037.

[14] (1883) 9 App.Cas. 1. See generally J. Getzler in Birks and Pretto (eds), *Breach of Trust* (Oxford: Hart Publishing, 2002), Ch.2.

> "[M]ust exercise such care and skill as is reasonable in the circumstances, having regard in particular (a) to any special knowledge or experience that he has or holds himself out as having, and (b) if he acts as trustee in the course of a business or profession, to any special knowledge or experience that it is reasonable to expect of a person acting in the course of that kind of business or profession."

In *Richards v Wood*,[15] Lewison LJ did not consider that s.1 "materially altered the test" in *Speight*.

It had been established by the courts prior to the Trustee Act 2000 that a higher standard was expected of paid trustees. For example, in *Bartlett v Barclays Bank Trust Co Ltd (No.1)*,[16] Brightman J said:

> "I am of opinion that a higher duty of care is plainly due from someone like a trust corporation which carries on a specialised business of trust management. A trust corporation holds itself out in its advertising literature as being above ordinary mortals. With a specialist staff of trained trust officers and managers... the trust corporation holds itself out, and rightly, as capable of providing an expertise which it would be unrealistic to expect and unjust to demand from the ordinary prudent man or woman who accepts, probably unpaid and sometimes reluctantly from a sense of family duty, the burdens of a trusteeship... so I think that a professional corporate trustee is liable for breach of trust if loss is caused to the trust fund because it neglects to exercise the special care and skill which it professes to have."[17]

As can be seen, the distinction between lay and professional trustees is maintained.

18–004 The duty of care, which may be excluded by the trust instrument,[18] applies to various functions of trustees listed in Sch.1 of the Act, whether arising by statute or by corresponding express provision in the trust instrument. The relevant functions are as follows: investment[19]; the acquisition of land[20]; the appointment of agents, nominees and custodians[21]; compounding liabilities[22]; insurance[23]; and powers relating to reversionary interests, valuations and audit.[24] It does not apply to dispositive powers of trustees, such as the power to select from a class of beneficiaries. Nor does it apply to the powers of maintenance and advancement which (as will be seen in Ch.21) are in essence dispositive. The duty of care is primarily concerned with powers, and applies to the manner of their exercise, not to the trustee's decision whether to exercise them or not. So far as duties are concerned, the question is simply whether the duty has been performed or not. If it has not, as where a distribution has been made to the wrong beneficiary, a

---

[15] [2014] EWCA Civ 327 at [31].

[16] [1980] Ch. 515 at 534. See also *Re Rosenthal* [1972] 1 W.L.R. 1273.

[17] See further *Gestrust SA v Sixteen Defendants* [2016] EWHC 3067 (Ch) (concerning a professional trustee company which sought directions with regard to the defence of pending litigation against companies owned by the Trust); cf. *Highmax Overseas Ltd v Chau Kar Hon* [2014] HKCA 248.

[18] Trustee Act 2000 Sch.1 para.7.

[19] Below, paras 19–005—19–021.

[20] Below, para.19–011.

[21] Below, paras 21–012—21–018.

[22] Below, para.21–010.

[23] Below, para.21–008.

[24] Below, para.21–011.

breach has been committed however careful the trustee was, although she may be relieved under s.61 of the Trustee Act 1925 if she acted honestly and reasonably.[25]

A further distinction between paid and unpaid trustees is maintained through the application of s.61, under which an unpaid family trustee is more likely to be relieved from liability than a professional trustee.[26] Further, a paid trustee will be expected to do more of the work herself and to delegate less; and a paid trustee will be given less opportunity to rely upon the fact that she acted upon legal advice.[27]

C. Trustee Exemption Clauses[28]

A question which has attracted much attention over the past two decades is whether and how far the settlor may effectively exempt a trustee from liability. Before considering the construction of express clauses, it should be noted that the Trustee Act 2000 does not deal specifically with trustee exemption clauses, but Sch.7 para.1, provides that the statutory duty of care is inapplicable "if or in so far as it appears from the trust instrument that the duty is not meant to apply". Further, as will be seen below, an exemption clause may be more strictly construed against a solicitor trustee than against a lay trustee.[29]

18–005

19th-century English[30] and Scottish[31] authorities indicated that exemption clauses, which are strictly construed against trustees,[32] would not protect them in cases of bad faith, recklessness or deliberate breach of duty.[33] To allow protection in cases of fraud would be contrary to public policy. The leading authority on this

---

[25] J. Lowry and R. Edmunds (2017) 133 L.Q.R. 223 and M. Haley (2017) 76 C.L.J. 537. See below, para.24–037.

[26] *National Trustee Co of Australasia Ltd v General Finance Co of Australasia* [1905] A.C. 373; *Re Pauling's ST* [1964] Ch. 303 at 338, 339. Below, paras 24-037—24-039. Much of the recent jurisprudence on s.61 of the Trustee Act 1925 has focused on its applicability to solicitors ensnared in fraudulent property transactions: below, para.24–039.

[27] *Re Windsor Steam Co (1901) Ltd* [1929] 1 Ch. 151. See also *Steel v Wellcome Custodian Trustees Ltd* [1988] 1 W.L.R. 167 at 174.

[28] See J. Getzler in Birks and Pretto (eds), *Breach of Trust* (2002), Ch.2.

[29] *Walker v Stones* [2001] Q.B. 902. See also *Breadner v Granville-Grossman (costs)* [2006] W.T.L.R. 411 at 420 (exemption clause does not protect a trustee against a court order that he should pay costs personally).

[30] *Wilkins v Hogg* (1861) 31 L.J. Ch. 41; *Pass v Dundas* (1880) 43 L.T. 665. See also *Rehden v Wesley* (1861) 29 Beav. 213.

[31] *Knox v Mackinnon* (1888) 13 App.Cas. 753; *Rae v Meek* (1889) 14 App.Cas. 558. See generally P. Matthews [1989] Conv. 42; P. Clifton (2001) 15 T.L.I. 194.

[32] This principle does not prevent a solicitor trustee who drafted the clause from relying on it; *Bogg v Raper, The Times*, 22 April 1998. See also *Wight v Olswang, The Times*, 18 May 1999.

[33] See *Walker v Stones* [2001] Q.B. 902.

point remains the Court of Appeal in *Armitage v Nurse*,[34] although as we shall see the issue has also been considered by the Privy Council.[35]

> In *Armitage*, the clause provided that the trustees should not be liable for loss or damage unless "caused by his own actual fraud. This, it was held, would protect the trustees so long as they did not act dishonestly, no matter how indolent, imprudent or negligent they were. As Millett LJ explained, the "irreducible core of obligations" owed by trustees included the duty to act honestly and in good faith but did not include any duty of skill or care, thus it was not repugnant to their duties, nor contrary to public policy, to allow exemption from liability for gross negligence, which differed only in degree from ordinary negligence.[36] The expression "actual fraud" excluded notions of constructive or equitable fraud, arising for example under the doctrine of "fraud on a power".[37] Older cases appearing to suggest that it was not possible to exclude liability for gross negligence turned on the wording of particular clauses. Reference was made, however, to the prevailing view that exemption clauses had gone too far.

It has since been held that an exemption clause covering defaults other than dishonesty could not be relied on, at least in the case of a solicitor trustee, where he had committed a deliberate breach of trust which no reasonable solicitor trustee could have thought was for the benefit of the beneficiaries, even if he genuinely believed that it was.[38] The recent decision in *Barnsley v Noble*[39] saw the Court of Appeal consider a clause in the following terms:

> "In the professed execution of the trusts and powers hereof no trustee shall be liable for any loss to the trust premises arising by reason of any improper investment made in good faith … or by reason of any other matter or thing except wilful and individual fraud or wrongdoing on the part of the trustee."

Applying *Armitage*, Sales LJ that this required conscious impropriety:

> "the phrase 'wilful fraud' means that it is a knowing and deliberate breach of a relevant equitable duty or reckless indifference to whether what is done is in breach of such duty which has to be shown … The same point applies in respect of the phrase 'wilful wrongdoing': it is the *wrong* doing, not the doing, which must be wilful."[40]

In 2011, the Privy Council considered this area in *Spread Trustee Co Ltd v Hutcheson*.[41] Although it was an appeal from Guernsey, the decision is important for dicta on English law from the Board, with each judge giving a separate opinion.[42] The case concerned alleged breaches of trust by a professional trustee

---

[34] [1998] Ch. 241; G. McCormack [1998] Conv. 100; N. McBride (1998) 57 C.L.J. 33. Leave to appeal to the House of Lords was refused; [1998] 1 W.L.R. 270. See also D. Pollard (1997) 11 T.L.I. 93; I. Greenstreet (2004) 18 T.L.I. 132; A Usilova (2016) 22 T. & T. 923; Law Com. No. 301 (2006) at para.2.15 and *Spread Trustee Co Ltd v Hutcheson* [2011] UKPC 13 (casting doubt on the views of Millett LJ on the Scottish cases).

[35] In *Spread Trustee Co Ltd v Hutcheson* [2011] UKPC 13; L. Aitken (2011) 127 L.Q.R. 503;

[36] His Lordship, writing extra-judicially, doubted the *propriety* of exemption clauses covering gross negligence; (1998) 114 L.Q.R. 214.

[37] Above, para.7–018.

[38] *Walker v Stones* [2001] Q.B. 902.

[39] [2016] EWCA Civ 799; E. Weaver (2017) 23 T. & T. 99

[40] [2016] EWCA Civ 799 at [38]–[39], approving the approach of Evans-Lombe J in *Bonham v Fishwick* [2007] EWHC 1859 (Ch); 10 I.T.E.L.R. 329.

[41] [2011] UKPC 13.

[42] The usual practice in the Privy Council is to issue a single judgment of the Board advising her Majesty.

in failing to investigate breaches by previous trustees. It was alleged that these breaches amounted to gross negligence. The trustees sought to rely on an exemption clause in the relevant settlements:

> "In the execution of the trusts and powers hereof no trustee shall be liable for any loss to the Trust Fund arising in consequence of the failure depreciation or loss of any investments made in good faith or by reason of any mistake or omission made in good faith or of any other matter or thing except wilful and individual fraud and wrongdoing on the part of the trustee who is sought to be made liable."

The question was whether at the relevant times it was possible as a matter of Guernsey law for a trustee to seek to rely on a clause such as this. The Trusts (Guernsey) Law 1989 s.34(7) originally provided that "nothing in the terms of a trust shall relieve a trustee of liability for a breach of trust arising from his own fraud or wilful misconduct". The Trusts (Amendment) (Guernsey) Law 1990, later amended[43] "or gross negligence" to the breaches for which liability could not be excluded. The Privy Council therefore had to consider what the customary law of Guernsey law was at the time of the 1989 Law to determine whether gross negligence could be excluded prior to the Amendment Law. The history of Guernsey means that it might either have looked to Scotland, where gross negligence ("culpa lata") cannot be excluded, or to England, where it could (assuming that *Armitage* is correct).

By a majority, the Privy Council held that Guernsey "would have looked to the law of England",[44] and also endorsed *Armitage*. Significantly, the Justices also doubted whether "gross negligence" negligence represents any distinct degree of fault in this area of English law,[45] and indeed "it is difficult to see why the line should be drawn between negligence and gross negligence".[46] Any reform, if it was thought necessary, should come from Parliament:

> "in relation to circumstances falling short of dishonesty or wilful misconduct, courts do best to leave the nature and extent of any intervention in parties' own arrangements to legislators."[47]

Lady Hale and Lord Kerr dissented, and Lady Hale markedly wished to keep open the issue of whether *Armitage* was correctly decided, since the Supreme Court had yet to consider it.[48] For her part, Lady Hale suggested that to prevent a trustee from excluding liability for gross negligence might be considered "a good thing—perhaps particularly in the light of the development of professional trustees and the modern approach to exemption clauses in consumer contracts".[49]

---

[43] By s.1(f), which came into force on 19 February 1991.

[44] [2011] UKPC 13 at [45].

[45] Of course, there are some contexts in which gross negligence is recognised in English law, as Lord Clarke recognised: [2011] UKPC 13 at [50]–[51].

[46] [2011] UKPC 13 at [62].

[47] [2011] UKPC 13, per Lord Mance at [111].

[48] [2011] UKPC 13 at [129]; "if this appeal succeeds, this Board will be taken to have decided a question which has never been decided at this level by the Courts of England and Wales. It will be taken to uphold in Guernsey law the decision of the English Court of Appeal in *Armitage v Nurse* although the Supreme Court of the United Kingdom has never had an opportunity to consider whether that case was rightly decided".

[49] [2011] UKPC 13 at [137].

There is a distinction between clauses which exempt from breach and those which prevent the duty from arising. Such a clause as the latter may be effective where there was no pre-existing fiduciary relationship between the parties, especially in the context of a commercial agreement between parties of equal status.[50]

It should be added that special rules apply to attempts to exclude the liability of trustee or manager for breach of duty of care in the case of pension trusts,[51] unit trusts[52] and debenture trusts.[53]

The Law Commission reviewed the matter and decided against recommending legislation to limit the use of exemption clauses; the proposal to do so had attracted little support during consultation and would restrict settlor autonomy. Instead it proposed that trustee exemption clauses should be regulated by professional bodies in order to ensure that settlors and testators were aware of the clauses.[54] It recommended that the regulatory and professional bodies should make and enforce regulations in accordance with their code of conduct, so that:

> "Any paid trustee who causes a settlor to include a clause in a trust instrument which has the effect of excluding or limiting liability for negligence must, before the creation of the trust, take such steps as are reasonable to ensure that the settlor is aware of the meaning and effect of the clause."[55]

A breach of the good practice rule, which of course applies only to new trusts, would not of itself render the trustee liable to damages, but would expose her to disciplinary measures. The Law Commission anticipated that "best practice will seep into the consciousness of the trust industry".[56] However, the Law Commission's conclusion was criticised as not going beyond existing good practice and doing nothing to address the wrongfulness of the continued existence of exemption clauses protecting paid trustees.[57] The division in *Spread Trustee* suggests that this area of the law, while apparently settled by *Armitage*, may be open to further review by the Supreme Court in the future.

---

[50] Law Com. No. 236, *Fiduciary Duties and Regulatory Rules* (1995). See also *Kelly v Cooper* [1993] A.C. 205 (Privy Council); *Citibank NA v MBIA Assurance SA* [2007] 1 All E.R. (Comm) 475; A. Trukhtanov (2007) 123 L.Q.R. 342.

[51] Pensions Act 1995 ss.33, 34(6) (investment functions); I. Greenstreet (2004) 18 T.L.I. 132; M. Howard (2011) 25 T.L.I. 99 (liability insurance). See recently *Dalriada Trustees Ltd v Mcauley* [2017] EWHC 202 (Ch); [2017] Pens. L.R. 8.

[52] Financial Services and Markets Act 2000 s.253 (exemption for negligence not permitted for manager or trustee).

[53] Companies Act 2006 s.750, re-enacting earlier legislation (exemption for negligence not permitted for trustee of debenture deed).

[54] Law Com. No. 301, *Trustee Exemption Clauses* (2006). Guidance for members has been published by the Law Society, the Society of Trust and Estate Practitioners (STEP) and the Institute of Chartered Accountants. The Government accepted the Report's recommendations (*Hansard*, 14 September 2010).

[55] Law Com. No. 301 (2006), para.7.2.

[56] Law Com. No. 301 (2006), para.6.117.

[57] A. Kenny [2007] Conv. 103; H. Delaney (2009) 23 T.L.I. 89 (contrasting the proposals of the Irish Law Reform Commission). See further Lady Hale's dissent in *Spread Trustee* [2011] UKPC 13 at [128]–[140].

3.   LIABILITY TO THIRD PARTIES

Persons entering into a contractual relationship with trustees, for example by supplying goods or by lending money, can enforce their rights against the trustees personally, but have no direct right to payment out of the trust assets. From the point of view of the trustees, they are entitled to an indemnity out of the trust fund for liabilities properly incurred, but this leaves them exposed to personal risk if the trust fund is insufficient,[58] unless they have limited their liability to the amount of the trust assets when dealing with the third party. From the point of view of third parties, although they may be subrogated to the trustees' right to an indemnity out of the trust fund, the difficulty is that the creditor cannot make any claim against the trust fund which the trustees could not have made.[59] If the trustees have committed a breach of trust, then of course they are not entitled to an indemnity,[60] and the creditor can be in no better position.

18–006

The absence of direct rights against the trust assets may cause difficulties with large commercial trusts, such as pension funds, wishing to borrow money on a large scale.

4.   UNANIMITY

Each trustee should be active in the administration of the trust. Equity does not recognise a "sleeping" trustee. A trustee who concurs with her co-trustees has, in so agreeing, as much "acted" as those others, and thus will be equally liable with them to beneficiaries who suffer loss if a breach results.[61] Nor will the concurring trustee necessarily escape liability when her co-trustee was a solicitor, unless she reasonably deferred to what could legitimately be regarded as superior knowledge.[62] But blind trust cannot safely be placed in a co-trustee. For although there is no rule that trustees are vicariously liable for the acts of co-trustees, a non-active trustee may herself be liable for neglecting to take the steps necessary to have prevented the breach.[63]

18–007

---

[58] See *Perring v Draper* [1997] E.G.C.S. 109 (trustees personally liable for £96,000 rent arrears on termination of lease vested in them as trustees); *Marston Thompson & Evershed Plc v Benn* [2007] W.T.L.R. 315 (£185,000 loan to fund development of rugby club clubhouse).

[59] See *Re Johnson* (1880) 15 Ch.D. 548; *Re Oxley* [1914] 1 Ch. 604; *Investec Trust (Guernsey) Ltd v Glenalla Properties Ltd* [2017] W.T.L.R. 205.

[60] See *Holding & Management Ltd v Property Holding & Investment Trust Plc* [1989] 1 W.L.R. 1313; *White v Williams* [2011] W.T.L.R. 899.

[61] *Bahin v Hughes* (1886) 31 Ch.D. 390; *Re Turner* [1897] 1 Ch. 536; *Wynne v Tempest* (1897) 13 T.L.R. 360. But the co-trustee who concurs may be able to obtain an indemnity from the active trustee; below, para.24–024.

[62] See *Head v Gould* [1898] 2 Ch. 250; *Bahin v Hughes* (1886) 31 Ch.D. 390.

[63] *Bahin v Hughes* (1886) 31 Ch.D. 390.

Trustees (other than trustees of charities and pension trusts[64]) cannot act by a majority, unless expressly authorised in the trust instrument.[65] A majority binds neither a dissenting minority nor the trust estate.[66] The consequences of this rule need to be appreciated.

> In *Re Mayo*,[67] for instance, one trustee of a trust for sale wished to sell, two to postpone. The trustees were by virtue of the trust to sell, under a *duty* to sell, but possessed *power* to postpone. Simonds J held that their duty to sell prevailed unless they were unanimous in exercising their power to postpone. They were not unanimous on this point; the view of the single trustee who wished to sell prevailed, and the other two were directed to join in the sale.

5. WHO MAY BE A TRUSTEE

18–008 In principle, any person who is able to hold property may be a trustee. Special rules apply to charity and pension trustees,[68] and other categories need special consideration.

18–009 **i. Children.** A child cannot hold a legal estate in land[69]; and the Law of Property Act 1925 s.20, provides that the appointment of a child to be a trustee in relation to any trust shall be void. A child of four years old was, however, held to be able to hold personalty on resulting trust.[70] As will be seen, if a child is a trustee of personalty, she may be replaced, whether or not she consents.

18–010 **ii. The Crown.** It is usually said that the Crown may be a trustee[71] "if it chooses deliberately to do so",[72] but attempts to claim funds in the hands of the Crown on the ground that the Crown should be treated as a trustee have not been successful.[73] The circumstances in which the Crown will accept a trusteeship

---

[64] Above, para.15–097 (charities) and para.17–012 (pensions).

[65] *Re Butlin's WT* [1976] Ch. 251; *Re Whiteley* [1910] 1 Ch. 600 at 608. See also Trustee Act 1925 s.63(3) on payments into court (and *Paratus AMC Ltd v Lewis* [2014] EWHC 933 (Ch) as an example of its application).

[66] *Luke v South Kensington Hotel Ltd* (1879) 11 Ch.D. 121. Again, unless the trust instrument provides otherwise, as in *ACLBDD Holdings Ltd, De Pury v Staechelin* [2018] EWHC 44 (Ch), where two out of three trustees had agreed to pay commission on the sale of a Gauguin painting. The third trustee had not been involved, but the Articles of the Trust Agreement provided for decision by a majority in any case: see at [137]–[149].

[67] [1943] Ch. 302; cf. *Tempest v Lord Camoys* (1882) 21 Ch.D. 571; but the unanimity rule did not affect the validity of a notice to quit served by only one of two joint tenants holding on trust for sale, because the characteristic of a periodic tenancy is that all parties must concur in its continuance; *Hammersmith and Fulham LBC v Monk* [1992] 1 A.C. 478.

[68] Above, para.15–096 (charities) and para.17–009 (pensions).

[69] Law of Property Act 1925 s.1(6).

[70] *Re Vinogradoff* [1935] W.N. 68; above, para.11–022.

[71] *Penn v Lord Baltimore* (1750) 1 Ves.Sen. 444, per Lord Hardwicke at 453; *Burgess v Wheate* (1757–59) 1 Eden 177.

[72] *Civilian War Claimants Association Ltd v R.* [1932] A.C. 14, per Lord Atkin at 27 (a claim by the Association for payment by the Crown of reparations money received from Germany: "There is nothing so far as I know, to prevent the Crown acting as agent or trustee if it chooses deliberately to do so.").

[73] *Re Mason* [1929] 1 Ch. 1; *Civilian War Claimants Association Ltd v R.* [1932] A.C. 14; *Tito v Waddell (No.2)* [1977] Ch. 106; above, para.2–035.

must be rare indeed, and there would be substantial difficulties in enforcing the trust if it did.[74] Henderson J has recently indicated that the same principles apply by analogy to foreign sovereign states assuming a trust obligation.[75]

iii. Judicial Trustees. The High Court may, on the application of a person creating or intending to create a trust, or by or on behalf of a trustee or beneficiary, appoint a person to be a judicial trustee of that trust.[76] The court may appoint any fit and proper person,[77] and, in the absence of the nomination of such person, may appoint an official of the court.[78] Remuneration may be paid,[79] and the court may direct an inquiry into the administration of the trust by a judicial trustee.[80] The court may give a judicial trustee any general or special directions in regard to the trust or to the administration thereof,[81] not, however, so as to:

18–011

> "[R]educe the administration of an estate by a judicial trustee to very much the same position as where an estate is being administered by the court and every step has to be taken in pursuance of the court's directions ... The object of the Judicial Trustees Act 1896... was to provide a middle course in cases where the administration of the estate by the ordinary trustees had broken down, and it was not desired to put the estate to the expense of a full administration... a solution was found in the appointment of a judicial trustee, who acts in close concert with the court and under conditions enabling the court to supervise his transactions."[82]

A judicial trustee may also be appointed in respect of the administration of an estate.[83] Originally, when there was no machinery whereby a personal representative could retire, this provided a method of replacing one who could no longer act. Since 1986, however, the court has been able to appoint a substitute executor or administrator, under s.50 of the Administration of Justice Act 1985. In an application under the 1896 Act for the appointment of a judicial trustee, the court may proceed as if it was an application under the 1985 Act, and vice versa.[84]

iv. The Public Trustee. The Public Trustee, established by the Public Trustee Act 1906, could be appointed as trustee alone or jointly with another or others,

18–012

---

[74] Hanbury, *Essays in Equity*, 1934, pp.87–89; Holdsworth H.E.L., Vol.IX, pp.30–32.

[75] *The High Commissioner for Pakistan in the United Kingdom v Prince Mukkaram Jah* [2016] EWHC 1465 (Ch) at [46]ff.

[76] Judicial Trustees Act 1896 s.1(1); Judicial Trustee Rules 1983 (SI 1983/370). The procedure has not been much used in practice, but was applied to a trust arising under mutual wills in *Thomas and Agnes Carvel Foundation v Carvel* [2008] Ch. 395.

[77] Judicial Trustees Act 1896 s.1(3); Public Trustee Act 1906 s.2(1)(d).

[78] Judicial Trustees Act 1896 s.1(3); usually the Official Solicitor of the court; Judicial Trustees Act 1896 s.5.

[79] Judicial Trustees Act 1896 s.1(5); Practice Direction (Judicial Trustees: Remuneration) [2003] 1 W.L.R. 1653.

[80] Judicial Trustees Act 1896 s.1(6), as amended by Administration of Justice Act 1982 s.57(1). On the auditing of accounts, see Judicial Trustees Act 1896 s.4(1), as amended by Administration of Justice Act 1982 s.57(2). See also Judicial Trustee Rules 1983 rr.2, 13.

[81] Judicial Trustees Act 1896 s.1(4); Judicial Trustee Rules 1983 r.8.

[82] *Re Ridsdel* [1947] Ch. 597 at 605.

[83] Judicial Trustees Act 1896 s.1(2).

[84] Administration of Justice Act 1985 s.50(4); Judicial Trustees Act 1896 s.1(7), added by the 1985 Act s.50(6).

and could act as a custodian trustee[85] or an ordinary trustee or as a judicial trustee. The Public Trustee is a corporation sole,[86] and is entitled to charge fees on a scale fixed by the Lord Chancellor.[87] One special function was the administration of small estates and, although he could decline to accept any trust, he could not do so on the ground "only of the small value of the trust property."[88] Another role of the Public Trustee is the holding of the property of a person who has died intestate, pending the appointment of an administrator.[89] Since the start of the present century, Government policy has been to wind down the work of the Public Trustee, and in 2006 the Lord Chancellor approved a proposal that the Public Trustee should retire in bulk from his current caseload in favour of an approved private sector corporate trustee.

18–013   **v.   Custodian Trustees.**[90]   The Public Trustee,[91] the Official Custodian for Charities[92] and a large number of other corporations[93] are authorised by statute to act as custodian trustees, and they may all charge fees not exceeding those chargeable by the Public Trustee.[94] Others may act under the terms of the trust instrument, outside the statutory schemes. The custodian trustee holds property and the documents relating thereto while leaving to the managing trustee the day-to-day administration of the trust.[95]

The advantage of the scheme of custodian trusteeship is that new managing trustees can be appointed without the necessity of undergoing the trouble and expense—which can be considerable in the case of a large trust—of vesting all the trust investments in new trustees whenever there is a death, retirement or new appointment. It should be noted that this advantage cannot be gained by appointing the holder of an office as trustee, as the investments must be transferred to the names of the new holders of the office when a change is made. This can be avoided if the trustee is a corporation sole.[96]

---

[85] Part 4, below.

[86] Public Trustee Act 1906 s.1.

[87] Public Trustee Act 1906 s.9; Public Trustee (Fees) Act 1957; Public Trustee (Liability and Fees) Act 2002.

[88] Public Trustee Act 1906 s.2(3).

[89] Law of Property (Miscellaneous Provisions) Act 1994 s.14, amending Administration of Estates Act 1925 s.9.

[90] S. Maurice (1960) 24 Conv.(N.S.) 196.

[91] Public Trustee Act 1906 s.4(3).

[92] Above, para.15–084.

[93] Public Trustee Rules 1912 r.30, as substituted by the Public Trustee (Custodian Trustee) Rules 1975 (SI 1975/1189) r.2; considered in *Various Incapacitated Persons v The Appointment of Trust Corporations as Deputies* [2018] EWCOP 3 See also Public Trustee (Custodian Trustee) Rules 1976 (SI 1976/836), 1981 (SI 1981/358) and 1994 (SI 1994/2519). Qualifying corporations include those of EU States which comply with the requirements and have a place of business in the UK carrying on trust business.

[94] Public Trustee Act 1906 s.4(3).

[95] For the relationship between custodian trustees and managing trustees, see Public Trustee Act 1906 s.4(2); *Forster v Williams Deacon's Bank Ltd* [1935] Ch. 359; *Re Brooke Bond and Co Ltd's Trust Deed* [1963] Ch. 357.

[96] *Bankes v Salisbury Diocesan Council of Education* [1960] Ch. 631 at 647–649.

In determining a number of trustees for the purpose of the Trustee Act 1925, the custodian trustee is not included.[97]

vi. Trust Corporations.   Trust corporations play a large part in the   **18–014**
administration of trusts. Their size, stability, dependability and expertise give
them advantages over individual trustees.[98]

They enjoy a special status in that they can often act alone in circumstances in which at least two trustees would otherwise be necessary.[99] A trust corporation can give a valid receipt for capital money arising from the sale of land[100]; and a trust of land has greater overreaching powers if a trust corporation is trustee.[101] Further, trustees may retire and leave a sole trustee only if that trustee is a trust corporation.[102]

In most private trusts, a trust corporation is typically a bank. The legal definition is:

> 'Trust corporation' means the Public Trustee or a corporation either appointed by the court in a particular case to be a trustee, or entitled by rules made under subs.(3) of s.4 of the Public Trustee Act 1906, to act as custodian trustee.[103]

The qualifications are contained in the Public Trustee (Custodian Trustee) Rules 1975.[104] The Law of Property (Amendment) Act 1926 s.3 added, amongst others, a trustee in bankruptcy,[105] the Treasury Solicitor, and the Official Solicitor. Some solicitors' practices satisfy the definition. A trust corporation has power to charge for reasonable remuneration under s.29 of the Trustee Act 2000, but express powers will normally be given for a fee to be charged for the service. In the context of the appointment of trust corporations as property and affairs deputies under mental capacity legislation, HHJ Hilder has provided detailed guidance on how such corporations can meet the standard of being "fit and proper persons".[106]

---

[97] Public Trustee Act 1906 s.4(2)(g).

[98] See, however, N. Johnson (1997/98) 4 *Trusts & Trustees* 6, as to the advantages of a private company as trustee.

[99] See *In Re Duxbury's ST* [1995] 1 W.L.R. 425; above, para.18–012 (Public Trustee).

[100] Trustee Act 1925 s.14; Law of Property Act 1925 s.27(2).

[101] Law of Property Act 1925 s.2(2).

[102] Trustee Act 1925 s.39; below, para.18–037.

[103] Trustee Act 1925 s.68(18); see also Law of Property Act 1925 s.205(1)(xxviii); Administration of Estates Act 1925 s.55(1)(xxvi); Senior Courts Act 1981 s.128.

[104] SI 1975/1189. They include any corporation which (i) is constituted under the law of the UK or of another Member State of the EU; and (ii) is empowered by its constitution to undertake trust business in England and Wales; (iii) has one or more places of business in the UK; and (iv) being a registered company has a capital (in stock or shares) for the time being issued of not less than £250,000 (or its equivalent in the currency of the state of registration), of which not less than £100,000 (or its equivalent) has been paid up in cash. See also the Public Trustee (Custodian Trustee) Rules 1976 (SI 1976/8836) and 1981 (SI 1981/358). Companies Act 2006 s.31 permits other companies to act as trustees but they will not be trust corporations.

[105] Amendments to these provisions were made by the Deregulation Act 2015 Sch.6(1) paras 1 and 2, which repealed the Deeds of Arrangement Act 1914, but they are not material for present purposes.

[106] *Various Incapacitated Persons v The Appointment of Trust Corporations as Deputies* [2018] EWCOP 3 at [35]–[37] and Schedule 2.

6. DISCLAIMER

18–015   Nobody can be compelled to accept the office of trustee against her will.[107] A person appointed as trustee who wishes to disclaim should do so by deed,[108] as this provides clear evidence of the disclaimer. However, a disclaimer may be implied; apathy will be evidence of an intention to disclaim, provided the apathy is consistent.[109] But if the trustee meddles with the estate, her conduct will be construed as an acceptance. Once she has disclaimed, she can no longer accept. Once she has accepted, she can no longer disclaim[110] but as we shall see, she may retire.[111]

7. NUMBER OF TRUSTEES

18–016   There is no restriction upon the number of trustees of personalty. It is inconvenient to have too many; and rare to have more than four, save in the case of charity and pension trustees, who can act by majority.[112] Where additional trustees are appointed under the statutory power, appointments may only be made up to a total of four.[113] A sole trustee is most unsatisfactory because of the opportunities for maladministration and fraud which then arise.

In trusts of land, the Trustee Act 1925 s.34 restricts the number of trustees to four. There are exceptions, the most important of which is that of land vested in trustees for charitable, ecclesiastical or public purposes.[114]

While a sole trustee of land is not forbidden,[115] the Trustee Act 1925 s.14(2) makes it impossible for a sole trustee (not being a trust corporation) to give a valid receipt for the proceeds of sale or other capital money arising under a trust of land, or capital money arising under the Settled Land Act 1925.[116]

8. APPOINTMENT OF TRUSTEES

A.   The First Trustees

18–017   The first trustees will ordinarily be appointed by the settlor or testator in the deed or will creating the trust. In the case of a trust created by a settlor, the trustees will ordinarily be parties to the deed, and the trust is constituted upon the conveyance of the trust property to them. In a will, the same persons may be appointed

---

[107] A person can, of course, become a constructive or resulting trustee against her will.

[108] *Re Schär* [1951] Ch. 280; *Holder v Holder* [1968] Ch. 353 (an executor).

[109] *Re Clout and Frewer's Contract* [1924] 2 Ch. 230; R. Crozier (2016) 166 N.L.J. 15.

[110] *Re Sharman's WT* [1942] Ch. 311; *Holder v Holder* [1968] Ch. 353.

[111] Below, para.18–035.

[112] Above, para.18–007. The special rules for the constitution of the trustees of pension funds are explained in Ch.17.

[113] Trustee Act 1925 s.36(6), below, para.18–022.

[114] Trustee Act 1925 s.34(3)(a).

[115] *Re Myhill* [1928] Ch. 100.

[116] Also Law of Property Act 1925 s.27(2); Law of Property (Amendment) Act 1926 Sch.

executors and trustees.[117] Where they are different persons, the trust is constituted upon the testator's death, for the title of the executors relates back to the death, and they hold on trust pending transfer to the persons appointed trustees in the will.

Trustees hold as joint tenants, and if one of several trustees dies, the survivors are the trustees, and they, and their successors, retain the same powers and duties as the original trustees.[118] On the death of a sole trustee, her personal representatives become trustees.[119] If she dies intestate, the trust estate will vest, pending the grant of administration, in the Public Trustee.[120] A trust does not normally fail for lack of a trustee; hence if the trustees disclaim, the trust still subsists, save in the rare cases where the settlor or testator has herself made the validity of the trust dependent upon the acceptance of office by particular trustees.[121] If all the nominated trustees predecease the testator in the case of a testamentary trust, the personal representatives of the testator will hold until such time as trustees are appointed.[122]

B. Who May Appoint New Trustees

i. Express Power. The trust instrument may include an express power to appoint new trustees, although it is normally sufficient to rely on the statutory power. Where an express power is given, it is often reserved to the settlor. The statutory power will be available in addition, unless a contrary intention appears in the instrument.[123]   **18–018**

ii. The Statutory Power: Trustee Act 1925 Section 36(1), (2).[124] The legislation provides: **18–019**

(1)   Where a trustee, either original or substituted, and whether appointed by the court or otherwise, is dead,[125] or remains out of the United Kingdom for more than 12

---

[117] And where this is the case, an application for removal in one capacity may extend to removal from their other role: *Re Folkes' Estate* [2017] EWHC 2559 (Ch) per Deputy Master Linwood at [236].

[118] Trustee Act 1925 s.18; *Rafferty v Philp* [2011] EWHC 709 (Ch). It is otherwise with a bare power given to two persons in their individual capacity: *Re Smith* [1904] 1 Ch. 139; *Re de Sommery* [1912] 2 Ch. 622; *Re Harding* [1923] 1 Ch. 182.

[119] Administration of Estates Act 1925 ss.1–3; Trustee Act 1925 s.18(2).

[120] Law of Property (Miscellaneous Provisions) Act 1994 s.14.

[121] *Re Lysaght* [1966] Ch. 191; *Re Woodhams (Deceased)* [1981] 1 W.L.R. 493.

[122] *Re Smirthwaite's Trust* (1870–71) L.R. 11 Eq. 251.

[123] Trustee Act 1925 s.69(2). See *Re Wheeler and De Rochow* [1896] 1 Ch. 315; *Re Sichel's Settlements* [1916] 1 Ch. 358.

[124] The statutory power does not apply to personal representatives; *Re King's WT* [1964] Ch. 542; above, para.2–019. The court, however, may appoint a substitute personal representative under Administration of Justice Act 1985 s.50; for recent examples of the application of the relevant principles, see *Harris v Earwicker* [2015] EWHC 1915 (Ch) and *Wilby v Rigby* [2015] EWHC 2394 (Ch). Special rules for the appointment of pension trustees are dealt with in Ch.17.

[125] Which includes the case of a person nominated trustee in a will but dying before the testator: Trustee Act 1925 s.36(8), and above, para.18–017.

months,[126] or desires to be discharged from all or any of the trusts or powers reposed in or conferred on him,[127] or refuses[128] or is unfit to act therein, or is incapable of acting therein,[129] or is an infant,[130] then, subject to the restrictions imposed by this Act on the number of trustees,—

(a) the person or persons nominated for the purpose of appointing new trustees by the instrument, if any, creating the trust; or

(b) if there is no such person, or no such person able and willing to act, then the surviving or continuing trustees or trustee for the time being, or the personal representatives of the last surviving or continuing trustee;

may, by writing,[131] appoint one or more other persons (whether or not being the persons exercising the power) to be a trustee or trustees in the place of the trustee so deceased, remaining out of the United Kingdom, desiring to be discharged, refusing, or being unfit or being incapable, or being an infant, as aforesaid.

(2) Where a trustee has been removed under a power contained in the instrument creating the trust, a new trustee or new trustees may be appointed in the place of the trustee who is removed, as if he were dead, or, in the case of a corporation, as if the corporation desired to be discharged from the trust, and the provisions of this section shall apply accordingly, but subject to the restrictions imposed by this Act on the number of trustees.

In favour of a purchaser of a legal estate in land, a statement in an instrument appointing a new trustee to the effect that a trustee is unfit, incapable or refuses to act, or has remained out of the UK for more than 12 months, is conclusive evidence of the matter. Similarly, any appointment of a new trustee depending on that statement, and the consequent vesting of the trust property in the new trustee, is valid in favour of such a purchaser.[132] It may be expected that any attempt to modify the statutory power will be clearly worded.[133]

18–020 iii. **Exercise of the Statutory Power.** It is common to appoint someone to exercise the statutory power.[134]

---

[126] The period must be continuous: *Re Walker* [1901] 1 Ch. 259; see also *Re Stoneham ST* [1953] Ch. 59. Trustee Act 1925 s.25, permits a trustee in such a case to delegate her duties by power of attorney for a period not exceeding 12 months; below, para.21–019.

[127] For retirement of a trustee, see below, para.18–035.

[128] This includes disclaimer.

[129] "Unfit" has a wider meaning than "incapable". "Incapable" refers to personal incapacity, such as illness or mental incapacity; see Trustee Act 1925 s.36(9). "Unfit" is more general and an absconding bankrupt has been held to be "unfit" but not "incapable": *Re Roche* (1842) 2 Dr. & War. 287. Removal may also be approved where the trustee is conflicted or professionally embarrassed: *Re Folkes' Estate* [2017] EWHC 2559 (Ch) per Deputy Master Linwood at [217](i). See s.36(3), providing that a corporation is "incapable" from the date of dissolution. Law of Property Act 1925 s.22(2) requires a mentally incapacitated trustee of land to be discharged before the legal estate is dealt with. This is not required where a donee of an enduring power of attorney is entitled to act for the incapable trustee; s.22(3), inserted by the Trustee Delegation Act 1999. This provision was further amended by the Mental Capacity Act 2005 to include the donee of a lasting power of attorney. See also Trusts of Land and Appointment of Trustees Act 1996 s.20; below, para.18–023.

[130] Law of Property Act 1925 ss.1(6), 20; *Re Parsons* [1940] Ch. 973.

[131] See below, para.18–027, and Trustee Act 1925 s.40.

[132] Trustee Act 1925 s.38.

[133] *Briggs v Gleeds (Head Office) (A Firm)* [2015] Ch. 212 per Newey J at [58].

[134] In *Bathurst v Bathurst* [2016] EWHC 3033 (Ch), Master Matthews approved the variation of the provision of the appointment of trustees to provide for the principal beneficiary should have the power to appoint, with the written consent of the trustees: below, para.23–022.

(a)   By Persons Appointed under s.36(1)(a).   If two or more persons are given power to exercise it jointly, the power is not, in the absence of a contrary intention, exercisable by the survivor. This is consistent with the usual rule relating to bare powers given to individuals.[135]

Complications can arise if the power is subjected to conditions and limitations.

> In *Re Wheeler and De Rochow*,[136] the settlor gave power to donees to appoint a new trustee if one of the existing trustees should be "incapable. One of the trustees was bankrupt, and absconded. This made him "unfit" but not "incapable".[137] The question was whether a new trustee should be appointed by the donees under s.36(1)(a) or by the continuing trustees under s.36(1)(b). It was held that the situation was not within the terms of the power given to the donees and that s.36(1)(b) applied.

(b)   By the Surviving or Continuing Trustees under s.36(1)(b).   In the case of   **18–021**
continuing trustees it is expressly provided by s.36(8) that the provisions of s.36 "relative to a continuing trustee include a refusing or retiring trustee, if willing to act in the execution of the provisions of this section." This provision enables a retiring sole trustee or a retiring group of trustees to appoint their successors.[138] It raises the question, however, whether their participation is essential; whether an appointment in which they did not participate would be void. Such an objection failed in *Re Coates to Parsons*[139]; the retiring trustee is only included if it is shown that she is competent and willing to act. The concurrence of a trustee who is removed on the ground that she remained outside the UK for more than 12 months[140] is not required.[141] It is advisable, in order to avoid these difficulties, that refusing or retiring trustees should participate in the appointment of new trustees if possible, and this is the usual practice.

Section 37(1)(c) requires the replacement of trustees who are being discharged unless there will be either a trust corporation or at least two persons[142] to act if the vacancy is not filled. The exception is where only one trustee was originally appointed and a sole trustee will be able to give a good receipt for capital money. It appears that the settlor may override this provision.[143]

The statutory power to appoint a new trustee can be exercised by the executor of a sole trustee appointed by will,[144] but not by the personal representative of the

---

[135]   *Re Harding* [1923] 1 Ch. 182; *Bersel Manufacturing Co Ltd v Berry* [1968] 2 All E.R. 552; above, para.7–002; it is otherwise where the power is given to persons as trustees: Trustee Act 1925 s.18(1).
[136]   [1896] 1 Ch. 315; followed reluctantly in *Re Sichel's Settlements* [1916] 1 Ch. 358; cf. *Re Brockbank* [1948] Ch. 206.
[137]   *Re Roche* (1842) Dr. & War. 287, above, para.18–019.
[138]   But two retiring trustees cannot be replaced by one, not being a trust corporation; *Adam and Company International Trustees Ltd v Theodore Goddard (A Firm)* [2000] W.T.L.R. 349; criticised in F. Barlow [2003] Conv. 15.
[139]   (1886) 34 Ch.D. 370.
[140]   Above, para.18–019.
[141]   *Re Stoneham ST* [1953] Ch. 59.
[142]   As amended by Trusts of Land and Appointment of Trustees Act 1996 Sch.3 para.3(12), substituting "persons" for "individuals". A corporate trustee (whether or not it is a "trust corporation") is a "person" but not an "individual". For problems arising before the amendment, see *Jasmine Trustees Ltd v Wells & Hind (A Firm)* [2008] Ch. 194.
[143]   *LRT Pensions Fund Trustee Co Ltd v Hatt* [1993] O.P.L.R. 225 at 260; *Adam & Co International Trustees Ltd v Theodore Goddard (A Firm)* [2000] W.T.L.R. 349.
[144]   *Re Shafto's Trusts* (1885) 29 Ch.D. 247.

survivor of a body of trustees named in a will, who has died in the testator's lifetime, as the Act does not contemplate the case of all the trustees named in the will predeceasing the testator.[145] Nor can the sole surviving trustee exercise the power by his will, so as thereby to appoint new trustees in succession to himself.[146] The aim of the Act of 1925 is to ensure the making of an appointment in all events. The executors who have proved the will need not have the concurrence of those who have not proved or intend to renounce probate.[147] A sole or last surviving executor who intends to renounce probate can nevertheless fulfil this one function without thereby accepting the office of executor,[148] but the title of an executor to exercise the statutory power can only be proved by a proper grant of administration.[149]

18–022   *(c)   Additional Trustees.*   A broad power is given by s.36(6),[150] restricted only by the limitation to a total number of four trustees, and by the fact that the power is to appoint "another person or other persons" and that consequently (and unlike appointments under subs.(1)) the appointor may not appoint himself.[151] Section 36(6) reads:

> Where, in the case of any trust, there are not more than three trustees—
> (a)   the person or persons nominated for the purpose of appointing new trustees by the instrument, if any, creating the trust; or
> (b)   if there is no such person, or no such person able and willing to act, then the trustee or trustees for the time being;
>   may, by writing, appoint another person or other persons to be an additional trustee or additional trustees, but it shall not be obligatory to appoint any additional trustee, unless the instrument, if any, creating the trust, or any statutory enactment provides to the contrary, nor shall the number of trustees be increased beyond four by virtue of any such appointment.

Section 36(6) was engaged by the facts of *Shergill v Khaira*,[152] in which the Supreme Court considered charitable trusts of two Sikh gurdwaras. The trust deeds gave the power to appoint and remove trustees to the First Holy Saint (a spiritual leader) or his successor, who was the Second Holy Saint. The case arose out of disputes over who was the next successor (and whether in any event the power extended to them), and thus over who had the power to order the removal and replacement of certain trustees. The defendants sought a permanent stay of proceedings on the basis that matters of religious faith were not justiciable. The Supreme Court[153] held that the claims were justiciable and the case should proceed to trial. For that reason, the Justices expressed themselves somewhat tentatively.[154] But the point for present purposes is that it was argued by the

---

[145] *Nicholson v Field* [1893] 2 Ch. 511.
[146] *Re Parker's Trusts* [1894] 1 Ch. 707.
[147] Trustee Act 1925 s.36(4).
[148] Trustee Act 1925 s.36(5).
[149] *Re Crowhurst Park* [1974] 1 W.L.R. 583.
[150] As amended by Trusts of Land and Appointment of Trustees Act 1996 Sch.3 para.3(11).
[151] *Re Power's ST* [1951] Ch. 1074.
[152] [2014] UKSC 33; [2015] A.C. 359; C. Gardner (2014) 2 *Oxford Journal of Law and Religion* 525; M. Herbert [2015] P.C.B. 137; F. Cranmer (2015) 17 Ecc.L.J. 123; S.S. Juss [2016] P.L. 198.
[153] The judgment of the court was given jointly by Lord Neuberger of Abbotsbury PSC, Lord Sumption and Lord Hodge JJSC (with whom Lord Mance and Lord Clarke JJSC agreed).
[154] [2015] A.C. 359 at [34].

defendants that, on the basis that the trust was formed when the property was transferred to the original trustees, then once the First Holy Saint died, s.36(1)(b) applied, so that the trustees at the time, could not delegate their power to appoint to anyone else. The Supreme Court noted that "the law in this area is surprisingly undeveloped",[155] but held, contrary to the defendants' argument, that it was arguable that "trustees must have the power to include new provisions in the trust deed which they would not normally have the power to impose in the case of a fully constituted trust."[156] It is submitted that the tentative view of the Justices is correct, as providing a viable solution to what would otherwise be a stalemate.

Section 36(6) was amended by the Trustee Delegation Act 1999 in order to give a limited power of appointing additional trustees to the donee of an enduring or lasting[157] power of attorney, to whom trustee functions relating to land or its proceeds of sale have been delegated under the 1999 Act or under s.25 of the Trustee Act 1925.[158] This is to ensure that there are at least two trustees to act, as required for the purpose of giving a good receipt for capital money. The amendment deals primarily with the situation where one co-owner of land has, prior to losing capacity, delegated her trustee functions to the other co-owner by enduring or lasting power of attorney.

iv. By Direction of the Beneficiaries. A new power was given to beneficiaries by s.19[159] of the Trusts of Land and Appointment of Trustees Act 1996, which applies to trusts of land and personalty, whenever created, unless excluded by the settlor.[160] Provided the beneficiaries are of full age and capacity and together absolutely entitled, and there is no person with an express power to appoint, the beneficiaries may direct the trustees in matters of retirement[161] and appointment. They may give directions of either or both of the following kinds: **18–023**

(a)   a written direction to a trustee or trustees to retire from the trust; and
(b)   a written direction to the trustees or trustee for the time being (or, if there are none, to the personal representative of the last person who was a trustee) to appoint by writing to be a trustee or trustees the person or persons specified in the direction.

The beneficiaries may give joint or separate directions, but they must specify the same person for appointment or retirement.[162] Section 19 has effect subject to

---

[155] [2015] A.C. 359 at [34](i).
[156] [2015] A.C. 359 at [33].
[157] Lasting powers of attorney were added by the Mental Capacity Act 2005.
[158] Trustee Delegation Act 1999 s.8, inserting s.36(6A)–(6D) into the 1925 Act. For powers of attorney, see below, para.21–020. The new provisions apply only to powers of attorney created after the commencement of the 1999 Act.
[159] This in effect reversed *Re Brockbank* [1948] Ch. 206. See also s.20 (replacement by direction of beneficiaries where trustee mentally incapacitated and no person entitled, willing and able to act under Trustee Act 1925 s.36(1)). Section 20 (unlike s.19) contains no provisions on vesting or indemnity. See M. Keppel-Palmer (1996) 146 N.L.J. 1779; N. Hopkins [1996] Conv. 411 at 428–430.
[160] s.21(5). Living settlors of trusts created before the 1996 Act may exclude the power by deed under s.21(6). The same applies to the power under s.20.
[161] Below, para.18–039.
[162] s.21(1), (2).

the restrictions imposed by the 1925 Act on the number of trustees. In the absence of the exercise of the new power by the beneficiaries, the trustees' power of appointment is exercisable in the usual way.

C. Appointment by the Court

18–024   **i. Trustee Act 1925 Section 41.**[163]   Subsection (1) provides:

> The court[164] may, whenever it is expedient to appoint a new trustee or new trustees, and it is found inexpedient difficult or impracticable so to do without the assistance of the court, make an order appointing a new trustee or new trustees either in substitution for or in addition to any existing trustee or trustees, or although there is no existing trustee.
>
> In particular and without prejudice to the generality of the foregoing provision, the court may make an order appointing a new trustee in substitution for a trustee who lacks capacity to exercise his functions as trustee or is a bankrupt, or is a corporation which is in liquidation or has been dissolved.

18–025   **ii. Circumstances in which the Jurisdiction will be Exercised.**   The section gives the court a discretion. Cases arise in a variety of circumstances, e.g. where a sole surviving trustee has died intestate, or where all the trustees of a testamentary trust predeceased the testator,[165] and difficulty is experienced in obtaining administration of his estate,[166] or where the donee is incapable of making an effective appointment by reason of being under age.[167] The court has power to replace a trustee against his will[168]; and also where the trustees were the life tenant and remainderman and there was friction between them; or where a trustee has, through age or infirmity,[169] become incapable of acting, or who permanently resides abroad.[170] The mere fact of friction between trustees is not however of itself a sufficient reason for removal and appointment of other trustees, unless the current administration of the trust is impeded.[171] It may be that the appointment of an extra professional trustee will improve the operation of a trust in such cases.[172] "Trusts, it can be said generally, are better administered in an atmosphere of harmony, not disharmony."[173]

---

[163] The section does not apply to the appointment of personal representatives (s.41(4)). Section 41(2), which relates to deeds of arrangement, was repealed by the Deregulation Act 2015 Sch.6 para.2. The rest of the section is unaffected.

[164] i.e. the High Court; or where the estate or trust fund does not exceed its financial jurisdiction, the County Court.

[165] *Re Smirthwaite's Trust* (1871) L.R. 11 Eq. 251.

[166] *Re Matthews* (1859) 26 Beav. 463.

[167] *Re Parsons* [1940] Ch. 973; REM (1941) 57 L.Q.R. 25.

[168] *Re Henderson* [1940] Ch. 764.

[169] *Re Lemann's Trust* (1883) 22 Ch.D. 633.

[170] *Re Bignold's ST* (1871–72) L.R. 7 Ch.App. 223.

[171] *In the Matter of the EA Scott 1991 Children's Settlement No.1* [2012] EWHC 2397 (Ch), per HH Judge Behrens at [139]–[147]. For a case on the other side of the line, *Riley v Seed* [2013] EWHC 4863 (Ch) per HHJ Hodge QC (sitting as a Judge of the High Court) at [76]–[81]. There is of course a connection between the circumstances of appointment and removal: see Part 12 below.

[172] [2012] EWHC 2397 (Ch) at [147].

[173] *James v Williams* [2015] EWHC 1166 (Ch) per HHJ Purle QC (sitting as a High Court Judge) at [59].

The statutory power of beneficiaries to direct appointments reduces the need to apply to court.[174]

It was held not to be "expedient" to appoint a new trustee of a pension fund on terms that it would be paid out of the fund in circumstances where the administrator of the employer company had sufficient expertise to administer the pension fund and could be paid only out of the company's free assets.[175]

The court should not be asked to exercise its jurisdiction where a statutory power can be exercised.[176] It has no jurisdiction to appoint a new trustee against the wishes of the persons who have a statutory power to appoint, even in a case where an application has been made to it by a majority of the beneficiaries.[177] Where the beneficiaries are of full capacity, absolutely entitled and unanimous, they may exercise the statutory power referred to above.

9. Vesting of the Trust Property in Trustees

A. Requirement of Vesting

The trust property must be vested in the trustees to enable them to deal with outside parties. Before and after the vesting, however, a trustee, whether appointed under s.36 or by the court under s.41, or by direction of the beneficiaries under ss.19 or 20 of the Trusts of Land and Appointment of Trustees Act 1996,[178] has:

> "[T]he same powers, authorities, and discretions, and may in all respects act as if he had been originally appointed a trustee by the instrument, if any, creating the trust.[179]"

18–026

B. Vesting Declaration under Section 40

i. Subsection (1). In order to avoid the necessity of a formal transfer of the trust property from the old trustees to the new, s.40 provides that the vesting may, with important exceptions, be effected automatically if the appointment of the trustees has been made by deed.[180] It does not apply, however, where the property is held by personal representatives and not by a trustee.[181]

Subsection (1) of s.40 provides that the deed of appointment shall operate to vest any land, chattel or chose in action subject to the trust in the new trustee, unless the deed expressly provides to the contrary.

18–027

ii. Exceptions under Subsection (4). These in outline are:

18–028

---

[174] Trusts of Land and Appointment of Trustees Act 1996 ss.19, 20; above, para.18–023.
[175] *Polly Peck International Plc (In Administration) v Henry* [1999] 1 B.C.L.C. 407.
[176] *Re Gibbon's Trusts* (1882) 30 W.R. 287 (where, however, such an appointment was made); cf. *Re May's WT* [1941] Ch. 109.
[177] *Re Higginbottom* [1892] 3 Ch. 132.
[178] Trusts of Land and Appointment of Trustees Act 1996 s.21(3) provides that Trustee Act 1925 ss.36(7) applies to trustees appointed under ss.19 and 20 of the 1996 Act.
[179] Trustee Act 1925 ss.36(7), 43.
[180] Above, para.18–019.
[181] *Re Cockburn's WT* [1957] Ch. 438; *Re King's WT* [1964] Ch. 542; above, para.2–019.

(a)   a mortgage of land to secure a loan of trust money;

(b)   land held under a lease which contains a covenant against assignment without consent, and the consent has not been obtained prior to the execution of the deed;

(c)   stocks and shares.[182]

These exceptions are necessary. Where trust money is lent on mortgage, no mention is made in the mortgage deed of the existence of the trust, nor upon a transfer of the mortgage, such as would occur on the appointment of a new trustee. If s.40(1) applied, the mortgagor on redeeming would have to investigate the appointments of new trustees to make sure he was paying the right persons. The second exception is included in order to avoid an unintended breach of covenant, such as could occur in the appointment of a new trustee. The most serious exception in practice is the third; for this is the most important and valuable form of property in modern settlements. The provision, however, was needed, because title to stocks and shares depends on the registration of the owners in the register of shareholders, and it is essential (unless the shares are held by a nominee) that the current trustees should be registered.[183]

It will be seen that vesting orders relating to registered land are not expressly excepted; however, the legal title cannot pass until effect is given on the register to any vesting order or vesting declaration made on the appointment or discharge of a trustee. The provisions of the Trustee Act 1925 relating to the appointment and discharge of trustees and the vesting of trust property apply to registered land subject to proper entry being made on the register.[184]

C.   Vesting Orders under Sections 44 to 56

18–029   Sections 44 to 56 contain the rules as to vesting orders by the court. These overlap with s.40, for vesting orders as to all kinds of property can be made not only where the appointment has been made by the court, but also where it has been made out of court under an express or statutory power. The court is given wide powers to make such orders in a variety of eventualities, which need not be detailed here.

10.   SELECTION OF TRUSTEES

A.   On Appointment by the Court under Section 41

18–030   The factors which a court will take into account when exercising its jurisdiction to appoint a trustee were discussed by Turner LJ in *Re Tempest*.[185] The court should always have regard to three prime requirements: the wishes of the person

---

[182] "Any share, stock, annuity or property which is only transferable in books kept by a company or other body, or in manner directed by or under an Act of Parliament." This includes money in a bank account, for example, but not bearer bonds.

[183] See M. Russell (1992) 142 N.L.J. 541. For electronic transfer, see above, para.5–014.

[184] See further R. Towns [1998] Conv. 380.

[185] (1865–66) L.R. 1 Ch. App. 485.

by whom the trust was created; the interests, which may be conflicting, of *all* the beneficiaries; and the efficient administration of the trust. It is important that the trustees act harmoniously together; but Turner LJ thought it would be going too far to say that the court should refuse to appoint a particular trustee on the ground that the continuing trustee refused to act with her. That would give the continuing trustee a veto; rather, the reasons for the refusal should be examined to see whether the objection is well founded.

The court is reluctant to appoint a person who, though not herself interested, is related to, or connected with, someone who is. Thus a relative of one of the beneficiaries is not a desirable appointment,[186] nor is one nominated by a relative of the testator with whom the testator was on bad terms.[187] Again, the solicitor to the trust,[188] or to one of the beneficiaries[189] or trustees, should not be appointed, as there might be a conflict of duties; unless, of course, no other person can be found to undertake the position.[190] If the solicitor to the trust is a continuing trustee, her partner should not be appointed.[191] Persons out of the jurisdiction will not be appointed[192] except in a case where circumstances require it, or where the beneficiaries are resident outside the jurisdiction also.[193] Even where the trust can be more conveniently administered by trustees resident abroad, the court may exact an undertaking from them that they will consult the court before proceeding to the appointment of new trustees out of the jurisdiction.[194] Trusts administered abroad have enjoyed a number of fiscal advantages, and this has encouraged the movement of many trusts to other jurisdictions.[195]

B. On Appointment under Express Power or under Section 36

i. Choice by Donee of Power. It is said that the above principles should guide persons exercising their power to appoint under s.36. In practice, however, it is common for beneficiaries and other members of the beneficiaries' families, and for solicitors to the beneficiaries, to be appointed. A conflict of interest and duty or of two duties should of course be avoided. However, even if the trustee appointed is one whom the court itself would not have selected, it seems that the court will not rectify it.[196]

18–031

---

[186] *Re Coode* (1913) 108 L.T. 94; *Re Parsons* [1940] Ch. 973 (where a child purported to appoint his mother).

[187] *Re Tempest* (1865–66) L.R. 1 Ch. 485.

[188] *Wheelwright v Walker* (1883) 23 Ch.D. 752; *Re Orde* (1883) 24 Ch.D. 271.

[189] *Re Earl of Stamford* [1896] 1 Ch. 288; *Re Spencer's SE* [1903] 1 Ch. 75; *Re Cotter* [1915] 1 Ch. 307.

[190] Alternatively, an independent professional trustee may be appointed alongside: *In the Matter of the EA Scott 1991 Children's Settlement No.1* [2012] EWHC 2397 (Ch) at [147].

[191] *Re Norris* (1884) 27 Ch.D. 333.

[192] *Re Weston's Settlements* [1969] 1 Ch. 223.

[193] *Re Liddiard* (1880) 14 Ch.D. 310; *Re Simpson* [1897] 1 Ch. 256; *Re Seale's Marriage ST* [1961] Ch. 574; *Re Windeatt's WT* [1969] 1 W.L.R. 692; *Re Whitehead's WT* [1971] 1 W.L.R. 833.

[194] *Re Freeman's ST* (1887) 37 Ch.D. 148.

[195] See above, para.3–003.

[196] In *Re Norris* (1884) 27 Ch.D. 333, the funds were being administered by the court; *Re Higginbottom* [1892] 3 Ch. 132; *Re Parsons* [1940] Ch. 973; REM (1941) 57 L.Q.R. 25.

18–032 **ii. Foreign Trusts.** Problems have arisen in relation to the appointment of foreign trustees with the intention of enjoying the tax advantages of offshore trusts. The tax advantages are now minimal unless there are beneficiaries who are resident abroad, or the settlor was domiciled[197] abroad at the date of the creation of the settlement. The court has been unwilling to appoint trustees resident abroad unless the beneficiaries have made their homes in the country in question.[198] It was said in *Re Whitehead's Will Trusts*[199] that trustees or persons with an express power should only appoint foreign resident trustees in similar circumstances (although an appointment inconsistent with this rule would be a valid appointment[200]). In a later case, however, Millett J held that the *Whitehead* approach is outdated.[201] Where the trustees are exercising their own discretion and are merely seeking the authorisation of the court for their own protection, the test is simply whether the proposed transaction is not so inappropriate that no reasonable trustee could entertain it. Thus Bermudan trustees were sanctioned although the trust had no Bermuda connection. Where it is clear that this test is satisfied, there is no need to apply to court. It is might be added that many settlements now expressly authorise the appointment of non-resident trustees.

18–033 **iii. Direction by Beneficiaries.** We saw that in certain circumstances, beneficiaries may give directions as to the exercise of the statutory power of appointment.[202] It appears that the beneficiaries are under no restrictions in the choice of person they direct to be appointed.

C. On Appointment by the Settlor

18–034 The settlor is under no restrictions in the selection of the original trustees, whether English or foreign. The question is not merely one of selecting efficient, businesslike and fair-minded trustees who will carry out their duties according to law. They are commonly given wide discretions. They therefore should be people who can be relied on to respect the wishes of the settlor on matters on which they are in law virtually uncontrolled; and in circumstances which may have greatly changed since the trust was created.

---

[197] Inheritance Tax Act 1984 s.267 (the right of an individual to elect to be treated as domiciled in the UK under ss.267ZA and 267ZB are excluded by s.267(5), added by the Finance Act 2013 s.177(2), and other revisions to s.267 made by the Finance (No.2) Act 2017 have similarly restricted flexibility as to domicile).

[198] Below para.23–017; *Re Weston's Settlements* [1969] 1 Ch. 223; cf. *Re Seale's Marriage ST* [1961] Ch. 574; *Re Windeatt's WT* [1969] 1 W.L.R. 692; *Re Whitehead's WT* [1971] 1 W.L.R. 833; T. Watkin (1976) 40 Conv.(N.S.) 295.

[199] [1971] 1 W.L.R. 833 at 838.

[200] *Meinertzhagen v Davis* (1844) 1 Coll. 353; PVB (1969) 85 L.Q.R. 15; *Re Whitehead's WT* [1971] 1 W.L.R. 833 at 837.

[201] *Richard v The Hon. AB Mackay* (1997) 11 T.L.I. 22; [2008] W.T.L.R. 1667 (decided 1987); R. Bramwell, The Offshore Tax Planning Review (1990/91), Vol.1, p.1. See also *Re Beatty's WT (No.2)* (1997) 11 T.L.I. 77.

[202] Trusts of Land and Appointment of Trustees Act 1996 ss.19–22; above, para.18–023.

11. RETIREMENT

A trustee may retire from a subsisting trust in any one of the ways explained below.[203] Retirement means a discharge from further responsibility and liability under the trust. A trustee should not retire when faced with disputes among beneficiaries and leave them to settle their differences among themselves. If she retires in order to facilitate a breach of trust by her successors, if she acts without due care, then she will remain liable, for in retiring and passing on the trust estate, she is still acting as a trustee.[204]   **18–035**

A. Under an Express Power in the Trust Instrument

This is rare, since (the predecessors of) ss.36 and 39 made express powers unnecessary.   **18–036**

B. Under Section 39

We saw that a trustee desiring to be discharged could be replaced by a newly appointed trustee.[205] She may retire, without being replaced, if she complies with s.39 of the Trustee Act 1925:   **18–037**

> (1) Where a trustee is desirous of being discharged from the trust, and after his discharge there will be either a trust corporation or at least two persons[206] to act as trustees to perform the trust, then, if such trustee as aforesaid by deed declares that he is desirous of being discharged from the trust, and if his co-trustees and such other person, if any, as is empowered to appoint trustees, by deed consent to the discharge of the trustee, and to the vesting in the co-trustees alone of the trust property, the trustee desirous of being discharged shall be deemed to have retired from the trust, and shall, by the deed, be discharged therefrom under this Act, without any new trustee being appointed in his place.

A retirement not complying with the statutory provisions is invalid, hence the trustee remains in office.[207]

---

[203] A personal representative may be discharged by the court; Administration of Justice Act 1985 s.50; *Heath v Heath*, unreported, 17 January 2018 per Carr J.

[204] *Head v Gould* [1898] 2 Ch. 250, per Kekewich J at 268–9.

[205] Trustee Act 1925 s.36(1); above, para.18–019. cf. Y. Tan (1989) 9 L.S. 323, suggesting that s.36 permits retirement without replacement.

[206] A sole trustee other than a trust corporation does not suffice even if he has power to give a valid receipt for capital money, in contrast with the position under Trustee Act 1925 s.37(1)(c). The word "persons" in s.39(1) was inserted by Trusts of Land and Appointment of Trustees Act 1996 Sch.3, para.3(13), in place of "individuals". A corporate trustee (whether or not a "trust corporation") is a "person" but not an "individual".

[207] *Mettoy Pension Trustees Ltd v Evans* [1990] 1 W.L.R. 1587; *Jasmine Trustees Ltd v Wells & Hind (A Firm)* [2008] Ch. 194. See also *Re Epona Trustees Ltd and Pentera Trustees Ltd* [2009] W.T.L.R. 87 (Jersey Royal Court).

C.   Under an Order of the Court

18–038   The court will only discharge a trustee under its statutory jurisdiction where it replaces her by a new appointment under s.41. It has however an inherent power to discharge her without replacement in the case of an action to administer the trust. While it will not, in the exercise of this jurisdiction, encourage capricious retirement,[208] it will allow a trustee to retire where it is entirely proper for her to do so.[209]

D.   By Direction of the Beneficiaries

18–039   It was seen above that s.19 of the Trusts of Land and Appointment of Trustees Act 1996 gives beneficiaries of full age and capacity and together absolutely entitled, the power to give directions to the trustees in matters of appointment and retirement.[210] Where a trustee has been given a direction to retire under s.19 and reasonable arrangements have been made for the protection of any rights of hers in connection with the trust, she must execute a deed declaring her retirement, provided that after her retirement there will be either a trust corporation or at least two persons to act, and either another person is to be appointed in her place (by direction of the beneficiaries or otherwise) or the continuing trustees by deed consent to her retirement.[211]

12.   REMOVAL

18–040   We have seen that the court[212] may, on the appointment of a new trustee, remove an existing trustee and that some appointments by a donee of a power will have this effect.[213] The power of beneficiaries to direct a trustee to retire was discussed above. The court has also an inherent jurisdiction in actions for the administration of trusts to remove a trustee compulsorily; but the principles on which this power is exercised are somewhat vague.[214]

Actual misconduct on the part of a trustee need not be shown, but the court must be satisfied that her continuance in office would be prejudicial to the due

---

[208] *Courtenay v Courtenay* (1846) 3 Jo. & La.T. 519 at 533.

[209] *Re Chetwynd's Settlement* [1902] 1 Ch. 692.

[210] Above, para.18–023. The power may be excluded by the settlor under ss.21(5), (6). For potential problems, see L. Clements (1998) 61 M.L.R. 56 at 67.

[211] s.19(3). For vesting and divesting of the trust property, see s.19(4) of the 1996 Act and Trustee Act 1925 s.40(2), as amended.

[212] Normally the Chancery Division, but the Family Division has such jurisdiction; *E v E* [1990] 2 F.L.R. 233 (post-nuptial settlement).

[213] Trustee Act 1925 ss.36, 41, above, paras 18–019, 18–030; *Re Stoneham ST* [1953] Ch. 59; as to removal of a charitable trustee, see Charities Act 2011 s.79 and *Trustees of the Celestial Church of Christ, Edward Street Parish v Lawson* [2017] EWHC 97 (Ch); above, para.15–098.

[214] *Letterstedt v Broers* (1884) 9 App.Cas. 371; *Re Wrightson* [1908] 1 Ch. 789; *Re Pauling's ST (No.2)* [1963] Ch. 576; *Jones v Attorney General* [1974] Ch. 148 (trustee of charitable trust); *Re Edwards' WT* [1982] Ch. 30; *In the Matter of the EA Scott 1991 Children's Settlement No.1* [2012] EWHC 2397 (Ch); *Re Folkes' Estate* [2017] EWHC 2559 (Ch) (claimant applied for the removal of executors of her mother's estate and replacement of them with an independent solicitor.).

performance of the trust, and so to the interests of the beneficiaries.[215] The court has a clear ground for removal in cases where a trustee is ignoring one of her duties.[216] Thus, though it will not necessarily constitute a breach of trust for a trustee of a will carrying on the business of his testator to set up a rival business, yet it will be a ground for her removal,[217] as she has put herself in a position wherein her duty and interest are bound to be in conflict. Similarly if trustees were to persist in an investment policy based on considerations other than the best interests of the beneficiaries.[218] Harman J suggested that a member of a discretionary class could procure the removal of a trustee who "deliberately refused to consider any question" relating to the qualification of members to receive payments.[219] Friction or hostility between the trustee and the beneficiaries is not a reason for removing the trustee unless the court is satisfied that it was impeding the proper execution of the trust.[220] An example of this is the decision of HH Judge Behrens in *In the Matter of the EA Scott 1991 Children's Settlement No.1*,[221] concerning a dispute between two brothers who were the sole trustees of a trust created by their mother. The hostility of one of the brothers, Andrew, was having "a deleterious effect on the administration of the trust" and was "affecting the welfare of the beneficiaries".[222] The court therefore ordered his removal.

In the case of a foreign settlement, the court has inherent jurisdiction to make in personam orders removing and replacing foreign trustees, whether or not the assets are in England, provided that the individual trustee is subject to the jurisdiction of the English courts.[223] However, where the applicable law of the trust is not English law, matters such as the appointment, resignation and removal of trustees are governed by the law of the relevant jurisdiction.[224]

In administration actions the powers of the court are very elastic.[225] The court can, at any time during such proceedings, remove the trustees, if it considers such removal necessary for the preservation of the trust estate or the welfare of the beneficiaries, notwithstanding that such removal has not been expressly asked for in the statement of case. But each case must be weighed carefully on its merits;

---

[215] See *E v E* [1990] 2 F.L.R. 233; *Isaac v Isaac* [2009] W.T.L.R. 265 (decided 2005); *Re Folkes' Estate* [2017] EWHC 2559 (Ch).

[216] See *Walker v Walker* [2010] W.T.L.R. 1617.

[217] *Moore v M'Glynn* [1894] 1 Ir.R. 74. The possibility of conflict may not suffice; *Isaac v Isaac* [2009] W.T.L.R. 265.

[218] *Cowan v Scargill* [1985] Ch. 270, below, para.19–019.

[219] *Re Gestetner Settlement* [1953] Ch. 672 at 688; see also per Lord Wilberforce in *McPhail v Doulton* [1971] A.C. 424 at 456; above, para.4–011.

[220] *Alkin v Raymond* [2010] W.T.L.R. 1117; *Kershaw v Micklethwaite* [2011] W.T.L.R. 413 (executor).

[221] [2012] EWHC 2397 (Ch).

[222] [2012] EWHC 2397 (Ch) at [145].

[223] By reason of service of the claim form in England, or because the trustee has submitted to the jurisdiction, or because the court has assumed jurisdiction under, CPR 1998, Pt 6.30–6.47.

[224] Recognition of Trusts Act 1987 Sch., art.8. For the applicable law, see arts 6, 7; see *C v C* [2015] EWHC 2699 (Ch); above, para.1–051.

[225] *Re Harrison's Settlement Trusts* [1965] 1 W.L.R. 1492. On the removal of an executor, see *IRC v Stype Investments (Jersey) Ltd* [1982] Ch. 456.

and the court will sometimes find it necessary to place in one scale a minor breach of trust, and in the other the certain expense to the trust estate of a change of trustees.[226]

Special rules relating to the suspension, removal, disqualification and replacement of pension trustees are discussed in Ch.17.

13.   CONTROL OF TRUSTEES[227]

18–041   The basic principle governing trustees is that, while duties must be discharged, the exercise of discretions needs only to be considered. The trustee is not obliged to exercise them in any particular manner, or indeed at all. Nor is a trustee bound only to reach what, with hindsight, may be said to be the "right" decision.[228] Thus in *Tempest v Lord Camoys*,[229] one trustee wished to take advantage of a power in a trust instrument to purchase land but his co-trustee would not agree. It could not be shown that he had failed to consider the matter, and the court refused to issue any directive to him.

Nor is there a general principle that trustees should consult beneficiaries, though they should inform them that they have certain rights.[230] Frequently consultation takes place as a matter of practice, but only occasionally does statute impose an obligation on them to do so,[231] and even then their wishes are not mandatory but must be related to the overall welfare of the trust.

But what is the position if trustees exercise a discretion in a manner that appears wholly unreasonable? Is it a satisfactory answer to state simply that the matter has been fully considered? The law on this subject is neither wholly clear not wholly satisfactory.

A.   Giving of Reasons

18–042   There is a basic rule that trustees cannot be compelled to explain their reasons for exercising or not exercising a discretionary power.

> In *Re Beloved Wilkes' Charity*,[232] trustees were directed to select a boy to be educated for Orders in the Church of England. Their freedom of choice was limited by a preference for certain parishes, if a fit and proper candidate from these parishes could be found.
>
> The trustees selected Charles Joyce, a boy who did not come from one of these parishes. It appeared that Charles' brother was a minister who had sought assistance on his behalf from one of the trustees. The trustees gave no reasons for their choice, but asserted that they had considered the candidates impartially.
>
> Lord Truro refused to set aside the trustees' selection, or to require the trustees to explain

---

[226] *Re Wrightson* [1908] 1 Ch. 789.

[227] See generally R. Nolan (2009) 68 C.L.J. 293.

[228] *Pitt v Holt* [2013] UKSC 26; [2013] 2 A.C. 108 per Lord Walker J.S.C. at [88].

[229] (1882) 21 Ch.D. 571. The statutory duty of care under Trustee Act 2000 s.1 (above, para.18–003) does not apply to the discretion whether or not to exercise a power.

[230] *Hawkesley v May* [1956] 1 Q.B. 304; *X v A* [2000] 1 All E.R. 490.

[231] e.g. for trusts of land: Trusts of Land and Appointment of Trustees Act 1996 s.11.

[232] (1851) 3 Mac. & G. 440.

how they had arrived at their conclusion.[233] However, this does not exclude the possibility of challenge if it appears that the trustees acted in breach of their duties, for example by failing to give a fair consideration to the question.[234]

No distinction exists in this context between oral and documentary evidence, which is a matter of some importance in view of the large amount of trust business which is conducted by correspondence or at meetings with written agenda and minutes.[235] In *Re Londonderry's Settlement*,[236] the court drew a sharp distinction between written material of this nature which related to management of the trust property (which should be disclosed to requesting beneficiaries) and material which related to the exercise of discretions (which need not be disclosed). But if trustees do give reasons, or if they may be inferred, then the courts will look into their adequacy.[237]

The principle that trustees need not give reasons for their decisions is based on the fact that trustees have a confidential role which, it is said, they cannot properly exercise if they are to be subjected to an investigation to see whether they have exercised it in the best possible manner.[238] Documents relating to the trust may contain confidential information, the disclosure of which could cause trouble in the family, out of all proportion to the benefit gained from inspecting them. Thus the principle is designed not to encourage secrecy but to avoid litigation and family disputes.[239]

Whether the principle is appropriate to pension trusts may be doubted,[240] but it was held to apply in *Wilson v Law Debenture Trust Corp Plc*,[241] even though pension trusts are in many ways treated differently from traditional trusts because the beneficiaries are not volunteers.[242] There the employees failed to obtain disclosure of the trustees' reasons for not transferring a surplus to another scheme to which the employees had been transferred. Any change, it was said, would

18–043

---

[233] For a discussion on policy grounds, see A. Samuels (1965) 28 M.L.R. 220; A. Hawkins and F. Taylor (1965) S.J. 239. For recent consideration of the issues, see *British Airways Plc v Airways Pension Scheme Trustee Ltd* [2017] EWHC 1191 (Ch) (pensions); *Children's Investment Fund Foundation (UK) v Attorney General* [2017] EWHC 1379 (Ch) (charitable company).

[234] As we shall see in *Pitt v Holt* [2013] UKSC 26; [2013] 2 A.C. 108; below, paras 18–046—18–048.

[235] In *Breakspear v Ackland* [2008] EWHC 220 (Ch); [2009] Ch. 32, the principle was held to extend to letters of wishes.

[236] [1965] Ch. 918; the facts are given below, para.20–020; *Butt v Kelson* [1952] Ch. 197. N. McLarnon (2016) 22 T. & T. 298; J. Finch [2014] P.C.B. 104

[237] *Klug v Klug* [1918] 2 Ch. 67 (where a mother refused to exercise an advancement in favour of her daughter, who had married without her consent).

[238] *Re Londonderry's Settlement* [1965] Ch. 918 at 935–936.

[239] *Hartigan Nominees Pty Ltd v Rydge* (1992) 29 N.S.W.L.R. 405, holding that *Londonderry* accorded with principle and common sense; J. Lehane [1994] 3 J.I.P. 60. cf. *Blenkinsop v Herbert (No.2)* [2016] WASC 280 per Master Sanderson at [13]. See J. Campbell (2009) 3 J. Eq. 97.

[240] Lord Browne-Wilkinson (1992) 6 T.L.I. 119 at 125; D. Schaffer (1994) 8 T.L.I. 27; Sir Robert Walker [1996] P.L.R. 107; D. Pollard (1997) 11 T.L.I. 11 and 42.

[241] [1995] 2 All E.R. 337; criticised D. Schaffer (1994) 8 T.L.I. 118; P. Clarke All E.R. Rev. 1995 at 321.

[242] Above, para.17–005.

require legislation.[243] The significance of member trustees (required by the Pensions Act 2004, replacing earlier provisions) in this context should not, however, be overlooked.[244]

It is otherwise where there is evidence of bad faith or other impropriety. The difficulty is that it may not be possible to establish impropriety without seeing the documents which the trustees are not obliged to disclose. The beneficiaries may obtain disclosure of documents to support their case, but may not use that process to ascertain if a case exists.[245] Indeed the order made in the *Londonderry* case was without prejudice to the beneficiary's right to disclosure in separate proceedings against the trustees.[246]

We shall see below in Ch 20 that this traditional trust law position in respect of access to trust documents, though well-established, has been challenged by beneficiaries using data protection legislation to seek access to information pertaining to the trust.[247]

B. Power of Decision

18–044   A trust deed may give the trustees or a third party power to decide a particular matter. We saw in Ch.4 that this may be a means of curing conceptual uncertainty,[248] in which case the question arises whether the court may intervene if the decision appears unreasonable or wrong. Lord Denning in *Re Tuck's Settlement Trusts* would only have accepted the decision of the Chief Rabbi "so long as he does not misconduct himself or come to a decision which is wholly unreasonable."[249]

The trustees cannot be given power to decide legal issues in such manner as to oust the jurisdiction of the court, as this would be contrary to public policy.[250] They may be given power to decide limited issues, such as where the beneficiaries reside, or what is their ancestry or faith. The House of Lords in *Dundee General Hospitals v Walker*[251] thought it possible that the decisions of trustees in such cases could be attacked on the grounds of perversity or failure to appreciate the issue, as well as on grounds of bad faith. Where a clause in a trust of a pension fund provided that the determination of matters such as eligibility and the construction of the instrument adopted by the trustees in good faith

---

[243] Regulations under the Pensions Act 1995 require the decisions of the trustees to be recorded, but do not impose any general duty to give reasons. For the implications of the Data Protection Act 1998, see M. Shillingford, The TACT Review, April 2000, p.3.

[244] P. O'Hagan (1995) 145 N.L.J. 1414.

[245] *Hartigan Nominees Pty Ltd v Rydge* (1992) 29 N.S.W.L.R. 405.

[246] [1965] Ch. 918 at 939. See also *Scott v National Trust for Places of Historic Interest or Natural Beauty* [1998] 2 All E.R. 705; P. Clarke All E.R. Rev. 1998 at 276–277.

[247] *Dawson-Damer v Taylor Wessing LLP (Information Commissioner intervening)* [2017] EWCA Civ 74; [2017] 1 W.L.R. 3255; below, para.20–022.

[248] Above, para.4–014.

[249] [1978] Ch. 49 at 62.

[250] *Re Wynn* [1952] Ch. 271. See also *Re Raven* [1915] 1 Ch. 673 (trustees cannot be given conclusive power to resolve doubts as to identity of beneficiary).

[251] [1952] 1 All E.R. 896 at 905. This was a Scottish appeal, but "of the highest persuasive value": per Lord Denning MR in *Re Tuck's ST* [1978] Ch. 49 at 61: support for this view was more recently offered by Morgan J in *Creasey v Sole* [2013] EWHC 1410 (Ch) at [66].

should be binding on all parties and beneficiaries, the British Columbia Court of Appeal held that its jurisdiction was not excluded where the trustees acted in breach of their duty of impartiality, although in good faith.[252]

The general principle that beneficiaries cannot control trustees in the manner in which they exercise their powers applies even though all the beneficiaries are ascertained and of full capacity and wish the power to be exercised in a particular way.[253] But in such a case the trust can of course be brought to an end.

C.   Intervention by the Court

The cases are not clear, however, on whether the courts will look into the exercise of a discretion that *appears* to be wholly unreasonable. The duty of care under s.1 of the Trustee Act 2000 does not apply to the exercise of dispositive powers. If there is an allegation of fraud or misconduct, the courts must investigate it; but the complainant is in a difficulty in that the evidence which he requires is the personal motivation of the trustees. If fraud is proved, or if the exercise of the discretion is shown to be "capricious",[254] or if the trustees have blindly followed the settlor's wishes,[255] the court will declare the trustees' decision void. Likewise if the trustees have improperly exercised a power for a collateral purpose, by analogy with the doctrine of "fraud on a power",[256] which can occur even though the trustees acted honestly in the sense that they thought their action was in the interests of the beneficiaries.[257] There is some authority that the court will not intervene in the absence of bad faith if the instrument provides that the trustees' discretion is "uncontrollable".[258] It is not clear how far the court has greater powers in the absence of such a statement.[259] Although some 19th century decisions[260] asserted a wide jurisdiction, it seems that the court will not intervene simply on the ground that the trustees have exercised their discretion in good faith but unreasonably. The House of Lords in the Scottish case of *Dundee General Hospital*[261] (which has been said to reflect also the law of England[262]) indicated that the court could intervene, whether or not the trustees had given their reasons, if it was clear that they had not applied their minds to the right question or had perversely shut their eyes to the facts.[263]

18–045

---

[252] *Boe v Alexander* (1988) 41 D.L.R. (4th) 520. See also *Jones v Shipping Federation of British Columbia* (1963) 37 D.L.R. (2d) 273.

[253] *Re Brockbank* [1948] Ch. 206; cf. *Re George Whichelow Ltd* [1954] 1 W.L.R. 5 at 8. See, however, s.19 of the Trusts of Land and Appointment of Trustees Act 1996; above, para.18–023.

[254] *Re Manisty's Settlement* [1974] Ch. 17; above, para.4–016.

[255] *Turner v Turner* [1984] Ch. 100.

[256] Above, para.7–018.

[257] *Hillsdown Holdings Plc v Pensions Ombudsman* [1997] 1 All E.R. 862 (transfer of surplus funds to employer).

[258] *Gisborne v Gisborne* (1877) 2 App.Cas. 300.

[259] See N. Parry [1989] Conv. 244.

[260] *Re Hodges* (1878) 7 Ch.D. 754; *Re Roper's Trust* (1879) 11 Ch.D. 272.

[261] *Dundee General Hospitals v Walker* [1952] 1 All E.R. 896. The trustees accepted that unreasonableness was the test, but this was doubted.

[262] *Scott v National Trust for Places of Historic Interest or Natural Beauty* [1998] 2 All E.R. 705.

[263] See also, for example, *British Airways Plc v Airways Pension Scheme Trustee Ltd* [2017] EWHC 1191 (Ch) per Morgan J at [492]: "It is clear that trustees must genuinely consider whether to, and

14. SETTING ASIDE TRUSTEES' DECISIONS: *PITT V HOLT*[264]

18–046 The Supreme Court in *Pitt v Holt* considered the circumstances in which the court may intervene where trustees exercise a discretionary dispositive power in good faith but their disposition does not have the full effect they intended because they were under some misapprehension, for example as to the tax consequences. It has now been definitively decided that the court may only intervene where a breach of duty has been established on the part of the trustees.[265] This Supreme Court decision has been for the most part a welcome resolution of a matter of considerable controversy.

Before substantive discussion, some points should first be noted. The principles to be discussed below cannot be invoked to correct a mistake in the drafting of the rules of a pension trust, as they apply to things done by trustees, not to things done by the settlor of a private trust or by an employer setting up a pension trust.[266] In other words, the principles cannot be used to circumvent the strict conditions of the doctrine of rectification.[267]

Where the court does intervene, the result is normally negative: the decision of the trustees may be set aside, or a future course of action restrained. Usually the court makes no positive direction that a discretion must be exercised in a particular way. However, this can be done in an appropriate case, as in *Klug v Klug*,[268] where a trustee refused to exercise a power of advancement for an extraneous reason (because the beneficiary, her daughter, had married without her consent). The court directed the trustee to agree to the advancement. Alternatively, a trustee may be persuaded by the prospect of removal.[269]

In order to understand the current law as decided in *Pitt*, we must briefly consider the unhappy history of the rule in *Re Hastings-Bass*.[270]

> In *Re Hastings-Bass*,[271] trustees exercised a power of advancement by creating a sub-trust but the remainder interests in it were void for perpetuity. This did not invalidate the exercise of the power as the primary intention was to create a life interest, and this had been achieved. The ratio was that trustees, when exercising a power of advancement, must consider whether it will

---

how to, exercise a discretion vested in them… It is less easy to find illustrations in the decided cases of circumstances where trustees have been held to have failed in their duty in this respect even though they have appeared to have gone through a decision-making process in relation to an issue."

[264] *Pitt v Holt* [2013] UKSC 26; [2013] 2 A.C. 108. See generally M. Ashdown, *Trustee Decision Making: The Rule in Re Hastings-Bass* (Oxford: Oxford University Press, 2015).

[265] [2013] UKSC 26; [2013] 2 A.C. 108, per Lord Walker JSC at [73].

[266] *Smithson v Hamilton* [2008] 1 W.L.R. 1453 (mistake enabling early retirement without reduction of benefits). P. Clarke and J. Edelman All E.R. Rev. 2008 at 300, 392. The principles may of course apply to an employee benefit trust, for example, once up and running: *Roadchef (Employee Benefits Trustees) Ltd v Timothy Ingram Hill* [2014] EWHC 109 (Ch).

[267] See Ch.29.

[268] [1918] 2 Ch. 67. See also *Re Hodges* (1878) 7 Ch.D. 754; *Re Roper's Trust* (1879) 11 Ch.D. 272. The appointment of new trustees is considered preferable to positive intervention (i.e. the judicial exercise of fiduciary discretions) by S. Gardner (1990) 107 L.Q.R. 214 at 219–220, discussing *Mettoy Pension Trustees Ltd v Evans* [1990] 1 W.L.R. 1587. See also D. Hayton [2005] Conv. 229, supporting positive intervention in pensions cases.

[269] Lord Walker stressed the range of options open to the court: [2013] UKSC 26; [2013] 2 A.C. 108 at [63].

[270] [1975] Ch. 25; below, para.21–043.

[271] [1975] Ch. 25.

operate for the benefit of the advancee. If one or more aspects cannot take effect, it does not follow that those which can take effect should not do so. Thus a misapprehension by the trustees as to the effect is not by itself fatal to the effectiveness of the advancement. If the provisions which can take effect cannot reasonably be regarded as for the benefit of the advancee, the exercise fails as not being within the scope of the power. Otherwise it takes effect to the extent that it can.

However, the case came to be regarded as authority for the principle (the so-called "rule in *Re Hastings-Bass*") which it did not actually decide,[272] namely that the court could set aside a disposition if it was clear that the trustees would (or possibly might) not have acted as they did had they not taken into account considerations which they should not have taken into account or failed to take into account considerations which they ought to have taken into account. The question whether the disposition was void or voidable was not resolved. This "seriously wrong turn"[273] was taken in *Mettoy Pension Trustees Ltd v Evans*,[274] and other cases followed suit.[275]

In 2011, the path of the law was "put back ... on the right course"[276] by the Court of Appeal in *Pitt v Holt*,[277] which was heard with the case of *Futter v Futter*. Lloyd LJ, who had previously applied the so-called rule in *Re Hastings-Bass* as a first instance judge himself,[278] gave the lead judgment for the court and held that the court could only intervene to set aside a disposition if it could be proved that the trustee(s) had acted in breach of duty.[279] The Supreme Court has now endorsed Lloyd LJ's fundamental analysis of this area.

First it is necessary to state the facts. In both cases, the Commissioners for HMRC were parties to the proceedings as these cases, like several others before them, involved the potential setting aside of a tax liability.[280]

18–047

> *Pitt v Holt* was an unusual case as it did not involve a trustee.[281] A receiver appointed to act for her husband by the Court of Protection under the Mental Health Act 1983[282] exercised a power (authorised by the court) to create a discretionary trust of a personal injury award for the benefit of her husband, but did not appreciate that it had adverse inheritance tax consequences. It was considered that, as she was a fiduciary, the principles relating to dispositions by trustees applied. In *Futter v Futter*, trustees exercised a power of advancement on the wrong

---

[272] *Pitt v Holt* [2011] 3 W.L.R. 19, per Lloyd LJ at [94]: "It has been said that *Re Hastings-Bass* did not involve applying what has come to be called the *Hastings-Bass* rule at all."

[273] *Pitt v Holt* [2011] 3 W.L.R. 19, per Longmore LJ at [227].

[274] [1990] 1 W.L.R. 1587.

[275] See *Edge v Pensions Ombudsman* [2000] Ch. 602; *Sieff v Fox* [2005] 1 W.L.R. 3811.

[276] [2011] 3 W.L.R. 19, per Longmore LJ at [227].

[277] [2011] 3 W.L.R. 19; R. Chambers [2011] 25 T.L.I. 17; M. Conaglen (2011) 70 C.L.J. 301; R. Nolan and A. Cloherty (2011) 127 L.Q.R. 499; P. Davies [2011] Conv. 406.

[278] In *Sieff v Fox* [2005] 1 W.L.R. 3811 (the case is reported as being decided by "Lloyd LJ" because his Lordship had been appointed to the Court of Appeal by the time of judgment).

[279] [2011] 3 W.L.R. 19 at [130].

[280] Indeed, the Supreme Court's published judgment, though not the Law Report, lists the appeal as *Futter v The Commissioners for HMRC; Pitt v Commissioners for HMRC*.

[281] Though for convenience, in the discussion which follows we shall generally refer to the "trustees'" decisions.

[282] Receivers have since been replaced by deputies under the current legislation, the Mental Capacity Act 2005. On the appointment of trust corporations as deputies, see *Various Incapacitated Persons v The Appointment of Trust Corporations as Deputies* [2018] EWCOP 3.

assumption that no capital gains tax would be payable. The question in both cases was whether the disposition could be set aside. This had been the result in the High Court, but the appeal by HMRC was successful in both cases.

The single judgment for the Supreme Court was given by Lord Walker JSC, in his final opinion as a serving Justice.[283] Lord Walker reviewed the authorities and agreed with Lloyd LJ in the Court of Appeal. The way in which previous cases such as *Mettoy Pension Trustees Ltd v Evans*[284] had interpreted the so-called "rule in *Re Hastings-Bass*" was not a correct statement of the law.[285] That interpretation of the "rule" took a quote from Buckley LJ in Re Hastings Bass and applied it inappropriately out of context.

The crucial distinction is between an error as to the scope of the trustees' power and an error in failing to give proper consideration to relevant matters.[286] The true *Re Hastings-Bass* principle is that the purported exercise of a discretionary power will be void if what is done is not within the scope of the power, for example if a necessary consent was not obtained or if the appointment was to a non-object.[287]

Cloutte v Storey,[288] a case on fraudulent appointments, was described as "difficult" and perhaps in need of revisiting in the future,[289] but Lord Walker left such points open for future decision,[290] noting that there may need to be a "separate pigeon-hole" for such cases.[291]

If there is some defect under the general law, for example perpetuity, the result depends on the extent of the invalidity. In advancement cases it depends on whether what remains can be considered to be for the benefit of the advancee, as in *Re Hastings-Bass*[292] itself, otherwise it will be void.

In contrast, Lord Walker confirmed that, where an exercise by trustees in within the terms of their power but the trustees have acted in breach of their duty, that exercise is not void but voidable at the instance of an affected beneficiary.[293] Where the exercise is voidable, it is subject to the usual equitable defences if a beneficiary seeks to set is aside, but remains valid if nobody with standing seeks to set it aside.

Lord Walker affirmed the approach to be adopted to cases involving inadequate deliberation by the trustees. For a transaction to be set aside:

"the inadequate deliberation on the part of the trustees must be sufficiently serious as to amount to a breach of fiduciary duty. Breach of duty is essential ... because it is only a breach

---

[283] Lord Walker had written extra-judicially, and critically, of the rule as it had developed: R. Walker, "The Limits of the Principle in Hastings-Bass" (2002) 13 K.C.L.J. 173.

[284] [1990] 1 W.L.R. 1587.

[285] [2013] UKSC 26; [2013] 2 A.C. 108 at [32].

[286] [2013] UKSC 26; [2013] 2 A.C. 108 at [60].

[287] See also *Breadner v Granville-Grossman* [2001] Ch. 523 (power of appointment expired at date of purported exercise).

[288] [1911] 1 Ch. 18.

[289] [2013] UKSC 26; [2013] 2 A.C. 108 at [62]. Indeed, Lord Walker in that paragraph described the case as having "bedevilled discussion of the true nature of the *Hastings-Bass* rule".

[290] [2013] UKSC 26; [2013] 2 A.C. 108 at [93]–[94].

[291] [2013] UKSC 26; [2013] 2 A.C. 108 at [62].

[292] [1975] Ch. 25.

[293] [2013] UKSC 26; [2013] 2 A.C. 108 at [93].

of duty on the part of the trustees that entitles the court to intervene… It is not enough to show that the trustees' deliberations have fallen short of the highest possible standards, or that the court would, on a surrender of discretion by the trustees, have acted in a different way. Apart from exceptional circumstances (such as an impasse reached by honest and reasonable trustees) only breach of fiduciary duty justifies judicial intervention."[294]

As Lloyd LJ put it, it is necessary for the beneficiaries to "grasp the nettle" and prove a breach of fiduciary duty on the part of the trustees.[295] *Pitt v Holt* further confirms that it is appropriate to take into account fiscal considerations.[296] Lord Walker also emphasised that the mere obtaining of apparently competent professional advice may not mean that the trustees avoid liability: they may commit breaches in other ways, such as by acting outside their powers.[297] There must always be an intense focus on the facts and ultimately a discretionary judgment by the court.[298]

Turning to the application of those principles to the facts of the instant appeals, neither disclosed a breach of duty. In *Futter v Futter*, the trustees had taken into account Capital Gains Tax, and "indeed, it was the paramount consideration, and the trustees thought about it a great deal".[299] They had sought advice but the advice turned out to be wrong because an amendment to the relevant tax legislation had been overlooked.[300] The trustees themselves had not acted in breach of duty, however, and so the transaction could not be set aside. In *Pitt v Holt*, the position was "even clearer"[301]:

"She had taken supposedly expert advice and followed it. There is no reason to hold that she personally failed in the exercise of her fiduciary duty. Unfortunately the advice was unsound."

Both appeals were therefore dismissed on this point. The Supreme Court did however go on to allow the appeal in *Pitt*, but relying on the equitable jurisdiction to set aside voluntary dispositions on the ground of mistake. In this respect, Lord Walker differed from Lloyd LJ's analysis of the gravity of the relevant mistake on the particular facts.[302] The point is noted for completeness here but considered more fully in Ch.29.[303]

---

[294] [2013] UKSC 26; [2013] 2 A.C. 108 at [73].

[295] [2011] 3 W.L.R. 19 at [130].

[296] [2013] UKSC 26; [2013] 2 A.C. 108 at [65]: "It might be said, especially by those who still regard family trusts as potentially beneficial to society as a whole, that the greater danger is not of trustees thinking too little about tax, but of tax and tax avoidance driving out consideration of other relevant matters."

[297] [2013] UKSC 26; [2013] 2 A.C. 108 at [80]. On the limits of this dictum, see *Davey v Money* [2018] EWHC 766 (Ch); [2018] W.L.R.(D) 219 per Snowden J at [447].

[298] [2013] UKSC 26; [2013] 2 A.C. 108 at [92].

[299] [2013] UKSC 26; [2013] 2 A.C. 108 at [95].

[300] Taxation of Chargeable Gains Act 1992 s.2(4).

[301] [2013] UKSC 26; [2013] 2 A.C. 108 at [97].

[302] [2013] UKSC 26; [2013] 2 A.C. 108 at [142], applying the test set out at [126].

[303] See further A. Burrows, *A Restatement of the English Law of Unjust Enrichment* (Oxford: Oxford University Press, 2012) at 66.

18–048   After *Pitt v Holt*, dispositions made by trustees under a misapprehension are harder to set aside than under the so-called "rule in *Re Hastings-Bass*", which had come to be regarded as some kind of "get out of jail free card".[304] Indeed, Lord Walker noted that it was

> "a striking feature of the development of the *Hastings-Bass* rule that it has led to trustees asserting and relying on their own failings, or those of their advisers, in seeking the assistance of the court … in general it would be inappropriate for trustees to take the initiative in commencing proceedings of this nature. They should not regard them as uncontroversial proceedings in which they can confidently expect to recover their costs out of the trust fund."[305]

The remedy, if any, is against professional advisers,[306] or against the trustees themselves.[307] In the alternative, as we shall see in Ch.29, the equitable mistake jurisdiction may be invoked to seek to set aside the disposition, as in *Pitt* itself.

The decision in *Pitt*, on the misadventures of the rule in *Re Hastings-Bass*, was broadly welcomed by commentators,[308] and was applied without difficulty in recent cases involving employee benefits trusts.[309] It has had a frostier reception in offshore jurisdictions,[310] with judicial criticism in the Isle of Man,[311] and legislative interventions in Jersey[312] and Bermuda[313] to pre-empt the *Pitt* approach being applied.

Most criticism[314] has focused on the persistence of discretion[315] and some of the issues left unresolved[316] by the Supreme Court given that no breach of duty was found in either of the instant cases.

One of those issues concerns when the court will intervene, where a breach of duty has been established. Is it enough to show that the trustees "might not" have

---

[304] Lord Neuberger of Abbotsbury (2009) 15 T. & T. 189 at 192.

[305] [2013] UKSC 26; [2013] 2 A.C. 108 at [69]. See also Lord Walker of Gestingthorpe (2015) 45 H.K.L.J. 417.

[306] Although such claims may not be straightforward, as recognised as a footnote by Lord Walker: [2013] UKSC 26; [2013] 2 A.C. 108 at [90]. See also T. Peacocke (2011) 25 T.L.I. 125.

[307] [2013] UKSC 26; [2013] 2 A.C. 108 at [89]. Lord Walker recognised that such claims may engage an exemption clause (above para.18–005), but other relief may be available, including the removal of the trustee.

[308] The case has been noted variously by R. Nolan (2013) 129 L.Q.R. 469; P.S. Davies and G. Virgo [2013] 21 R.L.R. 74; N. Lee [2014] Conv. 175; and F. Ng [2013] B.T.R. 566; M. Studer (2016) 22 T. & T. 971. M. Ashdown, *Trustee Decision Making: The Rule in Re Hastings-Bass* (2015), Ch.12. For international aspects, see S. Kempster [2016] P.C.B. 248 and R. Ham (2016) 22 T. & T. 971.

[309] *Roadchef (Employee Benefits Trustees) Ltd v Ingram Hill* [2014] EWHC 109 (Ch); *British Airways Plc v Airways Pension Scheme Trustee Ltd* [2017] EWHC 1191 (Ch) and *Wedgwood Pension Plan Trustee Ltd v Salt* [2018] EWHC 79 (Ch) per Penelope Reed QC.

[310] W. Redgrave [2014] P.C.B. 92; C. Mitchell [2017] P.C.B. 41 at 51–3.

[311] e.g. the decision of First Deemster Doyle in the Isle of Man case of *AB v CD*, unreported, CHP 2016/7.

[312] Trusts (Amendment No.6) (Jersey) Law 2013 s.47F(4), providing that the relevant decision may be set aside on the basis of a causative failure to take into account relevant considerations (whether or not in breach of duty).

[313] The Trustee Amendment Act 2014 (Bermuda) inserted a s.47A into the Bermudan Trustee Act 1974, which applies to the "Jurisdiction of court to set aside flawed exercise of fiduciary power".

[314] More criticism is directed at the approach to mistake, which again is considered in Ch.29, but see S. Watterson (2013) 72 C.L.J. 501; M. Ashdown, *Trustee Decision Making,* Ch.10.

[315] F. Ng [2013] B.T.R. 566 at 576.

[316] N. Lee [2014] Conv. 175 at 182–3.

made the decision that they did, or does it have to be shown that the trustees "would not" have made it? The "might not" approach is clearly a more generous test, and concerns about an overly broad scope may be allayed by the Supreme Court's clarification of the applicability of the rule, in that a breach must a priori have been established. However, Lord Walker declined to resolve the issue:

> "as a matter of principle there must be a high degree of flexibility in the range of the court's possible responses. To lay down a rigid rule of either 'would not' or 'might not' would inhibit the court in seeking the best practical solution in the application of the Hastings-Bass rule in a variety of different factual situations."[317]

It is perhaps to be regretted that the Supreme Court, having seized the opportunity to correct the erroneous interpretation of *Re Hastings-Bass*, did not go on to determine this point: nor have subsequent cases yet resolved the issues.[318] Overall, however, the judgments of Lloyd LJ and Lord Walker in the *Pitt* litigation have done much to clarify what had become a problematic enclave of equity.[319] As a result, the trend in litigation strategy in such cases since *Pitt* has been away from reliance on "the rule *Re Hastings Bass*" and towards the mistake claim.[320]

---

[317] [2013] UKSC 26; [2013] 2 A.C. 108 at [91]–[92].

[318] *Wedgwood Pension Plan Trustee Ltd v Salt* [2018] EWHC 79 (Ch) per Penelope Reed QC at [69]ff.

[319] For some of the implications for off-shore jurisdictions, see N. Lee [2014] Conv. 175 at 183 and M. Ashdown, *Trustee Decision Making* (2015), Ch.11.

[320] See e.g. *Freedman v Freedman* [2015] EWHC 1457 (Ch) and R. Lee [2018] Conv. 45.

CHAPTER 19

DUTIES OF TRUSTEES IN RELATION TO THE TRUST PROPERTY

1. DUTY TO COLLECT IN THE ASSETS

A. Duty on Accepting Office

TRUSTEES must, on their appointment, make themselves familiar with the terms of the trust and the state and the details of the trust property, check that the trust fund is invested in accordance with the provisions of the trust deed, and that the securities and any chattels are in proper custody.[1] They should not wait until the trust property is formally vested in them. The discharge of their duties will obviously depend upon circumstances. The trustees of a trust newly constituted, and with suitable assets, are in an easier situation than personal representatives who find, as part of the estate, assets which are highly speculative or precarious.

19–001

---

[1] *Re Miller's Deed Trust* (1978) 75 L.S.Gaz. 454.

In the latter case the duty is to consider the best method of protecting the value of the assets, and this may involve delaying a decision to dispose of them. Liability for loss will not be imposed on them if their decision to delay was reasonable, even though subsequent events show it to have been the less wise course.[2]

A replacement trustee must make all reasonable inquiries[3] to satisfy herself that nothing has been done by her predecessor and the continuing trustees which amounts to a breach of trust; and the continuing trustees must provide this information from trust documents.[4] Omission to inquire may render the new trustee liable, but she is not to be fixed with notice of matters that do not appear on any of the trust documents, though the matter may be known to the retiring trustee.[5] On a similar principle, if she is ignorant of the existence of some right forming part of the trust, she is not liable for loss of that right through non-enforcement unless she could have discovered its existence from materials at her disposal.[6]

B. Extent of Duty

19–002   The duty to safeguard trust assets is a stringent one; indeed, it has sometimes been almost too strictly applied.

> In *Re Brogden*,[7] the trustees of a marriage settlement took what they considered to be all reasonable steps to ensure that a covenant to pay £10,000 to them at the end of a stated period of five years was carried out. They did not sue because the covenantor's estate was the basis of the family partnership, the stability of which might have been imperilled by an action at a time of trade depression. The trustees were held liable. They should have taken every possible step to insist on payment, irrespective of the claims of sentiment within a family.
>
> In *Buttle v Saunders*,[8] trustees had orally agreed to sell a freehold reversion to the leaseholder. Then a beneficiary made a higher offer. The trustees declined to consider it, feeling themselves bound by commercial morality to complete the agreement. Wynn-Parry J held that, although there may be cases where a trustee should accept a lower offer—as where that offer may be lost if not honoured—and although the honourable course was to stand by the earlier offer, the trustees had an overriding duty to obtain the best price for their beneficiaries.

As we have seen above in Ch.13, however, trustees do have wide powers under the Trusts of Land and Appointment of Trustees Act 1996, which can lead

---

[2] *Buxton v Buxton* (1835) 1 My. & Cr. 80. *Pitt v Holt* [2013] UKSC 26; [2013] 2 A.C. 108 per Lord Walker JSC at [88].

[3] *Re Lucking's WT* [1968] 1 W.L.R. 866.

[4] *Tiger v Barclays Bank* [1951] 2 K.B. 556.

[5] *Hallows v Lloyd* (1888) 39 Ch.D. 686.

[6] *Youde v Cloud* (1874) L.R. 18 Eq. 634. A similarly reasonable rule governs the inquiries trustees should make in relation to covenants to settle after-acquired property: *Re Strahan* (1856) 8 De. G.M. & G. 291.

[7] (1888) 38 Ch.D. 546. See also *Harris v Black* (1983) 46 P. & C.R. 366.

[8] [1950] 2 All E.R. 193; E. Bodkin (1950) 14 Conv.(N.S.) 228; A. Samuels (1975) 30 Conv.(N.S.) 177; G. Lightman (2008) 22 T.L.I. 11. See also *Sergeant v National Westminster Bank* (1991) 61 P. & C.R. 518. cf. *Re Merchant Navy Ratings Pension Fund* [2015] EWHC 448 (Ch).

to the approval of innovative solutions in appropriate circumstances, even if they do not lead to the highest possible price being obtained.[9]

C.   Litigation

In *Re Brogden*,[10] the Court of Appeal laid down that the only excuse for not taking action to enforce payment was a well-founded belief on the part of the trustees that such action would be fruitless; and the burden of proof was on the trustees. Modern trustees have been given extensive powers of compounding (settling) liabilities, allowing time for the payment of debts, and compromising doubtful actions, etc. by the Trustee Act 1925 s.15.[11] Trustees are not liable for loss caused by any acts done by them in good faith in exercise of these powers, provided they have directed their minds to the problem and not just let the matter slide.[12] A trustee will be allowed the costs of litigation from the trust assets if properly incurred,[13] but not where the litigation results from an unreasonable withholding of property from those entitled to it,[14] nor where the litigation is speculative and turns out to be unsuccessful,[15] nor where the trustee has acted in a manner hostile to the beneficiaries,[16] nor where any trustees are in truth acting in another capacity.[17] In *Blades v Isaac*,[18] Master Matthews held that trustees were not be liable for the costs of a beneficiary who had successfully brought a claim for breach of duty, because they had acted out of concern about likely harm to family relationships from disclosing the relevant information. A beneficiary may sue a third party on behalf of the trust where the trustee unreasonably refuses to sue or has disabled herself from doing so.[19] (Where, however, the trustees are able and willing to sue, the beneficiary will be penalised in costs.[20]) Trustees who discontinue litigation against third parties because the trust fund could be

19–003

---

[9] Above, paras 13–028—13–029. See e.g. *Bagum v Hafiz* [2015] EWCA Civ 801; [2016] Ch. 241 (one of several beneficiaries being given the opportunity to buy pre-emptively the co-owned property at a price determined by the court); *Parkes v Wilkes* [2017] EWHC 1556 (Ch); [2017] 4 W.L.R. 123.

[10] (1888) 38 Ch.D. 546.

[11] Below, para.21–010.

[12] *Re Greenwood* (1911) 105 L.T. 509. cf. *Re Ezekiel's Settlements* [1942] Ch. 230.

[13] See generally *Alsop Wilkinson v Neary* [1996] 1 W.L.R. 1220; Lightman J (2006) 20 T.L.I. 151; *Granada Group Ltd v The Law Debenture Pension Trust Corp Plc* [2015] EWHC 1499 (Ch) per Andrews J at [91]–[97] (aff'd without comment on this point, [2016] EWCA Civ 1289); *Bonham v Blake Lapthorn Linnell* [2007] W.T.L.R. 189. As to how the costs are borne between capital and income, see *Close Trustees (Switzerland) SA v Vildosola* [2008] W.T.L.R. 1543.

[14] *Re Chapman* (1895) 72 L.T. 66.

[15] *Re Beddoe* [1893] 1 Ch. 547; *Re England's ST* [1918] 1 Ch. 24; *The Law Debenture Trust Corp Plc v Ukraine* [2017] EWHC 1902 (Comm) E. Campbell (2013) 19 T. & T. 442; M. Yip (2017) 31 T.L.I. 185; K. Davenport and T. Nelson (2017) 23 T. & T. 343.

[16] *Holding and Management Ltd v Property Holding and Investment Trust Plc* [1989] 1 W.L.R. 1313; *Breadner v Granville-Grossman* [2006] W.T.L.R. 411; *Shovelar v Lane* [2011] 4 All E.R. 669; *James v James* [2018] EWHC 242 (Ch).

[17] As where some of the trustees are also beneficiaries and defending a claim as such: *Pettigrew v Edwards* [2017] EWHC 8 (Ch); [2017] 1 P. & C.R. DG19.

[18] [2016] EWHC 601 (Ch); [2016] 2 P. & C.R. DG10.

[19] *Parker-Tweedale v Dunbar Bank Plc* [1991] Ch. 12; G. McCormack (1997) 11 T.L.I. 60. *Blades v Isaac* [2016] EWHC 601 (Ch); [2016] 2 P. & C.R. DG10.

[20] *D'Abo v Paget (No.2)* [2000] W.T.L.R. 863 (considering the position under the CPR 1998).

exhausted in indemnifying them for costs do not act unreasonably, and the beneficiaries may not take over the action.[21]

D.   A Continuing Duty

19–004   Trustees must regard their duty of safeguarding trust assets as a continuing one. In regard to investment in securities, the point is dealt with below. In regard to land, there is a duty to consider the maintenance and general welfare of the property, and in regard to deeds and chattels, a duty to see that they are kept securely.[22] There is no duty to insure unless required by the trust deed, but trustees have a power to insure.[23]

2.   DUTY TO INVEST[24]

A.   Meaning of Investment

19–005   A trustee is under a duty to invest trust money in her hands.[25] To invest means "to employ money in the purchase of anything from which interest or profit is expected".[26] Similarly, the Privy Council has observed that "the word 'investment' has no very precise legal meaning, but its natural meaning, in a financial context, is the acquisition of an asset to be held as a source of income".[27]

From the point of view of an individual investing her own money, she may not mind whether the profit comes from income earned by the investment or from capital appreciation. But trustees often have to consider the interests of a life tenant, who is entitled to the income, and also of the remaindermen who are interested in the capital. The trustees' duty is to act fairly between them. The investments should produce income, and maintain the capital, although investments are assessed according to the "portfolio theory", which permits some flexibility.[28] Thus premium bonds and chattels, such as antiques or silver, are not investments for this purpose. For this reason, a purchase of a house for occupation by a beneficiary, and which therefore produces no income, was held

---

[21] *Bradstock Trustee Services Ltd v Nabarro Nathanson (A Firm)* [1995] 1 W.L.R. 1405; *Re Nordea Trust Co (Isle of Man) Ltd* [2010] W.T.L.R. 1393.

[22] *Jobson v Palmer* [1893] 1 Ch. 71.

[23] Below, para.21–008.

[24] Trustees conducting investment business are required by Financial Services and Markets Act 2000 s.19, to be authorised under the Act or exempted.

[25] *Byrnes v Kendle* [2011] HCA 26, per Heydon and Crennan JJ at [119]: "it is the duty of a trustee to obtain income from the trust property if it is capable of yielding an income. If the property is money, it should be invested at interest or used to purchase income-yielding assets like shares." *Brudenell-Bruce, Earl of Cardigan v John Moore* [2014] EWHC 3679 (Ch) per Newey J at [88].

[26] *Shorter Oxford English Dictionary*; *Re Wragg* [1919] 2 Ch. 58 at 64, per P.O. Lawrence J who added: "and which property is purchased in order to be held for the sake of the income which it will yield."

[27] *Dominica Social Security Board v Nature Island Investment Co Ltd* [2008] UKPC 19 per Lord Walker of Gestingthorpe at [21].

[28] A. Hicks (2001) 15 T.L.I. 203. For the "portfolio theory", see below, para.19–014.

not to be an investment as a matter of common law,[29] but trustees have been given the power to make such a purchase by statute.[30] It remains the case that investments which yield a high rate of income because the capital is wasting away, or an unsecured loan,[31] should be avoided.

Mention should also be made of "total return" investment. This enables the selection of investments on the basis of the value of the returns they are expected to yield, without regard to the classification of these returns as capital or income. This gives more flexibility in the choice of investments, thereby enabling potentially higher returns. Trusts with interests in succession are not generally drafted to enable total return investment, and the tax implications are uncertain. In 2009, the Law Commission recommended that HMRC and HM Treasury should enter discussions with the trust industry as to the feasibility and mechanics of total return investment.[32] Section 4 of the Trusts (Capital and Income) Act 2013 introduces the power for charitable trustees to invest the endowment fund, or a portion of it, on a total return basis.[33]

Part II of the Trustee Act 2000, which confers wide investment powers on trustees, retains the traditional terminology of "investment" without elaboration. The Law Commission has considered that trustees may acquire assets for capital appreciation rather than income yield.[34] The Explanatory Notes (which accompany, but are not part of, the Act) state that the general power of investment permits the trustees to invest in a way which is expected to produce an income or capital return.[35] The exact scope remains somewhat uncertain, and it is to be expected that express clauses permitting the application of trust funds in a manner which may not strictly be an "investment" will continue to be used.

B.   Types of Investment

In most general terms, there are basically two types of investment. The first is a **19–006** loan at a rate of interest. The second is a participation in a profit-making activity; such as the purchase of ordinary shares in a company ("equities"). Ordinary shares were first included in the list of permitted investments for trustees by the Trustee Investments Act 1961. Mention should also be made of "derivatives", such as futures and options. A "future" obliges the holder to buy or sell (shares, currency, commodities, etc.) at a set price at a future date. An "option" gives the

---

[29] *Re Power* [1947] Ch. 572.

[30] Trusts of Land and Appointment of Trustees Act 1996 s.6(3); Trustee Act 2000 s.8; below, para.19–011.

[31] *Khoo Tek Keong v Ch'ng Joo Tuan Neoh* [1934] A.C. 529, endorsed on this point by Bean J in *Dalriada Trustees Ltd v Faulds* [2012] I.C.R. 1106.

[32] Law Com. No. 315, *Capital and Income in Trusts: Classification and Apportionment* (2009), para.5.104. The Law Commission's recommendations more specifically in this area resulted in the Trusts (Capital and Income) Act 2013, considered below, Ch.20. For charities, see above, para.15–093.

[33] By inserting ss.104A and B into the Charities Act 2011; see also The Charities (Total Return) Regulations 2013.

[34] No. 260, *Trustees' Powers and Duties* (1999), p.22; No. 315, *Capital and Income in Trusts: Classification and Apportionment* (2009), para.2.69. This view is supported in A. Hicks (2001) 15 T.L.I. 203 and in *Legal underpinning: Charities and Investment Matters* (Charity Commission, 2011).

[35] Trustee Act 2000: Explanatory Notes, para.22.

holder the right, but not the obligation, to buy or sell at a set price at a set date. Pension fund trustees and others with sufficiently wide powers may make use of derivatives in appropriate circumstances, but they are not within the traditional meaning of "investments".[36] Given their nature, dealing in derivatives can obviously be risky.

19–007   **i.   Loans at a Rate of Interest.**   In the case of an investment such as a deposit account at a bank or a building society, the capital sum does not alter (save by additions or withdrawals). Interest is earned at a rate which is normally variable.

Most fixed interest securities issued by the Government and local authorities are in the form of stock and pay a fixed rate of interest. The purchaser may sell the stock to other purchasers. The value of the stock is whatever a purchaser will give for it. That depends on many factors; essentially the current rate of interest chargeable on loans. Where interest rates have increased since the stock was issued, the value of the stock declines. A 3% stock, paying £3 per annum on an investment of £100, needs to pay the current rate of interest (if higher) in order to be saleable, but the interest is fixed at a lower rate. If the current market rate of return was 10%, a 3% stock would be worth £30. £3 per annum on an outlay of £30 is a 10% return.

Some stocks however are "dated"; that is, they will be repaid at "par" (100) at a stated date in the future. The nearer the date, the higher the price. Capital gains on certain government stocks are free of capital gains tax.[37] This and other factors contribute to the price.

A debenture is an acknowledgement of indebtedness by a company, supported in practice by a charge upon the undertaking and assets of a company. This is a floating, as opposed to a fixed, charge: the company is free to deal with any of its specific assets unaffected by the charge. The charge crystallises when the debenture holders take the necessary steps to enforce their security. The value of a debenture is dependent partly upon the ability of the assets and undertaking of the company to provide sufficient security for the loan, and it is therefore to some extent dependent upon the commercial stability of the company.

Preference shares are shares in a company which have a preference in relation to the payment of a fixed rate of dividend, and may have other preferential rights as well. Being dependent upon the earning by the company of sufficient profits to pay the dividends, they are less secure than government securities (gilts) or debentures, and consequently they normally carry a higher return. That does not mean that the rate of dividend rises. It is the price at which the shares can be purchased on the market which varies. If 5% preference shares, paying £5 per annum on their par value, were priced at 50, the dividend of £5 per annum on an outlay of £50 would put the shares on a return of 10%.

---

[36] cf. Law Com. No. 315, *Capital and Income in Trusts: Classification and Apportionment* (2009), para.2.69.
[37] Taxation of Chargeable Gains Act 1992 s.115; above, para.10–004.

ii. Equities.

(a) Ordinary Shares.   A company must provide a statement of its capital and **19–008**
initial shareholdings when applying for registration.[38] Shares are divided into
classes and normally include ordinary shares. Ownership of an ordinary share
entitles the purchaser to vote at the general meeting, to participate in dividends
when declared on the ordinary shares, and to participate in a winding up.

The Annual General Meeting will declare the dividend payable for the year, if
any. The value of ordinary shares varies with the fortunes of the company. They
necessarily contain an element of speculation, and it is for this reason that
ordinary shares were not authorised investments for trustees until 1961.

(b) Unit Trusts and Investment Trusts.[39]   The selection of ordinary shares for **19–009**
investment is a highly specialised matter. Further, it is important that the
investment of a trust should be spread over a wide range of companies. But a
small trust cannot provide a satisfactory spread by itself. This can be achieved by
participating in an investment fund which is managed by investment experts. Two
basic types are relevant. First the unit trust, in which the managers receive money
from investors, and form a single fund, divided up into units which are owned by
the investors. The investors have the advantage of investment expertise, and of
the spread of investments. Units in a trust can be bought and sold. Secondly, the
(misleadingly named) "investment trust". This is a limited company in which
shares can be bought and sold like other shares. The company buys shares in
other companies, and the investors receive their return in the form of dividends
from the investment trust.

C.   Express Powers of Investment

The starting point when considering the trustee's powers of investment should **19–010**
always be the trust document. A trustee may be given wide power by the trust
instrument to select investments; or her selection may be left to investments
authorised by the general law. Express clauses at one time were strictly construed,
reflecting the court's fear of investment in ordinary shares in the 19th century.
Thus it seemed to be established that words such as a "power to invest in such
securities as they might think fit"[40] gave power merely to select among securities
then authorised for trustee investment. This had changed by the time of *Re
Harari's Settlement Trusts*,[41] where the words "in or upon such investments as to
them may seem fit" permitted the trustees to invest in equities.

---

[38] Companies Act 2006 s.9 (the 2006 Act was amended by the Small Business, Enterprise and
Employment Act 2015 and now also requires a statement of initial significant control. The provisions
of the 2015 Act came into force from 30 June 2016).
[39] See A. Harris (1995) 92/09 L.S.Gaz. p.18.
[40] *Re Braithwaite* (1882) 21 Ch.D. 121; *Re Maryon-Wilson's Estate* [1912] 1 Ch. 55.
[41] [1949] 1 All E.R. 430.

It remains the usual practice to include a clause giving trustees wide powers of investment even though the Trustee Act 2000 greatly extended the range of investment powers; and the trustees, or other persons, may be given authority to amend the power.[42]

D.   The Purchase of Land

19–011   At common law, trustees could not purchase land unless the trust instrument so provided. Even where the instrument did authorise investment in land, we saw that the purchase of a house for the occupation of a beneficiary was not an "investment".[43] Indeed, the High Court of Australia has pointed to a "general proposition" that "it is the duty of the trustee to render the land productive", for example by leasing it.[44] A statutory power to purchase land was first given to trustees of land by the Trusts of Land and Appointment of Trustees Act 1996.[45] The power has since been widened and extended to trustees in general by the Trustee Act 2000 s.8 (although of course where the power is exercised, the trust would then become a trust of land and the 1996 Act would apply). Subject to any restriction or exclusion in the trust instrument,[46] trustees may acquire freehold or leasehold land in the UK:

(a)   as an investment, or

(b)   for occupation by a beneficiary, or

(c)   for any other reason.[47]

There is no restriction as to the length of any lease which may be acquired. Trustees who acquire land under this provision have all the powers of an absolute owner in relation to the land for the purpose of exercising their functions as trustees.[48] The statutory duty of care applies to trustees in the exercise of their powers under the Act in relation to land and also to the exercise of express powers relating to land.[49] Land outside the UK is excluded from the statutory power because such a purchase could create problems in a jurisdiction which does not recognise trusts. Trustees may, however, be given express power to purchase such land.

Trustees' power to invest in a mortgage of land is dealt with below.[50]

---

[42] [1949] 1 All E.R. 430 at 434.

[43] *Re Power* [1947] Ch. 572, above, para.19–005.

[44] *Byrnes v Kendle* [2011] HCA 26 per Gummow and Hayne JJ at [67].

[45] s.6(3).

[46] An example of a case involving such an exclusion of the power to acquire land is *Alexander v Alexander* [2011] EWHC 2721 (Ch).

[47] Trustee Act 2000 s.8. Only the acquisition of a legal estate in the land is permitted. The provision does not apply to settled land; s.10.

[48] Trustee Act 2000 s.8(3).

[49] Trustee Act 2000 Sch.1 para.2.

[50] Below, para.19–014.

E.   Authorised Investments

i.   Historical Rule.   The rules on investment by trustees have been governed   **19–012**
by the principles, first that trustees must avoid all risk to the capital of the fund,
and secondly, that the value of the pound will remain stable. Throughout the 19th
century, the system worked well enough. At first, trustees were restricted to
consols,[51] and were subsequently permitted to choose among a narrow range of
fixed interest investments, known as trustee securities. Investment was not then a
technical or specialised matter. The income beneficiaries were assured of an
income, and the capital was secure. But progressive inflation changed all that.

Much of the problem of the decline of the value of the currency should be
solved by investment in equities. A purchaser of a share in a company owns a
share of the operation. If the business prospers, its actual value may increase.
Assume, however, that the actual value of the business remains the same; if the
value of money is reduced to one-third, the value of the shares will treble,
providing "a hedge against inflation".

But in times of recession, the prices of ordinary shares fall even faster than
those of gilts. Prices on investment exchanges are established by buyers and
sellers, and a number of irrational factors play their part in establishing and
undermining confidence. The overall prices of shares are gauged by an index
called the *Financial Times Index*.[52] The fluctuations in prices underline the
dangers involved in investment in ordinary shares, and emphasise the need for
expertise in selecting investments; and the avoidance of speculation.

ii.   Trustee Investments Act 1961.   Authorised investments were extended by   **19–013**
the Trustee Investments Act 1961. The object of the Act was to permit trustees to
invest a proportion of trust funds in equities. The original permitted proportion
was one-half, but the Treasury increased this to three-quarters, pending a more
fundamental reform of trustee investments.[53]

The Act of 1961 had long been criticised as outdated, and it was invariably
side-stepped in any well-drawn trust by the provision of wider powers.
Nevertheless, the Act remained an obstacle in cases such as trusts arising on
intestacy or under home-made wills. The criticisms were broadly twofold. First,
the Act had not kept pace with the developments in the world of investments and
thus did not permit trustees to utilise many advantageous investments. Secondly,
its machinery was cumbersome as a result of the requirement of division of the
fund before any investment in equities could be made.

iii.   Trustee Act 2000.   The expansion of investment powers was one of the   **19–014**
major purposes of the Trustee Act 2000. This legislation substantially widened
investment powers so that trust income could be maximised without eroding the
capital. The beneficiaries remain protected by the requirement of professional
advice, the financial services legislation and the general law on investment duties.

---

[51] Fixed interest Government securities without redemption date.

[52] This is now the FT30-share index. There is also the broader-based, younger but more famous,
FTSE 100 Index. See also the Dow Jones (USA), Hang Seng (Hong Kong) and Nikkei (Japan).

[53] Trustee Investments (Division of Trust Fund) Order (SI 1996/845).

The major reform of the Act was to broaden significantly the investment powers of trustees, but to subject trustees to a series of duties when exercising those powers.

Before examining the investment provisions of the Act in detail, mention should be made of the modern "portfolio theory", whereby trustees' investment decisions must be evaluated not in relation to individual assets in isolation but in the context of the trust portfolio as a whole and as part of an overall investment strategy.[54] This theory has been approved by the Law Commission.[55] Although not expressly dealt with in the Act of 2000, it may now be regarded as part of the general law.[56]

Section 3 of the Trustees Act 2000 provides that, subject to the other provisions of Pt II of the Act, "a trustee may make any kind of investment that he could make if he were absolutely entitled to the assets of the trust". This is called "the general power of investment", and it applies to trusts whenever created.[57] The general power is additional to any express powers, but may be restricted or excluded by the trust instrument or by other legislation.[58] For example, a settlor may wish to exclude investments he does not consider ethical.[59] The general power does not apply to trustees of pension funds or authorised unit trusts, nor to trustees managing common investment or common deposit schemes under the Charities Act 2011.[60] Trustees in these categories are subject to their own statutory regimes.

Trustees' powers to acquire land have already been dealt with.[61] So far as mortgages are concerned, the limited powers contained in the Trustee Act 1925 and the Trustee Investments Act 1961 were replaced by a power to invest by way of a loan secured on land.[62] It appears from the general power to acquire land contained in s.8, which is confined to legal estates, that any secured loan must take effect by way of a legal mortgage, as under the previous law, although the point is unclear. While the power to acquire *land* is restricted to land in the UK,[63] there is no geographical limit on other investments.

---

[54] See Lord Nicholls (1995) T.L.I. 71; E. Ford (1996) 10 T.L.I. 102; I. Legair (2000) 14 T.L.I. 75; R. Thornton (2008) 67 C.L.J. 396 at 399–401. *Daniel v Tee* [2016] EWHC 1538 (Ch); [2016] 4 W.L.R. 115.

[55] Law Com. No. 260, *Trustees' Powers and Duties* (1999), p.23. It was also adopted in a Treasury consultation paper; *Investment Powers of Trustees* (May 1996), paras 35(ii), 40(iii).

[56] See Law Com. No. 315, *Capital and Income in Trusts: Classification and Apportionment* (2009), para.3.7: "The Trustee Act 2000 enables but does not require trustees to follow modern portfolio theory."

[57] Trustee Act 2000 s.7; s.4(3)(b) also recognises the "need for diversification of investments of the trust" as one of the "standard investment criteria": below, para.19–015. The Act of 1961 was substantially, although not entirely, repealed by the 2000 Act.

[58] Trustee Act 2000 s.6. No provision in a trust instrument made before 3 August 1961 is to be treated as a restriction or exclusion; s.7(2).

[59] Below, paras 19–019—19–020.

[60] Trustee Act 2000 ss.36–38.

[61] Above, para.19–011.

[62] Trustee Act 2000 s.3(3), (4).

[63] Trustee Act 2000 s.8(1).

F. Duties Relating to the Standard Investment Criteria

Section 4 of the Trustee Act 2000 imposes two duties on trustees when exercising **19–015** a power of investment (whether arising under the Act or from another source). Section 4(1) provides that trustees must have regard to the standard investment criteria when exercising any statutory or express power of investment. Second, trustees have a duty of periodic review of any investments: they must "from time to time review the investments of the trust and consider whether, having regard to the standard investment criteria, they should be varied". The standard investment criteria are listed in s.4(3):

"(a) the suitability to the trust of investments of the same kind as any particular investment proposed to be made or retained and of that particular investment as an investment of that kind, and (b) the need for diversification of investments of the trust, in so far as is appropriate to the circumstances of the trust".

These criteria are based on similar provisions in the Trustee Investments Act 1961 and, in conjunction with the duty to review, are consistent with the "portfolio theory" discussed above.[64] Diversification is particularly important with large funds.[65] The duty to consider the need for it arises in relation to investments held at the creation of the trust as well as to investments acquired later.[66] Thus trustees of a will trust were in breach of their duty to review investments where they decided to retain and refurbish a valuable but dilapidated property for six years without seeking professional advice, which would have been to sell it straight away in its unrepaired state.[67]

A small fund may achieve diversification by investing in unit trusts or shares in an investment trust company.[68] It is important to note that the standard investment criteria are not duties in themselves: the duties are contained in ss.4(1) and 4(2), and require regard to be had to the criteria. There is no "duty to diversify".[69]

The operation of s.4 is (by s.4(4)) subject to special provisions relating to social investment by charities, following the Charities (Protection and Social Investment) Act 2016.[70]

---

[64] Above, para.19–014.

[65] *Cowan v Scargill* [1985] Ch. 270; *Nestlé v National Westminster Bank Plc* [1993] 1 W.L.R. 1260.

[66] *Gregson v HAE Trustees Ltd* [2009] Bus. L.R. 1640.

[67] *Jeffery v Gretton* [2011] W.T.L.R. 809. However, the breach caused no loss to the trust; below, para.24–016.

[68] Above, para.19–009.

[69] *Gregson v HAE Trustees Ltd* [2009] Bus. L.R. 1640 per Robert Miles QC sitting as a deputy High Court judge at [90]; O. Court [2008] P.C.B. 298

[70] Below, para.19–021. The Charities (Protection and Social Investment) Act 2016 s.15(3) inserted s.4(4) into s.4 of the Trustee Act 2000: "This section has effect subject to section 292C(6) of the Charities Act 2011 (which disapplies the duties under this section in cases where they would otherwise apply in relation to a social investment within the meaning of Part 14A of that Act)."

G. Proper Advice

19–016 Section 5(1) of the Trustee Act 2000, following similar provisions in the previous legislation, requires trustees to obtain and consider proper advice about the way in which, having again regard to the standard investment criteria, the power of investment (whether express or statutory) should be exercised. Similarly, under s.5(2), when reviewing the investments, the trustees must obtain and consider proper advice as to whether the investments should be varied. It will be apparent that these provisions mirror the duties under s.4.

"Proper advice" is the advice of a person who is reasonably believed by the trustees to be qualified to give it by his ability in and practical experience of financial and other matters relating to the proposed investment.[71] The advice need not be written. By way of exception, trustees need not obtain such advice if they reasonably conclude that, in all the circumstances, it is unnecessary or inappropriate to do so.[72] An example may be when they propose to make a small and secure investment.

The trustees must, of course, consider the advice and then make their own decision.[73] They must not repose blind faith in the adviser. They may, however, delegate investment decisions, as discussed below. In the case of a trust corporation, there seems no reason why the advice should not be that of a competent officer, as under the previous law.

Although the provisions of the Act apply to trustees, it has been held by the Court of Protection that those with lasting powers of attorney should also follow the provisions relating to the standard investment criteria and the requirement to obtain and consider proper advice.[74]

Like s.4, s.5 has also been amended in respect of its application to charities by subsequent legislation, considered below.[75]

H. Duty of Care

19–017 Prior to the Trustee Act 2000, the standard of conduct required of a trustee was that of the "prudent man of business".[76] This was reformulated by s.1 of the Trustee Act 2000, which provides that a trustee must exercise such care and skill as is reasonable in all circumstances. As we have seen, what is reasonable will vary according to whether the trustee is a layman or a professional.[77] Neuberger J (as he then was) framed it as follows: "one simply looks at the ultimate action in

---

[71] Persons acting as investment advisers must be authorised under Financial Services and Markets Act 2000 s.19.

[72] Trustee Act 2000 s.5(3).

[73] *Shaw v Cates* [1909] 1 Ch. 389; *Martin v City of Edinburgh DC* [1988] S.L.T. 329; *Jones v AMP Perpetual Trustee Company NZ Ltd* [1994] 1 N.Z.L.R. 690.

[74] *Re Buckley* [2013] EWHC 2965 (COP), Judge Denzil Lush at [41].

[75] Below, para.19–021. The Trustee Act 2000 s.5(5) now provides that "This section has effect subject to section 292C(6) of the Charities Act 2011 (which disapplies the duties under this section in cases where they would otherwise apply in relation to a social investment within the meaning of Part 14A of that Act)".

[76] *Speight v Gaunt* (1883) 9 App. Cas. 1.

[77] Above, para.18–003.

relation to the shares ... and asks oneself whether or not that was something which a trustee, complying with the test laid down by Lord Watson [in *Learoyd v Whiteley*],[78] could reasonably have done."[79]

The duty of care applies to trustees in the exercise of statutory or express powers of investment, including their duty to have regard to the standard investment criteria and to obtain and consider proper advice.[80]

> In *Daniel v Tee*,[81] the claimant beneficiaries brought a claim for compensation for breach of trust arising from investments made by the defendants, professional solicitor trustees, from 2000 to 2002.[82] During this period, the defendants relied on advice by a particular firm: it was a time of particular market volatility in the technology sectors, in which the trust had invested. The claimants alleged that the defendants had failed in their duty to formulate an investment strategy and to review the investments. The court considered the extent to which such trustees, without personal experience or expertise in managing investments, could rely on independent financial advice which had turned out not to be correct. Richard Spearman QC, sitting as deputy judge of the High Court, held that some breaches of duty were established (applying the "no reasonable trustee" test), because the trustees had invested too heavily in equities. However, he held that the claimants had failed to show that the breaches had caused losses, because the trustees would likely have pursued similar investment strategies even had they discharged their duties.[83]

There had been a dearth of authority on the issues prior to *Daniel*,[84] and the judgment illustrates the challenges facing beneficiaries, outside of the most egregious examples, in establishing not only a breach of duty in such a case but also the extent of any losses (the latter is considered further below in Ch.24).

The duty also applies in relation to their power to acquire land.[85] So, for example, trustees may be in breach of duty if they invest by way of a secured loan which equals the value of the property, leaving no margin for depreciation, even though the former restrictions on the amount of the loan have gone. As will be seen in the following section, trustees may delegate investment decisions and may appoint nominees and custodians to hold the trust investments. The duty of care applies also to the exercise of these powers.[86]

I.   Delegation of Investment Powers

We have seen that investment normally needs expert advice. Trustees may wish to go further and delegate their investment powers to a professional such as an investment manager authorised under the financial services legislation. As this   **19–018**

---

[78] (1887) 12 App.Cas. 727
[79] *Wight v Olswang (No.2)* [2000] Lloyd's Rep. PN 662 at 665–666.
[80] Trustee Act 2000 Sch.1 para.1.
[81] [2016] EWHC 1538 (Ch); [2016] 4 W.L.R. 115.
[82] The claimants therefore relied on both the trustee's equitable duty and the statutory duty of care for the period after the Trustee Act 2000 came into force on 1 February 2001.
[83] [2016] EWHC 1538 (Ch) at [167] and [169].
[84] Richard Spearman QC recorded ([2016] EWHC 1538 (Ch) at [51]) that "counsel were unable to refer me to any decided case in which the claimants have proved loss flowing from an imprudent exercise of a trustee's power of investment" (relying on Lewin, 19th edn (2015), para.39–054) or on the extent to which trustees may rely on independent financial advice (at [58]).
[85] Trustee Act 2000 para.2.
[86] Trustee Act 2000 para.3.

involves the delegation of a discretion, it could not be done prior to the Trustee Act 2000 unless permitted by the trust instrument. An exception existed in the case of pension trustees,[87] but other trustees (in the absence of an express power) needed to apply to court for an extension of investment powers.[88] Alternatively, they could delegate by power of attorney under s.25 of the Trustees Act 1925.

Reform of this area was one of the major purposes of the Trustee Act 2000. Again, the Act adopts a framework of broadening the powers of trustees but then subjecting the trustees to a series of duties in respect of the exercise of those powers. Section 11 lists functions which may *not* be delegated, investment powers being omitted from the list. Where investment powers are delegated, the agent must satisfy the requirements relating to the standard investment criteria and the duty to review the investments from time to time.[89] She does not, however, need to obtain advice if she is the kind of person from whom the trustees could properly have obtained advice.[90] The delegation of asset management functions[91] must be done by an agreement in writing or evidenced in writing.[92] Further, the trustees must prepare a "policy statement" giving guidance as to how these functions should be exercised in the best interests of the trust, and the agent must agree to comply with it.[93]

Section 16 of the Trustee Act 2000 confers on trustees the power to appoint a nominee (save in regard to settled land) and to vest the trust property in question in the nominee. Section 17 permits the appointment of a custodian, to undertake safe custody of the assets in question or of any documents or records concerning them. Neither power applies to a trust which has a custodian trustee.[94] There are various restrictions as to who may be appointed as a nominee or custodian.[95] Normally the agent will be a person who carries on a business including acting as a nominee or custodian. The trustees may appoint one of their number if that one is a trust corporation, or may appoint two (or more) of their number if they are to act as joint nominees or joint custodians.[96] Charity trustees must act in accordance with guidance given by the Charity Commission concerning the selection of a nominee or custodian.[97]

The trustees may pay the nominee or custodian from the trust fund, and, if reasonably necessary, may appoint him on terms which permit him to appoint a substitute, restricting his liability, or permitting him to act in circumstances

---

[87] Pensions Act 1995 s.34. Thus the powers in the Trustee Act 2000 do not apply to pension trusts.

[88] See *Anker-Petersen v Anker-Petersen* (1998) 12 T.L.I. 166 (decided 1991).

[89] Trustee Act 2000 s.13(1).

[90] Trustee Act 2000 s.13(2).

[91] These are investment, the acquisition of property, the management of trust property and disposing of the property or of interests in it; s.15(5).

[92] Trustee Act 2000 s.15. In *Daniel v Tee* [2016] EWHC 1538 (Ch); [2016] 4 W.L.R. 115 (above, para.19–017), the deputy judge considered but rejected (at [189]–[198]) a claim in respect of impermissible delegation.

[93] Trustee Act 2000 s.15. This may refer to liquidity, the balance between capital and income, or ethical considerations.

[94] Trustee Act 2000 ss.16(3), 17(4). Nor do they apply to assets vested in the official custodian for charities. For bearer securities, see s.18.

[95] Trustee Act 2000 s.19.

[96] The trustee(s) so appointed must satisfy the conditions laid down in s.19, e.g. that he or they carry on a business including acting as a nominee or custodian.

[97] Current guidance may be found in the publication CC42 (February 2001).

capable of giving rise to a conflict of interest.[98] This reflects the fact that persons acting as nominees or custodians may in practice insist on the inclusion of such terms.

Unless the trust instrument provides otherwise, trustees who delegate to investment managers, nominees or custodians must keep the arrangements under review, including the review of any policy statement.[99] Trustees are not liable for the default of such agents unless they have failed to comply with the statutory duty of care when making the appointment or reviewing the arrangements.[100] The duty of care applies to the exercise of statutory or express powers to appoint agents, nominees or custodians. It applies in particular to the selection of the person who is to act, the terms upon which he is to act, and the preparation of a policy statement where asset management functions are delegated.[101] If, however, the trustees fail to act within their statutory powers of delegation, the appointment of the agent, nominee or custodian is not thereby invalidated.[102]

As in the case of other powers conferred by the Trustee Act 2000, the power to delegate to investment managers, nominees and custodians applies to trusts whenever created, but is subject to any restriction or exclusion in the trust instrument or other legislation.[103] Further details of the general power of delegation will be found in Ch.21.

J. General Duty in Choosing Investments; Ethical Investments

We have seen that the Trustee Act 2000 provides a framework for the exercise of trustee investment powers. The traditional standard of the "prudent man of business"[104] has been reformulated by s.1 of the Act as a duty to exercise such care and skill as is reasonable in the circumstances. No doubt it remains true that trustees must avoid investments "which are attended with hazard".[105] Although a trustee now has statutory power to "make any kind of investment that he could make if he were absolutely entitled to the assets of the trust",[106] the fact that he is *not* absolutely entitled places him in a different position from an absolute owner, who may speculate as he pleases. He must also consider the competing interests of the life tenant and the remainderman, investing so as to provide a reasonable income, and to keep secure the capital.[107] We have seen that the modern

19–019

---

[98] Trustee Act 2000 s.20.
[99] Trustee Act 2000 ss.21, 22.
[100] Trustee Act 2000 s.23. See s.23(2) for liability for substitute agents.
[101] Trustee Act 2000 Sch.1 para.3.
[102] Trustee Act 2000 s.24.
[103] Trustee Act 2000 ss.26, 27.
[104] *Speight v Gaunt* (1883) 9 App.Cas. 1; cf. *Nestlé v National Westminster Bank Plc* [1993] 1 W.L.R. 1260 (standard of prudence regarded as "undemanding" and likely to result in complacency and inactivity). See generally P. Pearce and A. Samuels [1983] Conv. 127.
[105] *Learoyd v Whiteley* (1887) 12 App.Cas. 727 at 733.
[106] Trustee Act 2000 s.3.
[107] Below, Ch.20. *Re Mulligan (Deceased)* [1998] 1 NZLR 481.

"portfolio theory"[108] requires the investment decisions of trustees to be made and evaluated in the context of the portfolio as a whole rather than in relation to individual assets.

These general investment duties were reviewed in *Nestlé v National Westminster Bank Plc*,[109] where the remainder beneficiary complained that the fund of £270,000 would have been worth over £1 million if properly invested. The claim failed because, although the trustees had failed to appreciate the scope of their investment power and to conduct regular reviews, the beneficiary had not proved that these failures had resulted in wrong investment decisions and resulting loss. Although the investments fell "woefully short" of maintaining the real value of the fund, failure to maintain the value was not in itself a breach of trust, as to do so would require extraordinary skill and luck, and would at times be impossible.[110] Investments may go down as well as up, after all. Further, the trustees were entitled and bound to consider tax implications, which justified investment in government stock rather than equities where the life tenant was non-resident. In the absence of such special factors, however, it was accepted that trustees should invest at least half of the fund in equities. If the case had arisen after the Trustee Act 2000, no doubt the trustees would have been held to be in breach of the statutory duty of care, but the issue of establishing loss would remain. A trustee who commits a mere error of judgment is unlikely to be held in breach of the duty of care.[111]

The question whether trustees may adopt non-financial investment criteria arose in *Cowan v Scargill*.[112]

> A mineworkers' pension fund with large assets and very wide powers of investment was managed by 10 trustees, of whom five, including the defendant, were appointed by the National Union of Mineworkers. They were assisted in investment decisions by an advisory panel of experts. An investment plan was submitted, which the union trustees, on the basis of union policy, refused to accept unless it was amended so that there should be no increase in overseas investments; those already made should be withdrawn; and there should be no investment in energies in competition with coal. Sir Robert Megarry VC held that the trustees would be in breach of duty if they refused to adopt the investment strategy. They must exercise their powers in the best interests of present and future beneficiaries. If the purpose of the trust was the provision of financial benefit, the best interests of the beneficiaries normally meant their best *financial* interests.[113] This duty to the beneficiaries was paramount. The trustees must exercise their investment powers so as to yield the best return, putting aside personal interests and social and political views. If investments in, for example, armaments or tobacco, were beneficial, they must not refrain because of their own views, however sincere. But financial benefit was not *inevitably* paramount. If all the beneficiaries were adults with strict

---

[108] Above, para.19–014. This is reflected in Pensions Act 1995 s.35; above, para.17–016.

[109] [1993] 1 W.L.R. 1260; J. Martin (1992) 142 N.L.J. 1279; A. Kenny [1993] Conv. 63; G. Watt and M. Stauch [1998] Conv. 352. See also Law Com. No. 315, *Capital and Income in Trusts, Classification and Apportionment* (2009), para.5.25.

[110] See *Jones v AMP Perpetual Trustee Company NZ Ltd* [1994] 1 N.Z.L.R. 690 (trustee is neither insurer nor guarantor of fund).

[111] See *Jones v AMP Perpetual Trustee Company NZ Ltd* [1994] 1 N.Z.L.R. 690 (not liable for mere error of judgment in retaining shares in a falling market).

[112] [1985] Ch. 270; P. Clarke [1984] All E.R. Rev. 306. See also Uniform Prudent Investor Act 1994 s.5 (USA), requiring investment solely in the interest of the beneficiaries; J. Langbein in D. Hayton (ed.), *Modern International Developments in Trust Law* (Kluwer Law International, 1999), Ch.11.

[113] [1985] Ch. 270 at 287.

views on, say, tobacco, it might not "benefit" them to make such investments.[114] Here, however, there was no justification for reducing the benefit because the trustees had an investment policy intended to assist the union or the industry. The trustees were pursuing union policy, and the ultimate sanction was removal.[115]

There are other ways of viewing *Cowan* and the outcome may have been different **19–020** if the union trustees had not argued their case on ideology rather than law.[116] Would the trustees be failing in their duties if they confined themselves to the investments proposed by the union trustees? In the case of a pension fund, maintenance of the prosperity of the industry might be thought to be in the financial interests of the beneficiaries, and to invest in a competing industry may be harmful.[117] Overseas investments may be risky, and there is an ample range of authorised investments at home: "no trust fund is so big as to exhaust the home market."[118]

Presumably there would be no breach if trustees were to pursue an ethical investment policy only after satisfying themselves that their selected investments were at least as financially sound as those rejected on ethical grounds (a "socially sensitive" policy).[119] The point is that they must not fetter their discretion by adopting a blinkered policy which excludes any consideration of the financial merits of a particular class of investments. Thus in *Martin v City of Edinburgh DC*,[120] the Scottish court granted a declaration that a policy to oppose apartheid by disinvesting in companies which had South African interests was a breach of duty, even though no loss was incurred. The trustees (the local authority) had failed to consider whether their policy was in the best financial interests of the beneficiaries. These principles should be adhered to whether the trustees have a negative investment policy (to avoid certain types of investments) or, less commonly, a positive investment policy (to make only certain types of investments). They must remember that their duty is the provision of financial benefits, "not the reform of the world".[121]

This approach has been supported in subsequent cases. Asplin J has more recently concluded that the appropriate approach is a reflexive one in the context: "the purpose of the trust defines what the best interests are and that they are

---

[114] [1985] Ch. 270 at 288.

[115] Damages would not be recoverable unless the policy was implemented and caused loss, which is unlikely.

[116] J. Farrar and J. Maxton (1986) 102 L.Q.R. 32. See also J. Langbein and R. Posner (1980) 79 Mich. L.Rev. 72.

[117] This argument was rejected by Megarry VC on the facts. The miners' pension fund was fully funded and unusual in that its value at that time far exceeded that of the declining coal industry, and there were many more pensioners than miners.

[118] P. Pearce and A. Samuels [1985] Conv. 52 at 53. Overseas investments are permitted by the Trustee Act 2000, with the exception of the purchase of land in foreign jurisdictions: s.8(1).

[119] See generally P. Docking and I. Pittaway (1990) 4 *Trust Law & Practice* 25; N. Convey (1990) 87/23 L.S.Gaz. 17; R. Ellison (1991) 5 T.L.I. 157; L. Irish and A. Kent (1994) 8 T.L.I. 10; Lord Nicholls (1995) 9 T.L.I. 71; P. Watchman, J. Anstee-Wedderburn and L. Shipway (2005) 19 T.L.I. 127 at 134; R. Thornton (2008) 67 C.L.J. 396.

[120] [1988] S.L.T. 329.

[121] (1991) 5 T.L.I. 157 at 165–166; *Harries v Church Commissioners for England* [1992] 1 W.L.R. 1241 (trustees must not make moral statements at the expense of the trust).

opposite sides of the same coin".[122] The "best interests" duty has been viewed as foundational and operating in combination with other duties of the trustee by Murphy J in a valuable recent judgment in the Federal Court of Australia (albeit in a particular statutory context).[123]

A settlor may secure ethical investments by providing in the instrument that the trustees must or must not make certain kinds of investments.[124] Where the trustees have delegated their investment powers, any such direction by the settlor will be reflected in the policy statement which they must prepare for the agent.[125] Where the trust instrument is silent on the matter, trustees may include ethical considerations in the policy statement, subject to their general law duties discussed above. The guidance in the policy statement must be formulated "with a view to ensuring that the functions will be exercised in the best interests of the trust",[126] and the statutory duty of care applies to its preparation.[127]

The investment policy of pension trustees must now be explicit as to the extent (if any) of ethical considerations.[128] Sir Ross Cranston, sitting as a Judge of the High Court, has recently considered the issues in respect of guidance for the investment strategy for the local government pension scheme.[129] It is acceptable to seek to impose "a base-line of risk and [to take] into account the role the legislative design gives local government pension scheme members through local pension boards and otherwise".[130] He concluded, however, that it is not permissible to single out certain non-financial factors or ethical considerations over others without justification.[131]

19–021   **i.   Charities.**   Different considerations apply to charities in this context, both as a matter of common law and (now) statute. In the case of a charity, an additional factor is that the trust is pursuing an aim, so that the question arises whether the trustees can invest in undertakings which are incompatible with their objective. For example, can trustees of a cancer charity invest in the tobacco industry?[132] As we have seen, trustees (including charity trustees) must have

---

[122] *Re Merchant Navy Ratings Pension Fund* [2015] EWHC 448 (Ch) at [229]. See M. Smith (2015) 29 T.L.I. 161; and D. Pollard (2016) 30 T.L.I. 71 and (2016) 30 T.L.I. 159.

[123] *Australian Securities and Investments Commission v Australian Property Custodian Holdings Ltd (Receivers and Managers Appointed) (In Liquidation) (Controllers Appointed) (No.3)* [2013] FCA 1342 at [464]–[484].

[124] Trustee Act 2000 s.6(1)(b); *Harries v Church Commissioners for England* [1992] 1 W.L.R. 1241.

[125] Trustee Act 2000 s.15(2).

[126] Trustee Act 2000 s.15(3).

[127] Trustee Act 2000 Sch.1 para.3.

[128] Pensions Act 1995 s.35. The investment provisions of the 1995 Act remain in force although much of the rest of the Act was repealed by Pensions Act 2004.

[129] *R. (on the application of Palestine Solidarity Campaign Ltd, Jacqueline Lewis) v Secretary of State for Communities and Local Government* [2017] EWHC 1502 (Admin).

[130] [2017] EWHC 1502 (Admin) at [31].

[131] [2017] EWHC 1502 (Admin) at [32] (in this case, the guidance sought to rule out pursuing boycotts, divestment and sanctions against foreign nations and UK defence industries, even where there was no significant financial risk involved).

[132] See BMA Report on Investment in the UK Tobacco Industry; H. Beynon (1982) 45 M.L.R. 268; J. Thurston (1987) 1 *Trust Law & Practice* 162; Annual Report of the Charity Commissioners 1987, paras 41–45; Annual Report 1996, paras 54–55 (pooled funds set up to exclude incompatible

regard to "the suitability to the trust of investments of the same kind as any particular investment proposed to be made or retained".[133]

> In *Harries v Church Commissioners for England*,[134] the claim was that the Commissioners, whose purpose was to promote the Christian faith through the Church of England, should not invest in a manner incompatible with that purpose even if this involved a risk of significant financial detriment. It was held that they could take non-financial ethical considerations into account only in so far as they could do so without jeopardising the profitability of investments. Their charitable purpose would be best served by seeking the maximum financial return. There might be rare cases where certain investments would directly conflict with the objects of the charity (as in the cancer/tobacco example).[135] In these cases the trustees should not make such investments even if this results in financial detriment, but this was unlikely to arise because of the width of other investments. There might also be rare cases where a particular investment might alienate potential donors or recipients.[136] The Commissioners already had a policy which excluded investment in armaments, gambling, tobacco, newspapers and South Africa, considering that there was an adequate width of alternative investments, and the propriety of this was not doubted.[137] The existing policy excluded around 13% of listed UK companies; the proposed policy which the plaintiffs sought would have excluded a further 24%. To exclude 37% would unduly restrict the Commissioners' ability to invest.

The Law Commission has in recent years undertaken projects on "Charity Law", beginning with its Eleventh Programme of Law Reform. The first phase of this considered Social Investment by Charities, and its recommendations were published in 2014, arguing for the introduction of various statutory powers and duties relating to social investment.[138] The Commission took the view that under the previous law:

> "charity trustees are not under a duty to seek the best financial return from social investments, but may consider the overall return, comprising both the financial return and the furtherance of the charity's purposes (which we call 'mission benefit')."[139]

The Law Commission thus sought to target a "misconception" that charity trustees must seek to maximise financial returns when making social investments,[140] by introducing a list of factors which may be taken into account by charity trustees.[141]

The Commission's proposals on this point became the Charities (Protection and Social Investment) Act 2016 s.15. This section introduces a new Part 14A

---

investments). Charity Commission guidance is given in publication CC14 (revised 2011). See also *Legal underpinning: Charities and Investment Matters)* (Charity Commission, 2011).

[133] Trustee Act 2000 s.4(3)(a).

[134] [1992] 1 W.L.R. 1241; R. Nobles [1992] Conv. 115; P. Luxton (1992) 55 M.L.R. 587; Lord Browne-Wilkinson (1992) 6 T.L.I. 119 at 123.

[135] [1992] 1 W.L.R. 1241 per Sir Donald Nicholls VC at 1246.

[136] [1992] 1 W.L.R. 1241 per Sir Donald Nicholls VC at 1247.

[137] The Commissioners appeared to have fettered their discretion, but this seems permissible where the excluded investments conflict with the charity's purpose, even if not directly incompatible.

[138] Law Commission, *Social Investment by Charities: The Law Commission's Recommendations* (September 2014).

[139] Law Commission, *Social Investment by Charities: The Law Commission's Recommendations* (September 2014), para.1.154.

[140] Law Commission, *Social Investment by Charities: The Law Commission's Recommendations* (September 2014), para.140.

[141] Law Commission, *Social Investment by Charities: The Law Commission's Recommendations* (September 2014), para.1.46ff.

("Social Investments) into the Charities Act 2011[142]: the new Part comprises three new sections, and follows a structure of conferring a broad power of investment constrained by associated duties which is similar to (though distinct from) that in the Trustee Act as seen above. Section 292A defines "social investment" as "when a relevant act of a charity[143] is carried out with a view to both (a) directly furthering the charity's purposes; and (b) achieving a financial return for the charity". Section 292B relates to the "general power to make social investments" and declares the following (so far as relevant for present purposes):

(1)   An incorporated charity has, and the charity trustees of an unincorporated charity have, power to make social investments.

(2)   The power conferred by this section may not be used to make a social investment involving—
(a)   the application or use of permanent endowment, or
(b)   taking on a commitment mentioned in section 292A(4)(b) that puts permanent endowment at risk of being applied or used,
unless the charity trustees expect that making the social investment will not contravene any restriction with respect to expenditure that applies to the permanent endowment in question.

(3)   The power conferred by this section—
(a)   may be restricted or excluded by the trusts of the charity;
(b)   is (subject to paragraph (a)) in addition to any other power to make social investments that the charity or charity trustees may have.[144]

Finally, s.292C then imposes duties upon charity trustees in relation to social investments: of considering whether to obtain advice before making a social investment and to obtain if it they consider they should; a duty of periodic review and a duty to consider advice when carrying out the review. The specific provisions are as follows (again so far as relevant):

(2)   The charity trustees of a charity must, before exercising a power to make a social investment—
(a)   consider whether in all the circumstances any advice about the proposed social investment ought to be obtained;
(b)   obtain and consider any advice they conclude ought to be obtained; and
(c)   satisfy themselves that it is in the interests of the charity to make the social investment, having regard to the benefit they expect it to achieve for the charity (by directly furthering the charity's purposes and achieving a financial return).

(3)   The charity trustees of a charity must from time to time review the charity's social investments.

(4)   When carrying out a review the charity trustees must—
(a)   consider whether any advice about the social investments (or any particular social investment) ought to be obtained; and
(b)   obtain and consider any advice they conclude ought to be obtained.

(5)   The duties under this section may not be restricted or excluded by the charity's trusts.

---

[142] As noted above, paras 19–015—19–016, the Charities (Protection and Social Investment) Act 2016 s.15(2)–(4) also makes consequential amendments, Trustee Act 2000 ss.4 and 5.

[143] Relevant act of charity is defined by Charities Act 2011 s.292A(3)–(8), broadly including the application of funds or property, or taking on liabilities putting funds at risk.

[144] s.292B(4) provides that "This section and section 292C do not apply in relation to—(a) charities established by, or whose purposes and functions are set out in, legislation; (b) charities established by Royal Charter; but they apply in relation to all other charities, whether established before or after this section comes into force."

Insofar as there were misconceptions as to the scope of charity trustees' powers and duties, the legislative clarification in this respect is to be welcomed.[145] It may also be observed that the duties imposed are not as onerous as those under the Trustee Act 2000 (there is no general requirement to obtain advice, nor for the advice to be "proper"), but as we have seen in Ch.15, charity trusteeship is already a burdensome office and the reforms in respect of social investment as intended to allow for flexibility. Furthermore, the reforms do not affect the principles above when it comes to making investments with a view solely to increasing the charities' funds, as opposed to investing in furtherance of the charitable aims.[146] The Charity Commission has published revised guidance for trustees in *Charities and Investment Matters*.[147] Section 16 of the 2016 Act provides that the Secretary of State must review the operation of the Act (including s.15) and consider how the Act affects "public confidence in charities, the level of charitable donations and people's willingness to volunteer".[148]

K.   Trustees Holding Controlling Interest in a Company

Difficult questions arise in relation to the trustees' duties where the trust owns a controlling interest in a company.[149] The first question is whether the shareholding is a proper investment at all. If the company is a private company, as is the usual case in this situation, express authorisation was needed prior to the Trustee Act 2000 to purchase such shares. At present, the issue is whether such a purchase satisfies the standard investment criteria laid down in s.4 of the Act.[150] Usually the question is one of retention. A provision expressly authorising retention is desirable (whether the holding is a majority or a minority), but the right to retain will be implied where the trust deed or will specifically refers to the property, as in the case of a specific bequest on trust.[151] A right to retain does not impliedly authorise a right to purchase more of the shares.[152]

19–022

But that is not the end of the matter. It is not sufficient for the trustees to determine that the investment is suitable, and leave it at that. For the company or its directors may engage in practices which are wholly unsuitable for a trust investment, such as speculative activities. Can the trustees shelter behind the directors, whose acts they are in a position to control?

> In *Bartlett v Barclays Bank Trust Co Ltd*,[153] the bank was trustee of the Bartlett trust. The sole asset of the trust was a shareholding amounting to virtually all the shares in a family property company, which held some £500,000 worth of rent-producing properties.
> Tax would need to be paid on the death of the life tenants, and a suggestion was made that cash would be more easily raised if the company went public; and merchant bankers advised

---

[145] N. Lee [2016] P.C.B. 267 at 269.

[146] N. Lee [2016] P.C.B. 267 at 269.

[147] *Charities and investment matters: a guide for trustees* (CC14, updated 1 August 2016).

[148] Charities (Protection and Social Investment) Act 2016 s.16(1)(a)–(c).

[149] A valuable consideration of the issues in this section has recently been offered by M. Yip (2017) 31 T.L.I. 185.

[150] Above, para.19–015.

[151] *Re Pugh* [1887] W.N. 143; *Re Van Straubenzee* [1901] 2 Ch. 779.

[152] [1887] W.N. 143.

[153] [1980] Ch. 515; *Walker v Stones* [2001] Q.B. 902. See Lord Nicholls (1995) 9 T.L.I. 71 at 76.

that a public issue would be more successful if the company were not only a manager of existing property, but a developer of new properties also. The bank agreed to a policy of active development, so long as the income available to the income beneficiaries was not prejudiced.

The board then embarked upon speculative developments, one of which was a disaster, because planning permission for the intended office development could not be obtained. This resulted in a large loss to the trust shareholding.

The Bank was held liable. It was not sufficient that they believed the directors to be competent and capable of running a profitable business. Their duty was "to conduct the business of the trust with the same care as an ordinary prudent man of business would extend to his own affairs."[154] To do that it was necessary, especially as the Bank was aware that the company was moving into speculative development, to get the fullest information on the conduct of the business; and not merely to be content with the supply of information which they received as shareholders. Cross J in *Re Lucking's Will Trusts*[155] held that a controlling shareholder should insist on being represented on the board; but Brightman J treated this as one convenient way of ensuring that all the necessary information was available.[156]

So the controlling shareholder must obtain the necessary information, as a means of "enabling the trustee to safeguard the interests of the beneficiaries."[157] How do the trustees do that? Ultimately, of course, the majority shareholder will get its way; as by adopting "the draconian course of threatening to remove, or actually removing, the board in favour of compliant directors",[158] which is asking a lot of the trust department of a bank. Brightman J was able to avoid the practical difficulties of such a course by finding that the members of the board were "reasonable persons, and would (as I find) have followed any reasonable policy desired by the bank had the bank's wishes been indicated to the board."[159] It is now common for the trust deed to contain a provision relieving the trustees of any duty to involve themselves in the affairs of the company in which they have a majority holding.

---

[154] [1980] Ch. 515 at 531, quoting *Speight v Gaunt* (1883) 9 App.Cas. 1. Now the question would be whether the trustees had complied with the duty of care under Trustee Act 2000 s.1: see *Daniel v Tee* [2016] EWHC 1538 (Ch), above para.19–017. The decision in *Bartlett* was endorsed by Lord Clarke of Stone-cum-Ebony for the Privy Council in *Spread Trustee Co Ltd v Hutcheson* [2011] UKPC 13; [2012] 2 A.C. 194 at [20].

[155] [1968] 1 W.L.R. 866 at 874.

[156] [1980] Ch. 515 at 533. "Other methods may be equally satisfactory and convenient depending upon the circumstances of the individual case. Alternatives which spring to mind are the receipt of copies of the agenda and minutes of board meetings if regularly held, the receipt of monthly management accounts in the case of a trading concern... the possibilities are endless...". See *Re Miller's Trust Deed* (1978) 75 L.S.Gaz. 454, where one of the trustees was a member of a firm of accountants which acted as auditors for the company.

[157] [1980] Ch. 515 at 534.

[158] [1980] Ch. 515 at 530.

[159] [1980] Ch. 515. The Virgin Islands Special Trusts Act 2003 removed this duty in relation to "VISTA trusts."

L. Extension of Investment Powers by the Court

Trustees may apply to court under s.57 of the Trustee Act 1925[160] or under the Variation of Trusts Act 1958[161] to widen investment powers. An application under s.57 is more convenient provided the beneficial interests are not affected.[162] Applications have been rare since the passing of the Trustee Investment Act 1961, the court taking the view (conveniently described as the *Re Kolb* principle[163]), that special circumstances have to be shown to justify an extension beyond the powers conferred by a modern statute. The question arose in *Mason v Farbrother*,[164] concerning a pension fund which had limited investment powers. By 1982, as a result of inflation, the fund had vastly increased, and the trustees wished to have wider powers. They applied to court under s.57 of the Trustee Act 1925.[165] It was held that there was no absolute rule that the court should not widen investment powers after the 1961 Act. The court approved a wide modern clause, as there were special circumstances, which included the effect of inflation and the fact that it was in the nature of a public fund.

19–023

A different approach was subsequently taken by Megarry VC in *Trustees of the British Museum v Attorney General*,[166] where the trustees were granted a relaxation of their existing scheme, made in 1960, as they needed a wider choice and a power to invest abroad. The trustees were eminent and responsible, and had highly skilled advice. The size of the fund (then £5 million–£6 million) made it unlike a private trust and more like a pension fund or large institutional investor. Referring to *Mason v Farbrother*,[167] where the court treated the *Re Kolb*[168] principle as still binding in the absence of special circumstances, Megarry VC disagreed that inflation could be called a special circumstance, and preferred to say that the *Re Kolb* principle had gone, although if the statutory powers were increased, the principle could apply again.

As we have seen, the Trustee Act 2000 revolutionised investment powers, making it unlikely that trustees will have much need to apply to court for extended powers. Should they do so, for example if they should wish to purchase land outside of England and Wales (which the Act of 2000 does not permit), the *Re Kolb* principle would again be relevant. It is more likely that applications to court would now involve attempts to lift specific restrictions and exclusions imposed by the settlor.[169] In such cases the *Re Kolb* principle would not apply, as

---

[160] Below, para.23–007.

[161] Below, para.23–012.

[162] *Anker-Petersen v Anker-Petersen*; (1998) 12 T.L.I. 166 (decided 1991).

[163] *Re Kolb's Will Trusts* [1962] Ch. 531; *Re Cooper's Settlement* [1962] Ch. 826; *Re Clarke's Will Trusts* [1961] 1 W.L.R. 1471.

[164] [1983] 2 All E.R. 1078; H. Norman [1984] Conv. 373.

[165] The application under the 1958 Act did not proceed because of difficulties with the representative parties. The aspect concerning the court's inherent jurisdiction to approve a compromise is dealt with below, para.23–005.

[166] [1984] 1 W.L.R. 418. See also *Steel v Wellcome Custodian Trustees Ltd* [1988] 1 W.L.R. 167; B. Dale [1988] Conv. 380.

[167] [1983] 2 All E.R. 1078.

[168] [1962] Ch. 531.

[169] It is also possible that there may be a desire to modernise or rationalise the powers given to the trustees: see e.g. *Re Portman Estate* [2015] 2 P. & C.R. DG10; below, para.23–007.

the trustees would not be seeking powers beyond those contained in the Trustee Act 2000. The issue for the court would be whether it would be justified in overturning the wishes of the settlor.

3. DUTY TO DISTRIBUTE. SATISFACTION OF CLAIMS

A. Liability for Wrongful Payments

19–024   A trustee is obliged to make payments of income and capital as they become due, and to make them to the persons properly entitled. Failure to do so is a breach of trust, which the trustee must normally make good, such as for example, a payment based on a forged document,[170] or upon an erroneous construction of a document,[171] even if legal advice was taken,[172] or without regard to the entitlement of illegitimate beneficiaries.[173]

Where a trustee makes an overpayment of income or of instalments of capital, the error may be adjusted in later payments.[174] If the payment is to a person who is not entitled, the trustee's right of recovery is governed by the law of restitution, and the money will (subject to defences) be recoverable if the mistake is one of fact or law.[175] An unpaid or underpaid beneficiary may, in addition to his right to sue the trustee, proceed against the property in the hands of the wrongly paid recipient not being a bona fide purchaser for value without notice.[176] A trustee-beneficiary who fails to pay himself in full has been held to have no remedy,[177] but this rule, if absolute, appears somewhat extreme.[178]

B. Doubtful Claims

19–025   **i. Application to Court for Directions.**   Where the trustees are in any doubt in relation to the claims of the beneficiaries, they may make an application to the court for directions; and will be protected if they obey the directions of the court.[179] This course can be taken with a minimum of complication.[180] In this way, problems of construction of the trust instrument and difficulties in administering the trust can be brought before the court, so that the trustees are not forced to take the risk of making decisions upon a false premise.[181] An

---

[170] *Eaves v Hickson* (1861) 30 Beav. 136.
[171] *Hilliard v Fulford* (1876) 4 Ch.D. 389.
[172] *National Trustees Company of Australasia Ltd v General Finance Company of Australasia Ltd* [1905] A.C. 373.
[173] Family Law Reform Act 1987 s.20.
[174] *Dibbs v Goren* (1849) 11 Beav. 483 (administration by the court); *Re Musgrave* [1916] 2 Ch. 417; P. Matthews [1994] 2 R.L.R. 44.
[175] *Kleinwort Benson Ltd v Lincoln City Council* [1999] 2 A.C. 349.
[176] *Re Diplock* [1948] Ch. 465.
[177] *Re Horne* [1905] 1 Ch. 76.
[178] It may have been overtaken by developments in the law of unjust enrichment.
[179] *Re Londonderry's Settlement* [1965] Ch. 918; *Finers v Miro* [1991] 1 W.L.R. 35.
[180] CPR 1998 Pts 8, 64.
[181] See also Administration of Justice Act 1985 s.48, giving the court power to authorise action to be taken in reliance on counsel's opinion respecting the construction of a will or trust.

application to the court can also be helpful in cases where the trustees are deadlocked or disabled by a conflict of interest in connection with the exercise of a discretion, for instance a discretionary power to make advancements. In such a case, the trustees surrender their discretion to the court, and must put all relevant information before it to enable the discretion to be exercised.[182] Trustees cannot, however, surrender the future exercise of discretions to the court.[183] Where, on the other hand, the trustees merely wish to obtain the blessing of the court for their proposed course of action, because it is for some reason momentous, their act of applying to court for directions does not involve a surrender of discretion.[184] Trustees or beneficiaries may apply for the trust to be administered by the court, but the court will only make an administration order if it considers that the issues cannot properly be resolved in any other way[185]: "the court is not there to act as a sort of bomb shelter" for trustees to avoid decisions.[186]

ii. Payment into Court. Where beneficiaries cannot be ascertained, or where **19–026**
for some exceptional reason trustees cannot obtain a good discharge from the trust, there is a residual power in trustees to pay the trust moneys into court.[187] The residue of the fund in *Re Gillingham Bus Disaster Fund*,[188] for instance, was eventually paid into court.

But this will not be tolerated by the court as a means of trustees evading their obligations when difficulties arise.[189] It is a last resort when all other methods of dealing with the problem have proved unsuccessful. Trustees who pay trust funds into court when a different course was preferable, may be liable for costs.[190]

iii. "Benjamin" Order. The court has a power to authorise distribution of **19–027**
the whole of the assets of an estate, although not all the beneficiaries or creditors have made themselves known so as to be able to receive their share. A typical situation is where the whereabouts or continued existence of a certain beneficiary is not known. The procedure is sometimes known as a "Benjamin" order, and its purpose is to protect those distributing the assets.[191] If those entitled who have received nothing under the distribution eventually come forward to establish their

---

[182] *Royal Society for the Prevention of Cruelty to Animals v Attorney General* [2002] 1 W.L.R. 448 (court has unfettered discretion to decide what to do).

[183] *Re Allen-Meyrick's WT* [1966] 1 W.L.R. 499.

[184] *Public Trustee v Cooper* [2001] W.T.L.R. 901, explaining *Marley v Mutual Security Merchant Bank and Trust Co Ltd* [1991] 3 All E. R. 198. The court will sanction the proposed exercise of discretion if the decision is one which a reasonable trustee could have reached and is not vitiated by any conflict of interest. See also *X v A* [2006] W.T.L.R. 171. For the position in respect of charities, see *Re Cup Trust* [2016] EWHC 876 (Ch); [2016] 3 W.L.R. 218 per Snowden J at [67]ff.

[185] CPR 1998 Pt 64 and Court Funds Rules 2011 (SI 2011/1734), rr.6–10.

[186] *In re T & D Industries Plc* [2000] 1 W.L.R. 646 per Neuberger J at 657 (speaking in the context of administrators making commercial and administrative decisions, but the sentiment applies broadly to trustees as well).

[187] Payment into court furnishes an exception to the rule that a majority of trustees cannot defeat a dissentient minority, for Trustee Act 1925 s.63, provides that the payment may in certain circumstances be made by a majority of the trustees.

[188] [1959] Ch. 62; above, para.11–007.

[189] See *Re Knight's Trust* (1859) 27 Beav. 45.

[190] *Re Cull's Trusts* (1875) L.R. 20 Eq. 561; A. Hawkins (1968) 84 L.Q.R. 64 at 65–67.

[191] *Re Benjamin* [1902] 1 Ch. 723; *Re Gess* [1942] Ch. 37; *Re Taylor* [1969] 2 Ch. 245.

claim, they may still be able to proceed, within the period of limitation, against the person wrongly paid,[192] or against the property itself. Such an order will of course only be made after all practicable inquiries have been instituted. An example is *Re Green's Will Trusts*,[193] where the testatrix left her property to her son, providing that it should go to charity if he did not claim it by the year 2020. The son had disappeared on a bombing raid in 1943, and all but his mother were satisfied that he was dead. A "Benjamin" order was made, allowing distribution to the charity, it being no bar to such an order that it was contrary to the intention of the testatrix.[194] "Missing beneficiary" insurance may be a preferable course, especially in the case of a small estate.[195]

In a commercial context, David Richards J considered the status of client money trusts held by a bank which went into special administration in *In Re MF Global UK Ltd (In Special Administration) (No.3)*.[196] No rules were provided for the distribution of the available funds, and so the bank and the administrators applied to the court for directions in dealing with various current, rejected and unknown claims. David Richards J held that it was within the court's inherent jurisdiction to give directions for the distribution of the trust property and authorised a scheme even though it involved an extension of *Re Benjamin* to dealing with unresolved claims:

> "In my judgment, these proposals properly balance both the interests of established clients to a timely return of their money and the interests of persons with serious but unresolved claims to be treated as clients."[197]

A similarly pragmatic approach has since been taken by Morgan J in the context of a scheme of distribution proposed by administrators in circumstances of imperfect knowledge.[198]

19–028   **iv. Distribution after Advertisement.**   Under the Trustee Act 1925 s.27, trustees have themselves the power to advertise for claimants[199] and, after compliance with certain formalities, the power to distribute the whole of their trust assets to claimants who have responded or of whom the trustees otherwise have notice. Those who subsequently demonstrate an entitlement are enabled to proceed against the property distributed, save when it is in the hands of a purchaser.[200] Section 27 applies to the trustees of pension funds, although in

---

[192] *Ministry of Health v Simpson* [1951] A.C. 251; *Re Lowe's WT* [1973] 1 W.L.R. 882 at 887. The overpaid beneficiary may be protected from this risk by "missing beneficiary" insurance; *Re Evans* [1999] 2 All E.R. 777.

[193] [1985] 3 All E.R. 455.

[194] Criticised on this point in P. Luxton [1986] Conv. 138.

[195] *Re Evans* [1999] 2 All E.R. 777.

[196] [2013] EWHC 1655 (Ch); [2013] 1 W.L.R. 3874; A. Zacaroli and A. Al-Attar (2014) 20 T. & T. 246. See also *Capita ATL Pension Trustees Ltd v Gellately* [2011] Pen. L.R. 153.

[197] [2013] EWHC 1655 (Ch); [2013] 1 W.L.R. 3874 at [32].

[198] *Allanfield Property Insurance Services Ltd (In Administration) v Aviva Insurance Ltd, AXA Insurance UK Plc* [2015] EWHC 3721 (Ch).

[199] Normally creditors, but also beneficiaries, for example claimants under an intestacy. Advertising is not sufficient protection against contingent debts; *Re Yorke* [1997] 4 All E.R. 907. See further *National Westminster Bank Plc v Lucas* [2014] EWCA Civ 1632.

[200] s.27(2)(a); *Re Aldhous* [1955] 1 W.L.R. 459.

practice it will be more difficult for them to show that they did not have notice of a particular claim. If they once had notice but have forgotten, they still have notice.[201]

v. Setting Aside a Fund. The Trustee Act 1925 s.26[202] provides a procedure **19–029** whereby trustees can set aside out of trust assets a sum to meet any potential liabilities under a lease or rentcharge, and then to distribute the remainder of the trust assets to those entitled. Again, should the sum set aside prove insufficient, those entitled to the extra sums may still follow the distributed property. In the case of contingent liabilities outside s.26, the trustees can either retain a fund, distribute under a court order, obtain insurance cover if available, or obtain an indemnity from the beneficiaries and then distribute.[203]

C. Relief under Section 61

A trustee who makes an erroneous distribution may be relieved from liability if **19–030** he acted honestly and reasonably and ought fairly to be excused.[204]

D. Discharge

On the termination of the trust, the trustees should present their final accounts and **19–031** obtain a discharge from the beneficiaries. The best protection is provided by a release by deed, for that places on a complaining beneficiary the burden of proving fraud, concealment, mistake or undue influence.[205] But a trustee is not entitled to a release by deed.[206] If the beneficiaries are unwilling to give one, the trustees may apply to the court for the accounts to be taken and approved.

---

[201] *MCP Pension Trustees Ltd v Aon Pension Trustees Ltd* [2011] 3 W.L.R. 455.
[202] As amended by Landlord and Tenant (Covenants) Act 1995 Sch.1.
[203] See Mellows, *The Law of Succession*, 5th edn (Butterworths, 1993), p.379; *Re Yorke* [1997] 4 All E.R. 907 (contingent liabilities of Lloyd's underwriter); *Re K* [2007] W.T.L.R. 1007 (estate distributed subject to retention of £50,000 for three years to fund defence of any proceedings by unpaid creditors whose claims were stale or disputed). See further Practice Note [2001] 3 All E.R. 765.
[204] Below, paras 24–037—24–039; *Re Evans* [1999] 2 All E.R. 777.
[205] *Fowler v Wyatt* (1857) 24 Beav. 232.
[206] *King v Mullins* (1852) 1 Drew. 308 at 311 per Kindersley VC.

CHAPTER 20

DUTIES OF TRUSTEES IN RELATION TO THE BENEFICIARIES

1. DUTY TO MAINTAIN EQUALITY BETWEEN THE BENEFICIARIES

A TRUSTEE is under a general duty to maintain equality between the **20–001** beneficiaries. This duty forms the basis of the specific rules of conversion and apportionment, discussed below, which apply as between life tenant and remainderman. It is not, however, confined to such cases. An example of the wider general duty is *Lloyds Bank Plc v Duker*,[1] where a testator's residuary estate included 999 company shares. He left 46/80 to his wife, and the rest to other beneficiaries. In spite of the general rule that a beneficiary is entitled in specie to his share of divisible personalty held on trust for sale, it was held that the wife could not claim 574 shares, as such a majority holding would be worth more than 46/80. The only fair solution was for the trustees to sell the shares and divide the proceeds in the specified proportions. Of course, where the trustees have a power to choose between various classes of beneficiaries, the duty to act impartially has no application. In such a case the trustees are entitled to prefer some beneficiaries over others, provided they do not take irrelevant matters into account.[2] However, so far as trustees' expenditure is concerned, if it is incurred for the benefit of the whole estate, it must be allocated to capital for income tax purposes and thus does not reduce the amount of income subject to the higher rates of tax applicable to the income of a discretionary trust.[3] Only those expenses which can be shown to relate solely to the discharge of the trustees' duties to the income beneficiaries may be attributed to income.

---

[1] [1987] 1 W.L.R. 1324. See also *Nestlé v National Westminster Bank Plc* [1993] 1 W.L.R. 1261; *X v A* [2000] 1 All E.R. 490; *Pagliaro v Thomas* [2008] W.T.L.R. 1417.
[2] *Edge v Pensions Ombudsman* [2000] Ch. 602.
[3] *Revenue and Customs Commissioners v Trustees of the Peter Clay Discretionary Trust* [2009] Ch. 296; M. Gunn (2017) 180 *Taxation* 16. See also *Close Trustees (Switzerland) SA v Vildosola* [2008] W.T.L.R. 1543 (how costs of litigation allocated to capital and income).

The current law is governed by the Trusts (Capital and Income) Act 2013,[4] which was enacted following proposals from the Law Commission.[5] The aim was to ensure that "complex and time-consuming calculations, generally affecting relatively small sums of money, will be avoided".[6] Section 1 of the 2013 Act is as follows:

1. Disapplication of apportionment etc. rules
   (1) Any entitlement to income under a new trust is to income as it arises (and accordingly section 2 of the Apportionment Act 1870, which provides for income to accrue from day to day, does not apply in relation to the trust).
   (2) The following do not apply in relation to a new trust—
      (a) the first part of the rule known as the rule in *Howe v. Earl of Dartmouth* (which requires certain residuary personal estate to be sold);
      (b) the second part of that rule (which withholds from a life tenant income arising from certain investments and compensates the life tenant with payments of interest);
      (c) the rule known as the rule in *Re Earl of Chesterfield's Trusts* (which requires the proceeds of the conversion of certain investments to be apportioned between capital and income);
      (d) the rule known as the rule in *Allhusen v. Whittell* (which requires a contribution to be made from income for the purpose of paying a deceased person's debts, legacies and annuities).
   (3) Trustees have power to sell any property which (but for subsection (2)(a)) they would have been under a duty to sell.

The reforms to the law on apportionment under s.1 only apply to "new trusts", which means a trust created or arising on or after the day on which this section comes into force (and includes a trust created or arising on or after that day under a power conferred before that day).[7] They are also subject to contrary intention appearing in a trust instrument.[8]

The relevant provisions of the Act came into force on 1 October 2013.[9] Since the provisions are not retrospective in application, the common law rules continue to apply to trusts created before that date and so will still be considered below. We shall term those trusts to which the old rules apply as "old trusts", and use the past tense to reflect their zombie status. It must be remembered throughout sections A and B, however, that for "new trusts" the 2013 Act will apply.[10]

---

[4] Helpfully noted by A. Palin [2013] P.C.B. 101 and (on the 2012 Bill) S. Shah (2012) 156 S.J. 10.

[5] Law Com. No. 315, *Capital and Income in Trusts: Classification and Apportionment* (2009). For previous reviews, see Law Reform Committee 23rd Report (1982); Trust Law Committee Consultation Paper, *Capital and Income of Trusts* (1998). The Explanatory Note to the 2013 Act is also to be commended as a readable guide.

[6] As Lord Henley the relevant Minister of State for the Home Office, put it at the Committee Stage in House of Lords: 25 April 2012: Column GC293.

[7] Trusts (Capital and Income) Act 2013 s.1(5).

[8] Trusts (Capital and Income) Act 2013 s.1(4)(a).

[9] Trusts (Capital and Income) Act 2013 (Commencement No.1) Order (SI 2013/676) art.4.

[10] There is as yet no case law on the Trusts (Capital and Income) Act 2013, but in *RBC Trustees (CI) Ltd v Stubbs* [2017] EWHC 180 (Ch), Rose J approved the rectification of two deeds of revocation and appointment dated 11 November 2008 and 22 April 2014, pertaining to existing trusts, and noted (at [66]) that the 2013 Act would govern any new trusts if created by the 2014 deed.

A. The Former Rule in *Howe v Earl of Dartmouth*

i. Life Tenant and Remainderman. A trustee must act impartially between life tenant and remainderman. This duty applies to the selection of investments[11]; and the rules governing investment by trustees are an attempt to strike a balance between the provision of income for the life tenant and the preservation of the capital for the remainderman.[12] So long as those rules are observed, a trustee is usually under no duty to rearrange the investments so as to balance equally the interests of the life tenant and remainderman.[13] Nor, if there are investments in the fund which have ceased to be authorised, are the trustees under any immediate duty to convert them into authorised investments. However the fund is invested, the normal rule is that the tenant for life takes all the income; the remainderman's interest is in the capital. The capital is not of course available until the life tenant's death; but the remainderman may, if she wishes, deal with or dispose of her reversionary interest in the fund.

    There are, as we shall see, some situations in which there is a duty to convert into authorised investments; and this duty carries with it a duty to apportion the income earned before the conversion is effected.

20–002

ii. The Duty to Convert. A duty to convert (i.e. sell) and re-invest in authorised investments may arise by reason of the existence of an express trust to sell, or, for old trusts, in the case of a bequest of residuary personalty, under the rule in *Howe v Earl of Dartmouth*.[14] Only an outline of the rule will be given, for several reasons. First, in the case of old trusts, the rule was almost invariably excluded in a professionally drafted will. Secondly, the investment powers of trustees are so wide after the Trustee Act 2000 that the duty to sell unauthorised investments now has little scope for application. Finally, the rule does not apply to new trusts.[15] *Howe v Earl of Dartmouth* established that, subject to a contrary provision in the will, there was a duty to convert where residuary personalty was settled by will in favour of persons in succession. The trustees were under a duty to convert all such parts of it as were of a wasting[16] or future or reversionary[17] nature or consisted of unauthorised securities,[18] into authorised investments.

20–003

---

[11] *Raby v Ridehalgh* (1855) 7 De G.M. & G. 104 at 109; *Re Dick* [1891] 1 Ch. 423 at 431.

[12] Above, para.19–005. There is no duty to preserve the real value of the capital: *Nestlé v National Westminster Bank Plc* [1993] 1 W.L.R. 1261 (suggesting also that trustees entitled to incline towards high income investments if rich remainderman and poor life tenant).

[13] "It is perhaps surprising that equity has not cast upon trustees, in every such case, a duty to convert the trust property as soon as practicable into something more likely to produce an equitable result", S. Bailey (1943) 7 Conv.(N.S.) 128 at 129; *Re Searle* [1900] 2 Ch. 829 at 834; cf. *Re Smith* (1971) 18 D.L.R. (3d) 405; (duty to reinvest where authorised shares producing low return because of company policy to pursue capital growth).

[14] (1802) 7 Ves.Jr. 137. The duty to sell the assets of an intestate was replaced by a power of sale; Administraton of Estates Act 1925 s.33, as amended by Trusts of Land and Appointment of Trustees Act 1996 Sch.2.

[15] Trusts (Capital and Income) Act 2013 ss.1(2)(a) and 1(2)(b).

[16] Such as mines or ships which will eventually become worthless; or patents or copyrights which expire.

[17] i.e. property which will only come into possession after the death of the life tenant.

[18] i.e. not authorised by the terms of the will, nor by Trustee Act 2000. cf. *Re Smith* (1971) 18 D.L.R. (3d) 405, above, para.20–002 (authorised securities).

Thus, under the old rule, property such as royalties and copyrights[19] should be converted in the interest of the remainderman, for these might be of reduced or of no value at the life tenant's death. On the other hand, "future" property such as a remainder or reversionary interest, or other property which at present produces no income, was of no immediate benefit to the tenant for life. In his interest therefore it should be converted into income-bearing properties.

On its terms, the rule was of limited application. It did not apply to life-time settlements[20]; nor to specific as opposed to residuary bequests[21] (for the settlor's or testator's intention in such cases is for the specific property settled to be enjoyed successively). Nor had it applied to leaseholds since the property legislation of 1925.

Subsection 1(2) of the 2013 Act, seen above, abolished the duty to sell, although trustees may still decide to do sell. If, in exercising their discretion, they do decide that it is appropriate still to sell, s.2(3) preserves their power to do so.

20–004   **iii. Apportionment.**   Where there was a duty to convert, there was, in the absence of an intention that the life tenant should enjoy the income until sale, a duty also to apportion fairly between the life tenant and the remainderman the original property pending conversion.

20–005   *(a) Wasting, Hazardous or Unauthorised Investments.*   It was assumed that wasting, hazardous and unauthorised securities produce income in excess of that which the life tenant should reasonably receive; and do so at the expense of the security of the capital. With such property therefore the object of the apportionment rule was to provide that the life tenant receives an income which represents the current yield on authorised investments,[22] and that the excess is added to capital.[23]

Now, under s.1(2)(b) of the 2013 Act, applicable to new trusts, the income beneficiary is simply entitled to the actual income from such investments as and when it arises.

20–006   *(b) Future, Reversionary or other Non-income Producing Property: The Former Re Earl of Chesterfield's Trusts.*   Where personalty which was subject to a duty to convert included reversionary property, it was necessary, in the interest of the life tenant, to provide for apportionment[24]; otherwise the life tenant would obtain no benefit from the property until it fell into possession. The reversion should be sold and the proceeds re-invested; until then there would be no way of producing income for the life tenant. When it had been sold, there was

---

[19] *Re Evans' WT* [1921] 2 Ch. 309; *Re Sullivan* [1930] 1 Ch. 84.

[20] *Re Van Straubenzee* [1901] 2 Ch. 779.

[21] [1901] 2 Ch. 779 at 782.

[22] The life tenant's income was fixed at 4% in *Re Baker* [1924] 2 Ch. 271. However, this became out of line with the return from gilt-edged investments, although interest rates are very low at the time of writing: for most of the last decade, the Monetary Policy Committee of the Bank England has maintained interest rates at 0.5% (the rate was at that level from 5 March 2009, lowered to 0.25% on 4 August 2016 and moved back to 0.5% on 2 November 2017). Trustees who have to decide what income to pay may be well advised to take instructions from the court.

[23] The life tenant will of course receive the income from the capital as thus increased.

[24] A reversionary interest in land is not within the rule (*Re Woodhouse* [1941] Ch. 332).

still the problem of determining how much of the proceeds of sale should be apportioned to capital and how much to the life tenant. This was done via the rule in *Re Earl of Chesterfield's Trusts*[25] by ascertaining the sum:

"[W]hich, put out at 4 per cent per annum… and accumulating at compound interest at that rate with yearly rests,[26] and deducting income tax at the standard rate, would, with the accumulation of interest, have produced, at the respective dates of receipt, the amounts actually received; and that the aggregate of the sums so ascertained ought to be treated as principal and be applied accordingly, and the residue should be treated as income."

In other words, the proceeds of sale of the reversion were treated as part principal, part interest. The principal was the sum which, if invested at 4% at the date of the testator's death, would have produced the sum now received. The balance went to the tenant for life.

Subsection 1(2)(c) of the 2013 Act disapplied this rule for new trusts, so that when such property as considered here comes into the possession of the trustees is to be treated as capital only.

iv. *Howe v Earl of Dartmouth* **and** *Re Earl of Chesterfield's Trusts* **in Modern Practice.**   The rules relating to conversion and apportionment demonstrated basic principles of equity. But they should be understood in their proper perspective, even insofar as they still apply to old trusts.   **20–007**

(a) *Exclusion of Duty to Apportion.*   Even for old trusts, the duty to apportion was in practice nearly always excluded, both in respect of income from unauthorised securities and in respect of reversionary interests. The duty to convert, where it existed, thus appeared in the context of a duty to change the investments.   **20–008**

(b) *Effect of Current Investment Situation.*   The utility of the rules of conversion and apportionment varied according to the current investment situation: **20–009**

"The dividend yield on the shares in the most regarded index of 100 leading equities has for years been far less than the interest yield obtainable on medium-dated fixed-interest government stock. In present-day circumstances, retaining unauthorised equities therefore tends to depress the life tenant's income, whereas when *Howe v Dartmouth* was decided the effect was the opposite. It no longer makes sense to say that the income of a life tenant from a fund of unauthorised equities ought to be limited to the yield of government stocks, since that would usually be higher, not lower."[27]

Thus the life tenant would want fixed interest investments when they provide a high income; the remainderman would want unauthorised securities for the preservation of the real value of the capital.[28] It would be the life tenant who

---

[25] (1883) 24 Ch.D. 643.

[26] i.e. the income is transferred to capital at the end of each year.

[27] Trust Law Committee Consultation Paper, *Capital and Income of Trusts* (1998).

[28] A good illustration of the tension is *Re Mulligan (Deceased)* [1998] 1 N.Z.L.R. 481.

would be pressing the trustees to convert urgently into gilt-edged securities at times when they could bring an income in excess of the 4% allowed to the life tenant by the rule of apportionment.

20–010   *(c)   New Trusts.*   As seen above, the Trusts (Capital and Income) Act 2013 s.1 abolished certain key equitable rules of apportionment, including the rules in *Howe v Earl of Dartmouth* and *Re Earl of Chesterfield's Trusts*,[29] for new trusts.

It had previously been proposed that the apportionment rules should be replaced by a statutory power of allocation, which would be an administrative power enabling trustees to allocate trust receipts and expenses to capital or income, so far as necessary to discharge their duty to maintain the balance between capital and income. Such a power would have given the trustees more freedom in choosing investments with a view to overall growth rather than capital and income returns, thus promoting a "total return" investment policy.[30] This reform was not implemented for all trusts, however; instead s.4 of the 2013 Act introduced this power for charitable trusts only.[31]

The Act therefore simply abolished the rules of apportionment without replacing them with any statutory power.[32]

Another way of maintaining the balance between beneficiaries is the "percentage trust", in which the settlor specifies that a percentage of the whole trust fund (valued annually after adding all receipts and deducting all outgoings) is to be given to the life tenant each year. The balance goes to the remainderman on termination of the life interest. It is not clear how the rules for the taxation of trusts apply to such a trust. The Law Commission recommended that more work to be done to develop percentage trusts, but this would be a task for the trust industry, in partnership with HM Treasury and HMRC.[33]

Even after the reforms, it remains possible for the settlor to make express provision for the approach to apportionment, including (if desired) the application of the former equitable rules.[34]

B.   Other Methods of Apportionment

20–011   Apportionment is necessary in other situations, and these will be mentioned in outline only, since many of the technicalities of the old law were removed by the 2013 Act.

20–012   **i.   Old Trusts: Apportionment Act 1870.**   When a testator or a life tenant dies, the question arises of the entitlement to periodical income, such as rents, interest and dividends, earned in whole or in part, but not paid, at the time of the death. In the case of old trusts, that which is treated as being earned before the

---

[29] And other equitable rules discussed in the following section of this chapter.

[30] Above, para.19–005.

[31] Above, para.19–005.

[32] Law Com. No. 315 (2009), paras 6.54–6.65.

[33] Law Com. No. 315 (2009), para.5.23. See also paras 3.17–3.22 of the Report, discussing USA models.

[34] Trusts (Capital and Income) Act 2013 s.1(4)(a).

death will be added to the estate, and that earned afterwards is payable as income to the income beneficiary under the will or, in the case of the death of a life tenant, to the next life tenant, or to the capital.

The division is governed by the Apportionment Act 1870 s.2, which provides that:

> "[A]ll rents, annuities, dividends, and other periodical payments in the nature of income… shall… be considered as accruing from day to day, and shall be apportionable in respect of time accordingly."

It was necessary therefore to ascertain the proportion of the earning period which expired prior to the death, and to divide the payment, when received, in the same proportion.[35] When rent was due, or a dividend earned, but not paid prior to the death, the whole income was paid to the testator's estate or to that of the life tenant. The 1870 Act could be excluded by an expression of an intention to do so. This was formerly common in order to avoid the complications which were introduced into the administration of an estate.

Section 2 of the 1870 Act no longer applies to new trusts, by virtue of s.1(1) of the 2013 Act. Instead, the simple rule is that "any entitlement to income under a new trust is to income as it arises".

ii. The Former Rule in *Allhusen v Whittell*. This rule attempted to strike a   **20–013** fair balance between life tenant and remainderman in respect of the payment of the debts of an estate. The life tenant under a will is entitled to income earned after the testator's death. The debts of the testator must also be paid; and it may take some time to do so. In the meantime the assets of the estate are earning income for the life tenant. It was thought that she should, in fairness, only have the income from the net estate. The rule in *Allhusen v Whittell*[36] provided that the life tenant should make a contribution. Romer LJ in *Corbett v Commissioners of Inland Revenue*[37] explained the rule as follows:

> "For the purposes of adjusting rights as between the tenant for life and the remainderman of a residuary estate, debts, legacies, estate duties, probate duties and so forth, are to be deemed to have been paid out of such capital of the testator's estate as will be sufficient for that purpose, when to that capital is added interest on that capital from the date of the testator's death to the date of the payment of the legacy or debt, or whatever it may have been, interest being calculated at the average rate of interest[38] earned by the testator's estate during the relevant period."

The rule could be excluded by an expression of contrary intent, or where its application would in the circumstances be inappropriate.[39] Witnesses to the Law Reform Committee in 1982 described the rule as "complex, fiddlesome and resulting in a disproportionate amount of work and expense," adding that where the rule was not excluded it was often simply ignored.[40]

---

[35] For class gifts, see *Re Joel* [1967] Ch. 14.
[36] (1867) L.R. 4 Eq. 295.
[37] [1938] 1 K.B. 567 at 584.
[38] *Re Wills* [1915] 1 Ch. 769.
[39] *Re McEuen* [1913] 2 Ch. 704; *Re Darby* [1939] Ch. 905.
[40] 23rd Report, above. See para.3.31.

It has been abolished for new trusts by s.1(4) of the 2013 Act. The effect now is that the payment of a deceased person's debts, legacies and annuities will be out of the capital alone.

20–014   **iii. The Rule in *Re Atkinson*.**   Where an authorised mortgage security is sold by the trustee mortgagees and the proceeds are insufficient to satisfy the principal and interest in full, it is necessary to determine the way in which the loss is to be shared between life tenant and remainderman. The sum realised must be apportioned between the life tenant and the remainderman in the proportion which the amount due for the arrears of interest bears to the amount due in respect of the principal.[41]

Reform of this rule (and the related rule in *Re Bird*, which need not be detailed here)[42] was also proposed by the Law Commission in its Report, and would have been a fifth subsection to s.1(2).[43] However, following Ministry of Justice consultation on the Law Commission's Bill, the reform was withdrawn from the Bill, on the basis that the rules

> "are less complex than the other rules set out in clause 1(2), [and] apply in fewer cases. The situations in which they do apply tend to be particularly unusual, where the need for legal advice is likely to be apparent in any case, and where the rules are more likely to be needed to achieve, and actually to achieve, fairness between capital and income beneficiaries."[44]

The rule in *Re Atkinson* thus continues to apply, subject to contrary provision in the trust instrument.

20–015   **iv. Interest on Compensatory Award.**   Where loss of the trust fund results in an award of equitable compensation, interest will be payable on the sum awarded from the date of the claim form until judgment. The interest should be apportioned between life tenant and remainderman. In *Jaffray v Marshall*,[45] a fair apportionment was considered to be half and half, taking a broad view.

20–016   **v. Purchase or Sale of Shares Cum Dividend.**   One of the factors which affects the price of shares is the date of payment of the next dividend. A share whose dividend will be paid tomorrow is worth more than it would be if the dividend had been paid yesterday. It would seem reasonable to require an apportionment when shares are bought or sold with the dividend, but the general rule is that there is none.[46] In this respect, the beneficiaries take "the rough with

---

[41] *Re Atkinson* [1904] 2 Ch. 160.

[42] [1901] 1 Ch 916.

[43] Law Com. No. 315, at 125: Draft Trusts (Capital and Income) Bill, cl.1(2)(e).

[44] Memorandum submitted by Professor Elizabeth Cooke, Law Commissioner, House of Lords Special Public Bill Committee, *Trusts (Capital and Income) Bill*: Written and Oral Evidence. HL Paper 42 21.

[45] [1993] 1 W.L.R. 1285 (overruled as to the underlying assessment of equitable compensation, but not the interest point, in *Target Holdings Ltd v Redferns (A Firm)* [1996] 1 A.C. 421); *Jeffery v Gretton* [2011] W.T.L.R. 809.

[46] *Bulkeley v Stephens* [1896] 2 Ch. 241; *Re Ellerman's ST* (1984) 81 L.S.Gaz. 430, where the decision to the contrary in *Re Winterstoke's WT* [1938] Ch. 158 was regarded as wrong; I. Pittaway (1986) 1 *Trust Law & Practice* 62. See Law Com. CP No. 175 (2004), paras 3.64–3.71.

the smooth".[47] This is probably more convenient overall than an insistence on an apportionment in every case. But an apportionment will be required if there would otherwise be "a glaring injustice".[48]

C. Company Distributions

Questions can also arise as to the entitlements of life tenant and remainderman to certain distributions by companies. The question of entitlement and that of the liability of the distribution to income tax are related questions, but are not identical.[49] The tax aspect is the reason for the attraction to shareholders generally of distributions as capital. The question whether the life tenant or remainderman is entitled (or whether an apportionment must be made) will arise, for example, where the company has taken steps to capitalise profits,[50] or where shareholders are given the right to choose between a cash dividend and an allotment of shares. The problem was that the rules derive from company law concepts of capital and income, which are different from the trust law classification.[51]

    20–017

The modern context in which the question arises is the company demerger, where a company in effect splits into two, and shares in the new company are given to shareholders in the original company. The demerger may be "direct", where the original company allocates to its shareholders the shares in the new company, or "indirect", where the new company allocates its own shares to shareholders of the original company. Whether these shares are to be treated as income or capital is relevant to beneficial entitlement and, as mentioned above, to taxation. When ICI transferred its bioscience business to a new company, Zeneca, and shares in the latter were given to ICI shareholders (the ICI shares being reduced in value by the demerger) in satisfaction of a dividend, it was held in *Sinclair v Lee*[52] that the new shares were capital assets, and hence did not pass under a gift by will of income from the ICI shares. The effect of the reconstruction was that two capital assets replaced one. Investment philosophy had greatly changed since the older cases,[53] and any other result would not reflect reality. *Sinclair* involved an "indirect" demerger. However, shares distributed under a "direct" demerger were still to be treated as income both for the purposes of entitlement and taxation.

The distinctions in the cases have been reformed by the Trusts (Capital and Income) Act 2013 ss.2 and 3. The effect of the reforms is to reclassify such

---

[47] *Re MacLaren's ST* [1951] 2 All E.R. 414 at 420.

[48] [1951] 2 All E.R. 414 at 420.

[49] *Re Bates* [1928] Ch. 682; *Re Doughty* [1947] Ch. 263; *Re Sechiari* [1950] 1 All E.R. 417; *Howell v Trippier (Inspector of Taxes)* [2004] W.T.L.R. 839; *Gilchrist v Revenue and Customs Commissioners* [2014] UKUT 169 (TCC); [2015] 2 W.L.R. 1; *Seddon v The Commissioners for Her Majesty's Revenue & Customs* [2015] UKFTT 0140 (TC).

[50] *Bouch v Sproule* (1887) 12 App.Cas. 385.

[51] Law Com. No. 315, *Capital and Income in Trusts: Classification and Apportionment* (2009), para.2.36.

[52] [1993] Ch. 497. See D. Hayton, *Modern International Developments in Trust Law* (Kluwer Law International, 1999), pp.288–291; P. Duffield (1995) 9 T.L.I. 55.

[53] Such as *Hill v Permanent Trustee Co of NSW* [1930] A.C. 720.

receipts, whether involving direct or indirect demergers, as capital rather than income with a power to compensate the income beneficiary who would otherwise be disadvantaged. Significantly, by s.2(6), the reforms apply "to any trust, whether created or arising before or after this section comes into force". The position is now, under s.2.(1):

> A receipt consisting of a tax-exempt corporate distribution[54] is to be treated for the purposes of any trust to which this section applies as a receipt of capital (even if it would otherwise be treated for those purposes as a receipt of income).

Section 3 of the 2013 Act applies where there has been a receipt of capital under s.2 and the trustees are satisfied that, were it not for that distribution, there would have been a receipt from the body corporate that would have been a receipt of income.[55] In such a case, the trustees may make a payment out of capital funds or transfer property to an income beneficiary,[56] for the purpose of

> placing the income beneficiary (so far as practicable) in the position in which the trustees consider that the beneficiary would have been had there been the receipt of income [as described in s.3(1)(b)].[57]

These reforms should be regarded as welcome, reflecting corporate practice and striking an appropriate balance between the competing interests involved without relying on undue technicality.

2. Duty to Provide Accounts and Information

A. Accounts

20–018 **i. Extent of Duty.** A trustee must keep accounts and be constantly ready to produce them for the beneficiaries.[58] It seems that a beneficiary is entitled only to see and inspect the accounts;[59] if he wants a copy himself, he must pay for it; but it is common practice to provide a copy for each of the beneficiaries.[60] An income beneficiary is entitled to full accounts, but a remainderman is entitled only to

---

[54] Defined in s.1(3) as exempt distributions under ss.1076, 1077 or 1078 of the Corporation Tax Act 2010 (or any other distribution if specified under a power by the Secretary of State, limited by ss.1(4) and (5).

[55] Trusts (Capital and Income) Act 2013 s.3(1).

[56] 2013 Act s.3(2).

[57] 2013 Act s.3(3).

[58] *Pearse v Green* (1819) 1 Jac. & W. 135 per Plumer MR at 140.

[59] As Master Matthews noted in *Royal National Lifeboat Institution v Headley* [2016] EWHC 1948 (Ch) at [11]: "When the books and cases talk about beneficiaries' 'entitlement to accounts' or to trustees being 'ready with their accounts' they are not generally referring to annual financial statements such as limited companies and others carrying on business (and indeed some large trusts) commonly produce in the form of balance sheets and profit and loss accounts, usually through accountants, and – in the case of limited companies – file at Companies House. Instead they are referring to the very notion of accounting itself. Trustees must be ready to account to their beneficiaries for what they have done with the trust assets. This may be done with formal financial statements, or with less formal documents, or indeed none at all. It is no answer for trustees to say that formal financial statements have not yet been produced by the trustees' accountants."

[60] *Ottley v Gilby* (1845) 8 Beav. 602; *Kemp v Burn* (1863) 4 Giff. 348.

such information as relates to capital transactions. A member of a class of discretionary beneficiaries is entitled to accounts,[61] but a person who is merely a potential object of a discretionary trust has no such right, at any rate where there is a large number of possible beneficiaries.[62]

ii. Audit. Apart from the cases of pension trusts and charitable trusts,[63] it is neither necessary nor, except in large and complicated trusts or where trouble with a beneficiary is foreseen, usual to have trust accounts audited. However, trustees may, in their absolute discretion, have the trust accounts examined and audited by an independent accountant, and may pay the costs out of income or capital. Audit should not be effected more than once in every three years, except in special cases.[64]   **20–019**

Any trustee or beneficiary may apply for the accounts of any trust to be investigated and audited by such solicitor or public accountant as may be agreed upon, or in default of agreement by the Public Trustee or by some person appointed by him.[65] The costs are usually borne by the trust, but the Public Trustee may order that the appellant or the trustees must pay them or share them.[66]

B. Information. Trust Documents

i. General. The beneficiaries are entitled to be informed about matters currently affecting the trust.[67] Beneficiaries of pension trusts have a statutory right to information.[68] A large trust will keep many documents, such as the   **20–020**

---

[61] *Chaine-Nickson v Bank of Ireland* [1976] I.R. 393; *Re Murphy's Settlements* [1999] 1 W.L.R. 282; J. Rimmer (2016) 22 T. & T. 451. *Royal National Lifeboat Institution v Headley* [2016] EWHC 1948 (Ch) per Master Matthews at [22]: "I do not think that it necessarily follows that all such documents must be disclosed to all beneficiaries. It must depend on what is needed in the circumstances for the beneficiaries to appreciate, verify and if need be vindicate their own rights against the trustees in respect of the administration of the trust. That will vary according to the facts of the case." *Patel v Patel* (2016) 19 I.T.E.L.R. 958 (Royal Court (Guernsey)) (disclosure of accounts).

[62] *Hartigan Nominees Pty Ltd v Rydge* (1992) 29 N.S.W.L.R. 405.

[63] Pensions Act 1995 s.41 and regulations thereunder; above, para.17–014; Charities Act 2011 ss.144–161; above, para.15–092.

[64] Trustee Act 1925 s.22(4). For the audit by the court of the accounts of a judicial trustee, see Administration of Justice Act 1982 s.57 (amending earlier legislation); Judicial Trustee Rules 1983 (SI 1983/370). By r.2 there is to be no automatic audit by the court of the accounts of a "corporate trustee," meaning the Official Solicitor, Public Trustee or a corporation appointed by the court to be a trustee, or which is entitled to be a custodian trustee by the Public Trustee Act 1906 s.4(3).

[65] Public Trustee Act 1906 s.13.

[66] See *Re Oddy* [1911] 1 Ch. 532.

[67] But this does not go so far as to put the trustees "under any duty to proffer information to their beneficiary, or to see that he has proper advice merely because they are trustees for him and know that he is entering into a transaction with his beneficial interest with some person or body connected in some way with the trustees, such as a company in which the trustees own some shares beneficially.": *Tito v Waddell (No.2)* [1977] Ch. 106 at 243, per Megarry VC.

[68] Pensions Act 1995 s.41 and regulations thereunder; above, para.17–024.

minutes of trustees' meetings. Documents connected with the trust are trust documents, and prima facie the property of the beneficiaries, and as such open to their inspection.[69]

We saw, however, in Ch.18, that trustees are not bound to give reasons for the exercise of their discretions. The policy of that principle has already been discussed.[70] In the present context, the problem is to reconcile that principle with the principle that beneficiaries are entitled to see the trust documents. If reasons for the exercise of discretionary powers are recorded in documents relating to the trust, are the beneficiaries entitled to see the documents?

> In *Re Londonderry's Settlement*,[71] the donees of a power under a discretionary trust decided to distribute the capital. One member of the discretionary class was dissatisfied with the sum which they intended to give her. She asked for copies of the minutes of trustees' meetings, documents prepared for the meetings, and correspondence between various interested persons. The trustees were willing only to show her documents giving the intended distributions and the annual trust accounts. They declined, in the general interest of the family, to disclose further documents, and brought a summons to determine the nature and extent of their duties in relation to disclosures.

The Court of Appeal found great difficulty in defining in general terms what were the "trust documents" which a beneficiary prima facie had a right to see. Salmon LJ said that the category of trust documents could not be defined. They have however:

> "[T]hese characteristics in common: (1) they are documents in the possession of the trustees as trustees; (2) they contain information about the trust, which the beneficiaries are entitled to know; (3) the beneficiaries have a proprietary interest[72] in the documents and, accordingly, are entitled to see them. If any parts of a document contain information which the beneficiaries are not entitled to know, I doubt whether such parts can be truly said to be integral parts of a trust document."[73]

20–021 Applying this reasoning, it was held in *Hartigan Nominees Pty Ltd v Rydge*[74] that the beneficiaries were not entitled to see the settlor's confidential memorandum of wishes, a document of no legal force setting out how he wished the trustees to exercise their discretions. This was more recently the issue in *Breakspear v Ackland*,[75] where the previous authorities (including those in the Commonwealth and Channel Islands) and academic commentaries were fully analysed. Briggs J applied the *Londonderry* principle and held that a beneficiary was not normally entitled to disclosure of a letter of wishes of the settlor of a family discretionary

---

[69] *O'Rourke v Darbishire* [1920] A.C. 581 at 619, 626. *Blades v Issac* [2016] EWHC 601 (Ch) at [51].

[70] Above, paras 18–042—18–043.

[71] [1965] Ch. 918; REM (1965) 81 L.Q.R. 192. See further D. Hayton in A. Oakley (ed.), *Trends in Contemporary Trust Law* (Oxford: Oxford University Press, 1996) 2 at 49.

[72] The right to information does not, however, depend on the beneficiary having a proprietary right, as explained below. See further *Lewis v Tamplin* [2018] EWHC 777 (Ch) (HHJ Matthews).

[73] [1965] Ch. 918 at 938.

[74] (1992) 29 N.S.W.L.R. 405; J. Lehane [1994] 3 J.Int.P. 60. The court may order the disclosure of a letter of wishes if there is good reason in a particular case; *Re Rabaiotti 1989 Settlements* (2001) 31 Fam. Law 808 (Royal Court of Jersey); *Breakspear v Ackland* [2009] Ch. 32.

[75] [2009] Ch. 32; D. Fox (2008) 67 C.L.J. 252; G. Griffiths [2008] Conv. 322; T. Tey (2008) 22 T.L.I. 126.

trust (leaving for another occasion the question whether the same applied to employee, pension and other commercial trusts). However, the trustees may disclose such a letter if they consider this to be in the interests of the sound administration of the trust, and their discretion to do so should not be fettered by the settlor.

Another question is whether a potential beneficiary of a discretionary trust has any right to information, at any rate if one of a large number of such persons. This was doubted in *Hartigan*. The question of a discretionary beneficiary's right to information arose again in *Re Murphy's Settlements*,[76] where a member of a class of beneficiaries of a discretionary trust sought to compel the settlor to disclose the names and addresses of the trustees. It was held that the court could make such an order, as a discretionary beneficiary was entitled to enquire as to the nature and value of the trust property, its income and how the fund had been invested and distributed. The court would be unlikely, however, to exercise its discretion in favour of a "remote" potential beneficiary, as it would be undesirable for the trustees to be "badgered" with claims by numerous beneficiaries for information.

The matter was considered and clarified by the Privy Council in *Schmidt v Rosewood Trust Ltd*,[77] where the question was whether (i) an unnamed discretionary beneficiary and (ii) the object of a power of appointment could require disclosure of trust documents. Lord Walker noted that trusts had changed radically, and it was often the case (for tax avoidance reasons) that the beneficiaries and their interests or expectations were not clearly identified.[78] It was fundamental to the law of trusts that the court had jurisdiction to supervise and intervene in the administration of trusts, including discretionary trusts.[79] The right to disclosure was an aspect of this inherent supervisory jurisdiction and did not depend on entitlement to a fixed and transmissible beneficial interest. A proprietary right was not necessary nor, in some cases, would it be sufficient. A discretionary beneficiary or an object of a mere power of appointment might be entitled, although the nature of their protection would depend on the court's discretion. The court might need to make a judgment in three areas: (a) whether a discretionary beneficiary or a beneficiary with a remote or wholly defeasible interest should be granted any relief; (b) what classes of documents should be disclosed, either totally or partially; and (c) what safeguards should be imposed to limit the use to be made of them. Where issues of confidentiality arose, the court might have to balance the competing interests of the beneficiaries, the trustees and third parties. The case was remitted to the lower court to decide whether disclosure should be ordered. It may also be relevant for the court to take into

---

[76] [1999] 1 W.L.R. 282; C. Mitchell (1999) 115 L.Q.R. 206.

[77] [2003] 2 A.C. 709 (Isle of Man); J. Davies (2004) 120 L.Q.R. 1. The case does not deal with the position of objects of a personal (non-fiduciary) power. See also *Foreman v Kingstone* [2004] 1 N.Z.L.R. 841; G. Griffiths [2005] Conv. 93; *Charman v Charman* [2006] 2 F.L.R. 422 (disclosure of assets of Bermuda trust in connection with divorce proceedings). W. East [2013] P.C.B. 106. On the considerations for trustees as to whether to disclose documents in a family context, see J. Finch [2014] P.C.B. 104.

[78] Indeed they were often barely perceptible behind "a web of camouflage" ([2003] 2 A.C. 709 at 724).

[79] Described as a "cardinal principle" by Horner J in *Re Hall (Deceased)* [2014] NICh 23.

account the terms of the trust document.[80] Newey J has recently held that, although *Schmidt* can be understood as liberalising the approach as a matter of discretion,

> "it must remain the case that a person must, at least normally, establish as a minimum a prima facie case that he is a beneficiary before there can be any question of the Court requiring a trustee or executor to disclose documents which would be protected by privilege if the applicant were not a beneficiary."[81]

Subject to the above, a trustee's duty is not merely one of answering questions; but also to provide beneficiaries with information concerning their interests under the trust; or, in the case of a child beneficiary, to inform him of his entitlement on coming of age.[82] There is, however, no duty to search out possible objects of a discretionary trust and inform them of their position.[83] Executors are under no positive duty, as a will is a public document.[84]

20–022   **ii. The Impact of Data Protection Legislation**   A significant question for the principles just discussed concerning a beneficiary's access to trust documents is the impact of data protection legislation, which (broadly) confers rights to access one's personal data held by another. This was considered recently by the Court of Appeal in *Dawson-Damer v Taylor Wessing LLP*[85]:

> Trustees of a settlement appointed over $400m to new trustees to hold on discretionary trusts in favour of the claimants' relatives. The claimants were a mother, who was a beneficiary of the original settlement, and her children, while the defendants were the solicitors of the Bahamian trust company which was the sole trustee of the same settlement. The claimants sought to challenge the validity of these appointments. In addition, they served a subject access request ("SAR") under section 7(2) of the Data Protection Act 1998 ("DPA") for personal data held by the defendants as solicitors for the trusts. The defendants refused to provide the data, on the basis that it was covered by legal professional privilege (LPP) and exempted under paragraph 10 of Schedule 7 to the DPA. The claimants also brought proceedings in the Bahamas, challenging the appointments. The defendants argued that LPP should extend to documents not disclosable to the beneficiary under principles of trusts law. The Court of Appeal adopted a narrow view of the LPP exemption and held that the data should be disclosed. The LPP extended only to proceedings in the United Kingdom, and the "DPA does not contain an exception for documents not disclosable to a beneficiary of a trust under trust law principles."[86]

There is a discretion under s.7(9) of the Act whether to make an order compelling compliance with a subject access request, and the judge at first instance had regard to trust law principles as a reason for not ordering

---

[80] As recently determined by the Court of Appeal in Bermuda: *Re Application for Information about a Trust* [2015] W.T.L.R. 559; 16 I.T.E.L.R. 955.

[81] *Birdseye v Roythorne* [2015] EWHC 1003 (Ch) at [24].

[82] *Hawkesley v May* [1956] 1 Q.B. 304; including, it seems, his rights under the rule in *Saunders v Vautier* (1841) Cr. & Ph. 240; below, para.23–001; A. Samuels (1970) 34 Conv.(N.S.) 29.

[83] *Hartigan Nominees Pty Ltd v Rydge* (1992) 29 N.S.W.L.R. 405.

[84] *Re Lewis* [1904] 2 Ch. 656; *Re Mackay* [1906] 1 Ch. 25; *Cancer Research Campaign v Ernest Brown & Co (A Firm)* [1997] S.T.C. 1425 (resulting in loss of opportunity to vary estate for inheritance tax purposes within statutory time limit).

[85] *Dawson-Damer v Taylor Wessing LLP (Information Commissioner intervening)* [2017] EWCA Civ 74; [2017] 1 W.L.R. 3255; D. Russell and T. Graham (2017) 23 T. & T. 967.

[86] [2017] EWCA Civ 74 per Arden LJ at [54].

compliance. However, Arden LJ disagreed, holding that the collateral intention of the claimants to use the information for the pursuit of their litigation against the trustee was not a barrier to an order being made in their favour, provided that it did not amount to an abuse of process.[87] This decision clearly may have major implications,[88] not least in the potential to increase the beneficiary's ability to access trust documents. It is important to note that the court took the view that in this case it was not exercising a jurisdiction in relation to the administration of the trust, nor was it "exercising any jurisdiction in relation to the administration of the trust, which is a matter for the Bahamian courts."[89] The impact of *Dawon-Damer* may therefore be particularly keenly felt in cases involving foreign jurisdictions, but requests under the data protection legislation may also involve a collateral attack on traditional trust law principles in this area.

---

[87] [2017] EWCA Civ 74 per Arden LJ at [108]–[114]: a mere collateral purpose will not usually amount to an abuse of process in these circumstances (at [109]).
[88] For consideration of the implications of *Dawson-Damer* (albeit outside the trust context), see *Ittihadieh v 5-11 Cheyne Gardens RTM Company Ltd* [2017] EWCA Civ 121.
[89] [2017] EWCA Civ 74 per Arden LJ at [113].

CHAPTER 21

POWERS OF TRUSTEES

1. INTRODUCTION

TRUSTEES may exercise such powers as are given to them by the trust **21–001** instrument or by statute. A power, as has been seen,[1] is to be distinguished from a duty, in that its exercise is not compulsory. In the absence of bad faith, the court will not interfere with the exercise of discretions. At most, the holder of a fiduciary power is under a duty to consider its exercise.[2]

---

[1] Above, para.2–021.

[2] As to whether trustees can fetter their powers by deciding in advance how to exercise them, see H. Arthur (1993) 7 T.L.I. 69.

[577]

Originally, it was necessary to spell out a trustee's powers in detail in the trust instrument. The Trustee Act 1925 (as amended) provided the basic powers needed by trustees. They may unless otherwise stated be excluded or amended as desired.[3] The 1925 Act became outdated in many respects, in particular with regard to delegation, insurance, remuneration, investment and the power to employ nominees and custodians. The powers were substantially modernised by the Trustee Act 2000, as will be explained in the relevant sections of this chapter. The Act came into force on 1 February 2001. Practitioners may continue to insert detailed provisions into the trust instrument, and many contemporary trust instruments give the trustees a power to amend the trust.[4]

2. TRUSTEES OF LAND

21–002 Section 6(1) of the Trusts of Land and Appointment of Trustees Act 1996 provides that:

> For the purpose of exercising their functions as trustees, the trustees of land have in relation to the land subject to the trust all the powers of an absolute owner.

Where the trust includes land and personalty, these powers are thus confined to the land. The width of the statutory powers is reduced by an important proviso: the powers conferred by s.6 "shall not be exercised in contravention of, or of any order made in pursuance of, any other enactment or any rule of law or equity."[5] The trustees, in exercising their powers under s.6, must also have regard to the rights of the beneficiaries,[6] and they have a general duty to consult adult beneficiaries with an interest in possession.[7] Thus trustees of land remain subject to the general duties imposed by equity on trustees and to restrictions on the statutory powers of trustees contained in other legislation or in other sections of the 1996 Act.[8] They are also subject to the statutory duty of care under s.1 of the Trustee Act 2000.[9]

Section 6 applies whether the trust of land is express, implied, resulting or constructive, and whether arising before or after the commencement of the 1996

---

[3] Trustee Act 1925 s.69(2). *Bullard v Bullard* [2017] EWHC 3 (Ch).

[4] See *Society of Lloyd's v Robinson* [1999] 1 W.L.R. 756; below, para.23–002.

[5] s.6(6). See also s.6(7).

[6] s.6(5). A purchaser of unregistered land is not concerned to see that this duty has been complied with; s.16(1). For registered land, see Land Registration Act 2002 s.26; G. Ferris and G. Battersby (2003) 119 L.Q.R. 94 and [2009] Conv. 39; S. Pascoe [2005] Conv. 140.

[7] s.11(1). This duty may be excluded by the settlor.

[8] See s.6(8). If a conveyance of unregistered land by the trustees (other than charity trustees) contravenes s.6(6) or (8), it is not invalid if the purchaser had no actual notice of the contravention; s.16(2). For registered land, see Land Registration Act 2002 s.26, above.

[9] s.6(9), introduced by Trustee Act 2000.

Act; trusts for sale and bare trusts are also included.[10] In the case of an expressly created trust of land, however, s.6 may be excluded by the settlor or the powers made exercisable subject to consent.[11]

In addition to the general powers described above, the 1996 Act confers certain specific powers on trustees of land. Under the general law, beneficiaries who are of full age and capacity and together absolutely entitled may call for a transfer of the trust property.[12] In the case of land, s.6(2) gives the trustees power to convey to such beneficiaries provided each is absolutely entitled,[13] even though they have not required the trustees to do so. If the beneficiaries do not co-operate, the court may order them to do whatever is necessary to secure that the land vests in them.

Where beneficiaries of full age are absolutely entitled as tenants in common, the trustees may partition the land or any part of it, obtaining the consent of each beneficiary and providing (by mortgage or otherwise) for the payment of any equality money.[14] This power may be excluded or made subject to other consents in an expressly created trust of land.[15] The delegation powers of trustees of land are dealt with later in this chapter.

3. POWER OF SALE[16]

A. Land

Land is held either by an owner absolutely entitled or under a trust of land or, in the case of a settlement created before the commencement of the Trusts of Land and Appointment of Trustees Act 1996, under a strict settlement. In the latter case, the tenant for life has the legal estate and a power of sale.[17] In the case of a trust of land, the legal estate is vested in the trustees, and they have a power of sale.[18] Where an express trust for sale is created, the trustees have power to postpone the sale indefinitely in the exercise of their discretion, despite any provision to the contrary in the trust instrument.[19] The receipt of at least two

21–003

---

[10] s.1. The Act came into force on 1 January 1997. For the application of the Act to personal representatives; see s.18.

[11] s.8. The settlor of a charitable trust may not exclude s.6. See G. Watt [1997] Conv. 263, discussing whether the power of sale may be excluded.

[12] *Saunders v Vautier* (1841) Cr. & Ph. 240; below, para.23–001.

[13] i.e. they are equitable co-owners. That their interests together add up to the whole does not otherwise suffice.

[14] Trusts of Land and Appointment of Trustees Act 1996 s.7. A purchaser of unregistered land is not concerned to see that the beneficiaries have consented; s.16(1). For registered land, see Land Registration Act 2002 s.26. The Law Commission has suggested some clarification: Law Com. CP No. 227, *Updating the Land Registration Act 2002: A Consultation Paper* (2016), para.5.63.

[15] Trusts of Land and Appointment of Trustees Act 1996 s.8.

[16] See generally R. Mitchell [1999] Conv. 84.

[17] Settled Land Act 1925 s.38(i).

[18] Trusts of Land and Appointment of Trustees Act 1996 s.6(1); above. This includes bare trusts; s.1(2). See G. Watt [1997] Conv. 263, as to whether the power of sale may be excluded. Personal representatives on intestacy have a power to sell land; Administration of Estates Act 1925 s.33, as amended by the 1996 Act.

[19] Trusts of Land and Appointment of Trustees Act 1996 s.4.

trustees or of a trust corporation is required for all capital money arising under a trust of land or strict settlement,[20] and the same rule applies to the overreaching of the beneficial interests.[21]

B.   Chattels

21-004   Where chattels or other personalty are held upon trust for sale, the position is the same as with land except that the receipt of a sole trustee is sufficient discharge to a purchaser.[22] The trust for sale may arise expressly or be implied, as we have seen, under the rule in *Howe v Earl of Dartmouth*,[23] although the latter rule does not now apply to trusts created after 1 October 2013.[24] Personal representatives have power to sell chattels (and other property) on intestacy.[25]

C.   Other Property

21-005   In the case of many other forms of property, a power of sale, if not given expressly, will usually be implied. Unauthorised investments, investments which the trustees think are not suitable for the trust, and trust property which is not in a state of investment at all, should be sold and invested in accordance with the express terms of the relevant investment power, or with the provisions of the Trustee Act 2000.[26]

Whenever trustees are authorised to pay or apply capital money for any purpose or in any manner, they have power to raise such money by sale, mortgage, etc. of the trust property then in possession.[27] But this does not authorise trustees to raise money by charging existing investments in order to purchase others.[28]

---

[20] Trustee Act 1925 s.14; Law of Property Act 1925 s.27(2); Serttled Land Act 1925 s.94(1).

[21] Law of Property Act 1925 s.2.

[22] Trustee Act 1925 s.14; below, para.21–007.

[23] (1802) 7 Ves.Jr. 137; above, para.20–003.

[24] Trusts (Capital and Income) Act 2013 s.1(a) and s.1(b); Trusts (Capital and Income) Act 2013 (Commencement No.1) Order (SI 2013/676) art.4.

[25] Administration of Estates Act 1925 s.33, as amended by Trusts of Land and Appointment of Trustees Act 1996 Sch.2. The definition of "personal chattels" in Administration of Estates Act 1925 s.55(1)(x), was amended by the Inheritance and Trustees' Powers Act 2014 s.3(1) to mean: "tangible movable property, other than any such property which—consists of money or securities for money, or was used at the death of the intestate solely or mainly for business purposes, or was held at the death of the intestate solely as an investment."

[26] Above, paras 19–014—19–021.

[27] Trustee Act 1925 s.16(1).

[28] *Re Suenson-Taylor* [1974] 1 W.L.R. 1280 (land).

D. Sales by Trustees

The detailed provisions relating to sales by trustees are contained in the Trustee Act 1925 s.12.[29] Trustees may sell all or any part of the property, by public auction or by private contract, subject to any such conditions respecting title or other matter as the trustee thinks fit.

    As we have seen, trustees are under an overriding duty to obtain the best price for the beneficiaries.[30] If they fail to do so, the beneficiaries may seek an injunction restraining the sale.[31] But if the sale has taken place, s.13 of the 1925 Act provides that it may not be impeached by a beneficiary on the ground that any of the conditions of the sale were unduly depreciatory, unless it also appears that the consideration for the sale was thereby rendered inadequate.[32] A purchaser will not be affected unless she was acting in collusion with the trustees.[33]

21–006

4. POWER TO GIVE RECEIPTS: TRUSTEE ACT 1925 SECTION 14

By the Trustee Act 1925 s.14, the written receipt by a trustee for money, securities, investments, etc. is a sufficient discharge to the person paying, and effectually exonerates him from being answerable for any loss or misapplication of the money. The section applies notwithstanding anything to the contrary in the trust instrument,[34] and applies to sole trustees, except in the case of proceeds of sale or other capital money arising under a trust of land or under the Settled Land Act where, unless the trustee is a trust corporation, the receipt of at least two trustees is necessary.[35] Where there is more than one trustee, all must sign, in accordance with the rule that they must act together.[36]

21–007

5. POWER TO INSURE: TRUSTEE ACT 1925 SECTION 19

A. Insurance

At common law trustees have a power to insure the trust property, and possibly a duty to do so (of uncertain scope) in accordance with their general duty of acting in the best interests of the trust.[37] As a general rule, however, they are not liable if

21–008

---

[29] As amended by Trusts of Land and Appointment of Trustees Act 1996 Sch.3.

[30] *Buttle v Saunders* [1950] 2 All E.R. 193; above, para.19–002. See also *Sergeant v National Westminster Bank* (1991) 61 P. & C.R. 518 and *Bagum v Hafiz* [2015] EWCA Civ 801; [2016] Ch. 241.

[31] *Wheelwright v Walker* (1883) 23 Ch.D. 752.

[32] Trustee Act 1925 s.13(1); *Dance v Goldingham* (1873) L.R. 8 Ch.App. 902. The trustee may, of course, be personally liable.

[33] Trustee Act 1925 s.13(2).

[34] Trustee Act 1925 s.14(3).

[35] Trustee Act 1925 s.14(2) as amended by Trusts of Land and Appointment of Trustees Act 1996 Sch.3; Settled Land Act 1925 s.94.

[36] Above, para.18–007; charitable and pension trustees may act by a majority.

[37] Law Com. No. 260, *Trustees' Powers and Duties* (1999), paras 6.7–6.8.

the property is destroyed; and if the trustees differ on the question whether the property should be insured, it seems that nothing can be done to compel them.[38]

Section 19 of the Trustee Act 1925 provided a power to insure, but it was limited and unsatisfactory. A new s.19 was substituted by the Trustee Act 2000.[39] This provides that a trustee may insure any trust property against risks of loss or damage due to any event and pay the premiums out of income or capital. In the case of property held on a bare trust (i.e. where the beneficiary is of full age and capacity and absolutely entitled or, where there is more than one beneficiary, each of them is of full age and capacity and they are together absolutely entitled), the power is subject to their directions.[40] The statutory duty of care[41] applies to the exercise of the power to insure, whether under s.19 or under an express power in the instrument.[42]

The policy moneys must be treated as capital and applied in accordance with the terms of the trust.[43]

B.   Reinstatement

21–009   Trustees may apply the policy money relating to land or other property in reinstatement, subject to the consent of any person whose consent is required by the trust instrument,[44] and without prejudice to the statutory or other right of any person to require the money to be spent in reinstatement.[45] Persons interested under the trust can, therefore, insist on having the premises rebuilt if they wish; or, if they do not wish it, they can prevent the trustees from using the money for that purpose, but in any case the money is capital money.

6.   POWER TO COMPOUND LIABILITIES: TRUSTEE ACT 1925 SECTION 15

21–010   Trustees are given a wide discretion in settling claims which may be made by third persons against the trust estate,[46] or by the trust estate against third persons. Adult beneficiaries who are under no disability may, of course, make any arrangement that they wish among themselves. Until the Variation of Trusts Act 1958[47] was passed, the court had no general power to approve adjustments in the beneficial interests. But the dividing line is difficult to draw. The court has inherent power to compromise a genuine dispute between beneficiaries[48] and s.15 has been held to authorise the settlement of a dispute with a person claiming to be

---

[38] *Re McEacharn* (1911) 103 L.T. 900.
[39] s.34. The substituted provision applies to trusts whenever created.
[40] Trustee Act 1925 s.19(2), (3).
[41] Trustee Act 2000 s.1; above, Ch.18.
[42] Trustee Act 2000 Sch.1 para.5.
[43] Trustee Act 1925 s.20.
[44] Trustee Act 1925 s.20(4).
[45] Trustee Act 1925 s.20(5).
[46] The section confers no power to make reasonable provision for satisfying contingent claims. See *Re Yorke (Deceased)* [1997] 4 All E.R. 907.
[47] Below, Ch.23.
[48] *Re Barbour's Settlement* [1974] 1 W.L.R. 1198; *Re Downshire SE* [1953] Ch. 218. Cf. *Re MK Airlines Ltd (In Liquidation)* [2012] EWHC 1018 (Ch); [2013] Bus. L.R. 169.

a beneficiary,[49] and also litigation between the trustees and beneficiaries on the question whether certain property was subject to the trust or not.[50] It was no objection to the jurisdiction under s.15 that the proposed compromise involved an adjustment of interests among the beneficiaries.[51] In *Re MF Global UK Ltd*,[52] David Richards J held, in the context of a bank going into special administration, that the trustee of a client money statutory trust had the power to compromise claims under s.15, as it would take express words to exclude the duty.[53]

Personal representatives and trustees may accept compositions for debts; allow time for payment of debts; compromise, abandon, submit to arbitration or otherwise settle any claim; and may enter into such agreements and execute such instruments as may be necessary for the efficient performance of these duties.[54] A wide power of this nature is of great practical importance in enabling the trustee to make a reasonable compromise instead of being obliged to litigate in respect of every possible claim, or risk liability for breach of trust if she fails to do so.[55] Trustees are not liable for loss caused by any act done by them in the exercise of the powers conferred by this section as long as they have discharged the statutory duty of care under the Trustee Act 2000,[56] and they have reached their decision by exercising their discretion and not by failing to consider the matter.[57] They may apply to the court to sanction a compromise. The court must consider what is the best from the point of view of everybody concerned, paying especial attention to the interests of child beneficiaries.[58]

7. POWER IN REGARD TO REVERSIONARY INTERESTS: TRUSTEE ACT 1925 SECTION 22[59]

Where part of the trust property consists of choses in action or reversionary interests the trustees may, on such interests falling into possession, "agree or ascertain the amount or value thereof in such manner as they think fit," without being responsible for any loss, if they have discharged the statutory duty of care under the Trustee Act 2000. But nothing in the section is to be construed as relieving trustees from the duty of getting in such interests as soon as possible after their falling into possession, for this is one of their primary duties.[60]

21–011

---

[49] *Eaton v Buchanan* [1911] A.C. 253; cf. *Abdallah v Rickards* (1888) 4 T.L.R. 622.

[50] *Re Earl of Strafford* [1980] Ch. 28.

[51] [1980] Ch. 28.

[52] *Re MF Global UK Ltd (In Special Administration) (No.5)* [2014] EWHC 2222 (Ch); [2014] Bus. L.R. 1156.

[53] [2014] EWHC 2222 (Ch) at [27]. *In re Nortel Networks UK Ltd* [2016] EWHC 2769 (Ch); *Re Cup Trust* [2016] EWHC 876 (Ch) (charities).

[54] See *Re Shenton* [1935] Ch. 651.

[55] *Re Brogden* [1948] Ch. 206; above, para.19–003. *Bradstock Group Pension Scheme Trustees Ltd v Bradstock Group Plc* [2002] I.C.R. 1427. *Re MF Global UK Ltd* [2014] EWHC 2222 (Ch) at [27]. *Trustees of the Singer & Friedlander Ltd Pension and Assurance Scheme v Corbett* [2015] Pens. L.R. 31.

[56] s.15(1), as amended by Trustee Act 2000. For the duty of care, see Ch.18.

[57] *Re Greenwood* (1911) 105 L.T. 509.

[58] *Re Ezekiel's ST* [1942] Ch. 230; *Re Earl of Strafford* [1980] Ch. 28.

[59] As amended by Trustee Act 2000.

[60] See above, para.19–001.

8. POWER TO DELEGATE

21–012 This is another area in which it is necessary to outline the historical background to the rules in order to understand their operation under the Trustee Act 2000.[61]

A. The Early Rule in Equity

The basic rule is that a person entrusted with a fiduciary duty does not fulfil it if she delegates it to someone else; she remains liable for the other person's default.[62] *Delegatus non potest delegare.*[63] But this rule was never inflexible, even in the times when the most rigorous views were being taken of the standard of conduct required from a trustee. Indeed, there are certain things which a business person would always delegate to a skilled agent. Thus, the employment of solicitors for legal, and brokers and bankers for financial, matters was sanctioned by ordinary business practice. This was recognised as early as 1754, by Lord Hardwicke in *Ex p. Belchier*,[64] and the trend of judicial decision, fortified by occasional statutory provisions, grew more and more tolerant of delegation in cases of commercial necessity. Following the two famous decisions of the House of Lords in *Speight v Gaunt*[65] and *Learoyd v Whiteley*,[66] it could be said that delegation was permissible if the trustees could show that it was reasonably necessary in the circumstances or was in accordance with ordinary business practice. The trustees had to exercise proper care in the selection of the agent, employ her in her proper field,[67] and exercise general supervision.[68] Trustees who delegated without authority remained vicariously liable for any resulting loss.[69] They were not vicariously liable for the acts of authorised agents, but incurred personal liability for failing to act prudently in matters of supervision and so forth.

A trustee's discretions could not, however, be delegated.[70] Further, exemption clauses expressly limiting his liability to cases of "wilful default" did not relieve him from the responsibility of acting as a prudent man of business.[71] Nor did the statutes of 1859 and 1893, the predecessors of the Trustee Act 1925 s.30(1) (now repealed), which restricted the liability of trustees to cases of wilful default, do more than change the onus of proof; these statutes placed the onus on:

---

[61] See below, para.21–014.

[62] *Turner v Corney* (1841) 5 Beav. 515 per Lord Langdale MR at 517.

[63] "Delegation cannot itself be delegated".

[64] (1754) Amb. 218.

[65] (1884) 9 App.Cas. 1.

[66] (1887) 12 App.Cas. 727.

[67] *Fry v Tapson* (1884) 28 Ch.D. 268.

[68] *Rowland v Witherden* (1851) 3 Mac. & G. 568.

[69] *Clough v Bond* (1838) 3 My. & Cr. 490 at 496–497; *Speight v Gaunt* (1884) 9 App.Cas. 1; *Target Holdings Ltd v Redferns (A Firm)* [1996] 1 A.C. 421 at 434.

[70] *Speight v Gaunt* (1884) 9 App.Cas. 1; below, para.21–019.

[71] *Re Chapman* [1896] 2 Ch. 763; *Re Brier* (1884) 26 Ch.D. 238; cf. *Armitage v Nurse* [1998] Ch. 241 at 252; below. Exemption clauses are discussed at para.18–005, above.

"[T]hose who seek to charge an executor or trustee with a loss arising from the default of an agent, when the propriety of employing the agent has been established."[72]

The kind of delegation referred to above is sometimes termed "collective delegation", meaning that all the trustees acting together appoint an agent to carry out some function. This may be contrasted with "individual delegation", where one trustee delegates all his functions to another person, which may be done by power of attorney.[73]

B. Trustee Act 1925

Under the Trustee Act 1925, trustees were no longer required to show a need to delegate. Delegation as such was accepted as a normal method of performing the duties incidental to trusteeship; but the overall duties of trusteeship remained in the trustees. Section 23(1) of the 1925 Act provided that a trustee could delegate acts (of an administrative nature) to agents, and that he would not be responsible for the default of the agent "if employed in good faith". Section 30(1) provided that a trustee was responsible for his own acts and defaults but not for those of any co-trustee or agent, nor for any other loss unless occasioned by "his own wilful default". The proper interpretation of, and the relationship between, these provisions remained a matter of doubt until their repeal by the Trustee Act 2000.

It was mentioned above that s.23(1) permitted the delegation of administrative acts. It did not permit the delegation of the exercise of discretions. That may be done by power of attorney under s.25 of the Trustee Act 1925,[74] but the trustee remains liable for the defaults of the attorney.

21–013

C. Trustee Act 2000

A major purpose of the Trustee Act 2000 was to reform trustees' powers of delegation.[75] First, it repealed the problematic ss.23 and 30 of the Act of 1925 and provided in their place a clearer framework for delegation. Secondly, it extended the circumstances in which discretionary *functions* may be delegated. This is particularly important in the context of investment, but is not confined to that. Other statutory provisions permitting the delegation of discretions are dealt with separately below.[76]

The wide powers of delegation introduced by the Act apply to trusts whenever created, but are subject to any restrictions or exclusions in the trust instrument or other legislation.[77] The powers apply to pension trusts, save that the trustees may not delegate investment functions nor appoint nominees and custodians under the

21–014

---

[72] *Re Brier* (1884) 26 Ch.D. 238 per Lord Selborne at 243; *Re Chapman* [1896] 2 Ch. 763 at 776.
[73] Below, para.21–019.
[74] Below, para.21–019.
[75] There is little authority on the statutory provisions, but an example is *Daniel v Tee* [2016] EWHC 1538 (Ch); [2016] 4 W.L.R. 115: considered above, para.19–017.
[76] Below, Sections D, E.
[77] Trustee Act 2000 ss.26, 27. For transitional provisions, see Sch.3.

new Act, as these matters should be dealt with under the pensions legislation.[78] The scope and effect of the power to delegate will now be considered.

21–015   **i.   General Power to Delegate.**   The approach taken in the Act of 2000 is that trustees may delegate any or all of their "delegable functions". Section 11 does not (save in the case of charitable trusts) provide a list of such functions, but instead lists those which may *not* be delegated. The delegable functions are those *other than*:

(a)   any function relating to whether or in what way any assets of the trust should be distributed;

(b)   any power to decide whether any fees or other payment due to be made out of the trust funds should be made out of income or capital;

(c)   any power to appoint a person to be a trustee of the trust; or

(d)   any power conferred by any other enactment or the trust instrument which permits the trustees to delegate any of their functions or to appoint a person to act as nominee or custodian.

Thus, the trustees cannot delegate their power of selection amongst the beneficiaries of a discretionary trust. They may, however, delegate investment decision-making,[79] and thereby obtain the benefit of the skilled professional service of an investment manager authorised under the financial services legislation. The detailed provisions of the Act in relation to the delegation of investment and other asset management functions were considered in Ch.19.[80] These statutory powers are additional to a trustee's power of individual delegation by power of attorney.[81] In the case of a charitable trust, s.11 lists the functions which may be delegated. Broadly, these are matters relating to income generation, including investment, but are otherwise administrative acts. These have already been mentioned.[82]

The trustees may delegate to one or more of their number, but not to a beneficiary, even if she is also a trustee.[83] If the same function is delegated to two or more persons, they must act jointly.

If it is reasonably necessary to do so, the trustees may delegate on terms permitting sub-delegation, restricting the liability of the agent, or permitting her to act in circumstances capable of giving rise to a conflict of interest.[84] This provision permits delegation to fund managers on their standard terms of business.

Whether the delegation is under the Act of 2000 or otherwise, the trustees may pay the agent from the trust funds if the terms of her appointment so provide, but

---

[78]   Trustee Act 2000 s.36. The delegation provisions do not apply to trustees of unit trusts or those managing a fund under a common investment or common deposit scheme for charities; ss.37, 38.

[79]   For a consideration of trustees' duties in this context, see *Daniel v Tee* [2016] EWHC 1538 (Ch); [2016] 4 W.L.R. 115 per Richard Spearman QC (sitting as a deputy judge of the High Court) at [192]–[198].

[80]   Above, para.19–018.

[81]   Below, Sections D, E.

[82]   Above, para.15–095.

[83]   Trustee Act 2000 s.12.

[84]   Trustee Act 2000 s.14.

the amount must not exceed what is reasonable for the services in question.[85] They may also reimburse her from the trust funds for expenses properly incurred.

Where the trustees have appointed an agent under the Act of 2000 or under the trust instrument or other legislation, they must keep the arrangement under review and must consider whether there is a need to revoke the appointment or to exercise any power they may have to give directions to the agent.[86]

ii. Nominees and Custodians. Prior to the Trustee Act 2000, it was doubtful whether trustees could appoint nominees or custodians in the absence of an express power to do so. This is a convenient practice which reduces delays in completing share transactions.

21–016

In order to allow trustees to benefit from modern investment practices, s.16 of the Trustee Act 2000 permits trustees to appoint nominees and vest trust assets in them, while s.17 permits the appointment of a custodian to undertake safe custody of the assets or of any documents or records concerning them.[87] The provisions already discussed concerning the terms of appointment of agents, remuneration and the duty to keep the arrangement under review apply also to nominees and custodians.

As mentioned above, a trustee may not vest trust assets in a third party unless authorised by the trust instrument or legislation. Thus, under the general law investments must be in the joint names of the trustees. If two trustees divide investments or invest separately, and one commits a breach of trust, the other will be equally liable for any loss.[88]

It is convenient also to mention here the related rule that trust capital should be received by all the trustees unless the trust instrument or legislation provides otherwise.[89] However, it has always been possible to delegate the receipt of income to one of several trustees,[90] although the co-trustees may be liable if they permit the payee to retain the money for longer than necessary.[91] In the case of company shares, the articles provide that trusts shall not be recognised.[92] In the case of joint ownership, the dividend is paid to the first named who can give a valid receipt.[93]

iii. Duty of Care. The statutory duty of care laid down in s.1 of the Trustee Act 2000[94] applies to a trustee when exercising the power of delegation under the Act or under any other power of delegation.[95] She is subject to the duty of care

21–017

---

[85] Trustee Act 2000 ss.14, 32. See also s.29(6) (remuneration of co-trustee appointed as agent).

[86] Trustee Act 2000 ss.21, 22. This is subject to any contrary intention in the trust instrument or other legislation.

[87] Above, para.20–018.

[88] *Lewis v Nobbs* (1878) 8 Ch.D. 591.

[89] See *Lee v Sankey* (1873) L.R. 15 Eq. 204; Trustee Act 1925 s.14; above, para.21–007.

[90] *Townley v Sherborne* (1634) J. Bridg. 35.

[91] *Carruthers v Carruthers* [1896] A.C. 659.

[92] Companies Act 2006 s.126.

[93] Companies (Tables A–F) Regulations 1985 (SI 1985/805), Table A, para.106. Further regulations have been made under the Companies Act 2006 s.19; The Companies (Model Articles) Regulations 2008 (SI 2008/3229).

[94] Above, para.18–003. *Daniel v Tee* [2016] EWHC 1538 (Ch); [2016] 4 W.L.R. 115.

[95] Trustee Act 2000 Sch.1 para.2.

when appointing an agent, nominee or custodian and when carrying out the obligation to keep the arrangement under review. In particular, she must comply with the duty when selecting the person to act, determining the terms on which she is to act, and, where asset management functions are delegated, when preparing the policy statement under s.15 of the Trustee Act 2000.[96] It appears that the duty of care applies to the selection of a person to act under a power of attorney, even though the delegating trustee in any event remains liable for any defaults of the attorney.[97]

21–018   **iv. Liability of Trustee.**   Section 23 of the Trustee Act 2000 provides that a trustee is not liable for any act or default of the agent, nominee or custodian unless she has failed to comply with the duty of care when entering into the arrangement or when keeping it under review. Where the arrangement permitted the agent to appoint a substitute, the trustee is not liable for the acts of the substitute unless she failed to comply with the duty of care when agreeing the term permitting substitution or when reviewing the arrangement. Section 23 applies whether the delegation was in the exercise of the power under the Act of 2000 or under an express power or pursuant to other legislation, unless it would be inconsistent with the trust instrument or other legislation. So, for example, s.23 will not apply to the question whether a trustee is liable for the acts of a person to whom she has granted a power of attorney, because s.25(5) of the Trustee Act 1925 provides that the trustee remains liable (irrespective of fault) for the acts and defaults of the donee of the power.

D.   Other Statutory Provisions Permitting Delegation of Discretions

21–019   We have seen that trustees cannot as a general rule delegate their discretions, for example the distribution of funds to beneficiaries of a discretionary trust. The delegation of discretions is permitted by Pt IV of the Trustee Act 2000, s.25 of the 1925 Act, s.9 of the Trusts of Land and Appointment of Trustees Act 1996, and under s.1 of the Trustee Delegation Act 1999.

Section 25[98] enables a trustee to delegate by deed[99] to any person[100] by power of attorney for 12 months or any shorter specified period "all or any of the trusts, powers and discretions vested in him as trustee either alone or jointly with any other person or persons." Written notice must be given within seven days to each of the other trustees and to each person who has the power to appoint new trustees.[101] It was previously doubted whether a trustee who was not himself entitled to remuneration could pay the delegate out of the trust fund. This was alleviated by the provisions of the Trustee Act 2000 enabling professional trustees

---

[96] Above, para.19–018.
[97] See Section D, below.
[98] As amended by Trustee Delegation Act 1999 s.5.
[99] In the case of delegation by a single donor, a prescribed form must be used; s.25(5), (6).
[100] Including a trust corporation; s.25(3).
[101] s.25(4). But failure to give notice does not, in favour of a person dealing with the donee of the power, invalidate any act done by the donee.

to charge even though the trust instrument does not so provide.[102] Delegation to a sole trustee is permitted, but this cannot circumvent the rule requiring payment of capital money to at least two trustees.[103] Following the Trustee Delegation Act 1999, a power of attorney under s.25 of the 1925 Act may be an enduring power or a lasting power of attorney under the Mental Capacity Act 2005. These powers survive the incapacity of the trustee.[104]

These provisions should only be used when such delegation is essential, for the donor of the power of attorney remains liable for the acts and defaults of the donee.[105]

The position relating to trusts of land is now found in s.9 of the Trusts of Land and Appointment of Trustees Act 1996, which permits the trustees to delegate any of their functions as trustees relating to the land, including sale, to any beneficiary (or beneficiaries) of full age and beneficially entitled to an interest in possession.[106] The delegation may be for any period or indefinite,[107] and must be by power of attorney[108] given by all the trustees jointly. It is revocable by any one or more of them, and will also be revoked if another person is appointed trustee.[109] Where a beneficiary ceases to be beneficially entitled, the delegation is revoked so far as it relates to him, but the functions remain exercisable by the remaining beneficiaries in the case of joint delegation.[110]

Beneficiaries to whom functions have been delegated under s.9 are in the same position as the trustees in relation to the exercise of the functions, but are not regarded as trustees for any other purpose. In particular, they cannot sub-delegate or give a valid receipt for capital money.[111] The provisions of the 1996 Act dealing with the trustees' liability for any defaults of the beneficiary to whom they have delegated were changed by the Trustee Act 2000. The duty of care under s.1 of the Act of 2000 applies to trustees of land in entering into an arrangement to delegate their functions under s.9 of the 1996 Act.[112] If the delegation is not irrevocable, they must keep the arrangement under review, including the need to exercise any power they have to revoke the delegation or to give directions to the beneficiary. The trustees are not liable for the acts or defaults of the beneficiary unless they have failed to comply with their duty of care in deciding to delegate or in reviewing the arrangement.[113]

A more general power of delegation applying to trustees of land who are also beneficiaries, in other words co-owners, is provided by s.1 of the Trustee

---

[102] Trustee Act 2000 s.29.

[103] Trustee Delegation Act 1999 ss.7, 8. Previously delegation to a sole co-trustee was not permitted.

[104] Trustee Delegation Act 1999 s.6, repealing s.2(8) of the Enduring Powers of Attorney Act 1985. The 1985 Act was repealed and re-enacted by the Mental Capacity Act 2005 (which also repealed s.6 of the 1999 Act). For enduring and lasting powers, see Section E, below.

[105] Trustee Act 1925 s.25(7).

[106] Where the trustees purport to delegate to a person who is not such a beneficiary, third parties dealing with that person in good faith are protected by s.9(2).

[107] s.9(5).

[108] s.9(6) provides that this cannot be an enduring power of attorney or a lasting power of attorney under the Mental Capacity Act 2005; below, para.21–020.

[109] s.9(3). It is not revoked if any grantor ceases to be a trustee.

[110] s.9(4).

[111] s.9(7).

[112] See s.9A of the 1996 Act, inserted by Trustee Act 2000 Sch.2.

[113] s.9A of the 1996 Act.

Delegation Act 1999. Such a trustee may delegate all trustee functions, including discretions, relating to the land or to income arising from it or to its proceeds of sale by power of attorney, which may be an enduring power of attorney or a lasting power of attorney under the Mental Capacity Act 2005.[114] Trustees who are not also beneficiaries do not fall within the scope of this provision. If they wish to delegate their discretions, they must do so under s.25 of the Trustee Act 1925.

E.   Delegation by Enduring or Lasting Power of Attorney

21–020   We have seen that s.25 of the Trustee Act 1925 permits a trustee to delegate all of her functions by power of attorney for a maximum of 12 months, subject to various procedural requirements.[115] This could be done, for example, if she was going abroad.

Prior to 1985, there was no possibility of a power of attorney which would continue in force after the donor had become mentally incapable, as such incapacity automatically revoked the power. The Enduring Powers of Attorney Act 1985, which introduced a power of attorney which would survive the donor's subsequent incapacity, was repealed and re-enacted by the Mental Capacity Act 2005.[116] Enduring powers of attorney created before 1 October 2007 remain valid and may be registered at any time, but no new enduring powers of attorney may be created as from 1 October 2007.

The Act of 2005 introduced the lasting power of attorney,[117] which may apply to property and financial affairs or to health and welfare matters. A lasting power of attorney which applies to property and financial affairs is similar to an enduring power of attorney. The main distinction is that a lasting power of attorney is not valid unless registered, whereas an enduring power of attorney needs to be registered only upon the onset of the donor's mental incapacity.

The Trustee Delegation Act 1999 draws a distinction between trustees who have a beneficial interest and those who do not. Its broad effect is first, to permit the delegation by power of attorney of all the functions of a trustee who also has a beneficial interest in the property. This is primarily directed to co-owners of land, who are normally both trustees and beneficiaries. Secondly, it ensures that a trustee who has no beneficial interest may only delegate trustee functions by power of attorney subject to the safeguards imposed by s.25 of the Trustee Act 1925. Thirdly, it ensures that the rule requiring capital money to be paid to at least two trustees cannot be circumvented by using a power of attorney.

In the case of a trustee who has a beneficial interest, s.1 of the 1999 Act permits the delegation by power of attorney of the trustee's powers and duties in relation to land, income from the land or its proceeds of sale. This may take the form of an enduring or lasting power of attorney.[118] The donor (the trustee) is

---

[114] See Section E, below, where the 1999 Act is more fully discussed.
[115] Above, para.21–019.
[116] The provisions of the 1985 Act are now found in Sch.4 of the Act of 2005.
[117] Mental Capacity Act 2005, ss.9–14.
[118] Such powers may not be created by trustees of land under s.9(1) of the Trusts of Land and Appointment of Trustees Act 1996; s.9(6), as amended by Sch.6 of the Mental Capacity Act 2005.

liable for the acts and defaults of the attorney, although not for the act of delegation itself. Section 1 applies only to powers of attorney created after the Act, although, by way of exception, it applies to enduring powers of attorney created before the commencement of the Act at the end of a transitional period during which s.3(3) of the 1985 Act (which subsection was otherwise repealed) could continue to apply to such a power.[119] Thus there was no need for the donor of an enduring power to execute a fresh power after the Act of 1999, which indeed she may have been unable to do by reason of loss of capacity. In favour of a purchaser dealing with the donee of a power of attorney, a signed statement by the donee at the time of the transaction or within the following three months to the effect that the donor trustee had a beneficial interest in the property is conclusive evidence of that fact.[120]

A co-owner may, therefore, delegate her trustee functions by power of attorney **21–021** without being subject to the restrictions contained in s.25 of the Trustee Act 1925, for example the 12-month time limit. An enduring or lasting power of attorney may be utilised to provide for the onset of mental incapacity. Where, however, one of two co-owners creates the power in favour of the co-trustee, the latter cannot give a good receipt for capital money.[121] In such a case another trustee must be appointed for the purpose,[122] but there is no need for the incapacitated trustee to be discharged.[123]

Prior to the 1999 Act it was not possible to delegate by way of enduring power of attorney under s.25 of the Trustee Act 1925. That restriction was removed by s.6 of the 1999 Act in relation to powers created after its commencement. A trustee who has no beneficial interest may delegate his trustee functions by way of an enduring or lasting power, but this may be done only by complying with s.25 of the 1925 Act, which is subject to more restrictions and safeguards than a co-owner's power of delegation under s.1 of the 1999 Act. As in the case of delegation by a trustee who is a co-owner, delegation under s.25 to a co-trustee cannot circumvent the rule requiring payment of capital money to at least two trustees.[124]

9.   POWERS OF MAINTENANCE AND ADVANCEMENT

Where any person has a contingent interest in property the question arises as to **21–022** the use which should be made of the income until the gift vests. Otherwise the income would not be put to any use during the period. The policy is to allow the gift to "carry the intermediate income" unless there are good reasons to the

---

[119]   Trustee Delegation Act 1999 s.4 (now covered by the Mental Capacity Act 2005).

[120]   Trustee Delegation Act 1999 s.2.

[121]   Trustee Delegation Act 1999 s.7. *Shah v Forsters LLP* [2017] EWHC 2433 (Ch) per Mr Jeremy Cousins QC (sitting as a Deputy Judge of the Chancery Division) at [98] (discussing the applicable propositions of law regarding joint tenancies in the context of a negligence claim against a firm of solicitors).

[122]   Such an appointment may be made by the donee of the power under s.36 of the Trustee Act 1925 (above, para.18–022), as amended by s.8 of the 1999 Act.

[123]   Law of Property Act 1925 s.22, as amended by s.9 of the 1999 Act and by Sch.6 of the Mental Capacity Act 2005.

[124]   Trustee Delegation Act 1999 ss.7, 8.

contrary. Generally speaking, all testamentary gifts except contingent pecuniary legacies carry the intermediate income unless it is otherwise disposed of.[125]

One of the most common contingencies is that of attaining the age of 21 or more. It is important to make provision for the use of the income for the maintenance and education of the beneficiary before the interest vests.

A similar question arises in the opposite case of children who have a vested interest in property; for it may then be desirable that they should not be entitled to draw the whole of the income. It is better that they should receive what is reasonably necessary for their maintenance and education, and that the balance should be invested for them until adulthood.

These matters may be expressly provided for in the trust instrument. If not, the court has an inherent power to approve the use of income, or even of capital for the maintenance of children.[126] But the statutory powers of maintenance[127] and advancement[128] about to be discussed are sufficient to meet the needs of most situations, and they can be amended as required to meet the needs of a particular trust. Such powers have commonly been used, not only, or mainly, for their original purposes, but rather for the fiscal advantages which they have been able to offer.[129] The duty of care under s.1 of the Trustee Act 2000 does not apply to these powers.

Both the powers of maintenance and advancement were broadened in terms of their application by the Inheritance and Trustees' Powers Act 2014,[130] although these reforms largely reflected typical drafting practice. Section 10 of the 2014 Act provides that s.9, with the exception of the key provision s.9(3)(b), applies in relation to trusts whenever created or arising. The reforms to the power of maintenance under s.8 apply only to trusts created or arising after 1 October 2014, or to an interest under a trust created or arising after the exercise of a power after 1 October 2014. The same commencement rule as applies to s.8 applies to s.9(3)(b). Bearing those points in mind, however, in what follows below the amended provisions (i.e. those currently in force) will be set out.

A. Maintenance: Trustee Act 1925 Section 31

21–023   **i. Subsection (1).**

> Where any property is held by trustees in trust for any person for any interest whatsoever, whether vested or contingent, then, subject to any prior interests or charges affecting that property—
> (i)   during the infancy of any such person, if his interest so long continues, the trustees may, at their sole discretion, pay to his parent or guardian, if any, or otherwise apply for or towards his maintenance, education, or benefit,[131] the whole or such part, if any, of the income of that property as the trustees may think fit, whether or not there is—

---

[125] Below, para.21–029.
[126] Below, para.21–045.
[127] Trustee Act 1925 s.31.
[128] Trustee Act 1925 s.32.
[129] *Pilkington v IRC* [1964] A.C. 612. See J. Brown (1994) 8 T.L.I. 49.
[130] Section 8 relates to maintenance and s.9 to advancement; D. Rees [2015] P.C.B. 20.
[131] See *Re Heyworth's Contingent Reversionary Interest* [1956] Ch. 364; *Pilkington v IRC* [1964] A.C. 612; *Re Pauling's ST* [1964] Ch. 303.

      (a)   any other fund applicable to the same purpose; or

      (b)   any person bound by law to provide for his maintenance or education[132]; and

  (ii)   if such person attaining the age of [18][133] years has not a vested interest in such income, the trustees shall thenceforth pay the income of that property and of any accretion thereto under subsection (2) of this section to him, until he either attains a vested interest therein or dies, or until failure of his interest.

Two amendments were made by the 2014 Act. The first, by s.8(a), was to substitute the former phrase "as may, in all the circumstances, be reasonable" for "as the trustees may think fit" in para.(i). This amendment makes it a matter of the trustees' discretion, to be exercised in good faith, rather than controlled by an objective standard of reasonableness. The second amendment was to remove what was formerly a proviso that the trustees should, so far as practicable, arrange for maintenance payments to be shared proportionately among various funds available for the purpose. Trustees are now able to pay out as much of the income as they think fit.

(a) *Prior Interests.* The power of maintenance can only arise where a person **21–024** is entitled to the income, whether by virtue of a vested interest, or by virtue of a contingent interest which carries the intermediate income.[134] If the income is applicable in favour of a prior interest, no question of its use for maintenance can arise. Similarly, a member of a discretionary class is not entitled to any income and the section does not therefore apply to payments made by the trustees in the exercise of their discretion.[135]

(b) *Child Beneficiary.* The question of application of income for the child's **21–025** maintenance, education or benefit, whether his interest is vested or contingent, is a matter for the trustees' discretion. The decision to apply income for such maintenance must be taken as a result of a conscious exercise of their discretion, and not automatically.[136] So long as the trustees have regard only to the interests of the children, it is no objection that the exercise of their discretion may incidentally benefit a parent.[137]

(c) *Adult Contingently Entitled.* A beneficiary contingently entitled to the **21–026** principal becomes entitled under para.(ii) of subs.(1) to the income at majority.[138] His entitlement to the capital must, of course, await the happening of the contingency. The entitlement to income at majority is subject to a contrary intention; and this has been found to exist where there is a direction to accumulate.

---

[132] See *Fuller v Evans* [2000] 1 All E.R. 636.

[133] Reduced from 21 by Family Law Reform Act 1969. See *Begg-McBrearty (Inspector of Taxes) v Stilwell* [1996] 1 W.L.R. 951; *Walker v Walker* [2010] W.T.L.R. 1617.

[134] Trustee Act 1925 s.31(3); below, paras 21–029—21–032.

[135] *Re Vestey's Settlement* [1951] Ch. 209.

[136] *Wilson v Turner* (1883) 22 Ch.D. 521.

[137] *Fuller v Evans* [2000] 1 All E.R. 636.

[138] *Re Jones' WT* [1947] Ch. 48.

In *Re Turner's Will Trusts*,[139] a testator provided interests in favour of his grandchildren contingently on their attaining the age of 28, and expressly gave the trustees power to apply the income for their maintenance, education and benefit until that time, and instructed the trustees to accumulate the surplus. One grandchild, Geoffrey, was 21 when the testator died; and himself died three years later aged 24. No income had been paid to him, and some £3,000 had been accumulated since the testator's death. The question was whether s.31(1) applied. If it did, Geoffrey's estate would have become entitled to the income. The Court of Appeal held that, in spite of the imperative terms of s.31, it gave way to an expression of a contrary intention in accordance with the Trustee Act 1925 s.69(2).

ii.   Subsection (2).

21–027   *(a)   Surplus Income to be Accumulated for Child Beneficiaries.*   Subsection (2) provides that the residue of the income, not applied for maintenance, shall be accumulated by investment until the person contingently entitled reaches majority. Income from such investments becomes available for future maintenance; and the accumulations themselves may be applied, before the beneficiary reaches majority, as if they were income arising in the then current year.

21–028   *(b)   Entitlement to Accumulations.*   On the majority (or earlier marriage or civil partnership) of a child, the question arises whether or not any accumulations should be given to him. As would be expected, he is entitled to the accumulations if he had a vested interest before reaching full age (for he was entitled all along to the income); or if, on attaining his majority, he "becomes entitled to the property from which the income arose in fee simple, absolute or determinable, or absolutely or for an entailed interest." In short, he is entitled to the accumulations on his majority (or earlier marriage or civil partnership) if he is then entitled to the capital.[140]

The question arose in *Re Sharp's Settlement Trusts*[141] whether the provision covered the case where the children of the settlor became entitled, subject to an overriding power of appointment, to the capital on attaining the age of 21. Were they then entitled absolutely? Pennycuick VC held that they were not: the fact that their interests could be defeated by the exercise of the power prevented their becoming entitled absolutely. It may be thought anomalous that "a person having a determinable interest in realty should qualify to take accumulations at 21,[142] but "a person having a like interest in personalty should not equally so qualify".[143] In all other cases, as for example the case of a contingent beneficiary whose

---

[139] [1937] Ch. 15; *Re Ransome* [1957] Ch. 348; J. Riddall [1979] Conv. 243; *Brotherton v IRC* [1978] 1 W.L.R. 610; *IRC v Bernstein* [1961] Ch. 399; *Re McGeorge* [1963] Ch. 544 (where the contrary intention was shown by deferring the gift to a daughter until after the death of a widow); *Re Erskine's ST* [1971] 1 W.L.R. 162; In *Bullard v Bullard* [2017] EWHC 3 (Ch), Master Matthews granted rectification of the trust deed in order to exclude the operation of s.31, which would have had detrimental fiscal consequences and was not intended by the settlor.

[140] Trustee Act 1925 s.31(2)(i).

[141] [1973] Ch. 331; D. Hayton (1972) 36 Conv.(N.S.) 436. See also *Re Delamere's Settlement Trusts* [1984] 1 W.L.R. 813.

[142] The words "fee simple, absolute or determinable," applying only to realty.

[143] [1973] Ch. 331 at 346. On the background development in this area, see JEM (1972) 36 Conv.(N.S.) 436 at 438. The accumulations of income were added to the share of each child, subject to the exercise of the power: *Re King* [1928] Ch. 330; *Re Joel's WT* [1967] Ch. 14; below, para.21–034.

interest never vests, or where the beneficiary, although having a vested interest, fails to reach majority, the accumulations are added to capital for all purposes.[144]

The provisions relating to the destination of accumulations in s.31(2) are also subject to a contrary intention in the trust instrument.[145] In *Re Delamere's Settlement Trusts*,[146] the trustees appointed income to beneficiaries "absolutely" in 1971. All the beneficiaries were then children. By 1981, £122,000 had been accumulated. The question arose whether s.31(2) applied, so that the share of any beneficiary dying before majority would devolve with the capital, or whether there was a contrary intention, so that the accumulations were held indefeasibly for the appointees. It was held that the word "absolutely" in the 1971 appointment indicated indefeasibility, thus excluding s.31(2). Clearly the mere fact that the interest is vested is not sufficient to achieve this result.[147]

iii. Gifts Carrying Intermediate Income. Section 31 only applies to contingent interests which carry the intermediate income; that is to say, to gifts which entitle the donee to claim the income earned by, or interest upon, the subject-matter of the gift between the date of the gift and the date of payment. Whether or not a gift should do so is not self-evident, and there are some complex and technical rules which do not provide any conceptual unity. Some rules are based on case law, and some on statute. It is unfortunate that there is not a single comprehensive code.

21–029

Vested gifts carry the intermediate income unless a contrary intention appears, as where the income is given to someone other than the donee for a period. A direction to accumulate the surplus income until majority, on the other hand, does not indicate that the gift does not carry the income, but merely that the power of maintenance is excluded.

With contingent gifts, the rules, subject always to an expression of contrary intention, are as follows.[148]

(a) Contingent Residuary Bequest. A contingent bequest of residuary personalty carries all income earned from the testator's death.[149] The undisposed of income "becomes part of the residue".[150] But it seems that, if a residuary bequest of personalty (whether vested or contingent) is postponed "to a future date which must come sooner or later,"[151] the intermediate income is undisposed of and therefore not carried by the gift.[152]

21–030

---

[144] Trustee Act 1925 s.31(2)(ii). On the distinction between contingent interests and interests subject to defeasance, see *Phipps v Ackers* (1842) 9 Cl. & F. 583; *Brotherton v IRC* [1978] 1 W.L.R. 610.

[145] Trustee Act 1925 s.69(2).

[146] [1984] 1 W.L.R. 813; R. Griffith [1985] Conv. 153.

[147] See Trustee Act 1925 s.31(2)(i)(a). See further, *Fine v Fine* [2012] EWHC 1811 (Ch), per David Donaldson QC, sitting as a Deputy Judge of the High Court.

[148] B. Ker (1953) 17 Conv.(N.S.) 273; PVB (1963) 79 L.Q.R. 184.

[149] *Re Adams* [1893] 1 Ch. 329.

[150] [1893] 1 Ch. 329 at 334.

[151] per Cross J in *Re McGeorge* [1963] Ch. 544 at 551; an example of such a date would be the death of an annuitant.

[152] *Re Oliver* [1947] 2 All E.R. 162; *Re Gillett's WT* [1950] Ch. 102; *Re Geering* [1964] Ch. 136; *Beard v Shadler* [2011] W.T.L.R. 1147.

21–031   *(b)   Contingent or Future Specific Gifts of Personalty or Realty and Contingent Residuary Devises of Freehold Land.*   The Law of Property Act 1925 s.175 provides that a contingent specific bequest of personalty or devise of realty and a contingent residuary devise of freehold land, and a devise of freehold land to trustees on trust for persons whose interests are contingent or executory shall carry the intermediate income. It will be noticed that the section does not affect a residuary gift of a leasehold interest, which ranks as personalty.[153]

21–032   *(c)   Contingent Pecuniary Legacy.*   A contingent pecuniary legacy does not carry the intermediate income.[154] To this rule there are three exceptions, in which cases the contingent pecuniary legacy will carry interest, and it will be available for the maintenance of a child.

First: where the legacy was given by the father of the child legatee, or by some person in loco parentis, so long as no other fund is provided for his maintenance,[155] and the contingency is the attainment of majority.[156]

Secondly: where the testator shows an intention to maintain.[157]

Thirdly: where the testator has set aside the legacy as a separate fund for the benefit of the legatee.[158]

21–033   **iv.   Aggregation of Income of Children with that of their Parents.**   It has been seen that an accumulation and maintenance settlement[159] giving contingent gifts to children with power to use the income for maintenance, and to accumulate that not so used, could offer tax advantages, both in the context of income tax and of inheritance tax, but that income so accumulated carries the income tax disadvantage of liability to the rate applicable to trusts (currently 45%).[160] This high rate of income tax, coupled with the restrictions imposed in relation to inheritance tax, have made these settlements less attractive. Where income is paid to the unmarried minor child of the settlor, the income is treated as that of his parent.[161] In other cases, the income is treated as part of the child's total income.

21–034   **v.   Gifts to Classes.**   Where there is a gift to a class contingently on attaining the age of 21, the trustees may treat separately, for these purposes, each person's presumptive share. That is to say, that when one member of the class attains 21 and becomes entitled to his share, the trustees may continue to exercise their powers of maintenance in respect of the other members.[162] Similarly, income may only be used for the maintenance of any member of the class if that income was

---

[153] *Re Woodin* [1895] 2 Ch. 309.
[154] *Re Raine* [1929] 1 Ch. 716; *Re George* (1877) 5 Ch.D. 837.
[155] *Re George (A Child)* (1877) 5 Ch.D. 837 at 843.
[156] *Re Abrahams* [1911] 1 Ch. 108.
[157] *Re Churchill* [1909] 2 Ch. 431. On the effect of s.31 of the Trustee Act 1925 in this respect, see (1953) 17 Conv.(N.S.) 273 at 279.
[158] *Re Medlock* (1886) 54 L.T. 828.
[159] Above, para.10–024.
[160] Above, para.10–002.
[161] Income Tax (Trading and Other Income) Act 2005 s.629. Similarly, where income is retained in a bare trust for the settlor's child.
[162] *Re King* [1928] Ch. 330.

earned during the lifetime of that member,[163] but if a member of a class dies without obtaining a vested interest, the accumulation of income representing his contingent share is added to the capital under s.31(2)(ii), although this means that future born members will thus benefit from it.[164]

B.   Advancement[165]

i.   The Meaning of Advancement.   We saw that maintenance was concerned with the payment of income for the benefit of child beneficiaries. Advancement is concerned with the payment or application of capital sums to the beneficiary's advantage before the time comes when he is entitled to demand the fund.[166] The scope of the power depends upon the terms of the instrument giving it,[167] and upon Trustee Act 1925 s.32.[168] Payments under the power have been made not only for the purpose of providing capital sums when needed, but also for the purpose of tax saving. **21–035**

Thus, suppose a fund is held on trust for A, the capital being payable to him on attaining 25. If A marries, or sets up in business or in a profession before that time, a power of advancement makes possible the payment to him of some or all of the capital of the fund to help with such a project. There is a similar but more complicated question if A's interest is subject to a prior life interest in X; for X's income will be affected by any payments out of the capital fund which produces it. Likewise if A's interest is contingent on his attaining 25; for if payments are made to A and A never attains 25 the capital payments will have been made to the wrong person.

The tax-saving question arises where trustees hold a large sum on trust for A for life and then to A's children equally at 21. Independently of the fund, A is rich enough to provide the children with all they need. It may be advantageous to make transfers of capital from the trust for the children. Inheritance tax will be avoided in some cases if the advancement was made more than seven years before A's death,[169] but the operation of this principle has been restricted by the Finance Act 2006.[170] Such a payment is certainly not an "advancement" within the usual meaning of the word, but no one could deny that the saving of tax on the trust is a benefit to the children. A further question arises, whether such sums must be held in trust for the children absolutely, or whether they may themselves be settled by the creation of sub-trusts for the benefit of themselves and also for other persons such as future dependants. These questions are dealt with below.

---

[163] *Re Joel's WT* [1967] Ch. 14. That decision was based on s.2 of the Apportionment Act 1870, which, as we have seen above, para.20–012, does not apply to trusts created after 1 October 2013: Trusts (Capital and Income) Act 2013 s.1(1). The point in the text however is unaffected.

[164] [1967] Ch. 14; not following *Re King* [1928] Ch. 330 on this point.

[165] It should be pointed out that the *power of advancement* is entirely distinct from the *presumption of advancement* seen earlier: paras 11–026—11–030.

[166] See *Fischer v Nemeske Pty Ltd* [2016] HCA 11; (2016) 257 C.L.R. 615.

[167] See *Re Collard's WT* [1961] Ch. 293. The point as to the wording of s.32 in *Re Collard's WT* has now been confirmed by the amendment of the section by s.9 of the 2014 Act.

[168] Below, para.21–038.

[169] Finance (No.2) Act 1987 s.96. This is because A was treated as owning the capital.

[170] Above, para.10–018.

21–036   ii. Original Meaning of Advancement.

> "The word 'advancement' itself meant in this context the establishment in life of the beneficiary who was the object of the power or at any rate some step that would contribute to the furtherance of his establishment.[171]... Typical instances of expenditure for such purposes under the social conditions of the nineteenth century were an apprenticeship or the purchase of a commission in the Army or of an interest in business. In the case of a girl there could be advancement on marriage."[172]

21–037   iii. Express Powers.   Until 1925, there was no statutory power of advancement. Express powers of advancement were given narrow scope consistent with the established meaning of the word.[173] So:

> "[T]o prevent uncertainties about the permitted range of objects for which moneys could be raised and made available, such words as 'or otherwise for his or her benefit' were often added to the word 'advancement'. It was always recognised that these added words were 'large words'[174] and indeed in another case[175] the same judge spoke of preferment and advancement of being 'both large words' but of 'benefit' as being the 'largest of all.'"[176]

The combined phrase "advancement or benefit" is read disjunctively.[177] It means "any use of the money which will improve the material situation of the beneficiary."[178] The scope of an express power depends of course upon its own language. The standard form of express power was incorporated in the Trustee Act 1925 s.32; and express provisions on the question of advancement are now usually confined to giving express powers to the trustees to create sub-trusts.[179]

21–038   iv. The Statutory Power: Trustee Act 1925 Section 32.

> Section 32—
> (1)   Trustees may at any time or times pay or apply any capital money subject to a trust, or transfer or apply any other property forming part of the capital of the trust property, for the advancement or benefit, in such manner as they may, in their absolute discretion, think fit, of any person entitled to the capital of the trust property or of any share thereof, whether absolutely or contingently on his attaining any specified age or on the occurrence of any other event, or subject to a gift over on his death under any specified age or on the occurrence of any other event, and whether in possession or in remainder or reversion, and such payment, transfer or application may be made notwithstanding that the interest of such person is liable to be defeated by the exercise of a power of appointment or revocation, or to be diminished by the increase of the class to which he belongs:

---

[171] See per Jessel MR in *Taylor v Taylor* (1875) L.R. 20 Eq. 155; *Lowther v Bentinck* (1874-75) L.R. 19 Eq. 166 (payment of debts); *Roper-Curzon v Roper-Curzon* (1870-71) L.R. 11 Eq. 452 (starting a career at the Bar); *Re Long's Settlement* (1868) 38 L.J.Ch. 125 (passage money to go to a colony); *Re Williams' WT* [1953] Ch. 138 (purchase of a house as a surgery); *Hardy v Shaw* [1976] Ch. 82 (shares in family company).

[172] *Pilkington v IRC* [1964] A.C. 612 per Lord Radcliffe at 634.

[173] *Molyneux v Fletcher* [1898] 1 Q.B. 648 per Kennedy LJ at 653.

[174] See Jessel MR in *Re Breeds' Will* (1875) 1 Ch.D. 226 at 228.

[175] *Lowther v Bentinck* (1874) L.R. 19 Eq. 166 at 169.

[176] per Lord Radcliffe in *Pilkington v IRC* [1964] A.C. 612 at 634; *Re Halsted's WT* [1937] 2 All E.R. 570 at 571; *Re Moxon's WT* [1958] 1 W.L.R. 165 at 168.

[177] *Lowther v Bentinck* (1874) L.R. 19 Eq. 166; *Re Halsted's WT* [1937] 2 All E.R. 570 at 571.

[178] per Lord Radcliffe in *Pilkington v IRC* [1964] A.C. 612 at 635.

[179] Below, para.21–042.

Provided that—

(a) property (including any money) so paid, transferred or applied for the advancement or benefit of any person must not, altogether, represent more than the presumptive or vested share or interest of that person in the trust property; and

(b) if that person is or becomes absolutely and indefeasibly entitled to a share in the trust property the money or other property so paid, transferred or applied shall be brought into account as part of such share; and

(c) no such payment, transfer or application shall be made so as to prejudice any person entitled to any prior life or other interest, whether vested or contingent, in the money [or other property paid, transferred or applied unless such person is in existence and of full age and consents in writing to such payment transfer or application.

(1A) In exercise of the foregoing power trustees may pay, transfer or apply money or other property on the basis (express or implied) that it shall be treated as a proportionate part of the capital out of which it was paid, transferred or applied, for the purpose of bringing it into account in accordance with proviso (b) to subsection (1) of this section.

The section does not apply to capital money arising under the Settled Land Act 1925.[180] Its application is always subject to the expression of a contrary intention[181] and it has been held to be excluded by provision for accumulation.[182] Most of the amendments to s.32 introduced by s.9 of the 2014 Act have effect in relation to the provisos, considered below.[183] But the opening of s.32 has been amended to make clear that the trustees are able to advance trust property as opposed only to capital monies.[184]

v. Continuing Problems in the Application of Section 32. The wide **21–039**
construction of the phrase "advancement" or "benefit" must have been carried into the statutory power created by s.32, since it adopts without qualification the accustomed wording, "for the advancement or benefit in such manner as they may in their absolute discretion think fit."[185] But this leaves open a number of questions; can payments be made for the "benefit" of a person who is not in any way in need? To what extent can an advancement re-settle the money advanced, the re-settlement changing the original trust? Can trustees, exercising the statutory power of advancement, delegate their discretion by giving a dispositive discretion to the trustees of the re-settlement; i.e. can they make an advancement on protective or discretionary trusts? These questions were discussed and largely settled in the long litigation over the will of William Pilkington.[186]

The testator left a share of his residuary estate on trust for his nephew Richard upon protective trusts during his life and after Richard's death upon trust for such of his children or remoter issue as he should by deed or will appoint and in default of appointment in trust for such of Richard's children as attained 21 (or, if female, married under that age) in equal shares.

---

[180] Trustee Act 1925 s.32(2), as substituted by Trusts of Land and Appointment of Trustees Act 1996 Sch.3 para.3(8).

[181] *Re Evans' Settlement* [1967] 1 W.L.R. 1294.

[182] *IRC v Bernstein* [1961] Ch. 399. This was so even if the direction for accumulation contravened statutory restrictions then in force; *Re Ransome* [1957] Ch. 348; *Brotherton v IRC* [1978] 1 W.L.R. 610.

[183] Below para.21–045.

[184] See previously *Re Collard's WT* [1961] Ch. 293.

[185] per Lord Radcliffe in *Pilkington v IRC* [1964] A.C. 612 at 635; *Re Pauling's ST* [1964] Ch. 303.

[186] *Pilkington v IRC* [1964] A.C. 612.

Richard had three children all born after the death of the testator of whom a two-year-old daughter Penelope was one. Richard's father (brother of the testator and grandfather of Penelope) proposed to make a settlement in favour of Penelope, providing that the trustees hold the property on trust to pay the income to Penelope at 21, and the capital for her absolutely at 30 and if Penelope died under 30 leaving children, on trust for such children at 21 with further family trusts in default. The trustees had power to apply the income for Penelope's maintenance until she reached the age of 21, and were to accumulate the surplus income. The trustees proposed to advance, with the consent of Richard, one-half of Penelope's expectant share under the testator's will, and pay it to the trustees of Richard's father's settlement. The House of Lords held that this proposal was within the trustees' power under s.32. They held also that the exercise of the power of advancement was analogous to the exercise of a special power of appointment and that in the circumstances the advancement would be void for perpetuity.

21–040   *(a)   Benefit.*   On the question of the benefit to Penelope, Lord Radcliffe held that it was immaterial that other persons, such as her future dependants, would benefit also.

> "[I]f the disposition itself, by which I mean the whole provision made, is for her benefit, it is no objection to the exercise of the power that other persons benefit incidentally as a result of the exercise."[187]

The relief from anxiety about the future maintenance of a wife and a family has been held to be a sufficient benefit[188]; as has the payment from a wife's fund to her husband to enable him to set up in business in England and prevent separation of the family.[189] The performance of the moral obligation felt by a wealthy man to contribute to a charitable trust where it would be a great burden to do so out of taxed income has been held to benefit him.[190] In that case the beneficiary would otherwise have made the contribution from his own resources and so there was a material benefit to him in the advancement. Where a beneficiary wished to have an advancement of capital in order to make a large charitable gift which she could not make from her own resources, it was held that the trustees should not exercise their power of advancement in this way: trust money could only be advanced to discharge a moral obligation if the beneficiary's material situation would be improved in some way.[191] Where the purpose of the advancement is to mitigate inheritance tax (or formerly estate duty) on the beneficiary's death, there is no need to show a material benefit to the beneficiary. The tax saving is a sufficient benefit.[192]

21–041   *(b)   Settlement of Funds Advanced. Sub-trusts.*   Nor was it any objection that the funds were being subjected to a settlement, and not paid for the sole benefit of

---

[187] *Pilkington v IRC* [1964] A.C. 612 per Lord Radcliffe at 636; *Re Halsted's WT* [1937] 2 All E.R. 570.

[188] *Re Halsted's WT* [1937] 2 All E.R. 570.

[189] *Re Kershaw's Trusts* (1868) L.R. 6 Eq. 322.

[190] *Re Clore's Settlement Trust* [1966] 1 W.L.R. 955. See also *Re Leigh's ST* [2006] W.T.L.R. 477 (decided 1980).

[191] *X v A* [2006] 1 W.L.R. 741.

[192] "if the advantage of preserving the funds of a beneficiary from the incidence of death duty is not an advantage personal to that beneficiary, I do not see what is"; per Lord Radcliffe in *Pilkington v IRC* [1964] A.C. 612 at 640; see also Upjohn J in *Re Wills WT* [1959] Ch. 1, 11–12; *Re Clore's ST* [1966] 1 W.L.R. 955.

Penelope; nor that her enjoyment was deferred. The settlement of advanced funds had many times been approved[193] and this inevitably meant that the trusts on which the funds would be held under the advancement were different from those laid down by the original settlor.

(c) Delegation. Closely connected with the question of resettlement is that of the extent to which trustees, in making an advancement on new trusts, can give discretionary powers to the trustees of the new settlement. In general, *delegatus non potest delegare*.[194] However: **21–042**

> "[T]he law is not that trustees cannot delegate: it is that trustees cannot delegate unless they have authority to do so. If the power of advancement which they possess is so read as to allow them to raise money for the purpose of having it settled, then they do have the necessary authority to let the money pass out of the old settlement into the new trusts. No question of delegation of their powers or trusts arises. If, on the other hand, their power of advancement is read so as to exclude settled advances, *cadit quaestio*."[195]

This does not, however, solve all the problems. The statutory power allows trustees to advance money by paying it to other trustees to hold on new trusts. Such trusts may include a power of advancement[196]; and presumably s.32 applies to the new trustees. Further, acting on the analogy of cases on special powers of appointment, it seems that the new trusts may include a protective and forfeitable life interest[197]; but that the discretionary trusts which come into effect upon the determination of the life interest may be invalid, because the duties of trustees of a discretionary trust involve dispositive (as opposed to administrative) discretions,[198] and these cannot be delegated without express authority.[199] This latter point is unaffected by the Trustee Act 2000.[200]

If that is correct, s.32 appears to give trustees no power to make an advancement upon a new settlement which takes the form of discretionary trusts. Such a situation appears necessarily to raise questions of delegation; and not to be covered by Lord Radcliffe's dictum quoted above. Whether a settlement on discretionary trusts would satisfy the test of "benefit" is another matter; for under such a trust no interest of course is technically given to the advanced beneficiary.[201] The delegation problem can be met by expressly empowering the trustees of the original settlement to delegate their powers in that manner.[202]

---

[193] *Re Halsted's WT* [1937] 2 All E.R. 570; *Re Moxon's WT* [1958] 1 W.L.R. 165; *Re Wills' WT* [1959] Ch. 1; *Re Abrahams' WT* [1969] 1 Ch. 463; *Re Hastings-Bass* [1975] Ch. 25 (see paras 18–046—18–048); F. Crane (1974) 38 Conv.(N.S.) 293.

[194] *Re May* [1926] Ch. 136; *Re Mewburn* [1934] Ch. 112; *Re Wills' WT* [1959] Ch. 1.

[195] *Pilkington v IRC* [1964] A.C. 612 per Lord Radcliffe at 639 ("cadit quaestio" means that "the argument falls", or that the point is no longer in issue).

[196] *Re Mewburn* [1934] Ch. 112; *Re Morris* [1951] 2 All E.R. 528; *Re Hunter's WT* [1963] Ch. 372.

[197] *Re Boulton's ST* [1928] Ch. 703; *Re Hunter* [1963] Ch. 372.; *Re Morris* [1951] 2 All E.R. 528.

[198] See A. Kiralfy (1953) 17 Conv.(N.S.) 285 at 289.

[199] *Re Boulton's ST* [1928] Ch. 703 per Eve J at 709.

[200] See Trustee Act 2000 s.11(2)(a); above, para.21–015.

[201] *Gartside v IRC* [1968] A.C. 553. This is not per se an objection; *Re Clore's Settlement Trust* [1966] 1 W.L.R. 955.

[202] For the view that *Pilkington v IRC* [1964] A.C. 612 does authorise the creation of discretionary trusts under the statutory power of advancement, see F. Crane (1963) 27 Conv.(N.S.) 65.

21–043 *(d) Perpetuity.* For the purposes of the perpetuity rule, the exercise of a power of advancement is treated, as has been seen,[203] on the analogy of a special power of appointment. Where a sub-trust is created by an advancement, the limitation in the sub-trust is tested for validity by being read back into the original instrument under which the power was exercised.[204] The advancements made in *Re Abrahams' Will Trusts*[205] and *Re Hastings-Bass*[206] failed, in part, to comply; as the intended advancement would have done in *Pilkington v IRC.*[207] In *Re Abrahams' Will Trusts*, the failure of the void parts of the sub-trust wholly changed the character of the benefit being conferred on the beneficiary, and the advancement was held void: there never was a valid exercise of the power by the trustees. In *Re Hastings-Bass*, however, the trustees' prime consideration was to create a life interest in the life tenant of the sub-trust in order to save estate duty on the death of his father, the life tenant of the original settlement. The fact that the interests in remainder in the sub-trust were void for perpetuity did not make the advancement itself void. The principles on which the exercise (or purported exercise) of a discretionary power such as the power of advancement may be held void or voidable have already been discussed.[208]

The Perpetuities and Accumulations Act 1964 introduced the "wait and see" rule, whereby the interests under the sub-trusts would be treated as valid until it became known that they would in fact vest outside the perpetuity period. This rule is preserved by the Perpetuities and Accumulations Act 2009 s.7.

21–044 *(e) Extension of the Scope of "Advancement"?* The High Court of Australia recently gave a particularly broad construction to the statutory power of advancement in *Fischer v Nemeske Pty Ltd*,[209] in which the Court reviewed the relevant English authorities, as the statutory power under s.44(1) of the Trustee Act 1925 (NSW) is modelled on the Trustee Act 1925 s.32.

> In *Fischer*, the trustee passed a resolution relating to an "asset revaluation reserve" (effectively the increase in value of the shares)[210] of nearly AU$4million in favour of two beneficiaries. The interest conferred upon the two beneficiaries could then be met by either the sale of the shares or transferring the shares to them. The trustees purported to make this arrangement pursuant to a power of advancement in the deed of settlement, but without affecting the instant ownership of the shares. No money was ever paid to the two beneficiaries. Their Honours, by a bare majority, held that the power could extend to the creation of a debt at common law, rather than any payment or transfer of property.

French CJ and Bell J held that

---

[203] *Pilkington v IRC* [1964] A.C. 612; above, para.21–039.
[204] *Re Paul* [1921] 2 Ch. 1.
[205] [1969] 1 Ch. 463.
[206] [1975] Ch. 25.
[207] [1964] A.C. 612.
[208] *Pitt v Holt* [2013] UKSC 26; [2013] 2 A.C. 108; above, paras 18–046—18–048.
[209] [2016] HCA 11 (per French CJ, Bell and Gageler JJ, Kiefel and Gordon JJ dissenting).
[210] This increase was treated as capital of the trust: [2016] HCA 11 per French CJ and Bell J at [14].

"Plainly there are many ways of achieving an advancement for the benefit of beneficiaries. The range of options available in any particular case depends upon the scope of the power conferred by the trust deed or by statute.[211] ... [*Pilkington*] should not be taken as excluding from the ambit of the power of advancement the creation of a creditor/debtor relationship between trustee and beneficiary by the creation of a vested, absolute equitable interest in capital realisable by an action for money had and received or otherwise."[212]

Some caution should be exercised over the breadth of this approach in *Fischer*, which was strongly criticised by the dissenting Justices.[213] Notwithstanding the reliance on English authorities, it may not be representative of English Law.[214]

vi. The Provisos.[215] It is in respect of the proviso that the main reforms from the 2014 Act can be seen: **21–045**

(a) Previously, only half the presumptive share of each beneficiary could be advanced under the statutory power.[216] The reason for this was that, if the contingent interest of the advanced beneficiary never vests, the fund in the hands of the person next entitled is reduced by the amount advanced. However, it may be advantageous to be able to advance the whole; and it was common to extend the statutory power so as to give the trustees power to advance the whole if they see fit.[217] The Law Commission proposed that the statutory power should be extended to the whole of the beneficiary's share.[218] Section 9(3)(b) of the 2014 Act gives effect to this provision, albeit only prospectively as set out above.[219] The statutory power has thus been brought into line with standard practice in drafting trusts, and would reduce the need for court applications to permit advances of more than half.

(b) This attempts to effect an equality between the members of a class of beneficiaries, by requiring those who have received benefits in advance of other members of a class of beneficiaries to count the advancement against their ultimate share.[220] Of course it is otherwise if the share never vests.[221]

---

[211] [2016] HCA 11 at [27].

[212] [2016] HCA 11 at [25].

[213] [2016] HCA 11 per Gordon J (dissenting) at [183]: "Unless provisions such as cl 4 are construed, are exercised and operate according to their terms, the potential for imprecise or wrongful dealings with trust property may be increased. Imprecise and wrongful dealings with trust property concern and affect not only a trust, its trustee and its beneficiaries but also third parties dealing with that trust."

[214] Some criticism has been expressed by the editors of *Lewin*: see *Lewin on Trusts*, 19th edn, Supplement para.32–043A.

[215] Set out above, para.21–038.

[216] See *Re Marquess of Abergavenny's Estate Act Trusts* [1981] 1 W.L.R. 843 (express power to pay life tenant any part or parts not exceeding one-half in value of the settled fund was exhausted by the advance of one-half, even though the remainder subsequently increased in value).

[217] In the absence of such an express power, the trust may be varied by the court to permit advancement of the whole in favour of a minor; *D (A Child) v O* [2004] 3 All E.R. 780; below, para.23–012.

[218] Law Com. No. 331, *Intestacy and Family Provision Claims on Death*, para.4.72. See also para.4.76 (property other than capital money).

[219] Above, para.21–022.

[220] The advance is brought into account at its value at the date of advancement. In times of inflation this can have capricious results. A form of indexation was therefore recommended by the Law Reform Committee, 23rd Report, *The Powers and Duties of Trustees* (1982 Cmnd. 8733), paras 4.43–4.47.

Section 9(6) of the 2014 Act introduces subs.(1A) into s.32: this subsection clarifies that the trustees can treat the money or property advanced to a beneficiary as a proportionate part of the capital of the trust as a whole.

(c) By advancing some or all of the capital, the fund which provides the income of the tenant for life is reduced. The consent of the tenant for life is therefore required for the exercise of the power. The court has no power to dispense with this consent.[222] A member of a discretionary class is not, however, a person whose consent is required.[223]

C. The Court's Inherent Power to Provide Maintenance and Advancement

21–046 The court has inherent power to order provision to be made for a child out of her property. This power is usually applied in respect of income,[224] but occasionally capital is used.[225] Also, the court has the statutory power to make an order authorising a person to make use of a child's property with a view to the application of the capital or income for the child's maintenance, education or benefit.[226]

D. Responsibility of the Trustees to See to the Application of the Money Advanced

21–047 We have seen that the trustees must be satisfied that the proposed advancement is for the benefit of the beneficiary. The final question is whether the trustees, in making an advancement, are under an obligation to see that the money is applied towards the purposes for which the payment was made. In *Re Pauling's Settlement Trusts*,[227] the Court of Appeal, dealing with an express power to advance one-half of an expected or presumptive share for the "absolute use" of a beneficiary, held that the power was fiduciary; the trustees could hand over a sum of capital quite generally to a beneficiary if they thought that he was the type of person who could be trusted with the money. Or, if the trustees made the advance for a particular purpose, which they stated, they could quite properly pay it over if they reasonably thought that he could be trusted to carry it out.

> "What they cannot do is prescribe a particular purpose, and then raise and pay the money over to the advancee leaving him or her entirely free, legally and morally, to apply it for that purpose or to spend it in any way he or she chooses without any responsibility on the trustees even to inquire as to its application."[228]

---

[221] *Re Fox* [1904] 1 Ch. 480 (express power).
[222] *Re Forster's Settlement* [1942] Ch. 199. See also *Henley v Wardell, The Times*, 29 January 1988.
[223] *Re Beckett's Settlement* [1940] Ch. 279.
[224] *Wellesley v Wellesley* (1828) 2 Bli.(N.S.) 124.
[225] *Barlow v Grant* (1684) 1 Vern. 255.
[226] Below, para.23–009; Trustee Act 1925 s.53.
[227] [1964] Ch. 303; below, para.24–029.
[228] [1964] Ch. 303 at 334.

CHAPTER 22

TRUSTEESHIP AND FIDUCIARY DUTIES

1.   REMUNERATION AND REIMBURSEMENT

THE basic principle of equity is that a trustee acts voluntarily and is not paid for her services.[1] It does not matter whether her services are of a professional nature, as where she is a solicitor, or whether they are personal. It follows, therefore, that a trustee can only claim remuneration if she can show a specific entitlement to it. The discussion that follows is essentially an account of how that entitlement can arise. Several of the principles to be considered here apply to fiduciaries more generally.

22–001

---

[1] *Robinson v Pett* (1734) 3 P. Wms. 249; *Re Barber* (1886) 34 Ch.D. 77; *Dale v IRC* [1954] A.C. 11 at 27. See also the Scottish cases of *Parks of Hamilton Holdings Ltd v Campbell* [2014] CSIH 36; 2014 S.C. 726 per Lord Drummond Young at [34]; *Kidd v Paull & Williamsons LLP* [2017] CSOH 16; 2017 G.W.D. 6–80 per Lord Tyre at [40]ff.

"It is not that reward for services is repugnant to the fiduciary duty, but that he who has the duty shall not take any secret remuneration or any financial benefit not authorized by the law, or by his contract, or by the trust deed under which he acts, as the case may be."[2]

It is a basic principle that a trustee may recover, by means of a lien over the trust property, for her legitimate out-of-pocket expenses, which include the payment of agents' fees wherever their employment is permitted,[3] and the proper costs of litigation,[4] including the costs of successfully (but not unsuccessfully) defending themselves from liability for breach of trust.[5] Trustees should seek the court's authorisation (a *Beddoe*[6] order) before suing or defending, to avoid the risk that their costs are found to have been improperly incurred,[7] but they may nevertheless recover their costs from the trust fund without such an order if the costs were properly incurred.[8] Where there is hostile litigation between rival claimants to the trust fund, the trustee should not become involved but should offer to submit to the court's direction; where the trustee is sued successfully by the beneficiaries, her costs will not come out of the trust fund; but where the dispute is with a third party, the trustee's duty is to protect the trust and she will be indemnified so long as the proceedings are properly brought or defended for the benefit of the trust, whether or not successfully.[9] Trustees do not fail in their duty where they discontinue litigation against a third party because the trust fund is likely to be exhausted in indemnifying them, leaving them personally exposed as to any insufficiency.[10] The trustee's lien over the fund extends to an indemnity against contingent liabilities.[11]

---

[2] *Dale v IRC* [1954] A.C. 11, per Lord Normand at 27.

[3] This must be borne in mind when considering the principle that the trustee's office is gratuitous. Her burden is alleviated to the extent that she can properly delegate the work to agents; above, para.21–012.

[4] Above, para.19–003. See *Re Spurling's Will Trusts* [1966] 1 W.L.R. 920; *Holding and Management Ltd v Property Holding and Investment Trust Plc* [1989] 1 W.L.R. 1313; *Breadner v Granville-Grossman (costs)* [2006] W.T.L.R. 411 (costs not recoverable where trustees had acted in a hostile or partisan manner); *McAteer v Lismore* [2015] NICh 3; *Ong v Ping* [2015] EWHC 3258 (Ch) (co-claimants did not need to have instructed two sets of solicitors); [2015] 6 Costs L.R. 997; *Blades v Isaac* [2016] EWHC 601 (Ch); [2016] 2 P. & C.R. DG10.

[5] *Armitage v Nurse* [1998] Ch. 241 at 262.

[6] [1893] 1 Ch. 547. See *Shovelar v Lane* [2011] 4 All E.R. 669. K. Davenport and T. Nelson (2017) 23 T. & T. 343. See also *Pettigrew v Edwards* [2017] EWHC 8 (Ch); [2017] W.T.L.R. 675 (no *Beddoe* order made where two of the trustees sought to defend claim by a life tenant in their capacities as capital beneficiaries).

[7] See *Singh v Basin, The Times*, 21 August 1998.

[8] *Bonham v Blake Lapthorn Linnell* [2007] W.T.L.R. 189. See also *Close Trustees (Switzerland) SA v Vildosa* [2008] W.T.L.R. 1543 (how litigation costs borne as between capital and income). *Granada Group Ltd v The Law Debenture Pension Trust Corp Plc* [2015] EWHC 1499 (Ch) per Andrews J at [91]–[97] (aff'd without comment on this point, [2016] EWCA Civ 1289); *Royal National Lifeboat Institution v Headley* [2016] EWHC 1948 (Ch); [2017] 1 P. & C.R. DG4 per Master Matthews at [37]–[40].

[9] *Alsop Wilkinson v Neary* [1996] 1 W.L.R. 1220. See also *McDonald v Horn* [1995] 1 All E.R. 961; *Chessels v British Telecommunications Plc* [2002] W.T.L.R. 719.

[10] *Bradstock Trustee Services Ltd v Nabarro Nathanson (A Firm)* [1995] 1 W.L.R. 1405.

[11] *X v A* [2000] 1 All E.R. 490; A. Kenny [2000] Conv. 560.

The right to reimbursement is statutory,[12] and prevails against trust property generally, both capital and income, and in some cases against the beneficiaries personally,[13] as in the case of a bare trust.[14]

A. Remuneration Authorised by the Trust Instrument

Express remuneration clauses are extremely common, and are frequently very widely drafted. Otherwise, prior to the reforms of the Trustee Act 2000 discussed in section B below, it would have been difficult to persuade professional people to act as trustees. While the principle of equity is that clauses authorising remuneration are to be strictly construed,[15] this has been relieved by s.28 of the Act of 2000. This provides that where there is an express clause permitting the trustee to be paid for his services, and the trustee is a trust corporation or is acting in a professional capacity, the trustee is entitled to be paid even if the services are capable of being provided by a lay trustee. The remuneration may take the form of the income from a part of the estate[16] or capital under a power of appointment,[17] or the trustee may be given power to make use of trust money in other ways.[18] A clause in a will authorising remuneration will also be valid.[19]

22–002

B. Trustee Act 2000

Part V of the Trustee Act 2000 facilitates the remuneration of professional trustees in cases where neither the trust instrument nor any other legislation provides for it. Section 29 (which applies whenever the trust was created) provides that a trust corporation[20] is entitled to receive reasonable remuneration out of the trust fund for services provided. A professional trustee who is neither a trust corporation nor a sole trustee is similarly entitled if each other trustee has agreed in writing that she may be remunerated. A sole trustee is excluded because the safeguard of collective scrutiny would be absent.

22–003

> In *Pullan v Wilson*,[21] the trustee was a qualified accountant appointed to be a third trustee of a set of family trusts. Some of the trust instruments provided for remuneration but not at all: it was however accepted that the trustee was only entitled to proper and reasonable remuneration. A beneficiary challenged the rates at which the trustee had been paid. His Honour Judge Hodge QC, sitting as a Judge of the High Court, held that appropriate reasonable figures would have been £330 and £165 respectively. His Honour held:

---

[12] Trustee Act 2000 s.31, replacing previous legislation. Interest is not payable (as the proceedings are not for the recovery of a debt or damages); *Foster v Spencer* [1996] 2 All E.R. 672.

[13] See generally *Stott v Milne* (1884) 25 Ch.D. 710; *Re Grimthorpe* [1958] Ch. 615.

[14] *Hurst v Bryk* [2002] 1 A.C. 185 at 196–197 (partners holding lease on trust for partnership).

[15] *Re Chalinder & Herington* [1907] 1 Ch. 58; *Re Gee* [1948] Ch. 284.

[16] *Public Trustee v IRC* [1960] A.C. 398. See J. Thurston (1988) 2 *Trust Law & Practice* 93.

[17] *Re Beatty's WT* [1990] 1 W.L.R. 1503.

[18] See *Space Investments Ltd v Canadian Imperial Bank of Commerce Trust Co (Bahamas) Ltd* [1986] 1 W.L.R. 1072 (settlement provided that bank trustee could deposit trust money with itself and use for own purposes, subject to normal obligation to repay).

[19] Trustee Act 2000 s.28.

[20] As defined in the Trustee Act 1925.

[21] [2014] EWHC 126 (Ch). D. Hayton (2014) 29 T.L.I. 51 at 63.

"a professional trustee is not necessarily entitled to charge by reference to his normal or standard charging rates (or those of his assistants), at least unless these have been specifically identified and approved before the relevant work is undertaken. To hold otherwise would be to deprive a court of equity of any effective control over a trustee's remuneration."[22]

On the facts, however, the Judge found that there had been agreement which meant that, for the trustee's rates, it was not possible for the claimant to resile from that rate (although the rate for the assistant's work was reduced).[23]

Section 29 extends to personal representatives acting professionally,[24] but does not apply to trustees of charitable trusts. The Secretary of State, however, may make provision by regulations for the remuneration of charity trustees.[25] The Charities Act 2011 permits remuneration for charity trustees in certain cases.[26]

C.   Other Statutory Provisions

22–004   Other statutory provisions enable fees to be charged by the Public Trustee,[27] by persons appointed to be Judicial Trustees,[28] and by corporations appointed as custodian trustees.[29] In this last case, the corporation concerned cannot also be a managing trustee.[30] But where a corporation is appointed to be a trustee by the court, the court has full discretion as to its fees, and is not restricted by this distinction.[31]

D.   Remuneration Authorised by the Court

22–005   The court has an inherent jurisdiction, which is exercisable retrospectively[32] and prospectively, but in exceptional cases only,[33] to authorise remuneration for trustees and other fiduciaries. The power has been exercised in favour of a fiduciary who was guilty of undue influence. In *O'Sullivan v Management*

---

[22] [2014] EWHC 126 (Ch) at [55].

[23] [2014] EWHC 126 (Ch) at [68].

[24] Trustee Act 2000 s.35.

[25] Trustee Act 2000 s.30. It was considered that to apply the general provision to charity trustees might undermine public confidence in the sector; Law Com. No. 260 (1999), para.7.22. See also s.32 (remuneration and reimbursement of agents, nominees and custodians).

[26] Above, para.15–099.

[27] Public Trustee Act 1906 s.9; Public Trustee (Fees) Act 1957; Public Trustee (Liability and Fees) Act 2002. He is paid such salary as the Lord Chancellor determines; Public Trustee Act 1906 s.8(1A).

[28] Judicial Trustees Act 1896 s.1.

[29] Public Trustee Act 1906 s.4.

[30] *Forster v Williams Deacon's Bank Ltd* [1935] Ch. 359; *Arning v James* [1936] Ch. 158.

[31] Trustee Act 1925 s.42.

[32] *Re Worthington* [1954] 1 W.L.R. 526; *Re Jarvis* [1958] 1 W.L.R. 815; *Phipps v Boardman* [1967] 2 A.C. 46; *Foster v Spencer* [1996] 2 All E.R. 672.

[33] *Brudenell-Bruce v Moore* [2014] EWHC 3679 (Ch) per Newey J at [235] (on the facts, no remuneration was approved, even though the trustee had acted in the belief that he was entitled to charge; the trustee had been appointed on the basis that he would not take a salary, that he did not have special qualifications and the estate was short of money) J. Hilliard and A. Mold (2015) 21 T. & T. 981.

Agency and Music Ltd,[34] a contract between a performer and his agent was set aside for undue influence and breach of fiduciary duty, but the agent was awarded remuneration (including a reasonable profit element) as he had contributed significantly to the claimant's success. The argument that the jurisdiction was exercisable only in favour of the morally blameless was rejected.[35]

The jurisdiction extends to increasing the rate of remuneration authorised by the settlor.[36] The court in such a case would have regard to the nature of the trust, the experience and skill of the trustee, and the sums claimed in comparison with the charges of other trustees. In *Re Portman Estate*,[37] the court approved an amendment to the schemes of the trusts in question so that "all trustees were entitled to be paid the same amounts for the same work",[38] and any increase in pay was still subject to a Remuneration Committee.

Factors in favour of the exercise of the court's discretion include the fact that the fiduciary's work has been of substantial benefit to the trust, as in *Boardman v Phipps*[39] (where the fiduciary's work transformed the fortunes of a company in which the trust held shares) and that if the work had not been done by the fiduciary it would have had to be done by someone else at the expense of the trust.[40] An example is where trustees (a surveyor and a building contractor) used special skills over many years to bring about a sale of trust land at a profit. They had not appreciated the extent of the task when appointed, otherwise they would have declined to act gratuitously. Remuneration was awarded for the work done, but not for remaining tasks, which required no special expertise.[41]

The House of Lords in *Guinness v Saunders*[42] refused a claim to remuneration by a company director who, it was assumed, had acted bona fide but in circumstances involving a clear conflict of interest and duty. It was doubted whether the jurisdiction would ever be exercised in favour of a director, as this would constitute interference by the court in the administration of the company's affairs. The company's articles gave the power to remunerate to the board of directors, to whom the claim should be addressed. Lord Goff considered that the jurisdiction could only be reconciled with the fundamental rule that a trustee is not entitled to remuneration to the extent that its exercise did not conflict with the policy underlying that rule.

---

[34] [1985] Q.B. 428; W. Bishop and D. Prentice (1986) 49 M.L.R. 118. See also *Warman International Ltd v Dwyer* (1995) 182 C.L.R. 544 (share of profits of business); R. Nolan (1996) 55 C.L.J. 201; *Cobbetts LLP v Hodge* [2010] 1 B.C.L.C. 30 (reimbursement of costs but no remuneration).

[35] Compare *Ball v Hughes* [2017] EWHC 3228 (Ch); [2018] 1 B.C.L.C. 58 and *Global Corporate Ltd v Hale* [2017] EWHC 2277 (Ch).

[36] *Re Duke of Norfolk's ST* [1982] Ch. 61; PVB (1982) 98 L.Q.R. 181. See also *Re Barbour's Settlement* [1974] 1 W.L.R. 1198 (application for increase should be made directly and not included as a term of a compromise of an unconnected dispute); cf. *Re Codd's WT* [1975] 1 W.L.R. 1139. The court will not appoint a paid trustee unless in the best interests of the beneficiaries; *Polly Peck International Plc (In Administration) v Henry* [1999] 1 B.C.L.C. 407.

[37] [2015] EWHC 536 (Ch); [2015] 2 P. & C.R. DG10.

[38] [2015] EWHC 536 (Ch); [2015] 2 P. & C.R. DG10

[39] [1967] 2 A.C. 46, below, para.22–022.

[40] *Re Berkeley Applegate (Investment Consultants) Ltd* [1989] Ch. 32 at 50–51; for the limits of the jurisdiction under *Re Berkeley Applegate*, see the consideration by Morgan J in two judgments in the litigation of *Gillan v Hec Enterprises Ltd (In Administration)* [2016] EWHC 3179 (Ch); [2017] 1 B.C.L.C. 340; and [2017] EWHC 462 (Ch); and by HHJ Pelling QC in *Re Birchall (A Bankrupt)* [2015] EWHC 1541 (Ch); [2017] 1 W.L.R. 667

[41] *Foster v Spencer* [1996] 2 All E.R. 672.

[42] [1990] 2 A.C. 663; J. Beatson and D. Prentice (1990) 106 L.Q.R. 365; J. Hopkins (1990) 49 C.L.J. 220; Law Com. CP No. 146 (1997), p.155. The facts are given at para.22–020, below.

Such a conflict would only be avoided if the exercise of the jurisdiction was restricted to cases where it could not have the effect of encouraging trustees to put themselves in a position of conflict of interest and duty.[43] *Boardman v Phipps* was such a case. There the merits of the claim were overwhelming, but *Guinness* was very different: the director had put himself in a position where his interests were in stark conflict with his duty. Also, he had received money which belonged to the company.

More recently, Asplin J has described the provision of such an allowance as "exceptional" and not applicable where the fiduciary has failed properly to account for the benefit obtained from the breaches of duty.[44]

E. Remuneration for Litigious Work by Solicitor-Trustees

22–006 Under the rule in *Cradock v Piper*,[45] a solicitor-trustee may charge costs if she has acted for a co-trustee as well as herself [46] in respect of business done in an action or matter in court, provided that her activities have not increased the expenses. It is not necessary that the court action should be hostile in character, but it must be some form of litigious matter.[47] The rule is exceptional and will not be extended by analogies.

It may also be noted here that a solicitor-trustee may employ her partner in cases where it would be proper to employ an outside solicitor, provided that she herself will derive no benefit, direct or indirect, from such an employment.[48] There must be complete separation of the trust work from the firm's general work, so as to make it clear that the solicitor-trustee is not involved in the former. This power is not restricted to matters in court, but it does not enable a solicitor-trustee to employ her own firm.[49]

F. Authorisation by Contract

22–007 Trustees may contract for remuneration with those beneficiaries who are of full age and capacity.[50] But such agreements may somewhat easily be brought under the head of undue influence,[51] and are neither encouraged nor common.

---

[43] [1990] 2 A.C. 663, at 701; cf. *O'Sullivan v Management Agency and Music Ltd* [1985] Q.B. 428, above, which was cited in argument but not referred to in the judgments of their Lordships. *Re Sunrise Radio* [2009] EWHC 2893 (Ch).

[44] *Global Energy Horizons Corp v Gray* [2015] EWHC 2232 (Ch) at [212].

[45] (1850) 1 Mac. & G. 664. See W. Bishop and D. Prentice (1983) 46 M.L.R. 289 at 306; C. Stebbings (1998) 19 Legal History 189.

[46] *Lyon v Baker* (1852) 5 De G. & Sm. 622.

[47] *Re Corsellis* (1887) 34 Ch.D. 675.

[48] *Clack v Carlon* (1861) 30 L.J.Ch. 639.

[49] *Christophers v White* (1847) 10 Beav. 523; *Re Hill* [1934] Ch. 623.

[50] If the beneficiaries are not all of full age and capacity, application must be made to court, as in *Re Duke of Norfolk's ST* [1982] Ch. 61 (living beneficiaries did not object, but some unborn).

[51] *Ayliffe v Murray* (1740) 2 Atk. 58; below, para.29–008 and following.

2.   TRUSTEES MUST NOT BE PURCHASERS

A.   Purchase of the Trust Property: The Self-Dealing Rule

This rule and those which follow are based on the principle that a trustee may not place herself in a position where her duty and her interest may conflict.[52] This means that trustees are not to become the owners or lessees of trust property. This rule is independent of any question of inadequacy of price, or unfairness, or undue advantage; the sale may have been at auction[53] and the trustee may have taken the bidding well above the reserve price, but she is still caught by the rule, which derives from her status and position and not from her conduct in the particular case.[54] The fairness of the transaction is irrelevant in the absence of informed consent of the beneficiaries. Nor does it matter that she left the decision to sell and the manner of sale wholly to her co-trustee; nor that she retired from the trust before making an offer.[55] Her responsibility as trustee is such that she must not contemplate the purchase at all.

22–008

> The rule was somewhat relaxed in *Holder v Holder*,[56] involving an executor who had purported to renounce the executorship, but invalidly, as he had already done some minor acts in the administration of the estate. After his purported renunciation, the executor took no further part in the administration. He later purchased at auction for a fair price some farmland belonging to the estate, of which he had previously been tenant. The Court of Appeal declined to set aside the purchase. The circumstances were special, because the executor had not interfered in the administration of the estate; nor had he taken part in organising the auction; nor was there any conflict of interest and duty, as the beneficiaries were not looking to him to protect their interests; and finally, any special knowledge he had about the property was acquired as tenant and not as executor. In any event, the claimant beneficiary had acquiesced in the sale.

As a general rule, however, a trustee or executor who has once involved herself in her office is affected by the rule for a considerable period after retirement.

The effect of the rule is that the purchase is voidable at the option of a beneficiary, who is allowed a generous time to discover the position.[57] The right to avoid the sale is effective against a purchaser with notice of the circumstances. The rule cannot be got around by sales to nominees,[58] for a repurchase by the trustee will be regarded as on behalf of the trust (unless the original sale was bona

22–009

---

[52] *Boardman v Phipps* [1967] 2 A.C. 46 at 123. This principle does not apply if it is the settlor who has placed the trustees in such a position; *Sargeant v National Westminster Bank Plc* (1991) 61 P. & C.R. 518; *Breakspear v Ackland* [2009] Ch. 32. See generally on loyalty, M. Conaglen, *Fiduciary Loyalty* (Oxford: Hart Publishing, 2010); J. Edelman in J. Glister & P. Ridge (eds), *Fault Lines in Equity* (Oxford: Hart Publishing, 2012), Ch.5; A.N. Licht (2017) 37 O.J.L.S. 770.
[53] See *Newgate Stud Co v Penfold* [2008] 1 B.C.L.C. 46.
[54] *Campbell v Walker* (1800) 5 Ves.Jr. 678; *Ex p. Lacey* (1802) 6 Ves.Jr. 625; *Movitex Ltd v Bulfield* [1988] B.C.L.C. 104; *Hall v Peck* [2011] W.T.L.R. 605.
[55] *Wright v Morgan* [1926] A.C. 788; *Re Boles and British Land Co's Contract* [1902] 1 Ch. 244.
[56] [1968] Ch. 353. cf. *Re Mulholland's WT* [1949] 1 All E.R. 460 (option to purchase acquired before trusteeship). *Alpstream AG v PK Airfinance Sarl* [2015] EWCA Civ 1318; [2016] 1 C.L.C. 135 (duty to obtain best price where mortgagee put aircraft up for sale and was the only bidder at the auction).
[57] For an illustration, see *Re Sherman* [1954] Ch. 653. See also *Walker v Walker* [2010] W.T.L.R. 1617; *Cardigan v Moore* [2012] EWHC 1024 (Ch).
[58] *Silkstone & Haigh Moor Coal Co v Edey* [1900] 1 Ch. 167.

fide).[59] A sale to the trustee's spouse is looked upon with suspicion,[60] and likewise a sale to a company in which the trustee has a substantial interest.[61] The rule was applied by analogy in *Kane v Radley-Kane*,[62] where a widow who was sole administratrix appropriated unquoted shares worth £50,000 to herself in satisfaction of the statutory legacy to which she was entitled on her husband's intestacy. This was done without the consent of her stepsons, who were entitled on the intestacy subject to her rights. The estate at that time was worth only £93,000, thus it appeared that the widow was entitled to it all. She sold the shares two years later for over £1 million. It was held that the appropriation of the shares breached the self-dealing rule and was equivalent to a purchase of trust property by a trustee. Thus the widow held the shares and their proceeds for the estate.

The court may in certain circumstances prefer to order a re-sale, and, if the price is higher than the previous sale price, the trustee must convey; otherwise she is held to her purchase. The trustee will not be allowed to bid at the new sale if this is objected to.[63]

The rule discussed above is subject to certain exceptions. The trust instrument may expressly permit the purchase by a trustee,[64] or otherwise losses resulting from breaches of the self-dealing rule may be covered by an exoneration clause.[65] Secondly, the court has a discretion to allow such a purchase in a proper case,[66] or to permit the trustee to bid at an auction.[67] Thirdly, a tenant for life of settled land, which she holds on trust, is permitted by statute to purchase the property.[68] A further exception was recently recognised in *Newman v Clarke*[69]:

> The defendant created a settlement. He was granted a lease by daughter and son-in-law of a house. That lease was capable of enfranchisement under the Leasehold Reform Act 1967, which enabled the tenant to purchase the freehold interest in the relevant property. The freehold reversion in the house was later sold to the trustees of the settlement. The defendant

---

[59] *Re Postlethwaite* (1888) 60 L.T. 514.

[60] See *Burrell v Burrell's Trustees* 1915 S.C. 333, where the sale was upheld; *Tito v Waddell (No.2)* [1977] Ch. 106; *Newgate Stud Co v Penfold* [2008] 1 B.C.L.C. 46.

[61] See *Re Thompson's Settlement* [1986] Ch. 99; C. Sherrin (1986) 1 *Trust Law & Practice* 66, where the contract for sale to a company of which the trustee was managing director and majority shareholder was held unenforceable; *Movitex Ltd v Bulfield* [1988] B.C.L.C. 104. A mortgagee is also debarred from selling the property to himself, but it has been held that he can sell to a company in which he has an interest if he acts in good faith and gets the best price reasonably obtainable; *Tse Kwong Lam v Wong Chit Sen* [1983] 1 W.L.R. 1349; *Close Brothers Ltd v AIS (Marine) 2 Ltd* [2017] EWHC 2782 (Admlty). See also *Farrar v Farrars Ltd* (1889) 40 Ch.D. 395; *Hall v Peck* [2011] W.T.L.R. 605.

[62] [1999] Ch. 274; C. Sherrin All E.R. Rev. 1998 at 463; S. Cretney (1998) 28 Fam. Law 526. The Law Commission invited views as to whether reform was needed in this context, but decided not to make any recommendation because the risks of reform outweighed the possible advantages; Law Com. No. 331, *Intestacy and Family Provision Claims on Death* (2011), para.5.67.

[63] See Cross J in *Holder v Holder* [1968] Ch. 353 at 371.

[64] See *Sargeant v National Westminster Bank Plc* (1991) 61 P. & C.R. 518.

[65] As in *Barnsley v Noble* [2016] EWCA Civ 799; [2017] Ch. 191. Sales LJ noted (at [29]) that the clause in question did not prevent the possibility of the remedy of rescission.

[66] *Farmer v Dean* (1863) 32 Beav. 327. Or the beneficiaries, all being of full age and capacity, may agree to it.

[67] *Holder v Holder* [1968] Ch. 353 at 398, 402. However, if they do bid, they must complete strictly with the terms: *Hall v Peck* [2011] W.T.L.R. 605.

[68] Settled Land Act 1925 s.68.

[69] [2016] EWHC 2959 (Ch); [2017] 4 W.L.R. 26; S. Kempster and R. Walker [2017] P.C.B. 79.

subsequently replaced one of the original trustees of the settlement. He sought to exercise his right under the 1967 Act, and the other beneficiaries objected, on the basis of the rule against self-dealing. The rule was held not to apply to the unilateral exercise of the right[70] in question, because it had been granted to the defendant before he became a trustee.[71]

While recognition of this exception may not be objectionable in principle, given the tenor of the cases already considered, it might be thought to be questionable on the facts given that the defendant had caused himself to become a trustee by exercising his own power of appointment under the original settlement and so put himself in the position of conflict.[72]

B.   Purchase of the Beneficial Interest: The Fair Dealing Rule

Equity's view is less stringent when dealing with a purchase by a trustee of the beneficial interest of a beneficiary.[73] This is a type of transaction which is carefully watched; the onus is on the trustee to show that she gave full value, and that the beneficiary gave informed consent.[74] The principles of undue influence apply; but it is open to a trustee in this type of case to show that the whole transaction was conducted at arm's length. This must however be very distinctly proved.[75]

22–010

3.   INCIDENTAL PROFITS

A.   Trustees

The rules discussed below apply in full force to trustees. Many of them apply also to other fiduciaries. Although we are mainly concerned here with trustees, it will be convenient to mention also, where relevant, the application of the rules to persons who are not strictly trustees but owe obligations in equity.

22–011

i.   **Rule in *Keech v Sandford*.**[76]   This rule prevents a trustee from keeping for her own benefit a renewal of a lease which she was able to obtain for herself by reason of her being the trustee of the original lease; and even though the trustee had tried unsuccessfully to obtain a renewal for the benefit of her beneficiary. In the leading case, from which the rule takes its name, the defendant held a lease of the profits of a market on trust for a child. Before the expiration of the lease, the

22–012

---

[70] It was held not to matter whether the rights were at common law or under statute: [2017] 4 W.L.R. 26 at [18].

[71] [2017] 4 W.L.R. 26 at [32].

[72] See Editor's Note [2017] P.C.B. 84 at 84–85.

[73] *Tito v Waddell (No.2)* [1977] Ch. 106 at 241; *Re Thompson's Settlement* [1986] Ch. 99; M. Conaglen (2006) 65 C.L.J. 366.

[74] *Thomson v Eastwood* (1877) 2 App.Cas. 215 at 236; *Hill v Langley, The Times*, 28 January 1988.

[75] See generally *Coles v Trecothick* (1804) 9 Ves.Jr. 234; *Morse v Royal* (1806) 12 Ves.Jr. 355; cf. *Williams v Scott* [1900] A.C. 499.

[76] (1726) Sel. Cas. t. King 61; A. Hicks (2010) 69 C.L.J. 287 (describing the decision at 319 as a "poorly reported decision of a less than distinguished Chancellor"); L. Smith (2014) 130 L.Q.R. 608; *Re Edwards' WT* [1982] Ch. 30; *Chan v Zacharia* (1984) 154 C.L.R. 178; cf. *Harris v Black* (1983) 46 P. & C.R. 366; P. Watts (2013) 129 L.Q.R. 527 at 530.

defendant asked the lessor to renew the lease in favour of the child. The lessor refused to grant a lease to the child on the grounds that, as the lease was of the profits of the market, he would be unable to distrain, and would be unable to enforce the covenant against the child. The trustee then took a lease for his own benefit.

Lord Chancellor King held that the trustee must hold the lease on trust for the child. He said[77]:

> "This may seem hard that the trustee is the only person of all mankind who might not have the lease; but it is very proper that the rule should be strictly pursued, and not in the least relaxed; for it is very obvious what would be the consequences of letting trustees have the lease, on refusal to renew to *cestui que use*."

A similar principle applies to the renewal of contracts.[78]

22–013   ii. Purchase of the Reversion.   Where the trustee acquires the freehold reversion, the position is unclear.[79] The trustee is liable if he has in any way made use of his position to get a personal benefit: thus if the lessor makes an offer to all his lessees giving them the right to enfranchisement on favourable terms, or if the lessee had any statutory right of enfranchisement, there could be no doubt that the trustee who sought to take the reversion for his own benefit would be liable. The courts have, however, vacillated in deciding whether there is any *absolute* liability in the absence of such abuse.[80]

> In *Protheroe v Protheroe*,[81] the Court of Appeal held that the rule was applicable, without qualification, to purchases of the freehold. A husband held the lease of the matrimonial home on trust for his wife and himself in equal shares. After the wife had petitioned for divorce, he purchased the freehold reversion. When he sold, the wife was held to be entitled to a share of the proceeds.[82] In earlier cases the courts had limited the rule to cases where the lease, the reversion on which was being purchased, was renewable by law or custom.[83] The rationale of that limitation was that if the lease were normally renewed in practice,[84] the lessee would suffer if the lease passed to a third party who might not follow the custom (particularly if the lease, as was commonly the case with church leases, was generally renewed at less than the market rent). Thus it was wrong to allow the trustee, who ought to be protecting his beneficiary's interests, to damage them.

Today, by statute, many lessees are given valuable rights of renewal or enfranchisement. It is submitted that the proper question in each case is: has the

---

[77] (1726) Sel. Cas. t. King 61 at 62.

[78] *Don King Productions Inc v Warren* [2000] Ch. 291.

[79] The converse situation where a trustee of the reversion purchases the lease was left open in *Re Thompson's Settlement* [1986] Ch. 99.

[80] *Norris v Le Neve* (1743) 3 Atk. 26; *Randall v Russell* (1817) 3 Mer. 190; cf. *Phillips v Phillips* (1885) 29 Ch.D. 673.

[81] [1968] 1 W.L.R. 519; P. Jackson (1968) 31 M.L.R. 707; F. Crane (1968) 32 Conv.(N.S.) 220; *Thompson's Trustee v Heaton* [1974] 1 W.L.R. 605; (1974) 38 Conv.(N.S.) 288; P. Jackson (1975) 38 M.L.R. 226; *Popat v Shonchhatra* [1997] 1 W.L.R. 1367.

[82] "It may be that there were facts in the case which indicated that the husband obtained the freehold by virtue of his position as leaseholder, but they are not apparent from the report"; L. Megarry (1968) 84 L.Q.R. 309 at 310.

[83] *Bevan v Webb* [1905] 1 Ch. 620; cf. *Griffith v Owen* [1907] 1 Ch. 195; *Phipps v Boardman* [1964] 1 W.L.R. 993 per Wilberforce J at 1009.

[84] See generally S. Cretney (1969) 33 Conv.(N.S.) 161, where the history of the doctrine is traced.

trustee taken advantage of his position to get a personal benefit? If so, he is liable, otherwise he is not. "It seems to me," said Pennycuick VC in *Thompson's Trustee in Bankruptcy v Heaton*,[85]

> "that apart from the fact that it binds me, this decision [*Protheroe v Protheroe*], like the rule in *Keech v Sandford*, is really in modern terms an application of the broad principle that the trustee must not make a profit out of the trust estate."

The onus would be on the trustee to satisfy the court, and it can be a very difficult one to discharge.

iii. Trustees as Company Directors. What is the position if a trustee receives remuneration from a directorship which she has obtained by virtue of her position as trustee?   **22–014**

> In *Re Macadam*,[86] trustees had power under the articles by virtue of their office to appoint two directors of a company. They appointed themselves, and were held liable to account for the remuneration which they received because they had acquired it by the use of their powers as trustees.

On the other hand, the remuneration may be retained if the trustees were directors before they became trustees,[87] or if the trustees were appointed directors independently of the votes of the shares of the trust,[88] or if the trustee did not obtain the remuneration by the use of his position as a trustee, but by an independent bargain with the firm employing him.[89] Indeed, as Cohen J said in *Re Macadam*,[90] "the root of the matter really is: Did [the trustee] acquire the position in respect of which he drew the remuneration by virtue of his position as trustee?" Trustees will not be liable even within that test if the terms of the trust authorised them to appoint themselves and receive remuneration.[91]

iv. Other Profits by Trustees. Incidental profits come to trustees in a variety of ways and must always be disgorged. The line traced throughout this chapter is consistent with the following proposition: **22–015**

> "Whenever it can be shewn that the trustee has so arranged matters as to obtain an advantage, whether in money or money's worth, to himself personally through the execution of his trust, he will not be permitted to retain, but will be compelled to make it over to his constituent."[92]

---

[85] [1974] 1 W.L.R. 605 at 606. See also *Don King Productions Inc v Warren* [2000] Ch. 291, favouring the *Protheroe* approach.
[86] [1946] Ch. 73; *Williams v Barton* [1927] 2 Ch. 9.
[87] *Re Dover Coalfield Extension Ltd* [1908] 1 Ch. 65; *Re Orwell's WT* [1982] 1 W.L.R. 1337.
[88] *Re Gee* [1948] Ch. 284.
[89] *Re Lewis* (1910) 103 L.T. 495, as explained in *Re Gee* [1948] Ch. 284.
[90] [1946] Ch. 73 at 82.
[91] *Re Llewellin's WT* [1949] Ch. 225. The court may sanction the retention of the fees; *Re Keeler's ST* [1981] Ch. 156.
[92] *Huntingdon Copper Co v Henderson* (1872) 4 R. (Court of Session) 294 at 308; cf. *Patel v Patel* [1981] 1 W.L.R. 1342 (no breach where trustees sought to live in the trust property where the beneficiaries were young children adopted by the trustees on the death of their parents).

The point can be applied to a few other examples of incidental profits. A trustee who introduced business of the trust to a firm, of which he was a member, was compelled to account for the profit[93]; similarly, a trustee who received a sum of £75 to induce him to retire[94]; and in another case a trustee who used trust funds in his own business was required to account for the profits he received[95]; and a trustee may be liable for profits which he ought reasonably to have received.[96] Some authorities indicated that trustees of pension funds who were also beneficiaries were excluded from benefit where they exercised a power to apply funds among a class of which they were members.[97] This over-strict interpretation of the principle, which has not been applied to trustee-beneficiaries of other trusts, was later overturned by statute.[98]

22–016   **v.   Trustee must not be in Competition with the Trust.**   One possible, and obvious, area of conflict of interest and duty is where the trustee operates in business in competition with the trust. Such competition was inevitable in *Re Thompson*,[99] where executors of a will were directed to carry on the business of the testator who had been a yacht broker. One of the executors was intending to set up on his own account as a yacht broker in competition. It was held that he must not set up in a competing business.

This rule applies to other fiduciaries who are not trustees. A partner is required by statute to "account for and pay over to the firm all profits made" by carrying on a business "of the same nature as and competing with that of the firm"[100] unless he has the consent of the other partners. It is a question of fact in each case whether or not the activity is in conflict with the fiduciary duty.[101]

B.   Other Fiduciaries[102]

22–017   **i.   The Principle.**   A similar rule applies to profits[103] made by other persons in breach of a fiduciary relation; indeed such persons are grouped with trustees in many formulations of the rule although there is no rule that they must act gratuitously.

---

[93] *Williams v Barton* [1927] 2 Ch. 9; endorsed by Lord Neuberger PSC in *FHR European Ventures LLP v Cedar Capital Partners LLC* [2014] UKSC 45; [2015] A.C. 250 at [16]. cf. *Jones v AMP Perpetual Trustee Company NZ Ltd* [1994] 1 N.Z.L.R. 690 (no breach where subsidiary placed trust business with parent company).

[94] *Sugden v Crossland* (1856) 3 Sm. & G. 192; *Re Smith* [1896] 1 Ch. 71.

[95] *Brown v IRC* [1965] A.C. 244 (a Scottish solicitor compelled to account for interest earned by deposits of clients' moneys).

[96] *Re Waterman's WT* [1952] 2 All E.R. 1054.

[97] Discussed in J. Mowbray (1996) 10 T.L.I. 49. See also, in the context of a family discretionary trust, *Breakspear v Ackland* [2009] Ch. 32.

[98] Pensions Act 1995 s.39; above, para.17–010. See *Edge v Pensions Ombudsman* [2000] Ch. 602.

[99] [1930] 1 Ch. 203; *Aberdeen Railway Co v Blaikie Bros* (1854) 1 Macq. 461; *Warman International Ltd v Dwyer* (1995) 182 C.L.R. 544; *Cheng Wai Tao v Poon Ka Man Jason* [2016] HKCFA 23; A.K. Koh and S.S. Tang [2016] L.M.C.L.Q. 358; P. Koh (2017) 80 M.L.R. 941.

[100] Partnership Act 1890 s.30.

[101] *Moore v M'Glynn* [1894] 1 Ir.R. 74.

[102] G. Jones (1968) 84 L.Q.R. 472; R. Goode (1976) 92 L.Q.R. 360 at 372; A. Oakley, *Constructive Trusts* (1996), 3rd edn, Ch.3; J. Shepherd (1981) 97 L.Q.R. 51; J.C. Shepherd, *The Law of Fiduciaries*

> "It is an inflexible rule of a Court of Equity that a person in a fiduciary position,... is not, unless otherwise expressly provided, entitled to make a profit; he is not allowed to put himself in a position where his interest and duty conflict."[104]

However, it is important to avoid the over-simplification of saying that a fiduciary must always account for all gains which come to him by reason of his fiduciary position. Indeed, Lord Herschell in the paragraph containing the above quotation "plainly recognised its limitations"[105]:

> "But I am satisfied that it might be departed from in many cases, without any breach of morality, without any wrong being inflicted, and without any consciousness of wrong-doing. Indeed, it is obvious that it might sometimes be to the advantage of the beneficiaries that their trustee should act for them professionally rather than a stranger, even though the trustee were paid for his services."[106]

It is not always easy, however, to determine whether a particular relationship should be classified as fiduciary. While some examples are well established, the boundaries of the category of fiduciary relationships are not clear, and the category is not closed.[107] Much will depend upon any agreement between the parties: the defining feature is the assumption of the duty of loyalty.[108] The category includes certain agents,[109] (including "self-appointed" agents[110]),

---

(Carswell, 1981); Snell, para.7–004; L. Smith in Getzler (ed.), *Rationalizing Property, Equity and Trusts* (Oxford: Oxford University Press, 2003), Ch.4; M. Conaglen. *Fiduciary Loyalty* (Oxford: Hart Publishing, 2010); J. Edelman (2010) 126 L.Q.R. 302. See Law Com. No. 236, *Fiduciary Duties and Regulatory Rules* (1995), examining the mismatch between general law obligations and regulatory rules. See chapters by A. Duggan (Ch.12), J. Edelman (Ch.13) and R. Nolan and M. Conaglen (Ch.14) in E. Bant and M. Harding (eds), *Exploring Private Law* (Cambridge: Cambridge University Press, 2010); L. Smith (2014) 130 L.Q.R. 608; K.F.K. Low (2016) 30 T.L.I. 3; P. Finn, *Fiduciary Obligations: 40th Anniversary Republication with Additional Essays* (Federation Press, 2016).

[103] For losses caused by breach of the duty of loyalty, see *Item Software (UK) Ltd v Fassihi* [2005] 2 B.C.L.C. 91 and *Wey Education Plc v Atkins* [2016] EWHC 1663 (Ch); A. Berg (2005) 121 L.Q.R. 213; J. Armour and M. Conaglen (2005) 64 C.L.J. 48; R. Lee [2009] Conv. 236; M. Conaglen (2010) 126 L.Q.R. 72; L. Smith in E. Bant and M. Harding (eds), *Exploring Private Law* (2010), Ch.16.

[104] Lord Herschell in *Bray v Ford* [1896] A.C. 44 at 51; see also Lord Cranworth in *Aberdeen Railway Co v Blaikie Bros* (1854) 1 Macq. 461 at 471; *Regal (Hastings) Ltd v Gulliver* [1942] 1 All E.R. 378; [1967] 2 A.C. 134n; *Breitenfeld UK Ltd v Harrison* [2015] EWHC 399 (Ch); [2015] 2 B.C.L.C. 275 per Norris J at [69]–[75].

[105] Lord Upjohn in *Boardman v Phipps* [1967] 2 A.C. 46 at 123.

[106] *Bray v Ford* [1896] A.C. 44 at 52.

[107] *English v Dedham Vale Properties Ltd* [1978] 1 W.L.R. 93; A. Duggan (1997) 113 L.Q.R. 601 at 619–626; Sir Anthony Mason (1997–98) 8 K.C.L.J. 1 at 6; Sir Peter Millett (1998) 114 L.Q.R. 214; S Worthington (1999) 58 C.L.J. 500; Birks (ed.), *Privacy and Loyalty* (Oxford: Clarendon Press, 1997) Chs 10, 11. Leggatt LJ has recently said that "it is exceptional for fiduciary duties to arise other than in certain settled categories of relationship" in *Nehayan v Kent* [2018] EWHC 333 (Comm) at [157].

[108] e.g. *Brown v Innovatorone Plc* [2012] EWHC 1321 (Comm) per Hamblen J at [1301]–[1304] (*Brown* was doubted by Lord Carnwath JSC in *Asset Land Investment Plc v The Financial Conduct Authority* [2016] UKSC 17; [2016] Bus. L.R. 524 at [94], but not on this point).

[109] *De Bussche v Alt* (1878) 8 Ch.D. 286; *New Zealand Netherlands Society v Kuys* [1973] 1 W.L.R. 1126 at 1129; *Conway v Eze* [2018] EWHC 29 (Ch). Not all agents are fiduciaries: *UBS AG (London Branch) v Kommunale Wasserwerke Leipzig GmbH* [2017] EWCA Civ 1567; [2017] 2 Lloyd's Rep. 621 per Lord Briggs of Westbourne and Hamblen LJ at [92] "There are no doubt many forms of non-fiduciary agency, just as there are forms of fiduciary agency in which the agent has no authority to affect the principal's relations with third parties." There are however dicta suggesting that there may

solicitors,[111] company directors,[112] partners,[113] confidential employees,[114] a pawnbroker,[115] and certain bailees,[116] but not a vendor of goods to which title has not yet passed to the purchaser.[117] There may be a fiduciary relationship between parties to a joint venture, but "only if after careful examination of the facts, the requisite fiduciary expectation of mutual trust and confidence is found to exist",[118] and caution will be applied between commercial joint venturers.[119]

22-018 Indeed, it may sometimes appear that the defendant may be classified as a fiduciary, or not, in order to achieve the desired result.

> In *Reading v Attorney General*,[120] a staff-sergeant in the British Army stationed in Cairo was bribed by Egyptians to ride in their civilian lorries carrying contraband goods, enabling the lorries to pass check posts without difficulty. The British authorities seized £20,000 from Reading; later he petitioned to recover it. He had obtained the money wrongfully, but he argued that this fact did not mean that the British Government was entitled to claim it. Reading failed, however, and one of the grounds for the decision in the House of Lords was that he, as a non-commissioned officer, was in a fiduciary relation to the Crown, and was therefore under a duty to account for the profit wrongfully made. Lord Porter recognised that "the words 'fiduciary relationship' in this setting are used in a wide and loose sense.[121]

Illegal or secret commissions or bribes obtained by a confidential servant or agent are recoverable by the principal or employer regardless of any quantifiable loss to

---

be a presumption that agents are fiduciaries; *Aluminium Industrie Vaassen BV v Romalpa Aluminium Ltd* [1976] 1 W.L.R. 676. *Australian Competition and Consumer Commission v Flight Centre Travel Group Ltd* [2016] HCA 49.

[110] *English v Dedham Vale Properties Ltd* [1978] 1 W.L.R. 93 (where the intending purchaser obtained planning permission in the vendor's name); A. Nicol (1978) 41 M.L.R. 474; G. Samuel (1978) 94 L.Q.R. 347.

[111] *Brown v IRC* [1965] A.C. 244; (1964) 80 L.Q.R. 480; *Longstaff v Birtles* [2002] 1 W.L.R. 470; *Ratiu v Conway* [2006] W.T.L.R. 101. See also *Hanson v Lorenz* [1987] 1 F.T.L.R. 23 (no liability to account to client for his profits from a joint venture where client had understood the agreement).

[112] *Regal (Hastings) Ltd v Gulliver* [1967] 2 A.C. 134n; *Industrial Development Consultants Ltd v Cooley* [1972] 1 W.L.R. 443; below, para.22–020. See also *Cullen Investments Ltd v Brown* [2017] EWHC 1586 (Ch).

[113] *Clegg v Fishwick* (1849) 1 Mac. & G. 294; *John Taylors (A Firm) v Masons* [2005] W.T.L.R. 1519.

[114] *Attorney General v Guardian Newspapers Ltd (No.2)* [1990] 1 A.C. 109 (The "Spycatcher" case; duty to account for profits). A former member of the security service does not owe a continuing fiduciary duty to the Crown in relation to information which is not confidential; *Attorney General v Blake* [2001] 1 A.C. 268 (although the defendant in *Blake* was accountable for profits on the basis of breach of contract). See also *Nottingham University v Fishel* [2000] I.R.L.R. 471; *Cobbetts LLP v Hodge* [2010] 1 B.C.L.C. 30; and *Marathon Asset Management LLP v Seddon* [2017] EWHC 300 (Comm); [2017] I.C.R. 791. On the duty of "fidelity", see R. Flannigan (2008) 124 L.Q.R. 274.

[115] *Mathew v TM Sutton Ltd* [1994] 1 W.L.R. 1455 (surplus proceeds of sale held on trust for pawnor and interest payable).

[116] *Aluminium Industrie Vaassen BV v Romalpa Aluminium Ltd* [1976] 1 W.L.R. 676; *Re Andrabell Ltd (In Liquidation)* [1984] 3 All E.R. 407.

[117] *Re Goldcorp Exchange Ltd (In Receivership)* [1995] 1 A.C. 74.

[118] [2017] EWHC 1586 (Ch) per Barling J at [257] (no fiduciary relationship was found on the facts).

[119] [2017] EWHC 1586 (Ch) per Barling J at [258] See, similarly, *Janus Capital Management LLC v Safeguard World International Ltd* [2016] EWHC 1355 (Ch), per Arnold J at [247]. cf. *Lac Minerals Ltd v International Corona Resources Ltd* [1989] 2 SCR 574.

[120] [1951] A.C. 507.

[121] [1951] A.C. 507 at 516.

her.[122] If the fiduciary relationship in this case is accepted, the result merely follows the earlier cases on agents. The application of the rule to a policeman[123] and a staff-sergeant may be an extension; indeed the speeches in the House of Lords in *Reading v Attorney General* suggest the extensiveness of fiduciary status.[124]

Where a fiduciary agent has taken a secret commission, it has been held that she forfeits her contractual remuneration.[125] In addition to paying no further fees, the principal is entitled to recover fees already paid as well as an account of profits, and the agent is not entitled to an allowance for the value of any work done. This principle could operate inequitably if the breach occurred towards the end of an agency relationship. It may be that a distinction should be drawn between long term fiduciary relationships and those of a "single transaction" character.[126]

Prior to the Supreme Court decision in *FHR European Ventures LLP v Cedar Capital Partners LLC*,[127] there was controversy over whether the remedy in such cases is purely personal or may be proprietary: this issue is considered in Part 3 below.

ii. Company Directors. Company directors are treated as fiduciaries[128] in so **22–019** far as they are prohibited from making a profit out of their office[129] unless the articles permit it or the shareholders or the board of directors consent. Following the recommendations of the Law Commission,[130] the fiduciary (and other) duties of directors were codified by the Companies Act 2006, in order to make the law more certain, accessible and comprehensible. The duties set out in the Act are based on and replace the previous common law rules and equitable principles

---

[122] *Attorney General for Hong Kong v Reid* [1994] 1 A.C. 324; below, para.22–029. See also *Brown v IRC* [1965] A.C. 244; *Logicrose Ltd v Southend United Football Club Ltd* [1988] 1 W.L.R. 1256 (principal can recover from agent whether he affirms or repudiates the transaction between the agent and the third party); G. Jones (1989) 48 C.L.J. 22; *Swindle v Harrison* [1997] 4 All E.R. 705 (undisclosed profit by solicitor from loan transaction arranged for client); *Murad v Al-Saraj* [2005] W.T.L.R. 1573; *FHR European Ventures LLP v Cedar Capital Partners LLC* [2014] UKSC 45; [2015] A.C. 250.

[123] *Attorney General v Goddard* (1929) 98 L.J.K.B. 743 (bribes received when on duty).

[124] See also *Swain v The Law Society* [1983] A.C. 598 (no fiduciary relationship between Law Society and solicitors).

[125] *Imageview Management Ltd v Jack* [2009] 2 All E.R. 666 (agent hired to negotiate contract for professional footballer); P. Watts (2009) 125 L.Q.R. 369.

[126] S. Oram [2010] L.M.C.L.Q. 95.

[127] [2014] UKSC 45; [2015] A.C. 250.

[128] The duty is owed to the company, not to the shareholders; *Percival v Wright* [1902] 2 Ch. 421. This is made statutory by Companies Act 2006 s.170(1). Directors do not thus owe, solely by virtue of their office, fiduciary duties to shareholders—there must be more to the relationship beyond the usual relationship between director and shareholders: *Sharp v Blank* [2015] EWHC 3220 (Ch).

[129] The office of director should not, however, be equated with that of trustee. The assets of the company, unlike trust property, are not vested in the director but in the company which is a separate legal entity and, more importantly, directors "are... commercial men managing a trading concern for the benefit of themselves and of all other shareholders in it...": per Jessell MR in *Re Forest of Dean Coal Mining Co Ltd* (1878) 10 Ch.D. 450, at 451–452.

[130] Law Com. No. 261; *Company Directors: Regulating Conflicts of Interest and Formulating a Statement of Duties.* See generally D. Ahern (2012) 128 L.Q.R. 114.

governing the duties owed by directors to the company.[131] The statutory duties are to be interpreted and applied by having regard to the common law rules and equitable principles, thus preserving existing case law.[132] The consequences of, and remedies for, breach of the fiduciary duties have not been codified and are, therefore, those provided by the general law on breach of fiduciary duty.[133]

While the statutory provisions for the most part reflect the rules laid down by the general law, one of the most important and to some extent controversial provisions of the Act is the express duty of a director to act in a way he considers, in good faith, would be most likely to promote the success of the company for the benefit of its members as a whole.[134] This went further than the law it replaced.[135] The duty to exercise reasonable care, skill and diligence is made statutory,[136] although the Act makes it clear that this is not a fiduciary duty.[137]

Fundamental to the codification of fiduciary duties is s.175[138] of the Act of 2006, which sets out the duty to avoid a situation in which the director has, or can have, a direct or indirect interest which conflicts, or possibly may conflict, with the interests of the company.[139] A director must not exploit any property, information or opportunity, and it is immaterial whether the company could take advantage of it.[140] There is no breach of duty if the situation could not reasonably be regarded as likely to give rise to a conflict of interest.[141] Importantly, the Act confirms that there is no breach if the matter has been authorised by the directors, although the manner of authorisation is subject to conditions.[142] The statutory

---

[131] Companies Act 2006 s.170. The duties apply, with any necessary adaptations, to former directors: s.170(2). By virtue of the Small Business, Enterprise and Employment Act 2015 s.89(1), the general duties apply to shadow directors (to the extent to which they are capable of some applying): see also C.R. Moore (2016) 36 L.S. 326 and the judgment of Morgan J in *Instant Access Properties Ltd v Rosser* [2018] EWHC 756 (Ch).

[132] Companies Act 2006 s.170(4), although caution may be observed in respect of older authorities if they took an anachronistically generous approach towards directors: see eg *Bishopsgate Investment Management Ltd (In Liquidation) v Maxwell (No.2)* [1994] All E.R. 261 per Hoffmann LJ at 264 and *Cheng Wai Tao v Poon Ka Man Jason* [2016] HKCFA 23 per Spigelman NPJ at [98].

[133] Companies Act 2006 s.178.

[134] Companies Act 2006 s.172.

[135] J. Lowry (2009) 68 C.L.J. 607.

[136] Companies Act 2006 s.174.

[137] Companies Act 2006 s.178(2).

[138] E. Lim (2013) 129 L.Q.R. 242.

[139] *Burns v Financial Conduct Authority* [2017] EWCA Civ 2140 at [74]–[76].

[140] Companies Act 2006 s.175(2). The reflects the strict rule of equity laid down in *Keech v Sandford* (1726) Sel. Cas. Ch. 61; above, para.22–012. *Cheng Wai Tao v Poon Ka Man Jason* [2016] HKCFA 23.

[141] Companies Act 2006 s.175(4)(a). This approach reflects Lord Upjohn's dissenting view in *Boardman v Phipps* [1967] 2 A.C. 46 at 124. It may also be regarded as lending support to the view that there is no breach where the board, being fully informed, has rejected the opportunity or venture; *Peso Silvermines Ltd v Cropper* (1966) 58 D.L.R. (2d) 1. See also *Foster Bryant Surveying Ltd v Bryant* [2007] B.C.L.C. 239; J. Payne All E.R. Rev. 2007, p.73 and *Cheng Wai Tao v Poon Ka Man Jason* [2016] HKCFA 23 per Spigelman NPJ at [104]–[105].

[142] Companies Act 2006 s.175(4)(b). The conditions are laid down in subss.(5) to (7). See also s.180 (consent, approval or authorisation by members).

no-conflict rule expresses in a single rule the previous distinct but overlapping no-conflict and no-profit rules. An objective test is applied, in line with the common law authorities.[143]

The rule against taking bribes and secret commissions is also statutory,[144] likewise the duty to declare to the other directors any interest, direct or indirect, which a director has in a proposed transaction or arrangement with the company.[145]

The statutory rules may be illustrated by the case law based on the equitable **22–020** principles which they codify. The leading case is the House of Lords decision in *Regal (Hastings) Ltd v Gulliver*.[146]

> R Ltd set up a subsidiary, A Ltd, to acquire the leases of two cinemas. A Ltd had a share capital of 5,000 £1 shares. The owner of the cinemas was only willing to lease them if the share capital of A Ltd was completely subscribed for. However, R Ltd had resources to subscribe for only 2,000 of the 5,000 shares and it was therefore agreed that the directors of R Ltd should subscribe for the rest. When the business of R Ltd was transferred to new controllers the directors made a profit from their holdings in A Ltd. The new controllers of R Ltd caused the company to sue the ex-directors of R Ltd for an account of the profit. The directors were held liable. They had made the profit out of their position as directors and, in the absence of shareholder approval, they were obliged to account.

There are a number of noteworthy features of *Regal*. First, the directors were found by the court to have acted bona fide, but the liability of a fiduciary to account for a profit made from his office "in no way depends on fraud, or absence of bona fides."[147] Secondly, the new controllers obtained a windfall.[148] Thirdly, it was arguable that the directors, by purchasing the shares in A Ltd had enabled R Ltd to enter into a transaction which it was otherwise commercially impossible for the company to enter into. While there is some truth in this, the decision that R Ltd did not have the necessary financial resources to enter into the transaction was made by the directors who were the very persons who benefited from this decision. As a result, a compelling argument can be made that a "reasonable man looking at the relevant facts and circumstances of the particular case would think that there was a real sensible possibility of conflict."[149]

A clear case of conflict of interest and duty arose in *Guinness Plc v Saunders*,[150] where a director (Ward) agreed to provide his services in connection with a proposed take-over of another company (Distillers), on terms that he would be paid a fee the size of which depended on the amount of the take-over

---

[143] *Richmond Pharmacology Ltd v Chester Overseas Ltd* [2014] EWHC 2692 (Ch); [2014] Bus. L.R. 1110, Stephen Jourdan QC sitting as a deputy High Court judge at [72]–[73].
[144] Companies Act 2006 s.176 (duty not to accept benefits from third parties). Some receipts of such benefits may also amount to a crime under the Bribery Act 2010 s.2.
[145] Companies Act 2006 s.177. See *Newgate Stud Co v Penfold* [2008] 1 B.C.L.C. 46 (involvement of fiduciary's wife).
[146] [1967] 2 A.C. 134n. For a review of this line of cases, see *Ultraframe (UK) Ltd v Fielding* [2007] W.T.L.R. 835; D. Prentice and J. Payne (2006) 122 L.Q.R. 558. See also R. Nolan in C. Mitchell and P. Mitchell (eds), *Landmark Cases in Equity* (Oxford: Hart Publishing, 2012), Ch.17.
[147] [1967] 2 A.C. 134 at 144.
[148] See D. Prentice (1979) 42 M.L.R. 215.
[149] *Boardman v Phipps* [1967] 2 A.C. 46 at 124, per Lord Upjohn.
[150] [1990] 2 A.C. 663; J. Beatson and D. Prentice (1990) 106 L.Q.R. 365; J. Hopkins (1990) 49 C.L.J. 220; S. Goulding [1990] Conv. 296.

bid if successful. The bid was successful, and the fee paid to Ward was £5.2 million. The claim by Guinness for summary judgment for the repayment of this sum was upheld in the House of Lords. Ward's interest in obtaining a fee calculated on the above basis conflicted with his duty as director, which was to give impartial advice concerning the take-over. The agreement for the fee, made with two other directors, but not the board of directors, was void for want of authority. Ward had no arguable defence to Guinness's claim that he had received the money, paid under a void contract, as a constructive trustee.

The courts have imposed liability on directors to account where the directors have made the profit out of an economic opportunity, or information, even though they acquired it in a personal capacity, if it was information which could have been exploited by their company.[151]

> In *Industrial Development Consultants Ltd v Cooley*,[152] the defendant was a director and general manager of the claimant company, which provided construction consultancy services. He attempted to interest a public Gas Board in a project, but was unsuccessful because the Gas Board's policy was not to employ development companies. The defendant was a distinguished architect who had worked in the gas industry for many years. For this reason, the Gas Board decided to offer the contract to him personally, which he accepted, obtaining a release from the claimant by falsely representing that he was ill. He was held to be liable to account to the claimant for the profits of the contract.

The significance of the case is twofold. First, the court rejected Cooley's defence that the information concerning the Gas Board's contract came to him in his private capacity, and not as director of the claimant company:

> "This is the first case in which it was decided that the prohibition on exploiting a corporate opportunity applies also to an opportunity which was presented to the director personally and not in his capacity with the company."[153]

Secondly, the decision whether or not the contract went to the company lay not with the fiduciary, Cooley, but with a third party, the Gas Board.[154] In *Cooley's* case there were special circumstances; this was exactly the type of opportunity which the company relied on Cooley to obtain; furthermore, the absence of bona fides was clear. Also, the imposition of liability provides directors with an incentive to channel opportunities to their companies and not exploit them for their personal advantage. A director's duty of undivided loyalty means that he must inform the company of a relevant business opportunity. It is not for the director to decide that the company would not be interested and then to appropriate the opportunity for himself.[155]

---

[151] See *Canadian Aero Service Ltd v O'Malley* (1973) 40 D.L.R. (3d) 371 SCC.

[152] [1972] 1 W.L.R. 443; [1972] 2 All E.R. 162 (the reports on the case are not identical); A. Yoran (1973) 89 L.Q.R. 187; J. Collier (1972) 30 C.L.J. 222. See also *CMS Dolphin Ltd v Simonet* [2001] 2 B.C.L.C. 704; *Re Bhullar Bros Ltd* [2003] 2 B.C.L.C. 241; D. Prentice and J. Payne (2004) 120 L.Q.R. 198; *Kingsley IT Consulting Ltd v McIntosh* [2006] B.C.C. 875.

[153] (1973) 89 L.Q.R. 187 at 189.

[154] Roskill J found that there was only a 10% chance that the Gas Board would have awarded the contract to the company. Thus the company only benefited because Cooley had breached his duty.

[155] *Re Allied Business and Financial Consultants Ltd* [2009] 2 B.C.L.C. 666; D. Ahern (2011) 74 M.L.R. 596. *Cheng Wai Tao v Poon Ka Man Jason* [2016] HKCFA 23.

There are other decisions which suggest a more benign attitude towards directors.

22–021

> In *Queensland Mines Ltd v Hudson*,[156] the claimant company had been interested in developing a mining operation and the defendant, the managing director, was successful in obtaining for the company the licences necessary to enable it to do so. However, because of financial problems it could not proceed. Hudson resigned as managing director and, with the knowledge of the company's board, successfully developed the mines. The Privy Council held that Hudson was not liable to account, for either of two reasons: (a) the rejection of the opportunity by the company because of cash difficulties took the venture outside the scope of Hudson's fiduciary duties or (b) because Hudson had acted with the full knowledge of the company's board, they should be taken to have consented to his activities.[157]

This decision was considered controversial. However, it now appears to be endorsed by the Companies Act 2006.[158]

An important point has been made more recently when considering claims against employees who are not directors.[159] Although such persons may owe fiduciary obligations, it should not be assumed that they are fiduciaries. Thus, in *Ranson v Customer Systems*,[160] a company claimed against its former employee for breach of a fiduciary duty of loyalty (as well as a contractual duty of fidelity), because the defendant, who had resigned, had made preparations for setting up his own business to compete with the company while still serving his notice period. Lewison LJ said: "Since fiduciary obligations are not 'one size fits all' it is, in my judgment, dangerous to reason by analogy from cases about company directors to cases about employees."[161] The starting point must always be the contract of employment: on the facts, no relevant fiduciary was owed.[162]

iii. ***Boardman v Phipps.*** Many of the difficulties relating to the application of the rule came to the fore in *Boardman v Phipps*.[163]

22–022

> The Phipps trust owned a substantial minority holding of shares in a private company. John Phipps, the claimant, was one of the beneficiaries under the trust, and the defendants were Boardman, a solicitor, and Tom Phipps, also a beneficiary. The trustees were an elderly widow who died in 1958, her daughter and an accountant. Boardman acted as solicitor to the trust. In

---

[156] (1978) 18 A.L.R. 1; W. Braithwaite [1980] Conv. 200; applied in *Jones v AMP Perpetual Trustee Company NZ Ltd* [1994] 1 N.Z.L.R. 690. See also *Island Export Finance Ltd v Umunna* [1986] B.C.L.C. 460 (defendant not liable for developing a business opportunity after resigning as managing director because company was not actively pursuing the venture when he resigned, and his resignation was influenced not by any wish to acquire the business opportunity but by dissatisfaction with the company). See also *In Plus Group Ltd v Pyke* [2002] 2 B.C.L.C. 201; P. Koh (2003) 62 C.L.J. 42, 403.

[157] (1978) 18 A.L.R. 1 at 10. Lord Upjohn's reasoning in *Boardman v Phipps* [1967] 2 A.C. 46 was adopted on the basis that he "dissented on the facts, but not on the law" (at 3).

[158] See s.175(4)(a), (b); above, para.22–019.

[159] *Ranson v Customer Systems Plc* [2012] EWCA Civ 841; *Threlfall v ECD Insight Ltd* [2012] EWHC 3543 (QB); *Airbus Operations Ltd v Paul Withey* [2014] EWHC 1126 (QB).

[160] [2012] EWCA Civ 841.

[161] [2012] EWCA Civ 841 at [24].

[162] [2012] EWCA Civ 841 at [67]–[68]. See also R. Flannigan [2015] J.B.L. 189; A. Frazer (2015) 131 L.Q.R. 53 at 74–77.

[163] [1967] 2 A.C. 46; G. Jones (1968) 84 L.Q.R. 472; B. Rider [1978] Conv. 114. For a valuable study of the papers in the case, see A. Hicks [2013] Conv. 232. The case was distinguished in *Satnam Investments Ltd v Dunlop Heywood & Co Ltd* [1999] 3 All E.R. 652, where the defendant, who took advantage of an opportunity arising from another's breach of fiduciary duty, was not himself a fiduciary; see also *University of London v Prag* [2014] EWHC 3564 (Ch).

1956, the defendants were dissatisfied with the way in which the company was managed. They made various inquiries on behalf of the trust, and in that capacity obtained confidential information about the company. They realised that it would be advantageous to sell some of the non-profit-making assets. They obtained control of the company by purchasing the remainder of the company's shares, and carried out the desired sales and reorganisation. The transaction was highly profitable. The trust gained in respect of its holding and the defendants gained in respect of the shares which they had purchased for the purpose of obtaining control.

Boardman had informed the beneficiaries and the two active trustees (the widow having lost mental capacity and taking no part in the affairs of the trust) giving them an outline of the negotiations and asking them whether they had any objection to his taking a personal interest, bearing in mind that his initial inquiry had been on behalf of the trust. Boardman acted bona fide throughout and thought that he had made a full disclosure and had the beneficiaries' consent. Wilberforce J however found that the claimant was justified in thinking that he had only been told half the truth. The trustees had been invited to consider whether the trust should find the money for the purchase of the shares; but the trustees were unable and unwilling to do so. John Phipps then called upon the defendants to account for the profits which they had made. The House of Lords (3–2) held that they must do so; but having acted bona fide, they were entitled to payment on a liberal scale for their work and skill.[164]

A number of points of importance arise from the case. First, Boardman was not a trustee. The fiduciary relation arose from his employment as solicitor by the trustees. He was not, however, employed to act for the trust in the dealings in question and he claimed, as he stated at the time, to have been acting in a private capacity. The members of the House of Lords took different views on this issue. In the early negotiations with the company, the defendants, who were not shareholders in their own right, purported to represent the trust, although strictly they did not do so. Lord Cohen, in the majority, said "that information and that opportunity they owed to their representing themselves as agents for the holders of the 8,000 shares held by the trustees."[165] Lord Upjohn, dissenting, said "though they portrayed themselves as representing the Phipps Trust, it is quite clear the offer was made by these two personally."[166]

22–023 Secondly, the liability of the defendants was unaffected by the fact that the trust had lost nothing; nor that the trust had greatly benefited; nor did it matter that the Phipps Trust could not have found the money; nor that the trustees would not have wished to use the money for that purpose even if they had it; nor that such use would have been in breach of trust, unless they had applied to the court and obtained consent to the investment.[167]

It is extremely difficult to determine the limits of this inflexible rule. Part of the difficulty stems from the lack of agreement as to whether the confidential information acquired by the appellants was trust property. The dissenting judges considered that it was not property. Of the majority, Lords Hodson and Guest considered that it was,[168] while Lord Cohen merely held that it was not property "in the strict sense of that word", so that liability to account for profits from its

---

[164] Above, para.22–005.

[165] [1967] 2 A.C. 46 at 103.

[166] [1967] 2 A.C. 46, at 120; see also Viscount Dilhorne at 91; and *New Zealand Netherlands Society v Kuys* [1973] 1 W.L.R. 1126; (1973) 37 Conv.(N.S.) 362.

[167] Lord Denning MR in the Court of Appeal mentioned this as a source of a potential conflict of interest and duty; [1965] Ch. 992 at 1020. The suggestion, however, seems unrealistic. See [1967] 2 A.C. 46 at 92, 124; cf. Lord Cohen at 103–104.

[168] Criticised G. Jones (1968) 84 L.Q.R. 472; A. Oakley, *Constructive Trusts*, 3rd edn (1996), p.170; Sir Peter Millett (1998) 114 L.Q.R. 214 at 222.

use depended on the facts of the case.[169] In *Aas v Benham*,[170] Lindley LJ laid down that information obtained in the course of a partnership business must not be used by the partners for their own benefit within the scope of the partnership business; but that they may make use of it for:

"[P]urposes which are wholly without the scope of the firm's business… It is not the source of the information, but the use to which it is applied, which is important in such matters."[171]

This was not disapproved in *Boardman v Phipps*,[172] but it seems that a stricter view there prevailed; the defendants were held accountable because they had obtained the information by purporting to represent the trust; notwithstanding that they were acting independently when they made the purchase. It is submitted that it is difficult to answer Lord Upjohn's argument in dissent[173]:

"I think, again, that some of the trouble that has arisen in this case, it being assumed rightly that throughout he was in such a [fiduciary] capacity, is that it has been assumed that it has necessarily followed that any profit made by him renders him accountable to the trustees. That is not so.… . It is perfectly clear that a solicitor can if he so desires act against his clients in any matter in which he has not been retained by them provided, of course, that in acting for them generally he has not learnt information or placed himself in a position which would make it improper for him to act against them. This is an obvious application of the rule that he must not place himself in a position where his duty and his interest conflict. So, in general, a solicitor can deal in shares in a company in which the client is a shareholder, subject always to the general rule that the solicitor must never place himself in a position where his interest and his duty conflict; and in this connection it may be pointed out that the interest and duty may refer (and frequently do) to a conflict of interest and duty on behalf of different clients and have nothing to do with any conflict between the personal interest and duty of the solicitor, beyond his interest in earning his fees."

His Lordship concluded:

"To extend the doctrines of equity to make the [defendants] accountable in such circumstances, is, in my judgment, to make unreasonable and inequitable applications of such doctrines."[174]

Where the rule applies, the only escape of the fiduciary is that she made full **22–024** disclosure, and obtained the consent of the other parties, and it is not open to her

---

[169] [1967] 2 A.C. 46 at 102. It was accepted in *Crown Dilmun Plc v Sutton* [2004] W.T.L.R. 497 that confidential information is not property. It may, however, be "sold in the market"; *Douglas v Hello! Ltd (No.3)* [2008] A.C. 1 (conjoined appeal with *OBG Ltd v Allan*). Information may now amount to property in certain statutory contexts, as decided by the Supreme Court in *Phillips v News Group Newspapers* [2012] UKSC 28; [2013] 1 A.C. 1 per Lord Walker of Gestingthorpe JSC at [20]: "The fact that technical and commercial information ought not, strictly speaking, to be described as property (the majority view of the House of Lords in *Phipps v Boardman* [1967] 2 A.C. 46…) cannot prevail over the clear statutory language. Whether or not confidential information can only loosely, or metaphorically, be described as property is simply irrelevant." L. Bently (2012) 71 C.L.J. 501.
[170] [1891] 2 Ch. 244.
[171] [1891] 2 Ch. 244 at 256.
[172] [1967] 2 A.C. 46.
[173] [1967] 2 A.C. 46 at 126.
[174] [1967] 2 A.C. 46 at 133–134, quoting Lord Selborne LC in *Barnes v Addy* (1874) 9 Ch.App. 244 at 251. See also *Chan v Zacharia* (1984) 154 C.L.R. 178 at 204, suggesting that there should be no liability if it would be unconscientious to assert it, or if there was no possible conflict of interest and duty and it was plainly in the interest of the beneficiary that the fiduciary obtain the rights for himself that he was absolutely precluded from seeking or obtaining for the beneficiary.

to argue that they would have consented if asked.[175] It is not, however, clear whether the "other parties" are the trustees or the beneficiaries. In the straightforward case of a profit made by a trustee, the relevant consent must be that of the beneficiaries, to whom the duty is owed. Difficulties will arise if any of the beneficiaries are children or unborn. *Boardman v Phipps*, however, was not such a case. Boardman was a fiduciary agent, the principals being the trustees. To whom did he owe his fiduciary duties? Presumably consent must be obtained from those persons. If the trustees had not consented, they would, as principals, have a right of recovery against their agent, any money thus recovered being held by them on trust for the beneficiaries. If the trustees had consented, the agent would nevertheless be liable to the beneficiaries if he owed fiduciary duties to *them*.[176]

The result of *Boardman v Phipps* was that the beneficiary successfully sued the agent, but the basis of this is not clear. Their Lordships spoke, rather ambiguously, of his being a fiduciary "to the trust".[177] Lord Guest spoke of the "knowledge and assent of the trustees".[178] Lord Hodson held that the relevant consent was that of the beneficiary; Boardman "was in a fiduciary position vis-à-vis the trustees, and through them vis-à-vis the beneficiaries."[179] Viscount Dilhorne regarded the consent of the principals as necessary, but also referred to the fact that the beneficiary was not fully informed.[180] Lord Upjohn said that Boardman was

> "in a fiduciary capacity at least to the trustees. Whether he was ever in a fiduciary capacity to the [claimant] was not debated before your Lordships and I do not think that it matters."[181]

This raises the question whether trustees can, if acting unanimously, give consent to dealings by their agent which would otherwise be a breach of his fiduciary obligations.[182] In the present case Boardman had obtained the consent of the two active trustees, but did not inform the third because she had lost mental capacity. Russell LJ in the Court of Appeal[183] had held that this was insufficient because two out of the three trustees

> "had no authority to turn this aspect of the trust property [the exploitation of the shares] over to the defendants, unless to be used exclusively for the benefit of the trust", and that the fiduciary could not "rid himself of the disqualification inherent in that position save with the informed consent of all three."

---

[175] *Murad v Al-Saraj* [2005] EWCA Civ 959; [2005] W.T.L.R. 1573, per Arden LJ at [71].

[176] Presumably the beneficiaries could sue the trustees in such circumstances even if they could not sue the agent.

[177] [1967] 2 A.C. 46 at 100, 104, 110.

[178] [1967] 2 A.C. 46 at 117.

[179] [1967] 2 A.C. 46 at 112. Lord Cohen also regarded the consent of the beneficiary as necessary, at 104. See further Law Com. CP No. 146, *Trustees' Powers and Duties* (1997), paras 3.29, 3.32, describing *Boardman v Phipps* as a "particularly difficult case in this regard".

[180] [1967] 2 A.C. 46 at 93.

[181] [1967] 2 A.C. 46 at 125–126.

[182] See D. Hayton (1990) 106 L.Q.R. 87 at 91–92, taking the view that prior specific (but not general) authority may be given if there is full disclosure by the agent and provided the "prudent businessman" test is satisfied.

[183] [1965] Ch. 992 at 1031.

It is submitted that the better view is that of Lord Upjohn, who replied that "not all the trustees acting together could do it for they cannot give away trust property."[184] On this view, it is only the beneficiaries or the settlor (by express provision in the trust instrument) who can authorise such dealings. The Law Commission doubted whether trustees can authorise others to do what they themselves have no power to do.[185] However, it is provided by s.14 of the Trustee Act 2000 that trustees may authorise their agent to act in circumstances capable of giving rise to a conflict of interest, provided it is reasonably necessary for the trustees to do so. This provision is primarily applicable to investment management functions.[186]

Finally, it is important to determine what remedy was decreed in *Boardman v Phipps*. This is discussed below.

iv. The Extent of the Fiduciary Principle. Essentially the problem is one of determining the limits of the rule.   **22–025**

> "Rules of equity have to be applied to such a great diversity of circumstances that they may be stated only in the most general terms and applied with particular attention to the exact circumstances of each case."[187]

If a fiduciary obtains a benefit for herself at the expense of her beneficiary, there is no difficulty. The position is more difficult where the beneficiary loses nothing; where she did not wish to make the profitable purchase which the trustee makes; where the fiduciary acted honestly; or even where the fiduciary conferred by her activities every possible benefit on the beneficiary, but received an additional benefit for herself. A windfall has been received through the exertions of the fiduciary; the beneficiary has risked nothing, and lost nothing; should she be entitled to the profits?[188] *Boardman v Phipps* answers this question in the affirmative but the Court of Appeal in 2005 suggested that the House of Lords might relax the severity of the inflexible rule in cases where it operates harshly and the remedy is disproportionate[189]: however, the invitation has not been taken up by the House of Lords or Supreme Court.

The law as it now stands might be criticised on the ground that, although intended as a deterrent, it fails to draw any distinction between the honest and the

---

[184] [1967] 2 A.C. 46 at 128.

[185] Law Com. CP No. 146, *Trustees' Powers and Duties* (1997), paras 3.26–3.33; Law Com. No. 260 (1999), para.4.27.

[186] The Law Commission has proposed further reform, (Law Com. No. 350, *Fiduciary Duties of Investment Intermediaries* (2014)), albeit not via a legislative scheme. Consequential amendments to the Occupational Pension Schemes (Investment) Regulations 2005/3378 were made by the Occupational Pension Schemes (Charges and Governance) Regulations 2015/879 and the Solvency 2 Regulations 2015/575.

[187] *Boardman v Phipps* [1967] 2 A.C. 46 at 123. See generally E. Simpson in Birks and Pretto (eds), *Breach of Trust* (Oxford: Hart Publishing, 2002), Ch.3.

[188] See generally G. Jones (1968) 84 L.Q.R. 472; A. Oakley, *Constructive Trusts*, 3rd edn (1996), pp.168–179.

[189] *Murad v Al-Saraj* [2005] EWCA Civ 959; [2005] W.T.L.R. 1573; M. McInnes (2006) 122 L.Q.R. 11; R. Cunnington (2008) 71 M.L.R. 559 at 583. However, no such relaxation could benefit the defendant on the facts of that case, who had not acted in good faith: [2005] EWCA Civ 959; [2005] W.T.L.R. 1573, per Arden LJ at [71].

dishonest fiduciary. Both are liable. However, it should be borne in mind that the honest fiduciary may be remunerated by order of the court, and on a liberal scale, as in *Boardman v Phipps*. A dishonest fiduciary, on the other hand, may be made to pay a higher rate of interest.[190]

But this still leaves open the question, to be determined on the facts of each case, whether the opportunity for profit arose by reason of the fiduciary position.[191] For example, suppose that a merchant banker, insurance broker, solicitor or company director learns through the proper course of her business information from a confidential source which may be of advantage to other clients in companies with which she is associated. Having satisfied the requirements of a particular client, is she precluded from making use of this information in respect of other trusts with which she is concerned or for herself? Similarly with the directors of several (non-competing) companies? Or, does her fiduciary duty to the second client place her under a duty to provide that client with the confidential information?[192] There is the danger that the rule, if applied inflexibly, may impose an impossible burden. As Lord Cohen said in *Boardman v Phipps*[193]:

> "[I]t does not necessarily follow that because an agent acquired information and opportunity while acting in a fiduciary capacity he is accountable to his principals for any profit that comes his way as the result of the use he makes of that information and opportunity. His liability to account must depend on the facts of the case."

Viscount Dilhorne[194] quoted Lindley LJ as saying "to hold that [one] partner can never derive any personal benefit from information which he obtains from [another] partner would be manifestly absurd."[195]

It is difficult to formulate any single test which may be applied to determine whether a fiduciary has incurred liability. It is submitted that liability will arise if any of the following factors is present:

(a)   the fiduciary has used trust property;
(b)   the profit has been made by use of or by reason of the fiduciary position or of an opportunity or knowledge resulting from it, even though no trust property was used; or
(c)   there was a conflict (or a significant possibility of a conflict) of interest and duty, even if no trust property was used, and the opportunity did not arise from the fiduciary relationship.[196]

---

[190]   Below, para.24–020.
[191]   G. Jones (1970) 86 L.Q.R. 463.
[192]   See B. Rider [1978] Conv. 114; *North and South Trust Co v Berkeley* [1971] 1 W.L.R. 470; M. Kay and D. Yates (1972) 35 M.L.R. 78; *Movitex Ltd v Bulfield* [1988] B.C.L.C. 104 (fiduciary must not place himself in a position where his duty to X conflicts with his duty to Y); M. Conaglen (2010) 126 L.Q.R. 72.
[193]   [1967] 2 A.C. 46 at 102–103; see also Lord Upjohn at 126.
[194]   [1967] 2 A.C. 46 at 90.
[195]   *Aas v Benham* [1891] 2 Ch. 244 at 255–256.
[196]   *Chan v Zacharia* (1984) 154 C.L.R. 178 at 198; *Industrial Development Consultants Ltd v Cooley* [1972] 1 W.L.R. 443. See also Stephenson LJ in *Swain v Law Society* [1982] 1 W.L.R. 17 at 31: there must be a possibility of a conflict of interest and duty, and a nexus between the fiduciary position and the profit made.

It should be noted that a claimant cannot have both an account of profits and damages for what she would have received had she been able to use the property for the period in question. These remedies are alternative, not cumulative, and the claimant must elect between them at the time of judgment in his favour, by which time it will be clear which remedy is the more advantageous.[197] A recent example is *Interactive Technology Corp Ltd v Ferster*, in which Morgan J held that the company had to elect between a remedy for repayment of the unauthorised remuneration and compensation for losses said to flow from that unauthorised remuneration.[198]

3.   PERSONAL AND PROPRIETARY REMEDIES[199]

A.   Accountability

It has often been said that a fiduciary who is required to account for profits becomes a "constructive trustee". But a duty to account is a personal liability; a constructive trust is a proprietary remedy. The significance of the distinction appears where the fiduciary is bankrupt, or where the assets in question have been profitably invested. A related question is whether tracing is available, which is discussed in Ch.26. Liability to account is not synonymous with constructive trusteeship, but the cases do not always maintain the distinction. Indeed, Lord Lane CJ once said "We find it impossible to reconcile much of the language used in these decisions."[200]

22–026

In *Boardman v Phipps*, Wilberforce J had held that the shares were held on constructive trust[201] for the beneficiaries; and that Boardman was accountable for profits he made, less a sum for his skill and effort. The House of Lords did not distinguish between accountability and constructive trust. Lord Guest concluded that the defendants held the shares as constructive trustees, and were bound to account to the claimant.[202] The other members spoke of accountability only.

---

[197] *Tang Man Sit (Personal Representatives) v Capacious Investments Ltd* [1996] A.C. 514 (secret profits from wrongful lettings of houses in breach of trust); P. Birks (1996) 112 L.Q.R. 375 See further *Mortgage Express v Lambert* [2016] EWCA Civ 555.

[198] *Interactive Technology Corp Ltd v Ferster* [2017] EWHC 217 (Ch) per Morgan J at [42]–[44]. See also *Instant Access Properties Ltd v Rosser* [2018] EWHC 756 (Ch).

[199] S. Worthington (2013) 72 C.L.J. 720; M. Harding (2013) 33 O.J.L.S. 81. On Scotland, see D.J. Carr (2014) 18 Edin.L.R. 29.

[200] *Re Att Gen's Reference (No.1 of 1985)* [1986] Q.B. 491 at 503 (the case itself was overruled in *FHR European Ventures LLP v Cedar Capital Partners LLC* [2014] UKSC 45; [2015] A.C. 250, as will be seen below, paras 22–028—22–033. On the historical background, see A. Hicks (2010) 69 C.L.J. 287.

[201] [1964] 2 All E.R. 187; cf. [1964] 1 W.L.R. 993.

[202] [1967] 2 A.C. 46 at 117. See D. Hayton (1990) 106 L.Q.R. 87 at 102, suggesting that the liability was personal only. See also *Ultraframe (UK) Ltd v Fielding* [2007] W.T.L.R. 881 (remedy in *Boardman* was not proprietary); cf. *Attorney General for Hong Kong v Reid* [1994] 1 A.C. 324, below, where Lord Templeman clearly regarded Boardman as a constructive trustee. See also *First Subsea Ltd (formerly BSW Ltd) v Balltec Ltd* [2017] EWCA Civ 186; [2018] Ch. 25, per Patten LJ at [37].

B.   Bribes and Secret Commissions

22–027   If the fiduciary has used or received trust property, then any profits made are held on constructive trust for the beneficiaries.[203] But what is the position if the disputed asset did not derive from the trust property but came from a third party, as in the case of a bribe or secret commission? This is a question which "reveals passions of a force uncommon in the legal world."[204] After over a century of doubt, it was authoritatively laid down by the Supreme Court in the 2014 decision of *FHR European Ventures LLP v Cedar Capital Partners LLC*[205] that "any benefit acquired by an agent as a result of his agency and in breach of his fiduciary duty is held on trust for the principal".[206] In order to understand the debate and its complications, which engage issues of policy, principle and precedent, it will be necessary to set out and consider the development of the law. However, it should be remembered throughout that the current legal position is as set out in *FHR European Ventures*, to which we return at the end of this Part.

C.   *Lister, Reid* and *Sinclair*

22–028   It was laid down by the Court of Appeal in *Lister & Co v Stubbs*[207] that where an agent or other fiduciary took a bribe, the principal's remedy was personal. The context was a claim against a foreman who had taken bribes to prefer certain suppliers. The fiduciary had to account for the bribe, but did not hold it on constructive trust. The result in that case was that the fiduciary could keep any profit made from investing the bribe money. This decision was long criticised[208] as contravening the principles of unjust enrichment and treating a dishonest fiduciary more leniently than an honest fiduciary such as Boardman in *Boardman v Phipps*.[209] It was, however, affirmed by the Court of Appeal in *Re Attorney General's Reference (No.1 of 1985)*,[210] although in a criminal law context, with the result that an employee who made a secret profit was not guilty of theft of his employer's property.

22–029   *Lister & Co v Stubbs* was disapproved by the Privy Council in a decision which concerned bribes but which is very significant in the wider area of profits made by fiduciaries.

---

[203] *Guinness Plc v Saunders* [1990] 2 A.C. 663, above, para.22–020; *Neptune (Vehicle Washing Equipment) Ltd v Fitzgerald* [1996] Ch. 274; *CMS Dolphin Ltd v Simonet* [2001] 2 B.C.L.C. 704 (business opportunity exploited by director treated as company property).

[204] *FHR European Ventures v Mankarious* [2013] EWCA Civ 17; [2014] Ch. 1 per Pill LJ at [61].

[205] [2014] UKSC 45; [2015] A.C. 250. M. Conaglen (2014) 73 C.L.J 490; W. Gummow (2015) 131 L.Q.R. 21; D. Whayman [2014] Conv. 518; D. Sheehan [2014] 22 R.L.R. 101.

[206] [2014] UKSC 45; [2015] A.C. 250 per Lord Neuberger PSC at [35] (quoting counsel's submission, which his Lordship adopted).

[207] (1890) 45 Ch.D. 1.

[208] Although supported in R. Goode (1987) 103 L.Q.R. 433; R. Goode in B. Rider (ed.), *Law at the Centre* (Kluwer Law International, 1999), p.185; A. Burrows (2001) 117 L.Q.R. 412 at 427.

[209] [1967] 2 A.C. 46.

[210] [1986] Q.B. 491.

In *Attorney General for Hong Kong v Reid*,[211] the defendant, a public prosecutor, took bribes of over $HK12 million to obstruct prosecutions, in breach of his fiduciary duty as a Crown servant. He failed to comply with an order to repay and was imprisoned. He had purchased three freehold properties with the money, which had since increased in value. The Privy Council decided that these properties were held on trust for the Crown.

Lord Templeman pointed out that bribes cause loss and damage to the principal, although it may not be quantifiable, as in the present case, where unquantifiable harm to the administration of justice had been done. A constructive trust of the bribe money arose because the fiduciary was under an immediate duty to pay it over to the principal. Applying the maxim "equity regards as done that which ought to be done", the money was the property of the principal in equity. The fiduciary's creditors should be in no better position than the fiduciary. If the bribe money was profitably invested, the profits belonged to the principal. If it decreased in value, the fiduciary was personally liable for the deficit. The constructive trust arose whether the fiduciary took property from the trust or from a third party in breach of duty. Any other result, it was said, would be inconsistent with the principle that a fiduciary must not profit from his office.[212]

The decision in *Reid* was framed in authoritative, indeed strident, terms, but certain difficulties remained. The Privy Council did not directly confront the policy issue of when proprietary remedies should be available and instead based its decision more narrowly on the equitable maxim, the application of which is controversial in that it is founded on the availability of specific performance, but an obligation to pay money is not normally specifically enforceable.[213] So far as the bribe has increased in value, the increase is a windfall to the claimant. By allowing the claimant to assert ownership of the bribe money and any profits made from it, to the detriment of a defendant's unsecured creditors, the decision was accused of amounting to "proprietary overkill".[214]

As *Attorney General for Hong Kong v Reid* was a decision of the Privy Council, **22–030** strongly disapproving *Lister*, a decision of the Court of Appeal of England and Wales, the question arose as to how far it was binding as a precedent. The Court of Appeal held that it was bound to follow *Lister* in *Sinclair Investments (UK) Ltd v Versailles Trade Finance Ltd (In Administration)*.[215]

---

[211] [1994] 1 A.C. 324. The person who bribed the agent is accountable to the principal for any resulting profit; *Fyffes Group Ltd v Templeman* [2000] 2 Lloyd's Rep. 643; A. Berg [2001] L.M.C.L.Q. 27 at 57. See also *Hurstanger v Wilson* [2007] 1 W.L.R. 2351; C. Miller [2007] All E.R. Rev. 98. Followed (pre-*FHR*) in the Jersey case of *Lloyds Trust Co (Channel Islands) Ltd v Fragoso* [2017] W.T.L.R. 103.

[212] [1994] 1 A.C. 324 at 336.

[213] Below, para.27–018; A. Oakley (1994) 53 C.L.J. 31; P. Clarke All E.R. Rev. 1994, at 252; cf. Sir Peter Millett (1998) 114 L.Q.R. 399 at 407; S. Worthington in Degeling and Edelman (eds), *Equity in Commercial Law* (Sydney: Lawbook Co, 2005), Ch.5; P. Millett in Burrows and Rodger (eds), *Mapping the Law* (Oxford: Oxford University Press, 2006), pp.274–275.

[214] D. Crilley [1994] 2 R.L.R. 57. See also G. Virgo in Getzler (ed.), *Rationalizing Property, Equity and Trusts* (2003), pp.96–98; R. Calnan [2004] 12 R.L.R. 1 at 21. cf. Lawrence Collins J in *Daraydan Holdings Ltd v Solland International Ltd* [2005] Ch. 119 who considered, however, that insolvency of the fiduciary should make no difference, as there would be no injustice to creditors in their not sharing an asset which the fiduciary should not have had. This view is supported in M. Halliwell [2005] Conv. 88 and P. Clarke All E.R. Rev 2005, 271.

[215] [2012] Ch. 453.

A director made a secret profit of nearly £30 million on the sale of his own shares at the top of the market. He had breached his fiduciary duty by entering into fraudulent dealings to increase the value of his own holding, which was in reality worthless. The question was whether the fiduciary held the profit on constructive trust for the principal (the company) or whether he was personally accountable only, in which case the principal would be in competition with other unsecured creditors. The director had not acquired the shares with company funds or money deriving from company funds, nor did he even acquire them as an indirect consequence of his misuse of those funds. Thus the claim was not to funds in respect of which the director owed fiduciary duties to the company, nor to any asset or proceeds of any asset purchased with those funds, nor to the proceeds of any right or opportunity belonging to the company. However, there was a close causal connection between the misuse of company funds and the money the director made on the sale of his shares. The profit derived from his fiduciary position and its receipt was a plain breach of fiduciary duty. The Court of Appeal considered that an unauthorised secret profit of this kind was to be treated in the same way as a bribe.

Lord Neuberger MR examined the cases before *Attorney General for Hong Kong v Reid*. He noted that the report in *Keech v Sandford* was unreasoned and unsatisfactory, but it could be treated as an example of a trustee seizing for his own benefit an opportunity effectively owned by the trust. Amongst the earlier cases was a decision of the House of Lords, *Tyrrell v Bank of London*,[216] which was inconsistent with the notion that a fiduciary held a bribe on trust for the principal, but the decision had not been cited in many cases and had been misinterpreted in *Reid*.[217]

Lord Neuberger was "far from satisfied" that the Supreme Court would follow *Reid*, adding that: "In any event it does not seem to me right to follow *Reid*."[218] His Lordship went on to give seven reasons why *Reid* should not be followed, including precedent, policy, poverty of reasoning and the possibility that equitable accounting could suffice[219]:

> "a beneficiary of a fiduciary's duties cannot claim a proprietary interest, but is entitled to an equitable account, in respect of any money or asset acquired by a fiduciary in breach of his duties to the beneficiary, unless the asset or money is or has been beneficially the property of the beneficiary or the trustee acquired the asset or money by taking advantage of an opportunity or right which was properly that of the beneficiary."[220]

Lord Neuberger MR thus considered that the policy question of preventing the false fiduciary from retaining the increase in value should be dealt with by extending the rules on equitable compensation, which were more flexible than the rules on proprietary interests. This would, in his Lordship's view, interfere less with the rights of other creditors than extending proprietary interests.

---

[216] (1862) 10 HL Cas. 26; P. Watts (2013) 129 L.Q.R. 527.

[217] [2012] Ch. 453 at [60]–[62].

[218] [2012] Ch. 453 at [76].

[219] [2012] Ch. 453 at [75]–[87].

[220] [2012] Ch. 453 per Lord Neuberger at [88]. This was also suggested as a compromise in the debate surrounding *Attorney General v Reid*: P. Birks, *An Introduction to the Law of Restitution*, revised edn (Oxford: Oxford University Press, 1989), p.389; P. Watts (1994) 110 L.Q.R. 178.

D. *FHR European Ventures*

The questions of policy and principle engaged by *Sinclair*[221] were revisited by the Court of Appeal in *FHR European Ventures v Cedar Capital Partners*.[222] The facts follow below when we consider the Supreme Court decision, but in the Court of Appeal it was held that where an opportunity properly belonging to the principal is exploited by the fiduciary to obtain a benefit for herself, it was possible to claim a proprietary interest, notwithstanding *Sinclair*:

22–031

> "the mere fact that the fiduciary obtains the benefit from a third party, or obtains a benefit that could never be or would never be obtained by the principal, or that the principal has obtained what he or she wanted or intended from the opportunity, is not necessarily a bar to a constructive trust of the benefit wrongly obtained by the fiduciary by taking advantage of the opportunity. Those are all features of bribe and secret commission cases."[223]

Significantly, the judgments in the Court of Appeal in *FHR European Ventures* also indicated judicial dissatisfaction with the position after *Sinclair*, which Etherton C described as "rendering the law more complex and uncertain and dependent on very fine factual distinctions".[224] Before considering how the Supreme Court resolved the appeal,[225] we must set out the facts:

> The case concerned a secret commission which had been made relating to the sale of the Monte Carlo Grand Hotel. FHR was a vehicle for the purchase of the share capital of the Hotel, and Cedar acted as agent negotiating the purchase, thus owing fiduciary duties to the claimants. However, Cedar had also made an agreement with the vendors of the Hotel, pursuant to which they received €10m when the sale completed. The appeal turned on whether or not the claimants were entitled to a proprietary remedy in respect of the €10 million, where the property was neither originally an asset of the principal nor the exploitation of an opportunity properly belonging to the principal. The Supreme Court dismissed the appeal, confirming that where an opportunity is exploited, there is indeed a constructive trust in favour of the principal.

Given what we saw in *Sinclair*,[226] it might initially seem surprising that the single judgment of the Court was delivered by Lord Neuberger PSC (as he by then was). The short opinion surveyed the authorities, concluding that there were decisions pointing in each direction, and that there was no "plainly right or plainly wrong answer to the issue of the extent of the rule".[227] Thus Lord Neuberger first considered "the arguments based on principle and practicality", before returning

[221] J. Edelman (2013) 129 L.Q.R. 66; K. Barnett (2015) 35 L.S. 302; P. Millett (2012) 71 C.L.J. 583.
[222] Also known as *FHR European Ventures v Mankarious* [2013] EWCA Civ 17; [2014] Ch. 1; endorsed obiter on this point by Proudman J in *Roadchef (Employee Benefits Trustees) Ltd v Hill* [2014] EWHC 109 (Ch) at [174]. L. Smith (2013) 72 C.L.J. 260; R. Chambers [2013] Conv. 241; R. Hedlund [2013] J.B.L. 747; P. Devonshire (2013) 24 K.L.J. 392; E. Granger and J. Goodwin [2013] 21 R.L.R. 85.
[223] [2013] EWCA Civ 17; [2014] Ch. 1 per Etherton C at [100].
[224] [2013] EWCA Civ 17; [2014] Ch. 1 at [116].
[225] [2014] UKSC 45; [2015] A.C. 250.
[226] Above, para.22–030.
[227] [2014] UKSC 45; [2015] A.C. 250 at [32].

to assess the decided case law.[228] In terms of principle, Lord Neuberger broadly endorsed the approach of Lord Templeman in *Reid*.[229]

> "The notion that the rule should not apply to a bribe or secret commission received by an agent because it could not have been received by, or on behalf of, the principal seems unattractive. The whole reason that the agent should not have accepted the bribe or commission is that it puts him in conflict with his duty to his principal."[230]

22-032 The line between policy and principle is not always clear, but we can identify some of the policy considerations which Lord Neuberger weighed in the balance. Drawing support from Lord Templeman in *Reid*,[231] Lord Neuberger argued that since

> "concern about bribery and corruption generally has never been greater than it is now ... one would expect the law to be particularly stringent in relation to a claim against an agent who has received a bribe or secret commission."[232]

Lord Neuberger considered the argument of policy that granting a proprietary remedy in such cases privileges the principal over other creditors of the fiduciary, since it will not form part of their available assets in the event of an insolvency.[233] However, the court felt that the point had "limited force"[234] in this context because the bribe should not be part of the agent's estate at all and arguably could have reduced the benefit of the transaction to the principal.[235] It appeared "just" to the court that an agent should be able to trace the proceeds of the bribe into other assets.[236]

Not being bound by *Lister v Stubbs*, as the Court of Appeal had been in *Sinclair*, the Supreme Court was able to confront the issues based on the reasoning in the conflicting decisions. But it was necessary to consider the House of Lords decision in *Tyrrell v Bank of London*,[237] which, as we saw above, was regarded by Lord Neuberger MR in *Sinclair* as being influential. Having concluded that policy and principle both required that there be a proprietary response, Lord Neuberger turned to the authorities, taking the view that "as a whole" they favoured the respondents' case.[238] The court departed from *Tyrrell*, which

---

[228] [2014] UKSC 45; [2015] A.C. 250.
[229] Even though, as we saw above, Lord Neuberger MR had, in *Sinclair*, been strongly critical of Lord Templeman's mode of reasoning in *Reid*: above, para.22–030.
[230] [2014] UKSC 45; [2015] A.C. 250 at [37].
[231] [1994] 1 AC 324 at 330H: "bribery is an evil practice which threatens the foundations of any civilised society".
[232] [2014] UKSC 45; [2015] A.C. 250 at [42], pointing to the Bribery Act 2010.
[233] [2014] UKSC 45; [2015] A.C. 250 at [43]–[44]. On the propriety of arguments based on the consequences in the event of insolvency, see C. Rotherham (2012) 65 C.L.P. 529; E. Houghton (2016) 22 T. & T. 956.
[234] [2014] UKSC 45; [2015] A.C. 250 at [43].
[235] [2014] UKSC 45; [2015] A.C. 250 at [43].
[236] [2014] UKSC 45; [2015] A.C. 250 at [44].
[237] (1862) 10 HL Cas. 26.
[238] [2014] UKSC 45; [2015] A.C. 250 at [46].

"should not stand in the way of the conclusion that the law took a wrong turn in *Heiron*[239] and *Lister*, and that those decisions, and any subsequent decisions (*Powell & Thomas*,[240] *Attorney General's Reference (No 1 of 1985)*[241] and *Sinclair*), at least in so far as they relied on or followed *Heiron* and *Lister*, should be treated as overruled."[242]

The Supreme Court therefore "restated"[243] the law and confirmed that the general equitable rule "that a bribe or secret commission accepted by an agent is held on trust for his principal."[244]

Overall, it is submitted that the outcome in *FHR European Ventures* is to be welcomed[245] as a clear, authoritative resolution of the debate, particularly in respect of the problems identified by the court below. The law no longer turns on fine distinctions between what may count as an "opportunity" and "artificialities and difficulties"[246] are avoided. The decision also, as Lord Neuberger noted, moves English law into step with the position in other common law jurisdictions.[247] However, the brevity of the judgment, in particular the lack of direct engagement with Lord Neuberger's own previous view in *Sinclair*, and the reasons for his Lordship's change of mind, mean that the welcome must necessarily be a qualified one.

The decision in *FHR* has been applied in relatively few subsequent decisions,[248] but the case of *Medsted Associates Ltd v Canaccord Genuity Wealth (International) Ltd*[249] is of particular interest as it illustrates the wider implications of the *FHR* approach:

22–033

> In *Medsted*, the claimant introduced clients to the defendant for purpose of trading contracts for difference. The defendant agreed to pay the claimant a share of the commission and funding rebate to be paid to the defendant by those clients. The clients were not told of split in

---

[239] Referring to the Court of Appeal decision in *Metropolitan Bank v Heiron* (1880) 5 Ex. D. 319.

[240] Referring to the Court of Appeal decision in *Powell & Thomas v Evan Jones & Co* [1905] 1 K.B. 11.

[241] Referring to the *Attorney General's Reference (No.1 of 1985)* [1986] Q.B. 491.

[242] [2014] UKSC 45; [2015] A.C. 250 at [49]–[50]. The court elsewhere in that paragraph went on to consider further reasons for departing from *Tyrrell*, which need not be detailed here.

[243] [2014] UKSC 45; [2015] A.C. 250 at [49].

[244] [2014] UKSC 45; [2015] A.C. 250 at [46]. Since the remedy is a proprietary one, change of position has been held not to operate as a defence: *SPL Private Finance (PF1) IC Ltd v Arch Financial Products LLP* [2014] EWHC 4268 (Comm) per Walker J at [353].

[245] For an assessment of the *FHR* case as part of broader trends in recent Supreme Court jurisprudence, see M. Yip and J. Lee (2017) 37 L.S. 647 and G. Virgo (2016) 14 Otago L.R. 257. For the subsequent litigation concerning the facts of the case, see *FHR European Ventures LLP v Mankarious* [2016] EWHC 359 (Ch), which raises difficulties of quantifying the profits made (see also *Torbay Holdings Ltd v Napier* [2015] NZHC 2477).

[246] [2014] UKSC 45; [2015] A.C. 250 at [38]: "The consequence of [*FHR*] is that a constructive trust will be imposed on fiduciaries in such cases regardless of whether it is possible to treat the benefit or payment received by the agent as derived from property in which the principal had a pre-existing interest" *First Subsea Ltd v Balltec Ltd* [2017] EWCA Civ 186; [2018] Ch. 25 per Patten LJ at [37].

[247] [2014] UKSC 45; [2015] A.C. 250 at [45]. See for example the Australian decisions in *Chan v Zacharia* (1984) 154 C.L.R. 178 and *Grimaldi v Chameleon Mining NL (No.2)* [2012] FCAFC 6; (2012) 200 F.C.R. 296; but cf. J. Campbell (2015) 39 Aust. Bar Rev. 320.

[248] See e.g. *Northampton Regional Livestock Centre Co Ltd v Cowling* [2015] EWCA Civ 651 and *Faichney v Aquila Advisory Ltd* [2018] EWHC 565 (Ch).

[249] *Medsted Associates Ltd v Canaccord Genuity Wealth (International) Ltd* [2017] EWHC 1815 (Comm); [2018] 1 W.L.R. 314.

commission. The defendant later dealt directly with clients, cutting the claimant out of the process and the claimant sued for breach of contract and claimed for the loss of commission. The defendant was found to have been in breach of contract, causing loss to the claimants. However, the claimant was held to have been in breach of fiduciary duty[250] to their clients in respect of the commissions. Relying on the policy in *FHR*, Teare J held that

> "the court should not assist Medsted to profit from its own breach of fiduciary duty to its clients. Were it to grant Medsted judgment for substantial damages to be assessed it would be doing so. For this reason the court cannot give such judgment."[251]

Before leaving the topic of *FHR*, we may note that the Supreme Court has subsequently addressed the difficulty in terms of precedent raised by *Reid*. In *Willers v Joyce (No.2)*,[252] the Court reiterated that the lower courts of England and Wales are bound by higher English courts, and should not generally follow a decision of the Privy Council that is inconsistent with such binding authority.[253] The Supreme Court did recognise an exception, which is where the Privy Council is expressly deciding a point of English law with a view to departing from prior authority.[254]

---

[250] The claimant owed fiduciary duties even though they did not have the authority to enter into legal relations on behalf of their clients: [2018] 1 W.L.R. 314 at [89] and [95], applying *McWilliam v Norton Finance Ltd* [2015] EWCA Civ 186; [2015] P.N.L.R. 22.

[251] [2018] 1 W.L.R. 314 at [135].

[252] [2016] UKSC 44; [2016] 3 W.L.R. 534; P. Mirfield (2017) 133 L.Q.R. 1.

[253] [2016] 3 W.L.R. 534 at [16]–[18].

[254] [2016] 3 W.L.R. 534 per Lord Neuberger PSC at [21] "it seems to me to be not only convenient but also sensible that the JCPC, which normally consists of the same judges as the Supreme Court, should, when applying English law, be capable of departing from an earlier decision of the Supreme Court or House of Lords to the same extent and with the same effect as the Supreme Court." The approach in *Willers* differs somewhat with the view of precedent that Lord Neuberger MR had taken in *Sinclair* [2012] Ch. 453 at [73]–[74].

CHAPTER 23

VARIATION OF TRUSTS

1. THE BACKGROUND

A TRUSTEE must administer the trust according to its terms. Any deviation is a breach of trust for which the trustee will be personally liable.[1] However, any adult beneficiary who does not lack capacity may deal with her equitable interest under the trust in any way she wishes; and may consent to the trustee dealing with the trust funds in a way which affects her interest. Further, adult beneficiaries who together are absolutely entitled to the trust property may terminate the trust and demand that the fund be handed over to them[2]; but not if any interests are outstanding,[3] nor if the trustees have no power to transfer the property.[4]

23–001

They may wish to do this for various reasons. In *Saunders v Vautier*,[5] the beneficiary wished to terminate an accumulation which was to continue until he reached 25; he was able to claim the fund at 21 (then the age of majority). If property is given to A for life and then to B, and both A and B are adult, they may each wish to have capital immediately available, and may agree to partition the fund. This was often done in order to reduce tax liability and especially liability

---

[1] Above, para.18–001; below, Ch.24.

[2] *Saunders v Vautier* (1841) Cr. & Ph. 240; *Re Smith* [1928] Ch. 915; *Re Nelson* [1928] Ch. 920n; *Re Becket's Settlement* [1940] Ch. 279. See also Trusts of Land and Appointment of Trustees Act 1996 s.6(2); above, para.21–002.

[3] *Berry v Green* [1938] A.C. 575; *Re Robb* [1953] Ch. 459; *Re Wragg* [1959] 1 W.L.R. 922; *Law Debenture Trust Corp Plc v Elektrim Finance NV* [2007] 1 P. & C.R. DG 6 (trustee's lien).

[4] *Don King Productions Inc v Warren* [2000] Ch. 291 (trust of benefit of non-assignable contracts). The point was not discussed on appeal.

[5] (1841) Cr. & Ph. 240; P. Matthews (2006) 122 L.Q.R. 266. For the meaning of "absolutely entitled" in a tax context, see *Figg v Clarke (Inspector of Taxes)* [1997] 1 W.L.R. 603 (class consisting of children of X not absolutely entitled for capital gains tax purposes until death of X, although X incapable of fathering more children); *Thorpe v Commissioners for HM Revenue and Customs* [2009] W.T.L.R. 1269.

for inheritance tax on the death of A. Inheritance tax, an outline of which was given in Ch.10, is chargeable on transfers on or within seven years before death. It is also chargeable on certain lifetime transfers even if the transferor survives for seven years, for example the creation of most trusts, although in such a case the rate is lower.[6] In the case of a life interest trust, the advantage of partitioning the fund between life tenant and remainderman before the Finance Act 2006 was that, provided the life tenant survived for seven years (which could be covered by insurance), no tax would be payable on the partition, whereas the whole capital was taxable if the life interest terminated on death.[7] The inheritance tax treatment of life interest trusts created on or after 22 March 2006 was changed by the Finance Act 2006.[8] The Act phased out the rule that life tenants were treated for inheritance tax purposes as owing the capital.

It may be advantageous in terms of income tax liability to share out the entitlement to income.[9] It appears that a variation is not a disposal for capital gains tax purposes.[10] As far as inheritance tax is concerned, trustees of a discretionary trust could formerly improve the tax position of the settlement by converting it to a trust with an interest in possession or to an accumulation and maintenance settlement, but the Finance Act 2006 removed the advantages of doing this.[11] The tax saving aspect of the matter is emphasised here because it was the motivating force in the passing of the Variation of Trusts Act 1958, and in the variations which have been made under it. "Nearly every variation," said Lord Denning MR, "that has come before the court has tax-avoidance for its principal object."[12] Even then, Lord Denning observed that "the avoidance of tax may be lawful, but it is not yet a virtue".[13] This aspect may give pause for thought in the light of comments by Lord Walker JSC in the Supreme Court's decision in *Pitt v Holt*[14]: that "there has been an increasingly strong and general recognition that artificial tax avoidance is a social evil". Variations have, of course, been made for other purposes, as will be seen.

23–002 One particular tax exemption should be noted. Where, not more than two years after a death of a person, testate or intestate, the disposition of his property taking effect upon his death is varied by an instrument in writing, such a variation is not a transfer of value for inheritance tax purposes,[15] nor a disposal for capital gains tax purposes,[16] and the variation takes effect as if made by the deceased. These

---

[6] Inheritance Tax Act 1984 s.7.

[7] Finance (No.2) Act 1987 s.96. See *Gibbon v Mitchell* [1990] 1 W.L.R. 1304.

[8] Above, para.10–018.

[9] For a recent example of a variation being approved for tax reasons, see the short judgment of HHJ Behrens in *Bailey v Bailey* [2014] EWHC 4411 (Ch), deferring the vesting date in order to avoid the likelihood of significant tax liabilities.

[10] *Wyndham v Egremont* [2009] W.T.L.R. 1473. There would be a disposal if the effect of the variation is to revoke the original settlement and to create a new one, but not if the original settlement continues as varied.

[11] Above, paras 10–018, 10–024.

[12] In *Re Weston's Settlements* [1969] 1 Ch. 223 at 245.

[13] [1969] 1 Ch. 223 at 245.

[14] *Pitt v Holt* [2013] 2 A.C. 108 at [135]. S. Evans [2015] Conv. 61; C. Mitchell [2017] P.C.B. 41 at 46–47; J. Lee (2018) 31 T.L.I. 219. Above, paras 18–046—18–048.

[15] Inheritance Tax Act 1984 ss.17, 142, as amended by Finance Act 2002 s.120.

[16] Taxation of Chargeable Gains Act 1992 s.62(6).

provisions used to be of great help where a wealthy testator wasted his nil-rate band by leaving everything to his wife.[17] They clearly apply both to an agreed variation by adult beneficiaries and to a variation under the Variation of Trusts Act 1958. A similar principle applies to an order under the Family Provision legislation.[18]

It should be added that, as seen earlier, the starting point should always be the trust instrument: the instrument itself may give the trustees a power to amend the trust. Such a power must be exercised for the purpose for which it was granted.[19] It has been said (in the context of a commercial trust) that, although the power must not be exercised beyond the reasonable contemplation of the parties, it would be going too far to say that such a power may never be exercised to alter rights or to bring a new class of property within the scope of the trust.[20]

2. VARIATIONS WHICH NEED THE APPROVAL OF THE COURT[21]

We have seen that children and persons lacking mental capacity are not able to deal with their property. If a situation arose where variations needed to be made to a trust in the interests of such persons, nothing could be done which involved any negotiation with or compromise by the persons under disability, without the approval of the court. The person under disability could be benefited at the expense of the other parties. The life tenant may be willing to agree to an advancement by the trustees,[22] or to surrender her life interest. But if the life tenant wanted something in return from the person under disability, there was no way in which she could negotiate it.

23–003

Yet, especially in the tax context, it was in the interest of the remaindermen that the variation should be made. Adult remaindermen could agree to a variation; it was hard for children, persons under a disability and unborn persons to be denied advantages which competent adults could obtain for themselves. The court, however, has no inherent general jurisdiction to vary a trust in favour of children and unborn persons.[23] But there are cases where the court can intervene, and these have been substantially increased by several statutes.

A. Inherent Jurisdiction

i. Salvage and Emergency.   A court has inherent power in the case of absolute necessity to sanction the mortgage of a child's property in order to protect the property which she retains. The jurisdiction is very narrow and is

23–004

---

[17] Unused nil-rate bands, including the new "residence" nil-rate band, may now be transferred to the spouse's estate: Inheritance Act 1984 s.8A; above, para.10–008.

[18] Inheritance Tax Act 1984 s.146. On intestacy, see now the Inheritance and Trustees' Powers Act 2014.

[19] *Hole v Garnsey* [1930] A.C. 472.

[20] *Society of Lloyd's v Robinson* [1999] 1 W.L.R. 756. See also Pensions Act 1995 ss.67–71.

[21] O. Marshall (1954) 17 M.L.R. 420; Harris, *Variation of Trusts*.

[22] *Pilkington v IRC* [1964] A.C. 612, above, para.21–039.

[23] *Chapman v Chapman* [1954] A.C. 429. See *CD v O* [2004] W.T.L.R. 751, discussing limited exceptions.

usual where expenditure is necessary to save buildings from collapse.[24] An extension of this jurisdiction allows the court in an emergency, not foreseen or anticipated by the settlor, to authorise the trustees to perform certain acts which are beyond the powers given to them in the trust instrument, where this is in the best interests of the trust estate and where the consent of all the beneficiaries cannot be obtained because they are not in existence or are under a disability.

In *Re New*,[25] the court approved a scheme of capital reconstruction of a company, splitting the shares into different and smaller denominations, and authorised the trustees to take the new shares, subject to an undertaking to apply for further authorisation to retain the shares after one year. This decision was said in *Re Tollemache*[26] to be the "high water-mark" of the emergency jurisdiction. Kekewich J and the Court of Appeal refused to sanction a widening of the trustees' investment powers merely because this would be for the advantage of the beneficiaries. There was no emergency. It is clear that the jurisdiction applies to administrative matters only, and does not cover schemes for the variation of beneficial interests.

23–005 **ii. Compromise.**[27] Prior to the decision of the House of Lords in *Chapman v Chapman*[28] in 1954, the courts had accepted a wide definition of the word "compromise" as the basis of a useful jurisdiction to approve a variation from the terms of a trust although there was no dispute between the parties in any real sense of the term. The cases were more akin to bargains or exchanges approved by the court as being fair to children or remaindermen, than to compromised litigation. There was a question whether the jurisdiction effected a variation of beneficial interests as distinct from varying the property subject to the trusts,[29] and the jurisdiction did not extend to the redrafting of a settlement as such—there had to be some element of composition of rights.[30] But this distinction was paper-thin. Denning LJ, the minority judge in the Court of Appeal in the *Chapman* case, would have got round the difficulty by accepting for the courts a general jurisdiction to vary trusts on behalf of those unascertained or under disability, but the House of Lords preferred the other solution—that of limiting the jurisdiction to sanction compromises to cases where there was a genuine dispute. Nor could matters that did not genuinely contain an element of dispute be made to look as if they did.[31] Where there is a genuine dispute, the court does have power to sanction a compromise, even if the compromise solution contains tax-saving advantages for the beneficiaries.

---

[24] *Re Jackson* (1882) 21 Ch.D. 786; *Conway v Fenton* (1888) 40 Ch.D. 512; *Re Montagu* [1897] 2 Ch. 8 at 11, per Lopes LJ.

[25] [1901] 2 Ch. 534. See also *Grender v Dresden* [2009] W.T.L.R. 379.

[26] [1903] 1 Ch. 457, affirmed at 955.

[27] O. Marshall (1954) 17 M.L.R. 427.

[28] [1954] A.C. 429.

[29] *Re Downshire Settled Estates* [1953] Ch. 218.

[30] *Re Chapman's ST* [1953] Ch. 218.

[31] *Re Powell-Cotton's Resettlement* [1956] 1 W.L.R. 23. Nor should the trustees, in their application to court for the exercise of the compromise jurisdiction, insert an unrelated claim for increased remuneration; *Re Barbour's Settlement Trusts* [1974] 1 W.L.R. 1198.

In *Allen v Distillers Co (Biochemicals) Ltd*,[32] the question was whether the court, in approving a settlement of the action of the child victims of the thalidomide drug, had jurisdiction to postpone the vesting of the capital in the children to an age greater than 18. Eveleigh J held that the court had no inherent jurisdiction to order a postponement; a beneficiary with a vested interest under a trust was entitled to demand possession on majority.[33] Nor was there a trust to which the Variation of Trusts Act 1958 applied; the payment out to trustees of sums paid into court did not give rise to the kind of trust contemplated by that Act. However, it was found that the terms of the settlement of the action were wide enough to authorise a postponement of payment.

An attempt to invoke the court's compromise jurisdiction occurred in *Mason v Farbrother*,[34] where trustees of a pension fund set up in 1929 for Co-operative Society employees had power to invest principally in the society itself and otherwise in authorised trustee securities. By 1982, as a result of inflation, the fund had increased to £127 million, and the trustees, who were anxious to have the wide powers of investment appropriate for modern pension funds, applied to the court for approval of an investment clause giving wider powers than those of the Trustee Investments Act 1961, which at that time governed trustee investments.[35] The trustees were uncertain as to the proper construction of the original investment clause, one view being that the whole fund should be invested in the society, and the other that the whole should be invested under the 1961 Act. This was sufficient to give the court jurisdiction, as genuine points of difference existed. It was not necessary that there should be a contested dispute. While a compromise need not be something between the two views, it was doubtful whether the court could substitute an entirely new investment clause. Thus the variation was not permitted under the court's jurisdiction to approve a compromise. (It was, however, authorised by s.57 of the Trustee Act 1925).[36]

23–006

B. Statutory Provisions (other than Variation of Trusts Act 1958)

i. Trustee Act 1925 Section 57(1).

23–007

> "Where in the management or administration of any property vested in trustees, any sale, lease, mortgage, surrender, release, or other disposition, or any purchase, investment, acquisition, expenditure, or other transaction, is in the opinion of the court expedient, but the same cannot be effected by reason of the absence of any power for that purpose vested in the trustees by the trust instrument, if any, or by law, the court may by order confer upon the trustees … the necessary power… on such terms… as the court may think fit… ."

This subsection overlaps with the "emergency" jurisdiction discussed above, and widens it by making the statutory jurisdiction available in cases of expediency rather than emergency. It operates as if its provisions were read into every

---

[32] [1974] Q.B. 384.

[33] *Saunders v Vautier* (1841) 4 Beav. 115; above, para.23–001.

[34] [1983] 2 All E.R. 1078; P. Clarke [1984] All E.R. Rev. at 308.

[35] But has since been overtaken by the provisions of the Trustee Act 2000; above, paras 19–013—19–014.

[36] Below, para.23–007.

settlement.[37] It is clear from the opening words of the section that it is only available in questions arising in the *management* or *administration* of property; it is not therefore available for the purpose of remoulding beneficial interests or for tax saving generally.[38] It is available, however, if the impact of the proposal on the beneficial interests is only incidental.[39]

Applications are usually heard in private, and it is not possible to learn from reported cases the full scope of the operation of the subsection. It has however been effectively used to authorise the sale of land where necessary consents had been refused[40]; to authorise borrowing and mortgaging[41]; and to authorise the purchase of a residence for the tenant for life,[42] the sale of a reversionary interest which under the terms of the trust instrument was not to be sold until it fell into possession,[43] and wider investment powers.[44] A recent application of the section was *Re English & American Insurance Co Ltd*,[45] in the context of an trust to deal with the insolvency of a company: Clive Freedman QC, sitting as a Deputy Judge, approved an apportionment of the funds to create two sub-trusts, balancing out the position between two groups of beneficiaries. It has been held that s.57 should be used in preference to the Variation of Trusts Act 1958 where wider investment powers are sought, provided the beneficial interests are not affected.[46] *Re Portman Estate*[47] involved an estate worth over £1.4billion held in various trusts, with Birss J noting that "the administrative powers relating to the various trusts make up a patchwork with different trusts having different powers". Birss J therefore approved a s.57 application which would essentially rationalise and harmonise the powers across the trusts. His Honour did however reject a suggestion that it would be appropriate to confer upon the trustees a power to amend their administrative powers in the future: to do so would be "to put the Court's power under s.57 of the Trustee Act into the hands of the trustees".

23–008   **ii.   Settled Land Act 1925 Section 64(1).**

"Any transaction affecting or concerning the settled land, or any part thereof, or any other land … which in the opinion of the court would be for the benefit of the settled land, or any part thereof, or the persons interested under the settlement, may, under an order of the court, be effected by a tenant for life, if it is one which could have been validly effected by an absolute owner."[48]

---

[37] *Re Mair* [1935] Ch. 562; see also *Re Salting* [1932] 2 Ch. 57.
[38] *Re Downshire SE* [1953] Ch. 218; cf. *Re Forster's Settlement* [1954] 3 All E.R. 714.
[39] *Southgate v Sutton* [2011] W.T.L.R. 1235 (partition authorised).
[40] *Re Beale's ST* [1932] 2 Ch. 15.
[41] *Page v West* [2010] W.T.L.R. 1811.
[42] *Re Power* [1947] Ch. 572; (1947) 91 S.J. 541.
[43] *Re Cockerell's ST* [1956] Ch. 372.
[44] *Re Shipwrecked Fishermen and Mariners' Royal Benevolent Society* [1959] Ch. 220; cf. *Re Powell-Cotton's Resettlement* [1956] 1 W.L.R. 23; *Mason v Farbrother* [1983] 2 All E.R. 1078.
[45] [2014] 1 P. & C.R. DG11.
[46] *Anker-Petersen v Anker-Petersen* (1998) 12 T.L.I. 166 (decided 1991).
[47] [2015] EWHC 536 (Ch); [2015] 2 P. & C.R. DG10.
[48] Settlements of land cannot be created after the Trusts of Land and Appointment of Trustees Act 1996.

It will be seen that this subsection is wider than Trustee Act s.57(1). "Transaction" is widely defined[49]; and there is no limitation restricting the court's powers to cases of management and administration.[50] The subsection enables the court to alter beneficial interests in such a way as to reduce tax liability[51] and was the most effective vehicle for this purpose before 1958. It applies however only to cases of settled land, and not to the ordinary case of a personalty settlement. In *Hambro v Duke of Marlborough*,[52] the Duke and the trustees considered that the second defendant, the Marquess of Blandford, who was tenant in tail in remainder, would be incapable of managing the Blenheim estate on the death of the Duke because of his "unbusinesslike habits" and lack of responsibility. They proposed a scheme whereby the estate would be conveyed to trustees of a new trust, to pay the income to the Duke for life, and then to hold on protective trusts for the second defendant for life, thereafter on the trusts of the existing settlement. This was held to be a "transaction" within s.64, which could vary the beneficial interests even where an ascertained adult beneficiary did not consent.[53]

iii. Trustee Act 1925 Section 53.[54]   Under s.53, the court is given power to **23–009** authorise certain dealings with a child's property "with a view to the application of the capital or income thereof for the maintenance, education, or benefit of the infant." As with s.57, the section overlaps and extends the inherent power to make provision for the maintenance of children. The word "benefit" has been widely construed, and the court has authorised transactions whose object was the reduction of estate duty for the child's benefit.[55] Thus, entails have been barred in order to exclude the interests of large numbers of remote beneficiaries with a view to raising money for the child's benefit[56] or to simplifying an application to the court under the Variation of Trusts Act 1958[57]; and reversionary interests have been sold to the tenant for life.[58] However, the proceeds of sale should be resettled; this will be an "application" for the child's benefit[59]; while an outright payment to her of the proceeds of sale will not be.[60]

---

[49] Settled Land Act 1925 s.64(2). See *Raikes v Lygon* [1988] 1 W.L.R. 281; *Hambro v Duke of Marlborough* [1994] Ch. 158.

[50] It has been used for such purposes; *Re White-Popham's SE* [1936] Ch. 725; *Re Scarisbrick's Re-Settlement Estates* [1944] Ch. 229. P. Reed [2010] P.C.B. 356.

[51] *Re Downshire SE* [1953] Ch. 218; *Raikes v Lygon* [1988] 1 W.L.R. 281.

[52] [1994] Ch. 158; E. Cooke [1994] Conv. 492.

[53] This was a preliminary issue. The scheme was subsequently approved; *The Times*, 23 July 1994.

[54] O. Marshall (1957) 21 Conv.(N.S.) 448.

[55] *Re Meux* [1958] Ch. 154.

[56] *Re Gower's Settlement* [1934] Ch. 365.

[57] *Re Bristol's SE* [1964] 3 All E.R. 939; *Re Lansdowne's WT* [1967] Ch. 603.

[58] *Re Meux* [1958] Ch. 154; cf. *Re Heyworth's Contingent Reversionary Interest* [1956] Ch. 364.

[59] *Re Meux* [1958] Ch. 154.

[60] *Re Heyworth's Contingent Reversionary Interest* [1956] Ch. 364; criticised O. Marshall (1957) 21 Conv.(N.S.) 448 at 450–454.

23–010   **iv. Matrimonial Causes Act 1973.**[61]   The court has wide power to make orders affecting the property of parties to matrimonial proceedings. It may order capital provision to be made, by cash payment, or property transfer, or by the making of a settlement for the benefit of the other spouse and the children of the family.[62] It may also effect the variation of ante-nuptial or post-nuptial settlements,[63] and the variation of orders for settlements made under the Act.[64]

The jurisdiction to vary a "post-nuptial settlement" under s.24 of the 1973 Act enabled the provision of a pension for a wife on divorce in *Brooks v Brooks*.[65] A company pension scheme of which the husband was the sole member provided that on retirement he could direct that part of his benefit should be used to make provision for his wife after his death, and that a lump sum would be payable at the discretion of the trustee to a class including the wife if he were to die prematurely. These factors made it a "marriage settlement", which had a wide meaning. The scheme could be varied so far as it constituted a settlement made by the husband. The trust was varied by directing that an immediate annuity and a deferred pension were to be provided in priority to and, if necessary, in diminution of the husband's pension. Had there been any other scheme members, the court would not have ordered a variation to their detriment, nor would it sanction a variation with adverse tax consequences.

This decision has been restricted by later legislation, and in any event it did not solve the problem of pension-splitting on divorce, which is dealt with by other legislation.[66]

23–011   **v. Mental Capacity Act 2005.**   Mental Capacity Act 2005 s.18(1)(h), re-enacting earlier legislation, gives to the Court of Protection a power to make a settlement of the property of a person who lacks capacity; and also, if the settlement contains a provision for variation or revocation, or if any material fact was not disclosed when the settlement was made, or where there has been any substantial change in circumstances, to vary the settlement in such manner as the judge thinks fit.[67]

---

[61] As seen previously, above para.13–003, the Marriage (Same Sex Couples) Act 2013 extended marriage to same sex couples (s.1 and s.11). There are various consequential amendments to matrimonial legislation, including the 1973 Act, but they do not affect the points here, beyond noting the extension to couples of the same sex.

[62] Matrimonial Causes Act 1973 ss.23 and 24. See also s.25, laying down the principles to be observed by the court in exercising its jurisdiction under ss.23, 24.

[63] s.24(1)(c), (d); M Bennett (2007) 37 Fam. Law 916. See *E v E* [1990] 2 F.L.R. 233; *C v C (Ancillary Relief: Nuptial Settlement)* [2005] Fam. 250; *N v N and F Trust* [2006] 1 F.L.R. 856. On the variation of Jersey trusts under the 1973 Act, see *Re B Trust* [2007] W.T.L.R. 1361; P. Matthews (2008) 22 T.L.I. 63; Trusts (Amendment No.4) (Jersey) Law 2006 art.9(4).

[64] s.31(2)(e). Further details must be obtained from Family Law books.

[65] [1996] 1 A.C. 375; M. Rae (1995) 145 N.L.J. 1009; M. Thomas [1997] Conv. 52.

[66] Welfare Reform and Pensions Act 1999. See also Pensions Act 1995, above, para.17–034 (earmarking).

[67] Mental Capacity Act 2005 Sch.2 para.6.

C.   Variation of Trusts Act 1958[68]

The Variation of Trusts Act 1958 gives to the court[69] a "very wide and, indeed,   **23–012**
revolutionary discretion"[70] to approve on behalf of four groups of persons[71]:

> "[A]ny arrangement... varying or revoking all or any of the trusts, or enlarging the powers of
> the trustees of managing or administering any of the property subject to the trusts."[72]

On its terms, this provision covers not only administrative matters, but also
variations in the beneficial interests; but the court may only approve such an
arrangement if it would be for the benefit of the person on whose behalf the
approval is given.[73] The Act applies to the statutory trusts arising on intestacy[74]
and to property in the course of administration by a personal representative.[75]

The courts have approved a wide variety of variations, and, in addition to
approving changes in the beneficial interests, have inserted a power of
advancement,[76] terminated an accumulation,[77] inserted an accumulation period[78]
and have widened the investment powers of trustees.[79] Recent cases have
established that the jurisdiction under the Act applies in principle to approving an
extension of the trust period,[80] provided that the settlement would still remain
"recognisably the same".[81] Investment clauses are rarely the subject of an
application, now that investment powers have been widened by the Trustee Act
2000.

It is of course in connection with schemes which vary beneficial interests for
tax saving purposes that the 1958 Act has been mainly applied. There has been
the suggestion that such applications are increasingly common.[82]

---

[68] Harris, *Variation of Trusts*, Ch.3; M. Mowbray (1958) 22 Conv.(N.S.) 373; D. Evans (1963) 27
Conv.(N.S.) 6; A. Maclean (1965) 43 Can.B.R. 181. The jurisdiction given by the Act is independent
of Trustee Act 1925 s.57, and Settled Land Act 1925 s.64, above. There may be technical reasons, e.g.
difficulties as to representative parties, why it is not possible to invoke the 1958 Act. See *Mason v
Farbrother* [1983] 2 All E.R. 1078.

[69] Proceedings under s.1 of the 1958 Act may be commenced and taken only in the High Court: High
Court and County Courts Jurisdiction Order 1991/724 art.6D, as amended by the High Court and
County Court Jurisdiction (Amendment) Order (SI 2014/821) art.2(8).

[70] per Evershed MR in *Re Steed's WT* [1960] Ch. 407 at 420–421.

[71] Below para.23–013.

[72] Variation of Trusts Act 1958 s.1(1). But see *Allen v Distillers Co (Biochemicals) Ltd* [1974] Q.B.
384, above, para.23–005.

[73] Except for persons in para.(d), below.

[74] *S v T1* [2006] W.T.L.R. 1461 (variation to prevent child of intestate father being disinherited by an
adoption order). *Wright v Gater* [2012] 1 W.L.R. 802; M. Flavin (2012) T. & T. 435.

[75] *Re Bernstein* [2010] W.T.L.R. 559; S. Evans [2011] Conv. 151.

[76] *Re Lister's WT* [1962] 1 W.L.R. 1441. See also *D (A Child) v O* [2004] 3 All E.R. 780 (extension of
power of advancement).

[77] *Re Tinker's Settlement* [1960] 1 W.L.R. 1011.

[78] *Re Lansdowne's WT* [1967] Ch. 603; *Re Holt's Settlement* [1961] Ch. 100.

[79] *Re Coates' Trusts* [1959] 1 W.L.R. 375; *Re Burney's ST* [1961] 1 W.L.R. 545.

[80] *Allfrey v Allfrey* [2015] EWHC 1717 (Ch); *DC v AC* [2016] EWHC 477 (Ch) per Sir Terence
Etherton C at [18]; *Pemberton v Pemberton* [2016] EWHC 2345 (Ch) per Judge Hodge QC at [28].

[81] *Pemberton v Pemberton* [2016] EWHC 2345 (Ch) per Judge Hodge QC at [28].

[82] S. Meadway (2016) T. & T. 886 at 886.

23–013   **i.   Persons on whose Behalf Approval may be Given.**   The principle is that the court is not asked to approve on behalf of ascertainable adults who can consent for themselves. The classes (as set out in Variation of Trusts Act 1958 s.1) are:

(a)   any person having, directly or indirectly, an interest, whether vested or contingent, under the trusts who by reason of infancy or other incapacity is incapable of assenting, or

(b)   any person (whether ascertained or not) who may become entitled, directly or indirectly, to an interest under the trusts as being at a future date or on the happening of a future event a person of any specified description or a member of any specified class of persons, so however that this paragraph shall not include any person[83] who would be of that description, or a member of that class, as the case may be, if the said date had fallen or the said event had happened at the date of the application to the court, or

(c)   any person unborn, or

(d)   any person in respect of any discretionary interest of his under protective trusts where the interest of the principal beneficiary has not failed or determined.[84]

Paragraph (b) may well of course include adults; but because the class is ascertainable only at a future time, its members cannot yet be known. Under the proviso, however, those who would qualify if the future event happened at the date of the application to the court must themselves consent. If however they are children, they come within para.(a).

In *Re Suffert*,[85] income was given under protective trusts to an unmarried woman for life, and, in the event of her having no issue, and subject to a general testamentary power, in trust for those who would become entitled under her intestacy. She had three adult cousins, who would be entitled in equal shares to her estate if she had died at the date of the application to the court. One cousin was made a party, and consented, but the others were not. In asking the court to approve the arrangement, it was argued that the court should approve on behalf of those who would be entitled on intestacy, as they came within para.(b). Buckley J however held that the proviso applied and that he could not approve on behalf of the two cousins. Otherwise he approved the arrangement.

23–014   The meaning of the words "may become entitled" in para.(b) were examined in *Knocker v Youle*.[86] Property was held on trust for the settlor's daughter for life under a settlement in which her cousins had very remote contingent interests. It was not practicable to get the approval of the cousins to the proposed variation because they were very numerous, and some were in Australia.[87] Approval was therefore sought on their behalf under subs.(1)(1)(b). The question was whether para.(b) included persons with an existing contingent interest, however remote. Warner J held that it did not. A person having a contingent interest was not a person who "may become entitled" to an interest. Paragraph (b) covered the case of a person who had a mere *spes* (an expectation) such as the prospective next of

---

[83] This presumably means any ascertained person; Harris, *Variation of Trusts*, 39–40.

[84] See *Gibbon v Mitchell* [1990] 1 W.L.R. 1304.

[85] [1961] Ch. 1.

[86] [1986] 1 W.L.R. 934; criticised J. Riddall [1987] Conv. 144, also discussing persons who are objects of mere powers and discretionary trusts.

[87] The Act does not deal with the problem of the beneficiary who must consent on his own behalf but who is untraceable. In such a case a *Benjamin* order (above, para.19–027) could be used. See P. Luxton (1986) 136 N.L.J. 1057.

kin of a living person in *Re Suffert*,[88] or a potential future spouse.[89] The adult cousins were in any event excluded by the proviso to para.(b).

ii. Parties.   In general, the settlor, if living,[90] and all beneficiaries under the   **23–015**
trusts, both adults and children, should be made parties. The children, unless their interests coincide with those of adult beneficiaries who consent, should be separately represented,[91] and a litigation friend must give full consideration to the way in which the proposed variation will affect the children's interests.[92] In the case of a class, those who are members of the class at the date of the application should be included[93]; but it is not necessary to join persons who may become members later[94]; nor persons who may become interested under discretionary trusts[95]; nor those who are possible objects of a power.[96] Persons unborn cannot of course be made parties, but their interests must be represented.[97] In *A v B*,[98] Warren J approved a scheme whereby the trustees executed partial releases of their power to benefit very remote beneficiaries, who therefore lost their right to challenge the proposed variation.[99] Where an adult who lacks capacity is involved the Court of Protection decides whether the proposed variation would be for her benefit.[100] Where, however, the beneficiary who lacks capacity is also under 18, Morgan J has recently concluded that the High Court retains jurisdiction, which sensibly avoids what would otherwise be a clash between jurisdictions.[101]

iii. Applicants.   The application should be made by a beneficiary, usually the   **23–016**
person currently receiving the income. But the settlor may also apply.[102] It is not usually satisfactory for the trustees to make the application because there might be an undesirable conflict of interest between their interest as an applicant, and as guardian of some of the beneficial interests for which they are responsible.[103]

---

[88] [1961] Ch. 1; *Re Moncrieff's ST* [1962] 1 W.L.R. 1344. But see J. Riddall [1987] Conv. 144 at p.146 for the view that such persons do have a contingent interest in the *settlement*, although not, of course, in the estate of their living relative.

[89] See *Re Clitheroe's ST* [1959] 1 W.L.R. 1159; *Re Lister's WT* [1962] 1 W.L.R. 1441.

[90] CPR 1998 Pt 64.4(2).

[91] *Re Whigham's ST* [1971] 1 W.L.R. 831.

[92] *Re Whittall* [1973] 1 W.L.R. 1027. See CPR 1998 Pt 21.

[93] *Re Suffert's Settlement* [1961] Ch. 1.

[94] *Re Moncrieff's ST* [1962] 1 W.L.R. 1344.

[95] *Re Munro's ST* [1963] 1 W.L.R. 145.

[96] *Re Christie-Miller's Marriage Settlement* [1961] 1 W.L.R. 462; Practice Direction [1976] 1 W.L.R. 884.

[97] The court must consider the position of any individual who may be born and become a beneficiary, not merely the class of unborn beneficiaries as a whole; *Re Cohen's ST* [1965] 1 W.L.R. 1229.

[98] *A v B* [2016] EWHC 340 (Ch); S. Meadway (2016) T. & T. 886.

[99] Warren J was satisfied that "on the facts of the present case, it is perfectly proper for the Trustees to effect the partial releases and that no fraud on a power is involved": [2016] EWHC 340 (Ch) at [32]. The wider class of remoter beneficiaries would still be eligible for consideration in the event of a "family catastrophe": at [24].

[100] Variations of Trusts Act 1958 s.1(3), as amended by the Mental Capacity Act 2005.

[101] *ET v JP* [2018] EWHC 685 (Ch); [2018] W.L.R.(D) 193 at [25]–[27], applying Variations of Trusts Act 1958 s.1(3).

[102] *Re Clitheroe's ST* [1959] 1 W.L.R. 1159.

[103] *Re Druce's ST* [1962] 1 W.L.R. 363.

They may apply if no-one else will do so, and the variation is in the interests of the beneficiaries.[104] The importance of independent scrutiny and instruction of separate counsel for each party and interest represented was emphasised by Norris J in *Wright v Gater*.[105]

The general principle is that applications under the Act should be made in open court, and any derogation from open justice must be justified by clear and cogent evidence.[106] Thus, in *V v T*,[107] Morgan J declined to hear a case in private when it concerned a wealthy family who wished to maintain a "modest and low-key unostentatious lifestyle for the children".[108] It was however appropriate to impose reporting restrictions and to deliver an anonymised judgment.[109]

23–017   **iv. Foreign Trusts.**   The court will not approve an agreement which provides for a settlement under the law of a foreign jurisdiction if the beneficiaries remain resident and domiciled in England; nor, as in *Re Weston's Settlement*,[110] where the connection with Jersey, the foreign jurisdiction, was recent and tenuous, and where the court doubted whether the living beneficiaries really intended to make Jersey their permanent home.[111] Trusts have, however, been "exported" in favour of a settlement with foreign trustees and governed by foreign law where the beneficiaries have emigrated permanently to the foreign country[112]; and approval has been given for the transfer of funds from a trust governed by English law to one governed by the law of Guernsey where the primary beneficiaries were resident and domiciled in France and the remainderman in Indonesia.[113] The advantages of trust exporting have been much reduced since the introduction of inheritance tax.[114]

It should be added that the appointment of a foreign trustee may be made in a proper case without the intervention of the court.[115]

---

[104] [1962] 1 W.L.R. 363 at 370. And in some cases, a trustee may also be a beneficiary, as in *Pemberton v Pemberton* [2016] EWHC 2345 (Ch).

[105] [2012] 1 W.L.R. 802 at [6]–[10].

[106] *V v T* [2014] EWHC 3432 (Ch), per Morgan J at [19]. See S. Taube [2015] P.C.B. 118 and S. Haren [2016] P.C.B. 15.

[107] [2014] EWHC 3432 (Ch).

[108] [2014] EWHC 3432 (Ch), per Morgan J at [23].

[109] [2014] EWHC 3432 (Ch), per Morgan J at [24]–[30].

[110] [1969] 1 Ch. 223.

[111] This is also considered under "Benefit" below, para.23–025.

[112] *Re Seal's Marriage Settlement* [1961] Ch. 574 (Canada); *Re Windeatt's WT* [1969] 1 W.L.R. 692 (Jersey); see also *Re Whitehead's WT* [1971] 1 W.L.R. 833.

[113] *Re Chamberlain* (unreported) discussed in J. Morcom (1976) 126 N.L.J. 1034; T. Watkin (1976) 40 Conv.(N.S.) 295.

[114] See Inheritance Tax Act 1984 ss.48(3), 201(1)(d), 267 (the last section as variously amended; most recently by the Finance (No.2) Act 2017).

[115] *Re Whitehead's WT* [1971] 1 W.L.R. 833. But an application will often be made to the court, and a variation will be necessary if the form of the trust needs to be altered in order to comply with the foreign law, if there is no power in the trust instrument to do this. See Parker and Mellows, *The Modern Law of Trusts*, 9th edn (London: Sweet & Maxwell, 2008), pp.620–626; R. Bramwell (1990/91) 1 *The Offshore Tax Planning Review*, p.1, discussing *Richard v The Hon, AB Mackay* Unreported, 1987, above, para.18–032.

Where the question is not one of exporting a trust to another jurisdiction but of varying a foreign trust, such a variation is governed by the applicable law of the trust.[116] This issue was considered recently by HHJ Hodge QC in *C v C*.[117]

> In *C v C*, the court was invited to approve variation to four family settlements, one of which was governed by the law of Kenya. The application was not contested, but the court had to determine the approach to be taken to varying a foreign trust. First,[118] it was held that the court should proceed with caution in deciding whether to assume jurisdiction in a case with foreign elements:[119] HHJ Hodge QC was satisfied on the facts that it was appropriate for the court to exercise the jurisdiction, not least since the other three settlements were governed by English law. Second,[120] the English court could "exercise its jurisdiction to vary a trust under the 1958 Act provided that the law of the country that applies to the trust has a similar power vested in its own courts".[121] Since the Kenyan courts would have such a power, HHJ Hodge QC approved the variation.

However, where the English court has jurisdiction to deal with an application for ancillary relief following divorce, it has jurisdiction to vary a nuptial settlement by way of ancillary relief even though the applicable law of the settlement is not English law.[122]

v. Effect of Approval by the Court. It appears that the arrangement is **23–018** effective from the time of the approval by the court. The reasons why this is so are not clear; and the result may be due to the practice established by *Re Viscount Hambledon's Will Trusts*.[123] Several, and in some cases conflicting, accounts have been given of the effect of approval by the court.

In *Re Joseph's Will Trusts*,[124] Vaisey J included in his order approving the variation a direction that the variation should be carried into effect. In *Re Viscount Hambleden's Will Trusts*,[125] Wynn-Parry J thought that he had no jurisdiction to make such a direction. Nor was it required. "I hold that the effect of my approval is effective for all purposes to vary the trusts."[126] In *Re Holt's Settlement*,[127] Megarry J was unconvinced. Before him, it was argued that the Act gives the court power to approve only on behalf of the persons mentioned in s.1(1); and the consent of the adults to a change in their beneficial interests was a "disposition", and ineffective unless in writing, as required by s.53(1)(c) of the Law of Property Act 1925.[128] Megarry J was reluctant to disturb what had

---

[116] Recognition of Trusts Act 1987 Sch., art.8. The applicable law is determined by arts 6, 7; above, para.1–051.

[117] [2015] EWHC 2699 (Ch), [2016] W.T.L.R. 223; J. MacDougald (2016) 22 T. & T. 1086.

[118] [2015] EWHC 2699 (Ch) at [30] (agreeing with the analysis in *Chester, North and Fawcett: Private International Law*, 14th edn (2008), pp.1323–4).

[119] See further *Re Paget's Settlement* [1965] 1 W.L.R. 1046, per Cross J.

[120] [2015] EWHC 2699 (Ch) at [30] and [43].

[121] [2015] EWHC 2699 (Ch) at [43].

[122] Recognition of Trusts Act 1987 art.15; *C v C (Ancillary Relief: Nuptial Settlement)* [2005] Fam. 250 (wife's claim under s.24(1)(c) of the Matrimonial Causes Act 1973); J. Harris (2005) 121 L.Q.R. 16.

[123] [1960] 1 W.L.R. 82; *Re Holt's Settlement* [1969] 1 Ch. 100 at 113.

[124] [1959] 1 W.L.R. 1019.

[125] [1960] 1 W.L.R. 82.

[126] [1960] 1 W.L.R. 82 at 86.

[127] [1969] 1 Ch. 100; PVB (1968) 84 L.Q.R. 162.

[128] Above, para.6–009; *Grey v IRC* [1960] A.C. 1.

become a very convenient practice based on *Re Viscount Hambleden*,[129] and searched for a theory to justify it. The suggestion that there was no "disposition" of the interests of the consenting adults, but a "species of estoppel"[130] operating against them was "unattractive". He was satisfied however that it could be explained on the ground that s.53(1)(c) was by necessary implication excluded; or that, where the variation was made for consideration, the consenting adults could be compelled to perform their contract and they held their original interests on constructive trusts, these being unaffected by s.53(1)(c).[131] The view that the variation obtains its effect by reason of the consent of the beneficiaries is supported by dicta in *IRC v Holmden*,[132] where however the question of s.53(1)(c) did not arise.

The arrangement coupled with the court's order is an "instrument" for the purposes of the Perpetuities and Accumulations Act 1964 s.15(5) and the Perpetuities and Accumulations Act 2009 s.15(1). This means that future interests permitted by the Acts may be provided for in an arrangement.[133] Because the variation does not owe its authority to the settlor, its provisions need not be such that the settlor could have created them.[134] The perpetuity period does not relate back to the original settlement. A variation which is inconsistent with the continuous existence of a power operates as a release of a power.[135]

23–019   **vi. Variation or Resettlement.**   The jurisdiction, as we have seen, is very wide. It is however a jurisdiction to "vary" and not to "resettle".[136] This is a difficult dividing line.[137] In *Re Ball's Settlement*, Megarry J laid down the general test as follows[138]:

> "If an arrangement changes the whole substratum of the trust, then it may well be that it cannot be regarded merely as varying the trust. But if an arrangement, while leaving the substratum, effectuates the purpose of the trust by other means, it may still be possible to regard that arrangement as merely varying the original trusts, even though the means employed are wholly different and even though the form is completely changed."

23–020   **vii. Fraud on a Power.**   Nor will the court approve a variation which involves a fraud on a power, as for example where property is held on trust for A for life and to such of A's children as he shall appoint, and A, in order to avoid tax

---

[129] [1960] 1 W.L.R. 82.

[130] [1969] 1 Ch. 100 at 114; *Spens v IRC* [1970] 1 W.L.R. 1173.

[131] Law of Property Act 1925 s.53(2); *Oughtred v IRC* [1960] A.C. 206; *Re Holt's Settlement* [1969] 1 Ch. 100 at 115–116.

[132] [1968] A.C. 685; cf. Trustee Act 1925 s.57; *Re Mair* [1935] Ch. 562.

[133] *Re Lansdowne's WT* [1967] Ch. 603; *Re Holt's Settlement* [1969] 1 Ch. 100.

[134] *Re Holt's Settlement* [1969] 1 Ch. 100. See also *Wyndham v Egremont* [2009] W.T.L.R. 1437.

[135] *Re Christie-Miller's Marriage Settlement* [1961] 1 W.L.R. 462; *Re Courtauld's Settlement* [1965] 1 W.L.R. 1385; *Re Ball's ST* [1968] 1 W.L.R. 899; above, para.7–031.

[136] *Re T's ST* [1964] Ch. 158; *Re Ball's ST* [1968] 1 W.L.R. 899; criticised PVB (1968) 84 L.Q.R. 458; *Re Holt's Settlement* [1969] 1 Ch. 100 at 117; *Allen v Distillers Co (Biochemicals) Ltd* [1974] Q.B. 384; *Wyndham v Egremont* [2009] W.T.L.R. 1473.

[137] See e.g. *Allfrey v Allfrey* [2015] EWHC 1717 (Ch), per Jeremy Cousins QC, sitting as a Deputy Judge of the Chancery Division, at [22].

[138] [1968] 1 W.L.R. 899 at 905. In *Wright v Gater* [2012] 1 W.L.R. 802, at [16], Norris J declined to approve an originally proposed "arrangement" which in his view came "dangerously close (if not to cross) the line between 'variation' and 'resettlement'."

liability on his death, appoints in favour of his living children, and does so with a view to partitioning the fund, with the court's approval, between his children and himself. Such an appointment has been held to be fraudulent and void on the ground that it was made so that the appointor may obtain a benefit for himself under the variation.[139]

viii. The Settlor's Intention. In giving approval, the court must be satisfied about the arrangement as a whole.[140] One relevant factor is whether or not the arrangement is consistent with the general plan of the settlor or testator. 23–021

> In *Re Steed's Will Trusts*[141] a testator had left property to a faithful housekeeper for her life on protective trusts and after her death as she should appoint, the trustee having power to pay capital moneys to her as they should think fit. The property included a farm which was let to the housekeeper's brother. The terms of the will were designed to give the maximum benefit in the property to the housekeeper, without giving her an absolute interest, because of the danger which the testator thought was real, of being, to use a common phrase, sponged upon by one of her brothers.[142]
>
> The trustees decided to sell the farm. The housekeeper started proceedings to stop them, exercised the power of appointment in favour of herself, and applied under the Variation of Trusts Act s.1, for the elimination of the protective element in her life interest. The result would be that she would become absolutely entitled to the property, because she would then be the life tenant, having appointed to herself the reversion. The only persons who might be prejudiced by such a variation would be those who might benefit under the discretionary trusts which would arise if the protective life interests were forfeited[143]; and under para.(d), the court is not concerned to see that they benefit from a variation. Was there any reason why approval should not be given?

The Court of Appeal refused:

> "It is the *arrangement* which has to be approved not just the limited interest of the person on whose behalf the court's duty is to consider it... the court must regard the proposal as a whole, and so regarding it, then ask itself whether in the exercise of its jurisdiction it should approve that proposal on behalf of the person who cannot give a consent... it was part of the testator's scheme... that this trust should be available for the [claimant] so that she should have proper provision made for her throughout her life, and would not be exposed to the risk that she might, if she had been handed the money, part with it in favour of another individual about whom the testator felt apprehension, which apprehension is plainly shared by the trustees."[144]

The question also arose in *Re Remnant's Settlement Trusts*,[145] where the proposed variation was the deletion of a forfeiture clause whereby beneficiaries who practised Roman Catholicism or married a Roman Catholic would lose their entitlement. The fact that the variation would defeat the settlor's intention was regarded as a serious matter, but not conclusive. As the forfeiture clause was 23–022

---

[139] *Re Robertson's WT* [1960] 1 W.L.R. 1050; *Re Brook's Settlement* [1968] 1 W.L.R. 1661; cf. *Re Wallace's Settlement* [1968] 1 W.L.R. 711. Compare *A v B* [2016] EWHC 340 (Ch), mentioned above, para.23–015.

[140] *Re Burney's ST* [1961] 1 All E.R. 856.

[141] [1960] Ch. 407; *Re Michelham's WT* [1964] Ch. 550.

[142] [1960] Ch. 407 at 415.

[143] Above, para.8–004; assuming that she would not now have children, this was only a prospective husband, described in the case of the "spectral spouse".

[144] [1960] Ch. 407 at 421–422.

[145] [1970] Ch. 560; below, para.23–027.

undesirable in the circumstances of the family (unlike the disputed provision in *Re Steed's Will Trusts*, which was not cited), it was fair and proper to delete it, notwithstanding the settlor's intention.

The testatrix in *Goulding v James*[146] had the clear intention that her daughter should have only a life interest and that her grandson should not have capital until aged 40 (because she mistrusted her son-in-law and her grandson had not "settled down"). A variation was sought whereby the daughter would have capital and the grandson would become entitled before the age of 40. As the proposed terms substantially increased the financial benefit to unborn beneficiaries, approval was given by the Court of Appeal, even though the proposal was contrary to the intention of the testatrix. Her wishes related only to the adult beneficiaries, and so carried little weight. *Re Steed's Will Trusts*, which laid down no general rule, was distinguishable because there the testator's purpose was evidenced in the will itself, and no benefit needed to be established for the class of beneficiaries on whose behalf consent was sought. In the present case extrinsic evidence of the wishes of the testatrix could not be allowed to outweigh considerations of benefit to the class of unborns, to whom this evidence had no relevance. The role of the court is not to stand in for the settlor but to consent on behalf of the beneficiaries who are unable to consent.

In *Bathurst v Bathurst*,[147] Master Matthews approved an arrangement varying the appointment process for new trustees. The settlor had reserved to himself the power to appoint new trustees during his lifetime, then after his death the statutory power applied.[148] All of the adult beneficiaries and three of the four trustees supported a proposed variation to give the power to appoint to the principal beneficiary, subject to written consent of the trustees; one trustee opposed it, preferring instead the power of nomination and appointment to remain with the trustees, with the principal beneficiary having a veto. Master Matthews held that it was relevant that the settlor had not entrusted the power of appointment to the trustees in the first place.[149]

23–023 **ix. Benefit.** It is necessary that the variation should be for the benefit of the persons in categories (a) or (c) on whose behalf approval is sought. There is no such requirement of benefit in respect of persons under category (d).[150]

23–024 *(a) Financial Benefit.* There is usually no difficulty in showing financial benefit.[151] But evidence must be presented to show that there is an advantage to each person required to be benefited.[152] Variations have commonly been made to save estate duty or inheritance tax,[153] capital gains tax,[154] and income tax.[155] Any

---

[146] [1997] 2 All E.R. 239; criticised P. Luxton (1997) 60 M.L.R. 719.
[147] [2016] EWHC 3033 (Ch); [2017] 1 P. & C.R. DG13.
[148] Trustee Act 1925 s.36.
[149] [2016] EWHC 3033 (Ch) at [4].
[150] Variations of Trusts Act 1958 s.1, proviso. See *Re Van Gruisen's WT* [1964] 1 W.L.R. 449.
[151] A straightforward and short example is *Bailey v Bailey* [2014] EWHC 4411 (Ch).
[152] *Re Clitheroe's ST* [1959] 1 W.L.R. 1159 at 1163.
[153] *Re Druce's ST* [1962] 1 W.L.R. 363; *Gibbon v Mitchell* [1990] 1 W.L.R. 1304.
[154] *Re Sainsbury's Settlement* [1967] 1 W.L.R. 476.
[155] *Re Clitheroe's ST* [1959] 1 W.L.R. 1159.

saving provides a larger sum for distribution, and remaindermen may also be benefited by the termination of an interest in possession as their interests will be accelerated. As stated above,[156] a partition of the settled fund between tenant for life and remainderman had inheritance tax advantages subject to changes made by the Finance Act 2006.[157] Provided the tenant for life survived for seven years, no tax would be payable, whereas the whole capital would be taxable if a life interest terminated on death. There may also be complications arising from deferments of interests under a trust.[158]

(b) Moral and Social Benefit. But benefit is not only financial. The court   **23–025** must also consider the general welfare of the persons on whose behalf approval is sought; this does not necessarily coincide with their financial interest.

> In *Re Weston's Settlements*,[159] two settlements had been made in 1964, one in favour of each of the settlor's sons (both young men and one still under age) and their children. The settlor moved to Jersey in 1967, and the sons followed him. The application was for the appointment of new trustees under Trustee Act 1925 s.41,[160] and for the insertion into the settlement of a power for the trustees to discharge the trust of the settlements and to create almost identical Jersey settlements. The object was to take advantage of the favourable fiscal situation in Jersey. The Court of Appeal refused. The variation would make the beneficiaries richer but would not be for their benefit, as Lord Denning MR noted in typical rhetorical style:
>
> "The court should not consider merely the financial benefit to the infant and unborn children, but also their educational and social benefit. There are many things in life more worthwhile than money. One of these things is to be brought up in this our England, which is still 'the envy of less happier lands.' I do not believe that it is for the benefit of the children to be uprooted from England and transported to another country simply to avoid tax ... many a child has been ruined by being given too much. The avoidance of tax may be lawful, but it is not yet a virtue. The Court of Chancery should not encourage or support it—it should not give its approval to it—if by so doing it would imperil the true welfare of the children, already born or yet to be born."[161]

Similarly, as has been seen, with the housekeeper who wished to become the absolute owner of a farm which would then have been at the mercy of her brother.[162] In *Re CL*,[163] it was held to be for the benefit of a person who lacked capacity to consent to the surrender of a protected life interest and a contingent remainder interest in favour of her daughter. It was what she would have done if she had not lacked capacity. Such persons should not be denied the opportunity of taking proper steps to preserve the family fortune.

(c) Postponing Vesting. It may be for the benefit of a child that the date of   **23–026** vesting of an interest in the capital should be postponed. In *Re T's Settlement*

---

[156] Above, para.23–001.

[157] Broadly, the inheritance tax rules discussed in the text apply to life interests arising before 22 March 2006 and those arising under a will or intestacy on or after that date; above, paras 10–017, 10–019.

[158] As in *Wright v Gater* [2012] 1 W.L.R. 802, in which the original proposal would have seen a substantial saving of inheritance tax (£89,000), but would have deprived the beneficiary of his right to income under the trust for some twelve years.

[159] [1969] 1 Ch. 223.

[160] Above, para.18–024.

[161] [1969] 1 Ch. 223 at 245.

[162] *Re Steed's WT* [1960] Ch. 407; above, para.23–021.

[163] [1969] 1 Ch. 587.

Trusts,[164] a beneficiary who was irresponsible and immature was entitled to a vested interest on attaining her majority, which she would do a few months after the application. The proposal was that her interest should be varied to become a protected life interest. Wilberforce J could not regard such protection as a "benefit in its own right"; but he made an order postponing the vesting of the capital until a specified age and providing that the property should be held on protective trusts in the meantime. In *Wright v Gater*,[165] Norris J declined to defer a three-year old toddler's interest in a substantial sum until he should reach the age of 30: significantly, there could be no particular indication of the beneficiary's likely attitude to money and his general level of responsibility.[166] Norris J did however accept that for a young man to become entitled to some £750,000 on his eighteenth birthday would expose him to risks and temptation. A revised arrangement was therefore approved, which staggered the beneficiary's entitlement: he would become entitled to the income from the fund at 18, to 10% of the fund at 21, and the remainder at 25.[167] In *Collins v Collins*,[168] Norris J applied similar care in approving the variation of a trust so that (amongst things) a beneficiary's interest vested at 18:

> "That does not of course mean [that] Charley is compelled to call for the transfer of the invested funds into her name: like many a wise young person she may feel it more prudent to leave it in the names of her erstwhile trustees as a protection against 'gold diggers'."[169]

23–027   *(d)   Trouble in the Family.*   Where a trust treats members of a family unequally, it may be for everyone's benefit, even for those who surrender a claim to property as a result, to vary the trust so as to treat each of them equally. Russell J thought not in *Re Tinker's Settlement*,[170] where, owing to the draftsman's oversight, the settlement provided that the share of the settlor's son should accrue to his sister's share if he died under the age of 30 years, even if he left children. It was not for the benefit of the sister's children to surrender their contingent interest.

A broader view was taken in *Re Remnant's Settlement Trusts*.[171] As mentioned above, a trust fund gave contingent interests to the children of two sisters, Dawn and Merrial, and contained a forfeiture provision in respect of any of the children who practised Roman Catholicism or was married to a Roman Catholic at the

---

[164] [1964] Ch. 158; *Re Holt's Settlement* [1969] 1 Ch. 100; *Re RGST Settlement* [2008] W.T.L.R. 527; *Wyndham v Egremont* [2009] W.T.L.R. 1473. See also *Allen v Distillers Co (Biochemicals) Ltd* [1974] Q.B. 384; above, para.23–005. It was reported in *The Times*, 16 February 1999, that a trust had been varied so that the son of the Duke of Northumberland would receive £250,000 a year from the age of 25 instead of 18.

[165] [2012] 1 W.L.R. 802.

[166] Norris J observed: "I pictured myself trying to explain to a 28-year-old Rory who was married and with children and who wanted to embark on a particular career why he could only do so with the approval of his mother and uncle (or the persons they had appointed to succeed them), and why I had taken away his access to his inherited funds": [2012] 1 W.L.R. 802 at [16].

[167] [2012] 1 W.L.R. 802 at [17] (various further provisions were included in the event of the beneficiary's death and other events, but they are immaterial for present purposes).

[168] [2016] EWHC 1423 (Ch).

[169] [2016] EWHC 1423 (Ch) per Norris J at [15].

[170] [1960] 1 W.L.R. 1011.

[171] [1970] Ch. 560; R. Cotterrell (1971) 34 M.L.R. 98.

time of vesting, with an accruer provision in favour of the children of the other. Dawn's children were Protestant, but Merrial's were Roman Catholic.

Pennycuick J approved the deletion of the forfeiture provision. This was clearly not for the financial benefit of Dawn's children, for they surrendered a very good chance of gaining by it. But it was overall for their benefit. "Obviously, a forfeiture provision of this kind might well cause very serious dissension between the families of the two sisters."[172] The forfeiture clause could also operate as a deterrent in the selection of a spouse. Freedom from such problems would be more important to the lives of the children than some more money.

In the Jersey case of *Re the Y Trust and the Z Trust*,[173] the Royal Court had to consider a trust established by a settlor who had strong personal views on illegitimacy, adoption, and same-sex marriage and partnerships and had included an interpretation provision to define "child" or "issue" or "descendant" under the trust, in order to reflect his views. The proposed variation would have broadened eligibility by changing certain of those restrictive definitions. The Royal Court endorsed what it took to be the "consistent theme" of the English cases that "where the Court is satisfied that a proposed arrangement is beneficial to those on whose behalf it is asked to sanction the variation, the fact that the variation might be contrary to the wishes of the settlor or testator is not material".[174]

(e) Taking a Chance. A difficulty arises where the proposed variation will almost certainly confer a benefit, but there may possibly be circumstances in which it will not. Thus, in *Re Cohen's Settlement Trust*,[175] an application was made to vary a settlement so as to make the interest of the grandchildren vest on a specified date, and not upon the death of a life tenant, in order to reduce estate duty. Although it was most unlikely (but not impossible) that the life tenant would live until the specified date, any children born after that date but before his death would lose their interests. Thus approval could not be given on behalf of unborn children. Where trustees wish to distribute on the footing that a middle-aged woman will not have further children, this may be sanctioned by court order (made in the exercise of its jurisdiction to secure the proper administration of a trust) without recourse to the 1958 Act.[176] Indeed, no application to court is needed where the woman is elderly,[177] although it is possible that assisted reproductive technology may challenge that proposition.[178]

The question is one of degree. The court will not give its approval where the benefit is a matter of chance, but it will not require absolute certainty of

23–028

---

[172] [1970] Ch. 560 at 566. Another benefit, of less weight, was to be freed from having to choose between one's religion and the entitlement under the will.

[173] [2017] JRC 100; M Herbert [2017] P.C.B. 206.

[174] [2017] JRC 100 at [35].

[175] [1965] 1 W.L.R. 1229.

[176] *Re Westminster Bank Ltd's Declaration of Trust* [1963] 1 W.L.R. 820 (over 50). The order did not extinguish the rights of any future child.

[177] *Re Pettifor's ST* [1966] Ch. 257 (over 70); cf. *Figg v Clarke (Inspector of Taxes)* [1997] 1 W.L.R. 603 (presumption of fertility until death in context of capital gains tax, where a deemed disposal occurs when beneficiaries become absolutely entitled to the trust property). See also *Re Levy Estate Trust* [2000] 5 C.L.Y. 635.

[178] See e.g. H. Legge (2001) 27 Tru. & E.L.J. 10 and (speaking about inheritance provisions in the context of the conception of a child after the death of its natural father) N. Maddox [2017] Conv. 408.

benefit,[179] if the risk is one which a "prudent and well advised adult would be prepared to take."[180] Most risks can be covered by insurance.

---

[179] *Re Holt's Settlement* [1969] 1 Ch. 100; *Re Robinson's ST* [1976] 1 W.L.R. 806.
[180] REM (1960) 76 L.Q.R. 22.

PART IV

PERSONAL AND PROPRIETARY CLAIMS

CHAPTER 24

CONSEQUENCES OF BREACH OF TRUST

1. PERSONAL LIABILITY

AS WE have seen in the preceding chapters, breaches of trust can take many forms. The trustee might fail to invest trust assets, or might fail to keep investments properly under review, or might invest in assets not authorised by the trust terms, or might disburse money to recipients who are not entitled to receive it, or might commit any number of other breaches of duty. Where a breach involves trust property being wrongly paid away by the trustees, the beneficiaries may seek to recover that property or its traceable substitutes. These proprietary claims will be dealt with in Ch.26. In this chapter, we discuss the personal claims that may be brought against trustees who breach their duties.   **24–001**

A trustee who fails to comply with her duties is liable to make good the loss to the trust estate. In this way liability is compensatory, and most of the discussion that follows will concern compensatory remedies. However, it must also be remembered that an express trustee owes a fiduciary obligation not to make an unauthorised profit from her position. The disgorgement of any profit can be effected through the proprietary mechanism of a constructive trust or through the personal award of an account of profits.[1] We have seen that a claimant must elect between compensatory and gain-based remedies if both are available on the same facts.[2]

A. General[3]

24–002 **i. Liability is Personal, not Vicarious.** A trustee is liable for her own breaches and not for those of her co-trustees.[4] The dividing line however is extremely difficult to draw; for if there is a breach by a co-trustee, the trustee may herself be at fault by leaving the matter in the hands of a co-trustee without inquiry, or for standing by while a breach of trust is being committed,[5] or for allowing trust funds to remain in the sole control of a co-trustee, or for failing to take steps to obtain redress on becoming aware of a breach of trust.

24–003 **ii. Breaches before Appointment.** A trustee is not liable for breaches of trust committed before her appointment in the absence of evidence indicating a breach of trust.[6] On appointment, however, she should examine the books and documents relating to the trust, and should ensure that the trust property is vested in her. If in the course of her inquiries she discovers a breach of trust, she should take steps against the former trustees; unless for some reason she can show that such proceedings would have been useless.[7]

24–004 **iii. Breaches after Retirement.** A trustee remains liable after retirement for breaches committed during her office, and similarly her estate remains liable after her death. She may however have been released by the other trustees, or by the beneficiaries if they are of full capacity and in possession of all the facts. She will not usually be liable in respect of breaches committed after retirement; but may be if she retired in order to facilitate a breach of trust.[8]

24–005 **iv. Trustee-Beneficiary.** Where the trustee in breach is also a beneficiary, her beneficial interest bears the loss against the other beneficiaries,[9] and, as we will see,[10] against the trustees.[11] This liability applies although the beneficial interest was acquired by her derivatively, even by purchase.[12]

---

[1] Above, para.22–026 and following.
[2] *Tang Man Sit (Personal Representatives) v Capacious Investments Ltd* [1996] 1 A.C. 514; above, para.22–025.
[3] See P. Birks and A. Pretto (eds), *Breach of Trust* (Oxford: Hart Publishing, 2002).
[4] *Townley v Sherborne* (1643) J. Bridg. 35 at 37–38.
[5] *Bahin v Hughes* (1886) 31 Ch.D. 390; below, para.24–023.
[6] *Re Strahan* (1856) 8 De G.M. & G. 291.
[7] *Re Forest of Dean Coal Co* (1878) 10 Ch.D. 450 at 452.
[8] *Head v Gould* [1898] 2 Ch. 250 at 272; *Re Whitehead's WT* [1971] 1 W.L.R. 833; above, para.18–032.
[9] *Re Dacre* [1915] 2 Ch. 480; [1916] 1 Ch. 344. Assignees are also bound, unless they took for value and without notice.
[10] Below, para.24–027.
[11] *Chillingworth v Chambers* [1896] 1 Ch. 685.
[12] *Re Dacre* [1915] 2 Ch. 480; [1916] 1 Ch. 344.

B. Equitable Compensation

The term "equitable compensation" is used in many senses.[13] Put at its broadest, **24–006**
it denotes any amount of money awarded to a claimant in the equity jurisdiction.
Although the name suggests a compensatory award, it has been said that
equitable compensation is payable pursuant to a defendant's liability to render an
account of profits.[14] As we shall see in Ch.25, awards of equitable compensation
have also been made in cases of knowing receipt or dishonest assistance, where
the response is not necessarily compensatory. The term is not used so broadly in
this chapter.

More narrowly, equitable compensation can refer to a compensatory award
that is available when it is shown that a defendant's breach of an equitable duty
has caused loss to the claimant. For example, in *Commonwealth Bank of
Australia v Smith*,[15] the claimants bought a pub on the recommendation of their
bank. The bank's advice in respect of the financial position of the pub was wrong,
and this amounted to a breach of fiduciary duty because the bank was also acting
for the vendors of the pub and thus in a conflicted position. The claimants were
awarded the difference between what the pub was worth and what they had paid
for it, together with interest.

In addition to the award payable in cases like *CBA v Smith*, equitable
compensation can also refer to an amount payable by a trustee following an
accounting exercise. The mechanism of the account is outlined in the next
section, but, briefly, it is a process through which the beneficiary enforces the
trustee's duties in respect of the trust. If the trustee has breached a duty, the trust
fund may be worth less than it ought to be worth. The account is taken on the
basis that the trustee did her job correctly, so the notional value of the fund is
greater than the actual value of the fund. The trustee must make up the difference
with a payment of money. Sometimes this payment of money is simply referred
to as part of the "accounting remedy", but it can also be called equitable
compensation, and will be so in this chapter.

The advantage of including both "accounting" awards and "discrete breach of
equitable duty" awards within the term "equitable compensation" is that these
two awards are closely linked in practice.[16] It is now common to claim "equitable
compensation for breach of trust", without reference to the accounting procedure.
A breach of trust that, in the past, may have been addressed by surcharging an

---

[13] It is a "category of concealed multiple reference": Meagher, Gummow and Lehane, 5th edn,
para.[23–015].

[14] *FHR European Ventures LLP v Cedar Capital Partners LLC* [2014] UKSC 45, [2015] A.C. 250 at
[6]; and see *Interactive Technology Corp Ltd v Ferster* [2017] EWHC 217 (Ch), where the proper
meaning of the term "equitable compensation" used in a court order was important.

[15] (1991) 42 F.C.R. 390. See also *Nocton v Lord Ashburton* [1914] A.C. 932. In fact the availability of
equitable compensation for breach of fiduciary duty is somewhat controversial, at least insofar as it is
not a straightforward substitute for rescission. But it now appears to be accepted in the cases. See P.
Birks, *An Introduction to the Law of Restitution* (Oxford: Oxford University Press, 1989), p.332; S.
Worthington (2000) 116 L.Q.R. 638 at 664; M. Conaglen, *Fiduciary Loyalty* (Oxford: Hart
Publishing, 2010), p.85 and following.

[16] Differences can still be seen. For example, the Limitation Act 1980 s.29(5)(a) applies to claims for
equitable compensation that are based on misapplication of trust property, but not to other claims for
equitable compensation: below, para.24–046.

account and ordering the trustee to pay the amount of the shortfall may now be addressed by simply ordering the trustee to pay equitable compensation.[17] It has recently been said by the highest authority that in such cases "the measure of compensation is ... the same as would be payable on an accounting, although the procedure is different".[18]

2.   BASIS AND MEASURE OF LIABILITY

A.   Trustee Accounting[19]

24–007   Trustee performance is traditionally ensured, and trustee breaches are traditionally addressed, through the mechanism of an account. The general principles were explained by Lewison J in *Ultraframe (UK) Ltd v Fielding*[20]:

> "The taking of an account is the means by which a beneficiary requires a trustee to justify his stewardship of trust property. The trustee must show what he has done with that property. If the beneficiary is dissatisfied with the way that a trustee has dealt with trust assets, he may surcharge or falsify the account. He surcharges the account when he alleges that the trustee has not obtained for the benefit of the trust all that he might have done, if he had exercised due care and diligence. If the allegation is proved, then the account is taken as if the trustee had received, for the benefit of the trust, what he would have received if he had exercised due care and diligence. The beneficiary falsifies the account when he alleges that the trustee has applied trust property in a way that he should not have done (e.g. by making an unauthorised investment). If the allegation is proved, then the account will be taken as if the expenditure had not been made; and as if the unauthorised investment had not formed part of the assets of the trust. Of course, if the unauthorised investment has appreciated in value, the beneficiary may choose not to falsify the account: in which case the asset will remain a trust asset and the expenditure on it will be allowed in taking the account."

An account may be a "common account", or it may be an account taken on the footing of "wilful default". The difference is that the common account is only concerned with assets that have actually been received and dealt with by the trustee. The trustee's liability to render a common account is inherent in the nature of trusteeship and does not depend on the beneficiary alleging wrongdoing.[21] If the account discloses that the trustee has made an unauthorised

---

[17] See Meagher, Gummow and Lehane, 5th edn, para.[23–030]. For an example of a breach of trust case being decided without any reference to accounting, see *Harris v Jones* [2011] EWHC 1518 (Ch) at [118] and following. See further S. Elliott (2002) 65 M.L.R. 588; C. Rickett (2003) 25 Syd. L.R. 31; J. Edelman (2010) 4 J.Eq. 122; *Halsbury's Laws of England Vol 98: Trusts and Powers*, 5th edn (2013) at [679]; *Nicholson v Morgan (No.3)* [2013] WASC 110 at [100]; C. Mitchell [2014] Conv. 211; *Agricultural Land Management Ltd v Jackson (No.2)* [2014] WASC 102 at [333] and following.
[18] *AIB Group (UK) Plc v Mark Redler & Co Solicitors* [2014] UKSC 58; [2015] A.C. 1503 at [91].
[19] Snell, para.20–003 and following.
[20] [2005] EWHC 1638 (Ch) at [1513]. See also *Pit v Cholmondeley* (1754) 2 Ves. Sen. 565 at 566; *Glazier v Australian Men's Health (No.2)* [2001] NSWSC 6 at [38]–[39] (reversed on appeal but not disagreeing on this point (2002) 54 N.S.W.L.R. 146); *Re Lehman Brothers International (Europe) (No.2)* [2009] EWHC 2141 (Ch) at [53]; *Libertarian Investments Ltd v Hall* [2013] HKCFA 93 at [168]–[172]; *AIB Group (UK) Plc v Mark Redler & Co Solicitors* [2014] UKSC 58 at [52]–[54], [90]; *Barnett v Creggy* [2016] EWCA Civ 1004; [2017] Ch. 273 at [22].
[21] *Partington v Reynolds* (1858) 4 Drew. 253. The court does have a discretion whether or not to order the account, however: *Campbell v Gillespie* [1900] 1 Ch. 225 at 229.

disbursement, the beneficiary may adopt the disbursement (if profitable),[22] or he may falsify the relevant entry in the account. The trustee is then required to replace the relevant property *in specie*, or, which is more likely, replace it with a payment of money. Traditionally, the amount of money necessary to reconstitute the fund was simply the current (i.e., judgment) value of the misapplied property.[23] This measure was implicit in the nature of a falsified account: the account was taken as if misapplied property was still in the trust fund.

If the beneficiary's complaint is instead that the trustee failed to acquire property for the trust, due to an absence of due care and diligence, then the beneficiary will seek to surcharge the account. The account will then be taken on the footing of "wilful default".[24] This type of account is "entirely grounded on misconduct",[25] and requires the beneficiary to allege that the trustee has committed a breach of duty. That alleged breach may be a failure to get the trust property in, or a failure to invest, or a failure to keep investments under review, etc. As Lord Millett NPJ said in *Libertarian Investments Ltd v Hall*[26]:

> "[If] the account is shown to be defective because it does not include property which the defendant in breach of his duty failed to obtain for the benefit of the trust, the plaintiff can surcharge the account by asking for it to be taken on the basis of 'wilful default', that is to say on the basis that the property should be treated as if the defendant had performed his duty and obtained it for the benefit of the trust. Since *ex hypothesi* the property has not been acquired, the defendant will be ordered to make good the deficiency by the payment of money, and in this case the payment of 'equitable compensation' is akin to the payment of damages as compensation for loss."

If a beneficiary is successful in an attempt to falsify or surcharge an account, the net effect will normally be that the account as taken does not tally with the funds available. The trustee will then be liable to make up the shortfall by a payment of money, which may be termed equitable compensation. In the case of a successful surcharge, as Lord Millett suggests, there is a close analogy with common law damages.[27] The surcharge will only be successful in the first place if the beneficiary can prove a breach of duty and causation of loss, and the amount of the surcharge will be the difference between what the trustee actually obtained and what a reasonable trustee acting with due care and diligence would have

24-008

---

[22] *Tang v Tang* [2017] HKCFA 3. An executor wrongly used estate money to part-fund the purchase of property. The claimants could adopt the disbursement and claim a proportionate share of the property (which of course included the increase in value).

[23] *Re Dawson* [1966] 2 N.S.W.L.R. 211.

[24] The beneficiary may also surcharge a common account, but, as the common account is only concerned with what the trustee has received, surcharging would only apply if property was received but not included in the account.

[25] *Partington v Reynolds* (1858) 4 Drew. 253 at 256.

[26] [2013] HKCFA 93 at [170].

[27] Although one difference is that any consequential loss suffered by the beneficiary cannot be addressed in the account: see J. Glister (2014) 8 J.Eq. 235. A distinction may also be drawn between breaches of equitable duties of skill and care (where the response is analogous to damages for negligence or breach of contract: see *Bartlett v Barclays Bank Trust Co Ltd (No.2)* [1980] Ch. 515; *Bristol and West Building Society v Mothew* [1998] Ch. 1) and breaches of the proscriptive fiduciary duties of loyalty. It may be that matters such as causation and foreseeability of loss are more claimant-friendly under the latter: see *Aequitas v AEFC* (2001) 19 A.C.L.C. 1006; cf. *Cassis v Kalfus (No.2)* [2004] NSWCA 315 at [99]–[113].

obtained.[28] The interesting point, however, concerns the payment that a trustee must make when a disbursement is falsified. The ability to falsify means that the beneficiary may be able to treat wrongly-disbursed property as still in the trust, and thereby avoid a loss that would have been suffered even if an unauthorised disbursement had instead been properly made. The following case is a good example.

> In *Cocker v Quayle*,[29] trustees of a marriage settlement were empowered to lend the trust assets to the husband in return for his bond. In breach of trust the trustees lent the money without taking any bond, and the husband then became bankrupt. The trust would have been in no better position even if the bond had been taken, since it would not have given any greater priority on the husband's bankruptcy than a simple claim in debt. Nonetheless, the trustees were liable to replace the trust fund.

The beneficiary can only falsify the account if the trustee has breached her duty. By definition, therefore, the trustee is at fault.[30] Nonetheless, it may still be thought surprising that a relatively innocent breach by a trustee in the early stages of what happens to be a disastrous investment can mean that the beneficiary avoids the consequences of that disastrous investment by falsifying the initial disbursement.[31] As will be seen in the discussion that follows, the proper response to this situation has been a matter of debate in recent years. The Supreme Court decision in *AIB Group (UK) Plc v Mark Redler & Co Solicitors*[32] has now confirmed that attention is to be turned towards the *consequences* of a trustee's breach. The crucial question is: What loss (if any) was caused by the breach of duty? Or, to put it another way: What would be the position if the trustee's duty had been properly performed?

B.   Modern Approach

24–009   **i.   Target Holdings**   The source of the recent controversy can be traced to the decision of the House of Lords in *Target Holdings Ltd v Redferns (A Firm)*.[33] The result of that case was undoubtedly correct, but Lord Browne-Wilkinson's reasoning has been questioned.

> A finance company, Target Holdings, agreed to lend money to Crowngate Developments to enable Crowngate to purchase two plots of land for £2 million. In fact Crowngate was participating in a fraud and the true value of the land was only £775,000.[34] In reliance on a surveyor's report prepared by another defendant, Target agreed to provide £1.7 million towards the supposed £2 million purchase price. That advance was to be secured by first legal

---

[28] *Nestlé v National Westminster Bank Plc* [1993] 1 W.L.R. 1260.

[29] (1830) 1 Russ. & M. 535. cf. the approach in the modern but similar case of *Main v Giambrone & Law (A Firm)* [2017] EWCA Civ 1193; below, para.24–013.

[30] If the trustee is not at fault then the account entry may not be falsified; e.g. if trust property is stolen without any fault on the part of the trustee and a reasonable trustee would not have insured against the theft.

[31] cf. *Youyang v Minter Ellison Morris Fletcher* (2003) 212 C.L.R. 484. See also the recent mortgage fraud cases; discussed below, para.24–039.

[32] [2014] UKSC 58.

[33] [1996] 1 A.C. 421.

[34] Under this "flipping" scam, the vendor would sell to P Ltd for £775,000, which would sell to K Ltd for £1.25 million, which in turn would sell to Crowngate for £2 million.

charges on the properties. Redferns solicitors were instructed to act for both Crowngate and Target.

Only £1.525 million of the £1.7 million loan was to be used for the purchase of the land. Target duly transferred £1.525 million to Redferns' client account, but £1.49 million was subsequently paid away in breach of trust before the proper securities were granted to Target. Those charges were eventually acquired some time later. Crowngate then defaulted on the mortgage repayments and was eventually wound up. Target sold the properties for £500,000 and claimed equitable compensation from Redferns of £990,000, being £1.49 million less the £500,000 obtained by the sale.

Target was successful before the Court of Appeal[35] but lost in the House of Lords. Lord Browne-Wilkinson, with whom the other Law Lords agreed, focused on the causation of loss rather than on the fact that the disbursements had been made without authority and in breach of trust. He said[36]:

"Target allege, and it is probably the case, that they were defrauded by third parties … to advance money on the security of the property. If there had been no breach by Redferns of their instructions and the transaction had gone through, Target would have suffered a loss in round figures of £1.2m (ie £1.7m advanced less £500,000 recovered on the realisation of the security). Such loss would have been wholly caused by the fraud of the third parties. The breach of trust committed by Redferns left Target in exactly the same position as it would have been if there had been no such breach: Target advanced the same amount of money, obtained the same security and received the same amount on the realisation of that security. In any ordinary use of words, the breach of trust by Redferns cannot be said to have caused the actual loss ultimately suffered by Target unless it can be shown that, but for the breach of trust, the transaction would not have gone through."

This focus on the causation of loss obscures the point that Redferns' initial disbursement had been made without authority. We have seen that, in cases of falsification, the fact that a disbursement could have been made correctly is not relevant; the point is that the trustee may not take credit in the account for the disbursement. That being so, why could Target not falsify the initial disbursement of £1.49 million, allow for the £500,000 received on sale, and receive their claimed £990,000? The answer to this question is, in simple terms, that Redferns fixed their mistake by eventually obtaining the proper charges. More properly, while Target could indeed falsify the initial disbursement, they were also obliged to accept the charges that Redferns acquired for them.[37] The later acquisition of these securities, being made within authority, meant that the account balanced.[38]

The result of the case—that Redferns were not liable to Target Holdings—can therefore be defended on two grounds. First, it can be said that Redferns' breach simply did not cause any loss to Target. This analysis was the basis of Lord

---

[35] [1994] 1 W.L.R. 1089.
[36] [1996] 1 A.C. 421 at 431; see also at 437, 439. In fact the early release of the money may well have been vital to the intermediate "flips" in the scheme. In that case Redferns' breach would have caused the loss, since otherwise the final transaction would not have gone through. Note that the case concerned a request for summary judgment and certain factors, such as duty-interest and duty-duty conflicts, were relevantly ignored. For the later history of the case see *Halsbury's Laws of England Vol 98: Trusts and Powers*, 5th edn (2013) at [682].
[37] P. Birks (1996) 26 U.W.A.L.R. 1 at 45–48; P. Millett (1998) 114 L.Q.R. 214 at 226; S. Elliott (2002) 65 M.L.R. 588.
[38] See M. Conaglen (2010) 4 J.Eq. 288 at 290: "the point is not that the disbursement was ever authorised, but rather that the trustee's conduct subsequent to that unauthorised disbursement was itself authorised and therefore needed to be reflected in the accounts".

Browne-Wilkinson's speech. Secondly, however, the same result can be achieved through the traditional trust accounting mechanism: although the disbursement was falsifiable, the later acquisition of the correct securities balanced the account so that no deficit remained owing.

24–010 **ii. AIB Group** Although the result in *Target Holdings* can be explained consistently with an orthodox trust accounting analysis, it remains true that Lord Browne-Wilkinson's approach focused on the causation of loss. The recent case of *AIB Group (UK) Plc v Mark Redler & Co Solicitors*[39] confirms that such a loss-focused inquiry is correct.

> AIB Group agreed to lend £3.3 million against a house valued at £4.5 million, but it naturally required a first legal charge. An existing mortgage, held by Barclays Bank, had to be redeemed. The borrowers executed a charge in favour of AIB Group, but the earlier Barclays security was never released. This was because the borrowers had two loan accounts with Barclays, with balances of £1.2 million and £300,000, but the solicitors only transferred enough money to close the first account. £300,000 was transferred to the borrowers instead of to Barclays, and despite repeated requests from the solicitors the borrowers did not return it. Thus £2.1 million was paid to the borrowers instead of the correct £1.8 million, and £1.2 million was paid to Barclays instead of the correct £1.5 million.
>
> Barclays was still owed £300,000 and so did not release its first charge. Eventually the AIB Group security was registered as a second charge. In due course the property was repossessed and sold for £1.2 million. The first £300,000 was paid to Barclays and AIB Group recovered the remaining £900,000.
>
> The solicitors' error meant that AIB Group lost £300,000, because, if the money had been disbursed correctly, Barclays would have released its mortgage and AIB Group would have recouped all of the £1.2 million sale proceeds. The solicitors admitted liability in this amount. However, AIB Group claimed equitable compensation in the amount of £2.4 million. They argued that all £3.3 million had been paid out in breach (and gave credit for the £900,000 recovered).

The solicitors, MRC, committed a clear breach of trust when they disbursed the money without properly arranging for the release of the Barclays charge. At trial,[40] the judge characterised this breach as *only* involving the £300,000 that should have been paid to Barclays but was instead paid to the borrowers. The other disbursements—£1.2 million to Barclays and £1.8 million to the borrowers—were not made in breach of trust. On appeal,[41] the Court of Appeal held that all £3.3 million had been paid away in breach of trust, but nonetheless limited AIB Group's recovery to £300,000. Although £3.3 million had been paid out in breach of trust, the only effect of that breach was that AIB Group had security worth £900,000 instead of £1.2 million. Most of AIB Group's loss was caused by the borrowers' default and the fact that the mortgaged property was worth much less than it was thought to be.

In contrast to the position in *Target Holdings*, the lenders in *AIB Group* never received the correct security. Assuming the Court of Appeal was correct that *all*

---

[39] [2014] UKSC 58; [2015] A.C. 1503; P. Davies (2015) 78 M.L.R. 681; P. Turner (2015) 74 C.L.J. 188; L. Ho (2015) 131 L.Q.R. 213; A. Televantos & L. Maniscalco [2015] Conv. 348; M. Conaglen (2016) 40 Melb.U.L.R 126.

[40] [2012] EWHC 35 (Ch) at [28]–[29], [32]–[34].

[41] [2013] EWCA Civ 45 at [40]–[43].

the money was paid out in breach of trust,[42] then, on an orthodox accounting analysis, in *AIB Group* there is no later entry in the account that would make the account balance. On the other hand, an award of £300,000 is clearly correct if the task is to identify the *consequences* of the solicitors' breach of trust, notwithstanding the point of how much money was actually paid out in breach. So, while the result in *Target Holdings* could be explained consistently with an accounting analysis, the same did not appear to be true of the Court of Appeal's decision in *AIB Group*.

The Court of Appeal's decision was upheld unanimously in the Supreme Court. Following a review of the authorities, Lord Toulson concluded[43]:   **24–011**

> "[A]bsent fraud, which might give rise to other public policy considerations that are not present in this case, it would not in my opinion be right to impose or maintain a rule that gives redress to a beneficiary for loss which would have been suffered if the trustee had properly performed its duties."

Lord Reed, giving the other reasoned judgment of the court, directly addressed the point of whether the result was consistent with accounting principles. He accepted that a wrongful disbursement could be disallowed in the trustee's account, but he also emphasised the distinction between liability and remedy.[44] A disbursement may be falsified, creating liability, but "an obligation to reconstitute the trust fund does not inexorably require a payment into the fund of the value of misapplied property".[45] Lord Reed concluded:

> "[T]he model of equitable compensation, where trust property has been misapplied, is to require the trustee to restore the trust fund to the position it would have been in if the trustee had performed his obligation. If the trust has come to an end, the trustee can be ordered to compensate the beneficiary directly. In that situation the compensation is assessed on the same basis, since it is equivalent in substance to a distribution of the trust fund. ... The measure of compensation should therefore normally be assessed at the date of trial, with the benefit of hindsight."[46]

If the solicitors in *AIB Group* had performed their obligation, the lenders would have received an additional £300,000 from the sale of the land. An award of £300,000 was therefore the appropriate remedy.

The state of the law following *Target Holdings* and *AIB Group* is clear: even in falsification cases, the courts are prepared to use hindsight to assess the consequences of a breach of trust. Sometimes, full repayment of the   **24–012**

---

[42] This is essentially a factual question that turns on the terms of the trust in question. In *AIB Group*, the point turned on a different view of the completion requirements applicable to remortgages. Lord Reed in fact preferred the view of the trial judge that only the payment of £300,000 to the borrowers instead of Barclays had been made in breach: [2014] UKSC 58 at [140]. On such an approach the outcome would be consistent with traditional accounting principles, since only that disbursement would have been unauthorised. But neither party had challenged the Court of Appeal's decision that all the money had been paid out in breach.

[43] [2014] UKSC 58 at [62] (with the agreement of Lord Neuberger, Lady Hale and Lord Wilson, and the general agreement of Lord Reed).

[44] [2014] UKSC 58 at [90].

[45] [2014] UKSC 58 at [107].

[46] [2014] UKSC 58 at [134]–[135].

wrongly-disbursed sum will still be appropriate. However, this will not be because of the nature of the accounting process; rather, it will be because the wrongful disbursement is seen as causing that amount of loss.[47] Attention is paid to the causation of loss, not to the fact of disbursement in breach.

We have seen that Lord Reed accepted the principle that a wrongful disbursement could be disallowed in an account. He went on, though, to say that the liability thus incurred must be distinguished from the remedy necessary to satisfy the liability. The one did not implicate the other. If that is indeed the correct model, it is doubtful that the notion of "falsification" now has any import beyond describing an instance of a breach of trust. As we have seen, on traditional principles falsification means that the account is taken on the basis that the misapplied property is still in the fund. It appears that, on the modern approach, falsification creates the liability to reinstate the fund to the position that it would have occupied if the trustee had performed her duty properly (which may include a properly-made disbursement from the fund).[48] These are subtly different positions.[49] The latter does not appear to say anything more than that the trustee must pay compensation for loss suffered as a result of her breach.

24–013   This shift towards a causation analysis is further shown by the recent Court of Appeal decision in *Main v Giambrone & Law (A Firm)*.[50]

> Investors in an Italian "holiday homes" property development paid deposits to a firm of solicitors, Giambrone, who practised in London and Italy. The solicitors were to hold the funds on trust pending the production by the property developers of bank loan guarantees that complied with a certain provision of Italian law. In the event, the solicitors released the trust monies to the developers in breach of trust and without the developers producing the appropriate guarantees. The development failed. Although the funds had been paid away in breach of trust, it was common ground that the investors would have been in no better position if proper bank guarantees had in fact been obtained.[51]

The defendant solicitors argued that no equitable compensation ought to be payable, since the investors would have been in the same position even with compliant guarantees. The claimant investors argued that the appropriate amount of compensation was the amount of the deposit paid away in breach of trust. The Court of Appeal found for the investors. Jackson LJ, with the agreement of Underhill and Moylan LJJ on the point, distinguished *Target Holdings* and *AIB Group* by noting that in *Main v Giambrone & Law* the solicitors were not

---

[47] See, e.g., *Main v Giambrone & Law (a firm)* [2017] EWCA Civ 1193; below, para.24–013. See generally M. Yip and J. Lee (2017) 37 L.S. 647 at 652–657.

[48] So, if the solicitors in *Target Holdings* had not eventually secured the charges, their liability would have been to reinstate the fund to the position it ought to have occupied. It ought to have included the charges. If the solicitors could not do that, the remedy would have been to pay compensation calculated on what those charges would have been worth. The charges would have been worth £500,000, since that is what the sales actually yielded. But a traditional falsification analysis would simply have taken the account on the basis that £1.49 million was still held on trust.

[49] For the view that the traditional approach to falsification still obtains, but that a "no causation" defence is now available to the trustee, see Meagher, Gummow and Lehane, 5th edn, para.[23–200]. The chapter ought to be read in full.

[50] [2017] EWCA Civ 1193; [2018] P.N.L.R. 2; P. Davies (2018) 134 L.Q.R. 165.

[51] This was because the events associated with the failure of the development did not trigger the guarantees (and would not have triggered compliant guarantees). This was "perhaps surprising": [2017] EWCA Civ 1193 at [47].

themselves required to take any positive steps to obtain the bank guarantees (in contrast to the duties of the solicitors in respect of the charges in *Target Holdings* and *AIB Group*). Instead, the duty of the solicitors in *Main v Giambrone & Law* was to do nothing until the developers produced appropriate guarantees.[52] Jackson LJ concluded[53]:

> "I would characterise the solicitors' obligation as an obligation to act as custodians of the deposit monies indefinitely. Compliant guarantees never appeared. Therefore Giambrone should have remained as custodians of the deposit monies until the preliminary contracts were rescinded, and then paid those monies back to their clients. In *Target* the plaintiff's claim failed on the 'but for' test. In the present case the claimants' claim passes the 'but for' test."

It is not clear that Jackson LJ's distinction between a duty to take positive steps and mere duty of custodianship is satisfactory; it is suggested that the proper duty on which to focus ought to be the trustee's duty to obey the terms of the trust. As one commentator has suggested, the case does not sit easily with *Target Holdings* and *AIB* Group; *Main v Giambrone & Law* may in fact be an early attempt to restrict the scope of the *AIB Group* decision.[54] In any case, *Main v Giambrone & Law* is a clear example of how the courts now use the language of causation in deciding such cases.

C. Particular Situations

Subsidiary rules applicable to particular situations will now be considered. **24–014**

i.   Purchase of Unauthorised Investments.   Most investments are authorised **24–015** for trustees,[55] so it will be rare for a trustee to make a disbursement that is properly characterised as an "unauthorised investment". A poorly-performing investment may suggest a breach of the trustee's duties relating to the selection of that investment, or in respect of keeping it under review; but the matter would be approached as the breach of one of those duties rather than as a simple unauthorised disbursement of trust money.

In the event that a trustee does make a disbursement without power (as opposed to within power but accompanied by a lack of care), the trustee will be liable for any loss incurred on the sale of that investment. Of course, the beneficiaries may adopt the unauthorised investment instead.[56]

ii.   Improper Retention of Investments.   A trustee who improperly retains an **24–016** investment is liable for the difference between the present value (or selling price) and the price which it would have raised if it had been sold at the proper time. How hard this can be on a trustee holding property in a falling market is shown

---

[52] [2017] EWCA Civ 1193 at [60]–[61].
[53] [2017] EWCA Civ 1193 at [62]–[63].
[54] P. Davies (2018) 134 L.Q.R. 165 at 167.
[55] See above, para.19–014.
[56] *Re Jenkin's and Randall's Contract* [1903] 2 Ch. 362; *Wright v Morgan* [1926] A.C. 788 at 799; *Tang v Tang* [2017] HKCFA 3.

by *Fry v Fry*[57] where trustees were liable for the difference between the price offered for a hotel in 1837 which they refused as inadequate, and the much lower price prevailing in 1859, the fall being largely due to the diversion of road traffic by the building of a railway.

A more modern example is *Ahmed v Ingram*,[58] where recipients of a share transfer that was void under the Insolvency Act 1986 s.284 were characterised as trustees who had improperly retained trust property. The recipients—who returned the shares shortly before the trial began—were made liable based on the difference between the value at return and the value that the transferor's trustee-in-bankruptcy would have realised.

We have seen that the Trustee Act 2000 s.5, following the pattern of earlier legislation, requires advice to be taken on the question of retaining investments.[59] Failure to do so will constitute a breach of the statutory duty of care.[60] However, there will be no liability if the improper retention caused no loss to the trust. In *Jeffery v Gretton*,[61] trustees of a will trust decided to retain and refurbish a valuable but dilapidated property without taking professional advice, but the repairs were sporadic and took nearly six years. Professional advice would have been to sell it in its unrepaired state in 2002, when it was worth £610,000. Although this was a breach of trust, the beneficiary's claim failed because her share of the proceeds after the eventual sale in 2008 for £885,000 was more than she would have received if the property had been sold in 2002 and her share invested. It was "a case of a thoughtless breach of trust that happens to have turned out well".[62]

24–017 **iii. Improper Sale of Authorised Investments.**   When an authorised investment is improperly sold, the beneficiaries may require the trustees either to account for the proceeds of sale or to replace the investment, valued as at the date of judgment.[63] Thus where trustees sold consols (a type of government bond) and invested in an unauthorised investment, the whole matter was treated as a single transaction and the trustees were held liable to replace the consols at the higher price then prevailing.[64] This is so even though the improper investment was realised without loss.[65]

---

[57] *Fry v Fry* (1859) 27 Beav. 144.
[58] [2018] EWCA Civ 519. Query whether recipients of a void transfer ought to be seen as bailees rather than trustees, and compare the analysis in *Jones (FC) & Sons (Trustee) v Jones* [1997] Ch. 159; below, para.26–005. On the calculation of loss, see further J. Glister [2014] L.M.C.L.Q. 511.
[59] Above, para.19–016.
[60] Trustee Act 2000 s.1; Sch.1 para.1.
[61] [2011] W.T.L.R. 809.
[62] [2011] W.T.L.R. 809 at 838.
[63] *Re Bell's Indenture* [1980] 1 W.L.R. 1217 (overruled on another point in *Dubai Aluminium Co Ltd v Salaam* [2003] 2 A.C. 366). But where the asset sold in breach of trust would have been properly sold at a later date, the trustee is liable to replace it at its value on that date, and not as at the date of judgment.
[64] *Phillipson v Gatty* (1848) 7 Hare 516.
[65] *Re Massingberd's Settlement* (1890) 63 L.T. 296.

iv. Failure to Invest. Trustees should invest within a reasonable time. Failure to do so will constitute a breach of the statutory duty of care.[66]   **24–018**

If a trustee is required to make a specific investment and fails to make any investment, and the price of the specific investment has risen, she will be liable to purchase as much of that investment as would have been purchased at the proper time.[67] Similarly if she chooses an investment other than that specified,[68] profit in the unauthorised investment being surrendered, of course, to the trust.[69] Where, as is nearly always the case in practice, the trustees may select investments at their discretion, it is not practicable to base recovery upon the price of a particular investment. The beneficiary will be entitled to any difference between the actual value of the trust fund and the value which a prudent trustee is likely to have achieved (by considering the average performance of ordinary shares during the period in question).[70]

v. Employment of Trust Fund in Trade. A trustee who employs trust funds in her trade or business is liable to account for the profits she makes,[71] or for the sums involved with interest, whichever is the greater. Difficult questions arise when she employs a mixed fund, being partly her own and partly trust money. Here the rule is that the beneficiaries may claim a proportionate share of the profits[72] or demand the return of the trust money with interest.[73]   **24–019**

vi. Interest.   **24–020**

> "It is well established in equity that a trustee who in breach of trust misapplies trust funds will be liable not only to replace the misapplied principal fund but to do so with interest from the date of the misapplication. This is on the notional ground that the money so applied was in fact the trustee's own money and that he has retained the misapplied trust money in his own hands and used it for his own purposes. Where a trustee has retained trust money in his own hands, he will be accountable for the profit which he has made or which he is assumed to have made with the use of the money. ... The defaulting trustee is normally charged with simple interest only,[74] but if it is established that he has used the money in trade he may be charged compound interest. ... Precisely similar equitable principles apply to an agent who has retained monies of his principal in his hands and used them for his own purposes."[75]

---

[66] Trustee Act 2000 s.1; Sch.1 para.1.

[67] *Byrchall v Bradford* (1822) 6 Madd. 235; *Robinson v Robinson* (1851) 1 De G.M. & G. 247.

[68] *Pride v Fooks* (1840) 2 Beav. 430.

[69] Below, para.24–021.

[70] *Nestlé v National Westminster Bank Plc* [1993] 1 W.L.R. 1260.

[71] *Re Davis* [1902] 2 Ch. 314; *Re Jarvis* [1958] 1 W.L.R. 815.

[72] Below, para.26–016.

[73] *Heathcote v Hulme* (1819) 1 Jac. & W. 122.

[74] *Belmont Finance Corp Ltd v Williams Furniture Ltd (No.2)* [1980] 1 All E.R. 393.

[75] *Burdick v Garrick* (1870) 5 Ch.App. 233. *Wallersteiner v Moir (No.2)* [1975] Q.B. 373 at 397; *Guardian Ocean Cargoes Ltd v Banco do Brasil (No.3)* [1992] 2 Lloyd's Rep. 193 (presumed used in investment business); *Mathew v TM Sutton Ltd* [1994] 1 W.L.R. 1455; cf. *O'Sullivan v Management Agency and Music Ltd* [1985] Q.B. 428; W. Bishop and D. Prentice (1986) 49 M.L.R. 118, above, para.22–005 (simple interest where profits used in trade, but trade benefited claimant, being in the nature of a joint venture).

If the trustee or agent has received a sum in excess of what the court would impose, he is accountable for what he has actually received, or the beneficiaries may adopt the investment.[76]

The rate of interest, and the choice between simple and compound,[77] is in the discretion of the court. The 19th century cases laid down four per cent[78] as the general rule, with an increase to five per cent where the trustee or other fiduciary was guilty of fraud[79] or active misconduct,[80] at any rate where the fraud or misconduct involved a profit for the trustee,[81] or where he ought to have received more than four per cent.[82]

In time these rates became out of line with commercial interest rates, which were considerably higher (although commercial interest rates have themselves become very low in recent years). More modern decisions have charged one per cent above the London clearing banks' base rate in force at the time[83]; or that allowed from time to time on the court's short-term investment account[84] (now called the court special account).[85] Compound interest is charged where that fairly represents what the trustee may reasonably be treated as having received,[86] or where there is a duty to accumulate,[87] and sometimes in cases of fraud or misconduct.[88] The traditional view, as mentioned above, has been that compound interest is awarded where the action is for disgorgement of profits but not in cases of compensation for loss. But the distinction is difficult to justify, since it is clear that simple interest does not adequately compensate a claimant for being out of his money.

The question which arose in *Westdeutsche Landesbank Girozentrale v Islington LBC*[89] was whether the equitable jurisdiction to award compound interest could be invoked in a common law personal action. The House of Lords, by a majority, held that it could not. Their Lordships revisited the matter in

---

[76] *Re Jenkins' and Randalls' Contract* [1903] 2 Ch. 362; *Wright v Morgan* [1926] A.C. 788 at 799.

[77] With yearly rests (*Jones v Foxall* (1852) 15 Beav. 388 at 393; *Guardian Ocean Cargoes Ltd v Banco do Brasil (No.3)* [1992] 2 Lloyd's Rep. 193; *El Ajou v Dollar Land Holdings Plc (No.2)* [1995] 2 All E.R. 213); and sometimes half-yearly rests (*Re Emmet's Estate* (1881) 17 Ch.D. 142).

[78] *Attorney General v Alford* (1855) 4 De G.M. & G. 843; *Fletcher v Green* (1864) 33 Beav. 426 at 430.

[79] *Attorney General v Alford* (1855) 4 De G.M. & G. 843 at 852.

[80] *Jones v Foxall* (1852) 15 Beav. 388 at 393; *Gordon v Gonda* [1955] 1 W.L.R. 885.

[81] S. Elliott [2001] Conv. 313.

[82] *Jones v Foxall* (1852) 15 Beav. 388 (calling in a mortgage which was returning 5%); see *Re Waterman's WT* [1952] 2 All E.R. 1054.

[83] *Wallersteiner v Moir (No.2)* [1975] Q.B. 373; JTF [1982] Conv. 93; *Belmont Finance Corp v Williams Furniture Ltd (No.2)* [1980] 1 All E.R. 393; *O'Sullivan v Management Agency and Music Ltd* [1985] Q.B. 428; *Guardian Ocean Cargoes Ltd v Banco do Brasil (No.3)* [1992] 2 Lloyd's Rep. 193 (1% above New York prime rate); *Rama v Millar* [1996] 1 N.Z.L.R. 257; *Re Duckwari Plc (No.2)* [1999] Ch. 268.

[84] *Bartlett v Barclays Bank Trust Co Ltd (No.2)* [1980] Ch. 515; cf. *Re Evans* [1999] 2 All E.R. 777 (lower rate of 8% against non-professional administrator in times of "more gentle" inflation). For discussion see S. Elliott [2001] Conv. 313.

[85] See The Court Funds Rules 2011 r.11. The current interest rate on the special account is 0.5%.

[86] *Wallersteiner v Moir (No.2)* [1975] Q.B. 373.

[87] *Re Emmet's Estate* (1881) 17 Ch.D. 142.

[88] *Jones v Foxall* (1852) 15 Beav. 388; *Gordon v Gonda* [1955] 1 W.L.R. 885; cf. *O'Sullivan v Management Agency and Music Ltd* [1985] Q.B. 428. As to costs, see Snell, para.30–021.

[89] [1996] A.C. 669.

Sempra Metals Ltd (formerly Metallgesellschaft Ltd) v IRC,[90] where the question was whether the court had jurisdiction to award compound interest in a common law claim for restitution. It had been conceded before the House of Lords in *Westdeutsche Landesbank* that no interest, compound or simple, was recoverable at common law in such a case, although either type could sometimes be recovered in equity. As the point had not been argued in the earlier case, their Lordships were free to re-examine the matter and held (by a majority) that compound interest could be awarded in the exercise of the common law restitutionary jurisdiction in appropriate circumstances. It is thus no longer necessary to consider whether equity should supplement the common law remedies to achieve full restitution.

vii. Profit in One Transaction; Loss in Another.   The general rule is that **24–021** any gains made out of the trust property belong to the beneficiaries while a loss incurred by reason of a breach of trust must be made good by the trustee. A trustee cannot set off a gain in one transaction against a loss made in another unauthorised transaction.

> In *Dimes v Scott*[91] trustees retained an unauthorised mortgage returning 10% all of which was paid to the tenant for life. When the mortgage was paid off, trustees were able to purchase more consols than they would have done if the reinvestment had taken place at the end of a year from the testator's death. Lord Lyndhurst held the trustees liable for the excess interest paid to the tenant for life[92] over that which would have been payable if the capital of the unauthorised investment had been invested in consols at the end of a year from the testator's death, and the trustees were unable to set off against this the gain arising from the fall in the price of consols.

The rule is harsh though logical. It has not been applied where the court finds that the gain and loss were part of the same transaction. There is often difficulty in determining whether the matter should or should not be regarded as a single transaction.

> In *Fletcher v Green*[93] trust money was lent on mortgage to a firm of which one trustee was a partner. The trustees reclaimed the money; the security was sold at a loss and the proceeds paid into court and invested in consols. The question was whether the trustees' accounts should credit them with the amount of the proceeds of sale or with the value of the consols, which had risen in price. They were held entitled to take advantage of the rise. No reasons were given. The case is usually explained on the ground that the whole matter was treated as one transaction. If that is so, they should logically have been at risk in relation to a possible fall in the price of consols; the trustees can hardly be allowed to take advantage of a rise but not the burden of a fall; but it would be hard on the trustees if they have to run the risk of loss on an investment made by the court.

---

[90] [2008] 1 A.C. 561; G. Virgo (2007) 66 C.L.J. 510; C. Nicholl (2008) 124 L.Q.R. 199; C. Mitchell (2008) 71 M.L.R. 290. See also *Hungerfords v Walker* (1989) 171 C.L.R. 125.

[91] (1828) 4 Russ. 195.

[92] The tenant for life was entitled only to 4% under the (now former) rule in *Howe v Earl of Dartmouth* (1802) 7 Ves.Jr. 137; above, para.20–002.

[93] (1864) 33 Beav. 426. See also *Hulbert v Avens* [2003] W.T.L.R. 387 (trustees entitled to offset interest on trust money which would not have been earned but for the breach).

The difficulty of laying down a clear rule was recognised in *Bartlett v Barclays Bank Trust Co Ltd (No.1)*[94] where the defendant bank was held liable as trustee for failing to exercise proper supervision of the board of directors of a private company whose shares were almost wholly owned by the trust. The board embarked on speculative ventures in property development: the Old Bailey project was a disaster; the Guildford project was a success. In finding the bank liable, Brightman J allowed the gain on the Guildford project to be set off against the Old Bailey. Without considering the cases in detail, he said,[95] after recognising the general rule:

> "The relevant cases are, however, not altogether easy to reconcile. All are centenarians and none is quite like the present. ... I think it would be unjust to deprive the bank of the element of salvage in the course of assessing the cost of the shipwreck."

Thus a gain can be set off against a loss if, even though not arising from the same transaction, they resulted from the same wrongful course of conduct; in the present case a policy of speculative investment.

3. LIABILITY INTER SE: CONTRIBUTION AND INDEMNITY

A. Joint and Several Liability

24–022   As we have seen, liability for breach of trust is personal and not vicarious.[96] However, where two or more trustees are liable for a breach of trust, their liability is joint and several. Thus a beneficiary may claim the whole loss by suing all or some or any one of those who are liable; and may levy execution for the whole sum against any one.[97]

B. Contribution

24–023   The rule used to be that the joint liability of trustees required an equal sharing of the liability, regardless of fault, and therefore that one trustee who had paid more than his share of the liability for a breach of trust was entitled to equal contribution from the other trustees who were also liable[98]; or from their estates after death.[99] The effect of this rule was shown dramatically in *Bahin v Hughes*,[100] where the Court of Appeal held that a passive trustee was liable with the active trustee. Cotton LJ said[101]:

---

[94] [1980] Ch. 515; above, para.19–022.
[95] [1980] Ch. 515 at 538.
[96] Above, para.24–002.
[97] *Fletcher v Green* (1864) 33 Beav. 426 at 430.
[98] *Fletcher v Green* (1864) 33 Beav. 426; *Ramskill v Edwards* (1885) 31 Ch.D. 100; *Robinson v Harkin* [1896] 2 Ch. 415.
[99] *Jackson v Dickinson* [1903] 1 Ch. 947.
[100] (1886) 31 Ch.D. 390; *Bishopsgate Investment Management Ltd v Maxwell (No.2)* [1994] 1 All E.R. 261 (no defence that blindly followed co-director's lead).
[101] (1886) 31 Ch.D. 390 at 396.

"Miss Hughes was the active trustee and Mr Edwards did nothing, and in my opinion it would be laying down a wrong rule to hold that where one trustee acts honestly, though erroneously, the other trustee is to be held entitled to indemnity who by doing nothing neglects his duty more than the acting trustee."

Although liability may still be equally shared,[102] the Civil Liability (Contribution) Act 1978 gives the court a discretion in relation to the amount to be recovered against two or more defendants who are liable in respect of the damage. The amount recoverable against any defendant shall be "such as may be found by the court to be just and equitable having regard to the extent of that person's responsibility for the damage in question",[103] and includes breach of trust as one of the forms of liability to which the Act applies.[104]

C.   Indemnity

There are a few cases where one trustee is not liable to contribute; that is, where he is entitled to an indemnity from his co-trustee against his own liability. Such cases are rare, for such relief: **24–024**

"would act as an opiate upon the consciences of the trustees; so that instead of the *cestui que trust* having the benefit of several acting trustees, each trustee would be looking to the other or others for a right of indemnity, and so neglect the performance of his duties."[105]

The situations are as set out below. The Civil Liability (Contribution) Act 1978 appears not to apply to these situations,[106] so they remain to be applied according to the general law.

i.   Fraud.   If one trustee alone has acted fraudulently, such as by misappropriating the trust money, the other will be entitled to an indemnity.[107] Of course, in some cases where one trustee alone is fraudulent, the other will not be liable at all, and so no question of contribution or indemnity will arise.[108] If all are fraudulent the rule used to be that the one who has paid the damages could not claim contribution from the others,[109] but this was because a claimant should not base a claim upon his wrong and not because the other trustees were entitled to indemnities. As these situations do not concern indemnities, the Civil Liability   **24–025**

---

[102] See *Brudenell-Bruce v Moore* [2014] EWHC 3679 (Ch) at [178].

[103] s.2(1). This may extend to a complete indemnity; s.2(2). See generally C. Mitchell [1997] 5 R.L.R. 27.

[104] s.6(1). See *Dubai Aluminium Co Ltd v Salaam* [2003] 2 A.C. 366; C. Mitchell (2003) 119 L.Q.R. 364; *Charter Plc v City Index Ltd* [2008] Ch. 313; G. Virgo (2008) 67 C.L.J. 254; *Purrunsing v A'Court & Co (A Firm)* [2016] EWHC 789 (Ch); [2016] 4 W.L.R. 81 at [62]–[67].

[105] *Bahin v Hughes* (1886) 31 Ch.D. 390 at 398, per Fry LJ.

[106] s.7(3); Law Commission Report on Contribution, No. 79 (1977), para.26. Even if the Act does apply, s.2(2) provides that contribution may amount to a complete indemnity, and on this the court would be guided by the general law.

[107] *Bahin v Hughes* (1886) 31 Ch.D. 390 at 395; *Thompson v Finch* (1856) 25 L.J.Ch. 681 (where trustee also a solicitor).

[108] *Re Smith* [1896] 1 Ch. 71 was an exceptional case of two trustees who acted together, but only one of whom was liable to the beneficiaries for the consequences. One trustee had chosen an investment honestly but the other had received a bribe in order to induce him to make it.

[109] *Attorney General v Wilson* (1840) Cr. & Ph. 1 at 28.

(Contribution) Act 1978 applies. No specific provision is made in that Act for the apportionment of liability among fraudsters.[110]

24–026 **ii. Solicitor and Trustee.**   Many of the cases of indemnity are cases where one trustee is a solicitor and has exercised such a controlling influence that the other trustee has been unable to exercise an independent judgment.[111] There is no rule, however, that:

> "a man is bound to indemnify his co-trustee against loss merely because he was a solicitor, when that co-trustee was an active participator in the breach of trust complained of, and is not proved to have participated merely in consequence of the advice and control of the solicitor."[112]

24–027 **iii. Beneficiary-Trustee.**   When a person who is a trustee and beneficiary participates in a breach of trust, he may not claim any share of the trust estate until he has made good his liability as trustee.[113] He will be required to indemnify his co-trustee to the extent of his beneficial interest; but this does not take away his right to contribution from his co-trustee. The rule in *Chillingworth v Chambers*[114] effects a compromise between these rules. A beneficiary-trustee must indemnify his co-trustee to the extent of his beneficial interest. That property is taken first to meet the claims; after that, their liability is shared equally. The non-beneficiary trustee is thus given a partial indemnity; partial in that it extends only to the value of the beneficiary-trustee's interest.

4.   CRIMINAL LIABILITY[115]

24–028 Breach of trust was not, at common law, a crime at all. The trustee was regarded as the owner of the trust property by the common law, which disregarded the rights of the beneficiary. But in 1857 breach of trust was made a statutory crime, and the law on the subject was incorporated in the Larceny Acts 1861 and 1916.

These Acts were repealed and replaced by the Theft Act 1968, which defines "theft" as the dishonest appropriation of property "belonging to another" with the intention of depriving the other of it permanently. By s.5(2) of the Act, "any person having a right to enforce the trust" is regarded as a person to whom the subject-matter of the trust "belongs" so that the criminal liability of trustees is in this way brought within the general law.[116] The objects of a discretionary trust can presumably be regarded as having a sufficient right of enforcement to bring

---

[110] See *K v P* [1993] Ch. 140 (although not a case on trustees).

[111] *Re Partington* (1887) 57 L.T. 654.

[112] *Head v Gould* [1898] 2 Ch. 250 at 265, per Kekewich J; above, para.18–007; *Lockhart v Reilly* (1856) 25 L.J. Ch. 697; *Re Turner* [1897] 1 Ch. 536 (involving two trustees, one a solicitor and one a linendraper).

[113] *Re Rhodesia Goldfields Ltd* [1910] 1 Ch. 239; *Selangor United Rubber Estates Ltd v Cradock (No.4)* [1969] 3 All E.R. 965.

[114] [1896] 1 Ch. 685; similarly if he becomes a beneficiary after the date of the breach, *Evans v Benyon* (1887) 37 Ch.D. 329, at 344.

[115] R. Brazier (1975) 39 Conv.(N.S.) 29.

[116] See *Re Attorney General's Reference (No.1 of 1985)* [1986] Q.B. 491; *R. v Clowes (No.2)* [1994] 2 All E.R. 316 (misappropriation of money held on trust for investors was theft).

s.5(2) into operation for such trusts. Section 4(2)(a) also brings within the definition of "theft" an appropriation by a trustee of "land or anything forming part of it," and s.2(1)(c) makes a trustee guilty of theft if he appropriates property though he believes that the equitable owners cannot be discovered.

The Fraud Act 2006 s.4 introduced a new criminal offence of fraud by abuse of position, which will be committed by a trustee who acts dishonestly for his own gain when occupying "a position in which he is expected to safeguard, or not to act against, the financial interests of another person".

5. PROTECTION OF TRUSTEES

A trustee who has committed a breach of trust may be able to escape personal **24–029** liability by bringing the case within one of the categories discussed below. Many of the relevant points arose in *Re Pauling's Settlement Trusts*.[117]

> The children of the Younghusband family sued to recover from the trustees of their mother's marriage settlement various payments which were alleged to have been made in breach of trust. The Younghusbands were often in financial difficulties. Their main source of money was Mrs Younghusband's marriage settlement under which she was tenant for life. The trustees had power, with her consent, to advance up to one-half of the presumptive share of each child in the trust fund. Several advances were made under this power to the children when they had attained ages varying from 27 (Francis) to 21 (Ann and Anthony). In most cases the advances were, to the knowledge of everyone concerned, applied for family purposes and usually towards the reduction of Mrs Younghusband's overdraft. On several occasions, but not on all, independent legal advice was obtained. The trustees relied on the consent and acquiescence of the advanced beneficiaries, and claimed an indemnity under the Trustee Act 1925 s.62, and asked for relief under s.61. Several of the payments were held to be in breach of trust and the defences set up by the trustees are considered in the following sections.

A. Participation in, or Consent to, a Breach of Trust[118]

A beneficiary who has participated in, or consented to, a breach of trust may not **24–030** sue. "It is clear to us," said Willmer LJ in *Re Pauling's Settlement Trusts*,[119]

> "that if the [trustee] can establish a valid request or consent by the advanced beneficiary to the advance in question, that is a good defence on the part of the [trustee] to the beneficiary's claim, even though it be plain that the advance was made in breach of trust."

A reversioner is not "less capable of giving ... assent when his interest is in reversion than when it is in possession,"[120] but he will not be treated as having given consent wherever he fails to take steps to remedy a breach of trust of which he has knowledge.[121]

---

[117] [1964] Ch. 303.

[118] See generally J. Payne in P. Birks and A. Pretto (eds), *Breach of Trust* (2002), Ch.10.

[119] [1964] Ch. 303, at 335; *Re Bucks Constabulary Widows' and Orphans' Fund Friendly Society (No.2)* [1979] 1 W.L.R. 936 at 955; *Allan v Rea Bros Trustees Ltd* [2002] W.T.L.R. 625.

[120] *Life Association of Scotland v Siddal* (1861) 3 De G.F. & J. 58 at 73.

[121] *Life Association of Scotland v Siddal* (1861) 3 De G.F. & J. 58.

24-031 **i. Knowledge.**   Consent is not a mere formality. It is a judgment upon the propriety of the proposed transaction.[122] For, if mere knowledge and a passive assent constituted consent, then a trustee could always escape liability by informing a beneficiary of what she proposed to do. The consent must be given by an adult of full capacity in circumstances in which he had a free choice. However, a child beneficiary may exceptionally be taken to have assented to a breach, for instance where he fraudulently misstated his age[123]:

> "The court has to consider all the circumstances in which the concurrence of the *cestui que trust* was given with a view to seeing whether it is fair and equitable that, having given his concurrence, he should afterwards turn around and sue the trustees: that, subject to this, it is not necessary that he should know what he is concurring in is a breach of trust, provided that he fully understands what he is concurring in, and that it is not necessary that he should himself have directly benefited by the breach of trust."[124]

Thus a beneficiary, who otherwise had a right to set aside a sale, was unable to do so when he had affirmed the sale, accepted part of the purchase money, and caused the purchaser to embark upon further liabilities which he could not repay.[125]

24-032 **ii. Benefit.**   It is not necessary that the beneficiary should have been motivated to derive a personal benefit from the breach, nor that he actually received one.[126] Where a beneficiary may recover even though he has received a benefit he must give credit for any benefit which he has received from the breach.[127]

24-033 **iii. Freedom of Decision.**   The decision must be freely taken by a person not under disability. Even where the beneficiary is an adult of full capacity, it may be possible to show that the consent was due to undue influence. Thus, in *Re Pauling*,[128] the advancements were in each case delayed until the child had become 21; but several of the payments which had been made to, or indirectly for, the benefit of the parents were presumed to have been the result of undue influence exercised by them over the children. Indeed it was clear that the advances were all made to meet the financial needs of the father. The Court of Appeal refused to accept the trustees' argument that undue influence was only relevant as between the children and their parents where the parents had acquired the benefit; they suggested that:

---

[122] *Re Massingberd's Settlement* (1890) 63 L.T. 296 at 299.
[123] See *Overton v Banister* (1884) 3 Hare 503.
[124] *Re Pauling's ST* [1962] 1 W.L.R. 86 at 108, per Wilberforce J, accepted by counsel in the Court of Appeal but not commented on by the court [1964] Ch. 303 at 339; approved in *Holder v Holder* [1968] Ch. 353 at 394, 399, 406. See also *Jeffery v Gretton* [2011] W.T.L.R. 809; *Pullan v Wilson* [2014] EWHC 126 (Ch) at [29]; *Brudenell-Bruce v Moore* [2014] EWHC 3679 (Ch) at [195].
[125] *Holder v Holder* [1968] Ch. 353.
[126] *Fletcher v Collis* [1905] 2 Ch. 24; *Allan v Rea Bros Trustees Ltd* [2002] W.T.L.R. 625.
[127] *Re Pauling's ST* [1964] Ch. 303. (The £300 received by Ann; and the policies received by Francis and George).
[128] [1964] Ch. 303.

> "[A] trustee carrying out a transaction in breach of trust may be liable if he knew, or ought to have known, that the beneficiary was acting under the undue influence of another, or may be presumed to have done so, but will not be liable if it cannot be established that he so knew, or ought to have known."[129]

It is impossible to say how long after the attainment of majority the presumption continues; this depends upon the circumstances of each case.[130]

B. Release and Acquiescence[131]

These defences relate to the conduct of the beneficiary after the breach has taken place; where they apply, they become equivalent to retrospective consent. A release may be, but need not be, formal; it may be inferred from conduct, as where a beneficiary accepted benefits under his mother's will which prohibited him from setting up any claim in respect of the administration of his father's estate.[132] Length of time in making a claim will not of itself be fatal, but will assist the trustee by requiring less evidence to establish a release.[133] Many of the points raised in connection with consent apply also here:

24–034

> "I ... agree that either concurrence in the act, or acquiescence without original concurrence, will release the trustees; but that is only a general rule, and the Court must inquire into the circumstances which induced concurrence or acquiescence."[134]

There will be no release for the trustees where the beneficiary acquiesced without knowledge of the facts; but, as with consent, it is not necessary that the beneficiary should have been aware of his legal rights.[135]

C. Impounding the Beneficiary's Interest: Trustee Act 1925 Section 62

i. Inherent Power. Independently of the Trustee Act 1925 s.62, the court has power to impound the interest of a beneficiary who has instigated or requested a breach of trust. The impounding of the beneficiary's interest means that it will be applied so far as it will go towards providing an indemnity to the trustee. The trustee must show that the beneficiary acted with knowledge of the facts,

24–035

---

[129] [1964] Ch. 303 at 338.

[130] *Huguenin v Baseley* (1807) 14 Ves.Jr. 273; *Allcard v Skinner* (1887) 36 Ch.D. 145 at 171.

[131] See generally J. Payne in P. Birks and A. Pretto (eds), *Breach of Trust* (2002), Ch.10; S. Degeling in P.S. Davies, S. Douglas and J. Goudkamp (eds), *Defences in Equity* (Oxford: Hart Publishing, 2018), Ch.6.

[132] *Egg v Devey* (1847) 10 Beav. 444. *Brudenell-Bruce v Moore* [2014] EWHC 3679 (Ch) at [197] (beneficiary acquiesced in the trustees allowing a relative of the beneficiary to live rent-free in a cottage).

[133] *Stackhouse v Barnston* (1805) 10 Ves.Jr. 453; *Life Association of Scotland v Siddall* (1861) 3 De G.F. & J. 58 at 77.

[134] *Walker v Symonds* (1818) 3 Swans. 1 at 64, per Lord Eldon; *Stackhouse v Barnston* (1805) 10 Ves.Jr. 453.

[135] *Holder v Holder* [1968] Ch. 353.

although she may not have known that these amounted to a breach of trust.[136] If the beneficiary instigated or requested the breach, it is not necessary to show that the beneficiary received a benefit[137]; but where a beneficiary merely concurred in or consented to a breach of trust, it seems necessary that a benefit be shown.[138] The trustee, as has been seen, is protected against an action from the consenting beneficiary in respect of the breach.

24–036   **ii.   Trustee Act 1925 Section 62.**   Section 62 extends this jurisdiction,[139] permitting the court to make an impounding order regardless of any question of benefit. As will be seen, consent, if it is to be effective, must be in writing.[140] Section 62(1) reads as follows:

> "Where a trustee commits a breach of trust at the instigation or request or with the consent in writing of a beneficiary, the court may, if it thinks fit, … make such order as to the court seems just, for impounding all or any part of the interest of the beneficiary in the trust estate by way of indemnity to the trustee or persons claiming through him."

The effect of an impounding order is not only that the beneficiary is unable to sue the trustee, but also that the liability to make up losses suffered by other beneficiaries will fall on her, rather than on the trustee. The liability cannot, however, be for a greater sum than the subsisting value of her own interest in the trust, and it is subject to the discretion of the court. The discretion is exercised in the light of the earlier cases on which s.62 is founded,[141] and generally speaking an indemnity will be given to a trustee against a beneficiary who has been at all active in inducing a breach. Again, however, the knowledge of the beneficiary must amount to a definite appreciation of what is being done. In *Re Somerset*,[142] an impounding order was refused to trustees who had invested trust funds on a mortgage of a particular property at the instigation of a beneficiary, since the beneficiary had no intention of being a party to a breach, which occurred only because the loan exceeded the authorised limit. He had left it entirely to the trustees to determine how much money to lend on the security.

The principle applies to a beneficiary who only becomes entitled to a beneficial interest after the breach.[143] The right to indemnity by impounding is available to former trustees after their resignation or replacement. The trustees in *Re Pauling's Settlement Trusts (No.2)*[144] claimed an indemnity out of the life

---

[136] See *Hillsdown Holdings Plc v Pensions Ombudsman* [1997] 1 All E.R. 862.

[137] *Fuller v Knight* (1843) 6 Beav. 205; *Chillingworth v Chambers* [1896] 1 Ch. 685 (a trustee beneficiary).

[138] *Chillingworth v Chambers* [1896] 1 Ch. 685. It has, however, been said that, even in the case of a beneficiary who requests a breach, the indemnity is limited to the benefit received by the beneficiary: *Raby v Ridehalgh* (1855) 7 De G.M. & G. 104.

[139] *Bolton v Curre* [1895] 1 Ch. 544 at 549, per Romer J.

[140] The requirement of writing applies only to consent; per Lindley MR in *Re Somerset* [1894] 1 Ch. 231 at 265–266.

[141] *Bolton v Curre* [1895] 1 Ch. 544 at 549.

[142] [1894] 1 Ch. 231; *Mara v Browne* [1895] 2 Ch. 69; cf. *Raby v Ridehalgh* (1855) 7 De G.M. & G. 104.

[143] *Evans v Benyon* (1888) 37 Ch.D. 329.

[144] [1963] Ch. 576; *Re Bucks Constabulary Widow's and Orphans' Fund Friendly Society (No.2)* [1979] 1 W.L.R. 936 at 955.

interest of the parents of the claimants, and Wilberforce J held that they were entitled to it, and would remain so entitled, although, as was intended, they would at a future time be replaced by new trustees.

D. Statutory Relief: Trustee Act 1925 Section 61[145]

Under this section the court may excuse trustees from the consequences of a breach of trust. It reads: **24–037**

> "If it appears to the court that a trustee, … is or may be personally liable for any breach of trust … but has acted honestly and reasonably, and ought fairly to be excused for the breach of trust and for omitting to obtain the directions of the court in the matter in which he committed such breach, then the court may relieve him either wholly or partly[146] from personal liability for the same."

The jurisdiction is available where a trustee "is or may be personally liable" for a breach of trust. There is thus no need to establish the liability; indeed it would put a trustee in a strange position if he had to prove his own liability in order to obtain relief. Several cases allowing relief have done so without reaching a conclusion on the question of liability.[147] However, "may be" has been interpreted as "indicating doubt, not futurity"[148]; the court will not commit itself in advance to giving relief in the case of a future breach of trust.[149]

Assuming that actual or potential liability exists, there are two stages in the application of the section:

> "The first is for the trustee to satisfy the court that he or she has acted honestly and reasonably. If the court is so satisfied, but only if the court is so satisfied, then, secondly, the court has to decide whether the trustee ought fairly to be excused, and whether to exercise its power to relieve the trustee wholly or partly from personal liability for the breach of trust."[150]

The trustee bears the onus of showing that he acted honestly and reasonably.[151] There is little authority on honesty, since dishonest trustees do not apply for relief.[152] However, Kekewich J once characterised as dishonest "a trustee who does nothing, swallows wholesale what is said by his co-trustee, never asks for

---

[145] L. Sheridan (1955) 19 Conv.(N.S.) 420n; D. Waters [1977] *Estates and Trusts Quarterly* 12; J. Lowry and R. Edmunds in P. Birks and A. Pretto (eds), *Breach of Trust* (2002), Ch.9; P. Davies [2015] Conv. 379; M. Haley (2017) 76 C.L.J. 537; J. Lowry and R. Edmunds (2017) 133 L.Q.R. 223. The section also applies to executors; Trustee Act 1925 s.68(17). The Charity Commission may relieve charity trustees from liability under the Charities Act 2011 s.191.

[146] See *Re Evans* [1999] 2 All E.R. 777; below, para.24–038.

[147] e.g. *Re Grindey* [1898] 2 Ch. 593.

[148] (1955) 19 Conv. (N.S.) 425.

[149] *Re Tollemache* [1903] 1 Ch. 457 at 465–466; affirmed at 953; *Re Rosenthal* [1972] 1 W.L.R. 1273. The court may, however, authorise an act so as to prevent it being a breach.

[150] *Santander UK Plc v RA Legal Solicitors* [2014] EWCA Civ 183; [2014] W.T.L.R. 813 at [106]; *National Trustees Co of Australasia v General Finance Co of Australasia* [1905] A.C. 373 at 381; *Marsden v Regan* [1954] 1 W.L.R. 423 at 434.

[151] *Re Stuart* [1897] 2 Ch. 583; *Santander UK Plc v RA Legal Solicitors* [2014] EWCA Civ 183.

[152] In *Perrins v Bellamy* [1898] 2 Ch. 521 at 527, Kekewich J noted that "the Legislature has made the absence of all dishonesty a condition precedent to the relief of the trustee from liability. But that is not the grit of the section."

explanation, and accepts flimsy explanations."[153] In respect of reasonableness, the usual standard is that of a prudent person of business managing his or her own affairs.[154] In the case of professional trustees the standard will be higher.[155] Unreasonable conduct will not bar the defence if it plays no part in the occasioning of the loss.[156] Of course, compliance with the reasonableness standard may mean there is no breach at all; but it is otherwise where, for example, payment has been made to the wrong person.[157]

24–038 It is not enough that the trustee's conduct is reasonable; there is the additional requirement of "ought fairly to be excused". In *Davis v Hutchings*[158] trustees, on the distribution of the trust fund, paid the share of one beneficiary to the solicitor to the trust (employed by them) in reliance upon the solicitor's statement that he was the assignee of the share. The share had in fact been mortgaged and assigned to him subject to the mortgage. Kekewich J held that the trustees were liable to the mortgagee. They had acted honestly and reasonably in relying on the solicitor, but they should not be excused.[159] Fairness should be considered in relation to all the parties, the trustees, the beneficiaries and the creditors, and is "essentially a matter within the discretion of the judge."[160] In *Re Evans*[161] the administratrix took out insurance to cover the share of a missing beneficiary and then distributed the estate. The beneficiary appeared and claimed his share, but the insurance covered only the capital sum to which he was entitled. The administratrix relied on s.61 as a defence to his claim for interest. It was held that she had acted reasonably, but ought fairly to be excused only to the extent that the claim could not be satisfied by assets retained by her which derived from the estate.

Little seems to be added to s.61 by the reference to omitting to obtain the directions of the court:

> "I do not see how the trustee can be excused for the breach of trust without being also excused for the omission referred to, or how he can be excused for the omission without also being excused for the breach of trust."[162]

24–039 Historically, applications for relief have most commonly arisen in connection with unauthorised investments.[163] Another situation is that of payment of the

---

[153] *Re Second East Dulwich, etc., Building Society* (1899) 79 L.T. 726 at 727.

[154] *Re Grindey* [1898] 2 Ch. 593 at 601; *Re Turner* [1897] 1 Ch. 536 at 542; *Re Lord de Clifford's Estate* [1900] 2 Ch. 707 at 716; *Re Stuart* [1897] 2 Ch. 583 at 590; *Re Rosenthal* [1972] 1 W.L.R. 1273; *Jeffery v Gretton* [2011] W.T.L.R. 809.

[155] *Bartlett v Barclays Bank Trust Co Ltd (No.1)* [1980] Ch. 515.

[156] *Davisons Solicitors v Nationwide Building Society* [2012] EWCA Civ 1626 at [50]; *Santander UK Plc v RA Legal Solicitors* [2014] EWCA Civ 183 at [21], [109].

[157] Below, para.24–039.

[158] [1907] 1 Ch. 356.

[159] Some of the dicta of Kekewich J were disapproved in *Re Allsop* [1914] 1 Ch. 1 at 11, 12; see also *Marsden v Regan* [1954] 1 W.L.R. 423 at 434–435.

[160] *Marsden v Regan* [1954] 1 W.L.R. 423 at 435.

[161] [1999] 2 All E.R. 777. See also *Dreamvar (UK) Ltd v Mishcon De Reya (A Firm)* [2016] EWHC 3316 (Ch) (relief under s.61 refused because the solicitor was insured and the effect of the breach on the claimant was "disastrous"). Reasoning upheld on appeal: [2018] EWCA Civ 1082 at [110]-[111].

[162] *Perrins v Bellamy* [1898] 2 Ch. 521 at 528.

[163] *Re Turner* [1897] 1 Ch. 536; *Re Stuart* [1897] 2 Ch. 583; *Re Dive* [1909] 1 Ch. 328; *Bartlett v Barclays Bank Trust Co Ltd (No.1)* [1980] Ch. 515.

funds to the wrong beneficiary,[164] or the payment of void claims by creditors.[165] More recently, several s.61 cases have involved mortgage frauds whereby banks are tricked into financing sham house purchases.[166] While the precise facts differ, these schemes usually involve a fraudster who tricks a bank into agreeing to lend money for a house purchase. In fact there is no such purchase, but the bank nonetheless instructs a solicitor and remits the loan funds to the solicitor's client account. On "completion" of the "purchase", the bank's solicitors send the funds to the vendor's solicitors. But the vendor's solicitors (if they are solicitors) are often rogues too, and the money and the fraudsters disappear. The bank sues its solicitor for breach of trust on the grounds that the money in the client account was held on trust for the bank; that it could only be disbursed on completion; and that—the whole affair being a sham—no completion ever took place. The primary cause of the bank's loss is clearly the fraud,[167] but the solicitors have also committed a breach of trust and they can only escape liability by persuading the court to grant relief under s.61.[168] In deciding whether or not to grant relief, the court assesses the solicitors' conduct against a standard of "reasonableness not of perfection".[169] However, the incentive to keep up to best practice is a strong one.

E.   Limitation and Laches[170]

i.   Six-Year Period Under Limitation Act 1980 Section 1(3).   Subject to exceptions discussed below, the Limitation Act 1980 s.21(3), provides a six-year limitation period. The subsection reads: **24–040**

---

[164] *Re Allsop* [1914] 1 Ch. 1; *National Trustees Co of Australasia v General Finance Co of Australasia* [1905] A.C. 373; *Re Windsor Steam Coal Co* [1929] 1 Ch. 151; *Re Wightwick's WT* [1950] Ch. 260; *Re Clapham* [2006] W.T.L.R. 203.

[165] *Re Lord de Clifford's Estate* [1900] 2 Ch. 707; *Re Mackay* [1911] 1 Ch. 300; cf. *Re Windsor Steam Coal Co Ltd* [1929] 1 Ch. 151.

[166] *Lloyds TSB Bank Plc v Markandan & Uddin* [2012] EWCA Civ 65; [2012] 2 All E.R. 884; *Davisons Solicitors v Nationwide Building Society* [2012] EWCA Civ 1626; *Santander UK Plc v RA Legal Solicitors* [2014] EWCA Civ 183; *Purrunsing v A'Court & Co (A Firm)* [2016] EWHC 789 (Ch); [2016] 4 W.L.R. 81; *Dreamvar (UK) Ltd v Mishcon De Reya (A Firm)* [2016] EWHC 3316 (Ch); J. Hall (2012) 26 T.L.I. 206.

[167] *Santander UK Plc v RA Legal Solicitors* [2014] EWCA Civ 183 at [24].

[168] The solicitors cannot rely on the principles in the *AIB Group* case, discussed above, paras 24–010 and following, to limit their liability. This is because, unlike in the *AIB Group* case, the solicitors in these mortgage fraud cases could never have made authorised disbursements: see [2013] EWCA Civ 45 at 46.

[169] *Davisons Solicitors v Nationwide Building Society* [2012] EWCA Civ 1626 at [48], highlighting the difference between the solicitor's conduct in that case and in *Lloyds TSB Bank Plc v Markandan & Uddin* [2012] 2 All E.R. 884. See also *Santander UK Plc v RA Legal Solicitors* [2014] EWCA Civ 183 at [107].

[170] See J. Weeks, *Preston and Newsom on Limitation of Actions*, 4th edn (London: Longman, 1989) Ch.7; H. McLean (1989) 48 C.L.J. 472; T. Prime and G. Scanlan, *The Law of Limitation*, 2nd edn (Oxford: Oxford University Press, 2001); W. Swadling and G. Watt in P. Birks and A. Pretto (eds), *Breach of Trust* (2002), Ch.11 and Ch.12 respectively.

> "Subject to the preceding provisions of this section, an action by a beneficiary[171] to recover trust property or in respect of any breach of trust, not being an action for which a period of limitation is prescribed by any other provision of this Act, shall not be brought after the expiration of six years from the date on which the right of action accrued.
>
> For the purposes of this subsection, the right of action shall not be treated as having accrued to any beneficiary entitled to a future interest in the trust property, until the interest fell into possession."

In this subsection, "trustee" includes personal representatives[172] and also certain fiduciary agents,[173] company directors[174] and a mortgagee in respect of the proceeds of sale,[175] but not a trustee in bankruptcy,[176] nor the liquidator of a company in voluntary liquidation.[177] It will also be noted that there is no distinction between the protection given to an express trustee and that given to an implied or constructive trustee. It will be seen that the subsection only applies to cases where an action is brought by a beneficiary in respect of the trust property.[178] Under the proviso, time only begins to run against remaindermen or reversioners when their interest falls into possession; and it has been held that this does not occur when improper advancements are made in favour of remaindermen.[179] If a beneficiary is entitled to two interests in the property, one in possession and one in remainder, he does not lose a claim in respect of the latter where time has run against him in respect of the former.[180]

ii. Exceptions to the Six-Year Rule.

24-041 *(a) Limitation Act 1980 Section 21(1).* There are some exceptions to the six-year rule.

> "(1) No period of limitation prescribed by this Act shall apply to an action by a beneficiary under a trust, being an action—
>
> (a) in respect of any fraud or fraudulent breach of trust to which the trustee was a party or privy; or
>
> (b) to recover from the trustee trust property or the proceeds of trust property in the possession of the trustee, or previously received by the trustee and converted to his use.[181]"

---

[171] The section does not apply to a claim by the Attorney General against the trustee of a charitable trust, which has no "beneficiary"; *Attorney General v Cocke* [1988] Ch. 414; J. Warburton [1988] Conv. 292. For the position of beneficiaries of a discretionary trust, see D. Hayton (2010) *Trusts and Estates Law & Tax Journal* 18.

[172] Limitation Act 1980 s.38(1); TA 1925 s.68(17).

[173] *Burdick v Garrick* (1870) L.R. 5 Ch.App. 233.

[174] *Belmont Finance Corp v Williams Furniture Ltd (No.2)* [1980] 1 All E.R. 393; *Gwembe Valley Development Company Ltd v Koshy* [2004] W.T.L.R. 97; *First Subsea Ltd v Balltec Ltd* [2017] EWCA Civ 186; [2018] Ch. 25; *Burnden Holdings (UK) Ltd v Fielding* [2018] UKSC 14 at [11].

[175] *Thorne v Heard* [1895] A.C. 495.

[176] *Re Cornish* [1896] 1 Q.B. 99.

[177] *Re Windsor Steam Coal Co* [1928] Ch. 609; affirmed on other grounds [1929] 1 Ch. 151.

[178] *Re Bowden* (1890) 45 Ch.D 444 at 451. In cases not involving strict trusts, the fiduciary's principal is the beneficiary.

[179] *Re Pauling's ST* [1964] Ch. 303.

[180] *Mara v Browne* [1895] 2 Ch. 69, reversed on another point [1896] 1 Ch. 199.

[181] But where a trustee is also a beneficiary and has received his share on a distribution of the trust property, para.(b) shall only apply in respect of the excess over his share, so long as the trustee acted honestly and reasonably in making the distribution; s.21(2).

This subsection reproduces, in the situations to which it applies, the rule of permanent liability which was applicable in equity to the case of express trustees.

In *North American Land Co v Watkins*,[182] an agent had been sent to America to buy land for his company. He bought it, and it was duly conveyed to the company, but the agent made and retained a profit for himself. After the expiration of the period applicable for the recovery of money had and received, the company successfully recovered the money on two grounds, first that the agent was in the position of a trustee and had retained trust money, and secondly that this conduct had been fraudulent.

But it seems that the fraud must be that of the trustee himself. In *Thorne v Heard*,[183] a trustee was protected where he had negligently left funds in the hands of a solicitor who had embezzled them; for the trustee to come within s.21(1) he must be "party or privy" to the fraud.

The two limbs of s.21(1) are distinct, and fraud is not relevant where a trustee is in possession of the trust property, or previously received the property and converted it to his use.

24–042

> In *James v Williams*,[184] X, who was entitled to a one-third share of a house on the intestacy of Y, treated the house as his own and purported to leave it by will to Z. It was held that X had been in the position of a constructive trustee, so that an action brought against Z by one of the other intestacy beneficiaries more than 12 years after the death of Y was not barred.

> In *Re Howlett*,[185] a trustee, who was income beneficiary until remarriage, continued in possession of a wharf until he died, and the remainderman was held able to sue the life tenant's representatives after his death for an occupation rent for the premises.

Conversion to the trustee's own use requires some wrongful application in his own favour. A trustee was held to escape from the subsection where he applied the trust funds for the maintenance of a child beneficiary,[186] or where the funds were dissipated by a co-trustee.[187]

As with s.21(3), the word "trustee" in s.21(1) has a wide meaning and includes, for example, company directors.[188] However, s.21(1) cannot be relied upon where there is no relevant relationship between the parties. Thus an action against a third party who has dishonestly assisted in a breach of trust, or who has knowingly received property in breach of trust, does not fall within s.21(1)(a)

---

[182] [1904] 1 Ch. 242; [1904] 2 Ch. 233. See also *First Subsea Ltd v Balltec Ltd* [2017] EWCA Civ 186; [2018] Ch. 25 (s.21(1)(a) applied to a director; s.21(1)(b) not engaged on the facts). Permission to appeal to the Supreme Court was granted in July 2017 but at the time of writing there have been no further developments.

[183] [1894] 1 Ch. 599; [1895] A.C. 495; *Re Fountaine* [1909] 2 Ch. 382.

[184] [2000] Ch. 1; cf. *Nolan v Nolan* [2004] W.T.L.R. 1261.

[185] [1949] Ch. 767. See also *Re Sharp* [1906] 1 Ch. 793.

[186] *Re Page* [1893] 1 Ch. 304; *Re Timmis* [1902] 1 Ch. 176.

[187] *Re Fountaine* [1909] 2 Ch. 382.

[188] Directors may commit a fraudulent breach of fiduciary duty, thus engaging s.21(1)(a), or may wrongly take company property, potentially engaging s.21(1)(b). However, s.21(1)(b) is not engaged when a director merely makes a gain in breach of fiduciary duty, even though that gain may be held on constructive trust. "This is because in such cases the director is not a trustee *virtute officii* in respect of the profit": *First Subsea Ltd v Balltec Ltd* [2017] EWCA Civ 186; [2018] Ch. 25 at [59], [62].

even though such a third party has sometimes been referred to as a "constructive trustee".[189] In these cases the action must be brought within the six-year period applicable to an action for damages for fraud.

24–043 The recent case of *Burnden Holdings (UK) Ltd v Fielding*[190] concerned the proper scope of s.21(1)(b) as it applies to company directors. On assumed facts,[191] the defendant directors had wrongly caused company assets to be transferred to certain other companies in which the defendant directors held majority shareholdings. A claim was brought six years and three days after the relevant transfer, and the question was whether that claim was barred by s.21(3) or fell within the exception in s.21(1)(b).

At trial, the defendants were successful in arguing that the claim was time-barred.[192] On appeal, the Court of Appeal held that s.21(1)(b) applied. The Court accepted that the defendant directors did not personally "receive" the misdirected assets, and nor were they ever "in possession of" them. But the Court held that receipt of those assets by companies that the defendants owned and controlled sufficed to bring the claim within s.21(1)(b).[193] On further appeal, the Supreme Court upheld the decision of the Court of Appeal but for different reasons. It was not necessary to construe s.21(1)(b) as including situations where trust property was received or possessed by companies that were controlled by the wrongdoing trustee. Instead, the Supreme Court held that company property will always have been relevantly "received" by that company's directors, regardless of into whose hands it may later have fallen. Company directors do not hold legal title to company property in the way that trustees hold legal title to trust property, but if property is owned by a company at all then that company's directors will have received it for the purposes of s.21(1)(b). Lord Briggs said, for the Court:

> "[I]n the context of company property, directors are to be treated as being in possession of the trust property from the outset. It is precisely because, under the typical constitution of an English company, the directors are the fiduciary stewards of the company's property, that they are trustees within the meaning of section 21 at all. Of course, if they have misappropriated the property before action is brought by the company (the beneficiary for this purpose) to recover it they may or may not by that time still be in possession of it. But if their misappropriation of the company's property amounts to a conversion of it to their own use, they will still necessarily have previously received it, by virtue of being the fiduciary stewards of it as directors."[194]

The only remaining question was whether the defendants had converted the transferred assets to their own use. On the assumed facts, they had done so: the wrongful transfer of the asset was a conversion, and it was to the defendants' use

---

[189] *Williams v Central Bank of Nigeria* [2014] UKSC 10; [2014] A.C. 1189 at [28], [57]–[68], and the authorities there cited; discussed S. Watterson (2014) 73 C.L.J. 253; P. Davies [2014] L.M.C.L.Q. 313; J. Lee (2015) 131 L.Q.R. 39.

[190] [2018] UKSC 14.

[191] The case concerned an appeal from an application for summary judgment.

[192] At trial the claimant company did not raise the s.21(1) point; it was permitted to do so on appeal.

[193] [2016] EWCA Civ 557 at [34]–[37], relying on *In re Pantone 485 Ltd; Miller v Bain* [2002] 1 B.C.L.C. 266.

[194] [2018] UKSC 14 at [19].

because of the benefit they stood to gain by the assets being transferred to companies in which they held shareholdings.[195]

(b) Claim to the Personal Estate of a Deceased Person. Under s.22, which is **24–044** subject to s.21(1), an action in respect of any claim to the personal estate of a deceased person must be brought within the period of 12 years from the date the right to receive the interest accrued. The better view is that this is the date on which the personal representatives are first in a position to distribute the residuary estate.[196] For historical reasons, s.22 does not apply to land, as it re-enacts provisions dating from a time when realty did not vest in the personal representatives. Difficult questions on the inter-relation of this section and s.21(3) can arise where the personal representatives administering an estate would normally be treated as having become trustees. In that case the question is whether the 12-year or six-year rule is applicable.[197] It was confirmed in *Davies v Sharples*[198] that s.22 does not apply to will trusts once the administration has been completed. The section deals with failures by personal representatives to administer the estate properly, but not with breaches of trust committed by trustees of the will trust (although they may be the same persons).

(c) Sections 28 and 32. Section 28 allows an extension of the period of **24–045** limitation in cases in which the claimant has been under a disability. Section 32 provides that where any action is based upon fraud or where the right of action is concealed by fraud or where the action is for relief from the consequences of a mistake, "the period of limitation shall not begin to run until the [claimant] has discovered the fraud, concealment or mistake … or could with reasonable diligence have discovered it." This section applies to actions against trustees.[199]

(d) Section 29. Section 29 is entitled "fresh accrual of action on **24–046** acknowledgement or part payment". Its effect is to restart the limitation clock whenever an acknowledgement or part payment is made in respect of claims to which the section applies. Subsection 29(5) provides:

> "[W]here any right of action has accrued to recover
>   (a) any debt or other liquidated pecuniary claim; or
>   (b) any claim to the personal estate of a deceased person or to any share or interest in any such estate;

---

[195] [2018] UKSC 14 at [22]. The conversion was to the defendants' use because of the gain they stood to make through their ownership of recipient companies. At the same time, the Court preferred not to say that the defendants received or were in possession of the assets by virtue of their control of the recipient companies. This is a narrow but defensible distinction. Similar considerations arise in other contexts, e.g. a director's personal liability for wrongful gains that are actually made by a company the director controls: see J. Glister (2017) 40 U.N.S.W.L.J. 4.

[196] *Re Loftus* [2007] 1 W.L.R. 591.

[197] *Re Timmis* [1902] 2 Ch. 176; *Re Richardson* [1920] 1 Ch. 423; *Re Oliver* [1927] 2 Ch. 323; *Re Diplock* [1948] Ch. 465; [1951] A.C. 251.

[198] [2006] W.T.L.R. 839.

[199] See *Kitchen v RAF Association* [1958] 1 W.L.R. 563; *Bartlett v Barclays Bank Trust Co Ltd* [1980] Ch. 515 at 537.

and the person liable or accountable for the claim acknowledges the claim or makes any payment in respect of it the right shall be treated as having accrued on and not before the date of the acknowledgment or payment."

A claim for equitable compensation against a trustee based on the misapplication of trust money will fall within s.29(5)(a). However, the provision does not cover all claims based on breach of trust or fiduciary duty.

In *Barnett v Creggy*,[200] the defendant, a solicitor, was a signatory to the bank accounts of two companies that were owned by the claimants. In 1998, the defendant caused US$1.2 million to be wrongly paid out of those company bank accounts. In 2006, the defendant sent a letter to one of the claimants saying, in effect, that if the misdirected money could not be recovered then the defendant would repay it himself. In 2012, the claimants brought an action against the defendant for US$1.2 million plus interest as equitable compensation for breach of fiduciary duty.

The 2012 action would have been time-barred unless it fell within s.29(5), with the 2006 letter grounding a fresh accrual. Putting aside the question of whether the defendant's letter truly did amount to an acknowledgement,[201] the action also needed to be one "to recover [a] debt or other liquidated pecuniary claim". The Court of Appeal held that the action in the present case was not of that nature.[202] The case did not involve a trustee misapplying trust property; rather, the duty that the solicitor breached was more properly characterised as a duty of skill and care.[203] That being so, the action did not relate to a debt or other liquidated pecuniary claim, even though the amount of compensation could be easily calculated[204]:

"Had [the solicitor] been sued in a straightforward way for compensation for breach of duty under his retainer, the compensation payable would not have been a liquidated sum, even if it was capable of easy assessment. I can see no reason to reach any different conclusion just because it is possible also to categorise what is in substance the same duty leading to the same result (payment of compensation for loss suffered) as fiduciary in character."

24-047 **iii. Assignees.** A transferee from the trustee is in the same position as the trustee was,[205] unless she is a bona fide purchaser for value without notice in which case she will presumably be treated as if she had purchased from someone who was not a trustee.

---

[200] [2016] EWCA Civ 1004; [2017] Ch. 273; D. Whayman [2017] Conv. 139.

[201] David Richards J held that it did: *Barnett v Creggy* [2014] EWHC 3080 (Ch); [2015] P.N.L.R. 13 at [109]. The point was not decided on appeal.

[202] The Court was unanimous in holding that the claim in the instant case did not fall within s.29(5)(a). Etherton MR and Sales LJ thought that claims for equitable compensation based on misapplication of trust property would fall within s.29(5)(a); Patten LJ thought that no claims for equitable compensation could fall within s.29(5)(a).

[203] [2017] Ch. 273 at [35], [55]. If the duty breached was properly characterised as one of skill and care, it may be questioned whether the breach was truly a breach of *fiduciary* duty: see *Bristol and West Building Society v Mothew* [1998] Ch. 1 at 17–18.

[204] [2017] Ch. 273 at [46], per Sales LJ.

[205] See *Baker v Medway Building and Supplies Ltd* [1958] 1 W.L.R. 1216; *Eddis v Chichester Constable* [1969] 2 Ch. 345.

iv. Where No Statutory Period is Applicable. In situations not covered by **24-048** the Limitation Act 1980, it is necessary to return to the law as it existed before the statutory protection was given. No provision is made, for example, either for claims for equitable relief by way of specific performance,[206] rescission or rectification, or injunction,[207] or in cases of redemption of a mortgage of pure personalty,[208] or the setting aside of a purchase of trust property by a trustee.[209] The rule of equity is that either no period is applicable, or that the relevant common law period is applied by analogy.[210]

v. Laches. The discussion above establishes when a limitation period will **24-049** apply. It is also necessary to consider the equitable doctrine of laches, and the interaction between laches and the statutory limitation periods.[211] Laches is a doctrine whereby the court will refuse relief to a claimant who has unconscionably delayed in bringing her claim.[212] Whether such a defence is available in a particular case is a matter for the discretion of the court, and will depend to a large extent upon the hardship caused to the defendant by the delay, any effect upon third parties, and generally upon the balance of justice in granting or refusing relief.[213] It must be emphasised that laches is not just about delay and effluxion of time; something more is required to ground the defence.

It is clear that the defendant may rely on the doctrine of laches in any situation for which no statutory period of limitation applies. This is obvious in those cases where the Limitation Act simply does not cover the type of claim in question at all, but it is also the position where the Act deals with the relevant type of claim but then disapplies the normal limitation period (e.g. the breach of trust claims that fall within s.21(1) and so are not subject to the usual six-year period).[214] A more difficult question is whether laches can be raised as a defence *within* a statutory limitation period. The Act provides in s.36(2) that "Nothing in this Act shall affect any equitable jurisdiction to refuse relief on the ground of acquiescence or otherwise". This was used in *Re Loftus*[215] to hold that laches can apply to claims that fall within s.21(1), but it ought to apply to all claims covered by the statute, including those to which a statutory period applies. In *P&O Nedlloyd BV v Arab Metals Co (No.2)*,[216] Moore-Bick LJ in obiter dicta could "see no reason in principle why, in a case where a limitation period does apply,

---

[206] See *P&O Nedlloyd BV v Arab Metals Co (No.2)* [2007] 1 W.L.R. 2288.

[207] See Limitation Act 1980 s.36(1); Law Com. C.P. 151 (1998); J. Weeks, *Preston and Newsom on Limitation of Actions* (1989) para.13.103. For criticisms of the present law, see *Cia de Seguros Imperio v Heath (REBX) Ltd* [2001] 1 W.L.R. 112 at 124.

[208] *Weld v Petre* [1929] 1 Ch. 33.

[209] *Baker v Read* (1854) 18 Beav. 398; *Morse v Royal* (1806) 12 Ves.Jr. 355.

[210] Limitation Act 1980 s.36(1). See *Knox v Gye* (1872) 5 App. Cas. 656 at 674.

[211] See C. Stanley and M. Ashdown (2014) 20 T. & T. 958.

[212] *Erlanger v New Sombrero Phosphate Co* (1878) 3 App. Cass. 1218 at 1279; *Re Sharpe* [1892] 1 Ch. 154 at 168; *Nelson v Rye* [1996] 1 W.L.R. 1378 at 1392.

[213] *Lindsay Petroleum Co v Hurd* (1874) L.R. 5 P.C. 221 at 239–241; *Weld v Petre* [1929] 1 Ch. 33 at 51–52.

[214] *Re Loftus* [2007] 1 W.L.R. 591 at [33]–[41], disapproving *Gwembe Valley Development Co Ltd v Koshy* [2004] W.T.L.R. 97.

[215] [2007] 1 W.L.R. 591 at [33].

[216] [2007] 1 W.L.R. 2288 at [61]; cf. *Re Pauling's Settlement Trusts* [1962] 1 W.L.R. 86; [1964] 1 Ch. 303.

unjustified delay coupled with an adverse effect of some kind on the defendant or a third party should not be capable of providing a defence in the form of laches even before the expiration of the limitation period". Again, though, something more than mere delay will be required—especially so since the statutory limitation has not yet expired.

24–050   **vi.   Actions for an Account.**   Section 23 of the 1980 Act provides:

> "[A]n action for an account shall not be brought after the expiration of any time limit under this Act which is applicable to the claim which is the basis of the duty to account."

This confirms that the period applicable to a particular cause of action—for example breach of trust—applies equally to the relief by way of account which flows from it. In *Coulthard v Disco Mix Club Ltd*[217] an action for an account arising out of a contractual fiduciary relationship was brought more than six years after the alleged breaches. The claimant sought to overcome this by arguing that no period of limitation applied to a dishonest breach by a fiduciary of his duty to account. It was held that there was no distinction in the limitation period applicable to a common law fraud action for damages and an action in equity for dishonest breach of fiduciary duty, unless the defendant had misappropriated trust property, in which case no period applied.[218] The present case involved no trust property, as the defendant was not obliged to keep the money in question separate from his own. The duty to account was contractual, even if owed by a fiduciary. It would have been "a blot on our jurisprudence" if the same facts gave rise to a time bar at common law but not in equity. The alleged dishonest breaches of fiduciary duty were simply the equitable counterparts of the common law claims, and so the common law period applied by analogy.

---

[217] [2000] 1 W.L.R. 707. See also *Paragon Finance Plc v DB Thakerar & Co (A Firm)* [1999] 1 All E.R. 400; *Raja v Lloyds TSB Bank Plc* [2000] Lloyd's Rep. Bank. 377; *Cia de Seguros Imperio v Heath (REBX) Ltd* [2001] 1 W.L.R. 112.

[218] Limitation Act 1980 s.21(1); above, para.24–041.

CHAPTER 25

PERSONAL CLAIMS AGAINST THIRD PARTIES

1. GENERAL

WHERE a trustee disburses trust property in breach of trust, or a company director misapplies company property, it is clear that the fault lies chiefly with the trustee or director. However, a claimant may also wish to pursue claims against third parties who were somehow involved in the trustee or director's breach of duty;[1] those third parties may have received the misdirected property, or induced or facilitated the breach. These claims may be made in addition to claims against the "first party" wrongdoer.[2]

25–001

There are many reasons why a claimant may wish to pursue third parties. Most obviously, the third party may have deeper pockets than the trustee herself and may be more able to satisfy a judgment (as in the case where the trustee is insolvent). In the case of frauds, the trustee may have disappeared. For these reasons, banks and solicitors (who have insurance policies) are popular targets. Another reason may be that the third party has made a profit as a result of the breach of trust, and a gain-based remedy against the third party would be more lucrative than a loss-based claim against the trustee.

The bulk of this chapter is concerned with the two main forms of third party personal liability; these are called "knowing receipt" and "dishonest assistance". The personal liability of a de facto trustee (also called a trustee *de son tort*) and

---

[1] See generally P. Davies, *Accessory Liability* (Oxford: Hart Publishing, 2015); J. Dietrich and P. Ridge, *Accessories in Private Law* (Cambridge: Cambridge University Press, 2015).

[2] Although, depending on the remedies sought, it may be that an election is ultimately required.

the strict liability action in *Re Diplock* are also discussed. First, however, it is necessary to outline the relationship between these personal claims and the proprietary claims that may also be made in respect of misdirected property.

A. Personal and Proprietary Claims

25–002 It is crucially important in this area to distinguish between personal claims and proprietary claims. Proprietary claims, which are addressed fully in Ch.26, are claims directly to assets in a defendant's hands. In the paradigmatic example of property transferred in breach of trust,[3] the basis of the proprietary claim is simply that the beneficiary's equitable rights persist in the property, even though the trustee has transferred legal title to a third party. The proprietary claim seeks to vindicate those existing rights.

A proprietary claim against a third party can be defeated in three ways. First, it may be shown that the transfer was not in breach of trust at all. In such a case, the beneficiary's equitable rights in the property are overreached and do not persist in the property when it is transferred to a new legal owner. Secondly, if the transfer was made in breach, the new legal owner can show that she is a bona fide purchaser for value without notice. The effect of this is to extinguish the beneficiary's prior equitable interest. Thirdly, the property may be dissipated in such a way as to leave no traceable substitutes. It may have been spent on a meal that has been eaten, or on a cruise that has been taken, or used to repay an unsecured debt.

It will be seen that the proprietary claim does not depend on the defendant's fault,[4] except to the extent that a lack of notice is a necessary ingredient of the bona fide purchase defence. Rather, the claim depends on the continued existence of property (including substitutes) that was and remains subject to a persisting equitable interest. A recipient of trust property who is vulnerable to such a claim may therefore properly be termed a "trustee" of the property. However, it is important to note that this label only recognises the persistence of the beneficiary's equitable interest; it does not of itself reveal anything about the duties that are owed by the trustee in respect of the property.[5] This is important because it shows that an innocent volunteer can take trust property subject to a prior equitable interest, thereby becoming a "trustee", and yet not be liable to account for her stewardship of that property. To put it another way, a recipient can be a trustee with no duties. Such a recipient would be able to dissipate the property with impunity. As Lloyd LJ said in *Independent Trustee Services Ltd v GP Noble Trustees*[6]:

---

[3] Most obviously an express trust, but property may also be transferred in breach of a constructive trust, with a proprietary claim available against the recipient. A recent example is *Keown v Nahoor* [2015] EWHC 3418 (Ch).

[4] *Ultraframe (UK) Ltd v Fielding* [2005] EWHC 1638 (Ch) at [1518].

[5] *Independent Trustee Services Ltd v GP Noble Trustees* [2012] EWCA Civ 195; [2013] Ch. 91 at [77]. Neither does it tell us if the person is relevantly a "trustee" for certain statutory purposes: see *Williams v Central Bank of Nigeria* [2014] UKSC 10; [2014] A.C. 1189; below, para.25–035.

[6] [2013] Ch. 91 at [75].

> "The beneficial title of the beneficiaries under the pension schemes would still have subsisted in the money after the payment to [the recipient] . Therefore, she would not have had a defence to a proprietary claim by the trustee for the recovery of the money. Being innocent, she would not, on the other hand, be liable to a personal claim."

Personal claims against third parties, on the other hand, generally *do* depend on fault. The third party may or may not have received trust property, but even if she has received it she will not be subject to a personal claim merely because of the fact of receipt.[7] As we have seen, the receipt of property subject to a prior equitable interest does not automatically mean that the recipient owes duties in respect of that prior interest. Instead, the personal liability is grounded on the receipt of property *with knowledge*.   **25–003**

Personal and proprietary claims must therefore be distinguished, but they do interrelate in several ways. First, although receipt-based personal liability requires fault, it does also require receipt of property in breach of trust or fiduciary duty. A person cannot be liable for knowing receipt if she never received tainted property, albeit that she may be liable on other grounds that do not depend on receipt. Secondly, someone who is a voluntary recipient of trust property (and thus subject to a proprietary claim) may also become subject to personal liability if she is subsequently made aware of the prior interest while the transferred property is still in her hands. That personal liability would only extend to property or substitutes that remained in her hands at the time she acquired knowledge; no liability would exist in respect of property already dissipated. Thirdly, both personal and proprietary claims may be made against the same person. If someone knowingly receives £50,000 in breach of trust, and dissipates £20,000, the beneficiaries may make a proprietary claim in respect of the remaining £30,000 and a personal claim in respect of the spent £20,000.

B.   A Note on Terminology

Prior to the twentieth edition of this work, the discussion of third party personal liability was contained in the chapter on constructive trusts. This was because persons who are found liable as de facto trustees, or for knowing receipt or dishonest assistance, are sometimes referred to as constructive trustees. Alternatively, they may be said to be liable to account as if they were constructive trustees. Following much judicial and academic criticism,[8] however, this usage may now be dying out. It is now more common to see references to knowing receipt and dishonest assistance as equitable wrongs in their own right, able to be   **25–004**

---

[7] The exception is the limited *Re Diplock* action, which only applies in respect of the maladministration of a deceased estate: below, para.25–032.
[8] See, e.g., P. Birks in E. McKendrick (ed.), *Commercial Aspects of Trusts and Fiduciary Obligations* (Oxford: Oxford University Press, 1992), Ch.8; D. Nicholls in W. Cornish et al (eds), *Restitution: Past, Present and Future* (Oxford: Hart Publishing, 1998), Ch.15; *Paragon Finance Plc v DB Thakerar & Co (A Firm)* [1999] 1 All E.R. 401 at 409, per Millett LJ; *Dubai Aluminium Co Ltd v Salaam* [2003] 2 A.C. 366 at 404, per Lord Millett.

remedied by awards of equitable compensation or accounts of profits.[9] It is no longer necessary to interpose a deemed trusteeship between the wrongful conduct and the remedy.[10]

Yet, as the discussion above shows, it is perfectly appropriate to term a recipient of trust property a "trustee" of that property. For as long as an innocent volunteer is unaware of the prior interest, she is a trustee with no duties. Accordingly, she is not liable to account for the property. Once she has been made aware of the prior interest then, to the extent trust property remains in her hands, she becomes subject to a duty not to dissipate it; in other words she becomes liable to account for it. (Of course, a recipient who knows about the prior interest from the start will always owe that duty not to dissipate.) This is real and not deemed trusteeship, even though the trustee's duties and protections are not the same as those of an express trustee. A similar analysis applies to de facto trustees.[11]

On the other hand, reference to trusteeship may be unhelpful, or at least unnecessary. In the case of dishonest assistants there is no property that can be held on trust by the assistant, so the trustee terminology seems inapt. And despite the argument just made in the previous paragraph, a knowing recipient is not treated as a trustee for the purposes of the Limitation Act 1980.[12] It has also been said that a knowing recipient is subject to a positive duty to reconvey the property on the grounds that her possession is always illegitimate.[13] This weakens any comparison with a bare express trustee who, while similarly only owing only a basic duty not to dissipate the property, is not obliged to convey it to the beneficiaries until their demand. Also unsettled are the existence and scope of fiduciary obligations (or obligations that mirror fiduciary obligations) that may be owed by third parties, and the calculation of accounts of profits that may be made against them.[14]

At all events, it seems reasonably clear that knowing receipt and dishonest assistance are now treated as wrongs in their own right. This development mirrors the demise of the accounting mechanism and the growth of direct claims for breach of trust discussed in Ch.24. For this reason, the material on third party liability (in this chapter) is separate from the discussion of constructive trusts (in Ch.12).

---

[9] See, e.g., *Aerostar Maintenance International Ltd v Wilson* [2010] EWHC 2032 (Ch); *Templeton Insurance Ltd v Brunswick* [2012] EWHC 1522 (Ch); *Independent Trustee Services Ltd v GP Noble Trustees* [2013] Ch. 91 at [22]; *Otkritie International Investment Management Ltd v Urumov* [2014] EWHC 191 (Comm); *Novoship (UK) Ltd v Nikitin* [2014] EWCA Civ 908; rep. sub. nom. *Novoship (UK) Ltd v Mikhaylyuk* [2015] Q.B. 499 at [66] and following. But one can still find references to the "constructive trustee" terminology; e.g. *Papadimitriou v Crédit Agricole Corp and Investment Bank* [2015] UKPC 13; [2015] 1 W.L.R. 4265 at [33], per Lord Sumption.

[10] D. Nicholls in W. Cornish et al (eds), *Restitution: Past, Present and Future* (1998) p.243.

[11] *Jasmine Trustees Ltd v Wells & Hind (A Firm)* [2008] Ch. 194 at [42].

[12] *Williams v Central Bank of Nigeria* [2014] A.C. 1189 at [13], [31]; see criticisms made in S. Watterson (2014) 73 C.L.J. 253.

[13] *Arthur v Attorney General of the Turks and Caicos Islands* [2012] UKPC 30 at [37]; *Williams v Central Bank of Nigeria* [2014] A.C. 1189 at [31]; C. Mitchell and S. Watterson in C. Mitchell (ed.), *Constructive and Resulting Trusts* (Oxford: Hart Publishing, 2010), Ch.4.

[14] See *Novoship (UK) Ltd v Mikhaylyuk* [2015] Q.B. 499; below, para.25–025.

2. KNOWING RECEIPT

In *El Ajou v Dollar Land Holdings*,[15] Hoffmann LJ outlined the requirements of a claim in knowing receipt[16]:   **25–005**

> "For this purpose the plaintiff must show, first, a disposal of his assets in breach of fiduciary duty; secondly, the beneficial receipt by the defendant of assets which are traceable as representing the assets of the plaintiff; and thirdly, knowledge on the part of the defendant that the assets he received are traceable to a breach of fiduciary duty."

A. Breach of Trust or Fiduciary Duty

The model knowing receipt case involves a misapplication of trust property by a trustee, but the principle is not confined to trusts. Knowing receipt liability can also be grounded on the misapplication of property by someone who—while not a trustee—owes fiduciary duties in respect of the property. The clearest examples are company directors and other agents, who owe fiduciary duties in respect of property that is legally owned by the company or the principal.[17]   **25–006**

i. Nature of the breach In cases that do concern trusts, a disposition may ground liability in knowing receipt if it was *either* made in breach of trust *or* made in breach of fiduciary duty. The requirement will be satisfied by a wholly innocent breach that was made in the absence of any conflict and which did not involve any profit for the trustee; it will also be satisfied by a disposition that, while made within the terms of the trust, was made in breach of fiduciary duty.   **25–007**

The position in respect of non-trustee fiduciaries is more complicated. The first question involves determining whether there is a valid contract, binding on the principal, under which the principal's property has been transferred to a third party. The principal's agent (for example the director of a company) may have breached fiduciary duties in entering into such a contract, but it does not follow that the agent did not have the requisite authority to bind the principal. If the relevant transfer of property was made pursuant to a contract binding on the principal, receipt of that property cannot ground liability in knowing receipt.[18]

Putting such cases aside, the breach of duty element of knowing receipt will certainly be satisfied if the relevant misapplication of the principal's property is made in breach of fiduciary duty. A more difficult question is whether liability can be grounded on dispositions of property that—although wrongful—are not tainted by a conflict of interest or by the making of an unauthorised profit. That

---

[15] [1994] 2 All E.R. 685.

[16] [1994] 2 All E.R. 685 at 700.

[17] *Belmont Finance Corp Ltd v Williams Furniture Ltd (No.2)* [1980] 1 All E.R. 393; *Agip (Africa) Ltd v Jackson* [1991] Ch. 547; *Ultraframe (UK) Ltd v Fielding* [2005] EWHC 1638 (Ch) at [1487]. The Full Court of the Federal Court of Australia has noted that alternative claims will be available to companies whose assets have been misdirected, so it would only be necessary to proceed in knowing receipt if particular remedies (beyond repayment of value paid away) were sought: *Great Investments Ltd v Warner* [2016] FCAFC 85; (2016) 243 F.C.R. 516 at [53].

[18] *Great Investments Ltd v Warner* (2016) 243 F.C.R. 516 at [56]. The principal may be able to rescind the contract; see below, para.25–014, and Ch.29. See generally M. Conaglen and R. Nolan (2013) 129 L.Q.R. 359; M. Yip (2017) 11 J. Eq. 293.

is, whether knowing receipt liability can exist in relation to breaches by fiduciaries of *non*-fiduciary equitable duties. The better view on this point is that receipt of property in breach of such non-fiduciary duties can indeed ground knowing receipt. This is so for two reasons. First, the equivalent duties do ground liability in knowing receipt when they are owed and breached by a trustee, and it would make sense to treat similarly all fiduciaries who have control another's property. Secondly, the terminology alone should not be allowed to determine the answer: although we might now confine "fiduciary" to the proscriptive duties to avoid unauthorised conflicts and profits, historically it had a wider meaning and simply meant "trustee-like".[19]

B. Beneficial Receipt of Traceable Assets

25–008 Liability in knowing receipt depends upon receipt by a defendant of property in respect of which the claimant has an equitable right. Two points appear from this. First, the property that the defendant receives does not have to be the same property as that which was misdirected from the claimant. Instead, the defendant must receive the *traceable proceeds* of the property that was lost by the claimant. The rules relating to tracing in equity, which are considered at length in Ch.26, are therefore relevant here.[20] It is not enough, however, that the defendant has benefitted in an abstract way from the breach of trust[21]:

> "[W]hat is required is a transactional link by which a new asset is exchanged for, and acquired with, the old one. The mere fact that a defendant has benefited from a breach of trust does not give rise to claims in knowing receipt".

Secondly, knowing receipt cannot lie when the claimant does not have an equitable right in property that the defendant receives. So, if a recipient takes property as a bona fide purchaser for value without notice of the breach of trust, she will be protected from a knowing receipt claim even if she is later made aware of the property's provenance.[22] She could even transfer the property on to someone who was always aware of the initial breach and that second recipient would not be liable in knowing receipt.[23] This is because the claimant's equitable right had already been extinguished.

---

[19] See *Westpac Banking Corp v Bell Group Ltd (No.3)* (2012) 44 W.A.R. 1 at [2714]–[2733]; M. Conaglen (2013) Co. and Sec. L.J. 403 at 407; A. Televantos (2017) 133 L.Q.R. 492.

[20] Although the claimant need only trace to the point of liability, which is either the moment of receipt or the moment of knowledge, whichever is the later (below, para.25–010). For knowing receipt it is not necessary to trace beyond that point, as it may be with a proprietary claim, considered in Ch.26.

[21] *OJSC Oil Company Yugraneft v Abramovich* [2008] EWHC 2613 (Comm) at [365]. See also *Criterion Properties Plc v Stratford* [2004] 1 W.L.R. 1846 at [27] (rights under an executory contract do not ground knowing receipt).

[22] Similarly with transfers of registered land under the Land Registration Act 2002 s.29: see M. Conaglen and A. Goymour in C. Mitchell (ed.), *Constructive and Resulting Trusts* (2010) Ch.5. In *Arthur v Attorney General of the Turks and Caicos Islands* [2012] UKPC 30, the Privy Council left open the question of whether the rights (if any) received by a transferee prior to registration could ground knowing receipt; see L. Bennett Moses (2013) 7 J. Eq. 74.

[23] An exception applies if the property is retransferred to the original trustee: *Re Stapleford Colliery Co* (1880) 14 Ch.D. 432.

An interesting question concerning beneficial receipt arose in *Akita Holdings Ltd v Attorney General of the Turks and Caicos Islands*.[24] Mr Hanchell, a government minister, had in breach of his fiduciary duty to the Crown arranged to sell a parcel of Crown land to a company that he controlled, Akita Holdings. The sale price was far below the true market value of the land. At trial, Goldsbrough CJ analysed the matter as follows[25]:

> "I regard this land as a mixed asset as described in *Foskett v McKeown* [2001] 1 A.C. 102.[26] The value in money which the defendant [Akita] put into the purchase of this asset represents but a proportion of its value. The balance of the value of the asset came from the property of the [Crown]. The proportions can be ascertained by mathematical calculation after one ascertains the value of the asset compared with the price paid."

On this analysis, which was not challenged in the Privy Council, Akita Holdings contributed the price it had actually paid, whereas the Crown 'contributed' the difference between that amount and the true value of the land. Akita had therefore received property in breach of fiduciary duty for the purposes of knowing receipt.[27]

The defendant must have received the property beneficially rather than ministerially (i.e. as agent).[28] The point often arises in relation to the receipt of money by banks, where the question is whether the bank has received the property beneficially or ministerially for the relevant account holder. It appears safe to say that a bank does receive money beneficially when it applies those funds to the reduction of an overdraft or repayment of a loan,[29] but beyond that the question is difficult and views differ.[30] Even a recipient who has only received property ministerially may still be liable for dishonest assistance,[31] of course, but the difference between the fault levels required for liability in knowing receipt and dishonest assistance may make the point of beneficial or ministerial receipt vital.

25–009

---

[24] [2017] UKPC 7; [2017] A.C. 590; J. Glister (2017) 11 J. Eq. 219.

[25] *Attorney General (Turks and Caicos Islands) v Akita Holdings Ltd* (Supreme Court of the Turks and Caicos Islands, 5 September 2014, unreported) at [41].

[26] Below, para.26–016.

[27] The Crown sought an account of profits rather than rescission, so the status of the contract under which the land was transferred to Akita was not discussed.

[28] *Trustor AB v Smallbone (No.2)* [2001] 1 W.L.R. 1177; C. Harpum (1986) 102 L.Q.R. 114; P. Birks (1989) 105 L.Q.R. 528; P. Millett (1991) 107 L.Q.R. 71.

[29] *Agip (Africa) Ltd v Jackson* [1990] Ch. 265 at 292, per Millett J; *Evans v European Bank Ltd* (2004) 61 N.S.W.L.R. 75 at [165]–[175]; *Papadimitriou v Crédit Agricole Corp and Investment Bank* [2015] 1 W.L.R. 4265 (a rare case where the bank had notice and so was not a bona fide purchaser for value of the funds).

[30] See Underhill, 19th edn, paras 98.18 and following; G. Virgo, *The Principles of Equity & Trusts*, 2nd edn (Oxford: Oxford University Press, 2016), pp.707–709; M. Bryan in F. Rose (ed.), *Restitution and Banking Law* (Oxford: Oxford University Press, 1998), Ch.10.

[31] *British America Elevator Co v Bank of British North America* [1919] A.C. 658; *Agip (Africa) Ltd v Jackson* [1990] Ch. 265, affirmed [1991] Ch. 547. A ministerial recipient could also act in such a way as to make him a de facto trustee (below, para.25–029) and could, if he dealt with the funds "inconsistent[ly] with the performance of trusts of which he is cognizant" be personally liable to the beneficiaries: *Lee v Sankey* (1873) L.R. 15 Eq. 204 at 211.

C.   Knowledge

25–010   The final requirement is that the recipient takes the relevant property with knowledge of the prior interest. That knowledge may be present at the time of receipt or, if the recipient has taken the property as an "innocent volunteer",[32] it may be acquired later while the received property is still in the recipient's hands. The defendant becomes subject to a personal liability to account once knowledge is acquired; if he later dissipates the property, that personal liability to account remains.

25–011   **i.   Knowledge of what?**   To be liable in knowing receipt, the defendant must know of the prior interest. However, this deceptively straightforward statement conceals a difficult area.[33]

In the first place, it is clear that a defendant can be liable even if he does not know what a trust is or what fiduciary duties are.[34] That said, it is also true that the defendant needs to know of the claimant's right to the relevant property. Knowledge of the existence of a claim in respect of that property can *indicate* knowledge of the existence of a right, but knowledge of a claim does not *automatically impute* knowledge of a right.[35] Hence, a solicitor was not accountable for moneys received in payment of costs and expenses paid by a client for work done in defending an action in which the claimant was asserting that the client was a trustee of the whole of its assets.[36] In the circumstances, the solicitor only knew of a "doubtful equity", but the outcome would be different if he knew that the claim was well-founded.

25–012   **ii.   Degrees of knowledge**   Closely linked to what the defendant must know is the question of to what degree he must know it. While constructive notice clearly suffices where the question is whether the recipient took the property subject to the trust, it does not follow that the same applies where the question is whether he has incurred the personal liability to account. Opinions have differed as to whether liability is based on actual knowledge, or constructive knowledge, or whether it is strict, so that even an innocent volunteer is liable. Formerly it appeared established that constructive notice sufficed.[37] Thus in *Belmont Finance*

---

[32] *Re Diplock* [1948] Ch. 465 at 478–479.

[33] It has been said that the decision whether recipients or assistants have the requisite level of fault is essentially a "jury question" that is not easily susceptible to legal analysis or categorisation: see *Agip (Africa) Ltd v Jackson* [1990] Ch. 265 at 293, per Millett J; W.M.C. Gummow (2013) 87 A.L.J. 311 at 319.

[34] *Barlow Clowes International Ltd (In Liquidation) v Eurotrust International Ltd* [2006] 1 W.L.R. 1476 at [28].

[35] *Carl Zeiss Stiftung v Herbert Smith & Co (No.2)* [1969] 2 Ch. 276 at 290; PVB (1969) 85 L.Q.R. 160; C. Harpum (1986) 102 L.Q.R. 267 at 287; *Sinclair Investments (UK) Ltd v Versailles Trade Finance Ltd (In Administrative Receivership)* [2011] EWCA Civ 347; [2012] Ch. 453 at [102]–[109]; *Papadimitriou v Crédit Agricole Corp and Investment Bank* [2015] 1 W.L.R. 4265 at [12]–[21].

[36] *Carl Zeiss Stiftung v Herbert Smith & Co (No.2)* [1969] 2 Ch. 276. A solicitor in doubt as to possible liability should apply to court for directions; *Finers v Miro* [1991] 1 W.L.R. 35. See also *United Mizrahi Bank Ltd v Doherty* [1998] 1 W.L.R. 435; *Bank of Scotland (Governor and Company) v A Ltd* [2001] 1 W.L.R. 751 (where bank suspects client).

[37] *Karak Rubber Co Ltd v Burden (No.2)* [1972] 1 W.L.R. 602.

Corp v Williams Furniture Ltd (No.2)[38] company directors who participated in an unlawful share purchase scheme were liable because they had knowledge of all the facts which established the improper use of the funds, and knew or ought to have known that the money which they received was impressed with a trust. It was immaterial that, as the judge found, the directors did not act fraudulently.

A different view was taken in *Re Montagu's Settlement Trusts*.[39]

> Trustees transferred certain settled chattels to the beneficiary (the tenth Duke of Manchester) absolutely, in breach of trust. The situation resulted from an "honest muddle" by all concerned. The Duke's solicitor had at an earlier stage been aware of the terms of the settlement. The Duke disposed of a number of the chattels during his lifetime. After his death, the eleventh Duke claimed that his predecessor had become a constructive trustee of them. In modern terminology, the eleventh Duke sued the tenth Duke's estate for knowing receipt.

Megarry VC held that, while the tenth Duke's estate must return any remaining chattels or their traceable proceeds, the Duke was not personally liable to account as a constructive trustee because he had no actual knowledge that the chattels were trust property transferred in breach of trust. Even if he had once understood the terms of the settlement, there was nothing to suggest that he remembered them so as to be aware at the date of receipt that the chattels were trust property. Nor was there any reason to impute the solicitor's knowledge to the Duke, by analogy with the doctrine of imputed notice.

The Vice-Chancellor emphasised that the relevant question was whether the recipient had *knowledge*, not whether he had *notice* according to the rules which dealt with the question whether an equitable interest was binding on a transferee. Constructive notice of a prior interest is certainly enough to make a purchaser for value still take property subject to previous equities. That, however, is only relevant to a *proprietary* claim:

> "I do not see why one of the touchstones for determining the burdens on property should be the same as that for deciding whether to impose a personal obligation on a man. The cold calculus of constructive and imputed notice does not seem to me to be an appropriate instrument for deciding whether a man's conscience is sufficiently affected for it to be right to bind him by the obligations of a constructive trustee."[40]

Instead, the question in the present context was whether a person was to have imposed on him a personal liability to account. Megarry VC held that liability should not be imposed unless the conscience of the recipient was affected; this required "want of probity", which includes actual knowledge, shutting one's eyes to the obvious, or wilfully and recklessly failing to make such enquiries as a reasonable and honest person would make; it does not include knowledge of circumstances which would indicate the facts to an honest and reasonable person or would put the latter on enquiry.[41]

---

[38] [1980] 1 All E.R. 393; see also *(No.1)* [1979] Ch. 250; *International Sales and Agencies Ltd v Marcus* [1982] 3 All E.R. 551 at 558.

[39] [1987] Ch. 264; C. Harpum (1986) 102 L.Q.R. 267 and (1987) 50 M.L.R. 217.

[40] [1987] Ch. 264 at 272–273.

[41] *Re Montagu's ST* [1987] Ch. 264 at 285. Megarry VC was locating "want of probity" within the five-fold classification that appears in *Baden, Delvaux and Lecuit v Société Générale pour Favoriser le Développement du Commerce et de l'Industrie en France SA* [1983] B.C.L.C. 325, viz. (i) actual

25–013   The question was examined by the Court of Appeal in *Bank of Credit and Commerce International (Overseas) Ltd v Akindele*,[42] which states the current test. The defendant had received $6.68 million in 1988 as a return on $10 million he had paid to the bank in 1985 under an artificial loan agreement. The transaction involved a fraudulent breach of the fiduciary duties owed to the bank by certain parties, but the defendant knew nothing of the frauds within the BCCI group at that time nor of the fraudulent aspect of the particular agreement. Nourse LJ reviewed the authorities (including Commonwealth decisions) and academic commentaries on the degree of knowledge required to found recipient liability. First, his Lordship confirmed that dishonesty had never been required. There was considerable authority supporting the view that constructive notice sufficed,[43] although in much of it the question had not been examined in depth because the defendant had actual knowledge, or the decisions were based on assistance rather than receipt. Other authorities favoured the view that constructive notice did not suffice, at any rate in the case of commercial transactions, where (in cases not involving title to land) there was no duty to investigate. In such cases, purchasers have been held not liable unless they had actual knowledge of the impropriety or acted with wilful or reckless disregard.[44]

Nourse LJ regarded *Re Montagu's ST* as the "seminal judgment". So far as the five categories of knowledge elaborated in the *Baden*[45] case were concerned, they had been formulated with "assistance" rather than "receipt" in mind. There were grave doubts as to the utility of this categorisation in receipt cases. The purpose of such a categorisation could only be to enable the court to determine whether the defendant's conscience was sufficiently affected to bind him as constructive trustee. There was, therefore, no need for the categorisation. There was a single test of dishonesty for assistance liability,[46] and there should be a single test of knowledge for recipient liability: "The recipient's state of knowledge must be such as to make it unconscionable for him to retain the benefit of the receipt".[47]

---

knowledge; (ii) wilfully shutting one's eyes to the obvious; (iii) wilfully and recklessly failing to make such inquiries as an honest and reasonable person would make; (iv) knowledge of circumstances which would indicate the facts to an honest and reasonable person; (v) knowledge of circumstances which would put an honest and reasonable person on inquiry. This classification may still be helpful: see *Armstrong DLW GmbH v Winnington Networks Ltd* [2012] EWHC 10 (Ch); [2013] Ch. 156 at [130]–[132].

[42] [2001] Ch. 437; R. Nolan (2000) 59 C.L.J. 447; J. Penner (2000) 14 T.L.I. 229; P. Birks and W. Swadling [2000] All E.R. Rev. at.319; J. Stevens [2001] 9 R.L.R. 99.

[43] *Belmont Finance Corp v Williams Furniture Ltd (No.2)* [1980] 1 All E.R. 393; *Agip (Africa) Ltd v Jackson* [1990] Ch. 265 (not dealt with on appeal at [1991] Ch. 547); *Polly Peck International Plc v Nadir (No.2)* [1992] 4 All E.R. 769; *Houghton v Fayers* [2000] 1 B.C.L.C. 511.

[44] See *Eagle Trust Plc v SBC Securities Ltd* [1993] 1 W.L.R. 484; *Cowan de Groot Properties Ltd v Eagle Trust Plc* [1992] 4 All E.R. 700; *El Ajou v Dollar Land Holdings Plc* [1993] 3 All E.R. 717 (reversed on another point at [1994] 2 All E.R. 685). Banks and other financial institutions must, however, satisfy the money laundering regulations. See also the dissenting comments of Rix LJ on "commercially acceptable conduct" of banks in the context of money laundering in *Abou-Rahmah v Abacha* [2007] W.T.L.R. 1 at [48]–[58] (albeit considering the defence of good faith change of position in unjust enrichment).

[45] Above, fn.41.

[46] Discussed below, para.25–022.

[47] [2001] Ch. 437 at 455.

Applying the test in *Akindele* itself, the defendant's knowledge was not such as to make it unconscionable for him to enter into the agreement in 1985, when the integrity of BCCI was not doubted. At the time of the receipt of $6.68 million in 1988 he had suspicions, but his state of knowledge was not such as to make it unconscionable for him to retain the money. His knowledge in 1988 concerned the general reputation of the BCCI group from late 1987 onwards, and not the particular transaction entered into in 1985. Nor was the very high interest rate of itself sufficient to fix the defendant with knowledge that would make his retention of the benefit unconscionable. If Nourse LJ had thought that it was still the appropriate test, he would have held that the defendant did not have actual or constructive knowledge that his receipt was traceable to a breach of fiduciary duty.

The requirement that the recipient's knowledge "be such as to make it unconscionable for him to retain the benefit" has been reaffirmed and applied on several occasions,[48] and seems to have settled the law in England and Wales.[49] One possible caveat involves the decision in *Criterion Properties Plc v Stratford UK Properties LLC*,[50] where the House of Lords explained that the equitable principles governing liability for receipt of trust property do not apply to liability for receipt of property under a contract which is set aside (as was the case in *Akindele*). In fact, however, this does not undermine the authority of *Akindele*. First, the Court of Appeal's decision in *Criterion Properties* makes clear that the *Akindele* test still applies to cases that do involve relevant receipts.[51] Secondly, as Conaglen and Nolan point out,[52] a close look at the facts of *Akindele* reveals that Chief Akindele did not actually receive payment from the person with whom he had contracted. Akindele received funds from BCCI (Overseas) Ltd, but he had contracted with another company in the same group, ICIC (Overseas) Ltd. Since BCCI (Overseas) did not owe any money to Akindele, it was a breach of duty for the directors to cause any money to be paid to him. It was this transfer in breach of duty that grounded the claim in knowing receipt.

25–014

D. Remedies[53]

If the transferred property or its traceable substitutes are still in the hands of the recipient, the claimant can bring a proprietary claim in respect of those assets. As we have seen, the recipient's knowledge is irrelevant to that action except to the extent that it disallows him from raising the defence of bona fide purchase.

25–015

---

[48] *Charter Plc v City Index Ltd* [2008] Ch. 313; *Templeton Insurance Ltd v Brunswick* [2012] EWHC 1522 (Ch) at [79]–[83]; *Armstrong DLW GmbH v Winnington Networks Ltd* [2013] Ch. 156 at [130]–[132] (where "unconscionable" was mapped onto the *Baden* scale of knowledge); *Group Seven Ltd v Nasir* [2017] EWHC 2466 (Ch) at [473]–[478] (where Morgan J followed the approach in *Armstrong v Winnington*).

[49] Of course, the application of that law to the facts of a particular case may still be very difficult.

[50] [2004] 1 W.L.R. 1846; R. Stevens (2004) L.M.C.L.Q. 421; J. Yap (2011) 127 L.Q.R. 350.

[51] [2003] 1 W.L.R. 2108.

[52] M. Conaglen and R. Nolan (2013) 129 L.Q.R. 359 at 373, making reference to Carnwath J's findings of fact at trial: *BCCI (Overseas) Ltd v Chief Akindele* [1999] B.C.C. 669.

[53] See C. Mitchell and S. Watterson in C. Mitchell (ed.), *Constructive and Resulting Trusts* (2010), Ch.4.

Similarly, any order to retransfer property on the basis that the claimant has persisting equitable rights in that property is not a remedy *for* knowing receipt, even if it may be awarded against someone who would also be liable as a knowing recipient.

The traditional position is that a finding of knowing receipt gives rise to a liability to account as if the defendant were a constructive trustee. Although this language of constructive trusteeship may be dying out,[54] it remains true that a knowing recipient's liability to account is similar to the personal liability to account owed by a normal express trustee. In this way a knowing recipient can be liable for equitable compensation in the same way as an express trustee.[55] If, for example, a recipient has knowingly received property and has subsequently dissipated it, the recipient will be personally liable for the judgment value of the property that was received. The difference between the receipt value and the judgment value may go unnoticed in cases where money is received and dissipated, but not in cases involving different types of property. In *Re Rothko*,[56] paintings by the famous painter Mark Rothko were wrongly transferred to third parties. Those third parties disposed of the paintings, which later rose in value. The third parties were held liable for the market value of the paintings at judgment, not at the point of receipt.

This award of equitable compensation may be seen as a remedy for breach of the duty not to dissipate the property. There is no doubt that recipients owe such a duty if they take property subject to a prior interest with knowledge of that interest. However, the position is more difficult in respect of other, extended duties that are normally owed by express trustees but which may not be owed by knowing recipients. For example, most express trustees owe duties to invest the trust property and can be sued for equitable compensation if they fail to do so.[57] Yet to require the same of knowing recipients would be inconsistent with what is said to be the recipient's paramount duty to restore the property immediately.[58] It therefore appears that claimants cannot surcharge the "account" of a knowing recipient in the way that they could surcharge the accounts rendered by most express trustees.[59] The knowing recipient is instead in a similar position to the trustee of a "bare" express trust, whose only duty is not to dissipate the property.[60]

---

[54] Above, para.25–004.

[55] It may be that, in an exceptional case, a knowing recipient could even be excused from liability under Trustee Act 1925 s.61: see P. Davies [2015] Conv. 379 at 382. On s.61 generally, see above, para.24–037.

[56] 43 N.Y. 2d 305 (1977), cited in Underhill, 19th edn, para.98.35.

[57] *Nestlé v National Westminster Bank Plc* [1993] 1 W.L.R. 1260.

[58] *Arthur v Attorney General of the Turks and Caicos Islands* [2012] UKPC 30 at [37]; *Williams v Central Bank of Nigeria* [2014] A.C. 1189 at [31]: a knowing recipient "does not have the powers or duties of a trustee, for example with regard to investment or management"; but see the discussion of *Evans v European Bank Ltd* (2004) 61 N.S.W.L.R. 75 in C. Mitchell and S. Watterson in C. Mitchell (ed.), *Constructive and Resulting Trusts* (2010), p.139.

[59] Above, para.24–007.

[60] See *Herdegen v FCT* (1988) 84 A.L.R. 271 at 281–282; P. Matthews [2005] P.C.B. 266 and 271.

Accounts of profits may also be awarded against most express trustees. This is not on the basis that the trustee has committed a breach of trust,[61] but rather that she has committed a breach of fiduciary duty by making an unauthorised profit. Whether an account of profits ought to be available against a knowing recipient does not seem susceptible of a blanket answer. On one hand, it is generally thought that trustees of "bare" express trusts do not owe fiduciary obligations and are therefore not liable to account for profits. If that is true,[62] it may be argued that knowing recipients do not either. On the other hand, a recipient who had actual knowledge of the prior interest ought not to be able to benefit in any way from her receipt of the property.[63]

Consider the following example:

> A trustee pays money to a third party in breach of trust. The recipient is suspicious of the gift, so places the money in a separate interest-bearing account and does not make any withdrawals. Because of the presence of those funds, the recipient's bank agrees to lend money to the recipient at a more advantageous interest rate than would otherwise have been offered. This enables the recipient to buy a nicer house, which appreciates more rapidly. Throughout, the trust money is still sitting in the separate account. Is the recipient liable to account for the gain made by borrowing money at the lower rate? Is she liable for the increased gain made by buying a house that has appreciated more rapidly than others she could have bought? Is she liable for the entire increase in value of her house?

It should be emphasised that this discussion is concerned with discrete profits made by the recipient; if the "profit" instead consisted of an accretion to the trust property, or of a rise in its value, then that profit would simply involve an increase in the value of the property that the recipient must not dissipate (and in respect of which she would be liable to pay equitable compensation for breach of that duty not to dissipate).[64]

i. Contribution. It has been held that the Civil Liability (Contribution) Act 1978 may enable recipients to recover a contribution from other persons responsible for the loss to the trust. In *Charter Plc v City Index Ltd*,[65] a knowing recipient was liable "in respect of the same damage"[66] as were other defendants who were liable in negligence. Although the gain-based remedy of an account of profits can be awarded against a knowing recipient, the loss-based remedy of equitable compensation can be awarded too. Thus a liability to compensate for

25–016

---

[61] Although in some cases a similar outcome might be achieved by surcharging a common account and claiming that the sums received were received on behalf of the trust.

[62] It has been doubted: see M. Conaglen, *Fiduciary Loyalty* (Oxford: Hart Publishing, 2010), pp.197–201.

[63] Writing extra-judicially, Lord Nicholls thought that an account of profits was currently available against all knowing recipients but ought only to be available against dishonest ones: D. Nicholls in W. Cornish et al (eds), *Restitution: Past, Present and Future* (1998), pp.231, 233, 237, 243–4.

[64] In *Akita Holdings Ltd v Attorney General of the Turks and Caicos Islands* [2017] A.C. 590, the defendant company was liable for the current (increased) value of the transferred land and was also liable for the benefit received by its use of the land for the purpose of raising finance. See further J. Glister (2017) 11 J. Eq. 219 at 223–224.

[65] [2008] Ch. 313; G. Virgo (2008) 67 C.L.J. 254; A. Goymour [2008] 16 R.L.R. 113; J. Edelman and C. Mitchell [2008] All E.R. Rev. at 398; S. Gardner (2009) 125 L.Q.R. 20.

[66] Civil Liability (Contribution) Act 1978 s.1.

losses always attends a knowing receipt claim, although it may be different if the claimant has already elected for an account of profits.[67]

3. DISHONEST ASSISTANCE

25–017   The second form of third party personal liability is "dishonest assistance". Under this head, a third party will be liable to the beneficiary or principal if he dishonestly assists in a breach of trust or fiduciary duty.

Subject to the requirement to elect between remedies, it is possible for a recipient to be liable for both knowing receipt and dishonest assistance. That is, the fact of receipt does not prevent liability for dishonest assistance. This will be important in the event that the beneficiary's loss as a result of the breach outweighs the value of the property that was received by the third party.

A.   Breach of Trust or Fiduciary Duty

25–018   In *Barnes v Addy*,[68] Lord Selborne laid down the test of liability as that of as assisting "with knowledge in a dishonest and fraudulent design on the part of the trustees". This statement was obiter, but the principle that the third party could not be liable under this head unless the breach of trust in which he assisted was dishonest on the part of the trustee became entrenched in the law until clarified by the Privy Council in *Royal Brunei Airlines Sdn Bhd v Tan*.[69]

> The claimant appointed a company ("BLT") to act as its travel agent and to account for the proceeds of ticket sales. It was conceded that BLT committed a breach of trust by using the money in its business. BLT fell into arrears in accounting and the contract was terminated. As BLT was insolvent, the claimant sued Tan, the principal shareholder and director. It was conceded that Tan had assisted in the breach with actual knowledge. The Brunei Court of Appeal found for Tan, holding that the breach in which he had assisted had not been shown to be fraudulent on the part of BLT. The appeal to the Privy Council centred upon the question whether accessory liability requires the breach of trust itself to be fraudulent. Tan was held personally liable for dishonestly assisting BLT's breach. There was no further requirement of dishonesty by BLT.[70]

Lord Nicholls of Birkenhead reviewed the authorities prior to *Barnes v Addy*. Those authorities did not require dishonesty on the part of the trustee whether the third party had procured the breach[71] or had merely assisted in it. The law had taken a wrong turning in reliance on Lord Selborne's dictum in *Barnes v Addy*. The trustee would be liable whether or not the breach was dishonest, but it would make no sense for a dishonest accessory, whose liability is fault-based, to escape

---

[67] See the judgment of Arden LJ on this point: [2008] Ch. 313 at [64]–[71].

[68] (1874) L.R. 9 Ch.App. 244 at 251, 252.

[69] [1995] 2 A.C. 378; M. Halliwell [1995] Conv. 339; C. Harpum (1995) 111 L.Q.R. 545; R. Nolan (1995) 54 C.L.J. 505; J. Stevens (1995) 3 R.L.R. 105; S. Gardner (1996) 112 L.Q.R. 56. For criticisms, see P. Birks [1996] L.M.C.L.Q. 1; A. Berg (1996) 59 M.L.R. 443.

[70] In fact BLT's breach was dishonest because Tan's state of mind could be imputed to it: see *El Ajou v Dollar Land Holdings Plc* [1994] 2 All E.R. 685 ("directing mind and will").

[71] See *Eaves v Hickson* (1861) Beav. 136 (trustees innocently deceived by forgery made wrongful distribution which the party responsible for the deceit was liable to restore). A modern authority not requiring dishonesty by the trustees is *Powell v Thompson* [1991] 1 N.Z.L.R. 597.

simply because the trustee did not also act dishonestly. The current position in England and Wales, therefore, is that the underlying breach by the trustee or fiduciary does not itself have to be dishonest or fraudulent.[72]

Liability for dishonest assistance can attach to breaches of fiduciary duty as well as to breaches of trust.[73] As mentioned above in the case of knowing receipt,[74] the better view is that liability can also exist in respect of breaches of non-fiduciary duties that are owed by, for example, company directors.[75]

B.   Assistance

The principle here is simply that the third party's actions have assisted the trustee or fiduciary to commit the breach of trust. Acts done prior to the breach can obviously amount to assistance in the breach. Acts done after the breach can also count if, for example, the third party "assisted in moving the assets further away from the original beneficial owners".[76] The third party's actions must have factually assisted the trustee in some significant way,[77] but "it is not necessary to show a precise causal link between the assistance and the loss".[78]

25–019

C.   Dishonesty

The level of fault that is required of the third party is a matter of great importance because frauds and other breaches of duty in the commercial context are complex and can involve participants who are unaware of the wrongdoing. As the name of the head of liability suggests, the law now requires "dishonesty" on the part of the third party. The leading authority on the point is again *Royal Brunei Airlines Sdn Bhd v Tan*.[79]

Although the main issue, as we have seen, was whether the breach must be dishonest on the part of the trustee, the Privy Council considered also the question whether the assistant must have acted dishonestly. In confirming that requirement, Lord Nicholls rejected the old label "knowing assistance" because "knowledge" has too many shades of meaning. The five categories of knowledge

25–020

---

[72] In Australia, the breach itself must still be dishonest and fraudulent: *Consul Development Pty Ltd v DPC Estates Pty Ltd* (1975) 132 C.L.R. 373; *Farah Constructions Pty Ltd v Say-Dee Pty Ltd* (2007) 230 C.L.R. 89. If an accessory is dishonest but the trustee herself is not, the accessory will be liable under another head: *Hasler v Singtel Optus Pty Ltd* [2014] NSWCA 266 at [64] and following.

[73] *Fiona Trust & Holding Corp v Privalov* [2010] EWHC 3199 (Comm) at [61]; *Goldtrail Travel Ltd v Aydin* [2014] EWHC 1587 (Ch) at [128]; *Novoship (UK) Ltd v Mikhaylyuk* [2015] Q.B. 499 at [92].

[74] Above, para.25–007.

[75] See W.M.C. Gummow (2013) 87 A.L.J. 753 at 758, warning that equity should follow the law and not "fix criteria more severe for the third party than those (if any) for which [a relevant] statute provides".

[76] *Independent Trustee Service Ltd v GP Noble Trustees Ltd* [2010] EWHC 1653 (Ch) at [242] (not considered on appeal [2013] Ch. 91). See also *Twinsectra Ltd v Yardley* [2002] 2 A.C. 164 at [107]; *Heinl v Jyske Bank (Gibraltar) Ltd* [1999] Lloyd's Rep. Bank. 511 at 523.

[77] cf. *Brinks Ltd v Abu-Saleh* [1996] C.L.C. 133 at 149, per Rimer J, finding no liability in the absence of an act "in furtherance of the breach of trust".

[78] *Casio Computer Co Ltd v Sayo* [2001] EWCA Civ 661 at [16], approving *Grupo Torras SA v Al-Sabah* [2001] C.L.C. 221 at [119].

[79] [1995] 2 A.C. 378.

elaborated by Peter Gibson J in the *Baden* case[80] were "best forgotten". The word "dishonesty" was also to be preferred to "unconscionable conduct".[81] Lord Nicholls summarily rejected the view that an accessory could never be directly liable to the beneficiaries, because they are entitled to expect that others will refrain from intentionally intruding in the trustee-beneficiary relationship. Similarly rejected was the view that even an innocent third party could be liable, as that would make commerce impossible. In rejecting the view that negligence was a sufficient basis for liability, Lord Nicholls observed that in the commercial context persons such as bankers, advisers and many other agents would be liable to the trustees if they acted negligently. There was no reason why they should also be liable to the beneficiaries.[82] Thus the conclusion was that dishonesty is the basis of assistance liability.

25–021   It remains to be considered what is meant by "dishonesty". Lord Nicholls explained that it combines the objective standard of not acting as an honest person would in the circumstances with a strong subjective element: the court will assess the conduct in the light of what the defendant actually knew, not what a reasonable person would have known, and will have regard to the defendant's experience, intelligence and reasons for acting as he did. The broad meaning is conscious impropriety.[83]

The House of Lords revisited the issue in *Twinsectra Ltd v Yardley*,[84] where the words of Lord Nicholls in *Royal Brunei Airlines Sdn Bhd v Tan* were closely analysed. Their Lordships described three tests of dishonesty:

(i)   the purely subjective "Robin Hood test", where the defendant is judged by their own standards of honesty, which the courts have rejected;
(ii)   the purely objective test; and
(iii) the "combined test", said by the majority to be favoured by Lord Nicholls, whereby the conduct must be dishonest by ordinary standards and the defendant also realised that, by those standards, his conduct was dishonest.

The majority of their Lordships adopted the "combined test" and held that dishonesty required subjective awareness that the conduct was dishonest by the objective standards of reasonable and honest people. Lord Millett, in a dissenting speech, considered that the correct reading of the decision in *Royal Brunei Airlines* did not involve a truly combined objective and subjective test. Instead, Lord Millett thought that the only subjective elements allowed were the defendant's experience, intelligence and actual state of knowledge. There was no requirement that he must have subjectively realised he was acting dishonestly.

---

[80] *Baden, Delvaux and Lecuit v Société Générale pour Favoriser le Développement du Commerce et de l'Industrie en France SA* [1983] B.C.L.C. 325; above, fn.41.

[81] Although an "unconscionable" standard was later applied to knowing receipt in *Akindele*; above, para.25–013.

[82] cf. G. McCormack (1995) 9 T.L.I. 102, suggesting that an accessory to fraud should be liable if negligent.

[83] See also *Heinl v Jyske Bank (Gibraltar) Ltd* [1999] Lloyd's Rep. Bank. 511 (high standard of proof of dishonesty required).

[84] [2002] A.C. 164; T. Yeo and H. Tjio (2002) 118 L.Q.R. 502. See also *Papamichael v National Westminster Bank Plc* [2003] 1 Lloyd's Rep. 341.

Lord Millett preferred an objective approach, adding that, so far as the defendant's state of knowledge was concerned, he did not need to know the details of the trust. It sufficed if he knew that the money was not at the free disposal of the person whose breach he assisted.

The meaning of dishonesty was re-examined by the Privy Council in *Barlow Clowes International Ltd v Eurotrust International Ltd*.[85] Lord Hoffmann confirmed that the test laid down in *Royal Brunei Airlines Sdn Bhd v Tan* was that the defendant must either have known that the transaction was not one in which he could honestly participate or have suspected this and decided not to make enquiries. Although a dishonest state of mind is subjective, the standard by which it is judged is objective: if, by ordinary standards, it would be considered dishonest, it is irrelevant that the defendant's standards are different. **25–022**

Lord Hoffmann sought to interpret the majority's decision in *Twinsectra Ltd v Yardley* as not introducing a different test from *Royal Brunei Airlines*. He considered that Lord Hutton's remarks in that case (and indeed some of his own), although ambiguous, had been misinterpreted by academic writers. In his Lordship's view, Lord Hutton had not meant that, in order to be dishonest, the defendant must have thought about what normally accepted standards were. Lord Hoffmann in *Barlow Clowes* was thus able to conclude that the principles laid down by the House of Lords in *Twinsectra Ltd v Yardley* were in fact no different from those laid down by the Privy Council in *Royal Brunei Airlines*. The subjective element is what the defendant knew. The objective element is that his conduct was dishonest by the ordinary standards of honest people. It is not necessary for him to have formed a view on the propriety of his conduct in the light of those standards.

Whether or not this re-interpretation of *Twinsectra* can be seen as convincing,[86] it is clear that the law now applies an objective test of dishonesty. The recent case of *Ivey v Genting Casinos (UK) Ltd (trading as Crockford Clubs)*[87] concerned the offence of cheating at gambling under the Gambling Act 2005 s.42. The case therefore involved a criminal offence rather than the civil action of dishonest assistance. However, Lord Hughes said for a unanimous Supreme Court[88]:

> "Successive cases at the highest level have decided that the test of dishonesty is objective. After some hesitation in *Twinsectra Ltd v Yardley*, the law is settled on the objective test set out by Lord Nicholls of Birkenhead in *Royal Brunei Airlines Sdn Bhd v Tan*. ... The test now clearly established was explained thus in the *Barlow Clowes* case by Lord Hoffmann, who had been a party also to the *Twinsectra* case:

---

[85] [2006] 1 W.L.R. 1476.

[86] For criticism see T. Yeo (2006) 122 L.Q.R. 171; J. Penner (2006) 20 T.L.I. 122; G. Virgo in A. Burrows and A. Rodger (eds), *Mapping the Law, Essays in memory of Peter Birks* (Oxford: Oxford University Press, 2006), p.86; J. Lee (2008) 28 L.S. 1.

[87] [2017] UKSC 67; [2017] 3 W.L.R. 1212; G. Virgo (2018) 77 C.L.J. 18.

[88] [2017] UKSC 67 at [62]–[63], referring to *Barlow Clowes International Ltd v Eurotrust International Ltd* [2006] 1 WLR 1476; *Abou-Rahmah v Abacha* [2006] EWCA Civ 1492; [2007] Bus. L.R. 220; *Starglade Properties Ltd v Nash* [2010] EWCA Civ 1314; [2011] Lloyd's Rep. F.C. 102. The comments on the meaning of dishonesty were strictly made obiter, as the Court concluded that cheating did not require dishonesty. For a very useful review of the authorities on dishonesty, see *Group Seven Ltd v Nasir* [2017] EWHC 2466 (Ch) at [411]–[440] (but note the case predated *Ivey*).

"Although a dishonest state of mind is a subjective mental state, the standard by which the law determines whether it is dishonest is objective. If by ordinary standards a defendants mental state would be characterised as dishonest, it is irrelevant that the defendant judges by different standards."

Although the House of Lords and Privy Council were careful in these cases to confine their decisions to civil cases, there can be no logical or principled basis for the meaning of dishonesty (as distinct from the standards of proof by which it must be established) to differ according to whether it arises in a civil action or a criminal prosecution. Dishonesty is a simple, if occasionally imprecise, English word. It would be an affront to the law if its meaning differed according to the kind of proceedings in which it arose."

25-023 Clearly dishonesty includes deliberately closing one's eyes or deliberately not asking questions, of which an example is *Agip (Africa) Ltd v Jackson*[89]:

Payment orders from Agip to third parties were fraudulently altered by Agip's accountant, Z, who changed the name of the payees to that of B Co and other companies. B Co (and the other companies) had been formed by the defendants, who were two accountants in partnership (Jackson & Co) and their employee. Two of the defendants were the sole directors and shareholders of B Co. The money was transferred to the account of B Co and thence to Jackson's client account in the Isle of Man. It was then paid to various recipients abroad who had no connection with Agip. B Co was then put into liquidation. Agip sought to recover from the defendants, who had throughout followed the instructions of their client, a French lawyer acting for unidentified principals.

The claim based on assistance in the breach was successful before Millett J. Z had committed a breach of his duty to Agip, which the defendants must have realised was going on. They obviously knew they were "laundering" money, and were consciously helping Z to conceal the fraud. At best, they had been indifferent to it, which amounted to dishonesty. One partner and the employee were liable for assisting the breach, and the other partner was vicariously liable for their acts. The judgment of Millett J was upheld on appeal[90]: the defendants were liable because they did not act honestly.

D. Remedies

25-024 It has been held that a dishonest assistant is jointly and severally liable with the trustee for any loss, but is accountable only for his own share of any profit from the breach.[91] Although this position is easy to state as a matter of doctrine, it conceals an interesting theoretical point.

A dishonest assistant is jointly and severally liable with the trustee for losses suffered as a result of the breach. Importantly, the assistant's liability for that loss does not depend on his or her conduct *causing* the loss. Of course, a third party will not be liable under the head of dishonest assistance if the beneficiary cannot prove factual assistance in the breach. But once that assistance is established, along with the other requirements of an underlying breach by the trustee and

---

[89] [1990] Ch. 265; P. Millett (1991) 107 L.Q.R. 71.
[90] [1991] Ch. 547.
[91] *Fyffes Group Ltd v Templeman* [2000] 2 Lloyd's Rep. 643; *Ultraframe (UK) Ltd v Fielding* [2005] EWHC 1638 (Ch) at [1589]–[1600]; S. Baughen [2007] L.M.C.L.Q. 545; A. Goymour [2008] 16 R.L.R. 113.

dishonesty on the part of the third party, the assistant will be liable for any loss suffered as a result of the underlying breach of trust. It will not be necessary for the beneficiary to prove that the third party's assistance was a necessary cause of that loss.[92] To put the point from the other side: the third party cannot escape liability by showing that the beneficiary would have suffered the same loss even without the third party's assistance. The assistant is liable for losses suffered as a result of the underlying breach, not merely losses suffered as a result of the assistance.[93]

This suggests that the assistant's liability duplicates that of the trustee.[94] Yet, if that is true, it ought to follow that the assistant is also liable for the amount of any profit made by the trustee. This proposition was, however, rejected in *Ultraframe (UK) Ltd v Fielding*,[95] where Lewison J thought that such a response would be penal. Instead, it was held that dishonest assistants are only liable to account for their own shares of any profits made as a result of the breach of trust.

The general position is therefore that dishonest assistants are jointly and severally liable with the trustee for losses suffered as a result of the breach, but that assistants are liable only for their own gains and not gains made by other wrongdoers.[96]

Although accounts of profits may be awarded against dishonest assistants, they will be assessed on a different basis from those awarded against trustees and fiduciaries. So held the Court of Appeal in *Novoship (UK) Ltd v Mikhaylyuk*.[97]

25–025

> Ship charterers paid bribes to Mr Mikhaylyuk, the manager of a ship-owning company, who was responsible for negotiating charters. The scheme was complicated and involved several parties, but in essence Mr Mikhaylyuk breached his fiduciary duty to the ship owners and the bribing charterers dishonestly assisted him to do so. At trial, the charterers were ordered to account for the profits they had made under the charters. This was an enormous sum because the market had changed and the charterers were able to sub-charter their ships at great profit. The Court of Appeal reversed the award and held that those profits had not been caused by the act of dishonest assistance.

---

[92] *Grupo Torras SA v Al-Sabah* [2001] C.L.C. 221 at [119]; *Casio Computer Co Ltd v Sayo* [2001] EWCA Civ 661 at [16]; *Madoff Securities International Ltd v Raven* [2013] EWHC 3147 (Comm) at [339].

[93] See J. Glister (2016) 42 Aust. Bar. Rev. 152. cf. the comment in *Central Bank of Ecuador v Conticorp SA* [2015] UKPC 11; [2016] 1 B.C.L.C. 26 at [170], but the distinction was not there in issue.

[94] See S. Elliott and C. Mitchell (2004) 67 M.L.R. 16; cf. P. Ridge (2008) 124 L.Q.R. 445. Also see the discussion in G. Virgo, *The Principles of Equity & Trusts*, 2nd edn (2016), pp.734–737.

[95] [2005] EWHC 1638 (Ch) at [1589]–[1600]. Lewison J did not follow a Canadian line of authority that provided for an assistant to be liable for the profit made by the primary wrongdoer.

[96] A caveat is that the disgorgeable gain of an individual wrongdoer, whether a fiduciary or a third party, may be calculated by reference to gains actually made by companies controlled by the wrongdoer: see J. Glister (2017) 40 U.N.S.W.L.J. 4.

[97] [2015] Q.B. 499; P. Davies (2015) 131 L.Q.R. 173; W. Gummow (2015) 74 C.L.J. 405. See also *Fyffes Group Ltd v Templeman* [2000] 2 Lloyd's Rep. 643. *Novoship* is an example of the point made in fn.96 above. At trial, Christopher Clarke J found the assistant Mr Nikitin liable for profits actually made by a company he controlled: [2012] EWHC 3586 (Comm) at [529]. The appeal was allowed, but the Court of Appeal assumed that the assistant would indeed have been liable for any relevant gains made by his company: [2015] Q.B. 499 at [62].

The third parties were not themselves fiduciaries and so did not owe the fiduciary obligation not to make a profit, even though they were susceptible to an award of an account of profits being made against them[98]:

> "Mr Nikitin [one of the charterers] was not a fiduciary either as regards [*Novoship*] or the ship owning companies. He is not sued for a breach of fiduciary duty. He is sued because he has committed an equitable wrong. Where a claim based on equitable wrongdoing is made against one who is not a fiduciary, we consider that, as in the case of a fiduciary sued for breach of an equitable (but non-fiduciary) obligation, there is no reason why the common law rules of causation, remoteness and measure of damages should not be applied by analogy. We recognise that these rules do not apply to the case of a fiduciary sued for breach of a fiduciary duty; but that is because the two cases are different."

Unlike in the case of a fiduciary being made to disgorge profits,[99] the third parties in this case were able to avoid liability on the grounds that "the real or effective cause of the profits was the unexpected change in the market".[100] Their profits were not attributable, as a matter of causation, to their wrong of dishonest assistance.

25–026 The distinction, recognised in *Novoship*, between accounts of profits awarded against trustees and those awarded against wrong-doing third parties may not yet be firmly entrenched. The distinction has been criticised at appellate level in Australia, where the Full Court of the Federal Court noted that "the principles and informing policy to hold the dishonest participant to account are no different to the holding of the fiduciary to account".[101] Furthermore, in *Central Bank of Ecuador v Conticorp SA*, Lord Mance said for the Privy Council[102]:

> "[T]he Court [in *Novoship*] refused to distinguish between the liability in equity of the fiduciary and that of a knowing recipient or a dishonest assister. The Board considers that this is in principle correct."

As we have seen, the Court of Appeal in *Novoship* did indeed hold that accounts of profits were available against wrongdoing third parties as well as against wrongdoing fiduciaries. But the whole point of difference between the Court of Appeal and Christopher Clarke J in *Novoship*—and the very reason the appeal was allowed—was that the Court of Appeal thought the principles governing those accounts would differ between wrongdoing fiduciaries and wrongdoing third parties.

25–027 Awards of equitable compensation or accounts of profits are not the only possible consequences of a finding of dishonest assistance. In *UBS AG (London Branch) v Kommunale Wasserwerke Leipzig GmbH*,[103] UBS dishonestly assisted another company, Value Partners, to breach fiduciary duties owed to its clients. The scheme involved Value Partners advising their clients to do business with UBS,

[98] [2015] Q.B. 499 at [107]. cf. at [82].
[99] See *Murad v Al-Saraj* [2005] W.T.L.R. 1573.
[100] [2015] Q.B. 499 at [114].
[101] *Lifeplan Australia Friendly Society Ltd v Ancient Order of Foresters in Victoria Friendly Society Ltd* [2017] FCAFC 74 at [68]. At the time of writing an appeal to the High Court of Australia is pending.
[102] [2015] UKPC 11 at [9] in the unreported interest and costs judgment.
[103] [2017] EWCA Civ 1567; [2017] 2 Lloyd's Rep. 621.

regardless of their clients' true interests. Those clients, one of which was KWL, were persuaded to enter into certain high-risk derivative agreements with UBS. The conduct of UBS was dishonest because it was "both deliberate (i.e. carried out in the knowledge that Value Partners was abusing its fiduciary duty to KWL) and secretive, in the sense that UBS knew that KWL was ignorant of the corrupt arrangement".[104] The actual breach of fiduciary duty was committed by Value Partners, but the Court of Appeal held by majority that UBS's dishonest assistance meant that it could not resist rescission of its contract with KWL.[105] Rescission allowed KWL to avoid large losses that it would otherwise have suffered under the derivative products.

i. Contribution and Vicarious Liability. Like a knowing recipient,[106] a dishonest assistant may be liable in respect of the same damage as another person. Contribution may lie between them under the Civil Liability (Contribution) Act 1978.

25–028

It may be that the other liable person is not herself a wrongdoer but is instead vicariously liable for the acts of another wrongdoer. The circumstances in which a firm of solicitors will be vicariously liable for the acts of a partner who has dishonestly assisted in a breach of trust were clarified by the House of Lords in *Dubai Aluminium Co Ltd v Salaam*.[107] In that case a dishonest partner had planned, drafted and signed sham agreements giving effect to a scheme involving over $50 million which he knew to be fraudulent. The question was whether s.10 of the Partnership Act 1890 applied, under which a firm is liable for any wrongful act or omission of a partner acting in the ordinary course of the business of the firm, or with the authority of his partners. If that provision did apply, contribution could be sought from the partners.

The firm was held liable on the ground that, although the wrongful acts had not been authorised, the fraudulent scheme was so closely connected with the acts the dishonest partner was authorised to do that he could be said to have been acting in the ordinary course of the firm's business when he committed them. It is not within the ordinary course of a solicitor's practice to act as an express trustee,[108] nor to act as a trustee when not appointed as such and so incur liability as a constructive trustee in the sense of a de facto trustee.[109] However, the present case was not of that kind, despite the fact that the solicitor could be termed "liable to account as a constructive trustee". Given that a solicitor may be guilty of dishonest conduct while acting within the ordinary scope of his practice, there was no reason why his firm should not incur vicarious liability for loss caused by

---

[104] [2017] EWCA Civ 1567 at [93].

[105] [2017] EWCA Civ 1567 at [156] per Lord Briggs and Hamblen LJ; Gloster LJ disagreed that UBS acted as a dishonest assistant and concluded that KWL was not entitled to rescind. On rescission see below, Ch.29.

[106] Above, para.25–016, discussing *Charter Plc v City Index Ltd* [2008] Ch. 313.

[107] [2003] 2 A.C. 366; C. Mitchell (2003) 119 L.Q.R. 364. *Re Bell's Indenture* [1980] 1 W.L.R. 1217 was overruled in part. See also *Agip (Africa) Ltd v Jackson* [1991] Ch. 547. For vicarious liability to account for a profit, see J. Edelman (2008) 124 L.Q.R. 21.

[108] See *Walker v Stones* [2001] Q.B. 902.

[109] This was the sense in which the term "constructive trustee" was used in *Mara v Browne* [1896] 1 Ch. 199, where Lord Herschell said that it was not within a partner's implied authority to make himself a constructive trustee and thereby subject his partners to the same liability.

conduct which constituted him a constructive trustee in the sense of a person who was personally accountable for dishonest assistance in a breach of trust.

Another question is whether a firm is vicariously liable for an act of dishonest assistance in a breach of trust committed by its employee (as opposed to a partner). The firm will be liable where the victim of the employee's dishonesty was the firm's own client, but not where the victim was not its client.[110]

4. DE FACTO TRUSTEES

25–029   This head of liability concerns third parties who are not properly trustees but who take it upon themselves to act as such. In *Mara v Browne*,[111] A.L. Smith LJ said:

> "Now, what constitutes a trustee de son tort? It appears to me if one, not being a trustee and not having authority from a trustee, takes upon himself to intermeddle with trust matters or to do acts characteristic of the office of trustee, he may thereby make himself what is called in law a trustee of his own wrong—i.e., a trustee de son tort, or, as it is also termed, a constructive trustee."

Care must be taken in respect of "constructive trustee". What the court does is to construe the person as an express trustee on the basis that they have acted as such. In *Soar v Ashwell*,[112] Lord Esher MR said:

> "The cases seem to me to decide that, where a person has assumed, either with or without consent, to act as a trustee of money or other property, i.e., to act in a fiduciary relation with regard to it, and has in consequence been in possession of or has exercised command or control over such money or property, a Court of Equity will impose upon him all the liabilities of an express trustee, and will class him with and will call him an express trustee of an express trust."

As the passage from *Mara v Browne* indicates, the traditional name for this liability is trusteeship *de son tort* ("of his own wrong").[113] But in *Dubai Aluminium Co Ltd v Salaam*, Lord Millett said: "Substituting dog Latin for bastard French, we would do better today to describe such persons as de facto trustees."[114]

25–030   An example of a de facto trustee can be found in *Life Association of Scotland v Siddal*,[115] where a trustee of land devised the land to his sister Gertrude. The devise was subject to the payment of a legacy, which was not made, so the land did not in fact pass to Gertrude. Gertrude nonetheless acted as if she was trustee of the land, and proceeded to sell it. Instead of collecting the proceeds of sale she allowed them to be paid to a third party. After Gertrude's death her estate was made liable to restore the proceeds of sale plus interest.

---

[110] *Balfron Trustees Ltd v Peterson* [2002] W.T.L.R. 157; S. Baughen [2007] L.M.C.L.Q. 545.
[111] [1896] 1 Ch. 199 at 209.
[112] [1893] 2 Q.B. 390 at 394.
[113] The phrase is a development from executor *de son tort*.
[114] [2003] 2 A.C. 366 at [138]; see also *Williams v Central Bank of Nigeria* [2014] A.C. 1189 at [9].
[115] (1861) 3 De G.F. & J. 58.

Agents of true trustees may also be liable as de facto trustees if they do acts characteristic of a trustee and outside the duties of an agent.[116]

Although de facto trustees are discussed here, in the context of personal claims against third parties, de facto trusteeship is properly characterised as a form of "first party" liability.[117] The actions of third parties justify treating these strangers to the trust in the same way as if they had been properly appointed as trustees. They will be subjected to the same duties and liabilities as trustees,[118] including fiduciary duties,[119] and will be treated the same way for limitation purposes.[120] A person who has already done acts sufficient to constitute him a de facto trustee, and who then does an act that would be a breach of trust if done by a properly-appointed trustee, may even be entitled to ask the court for relief from the consequences of a breach of trust under s.61 of the Trustee Act 1925.[121] Not all de facto trustees are wrongful intermeddlers in a pejorative sense, even though by definition they are not entitled to act as they have done. A person may have become only a de facto trustee because of some innocent defect in their purported appointment as a true trustee.[122]

25–031

5. THE PERSONAL ACTION IN RE DIPLOCK

In *Re Diplock*,[123] executors distributed large sums of money to numerous charities under the terms of a residuary bequest which was subsequently held to be invalid.

25–032

> By his will Diplock gave the residue of his property on trust for such "charitable or benevolent ... objects in England as my ... executors ... may in their ... absolute discretion select." He and the executors thought that this was a valid charitable gift, but it was not.[124] The executors distributed £203,000 among a considerable number of charitable institutions. When the invalidity of the charitable gift was discovered, the next-of-kin settled their claim against the executors for £15,000 with the approval of the court. The next-of-kin then attempted to recover the rest of the money from the charities directly.

---

[116] *Williams-Ashman v Price and Williams* [1942] Ch. 219 at 228. See also *Williams v Williams* (1881) 17 Ch.D. 437; *Competitive Insurance Co Ltd v Davies Investments Ltd* [1975] 1 W.L.R. 1240.

[117] *Taylor v Davies* [1920] A.C. 636 at 651. Personal claims against trustees are discussed in Ch.24.

[118] *Soar v Ashwell* [1893] 2 Q.B. 390 at 394.

[119] *Taylor v Davies* [1920] A.C. 636.

[120] *Cattley v Pollard* [2007] Ch. 353; *Williams v Central Bank of Nigeria* [2014] A.C. 1189. They are not, however, "trustees of the settlement" within the meaning of the Taxation of Chargeable Gains Act 1992 s.69: *Jasmine Trustees Ltd v Wells & Hind (A Firm)* [2008] Ch. 194.

[121] Above, para.24–037. It seems that this possibility ought to exist, given that de facto trustees may be entirely innocent and may even have assumed control of the relevant property with the consent of the beneficiaries. See *Agusta Pty Ltd v Provident Capital Ltd* [2012] NSWCA 26 at [36]. But note the words of s.61: "a trustee, whether appointed by the court or otherwise".

[122] *Pearce v Pearce* (1856) 22 Beav. 248.

[123] [1948] Ch. 465 (CA); [1951] A.C. 251 (HL) (where the earlier authorities are extensively reviewed). See S. Whittaker (1983) 4 *Journal of Legal History* 3; T. Akkouh and S. Worthington in C. Mitchell and P. Mitchell (eds), *Landmark Cases in the Law of Restitution* (Oxford: Hart Publishing, 2006), Ch.11.

[124] *Chichester Diocesan Fund v Simpson* [1944] A.C. 341.

The next-of-kin brought both proprietary and personal actions against the charities. The proprietary claims were successful where the donations could still be identified in the hands of the recipients but not where the money had already been spent. These tracing questions are considered in Ch.26.

The next-of-kin claimed alternatively that a direct personal action lay against the innocent recipients in equity. This claim succeeded in the Court of Appeal, whose judgment was unanimously affirmed by the House of Lords.[125] Such an action may be brought by an unpaid or underpaid creditor, legatee or next-of-kin against the recipient, whether the latter is an overpaid creditor or beneficiary or a "stranger" having no claim to any part of the estate.[126] While the common law action for money had and received was then confined to mistakes of fact,[127] it was held that the action in equity lay whether the mistake was of fact or, as in the present case, of law. The mistake in such a case is not that of the claimant, but that of the personal representative, who is not a party to the action. The claimant has no way of finding out whether the mistake was of fact or law, nor whether it was a mistaken or deliberate misapplication,[128] hence:

> "[I]t would be a strange thing if the Court of Chancery, having taken upon itself to see that the assets of a deceased person were duly administered, was deterred from doing justice to a creditor, legatee or next-of-kin because the executor had done him wrong under a mistake of law."[129]

25–033 The action will not lie against a bona fide purchaser for value without notice, but, as far as a volunteer is concerned, it is no defence that she was unaware of the mistake.[130] This strict liability is therefore different from liability in knowing receipt. Knowing receipt could also be grounded on a mistaken payment by an executor, but, as we have seen, the liability there depends on the recipient having a level of knowledge such as to make it unconscionable for her to retain the benefit of the receipt.[131] Although liability under the personal *Re Diplock* action is strict, the claim will still fail if the claimant has acquiesced in the wrongful payment,[132] or has failed to bring his action within the time permitted by the Limitation Act 1980.[133] It is not settled whether the action lies against the recipient's successor in title.[134]

---

[125] [1951] A.C. 251 (sub nom. *Ministry of Health v Simpson*).

[126] [1948] Ch. 465 at 502; [1951] A.C. 251 at 269.

[127] The action now lies for recovery of money paid by mistake of law; *Kleinwort Benson Ltd v Lincoln CC* [1999] 2 A.C. 349.

[128] It seems that the action will lie where the wrongful payment was deliberate: [1951] A.C. 251 at 270.

[129] [1951] A.C. 251 at 270, per Lord Simonds. The personal representative can now himself recover from the recipient whether the mistake was of fact or law: *Kleinwort Benson Ltd v Lincoln CC* [1999] 2 A.C. 349.

[130] [1948] Ch. 465 at 503.

[131] Above, para.25–013.

[132] [1951] A.C. 251 at 276.

[133] Below, para.25–036.

[134] See the discussion in Goff and Jones, 7th edn, p.707 (the point is not directly discussed in subsequent editions).

The *Re Diplock* personal action lies for the principal sum only, without interest,[135] and is subject to two further important qualifications. First, the direct claim against the recipient is limited to the amount which cannot be recovered from the personal representative, who is primarily liable.[136] Thus the recipient will only be liable in respect of the whole sum if nothing can be recovered from the personal representative, for example because he is insolvent, or cannot be found, or acted under a court order,[137] or is protected by s.27 of the Trustee Act 1925.[138] This limitation has been criticised.[139] Why should the recipient's liability depend on the personal representative's solvency? The solution adopted in *Re Diplock* benefits the recipient at the expense of the personal representative, who, on paying the claimant, should be subrogated to the claimant's right to sue the recipient. Another solution might be to require the claimant to exhaust his remedies against the recipient before suing the personal representative.[140]

The second qualification is that the action appears to be limited to claims arising out of the administration of estates and does not apply in respect of inter vivos trusts.[141] The action originated at a time when the Court of Chancery was attempting to acquire the jurisdiction then exercised by the ecclesiastical courts over the administration of assets,[142] and is not necessarily available to beneficiaries of lifetime trusts.[143] Some cases do indicate that the court is not unwilling to extend the action beyond the administration of estates.[144] However, even if the *Re Diplock* action is widened to include lifetime trusts, it would not simply usurp the role of knowing receipt. This is because the remedies available against a knowing recipient are more extensive than those available under the *Re Diplock* principle. Liability under *Re Diplock* is confined to the amount of receipt, without interest, and only insofar as that amount cannot be recovered from the primary wrongdoer. Under knowing receipt, on the other hand, the defendant may be liable to an award of an account of profits, or for the value of the assets at judgment.[145] A knowing receipt claim was made in *Re Diplock* itself,

---

[135] This was described as an anomaly by Lord Walker in *Sempra Metals Ltd (formerly Metallgesellschaft Ltd) v IRC* [2008] 1 A.C. 561 at 626.

[136] [1948] Ch. 465 at 503. Here the executors paid £15,000 under a compromise approved by the court.

[137] For example, a *Benjamin* order (*Re Benjamin* [1902] 1 Ch. 723), giving him liberty to distribute on the footing that a particular person is dead.

[138] Above, para.19–028.

[139] See A. Denning (1949) 65 L.Q.R. 37 at 44; S. Whittaker (1983) 4 J.L.H. 3; Goff and Jones, 9th edn, para.8–123.

[140] As is required in Western Australia by the Trustees Act 1962 s.65(7).

[141] See [1951] A.C. 251 at 265–266, per Lord Simonds.

[142] See C. Harpum (1990) 49 C.L.J. 217 at 219.

[143] Although if a trustee pays trust money under a mistake of fact (or now, by mistake of law) he may recover it, and may be compelled by the beneficiaries to do so: *Re Robinson* [1911] 1 Ch. 502.

[144] See *Butler v Broadhead* [1975] Ch. 97; *GL Baker Ltd v Medway Building and Supplies Ltd* [1958] 1 W.L.R. 1216; *Nelson v Larholt* [1948] 1 K.B. 339; *Eddis v Chichester Constable* [1969] 1 All E.R. 566 (affirmed, without discussing this point, [1969] 2 Ch. 345); *Davies v Sharples* [2006] W.T.L.R. 839 (will trust).

[145] Above, para.25–015.

but was defeated because the recipients were innocent.[146] If it had been successful, the recipients would have been liable pay interest on the sum received.

25–034 Much criticism has centred around the apparent refusal of the House of Lords in *Re Diplock* to recognise the defence of change of position. Where the volunteer has received the money in good faith, his liability to repay it could cause hardship if he has acted to his detriment by spending the money in an exceptional and irretrievable manner. The most famous donation in *Re Diplock* involved money being paid to a hospital charity and used in the erection of new buildings. This, it was considered, made it inequitable to allow tracing,[147] but was no defence to the personal action. However, it may be that a change of position defence now applies to the personal claim: this was suggested by Lord Goff in *Lipkin Gorman v Karpnale Ltd*,[148] and the defence was assumed to be available in *Davies v Sharples*.[149]

6. LIMITATION AND THIRD PARTIES

25–035 We saw in Ch.24 that a six-year limitation period generally applies to "an action by a beneficiary to recover trust property or in respect of any breach of trust".[150] That six-year period does not apply, however, to actions that fall within the following exception contained in the Limitation Act 1980 s.21(1):

> "No period of limitation prescribed by this Act shall apply to an action by a beneficiary under a trust, being an action—
> (a) in respect of any fraud or fraudulent breach of trust to which the trustee was a party or privy; or
> (b) to recover from the trustee trust property or the proceeds of trust property in the possession of the trustee, or previously received by the trustee and converted to his use."

The question in *Williams v Central Bank of Nigeria*[151] was whether or not actions in knowing receipt and dishonest assistance fell within s.21(1). If they did, no period of limitation would be imposed by the Act. If they did not, the general six-year period in s.21(3) would apply and the claims would be time-barred. There were two ways in which the claims could fall within s.21(1) and so not be subject to limitation. First, a knowing recipient could be a "trustee" within the meaning of s.21(1)(a).[152] Secondly, an action "in respect of any fraud or

---

[146] [1948] 1 Ch. 465 at 477–479.
[147] Below, para.26–031. It may be better to say that tracing was allowed but claiming was not.
[148] [1991] 2 A.C. 548 at 580; W. Cornish (1991) 50 C.L.J. 407; below, para.26–031.
[149] [2006] W.T.L.R. 839.
[150] Limitation Act 1980 s.21(3); above, para.24–040.
[151] [2014] A.C. 1189; S. Watterson (2014) 73 C.L.J. 253; P. Davies [2014] L.M.C.L.Q. 313; J. Lee (2015) 131 L.Q.R. 39.
[152] Counsel apparently acknowledged that a dishonest assistant could not relevantly be a "trustee" (at [30]), although Lord Neuberger expressly decided the question in respect of both knowing recipients and dishonest assistants (at [90]). If a knowing recipient is not a trustee then it would certainly appear that a fortiori a dishonest assistant is not.

fraudulent breach of trust to which the trustee was a party or privy" may include an action against a third party who is not herself a trustee.

The first argument failed on the grounds that a knowing recipient is not a true trustee. The word "trustee" in the Act relevantly includes constructive trustees, but the majority interpreted this to mean "true" constructive trustees, such as de facto trustees,[153] and not people who may be liable to account as if they were trustees.[154] The main reason for this seems to be that no trust or confidence is ever placed in a knowing recipient,[155] even though knowing recipients do acquire property that could form the subject-matter of a trust. However, as Watterson points out,[156] if a lack of reposition of trust and confidence stops a person from being a trustee then many trusts that are imposed by operation of law ought to be excluded. Indeed, de facto trustees may not have trust and confidence reposed in them; yet de facto trustees were given as examples of third parties who *were* true trustees and who could therefore fall within s.21(1).[157]

The second argument also failed, with Lord Sumption holding that s.21(1)(a) "is concerned only with actions *against trustees* on account of their own fraud or fraudulent breach of trust".[158] In addition to other reasons based on legislative history[159] and statutory construction,[160] the majority thought the alternative would lead to an anomaly because identical conduct on the part of a dishonest assistant would be treated differently by the limitation regime according to whether the underlying breach by the trustee was dishonest or not.[161] Only those actions where the trustee was dishonest would fall within s.21(1), yet it has been clear since *Royal Brunei Airlines Sdn Bhd v Tan*[162] that the focus is on the conduct of the assistant and that dishonesty on the part of the trustee is not required. For the majority there was "no rational reason" why identical conduct on the part of the assistant should attract a different limitation period dependent upon the trustee's own honesty, when it is irrelevant to the assistant's liability.[163]

The majority's approach does have the advantage of avoiding that anomaly. However, and as Lord Clarke noted in his dissent on this point,[164] it is somewhat difficult to reconcile with the text of the section. This is because the majority

---

[153] Above, para.25–029.

[154] Lord Sumption and Lord Neuberger each wrote substantive judgments but also expressed their agreement with each other. Lord Hughes also agreed with Lord Sumption and Lord Neuberger. Lord Clarke concurred "somewhat reluctantly" on this point. Lord Mance dissented.

[155] [2014] A.C. 1189 at [31], per Lord Sumption; [64], per Lord Neuberger; [165], per Lord Clarke.

[156] S. Watterson (2014) 73 C.L.J. 253 at 256.

[157] [2014] A.C. 1189 at [7]–[11], citing *Selangor United Rubber Estates Ltd v Cradock (No.3)* [1968] 1 W.L.R. 1555 and *Paragon Finance Plc v DB Thakerar & Co (A Firm)* [1999] 1 All E.R. 400.

[158] [2014] A.C. 1189 at [32] (emphasis added); see also at [102].

[159] The forerunners of s.21(3) were intended to relieve trustees from the previous position that no limitation period applied to any claims against them, and the exceptions to that change "must apply to the same persons as the rule" ([2014] A.C. 1189 at [33]).

[160] These concerned the weight to be given to, first, the inclusion of "to which the trustee was a party or privy" in s.21(1)(a); and second, the fact that the exception in s.21(1)(b) clearly applies only to trustees themselves ([2014] A.C. 1189 at [34], [36]).

[161] [2014] A.C. 1189 at [35]; see also at [99], per Lord Neuberger.

[162] [1995] 2 A.C. 378; above, para.25–018.

[163] [2014] A.C. 1189 at [35]. Lord Mance in dissent saw this difference in treatment as coherent: at [157].

[164] [2014] A.C. 1189 at [173]–[174]. Compare Lord Neuberger's views at [97].

accepted that actions against third parties do fall within s.21(3) and are therefore covered by the standard six-year period. The words that operate to include them within s.21(3) are the words "in respect of any breach of trust". It appears inconsistent to interpret those words as including claims against third parties for the purposes of s.21(3), yet to interpret "in respect of any fraud or fraudulent breach of trust" as excluding such claims for the purposes of s.21(1).

25–036 For better or worse, the law now appears clear on the point: claims in knowing receipt and dishonest assistance will attract a six-year limitation period under s.21(3).[165] Claims against de facto trustees will normally be subject to the six-year period but may fall within s.21(1) if the facts allow. *Re Diplock* claims made by unpaid beneficiaries of the will or intestacy attract a longer limitation period of 12 years under s.22.[166]

Although the limitation period applicable to *Re Diplock* claims by unpaid beneficiaries is clear, the period applicable to claims by unpaid creditors is not. The same 12 year period could apply if the s.22 words "in respect of any claim to the personal estate of a deceased person or to any share or interest in any such estate" apply to actions by unpaid creditors in the same way as they apply to actions by unpaid beneficiaries. This is possible on a wide reading,[167] although the claim of the unpaid creditor is not exactly that she is entitled to the estate itself (unlike the claim of the unpaid beneficiary).[168] If the creditor's claim is not covered by s.22 then there are three options. First, it may be covered by s.5 and therefore subject to a six-year period.[169] This section is headed "actions on simple contract", but it has acquired a much wider meaning that the name suggests and in particular is the general rule for claims for unjust enrichment.[170] Secondly, and which is perhaps more likely, the *Re Diplock* creditor claim could be seen as sufficiently analogous to the claims that fall within s.5 to justify equity applying a six-year period by analogy.[171] Thirdly, the claim may not be covered by the Act either directly or by analogy. In that case the matter will be left to the doctrine of laches.[172]

There is also a practical reason to favour a six-year period. If the creditor's claim against the third party does indeed fall within s.22, then so ought the creditor's claim against the executor. However, it is clear that the claims against the executor do not fall within s.22. Claims brought by unpaid creditors against executors who have distributed the estate in such a way as to leave the creditors

---

[165] Although time will not begin to run immediately if the action falls within s.32 (postponement in cases of fraud, concealment or mistake).

[166] *Re Diplock* [1948] Ch. 465 at 514 (considering s.20 of the 1939 Act; the forerunner of s.22 of the 1980 Act).

[167] This is the view taken in M. Franks, *Limitation of Actions* (London: Sweet & Maxwell, 1959), p.259.

[168] See *Re Blow* [1914] 1 Ch. 233.

[169] This is the view taken in R. Kerridge, *Parry and Kerridge: The Law of Succession*, 13th edn (London: Sweet & Maxwell, 2016), para.24–44, although the text may elide the creditor's claim against the deceased (i.e., the reason why the claimant is a creditor in the first place) with the *Re Diplock* claim against the third party.

[170] *Kleinwort Benson Ltd v Sandwell BC* [1994] 4 All E.R. 890 at 942–943.

[171] The ability of equity to apply limitation periods by analogy is preserved in s.36.

[172] Above, para.24–049.

unpaid are still treated actions in *devastavit*.[173] For limitation purposes, *devastavit* is considered a tort and so the action is subject to a six-year period under s.2.[174] Under the *Re Diplock* principle, that claim must be brought first and the remedies against the executor exhausted. It therefore makes sense for the limitation periods to be the same,[175] or at least for the limitation period against the third party not to exceed that which applies against the executor. Otherwise a claim could be barred against the executor but could still lie against the recipient. Although this is not problematic in itself, it does not fit well with the requirement that remedies against the executor be exhausted first.

---

[173] See A. McGee, *Limitation Periods*, 2nd edn (London: Sweet & Maxwell, 1994), pp.255–256; T. Prime and G. Scanlan, *The Law of Limitation*, 2nd edn (Oxford: Oxford University Press, 2001), pp.317–318.

[174] *Lacons v Warmoll* [1907] 2 K.B. 350. The six-year period is still applied if the action is for an account, since the *devastavit* is the basis of the liability to account: see s.23.

[175] See, on this point in relation to the beneficiary's claim, *Re Diplock* [1948] Ch. 465 at 514.

1.   INTRODUCTION

MOST actions at law and in equity are personal. We now have to consider the   **26–001**
occasions on which a claimant has the right to proceed against a particular asset
in the defendant's hands. Such proprietary claims exist to a very limited extent at
law; and these, for convenience and for the sake of comparison, will be described
here.[1] In equity the right to follow or trace property is more extensive. We will
see that proprietary rights may be asserted where the claimant is making a claim
at law or in equity to a specific piece of property, and also where she is making a
claim in equity against a mixed fund to which property of hers (in equity) has
contributed.

There are two main advantages of a proprietary over a personal claim. First
and foremost, satisfaction of the claimant's demand does not depend on the
solvency of the defendant. If the property traced is the claimant's in equity, it
escapes the defendant's bankruptcy.[2] Secondly, in some cases, the claimant will
be able to take advantage of increases in the value of the property. For these
reasons a claimant will want to make a proprietary claim if she can, and to do so
she will need to locate the property by following or tracing it.

Following and tracing are normally used to identify assets in respect of which
a proprietary claim may lie. However, they are also relevant to some personal
actions. For example, a tracing analysis may be employed to determine whether
or not trust property was received by the defendant for the purposes of liability in
knowing receipt.[3]

---

[1] Below, paras 26–002, 26–004—26–006.
[2] Insolvency Act 1986 s.283.
[3] *Relfo Ltd (In Liquidation) v Varsani* [2014] EWCA Civ 360; [2015] 1 B.C.L.C. 14; below,
para.26–025.

A. Tracing, Following and Claiming

26–002 The concepts of tracing and following are distinct. In *Foskett v McKeown*,[4] Lord Millett said:

> "[Tracing and following] are both exercises in locating assets which are or may be taken to represent an asset belonging to the plaintiffs and to which they assert ownership. The processes of following and tracing are, however, distinct. Following is the process of following the same asset as it moves from hand to hand. Tracing is the process of identifying a new asset as the substitute for the old. Where one asset is exchanged for another, a claimant can elect whether to follow the original asset into the hands of the new owner or to trace its value into the new asset in the hands of the same owner. In practice his choice is often dictated by the circumstances."[5]

As following involves tracking the same asset as it moves from hand-to-hand, it rarely presents evidential difficulties. Problems only arise if the asset is mixed with another asset in a way that renders the original asset no longer identifiable, or if the asset is joined to another asset in such a way that it is impractical to separate them. In most cases the law's response to these situations is to treat the mixed property as co-owned by the owners of the contributing assets.[6] For example, in *Spence v Union Marine Insurance Co Ltd*,[7] cotton bales belonging to several different consignees became indistinguishable when their markings were washed away in a shipwreck. Although such loss of marking should not strictly alter the ownership of the individual bales, the court held the remaining bales to be co-owned. The original bales could be followed into co-ownership of the remaining bales.

Even though following itself may be a straightforward process, this does not mean that a claim can easily be made in respect of the followed property. This is because in many cases the original item will have been exchanged for another, and the person who now holds the original item will have a good defence to any claim made in respect of it. If a trustee wrongly misuses trust money to buy a car in her daughter's name, it is easy to follow the trust money into the hands of the car dealer. However, the dealer will almost certainly be a bona fide purchaser of the money and no claim will succeed against him.[8] Instead, the claimant beneficiary will trace the value into the substituted asset—the car in the hands of the trustee's daughter—and claim that property instead. The important point here

---

[4] [2001] 1 A.C. 102. See also *Ultraframe (UK) Ltd v Fielding* [2005] EWHC 1638 (Ch) [1464]; L. Smith, *The Law of Tracing* (Oxford: Oxford University Press, 1997), pp.6–14.

[5] [2001] 1 A.C. 102 at 127.

[6] The two exceptions to this are the doctrines of accession (where a junior item accedes to a dominant item and thereby ceases to exist) and specification (where an item is transformed into a completely new item of property). See generally P. Birks in N. Palmer & E. McKendrick (eds), *Interests in Goods*, 2nd edn (London: LLP, 1998), Ch.9. When accession involves land, it is known as the doctrine of fixtures: see *Elitestone Ltd v Morris* [1997] 1 W.L.R. 687.

[7] (1868) L.R. 3 C.P. 427. For a more modern example see *Hill v Reglon Pty Ltd* [2007] NSWCA 295 (indistinguishable scaffolding poles).

[8] *Thorndike v Hunt* (1859) 3 De G. & J. 563; *Thomson v Clydesdale Bank* [1893] A.C. 282. See also *Independent Trustee Services Ltd v GP Noble Trustees* [2012] EWCA Civ 195; [2013] Ch. 91 (money paid under consent order in divorce proceedings); T. Cutts [2013] L.M.C.L.Q. 17.

is that tracing and following are merely processes; they are *not* claims or remedies in themselves. In *Foskett v McKeown*, Lord Millett continued[9]:

> "[Tracing] is merely the process by which a claimant demonstrates what has happened to his property, identifies its proceeds and the persons who have handled or received them, and justifies his claim that the proceeds can properly be regarded as representing his property. Tracing ... identifies the traceable proceeds of the claimant's property. It enables the claimant to substitute the traceable proceeds for the original asset as the subject matter of his claim. *But it does not affect or establish his claim.*"

The discussion which follows shows that different tracing rules currently operate at law and in equity. There is arguably little point in maintaining this distinction, since in either case a tracing exercise simply identifies property over which a claim may be made. Both Lord Steyn and Lord Millett took this view in *Foskett v McKeown*,[10] although their comments were obiter dicta. Subsequent cases have acknowledged these comments,[11] but they have not been treated as actually settling the law in favour of a unified tracing process.[12] Notably, the Supreme Court made reference to the separate common law and equitable tracing rules in *FHR European Ventures LLP v Cedar Capital Partners LLC*.[13] The current position is that discrete common law and equitable tracing rules remain, although it seems possible that a unified process will eventually evolve. The expansion of the circumstances in which a constructive trust may be found also means that it is often easy to establish an entitlement to trace in equity.[14]

26–003

2. TRACING AT COMMON LAW[15]

The point of tracing in equity is normally to identify property in respect of which a proprietary remedy may be sought. That remedy may be a declaration that certain property is held on constructive trust, or is charged to secure a debt owed to the claimant. It is true that the claimant's ultimate aim is rarely to acquire the property in the sense of it being transferred to him. Rather, the point is to establish the proprietary right and then to realise that right by collecting the proceeds of sale of the property. But the claimant is still making a proprietary claim in respect of proprietary rights.

26–004

The position at common law is slightly different. Claimants still trace in order to identify assets in respect of which they can assert proprietary rights, but they do not seek proprietary remedies. This is because the common law never developed an action for chattels that entitled a claimant to seek specific

---

[9] [2001] 1 A.C. 102 at 128 (emphasis added).

[10] [2001] 1 A.C. 102 at 113 (Lord Steyn), 128 (Lord Millett). See Lord Millett's extra-judicial views in (1998) 114 L.Q.R. 399 at 409 and [1999] 14 *Amicus Curiae* 4. See also L. Smith, *The Law of Tracing* (1997), pp.278–279; R. Walker [2000] R.L.R. 573; Goff and Jones, 9th edn, para.7–18.

[11] See *Shalson v Russo* [2005] Ch. 281 at [103]–[104].

[12] See *London Allied Holdings Ltd v Lee* [2007] EWHC 2061 (Ch) at [246]–[247].

[13] [2014] UKSC 45; [2015] 1 A.C. 250 at [45].

[14] Although the Supreme Court has recently sounded a note of caution here: below, para.26–012.

[15] M. Scott (1966) 7 W.A.L.R. 463; S. Khurshid and P. Matthews (1979) 95 L.Q.R. 78; P. Matthews in P. Birks (ed.), *Laundering and Tracing* (Oxford: Clarendon Press, 1995), p.23; D. Fox, *Property Rights in Money* (Oxford: Oxford University Press, 2008). See P. Birks, *An Introduction to the Law of Restitution,* revised edn (Oxford: Oxford University Press, 1989), p.358.

recovery.[16] Historically, the point of tracing at common law was to establish rights in an asset sufficient to allow the claimant to sue in conversion or to bring an action for money had and received. Both of these are personal claims, and personal actions as a general rule abate on bankruptcy. This is indeed the case with money had and received, where the claimant will only receive an insolvency dividend. However, an action in conversion is comparable to a proprietary claim in one important respect. This is because the claimant's entitlement is to the chattel or to its value—its full value that is, even if the defendant is insolvent, and not merely to a dividend in the insolvency.[17] Nowadays cases will often not refer to the action in conversion. Instead it is simply said that a claimant can bring a proprietary claim.[18] However, the analysis remains the same on the essential point; namely, *when* will a claimant be able to trace property in order to sue in conversion, or in order to bring a proprietary claim? One advantage of the new terminology is also that the action can be seen as available in respect of intangible property.[19]

26–005 There is no doubt that a claimant can bring an action in respect of a chattel owned by him. The question then arises whether this right is limited to the case of a specific chattel. Should this right not continue if the defendant had exchanged one chattel for another; or the chattel for a sum of money; or had spent that money on another chattel? The answer was given by Lord Ellenborough in *Taylor v Plumer*[20]:

> "It makes no difference in reason or law into what other form, different from the original, the change may have been made, whether it be into that of promissory notes for the security of the money which was produced by the sale of the goods of the principal, as in *Scott v Surman*,[21] or into other merchandise, as in *Whitecomb v Jacob*,[22] for the product of or substitute for the original thing still follows the nature of the thing itself, as long as it can be ascertained to be such, and the right only ceases when the means of ascertainment fail, which is the case when the subject is turned into money, and mixed and confounded in a general mass of the same description. The difficulty which arises in such a case is a difficulty of fact and not of law, and the dictum that money has no ear-mark must be understood in the same way; i.e. as predicated only of an undivided and undistinguishable mass of current money. But money in a bag or otherwise kept apart from other money, guineas, or other coin marked (if the fact were so) for the purpose of being distinguished, are so far ear-marked as to fall within the rule on this subject, which applies to every other description of personal property whilst it remains (as the property in question did) in the hands of the factor [the bankrupt] or his general legal representatives."

---

[16] A discretion to award specific recovery in an action in detinue was given to the court in 1854: Common Law Procedure Act 1854 s.78. Detinue was abolished by the Torts (Interference with Goods) Act 1977 s.2; but the discretionary power of the court to order specific recovery in an action in conversion is retained by s.3.

[17] S. Khurshid and P. Matthews (1979) 95 L.Q.R. 78; M. Scott (1966) 7 W.A.L.R. 463. See *Giles v Perkins* (1807) 9 East. 12; *Scott v Surman* (1742) Willes 400.

[18] See *Jones (FC) & Sons (Trustee) v Jones* [1997] Ch. 159 at 168: "The trustee must bring his claim at common law. It follows that, if he has to trace his money, he must rely on common law tracing rules, and that he has no proprietary *remedy*. But it does not follow that he has no proprietary *claim*." (original emphasis).

[19] By contrast, conversion does not apply in respect of intangible property: *OBG Ltd v Allan* [2008] 1 A.C. 1.

[20] (1815) 3 M. & S. 562 at 575; *Re J Leslie Engineers Co Ltd* [1976] 1 W.L.R. 292 at 297.

[21] (1742) Willes 400.

[22] (1710) Salk. 160.

In *Taylor v Plumer*, the defendant handed money to a stockbroker, Walsh, to purchase bonds. Walsh instead purchased American investments and bullion and hurried off to Falmouth to sail to America. He was caught, and the investments and bullion were seized by the defendant. On Walsh's bankruptcy, his assignees in bankruptcy sought to recover them from the defendant. They failed. The investments were the ascertainable product of the defendant's money and owned by him. If the parties had been reversed, and the defendant had been suing for the recovery of the securities and bullion, his action would have succeeded, but the assignees would have had the choice of returning them or of paying their full value in damages; just as if Walsh had taken the defendant's coach and horses and had them in his possession on his bankruptcy.

The crucial question at common law is whether identifiable property exists, the title to which has not passed to the defendant.[23] In *Banque Belge pour L'Etranger v Hambrouck*[24] money passing through substantially unmixed bank accounts was treated by the majority of the Court of Appeal as still identifiable. In *Lipkin Gorman v Karpnale Ltd*,[25] the House of Lords considered that the claimant firm could have traced at common law where money was drawn out of its client account by a partner, Cass, and paid to the Playboy Club. Although the claimant had no proprietary interest in the money in the account, the bank's debt was a chose in action which was the legal property of the claimant. This could be traced into its product, the money withdrawn (apparently even though Cass had legal title to that), and followed into the hands of the volunteer recipient. In *Jones (FC) & Sons (Trustee) v Jones*[26] a partner withdrew £11,700 from a partnership account by cheques in favour of his wife after an act of bankruptcy on the part of the firm and the wife opened an account with a broker, into which the money was paid. The money was profitably invested in potato futures and the wife received cheques from the broker for £50,760 which she paid into another account she had opened with R Bank. The wife conceded that the trustee in bankruptcy was entitled to £11,700 but claimed to keep the profit. Her claim was rejected by the Court of Appeal. She had taken possession of money (£11,700) the legal title to which was vested in the trustee in bankruptcy under the insolvency legislation. He was entitled at common law not only to trace his property into its exchange product but also to trace any profit made from it.

It has been persuasively argued that *Taylor v Plumer* was in fact a decision on tracing in equity and thus not authority for the proposition that tracing into an

26–006

---

[23] See M. Scott (1966) 7 W.A.L.R. 463 at 481.

[24] [1921] 1 K.B. 321.

[25] [1991] 2 A.C. 548 (a personal action); P. Watts (1991) 107 L.Q.R. 521; M. Halliwell [1992] Conv. 124; E. McKendrick (1992) 5 M.L.R. 377; L. Smith (2009) 125 L.Q.R. 338. It was conceded (p.572) that the claimant's legal title to the money was not defeated by any mixing by Cass with his own money before payment to the club (cf. *Bank of America v Arnell* [1999] Lloyd's Rep. Bank. 399). Presumably mixing by the club would defeat a common law tracing claim.

[26] [1997] Ch. 159; P. Birks and W. Swadling [1996] All E.R. Rev., p.366; P. Birks (1997) 11 T.L.I. 2; D. Fox (1997) 56 C.L.J. 30; C. Mitchell (1997–98) 8 K.C.L.J. 123; L. Smith, *The Law of Tracing* (1997), pp.320–340; P. Millett in A. Burrows and A. Rodger (eds), *Mapping the Law* (Oxford: Oxford University Press, 2006), Ch.14.

"exchange product" is possible at common law.[27] It is clear, however, that *Taylor v Plumer* has been accepted in the subsequent case law as authority for that proposition.[28] In the *Jones* case Millett LJ acknowledged that *Taylor v Plumer* was concerned with the rules of equity but held that this did not mean that the common law did not recognise claims to substitute assets or their products. Thus the trustee in bankruptcy could follow the chose in action constituted by the partnership account into the cheques drawn on it, and could follow those cheques into the account with the broker, the cheques from the broker, and ultimately the chose in action constituted by the account with R Bank. He was entitled at law to the balance in that account, whether greater or less than the original amount withdrawn from the partnership account.[29]

What the common law cannot do is to provide full protection to the claimant in the most important type of case in which these questions arise: where the defendant has received the claimant's money, mixed it with other money in a bank account, and has gone bankrupt.[30] In *Agip (Africa) Ltd v Jackson* the claimant sought to trace money transferred to the defendants as a result of the fraud of the claimant's accountant, who had changed the names on payment orders. The money had been paid out (to B Co and thence to the defendants) by a London bank on the telexed instructions of a Tunis bank (where the claimant maintained an account), which then instructed a New York bank to reimburse the London bank. The defendants had paid most of the money away, but part of it remained and was paid into court. Millett J[31] rejected the claim based on common law tracing on the ground that no physical asset of the claimant (such as a cheque or its proceeds) could be identified in the defendant's hands. Nothing but a stream of electrons passed between the banks as a result of the telegraphic transfers. The London bank paid with its own money, subject to reimbursement, and not with anything identifiable as the product of the claimant's property. It was not possible to show the source from which the London bank was reimbursed without tracing the money through the New York clearing system. There it was mixed, which defeated the common law claim. The decision was upheld on appeal on the basis that mixing defeated the claim.[32] Lord Millett subsequently restated the view that the common law cannot trace money transferred electronically both judicially and

---

[27] S. Kurshid and P. Matthews (1979) 95 L.Q.R. 78; L. Smith [1995] L.M.C.L.Q. 240; P. Matthews and P. Birks in P. Birks (ed.), *Laundering and Tracing* (1995), pp.49–51 and 297–298 respectively.

[28] *Banque Belge pour L'Etranger v Hambrouck* [1921] 1 K.B. 321; *Lipkin Gorman v Karpnale Ltd* [1991] 2 A.C. 548; *Agip (Africa) Ltd v Jackson* [1991] Ch. 547.

[29] cf. *SmithKline Beecham v Apotex Europe Ltd* [2007] Ch. 71 at 88, where Jacob LJ said that he could not see why equity had no role to play in the *Jones* case: "it looks like a plain case of constructive trusteeship."

[30] P. Birks (1992) 45 C.L.P. 69. For the view that mixing does not prevent common law tracing, see L. Smith, *The Law of Tracing* (1997), pp.162–174.

[31] [1990] Ch. 265 at 286; P. Birks (1989) 105 L.Q.R. 528; P. Millett (1991) 107 L.Q.R. 71. See also *Bank of America v Arnell* [1999] Lloyd's Rep. Bank. 399; D. Fox (2000) 59 C.L.J. 28.

[32] [1991] Ch. 547 at 565. Tracing in equity was allowed. In *Jones (FC) & Sons (Trustee) v Jones* [1997] Ch. 159, it was not necessary to trace the passage of the money through a clearing system.

extra-judicially,[33] and it found support elsewhere.[34] It may be, however, that such money remains traceable at common law if it has not been mixed by passing through an inter-bank clearing system.[35]

Whether or not the common law can trace electronic money, the most important point is that the common law does not allow tracing through mixtures. As we will see, mixing does not prevent tracing in equity. In practical terms, most of the situations in which a claim to trace arises are cases of money in mixed bank accounts, in which the common law remedy is not available. Tracing at common law therefore has limited practical importance today. It is much more advantageous to trace in equity if it is possible to do so.

3.   TRACING IN EQUITY

Equity has developed more sophisticated methods of tracing. The rules have developed, and are usually applied, in the context of property in the hands of trustees or other fiduciaries, and often on the bankruptcy of the fiduciary. But the rules can also be relevant to third parties; for example, in *Relfo Ltd (In Liquidation) v Varsani*,[36] the point of the tracing exercise was to establish whether or not a third party had received property for the purposes of liability in knowing receipt.

26–007

A.   **Entitlement to Trace**

A claimant who wishes to trace in equity must establish his entitlement to do so. The easiest way to do this is by showing that he had some pre-existing equitable proprietary interest in the original asset before it was misdirected; the asset may have been held on trust for the claimant, or he may have held an equitable charge[37] over it.

26–008

Where the claimant is initially the legal and beneficial owner of property, on the other hand, he does not hold an equitable interest in it. In these cases it used to be thought that the ability to trace depended on the property being misdirected in

---

[33] *El Ajou v Dollar Land Holdings Plc* [1993] 3 All E.R. 717 at 733 (not discussed on appeal at [1994] 2 All E.R. 685); (1991) 107 L.Q.R. 71 at 74; (1995) 9 T.L.I. 35 at 39; [1999] 14 *Amicus Curiae* 4.

[34] *Nimmo v Westpac Banking Corp* [1993] 3 N.Z.L.R. 218; *Bank Tejarat v Hong Kong and Shanghai Banking Corp (CI) Ltd* [1995] 1 Lloyd's Rep. 239. Cf. *BMP Global Distribution Inc v Bank of Nova Scotia* [2009] 1 S.C.R. 504; noted D. Fox (2010) 69 C.L.J. 28. Where a payment is made between two bank accounts telegraphically, electronically or by cheque, one chose in action is reduced or extinguished and another created, thus no property of the payer is obtained by the payee within the Theft Act 1968; *R. v Preddy* [1996] A.C. 815. Following *Preddy*, a new Theft Act 1968 s.15A was inserted, creating the offence of obtaining a money transfer by deception. That offence was repealed for actions taking place after 15 January 2007 and the area is now covered by the Fraud Act 2006.

[35] A. Oakley (1995) 54 C.L.J. 377. See also L. Smith, *The Law of Tracing* (1997), pp.253–258; L. Smith in F. Rose (ed.), *Restitution and Banking Law* (Oxford: Mansfield Press, 1998), Ch.8; J. Ulph [2007] 15 R.L.R. 76.

[36] [2014] EWCA Civ 360; [2015] 1 B.C.L.C. 14.

[37] *Dick v Harper* [2006] B.P.I.R. 20.

breach of a fiduciary duty owed to the claimant[38]; this explained why claimants could trace property misdirected by company directors and agents.[39] More recently, however, the need for a fiduciary relationship has been questioned.[40] Although it has never been formally abandoned, the current approach of the law is to ground a claimant's entitlement to trace on an equitable interest in the relevant property, even if that interest did not pre-date the misdirection of the property from its owner.

This is a welcome development in that the requirement of a fiduciary relationship may be quietly forgotten. That requirement was superfluous in the case of express trusts, difficult to apply in respect of resulting and constructive trusts, absurd in the case of thieves, and it could not explain why the holder of an equitable charge can trace. On the other hand, it is arguable that the nature of the claimant's interest (a point relevant to claiming) is now being conflated with the separate point of his entitlement to trace in equity.[41] Indeed, it is arguable that a desire to allow claimants to trace in equity has led to an increase in the circumstances in which an equitable interest may be created, and also some historical distortion of fiduciary principles. Nonetheless, it cannot be denied that the nature of the claimant's interest and his entitlement to trace are closely linked in the current law.

26–009   **i. Pre-Existing Equitable Proprietary Interests.**   A beneficiary holding an equitable interest under an express trust is clearly entitled to trace the value of trust property that is wrongly disbursed from the trust.[42] The same applies to beneficiaries of resulting and constructive trusts where the property is held on pre-existing trusts before the relevant misapplication.[43] For example, it has now been settled by the Supreme Court that secret commissions obtained in breach of fiduciary duty are held on constructive trust for the fiduciary's principal.[44] The

---

[38] *Sinclair v Brougham* [1914] A.C. 398; *Re Hallett's Estate* (1880) 13 Ch.D. 696; *Agip (Africa) Ltd v Jackson* [1991] Ch. 547. Televantos argues that "fiduciary" in this context did not refer to duties to avoid unauthorised conflicts and profits, but instead merely identified a person who had control of assets in which another party held proprietary rights. Those proprietary rights may have been legal (as in the case of bailment or theft) or equitable (as in the case of a trust): A. Televantos (2017) 133 L.Q.R. 492.

[39] Also executors; *Re Diplock* [1948] Ch. 465. This category differs because people entitled under a will or intestacy do not hold a proprietary interest in the assets of the estate, at least for most purposes: *Commissioner of Stamp Duties (Queensland) v Livingston* [1965] A.C. 694; above, para.2–020. However, it can be argued that they do hold a proprietary interest sufficient for the purposes of tracing, and are analogous to the objects of discretionary trusts: see R. Nolan (2006) 122 L.Q.R. 232; M. Conaglen [2008] I.P.Q. 82 at 89. cf. D. Salmons (2017) 76 C.L.J. 399, arguing that a proprietary claim ought not to have been available in *Re Diplock*.

[40] P. Birks (1995) 9 T.L.I. 124; *Bristol and West Building Society v Mothew* [1998] Ch.1 at 23; L. Smith, *The Law of Tracing* (1997), pp.123–130, 340–347; *Foskett v McKeown* [2001] 1 A.C. 102 at 128; A. Televantos (2017) 133 L.Q.R. 492 (arguing the requirement can be traced to Lord Greene MR's misreading of earlier authorities in *Re Diplock* [1948] Ch. 465, and concluding that modern courts are not bound by it).

[41] See *Bristol & West Building Society v Mothew* [1998] Ch. 1 at 23; *Foskett v McKeown* [2001] 1 A.C. 102 at 128.

[42] *Foskett v McKeown* [2001] 1 A.C. 102.

[43] See Chs 11 and 12 above.

[44] *FHR European Ventures LLP v Cedar Capital Partners LLC* [2015] 1 A.C. 250. cf. *Clegg v Pache (deceased)* [2017] EWCA Civ 256 at [87]–[90] (analysis extended to gains made by a company

trust arises at the point of receipt. If the fiduciary then invests those funds on his own account, the principal can trace into the fruits of that investment.[45]

When a trustee disposes of property in an unauthorised fashion the beneficiary's equitable interest still encumbers the property.[46] That interest will be extinguished if the trustee wrongly transfers the property to a bona fide purchaser for value without notice. The interest will still bind the property in the hands of an innocent recipient who does not give value, but it is important to note that such a volunteer is not subjected to any duties in respect of that property unless and until she becomes aware of the prior interest. If the property is dissipated before the recipient is made aware of the interest, the recipient owes no liability in equity in respect of it. On the other hand, if the property still exists (albeit in altered form, or mixed with the recipient's own property) the beneficiary can trace into the substitutes.[47]

ii. Newly-Created Equitable Proprietary Interests.

(a) Rescission, Intention and Resulting Trusts.   We now turn to property that **26–010** is not held subject to pre-existing equitable interests. It is well-established that a claimant who elects to rescind a voidable transaction, such as a contract induced by misrepresentation or undue influence, can trace the property that has passed under that contract. This is on the basis that the property revests in equity in the claimant on rescission.[48] The transferor then becomes entitled under a resulting[49] trust. This equitable interest vests retrospectively for the purpose of allowing the claimant to trace in equity, although not for all purposes.[50]

It is important to note that the recipient acquires a full title until the transferor exercises her "mere equity" and rescinds.[51] The transferor intends that full legal title to the relevant property should pass to the recipient, although the vitiating

---

controlled by the wrongdoing fiduciary, thus enabling a proprietary claim in respect of some of those gains that were subsequently paid to a third party).

[45] *Attorney General for Hong Kong v Reid* [1994] 1 A.C. 324. See also *Keown v Nahoor* [2015] EWHC 3418 (Ch) (property transferred to third party in breach of a constructive trust).

[46] *Independent Trustee Services Ltd v GP Noble Trustees Ltd* [2012] EWCA Civ 195; [2013] Ch. 91 at [104]; *Akers v Samba Financial Group* [2017] UKSC 6; [2017] A.C. 424 at [51]. See generally D. Fox in P. Birks and A. Pretto (eds) *Breach of Trust* (Oxford: Hart Publishing, 2002) Ch.4.

[47] It does not necessarily follow that the beneficiary can successfully *claim* the substitutes: see *Re Diplock* [1948] Ch. 465 at 546–548.

[48] *Daly v Sydney Stock Exchange* (1986) 160 C.L.R. 371; *Lonrho Plc v Fayed (No.2)* [1992] 1 W.L.R. 1; *El Ajou v Dollar Land Holdings Plc* [1993] 3 All E.R. 717 at 734 (reversed on other grounds [1994] 2 All E.R. 685); *Bristol & West Building Society v Mothew* [1998] Ch. 1 at 22; *Shalson v Russo* [2005] Ch. 281 at 317–318, 321–324; *Independent Trustee Services Ltd v GP Noble Trustees Ltd* [2013] Ch. 91 at [104]; *National Crime Agency v Robb* [2014] EWHC 4384 (Ch); [2015] Ch. 520 at [49]; *Bainbridge v Bainbridge* [2016] EWHC 898 (Ch) at [24]; P. Millett (1998) 114 L.Q.R. 399 at 416 and [1998] 6 R.L.R. 283.

[49] It has been suggested that the trust is properly characterised as constructive, and is a species of the "unconscionable retention" trust discussed below at para.26–011: see *National Crime Agency v Robb* [2015] Ch. 520 at [44].

[50] *Bristol & West Building Society v Mothew* [1998] Ch. 1 at 23; *Shalson v Russo* [2005] Ch. 281 at [125]–[127]; *Independent Trustee Services Ltd v GP Noble Trustees Ltd* [2013] Ch 91 at [53]. cf. P.G. Turner (2016) 75 C.L.J. 206.

[51] *Guinness Plc v Saunders* [1990] 2 A.C. 663 at 698; *Re Ciro Citterio Menswear Plc* [2002] 1 W.L.R. 2217 at 2231.

factor means that she is allowed to change her mind. If and when she does, the property revests in equity (and does so retrospectively for the purposes of tracing).

The importance of the transferor's intention can also be seen in *Westdeutsche Landesbank Girozentrale v Islington LBC*.[52] One question in that case was whether the claimant bank retained an equitable proprietary interest in money paid to the defendant local authority under a transaction (an "interest rate swap") that was ultra vires (so far as the defendant was concerned) and void. Tracing would in any event have been impossible because the money had been mixed with other money in an account and used for general expenditure, the account having been subsequently overdrawn several times.[53] The defendant conceded personal liability to repay, but the issue was whether compound interest could be awarded to the bank. Their Lordships unanimously agreed that the bank retained no equitable proprietary interest in the money, which, according to the majority, meant that there was no jurisdiction to award compound interest.[54] *Sinclair v Brougham*,[55] where the House of Lords had permitted tracing by creditors (depositors) of a bank whose business was ultra vires, was overruled. Although in *Westdeutsche* the bank's belief in the validity of the transaction was mistaken, it intended the money to become the absolute property of the defendant and had been prepared to take the risk of insolvency. As a general rule, property in money passes even though a contract is void, although there may be limited exceptions in the case of "fundamental mistake" in the orthodox sense.[56] Thus there was considered to be no moral or legal reason why, had there been an insolvency, the claimant should have had priority over general creditors. The defendant received the money neither as a resulting trustee (because the property had passed as intended) nor as a constructive trustee (because it was unaware of the invalidity until after the money had been spent and its conscience was thus unaffected) but was merely subject to personal liability at common law to repay.

26–011   *(b)   Conscience and Constructive Trusts.*   As an alternative to a resulting trust, it may be possible for a claimant to establish that the recipient holds the transferred property on constructive trust. Constructive trusts respond to the recipient's conscience rather than to the transferor's intention.

As we have seen, no resulting or constructive trust was found in *Westdeutsche*. There was no constructive trust because the money had been spent by the time the recipient's conscience was affected.[57] However, there are similar cases where the recipient has been found to hold transferred property on constructive trust. In

---

[52] [1996] A.C. 669. M. Cope (1996) 112 L.Q.R. 521; P. Birks [1996] R.L.R. 3; G. Jones (1996) 55 C.L.J. 432; C. Mitchell (1996) 10 T.L.I. 84; S. Gardner [2008] 16 R.L.R. 107.

[53] See below, para.26–023.

[54] This aspect has now been overtaken by the decision in *Sempra Metals Ltd (formerly Metallgesellschaft Ltd) v IRC* [2008] 1 A.C. 561.

[55] [1914] A.C. 398.

[56] [1996] A.C. 669 at 690; *Angove's Pty Ltd v Bailey* [2016] UKSC 47; [2016] 1 W.L.R. 3179 at [30].

[57] [1996] A.C. 669 at 700. Interest rate swaps were found to be ultra vires the powers of local authorities in *Hazell v Hammersmith & Fulham LBC* [1992] 2 A.C. 1. The first instance decision in that case was delivered in November 1989, over two years after Westdeutsche had paid the money to Islington LBC.

Chase Manhattan Bank NA v Israel-British Bank (London) Ltd,[58] Goulding J allowed the claimant to trace money paid by mistake of fact to the defendant (now insolvent) on the basis that the claimant retained an equitable proprietary interest in the money. Although this reasoning cannot be supported—as a full legal owner the claimant had no equitable interest prior to the payment[59] —the result of the case can be supported on the basis that the defendant bank became aware of the mistake within two days and retained the money in traceable form. Thus the bank's conscience was sufficiently affected to found a constructive trust. Lord Browne-Wilkinson explained it in the following way in *Westdeutsche*[60]:

> "[In *Chase Manhattan*] the defendant bank knew of the mistake made by the paying bank within two days of the receipt of the moneys. The judge treated this fact as irrelevant... but in my judgment it may well provide a proper foundation for the decision. Although the mere receipt of the moneys, in ignorance of the mistake, gives rise to no trust, the retention of the moneys after the recipient bank learned of the mistake may well have given rise to a constructive trust."

On this analysis, where a recipient takes property innocently, then for as long as that property remains identifiable the claimant can give the recipient notice of her claim and thereby turn it into an "unconscionable retention" case. At that point, the claimant gains an equitable interest in the transferred property. In *Clark v Cutland*,[61] for example, a director transferred company assets in breach of fiduciary duty to his pension trustees. The pension trustees were innocent volunteers, but a constructive trust clothed the transferred assets once they had been notified of the company's claim.[62]

When the recipient learns of the claim the law behaves rather like it does on rescission of a voidable transaction. The claimant's interest vests retrospectively for the purposes of tracing, but it must be remembered that the title passed fully until the revesting. This means that no liability will exist in respect of property that has already been dissipated.[63] But it is still important that the interest vests retrospectively for tracing purposes, because this enables the claimant to treat substitutes that were made before the revesting as subject to her claim (if they can still be identified). Once again, though, it does not automatically follow that a claim in respect of those substitutes will be successful.

Lord Browne-Wilkinson's "unconscionable retention" analysis in *Westdeutsche*   **26–012**
has been applied several times in subsequent cases,[64] although the reception has

---

[58] [1981] Ch. 105; W. Swadling (1996) 16 L.S. 110; G. McCormack [1996] Conv. 86; A. Burrows (2001) 117 L.Q.R. 412 at 426.

[59] It may be added that the payment was intended, although mistaken; so no resulting trust arose on transfer.

[60] [1996] A.C. 669 at 715.

[61] [2004] 1 W.L.R. 783.

[62] [2004] 1 W.L.R. 783 at 792–793.

[63] Specifically, there will be no liability specifically for dissipating the claimant's property (because it was not at the relevant time the claimant's property). But there may still be liability under a claim for money had and received.

[64] *Papamichael v National Westminster Bank Plc* [2003] 1 Lloyd's Rep. 341; *Clark v Cutland* [2004] 1 W.L.R. 783; *Commerzbank Aktiengesellschaft v IMB Morgan Plc* [2005] W.T.L.R. 1485 at 1495; *Re Farepak Food and Gifts Ltd* [2006] EWHC 3272 (Ch) at [40]; *Wambo Coal Pty Ltd v Ariff* [2007]

not been universally positive.[65] Some further recent doubt has been cast on the matter by Lord Sumption's judgment in *Angove's Pty Ltd v Bailey*.[66] That case did not involve any form of mistake. Instead, it concerned an argument that an agent collecting customer payments for a principal would hold the funds on constructive trust if the agent knew when it collected the payments that it would be unable properly to account for them because of the agent's imminent insolvency. Lord Sumption disapproved of an earlier case, *Neste Oy v Lloyd's Bank Plc*,[67] where a recipient who knew at the time of receipt that it was insolvent was found to hold the sums on trust for the transferor. He said[68]:

> "[W]here money is paid with the intention of transferring the entire beneficial interest to the payee, the least that must be shown in order to establish a constructive trust is (i) that that intention was vitiated, for example because the money was paid as a result of a fundamental mistake or pursuant to a contract which has been rescinded, or (ii) that irrespective of the intentions of the payer, in the eyes of equity the money has come into the wrong hands, as where it represents the fruits of a fraud, theft or breach of trust or fiduciary duty against a third party. .. [But] the prospect of a total failure of consideration, however inevitable, is not a circumstance which could [vitiate] the intention of [a payer] to part with its entire interest in the money."

These comments do not conflict directly with the unconscionable retention analysis, since the case did not concern mistake (and indeed Lord Sumption expressly allowed that "fundamental mistake"[69] could still ground a constructive trust). However, to the extent that the unconscionable retention analysis turns on the conscience of the recipient, and not on the vitiated intention of the transferor, the comments in *Angove's v Bailey* do sound a note of caution. Lord Browne-Wilkinson suggested in *Westdeutsche* that it was the recipient's knowledge of the mistake that mattered.[70] That is not immediately easy to reconcile with Lord Sumption's comment in *Angove's v Bailey* that "Property rights are fixed and ascertainable rights. Whether they exist in a given case depends on settled principles, even in equity."[71]

26–013 Whether or not a constructive trust over a mistaken payment can be enlivened by the recipient's knowledge that it was paid under mistake, it is clear that a constructive trust may be found when the recipient acquires property fraudulently in the first place.[72] It will be a case of unconscionable acquisition, not merely of

---

NSWSC 589 at [32]–[44]. For academic support see B. McFarlane in J. Glister and P. Ridge (eds), *Fault Lines in Equity* (Oxford: Hart Publishing, 2012), Ch.8.

[65] P. Millett (1998) 114 L.Q.R. 399 at 413; *Wuhan Guoyu Logistics Group Co Ltd v Emporiki Bank of Greece SA* [2013] EWCA Civ 1679 at [19]; Goff and Jones, 9th edn, para.37–24.

[66] [2016] UKSC 47; [2016] 1 W.L.R. 3179; above, para.12.030.

[67] [1983] 2 Lloyd's Rep. 658 (only the final payment of several was held on trust).

[68] [2016] 1 W.L.R. 3179 at [30]. The comments were obiter dicta because the Court held that the agency agreement had been validly terminated. There being no authority to collect any moneys, no question of a trust over them could arise.

[69] As Professor Watts has observed, absent further refinement, "the concept of 'fundamentality' is going to be asked to do a lot of work": P. Watts (2017) 133 L.Q.R. 11 at 14.

[70] [1996] A.C. 669 at 715.

[71] [2016] 1 W.L.R. 3179 at [28].

[72] *Westdeutsche Landesbank Girozentrale v Islington LBC* [1996] A.C. 669 at 716. Lord Sumption did not doubt that property acquired through fraud or theft could be held on constructive trust: *Angove's Pty Ltd v Bailey* [2016] 1 W.L.R. 3179 at [30].

unconscionable retention. Of course, fraud in the acquisition of property may—depending on the transaction in question—also give the claimant the ability to rescind and acquire an interest under a resulting trust.[73] Either way, the claimant will have a sufficient equitable interest to enable her to trace the property. A difficulty arises, however, with stolen property. A thief does not acquire the victim's title, and the victim remains the full legal owner of stolen property. Yet it seems absurd that a victim of theft should be left to a personal remedy against the thief, as the following example demonstrates:

> X owes £1,000 to his creditors and has only £100. He steals £1,000 from Y and mixes that money in his account which now has £1,100. He now "owes" £2,000. Should the available money be shared rateably between Y and the creditors, or should Y get back first her £1,000, which X should never have had? Common law tracing is not available because the funds are mixed. Neither is equitable tracing, unless—as would be unlikely—X was initially Y's fiduciary.

Equity's response has been to say that a thief holds stolen property on trust for his victim.[74] Although this ignores rather than answers the question about the thief's title,[75] it does provide a basis for the victim of theft to trace and claim the stolen property.

B.   Unmixed Funds

The easy case is that in which there has been no mixing of the trust funds with the trustee's own money. If the trustee has sold the trust property, the beneficiary may take the proceeds if he can identify them. (If the purchaser from the trustee had notice, the beneficiary may elect to take either the property or the proceeds as the purchaser will not be able to raise the defence of bona fide purchase.[76]) If the proceeds of sale have been used to purchase other property the beneficiary may

26–014

> "elect either to take the property purchased, or to hold it as a security for the amount of trust money laid out in the purchase; or, as we generally express it, he is entitled at his election either to take the property, or to have a charge on the property for the amount of the trust money."[77]

---

[73] See *Halley v Law Society* [2003] EWCA Civ 97 at [45]–[48].

[74] *Black v S Freedman & Co* (1910) 12 C.L.R. 105; *Lennox Industries (Canada) Ltd v The Queen* (1987) 34 D.L.R. 297; *Bishopsgate Investment Management Ltd v Maxwell* [1993] Ch. 1 at 70; *Westdeutsche Landesbank Girozentrale v Islington LBC* [1996] A.C. 669 at 715–716; *Armstrong DLW GmbH v Winnington Networks Ltd* [2013] Ch. 156 at 220–221. But see doubts expressed in *Shalson v Russo* [2005] Ch. 281 at [110].

[75] See R. Chambers, *Resulting Trusts* (1997), p.117, and in E. Bant and M. Harding, *Exploring Private Law* (Cambridge: Cambridge University Press, 2010), Ch.10, preferring a resulting trust analysis; L. Smith, *The Law of Tracing* (1997), pp.343–347; S. Barkehall Thomas (2009) 3 J.Eq. 52; J. Tarrant (2009) 3 J.Eq. 170. Of course, if a legal owner could trace in equity there would be no need for the trust: see A. Televantos (2017) 133 L.Q.R. 492, 494.

[76] Above, para.1–039.

[77] *Re Hallett's Estate* (1880) 13 Ch.D. 696 at 709, per Jessel MR.

The beneficiary is entitled to any increase in value even though the trustee could have made the purchase with his own money.[78] However, an increase in value must be distinguished from discrete profits made as a result of the use of the property. The existence and amount of these profits may be relevant to an action for breach of fiduciary duty, but those profits do not represent the traceable substitutes of the original property.[79]

C. Mixed Funds

26–015   The position is more complicated where the trustee has mixed the trust funds with other money, and possibly converted the mixed funds into other property. The position differs according to whether the claim is against the trustee (or his successors), or whether the ownership of the mixed fund must be apportioned between two trusts or a trust and an innocent volunteer. Also, there are special rules applicable to cases of mixed funds in bank accounts.

26–016   **i.   Position as Against the Trustee.**   The rule here is that the beneficiaries have a first claim over the mixed fund or any property purchased with it. The onus is on the trustee to prove that part of the mixed fund is his own.

> "[I]f a trustee amalgamated [trust property] with his own, his beneficiary will be entitled to every portion of the blended property which the trustee cannot prove to be his own."[80]

Assuming the trustee can prove his contribution, the beneficiaries share any property purchased from the mixed fund with the trustee (or his successors), the shares being proportionate to the contributions. In *Foskett v McKeown*,[81] the trustee used his own money to pay the first three premiums on a life assurance policy and trust money to pay the fourth and fifth, after which he died. It was held by a majority of the House of Lords that the beneficiaries were entitled to a 40% share in the policy proceeds. The trustee had settled the policy on his children but they, being volunteer successors, could be in no better position than the trustee. Lord Millett expressed the rule as follows:

> "Where a trustee wrongfully uses trust money to provide part of the cost of acquiring an asset, the beneficiary is entitled *at his option* either to claim a proportionate share of the asset or to enforce a lien upon it to secure his personal claim against the trustee for the amount of the misapplied money. It does not matter whether the trustee mixed the trust money with his own

---

[78] See the example of the winning lottery ticket in *Foskett v McKeown* [2001] 1 A.C. 102 at 134; and below, para.26–032.

[79] *Ultraframe (UK) Ltd v Fielding* [2005] EWHC 1638 (Ch) at [1470]–[1475]. cf. *Jones (FC) & Sons (Trustee) v Jones* [1997] Ch. 159, a case on common law tracing, which may be explained as an "increase in value" case.

[80] *Re Tilley's WT* [1967] Ch. 1179 at 1182, quoting *Lewin on Trusts*, 16th edn (1964), p.223; *Lupton v White* (1808) 15 Ves.Jr. 432; *Indian Oil Corp Ltd v Greenstone Shipping SA* [1987] 2 Lloyd's Rep. 286; P. Stein (1987) 46 C.L.J. 369; *Coleman v Harvey* [1989] 1 N.Z.L.R. 723; *Glencore International AG v Metro Trading International Inc* [2001] 1 Lloyd's Rep. 284; *Sinclair Investments (UK) Ltd v Versailles Trade Finance Ltd (In Administrative Receivership)* [2011] EWCA Civ 347; [2012] Ch. 453 at [138] ("maelstrom account").

[81] [2001] 1 A.C. 102; P. Birks and W. Swadling [2000] All E.R. Rev. 2000, p.320; R. Walker [2000] R.L.R. 573; A. Burrows (2001) 117 L.Q.R. 412; D. Fox [2001] L.M.C.L.Q. 1.

in a single fund before using it to acquire the asset, or made separate payments (whether simultaneously or sequentially) out of the differently owned funds to acquire a single asset ... As against the wrongdoer and his successors, the beneficiary is entitled to locate his contribution in any part of the mixture and to subordinate their claims to share in the mixture until his own contribution has been satisfied. This has the effect of giving the beneficiary a lien for his contribution if the mixture is deficient."[82]

The dissenting judgments proceeded on the basis that, on the particular facts, the premiums paid with trust money did not add to the value of the policy, so that the beneficiaries were entitled only to the return of the sums paid with their money.

It may be argued that the trustee ought not to receive any benefit from property bought from a mixed fund that has increased in value, at least in cases where the asset is not severable and so there is no possibility that the trustee could have bought only his share (a boat, for example, as opposed to company shares). In *Scott v Scott*,[83] a trustee had mixed personal and trust money to buy a house. The trustee unsuccessfully sought to keep all of the increase in value, but there was no occasion to consider whether the same claim by the beneficiaries would have been successful.[84] *Foskett v McKeown* indicates that the trustee will retain the increase in value associated with his share of the mixed asset, although again the contrary position was not argued and on the facts the insurance policy would still have paid out even without the later trust fund contributions.[85] This is a difficult point of principle: while there is an obvious reluctance to allow the trustee to profit in any way from the misuse of trust money, it can be argued that by choosing to claim a proportionate share of the asset bought from mixed funds the beneficiaries adopt the trustee's "investment".[86] It would be inconsistent also to claim the increase in value associated with the trustee's share on the grounds that it was the fruit of a breach of fiduciary duty.

Finally, the beneficiaries must be able to trace into a particular mixed fund, or to property bought from a particular mixed fund, in order to make a claim. The contrary was suggested in *Space Investments Ltd v Canadian Imperial Bank of Commerce Trust Co (Bahamas) Ltd*, where Lord Templeman said that if a bank trustee misappropriated trust money for its own benefit it would be possible

26–017

"to trace the trust money to all the assets of the bank and to recover the trust money by the exercise of an equitable charge over all the assets of the bank."[87]

The difficulty with this is that it suggests that if a mixed fund has been lost, the beneficiaries still have a proprietary claim to the trustee's remaining assets, which

---

[82] [2001] 1 A.C. 102 at 131. In fact the provenance of the third premium was disputed; if the third premium had been paid with trust funds, the beneficiaries would have been entitled to 60% of the proceeds.
[83] (1963) 109 C.L.R. 649.
[84] Such a claim had been rejected at trial and the beneficiaries did not cross-appeal on the point.
[85] The policy would have been kept on foot by, in effect, dipping into its own profits to pay the premiums due.
[86] Compare *Paul A Davies (Australia) Pty Ltd (In Liquidation) v Davies* [1983] 1 N.S.W.L.R. 440.
[87] [1986] 1 W.L.R. 1072 at 1074. The point did not arise on the facts because the mixing had been done lawfully.

are impressed with a charge. Such a view would be unfair to the general creditors, and is supported neither by principle nor by policy.[88]

Lord Templeman's comments have not been well-received in subsequent cases.[89] If they still carry any weight, it is only in the specific context of bank trustees. In *Serious Fraud Office v Lexi Holdings*,[90] the Court of Appeal rejected the argument that a charge could be imposed on all of the defendant's assets (including his share of the matrimonial home bought some years earlier) where the trust funds could no longer be identified:

> "This cannot be right, in our view. For the equitable charge to attach it must attach to assets in existence which derive from the misappropriated trust funds. There must be a nexus. Were it otherwise the principles of following and tracing could become otiose."[91]

26–018   **ii.   Position as Between Two Trusts, or Trust and Third Party.**   It may be, however, that the trustee has mixed the funds of two trusts, whether or not with his own, or has transferred the funds to an innocent volunteer,[92] who has mixed them with her own.[93] The rule here is that the two trusts, or the trust and the volunteer, share pari passu (i.e. rateably) in the mixed funds or any property purchased out of them.[94]

Where there have been several victims but there is no realistic possibility that other claimants will seek to assert a charge ranking rateably with the claimant's, the claimant may be permitted to trace an amount in excess of that which she would obtain on a rateable division. Whether the rights of third parties may be raised as a partial defence to a tracing claim depends on the circumstances of each case.[95]

26–019   **iii.   Bank Accounts.**   Any mixing is likely, however, to occur in the context of a banking account, to which special rules apply. Again, it is necessary to distinguish the position as between trustee and beneficiary and as between two trusts or trust and innocent volunteer. These rules govern the allocation of payments out of the mixed fund.

---

[88] See the criticisms in R. Goode (1987) 103 L.Q.R. 433.

[89] Later cases have often distinguished *Space Investments* rather than expressly disapproved it: see *Re Goldcorp Exchange Ltd* [1995] 1 A.C. 74; *Bishopsgate Investment Management Ltd v Homan* [1995] Ch. 211; *Fortex Group Ltd v MacIntosh* [1998] 3 N.Z.L.R. 171; *Re BA Peters Plc (In Administration)* [2010] 1 B.C.L.C. 142. But the general reception is negative: *Lehman Brothers International (Europe) v CRC Credit Fund Ltd* [2010] 2 B.C.L.C. 301 at [184]–[192].

[90] [2009] Q.B. 376

[91] [2009] Q.B. 376 at 393.

[92] A recipient who, although not dishonest, ought to have known that the money was not his is not an innocent volunteer: *Boscawen v Bajwa* [1996] 1 W.L.R. 328 at 337.

[93] In *Foskett v McKeown* [2001] 1 A.C. 102 at 132 their Lordships distinguished innocent volunteers who were contributors from those who were merely successors in title to the wrongdoer and in no better position.

[94] *Re Diplock* [1948] Ch. 465; *Foskett v McKeown* [2001] 1 A.C. 102.

[95] *El Ajou v Dollar Land Holdings Plc (No.2)* [1995] 2 All E.R. 213.

(a) Re Hallett's Estate. In *Re Hallett's Estate*,[96] Mr Hallett, a solicitor, mixed **26–020** with his own money certain funds from two trusts. One of the trusts was his own marriage settlement of which he was trustee. The other was a trust of which a client, Mrs Cotterill, was beneficiary, but Mr Hallett was not the trustee. At his death there were insufficient funds to pay Mr Hallett's personal debts and to meet these claims. The question was how to allocate the withdrawals that had been made from the fund as between Mr Hallett and the claimants. This would determine entitlement to the money that remained.

The Court of Appeal held that the payments out of the fund must be treated as payments of Mr Hallett's own money. This left sufficient money to satisfy the claims of Mrs Cotterill and of the beneficiaries under the marriage settlement, so the question of how to allocate the payments between the claimants inter se did not arise.[97] The reason given by Jessel MR for allocating payments to Mr Hallett's money and not to the trust was that wherever an act, "can be done rightfully, [a man] is not allowed to say, against the person entitled to the property or the right, that he has done it wrongfully."[98]

(b) Re Oatway. The principle in *Re Hallett's Estate* operates in the context of **26–021** a claim against a balance in the account,[99] and does not derogate from the general principle that the beneficiaries have a first claim on any property bought out of a mixed fund.

In *Re Oatway*,[100] the trustee withdrew money from the mixed fund and invested it. Later he withdrew the balance of the fund and dissipated it. Joyce J rejected the argument that the money drawn out first must be treated as his own, holding that the beneficiaries' claim must be satisfied from any identifiable part of the mixed fund before the trustee could set up his own claim. Thus the beneficiaries were entitled to the investments in priority to the creditors of the trustee.

The balance of the money was dissipated in *Re Oatway*. More difficult is the case where property has been purchased from a mixed fund, but where sufficient balance remains to satisfy the beneficiary's claim. The point will be significant where the property purchased has increased in value, or if the balance has been spent on a property which has increased by a smaller amount. *Re Tilley's Will Trusts*[101] suggests that the beneficiaries must be content with a claim to the balance (or the second property, as the case may be).[102] It was also held in *Turner*

---

[96] (1880) 13 Ch.D. 696. The principle has been applied to a common law claim to wrongly mixed oil; *Glencore International AG v Metro Trading International Inc* [2001] 1 Lloyd's Rep. 284; J. Ulph [2001] L.M.C.L.Q. 449.

[97] In the court below, where, on the view taken by Fry J, this question did arise, it was solved by applying the rule in *Clayton's Case* (1817) 1 Mer. 572.

[98] (1880) 13 Ch.D. 696 at 727.

[99] Thus it cannot be relied on in a criminal case to show that the accused was withdrawing his own money; *R. v Clowes (No.2)* [1994] 2 All E.R. 316.

[100] [1903] 2 Ch. 356; *Re Tilley's WT* [1967] Ch. 1179 at 1185.

[101] [1967] Ch. 1179.

[102] See P. Birks, *An Introduction to the Law of Restitution* (Oxford: Oxford University Press, 1995), p.370; A. Oakley (1995) 54 C.L.J. 377 at 416; cf. D. Hayton in P. Birks (ed.), *Laundering and Tracing* (1995), p.6.

v Jacob[103] that, where a trustee had mixed trust funds with her own in a deposit account, and a sum equal to the trust fund remained in the account, the beneficiary had no beneficial interest in property purchased with funds from the account but could claim only against the account.

The better view, however, is that the beneficiary should be allowed to "cherry pick" if the only contest is between the beneficiary and the wrongdoer. This avoids the wrongdoer being "left with all the cherries".[104] The rule may also be understood as being that the situation is to be interpreted whichever way is less favourable to the trustee. The point was explained by Campbell J in the Supreme Court of New South Wales[105]:

> "When a trustee has wrongfully taken property from a trust fund, his first obligation is, so far as the trust property can be seen as remaining in his hands, to make restitution—i.e. to put back *in specie* into the trust fund whatever of the trust property he still retains. Until he has performed that obligation, equity will not permit him to assert that he has unfettered ownership of *any* of the property into which any part of the trust property has been converted or mixed. In this way, there is a potential for any of the property into which the trust property has been converted or mixed to be the subject of, eventually, an order for restitution *in specie*."

The point did not arise in *Foskett v McKeown*, although the tenor of the majority judgments supports the view that beneficiaries may treat a mixed fund as charged in their favour,[106] and may then elect to trace the value of their interest into any property bought from that fund. The presumption in *Re Hallett's Estate* is accordingly limited to apportioning to the trustee any non-traceable withdrawals from a mixed fund.

26–022   (c)   *Clayton's Case.*   It remains to consider the position where the mixed funds in the bank account represent the funds of two trusts, or of a trust and an innocent volunteer. Here the rule in *Clayton's Case*[107] lays down that, in the case of a current bank account, the first payment in is appropriated to the earliest debt which is not statute-barred; in other words, first in, first out. This is a rule which has some relevance and convenience in commercial matters, such as when a debtor makes a payment to a creditor that could be applied to one of several debts, and neither the debtor not creditor expressly allocates the payment. However, we have seen that it does not apply to accounts between trustee and beneficiary.

The "first in, first out" rule in *Clayton's Case* has been applied as a means of determining entitlement in a mixed banking account between rival persons with a

---

[103] *Turner v Jacob* [2008] W.T.L.R. 307 at [102].

[104] *Shalson v Russo* [2005] Ch. 281 at [144]; D. Hayton in P. Birks and A. Pretto (eds), *Breach of Trust* (2002), pp.386–387. But the beneficiary can at most cherry-pick among assets bought *from* the mixed fund: *FHR European Ventures LLP v Mankarious* [2016] EWHC 359 (Ch) at [36]–[42].

[105] *Re French Caledonia Travel Service Pty Ltd (In Liquidation)* (2003) 59 N.S.W.L.R. 361 at 386.

[106] Care must be taken with the use of the word "charge" here. The fact that property is purchased with "charged funds" does not mean that the beneficiary is limited to claiming a "charge" over that property: see *Re French Caledonia Travel Service Pty Ltd (In Liquidation)* (2003) 59 N.S.W.L.R. 361 at 386.

[107] *Clayton's Case, Devaynes v Noble* (1817) 1 Mer. 572; cf. *Re British Red Cross Balkan Fund* [1914] 2 Ch. 419 (where later subscribers to a fund could not claim surplus to the exclusion of earlier subscribers).

right to trace,[108] and also between a person with a right to trace and an innocent volunteer.[109] But it is not the only approach that may be taken. In *Barlow Clowes International Ltd v Vaughan*, Woolf LJ said[110]:

> "[I]t is settled law that the rule in *Clayton's Case* can be applied to determine the extent to which as between each other, equally innocent claimants are entitled in equity to monies which have been paid into a bank account and then subject to the movements within that account. However, it does not … follow that the rule has always to be applied for this purpose. In a number of different circumstances the rule has not been applied. The rule need only be applied when it is convenient to do so and when its application can be said to do broad justice having regard to the nature of the competing claims."

The *Barlow Clowes* case concerned a failed investment company that had gone into liquidation and the question was how to distribute the remaining assets among the unpaid investors. The Court of Appeal confirmed the default status of the rule in *Clayton's Case*, but recognised that the rule ought not to apply if its application would be impractical or would cause injustice. In *Barlow Clowes*, the rule was not applied because it would have been contrary to the presumed intention of the investors, who knew their money was to be pooled. Instead, a pari passu (rateable) distribution was ordered.

Cases since *Barlow Clowes* confirm that the modern approach is to distinguish *Clayton's Case* rather than to apply it.[111] Indeed, in *Russell-Cooke Trust Co v Prentis*,[112] Lindsay J said that it might now be "more accurate to refer to the exception that is, rather than the rule in, *Clayton's Case*." Although it is "probably"[113] still the default rule, very little is required to displace it in favour of the rateable approach.

(d)   Lowest Intermediate Balance.   So far as claims against a bank balance are concerned, the rule is that tracing can succeed against a mixed fund in the bank account to the extent that the trust funds can still be shown to be there. If the account falls below that sum, that part of the trust money must have been spent.[114] Later payments in are not treated as repayments of the trust fund unless the trustee shows an intention to do so.[115] This means it is important to ascertain from the accounts the lowest balance in the fund; to that extent tracing is

26–023

---

[108] *Re Hallett's Estate* (1879) 13 Ch.D. 696 (Fry J); *Re Stenning* [1895] 2 Ch. 433; *Re Diplock* [1948] Ch. 465 (the National Institute for the Deaf).

[109] *Re Stenning* [1895] 2 Ch. 433; *Mutton v Peat* [1899] 2 Ch. 556 at 560; *Re Diplock* [1948] Ch. 465 at 559–563.

[110] *Barlow Clowes International Ltd v Vaughan* [1992] 4 All E.R. 22 at 39.

[111] *Russell-Cooke Trust Co v Prentis* [2003] 2 All E.R. 478; *Re International Investment Unit Trust* [2005] 1 N.Z.L.R. 270; *Commerzbank Aktiengesellschaft v IMB Morgan Plc* [2005] W.T.L.R. 1485; *National Crime Agency v Robb* [2015] Ch. 520 at [64]; *Charity Commission for England and Wales v Framjee* [2015] 1 W.L.R. 16 at [49].

[112] [2003] 2 All E.R. 478 at [55].

[113] *Charity Commission for England and Wales v Framjee* [2015] 1 W.L.R. 16 at [49].

[114] In *James Roscoe (Bolton) Ltd v Winder* [1915] 1 Ch. 62, 69 Sargant J said that tracing extended to "such an amount of the balance ultimately standing to the credit of the trustee as did not exceed the lowest balance of the account during the intervening period".

[115] *James Roscoe (Bolton) Ltd v Winder* [1915] 1 Ch. 62; *Re Goldcorp Exchange Ltd* [1995] 1 A.C. 74. See also *Glencore International AG v Metro Trading International Inc* [2001] 1 Lloyd's Rep. 284 (wrongly mixed oil).

available. Of course the personal claim remains as to any shortfall, in cases where the trust money withdrawn cannot be traced into other property.

If tracing is not permitted beyond the "lowest intermediate balance" of an account, then it may be thought that a fortiori there can be no tracing when an account is operated in overdraft. This indeed is the traditional position: if trust money is paid into an overdrawn account it will repay—in part or in full—a debt due from the customer to the bank. The bank will in normal circumstances be a bona fide purchaser for value without notice, so no claim will lie against it, and there will at that point be no traceable substitute of the money. The bank may subsequently allow further drawing on the overdraft, but any property bought with that new money cannot be seen to have been bought with trust money.[116]

However, considerable doubt has been cast on this position (and by extension on the lowest intermediate balance rule) by the Privy Council's decision in *Brazil v Durant*.[117] That case is considered in more detail in the next section, but it is relevant for present purposes because Lord Toulson reviewed the authorities concerning tracing through an overdraft and noted that

"An account may be used as a conduit for the transfer of funds, whether the account holder is operating the account in credit or within an overdraft facility. The Board therefore rejects the argument that ... the court can never trace the value of an asset whose proceeds are paid into an overdrawn account."[118]

Lord Toulson was careful not to doubt the outcomes in *Roscoe v Winder*[119] and *Re Goldcorp*,[120] the leading cases concerning the lowest intermediate balance rule. Nonetheless, the future of the rule remains uncertain.[121]

D. Tracing and Debts

26–024   The purpose of tracing is to identify substitutes of trust property in respect of which claims may be made. If a trustee wrongly uses trust money to buy a house in her daughter's name, the beneficiaries can trace into and claim the house. Tracing works straightforwardly in situations like this, where one asset has been directly exchanged for another.

Credit and clearing facilities present a potential problem. When a credit card is used to buy goods, the cardholder borrows money from the credit card company to fund the purchase. That debt is repaid in due course. But if trust money is subsequently used to repay the debt it cannot strictly be said that the trust money

---

[116] *Re Goldcorp Exchange Ltd* [1995] 1 A.C. 74; *Re Registered Securities Ltd* [1991] 1 N.Z.L.R. 545 at 554.

[117] *Federal Republic of Brazil v Durant International Corp* [2015] UKPC 35; [2016] A.C. 297; below, para.26–026.

[118] [2016] A.C. 297 at [39]–[40]. Some earlier cases had similar points; e.g. *Hagan v Waterhouse* (1991) 34 N.S.W.L.R. 308 at 358.

[119] *James Roscoe (Bolton) Ltd v Winder* [1915] 1 Ch. 62.

[120] *Re Goldcorp Exchange Ltd* [1995] 1 A.C. 74.

[121] The Jersey Courts in *Brazil v Durant* had been able to say that the lowest intermediate balance rule simply did not form part of the laws of Jersey: [2012] JRC 211 at [219]; [2013] JCA 71 at [62]. While the future of the rule in England is uncertain, it cannot be said that the rule does not exist.

itself was used to buy the goods.[122] In *Bishopsgate Investment Management Ltd v Homan*[123] Leggatt LJ firmly rejected the concept of tracing into an asset acquired by the trustee before the trust money was misappropriated and thus without its aid.[124] Dillon LJ, however, regarded it as arguable that the beneficiary could claim in respect of an asset if there was a connection between the misappropriated money and the acquisition of the particular asset, as where the asset was bought with borrowed money and at the time of the borrowing it could be inferred that the trustee intended to repay with trust money.[125]

Although in such cases the trust money is not strictly used to acquire the asset, **26–025** more recent authorities have taken a wider view of the connection necessary between the misapplied trust money and the asset sought to be traced. In *Relfo v Varsani*,[126] a director of Relfo Ltd wrongly caused the company to pay £500,000 to an account in the name of Mirren Ltd. The transfer was made on 5 May. On the same day, another company called Intertrade LLC paid the dollar equivalent of £500,000 to Mr Varsani. Beyond that the facts were unclear: it appeared that Mirren had reimbursed the money used to make the Intertrade payment to Mr Varsani, but that it had done so after the Intertrade payment had already been made. In particular, Relfo accepted that it could not

> "point to specific transactions passing between the Mirren and Intertrade accounts to show how the Relfo/Mirren payment was translated into the Intertrade payment which went to Mr Varsani's account".[127]

Nonetheless, both Sales J and the Court of Appeal allowed Relfo to trace the misapplied money into the hands of Mr Varsani. The Court of Appeal found that Sales J had been entitled to draw the inference that the money misdirected from Relfo had been used to put Intertrade in funds and had then been used to pay Mr Varsani. That conclusion could validly be drawn even if it did not accord with the strict chronology of the payments into and out of the various accounts.[128]

A similar point arose in *Brazil v Durant*,[129] where the mayor of Sao Paulo had **26–026** accepted bribes amounting to $10.5 million in relation to infrastructure contracts. Those bribes were held on constructive trust under the principle in *Attorney General for Hong Kong v Reid*.[130] The mayor channelled the bribe money from a New York bank account to accounts in Jersey held in the names of two companies, Durant International and Kildare Finance. Those two companies were controlled by the mayor and his son. The claimant, which was in effect the

---

[122] If the repaid debt had been secured, subrogation to the security may be possible; below, para.26–027.

[123] [1995] Ch. 211. The purchaser had incurred a debt through drawing down an overdraft, had used that money to buy the goods, and had then repaid the overdraft with trust money.

[124] [1995] Ch. 211 at 221–222.

[125] [1995] Ch. 211 at 217. Henry LJ agreed with both judgments.

[126] *Relfo Ltd (In Liquidation) v Varsani* [2014] EWCA Civ 360; S. Watterson (2014) 37 C.L.J. 496; R. Nolan (2015) 131 L.Q.R. 8.

[127] [2014] EWCA Civ 360 at [13].

[128] [2014] EWCA Civ 360 at [63].

[129] *Federal Republic of Brazil v Durant International Corp* [2015] UKPC 35; [2016] A.C. 297; P.G. Turner (2016) 75 C.L.J. 462. J. Campbell (2016) 42 Aust. Bar Rev. 32.

[130] [1994] 1 A.C. 324; above, para.22–029.

Municipality of Sao Paulo, successfully sought a declaration that the companies held those funds on constructive trust in the amount of $10.5 million.

The defendant companies appealed to the Privy Council, arguing that the constructive trust ought to be limited to $7.7 million rather than the full $10.5 million. The basis for this argument was that some payments had been credited to the Jersey accounts before the relevant money had left the New York account. But Lord Toulson concluded that the lower courts had been justified in allowing the claimant to trace to the full amount of $10.5 million[131]:

> "If the court is satisfied that the various steps are part of a coordinated scheme, it should not matter that, either as a deliberate part of the choreography or possibly because of the incidents of the banking system, a debit appears in the bank account of an intermediary before a reciprocal credit entry. ... But the claimant has to establish a coordination between the depletion of the trust fund and the acquisition of the asset which is the subject of the tracing claim, looking at the whole transaction, such as to warrant the court attributing the value of the interest acquired to the misuse of the trust fund."

While tracing will not be forestalled by arrangements of the type seen in *Brazil v Durant* and *Relfo v Varsani*, the Privy Council rejected as too broad the proposition that money used to pay a debt may be traced into whatever was acquired in return for the debt.[132] What is required is a "coordination"; a "close causal and transactional link between the incurring of a debt and the use of trust funds to discharge it".[133] Future cases will explore and explain the nature of the link that is required, but it appears that attention will be focused on whether the trustee incurred the debt already intending to use trust money to repay it.[134]

4. SUBROGATION

26–027 This is a doctrine with common law and equitable origins whereby one person is entitled to stand in the shoes of another and assert that other's rights.[135] The most common examples are insurance and suretyship. An insurer who pays the loss is entitled to stand in the shoes of the insured and assert his rights against the wrongdoer. The House of Lords in *Napier and Ettrick (Lord) v Hunter*[136] held that an insurer's subrogation rights should have proprietary protection in the form of a lien (rather than a more onerous constructive trust) over damages paid to the

---

[131] [2016] A.C. 297 at [38]–[40].

[132] [2016] A.C. 297 at [33], rejecting the argument made in L. Smith (1995) 54 C.L.J. 290.

[133] [2016] A.C. 297 at [34]. The required link was not present in *Labrouche v Frey* [2016] EWHC 268 (Ch) at [277].

[134] See *Foskett v McKeown* [1998] Ch. 265 at 283 per Scott VC, quoted with approval in *Federal Republic of Brazil v Durant International Corp* [2016] A.C. 297 at [24], [38]; T. Cutts (2016) 79 M.L.R. 381; R. Nolan in P.G. Turner (ed.), *Equity and Administration* (Cambridge: Cambridge University Press, 2016) Ch.4. cf. M. Conaglen (2011) 127 L.Q.R. 432.

[135] See C. Mitchell and S. Watterson, *Subrogation: Law and Practice* (Oxford: Oxford University Press, 2007); Goff and Jones, 9th edn, Ch.39; L. Smith (1995) 54 C.L.J. 290; C. Mitchell in A. Burrows and A. Rodger (eds), *Mapping the Law* (2006), Ch.6.

[136] [1993] A.C. 713. See also *Lonrho Exports Ltd v Export Credits Guarantee Department* [1999] Ch. 158 (if insurer recovers from third party a sum greater than its entitlement by subrogation, surplus is held on trust for the insured).

insured by the wrongdoer. Thus unsecured creditors would not benefit from the double payment at the expense of the insurer on the bankruptcy of the insured.

In the insurance cases the payer is subrogated to the rights of the payee against third parties.[137] In other cases the payer is subrogated to the rights of third parties against the payee, as where the payee has used the money to pay off creditors.

In the context of tracing, the question is whether the claimant may be subrogated to the position of a secured creditor paid off by the defendant with the claimant's money. (If the creditor was unsecured, subrogation will not improve the claimant's position). In *Re Diplock*[138] the next of kin's money had been wrongly paid to hospital charities, two of which used it (innocently) to pay off secured and unsecured debts. It was held that there was no right of subrogation, because that would require reviving debts and securities which had been extinguished. This outcome was criticised as allowing the unjust enrichment of the charities at the expense of the next of kin, and the position was eventually reviewed by the Court of Appeal in *Boscawen v Bajwa*.[139] A building society advanced money for the purchase of property and the discharge of a legal charge on that property. The society intended to have a first legal charge on completion. It sent the money to the solicitor acting for itself and the purchaser, intending to retain the beneficial interest in the money until the security was in place, but its instructions were not carried out. The purchase was not completed, but the society's money was used to redeem the existing charge. It was held that the society was entitled to be subrogated to the position of the legal chargee. It would be unconscionable to assert that the charge had been redeemed for the landowner's benefit.

The application of the doctrine to a loan which is valid, intended to be secured, **26–028** and which is used to pay off a secured loan, is not surprising. However, the Court of Appeal took the opportunity to state that the doctrine applied in circumstances such as those of *Re Diplock*. The passage in that case which denied the remedy was considered difficult and in need of review in the light of later developments in the law of restitution. It could not be objected that the creditor's security had been extinguished: that was not a bar to subrogation but a precondition. What had motivated the Court of Appeal to deny the remedy in *Re Diplock* was a desire to avoid injustice to a charity which had redeemed a mortgage which the bank was content to leave outstanding indefinitely.

> "It may be doubted whether in its anxiety to avoid injustice to the hospital the court may not have done an even greater injustice to the next of kin, who were denied even the interest on their money."[140]

---

[137] R. Merkin and J. Steele, *Insurance and the Law of Obligations* (Oxford: Oxford University Press, 2013), Ch.5.
[138] [1948] Ch. 465.
[139] [1996] 1 W.L.R. 328; P. Birks (1995) 9 T.L.I. 124; N. Andrews (1996) 55 C.L.J. 199; A. Oakley [1997] Conv. 1; P. Matthews (1997) 3 T. & T. 18. See also *Castle Phillips Finance v Piddington* [1995] 1 F.L.R. 783; *Anfield (UK) Ltd v Bank of Scotland Plc* [2011] 1 W.L.R. 2414.
[140] [1996] 1 W.L.R. 328 at 341, per Millett LJ.

Millett LJ, with the agreement of Waite and Stuart-Smith LJJ, thought the solution should have been to delay enforcement of the revived security until the charity had had a reasonable opportunity to obtain a fresh loan on suitable terms.

The House of Lords examined the role of intention in subrogation in *Banque Financière de la Cité v Parc (Battersea) Ltd*.[141] It was considered that in cases where the doctrine rested upon a contractual basis, as in the insurance cases, it was based on the common intention of the parties. However, no such intention was required where the claim was founded on the law of restitution (as in *Boscawen v Bajwa*[142]), where the aim was to reverse or prevent unjust enrichment. Where the claimant's money had been used to pay off a first chargee, the availability of subrogation did not depend on any common intention between the claimant and the second chargee or between the claimant and the payee that the claimant should be subrogated to the security of the first chargee. This issue was whether the second chargee would be unjustly enriched at the claimant's expense in the absence of such subrogation. Intention was, however, relevant to the question whether the enrichment would be unjust: it would not be if the transaction had been intended to create merely an unsecured loan.

26–029 In *Menelaou v Bank of Cyprus UK Ltd*,[143] Mr and Mrs Menelaou wanted to sell their own house and use some of the proceeds to buy a house in their daughter's name. The Bank of Cyprus, which held a charge over the parents' house, agreed to release that security in return for a new charge over the daughter's house. In fact, however, the bank never acquired a valid charge over the daughter's house. The question was whether the bank could be subrogated to the unpaid vendor's lien that had briefly encumbered the daughter's house before it had been paid off with the proceeds of sale of the parents' house.

The Supreme Court held unanimously that the bank could indeed be subrogated to the unpaid vendor's lien, although the Justices differed in their reasons for reaching that result. Lords Clarke, Neuberger, Kerr and Wilson applied an unjust enrichment analysis and held that subrogation would apply to prevent the daughter being unjustly enriched at the expense of the bank.[144] Even assuming that the funds used to discharge the lien were not actually the bank's money, a "sufficient causal connection"[145] still existed on the facts to mean that the daughter's enrichment would be at the expense of the bank. This unjust enrichment would be prevented by subrogating the bank to the unpaid vendor's lien. Lord Carnwath, by contrast, held that subrogation would only be an appropriate remedy if the bank could show that it had a proprietary interest in the

---

[141] [1999] 1 A.C. 221. Subrogation was held to apply only as between the claimant and the second chargee. See P. Watts (1998) 114 L.Q.R. 341; C. Mitchell [1998] 6 R.L.R. 144; M. Bridge [1998] J.B.L. 323; D. Friedmann (1999) 115 L.Q.R. 195. See also *Cheltenham and Gloucester Plc v Appleyard*, The Times, 29 March 2004.

[142] [1996] 1 W.L.R. 328. See also *Halifax Plc v Omar* (2002) 2 P. & C.R. 26; *Anfield (UK) Ltd v Bank of Scotland Plc* [2011] 1 W.L.R. 2414 at 2417.

[143] [2015] UKSC 66; [2016] A.C. 176; S. Watterson [2016] C.L.J. 209; C. Buckingham and L. Chambers [2016] Conv. 219; M. Cleaver (2018) 29 J.B.F.L.P 34, Goff and Jones, 9th edn, paras 7–03—7–11.

[144] For trenchant criticism of the Supreme Court's unjust enrichment analysis, see G. Virgo (2016) University of Cambridge Faculty of Law Research Paper No. 10/2016.

[145] [2016] A.C. 176 at [27]. See further on this point *Investment Trust Companies v Revenue and Customs Comrs* [2017] UKSC 29; [2018] A.C. 275 at [37]–[66].

funds used to discharge the lien. His Lordship held that a proprietary interest did exist on the facts: in an application of "the *Quistclose* principle",[146] it could be said that the proceeds of sale of the parents' house, when received by the solicitors, were held on trust such that the bank had a proprietary interest.[147] Those funds were used to purchase the daughter's house, and to discharge the unpaid vendor's lien, thus establishing the necessary "tracing link" between the bank's property and the discharge of the security to which the bank now sought to be subrogated.

Lords Clarke, Neuberger, Kerr and Wilson agreed that the result could be reached in the way suggested by Lord Carnwath (unlike Lord Carnwath, the other Justices did not think the result could *only* be reached in that way). In addition to deciding that subrogation is an available remedy for unjust enrichment,[148] the case is therefore a further illustration that subrogation to an unpaid vendor's lien is an available remedy when a claimant's property can be traced into the funds used to discharge that lien.

5. CHANGE OF POSITION[149]

We have seen that a person into whose hands the claimant's property has been traced or followed may be able to raise the defence of bona fide purchase.[150] There may also be another defence open to the recipient: that of change of position.[151] It should be emphasised that both the bona fide purchase and change of position doctrines are defences to *claims*; they are not directly concerned with the tracing process itself.

26–030

The doctrine of change of position provides that a defendant's liability may be reduced pro tanto,[152] or eliminated, if his "position has so changed that it would be inequitable in all the circumstances to require him to make restitution, or alternatively restitution in full".[153] A causal link between the receipt and the

---

[146] [2016] A.C. 176 at [133]–[140]. referring to *Barclays Bank Ltd v Quistclose Investments Ltd* [1970] A.C. 567; above, para.2–009.

[147] Alternatively, the bank may have had proprietary interest through a charge over the proceeds of sale: see *Buhr v Barclays Bank plc* [2001] EWCA Civ 1223, [2002] B.P.I.R. 25 at [45].

[148] See *Swynson Ltd v Lowick Rose LLP (formerly Hurst Morrison Thomson LLP) (In Liquidation)* [2017] UKSC 32; [2018] A.C. 313 at [29].

[149] See L. Smith, *The Law of Tracing* (1997), pp.34–38; G. Virgo and J. Palmer [2005] 13 R.L.R. 34 and 53 respectively; C. Mitchell [2005] L.M.C.L.Q. 168; T. Wee [2006] 14 R.L.R. 55; G. Jones in A. Burrows and A. Rodger (eds), *Mapping the Law* (2006) Ch.4; E. Bant, *The Change of Position Defence* (Oxford: Hart Publishing, 2009); A. Burrows, *A Restatement of the English Law of Unjust Enrichment* (Oxford: Oxford University Press, 2012), pp.117–122.

[150] A purchaser in an arm's length transaction not involving investigation of title to land will not normally have constructive notice: *Sinclair Investments (UK) Ltd v Versailles Trade Finance Ltd (in administrative receivership)* [2011] EWCA Civ 347; [2012] Ch. 453 (this point not affected by *FHR European Ventures LLP v Cedar Capital Partners LLC* [2015] 1 A.C. 250).

[151] Bona fide purchase is not a species of the change of position defence because the consideration does not need to be adequate: *Lipkin Gorman v Karpnale Ltd* [1991] 2 A.C. 548; K. Barker [1999] 7 R.L.R. 75.

[152] *David Securities Pty Ltd v CBA* (1992) 175 C.L.R. 353 at 385.

[153] *Lipkin Gorman v Karpnale Ltd* [1991] 2 A.C. 548 at 580.

change of position is required.[154] The defence normally operates where the defendant has disposed of money or other property in an exceptional and irretrievable manner in reliance upon the validity of his receipt of the claimant's property.[155] It is not limited to disposals of money or property, however, and could also apply in rare cases where the defendant has given up his job[156] or performed services in reliance on entitlement to payment. In a 2014 Australian case, the defence was accepted when, in reliance on the receipt of a mistaken payment, the recipient chose to forgo legal action against third parties.[157]

The defence is available to an innocent defendant but not to a wrongdoer.[158] Differing views have been expressed as to whether a defendant who, although honest, ought to have known that the property was not hers is "innocent" for this purpose.[159] Mere carelessness on the part of the defendant is not a bar to the defence. Often the claimant has been careless in making the payment, and the court will not balance the fault of each party.[160] On the other hand, conduct short of dishonesty may bar the defendant from relying on the defence, as where she suspected a mistake but made no enquiries.[161] General suspicions unrelated to the transaction in question may not bar the defence.[162] The question is not whether she was dishonest but whether, in the circumstances, it would be inequitable to allow the recipient to deny restitution.[163] The recipient cannot rely on an illegal act as a change of position, even if she was unaware of the illegality.[164]

---

[154] *Scottish Equitable Plc v Derby* [2001] 3 All E.R. 818; *Dextra Bank & Trust Co Ltd v Bank of Jamaica* [2002] 1 All E.R. (Comm) 193 at 203; M. McInnes (2002) 118 L.Q.R. 209; P. Watts (2002) 61 C.L.J. 301; P. Birks and W. Swadling [2002] All E.R. Rev., p.316; T. Akkouh and C. Webb [2002] 10 R.L.R. 107.

[155] See *Philip Collins Ltd v Davis* [2000] 3 All E.R. 808 (overpaid royalties: partial defence where defendants had geared their outgoings to income over an extended period); cf. *Hillsdown Holdings Plc v Pensions Ombudsman* [1997] 1 All E.R. 862 at 904 (no defence where money used to pay tax which was recoverable).

[156] See the discussion in *Commerzbank AG v Price-Jones* [2003] All E.R. (D) 303; P. Birks (2004) 120 L.Q.R. 373.

[157] *Australian Financial Services and Leasing Pty Ltd v Hills Industries Ltd* [2014] HCA 14; (2014) 253 C.L.R. 560.

[158] *Lipkin Gorman v Karpnale Ltd* [1991] 2 A.C. 548; *Cressman v Coys of Kensington (Sales) Ltd* [2004] 1 W.L.R. 2775 (no defence where property given away after knowledge of mistake). On the wrongdoer bar, see P. Birks, *Unjust Enrichment* (2005), Ch.9; E. Bant [2009] L.M.C.L.Q. 166; E. Bant, *The Change of Position Defence* (2009), Ch 6; and E. Bant [2012] L.M.C.L.Q. 122; cf. Y. Hu [2011] 19 R.L.R. 112 at 124.

[159] Law Com. No. 227 (1994), para.2.23; *South Tyneside MBC v Svenska International Plc* [1995] 1 All E.R. 545 at 569; R. Nolan and P. Birks in P. Birks (ed.), *Laundering and Tracing* (1995), pp.158 and 325; M. Jewell [2000] R.L.R. 1 at 16; cf. R. Chambers [1996] R.L.R. 103; P. Birks (2000) 14 T.L.I. 217 at 223–227.

[160] *Dextra Bank & Trust Co Ltd v Bank of Jamaica* [2002] 1 All E.R. (Comm) 193.

[161] See *Fea v Roberts* [2006] W.T.L.R. 255 (legacy paid to wrong person).

[162] *Abou-Rahmah v Abacha* [2007] W.T.L.R. 1 (suspicions of money-laundering); G. Virgo (2007) 66 C.L.J. 22; J. Lee [2007] 15 R.L.R. 135.

[163] *Niru Battery Manufacturing Co v Milestone Trading Ltd* [2004] Q.B. 985; A. Tettenborn [2003] 11 R.L.R. 98. The approach of the Court of Appeal is criticised as muddying the waters in P. Birks (2004) 120 L.Q.R. 373 at 377, and also in A. Burrows (2004) 63 C.L.J. 276; A. Tettenborn [2004] 12 R.L.R. 155; E. Ellinger (2005) 121 L.Q.R. 51.

[164] *Barros Mattos Jnr v MacDaniels Ltd* [2005] 1 W.L.R. 247. The effect of *Patel v Mirza* [2016] UKSC 42; [2017] A.C. 467 on this point remains to be seen; above, para.14–014.

A. Potential Application to Proprietary Claims

The change of position defence was accepted by the House of Lords in *Lipkin*   **26–031**
Gorman v Karpnale Ltd.[165] However, that case involved a personal action for
money had and received, and it is not clear how far the defence will be generally
available. Specifically, it is not clear if the defence applies where the claimant is
asserting property rights in respect of assets in the defendant's hands.

An earlier version of the defence can perhaps be seen in *Re Diplock*,[166] where
innocent volunteers (charities) had spent the claimant's money on improvements
and alterations to their own land. It was held that no charge should be imposed,
because a charge is enforceable by sale and it would be harsh to make the
volunteers sell their land.

On the other hand, the difficulty with allowing a change of position defence to
operate in the context of proprietary claims is that, as Professor Fox has
written[167]:

> "It is alien to the security of property interests that the conduct of a person who receives the
> plaintiff's asset should affect the plaintiff's right to enforce his property in it. It is in the nature
> of a proprietary interest that it should remain enforceable against persons generally, provided
> that the conditions for its continued survival are fulfilled. ... [T]he defence should not be
> available in restitutionary actions which aim directly at the vindication of title, other than
> those where the plaintiff's title is itself created in response to unjust enrichment."

In *Foskett v McKeown*, Lord Millett commented[168]:

> "[A] claim in unjust enrichment is subject to a change of position defence, which usually
> operates by reducing or extinguishing the element of enrichment. An action like the present is
> subject to the bona fide purchaser for value defence, which operates to clear the defendant's
> title."

The application of the change of position defence may therefore depend on the
genesis of the proprietary right that is being asserted.[169] This position seems to
balance appropriately the security of property interests and the security of
receipts.[170] Quite simply, however, the point is not settled.

Finally, it is worth noting the limited effect of any recognition of change of   **26–032**
position. The defence, if it applies to proprietary claims, only reduces liability by
the amount of an exceptional expense that would otherwise not have been
incurred. The defence is not, therefore, concerned with situations when the
expense *would* normally have been incurred, but where it just happened to be

---

[165] [1991] 2 A.C. 548; G. Jones (1993–94) 4 K.C.L.J. 93.
[166] [1948] Ch. 465 at 546–548; see *Boscawen v Bajwa* [1996] 1 W.L.R. 328 at 341.
[167] D. Fox [2000] R.L.R. 465 at 488.
[168] [2001] 1 A.C. 102 at 129.
[169] See also R. Nolan in P. Birks (ed.), *Laundering and Tracing* (1995) Ch.6 at pp.175–185; A.
Burrows in S. Degeling and J. Edelman (eds), *Unjust Enrichment in Commercial Law* (Sydney:
Thomson Reuters, 2008) Ch.17 pp.352–357; cf. Goff and Jones, 9th edn, para.27–68; E. Bant, *The
Change of Position Defence* (2009), pp.204–208; A. Burrows, *A Restatement of the English Law of
Unjust Enrichment* (2012), p.118.
[170] See *National Bank of New Zealand Ltd v Waitaki International Processing (NI) Ltd* [1999] 2
N.Z.L.R. 211; *Kleinwort Benson Ltd v Lincoln CC* [1999] 2 A.C. 349 at 382.

incurred out of the claimant's property. In these situations, the defendant cannot be said to have changed his or her position.

An example might be a winning lottery ticket bought with funds traceable by the claimant, but which could just as easily have been bought with the innocent defendant's own funds.[171] This is not a case of change of position at all. Any amelioration of harsh results must instead depend on judicious findings of fact (which facts oust the tracing presumptions), or on the ability to award the defendant an allowance. The irony of the lottery ticket example is that, if the ticket had not won and the money had therefore been dissipated and become untraceable, the innocent defendant would not have owed any personal liability in equity in respect of the claimant's lost £2.

---

[171] See *Foskett v McKeown* [2001] 1 A.C. 102 at 134. In Lord Millett's example the defendant was a wrongdoer, but that does not matter.

PART V

MISCELLANEOUS EQUITABLE
REMEDIES AND DOCTRINES

CHAPTER 27

SPECIFIC PERFORMANCE

1. GENERAL PRINCIPLES[1]

27–001 AN OUTLINE of the nature of equitable remedies has already been given.[2] Their characteristics, in relation to specific performance in particular, must now be examined.

A. Discretionary

27–002 Specific performance, like other equitable remedies, is only given as a matter of discretion, although the discretion is exercised in accordance with settled principles.[3] Thus, there are some cases, notably contracts for the sale of land,[4] where the claimant may expect to obtain specific performance as a matter of course, and other cases, such as contracts for personal services,[5] where she may expect not to. The discretionary nature of the remedy is well illustrated by a consideration of the matters, such as the conduct of the claimant, which the court may regard as a bar to specific performance.[6]

B. Common Law Remedies Inadequate

27–003 Specific performance is only available where the common law remedy of damages for breach of contract is inadequate[7]; for example where the obligation is a continuing one, necessitating a series of actions at law for damages,[8] or where the loss would be difficult to quantify.[9] But specific performance will not be available if, on the true construction of the contract, the parties have agreed that a specific sum of money is to be paid as an alternative to performing the contract.[10]

---

[1] See Fry, *Specific Performance*, 6th edn (1921); Jones and Goodhart, *Specific Performance*, 2nd edn (London: Butterworths, 1996); Spry, *Equitable Remedies*, 9th edn (2014).
[2] Above, para.1–037.
[3] *Lamare v Dixon* (1873) L.R. 6 H.L. 414; *Haywood v Cope* (1858) 25 Beav. 140 at 151 (Romilly MR).
[4] Below, para.27–014.
[5] Below, para.27–024.
[6] Below, para.27–033.
[7] *Beswick v Beswick* [1968] A.C. 58, below, para.27–047.
[8] *Beswick v Beswick* [1968] A.C. 58, but see below, para.27–049.
[9] See, however, *Co-operative Insurance Society Ltd v Argyll Stores (Holdings) Ltd* [1998] A.C. 1.
[10] *Legh v Lillie* (1860) 6 H. & N. 165.

C.   Specific Performance is a Remedy in Personam[11]

An order of specific performance issues against the individual defendant. If the **27–004** defendant is within the jurisdiction of the court and can be compelled personally to carry out his obligation, the court may order him to do so even though the subject-matter of the contract is outside the jurisdiction of the court.

> In *Penn v Lord Baltimore*,[12] the parties had entered into a written agreement fixing the boundaries of Pennsylvania and Maryland, the former of which belonged to the claimants and the latter to the defendant. The claimants sued the defendant in England to have the agreement specifically performed, and one of the objections taken by the defendant was to the jurisdiction of the court. This objection was overruled by Lord Hardwicke on the ground that:
>
> > "[T]he conscience of the party was bound by this agreement; and being within the jurisdiction of this court, which acts *in personam*, the court may properly order it as an agreement."[13]
>
> Although the land was not within the jurisdiction, the defendant was, and the court would hold him in contempt unless he complied.

D.   Ensuring Observance

Equitable remedies will never issue unless the court can ensure that they will be **27–005** observed. As equity does not act in vain, specific performance will be ordered only where the defendant is in a position to comply.

> In *Jones v Lipman*,[14] the defendant entered into a contract to sell some land to the claimant, but then sought to avoid specific performance by selling the land to a company acquired by him solely for this purpose and controlled by him. While specific performance would not normally be ordered against a vendor who no longer owned the property, here the defendant was still in a position to complete the contract, because the company was:
>
> > "the creature of the vendor, a device and a sham, a mask which he holds before his face in an attempt to avoid recognition by the eye of Equity."[15]
>
> Thus specific performance was ordered against the vendor (and, somewhat controversially,[16] the company).

---

[11] Above, paras 1–008, 1–018.

[12] (1750) 1 Ves.Sen. 444; *Richard West and Partners (Inverness) Ltd v Dick* [1969] Ch. 424. It does, however, appear that the tendency of modern decisions is to restrict the limits within which this jurisdiction will be exercised: see Dicey, Morris and Collins, *The Conflict of Laws*, 15th edn (London: Sweet & Maxwell, 2012), paras 23–042–23–051; J. Wass (2014) 63 I.C.L.Q. 103.

[13] (1750) 1 Ves. Sen. 444 at 447.

[14] [1962] 1 W.L.R. 832. See also *Elliott v Pierson* [1948] Ch. 452.

[15] [1962] 1 W.L.R. 832 at 836, per Russell J.

[16] See *VTB Capital Plc v Nutritek International Corp* [2012] EWCA Civ 808; [2012] 2 Lloyd's Rep. 313 at [64]–[66] (CA: Lloyd LJ); [2013] UKSC 5; [2013] 2 A.C. 337 at [135] (SC: Lord Neuberger); *Prest v Petrodel Resources Ltd* [2013] UKSC 34; [2013] 2 A.C. 415 at [30] (Lord Sumption), [73] (Lord Neuberger).

E. The Enforcement of Positive Contractual Obligations

27–006   Unlike injunctions, the remedy of specific performance is confined to the enforcement of positive contractual obligations. A prohibitory injunction is appropriate to restrain the breach of a negative contract, while a mandatory injunction is used to force the defendant to take positive steps to undo an act already done in breach of contract. But this classification is not inflexible. Even where the claimant wishes to enforce a positive contractual obligation, he may ask for an injunction instead of specific performance. The advantage of such a course is that an injunction can be obtained on an interlocutory basis, while specific performance cannot.[17] It should also be added that specific performance does not lie against the Crown.[18]

F. Time for Performance

27–007   While specific performance is a remedy for breach of contract, it may in some circumstances be obtained before the time for performance has arrived. In *Marks v Lilley*[19] the claimant commenced an action for specific performance of a contract for the sale of land after the contractual completion date but without first having served a notice making time of the essence of the contract.[20] It was held that this action was not premature, as the equitable right to specific performance, based on the defendant's equitable duty to perform his contract, had already accrued. Indeed, it may be wise for the purchaser in such a situation *not* to serve a notice to complete. In *Clarke Investments Ltd v Pacific Technologies*,[21] the claimant served a notice to complete, but on the due date was itself no longer in a position to complete. The vendor rescinded the contract and kept the deposit.[22] In *Hasham v Zenab*[23] specific performance of a contract for the sale of land was granted even before the contractual completion date where the defendant had been guilty of anticipatory breach of contract.[24] The order would not, of course, take effect before the fixed date.

---

[17] See *Sky Petroleum Ltd v VIP Petroleum Ltd* [1974] 1 W.L.R. 576; *Astro Exito Navegacion SA v Southland Enterprise Co Ltd (No.2)* [1983] 2 A.C. 787; *Peninsular Maritime Ltd v Padseal Ltd* (1981) 259 E.G. 860; *Parker v Camden LBC* [1986] Ch. 162; *Ashworth v Royal National Theatre* [2014] EWHC 1176 (QB); [2014] I.R.L.R. 526.

[18] Crown Proceedings Act 1947 s.21(1)(a). The proper remedy is a declaration.

[19] [1959] 1 W.L.R. 749. There is a breach of contract at law and in equity if completion does not occur on the contractual date, even though time has not become of the essence: *Raineri v Miles* [1981] A.C. 1050, below, para.27–036.

[20] On the serving of notices to complete, see *Samarenko v Dawn Hill House Ltd* [2011] EWCA Civ 1445; [2013] Ch. 36.

[21] [2013] EWCA Civ 750; [2013] 2 P. & C.R. 20.

[22] It appears that the purchaser made no application for the return of the deposit under Law of Property 1925 s.49(2), which on the facts would probably have been granted. On the return of deposits see *Midill (97PL) Ltd v Park Lane Estates Ltd* [2009] 1 W.L.R. 2460.

[23] [1960] A.C. 316; R.E.M. (1960) 76 L.Q.R. 200. This is similar to the position at law, where an immediate right to damages accrues upon an anticipatory breach of contract: *Hochster v De la Tour* (1853) 2 E. & B. 678.

[24] Anticipatory breach is not essential, but there must be a sufficient likelihood of breach; Spry, *Equitable Remedies*, 9th edn (2014), pp.80–81. See further *Oakacre Ltd v Claire Cleaners (Holdings) Ltd* [1982] Ch. 197; *Airport Industrial GP Ltd v Heathrow Airport Ltd* [2015] EWHC 3753 (Ch).

G.   Specific Performance and Damages or Compensation

Damages may be awarded either in addition to or in substitution for specific performance.[25] Similarly, there are some cases, involving misdescription in contracts for the sale of land, where the court may grant specific performance with compensation in the form of an abatement of the purchase price.[26]   **27–008**

2.   EFFECT OF ORDER ON OTHER REMEDIES

If specific performance is granted, but enforcement subsequently becomes impossible, what remedies are available to the claimant?   **27–009**

A.   Common Law Remedy not Excluded

In *Johnson v Agnew*,[27] the claimant, having contracted to sell mortgaged properties to the defendant, obtained an order of specific performance. Subsequently, owing to the defendant's delay, the properties were sold by the mortgagees so that it became impossible to comply with the order. The price obtained by the mortgagees was lower than the contract price, so the claimant sought damages from the defendant at common law for breach of contract.[28] The defendant claimed that the claimant's election to seek specific performance was irrevocable, so that he could not claim damages at common law. The House of Lords found in favour of the claimant. Lord Wilberforce explained the vendor's position as follows.   **27–010**

If a purchaser fails to complete, the vendor can treat this as a repudiation and claim damages for breach of contract, or he may seek specific performance. If he proceeds for these remedies in the alternative, he must elect at trial.[29] If an order for specific performance is made, the contract still exists and is not merged in the judgment. If the defendant then fails to comply with the order, the claimant may apply either to enforce or to dissolve the contract. It follows from the fact that the contract still exists that the claimant can recover damages at common law. The argument based on irrevocable election is unsound:

> "A vendor who seeks (and gets) specific performance is merely electing for a course which may or may not lead to implementation of the contract; what he elects for is not eternal and unconditional affirmation, but a continuance of the contract under control of the court, which

---

[25] Lord Cairns' Act 1858; Judicature Act 1873; Senior Courts Act 1981 s.50; below, para.27–044.

[26] Below, para.27–044 (damages), and para.27–039 (compensation). See also *Seven Seas Properties Ltd v Al-Essa* [1988] 1 W.L.R. 1272 (specific performance and damages combined with asset-freezing injunction).

[27] [1980] A.C. 367; P. Baker (1979) 95 L.Q.R. 321; F. Crane [1979] Conv. 293; G. Woodman (1979) 42 M.L.R. 696; M. Hetherington (1980) 96 L.Q.R. 403; A. Oakley (1980) 39 C.L.J. 58; D. Jackson (1981) 97 L.Q.R. 26.

[28] Or, alternatively, damages under Lord Cairns' Act; below, para.27–044.

[29] See further *Meng Leong Development Pte Ltd v Jip Hong Trading Co Pte Ltd* [1985] A.C. 511 (PC); (1985) 101 L.Q.R. 309.

control involves the power, in certain events, to terminate it. If he makes an election at all, he does so when he decides not to proceed under the order for specific performance; but to ask the court to terminate the contract."[30]

If the claimant accepts a repudiation, he cannot afterwards seek specific performance, because the defendant has been discharged from further performance by the claimant's acceptance of the repudiation. But if the claimant obtains an order of specific performance, and enforcement becomes impossible, there is no reason why the claimant should be precluded from seeking a remedy at common law.[31]

B.   The Court's Discretion

27–011   As noted, the remedy is discretionary. The control of the court is thus exercised according to equitable principles: the relief sought by the claimant will be refused if it would be unjust to the other party to grant it. In *Johnson v Agnew*,[32] it was the purchaser's fault that it had become impossible to enforce the order, therefore the vendor was entitled not only to the discharge of the order and the termination of the contract, but to damages at common law for breach of contract.

C.   Subsequent Performance Regulated by Terms of Order

27–012   Although the contract still exists after specific performance is granted and does not merge into the order until the legal title has been conveyed, the rights under the contract may be affected by the order. By applying for specific performance, the claimant puts into the hands of the court how the contract is to be carried out: the performance of the contract is regulated by the provisions of the order and not those of the contract. In *Singh v Nazeer*,[33] a purchaser was granted specific performance of a contract for the sale of land. The purchaser then delayed, so the vendor served a completion notice and claimed damages and forfeiture of the deposit. Megarry J held that the completion notice was invalid. The machinery provisions of the contract, for example as to mode and date of completion, were intended to apply to performance out of court. Once specific performance was granted, they must yield to any directions in the order. Unless the parties agree, the working out, variation or cancellation of an order for specific performance is a matter for the court. Applying these principles, a vendor who obtains specific performance is not free to sell to a third party if the purchaser fails to comply

---

[30] [1980] A.C. 367 at 398 (per Lord Wilberforce). See also *Hillel v Christoforides* (1992) 63 P. & C.R. 301; *Homsy v Murphy* (1997) 73 P. & C.R. 26.
[31] Damages are also available in lieu of specific performance under Lord Cairns' Act (below, para.27–044); *Biggin v Minton* [1977] 1 W.L.R. 701.
[32] [1980] A.C. 367.
[33] [1979] Ch. 474. See also *Jones v Mahmut* [2017] EWCA Civ 2362 (order made under Landlord and Tenant Act 1987 s.19, rather than order of specific performance, but same principles apply).

with the order. Unless the purchaser agrees to the resale, the vendor's remedy in such a case is to apply to court either for enforcement of the order or for an order terminating the contract.[34]

3. SPECIFIC PERFORMANCE IN PARTICULAR SITUATIONS

It is a fundamental rule that specific performance will not be granted where the claimant would be adequately compensated by the common law remedy of damages.[35] There are some situations, few in number, in which it is settled that the claimant may expect to obtain specific performance.[36] There are also numerous situations in which it can firmly be said that the claimant will *not* be awarded specific performance. That said, it may be that many of the arguments for restricting specific performance are no longer wholly convincing.[37]

27–013

A. Contracts for the Sale of Land[38]

A claimant seeking specific performance of a contract for the sale (or other disposition) of land must first satisfy the requirements of s.2 of the Law of Property (Miscellaneous Provisions) Act 1989. These requirements apply also to a claim for damages. Section 2 provides that a contract for the sale or other disposition of an interest in land can only be made in writing incorporating all the terms which the parties have agreed. The document must be signed by or on behalf of each party. Under the previous law, the contract needed only to be *evidenced in* writing, and an oral contract could be enforced under the doctrine of part performance. The present rule leaves no scope for part performance, which can only cure *evidential* defects.[39]

27–014

Assuming s.2 is satisfied, specific performance is readily granted to enforce a contract to create or convey a legal estate in land (for example, to sell land[40] or to grant a lease) unless some special consideration arises to prevent it. It cannot however be said that the claimant is *entitled* to specific performance, as the order is always subject to the discretion of the court.

---

[34] *GKN Distributors Ltd v Tyne Tees Fabrication Ltd* [1985] 2 E.G.L.R. 181 (vendor's claim against purchaser for declaration, forfeiture of deposit and damages dismissed).

[35] *Hutton v Watling* [1948] Ch. 26 at 36, affirmed [1948] Ch. 398. On the effect on the defendant's insolvency, see *Freevale Ltd v Metrostore (Holdings) Ltd* [1984] Ch. 199; D. Milman and S. Coneys [1984] Conv. 446; *Amec Properties Ltd v Planning Research & Systems Plc* [1992] 1 E.G.L.R. 70; *Bristol Alliance Nominee No.1 Ltd v Bennett* [2013] EWCA Civ 1626.

[36] See *Haywood v Cope* (1858) 25 Beav. 140, per Romilly MR at 151; *Lamare v Dixon* (1873) L.R. 6 HL 414.

[37] e.g. *Geys v Société Générale, London Branch* [2012] UKSC 63; [2013] 1 A.C. 523 at [77] (Lord Wilson questioning the reluctance to specifically enforce personal service contracts).

[38] See R. Chambers in S. Degeling and J. Edelman (eds), *Equity in Commercial Law* (Sydney: Lawbook Co, 2005) Ch.17.

[39] cf. *Singh v Beggs* (1996) 71 P. & C.R. 120 at 122, where this point was not taken.

[40] On specific performance of options and rights of pre-emption, see *Pritchard v Briggs* [1980] Ch. 338; *Sudbrook Trading Estate Ltd v Eggleton* [1983] 1 A.C. 444; *Sparks v Biden* [2017] EWHC 1994 (Ch) (specific performance of an implied term in an option). See also *Berkley v Poulett* (1976) 120 S.J. 836 (sub-purchaser).

Each piece of land is unique, and it is accepted as a general rule that an award of damages is not adequate compensation for the purchaser or lessee.[41] If the purchaser does not acquire the land he will not have to pay the price, thus:

> "[T]he damages for loss of such a bargain would be negligible and, as in most cases of breach of contract for the sale of land at a market price by refusal to convey it, would constitute a wholly inadequate and unjust remedy for the breach. That is why the normal remedy is by a decree for specific performance by the vendor of his primary obligation to convey, on the purchaser's performing or being willing to perform his own primary obligations under the contract."[42]

The court, treating each party equally, will also give specific performance to the vendor or lessor,[43] although a monetary payment might be adequate compensation.

If a vendor fails to comply with the order, the purchaser may apply to the court for an order nominating some person to execute the conveyance in the vendor's name.[44]

B.   Contractual Licences

27–015   It was at one time thought that specific performance would not be granted of a contractual licence to occupy land, on the ground that the licence created no estate in the land.[45] This view was later seen to be inconsistent with the court's power to grant an injunction to restrain the wrongful revocation of a contractual licence.[46] Thus in *Verrall v Great Yarmouth BC*[47] the Court of Appeal affirmed the grant of specific performance to enforce a contractual licence whereby the National Front was to occupy the defendant's premises for the purpose of its annual conference. The remedy of damages would be inadequate as the claimant could not find any other premises. Roskill LJ held it to be the duty of the court:

> "to protect, where it is appropriate to do so, any interest, whether it be an estate in land or a licence, by injunction or specific performance as the case may be."[48]

---

[41] See, e.g., *Mungalsingh v Juman* [2015] UKPC 38 per Lord Neuberger at [33]. But cf. J.D. Heydon and M.J. Leeming, *Cases and Materials on Equity and Trusts*, 8th edn (Sydney: LexisNexis Butterworths, 2011), p.1146, preferring the explanation that "the process of looking for, negotiating for and completing the purchase of land is a lengthy and irritating one; ... so that it is better to get specific performance ... rather than get damages and use them to buy something similar." See also Law Com. No. 238 (1996), para.9.3, fn.5.

[42] *Sudbrook Trading Estate Ltd v Eggleton* [1983] 1 A.C. 444 at 478.

[43] *Cogent v Gibson* (1864) 33 Beav. 557.

[44] Senior Courts Act 1981 s.39; Trustee Act 1925 ss.44(vi), 50; Administration of Estates Act 1925 s.43(2).

[45] *Booker v Palmer* [1942] 2 All E.R. 674 at 677, per Lord Greene MR.

[46] *Winter Garden Theatre (London) Ltd v Millennium Productions Ltd* [1948] A.C. 173.

[47] [1981] Q.B. 202; A. Briggs [1981] Conv. 212. See also *Tanner v Tanner* [1975] 1 W.L.R. 1346 at 1350.

[48] [1981] Q.B. 202 at 220.

C.   Contracts for the Sale of Personal Property

Chattels and stocks and shares do not usually possess such individual character as land. Most commercial contracts for the purchase of goods,[49] or for a loan of money,[50] or contracts for the purchase of government stock, will not be specifically performed.[51] But if stocks or shares cannot always be bought in the market, the court may order specific performance[52]; or where a chattel has especial value by reason of its individuality, beauty or rarity.[53] Indeed, in such situations, there is an ancient jurisdiction to order the specific recovery of such a chattel if wrongly detained.[54] Where specific performance of a contract to sell a house is granted, the remedy is also available in respect of a related contract to sell the chattels in it.[55]

27–016

Further, the Sale of Goods Act 1979[56] s.52 (replacing earlier legislation) enables the court to order specific performance of a contract for the sale of specific or ascertained goods, either unconditionally, or upon such terms as to damages, payment of the price or otherwise as to the court may seem just. The power is discretionary, and it must still be shown that the remedy of damages is inadequate. It was intended to broaden the scope of the remedy of specific performance in connection with the purchase of chattels, but less use has been made of it than might have been expected.[57] In *Cohen v Roche*,[58] the claimant agreed to purchase from the defendants a set of eight Hepplewhite[59] chairs. This was a contract for the sale of specific goods; but McCardie J, finding that the chairs were "ordinary articles of commerce and of no special value or interest," refused to order specific performance and awarded damages. In *Behnke v Bede Shipping Co*,[60] Wright J made an order for specific performance of a contract for the sale of a ship, being satisfied that the ship was of peculiar and practically unique value to the claimant.

---

[49] *Dominion Coal Co Ltd v Dominion Iron and Steel Co Ltd* [1909] A.C. 293; *Cohen v Roche* [1927] 1 K.B. 169; *Société Des Industries Metallurgiques SA v The Bronx Engineering Co Ltd* [1975] 1 Lloyd's Rep. 465. See the examples given by Goff LJ in *Price v Strange* [1978] Ch. 337 at 359.

[50] *South African Territories Ltd v Wallington* [1898] A.C. 309.

[51] *Cud (or Cuddee) v Rutter* (1720) 1 P.Wms. 570 (South Sea Bubble Stock); *Mason v Armitage* (1806) 13 Ves.Jr. 25.

[52] *Duncuft v Albrecht* (1841) 12 Sim. 189; *Mills v Sportsdirect.com Retail Ltd* [2010] 2 B.C.L.C. 143; *Watson v Watchfinder.co.uk Ltd* [2017] EWHC 1275 (Comm); [2017] Bus. L.R. 1309 (share option agreement).

[53] *Falcke v Gray* (1859) 4 Dr. 651 (ornamental jars, although order refused on grounds of hardship); *Phillips v Lamdin* [1949] 2 K.B. 33 (ornamental door).

[54] *Pusey v Pusey* (1684) 1 Vern. 273 (an antique horn, supposedly given by King Canute); *Duke of Somerset v Cookson* (1735) 3 P.Wms. 390 (an altar piece); *Fells v Read* (1796) 3 Ves.Jr. 70; (the tobacco box of a club).

[55] *Record v Bell* [1991] 1 W.L.R. 853.

[56] The Act has been amended to allow specific performance of the seller's duty to repair or replace goods (Pt 5A); D. Harris (2003) 119 L.Q.R. 541.

[57] [1969] J.B.L. 211; *Société Des Industries Metallurgiques SA v The Bronx Engineering Co Ltd* [1975] 1 Lloyd's Rep. 465.

[58] [1927] 1 K.B. 169.

[59] George Hepplewhite is regarded alongside Thomas Sheraton and Thomas Chippendale as the leading English furniture-makers of the 18th century.

[60] [1927] 1 K.B. 649 at 661; cf. *Hart v Herwig* (1873) L.R. 8 Ch.App. 680.

27–017 A bold exercise of jurisdiction can be seen in *Sky Petroleum Ltd v VIP Petroleum Ltd*.[61] A contract had been entered into whereby the claimant company would buy all the petrol needed for its garages from the defendant company, which would supply the claimant with all its requirements. The defendant, alleging breach, purported to terminate the contract in November 1973, at a time when petrol supplies were limited, so that the claimant would have little prospect of finding an alternative source. An interlocutory injunction was granted to restrain the withholding of supplies.

Goulding J acknowledged that it amounted to specific performance, the matter being one of substance, and not of form; but held that the court had jurisdiction to order specific performance of a contract to sell chattels, although they were not specific or ascertained, where the remedy of damages was inadequate. The usual rule that specific performance was not available to enforce contracts for the sale of chattels was well established and salutary; but it was based on the adequacy of damages, and was therefore not applicable to the present case, where the company might be forced out of business if the remedy was not granted.[62]

D. Contracts to Pay Money

27–018 Contracts to pay money are normally not specifically enforceable, because damages will usually be an adequate remedy. So, for example, specific performance of a contract of loan will not be awarded against the borrower, because the remedy of damages is adequate.[63] Exceptionally, however, specific performance may be obtainable in the following situations:

i.　where the contract is to pay money to a third party, so that any damages awarded would probably be nominal[64];

ii.　where the contract is for the payment of an annuity[65] or other periodical sums. This exception is based on two grounds: first that specific performance avoids the inconvenience of a series of actions for damages every time payment is not made; and, secondly, even if substantial damages were available, it has been suggested that the common law remedy would still be inadequate as the amount in the case of an annuity would be conjectural[66];

iii.　a contract with a company to take up and pay for debentures[67];

iv.　a contract of indemnity, if, on its true construction, the obligation is to relieve a debtor by preventing him from having to pay his debt. Instead of compelling the debtor first to pay the debt and perhaps to ruin himself in

---

[61] [1974] 1 W.L.R. 576. See also *Howard E. Perry & Co Ltd v British Railways Board* [1980] 1 W.L.R. 1375 (contract for supply of steel specifically enforced); J. Thornely (1980) 39 C.L.J. 269.

[62] [1974] 1 W.L.R. 576 at 578.

[63] See *Locabail International Finance Ltd v Agroexport* [1986] 1 W.L.R. 657 (no mandatory injunction).

[64] *Beswick v Beswick* [1968] A.C. 58; below, para.27–047. The third party may now be able to enforce the contract under the Contracts (Rights of Third Parties) Act 1999.

[65] *Beswick v Beswick* [1968] A.C. 58.

[66] *Adderley v Dixon* (1824) 1 Sim. & St. 607 at 611. But see below, para.27–049.

[67] Companies Act 2006 s.740 (re-enacting previous legislation).

doing so, equity will order the indemnifier to pay the debt. It will be otherwise if the obligation is merely to repay the debtor a sum of money after he has paid it. Damages will then be an adequate remedy[68];

v.   as has been seen, in the case of a contract for the sale of land, the vendor will be granted specific performance of the purchaser's obligation to make a money payment. Although the remedy of damages may be adequate, specific performance is allowed because of the mutuality principle;

vi.   a contract to pay a debt out of specific property segregated by the debtor for that purpose is specifically enforceable, and creates an equitable interest in the specific property, unless there is evidence of a contrary intention.[69]

E.   Volunteers

Specific performance will not be awarded to a volunteer. Indeed, unless the contract is by deed, consideration is necessary for the validity of the contract itself. Parties to a deed of covenant may sue at law, even though there is no consideration, but they will not be able to obtain specific performance.[70] Problems commonly arose in this connection in relation to covenants to make family settlements.[71] Inadequacy of consideration is not a bar to specific performance, but may be relevant to the exercise of the court's discretion.[72]

27–019

The Contracts (Rights of Third Parties) Act 1999 permits a third party in certain circumstances to enforce a term of a contract which is for his benefit. Section 1(5) provides that:

> "[T]here shall be available to the third party any remedy that would have been available to him in an action for breach of contract if he had been a party to the contract (and the rules relating to damages, injunctions, specific performance and other relief shall apply accordingly)."

This provision arguably enables the third party to obtain specific performance in a case where the remedy of damages would be inadequate. However, the volunteer principle, which is one of the "rules relating to… specific performance",[73] may mean that the third party should be confined to damages, as in the case of a volunteer who is a party to a covenant.[74]

It is no objection, provided that the party seeking specific performance is not a volunteer, that the order will have the direct consequence of benefiting a

---

[68] *McIntosh v Dalwood (No.4)* (1930) 30 S.R.(NSW) 415 at 418.

[69] *Swiss Bank Corp v Lloyds Bank Ltd* [1982] A.C. 584 at 613 (per Lord Wilberforce); *Napier and Ettrick (Lord) v Hunter* [1993] A.C. 713.

[70] See *Cannon v Hartley* [1949] Ch. 213; cf. N. Andrews (2001) 60 C.L.J. 250, suggesting that s.1(5) is an exception to the volunteer rule.

[71] Above, para.5–022.

[72] Spry, *Equitable Remedies*, 9th edn (2014), pp.59–61, See below, para.27–038.

[73] See Law Commission, *Privity of Contract: Contracts for the Benefit of Third Parties* (LC242, 1999), paras 3.33(iii) and 10.2.

[74] *Cannon v Hartley* [1949] Ch. 213.

volunteer[75]; nor, in the case of the due exercise of an option to purchase land, that the option was granted for a token payment or for no payment at all.[76]

F. Contracts Requiring Supervision

27–020   **i. The Principle.**   It is settled law that a court will not grant specific performance where the order would require constant supervision by the court.[77] The reason is that supervision would be impracticable. Equity does nothing in vain; and will not issue orders which the court cannot be certain to enforce. Of course, the threat of imprisonment would be effective in many cases; but imprisonment of the defendant for contempt, if he proves recalcitrant, is a "heavy-handed" mechanism which will not get the duty performed.[78]

Orders for the specific performance of contracts to create or convey a legal estate in land do not meet with this difficulty. All that the defendant needs to do to perform such a contract is to execute the document; and, as has been seen, if he refuses, he may be threatened with imprisonment for contempt; and if he still refuses, the court may nominate any person to effect the conveyance.[79]

One important question is whether there is a sufficient definition of what has to be done in order to comply with the order of the court.[80]

> In *Posner v Scott-Lewis*,[81] a lease contained a landlord's covenant to employ a resident porter, whose duties were to clean the common parts, to look after the heating and to carry rubbish to the dustbins. Specific performance of this covenant was granted, to procure the appointment of a porter. The earlier decision to the contrary in *Ryan v Mutual Tontine Westminster Chambers Association*,[82] was difficult to distinguish, but the authority of that case had been weakened by later decisions.[83] The relevant questions were: (a) was there a sufficient definition of what had to be done? (b) would an unacceptable degree of superintendence be involved? (c) what would be the respective hardship to the parties if the order was made or refused? The answer to these questions supported a grant of specific performance; the remedy of damages was clearly inadequate.

27–021   Other illustrations include *Beswick v Beswick*,[84] where specific performance was ordered of a contract to make a regular payment to the claimant for life. In *Sky*

---

[75] See *Beswick v Beswick* [1968] A.C. 58, below, para.27–047.

[76] *Mountford v Scott* [1975] Ch. 258, affirming on different grounds the decision of Brightman J; F. Crane (1975) 39 Conv.(N.S.) 270; *Midland Bank Trust Co Ltd v Green* [1980] Ch. 590 CA; F. Crane [1979] Conv. 441.

[77] *Ryan v Mutual Tontine Westminster Chambers Association* [1893] 1 Ch. 116; *Blackett v Bates* (1865) L.R. 1 Ch. App. 117 (maintenance of railway); *Joseph v National Magazine Co* [1959] Ch. 14; *Re C (A Minor)* [1991] 2 F.L.R. 168 (schooling).

[78] *Co-operative Insurance Society Ltd v Argyll Stores (Holdings) Ltd* [1998] A.C. 1.

[79] Above, para.27–014.

[80] *Tito v Waddell (No.2)* [1977] Ch. 106 at 322, per Megarry VC; F. Crane (1977) 41 Conv.(N.S.) 432 at 436.

[81] [1987] Ch. 25; G. Jones (1987) 46 C.L.J. 21.

[82] [1893] 1 Ch. 116.

[83] *Giles (CH) & Co Ltd v Morris* [1972] 1 W.L.R. 307 at 318; *Shiloh Spinners Ltd v Harding* [1973] A.C. 691 at 724; *Tito v Waddell (No.2)* [1977] Ch. 106 at 321. The House of Lords in *Co-operative Insurance Society Ltd v Argyll Stores (Holdings) Ltd* [1998] A.C. 1, however, considered that the dicta in *Shiloh Spinners* had been too widely interpreted.

[84] [1968] A.C. 58.

Petroleum Ltd v VIP Petroleum Ltd[85] an interlocutory injunction, which was regarded as tantamount to specific performance, was granted to enforce the defendant's obligation to supply petrol regularly to the claimant. In the related area of mandatory injunctions, the requirement of supervision has not been regarded as an unsurmountable obstacle.[86] Specific performance is more likely to be granted, in spite of supervision difficulties, against a defendant who has had some or all of the benefit to which he was entitled under the contract.[87]

The principle was reviewed by the House of Lords in *Co-operative Insurance Society Ltd v Argyll Stores (Holdings) Ltd.*[88] The question was whether specific performance should be granted of a covenant in a lease of a supermarket (which was the focal point of a shopping centre) to keep open during the usual hours of business. The supermarket had been trading at a loss and the lease had 19 years to run. The House of Lords, reversing the Court of Appeal, rejected the landlord's claim for specific performance, even though any damages would be difficult to quantify. Although the breach was deliberate, specific performance would be oppressive to the tenant, whose loss in complying might be far greater than the loss to the landlord should the covenant be broken. As in the analogous sphere of mandatory injunctions, it was not in the public interest to require the carrying on of a business at a loss if there was some other plausible means of compensation. In any event, the covenant was not sufficiently certain for an order of specific performance. The supervision principle remained important, although there were fewer objections where an order simply required the defendant to achieve a specified result[89] (as in the repairs cases, discussed below) than where an order was sought to require the defendant to carry on an activity.[90]

ii. Construction Cases. The court does not generally order specific   **27–022**
performance of a contract to build or repair[91]; but there are certain exceptional
cases.

> "The first [requirement] is that the building work, of which he seeks to enforce the performance, is defined by the contract; that is to say, that the particulars of the work are so far definitely ascertained that the court can sufficiently see what is the exact nature of the work of which it is asked to order the performance. The second is that the claimant has a substantial interest in having the contract performed, which is of such a nature that he cannot adequately be compensated for breach of the contract by damages. The third is that the defendant has by the contract obtained possession of land on which the work is contracted to be done."[92]

---

[85] [1974] 1 W.L.R. 576.

[86] *Redland Bricks Ltd v Morris* [1970] A.C. 652; *Gravesham BC v British Railways Board* [1978] Ch. 379, below, para.28–018.

[87] *Tito v Waddell (No.2)* [1977] Ch. 106 at 322.

[88] [1998] A.C. 1. G. Jones (1997) 56 C.L.J. 488; A. Phang (1998) 61 M.L.R. 421; A. Tettenborn [1998] Conv. 23; P. Luxton [1998] Conv. 396.

[89] This was the context of Lord Wilberforce's rejection of supervision difficulties in *Shiloh Spinners Ltd v Harding* [1973] A.C. 691 at 724, which had been too widely interpreted in other cases.

[90] [1998] A.C. 1 at 11–12.

[91] *Wheatley v Westminster Brymbo Coal Co* (1869) L.R. 9 Eq. 538; *Haywood v Brunswick Building Society* (1881) 8 Q.B.D. 403.

[92] *Wolverhampton Corp v Emmons* [1901] 1 K.B. 515 at 525, per Romer LJ; *Hounslow LBC v Twickenham Developments Ltd* [1971] Ch. 233.

In *Wolverhampton Corp v Emmons*[93] a plot of land had been sold by an urban sanitary authority, in pursuance of a scheme of street improvement, to the defendant, who agreed to erect buildings on it, and went into possession. A later agreement provided for the erection of the buildings in accordance with detailed plans. The Court of Appeal ordered specific performance.

This exception is said to be based on a "balance of convenience". Historically it originates in a series of cases relating to the early days of railways.[94] Where a railway was built through a farmer's land and the railway company undertook to provide a bridge or tunnel to connect the separated parts of the farmer's land, it would have been most unjust to leave the farmer to a remedy in damages. These specialised cases have been given more general application, and the formulation in *Wolverhampton Corp v Emmons*[95] was further extended in *Carpenters Estates v Davies*,[96] where Farwell J held that it was sufficient that the defendant was in possession of the land, whether he came in by the contract or not. After all, the defendant's possession is the material factor; for the claimant cannot then enter to perform the construction or repair work himself.

27–023   **iii. Enforcement of Leasehold Covenants.**   The "construction contracts" exception was extended to cover a landlord's repairing covenant in *Jeune v Queens Cross Properties Ltd*,[97] where a balcony which was not part of the demised premises fell into disrepair. The three conditions laid down in *Wolverhampton Corp v Emmons*[98] were satisfied, as the landlord was in possession of the balcony, and the work involved was specific. There was a clear breach, and no doubt as to what was required to be done to remedy it. A mandatory order was much more convenient than an award of damages, leaving it to the tenant to do the work. The decision was extended by statute, now Landlord and Tenant Act 1985 s.17, which provides that the court may order specific performance of a landlord's repairing covenant relating to any part of the premises in which the tenant's dwelling is comprised, notwithstanding any equitable rule restricting this remedy.

It has since been established that, contrary to the previous understanding, specific performance of a tenant's repair covenant may be granted in rare cases where there is no other adequate remedy. *Rainbow Estates Ltd v Tokenhold Ltd*[99] was such a rare case, as the property (a listed building) was in serious disrepair and deteriorating but the lease contained no right of forfeiture nor any right for the landlord to have access to do the repairs at the tenant's expense. The schedule of works was sufficiently certain to be enforceable, and objections based on

---

[93] [1901] 1 K.B. 515. See also *Price v Strange* [1978] Ch. 337 at 359.
[94] *Ryan v Mutual Tontine Westminster Chambers Association* [1893] 1 Ch. 116 at 128.
[95] [1901] 1 K.B. 515.
[96] [1940] Ch. 160.
[97] [1974] Ch. 97; *Francis v Cowcliff Ltd* (1977) 33 P. & C.R. 368; *Gordon v Selico Ltd* [1985] 2 E.G.L.R. 79; *Hammond v Allen* [1994] 1 All E.R. 307. If the matter is urgent, a mandatory interlocutory injunction may be granted; *Parker v Camden LBC* [1986] Ch. 162 (boiler strike threatened tenants' health).
[98] [1901] 1 K.B. 515.
[99] [1999] Ch. 64; M. Pawlowski and J. Brown [1998] Conv. 495; S. Bridge (1999) 58 C.L.J. 283.

mutuality[100] or difficulties of supervision were of little force. The order simply required the tenant to achieve a result rather than carry on an activity.[101]

G. Contracts for Personal Services

It is well established that contracts which are personal in nature or which involve the performance of personal services will not normally be specifically enforced.[102] In this respect, it is necessary to distinguish contracts of employment from other contracts for personal services. The former are governed by a firm prohibition against specific enforcement by Trade Union and Labour Relations (Consolidation) Act 1992 s.236, which provides that:

27–024

> "No court shall ... by way of an order for specific performance ... compel an employee to do any work or to attend at any place for the doing of any work."

A contract of employment is defined in s.295(1).[103] Not every contract for personal services constitutes a contract of employment; for it may be a contract between an employer and an independent contractor.

In cases of contracts not covered by the Act, or where enforcement is sought by an employee against an employer,[104] the equitable principle applies. The reasons traditionally given for the rule are first, that such contracts would require constant supervision, and would in practice be impossible to enforce; and secondly, that it is contrary to public policy to compel one person to submit to the orders of another. "The courts," said Fry LJ, "are bound to be jealous, lest they should turn contracts of service into contracts of slavery."[105] Megarry J hoped that the court might look again at this "so-called rule". It was not based on these difficulties alone; but was rather a question of human nature.

> "If a singer contracts to sing, there could no doubt be proceedings for committal if, ordered to sing, the singer remained obstinately dumb. But if instead the singer sang flat, or sharp, or too fast, or too slowly, or too loudly, to too quietly, or resorted to a dozen of the manifestations of temperament traditionally associated with some singers, the threat of committal would reveal itself as a most unsatisfactory weapon, for who could say whether the imperfections of performance were natural or self induced? To make an order with such possibilities of evasion would be vain, and so the order will not be made ... the matter is one of balance and advantage and disadvantage in relation to the particular obligations in question, and the fact that the balance will usually lie on one side does not turn this probability into a rule."[106]

---

[100] Below, para.27–030.

[101] See *Co-operative Insurance Society Ltd v Argyll Stores (Holdings) Ltd* [1998] A.C. 1; above, para.27–021.

[102] Fry, *Specific Performance*, 6th edn (1921), pp.50–51; *Lumley v Wagner* (1852) 1 De G.M. & G. 604, below, para.28–062; *Thomas Marshall (Exports) Ltd v Guinle* [1979] Ch. 227; *Provident Financial Group Plc v Haywood* [1989] 3 All E.R. 298 at 302. See A. Burrows (1984) 4 L. S. 102 at 112–114.

[103] "Contract of employment" means "a contract of service or of apprenticeship".

[104] If an employee is unfairly dismissed the Employment Rights Act 1996 ss.114, 115 empower an employment tribunal to order reinstatement or re-engagement. But if the order is not complied with the sanction is an award of compensation; s.117.

[105] *De Francesco v Barnum* (1890) 45 Ch.D. 430.

[106] *Giles (CH) & Co Ltd v Morris* [1972] 1 W.L.R. 307 at 318. This passage was approved by Goff LJ in *Price v Strange* [1978] Ch. 337 at 359; cf. Buckley LJ at 369. But the House of Lords in

Nor, as we will see, can the rule be avoided by seeking an injunction instead of specific performance, where the injunction would in effect compel performance.[107] However, this principle is not inflexible. An injunction may be granted where its effect would be to make performance of the contract the only realistic course open to the defendant, although not actually compelled.[108]

In *Giles (CH) & Co Ltd v Morris*,[109] a distinction was drawn between the performance of a contract of service and the execution of such a contract which provided for the claimant to be appointed managing director of a company for a period of five years. As we have seen, this approach was also adopted in *Posner v Scott-Lewis*,[110] where specific performance was granted of a covenant in a lease to appoint a resident porter. Nor should it be assumed that as soon as any element of personal service or continuous services can be discerned in a contract, the court will always refuse an order. In *Beswick v Beswick*,[111] Lord Upjohn said that a small element of personal services in a contract did not warrant the refusal of specific performance on the ground of want of mutuality.

> In *Hill v CA Parsons & Co Ltd*,[112] the claimant was a senior engineer in the employment of the defendant. In May 1970 a trade union successfully introduced a closed shop, under which it became a term of employment that all the defendant's employees were to be members of the union. The claimant refused, and received a month's notice of dismissal. He obtained an interlocutory injunction restraining the termination. The circumstances were special, in that the notice was short; a reasonable notice would probably have given him certain legislative protections; and the employee and employer retained their mutual confidence.
>
> Lord Denning MR said[113]:
>
> > "It may be said that, by granting an injunction in such a case, the court is indirectly enforcing specifically a contract for personal services. So be it. Lord St. Leonards L.C. did something like it in *Lumley v Wagner*.[114] And I see no reason why we should not do it here."
>
> Stamp LJ, dissenting, felt that the rule against specific performance of service contracts, while not without exceptions, was deeply embedded in the law. The rule, he said, was a salutary one, which benefited the employer and employee equally.[115]

Scandinavian Trading Tanker Co A/B v Flota Petrolera Ecuatoriana [1983] 2 A.C. 694, concerning a time charter, took the view that there was no jurisdiction to grant specific performance of a service contract.

[107] Below, para.28–062.

[108] *Lauritzencool AB v Lady Navigation Inc* [2005] 1 W.L.R. 3686 (time charter); R. Grime [2005] All E.R. Rev. p.385; P. Devonshire (2005) 121 L.Q.R. 560.

[109] [1972] 1 W.L.R. 307.

[110] [1987] Ch. 25; G. Jones (1987) 46 C.L.J. 21; above, para.27–020.

[111] [1968] A.C. 58 at 97.

[112] [1972] Ch. 305; below, para.28–063. cf. *Chappell v Times Newspaper Ltd* [1975] 1 W.L.R. 482, where the employer "had every reason to suspect the plaintiff's loyalty"; *Wishart v National Association of Citizens Advice Bureaux Ltd* [1990] I.C.R. 794.

[113] [1972] Ch. 305 at 315.

[114] (1852) 1 De G.M. & G. 604; below, para.28–062.

[115] [1972] Ch. 305 at 324.

More recently, Lord Wilson questioned "whether nowadays the more impersonal, less hierarchical, relationship of many employers with their employees requires review of the usual unavailability of specific performance".[116]

Cranston J reviewed the authorities in *Ashworth v Royal National Theatre*,[117] where certain musicians who had been made redundant sought reinstatement through an award of specific performance. The defendant theatre had decided to replace the musicians with recorded music, in probable breach of the musicians' contracts. At an interim relief hearing, Cranston J decided that the claimants had little prospect of obtaining an order for specific performance, so he refused to grant an interim injunction. Among other things, Cranston J placed weight on the theatre's right to freedom of expression under art.10 of the European Convention on Human Rights.[118]

H.   Contracts for the Creation of Transient or Terminable Interests

As equity does not act in vain, specific performance will not be granted of an agreement for a lease which has already expired by the date of the hearing,[119] nor of an agreement for a tenancy at will or a partnership at will.[120] However, the mere fact that the interest is of a short duration is not a necessary bar to specific performance.

27–025

As mentioned above, in *Verrall v Great Yarmouth BC*,[121] the defendant council had granted a contractual licence to the National Front to occupy its premises for two days (on a date which had not yet occurred) for an annual conference. The defendant wrongfully repudiated the contract, but sought to avoid specific performance, partly on the ground that the licence was a transient interest. This argument was rejected by the Court of Appeal. It was held that there was no reason why the court could not order specific performance of a contractual licence of short duration. Authorities to the contrary were inconsistent with the decision of the House of Lords in *Winter Garden Theatre (London) Ltd v Millennium Productions Ltd*,[122] whereby an injunction could be granted to restrain the wrongful revocation of the licence[123]:

---

[116] *Geys v Société Générale, London Branch* [2013] 1 A.C. 523 at [77]. His Lordship did not quite use the phrase "gig economy".

[117] [2014] I.R.L.R. 526.

[118] [2014] I.R.L.R. 526 at [27] and [33]; Human Rights Act 1998 s.12 requires that the court, when considering granting any relief which may affect the right of freedom of expression, must have particular regard to the right's importance.

[119] *Turner v Clowes* (1869) 20 L.T. 214. But the doctrine of *Walsh v Lonsdale* (1882) 21 Ch.D. 9, above, para.1–016, will govern the rights and obligations of the parties if specific performance of a contract for a lease would have been available during its currency, even though it has terminated by the date of the hearing: *Industrial Properties (Barton Hill) Ltd v Associated Electrical Industries Ltd* [1977] Q.B. 580. See also *Tottenham Hotspur Football and Athletic Co v Princegrove Publishers* [1974] 1 W.L.R. 113; *Darjan Estate Co Plc v Hurley* [2012] 1 W.L.R. 1782.

[120] *Hercy v Birch* (1804) 9 Ves. 357. Even if not merely at will, a partnership agreement involves the difficulty of supervision.

[121] [1981] Q.B. 202, above, para.27–015.

[122] [1948] A.C. 173.

[123] [1981] Q.B. 202 at 220, per Roskill LJ. See also the comments of Lord Denning MR at 215.

"In my judgment the old view,[124] such as it was, that courts of equity would not protect a so-called transient interest can no longer be supported, at any rate to its full extent."

Thus specific performance remains inappropriate in respect of an interest which has already expired or which is revocable at the will of the defendant, but it may be granted at the discretion of the court in an appropriate case involving an interest of short duration.

I. Contracts to Leave Property by Will

27-026 The remedy for breach of such a contract is normally damages, recoverable from the testator's estate.[125] Specific performance might be ordered, as was indicated obiter by the Court of Appeal in *Synge v Synge*.[126] In that case a husband promised to leave property to his wife in consideration of their marriage. When the husband died, failing to leave the relevant property to her, his wife sought damages against the estate. She did not seek specific performance because her husband had conveyed away the relevant land to someone who was probably an innocent purchaser. But, speaking of the general case, the Court of Appeal had "no doubt of the power of the Court to decree a conveyance of ... property after the death of the person making the proposal against all who claim under him as volunteers".[127]

In *Schaefer v Schuhmann*,[128] Lord Cross treated it as established that where there is a contract to leave specific property by will, the claimant:

"can obtain a declaration of his right to have it left to him by will and an injunction to restrain the testator from disposing of it in breach of contract: *Synge v Synge*. No doubt if the property is land he could also register the contract or a caution against the title."[129]

If the testator retains the property until his death, but dies insolvent, the promisee can only rank as a creditor for value in competition with other such creditors.[130]

Finally, it seems that specific performance will not be granted of a contract by the donee of a testamentary power of appointment to exercise the power in favour of the claimant.[131]

---

[124] Exemplified in cases such as *Lavery v Pursell* (1888) 39 Ch.D. 508 at 519 (specific performance of an agreement for a lease for one year refused).

[125] *Hammersley v De Biel* (1845) 12 Cl. & F. 45; *Schaefer v Schuhmann* [1972] A.C. 572.

[126] [1894] 1 Q.B. 466. See also *Wakeham v Mackenzie* [1968] 1 W.L.R. 1175.

[127] [1894] 1 Q.B. 466 at 471.

[128] [1972] A.C. 572 (PC). See also Inheritance (Provision for Family and Dependants) Act 1975 s.11.

[129] [1972] A.C. 572 at 586. If the contract relates to land, it must be writing, in order to satisfy s.2 of the Law of Property (Miscellaneous Provisions) Act 1989; *Taylor v Dickens* [1998] 1 F.L.R. 806.

[130] [1972] A.C. 572. See also *Beyfus v Lawley* [1903] A.C. 411.

[131] *Re Parkin* [1892] 3 Ch. 510. The proper remedy is damages. See also *Robinson v Ommanney* (1883) 23 Ch.D. 285.

J. Contracts to Transfer Goodwill

A contract to sell the goodwill of a business alone is not specifically enforceable, because the subject-matter of the contract is too uncertain.[132] But specific performance will be granted of a contract to transfer the goodwill together with the premises or other assets of a business.[133]

27–027

K. Contracts to Refer to Arbitration

Such a contract is not specifically enforceable.[134] But if the claimant sues on a contract which includes an arbitration provision, the defendant may ask for a stay of proceedings under the Arbitration Act 1996 s.9 so that the claimant must proceed with the arbitration or be left with no remedy.[135] The court will, however enforce the arbitrator's award.[136]

27–028

L. No Specific Performance of Part of a Contract[137]

A court will not usually order specific performance of any part of a contract unless it can order performance of the whole. In *Ogden v Fossick*,[138] an agreement between the parties provided that the defendant would grant to the claimant a lease of a coal wharf, and that the defendant should be appointed manager of the wharf. In an action for specific performance of the agreement to grant the lease, specific performance was denied on the ground that the part of the agreement which the court could enforce was inseparably connected with the contract of employment which it would not.

27–029

But the rule is not absolute.[139] It may be possible to construe a contract which contains several parts as being in effect several separate and distinct contracts, so that the enforcement of one part is independent of the others.[140] This question often arises where several lots of land are sold and the question is whether there is one sale of several lots,[141] or several sales of individual lots.[142]

---

[132] *Darbey v Whitaker* (1857) 4 Drew. 134.

[133] (1857) 4 Drew. 134 at 140. And see *Beswick v Beswick* [1968] A.C. 58; below, para.27–048.

[134] *Doleman & Sons v Ossett Corp* [1912] 3 K.B. 257 at 268.

[135] See also s.86. As to the court's jurisdiction to intervene by way of injunction, see below, para.28–071.

[136] *Wood v Griffith* (1818) 1 Swans. 43. See also *Sudbrook Trading Estate Ltd v Eggleton* [1983] 1 A.C. 444, as to the possibility of specific performance of a contract to appoint a valuer or arbitrator to fix the price in an option to renew a lease.

[137] Fry, *Specific Performance*, 6th edn (1921), Ch.16. Compare the doctrine of partial performance; *Thames Guaranty Ltd v Campbell* [1985] Q.B. 210.

[138] (1862) 4 De G.F. & J. 426.

[139] *Beswick v Beswick* [1968] A.C. 58; *CH Giles & Co Ltd v Morris* [1972] 1 W.L.R. 307 at 317–318; *Astro Exito Navegacion SA v Southland Enterprise Co Ltd (No.2)* [1983] 2 A.C. 787. The judge ordered specific performance of part of a contract in *Thevarajah v Riordan* [2014] EWHC 725 (Ch), but the defendants did not object.

[140] *Wilkinson v Clements* (1872) L.R. 8 Ch. App. 96, below, para.27–031.

[141] *Roffey v Shallcross* (1819) 4 Madd. 227.

[142] *Lewin v Guest* (1826) 1 Russ. 325.

4. MUTUALITY

A. Refusal of Specific Performance for Lack of Mutuality[143]

27–030   It has been seen that where specific performance may be ordered in favour of a purchaser or lessee, the remedy will be available also in favour of the vendor or lessor.[144] Such a person can compel the other party to take the property even though in many cases an award of damages would be adequate compensation for her loss. She can obtain specific performance under a principle of mutuality.

A similar principle applies to deny specific performance, on grounds of lack of mutuality, where the situation is one in which that remedy could not be available to the other party.[145] "It is not disputed," said Leach MR, "that it is a general principle of courts of equity to interpose only where the remedy is mutual."[146] Thus one party is not compelled specifically to perform her obligation if she would herself be left with only a remedy in damages. In *Flight v Bolland*,[147] the claimant failed to obtain specific performance because, as he was below the age of majority, it could not be obtained against him.[148] Nor can a person whose own obligation is to perform personal services obtain specific performance, as it could not be obtained against him.[149]

The Landlord and Tenant Act 1985 s.17, allows a court to order specific performance of a landlord's repairing covenant, notwithstanding any equitable rule restricting this remedy, "whether based on mutuality or otherwise."[150] A lack of mutuality is not, therefore, a bar to a tenant seeking specific performance. It was subsequently held in *Rainbow Estates Ltd v Tokenhold Ltd*[151] that specific performance of a *tenant's* repairing covenant is possible under the general law, although it would only be awarded rarely. It might be added that the claimant may be able to overcome the absence of mutuality by waiving the benefit of a term,[152] or submitting to perform an obligation, which could not be specifically enforced against him.[153]

Finally, the mutuality principle goes only to discretion, not to jurisdiction. Thus the absence of mutuality does not deprive the court of jurisdiction to award damages in lieu of specific performance under Lord Cairns' Act 1858.[154]

---

[143] See Spry, *Equitable Remedies*, 9th edn (2014), pp.7–12, 95–107.

[144] Above, para.27–014.

[145] This defence based on lack of mutuality may be waived by the conduct of the defendant: *Price v Strange* [1978] Ch. 337.

[146] (1828) 4 Russ. 298 at 301.

[147] (1828) 4 Russ. 298.

[148] *Lumley v Ravenscroft* [1895] 1 Q.B. 683.

[149] *Pickering v Bishop of Ely* (1843) 2 Y. & C. Ch. 249; *Ogden v Fossick* (1862) 4 De G.F. & J. 426; above, para.27–029.

[150] Above, para.27–027.

[151] [1999] Ch. 64.

[152] *Heron Garage Properties Ltd v Moss* [1974] 1 W.L.R. 148.

[153] *Scott v Bradley* [1971] Ch. 850; R.E.M. (1951) 67 L.Q.R. 300.

[154] *Price v Strange* [1978] Ch. 337. For Lord Cairns' Act, see below, para.27–044.

B.   The Time at which the Remedy must be Mutual

Must the requirement of mutuality be satisfied at the date of the contract, or will it suffice that the remedy has become mutually available by some later date, such as the date of the hearing? This question has been the source of much academic disagreement. Fry's proposition was that, subject to certain exceptions, the contract must be mutual when entered into.[155] Ames, on the other hand, considered that:

> "Equity will not compel specific performance by a defendant if, after performance, the common law remedy of damages would be his sole security for the performance of the [claimant's] side of the contract."[156]

27–031

The courts, it must be said, had never applied a principle as rigid as that propounded by Fry. It was laid down in *Hoggart v Scott*[157] that a vendor may obtain specific performance if he can show a good title at the time of the hearing, even though he had none when the contract was made. We saw that there could generally be no specific performance of a contract where the obligation of one party was the performance of services. It was held, however, in *Wilkinson v Clements*[158] that if the claimant has already performed the services, he may enforce the contract.

The formulation of Ames was adopted by the Court of Appeal in preference to Fry's rule.

> In *Price v Strange*[159] D contracted to grant an underlease of a flat to P, and the agreement contained an undertaking by P to execute internal and external repairs. P did the internal repairs, and was ready and willing to complete the external; but D repudiated the contract, and did the external repairs herself. P sued for specific performance of the contract to grant the underlease. D claimed that P was not entitled to specific performance because, relying on Fry's rule, there was no mutuality at the date of the contract: P's repair obligations were not specifically enforceable. It was held that Fry's rule was wrong; the time for considering mutuality was the date of the judgment. If by that time those obligations which were not specifically enforceable had been performed, P could obtain specific performance.

27–032

The principle is that the court will not compel a defendant to perform her obligations specifically if it cannot at the same time ensure that any unperformed obligations of the claimant will be specifically performed, unless, perhaps, damages would be an adequate remedy to the defendant for any default on the

---

[155] Fry, *Specific Performance*, 6th edn (1921), p.219.

[156] Ames, *Lectures in Legal History* (1913), p.370.

[157] (1830) 1 Russ. & M. 293; *Joseph v National Magazine Co Ltd* [1959] Ch. 14 (a case of personal property); *Price v Strange* [1978] Ch. 337 at 355 and 364. See C. Emery (1977) 41 Conv.(N.S.) 18.

[158] (1872) L.R. 8 Ch.App. 96. If the claimant has not performed all the obligations, justice can be done by granting specific performance on terms of a monetary readjustment. See also *Wakeham v Mackenzie* [1968] 1 W.L.R. 1175.

[159] [1978] Ch. 337; F. Glover (1978) 128 N.L.J. 569; applied in *Sutton v Sutton* [1984] Ch. 184 (wife agreed to consent to divorce and not to seek maintenance in return for a transfer of the home. Husband could not have enforced her promises, but once she had performed an appreciable part by giving formal consent to the petition, he could not rely on absence of mutuality).

claimant's part.[160] Specific performance was, accordingly, granted on terms that P should pay compensation to D for the cost of the repairs done by D.

5. DEFENCES TO SPECIFIC PERFORMANCE

27–033 The situations discussed below are those in which the discretion of the court is unlikely to be exercised in favour of specific performance, although the contract is of a type to which the remedy is appropriate. Most of the illustrations relate to land, for, as we have seen, few contracts outside this area are specifically enforceable. It will be noted that, in some of the circumstances discussed below, such as hardship or delay, the contract is unaffected, and the defendant remains liable in damages; the claimant is merely denied specific performance. In others, as in some cases of mistake and misrepresentation, the contract may be rescinded in equity, which is of course a defence to specific performance, and which will preclude enforcement at law.[161] In cases of substantial misdescription or lack of good title, the vendor may be in breach; not only is the vendor unable in such circumstances to obtain specific performance; he may be liable in damages to the purchaser.

A. Mistake and Misrepresentation

27–034 There are situations in which equity, although refusing to rescind a contract or cancel a deed for mistake or misrepresentation, will not give the other party positive equitable help in enforcing it. The claimant will be left to her remedy in damages.[162] The court is not bound to order specific performance in every case in which it will not set aside the contract, nor to set aside every contract that it will not specifically enforce.[163]

A defendant cannot usually resist specific performance by alleging merely his own fault and mistake,[164] nor on the ground that he was mistaken as to the legal effect of the agreement,[165] although "unilateral mistake may, in some circumstances, afford an answer to a claim for specific performance."[166] Generally, equity will hold the defendant to enforcement of his bargain unless it can be shown that this would involve real hardship amounting to injustice.[167]

---

[160] [1978] Ch. 337 at 367–378.

[161] Above, para.1–038.

[162] See *Mortlock v Buller* (1804) 10 Ves.Jr. 292, per Lord Eldon.

[163] e.g. *Wood v Scarth* (1855) 2 K. & J. 33 (in equity); 1 F. & F. 293 (at law). A modern example is *Heath v Heath* [2010] 1 F.L.R. 610 (both parties to a contract to sell the wife's share to the husband mistakenly thought that their son would inherit the property).

[164] *Duke of Beaufort v Neeld* (1845) 12 Cl. & F. 248 at 286.

[165] *Powell v Smith* (1872) L.R. 14 Eq. 85; *Hart v Hart* (1881) 18 Ch.D. 670.

[166] *Mountford v Scott* [1975] Ch. 258 at 261, per Brightman J; *Malins v Freeman* (1837) 2 Keen 25; *Riverlate Properties Ltd v Paul* [1975] Ch. 133 at 140, per Russell LJ; *Watkin v Watson-Smith*, *The Times*, 3 July 1986.

[167] *Van Praagh v Everidge* [1902] 2 Ch. 266; reversed on another ground [1903] 1 Ch. 434.

In *Webster v Cecil*,[168] A, by letter, offered to sell some property to B. He intended to offer it at £2,250 but by mistake wrote £1,250. B agreed to buy at £1,250. A immediately gave notice of the error and was not compelled to carry out the sale.

In *Tamplin v James*,[169] an inn was offered for sale, and was correctly described with reference to plans. At the rear of the inn was a piece of land, not belonging to the vendors, and so not included in the sale, which had commonly been occupied with the inn. The defendant knew the premises, but did not consult the plans, and he agreed to purchase in the belief that he was buying both the inn and the land at the rear. Specific performance was ordered against him.

A case that goes further, and perhaps too far, is *Malins v Freeman*,[170] where an estate was purchased at an auction and the defendant bid under a mistake as to the lot put up for sale. Specific performance was refused although the mistake was due entirely to the defendant's fault and not in any way caused by the vendor; and the defendant waited until the auction was over before declaring the mistake.

Where the mistake is in the written record of the contract, the claimant may obtain rectification and specific performance in the same action.[171]

B. Conduct of the Claimant

The claimant must come to equity with clean hands.[172] Before specific performance can be ordered in her favour, she must show that she has performed all her own obligations under the contract,[173] or has tendered performance, or is ready and willing to perform them.[174] Thus a person holding under an agreement for a lease is not entitled to specific performance of the lease if she is herself in breach of one of its covenants.[175] Nor could a purchaser obtain specific performance if she had taken advantage of the illiteracy of a defendant who was not separately advised.[176] The conduct in question must be connected to the contract of which specific performance is sought.[177]

27–035

---

[168] (1861) 30 Beav. 62; *Day v Wells* (1861) 30 Beav. 220; cf. *Hartog v Colin and Shields* [1939] 3 All E.R. 566. See also *Watkin v Watson-Smith, The Times*, 13 July 1986 (no specific performance where elderly vendor offered bungalow for sale at £2,950 by mistake, intending £29,500. There was no contract).

[169] (1880) 15 Ch.D. 215; cf. *Denny v Hancock* (1870) L.R. 6 Ch.App. 1, where specific performance was refused because the mistake was induced unintentionally by the claimant. See also *Bashir v Ali* [2011] EWCA Civ 707; [2011] 2 P. & C.R. 12 (specific performance ordered where common mistake as to inclusion of studio flat).

[170] (1837) 2 Keen 25.

[171] *Craddock Bros v Hunt* [1923] 2 Ch. 136. Rectification is considered in Ch.29 below.

[172] This doctrine cannot be ousted by the terms of the contract; *Quadrant Visual Communications Ltd v Hutchison Telephone (UK) Ltd* [1993] B.C.L.C. 442.

[173] Except the most trivial ones; *Dyster v Randall* [1926] Ch. 932 at 942–943. See also *Sport International Bussum BV v Inter-Footwear Ltd* [1984] 1 W.L.R. 776.

[174] *Lamare v Dixon* (1873) L.R. 6 HL 414; *Australian Hardwoods Pty Ltd v Railways Commissioner* [1961] 1 W.L.R. 425; *Cornish v Brook Green Laundry* [1959] 1 Q.B. 391; *Mungalsingh v Juman* [2015] UKPC 38 at [31].

[175] *Walsh v Lonsdale* (1882) 21 Ch.D. 9; *Coatsworth v Johnson* (1886) 55 L.J.Q.B. 220.

[176] *Mountford v Scott* [1975] Ch. 258.

[177] *van Gestel v Cann, The Times*, 7 August 1987 (no defence where alleged fraudulent expenses claims not connected to contract).

The "clean hands" defence is traditionally concerned with the conduct of the claimant alone, although all the circumstances, including the conduct of the defendant, are relevant to the exercise of the discretion.[178]

C.   Laches or Delay

27–036   Generally, in equity, time is not held to be of the essence of a contract,[179] thus specific performance may be ordered although the contractual date for performance has passed. Failure to complete on the contractual date may, however, render the delaying party liable to damages for breach of contract. The fact that time is not of the essence in equity does not negative a breach of contract in such a case. It means that the breach does not amount to a repudiation of the contract. Thus the delaying party, although liable to damages, does not lose the right to seek specific performance, nor will he forfeit his deposit, provided he is ready to complete within a reasonable time.[180]

There is no statutory period of limitation barring claims to specific performance or to the refusal of relief on the ground of acquiescence.[181] The six-year rule which governs claims for damages for breach of contract does not apply by analogy to claims for specific performance.[182] This means that a claim for specific performance could be successful even if brought more than six years after the breach of contract, although such cases would be rare in the absence of fraud. The defendant may rely on the doctrine of laches, so that a claimant who delays unreasonably in bringing an action for specific performance may lose her claim.[183] There is no rule to lay down what is meant by unreasonable delay. One relevant factor is the subject-matter of the contract. If it has a speculative or fluctuating value, the principle of laches will be especially applicable.[184] Another factor is whether cross-examination is still possible.[185]

---

[178] *Sang Lee Investment Co Ltd v Wing Kwai Investment Co Ltd, The Times*, 14 April 1983. This position may change as the law develops following *Patel v Mirza* [2016] UKSC 42; [2017] A.C. 467; considered above, para.14–012.

[179] This rule now applies also at law; Law of Property Act 1925 s.41. (Time may be made of the essence in a contract for the sale of land by the service of a notice to complete.) See T. Etherton [2013] Conv. 355.

[180] *Raineri v Miles* [1981] A.C. 1050; *Oakacre Ltd v Claire Cleaners (Holdings) Ltd* [1982] Ch. 197; cf. *United Scientific Holdings Ltd v Burnley BC* [1978] A.C. 904 (as to rent review clauses). See J. Thomson (1980) 96 L.Q.R. 481; A. Samuels (1981) 44 M.L.R. 100.

[181] Limitation Act 1980 s.36(1), (2). For criticisms of the present law, see *Cia de Seguros Imperio v Heath (REBX) Ltd* [2001] 1 W.L.R. 112 at 124.

[182] *P&O Nedlloyd BV v Arab Metals Co (No.2)* [2007] 1 W.L.R. 2288.

[183] *Southcomb v Bishop of Exeter* (1847) 6 H. 213; *Eads v Williams* (1854) 4 De G.M. & G. 674; *MEPC Ltd v Christian-Edwards* [1981] A.C. 205. cf. *Cenac v Schafer* [2016] UKPC 25 at [31]: "in order to resist a claim for specific performance on the ground of delay, it is necessary to show that prejudice has resulted from the delay". There are cases where even a delay for which neither party is to blame may be a reason for leaving the purchaser to damages; *Patel v Ali* [1984] Ch. 283, below, para.27–038.

[184] *Mills v Haywood* (1877) 6 Ch.D. 196.

[185] *Heath v Heath* [2010] 1 F.L.R. 610 (one party deceased).

In *Lazard Bros & Co Ltd v Fairfield Property Co (Mayfair) Ltd*,[186] a contract was entered into on 12 March 1975. The claimants commenced an action for specific performance on 14 May 1977. In ordering specific performance, Megarry VC said that if specific performance was to be regarded as a prize, to be awarded by equity to the zealous and denied to the indolent, then the claimants should fail. But whatever might have been the position over a century ago[187] that was the wrong approach today. If between the parties it was just that the claimant should obtain the remedy, the court ought not to withhold it merely because he had been guilty of delay. There was no ground here on which delay could properly be said to be a bar to an order of specific performance.

Special considerations apply where the claimant has taken possession under the contract,[188] so that the purpose of specific performance is merely to vest the legal estate in her. In *Williams v Greatrex*,[189] a delay of 10 years in such circumstances did not bar specific performance. But a significant factor there was that the transaction creating the proprietary interest was not in issue. It is otherwise where the contract itself is disputed. In such a case, the doctrine of laches does apply.[190]

Where the claimant has delayed, but specific performance is refused for another **27–037** reason, the effect of her delay may be that the date for assessing damages in lieu of specific performance under Lord Cairns' Act is moved back from the date of judgment to the date upon which the matter might have been disposed of.[191]

The situation discussed above is where the delay has occurred before the claimant has sought specific performance. Where the claimant commences the action for specific performance promptly but then delays in bringing the matter to trial, she may, in a clear case, be disentitled to the remedy.[192] Where she obtains an order for specific performance but then delays in enforcing it for a long period, leave to enforce it will be refused only if there is an insufficient explanation and if there has been detriment to the defendant. Thus, in *Easton v Brown*,[193] a delay of eight years in seeking to enforce the order was no bar where the defendant's former wife and children had remained in occupation and the claimant had been legally advised that it would be difficult to remove them. The claimant had an explanation for the delay and had acted reasonably; detriment to the defendant was not on its own a ground for refusing leave to enforce the order.

Finally, in cases where time is of the essence, specific performance is not normally available after the stipulated date. It has been held in Australia, however, that the court may, in the exercise of its equitable jurisdiction to relieve against forfeiture, grant specific performance to prevent the "forfeiture" of the

---

[186] (1977) 121 S.J. 793; [1978] Conv. 184.

[187] See, e.g., *Huxham v Llewellyn* (1873) 21 W.R. 570 (delay of five months in the case of commercial premises prevented specific performance).

[188] It is otherwise if possession has been taken other than pursuant to the contract: *Mills v Haywood* (1877) 6 Ch.D. 196. The principle applies, however, where the claimant remains in possession after buying the co-owner's share, but the legal title has not been conveyed into his sole name; *Frawley v Neill, The Times*, 5 April 1999 (rights under 1975 contract not barred by laches).

[189] [1957] 1 W.L.R. 31.

[190] *Joyce v Joyce* [1979] 1 W.L.R. 1170.

[191] *Malhotra v Choudhury* [1980] Ch. 52.

[192] *Du Sautoy v Symes* [1967] Ch. 1146 at 1168. *Towli v Fourth River Property Co Ltd, The Times*, 24 November 1976 (delay of nine years between writ and hearing) was such a clear case.

[193] [1981] 3 All E.R. 278. The claimant also obtained an order for inquiry as to damages arising from the defendant's failure to complete.

purchaser's equitable interest under the contract.[194] The Privy Council has rejected the Australian approach, although leaving open the possibility of relief based on restitution or estoppel if injustice would otherwise result.[195]

D. Hardship

27–038 In general, specific performance may be refused in the discretion of the court where it would cause unnecessary hardship to either of the parties,[196] or to a third party.[197] Inadequacy of price is not, standing by itself, a ground for refusing specific performance; but it may be evidence of other factors, such as fraud[198] or undue influence,[199] which would render enforcement inequitable.

These matters arose in *Patel v Ali*,[200] where the vendor and her husband were co-owners of a house which they contracted to sell in 1979. The husband's bankruptcy caused a long delay in completion, for which neither the vendor nor the purchaser was to blame. After the contract, the vendor had a leg amputated. She later gave birth to her second and third children. The purchaser obtained an order for specific performance, against which the vendor appealed on the ground of hardship. She spoke little English, and relied on help from nearby friends and relatives, hence it would be a hardship to leave the house and move away. Goulding J held that the court in a proper case could refuse specific performance on the ground of hardship subsequent to the contract, even if not caused by the claimant and not related to the subject-matter. On the facts, there would be hardship amounting to injustice, therefore the appropriate remedy was damages.

A recent case going the other way is *Shah v Greening*.[201] The vendors of a house, Mr and Mrs Greening, had been planning to sell and downsize to another property they owned. Mr Greening sadly died between the exchange of contracts and the date set for completion. Shortly before completion, Mrs Greening wrote to the purchasers stating that she did not wish to proceed and offering the return

---

[194] *Legione v Hateley* (1983) 152 C.L.R. 406; (1983) 99 L.Q.R. 490.

[195] *Union Eagle Ltd v Golden Achievements Ltd* [1997] A.C. 514; J. Heydon (1997) 113 L.Q.R. 385; M. Thompson [1997] Conv. 382; J. Stevens (1998) 61 M.L.R. 255.

[196] *Denne v Light* (1857) 8 De G.M. & G. 774; *Warmington v Miller* [1973] Q.B. 877 (no specific performance of contract to sublet if result would be to expose tenant to liability for breach of covenant against subletting); *Wroth v Tyler* [1974] Ch. 30 (no specific performance where it would force a man to bring proceedings against his wife); *Shell UK Ltd v Lostock Garage Ltd* [1976] 1 W.L.R. 1187 at 1202; *Bower Terrace Student Accommodation Ltd v Space Student Living Ltd* [2012] EWHC 2206 (Ch); *SC Johnson & Son Inc v Hillshire Brands Co* [2013] EWHC 3080 (Ch) at [43]. See Fry, *Specific Performance*, Ch.16; Spry, *Equitable Remedies*, pp.202–208. See also A. Dowling [2011] Conv. 209, as to the position where the buyer cannot raise the money.

[197] *Earl of Sefton v Tophams Ltd* [1966] Ch. 1140; *Sullivan v Henderson* [1973] 1 W.L.R. 333; *Watts v Spence* [1976] Ch. 165; *Cedar Holdings Ltd v Green* [1981] Ch. 129 at 147. This case was disapproved on another point in *Williams and Glyn's Bank Ltd v Boland* [1981] A.C. 487 at 507. See also *Thames Guaranty Ltd v Campbell* [1985] Q.B. 210; cf. *Patel v Ali* [1984] Ch. 283, below, (interests of vendor's children in their own right not material, but relevant to hardship of vendor).

[198] *Coles v Trecothick* (1804) 9 Ves.Jr. 234 at 246; *Callaghan v Callaghan* (1841) 8 Cl. & F. 374.

[199] *Fry v Lane* (1888) 40 Ch.D. 312 (sale set aside).

[200] [1984] Ch. 283. cf. *Twinsectra Ltd v Sander* (unreported, Ch.D. 10 September 2016) (specific performance granted, but difficult circumstances of vendor taken into account in precise timing and terms of the order).

[201] [2016] EWHC 548 (Ch).

of their deposit. The purchasers expressed their sympathy but wished to proceed and, on the day completion was due, served notice to complete. In granting specific performance, Master Bowles considered Mrs Greening's personal situation but ultimately concluded that—unlike in *Patel v Ali*—there were no "extraordinary and persuasive circumstances such as to take the case away from the normal situation, in which the contracting parties undertake the risk of such hardship as may arise in the supervening period between exchange and completion".[202]

E. Misdescription of Subject-matter

i. Specific Performance Subject to Compensation.[203] If the property agreed to be sold is incorrectly described in the contract, the vendor cannot fulfil his promise to transfer property which corresponds exactly with that which he contracted to convey. A frequent instance is an inaccurate measurement in the plan.[204] A misdescription is a term of the contract; the vendor is therefore in breach. To deny him specific performance on that account would introduce a rigid rule capable of producing injustice. Equity adopts a more flexible approach; the circumstances may be such that justice will be done by compelling completion, notwithstanding the error, compensating the purchaser by allowing him a reduction in the price he had agreed to pay ("abatement").[205] This course will not be followed if it would prejudice the rights of a third party interested in the estate.[206] On the other hand, the misdescription may be so serious that to order specific performance would be in effect to force the purchaser to take something wholly different from what he intended.[207] If so, the only way of achieving justice may be to permit the purchaser to rescind; or to refuse to grant specific performance to the vendor.

27–039

ii. Refusal of Specific Performance. The rule is thus that a purchaser will not be forced to take something which is *different in substance* from that which he agreed to buy.[208] Differences of quality or quantity will not *by themselves* suffice as a defence to an action for specific performance (although of course they will give rise to a claim for compensation) unless they can fairly be said to make the property, as it in fact is, different in substance from that contracted to be sold.[209] A misdescription is substantial for this purpose if it so far affects:

27–040

---

[202] [2016] EWHC 548 (Ch) at [84].

[203] See C. Harpum (1981) 40 C.L.J. 47, taking the view that this should not be distinguished from specific performance with damages under Lord Cairns' Act, below, para.27–044.

[204] See, e.g. *Watson v Burton* [1957] 1 W.L.R. 19; *Topfell Ltd v Galley Properties Ltd* [1979] 1 W.L.R. 446 (inability to give vacant possession).

[205] If the misdescription goes against the vendor, he cannot increase the price: *Re Lindsay and Forder's Contract* (1895) 72 L.T. 832 (but specific performance might be refused on the ground of hardship). See also *Seven Seas Properties Ltd v Al-Essa* [1988] 1 W.L.R. 1272.

[206] *Cedar Holdings Ltd v Green* [1981] Ch. 129.

[207] See *Cedar Holdings Ltd v Green* [1981] Ch. 129 (specific performance with abatement not appropriate where vendor's interest merely a co-ownership share).

[208] *Flight v Booth* (1834) 1 Bing.N.C. 370; *Watson v Burton* [1957] 1 W.L.R. 19.

[209] If a vendor contracts to sell a lease of Blackacre, a purchaser cannot be compelled to take an underlease: *Madeley v Booth* (1845) 2 De G. & Sm. 718; nor if he contracts to sell a "registered

"the subject-matter of the contract that it may be reasonably supposed, that, but for such misdescription, the purchaser might never have entered into the contract at all."[210]

This will always be a question of fact in each case: obviously A, who has contracted to sell Blackacre to B, cannot force him to take Whiteacre, even if Whiteacre is larger, more valuable, and better suited to B's purposes. It is often difficult to say whether a misdescription of the area of land involves a difference of substance or of quantity; the rule is "easy to be understood, though often difficult of application."[211] However, although the vendor cannot compel a purchaser to take something different from that contracted to be sold, it is only just to give the purchaser the option of insisting on completion, and being paid compensation[212] for what he has lost. If it were not so, a person in default could in effect take advantage of his own wrong. Thus the purchaser has a choice: he may elect to take the property,[213] notwithstanding that it may be substantially different from the contract description.

27–041   **iii.   Conditions of Sale.**   The above is true of "open" contracts, but the parties are free to make their own conditions to regulate what is to happen if there is a misdescription. In the case of contracts for the sale of land, most contracts prepared by a solicitor will now be made subject to the Law Society's Standard Conditions of Sale or Standard Commercial Property Conditions. In every case, therefore, the first question must be: what does the contract provide? But even then caution is necessary, since the courts have been reluctant to permit either party to contract out of the rights conferred on them by equity.[214]

27–042   **iv.   Want of Good Title.**   The court will not force a doubtful title on a purchaser. The phrase "defect in title" is loosely used in some of the cases to indicate that the vendor, through some material error in description, fails in effect to convey to the purchaser the property he intended to buy. In other cases the expression may be used in a more literal sense; where, for example, the vendor's land is burdened with restrictive covenants.[215] Yet there are other cases where there is not merely a defect in the vendor's title, but no title at all. Clearly the purchaser cannot be compelled to take a bad title, nor be allowed to refuse a good one. Between the good and the bad is an infinite variety of doubtful titles, and the question inevitably arises of drawing a line between those titles which a purchaser will, and those which he will not, be compelled to accept. The test is

freehold property," can he compel the purchaser to take a possessory (as distinct from *absolute*) freehold title; *Re Brine and Davies' Contract* [1935] Ch. 388.

[210] *Flight v Booth* (1834) 1 Bing.N.C. 370 at 377, per Tindal CJ.

[211] *Re Fawcett and Holmes' Contract* (1889) 42 Ch.D. 150 at 156, per Lord Esher MR; cf. *Watson v Burton* [1957] 1 W.L.R. 19.

[212] *Mortlock v Buller* (1804) 10 Ves.Jr. 292 at 316. The compensation must generally be claimed before completion: *Joliffe v Baker* (1883) 11 Q.B.D. 255.

[213] In the absence of special circumstances, e.g. if he was himself aware of the misdescription at the date of the contract; *Castle v Wilkinson* (1870) L.R. 5 Ch. 534. See C. Emery [1978] Conv. 338 at 340.

[214] See *Topfell Ltd v Galley Properties Ltd* [1979] 1 W.L.R. 446; *Rignall Developments Ltd v Halil* [1988] Ch. 190. Conditions of sale are subject to the Unfair Contract Terms Act 1977; *Walker v Boyle* [1982] 1 W.L.R. 495.

[215] *Re Nisbet and Potts' Contract* [1906] 1 Ch. 386; *Faruqi v English Real Estates Ltd* [1979] 1 W.L.R. 963.

whether there is likely to be litigation. If the doubt is one of law, the court will normally resolve it.[216] If the doubt is one of fact, it is the court's duty, unless there are exceptional circumstances, to decide the question of title as between the vendor and purchaser. If the court concludes that the purchaser will not be at risk of a successful assertion against him of an incumbrance, then the court should declare in favour of a good title, and should not be deterred by the mere possibility of future litigation by a claimant to an incumbrance who is not bound by the declaration.[217] But if good title is not shown, the purchaser will be entitled to rescind, unless the vendor removes the doubt. The court will not compel a party to purchase a law suit.[218]

F.   Public Policy

The court will not order specific performance of a contract where the result **27–043** would be contrary to public policy. Some contracts will be wholly unenforceable by courts, as where a contract requires one of the parties to commit a crime. As Lord Neuberger said in *Patel v Mirza*,[219] neither an award of specific performance nor damages would be appropriate here. An award of specific performance would involve the court ordering a party to act illegally, which a court could not do. An award of damages would be similarly problematic, because "conceptually, damages are a substitute for non-performance, and performance is not something the court can award".[220]

On other occasions the contract itself may be unobjectionable but an award of specific performance would be inappropriate. In *Wroth v Tyler*,[221] a husband, the owner of the matrimonial home, entered into a contract to sell with vacant possession. Before completion, his wife registered a charge under the Matrimonial Homes Act 1967.[222] The purchasers sued for specific performance, and failed on two grounds. First, the husband could only carry out his obligation by obtaining a court order terminating the wife's right of occupation, and this would depend on the discretion of the court. To grant specific performance would compel the husband to embark on difficult and uncertain litigation. He had attempted to obtain the wife's consent by all reasonable means short of litigation, and it would be most undesirable to require a husband to take proceedings against his wife, especially where they were still living together. Secondly, nor would it be appropriate to grant the purchasers specific performance subject to the wife's

---

[216] *Wilson v Thomas* [1958] 1 W.L.R. 422.

[217] *MEPC Ltd v Christian-Edwards* [1981] A.C. 205 (doubt as to abandonment of 1912 contract: good title established). See also *Re Handman and Wilcox's Contract* [1902] 1 Ch. 599; *Selkirk v Romar Investments Ltd* [1963] 1 W.L.R. 1415.

[218] *Re Nichols and Von Joel's Contract* [1910] 1 Ch. 43 at 46. See also *Pips (Leisure Productions) Ltd v Walton* (1981) 260 E.G. 601 (purchaser entitled to rescind contract for sale of lease which was already forfeited).

[219] [2016] UKSC 42; [2017] A.C. 467.

[220] [2017] A.C. 467 at [160].

[221] [1974] Ch. 30. See also *Malhotra v Choudhury* [1980] Ch. 52 at 71; *Verrall v Great Yarmouth BC* [1981] Q.B. 202, above, para.27–015 (specific performance of contract to hire conference hall to National Front), where this defence failed: the risk of public disorder was outweighed by the freedom of speech and assembly and the sanctity of contract; *Sutton v Sutton* [1984] Ch. 184.

[222] Now Family Law Act 1996.

right of occupation. The husband and daughter would remain liable to eviction by the purchasers, and the family would be split up. The court would be slow to order specific performance in such circumstances.

6. THE JURISDICTION UNDER LORD CAIRNS' ACT

A. Award of Damages under Lord Cairns' Act

27–044
The Chancery Amendment Act 1858, commonly known as Lord Cairns' Act, gave to the Court of Chancery discretionary power to award damages either in addition to or in substitution for specific performance.[223] It provided in s.2:

> "In all cases in which the Court of Chancery has jurisdiction to entertain an application for an injunction against a breach of any covenant, contract, or agreement, or against the commission or continuance of any wrongful act, or for the specific performance of any covenant, contract, or agreement, it shall be lawful for the same Court, if it shall think fit, to award damages to the party injured, either in addition to or in substitution for such injunction or specific performance; and such damages may be assessed in such manner as the Court shall direct."

The modern version, which may have a wider effect,[224] appears in the Senior Courts Act 1981 s.50:

> "Where the Court of Appeal or the High Court has jurisdiction to entertain an application for an injunction or specific performance, it may award damages in addition to, or in substitution for, an injunction or specific performance."

Before Lord Cairns' Act, it was only in the common law courts that damages were awarded.[225] The Act gave power to award damages where none would be available at law.[226] But it did not give the Court of Chancery power to award common law damages.[227] It applied only to cases where the court had jurisdiction to award specific performance. Thus Lord Cairns' Act does not apply where the

---

[223] See generally J. Jolowicz (1975) 34 C.L.J. 224; T. Ingman and J. Wakefield [1981] Conv. 286; T. Ingman [1994] Conv. 110; P. McDermott, *Equitable Damages* (Butterworths, 1994); K. Barnett and M. Bryan (2015) 9 J. Eq. 150.

[224] In that the reference to injunction may include breaches of equitable duties. In *Giller v Procopets* (2008) 24 V.R. 1, the Victorian Court of Appeal awarded Lord Cairns' Act damages for breach of the equitable duty of confidence. Victoria's modern Lord Cairns' Act provision is relevantly identical to Senior Courts Act 1981 s.50.

[225] It appears that the Court of Chancery had inherent power to award damages in equity, but this was rarely exercised. See Spry, *Equitable Remedies*, pp.647–649; P. McDermott (1992) 108 L.Q.R. 652; cf. *Surrey v Bredero Homes Ltd* [1993] 1 W.L.R. 1361 at 1368, where Dillon LJ said that the Court of Chancery had "no power to award damages" before the 1858 Act. For the Court of Chancery's ancient statutory jurisdiction to award damages, see McDermott, *Equitable Damages* (1994), p.8.

[226] See *Johnson v Agnew* [1980] A.C. 367 (Lord Wilberforce); *Price v Strange* [1978] Ch. 337; *Oakacre Ltd v Claire Cleaners (Holdings) Ltd* [1982] Ch. 197 (cause of action for damages at law not accrued when action commenced).

[227] But see *Price v Strange* [1978] Ch. 337 at 358, where Goff LJ said: "One purpose and a very important purpose of that Act was, of course, to avoid circuity of action by enabling the old Court of Chancery to award damages at law."

contract is of a type which is not specifically enforceable[228]; but it does apply where the contract is of a type which is, even though specific performance is refused on some discretionary ground, such as the absence of mutuality.[229] There is no jurisdiction under Lord Cairns' Act if specific performance is no longer possible, as where the land has been sold to a third party. However, the jurisdiction exists if, when the proceedings were begun, the court could have granted specific performance, notwithstanding that thereafter, but before judgment, specific performance has become impossible.[230]

It was not until the Judicature Act 1873 that common law damages were available in the Chancery Division. Today it is only necessary to rely on Lord Cairns' Act if no damages would be available at law.[231]

B.   Measure of Damages under Lord Cairns' Act

It was at one time thought that it could be advantageous to the claimant to rely on Lord Cairns' Act even where common law damages were available, as the measure of damages might be different. In *Wroth v Tyler*,[232] the contract price of the property was £6,000 and it was worth £7,500 on the date at which completion was due. By the date of judgment, eighteen months later, its value had risen to £11,500. Megarry J refused specific performance for reasons mentioned above,[233] so the main issue was the measure of damages. It was "common ground" that the normal rule is that damages for breach of a contract for the sale of land are measured by the difference (if any) between the contract price and the market price at the date of the breach, which is normally the completion date (with interest from that date until judgment). Applying that rule, damages would be £1,500. Although Fry had said that "the measure would be the same under Lord Cairns' Act",[234] Megarry J held that damages under the Act may be assessed on a basis which is not identical with that of the common law[235]: they should be a true substitute for specific performance, and must put the claimants in as good a position as if the contract had been performed. Damages could be measured as at the date of judgment, and the purchasers were awarded £5,500.

27–045

---

[228] *Lavery v Pursell* (1888) 39 Ch.D. 508 (tenancy for one year; above para.27–025). As to whether contracts for personal services come into this category, see the different views expressed in *Price v Strange* [1978] Ch. 337 at 359 (Goff LJ) and at 369 (Buckley LJ). The House of Lords in *Scandinavian Trading Tanker Co AB v Flota Petrolera Ecuatoriana* [1983] 2 A.C. 694 took the view that there was no jurisdiction to grant specific performance of a contract for services.

[229] *Price v Strange* [1978] Ch. 337. Even where the contract concerns building or repair works, the court has jurisdiction under the 1858 Act: at 359. See also *Wroth v Tyler* [1974] Ch. 30; *Malhotra v Choudhury* [1980] Ch. 52.

[230] *Johnson v Agnew* [1978] Ch. 176, CA.

[231] See *Oakacre Ltd v Claire Cleaners (Holdings) Ltd* [1982] Ch. 197 (cause of action for damages not yet accrued).

[232] [1974] Ch. 30; applied in *Grant v Dawkins* [1973] 1 W.L.R. 1406. See also *Oakacre Ltd v Claire Cleaners (Holdings) Ltd* [1982] Ch. 197 (damages awarded in addition to specific performance not limited to those accrued when action commenced).

[233] Above, para.27–043.

[234] Fry, *Specific Performance*, 6th edn (1921), p.602.

[235] [1974] Ch. 30 at 58–60.

This reasoning is questionable because the damages awarded in *Wroth v Tyler* could equally have been awarded at common law. There is no inflexible rule at common law that damages must be assessed as at the date of the breach of contract.[236] The principle is that the claimant should be put in the same position as if the contract had been duly performed. This is shown by considering mitigation. In the case of chattels, damages will usually be assessed at the breach, because at that date the claimant could have acquired an equivalent chattel elsewhere. But in the case of a specifically enforceable contract, such as a contract to buy land, the purchaser cannot reasonably be expected to mitigate the damages by seeking an equivalent property elsewhere as soon as the breach occurs, because she will normally wish to wait and see if specific performance is obtainable.[237] In such a case, the common law principle of putting the claimant in the same position as if the contract had been performed is only adhered to in times of rising property prices by assessing the damages at a date subsequent to the breach.[238]

27-046 In the subsequent case of *Johnson v Agnew*,[239] Lord Wilberforce agreed that damages at common law are not necessarily calculated by reference to breach-date values. In doing so, his Lordship rejected the view that damages under Lord Cairns' Act and damages under the general law would be calculated differently: "I find in the Act no warrant for the court awarding damages differently from common law damages".[240] Read in the context in which it was made, the comment is uncontroversial: in the normal run of things there will obviously be little difference between damages as a substitute for specific performance and damages which aim to put the claimant in the same position as if the contract had been performed. After all, the general purpose of contract damages is to award a substitute for performance. But Lord Wilberforce's comment must not be taken too broadly and must not be allowed to obscure the point that damages under Lord Cairns' Act are available in many instances where damages at law are not.[241]

This is most clearly seen when Lord Cairns' Act damages are awarded in lieu of an injunction, rather than when they are awarded in lieu of specific performance.[242] Damages awarded in lieu of an injunction may be awarded in a

---

[236] *Wroth v Tyler* [1974] Ch. 30 at 57; *Horsler v Zorro* [1975] Ch. 302 at 316 (a decision of Megarry J); *Radford v De Froberville* [1977] 1 W.L.R. 1262; *Malhotra v Choudhury* [1980] Ch. 52; *Johnson v Agnew* [1980] A.C. 367; *Suleman v Shahsavari* [1988] 1 W.L.R. 1181; *Hooper v Oates* [2013] EWCA Civ 91; [2014] Ch. 287; A. Dyson and A. Kramer (2014) 131 L.Q.R. 259; *Morris-Garner v One Step (Support) Ltd* [2018] UKSC 20 at [47].

[237] Specific performance of contracts involving land is not always awarded in Canada: *Semelhago v Paramadevan* [1996] 2 S.C.R. 415. This means a purchaser has to mitigate, even if he or she seeks specific performance: *Southcott Estates Inc v Toronto Catholic School Board* [2012] 2 S.C.R. 675; J. O'Sullivan (2013) 72 C.L.J. 253. See generally A. Summers, *Mitigation in the Law of Damages* (Oxford: Oxford University Press, 2018).

[238] See *Hooper v Oates* [2014] Ch. 287.

[239] [1980] A.C. 367. The facts have been given, above, para.27-010. See also *Malhotra v Choudhury* [1980] Ch. 52 (claimant had delayed, so damages calculated according to earlier valuation date).

[240] [1980] A.C. 367 at 400.

[241] *Morris-Garner v One Step (Support) Ltd* [2018] UKSC 20 at [47].

[242] Although see *Oakacre Ltd v Claire Cleaners (Holdings) Ltd* [1982] Ch. 197 (award of damages in lieu when cause of action for damages not yet accrued).

wide variety of situations. These include breaches of negative obligations as well as positive obligations; ongoing breaches of obligations; and even future breaches of obligations that have not happened yet. In all of these situations, any damages awarded in lieu of an injunction will be awarded as a true substitute for that injunction.[243] But what that requires in any given case may well be more difficult to work out than when damages are awarded in lieu of specific performance. These matters are considered more fully in Ch.28.[244]

7. SPECIFIC PERFORMANCE AND THIRD PARTIES

Claims for specific performance are usually made between the parties to the contract.[245] In such a case, all the parties to the contract must be parties to the action.[246]

27–047

A different question is whether specific performance may be obtained by a party to the contract but for the benefit of a third party, as where A has contracted with B to confer a benefit on C. As discussed below, C may be able to enforce the contract in her own right under the Contracts (Rights of Third Parties) Act 1999. If, however, because the contract was entered into before the application of the 1999 Act, C cannot enforce the contract herself, the question is whether B may obtain specific performance, compelling A to confer the benefit on C.

> In *Beswick v Beswick*,[247] one Peter Beswick, a coal merchant who wished to retire, made an arrangement with his nephew under which the business was transferred to the nephew, and the nephew promised to employ Peter as consultant for a weekly wage, and after his death to pay to Peter's widow £5 per week for her life. Payments were made to Peter during his lifetime, but soon after his death ceased to be paid to his widow. The widow took out letters of administration of Peter's estate and sued both as administratrix and in her own right under the contract.

The House of Lords held that she was entitled as administratrix to specific performance of the promise to make the weekly payments to her as Peter's widow. She was unable to sue in her own right because of the rule of privity.

The difficulties which faced the widow in her action as administratrix were essentially threefold: (a) Peter's estate, which she represented, had lost nothing by the breach; (b) the widow, in her own capacity, had suffered the loss but had no right of action; and (c) the agreement was for the payment of money and was not the type of agreement where breach is usually remedied by an order of specific performance.[248]

27–048

The widow, as administratrix, overcame them all. Lord Upjohn thought that (a) was an argument in favour of specific performance; "the court ought to grant

---

[243] *Morris-Garner v One Step (Support) Ltd* [2018] UKSC 20 at [44], [95].

[244] Below, para.28–053.

[245] For the rights of a sub-purchaser to obtain specific performance of the head contract, see *Berkley v Poulett* (1976) 120 S.J. 836, above para.12–008. On the rights of assignees of agreements for lease, see Landlord and Tenant (Covenants) Act 1995. On the rights of assignees of contracts for the sale of land, see Land Charges Act 1972 s.2(4); Land Registration Act 2002 s.3(2).

[246] See *Tito v Waddell (No.2)* [1977] Ch. 106 at 324 (Megarry VC).

[247] [1968] A.C. 58; N. Andrews (1988) 8 L.S. 14.

[248] Above, para.27–018.

a specific performance order all the more because damages *are* nominal."[249] She had no other effective remedy; "justice demands that [the promisor] pay the price and this can only be done in the circumstances by equitable relief."[250] Yet this rather disregards the principle that equitable remedies are available where the legal remedy is inadequate to compensate for the loss. It is not that equitable remedies are available where the claimant has suffered no loss,[251] nor where an independent person has suffered a loss for which there is no cause of action.

Their Lordships found no difficulty in treating the case as a suitable one for specific performance. "Had [the promisor] repudiated the contract in the lifetime of [the promisee] the latter would have had a cast-iron case for specific performance."[252] The orthodox view has been that specific performance will not be ordered in cases where the promise is to pay money unless the claimant is a vendor or lessor against whom the purchaser or lessee could have demanded specific performance. *Beswick v Beswick* may have been regarded as such a case, for the nephew "could on his part clearly have obtained specific performance of it if Beswick senior or his administratrix had defaulted."[253] That, it is submitted, is questionable; for the contract was essentially for the sale of the goodwill of the business; such a contract is not normally specifically enforceable, in contrast to a contract to sell premises along with the goodwill.[254]

27–049 It was said also that a contract to pay an annuity is specifically enforceable. In *Adderley v Dixon*,[255] Leach MR gave the reason that the amount of damages would be conjectural. While such a proposition may have been sound in 1824, the development of life assurance and of actuarial valuation of life interests has made an annuity and a capital sum in effect interchangeable. Annuities are freely purchased from insurance companies in exchange for capital payments and can similarly be freely sold for a capital sum. Thus the conjectural element is less marked than it was in earlier times. If the claimant was awarded damages, and desired the annuity, all she need do is buy one.

The cases on which their Lordships relied to support the view that the contract to pay was specifically enforceable, at the instance of a personal representative, were all cases either of a contract to transfer land or contracts to pay an annuity. It is possible to treat *Beswick v Beswick* as consistent with authority by saying that there was mutuality, that the contract (being to pay an annuity) was capable of specific performance, and that the common law remedy of damages (assuming them to be nominal) was inadequate. The claimant barely succeeds on the first two; and only on the third by relying on cases which uphold it without explaining the logical dilemma of holding an award of nominal damages inadequate where no loss was suffered by the party able to sue.

---

[249] [1968] A.C. 58 at 102; cf. *Re Cook's ST* [1965] Ch. 902; above, para.5–025.

[250] [1968] A.C. 58 at 102.

[251] cf. *Marco Productions Ltd v Pagola* [1945] 1 K.B. 111; injunction available to restrain breach of negative covenant even though the breach causes no loss to claimant; or if only nominal damages would be available at law; *Rochdale Canal Co v King* (1851) 2 Sim.(N.S.) 78.

[252] [1968] A.C. 58 at 98.

[253] [1968] A.C. 58 at 89, per Lord Pearce.

[254] *Darbey v Whitaker* (1857) 4 Drew. 134 at 139, 140; above, para.27–027.

[255] (1824) 1 Sim. & St. 607 at 611; G. Treitel (1966) 29 M.L.R. 657 at 663.

In spite of these criticisms, the broad equitable view of the situation taken by the House of Lords should be commended. There was "an unconscionable breach of faith [and] the equitable remedy sought is apt."[256] Lord Pearce and Lord Upjohn both approved the dictum of Windeyer J in *Coulls v Bagot's Executor and Trustee Co Ltd*, in which he said[257]:

> "It seems to me that contracts to pay money or transfer property to a third person are always, or at all events very often, contracts for breach of which damages would be an inadequate remedy—all the more so if it be right (I do not think it is) that damages recoverable by the promisee are only nominal ... I see no reason why specific performance should not be had in such cases ... There is no reason today for limiting by particular categories, rather than by general principle, the cases in which orders for specific performance will be made."

There were in *Beswick* no technical or practical difficulties preventing an award of specific performance and "justice demands that [the promisor] pay the price and this can only be done in the circumstances by equitable relief."[258]

Today, the widowed Mrs Beswick would be able to enforce the contract in her own right if it were entered into after the Contracts (Rights of Third Parties) Act 1999. Whether she would be able to obtain specific performance by virtue of s.1(5) is less clear.[259] This depends on whether the subsection must be taken to override the principle that specific performance is not available to a volunteer. The Law Commission simply stated that the widow would have "the right of enforcement", without reference to specific performance.[260] Even if specific performance would not be available, at least the widow would be able to obtain substantial damages, being a person with a cause of action who has suffered a loss by the breach. To that extent, the remedy of damages is adequate. **27–050**

8.   JURISDICTION

Both the High Court and the County Court have jurisdiction to grant specific performance, but the jurisdiction of the County Court,[261] in cases of specific performance of contracts to sell or to let land, is limited to cases where the purchase money, or the value of the property in the case of a lease, does not exceed the County Court limit. This is currently £350,000.[262] **27–051**

The County Court must give effect to every defence or counterclaim to which effect would be given in the High Court.[263] Thus, in *Kingswood Estate Co Ltd v*

---

[256] [1968] A.C. 58 at 83, per Lord Hodson.

[257] (1967) 119 C.L.R. 460 at 503.

[258] [1968] A.C. 58 at 102, per Lord Upjohn.

[259] Discussed above, para.27–048.

[260] Law Com. No. 242, para.7.46.

[261] County Courts Act 1984 s.23(d). There is now a single County Court, notwithstanding the name of the governing Act: County Courts Act 1984 s.A1, inserted by Crime and Courts Act 2013.

[262] The County Court Jurisdiction Order 2014. The parties may agree to submit to the jurisdiction of the County Court in cases above the limit, and the High Court has power to transfer any proceedings to the County Court under s.40(2) of the 1984 Act. See also *Joyce v Liverpool City Council* [1996] Q.B. 252 (small claims).

[263] County Courts Act 1984 s.38.

Anderson,[264] where the landlord brought an action for possession based on the termination of a common law periodic tenancy, the County Court gave effect to the tenant's defence that she held the property under a specifically enforceable agreement for a lease for life, even though it had no jurisdiction to grant specific performance of that agreement. Similarly, in *Rushton v Smith*,[265] the County Court had no jurisdiction to grant specific performance of an agreement for a business tenancy where the value of the property exceeded the County Court limit, but it nevertheless had jurisdiction to decide whether or not the tenant would be entitled to such an order.

---

[264] [1963] 2 Q.B. 169. See also *Cornish v Brook Green Laundry Ltd* [1959] 1 Q.B. 394.
[265] [1976] Q.B. 480.

CHAPTER 28

INJUNCTIONS

1. JURISDICTION

A. The High Court

28–001 AN INJUNCTION is an order by the court to a party to do or refrain from doing a particular act. Originally the Court of Chancery alone[1] could grant injunctions. This inevitably led to much duplication of proceedings; as where a claimant required an injunction in aid of a legal right. The Common Law Procedure Act 1854 gave to common law courts a power to grant injunctions in certain cases. The present jurisdiction is governed by the Senior Courts Act 1981, replacing the Judicature Acts, which vested the jurisdiction of the Court of Chancery and of the common law courts in the High Court. The Senior Courts Act 1981 provides in s.37(1):

> "The High Court may by order (whether interlocutory or final) grant an injunction ... in all cases in which it appears to the court to be just and convenient to do so."[2]

28–002 Care must be taken when discussing the "jurisdiction" to award injunctions. In a strict sense, the court has jurisdiction to grant an injunction against a person simply by virtue of that person being subject to the in personam jurisdiction of the court.[3] However, that jurisdiction is exercised, not on the individual preference of the judge, but "according to sufficient legal reasons or on settled legal principles."[4] It is therefore necessary to distinguish between the *power* of the court to award an injunction and the *practice* of the court only to do so in certain circumstances. In *Fourie v Le Roux*,[5] Lord Scott referred to the latter as "the restrictions and limitations which have been placed by a combination of judicial precedent and rules of court on the circumstances in which the injunctive relief in question can properly be granted."

Clearly, these restrictions and limitations may change and develop over time.[6] A modern case exemplifying this is *Cartier International AG v British Sky*

---

[1] Or the Court of Exchequer in its equity jurisdiction: see *Halsbury's Laws of England*, 5th edn, Vol.24, para.699, fn.4. See generally Sharpe, *Injunctions and Specific Performance*; I.C.F. Spry, *Equitable Remedies*, 9th edn (2014), Chs 4 and 5.

[2] This consolidates the previous legislation. Compare the wording of s.25(8) of the Supreme Court of Judicature Act 1873 and s.45 of the Act of 1925: "just or convenient"; *Day v Brownrigg* (1878) 10 Ch.D. 294; *L v L* [1969] P. 25.

[3] *Fourie v Le Roux* [2007] 1 W.L.R. 320 at [30].

[4] *Beddow v Beddow* (1878) 9 Ch.D. 89 at 93, per Jessel MR.

[5] [2007] 1 W.L.R. 320 at [25]. See also *Masri v Consolidated Contractors International (UK) Ltd (No.2)* [2009] Q.B. 450 at [175].

[6] *Broadmoor Special Hospital Authority v Robinson* [2000] Q.B. 775 at [20].

Broadcasting Ltd,[7] where an injunction was granted requiring internet service providers to block access to certain websites that advertised and sold counterfeit goods. The claimants were trade mark holders who claimed that their trade marks were being infringed by the sale of the counterfeit goods. The injunction was granted even though the internet service providers had not themselves infringed any rights of the claimants. Although a statutory power exists under the Copyright, Designs and Patents Act 1988 to enable the High Court to issue injunctions against service providers, that statutory power is limited to cases involving copyright infringement by third parties.[8] In the *Cartier* case, the court was able to interpret s.37(1) of the Senior Courts Act as authorising a similar practice in respect of trade mark infringement.

B.   The County Court

Section 38 of the County Courts Act 1984 provides that (subject to exceptions) the court may make any order which could be made by the High Court. One such exception involves search orders,[9] which cannot be granted in the County Court unless a judge of the High Court or Court of Appeal is presiding. Formerly the County Court could not issue freezing injunctions[10] either, but this restriction has been removed.[11]   **28–003**

2.   TYPES OF INJUNCTIONS

A.   Prohibitory and Mandatory Injunctions

The most common form of an injunction, as the name implies, is one which is prohibitory or restrictive. However, if the unlawful act has been committed and an order restraining its commission is therefore meaningless, justice can sometimes be done by issuing a mandatory injunction ordering the act to be undone. At one time the negative character of an injunction used to be insisted upon; if the court intended to order a party to pull down a building, the order would be that he should refrain from permitting the building to remain on his land. Such an injunction may have a positive effect, as in *Sky Petroleum Ltd v VIP Petroleum Ltd*,[12] where an injunction restraining the defendant from   **28–004**

---

[7] [2016] EWCA Civ 658; [2017] 1 All E.R. 700; affirming [2015] 1 All E.R. 949 at [92]–[111]. The point was no longer an issue before the Supreme Court: see [2018] UKSC 28 at [5]. See also *Google Inc v Equustek Solutions Inc* 2017 SCC 34; [2017] 1 S.C.R. 824, where the Supreme Court of Canada upheld a worldwide interlocutory injunction that required Google to "de-index" the webpages of defendants in separate intellectual property litigation; M. Douglas (2018) 134 L.Q.R. 181.
[8] Copyright, Designs and Patents Act 1988 s.97A: "The High Court … shall have power to grant an injunction against a service provider, where that service provider has actual knowledge of another person using their service to infringe copyright."
[9] Below, para.28–072; see The County Court Remedies Regulations 2014.
[10] Below, para.28–075.
[11] The County Court Remedies Regulations 2014.
[12] [1974] 1 W.L.R. 576.

withholding supplies of petrol was equivalent to specific performance of the contract. There is now no objection to mandatory injunctions being couched in positive form.

B. Perpetual and Interlocutory (or Interim) Injunctions

28–005 Prohibitory or mandatory injunctions may be perpetual or interlocutory. "Perpetual" does not mean necessarily that the effect of the order must endure forever; it means that the order will finally settle the present dispute between the parties, being made as the result of an ordinary action, the court having heard in the ordinary way the arguments on both sides. But a claimant may not always be able to wait for the action to come on in the normal course; it may be that irreparable damage will be done if the defendant is not immediately restrained. In such cases the claimant will serve on the defendant a notice that an application is being made to the court for an interlocutory injunction. The service of this notice will enable the defendant also to be heard, if he or she wishes, but the hearing will not be a final decision on the merits of the case. If the claimant has made out a sufficient case, the judge will grant an interlocutory injunction, which is effective only until the trial of the action or some earlier specified date.

C. Injunctions Without Notice[13]

28–006 An application may be made without notice if notice would enable the defendant to take steps to defeat the purpose of the injunction, for example by taking assets out of the jurisdiction, or if the claimant had no time to give notice before the threatened wrongful act. But the latter would be rare, as the claimant could normally at least give notice by telephone: "Any notice is better than none."[14] If an injunction is granted without notice, notice will then be served on the defendant, who will then have a chance of having the order set aside or varied.[15] Obviously only interlocutory injunctions can be granted without notice.

D. Quia Timet Injunctions

28–007 A quia timet injunction is one which issues to prevent an infringement of the claimant's rights where the infringement is threatened, but has not yet occurred. The jurisdiction exists in relation to both perpetual and interlocutory injunctions, and to both prohibitory and mandatory injunctions. The claimant must show a very strong probability of a future infringement, and that the ensuing damage will be of a most serious nature.[16]

---

[13] Called ex parte injunctions before the CPR 1998 came into operation.
[14] *National Commercial Bank Jamaica Ltd v Olint Corp Ltd (Practice Note)* [2009] 1 W.L.R. 1405 at 1408 (PC).
[15] CPR 23.9, 23.10.
[16] *Fletcher v Bealey* (1885) 28 Ch.D. 688; *Attorney General v Nottingham Corp* [1904] 1 Ch. 673; *Redland Bricks Ltd v Morris* [1970] A.C. 652; below, para.28–042.

3. GENERAL PRINCIPLES

A. Nature of Remedy

i. Discretionary Remedy. While the injunction is a much wider remedy than specific performance, the two remedies share characteristics. Thus, the injunction is a discretionary remedy,[17] based on the inadequacy of common law remedies. Similar principles also apply to the exercise of the discretion of the court. As in the case of specific performance, the court may award damages under Lord Cairns' Act, either in lieu of, or in addition to, an injunction.[18] In a rare case, the court will grant a declaration that a person who has yet to seek an injunction has no entitlement to it.[19]

28–008

ii. Remedy in Personam. Like specific performance, the injunction is a remedy in personam. It is possible to enjoin a defendant who is not personally within the jurisdiction, provided service out of the jurisdiction can properly be done under the civil procedure rules.[20] But, as a general rule, no injunction will be granted in connection with the title to land outside the jurisdiction, even if the defendant is within the jurisdiction.[21] It is otherwise in the case of chattels, and, even in the case of land, the rule is subject to exceptions.[22] Finally, an injunction may be granted against an unnamed defendant,[23] or against all the members of a class or organisation to restrain the unlawful acts of unidentified members.[24]

28–009

iii. Contempt. Non-compliance with an injunction (or an undertaking given in lieu[25]) is a contempt of court,[26] punishable by imprisonment,[27] sequestration of property (in the case of a corporation) or a fine.[28] Acts done in breach of an

28–010

---

[17] Unless it is a statutory remedy to enforce a right for which there is no common law remedy; *Bristol City Council v Lovell* [1998] 1 W.L.R. 446 at 453 (right to buy). Similarly, a claimant who has been totally dispossessed by trespass is entitled to an injunction as of right; *Harrow LBC v Donohue* [1995] 1 E.G.L.R. 257; below, para.28–066.

[18] Below, para.28–050.

[19] *Greenwich Healthcare NHS Trust v London Quadrant Housing Trust* [1998] 1 W.L.R. 1749.

[20] CPR Pt 6; Practice Direction 6B.

[21] *Deschamps v Miller* [1908] 1 Ch. 856; *Re Hawthorne* (1883) 23 Ch.D. 743. See Dicey, Morris and Collins, *The Conflict of Laws*, 15th edn (London: Sweet & Maxwell, 2012), paras 23–042—23–051, discussing also the effect of Civil Jurisdiction and Judgments Act 1982 s.30. This principle applies also to foreign intellectual property; *Tyburn Productions Ltd v Conan Doyle* [1991] Ch. 75.

[22] See *Penn v Lord Baltimore* (1750) 1 Ves.Sen. 444, above, para.27–004; *Hamlin v Hamlin* [1986] Fam. 11.

[23] *Bloomsbury Publishing Group Plc v News Group Newspapers Ltd* [2003] 1 W.L.R. 1633.

[24] *M. Michaels (Furriers) Ltd v Askew, The Times*, 25 June 1983 (nuisance by members of "Animal Aid"); cf. *United Kingdom Nirex Ltd v Barton, The Times*, 14 October 1986. See further J. Seymour (2007) 66 C.L.P. 605.

[25] *Hussain v Hussain* [1986] Fam. 134; *Roberts v Roberts* [1990] 2 F.L.R. 111.

[26] Contempt of Court Act 1981. See also *Parker v Camden LBC* [1986] Ch. 162. As to children and persons who lack capacity, see *Wookey v Wookey* [1991] Fam. 121; *Re H (Respondent under 18: Power of Arrest)* [2001] 1 F.L.R. 641.

[27] *Hale v Tanner* [2000] 1 W.L.R. 2377; *JSC BTA Bank v Solodchenko* [2011] EWCA Civ 1241; [2012] 1 W.L.R. 350.

[28] As to a company's liability for employee's breach, see *Re Supply of Ready Mixed Concrete (No.2)* [1995] 1 A.C. 456. For liability of directors, see *Director General of Fair Trading v Buckland* [1990]

injunction may be void for illegality.[29] As disobedience may lead to imprisonment, the injunction must be expressed in exact terms, so that the defendant knows precisely what to do, or refrain from doing.[30] As committal proceedings are equivalent to a criminal charge, the breach of injunction must be established beyond reasonable doubt.[31]

A question which has become prominent is whether third parties commit contempt if they knowingly act contrary to an injunction. A third party who aids and abets a breach of injunction is guilty of contempt.[32] An agent of the party enjoined is also bound by the injunction.[33] The court has jurisdiction in wardship and other special cases to make an injunction against the world at large,[34] although a person who contravened the order in good faith and without notice of its terms would not commit contempt.[35] In *Attorney General v Times Newspapers Ltd*,[36] newspapers which published confidential material which other newspapers had been enjoined from publishing were guilty of contempt. The House of Lords held that strangers who knowingly took action to damage or destroy confidentiality before the trial committed contempt by nullifying the purpose of the trial. The question was not whether third parties were bound by the injunction, but whether they could commit contempt even though they were not bound. As they were not parties to the order, the basis of the contempt would not be a breach of the order (unless they had aided and abetted a breach) but knowing interference with the administration of justice.[37]

28–011   **iv. Crown Proceedings.**   An injunction will not normally lie against the Crown.[38] The proper remedy in such a case is the declaration. A former disadvantage that an interim declaration could not be granted has now gone.[39] The position at the time of writing is that an interlocutory injunction may, exceptionally, be granted against the Crown to protect rights enforceable under

---

1 W.L.R. 920; *Attorney General for Tuvalu v Philatelic Distribution Corp Ltd* [1990] 1 W.L.R. 926. Non-compliance with an injunction may be an element in a subsequent award of exemplary damages: *Drane v Evangelou* [1978] 1 W.L.R. 455.

[29] *Clarke v Chadburn* [1985] 1 W.L.R. 78 (union rules). Compliance with a statute affords a defence; *A v B Bank (Governor and Company of the Bank of England intervening)* [1993] Q.B. 311.

[30] *Redland Bricks Ltd v Morris* [1970] A.C. 652; *Co-operative Insurance Society Ltd v Argyll Stores (Holdings) Ltd* [1998] A.C. 1; *O (A Child) v Rhodes* [2015] UKSC 32; [2016] A.C. 219 at [79].

[31] *Re Bramblevale Ltd* [1970] Ch. 128; *Kent CC v Batchelor* (1977) 33 P. & C.R. 185.

[32] *Acro (Automation) Ltd v Rex Chainbelt Inc* [1971] 1 W.L.R. 1676.

[33] *Cretanor Maritime Co Ltd v Irish Marine Management Ltd* [1978] 1 W.L.R. 966. See the asset-freezing cases, below, para.28–075, particularly the "world-wide assets" cases.

[34] *Venables v News Group Newspapers* [2001] Fam. 430.

[35] *Re X (A Minor)* [1984] 1 W.L.R. 1422; *Attorney General v Times Newspapers Ltd* [1992] 1 A.C. 191 at 224; *Kelly v BBC* [2001] Fam. 59; *Attorney General v Harris* [2001] 2 F.L.R. 895; *BBC v CAFCASS Legal* [2007] 2 F.L.R. 765.

[36] [1992] 1 A.C. 191 (the *Spycatcher* case).

[37] *Attorney General v Punch* [2003] 1 A.C. 1046; P. Devonshire (2003) 119 L.Q.R. 384. For the position of third parties in relation to final injunctions, see *Jockey Club v Buffham* [2003] Q.B. 462; A. Smith (2003) 62 C.L.J. 241.

[38] Crown Proceedings Act 1947 s.21; *R. v Secretary of State for Transport, Ex p. Factortame Ltd* [1990] 2 A.C. 85.

[39] CPR 25.1. See *R. v R. (Interim Declaration: Adult's Residence)* [2000] 1 F.L.R. 451; *Bank of Scotland (Governor and Company) v A Ltd* [2001] 1 W.L.R. 751; *NHS Trust v T (Adult Patient: Refusal of Medical Treatment)* [2005] 1 All E.R. 387.

EU law.[40] Further, an injunction, final or interlocutory, may be granted against ministers and other officers of the Crown, and a minister can be liable for contempt.[41]

B. Locus Standi

"It is a fundamental rule that the court will only grant an injunction at the suit of a private individual to support a legal right."[42] The type of right which may be protected by injunction in the field of private law is dealt with below, but the question also arises as to who may seek an injunction to protect a public right. This requires a consideration of the extent to which the civil courts may restrain a breach of the criminal law by injunction. The general rule is that public rights are protected by the Attorney General, acting either on his or her own initiative, or on the relation of a member of the public. The Attorney may obtain an injunction to restrain breaches of the criminal law even if there is a statutory remedy, where that remedy is inadequate,[43] and the view of the court is that injunctions should be granted at his or her request to prevent clear breaches of the law irrespective of the weighing of benefits and detriments which characterises most other injunctions.[44]

28–012

By way of exception to this general rule, an individual may seek an injunction if interference with a public right, created by statute or existing at common law, would also infringe some private right of his or would inflict special damage on him,[45] save where statute has, for instance by providing an exclusive remedy, excluded it.[46] But an individual who does not come within the established exceptions has no remedy, for it is no part of English law that a person who suffers damage by reason of another person's breach of statute has a civil action against that person.[47] Thus a record company could not get an injunction against a defendant who traded in "bootleg" records in breach of statute, as there is no

---

[40] *R. v Secretary of State for Transport, Ex p. Factortame Ltd (No.2)* [1991] 1 A.C. 603; W. Wade (1991) 107 L.Q.R. 4.

[41] *M v Home Office* [1994] 1 A.C. 377.

[42] *Thorne v British Broadcasting Corp* [1967] 1 W.L.R. 1104 at 1109, per Lord Denning MR ("legal" is here taken to include "equitable"). Lord Denning expressed different views in *Chief Constable of Kent v V* [1983] Q.B. 34 (following the Supreme (now Senior) Courts Act 1981), but these were rejected in *P v Liverpool Daily Post and Echo Newspapers Plc* [1991] 2 A.C. 370.

[43] *Attorney General v Sharp* [1931] 1 Ch. 121; *Attorney General v Chaudry* [1971] 1 W.L.R. 1614.

[44] *Attorney General v Bastow* [1957] 1 Q.B. 514; *Attorney General v Harris* [1961] 1 Q.B. 74. The role of the Attorney General was reviewed in 2007 but the law was not changed.

[45] *Gouriet v Union of Post Office Workers* [1978] A.C. 435; *Lonrho Ltd v Shell Petroleum Co Ltd* [1982] A.C. 173; *RCA Corp v Pollard* [1983] Ch. 135. An action also lies if the claimant can show that he or she is a member of the class for whose benefit the statute was passed and upon whom Parliament intended to confer a cause of action; *R. v Deputy Governor of Parkhurst Prison, Ex p. Hague* [1992] 1 A.C. 58.

[46] *Stevens v Chown* [1901] 1 Ch. 894; cf. *Meade v Haringey LBC* [1979] 1 W.L.R. 637.

[47] *Lonrho Ltd v Shell Petroleum Co Ltd* [1982] A.C. 173; *CBS Songs Ltd v Amstrad Consumer Electronics Plc* [1988] A.C. 1013; *P v Liverpool Daily Post and Echo Newspapers Plc* [1991] 2 A.C. 370.

principle that a person can restrain a crime affecting his property rights by injunction where the statute was not designed for the protection of the class of which he is a member.[48]

28–013 Another important question is whether a private individual may obtain an injunction to restrain a threatened criminal offence which would interfere with a public right when the Attorney General has refused consent to a relator action, the case not being one where private rights or special damage to the claimant are involved.[49] In *Gouriet v Union of Post Office Workers*,[50] the claimant, a member of the public, sought an injunction to restrain a threatened boycott of postal communications between Britain and South Africa, in breach of statute. The Attorney General had refused consent to a relator action, without giving reasons. It was unanimously held in the House of Lords that the court had no jurisdiction to grant such an injunction, nor to control the exercise of the Attorney General's discretion in any way.

In the case of a crime which has already been committed, it has been held that the police have locus standi to seek an injunction to "freeze" money in a bank account which is reasonably believed to be the proceeds of a crime.[51] This principle is not without difficulty, and is confined to an asset which can be identified as the stolen item or as property representing it.[52] No such injunction is available in respect of moneys not themselves obtained by fraud but which were profits made by means of a loan obtained by fraud.[53] The House of Lords in *Attorney General v Blake*[54] considered that the Attorney General had no entitlement to an injunction which effectively froze the proceeds of crime (royalties from a book written by a former KGB spy), because this would amount to confiscation outside the statutory provisions permitting confiscation orders. Their Lordships decided that the private law remedy of an account of profits was available, and thus the point did not arise. No view was expressed as to the correctness of the police cases, which were distinguishable.

Finally, the rule that only the Attorney General may enforce public rights is subject to certain statutory exceptions, enabling a local authority to seek an

---

[48] *RCA Corp v Pollard* [1983] Ch. 135; *Rickless v United Artists Corp* [1988] Q.B. 40. See now Copyright, Designs and Patents Act 1988 s.194.

[49] The right to bring a private prosecution, once the offence is committed, is a different matter, but the Attorney General has power to veto such proceedings.

[50] [1978] A.C. 435; D. Williams (1977) 36 C.L.J. 201; H.W.R. Wade (1978) 94 L.Q.R. 4; T. Hartley (1978) 41 M.L.R. 58; R. Simpson (1978) 41 M.L.R. 63; D. Feldman (1979) 42 M.L.R. 369.

[51] *Chief Constable of Kent v V* [1983] Q.B. 34; *West Mercia Constabulary v Wagener* [1982] 1 W.L.R. 127.

[52] *Chief Constable of Hampshire v A Ltd* [1985] Q.B. 132. See also *Malone v Metropolitan Police Commissioner* [1980] Q.B. 49.

[53] *Chief Constable of Leicestershire v M* [1989] 1 W.L.R. 20; cf. *Securities and Investments Board v Pantell SA* [1990] Ch. 426.

[54] [2001] 1 A.C. 268.

injunction in its own name to protect public rights in the locality,[55] or to enforce planning control.[56] Various public authorities may also seek injunctions to prevent anti-social behaviour.[57]

C. Protection of Legal or Equitable Rights

A right that is to be protected by an injunction must be one that is known to law or equity. The point was firmly made in *Day v Brownrigg*.[58] **28–014**

> The claimant lived in a house that had been called "Ashford Lodge" for 60 years. The defendant lived in a smaller neighbouring house called "Ashford Villa". The defendant started to call his house "Ashford Lodge" and the claimant sought an injunction to restrain him from doing so. The Court of Appeal took the view that there was no violation of a legal or equitable right of the claimant so that no injunction would be granted.

Similarly, in *Paton v Trustees of British Pregnancy Advisory Service*,[59] it was held that a husband could not obtain an injunction to prevent his wife from having, or a registered medical practitioner from performing, a legal abortion: the husband had "no legal right enforceable at law or in equity."

Injunctions have proved particularly valuable in protecting confidential or private material.[60] Other rights which may be protected by injunction include the right (contractual or otherwise) not to be subjected to arbitration proceedings which could not lead to a fair trial[61]; the right (contractual or otherwise) not to be sued in a foreign court[62]; the right to restrain a breach of European Union law[63]; the right to restrain the export of works of art by means of forged documents[64]; the right to refuse surgery[65]; the right not to be harassed[66]; the right of a public body to prevent interference with the performance of its statutory responsibilities[67]; **28–015**

---

[55] Local Government Act 1972 s.222. See *Mayor of London (on behalf of the Greater London Authority) v Hall* [2011] 1 W.L.R. 504 (injunction against demonstrators camped opposite Parliament).

[56] Town and Country Planning Act 1990 s.187B. See *South Bucks DC v Porter* [2003] 2 A.C. 558.

[57] Anti-Social Behaviour, Crime and Policing Act 2014 s.5. See *Chief Constable of the Bedfordshire Police v Golding* [2015] EWHC 1875 (QB) (injunctions sought against the leaders of "Britain First" to prevent a march during Ramadan; not granted).

[58] (1878) 10 Ch.D. 294; *Beddow v Beddow* (1878) 9 Ch.D. 89 at 93; see also *Montgomery v Montgomery* [1965] P. 46.

[59] [1979] Q.B. 276. For a discussion of the position if the proposed abortion would be illegal, see I. Kennedy (1979) 42 M.L.R. 324; *C v S* [1988] Q.B. 135; A. Grubb and D. Pearl (1987) 103 L.Q.R. 340.

[60] Below, para.28–068.

[61] *Bremer Vulkan Schiffbau und Maschinenfabrik v South India Shipping Corp* [1981] A.C. 909.

[62] *British Airways Board v Laker Airways Ltd* [1985] A.C. 58; *South Carolina Insurance Co v Assurantie Maatschappij "De Zeven Provincien" NV* [1987] A.C. 24.

[63] *Cutsforth v Mansfield Inns Ltd* [1986] 1 W.L.R. 558; *Taittinger v Allbev Ltd* [1994] 4 All E.R. 75.

[64] *Kingdom of Spain v Christie, Manson & Woods Ltd* [1986] 1 W.L.R. 1120.

[65] *Re C (Adult: Refusal of Treatment)* [1994] 1 W.L.R. 290.

[66] Protection from Harassment Act 1997 s.3; see *Levi v Bates* [2015] EWCA Civ 206 (injunction refused).

[67] *Broadmoor Special Hospital Authority v Robinson* [2000] Q.B. 775.

and the right to ensure the effectiveness of a court order.[68] The latter right is the basis of the use of the injunction to prevent the defendant from leaving the country.[69] More examples are given throughout this chapter, and particularly in Part 9 below.[70]

4. PERPETUAL INJUNCTIONS

28–016 It is axiomatic that the jurisdiction to grant injunctions is discretionary. But, as with specific performance, the court, in exercising its discretion, pays attention to certain factors established by the precedents as being of particular relevance.

A. Prohibitory Injunctions

28–017 If a claimant has established the existence of a right, infringement of that right should be restrained, but injunctions will not be granted where an award of damages would be sufficient. Damages will not be an adequate remedy if they are not quantifiable, or if money could not properly compensate the claimant, as in the case of nuisance and other continuous or repeated injuries requiring a series of actions for damages.

The extent of the damage is not the crucial point. An injunction may be granted even if only nominal damages would be recoverable at law.[71] The smallness of the damage and the fact that a monetary sum could easily be assessed to compensate for it, is no reason for withholding an injunction if the consequence is that the defendant is in effect compulsorily "buying" a right which is the claimant's to sell only if she wants to.[72] This principle was applied in *Express Newspapers Ltd v Keys*.[73]

> Certain trade unions had issued instructions to their members to support a "Day of Action" in protest against Government policies. The claimants sought an injunction to restrain the unions from inducing a breach of contract between the members and their employers. Griffiths J, in granting the injunction, held that damages would be inadequate. The employers did not want money; they wanted their newspapers to be published. To refuse the injunction would be giving a licence to the unions to commit an unlawful act merely because they could afford to pay the damages.

---

[68] *Maclaine Watson & Co Ltd v International Tin Council (No.2)* [1989] Ch. 286 (unpaid judgment debt).

[69] *Bayer AG v Winter* [1986] 1 W.L.R. 497; *JSC Mezhdunarodny Promyshlenniy Bank v Pugachev* [2015] EWCA Civ 1108.

[70] Below, para.28–055 and following ("Injunctions in Particular Situations").

[71] *Rochdale Canal Co v King* (1851) 2 Sim.(n.s.) 78; *Woollerton and Wilson Ltd v Richard Costain Ltd* [1970] 1 W.L.R. 411.

[72] *Wood v Sutcliffe* (1851) 2 Sim.(N.S.) 163. In *Express Newspapers Ltd v Keys* [1980] I.R.L.R. 247, and *Patel v WH Smith (Eziot) Ltd* [1987] 1 W.L.R. 853, it was held that this principle applied equally to interlocutory injunctions, and was not affected by *American Cyanamid Co v Ethicon Ltd* [1975] A.C. 396, below, para.28–029.

[73] [1980] I.R.L.R. 247. The injunction was interlocutory but the judgment on this aspect is of general application.

Similarly in cases in which the defendant has trespassed on the claimant's property: actual loss does not need to be shown before an injunction is granted.[74] But there may be cases in which injunctions will be refused, for example if the infringement is occasional or temporary, or if it is a trivial matter. One such case was *Armstrong v Sheppard and Short*,[75] where the claimant had misled the court and had suffered no real damage. Lord Evershed MR said:

> "A proprietor who establishes a proprietary right is ex debito justitiae entitled to an injunction unless it can be said against him that he has raised such an equity that it is no longer open to him to assert his legal or proprietary rights."[76]

In *Behrens v Richards*[77] an injunction was not granted to restrain the public from using tracks on the claimant's land on an unfrequented part of the coast, causing no damage to him. Such cases are, however, to be regarded as exceptional.[78]

It is obvious that these various factors are not to be considered in isolation and no complete list can be given of instances where an injunction will be refused. The principle applied by the courts is the protection of existing rights which are recognised by the law. But an injunction will not issue in every such case; it may be refused where damages are an adequate remedy, or where the claimant has by her conduct disentitled herself from injunctive relief, or where the defendant gives to the court an undertaking not to do the act complained of[79]; or where, even if there is no other suitable remedy, the court considers that the claimant has suffered no injustice.[80]

B. Mandatory Injunctions

These are governed by the same general principles as prohibitory injunctions, **28–018** save that the problems of enforcement, supervision and hardship may be more acute. Mandatory injunctions are less frequently granted than prohibitory injunctions, and, as Lord Upjohn stated in *Redland Bricks Ltd v Morris*,[81] are entirely discretionary, although it has been held that the court has no real discretion in cases involving trespass by total dispossession.[82]

There are two broad categories of mandatory injunctions: the first is the "restorative" injunction, requiring the defendant to undo a wrongful act in situations where a prohibitory injunction might have been obtained to prevent the

---

[74] *Goodson v Richardson* (1874) L.R. 9 Ch.App. 221; *Trenberth (John) Ltd v National Westminster Bank Ltd* (1979) 39 P. & C.R. 104.
[75] [1959] 2 Q.B. 384.
[76] [1959] 2 Q.B. 384 at 394. See *Harrow LBC v Donohue* [1995] 1 E.G.L.R. 257.
[77] [1905] 2 Ch. 614.
[78] *Patel v WH Smith (Eziot) Ltd* [1987] 1 W.L.R. 853; *Anchor Brewhouse Developments Ltd v Berkley House (Docklands Developments) Ltd* [1987] 2 E.G.L.R. 173.
[79] *Halsey v Esso Petroleum Co Ltd* [1961] 1 W.L.R. 683; *British Broadcasting Corp v Hearn* [1977] 1 W.L.R. 1004. cf. *Weller v Associated Newspapers Ltd* [2015] EWCA Civ 1176; [2016] 1 W.L.R. 1541 where an injunction was granted because the defendant refused to provide a formal undertaking.
[80] See *Glynn v Keele University* [1971] 1 W.L.R. 487.
[81] [1970] A.C. 652 at 655. See also *Leakey v National Trust for Places of Historic Interest or Natural Beauty* [1980] Q.B. 485; *Re C (A Minor)* [1991] 2 F.L.R. 168.
[82] *Harrow LBC v Donohue* [1995] 1 E.G.L.R. 257.

commission of the act.[83] In such a case failure to seek a prohibitory injunction does not preclude the subsequent grant of a mandatory injunction, but it is a factor to be taken into account: a final injunction is unlikely if the claimant "stood by" during building works in breach of covenant, but he may succeed if he made his objections clear.[84] The other category is the mandatory injunction to compel the defendant to carry out some positive obligation. If the matter is one of contract, specific performance is more usual in the latter situation, but an injunction may be granted.[85] We have already seen that the terms of an injunction must be certain. It follows from this that a duty which is itself uncertain cannot be enforced by injunction.[86]

Problems of supervision may arise with mandatory injunctions as with specific performance.[87] This will not normally prevent the grant of a "restorative" mandatory injunction, which merely requires an act of restoration, but a mandatory injunction is unlikely to be granted in cases involving the continuous performance of a positive obligation.

> In *Gravesham BC v British Railways Board*,[88] the defendant planned to curtail the services of its ferry. As this would cause inconvenience to some local workers, a mandatory injunction was sought to compel the defendant to maintain existing timetables, even though this would cause the ferry to be run at a loss. It was held that in fact there was no breach of the defendant's common law duty to operate the ferry, but even if there had been, a mandatory injunction would not be appropriate, because of enforcement difficulties and financial hardship to the defendant. Slade J said that there was no absolute and inflexible rule that the court will never grant an injunction requiring a series of acts involving the continuous employment of people over a number of years. But the jurisdiction to grant such an injunction would be exercised only in exceptional circumstances.

28–019   As in the case of prohibitory injunctions, it is not necessary for the claimant to show grave damage or inconvenience. In *Kelsen v Imperial Tobacco Co Ltd*[89] a mandatory injunction was granted to enforce the removal of a sign which trespassed in the airspace above the claimant's premises, causing no real damage to him, save in so far as he could have charged for the use of the space.

> In *Wrotham Park Estate v Parkside Homes Ltd*,[90] the defendant had erected houses in breach of a restrictive covenant which it had thought was unenforceable. Although purchasers were now in occupation, the claimants sought a mandatory injunction for the demolition of the

---

[83] *Charrington v Simons & Co Ltd* [1971] 1 W.L.R. 598; *Pugh v Howells* (1984) 48 P. & C.R. 29; *Jones v Stones* [1999] 1 W.L.R. 1739.

[84] See *Wrotham Park Estate v Parkside Homes Ltd* [1974] 1 W.L.R. 798, below; *Gafford v Graham* (1999) 77 P. & C.R. 73; *Mortimer v Bailey* [2005] 1 E.G.L.R. 75; G. Watt [2005] Conv. 460.

[85] See *Evans v BBC and IBA, The Times*, 26 February 1974 (interlocutory).

[86] *Bower v Bantam Investments Ltd* [1972] 1 W.L.R. 1120 (interlocutory); cf. *Acrow (Automation) Ltd v Rex Chainbelt Inc* [1971] 1 W.L.R. 1676; *Peninsular Maritime Ltd v Padseal Ltd* (1981) 259 E.G. 860.

[87] Above, para.27–020.

[88] [1978] Ch. 379. See also *Dowty Boulton Paul Ltd v Wolverhampton Corp* [1971] 1 W.L.R. 204 (no injunction to enforce a covenant to maintain land as an airfield); cf. *Co-operative Insurance Society Ltd v Argyll Stores (Holdings) Ltd* [1998] A.C. 1 (no specific performance of covenant in lease to keep a shop open in trading hours); above, para.27–021.

[89] [1957] 2 Q.B. 334.

[90] [1974] 1 W.L.R. 798; distinguished in *Wakeham v Wood* (1982) 43 P. & C.R. 40, where the building was in flagrant disregard of the covenant.

houses. For various reasons, they had not sought interlocutory relief to prevent the erection of the houses, but this was not fatal to the grant of a mandatory injunction.[91] The fact that the action was commenced before much building had been done was a relevant but not a conclusive factor. The injunction was refused, as it would result in the unpardonable waste of needed houses. Instead, damages were awarded under Lord Cairns' Act.

Finally, it has been held that the court should be reluctant to intervene in industrial disputes by the grant of a mandatory injunction. **28–020**

In *Harold Stephen and Co Ltd v Post Office*,[92] an industrial dispute had arisen whereby postal workers were suspended. This resulted in the claimant company's mail being held up and its business seriously disrupted. The company sought a mandatory injunction against the Post Office to release its mail. The Court of Appeal refused the injunction, which would require the Post Office to take back the suspended workers, who would be likely to continue the unlawful action. The injunction would, therefore, have the effect of revoking the Post Office's disciplinary measures.

"It can only be in very rare circumstances and in the most extreme circumstances that this court should interfere by way of mandatory injunction in the delicate mechanism of industrial disputes and industrial negotiations."[93]

Such an extreme case was *Parker v Camden LBC*,[94] where a strike of boilermen employed by the landlord council meant that the tenants, many of whom were elderly or had young children, had no heating or hot water. In these exceptional circumstances, involving risk to life and health, the court was prepared to grant a mandatory injunction to turn on the boiler even though industrial action was involved.

The principles applicable to the grant of mandatory interlocutory injunctions and mandatory quia timet injunctions are discussed below.[95]

C.   Suspension of Injunctions

If it would be very difficult for the defendant to comply immediately with the injunction, he or she will not be made to do the impossible. The injunction may be granted but suspended for a reasonable period, particularly if such a course will not result in financial damage to the claimant. The defendant may be required to undertake to pay damages to the claimant for any loss. Suspension may be appropriate where the defendant is a local authority, which must make alternative arrangements for the performance of its duties. Thus, in *Pride of Derby Angling Association v British Celanese Co*,[96] an injunction was granted against a local authority to restrain the pollution of a river, but was suspended for a reasonable time, with the possibility of further suspension should the circumstances require it. **28–021**

[91] See also *Shaw v Applegate* [1977] 1 W.L.R. 970 at 978.

[92] [1977] 1 W.L.R. 1172.

[93] [1977] 1 W.L.R. 1172 at 1180. See also *Meade v Haringey LBC* [1979] 1 W.L.R. 637.

[94] [1986] Ch. 162 (interlocutory).

[95] Below, paras 28–040, 28–042.

[96] [1953] Ch. 149. See also *Halsey v Esso Petroleum Co Ltd* [1961] 1 W.L.R. 683 (suspension for six weeks in nuisance case).

5. INTERLOCUTORY (OR INTERIM) INJUNCTIONS

A. General

28–022   Interlocutory injunctions raise somewhat different considerations. The object of an interlocutory injunction is "to prevent a litigant, who must necessarily suffer the law's delay, from losing by that delay the fruit of his litigation."[97] Or, in the words of the Privy Council, its purpose is "to improve the chances of the court being able to do justice after a determination of the merits at the trial."[98]

Interlocutory injunctions may be prohibitory, mandatory, or quia timet. Normally such an injunction remains in force until the trial of the action, but it may be granted for some shorter specified period. If the parties consent, the interlocutory hearing may be treated as a final trial if the dispute is of law. But this will not be possible if the dispute is of fact, as affidavit evidence is unsuitable for such issues.

As we have seen, failure to seek an interlocutory injunction to restrain the commission of a wrongful act will not necessarily preclude the claimant from later obtaining a final mandatory injunction to compel the defendant to undo the act.[99]

28–023   **i. Without Notice Procedure.**   The claimant should give at least three clear days' notice, so that, when the application is heard, the defendant can oppose it. But exceptionally an injunction may be granted without serving notice on the defendant, if the matter is one of such urgency that irreparable damage would be caused if the claimant had to go through the normal procedure.[100] The "without notice" injunction may be subsequently set aside or varied on the defendant's application.[101] Such an injunction may be granted even before the proceedings have started. In *Re N (No.2)*,[102] an injunction was granted without notice by a High Court judge at his residence on a Sunday, to prevent the applicant's husband from taking their children to Australia.

The "without notice" procedure has been found most useful in the search order and asset-freezing cases, where there is a danger that the defendant, if aware of the application, would destroy or remove vital evidence, or move assets out of the jurisdiction. These developments are discussed below.[103]

28–024   **ii. Discharge of Interlocutory Injunctions.**   The court has inherent jurisdiction to discharge an interlocutory injunction, even when the defendant has

---

[97] *Hoffman-La Roche (F) & Co v Secretary of State for Trade and Industry* [1975] A.C. 295 at 355, per Lord Wilberforce.

[98] *National Commercial Bank Jamaica Ltd v Olint Corp Ltd (Practice Note)* [2009] 1 W.L.R. 1405 at 1409.

[99] *Wrotham Park Estate v Parkside Homes Ltd* [1974] 1 W.L.R. 798. But such an omission may be relevant to the defence of acquiescence: *Shaw v Applegate* [1977] 1 W.L.R 970, below, para.28–045.

[100] CPR 25.3. See *National Commercial Bank Jamaica Ltd v Olint Corp Ltd (Practice Note)* [2009] 1 W.L.R. 1405 at 1408. Where a trade dispute is involved, see the Trade Union and Labour Relations (Consolidation) Act 1992 s.221(2).

[101] CPR 23.9, 23.10.

[102] [1967] Ch. 512.

[103] Below, paras 28–072, 28–075.

not applied for its discharge.[104] Furthermore, where an injunction has been granted which affects someone who was not a party to the action, that person can apply to court for the variation or discharge of the injunction.[105]

iii. Injunctions Pending Appeal.   Where a claim for an interlocutory **28–025** injunction is dismissed, the judge has jurisdiction to grant a limited injunction pending an appeal, on the claimant's without notice application.[106] Such an injunction may be granted in order that the appeal, if successful, is not nugatory.

iv. Complete Relief.   It is no objection that the grant of an interlocutory **28–026** injunction gives complete relief to the claimant without requiring her to prove her case, so that she need bring no final action. In *Woodford v Smith*,[107] Megarry J granted an interlocutory injunction to restrain a residents' association from breaking its contract by holding a meeting without the claimant members. There was nothing to prevent the court in a proper case from granting on an interim application all the relief claimed in the action. In *Evans v BBC and IBA*,[108] a mandatory interlocutory injunction was granted to enforce the Welsh Nationalist Party's alleged contractual right to a Party Political Broadcast on television just before an election. The interlocutory injunction was thus a complete remedy, making it unnecessary to continue to trial and prove the case.

v. Injunction Ineffective.   As equity does not act in vain, an interlocutory **28–027** injunction will not be granted where it would be of no effect.[109] In *Bentley-Stevens v Jones*,[110] a director was removed by irregular proceedings. This was not a case for an interlocutory injunction, as the irregularities could be cured by going through the proper processes; the result therefore would be the same.

B.   Principles Applicable to the Issue of Interlocutory Injunctions

As in the case of mandatory injunctions, the interlocutory injunction is **28–028** discretionary and is not granted as of course. Prior to the decision of the House of Lords in *American Cyanamid Co v Ethicon Ltd*,[111] discussed below, the claimant

---

[104] *RD Harbottle (Mercantile) Ltd v National Westminster Bank Ltd* [1978] Q.B. 146.
[105] *Cretanor Maritime Co Ltd v Irish Marine Management Ltd* [1978] 1 W.L.R. 966; *Iraqi Ministry of Defence v Arcepey Shipping Co SA* [1981] Q.B. 65, below, para.28–080 (asset-freezing injunctions).
[106] *Erinford Properties Ltd v Cheshire CC* [1974] Ch. 261; *Chartered Bank v Daklouche* [1980] 1 W.L.R. 107. See also *Ketchum International Plc v Group Public Relations Holdings Ltd* [1997] 1 W.L.R. 4 (jurisdiction to restrain disposal of assets pending appeal if good arguable appeal); *Belize Alliance of Conservation Non-Govermental Organisations v Department of the Environment of Belize* [2003] 1 W.L.R. 2839 (Privy Council has such jurisdiction).
[107] [1970] 1 W.L.R. 806; see also *Manchester Corp v Connolly* [1970] Ch. 420, where there was plainly no defence.
[108] *The Times*, 26 February 1974. See also *Shepherd Homes Ltd v Sandham* [1971] Ch. 340 at 347, and *Acrow (Automation) Ltd v Rex Chainbelt Inc* [1971] 1 W.L.R. 1676 at 1683.
[109] Similarly with final injunctions: *Attorney General v Guardian Newspapers Ltd (No.2)* [1990] 1 A.C. 109. A declaration may be appropriate; *Love v Herrity* (1991) 23 H.L.R. 217.
[110] [1974] 1 W.L.R. 638.
[111] [1975] A.C. 396.

had to show a strong prima facie case that his rights had been infringed.[112] He was then required to show that damages would not be an adequate remedy if he succeeded at the trial, and that the balance of convenience favoured the grant. In other words, an interlocutory injunction would not be granted unless the claimant could show that it was more likely than not that he would succeed in obtaining a final injunction at the trial.

28–029 **i. *American Cyanamid Co v Ethicon Ltd.*** The principles mentioned above were replaced by the rules laid down by Lord Diplock in *American Cyanamid*,[113] which were designed to circumvent the necessity of deciding disputed facts or determining points of law without hearing sufficient argument.[114] The case concerned an application for a quia timet interlocutory injunction to restrain the infringement of a patent. It was unanimously held that there was no rule requiring the claimant to establish a prima facie case.[115] The rule is that the court must be satisfied that the claimant's case is not frivolous or vexatious and that there is a serious question to be tried. Once that is established, the governing consideration is the balance of convenience. The court should not embark on anything resembling a trial of the action. At the interlocutory stage it is no part of the court's function to resolve conflicts of evidence on affidavit nor to resolve difficult questions of law.[116] These are matters for the trial. At the interlocutory stage the facts may be disputed and the evidence incomplete and there is no cross-examination; the court's discretion would be stultified if, on untested and incomplete evidence, it could only grant the injunction if the claimant had shown that he was more than 50% likely to succeed at trial.

While the balance of convenience is the governing consideration, a significant factor in assessing it is the inadequacy of damages to each party. If that does not provide an answer, then other aspects of the balance of convenience will arise. If the balance of convenience does not clearly favour either party, then the preservation of the status quo will be decisive. Only as a last resort is it proper to consider the relative strength of the cases of both parties, and only then if it appears from the facts set out in the affidavit evidence, as to which there is no credible dispute, that the strength of one party's case is disproportionate to that of the other.[117] Finally, other special factors may have to be considered in individual

---

[112] See *JT Stratford & Son Ltd v Lindley* [1965] A.C. 269, especially at 338 (Lord Upjohn). The contrary was not there argued. The decision was not cited in *American Cyanamid*.

[113] *American Cyanamid Co v Ethicon Ltd* [1975] A.C. 396.

[114] *Smith v Inner London Education Authority* [1978] 1 All E.R. 411 at 426.

[115] But Lord Diplock himself had said that an applicant for an interlocutory injunction had to show a "strong prima facie case" that he would succeed at trial: *Hoffman-LaRoche (F) & Co v Secretary of State for Trade and Industry* [1975] A.C. 295 at 360. For an explanation, see *Series 5 Software Ltd v Clarke* [1996] 1 All E.R. 853.

[116] *Derby & Co Ltd v Weldon* [1990] Ch. 48.

[117] See *Cambridge Nutrition Ltd v British Broadcasting Corp* [1990] 3 All E.R. 523; cf. *Series 5 Software Ltd v Clarke* [1996] 1 All E.R. 853. Also compare the position in Australia: *ABC v O'Neill* (2006) 227 C.L.R. 57.

cases. It has been said by the Privy Council that "The basic principle is that the court should take whichever course seems likely to cause the least irremediable prejudice to one party or the other."[118]

The principles laid down by Lord Diplock in *American Cyanamid* were these:

(a) Claimant's Case not Frivolous or Vexatious. This requirement was designed to remove "any attempt by [claimants] to harass defendants, any case which was futile and any case which was misconceived or an abuse of the process of the court."[119] Such claims fail at the threshold. The claimant must show that there is a serious question to be tried, which means that she must have a good arguable case, or, in other words, a real prospect of success at the trial.[120] The hurdle "is a relatively low one".[121] **28–030**

(b) The Balance of Convenience. We have seen that the inadequacy of damages is a significant factor in assessing the balance of convenience. The court must first of all consider the adequacy of damages to each party, namely whether damages would adequately compensate the claimant for any loss caused by the acts of the defendant prior to the trial[122] and whether, should the claimant fail at the trial, any loss caused to the defendant by the grant of the injunction could be adequately compensated by the claimant's undertaking in damages.[123] **28–031**

An example of irreparable loss is the distribution of a dividend to shareholders on the basis of supposedly erroneous calculations.[124] Another is the loss of trade when members of the public picketed the claimant's business premises,[125] or when a trade union proposed unlawfully to induce the claimant's employees to break their contracts by supporting a political strike[126]; the loss cannot be measured, but it may be great. Similarly, the publication of confidential material,[127] or the loss of a job with good prospects.[128] Damages will also be inadequate where, if a doctor did not obtain an injunction to restrain the termination of his contract, he would lose the chance to clear his name at disciplinary proceedings.[129] Likewise if the defendant does not have the means to

---

[118] *National Commercial Bank Jamaica Ltd v Olint Corp Ltd (Practice Note)* [2009] 1 W.L.R. 1405 at 1409.

[119] *Honeywell Information Systems Ltd v Anglian Water Authority, The Times,* 29 June 1976 (Geoffrey Lane LJ).

[120] *Re Lord Cable* [1977] 1 W.L.R. 7 at 20; *Smith v Inner London Education Authority* [1978] 1 All E.R. 411; *Cayne v Global Natural Resources Plc* [1984] 1 All E.R. 225.

[121] *Haque v Raja* [2016] EWHC 1950 (Ch) at [26].

[122] See *Lion Laboratories Ltd v Evans* [1985] Q.B. 526.

[123] *Chancellor, Masters and Scholars of the University of Oxford v Pergamon Press Ltd* (1977) 121 S.J. 758. See also *Laws v Florinplace Ltd* [1981] 1 All E.R. 659 (injunction to restrain nuisance by running "sex shop" in residential area).

[124] *Bloxham v Metropolitan Ry* (1868) L.R. 3 Ch.App. 337.

[125] *Hubbard v Pitt* [1976] Q.B. 142, below, para.28–032. See also *Cutsforth v Mansfield Inns Ltd* [1986] 1 W.L.R. 558.

[126] *Express Newspapers Ltd v Keys* [1980] I.R.L.R. 247.

[127] *Attorney General v Guardian Newspapers Ltd* [1987] 1 W.L.R. 1248 (*Spycatcher*). But the perpetual injunction was refused: *Attorney General v Guardian Newspapers (No.2)* [1990] 1 A.C. 109.

[128] *Fellowes & Son v Fisher* [1976] Q.B. 122; *Powell v Brent LBC* [1987] I.R.L.R. 466.

[129] *Kircher v Hillingdon Primary Care Trust* [2006] Lloyd's Rep. Med. 215.

pay any appreciable damages,[130] or if the damages would be unquantifiable,[131] as in the case of injury to goodwill[132] or reputation.[133]

In *AB v CD*,[134] one party, CD, sought to breach a licensing agreement. AB commenced arbitration proceedings and sought an interim injunction that would, in effect, require CD to honour the agreement in the meantime. That injunction was refused at trial because of a clause in the licensing agreement which provided that CD would not be liable for AB's lost profits or other consequential losses. The trial judge reasoned that, although AB may indeed suffer such losses, they could not weigh on the balance of convenience because those losses would not ultimately be recoverable even if AB were successful in the substantive action. The Court of Appeal allowed AB's appeal and granted the injunction:

> "The primary obligation of a party is to perform the contract. The requirement to pay damages in the event of a breach is a secondary obligation, and an agreement to restrict the recoverability of damages in the event of a breach cannot be treated as an agreement to excuse performance of that primary obligation."[135]

While the adequacy of damages is a most significant factor, other considerations may be taken into account in assessing the balance of convenience. Indeed, Lord Diplock concluded his exposition of the guiding principles in *American Cyanamid* by referring to "other special factors" that may have to be considered in individual cases.[136] Where the dispute between the parties is a political one, the damage to both parties may not be calculable in monetary terms.[137] All the circumstances must be considered, including difficulties of compliance or enforcement, and the principle that the court should be reluctant to interfere in industrial disputes or political decisions by injunction.[138] In *Smith v Inner London Education Authority*,[139] where an interlocutory injunction was sought to restrain an alleged breach of statutory duty, it was said that where the defendant is a public body, the balance of convenience

---

[130] *De Falco v Crawley BC* [1980] Q.B. 460 (no injunction where claimant could not give worthwhile undertaking in damages); cf. *Bunn v British Broadcasting Corp* [1998] 3 All E.R. 552 at 558.

[131] *Araci v Fallon* [2011] EWCA Civ 668; [2011] All E.R. (D) 37 (breach of contract not to ride horse other than claimant's in the Derby).

[132] *Chancellor, Masters and Scholars of the University of Oxford v Pergamon Press Ltd* (1977) 121 S.J. 758.

[133] *British Broadcasting Corp v Hearn* [1977] 1 W.L.R. 1004 (injunction to restrain interference with claimant's broadcast of the Cup Final to South Africa); *Schering Chemicals Ltd v Falkman Ltd* [1982] Q.B. 1.

[134] [2014] EWCA Civ 229; [2015] 1 W.L.R. 771; P. Turner (2014) 73 C.L.J. 493. See also *Bath and NE Somerset DC v Mowlem Plc* [2004] EWCA Civ 115; [2015] 1 W.L.R. 785n.

[135] [2015] 1 W.L.R. 771 at [27].

[136] [1975] A.C. 396 at 409. See *Hubbard v Pitt* [1976] Q.B. 142 at 185 (these special factors are matters to be weighed on the balance of convenience, not factors allowing the case to fall outside the *American Cyanamid* principles).

[137] See *Lewis v Heffer* [1978] 1 W.L.R. 1061. Geoffrey Lane LJ, at 1078, found great difficulty in applying *American Cyanamid* in such a case.

[138] *Meade v Haringey LBC* [1979] 1 W.L.R. 637; *Jakeman v South West Thames Regional Health Authority and London Ambulance Service* [1990] I.R.L.R. 62.

[139] [1978] 1 All E.R. 411 (injunction to restrain phasing out of grammar schools refused). See also *R. v Ministry of Agriculture Fisheries and Food, Ex p. Monsanto Plc* [1999] Q.B. 116; *Belize Alliance of Conservation Non-Governmental Organisations v Department of the Environment of Belize* [2003] 1 W.L.R. 2839.

must be looked at more widely; the court must consider the interests of the general public to whom the duty is owed. Similarly where an injunction is sought to prevent a public authority from enforcing a law which is claimed to be invalid (as being incompatible with EU law). In such an exceptional case, an injunction should not be granted unless there is firm ground for the challenge, and the public interest must be considered when assessing the balance of convenience.[140] Special considerations affecting the grant of search orders and asset-freezing interlocutory injunctions are discussed elsewhere.[141]

If the balance of convenience does not clearly favour either party, then the deciding factor will be the preservation of the status quo.[142] This means the circumstances prevailing when the defendant began the activity which the claimant seeks to restrain,[143] "but it is of course impossible to stop the world pending trial."[144]

28–032

We have also seen that the relative strength of each party's case is a factor to be considered as a last resort, and only then if the strength of one party's case is disproportionate to that of the other.[145]

ii. Exceptional cases. The following are cases where the *American Cyanamid* principles do not apply, or apply in modified form. Other exceptional cases may arise outside these categories.[146] Thus it has been held that *American Cyanamid* is inapplicable to an order to give life-sustaining treatment to a child.[147] Nor does it apply where there is a clear statutory power to grant an injunction.[148] Indeed, the number of exceptions may indicate that the *American Cyanamid* principles are flawed.[149]

28–033

(a) Where Trial of the Action Unlikely or Delayed. In *Cayne v Global Natural Resources Plc*,[150] the Court of Appeal held that the *American Cyanamid*

28–034

---

[140] *R. v Secretary of State for Transport, Ex p. Factortame (No.2)* [1991] 1 A.C. 603.

[141] Below, paras 28–072, 28–075.

[142] See *Lewis v Heffer* [1978] 1 W.L.R. 1061; *Chancellor, Masters and Scholars of the University of Oxford v Pergamon Press Ltd* (1977) 121 S.J. 758.

[143] *Fellowes & Son v Fisher* [1976] Q.B. 122 at 141; *Garden Cottage Foods Ltd v Milk Marketing Board* [1984] A.C. 130. But delay by the claimant will be taken into account in considering this principle: *Shepherd Homes Ltd v Sandham* [1971] Ch. 340.

[144] *National Commercial Bank Jamaica Ltd v Olint Corp Ltd (Practice Note)* [2009] 1 W.L.R. 1405 at 1409.

[145] Relative strength was decisive in *Cambridge Nutrition Ltd v British Broadcasting Corp* [1990] 3 All E.R. 523, where the timing of a broadcast was vital and a contract to restrain it was doubtful.

[146] *R. v Secretary of State for Health, Ex p. Generics (UK) Ltd* [1998] Eu. L.R. 146. For EU law considerations, see *R. v Secretary of State for Health, Ex p. Imperial Tobacco Ltd* [2001] 1 W.L.R. 127.

[147] *Re J (A Minor) (Medical Treatment)* [1993] Fam. 15.

[148] *Runnymede BC v Harwood* (1994) 68 P. & C.R. 300 (Town and Country Planning Act 1990 s.187B).

[149] See J. Martin (1993) 3 Carib. L.R. 76 and (1993–94) 4 K.C.L.J. 52; A. Zuckerman (1993) 56 M.L.R. 325 at 328.

[150] [1984] 1 All E.R. 225, applying *NWL Ltd v Woods* [1979] 1 W.L.R. 1294; *Thomas v National Union of Mineworkers (South Wales Area)* [1986] Ch. 20; *Cambridge Nutrition Ltd v British Broadcasting Corp* [1990] 3 All E.R. 523. See also *Araci v Fallon* [2011] EWCA Civ 668; [2011] All E.R. (D) 37 (to restrain breach of contract not to ride horse other than claimant's in the Derby).

principles do not apply to cases where no trial is likely to take place. Likewise in a restraint of trade case if the trial is unlikely to come on before the end of the period of the restraint.[151] Where the question is whether information can be published in spite of its confidentiality, delay in coming to trial could result in the stifling of legitimate comment until it is no longer important if only an arguable case is required.[152] In these cases it is best to decide on the basis of relative strength, otherwise the defendant might be effectively precluded at the interlocutory stage from disputing the claim at trial.

28–035 *(b) Where no Arguable Defence.* It has been held that the *American Cyanamid* rules do not apply where the defendant has no arguable defence.[153] In such a case it is not necessary to consider the balance of convenience. Thus the claimant may obtain an interlocutory injunction to restrain a clear trespass even where it causes no damage[154]; or to restrain a clear misapplication of union funds.[155] The principle that the claimant is entitled almost as of right to an injunction to restrain a plain breach of a negative contract provides another example.[156]

28–036 *(c) Human Rights Act 1998: Freedom of Expression.* Article 10 of the European Convention on Human Rights protects the right to freedom of expression, subject to certain qualifications. Section 12 of the Human Rights Act 1998 applies where a court is considering whether to grant any relief which, if granted, might affect the exercise of the Convention right to freedom of expression. Section 12(3) provides that no such relief is to be granted so as to restrain publication before trial unless the court is "satisfied that the applicant is likely to establish that publication should not be allowed". This means that a final injunction must be the likely outcome, not merely that publication must likely be found to be wrongful.

Under s.12(4), the court must have particular regard to the importance of the Convention right to freedom of expression and, where the proceedings relate to material which appears to be journalistic, literary or artistic, to the extent to which the material has or is about to become available to the public, or to which publication is or would be in the public interest, and to any relevant privacy code.

Thus where interlocutory injunctions are sought to restrain publication before trial in cases involving breach of confidence, privacy or libel, the court must look at the strength of the case and not apply *American Cyanamid*. The word "likely" in s.12(3) means that the claimant must normally show that he will probably succeed at the trial, although a lesser degree of likelihood will suffice in some

---

[151] *David (Lawrence) Ltd v Ashton* [1991] 1 All E.R. 385; *Lansing Linde Ltd v Kerr* [1991] 1 W.L.R. 251 (treated as a "wider view of the balance of convenience").

[152] *Attorney General v Times Newspapers Ltd* [1992] 1 A.C. 191 at 226.

[153] *Official Custodian for Charities v Mackey* [1985] Ch. 168; *Love v Herrity* (1991) 23 H.L.R. 217.

[154] *Patel v WH Smith (Eziot) Ltd* [1987] 1 W.L.R. 853; *Anchor Brewhouse Developments Ltd v Berkley House (Docklands Developments) Ltd* [1987] 2 E.G.L.R. 173; *London & Manchester Assurance Co Ltd v O&H Construction Ltd* [1989] 2 E.G.L.R. 185.

[155] *Taylor v National Union of Mineworkers (Derbyshire Area), The Times*, 29 December 1984.

[156] *Doherty v Allman* (1878) 3 App.Cas. 709; below, para.28–056, applied to interlocutory injunctions in *Hampstead & Suburban Properties Ltd v Diomedous* [1969] 1 Ch. 248; *Attorney General v Barker* [1990] 3 All E.R. 257; *Araci v Fallon* [2011] EWCA Civ 668; [2011] All E.R. (D) 37.

cases, for example where the consequences of publication would be particularly grave.[157] In any event, even if the claimant does satisfy this test, it does not follow that the injunction must be granted, as factors such as the balance of convenience must still be considered. So in *Douglas v Hello! Ltd*,[158] where a celebrity couple sought to restrain publication of wedding photographs by the defendant magazine in breach of exclusive rights agreed with a rival magazine, no interim injunction was granted. Although the test in s.12(3) was satisfied, the balance of convenience favoured the defendant in view of the publicity organised by the claimants.[159]

In *PJS v News Group Newspapers Ltd*,[160] a newspaper sought to publish details of the private sexual activities of one member of a famous celebrity couple. The couple had young children. The question before the Supreme Court was whether an interlocutory injunction restraining publication ought to be granted. Lord Mance analysed the question through the lens of s.12(4) of the Human Rights Act 1998 and concluded that an injunction should be issued. While the court must pay particular regard to the right of freedom of expression, this does not enhance the weight given to art.10 rights as against other ECHR rights (in this case art.8).[161] Given that the proposed information was simply a "kiss and tell" story, there would be no public interest in its publication.[162] There was a little more to be said on the point of the material being available to the public. It was easy to discover the identities of the couple through an internet search, and newspaper stories had been published in other jurisdictions (including Scotland). However, the court could still take account of differences in the way the material would be available: there is a distinction between information being prominently displayed in a major national newspaper and information being accessible only to those who seek it out on the internet.[163]

(d) Trade Disputes.   After the decision in *American Cyanamid*, provisions   **28–037**
now found in s.221(2) of the Trade Union and Labour Relations (Consolidation) Act 1992 were enacted, providing that where, in an application for an interlocutory injunction, the defendant claims that he acted in contemplation or furtherance of a trade dispute, the court in exercising its discretion is to have regard to the likelihood of the defendant's establishing at the trial any of the matters which, under the Act, confer immunity from tortious liability.[164] Thus *American Cyanamid* is modified in trade dispute cases by the opportunity for the defendant to prove a prima facie defence under the labour relations legislation.

The reason for this amendment was that applications for injunctions in industrial disputes rarely went beyond the interlocutory stage, and if *American*

---

[157] *Cream Holdings Ltd v Banerjee* [2005] 1 A.C. 253; *CC v AB* [2007] 2 F.L.R. 301; *Browne of Madingley (Lord) v Associated Newspapers Ltd* [2008] Q.B. 103.

[158] [2001] Q.B. 967; N. Moreham (2001) 64 M.L.R. 767.

[159] This outcome was later criticised: *Douglas v Hello! Ltd (No.3)* [2006] Q.B. 125 at [253].

[160] [2016] UKSC 26; [2016] A.C. 1081; J. Rowbottom (2017) 133 L.Q.R. 177; O. Butler (2016) 75 C.L.J. 452.

[161] [2016] A.C. 1081 at [19]–[20]; *Re S (A Child) (Identification: Restrictions on Publication)* [2005] 1 A.C. 593.

[162] [2016] A.C. 1081 at [21]–[24]. Contrast *Campbell v MGN Ltd* [2004] 2 A.C. 457.

[163] [2016] A.C. 1081 at [34]. Lord Toulson dissented on this point: at [89]–[90].

[164] See s.219 of the 1992 Act.

Cyanamid was applied without modification, the balance of convenience would invariably favour the claimant (i.e. the employer),[165] thus denying the trade unions their power to pressurise employers. Industrial action is unlikely to be effective if it has to be postponed, thus the unions' bargaining counter would disappear.

Section 221(2) of the 1992 Act requires the court to "have regard" to the likelihood of the defence of statutory immunity succeeding at the trial. Thus the injunction will not normally be granted where the likelihood is that this defence would succeed.[166] But even in such a case the court retains a residual discretion which it may exercise in favour of granting the injunction, for example if the industrial action "endangers the nation or puts at risk such fundamental rights as the right of the public to be informed and the freedom of the Press,"[167] or "would probably have an immediate and devastating effect on the applicant's person or property" or would "cause immediate serious danger to public safety or health."[168] But such cases would be "altogether exceptional", because, "When disaster threatens, it is ordinarily for the government, not the courts, to act to avert it."[169]

28-038   *(e)   Injunctions to Restrain the Presentation of a Winding-up Petition.*   It has been held that a prima facie case (of abuse of process) is still required where a company seeks to restrain a creditor from presenting a winding-up petition.[170] If a prospective petitioner intends to petition on the basis of a debt alleged to be presently due, and there is a bona fide dispute as to whether it is presently due, it has been held by the Court of Appeal that the company is entitled as of right to an interlocutory injunction restraining the presentation of the petition, other than on the basis of a contingent or future debt.[171]

Difficulty was also experienced in applying the *American Cyanamid* rules where a company sought an interlocutory injunction to restrain a takeover bid.[172]

28-039   *(f)   Search Orders.*   The search order, formerly known as an *Anton Piller* injunction,[173] has been held to require an extremely strong prima facie case.[174]

---

[165] Especially in public service disputes, where public interest is relevant to the balance of convenience; see *Beaverbrook Newspapers Ltd v Keys* [1978] I.R.L.R. 34.

[166] As to the degree of likelihood necessary to produce this result, see *Duport Steels Ltd v Sirs* [1980] 1 W.L.R. 142; *Hadmor Productions Ltd v Hamilton* [1983] 1 A.C. 191.

[167] *Express Newspapers Ltd v MacShane* [1980] A.C. 672 at 695, per Lord Scarman. See also the views of Lords Diplock and Scarman in *NWL Ltd v Woods* [1979] 1 W.L.R. 1294.

[168] *Duport Steels Ltd v Sirs* [1980] 1 W.L.R. 142 at 166, per Lord Fraser.

[169] [1980] 1 W.L.R. 142 at 171. The existence of this residual discretion has been challenged; Lord Wedderburn and R. Simpson (1980) 43 M.L.R. 319 at 326–327.

[170] *Bryanston Finance Ltd v De Vries (No.2)* [1976] Ch. 63. Buckley LJ, at 78, regarded this as a "special factor". The other members of the Court of Appeal said that *American Cyanamid* did not apply.

[171] *Stonegate Securities Ltd v Gregory* [1980] Ch. 576 (*American Cyanamid* was not cited).

[172] *Dunford & Elliott Ltd v Johnson & Firth Brown Ltd* [1977] 1 Lloyd's Rep. 505. Lord Denning MR held that the *American Cyanamid* principles did not apply, but Lawton and Roskill LJJ preferred to apply those principles, notwithstanding the difficulties.

[173] *Anton Piller KG v Manufacturing Processes Ltd* [1976] Ch. 55.

[174] Below, para.28–072.

The order is an exceptional case because such applications are usually without notice, and because of the "draconian" nature of the injunction.[175]

C. Mandatory Interlocutory Injunctions

American Cyanamid itself involved a prohibitory injunction, but the principles there expressed were not confined to such applications and the Privy Council has confirmed that they apply generally to mandatory interlocutory injunctions.[176] Their Lordships commented that arguments over the prohibitory or mandatory classification of injunctions were "barren", and held that the "least irremediable prejudice" principle applies to both. However, it is still the case that manadatory interlocutory injunctions will be granted less readily[177]:

28–040

> "What is true is that the features which ordinarily justify describing an injunction as mandatory are often more likely to cause irremediable prejudice than in cases in which a defendant is merely prevented from taking or continuing with some course of action."

If it appeared likely that the injunction would cause irremediable prejudice to the defendant, the court would be reluctant to grant it unless satisfied that the chances that it would turn out at the trial to have been wrongly granted were low.[178]

Mandatory interlocutory injunctions will be granted in a suitable case, for example, to compel the demolition of a building where the defendant has deliberately hurried on with the building,[179] to reinstate a wrongfully evicted occupier to possession[180]; to enforce the return of passports wrongfully detained by the police[181]; to compel performance of a landlord's obligations[182]; to enforce the planning legislation[183]; to compel surrender of an unlawful sublease[184]; or, in the search order cases,[185] to compel the defendant to submit articles for inspection.

The court will be reluctant to grant such an injunction where the case involves an industrial dispute,[186] but will do so in exceptional circumstances if the balance

---

[175] See *Yousif v Salama* [1980] 1 W.L.R. 1540 at 1544; below, para.28–072; *Derby & Co Ltd v Weldon (No.7)* [1990] 1 W.L.R. 1156 at 1173.

[176] *National Commercial Bank Jamaica Ltd v Olint Corp Ltd (Practice Note)* [2009] 1 W.L.R. 1405.

[177] *National Commercial Bank Jamaica Ltd v Olint Corp Ltd (Practice Note)* [2009] 1 W.L.R. 1405 at 1409.

[178] cf. *Shepherd Homes Ltd v Sandham* [1971] Ch. 340, where Megarry J said that, in the case of a mandatory interlocutory injunction, the court must feel "a high degree of assurance" that at the trial it will appear that the injunction was rightly granted.

[179] *Von Joel v Hornsey* [1895] 2 Ch. 774; *London & Manchester Assurance Co Ltd v O&H Construction Ltd* [1989] 2 E.G.L.R. 185.

[180] *Luganda v Service Hotels* [1969] 2 Ch. 209; *Parsons v Nasar* (1991) 23 H.L.R. 1.

[181] *Ghani v Jones* [1970] 1 Q.B. 693; cf. *Malone v Metropolitan Police Commissioner* [1980] Q.B. 49.

[182] *Hart v Emelkirk Ltd* [1983] 1 W.L.R. 1289; *Peninsular Maritime Ltd v Padseal Ltd* (1981) 259 E.G. 860. See also *Cork v Cork* [1997] 1 E.G.L.R. 5.

[183] *Croydon LBC v Gladden* (1994) 68 P. & C.R. 300 (removal of replica spitfire from roof).

[184] *Hemingway Securities Ltd v Dunraven Ltd* [1995] 1 E.G.L.R. 61.

[185] Below, para.28–072.

[186] *Meade v Haringey LBC* [1979] 1 W.L.R. 637 (no injunction to reopen schools closed by a strike); cf. *Express Newspapers Ltd v Keys* [1980] I.R.L.R. 247, where the dispute was political.

of convenience so requires. Such a case was *Parker v Camden LBC*,[187] where a strike of boilermen was endangering the life and health of council tenants. The court was prepared to grant a mandatory interlocutory injunction to resume the supply of heating and hot water.

It has been held, in a case concerning trespass by building operations, that if the claimant could have got a prohibitory quia timet injunction to restrain the commission of the wrongful act, had she known about it in time, then the defendant should be in no better position if he in fact commits the act: a mandatory interlocutory injunction should be granted to enforce the removal of the building works.[188]

The following are cases where a mandatory interlocutory injunction was clearly required:

> In *Esso Petroleum Co Ltd v Kingswood Motors*,[189] the defendant agreed with the claimant not to sell a garage without first procuring that the purchaser would enter a solus agreement[190] with the claimant. The land was sold to a purchaser who conspired with the defendant to effect a breach. A mandatory interlocutory injunction was granted to compel a retransfer of the land to the defendant. There could be no clearer case of inducing breach of contract, and damages would be wholly inadequate.

> In *Sky Petroleum v VIP Petroleum Ltd*,[191] such an injunction was granted to enforce a contract to supply petrol to the claimant. As there was no alternative supply, damages would be inadequate, and the claimant might be forced out of business unless the court intervened.

> In *Evans v BBC and IBA*,[192] an order was made to compel the television authorities to show a party political broadcast. On the balance of probabilities there was a contract with the Welsh Nationalist Party to broadcast it. Damages would be manifestly useless, as the election was about to take place. In such a case the court should take the risk of it turning out that there was no contract.

D. Conditions and Undertakings

28–041 On the grant of an interlocutory injunction, the claimant is normally required to give an undertaking in damages[193] in the event that the injunction is discharged at the trial as having been granted without good cause[194]; but a defendant may also be put on similar terms as a condition of an injunction not being granted.[195] One reason for the practice of undertakings is that it aids the court in achieving its object of abstaining from expressing any opinion on the merits until the hearing.[196] While an undertaking by the claimant is exacted for the benefit of the

---

[187] [1986] Ch. 162.
[188] *Trenberth (John) Ltd v National Westminster Bank Ltd* (1979) 39 P. & C.R. 104.
[189] [1974] Q.B. 142; *Hemingway Securities Ltd v Dunraven Ltd* [1995] 1 E.G.L.R. 61.
[190] A solus agreement would provide that the purchaser would deal only with the claimant.
[191] [1974] 1 W.L.R. 576 (the injunction was negative in form, but mandatory in substance).
[192] *The Times*, 26 February 1974.
[193] Or to do some other act; *PS Refson & Co Ltd v Saggers* [1984] 1 W.L.R. 1025. See generally A. Zuckerman (1994) 53 C.L.J. 546; S. Gee [2006] L.M.C.L.Q. 181.
[194] Search orders and asset-freezing injunctions, below, paras 28–072, 28–075, provide good examples of the need for undertakings. See *Digital Equipment Corp v Darkcrest Ltd* [1984] Ch. 512.
[195] *Elwes v Payne* (1879) 12 Ch.D. 468.
[196] *American Cyanamid Co v Ethicon Ltd* [1975] A.C. 396 at 407.

defendant, it is not a contract with the defendant. The undertaking is given to the court, so that non-performance is a contempt of court and not a breach of contract.[197] Enforcement is at the court's discretion.[198] Damages will normally become payable if the claimant is unsuccessful at the trial, either because she cannot establish her case or because the judge who granted the interlocutory injunction took a wrong view of the law. The claimant may be required to give security or to pay the money into court. Any damages will be assessed on the same basis as damages for breach of contract.[199] Aggravated and exemplary damages may be awarded if appropriate.[200] A claimant's refusal to seek an interlocutory injunction, in order to avoid the need to give an undertaking, is not a ground for striking out her application for a final injunction,[201] but is a factor to be taken into account.[202]

In *Hoffman-La Roche (F) & Co v Secretary of State for Trade and Industry*,[203] the question arose whether the Crown should be required to give an undertaking as a condition of the grant of an interlocutory injunction to restrain the company from charging prices for drugs in excess of those specified in an order (which the company claimed was ultra vires). The House of Lords held that the undertaking should not be required.

Their Lordships held that a distinction had to be drawn between two cases: first, where the Crown was asserting a proprietary or contractual right, the ordinary rule applied and the Crown should give an undertaking; but, secondly, where an injunction was sought to enforce the law, the defendant must show special reason why justice required that it should not be granted, or should only be granted on terms. The present case was within the second category. The reason for this distinction is that where a person is prosecuted and acquitted, he may suffer loss but cannot normally recover from the prosecutor. There is therefore no reason why the Crown should incur liability when an injunction is sought to enforce the law.

This principle has been applied to a local authority seeking a law-enforcement injunction,[204] to the former Financial Services Authority while acting in its capacity as a regulator,[205] and to a foreign regulatory body.[206] It also applies

---

[197] See *Hussain v Hussain* [1986] Fam. 134; *Mid Suffolk DC v Clarke* [2007] 1 W.L.R. 980. But the undertaking may include a contractual obligation to the other party; *Midland Marts Ltd v Hobday* [1989] 1 W.L.R. 1143.

[198] *Cheltenham and Gloucester Building Society v Ricketts* [1993] 1 W.L.R. 1545.

[199] *Hoffman-La Roche (F) & Co v Secretary of State for Trade and Industry* [1975] A.C. 295 at 361, per Lord Diplock. See generally S. Ralston (2011) 127 L.Q.R. 180.

[200] *Al-Rawas v Pegasus Energy Ltd* [2009] 1 All E.R. 346.

[201] *Oxy Electric Ltd v Zainuddin* [1991] 1 W.L.R. 115, doubting *Blue Town Investments Ltd v Higgs & Hill Plc* [1990] 1 W.L.R. 696. The final injunction in *Oxy Electric* was later refused; [1990] E.G.C.S. 128.

[202] *Snell & Prideaux Ltd v Dutton Mirrors Ltd* [1995] 1 E.G.L.R. 259.

[203] [1975] A.C. 295. The statute in question expressly provided for the grant to the Crown of an injunction as the only means of enforcing the statute.

[204] *Kirklees BC v Wickes Building Supplies Ltd* [1993] A.C. 227 (Sunday trading); *Director General of Fair Trading v Tobyward* Ltd [1989] 1 W.L.R. 517. See also *Securities and Investments Board v Lloyd-Wright* [1993] 4 All E.R. 210; *Customs and Excise Commissioners v Anchor Foods Ltd* [1999] 1 W.L.R. 1139.

[205] *FSA v Sinaloa Gold Plc* [2013] UKSC 11; [2013] 2 A.C. 28; J. Varuhas and P. Turner (2014) 130 L.Q.R. 33.

where the Attorney General acts ex officio to enforce the law by injunction. But where the Attorney General brings the action under the relator procedure, the relator must give the usual undertaking,[207] as must a local authority acting as a relator.[208]

6.   QUIA TIMET INJUNCTIONS

28–042   A quia timet injunction may be available where the injury to the claimant's rights has not yet occurred, but is feared or threatened. The injunction may be perpetual or interlocutory, prohibitory or mandatory. It may further be subdivided into two broad categories:

> "[F]irst, where the defendant[209] has as yet done no hurt to the [claimant] but is threatening and intending (so the [claimant] alleges) to do works which will render irreparable harm to him or his property if carried to completion ... those cases are normally, though not exclusively, concerned with negative injunctions. Secondly, the type of case where the [claimant] has been fully recompensed both at law and in equity for the damage he has suffered but where he alleges that the earlier actions of the defendant may lead to future causes of action... It is in this field that the undoubted jurisdiction of equity to grant a mandatory injunction ... finds its main expression."[210]

How serious must the fears of the claimant be, and how grave the suspected damage? As Lord Dunedin said, it is not sufficient to say "timeo".[211] The requirements have been described in the following terms: a strong case of probability[212]; proof of imminent danger; and there must also be proof that the apprehended damage will, if it comes, be very substantial.[213] Thus, in *Attorney General v Nottingham Corp*,[214] a quia timet injunction was not granted to restrain the corporation from building a smallpox hospital, as there was no proof of genuine danger to nearby residents.

The principles applicable to the grant of a mandatory quia timet injunction were laid down by the House of Lords in *Redland Bricks Ltd v Morris*.[215]

---

[206] *United States Securities & Exchange Commission v Manterfield* [2010] 1 W.L.R. 172.

[207] *Hoffman-La Roche (F) & Co v Secretary of State for Trade and Industry* [1975] A.C. 295 at 363.

[208] *Kirklees BC v Wickes Building Supplies Ltd* [1993] A.C. 227.

[209] The defendant must have threatened the act in question: see *Celsteel Ltd v Alton House Holdings Ltd* [1986] 1 W.L.R. 512 (no injunction against freeholder where act threatened by tenant).

[210] *Redland Bricks Ltd v Morris* [1970] A.C. 652 at 665, per Lord Upjohn. See also *Hooper v Rogers* [1975] Ch. 43; *Allen v Greenhi Builders Ltd* [1979] 1 W.L.R. 136 (registration as "pending land action").

[211] *Attorney General for the Dominion of Canada v Ritchie Contracting and Supply Co Ltd* [1919] A.C. 999 at 1005: (timeo is Latin for "I am afraid"); *ERY v Associated Newspapers Ltd* [2016] EWHC 2760 (QB) at [41].

[212] *Attorney General v Manchester Corp* [1893] 2 Ch. 87 at 92.

[213] *Fletcher v Bealey* (1885) 27 Ch.D. 688 at 698. cf. *Trenberth (John) Ltd v National Westminster Bank Ltd* (1979) 39 P. & C.R. 104.

[214] [1904] 1 Ch. 673; *Attorney General v Guardian Newspapers (No.2)* [1990] 1 A.C. 109 (no general injunction against publication of any material the media might obtain from Crown servants in breach of confidence). See also *British Data Management Plc v Boxer Commercial Removals Plc* [1996] 3 All E.R. 707 (libel); *Re Q's Estate* [1999] 1 Lloyd's Rep. 931 (asset freezing).

[215] [1970] A.C. 652.

The defendant company's digging activities caused landslips on the claimants' adjoining property, which they used as a market garden. The claimants' land, of which about one-tenth of an acre was affected, was worth about £12,000, but the cost of remedying the landslips would be about £30,000. The claimants were awarded damages, a prohibitory injunction to restrain further withdrawal of support, and a mandatory injunction that the defendants "take all necessary steps to restore support within six months. But the House of Lords allowed the defendant's appeal against the grant of the mandatory injunction on the ground that it did not specify exactly what it had to do.

Lord Upjohn set out the following four principles applicable to the grant of a mandatory quia timet injunction.[216]

    i.   The claimant must show a very strong probability that grave damage will accrue to him in the future. It is a jurisdiction to be exercised sparingly and with caution, but, in the proper case, unhesitatingly.

    ii.   Damages will not be an adequate remedy if such damage does happen, applying the general principle of equity.

    iii.   Unlike the case where a negative injunction is granted to prevent the continuance or recurrence of a wrongful act, the cost to the defendant to do works to prevent or lessen the likelihood of a future apprehended wrong must be taken into account:

        (a)   where the defendant has acted wantonly and quite unreasonably, he may be ordered to do positive work even if the expense to him is out of all proportion to the advantage thereby accruing to the claimant;

        (b)   but where the defendant has acted reasonably, although wrongly, the cost of remedying his earlier activities is most important. If it seems unreasonable to inflict such expenditure on one who is no more than a potential wrongdoer the court must exercise its jurisdiction accordingly. The court may order works which may not remedy the wrong but may lessen the likelihood of further injury. It must be borne in mind that the injury may never in fact occur, and that, if it does, the claimant may then seek the appropriate legal or equitable remedy.

    iv.   If a mandatory injunction is granted, the court must see that the defendant knows exactly in fact what he has to do.[217]

7.   DEFENCES

A.   Delay

As in the case of specific performance, laches may be a defence even though the claimant's rights have not become statute-barred.[218] But a smaller degree of delay will defeat a claim for an interlocutory injunction than is necessary in the case of a perpetual injunction.[219] This is because, if an interlocutory claim is dismissed, the claimant is not unduly prejudiced, as she can still seek a perpetual injunction. But the refusal of a perpetual injunction amounts to a final dismissal.

28–043

The claimant must act promptly in the case of an injunction without notice, as any delay illustrates that her case is not urgent.[220] Where the claimant has delayed her application for an interlocutory injunction, she is unlikely to establish that it

---

[216] [1970] A.C. 652 at 665–666 (the text is a close paraphrasing of Lord Upjohn's speech).

[217] See also *Harold Stephen & Co Ltd v Post Office* [1977] 1 W.L.R. 1172; *Parsons v Nasar* (1991) 23 H.L.R. 1; *Co-operative Insurance Society Ltd v Argyll Stores (Holdings) Ltd* [1998] A.C. 1.

[218] See Limitation Act 1980 s.36.

[219] *Johnson v Wyatt* (1863) 2 De G.J. & S. 18.

[220] *Bates v Lord Hailsham of St Marylebone* [1972] 1 W.L.R. 1373.

would be unreasonable to make her wait until trial. An unexplained delay of five months prevented the grant of an interlocutory injunction in *Shepherd Homes Ltd v Sandham*,[221] where Megarry J explained that if the injunction is also mandatory, any delay by the claimant will mean that the injunction, if granted, would disturb rather than preserve the status quo.[222] It may be otherwise, however, if there is no arguable defence.[223]

The authorities are not reconcilable on the question of delay in perpetual injunctions. It is sometimes said that laches is no defence,[224] or, to go to the other extreme, that mere lapse of time is a bar.[225] In *Kelsen v Imperial Tobacco Co Ltd*[226] a mandatory injunction was granted to restrain a trespass even though it appeared that the state of affairs had existed for seven years. In *Fullwood v Fullwood*,[227] Fry J held that a delay of two to three years was no defence, on the ground that mere lapse of time unaccompanied by acquiescence was no bar unless the legal right itself was barred.

28-044   In *HP Bulmer Ltd & Showerings Ltd v Bollinger SA*,[228] the appellants had described their products as "champagne perry" and "champagne cider" since 1950 and 1906 respectively. The latter usage had been known to the respondents since about 1930. Injunctions were granted in the High Court to restrain both descriptions. The defence of delay failed. This was a continuing wrong, and the right in question was legal. Whitford J held that in such a case the delay must be "inordinate" if it is to prevent the grant of an injunction. Here it was not, because advice had to be sought, and interests consulted. One injunction was discharged by the Court of Appeal because passing-off was not established, but their Lordships considered that the injunction would not have been refused on account of delay. Goff LJ thought that "inordinate" delay would be a ground for refusing an injunction, even in the case of a legal right, but that delay in the present case was not of that order. The issue was also aired in one of the final decisions of the House of Lords, in a case where the claimant sought a declaration to recognise his entitlement to royalties in connection with his organ solo in 1967 in the highly successful recording of the song "A Whiter Shade of Pale".[229] There was no statutory limitation period, but he had delayed 38 years in making the claim. As a declaration as to the existence of a long term property right was not equitable relief, it could not be barred by laches or acquiescence. In any event, no prejudice to the defendants resulting from the delay, which would be necessary if the defence had been available, had been shown.

---

[221] [1971] Ch. 340; cf. *Texaco Ltd v Mulberry Filling Station Ltd* [1972] 1 W.L.R. 814; *Express Newspapers Plc v Liverpool Daily Post and Echo Plc* [1985] 1 W.L.R. 1089; *Newport Association Football Club Ltd v Football Association of Wales Ltd* [1995] 2 All E.R. 87 (explanation for delay).

[222] See *Shotton v Hammond* (1976) 120 S.J. 780 (mandatory interlocutory injunction granted in spite of delay of six weeks by the claimant, who was not legally aided).

[223] See *Patel v WH Smith (Eziot) Ltd* [1987] 1 W.L.R. 853.

[224] *Archbold v Scully* (1861) 9 H.L.C. 360 at 383.

[225] *Brooks v Muckleston* [1909] 2 Ch. 519.

[226] [1957] 2 Q.B. 334; cf. *Lester v Woodgate* [2010] 2 P. & C.R. 21.

[227] (1878) 9 Ch.D. 176.

[228] [1977] 2 C.M.L.R. 625; cf. *Vine Products Ltd v McKenzie & Co Ltd* (1969) R.P.C. 1 (no injunction to restrain description as "sherry", the usage having been common knowledge for 100 years). See also *Erlanger v New Sombrero Phosphate Co* (1873) 3 App.Cas. 1218 at 1279–1280.

[229] *Fisher v Brooker* [2009] 1 W.L.R. 1764.

Laches may be regarded more strictly if third parties would be affected. It is possible that a claimant who has delayed will be awarded damages in lieu of an injunction under Lord Cairns' Act.[230]

It has been suggested that a longer delay is required before a claimant will be refused an injunction where the right is legal than where it is equitable[231]; or alternatively that a less strict view of laches might be taken as to matters within equity's exclusive jurisdiction, such as a breach of trust, where there is no alternative remedy at law.[232] But the Court of Appeal has described the distinction between legal and equitable rights in this context as archaic and arcane.[233]

Finally, where an injunction is sought in a claim for judicial review, it is provided that, in the case of "undue delay", the injunction may be refused if the granting of relief "would be likely to cause substantial hardship to, or substantially prejudice the rights of, any person or would be detrimental to good administration."[234]

B.   Acquiescence[235]

Lapse of time will be taken into account in that it may indicate acquiescence. It is, **28–045** of course, possible to find acquiescence without delay and delay without acquiescence but there is normally some overlap.[236] As in the case of laches, a greater degree of acquiescence is needed to defeat a claim for a final injunction than an interlocutory injunction. In *Richards v Revitt*,[237] it was said that the fact that the claimant has previously overlooked trivial breaches of covenant does not debar him, on the ground of acquiescence, from acting on a serious breach. A leading authority is *Sayers v Collyer*,[238] where a house was being used as a beershop in breach of covenant. The claimant could not get an injunction, as he had known of the breach for three years, and, furthermore, had bought beer there. This was sufficient to bar any remedy. But a lesser degree of acquiescence, while not sufficient to bar the action completely, might be a reason for giving damages in lieu of an injunction under Lord Cairns' Act.

In *Shaw v Applegate*,[239] the claimant sought to enforce a covenant entered into by the defendant in 1967 not to use his land as an amusement arcade. Breaches of covenant occurred from about 1971. The claimant was aware of the facts but was unsure whether they constituted

---

[230] *Shelfer v City of London Electric Lighting Co* [1895] 1 Ch. 287 at 322; see also *Bracewell v Appleby* [1975] Ch. 408; *Ketley v Gooden* (1997) 73 P. & C.R. 305.

[231] *Cluett Peabody & Co Inc v McIntyre Hogg Marsh and Co Ltd* [1958] R.P.C. 335 at 354, per Upjohn J; *HP Bulmer and Showerings Ltd v J Bollinger SA* [1977] 2 C.M.L.R. 625.

[232] See Spry, *Equitable Remedies*, 9th edn (2014), p.453; *Knight v Bowyer* (1858) 2 De G. & J. 421; cf. *Oxy Electric Ltd v Zainuddin* [1990] E.G.C.S. 128 (final injunction to enforce restrictive covenant refused because of seven month delay).

[233] *Habib Bank Ltd v Habib Bank AG Zurich* [1981] 1 W.L.R. 1265 at 1285 and 1287; cf. Spry, p.452.

[234] Senior Courts Act 1981 s.31(6); CPR 1998, Pt 54.5.

[235] See Limitation Act 1980 s.36(2). The Act does not affect this defence.

[236] See the discussion in *Fisher v Brooker* [2009] 1 W.L.R. 1764.

[237] (1877) 7 Ch.D. 224 at 226.

[238] (1885) 28 Ch.D. 103.

[239] [1977] 1 W.L.R. 970. See also on this point *Sayers v Collyer* (1885) 28 Ch.D. 103 at 110.

a breach of covenant. He began proceedings for an injunction in 1973, but did not seek interlocutory relief, so that the defendant continued to carry on his business, investing money and building up goodwill, until the trial in 1976. It was held that the claimant was not guilty of such a degree of acquiescence as to bar all remedies, the real test being whether, on the facts of the particular case, it would be dishonest or unconscionable for him to seek to enforce his rights.[240] This was not the case, because of the claimant's doubts as to his legal rights. But there was sufficient acquiescence to bar the remedy of an injunction because the defendant had been lulled into a false sense of security by the claimant's inactivity and failure to seek interlocutory relief. Thus the appropriate remedy was damages in lieu of an injunction under Lord Cairns' Act.

Similarly in *Gafford v Graham*,[241] where the claimant sought mandatory and prohibitory injunctions to demolish a building erected in breach of covenant and to restrain an unlawful use of the land. In the case of one breach where, knowing of his rights, he had failed to complain for three years, all relief was barred by acquiescence. In the case of another breach, the claimant had acted promptly but had not sought interlocutory relief. This was an important factor which made a final injunction inappropriate, thus damages were awarded.

The modern approach to acquiescence is to enquire:

(a)   whether the defendant was encouraged to believe he was entitled to act as he did; and

(b)   if so, whether the encouragement caused detriment; and

(c)   if so, whether it was unconscionable in all the circumstances for the claimant to assert his legal rights.[242]

C.   Hardship

28–046   Hardship to the defendant is a relevant consideration in injunctions, as we also saw in specific performance.[243] It is perhaps of more weight in the case of an interlocutory injunction than in the case of a final injunction, where the infringement of the claimant's rights has been established. Hardship may also carry more weight in the case of mandatory injunctions.[244] Damages may be awarded in lieu of an injunction under Lord Cairns' Act if the injunction would be oppressive to the defendant.[245]

The element of hardship to the defendant might be overcome in appropriate cases by granting an injunction but suspending its operation.[246] Even if there is no hardship to the defendant, an injunction may be refused if it would prejudice an innocent third party.[247]

---

[240] [1977] 1 W.L.R. 970 at 978. See also *HP Bulmer & Showerings Ltd v J Bollinger SA* [1977] 2 C.M.L.R. 625 at 682; *Blue Town Investments Ltd v Higgs and Hill Plc* [1990] 1 W.L.R. 696.

[241] (1999) 77 P. & C.R. 73.

[242] *Jones v Stones* [1999] 1 W.L.R. 1739; *Harris v Williams-Wynne* [2006] 2 P. & C.R. 27.

[243] Above, para.27–038. See *Shell UK Ltd v Lostock Garages Ltd* [1976] 1 W.L.R. 1187.

[244] *Attorney General v Colchester Corp* [1955] 2 Q.B. 207; *Gravesham BC v British Railways Board* [1978] Ch. 379 (a mandatory injunction would not be granted to compel the running of a ferry at a heavy loss, which would benefit few passengers).

[245] See *Shaw v Applegate* [1977] 1 W.L.R. 970 at 978–979.

[246] Above, para.28–021.

[247] *Maythorn v Palmer* (1864) 11 L.T. 261; cf. *PSM International Plc v Whitehouse and Willenhall Automation Ltd* [1992] I.R.L.R. 279.

It has previously been noted that the disproportionate cost of complying with a mandatory quia timet injunction may be a ground for refusing the grant if the defendant has acted reasonably.[248] Lord Upjohn, however, thought that such considerations would not be taken into account in the case of a negative injunction to prevent the continuance or recurrence of a wrongful act; any argument by the wrongdoer that the injunction would be very costly to him, perhaps by preventing him from carrying out a contract with a third party, would carry little weight.

D. Conduct of the Claimant

The claimant must come to equity with clean hands. If, therefore, he is in breach of his own obligations, or otherwise guilty of unfair conduct,[249] he will not be granted an injunction, although trifling breaches may not disentitle him.[250] Similarly, he who comes to equity must do equity, therefore the claimant will not succeed if he is unable or unwilling to carry out his own future obligations.[251]   **28–047**

But the defence of "clean hands" must be related to the subject-matter of the dispute, and does not embrace the claimant's general conduct. Thus in *Argyll (Duchess) v Argyll (Duke)*,[252] the fact that the wife's conduct had caused the divorce was no answer to her claim to an injunction to restrain a breach of confidence by her husband. In *Hubbard v Vosper*,[253] one reason for refusing the interlocutory injunction was that the claimant had not come with clean hands, in that he had protected his secrets by deplorable means, namely by a private criminal code for dealing with the "enemies" of Scientology.

E. The Public Interest

In *Miller v Jackson*,[254] a cricket club committed the torts of nuisance and negligence in allowing cricket balls to land on the claimants' property. An injunction was refused by the Court of Appeal because the public interest in enabling the inhabitants of the area to enjoy the benefits of outdoor recreation prevailed over the claimants' private right to quiet enjoyment of their house and garden. Damages of £400 for past and future inconvenience were awarded instead.[255]   **28–048**

---

[248] *Redland Bricks Ltd v Morris* [1970] A.C. 652 at 666.

[249] *Shell UK Ltd v Lostock Garages Ltd* [1976] 1 W.L.R. 1187. See also *Royal Bank of Scotland Plc v Highland Financial Partners LP* [2013] EWCA Civ 328.

[250] *Besant v Wood* (1879) 12 Ch.D. 605.

[251] *Measures v Measures* [1910] 2 Ch. 248; *Chappell v Times Newspapers Ltd* [1975] 1 W.L.R. 482 (employees failed to obtain injunction to restrain their dismissal where they refused to give an undertaking not to strike).

[252] [1967] Ch. 302. See also *Fiona Trust & Holding Corp v Privalov* [2008] EWHC 1748 (Comm).

[253] [1972] 2 Q.B. 84.

[254] [1977] Q.B. 966.

[255] Under Lord Cairns' Act; below, para.28–050.

In *Lawrence v Fen Tigers Ltd*,[256] the Supreme Court held that the public interest is not relevant to the initial question of whether or not an activity could constitute a legal nuisance. However, the public interest may well be relevant to the next question of whether to grant an injunction or award damages in lieu. In *Lawrence v Fen Tigers*, the existence of planning permission in respect of a sports stadium did not mean that the noise emitted from that stadium was not a nuisance actionable by local residents. Nonetheless, that planning permission would indicate that an award of damages may be preferred to the granting of an injunction.

28–049 The existence and scope of the public interest defence has been of particular importance in cases concerning confidential information and privacy. We have already seen that, in cases where the material in question is journalistic, literary or artistic, the court must have particular regard to the public interest in deciding whether to award an injunction.[257] More generally, injunctions will be refused if the public interest in the preservation of confidence is overridden by some other public interest. It is not enough that the information is a matter of public interest: the test is whether it is in the public interest that the duty of confidence should be breached.[258] Matters such as confidentiality or national security[259] must be balanced against the public interest in freedom of speech and the press and the right to receive information.

Under the general law there is no confidence in "iniquity".[260] This principle was discussed by the House of Lords in *Attorney General v Guardian Newspapers Ltd (No.2)*,[261] where the question was whether newspapers should be enjoined from publishing *Spycatcher* (the memoirs of Peter Wright, a former member of the security services). It was said that the "iniquity" defence was subject to two limitations. First, the disclosure of confidential information revealing wrong-doing should in some cases be to interested parties such as the police rather than to the public at large.[262] Secondly, the duty of confidence was not overridden by mere allegations of wrong-doing. While the wrong-doing need not be proved, there must be at least a prima facie case. Further, it was not the

---

[256] *Coventry v Lawrence* [2014] UKSC 13; rep. sub. nom. *Lawrence v Fen Tigers Ltd* [2014] A.C. 822; D. Howarth (2014) 73 C.L.J. 247; E. Lees [2014] Conv. 449; below, para.28–052.

[257] Human Rights Act s.12(4); above, para.28–036. The subsection applies to interlocutory and perpetual injunctions.

[258] *Prince of Wales v Associated Newspapers Ltd* [2008] Ch. 57 (publication of private diaries); *Mosley v News Group Newspapers Ltd* [2008] E.M.L.R. 20 (disclosure of sado-masochistic activities); K. Hughes (2009) 125 L.Q.R. 244.

[259] *Attorney General v Guardian Newspapers Ltd* [1987] 1 W.L.R. 1248, and *(No.2)* [1990] 1 A.C. 109 (*Spycatcher*).

[260] *Gartside v Outram* (1857) 26 L.J. Ch. 113.

[261] [1990] 1 A.C. 109. The "iniquity" involved alleged plots to overthrow the Wilson government and to kill President Nasser. See also *Finers v Miro* [1991] 1 W.L.R. 35 (fraud); *Commissioner of Police of Bermuda v Bermuda Broadcasting Co Ltd, The Times*, 24 January 2008 (corruption allegations about public figures).

[262] See *Francome v Mirror Group Newspapers* [1984] 1 W.L.R. 892 (injunction to restrain publication of illegally taped telephone conversations revealing possible criminal offences and breaches of Jockey Club regulations; public interest could be served by making tapes available to police or Jockey Club); cf. *Cork v McVicar, The Times*, 31 October 1984 (exposure of corrupt practices in the administration of justice not to be restrained by injunction; argument that disclosure should only be to the appropriate authorities rejected). See also *Re a Company's Application* [1989]

case that *any* breach of the law was within the "iniquity" defence. In the present case, the publication of the entire book or substantial extracts could not be within this defence when the allegations of "iniquity" covered only a few pages. The final injunction was, however, refused because the information was by this time within the public domain.

Where there is no wrong-doing by the claimant the public interest defence will succeed only in exceptional cases. Such a case was *Lion Laboratories Ltd v Evans*,[263] where the claimant failed to restrain the publication of confidential documents concerning the accuracy of a "breathalyser" device manufactured by the claimant. Confidentiality had to be weighed against the public interest in the accuracy of a device upon which depended liability to criminal penalties.

8. THE JURISDICTION UNDER LORD CAIRNS' ACT

The Chancery Amendment Act 1858, commonly known as Lord Cairns' Act, **28–050** gave to the Court of Chancery discretionary power to award damages either in addition to or in substitution for an injunction or specific performance.[264] The jurisdiction now derives from the Senior Courts Act 1981 s.50.

> "Where the Court of Appeal or the High Court has jurisdiction to entertain an application for an injunction or specific performance, it may award damages in addition to, or in substitution for, an injunction or specific performance."

The Chancery Division has, of course, been able, since the Judicature Act 1873, to award damages in any case where the common law courts could have done so, but these are common law damages. It will still be necessary to rely on Lord Cairns' Act where no damages would be available at law, for example in lieu of a quia timet injunction where no legal injury has yet occurred[265]; or if some damage has occurred but may continue in the future, and damages are awarded to cover future loss[266]; or where the claimant's right is exclusively equitable, as in the case of a restrictive covenant.[267] In other cases it will not be necessary to invoke Lord Cairns' Act and damages may be awarded at common law.

The discretion exercisable under Lord Cairns' Act is similar to the discretion which the court has had since the Judicature Act to grant injunctions or damages

---

Ch. 477; (no injunction to restrain disclosure to tax and regulatory authorities); *Woolgar v Chief Constable of Sussex Police* [2000] 1 W.L.R. 25 (no injunction to restrain disclosure to nursing regulatory body).

[263] [1985] Q.B. 526 (interlocutory).

[264] See generally J. Jolowicz (1975) 34 C.L.J. 224; T. Ingman and J. Wakefield [1981] Conv. 286; T. Ingman [1994] Conv. 110; P. McDermott, *Equitable Damages* (1994); K. Barnett and M. Bryan (2015) 9 J. Eq. 150.

[265] *Leeds Industrial Co-operative Society v Slack* [1924] A.C. 851; establishing the point after some doubt; *Hooper v Rogers* [1975] Ch. 43; *Johnson v Agnew* [1980] A.C. 367 at 400.

[266] See *Kennaway v Thompson* [1981] Q.B. 88. For the position under the Human Rights Act 1998 where the defendant is a public authority, see *Marcic v Thames Water Utilities Ltd (No.2)* [2002] Q.B. 1003.

[267] *Baxter v Four Oaks Properties Ltd* [1965] Ch. 816; *Wrotham Park Estate Ltd v Parkside Homes Ltd* [1974] 1 W.L.R. 798.

at common law, in cases where they are available. The principle is the same; the court will not give damages instead of an injunction if damages will not be adequate to protect the claimant's rights. The court will consider the principles set out in *Shelfer v City of London Electric Lighting Co*,[268] as clarified in *Lawrence v Fen Tigers Ltd*,[269] governing the award of damages under Lord Cairns' Act even where the claimant has a cause of action at law, and there is jurisdiction to award damages at law.[270]

Lord Cairns' Act enables the award of damages in lieu of a final (not interlocutory) injunction only if there is *jurisdiction* to grant one,[271] in the sense that the claimant has established a prima facie case for equitable relief. It does not matter that the injunction is refused on some discretionary ground, such as, for example, delay or acquiescence,[272] although delay may be a reason for moderation when assessing the damages.[273] Nor is it necessary for an injunction to have been claimed.[274] But if, by the time the action is commenced, the court could not award an injunction, then there will be no jurisdiction to award damages under Lord Cairns' Act either.[275] In such a case the claimant can be awarded common law damages, provided she has a cause of action at law.

A. Award of Damages under Lord Cairns' Act

28–051 If the claimant can establish that her rights have been infringed, she is prima facie entitled to an injunction.[276] Damages will only be awarded in lieu in special circumstances; otherwise the defendant would be allowed to "buy" the right to continue the wrongful act.[277] But when do such special circumstances exist?

The leading case is *Shelfer v City of London Lighting Co*,[278] a case of nuisance. A.L. Smith LJ laid down a "good working rule" that damages should only be awarded in lieu if all the following requirements were satisfied:

(i)   the injury to the claimant is small; and

(ii) the injury is capable of being estimated in monetary terms; and

---

[268] [1895] 1 Ch. 287; below para.28–051.

[269] [2014] A.C. 822; below, para.28–052.

[270] See *Kelsen v Imperial Tobacco Co Ltd* [1957] 2 Q.B. 334; *Woollerton and Wilson Ltd v Richard Costain Ltd* [1970] 1 W.L.R. 411.

[271] *Hooper v Rogers* [1975] Ch. 43 at 48; *Jaggard v Sawyer* [1995] 1 W.L.R. 269 at 285; *Morris-Garner v One Step (Support) Ltd* [2018] UKSC 20 at [45], [95(3)].

[272] *Shaw v Applegate* [1977] 1 W.L.R. 970; *Gafford v Graham* (1999) 77 P. & C.R. 73. Distinguish a case of *jurisdiction* being lost through the passage of time. See generally *Lavery v Pursell* (1883) 39 Ch.D. 508 at 519. The position is the same for specific performance, above, para.27–044.

[273] *Pell Frischmann Engineering Ltd v Bow Valley Iran Ltd* [2011] 1 W.L.R. 2370 at [54].

[274] *Pell Frischmann Engineering Ltd v Bow Valley Iran Ltd* [2011] 1 W.L.R. 2370 at [48]. Lord Reed expressed some doubt about this in *Morris-Garner v One Step (Support) Ltd* [2018] UKSC 20 at [45], but the point was not decided.

[275] *Surrey CC v Bredero Homes Ltd* [1993] 1 W.L.R. 1361; *Jaggard v Sawyer* [1995] 1 W.L.R. 269 at 285.

[276] *Lawrence v Fen Tigers Ltd* [2014] A.C. 822 at [101]; *D v P* [2016] EWCA Civ 87 at [13]–[23].

[277] See *Wakeham v Wood* (1982) 43 P. & C.R. 40; *Sampson v Hodson-Pressinger* [1981] 3 All E.R. 710; *Oxy Electric Ltd v Zainuddin* [1991] 1 W.L.R. 115; *Elliott v Islington LBC* [1991] 1 E.G.L.R. 167; *Harrow LBC v Donohue* [1995] 1 E.G.L.R. 257.

[278] [1895] 1 Ch. 287.

(iii) the injury would be adequately compensated by a small payment[279]; and

(iv) it would be oppressive to grant an injunction.[280]

In subsequent cases these principles were applied with varying degrees of stringency. The following cases provide examples.

> In *Fishenden v Higgs and Hill Ltd*,[281] the defendant erected a building which obstructed the claimant's light in a manner that justified substantial damages, but not, by reason of the very high property values involved and the conduct of the defendant, an injunction. The Court of Appeal said that the principles of *Shelfer's* case were a useful guide, but not intended to be exhaustive or rigidly applied, and not a universal or even a sound rule in the case of rights to light. Romer LJ agreed that an injunction should be refused if the four requirements were satisfied, but said that it did not follow that an injunction should be granted if they were not.

> In *Kennaway v Thompson*,[282] the claimant sought an injunction to restrain a nuisance by excessive noise against a motor boat racing club. The Court of Appeal granted the injunction, holding that the jurisdiction to award damages in lieu of an injunction should be exercised only in very exceptional circumstances in cases of continuing nuisance. In the present case the injury to the claimant was not small, nor was it capable of estimation in monetary terms, nor could the sum awarded in the High Court (£16,000) be called a "small payment."

> In *Gafford v Graham*,[283] damages were awarded in lieu of an injunction to demolish a building put up in breach of covenant and to restrain a prohibited use of the land, even though the injury was not "small", nor could it be remedied by a "small payment". Thus damages of £25,000 were awarded, as the essential prerequisite that it would be oppressive to grant an injunction was satisfied. The claimant had previously shown that he was willing to settle for money, and this tipped the balance in favour of damages. *Shelfer's* case provided only a "working rule", and the principles must be adaptable to the facts of individual cases.

> In *Regan v Paul Properties DPF No.1 Ltd*,[284] the defendant's building significantly reduced the light to the claimant's living room. This interference reduced the value of the property by only £5,000, but it would cost the defendant £175,000 to comply with an injunction to remove the upper level of the building, which had been constructed after the claimant had protested. The injunction was granted, because the injury was not "small", nor would the loss to the defendant make it oppressive to grant the injunction. The court held that it was still the law that damages in lieu of an injunction to restrain a continuing wrong should be granted only in very exceptional cases, and there was no onus on the claimant to persuade the court that damages would be inadequate.

The area was reviewed by the Supreme Court in *Lawrence v Fen Tigers Ltd*,[285]   **28–052**
where the claimants bought a house near to an existing speedway circuit and

---

[279] The jurisdiction to grant injunctions is based on the inadequacy of common law damages. It might be argued that compliance with the third requirement should alone be sufficient to prevent the grant of an injunction. But common law damages may not be available, and cannot be awarded for the future; *Jaggard v Sawyer* [1995] 1 W.L.R. 269. See J. Jolowicz (1975) 34 C.L.J. 224.

[280] See *Jaggard v Sawyer* [1995] 1 W.L.R. 269 (injunction would prevent access to defendants' house).

[281] (1935) 153 L.T. 128; *Colls v Home and Colonial Stores Ltd* [1904] A.C. 179; *Lyme Valley Squash Club Ltd v Newcastle under Lyme BC* [1985] 2 All E.R. 405.

[282] [1981] Q.B. 88; *Elliott v Islington LBC* [1991] 1 E.G.L.R. 167; *Watson v Croft Promosport Ltd* [2009] 3 All E.R. 249.

[283] (1999) 77 P. & C.R. 73.

[284] [2007] Ch. 135; cf. *Tamares (Vincent Square) Ltd v Fairpoint Properties (Vincent Square) Ltd* [2007] 1 W.L.R. 2148 (no injunction for loss of light to office building).

[285] [2014] A.C. 822; D. Howarth (2014) 73 C.L.J. 247; E. Lees [2014] Conv. 449.

motocross track but found the levels of noise to be unacceptable. They brought a successful action in nuisance and the trial judge granted an injunction restricting the motor racing activities to 12 days per year. The Court of Appeal allowed an appeal on the basis that the noise was an established part of the locality and so did not constitute a nuisance. The Supreme Court allowed the claimants' appeal and restored the order of the trial judge. However, although the injunction was reinstated, Lord Neuberger emphasised that the defendants could apply to the trial judge to discharge the injunction and award damages instead.

Following a full review of the authorities, Lord Neuberger concluded that the question of whether to award an injunction or damages must not be reduced to a mechanistic application of the *Shelfer* principles. His Lordship adopted the observation of Millett LJ in *Jaggard v Sawyer*[286] that the decision to award damages in lieu involves an exercise of discretion, which means that no earlier case can amount to a binding authority on how that discretion should be exercised. He concluded[287]:

> "Where does that leave A L Smith L.J.'s four tests? While the application of any such series of tests cannot be mechanical, I would adopt a modified version of the view expressed by Romer L.J. in *Fishenden*. First, the application of the four tests must not be such as 'to be a fetter on the exercise of the court's discretion'. Secondly, it would, in the absence of additional relevant circumstances pointing the other way,[288] normally be right to refuse an injunction if those four tests were satisfied. Thirdly, the fact that those tests are not all satisfied does not mean that an injunction should be granted."

Lord Clarke would have simply abandoned the *Shelfer* principles.[289] The other Justices did not go quite this far,[290] and subsequent cases suggest that *Shelfer* will remain relevant.[291] However, the Supreme Court certainly rejected any application of those principles as strict criteria or hurdles to be overcome, rather than as (at most) useful guidelines.

B. Measure of Damages under Lord Cairns' Act

28–053 In *Pell Frischmann Engineering Ltd v Bow Valley Iran Ltd*,[292] Lord Walker said:

---

[286] [1995] 1 W.L.R. 269 at 288; adopted [2014] A.C. 822 at [120].

[287] [2014] A.C. 822 at [123].

[288] Lord Neuberger did not directly expand upon this point, but injunctions have been granted even when the *Shelfer* criteria have been satisfied if the defendant acted in reckless disregard of the claimant's rights: see *Pugh v Howells* (1984) 48 P. & C.R. 298; but cf. *Ketley v Gooden* (1997) 73 P. & C.R. 305 (no injunction if injury small, even if reckless disregard by defendant). Lord Neuberger may also have had in mind the "neighbourly" or otherwise spirit of the defendant: see *Colls v Home and Colonial Stores Ltd* [1904] A.C. 179 at 193; [2014] A.C. 822 at [105], [109].

[289] [2014] A.C. 822 at [171].

[290] Lord Sumption considered *Shelfer* to be out of date and thought that the whole area required a thorough review, although not in the present case: [2014] A.C. 822 at [161].

[291] See *Higson v Guenault* [2014] EWCA Civ 703 at [51]; *Gott v Lawrence* [2016] EWHC 68 (Ch) at [70]; *Kerry Ingredients (UK) Ltd v Bakkavor Group Ltd* [2016] EWHC 2448 (Ch) (though it appears *Lawrence v Fen Tigers Ltd* was not there cited).

[292] [2011] 1 W.L.R. 2370 at [48]. See, to the same effect, *Leeds Industrial Co-operative Society v Slack* [1924] A.C. 851 at 870; *Wroth v Tyler* [1974] Ch. 30 at 58 (specific performance); *Attorney General v Blake* [2001] 1 A.C. 268 at 281; *Morris-Garner v One Step (Support) Ltd* [2018] UKSC 20 at [44].

"Damages under Lord Cairns' Act are intended to provide compensation for the court's decision not to grant equitable relief in the form of an order for specific performance or an injunction in cases where the court has jurisdiction to entertain an application for such relief."

Damages awarded under Lord Cairns' Act need not necessarily be measured in the same way as damages awarded at common law. Damages are recoverable under Lord Cairns' Act where none would be obtainable at law; for example, in lieu of a quia timet injunction.[293] They are also recoverable for continuing wrongs, because a refusal to grant an injunction means the defendant is, as a practical matter, permitted to "perpetuate the wrongful state of affairs he has brought about".[294] Nonetheless, Lord Cairns' Act damages must still be awarded with the aim of compensating the claimant for the court's decision not to grant injunctive relief.[295]

As a general matter, and putting aside Lord Cairns' Act for a moment, the law recognises more than one type of loss. In *The Mediana*, Lord Halsbury famously asked[296]:

"Supposing a person took away a chair out of my room and kept it for twelve months, could anybody say you had a right to diminish the damages by shewing that I did not usually sit in that chair, or that there were plenty of other chairs in the room?"

The owner of the chair has not suffered any economic loss in the usual sense; however, she has suffered through the infringement of a valuable right that she possesses. For this reason, substantial damages will be available. The point is clearly seen in the law of trespass, where substantial damages may be awarded at common law without proof of damage,[297] and also in the law of conversion.[298] The damages awarded in such cases may be termed "user damages", because they are assessed by reference to the value of the use wrongfully made of property.[299]

The question is when damages ought to be assessed by reference to this principle, or something like it, and when they ought to be assessed by reference to a comparison between the claimant's position as it is and the claimant's position had the wrong in question not been committed. This point was recently addressed by the Supreme Court in *Morris-Garner v One Step (Support) Ltd*,[300] a case where the defendant breached a restrictive covenant (a "non-compete clause") in a contract for the sale of a business. Rather than seeking damages based on the profits that the claimant would have made if the defendant had not breached the

---

[293] As in *Hooper v Rogers* [1975] Ch. 43.
[294] *Attorney General v Blake* [2001] 1 A.C. 268 at 281.
[295] *Morris-Garner v One Step (Support) Ltd* [2018] UKSC 20 at [95(3)].
[296] [1900] A.C. 113 at 117.
[297] e.g. *Whitwham v Westminster Brymbo Coal & Coke Co* [1896] 2 Ch. 538. Thus substantial damages may also be awarded under Lord Cairns' Act when an injunction preventing trespass is refused: *Bracewell v Appleby* [1975] Ch. 408; *Jaggard v Sawyer* [1995] 1 W.L.R. 269.
[298] e.g. *Solloway v McLaughlin* [1938] A.C. 247; *BBMB Finance (Hong Kong) Ltd v Eda Holdings Ltd* [1990] 1 W.L.R. 409.
[299] *Kuwait Airways Corp v Iraqi Airways Co (Nos 4 and 5)* [2002] 2 A.C. 883 at [87]; *Morris-Garner v One Step (Support) Ltd* [2018] UKSC 20 at [95(1)].
[300] [2018] UKSC 20.

non-compete clause, the claimant instead sought damages calculated on the price it would have demanded to relax the non-compete clause (which was a higher amount).

Morris-Garner v One Step (Support) Ltd is relevant to the present discussion because, while not itself a Lord Cairns' Act case, the line of authority that the claimant relied upon involved damages awarded under the Act. In *Wrotham Park Estate Ltd v Parkside Homes Ltd*,[301] the defendant had erected and sold houses in breach of covenant. There was jurisdiction to grant a mandatory injunction against the defendant and the purchasers, who had aided and abetted the breach. But the injunction was refused, in order to avoid the demolition of valuable houses. As a restrictive covenant was involved, damages were available only under Lord Cairns' Act and not at common law. The value of the claimant's estate was not diminished by the breach, but it did not follow that only nominal damages were available. Brightman J held that a just substitute for the injunction would be such sum as the claimant could reasonably have demanded to relax the covenant, assessed at £2,500.

The matter arose again in *Jaggard v Sawyer*,[302] where the defendant built a house in breach of covenant and trespassed upon a private road to gain access to it. The claimant sought an injunction to restrain the trespass (which caused little injury), or damages in lieu. The judge below refused the injunction, which would have rendered the property landlocked, and awarded a sum under Lord Cairns' Act reflecting what the defendant should have paid for a right of way and a release of the covenant. This was upheld by the Court of Appeal, applying *Wrotham Park*.

Both *Wrotham Park* and *Jaggard v Sawyer* were cases where it could be said that a valuable property right of the claimant's was infringed.[303] Following *Attorney General v Blake*,[304] however, courts began awarding damages calculated on this basis even in cases of breach of contract. In the words of Lord Nicholls:

> "The *Wrotham Park* case [shows] that in contract as well as in tort damages are not always narrowly confined to recoupment of financial loss. In a suitable case damages for breach of contract may be measured by the benefit gained by the wrongdoer from the breach."[305]

28-054   Hence the central question in *Morris-Garner v One Step (Support) Ltd*: when is it appropriate to calculate damages based on a hypothetical negotiation between claimant and defendant, and when must the law follow the more usual process of comparing the claimant's actual economic position with the position she would

---

[301] [1974] 1 W.L.R. 798. See also *Amec Developments Ltd v Jury's Hotel Management (UK) Ltd* (2001) 82 P. & C.R. 286; D. Halpern [2001] Conv. 453; A.W-L. See [2017] Conv. 339.

[302] [1995] 1 W.L.R. 269. The decision was applied in *Gafford v Graham* (1999) 77 P. & C.R. 73; above, para.28–051.

[303] Although cf. Lord Sumption's view of *Wrotham Park* in *Morris-Garner v One Step (Support) Ltd* [2018] UKSC 20 at [114] ("for practical purposes a contract case").

[304] [2001] 1 A.C. 268; above, para.1–022. The precise question in *Blake* was whether an account of profits could, in exceptional circumstances, be awarded for breach of contract. That decision (in the affirmative) was not affected by *Morris-Garner v One Step (Support) Ltd* [2018] UKSC 20.

[305] [2001] 1 A.C. 268 at 283–284. Subsequent case examples include *Experience Hendrix LLC v PPX Enterprises Inc* [2003] 1 All E.R. (Comm) 830; *WWF World Wide Fund for Nature v World Wrestling Federation Entertainment Inc* [2008] 1 W.L.R. 445; *Field Common Ltd v Elmbridge BC* [2009] 1 P. & C.R. 1.

have occupied if the contract had been performed?[306] Lord Reed JSC concluded, as far as general damages for breach of contract are concerned, that the normal method would involve a comparison between the claimant's actual and notional economic positions. The availability of hypothetical "negotiating damages" was not a matter for claimant election,[307] and it did not involve questions of what would be a "just response".[308] Instead, such damages would only be available when the claimant's loss could be appropriately measured by reference to "the economic value of the right which has been breached, considered as an asset".[309] The present case was not of that nature because the breach of the non-compete clause did not result in the loss of a valuable asset.

Relevantly for the current discussion of Lord Cairns' Act damages, Lord Reed concluded[310]:

> "Damages can be awarded under Lord Cairns' Act in substitution for specific performance or an injunction, where the court had jurisdiction to entertain an application for such relief at the time when the proceedings were commenced. Such damages are a monetary substitute for what is lost by the withholding of such relief.
>
> "One possible method of quantifying damages under this head is on the basis of the economic value of the right which the court has declined to enforce, and which it has consequently rendered worthless. Such a valuation can be arrived at by reference to the amount which the claimant might reasonably have demanded as a quid pro quo for the relaxation of the obligation in question. The rationale is that, since the withholding of specific relief has the same practical effect as requiring the claimant to permit the infringement of his rights, his loss can be measured by reference to the economic value of such permission.
>
> "That is not, however, the only approach to assessing damages under Lord Cairns' Act. It is for the court to judge what method of quantification, in the circumstances of the case before it, will give a fair equivalent for what is lost by the refusal of the injunction."

Thus it must always be borne in mind that Lord Cairns' Act damages are awarded as a substitute for the injunction that the court withholds, and so attention must remain focused on what the claimant has lost by the refusal of that injunction.

9. INJUNCTIONS IN PARTICULAR SITUATIONS

A. To Restrain a Breach of Contract

An injunction is the appropriate remedy to restrain the breach of a negative undertaking in a contract. In some measure it corresponds to specific performance in the area of positive undertakings.[311] But, as will be seen,[312] the jurisdiction to grant an injunction is wider.

28–055

---

[306] [2018] UKSC 20 at [1].

[307] As Phillips J had held: [2014] EWHC 2213 (QB).

[308] As the Court of Appeal had held: [2016] EWCA Civ 180; [2017] Q.B. 1.

[309] [2018] UKSC 20 at [95(10)].

[310] [2018] UKSC 20 at [95(3)]–[95(5)].

[311] Above, para.27–006. Mandatory injunctions may also be available.

[312] Below, para.28–057.

28–056   **i. Contract Wholly Negative**   Where the essence of the contractual undertaking is negative, the court will grant an injunction to restrain a breach almost as a matter of course. As Lord Cairns LC explained in *Doherty v Allman*,[313] if the parties

> "contract that a particular thing shall not be done, all that a Court of Equity has to do is to say, by way of injunction, that which the parties have already said by way of covenant, that the thing shall not be done."

It is not necessary even to prove damage,[314] except where the action is by a reversioner.[315]

In *Araci v Fallon*,[316] the defendant, a famous jockey, had contracted to ride the claimant's horse when asked, and not to ride a rival owner's horse. An interlocutory injunction was granted to prevent him from riding a rival owner's horse in the Derby.

But the *Doherty v Allman* principle must be applied "in the light of the surrounding circumstances in each case,"[317] and it does not prevent the court from considering the effect of delay or other supervening circumstances.[318] Thus an injunction was refused in *Baxter v Four Oaks Properties Ltd*,[319] where the defendants, innocently, but in breach of the covenant, intended to use a new building as flats.

> "The effect of granting such an order would ... be to put the [claimants] in a very strong bargaining position, for unless the defendants were prepared to leave the building unused, they would be forced to buy a release of the injunction ... what the [claimants] would get in the end would be damages—though, no doubt, more damages than they would get if no injunction were granted."[320]

28–057   **ii. Positive and Negative Terms.**   Where a contract contains both positive and negative stipulations, and the positive ones are not susceptible to specific performance, the question arises whether the claimant can restrain the breach of the negative stipulation by injunction. In suitable cases, this can be done: the jurisdiction to grant an injunction is wider than that to order specific performance.[321] However, the principle is that an injunction will not be granted if that would amount to indirect specific performance of the positive terms.

28–058   **iii. No Express Negative Stipulation.**   Where a contract, drafted in positive form, contains no express negative stipulation, it may be possible to discover in

---

[313] (1878) 3 App.Cas. 709 at 720; *Sefton v Tophams Ltd* [1967] A.C. 50; *Sutton Housing Trust v Lawrence* (1988) 55 P. & C.R. 320 (granted to prevent tenant keeping dog in breach of covenant).

[314] *Grimston v Cuningham* [1894] 1 Q.B. 125; *Marco Productions Ltd v Pagola* [1945] K.B. 111, where dancers agreed not to perform for another producer; injunction granted although the claimants could not show that they would suffer greater damage if the dancers performed elsewhere than if they remained idle.

[315] *Johnstone v Hall* (1856) 2 K. & J. 414; *Martin v Nutkin* (1724) 2 P.Wms. 266.

[316] [2011] EWCA Civ 668; [2011] All E.R. (D) 37.

[317] *Shaw v Applegate* [1977] 1 W.L.R. 970 at 975, per Buckley LJ.

[318] [1977] 1 W.L.R. 970 at 980, per Goff LJ.

[319] [1965] Ch. 816.

[320] [1965] Ch. 816 at 829, per Cross J.

[321] See *Thomas Marshall (Exports) Ltd v Guinle* [1979] Ch. 227 at 243.

the contract, on its proper construction, an implied negative undertaking which can be remedied by injunction.[322] This is especially important where the positive obligation is not specifically enforceable. It is not possible to lay down a rule to determine the circumstances in which an injunction may be obtained. The question in each case depends upon the construction which the court places upon the particular contract.

The principle was laid down by Lord Selborne LC in *Wolverhampton and Walsall Railway Co Ltd v LNW Ry Ltd*[323] as being that the court should:

> "[L]ook in all such cases to the substance and not to the form. If the substance of the agreement is such that it would be violated by doing the thing sought to be prevented, then the question will arise, whether this is the court to come to for a remedy. If it is, I cannot think that ought to depend on the use of a negative rather than an affirmative form of expression."

A negative stipulation is rarely implied in contracts of personal service, for to do so might allow the indirect enforcement of a contract which is not specifically enforceable. Thus, it will not be implied although the servant has contracted to devote the whole of his time to his employer,[324] nor where there was a contract to sell to a purchaser all the "get" of a colliery for five years[325]; nor where a boxer agreed that his manager should have the "sole arrangements" for his boxing and other engagements.[326] However, in *Metropolitan Electric Supply Co v Ginder*,[327] the defendant applied for a supply of electricity on terms which provided that the defendant agreed to take all the electricity required by his premises from the claimant for a stated period. The claimant was not bound to supply, nor the defendant to take, any electricity. The contract was construed as an undertaking not to take electricity from any other persons, and the defendant was restrained by injunction from doing so. In *Manchester Ship Canal v Manchester Racecourse Co*,[328] the grant of a "first refusal" was construed as an undertaking enforceable by injunction, not to sell to anyone else in contravention of the undertaking.

It is established that a negative term may be implied in the following types of case.

(a) Contracts Affecting the Use of Land. A covenant which touches and concerns the land so as to be binding in equity upon successors in title under the **28–059**

---

[322] *Tulk v Moxhay* (1848) 2 Ph. 774; *Jones & Sons Ltd v Tankerville* [1909] 2 Ch. 440. Breach of an obligation imposed by law can be restrained by injunction even though the contract contains no express negative term: *Hivac v Park Royal Scientific Instruments* [1946] Ch. 169; *Provident Financial Group Plc v Hayward* [1989] I.C.R. 160 (confidential information).

[323] (1873) L.R. 16 Eq. 433 at 440; *Whitwood Chemical Co Ltd v Hardman* [1891] 2 Ch. 416 at 441, per Lindley LJ; *Bower v Bantam Investments Ltd* [1972] 1 W.L.R. 1120.

[324] *Whitwood Chemical Co Ltd v Hardman* [1891] 2 Ch. 416; *Bower v Bantam Investments Ltd* [1972] 1 W.L.R. 1120.

[325] *Fothergill v Rowland* (1873) L.R. 17 Eq. 132.

[326] *Mortimer v Beckett* [1920] 1 Ch. 571. See also *Fraser v Thames Television Ltd* [1984] Q.B. 44.

[327] [1901] 2 Ch. 799. See also *Sky Petroleum Ltd v VIP Petroleum Ltd* [1974] 1 W.L.R. 576.

[328] [1901] 2 Ch. 37. See also *Gardner v Coutts & Co* [1968] 1 W.L.R. 173 (implied term in right of pre-emption that property will not be given to another); cf. *Pritchard v Briggs* [1980] Ch. 338.

doctrine of *Tulk v Moxhay*[329] will be construed as negative and subjected to an injunction if it is negative in substance although positive in form. Indeed, in *Tulk v Moxhay* itself, the covenant was to:

> "[K]eep and maintain the said piece of ground in its then form, and in sufficient and proper repair ... in an open state, uncovered with any buildings in neat and ornamental order."[330]

The fact that a court was powerless to interfere against third parties except by the use of an injunction no doubt encouraged the courts to extend its use of the concept.

28–060   *(b) Contractual Licences.*   After a long search for the proper solution to the problem of the revocation by a licensor of a contractual licence in breach of contract, the courts found it in the issue of an injunction to restrain the breach of contract.[331] Where the wrongful revocation occurs before the licensee has entered, the court may, in an appropriate case, grant specific performance or a mandatory injunction to compel performance of the licensor's obligations.[332] A contractual licence is commonly in positive form—permitting the licensee to occupy premises. But where the licence on its proper construction gives no right to the licensor to revoke in the way in which he has purported to do, the court will treat the matter as one in which the licensor has contracted not to revoke inconsistently with the terms of the licence, and will restrain him from doing so.[333]

28–061   **iv. Contracts for Personal Services.**   It has been seen that contracts for personal services would not be specifically enforced either by specific performance or by an injunction.[334] In the case of contracts of employment, the Trade Union and Labour Relations (Consolidation) Act 1992 s.236 provides that:

> "[N]o court shall ... by way of ... injunction ... restraining a breach or threatened breach of [a contract of employment] compel an employee to do any work or to attend at any place for the doing of any work."

This provision, as with the corresponding provision relating to specific performance, applies only to contracts of employment[335] and only to enforcement against an employee. The equitable principle which denies specific enforcement of contracts of service has in appropriate circumstances permitted the issue of an injunction to restrain a negative undertaking in a contract for personal services, and this may have the effect indirectly of causing a contract to be performed. Two aspects of the question of the issue of an injunction in this circumstance need to be examined.

---

[329] (1848) 2 Ph. 774.
[330] (1848) 2 Ph. 774 at 775.
[331] Below, para.30–007 and following.
[332] *Verrall v Great Yarmouth BC* [1981] Q.B. 202, above, para.27–015.
[333] See *Jones (James) and Sons Ltd v Earl of Tankerville* [1909] 2 Ch. 440.
[334] Above, para.27–024.
[335] cf. independent contractors.

(a)   Restraining Breach by Employee or Independent Contractor.   **28–062**

> In *Lumley v Wagner*,[336] Miss Wagner, an opera star, had agreed with Lumley that she would sing at Her Majesty's Theatre during a certain period, and would not sing anywhere else without his written permission. She made another engagement with Gye to sing at Covent Garden and abandoned her previous commitment to Lumley, who sought an injunction to restrain her from singing for Gye. Lord St Leonards held that an injunction should be granted to restrain the breach of the negative stipulation; it would not of course have been possible to obtain specific performance of the promise to sing.

The principle of *Lumley v Wagner* has been much criticised.[337] It is said that the issue of an injunction in this situation is the equivalent of specific performance; and that a number of principles are thereby disregarded, especially the rule that the court will not supervise the performance of contracts; and the principle that the contracting parties must not become tied together in a relationship involving a status of servitude. However, where the contract does not involve very personal skills or talents, there is no objection to an injunction which might indirectly compel performance.[338]

It is submitted that the correct approach in these situations, as in other cases of injunctions, is that the injunction should issue to restrain the breach of a negative undertaking, unless the defendant can show that the court should in its discretion refuse on the ground that undesirable consequences may follow. Each case, in other words, should be treated on its merits.

Thus an employee should not be put into a position in which she must either perform the contract or do nothing. In *Warner Bros v Nelson*,[339] a well-known actress, Bette Davis, contracted to work for the claimants and not to work as a film actress for any other film company for the period of her contract, "or to be engaged in any other occupation". The term was not held void under the restraint of trade doctrine, and the question was whether an injunction was an appropriate remedy.

> "[I]t would, of course, be impossible to grant an injunction covering all the negative covenants in the contract. That would, indeed, force the defendant to perform her contract or remain idle; but this objection is removed by the restricted form in which the injunction is sought. It is confined to forbidding the defendant, without the consent of the [claimants], to render any services for or in any motion picture or stage production for any one other than the [claimants]."[340]

An injunction was given on these terms.[341] Miss Davis was still free to earn a living in other ways, even if they were less lucrative.

---

[336] (1852) 1 De G.M. & G. 604; S. Waddams (2001) 117 L.Q.R. 431.

[337] Ames, *Lectures on Legal History* (1913), p.370; *Whitwood Chemical Co v Hardman* [1891] 2 Ch. 416 at 428, per Lindley LJ: "I think that the court ... will generally do much more harm by attempting to decree specific performance in cases of personal service than by leaving them alone; and whether it is attempted to enforce these contracts directly by a decree of specific performance, or indirectly by an injunction, appears to me to be immaterial."

[338] *Lauritzencool AB v Lady Navigation Inc* [2005] 1 W.L.R. 3686 (time charter).

[339] [1937] 1 K.B. 209.

[340] [1937] 1 K.B. 209 at 219, per Branson J.

[341] *Robinson & Co Ltd v Heuer* [1898] 2 Ch. 451.

In *Evening Standard Co Ltd v Henderson*[342] an employee had failed to give the required notice. The Court of Appeal was prepared to grant an interlocutory injunction to prevent him from working for a rival paper during the notice period. As the employer had undertaken to pay his salary for that period even if he did not work ("gardening leave"), the injunction did not compel him to perform the contract or starve, but was rather a means of enforcing the notice requirement. It may be otherwise if the "garden leave" is so long that the employee may lose his skills.[343]

28–063 *(b) Compelling Employer to Employ.*

> In *Page One Records v Britton*,[344] a group of musicians appointed the claimant as their manager for five years, contracting not to engage anyone else as manager. They wished to change, and the claimant sought an injunction to prevent the employment of another manager, arguing on the lines of *Warner Bros v Nelson* that the defendants could retain him or continue without a manager. The injunction was refused, as it would *persuade* them to retain the claimant, which would be undesirable in a personal and fiduciary relationship in which the defendants had lost confidence in him.

Although the group could have earned their living in another way, just as Bette Davis could have done, it would be unrealistic to expect any of them to do so. Unless the period of the injunction is short, it puts economic pressure on the defendant to perform an obligation which is not specifically enforceable. The Court of Appeal subsequently held in *Warren v Mendy*[345] that *Page One Records* is preferable to *Warner*. The claimant was refused an injunction which in effect would have compelled a boxer to retain him as manager for at least two years. In relationships involving skill or talent and a high degree of mutual confidence,[346] the court should not enforce negative terms of a contract if this would in effect compel performance of the positive terms.

In *Hill v CA Parsons & Co Ltd*,[347] we saw that the Court of Appeal granted an injunction restraining an employer from acting on a wrongful dismissal. This amounted to indirect specific performance of a service contract; but the circumstances were special. Personal confidence still existed between the parties; a proper length of notice would have safeguarded the claimant's right under the Industrial Relations Act 1971; also the claimant was due to retire in two years, and his pension depended on his average salary during the last three years of employment. Stamp LJ dissented, and would have allowed the pension claim to be included in an award of damages. The question arose again in *Chappell v*

---

[342] [1987] I.R.L.R. 64. See also *Elsevier Ltd v Munro* [2014] EWHC 2648 (QB); [2014] I.R.L.R. 766; but cf. *Sunrise Brokers LLP v Rodgers* [2014] EWCA Civ 1373; [2015] I.R.L.R. 57, where the defendant unilaterally left work and so was not entitled to be paid (as he would have been if he had remained and been placed on garden leave by his employer).

[343] *Provident Financial Group Plc v Hayward* [1989] I.C.R. 160; *William Hill Organisation Ltd v Tucker* [1999] I.C.R. 291.

[344] [1968] 1 W.L.R. 157.

[345] [1989] 1 W.L.R. 853.

[346] The obligation of the claimants in *Warner Bros v Nelson* [1937] 1 K.B. 209, and *Lumley v Wagner* (1852) 1 De G.M. & G. 604; above, para.28–062, was merely to pay money.

[347] [1972] Ch. 305; above, para.27–024. See also *Jones v Lee* [1980] I.R.L.R. 67.

Times Newspapers Ltd,[348] where employees sought an injunction to restrain their dismissal during an industrial dispute. As mutual confidence no longer existed between the parties, the case was not within the *Hill v Parsons* exception. The fact that unfair dismissal was unlawful did not mean that a service contract was enforceable by injunction. That would be a "plain recipe for disaster".[349]

It appears that the grant of an injunction within the *Hill v Parsons* exception is not a rarity. Although the claimant must normally show that mutual confidence still exists,[350] this is not inevitably precluded by the fact that the employer opposes the claim. It suffices to establish that the employer has no rational ground to lack confidence, as where there has been no friction at the workplace.[351]

B. To Restrain a Breach of Trust

There are many examples of the issue of an injunction to restrain a breach of an equitable obligation, and a few must suffice here. Trustees have been restrained from distributing an estate inconsistently with the terms of the instrument,[352] or from selling under depreciatory conditions of sale[353]; or for a price below that offered firmly by a prospective purchaser[354]; or selling land without appointing a second trustee and without consulting the beneficiary.[355] Where the claimant has the entitlement to trace and claim property in equity,[356] an injunction may be granted to restrain the defendant from disposing of the property.[357]

28–064

C. To Restrain the Commission or Continuance of a Tort

i. Nuisance.   The act complained of must constitute a nuisance at law. "There is no such thing as an equitable nuisance."[358] The interference must cause or threaten damage.[359] No injunction will issue to deal with a trifling interference.[360]

28–065

---

[348] [1975] 1 W.L.R. 482; see also *GKN (Cwmbran) Ltd v Lloyd* [1972] I.C.R. 214; *Ali v Southwark LBC* [1988] I.R.L.R. 100; *Wishart v National Association of Citizens Advice Bureaux Ltd* [1990] I.C.R. 794.

[349] [1975] 1 W.L.R. 482 at 506. See also the Employment Rights Act 1996 s.117: an employment tribunal may order reinstatement, but the sanction in the event of non-compliance is only an award of compensation.

[350] cf. *Robb v Hammersmith and Fulham LBC* [1991] I.R.L.R. 72 (no dismissal prior to disciplinary procedure even though loss of confidence); *Jones v Gwent CC* [1992] I.R.L.R. 521; *Gryf-Lowczowski v Hinchingbrooke Healthcare NHS Trust* [2006] Lloyd's Rep. Med. 199.

[351] *Powell v Brent LBC* [1987] I.R.L.R. 466; *Hughes v Southwark LBC* [1988] I.R.L.R. 55.

[352] *Fox v Fox* (1870) L.R. 11 Eq. 142.

[353] *Dance v Goldingham* (1873) L.R. 8 Ch.App. 902.

[354] *Buttle v Saunders* [1950] 2 All E.R. 193 (above, para.19–002) where the trustee had promised (but not in binding form) to sell land to another purchaser.

[355] *Waller v Waller* [1967] 1 W.L.R. 451.

[356] Ch.26.

[357] *A v C* [1981] Q.B. 956n.; *Polly Peck International Plc v Nadir (No.2)* [1992] 4 All E.R 769.

[358] *Soltau v de Held* (1851) 2 Sim.(N.S.) 133 at 151, per Kindersley VC.

[359] It is otherwise where the nuisance is actionable without proof of damage; *Sevenoaks DC v Pattullo & Vinson Ltd* [1984] Ch. 211; *Halton BC v Cawley* [1985] 1 W.L.R. 15 (right to hold market).

[360] *Ankerson v Connelly* [1907] 1 Ch. 678.

That said, if the claimant can establish that her rights have been infringed, she is prima facie entitled to an injunction.[361] Damages may be awarded in lieu under Lord Cairns' Act,[362] and the public interest in the activity continuing may be relevant in deciding whether to award damages or grant an injunction.[363]

28–066 **ii. Trespass.** An injunction will issue to restrain a threatened or existing trespass. In minor cases, the court will leave the claimant to such remedy as he has at law; as where a clergyman of the Church of England held services on the seashore between high and low water mark which was leased by the Crown to the Corporation[364]; or where collectors chased a butterfly on to the claimant's land.[365] Where, however, the defendant entered the claimant's wood, cut down trees and clearly intended to cut more, he was restrained.[366] Indeed, there is no real discretion to refuse in cases of total dispossession.[367] Even if the injunction would be difficult to enforce, as where the defendants had no assets and imprisonment would be disproportionate, it may still be granted if it could have a real deterrent effect.[368]

Where the defendant has no arguable defence, the claimant may be granted an interlocutory injunction even where the trespass has caused no damage.[369]

A mandatory injunction will be granted where necessary, for example requiring the removal of an advertising sign which projected into the airspace above the claimant's single-storey shop.[370]

28–067 **iii. Libel.** When seeking an injunction to restrain publication of a libel, the claimant must satisfy the court of the falsity of the statements, and, where they are privileged, the presence of malice.

> "The court will not restrain the publication of an article, even though it is defamatory, when the defendant says that he intends to justify it or to make fair comment on a matter of public interest. ... The reason sometimes given is that the defences of justification and fair comment are for the jury, which is the constitutional tribunal, and not for a judge; but a better reason is the importance in the public interest that the truth should out."[371]

---

[361] *Lawrence v Fen Tigers Ltd* [2014] A.C. 822 at [101].

[362] Above, para.28–050.

[363] *Lawrence v Fen Tigers Ltd* [2014] A.C. 822; above, para.28–048.

[364] *Llandudno UDC v Woods* [1899] 2 Ch. 705. Refusal terminates self-help remedies; *Burton v Winters* [1993] 1 W.L.R. 1077.

[365] *Fielden v Cox* (1906) 22 T.L.R. 411; *Behrens v Richards* [1905] 2 Ch. 614.

[366] *Stanford v Hurlstone* (1873) L.R. 9 Ch.App. 116. See also *League Against Cruel Sports Ltd v Scott* [1986] Q.B. 240 (persistent trespass by hunt).

[367] *Harrow LBC v Donohue* [1995] 1 E.G.L.R. 257.

[368] *Secretary of State for the Environment, Food and Rural Affairs v Meier* [2009] 1 W.L.R. 2780 (travellers).

[369] *Patel v WH Smith (Eziot) Ltd* [1987] 1 W.L.R. 853; *Anchor Brewhouse Developments Ltd v Berkley House (Docklands Developments) Ltd* [1987] 2 E.G.L.R. 173.

[370] *Kelsen v Imperial Tobacco Co Ltd* [1957] 2 Q.B. 334. See also *Trenberth (John) Ltd v National Westminster Bank Ltd* (1979) 39 P. & C.R. 104; *London & Manchester Assurance Company Ltd v O&H Construction Ltd* [1989] 2 E.G.L.R. 185 (interlocutory).

[371] *Fraser v Evans* [1969] 1 Q.B. 349 at 360, per Lord Denning MR; *Bryanston Finance Ltd v de Vries* [1975] Q.B. 703 (privileged occasions); *Khashoggi v IPC Magazines Ltd* [1986] 1 W.L.R. 1412; *Attorney General v News Group Newspapers Ltd* [1987] Q.B. 1; *Holley v Smyth* [1998] Q.B. 726.

The interest of the public in knowing the truth outweighs the interest of a claimant in maintaining his reputation.[372] Thus, it was laid down in *Bonnard v Perryman*[373] as a working rule that an interlocutory injunction ought never to be granted except in the clearest cases, in which, if a jury did not find the matter complained of to be libellous, the court would set aside the verdict as unreasonable. But in *Hubbard v Pitt*,[374] the Court of Appeal upheld the grant of an interlocutory injunction to restrain, amongst other things, the display of allegedly libellous placards and leaflets outside the claimants' business premises. The necessity of preserving the freedoms of speech, assembly and demonstration should "not constrain the court to refuse a [claimant] an injunction to prevent defendants exercising these liberties in his front garden."[375] The injunction may also be granted if there is a clear case that publication is part of a concerted plan to inflict deliberate damage without just cause.[376] In *Monson v Tussaud's*,[377] an injunction was refused because it appeared that there might be a question at the trial whether the claimant had agreed to the publication. The court will only intervene where the issue is clear and certain. It "will not prejudice the issue by granting an injunction in advance of publication."[378] It has been held that the principles laid down in *American Cyanamid Co v Ethicon Ltd*[379] governing the grant of an interlocutory injunction have no application to libel injunctions, thus preserving the rule in *Bonnard v Perryman*.[380] This rule is unaffected by s.12(3) of the Human Rights Act 1998, which has already been considered.[381]

Once libel has been proved at the trial, the claimant may obtain an injunction to restrain its repetition. Section 13 of the Defamation Act 2013 also makes clear that, where a claimant succeeds in a defamation action, the court has the power to order the removal of the statement from a website, or the ceasing of the distribution, sale or exhibition of material containing the statement.

---

[372] *Woodward v Hutchins* [1977] 1 W.L.R. 760 at 764 (per Lord Denning MR).

[373] [1891] 2 Ch. 269.

[374] [1976] Q.B. 142; (Lord Denning MR dissenting).

[375] [1976] Q.B. 142 at 187, per Stamp LJ.

[376] *Gulf Oil (Great Britain) Ltd v Page* [1987] Ch. 327 (airborne sign over Cheltenham racecourse); *Femis-Bank (Anguilla) Ltd v Lazar* [1991] Ch. 391.

[377] [1894] 1 Q.B. 671. The claimant, who had been tried in Scotland for murder, where the jury had returned a verdict of "not proven", complained of the exhibition of a figure of himself in a room next to the "Chamber of Horrors".

[378] *Fraser v Evans* [1969] 1 Q.B. 349 at 361, per Lord Denning MR.

[379] [1975] A.C. 396, above, para.28–029.

[380] *Bestobell Paints Ltd v Bigg* (1975) 119 S.J. 678; *J Trevor & Sons v PR Solomon* (1978) 248 E.G. 779; *Herbage v Pressdram Ltd* [1984] 1 W.L.R. 1160; *Gulf Oil (Great Britain) Ltd v Page* [1987] Ch. 327.

[381] Above, para.28–036; *Greene v Associated Newspapers Ltd* [2005] Q.B. 972. See also I. Leigh and L. Lustgarten (1999) 58 C.L.J. 509 at 531–536.

D. Breach of Confidence and Misuse of Private Information

28–068   An injunction will be available to restrain a breach of confidence, whether arising out of a personal,[382] commercial[383] or other[384] relationship. An injunction will also be available to restrain a misuse of private information, if the claimant has a reasonable expectation of privacy.[385]

The causes of action in breach of confidence and misuse of private information are separate, although the latter did begin life as part of the former. While breach of confidence is an equitable claim, misuse of private information is classified as a tort. In *Google v Vidal-Hall*,[386] the Court of Appeal said:

> "Misuse of private information is a civil wrong without any equitable characteristics. We do not need to attempt to define a tort here. But if one puts aside the circumstances of its 'birth', there is nothing in the nature of the claim itself to suggest that the more natural classification of it as a tort is wrong. ... We are conscious of the fact that there may be broader implications from our conclusions, for example as to remedies, limitation and vicarious liability, but these were not the subject of submissions, and such points will need to be considered as and when they arise."

The precise question in the *Google* case was whether a claim for misuse of private information was a claim "made in tort" for the purposes of allowing service out of the jurisdiction. The Court of Appeal held that it was, but also recognised that its decision may have "broader implications".[387]

28–069   In cases of breach of confidence, injunctions may be granted against a party to a confidential relationship or against third parties, such as the press, who seek to publish confidential information knowing it to be such.[388] The third party, however, is not necessarily in the same position as the original confidant, as their respective duties may be different.[389] Worldwide publication releases third parties[390] (but probably not the original confidant[391]) from any duty of confidence, although in exceptional cases publication on the internet after the

---

[382] *Argyll v Argyll* [1967] Ch. 302 (communications between husband and wife).

[383] *Peter Pan Manufacturing Corp v Corsets Silhouette Ltd* [1964] 1 W.L.R. 96 (underwear designs); *Seager v Copydex* [1967] 1 W.L.R. 923 (carpet grips) *Fraser v Thames Television Ltd* [1984] Q.B. 44 (idea for television show).

[384] *Attorney General v Guardian Newspapers* Ltd [1987] 1 W.L.R. 1248 (*Spycatcher* at the interlocutory stage).

[385] *McKennit v Ash* [2008] Q.B. 73; *Campbell v MGN Ltd* [2004] 2 A.C. 457; *Mosley v News Group Newspapers Ltd, The Times*, 30 July 2008; *Weller v Associated Newspapers Ltd* [2015] EWCA Civ 1176; [2016] 1 W.L.R. 1541 (a family outing to a café, so in public); *PJS v News Group Newspapers Ltd* [2016] A.C. 1081.

[386] [2015] EWCA Civ 311; [2016] Q.B. 1003 at [43], [51]. The Supreme Court gave permission to appeal, but not on the ground relevant to the present discussion. The appeal was later withdrawn.

[387] For discussion of some of the effects of characterising the claim as a tort, see B. McDonald in A. Dyson et al (eds), *Defences in Tort* (Oxford: Hart Publishing, 2015), Ch.15.

[388] *Attorney General v Guardian Newspapers Ltd* [1987] 1 W.L.R. 1248, and (*No.2*) [1990] 1 A.C. 109 (*Spycatcher*).

[389] *Attorney General v Guardian Newspapers Ltd (No.2)* [1990] 1 A.C. 109.

[390] *Attorney General v Guardian Newspapers Ltd (No.2)* [1990] 1 A.C. 109 (*Spycatcher* final injunction refused). See also *Lord Advocate v The Scotsman Publications Ltd* [1990] 1 A.C. 812.

[391] *Attorney General v Guardian Newspapers Ltd (No.2)* [1990] 1 A.C. 109 (because he must not profit from his own wrong).

injunction has been issued may not bring this principle into play, as the injunction could still prevent wider circulation of the information.[392]

While publication of material usually destroys the confidence in that material, with the result that an injunction to protect that confidence will no longer issue,[393] the same is not true in the context of misuse of private information. As seen above,[394] in *PJS v News Group Newspapers*, the identity of a celebrity who had engaged in certain private extra-marital sexual activities was widely available on the internet. An injunction would not issue in support of a claim in breach of confidence. However, in respect of misuse of private information[395]:

> "[R]epetition of such a disclosure or publication on further occasions is capable of constituting a further tort of invasion of privacy, even in relation to persons to whom disclosure or publication was previously made—especially if it occurs in a different medium."

An injunction may still be available to restrain these further breaches.[396] In appropriate cases, the court must apply the Human Rights Act 1998 s.12, considered above.[397]

E.   Family Matters

The court has a statutory jurisdiction to grant injunctions to restrain a husband **28–070** from dealing with property so as to defeat his wife's claim to maintenance.[398] Injunctions are commonly granted in relation to occupation of the home under the provisions of the matrimonial homes legislation.[399] Thus injunctions have been granted to restrain a husband from installing his lover in the matrimonial home,[400] or to exclude the husband from the home,[401] or to restrain a man from living near his former wife,[402] or, in a grave case, to exclude an adult child from

---

[392] *Venables v News Group Newspapers* [2001] Fam. 430, an exceptional case where an injunction was ordered against the world.

[393] *Attorney General v Guardian Newspapers Ltd (No.2)* [1990] 1 A.C. 109 (*Spycatcher* final injunction refused). The European Court of Human Rights held that the Government had violated art.10 of the Convention in maintaining the injunctions after publication abroad.

[394] Above, para.28–036.

[395] *PJS v News Group Newspapers Ltd* [2016] A.C. 1081 at [32]. The Court used "misuse of private information" and "invasion of privacy" interchangeably. Some years earlier the House of Lords had decided there was no general tort of invasion of privacy: *Wainwright v Home Office* [2004] 2 A.C. 430; *Campbell v MGN Ltd* [2004] 2 A.C. 457.

[396] *Weller v Associated Newspapers Ltd* [2016] 1 W.L.R. 1541 at [88] (Mail Online refused to provide an undertaking not to republish photographs).

[397] Above, para.28–036.

[398] Matrimonial Causes Act 1973 s.37; Matrimonial and Family Proceedings Act 1984 s.24.

[399] Now the Family Law Act 1996.

[400] *Pinckney v Pinckney* [1966] 1 All E.R. 121.

[401] *Hall v Hall* [1971] 1 W.L.R. 404; *Phillips v Phillips* [1973] 1 W.L.R. 615.

[402] *M v M* (1983) 13 Fam.Law 110; *Burris v Azadani* [1995] 1 W.L.R. 1372.

his parents' home.[403] But the jurisdiction is sparingly exercised; it must be necessary to protect the applicant or a relevant child and should never be regarded as routine.[404]

The remedy of injunction is also employed in the protection of children[405]; for example, to restrain persons who had enticed a girl of 16 away from her father from continuing to harbour her[406]; in support of a custody order[407]; to protect a child from publicity[408] (although press freedom should not be restricted any more than is essential); or to restrain the mother of a ward from leaving the jurisdiction before submitting to a test to establish its paternity.[409]

As we have seen, a husband cannot obtain an injunction to prevent his wife from having an abortion.[410]

F. Judicial Proceedings

28–071   In proper cases, judicial proceedings in inferior courts[411] and private prosecutions[412] may be restrained. So also the initiation of proceedings in the High Court,[413] but once commenced, proceedings in the High Court are not subject to injunction.[414] Judicial proceedings in foreign courts may be restrained by injunction, where this is appropriate to avoid an injustice, but this is a jurisdiction to be exercised with great caution.[415] Such an injunction will only be issued against a party who is amenable to the jurisdiction of the English court. It is

---

[403] *Egan v Egan* [1975] Ch. 218 (a clear history of assaults, and threats of more). See also *Re L (Vulnerable Adults with Capacity: Court's Jurisdiction)* [2011] Fam. 189.

[404] *Des Salles d'Epinoix v Des Salles d'Epinoix* [1967] 1 W.L.R. 553; *Wiseman v Simpson* [1988] 1 W.L.R. 35; Family Law Act 1996 ss.33, 35, 36.

[405] For the practical limitations on the exercise of the jurisdiction, see *Re C (A Minor)* [1991] 2 F.L.R. 168. For the protection of vulnerable adults, see *Re HM (Vulnerable Adult: Abduction) (No.2)* [2011] 1 F.L.R. 97.

[406] *Lough v Ward* [1945] 2 All E.R. 338.

[407] *Re W (A Minor)* [1981] 3 All E.R. 401. As to adoption orders, see *Re D (A Minor)* [1991] Fam. 137.

[408] *Re S (A Child) (Identification: Restrictions on Publication)* [2005] 1 A.C. 593.

[409] *Re I (A Minor), The Times*, 22 May 1987.

[410] *Paton v Trustees of British Pregnancy Advisory Service* [1979] Q.B. 276; above, para.28–014; *C v S* [1988] Q.B. 135.

[411] *Re Connolly Bros Ltd* [1911] 1 Ch. 731 (Lancaster Palatine Court); *Thames Launches v Trinity House Corp (Deptford Strond)* [1961] Ch. 197 (magistrates' court); *Murcutt v Murcutt* [1952] P. 266 (county court).

[412] *Thames Launches v Trinity House Corp (Deptford Strond)* [1961] Ch. 197.

[413] *McHenry v Lewis* (1882) 22 Ch.D. 397; *Ellerman Lines v Read* [1928] 2 K.B. 144; *Settlement Corp v Hochschild* [1966] Ch. 10. See also *Bryanston Finance Ltd v de Vries (No.2)* [1976] Ch. 63 (winding-up petition).

[414] *Attorney General v Times Newspapers Ltd* [1974] A.C. 273. But this decision was held by the European Court (26 April 1979) to infringe art.10 of the European Convention on Human Rights, which guarantees freedom of expression. See also *Attorney General v London Weekend Television Ltd* [1973] 1 W.L.R. 202; *Attorney General v Ebert* [2002] 2 All E.R. 789 (injunction to prevent vexatious litigant from interfering with the proper administration of justice).

[415] See the outline of the principles given in *Deutsche Bank AG v Highland Crusader Offshore Partners LP* [2010] 1 W.L.R. 1023 at [50].

directed not to the foreign court, but to the parties.[416] Generally comity requires that the English court should have a sufficient interest in, or connection with, the matter to justify indirect interference.[417] At the time of writing, an anti-suit injunction may not be granted to restrain proceedings in another EU Member State.[418]

Where a dispute is subject to an arbitration agreement, the court will stay domestic proceedings that fall within the scope of the arbitration agreement.[419] It will also grant injunctions to restrain foreign proceedings that are within that scope, and are therefore in breach of the arbitration agreement.[420]

G.   To Prevent Removal or Destruction of Evidence: Search Orders

This type of injunction is designed to secure that, pending trial,[421] the defendant does not dispose of any articles in his possession which could be prejudicial at the trial. It is "an illustration of the adaptability of equitable remedies to new situations."[422] It is particularly useful to the victims of commercial malpractice, such as breach of confidence, breach of copyright and passing off, although it has also been used in the family context.[423] It is essential that such an order be available without notice, so that the defendant is not forewarned:

28–072

> "If the stable door cannot be bolted, the horse must be secured. ... If the horse is liable to be spirited away, notice of an intention to secure the horse will defeat the intention."[424]

Search orders were formerly known as *Anton Piller* orders, taking their name from the case (discussed below) in which the Court of Appeal confirmed the practice. They were put on a statutory footing by s.7 of the Civil Procedure Act 1997, and are governed also by the Civil Procedure Rules 1998.[425] They are now called "search orders", although of course they are referred to as *Anton Piller* orders or injunctions in the case law preceding these developments.

The search order has been variously described as "a draconian power which should be used only in very exceptional cases",[426] and as "an innovation which

---

[416] *Société Nationale Industrielle Aerospatiale v Lee Kui Jak* [1987] A.C. 871; *Donohue v Armco Inc* [2002] 1 All E.R. 749. See Civil Jurisdiction and Judgments Act 1982 s.49.

[417] *Airbus Industrie GIE v Patel* [1999] 1 A.C. 119.

[418] See Brussels I Regulation 44/2001 (and now Regulation 1215/2012); *Turner v Grovit* [2005] 1 A.C. 101; A. Briggs (2004) 120 L.Q.R. 529; A. Dickinson [2004] L.M.C.L.Q. 273; C. Hare (2004) 63 C.L.J. 570; *West Tankers Inc v Allianz SpA* [2009] 1 A.C. 1138 at [28]; E. Peel (2009) 125 L.Q.R. 365; R. Fentiman (2009) 68 C.L.J. 278.

[419] Arbitration Act 1996 s.9.

[420] *The Angelic Grace* [1995] 1 Lloyd's Rep. 87; *AES Ust-Kamenogorsk Hydropower Plant LLP v Ust-Kamenogorsk Hydropower Plant JSC* [2013] UKSC 35; [2013] 1 W.L.R. 1889.

[421] Or after judgment, in aid of execution; CPR 25.2.

[422] *Rank Film Distributors Ltd v Video Information Centre* [1982] A.C. 380 at 439 (per Lord Wilberforce).

[423] *Emanuel v Emanuel* [1982] 1 W.L.R. 669. It remains a rare weapon in family cases; *Burgess v Burgess* [1996] 2 F.L.R. 34.

[424] *Rank Film Distributors Ltd v Video Information Centre* [1982] A.C. 380 at 418.

[425] Part 25 (Interim Remedies). See also Senior Courts Act 1981 s.33(1).

[426] *Yousif v Salama* [1980] 1 W.L.R. 1540 at 1544, per Donaldson LJ.

has proved its worth time and time again".[427] The first reported decision was *EMI Ltd v Pandit*,[428] where an order was made without notice in a breach of copyright action to enable the claimant to enter the defendant's premises to inspect, photograph and remove infringing articles. The jurisdiction to make such an order was confirmed by the Court of Appeal in *Anton Piller KG v Manufacturing Processes Ltd*.[429]

> The defendants had received confidential information and plans concerning the claimant's electrical equipment in their capacity as the claimant's selling agents in England. The claimant had reason to believe that the defendants were selling the information to competitors, but were unable to prove this without access to documents situated on the defendants' premises.

The Court of Appeal made an order without prior notice to the defendants, requiring them to permit the claimant to enter their premises and inspect documents relating to the equipment. Such an order would only be made in exceptional circumstances, where it was essential that the claimant should inspect the documents to enable justice to be done between the parties, and there was a danger that vital evidence would otherwise be destroyed.

28–073 Unlike a search warrant, the order does not authorise the claimant to enter against the defendant's will. But it does order the defendant to permit the claimant to enter, so that, if the defendant does not comply, not only does he commit a contempt of court, but adverse inferences will be drawn against him at the trial. Ormrod LJ laid down three conditions for the grant of the order.[430] The claimant must:

(i)   have an extremely strong prima facie case;
(ii) show actual or potential damage of a very serious nature;
(iii) have clear evidence that the defendant has incriminating documents or things and a real possibility of their destruction before an application with notice can be made.[431]

It might be added that the order should not be sought as a "fishing expedition".[432]

In the enforcement of the order, the claimant must act with circumspection. She should be attended by her solicitor, and must undertake in damages (giving security in appropriate cases), so as to safeguard the defendant's rights. Because of the draconian nature of the order, the applicant is under a strict duty to make full and frank disclosure of all relevant matters to the court.[433] Strict requirements

---

[427] *Rank Film Distributors Ltd v Video Information Centre* [1982] A.C. 380 at 406, per Lord Denning MR.
[428] [1975] 1 W.L.R. 302.
[429] [1976] Ch. 55.
[430] In *Anton Piller KG v Manufacturing Processes Ltd* [1976] Ch. 55. For further guidelines, see *CBS United Kingdom Ltd v Lambert* [1983] Ch. 37; *Digital Equipment Corp v Darkcrest Ltd* [1984] Ch. 512.
[431] See *Yousif v Salama* [1980] 1 W.L.R. 1540.
[432] i.e. as a means of finding out what charges can be made.
[433] *Behbehani v Salem* [1989] 1 W.L.R. 723; *Lock International Plc v Beswick* [1989] 1 W.L.R. 1268; *Tate Access Floors Inc v Boswell* [1991] Ch. 512; *Elvee Ltd v Taylor* [2001] EWCA Civ 1943; [2002] F.S.R. 48.

have been developed to avoid oppression.[434] For example, the order must be executed in office hours so that legal advice is available; a woman must be present at a search of a private house where a woman may be alone; and a list of items must be prepared before they are removed, which the defendant may check. Where the claimant or her solicitor has acted improperly the court may set aside the order.

The utility of the search order suffered a set-back when the House of Lords held in *Rank Film Distributors Ltd v Video Information Centre*,[435] a copyright case, that the defendant could invoke the privilege against self-incrimination. But the privilege was subsequently withdrawn by s.72 of the Senior Courts Act 1981, in the case of proceedings to obtain disclosure of information relating to the infringement of rights pertaining to any intellectual property[436] or passing-off. Matters disclosed as a result of such proceedings are not admissible in evidence against the defendant in proceedings against him for a related offence.[437] Other exceptions have been added.[438] The defendant may still invoke the privilege against self-incrimination in a case outside the statutory exceptions.[439] The House of Lords elsewhere suggested further reforms.[440] Although the privilege may still be invoked in many areas, it does not extend to "independent matters" coming to light in the course of executing a search order, as where pornographic material was found during a search for other items.[441]

28–074

H.   To Prevent Removal of Assets: Freezing Injunctions

i.   General Principles.   This injunction was for many years known as a *Mareva* injunction, taking its name from *Mareva Compania Naviera SA v International Bulkcarriers SA*,[442] although the first reported exercise of the jurisdiction occurred in *Nippon Yusen Kaisha v Karageorgis*.[443] It is now called a

28–075

---

[434] *Universal Thermosensors Ltd v Hibben* [1992] 1 W.L.R. 840; CPR 25A *Practice Direction*, para.7. In some earlier cases the order appears to have been oppressive, e.g. *Lock International Plc v Beswick* [1989] 1 W.L.R. 1268.

[435] [1982] A.C. 380. Templeman LJ in the Court of Appeal, at 423, thought the court would award high damages where the defendant sought to rely on the privilege.

[436] Defined by s.72(5). See *Cobra Golf Inc v Rata* [1998] Ch. 109; *Gray v News Group Newspapers Ltd* [2011] 2 W.L.R. 1401.

[437] s.72(3). It is otherwise in the case of proceedings for contempt or perjury, s.72(4).

[438] See CPR 25A Practice Direction, para.7.9; *Kensington International Ltd v Republic of Congo* [2008] 1 W.L.R. 1144 (Fraud Act 2006 s.13).

[439] *Emanuel v Emanuel* [1982] 1 W.L.R. 669 (Revenue offences); *Tate Access Floors Inc v Boswell* [1991] Ch. 512; *IBM United Kingdom Ltd v Prima Data International Ltd* [1994] 1 W.L.R. 719 (conspiracy).

[440] *Istel (AT&T) Ltd v Tully* [1993] A.C. 45. The position is not changed by the Civil Procedure Act 1997; s.7(7).

[441] *C Plc v P (Attorney General intervening)* [2008] Ch. 1; R. Moules (2007) 66 C.L.P. 528.

[442] [1975] 2 Lloyd's Rep. 509; D. Powles (1978) J.B.L. 11; A. Bland (1980) 2 W.I.L.J. 60; R. Horsfall [1982] Conv. 265; C. Hodgekiss (1982) 99 L.Q.R. 7; A. Zuckerman (1993) 56 M.L.R. 325 and (1993) 109 L.Q.R. 432.

[443] [1975] 1 W.L.R. 1093. See *The Siskina* [1979] A.C. 210 at 229, where Lord Denning MR described this injunction as a "rediscovery" of the procedure known as foreign attachment; *Z Ltd v A-Z and AA-LL* [1982] Q.B. 558.

freezing injunction.[444] It was described by Lord Denning MR as "the greatest piece of judicial law reform in my time."[445]

> "A *Mareva* injunction is interlocutory, not final; it is ancillary to a substantive pecuniary claim for debt or damages; it is designed to prevent the judgment … for a sum of money being a mere 'brutum fulmen.'"[446]

The usual purpose of a freezing injunction is to prevent the dissipation or removal of assets before trial, so that if the claimant succeeds in the action, there will be property of the defendant available to satisfy the judgment. It may also be granted after final judgment if the claimant can show grounds for believing that the defendant will dispose of his assets to avoid execution.[447] In such a case the injunction may even be granted against the defendant's spouse.[448] Now that electronic banking is the norm, the significance of the injunction will be readily appreciated. Its effectiveness is assisted by ancillary orders to enable the claimant to obtain disclosure of documents and information as to assets,[449] and by the availability of contempt proceedings against third parties.

The freezing injunction is usually sought as an interlocutory measure and without notice: speed is of the essence.[450] It is frequently sought in conjunction with a search order. The basis of the jurisdiction is now the Senior Courts Act 1981 s.37: the injunction may be granted whenever it is "just and convenient" to do so, but with "great circumspection".[451] It is unlimited as to its subject-matter and the nature of the proceedings.[452] It may be granted, although rarely, in matrimonial cases.[453] As in the case of interlocutory injunctions generally, the claimant must satisfy the conditions laid down by the House of Lords in *American Cyanamid Co v Ethicon Ltd*: she must have a good arguable case and the balance of convenience must favour the grant.[454] The claimant must give an undertaking in damages in case she should be unsuccessful at the trial,[455] and the defendant may apply within seven days of service of the order on him for it to be discharged.[456] The defendant may be able to rely on the privilege against

---

[444] CPR 25.1(1)(f).

[445] *The Due Process of Law* (1980), p.134; Lord Denning, *The Closing Chapter* (1983), p.225. See also Donaldson LJ in *Bank Mellat v Nikpour* [1985] F.S.R. 87 at 91–92, describing the freezing injunction, along with the search order, as "one of the law's two 'nuclear' weapons."

[446] *The Siskina* [1979] A.C. 210 at 253, per Lord Diplock.

[447] *Babanaft International Co SA v Bassatne* [1990] Ch. 13; CPR 25.2.

[448] *Mercantile Group (Europe) AG v Aiyela* [1994] Q.B. 366.

[449] *Bekhor (AJ) & Co Ltd v Bilton* [1981] Q.B. 923; *Bankers Trust Co v Shapira* [1980] 1 W.L.R. 1274; CPR 25.1(1)(g).

[450] *Third Chandris Shipping Corp v Unimarine SA* [1979] Q.B. 645.

[451] *Mercedes-Benz AG v Leiduck* [1996] 1 A.C. 284 at 297, per Lord Mustill.

[452] *Z Ltd v A-Z and AA-LL* [1982] Q.B. 558. It may be combined with specific performance; *Seven Seas Properties Ltd v Al-Essa* [1988] 1 W.L.R. 1272.

[453] *C v C (Without Notice Orders)* [2006] 1 F.L.R. 936; *Re M (Freezing Injunction)* [2006] 1 F.L.R. 1031.

[454] [1975] A.C. 396; above, para.28–029. cf. *Polly Peck International Plc v Nadir (No.2)* [1992] 4 All E.R. 769 at 786.

[455] Unless the claimant is the Crown acting in a public capacity: see *FSA v Sinaloa Gold Plc* [2013] UKSC 11; [2013] 2 A.C. 28; J. Varuhas and P. Turner (2014) 130 L.Q.R. 33.

[456] *Mareva Compania Naviera SA v International Bulkcarriers SA* [1975] 2 Lloyd's Rep. 509; CPR 23.10.

self-incrimination to avoid compliance with the injunction or a disclosure order, unless he is adequately protected by a term of the order preventing the use of the disclosures in a prosecution. The application of the privilege has already been discussed.[457]

It has been held that the old writ *ne exeat regno*[458] may be granted in support of a freezing injunction,[459] or, if its requirements are not satisfied, an interlocutory injunction under s.37(1) of the Senior Courts Act 1981 to restrain the defendant from leaving the country.[460]

ii. Guidelines for the Grant of the Injunction. While the discretion of the court is not fettered by rigid rules, Lord Denning MR suggested the following guidelines[461]: **28–076**

(a) the claimant must have a good arguable case[462];
(b) where the injunction applies to goods, caution is required to avoid bringing the defendant's business to a standstill[463];
(c) the court should favour the grant if it would be likely to compel the defendant to provide security;
(d) the claimant must make full and frank disclosure of all material matters[464];
(e) he should give particulars of his claim and its amount, and (in an application without notice) he should fairly state the points made against it by the defendant;
(f) he must undertake in damages, giving security in suitable cases, in case he is unsuccessful in the action.[465]

Lord Denning added that the claimant had to establish that there was a risk of the removal of assets from the jurisdiction. It is no longer necessary for the claimant to establish in all cases that there is such a risk, as s.37(3) of the Senior

---

[457] Above, para.28–074.
[458] Above, para.1–037. "Writ" has now been replaced by "claim form"; CPR 7.
[459] *Al Nahkel for Contracting and Trading Ltd v Lowe* [1986] Q.B. 235; cf. *Allied Arab Bank Ltd v Hajjar* [1988] Q.B. 787.
[460] *Bayer AG v Winter* [1986] 1 W.L.R. 497; *JSC Mezhdunarodny Promyshlenniy Bank v Pugachev* [2015] EWCA Civ 1108. A freezing order was also made, which controversially required Mr Pugachev to disclose information about discretionary trusts of which he was an object: [2015] EWCA Civ 139; [2016] 1 W.L.R. 160 at [60].
[461] *Rasu Maritima SA v Perusahaan* [1978] Q.B. 644; *Third Chandris Shipping Corp v Unimarine SA* [1979] Q.B. 645. See also *Barclay-Johnson v Yuill* [1980] 1 W.L.R. 1259; *Z Ltd v A-Z and AA-LL* [1982] Q.B. 558; *Derby & Co Ltd v Weldon* [1990] Ch. 48; *Flightwise Travel Services Ltd v Gill, The Times*, 12 December 2003. See Practice Direction [1996] 1 W.L.R. 1552.
[462] See *Etablissement Esefka International Anstalt v Central Bank of Nigeria* [1979] 1 Lloyd's Rep. 445; *Barclay-Johnson v Yuill* [1980] 1 W.L.R. 1259; *Kazakhstan Kagazy Plc v Arip* [2014] EWCA Civ 381.
[463] As to chattels, see *CBS United Kingdom Ltd v Lambert* [1983] Ch. 37.
[464] Failure to make full disclosure may result in discharge. See *Columbia Picture Industries Inc v Robinson* [1987] Ch. 38; *Lloyds Bowmaker Ltd v Britannia Arrow Holdings Plc* [1988] 1 W.L.R. 1337; *Brink's-MAT Ltd v Elcombe* [1988] 1 W.L.R. 1350; *Behbehani v Salem* [1989] 1 W.L.R. 723; *Memory Corp Plc v Sidhu (No.2)* [2000] 1 W.L.R. 1443; *UL v BK* [2013] EWHC 1735 (Fam); [2014] Fam. 35 at [50].
[465] This will not normally be required in a post-judgment case unless leave to appeal has been granted; *Gwembe Valley Development Co Ltd v Koshy (No.4), The Times*, 28 February 2002.

Courts Act 1981 provides that the injunction may be granted to prevent the defendant from removing from the jurisdiction "or otherwise dealing with" the assets. Thus a risk of dissipation within the jurisdiction[466] (or, in an extreme case, damage or destruction[467]) is sufficient. The developments as to foreign assets are discussed below.

Exceptionally, the injunction may be made against all the defendant's assets; but usually a limit will be specified.[468] In rare cases it may be made in respect of a joint account,[469] but not assets of the defendant's spouse or another third party,[470] save in aid of enforcement of a judgment.[471] In the context of the standard Commercial Court freezing order, an order made in relation to "his assets" includes those that the defendant holds on trust for a third party.[472] In addition, "assets" includes the right of a defendant to draw down on unsecured loans.[473] The injunction should rarely be granted where the defendant is a bank, otherwise its business could be irreparably harmed.[474]

It has recently been held that the claimant must demonstrate "grounds for belief" that the defendant has assets on which the freezing injunction will bite. It is not enough merely to assert that the defendant is a wealthy person who must have assets somewhere.[475]

28–077   **iii. The Jurisdiction of the Court.**   The House of Lords in *The Siskina*[476] emphasised that the injunction had to be ancillary to substantive relief which the High Court had jurisdiction to grant; and that there was no power to grant the injunction save in protection or assertion of some legal or equitable right which the High Court had jurisdiction to enforce by final judgment. *The Siskina* was reversed on this point for cases within s.25 of the Civil Jurisdiction and Judgments Act 1982,[477] "but it remains an influential and controversial decision,

---

[466] See *Z Ltd v A-Z and AA-LL* [1982] Q.B. 558.

[467] *Standard Chartered Bank v Walker* [1992] 1 W.L.R. 561.

[468] *Z Ltd v A-Z and AA-LL* [1982] Q.B. 558. After-acquired assets may be included; *TDK Tape Distributors (UK) Ltd v Videochoice Ltd* [1986] 1 W.L.R. 141. The claimant may alternatively seek a "notification injunction" whereby the defendant must give notice if he intends to dispose or deal with certain assets (or assets amounting to a certain value). Such an injunction is effectively a modified freezing order and can only be granted if the requirements for a freezing order are met: *Holyoake v Candy* [2017] EWCA Civ 92; [2017] 3 W.L.R. 1131.

[469] *Z Ltd v A-Z and AA-LL* [1982] Q.B. 558.

[470] *SCF Finance Co Ltd v Masri* [1985] 1 W.L.R. 876; *Allied Arab Bank Ltd v Hajjar* (1989) 19 Fam.Law 68; cf. *TSB Private Bank International SA v Chabra* [1992] 1 W.L.R. 231.

[471] *Mercantile Group (Europe) AG v Aiyela* [1994] Q.B. 366. See also *C Inc Plc v L* [2001] 2 Lloyd's Rep. 459.

[472] *JSC BTA Bank v Solodchenko* [2011] 1 W.L.R. 888 at [49]; *Lakatamia Shipping Co Ltd v Su* [2014] EWCA Civ 636; [2015] 1 W.L.R. 291 (Rimer LJ dissented, noting that property held on trust cannot be used to satisfy a judgment); cf. the earlier standard form considered in *Federal Bank of the Middle East v Hadkinson* [2000] 1 W.L.R. 1695.

[473] *JSC BTA Bank v Alyazov (No.10)* [2015] UKSC 64; [2015] 1 W.L.R. 4754 at [39]. Again the point turned on new wording inserted into the standard form.

[474] *Polly Peck International Plc v Nadir (No.2)* [1992] 4 All E.R. 769; A. Zuckerman (1992) 108 L.Q.R. 559. See also *Themehelp Ltd v West* [1996] Q.B. 84 (guarantee).

[475] *Ras al Khaimah Investment Authority v Bestfort Development LLP* [2017] EWCA Civ 1014; [2018] 1 W.L.R 1099 at [39].

[476] [1979] A.C. 210.

[477] See *Haiti (Republic of) v Duvalier* [1990] 1 Q.B. 202.

and has had considerable effect on the development of the law of anti-suit injunctions."[478] Section 25 was originally confined to proceedings in countries which were parties to the Brussels and Lugano Conventions, but was extended in 1997[479] to proceedings in countries which are party to neither Convention. In cases where the court has no independent jurisdiction as to the subject-matter of the proceedings, it may refuse to grant the injunction on the basis of inexpedience.[480]

It has been held that a freezing injunction may not be granted unless the cause of action has accrued,[481] but the current view is that equity will "lend a hand" in advance of the appropriate time at law, to prevent injustice.[482] However, the claimant must at least have formulated a case for substantive relief which she intends to seek.[483]

iv. The English-based Defendant.

iv. The English-based Defendant. The freezing injunction evolved as a remedy against a foreign-based defendant having assets within the jurisdiction. It was assumed in the early decisions that there was no power to grant such an injunction against an English-based defendant, although the merit of such a distinction was questioned.[484]

28–078

The difficulty in the way of extending the freezing injunction to English-based defendants was the clear line of authority to the effect that there was "no statutory or other power in the Court to restrain a person from dealing with his property at a time when no order against him has been made."[485]

Eventually the jurisdiction to enjoin an English-based defendant became established.[486] It was confirmed by s.37(3) of the Senior Courts Act 1981, providing that the court's power to grant an interlocutory injunction restraining a party to any proceedings from removing from the jurisdiction, or otherwise dealing with, assets located within the jurisdiction shall be exercisable whether or not that party is domiciled, resident or present within the jurisdiction.

v. Assets outside the Jurisdiction.

v. Assets outside the Jurisdiction. The freezing injunction was originally confined to assets within the jurisdiction. It is now established that the injunction (and ancillary disclosure order) may be granted against a defendant who is amenable to the jurisdiction of the court in respect of assets outside the jurisdiction, even on a worldwide basis. The objections to extending the

28–079

---

[478] *Masri v Consolidated Contractors International (UK) Ltd (No.3)* [2009] Q.B. 503 at 518.
[479] Civil Jurisdiction and Judgments Act 1982 (Interim Relief) Order 1997 (SI 1997/302). See also Civil Jurisdiction and Judgments Regulation 2009 (SI 2009/3131).
[480] Civil Jurisdiction and Judgments Act 1982 s.25(2); *Crédit Suisse Fides Trust SA v Cuoghi* [1998] Q.B. 818 at 829, 831. See also *Refco Inc v Eastern Trading Co* [1999] 1 Lloyd's Rep. 159; *Motorola Credit Corp v Uzan (No.2)* [2004] 1 W.L.R. 113; *Rhode v Rhode and Pembroke Square Ltd* [2007] 2 F.L.R. 971.
[481] *Veracruz Transportation Inc v VC Shipping Co Inc* [1992] 1 Lloyd's Rep. 353.
[482] *Re Q's Estate* [1999] 1 Lloyd's Rep. 931.
[483] *Fourie v Le Roux* [2007] 1 W.L.R. 320; P. Devonshire (2007) 123 L.Q.R. 361.
[484] See *The Siskina* [1979] A.C. 210.
[485] *Jagger v Jagger* [1926] P. 93 at 102, per Scrutton LJ. See also *Lister & Co v Stubbs* (1890) 45 Ch.D. 1.
[486] See *AJ Bekhor & Co Ltd v Bilton* [1981] Q.B. 923; Lord Denning, *The Due Process of Law* (1980), pp.147–149.

injunction to foreign assets were that the order would be oppressive and unenforceable, and that the territorial limitations were confirmed by s.37(3) of the Senior Courts Act 1981. But the Court of Appeal held in *Babanaft International Co SA v Bassatne*[487] that s.37(3) did not restrict the scope, geographical or otherwise, of s.37(1). This case involved a post-judgment freezing injunction. Such an order would more readily be made against assets abroad than in a pre-judgment case, but would nevertheless be rare. A personal order binding the defendant alone was made. It is now provided in the Civil Procedure Rules that the injunction may be granted in relation to assets "whether located within the jurisdiction or not",[488] but the decisions on "worldwide assets" remain important.

The issue next arose in the Court of Appeal in *Haiti (Republic of) v Duvalier*,[489] which concerned the alleged embezzlement of $120 million from Haiti during the presidency of Jean-Claude Duvalier. No substantive relief in England was sought. The court granted a pre-judgment freezing injunction in respect of worldwide assets, although recognising that this was a most unusual measure which should very rarely be granted. While the court would be more willing in a post-judgment case, or where the claimant had a tracing or other proprietary claim, the injunction could be granted in respect of a pre-judgment money claim such as the present case, where international co-operation was demanded. Previous limitations arose from practice rather than from any restriction on the court's power. The injunction was granted subject to a "*Babanaft* proviso"[490] in respect of the foreign assets, to protect third parties outside the jurisdiction save to the extent that the order might be enforced by the local court.

Even stricter safeguards were required by the Court of Appeal in *Derby & Co Ltd v Weldon*,[491] where a pre-judgment worldwide freezing injunction was granted. It was emphasised that, in addition to a good arguable case, the claimant must show that any English assets are insufficient, that there are foreign assets, and that there is a real risk of disposal of the latter. The injunction will not be granted if it would be oppressive. The court must be satisfied, by means of undertaking or proviso, that (a) the defendant will not be oppressed by exposure to a multiplicity of proceedings[492]; (b) the defendant will be protected against misuse of information gained from the order for disclosure of assets; and (c) third parties are protected. The present case was sufficiently exceptional because a very large sum was involved (£15 million), the English assets were totally inadequate, and there was a high risk of dissipation of the foreign assets through

---

[487] [1990] Ch. 13.

[488] CPR 25.1(1)(f).

[489] [1990] 1 Q.B. 202. It has been said that *Duvalier* "goes to the very edge of what is permissible"; L. Collins (1989) 105 L.Q.R. 262 at 281. This comment was noted by Millett LJ in *Crédit Suisse Fides Trust SA v Cuoghi* [1998] Q.B. 818. For other criticisms of worldwide orders, see T. Hartley (2010) 126 L.Q.R. 194 at 210–221.

[490] For the current form of the proviso, see CPR 25A Practice Direction (Annex). The applicant must undertake not to enforce outside the jurisdiction without permission of the court. Guidelines for the grant of permission were given in *Dadourian Group International Inc v Simms (Practice Note)* [2006] 1 W.L.R. 2499. See also *Taurus Petroleum Ltd v State Oil Company of the Ministry of Oil, Republic of Iraq* [2015] EWCA Civ 835; [2016] 1 Lloyd's Rep 42.

[491] [1990] Ch. 48.

[492] See *Re Bank of Credit and Commerce International SA* [1994] 1 W.L.R. 708.

inaccessible overseas companies. In *Derby & Co Ltd v Weldon (No.3 and No.4)*[493] a similar injunction was granted against companies in Luxembourg and Panama which had no assets within the jurisdiction. The Luxembourg company was subject to the jurisdiction of a court which would enforce the orders of the English court under the Civil Jurisdiction and Judgments Act 1982. Concerning the Panama company, the fact that the order could not be specifically enforced was no bar. The order would not be made if there was no effective sanction, but the sanction of being debarred from defending in the event of disobedience normally sufficed.[494]

It has since been explained that, where an injunction is sought in aid of foreign proceedings, the focus is on whether it is expedient to grant it, in view of the court's lack of jurisdiction over the subject-matter of the proceedings, and not whether the circumstances are exceptional.[495] However, a worldwide order should not be granted routinely or without very careful consideration. Indeed, the Court of Appeal has emphasised that a worldwide order should not be made in the absence of a "real connecting link" between the defendant and the territorial jurisdiction of the court, such as the defendant being a British national or based in the jurisdiction or where the main proceedings will be in this jurisdiction.[496] Finally, the court may, in exceptional cases, order the transfer of assets from one foreign jurisdiction to another to prevent their dissipation.[497]

vi. Operation in Personam.   The usual subject-matter of a freezing injunction is a sum of money, often in a bank account. But there is no reason why other assets, such as a ship,[498] or an aeroplane,[499] should not be "frozen" by this method. It is important to note, however, that such an injunction, even if related to a specified asset, operates only in personam. It is not a form of pre-trial attachment. It does not effect seizure of the asset, nor is it analogous to a lien. It merely prohibits the defendant personally from removing or transferring the asset. It gives no proprietary right in the asset, nor priority over other creditors.[500] The claimant's right is merely to have the asset preserved so that, if she succeeds in her action, judgment may be executed against it, but the rights of a third party with an interest in the asset will not be prejudiced.[501] The injunction may (initially or by variation) permit the assets to be used for living expenses or to

28–080

---

[493] [1990] Ch. 65.

[494] See L. Collins (1989) 105 L.Q.R. 262 at 296.

[495] *Crédit Suisse Fides Trust SA v Cuoghi* [1998] Q.B. 818; Civil Jurisdiction and Judgments Act 1982 s.25(2); *Motorola Credit Corp v Uzan (No.2)* [2004] 1 W.L.R. 113.

[496] *Banco Nacional De Comercio Exterior SNC v Empresa De Telecommunicaciones De Cuba SA* [2008] 1 W.L.R. 1936. See also the guidelines in *Dadourian Group International Inc v Simms (Practice Note)* [2006] 1 W.L.R. 2499.

[497] *Derby & Co Ltd v Weldon (No.6)* [1990] 1 W.L.R. 1139.

[498] *The Rena K* [1979] Q.B. 377.

[499] *Allen v Jambo (Holdings) Ltd* [1980] 1 W.L.R. 1252.

[500] See *Sanders Lead Co Inc v Entores Metal Brokers Ltd* [1984] 1 W.L.R. 452; *Bank Mellat v Kazmi* [1989] Q.B. 541. Assets subject to tracing and eventual claim may be protected by an ordinary interlocutory injunction; *Polly Peck International Plc v Nadir (No.2)* [1992] 4 All E.R. 769.

[501] *Cretanor Maritime Co Ltd v Irish Marine Management Ltd* [1978] 1 W.L.R. 966; *Taylor v Van Dutch Marine Holding Ltd* [2017] EWHC 636 (Ch); [2017] 1 W.L.R. 2571 (where the order was varied to make clear that a secured creditor could still enforce its security over "frozen" assets, but such amendment was not strictly necessary).

make payments in good faith in the ordinary course of business.[502] Such a term does not, however, protect the recipient of the payments in a case where the claimant establishes proprietary rights over the assets.[503]

28-081 **vii. Position of Third Parties.**   As far as the liabilities of a third party are concerned, we have seen that a third party who aids and abets the breach of an injunction by the defendant is guilty of contempt.[504] So in the case of a freezing injunction against a sum of money in a bank account, the bank, once it has notice, must not facilitate the disposal of the money without a court order.[505] If it does so, it may commit contempt but the claimant has no action against the bank in negligence.[506] It is clear that any expenses incurred by a bank or other third party in complying with the injunction must be met by the claimant.[507]

Similarly, the injunction must not interfere with the convenience or freedom of action of a third party. So in *Galaxia Maritime SA v Mineralimportexport*,[508] where a freezing injunction had been obtained as to a ship's cargo, the shipowner obtained its discharge, as it would interfere with the crew's arrangements for Christmas.

---

[502] *Iraqi Ministry of Defence v Arcepey Shipping Co SA* [1981] Q.B. 65; *Z Ltd v A-Z and AA-LL* [1982] Q.B. 558; *TDK Tape Distributors (UK) Ltd v Videochoice Ltd* [1986] 1 W.L.R. 141; *Atlas Maritime Co SA v Avalon Maritime Ltd* [1991] 4 All E.R. 769 and *(No.3)* [1991] 1 W.L.R. 917.

[503] *United Mizrahi Bank Ltd v Doherty* [1998] 1 W.L.R. 435.

[504] Above, para.28–010. See *Bank Mellat v Kazmi* [1989] Q.B. 541. A post-judgment freezing injunction may be granted against the defendant's spouse; *Mercantile Group (Europe) AG v Aiyela* [1994] Q.B. 366; above, para.28–076.

[505] *Z Ltd v A-Z and AA-LL* [1982] Q.B. 558; cf. *Law Society v Shanks* [1988] 1 F.L.R. 504. The injunction should not be granted against a bank as defendant; above, para.28–076.

[506] *Commissioners of Customs and Excise v Barclays Bank Plc* [2007] 1 A.C. 181; S. Gee (2006) 122 L.Q.R. 535.

[507] *Rahman (Prince Abdul) Bin Turki Al Sudairy v Abu-Taha* [1980] 1 W.L.R. 1268; *Searose Ltd v Seatrain (UK) Ltd* [1981] 1 W.L.R. 894. Undertakings will normally be given in this respect; *Z Ltd v A-Z and AA-LL* [1982] Q.B. 558.

[508] [1982] 1 W.L.R. 539. See also *Clipper Maritime Co Ltd of Monrovia v Mineralimportexport* [1981] 1 W.L.R. 1262; *Arab Monetary Fund v Hashim (No.2)* [1990] 1 All E.R. 673 (where compliance with disclosure order might incriminate third parties abroad).

CHAPTER 29

RESCISSION AND RECTIFICATION

1.   RESCISSION

A.   General

THE right to rescind is the right of a party to a contract to have it set aside and to be restored to her former position. The contract remains valid unless and until rescinded, so that, as we shall see, third parties may acquire interests under it in the meantime. This is rescission in the strict sense, and must be distinguished on the one hand from contracts void ab initio, for example on the ground of illegality, and on the other hand from contracts with no inherent invalidity which are subsequently discharged by breach.[1] Rescission is not a judicial remedy as such, for it may be achieved by act of the parties, nevertheless the assistance of the court is often invoked,[2] for example to secure restitution of any property. Equity has traditionally been more flexible than the common law in its view of restitutio in integrum, although the distinction is becoming harder to maintain.[3]

29–001

---

[1] See *Johnson v Agnew* [1980] A.C. 367. On the right to rescind for fraud, see *Logicrose Ltd v Southend United Football Club Ltd* [1988] 1 W.L.R. 1256 and the principles in cases of bribery *Conway v Eze* [2018] EWHC 29 (Ch) (where an agent of one party to the contract is bribed by the other party) and *Chancery Client Partners Ltd v MRC 957 Ltd* [2016] EWHC 2142 (Ch) (rescission not available where the agent was bribed by someone who was not party to the contract and the other contractor is innocent: damages are the appropriate remedy). A majority of the Court of Appeal has recently taken a broad view of the right to rescind where the other party's conscience is affected by a bribe: *UBS AG (London Branch) v Kommunale Wasserwerke Leipzig GmbH* [2017] EWCA Civ 1567; [2017] 2 Lloyd's Rep. 621.

[2] *Peak Hotels and Resorts Ltd v Tarek Investments Ltd* [2015] EWHC 1997 (Ch) at [131]–[138].

[3] *Halpern v Halpern (Nos 1 and 2)* [2008] Q.B. 195; L. Pearce [2008] 16 R.L.R. 124. See generally O'Sullivan, Elliott and Zakrzewski, *The Law of Rescission*, 2nd edn (Oxford: Oxford University Press, 2014); *UBS AG (London Branch) v Kommunale Wasserwerke Leipzig GmbH* [2017] EWCA Civ 1567; [2017] 2 Lloyd's Rep. 621.

Equity can effect what is necessary, for example by ordering accounts and inquiries[4] or an allowance for services rendered.[5]

The party rescinding is entitled to be restored to the position she would have been in had the contract not been entered into. She cannot recover damages, as that would put her in the position she would have been in had the contract been performed.[6]

B.   Grounds for Rescission[7]

i.   Mistake.[8]

29–002   *(a)   Voluntary Dispositions.*   A voluntary disposition, such as a gift or settlement,[9] may be set aside in equity on the ground of mistake. The principles were recently reviewed by the Supreme Court in *Pitt v Holt*.[10] The case has been considered above in the context of trustees' decision-making,[11] where it was seen that the challenge to the transactions on the basis of what was once thought to the rule in *Re Hastings-Bass*[12] failed. But in the *Pitt* appeal,[13] the Supreme Court also considered the possibility of a relief on the basis of equity's jurisdiction to rescind a voluntary transaction in the case of mistake. First, we may return to the facts:

> The settlor, who had a personal injury award, created a "special needs" discretionary trust, of which he was the primary beneficiary, but professional advisers did not appreciate that inheritance tax would be payable. This could have been avoided if a different form of trust had been used. An application was made to set aside the settlement on the ground of mistake, and HMRC joined the proceedings.

Modern cases had drawn a distinction between mistakes as to the legal "effect" of the disposition,[14] which may be sufficient, and as to its "consequences", which is not. The impact of taxation on a transaction is a consequence rather than a legal

---

[4] *Erlanger v New Sombrero Phosphate Co* (1878) 3 App.Cas. 1218. If all that was required was a return of money or other property without any adjustments, this could be achieved by the common law action for money had and received.

[5] *Guinness Plc v Saunders* [1990] 2 A.C. 663 at 698.

[6] *Redgrave v Hurd* (1881) 20 Ch.D. 1.

[7] See generally J. Cartwright, *Misrepresentation, Mistake and Non-Disclosure* (London: Sweet & Maxwell, 2016); E. Bant (2012) 32 O.J.L.S. 467.

[8] A. Burrows, *A Restatement of the English Law of Unjust Enrichment* (Oxford: Oxford University Press, 2012), pp.63–69.

[9] On what counts as a voluntary disposition, see *Co-operative Bank Plc v Hayes Freehold Ltd* [2017] EWHC 1820 (Ch) (considering a deed involving the surrender of an underlease and the consequent release from the landlord's obligations under that lease).

[10] [2013] UKSC 26; [2013] 2 A.C. 108. P.S. Davies and G. Virgo [2013] 21 R.L.R. 74; N. Lee [2014] Conv. 175; F. Ng [2013] B.T.R. 566; S. Watterson (2013) 72 C.L.J. 501; I. Dodds [2016] 24 R.L.R. 129. See generally M. Ashdown, *Trustee Decision Making: The Rule in Re Hastings-Bass* (Oxford: Oxford University Press, 2015).

[11] Above, paras 18–046—18–048.

[12] [1975] Ch. 25.

[13] There was no similar alternative claim in the *Futter* appeal which the Supreme Court also considered.

[14] *Gibbon v Mitchell* [1990] 1 W.L.R. 1304; *Anker-Petersen v Christensen* [2002] W.T.L.R. 313; *Wolff v Wolff* [2004] W.T.L.R. 1349.

effect, and so is outside the scope of factors enabling a disposition to be set aside. However, although in general "a mistake as to the essential nature of a transaction is likely to be more serious than a mistake as to its consequences",[15] that did not justify the limitation of the mistake to mistakes about "effects" alone.[16] Instead, a broader approach was to be adopted, reaffirming the approach of Lindley LJ in *Ogilvie v Littleboy*[17]:

> "In the absence of all circumstances of suspicion a donor can only obtain back property which he has given away by showing that he was under some mistake of so serious a character as to render it unjust on the part of the donee to retain the property given to him."[18]

The focus is therefore on the gravity of the causative mistake and the unconscionability of the situation. Lord Walker stressed that the inquiry must always be fact-specific:

> "The court cannot decide the issue of what is unconscionable by an elaborate set of rules. It must consider in the round the existence of a distinct mistake (as compared with total ignorance or disappointed expectations), its degree of centrality to the transaction in question and the seriousness of its consequences, and make an evaluative judgment whether it would be unconscionable, or unjust, to leave the mistake uncorrected."[19]

Applying that test to the present case, Lord Walker held that the settlement should be set aside because of the gravity of Mrs Pitt's mistake as to the adverse tax consequences of the arrangement.[20]

It will be apparent that Lord Walker's deliberately broad approach here left many questions unresolved.[21] Most immediately, it is not clear how or to what extent (or why) the equitable jurisdiction to relieve a mistake is more limited than its common law counterpart.[22] The jurisdiction has been examined in several subsequent cases. In *Wright v National Westminster Bank*,[23] Norris J was satisfied that a husband and wife had made "grave mistake[s]" in misunderstanding the arrangement under a trust declared by the husband. Mrs Wright had contributed to the settlement directly, but under the terms of the trust this meant that she was deprived of income both before and after Mr Wright's death. That result was unconscionable, in Norris J's view:

---

[15] [2013] UKSC 26 at [103].

[16] *Lobler v The Commissioners for Her Majesty's Revenue and Customs* [2015] UKUT 152 (TCC) per Proudman J at [70].

[17] (1897) 13 TLR 399.

[18] (1897) 13 TLR 399 at 400.

[19] [2013] UKSC 26 at [128].

[20] [2013] UKSC 26 at [142].

[21] Some further questions are raised by S. Watterson (2013) 72 C.L.J. 501 at 503.

[22] See Goff and Jones, 9th edn, Ch.9.

[23] [2014] EWHC 3158 (Ch).

"This was in my judgment an explicit and apparent mistake as to the nature of the transaction and its effects into which Mr Wright and Mrs Wright were being invited by the bank to enter. The mistake has serious consequences for Mr and Mrs Wright. I am satisfied that I ought to rescind the discretionary trust."[24]

29–003 Though not applicable in *Pitt* itself, Lord Walker raised the possibility that, since the jurisdiction may permit dispositions to be set aside so as to avoid tax liabilities, the court may in some circumstances consider whether to refuse relief:

"In some cases of artificial tax avoidance the court might think it right to refuse relief, either on the ground that such claimants, acting on supposedly expert advice, must be taken to have accepted the risk that the scheme would prove ineffective, or on the ground that discretionary relief should be refused on grounds of public policy."[25]

It is not clear when such public policy would be engaged outside of the most egregious case of tax avoidance. In *Kennedy v Kennedy*,[26] Sir Terence Etherton C granted rescission of an appointment of shares in favour of a settlor under what was intended to be a tax efficient arrangement, which in fact result in a significant Capital Gains Tax liability. The Chancellor held that the mistakes were "causative and very serious"[27]: significantly, although the arrangement engaged tax considerations, it

"was not an artificial tax avoidance arrangement or part of one. It was executed as a perfectly legitimate way of conferring benefit on Mr and Mrs Kennedy's children and grandchildren in a tax efficient manner that was contemplated by express provisions in [Finance Act] 2006."[28]

Indeed, there may be cases where the tax liabilities are incurred without the claimant appreciating that there are tax consequences at all.[29] The possibility of taking into account tax avoidance in the exercise of the court's discretion was raised in *Van der Merwe v Goldman*[30]:

A husband and wife, who jointly owned a house in Oxford, endeavoured to arrange their affairs in a tax efficient manner, anticipating changes to domicile provisions (they were both domiciled in South Africa for tax purposes). The wife transferred her share in the house to the husband, who in turn then declared himself trustee along with his wife, and transferred title into both of their names. The trust was in favour of the couple and their children. Unbeknownst to the couple, various changes to the inheritance tax regime had been announced shortly before they entered into these arrangements, which gave rise to significant tax liabilities. The claimant sought to set aside the settlement and transfer, which Her Majesty's Revenue and Customs opposed. Morgan J granted rescission.

---

[24] [2014] EWHC 3158 (Ch) at [22]. Norris J also held that the particular deed of gift by which Mrs W had purported to transfer units to Mr W had been uncertain in any case. Norris J required, upon setting aside the transaction, that Mr and Mrs W submit appropriate revised tax returns to reflect the income which was purportedly vested in the trusts.

[25] [2013] UKSC 26 at [135]. S. Evans [2015] Conv. 61.

[26] [2014] EWHC 4129 (Ch); T.K.C. Ng [2015] Conv. 266. At [36], the Chancellor offered a helpful summary of the appropriate principles after *Pitt v Holt*.

[27] [2014] EWHC 4129 (Ch) at [36].

[28] [2014] EWHC 4129 (Ch) at [39].

[29] *Lobler v The Commissioners for Her Majesty's Revenue and Customs* [2015] UKUT 152 (TCC).

[30] [2016] EWHC 790 (Ch); [2016] 4 W.L.R. 71 and [2016] EWHC 926 (Ch). See also *Bainbridge v Bainbridge* [2016] EWHC 898 (Ch); [2016] 2 P. & C.R. DG16 (Master Matthews).

Somewhat surprisingly, "HMRC accepted that it was unrealistic for them to ask a judge at first instance to give effect to Lord Walker's suggested possibility on the facts of this case," and Morgan J agreed.[31]

However, given that Lord Walker's approach in *Pitt* is predicated upon "an intense focus... on the facts of the particular case", it is clearly appropriate an appropriate point for a first instance judge to consider.[32]

This tax avoidance point in *Pitt* has received a decidedly frosty welcome in offshore jurisdictions.[33] The academic literature has been divided in its attitude towards Lord Walker's tax avoidance caveat: some writers have expressed concern that the approach penalises claimants and that avoidance which does not amount to abuse should not bar relief.[34] Others have considered that the fact that a disposition occurs during an attempt at tax avoidance can be a relevant factor in the exercise of the court's discretion whether to set that disposition aside.[35] As summarised by Proudman J in *Freedman v Freedman*[36]:

"in order for relief to be given, there must be a distinct mistake, a serious mistake, and it must be unconscionable not to set the settlement aside. In addition, it is likely that relief will not be given if the transaction is part of a tax avoidance scheme".

Although it is a broad discretion dependent upon the facts, factors which have so far been taken into account in assessing unconscionability under *Pitt* include the availability of an alternative remedy,[37] the size of the unintended tax liability,[38] and the effect on any other parties or obligations if the disposition were not set aside.[39] Finally, it should be noted that a voluntary disposition may also be set aside if there was a fundamental mistake as to an existing fact which was basic to the transaction. An example is *Re Griffiths*,[40] where a gift was set aside where the donor would not have made it had he been aware of his terminal illness, which made the intended tax saving impossible to achieve.

---

[31] [2016] 4 W.L.R. 71 at [42].

[32] [2013] UKSC 26 at [126]; for further criticism, see J. Lee (2017) 31 T.L.I. 219.

[33] *AB v CD*, unreported, CHP 2016/7 (Isle of Man); *Nourse v Heritage Corporate Trustees Ltd*, Royal Court of Guernsey, Judgment 1/2015; *Boyd v Rozel Trustees (Channel Islands) Ltd* [2014] JRC 056 (Jersey, which has also seen legislation: Trusts (Amendment No.6) (Jersey) Law 2013 s.47E) and The Hon Anthony Smellie CJ (of the Cayman Islands) (2014) 20 T. & T. 1101; R. Lee [2018] Conv. 45.

[34] F. Ng [2013] B.T.R. 566, 575-6; N. Lee [2014] Conv. 175; C. Mitchell [2017] P.C.B. 41. The Finance Act 2013 s.206, and collectively Part 5 introduced a "general anti-abuse rule" which enables courts to disregard "contrived or abnormal steps" in tax arrangements deemed to be abusive.

[35] M. Yip (2014) J. Eq. 46; J. Lee (2017) 31 T.L.I. 219.

[36] [2015] EWHC 1457 (Ch) at [18].

[37] *Co-operative Bank Plc v Hayes Freehold Ltd* [2017] EWHC 1820 (Ch) per Henry Carr J at [139] (cause of action in negligence against solicitors who advised on the relevant deal; rescission was denied on the facts)

[38] *Kennedy v Kennedy* [2014] EWHC 4129 (Ch); *Freedman v Freedman* [2015] EWHC 1457 (Ch).

[39] *Gresh v RBC Trust Co* Royal Court of Guernsey, Judgment 6/2016; *Pitt* (at [142]).

[40] [2009] Ch. 162. The Court of Appeal in *Pitt v Holt* [2011] 3 W.L.R. 19 had reservations about the result in that case (although not the principle) because the donor had not followed advice to take out insurance. As he had taken the risk, it would not be against conscience for the recipient to retain the gift.

29–004　　*(b)　Contracts.*　　While mistake alone may justify refusal of an order for specific performance,[41] mistake alone is not an automatic ground for rescission, although a mistake induced by fraud, or by misrepresentation, or deliberately not corrected in a situation that called for full disclosure[42] is a more compelling case than a mistake arising without the responsibility of the other party. If two parties enter into a contract and one makes a mistake concerning it, the general principle is that behind the maxim caveat emptor; a party who knows she is making a better bargain than the other is under no duty to divulge the fact. A party who wishes to secure a form of guarantee as to any aspect of the transaction must raise the matter at the time and have it dealt with on the basis of representation or a term of the contract. All this is inherent in freedom of contract; but it is subject to some limits even at common law. For instance, a party cannot remain silent when he knows the other party is mistaken as to what the actual terms of the contract are[43]; or in certain cases of mistake as to the identity of the person contracted with.[44]

It was at one time thought that there was a jurisdiction in equity to rescind a contract on the ground of mistake common to both parties in circumstances where the contract was valid at common law. This has now been discredited as inconsistent with the decision of the House of Lords in *Bell v Lever Bros Ltd.*[45]

> A company gave Bell a "golden handshake" to compensate him for the early termination of his contract of service. The company then discovered that the contract of service was voidable by reason of Bell's breach of fiduciary duty, so that he could have been dismissed without compensation. There was no fraudulent concealment, as Bell's mind was not directed to his breach of duty at the time of the compensation agreement. The House of Lords declined to rescind the latter agreement.

After *Bell*, the Court of Appeal, in particular Lord Denning (as Denning LJ in *Solle v Butcher*)[46], asserted a wide equitable jurisdiction to rescind a contract where the mistake was not of a character to make the contract void at law. For the next half century the courts struggled to define equity's supposed jurisdiction, which required the mistake to be common and sufficiently fundamental, and the claimant not to have been "at fault". The decision in *Bell v Lever Bros Ltd* was treated as dealing only with the position at common law. However, it did not prove possible to define the two different kinds of mistake, one operating at law and one in equity, and the attempts to do so merely emphasised the confusion. The Court of Appeal rejected equity's supposed jurisdiction in *Great Peace Shipping Ltd v Tsavliris Salvage (International) Ltd.*[47]

---

[41] e.g. *Wood v Scarth* (1855) 2 K. & J. 33, above, para.27–034.

[42] e.g. *Gordon v Gordon* (1816) 3 Swan. 400, below, para.29–006.

[43] *Smith v Hughes* (1870-71) L.R. 6 Q.B. 597 (endorsed by Lord Neuberger PSC in *VTB Capital Plc v Nutritek International Corp* [2013] UKSC 5; [2013] 2 A.C. 337 at [140]); *Hartog v Colin & Shields* [1939] 3 All E.R. 566; *Dresdner Kleinwort Ltd, Commerzbank AG v Richard Attrill* [2013] EWCA Civ 394 per Elias LJ at [86].

[44] *Cundy v Lindsay* (1878) 3 App.Cas. 459; *Ingram v Little* [1961] 1 Q.B. 31; cf. *Lewis v Averay* [1972] 1 Q.B. 198.

[45] [1932] A.C. 161; C. MacMillan (2003) 119 L.Q.R. 625.

[46] [1950] 1 K.B. 671.

[47] [2003] Q.B. 679. See also *Statoil ASA v Louis Dreyfus Energy Services LP* [2008] 2 Lloyd's Rep. 685 (unilateral mistake).

The parties entered into a contract to hire a ship to escort a damaged ship to port. Both parties wrongly thought that the two ships were in close proximity. On discovering that this was not so, the defendant repudiated the contract and hired a closer ship, refusing to pay the claimant the contractual cancellation fee on the ground that the contract could be set aside in equity. The Court of Appeal held that equity had no jurisdiction to rescind a contract for common mistake. The cancellation fee was, therefore, payable.

It was, however, inconceivable that the House of Lords in *Bell* would have overlooked a right to rescind in equity. The reality was that equity did not have the jurisdiction claimed by Lord Denning.[48] The effect of *Solle v Butcher* was not to supplement or mitigate *Bell*, but to say that it was wrongly decided. Thus *Solle v Butcher* could not stand with *Bell*.

This rejection of equity's "intrusion" into the law on rescission of a contract for mistake was welcomed, although the decision in *Great Peace Shipping* was criticised in some respects.[49] The court will also be alert to whether the risk of mistake has been allocated by the parties to the contract.[50] It of course remains possible to establish a common mistake applying *Bell*.[51]

ii. Other Grounds. Mistake in a wider sense may give rise to the right to rescind, as where the mistake results from a misrepresentation; similarly in a case of constructive fraud, which embraces the doctrines of undue influence and unconscionable bargains. These will be discussed below. The right to rescind may also be granted expressly by the terms of the contract, which will then govern its exercise. The right to rescind where there has been a substantial misdescription in a contract for the sale of land has already been discussed.[52]

29–005

(a) Misrepresentation.[53] Where the misrepresentation was fraudulent, the contract could be set aside both at common law and in equity. "Fraudulent" here means that the misrepresentation was made knowingly or recklessly.[54] It must have been intended to be acted upon, and actually have had this result. Equity alone, however, gave relief where the misrepresentation was not fraudulent. Such an "innocent misrepresentation" was not recognised at common law unless it had become a term of the contract.[55] The Supreme Court has considered misrepresentation in several recent cases.

29–006

---

[48] Lord Millett described Lord Denning's approach as "heresy", saying "The less said about it the better." See (2007) 123 L.Q.R. 159 at 163.

[49] G. McMeel [2002] L.M.C.L.Q. 449; F. Reynolds and S. Midwinter (2003) 119 L.Q.R. 177 and 180 respectively; C. Hare (2003) 62 C.L.J. 29; A. Phang [2003] Conv. 247; J. Cartwright [2003] 11 R.L.R. 93; T. Yeo (2005) 121 L.Q.R. 393; G. McMeel [2006] L.M.C.L.Q. 49 at 62.

[50] *Dana Gas PJSC v Dana Gas Sukuk* [2017] EWHC 2928 (Comm) per Leggatt J at [61]–[62].

[51] For a recent example of an agreement being held to have been void on the basis of common mistake, see *The British Red Cross v Werry* [2017] EWHC 875 (Ch) (the parties were shown to have been mistaken by the belated discovery of a will).

[52] Above, para.27–039.

[53] Only an outline will be given here, and reference should be made to the standard works on contract.

[54] *Derry v Peek* (1889) 14 App.Cas. 337; *ECO3 Capital Ltd v Ludsin Overseas Ltd* [2013] EWCA Civ 413 at [77]–[82]. *Beacon Insurance Co Ltd v Maharaj Bookstore* [2014] UKPC 21 per Lord Hodge at [36]: "The boundary between an incompetent mistake and a lie may be a matter of impression which is usually best left to the trial judge who sees the witness give evidence." Damages for deceit are also available: *Archer v Brown* [1985] Q.B. 401; *Saunders v Edwards* [1987] 1 W.L.R. 1116.

[55] See *Heilbut Symons & Co v Buckleton* [1913] A.C. 30.

It is necessary not only for there to be a misrepresentation, but also for the representee to have been induced to act to their detriment. In *Hayward v Zurich Insurance Co*,[56] the claimant insurers sought to have set aside the settlement of an insurance claim on the basis that the defendant had fraudulently exaggerated his injuries, as had been subsequently revealed. The claimants had suspected that the defendant had been lying throughout but nevertheless settled the claim. It was held that they were entitled to set aside the settlement. Lord Clarke held that "questions of inducement and causation are questions of fact"[57] and rejected the suggestion that belief is a requisite element of the tort:

> "The fact that the representee (Zurich) does not wholly credit the fraudster (Mr Hayward) and carries out its own investigations does not preclude it from having been induced by those representations. Qualified belief or disbelief does not rule out inducement, particularly where those investigations were never going to find out the evidence that subsequently came to light."[58]

Nor is it necessary for the representation to be the sole cause of inducement.[59]

It should be noted that mere silence does not constitute a misrepresentation unless it creates a false impression by distorting the meaning of any positive statement.[60] Further, there are duties relating to disclosure in the case of a contract uberrimae fidei (of the utmost good faith),[61] such as contracts of insurance of all kinds,[62] and contracts for family settlements.[63] Breach of such a

---

[56] [2016] UKSC 48; [2017] A.C. 142; Lindeman (2017) 36 C.J.Q. 273; K.C.F. Loi [2017] J.B.L. 598; R. Lee [2017] L.M.C.L.Q. 150; P.J. Rawlings and J.P. Lowry (2017) 80 M.L.R. 524.

[57] [2017] A.C. 142 at [25]; see also Lord Toulson JSC at [71].

[58] [2016] UKSC 48 per Lord Clarke at [40]. The question whether a representee who is aware of the full facts and knows that the relevant representation is false could seek rescission was left open, as Zurich merely suspected that Mr Hayward's claim was fraudulent: at [44]–[48]: but in *Holyoake v Candy* [2017] EWHC 3397 (Ch), Nugee J, distinguished Hayward and held (at [388]) that "it is difficult to see how [a claimant] can say that he has been induced to enter into a contract by a lie if he knows that it is untrue". See also Law Com. No. 353/Scot Law Com. No. 238, *Insurance Contract Law: Business Disclosure; Warranties; Insurers' Remedies for Fraudulent Claims; and Late Payment* (2014) at para.23.21.

[59] [2016] UKSC 48 per Lord Clarke at [33] (relying on *Barton v Armstrong* [1976] A.C. 104).

[60] *Oakes v Turquand* (1867) L.R. 2 H.L. 325.

[61] Or where a fiduciary or other similar special relationship exists between the contracting parties; *van Gestel v Cann, The Times*, 7 August 1987; *Guinness Plc v Saunders* [1990] 2 A.C. 663; *Conlon v Simms* [2008] 1 W.L.R. 484 (partnership agreement).

[62] Insurance contract law has been reformed as a result of work by the Law Commissions: leading to the Consumer Insurance (Disclosure and Representations) Act 2012 (see M. Clarke [2012] L.M.C.L.Q. 611) and the Insurance Act 2015. The 2015 Act abolishes the general right of an avoidance for breach of the duty of good faith, but see B. Soyer and A.M. Tettenborn (2016) 132 L.Q.R. 618 and R. Merkin and O. Gurses (2015) 78 M.L.R. 1004. Nevertheless, "exacting duties of disclosure are still imposed on the applicant for insurance at the pre-contract stage": *Versloot Dredging BV v HDI Gerling Industrie Versicherung AG* [2016] UKSC 45; [2017] A.C. 1 per Lord Hughes at [54].

[63] Also company prospectuses: see *London Assurance Co v Mansel* (1879) 11 Ch.D. 363 and *The New Brunswick and Canada Railway and Land Co v Muggeridge* (1860) 1 Dr. & Sm. 363 at 381. "[There] is no general doctrine of 'good faith' in English contract law, although a duty of good faith is implied by law as an incident of certain categories of contract" per Jackson LJ at *Mid Essex Hospital Services NHS Trust v Compass Group UK and Ireland Ltd* [2013] EWCA Civ 200 at [105]; J.W. Carter and W. Courtney (2016) 75 C.L.J. 608; S Saintier [2017] J.B.L. 441; Z.X. Tan [2016] J.B.L. 420.

duty of disclosure is not a misrepresentation within the Misrepresentation Act 1967, nor does it sound in damages,[64] the proper remedy being rescission.[65]

Similar duties may be owed to the court.[66] In *Jenkins v Livesey (formerly Jenkins)*,[67] a divorcing couple agreed that the husband would transfer his half-share of the home to the wife, who would give up all claims to financial provision. Shortly after this agreement, the wife became engaged to marry a man she had met before the agreement. This was not disclosed to the husband nor to her own solicitor. The agreement was then embodied in a consent order under s.25(1) of the Matrimonial Causes Act 1973. Two days after the husband conveyed his share of the home, the wife remarried. The House of Lords set aside the consent order. The remarriage ended the wife's right to financial provision, thus the husband would not have entered into the agreement had it been disclosed. The test for whether the order should be set aside was whether the order was substantially different from that which would have been made upon full disclosure.

The position in respect of fraudulent non-disclosure was considered by the Supreme Court in a pair of appeals[68] in 2015: *Sharland v Sharland*[69] and *Gohil v Gohil*.[70]

> In *Sharland*, the divorcing couple had agreed a financial settlement. Before the consent order was sealed, the wife discovered that the husband had failed to disclose the true extent of his dealings in respect of his shareholding in a company. This amount to dishonest non-disclosure as the value of the shareholding was much higher than he had maintained during the hearing. The judge at first instance however perfected the consent order as he held that the same order would have been made in any event and so the non-disclosure was not material. The Supreme Court considered that the consent order should be set aside and the matter remitted to the High Court for a further hearing[71]:
>
>> "It is clear from ... *Livesey* that the misrepresentation or non-disclosure must be material to the decision that the court made at the time. But this is a case of fraud. It would be extraordinary if the victim of a fraudulent misrepresentation, which had led her to compromise her claim to financial remedies in a matrimonial case, were in a worse position than the victim of a fraudulent misrepresentation in an ordinary contract

---

[64] *Banque Keyser Ullman SA v Skandia (UK) Insurance Co Ltd* [1990] 1 Q.B. 665 at 789–790; affirmed [1991] 2 A.C. 249. Damages are recoverable in cases of fraud; *Conlon v Simms* [2008] 1 W.L.R. 484.

[65] *Gordon v Gordon* (1816) 3 Swan 400 (a deed of settlement of property within a family was entered into by an eldest son in the belief that he was illegitimate; the deed was set aside because the younger son knew, but had not disclosed, that the parents had entered into a secret marriage)

[66] "Family proceedings are different from ordinary civil proceedings in two respects. First, in family proceedings ... a consent order derives its authority from the court and not from the consent of the parties, whereas in ordinary civil proceedings, a consent order derives its authority from the contract made between the parties... Second, in family proceedings there is always a duty of full and frank disclosure, whereas in civil proceedings this is not universal": [2016] A.C. 871 per Baroness Hale of Richmond DPSC at [27] (citations omitted).

[67] [1985] A.C. 424. See R. Ingleby (1985) 44 C.L.J. 202. The decision is based on the requirements of s.25, rather than the concept of uberrima fides in the agreement for a consent order.

[68] The appeals were heard together by the same seven-Justice panel and judgments delivered on the same day. P. Way and A. Tarasiewicz [2016] P.C.B. 36

[69] [2015] UKSC 60; [2016] A.C. 871.

[70] [2015] UKSC 61; [2016] A.C. 849.

[71] [2016] A.C. 871 at [32].

case, including a contract to settle a civil claim … [A] party who has practised deception with a view to a particular end, which has been attained by it, cannot be allowed to deny its materiality."

In *Gohil*, the husband and wife's ancillary relief proceedings were resolved by a consent order, which recorded that the wife believed that the husband had not frankly disclosed the full extent of his assets. The wife subsequently applied to set aside the consent order on the basis of non-disclosure.[72] The first instance judge had set aside the consent order, but was reversed by the Court of Appeal. The Supreme Court reinstated the judge's original decision. Lord Wilson emphasised that "the spouse has a duty to the court to make full and frank disclosure of his resources" and "[one] spouse cannot exonerate the other from complying with his or her duty to the court"[73]: the express inclusion of the wife compromising in the teeth of her disbelief did not prevent the setting aside of the consent order. Summarising the position after *Sharland* and *Gohil*, Lord Neuberger observed in the latter:

"where a party's non-disclosure was inadvertent, there is no presumption that it was material and the onus is on the other party to show that proper disclosure would, on the balance of probabilities, have led to a different order; whereas where a party's non-disclosure was intentional, it is deemed to be material, so that it is presumed that proper disclosure would have led to a different order, unless that party can show, on the balance of probabilities, that it would not have done so.[74]"

The general effect of the Supreme Court's recent jurisprudence on misrepresentation is to reaffirm the judicial policy against fraud in the context of litigation: King LJ has described *Gohil* as being "unequivocal" on the point.[75] An exception is *Versloot Dredging BV v HDI Gerling Industrie Versicherung AG*,[76] a case concerning "collateral lies"—those which are irrelevant to the merits of the claim—in insurance claims. By a majority, the Supreme Court held that the fraudulent claims rule does not apply to such claims:

---

[72] There were further complications, not material for present purposes, in the light of the husband's subsequent conviction in respect of money laundering and conspiracy to defraud, as the wife sought to rely on evidence obtained the criminal proceedings.

[73] [2016] A.C. 849 at [22].

[74] [2016] A.C. 849 at [44]. On the setting aside of orders after *Sharland* and *Gohil*, see *GW v GW* [2016] EWHC 3000 (Fam); [2017] 4 W.L.R. 13 (rehearing after material non-disclosure by husband); *Norman v Norman (No.2): Practice Note* [2017] EWCA Civ 120; [2017] 1 W.L.R. 2554; *Re W (A Child)* [2017] EWHC 1760 (Fam) (refusal to set aside adoption order where no fraud established, which would not have been material in any event); *Taylor v The Secretary of State for Business, Innovation and Skills* [2016] EWHC 1953 (Ch) (refusal to set aside undertaking not to act as a director); *AB v CD (Financial Provision) (Consent Order: Non-disclosure)* [2016] EWHC 10 (Fam); [2016] 4 W.L.R. 36 per Roberts J at [165] and [167]: "it is not for a litigant to judge the ambit of the duty to disclose or the consequences of disclosure… The duty of confidence which exists between the court and the parties will usually mean that disclosure is the safest route in cases of doubt." *Salekipour v Parmar* [2017] EWCA Civ 2141 (County Court judge has power to set aside an earlier final order of the County Court obtained by perjury or fraud). On the position in Australia in cases not amounting to fraud, see *Clone Pty Ltd v Players Pty Ltd* [2018] HCA 12.

[75] *Roocroft v Ball* [2016] EWCA Civ 1009 (order on dissolution after civil partnership) per King LJ at [65].

[76] [2017] A.C. 1.

"Even in the law of insurance a material misrepresentation or non-disclosure in the making of the contract, whether honest or dishonest, will not give rise to a right of avoidance unless it induced the insurer to accept the risk or to do so on the particular terms."[77]

As far as innocent misrepresentation was concerned, equity's jurisdiction depended on the force of the misrepresentation on the claimant's mind rather than the mental state of the defendant when she made it, or on the relative importance of the fact misrepresented to the contract as a whole. Thus a claimant seeking rescission on this ground did not have to prove negligence or any other degree of fault in the defendant but only the fact of her own reliance on the statement, and its untruth.

29–007

Prior to the Misrepresentation Act 1967 the claimant could rescind,[78] or possibly resist specific performance, but she could not recover damages on the basis of an innocent misrepresentation. Since that Act, however, the claimant may recover damages under s.2(1) for an innocent misrepresentation unless the defendant had reasonable grounds to believe and did believe that the statement was true.[79] The measure of damages is the same as that which applies to a fraudulent misrepresentation.[80] By s.2(2), damages may be awarded in lieu of rescission wherever the court thinks it would be equitable to do so, having regard to the nature of the misrepresentation and the loss that would be caused by it if the contract were upheld, as well as the loss that rescission would cause to the defendant. Damages may be awarded under s.2(2) although the misrepresentation was wholly innocent, (i.e. non-negligent). The measure is as in contract, and is thus different from the measure of damages under subs.(1).[81] The result intended would seem to be that damages are the most suitable remedy in cases of misrepresentations inducing a contract, save where the facts reveal a real justification for there being rescission of the contract as well. The Court of Appeal considered the scope and meaning of s.2(2) in *Salt v Stratstone Specialist Ltd*[82]: where Longmore LJ held that[83]

---

[77] [2017] A.C. 1 at [35]. His Lordship continued that to hold otherwise and to allow the insurer to avoid the contract, would be "disproportionately harsh to the insured and goes further than any legitimate commercial interest of the insurer can justify".

[78] See generally *Redgrave v Hurd* (1881) 20 Ch.D. 1.

[79] See *Laurence v Lexcourt Holdings Ltd* [1978] 1 W.L.R. 1128; *Walker v Boyle* [1982] 1 W.L.R. 495; *Government of Zanzibar v British Aerospace (Lancaster House) Ltd* [2000] 1 W.L.R. 2333.

[80] *Royscot Trust Ltd v Rogerson* [1991] 2 Q.B. 297; R. Hooley (1991) 107 L.Q.R. 547. But the correctness of *Royscot* was left open in *Smith New Court Securities Ltd v Scrimgeour Vickers (Asset Management) Ltd* [1997] A.C. 254; J. Payne (1997) 56 C.L.J. 17. See also *East v Maurer* [1991] 1 W.L.R. 461 (loss of profits); *Clef Aquitaine SARL v Laporte Materials (Barrow) Ltd* [2001] Q.B. 488 (reduced profits); *Yam Seng Pte Ltd v International Trade Corp Ltd* [2013] EWHC 111 (QB); [2013] 1 C.L.C. 662 at [205]–[221] (looking at net loss); *Dhaliwal v Hussain* [2017] EWHC 2655 (Ch) (losses from fraudulent misrepresentation in respect of sale of dental practice). On causation in misrepresentation, see K.R. Handley (2015) 131 L.Q.R. 275.

[81] *William Sindall Plc v Cambridgeshire CC* [1994] 1 W.L.R. 1016; H. Beale (1995) 111 L.Q.R. 60; A. Oakley (1995) 54 C.L.J. 17.

[82] *Salt v Stratstone Specialist Ltd (t/a Stratstone Cadillac Newcastle)* [2015] EWCA Civ 745; P.S. Davies (2016) 75 C.L.J. 15; P.G. Turner (2016) 132 L.Q.R. 388.

[83] [2015] EWCA Civ 745 at [17]. "This may seem harsh on the misrepresentee who has, through no fault of his own, lost the right to rescind, but the wording of the statute does not sensibly lead to any other interpretation." P.S. Davies (2016) 75 C.L.J. 15 at 17; cf. P.G. Turner (2016) 132 L.Q.R. 388.

"the words 'in lieu of rescission' must… carry with them the implication that rescission is available (or was available at the time the contract was rescinded). If it is not (or was not available in law) because e.g. the contract has been affirmed, third party rights have intervened, an excessive time has elapsed or restitution has become impossible, rescission is not available and damages cannot be said to be awarded 'in lieu of rescission'."

A term in the contract purporting to restrict or exclude liability for misrepresentation is of no effect except insofar as it satisfies the requirement of reasonableness as stated in s.11(1) of the Unfair Contract Terms Act 1977.[84]

Equity's remedy of rescission now forms part of a hierarchy of remedies for misrepresentation that are available generally to a claimant, instead of being the only and not always very apposite remedy available in the absence of fraud. It is thus now more important as a supplementary than as a basic remedy. The history and rationale of the remedy are, however, of interest in considering rescission for mistakes not induced by misrepresentation, discussed in the earlier part of this section.

29-008   (b)   *Undue Influence.*[85]   Under the head of constructive fraud,[86] equity recognises a wide variety of situations in which intervention is justified by reason of a defendant's influence or dominance over the claimant in procuring his execution of a document (such as a settlement) or his entering into an obligation; equity's intervention here is independent of any question of the accuracy of information supplied to the claimant. Equity intervenes in such cases, not because, as is the case with misrepresentations, the defendant has positively (albeit innocently) misled the claimant on a particular and relevant point of fact, but because the defendant had caused the claimant's judgment to be clouded, with the result that he has failed to consider the matter as he ought. The right to set aside the transaction arises without the claimant having to show that he or she would have acted differently in the absence of undue influence.[87]

Actual threats, or physical duress, are remedied both at law[88] and in equity, but equity's view is the wider. Where threats have made it impossible for the claimant either to consider the relevant matter normally or to feel a free agent, as when a son was threatened with disclosure to his sick father of the forging of the father's

---

[84] s.3, as amended by the 1977 Act. See *Walker v Boyle* [1982] 1 W.L.R. 495; *Taberna Europe CDO II Plc v Selskabet AF1* [2016] EWCA Civ 1262; [2017] Q.B. 633.

[85] See generally Halliwell, *Equity and Good Conscience in a Contemporary Context* (London: Old Bailey Press, 1997), Ch.3; Enonchong, *Duress, Undue Influence and Unconscionable Dealing* (London: Lloyd's of London Press, 1998); K. Lewison [2011] 19 R.L.R. 1. N. Enonchong, *Duress, Undue Influence and Unconscionable Dealing* (London: Sweet & Maxwell, 2012); A. Burrows, *A Restatement of the English Law of Unjust Enrichment* (Oxford: Oxford University Press, 2012), 72–9; M. Chen-Wishart (2013) 62 I.C.L.Q. 1, comparing England and Singapore.

[86] See *O'Sullivan v Management Agency and Music Ltd* [1985] Q.B. 428, at 455; *Mander v Evans* [2001] 1 W.L.R. 2378. See also *Re Edwards* [2007] W.T.L.R. 1387 (will may be set aside in equity on the ground of "fraudulent calumny"); *Edkins v Hopkins* [2016] EWHC 2542 (Ch) (will not set aside as deceased acted as free agent notwithstanding influence of key legatee); *Kunicki v Haywards* [2016] EWHC 3199 (Ch). M. Allardice (2017) 7 Elder L.J. 10 and Law Com. CP No. 231, *Making a Will* (2017), paras 7.61–7.63.

[87] *UCB Corporate Services Ltd v Williams* (2003) 1 P. & C.R. 12. However, this question is relevant to the quantification of any loss.

[88] See A.F.H. Loke (2017) 37 L.S. 418.

signature by his brother, equity will intervene.[89] But influence by means other than threats is the more usual type of case. As the High Court of Australia has recently noted in *Thorne v Kennedy*[90]:

> "One reason for the difficulty of defining undue influence is that the label "undue influence" has been used to mean different things. It has been used to include abuse of confidence, misrepresentation, and the pressure which amounts to common law duress. Each of those concepts is better seen as distinct. Nevertheless, the boundaries, particularly between undue influence and duress, are blurred. One reason why there is no clear distinction is that undue influence can arise from widely different sources, one of which is excessive pressure. Importantly, however, since pressure is only one of the many sources for the influence that one person can have over another, it is not necessary that the pressure which contributes to a conclusion of undue influence be characterised as illegitimate or improper."

It is possible for a defendant to have obtained almost complete domination over the mind of another,[91] but in most cases the undue[92] influence is exerted only to secure a specific objective.[93] The varieties of methods are infinite also; they may range from developing a sense of complete confidence[94] over many years to quick seizure of an opportunity presented by a defendant's weakness.

There are two categories of cases; first, those in which equity presumes undue influence. While the presumption does not apply to every relationship of trust and confidence,[95] it does arise in certain well defined cases such as parent and child, guardian and ward, doctor and patient, solicitor and client, religious adviser and pupil,[96] and other situations where it is shown that a similar relationship of

29–009

---

[89] *Mutual Finance Co v Wetton* [1937] 2 K.B. 389; *Barton v Armstrong* [1976] A.C. 104. See W. Winder (1939) 3 M.L.R. 97.

[90] [2017] HCA 49 at [31], See also *Tufton v Sperni* [1952] 2 T.L.R. 516. cf. *Evans v Lloyd* [2013] EWHC 1725 (Ch); [2013] W.T.L.R. 1137 (transferor found to have made free and informed decision).

[91] *Smith v Kay* (1859) 7 H.L.Cas. 750; *Morley v Loughnan* [1893] 1 Ch. 736; *Cramaso LLP v Viscount Reidhaven's Trustees* [2014] UKSC 9; [2014] A.C. 1093; L. Macgregor (2015) 19 Edin. L.R. 112.

[92] It may be undue without being for personal gain, as where a parent's influence leads to an improvident settlement by a child that is only of marginal benefit to the parent: *Bullock v Lloyds Bank* [1955] Ch. 317. cf. *Howard v Howard-Lawson* [2012] EWHC 3258 (Ch).

[93] *Lyon v Home* (1868) L.R. 6 Eq. 655 (a spiritual medium induced a widow into believing her deceased husband wished her to make various gifts to the medium).

[94] *Tate v Williamson* (1866–67) L.R. 2 Ch. App. 55.

[95] *National Westminster Bank Plc v Morgan* [1985] A.C. 686; *Goldsworthy v Brickell* [1987] Ch. 378.

[96] *Allcard v Skinner* (1887) 36 Ch.D. 145 (nun and mother superior); *Huguenin v Baseley* (1807) 14 Ves. 273. For the view that there are not two categories, see K. Lewison [2011] 19 R.L.R. 1. On undue influence in the spiritual context, see R. Hedlund (2016) 5 O.J.L.R. 298.

confidence existed.[97] It is unlikely to arise in a "purely commercial relationship".[98] Here equity requires positive evidence that no undue influence was in fact exerted, and it is not enough to show that there was no "sinister" conduct on the part of the defendant.[99] As Sir Terence Etherton C has explained:

> "The relationship between two individuals may be such that, without more, one of them is disposed to agree a course of action proposed by the other. Typically this occurs where one person places trust in another to look after their affairs and interests, and the latter betrays that trust by preferring their own interests. It is a matter of evidence whether one party has reposed sufficient trust and confidence in the other to give rise to a presumption of undue influence. The principle is not confined, however, to cases of abuse of trust and confidence. It also includes, for example, cases where a vulnerable person has been exploited."[100]

Secondly, in cases outside this category equity requires positive proof of influence having actually been exerted.[101] But in all cases the question is whether a defendant has taken advantage of her position,[102] which includes breaching a duty of candour and fairness arising from the relationship,[103] or has been assiduous not to do so. Many cases turn on whether a defendant discouraged independent legal advice or proceeded in such a way as to make it unlikely that

---

[97] *Re Craig* [1971] Ch. 95 (aged widower and secretary); *Lloyd's Bank Ltd v Bundy* [1975] Q.B. 326 (banker and aged customer); *O'Sullivan v Management Agency and Music Ltd* [1985] Q.B. 428 (manager and entertainer); *Re Brocklehurst* [1978] Ch. 14 at 42; *Simpson v Simpson* [1992] 1 F.L.R. 601 (incapacitated elderly husband and younger wife); *Cheese v Thomas* [1994] 1 W.L.R. 129 (elderly uncle and great nephew); *Hammond v Osborn* [2002] W.T.L.R. 1125 (elderly man and carer); *Curtis v Curtis* [2011] EWCA Civ 1602 ("Self Realisation Mediation Healing Centre Charitable Trust" exercised undue influence in receiving property from devotee). The court may also have a residual jurisdiction in the case of vulnerable adults: *Re L (Vulnerable Adults with Capacity: Court's Jurisdiction)* [2012] EWCA Civ 253. See also *Birmingham City Council v Beech (aka Howell)* [2014] EWCA Civ 830; [2015] 1 P. & C.R. 1.

[98] *Maxted v Investec Bank* [2017] EWHC 1997 (Ch) per Mr Registrar Briggs at [26], also concluding "The Applicants are men of business and, in my judgment, capable of looking after themselves, understanding the risks involved in the giving of guarantees."

[99] *Hammond v Osborn* [2002] W.T.L.R. 1125; K. Scott [2003] L.M.C.L.Q. 145; P. Birks (2003) 119 L.Q.R. 34 at 36 and (2004) 120 L.Q.R. 34; *Niersmans v Pesticcio* [2004] W.T.L.R. 699; N. Enonchong (2005) 121 L.Q.R. 29. See generally M. Chen-Wishart (2006) 59 C.L.P. 231.

[100] *Birmingham City Council v Beech (aka Howell)* [2014] EWCA Civ 830 at [59]. See also *Hart v Burbidge* [2014] EWCA Civ 992; [2015] 1 P. & C.R. DG9 (daughter exercising influence over mother) per Vos LJ at [48]: "Disposing of almost the entirety of the deceased's cash by way of gift would seem obviously to call for an explanation, since it deprived the deceased of security, an income, and the ability to live alone."

[101] As in the case of gifts by will, where no presumption of undue influence arises by reason of the relationship of the parties. P. Ridge (2004) 120 L.Q.R. 617; Law Com. CP No. 231, *Making a Will* (2017), Ch.7. There is no presumption of undue influence between husband and wife, although a transaction may be set aside if a relationship of confidence is shown to have existed, or failing that, on proof of undue influence; *Bank of Montreal v Stuart* [1911] A.C. 120; *Kingsnorth Trust Ltd v Bell* [1986] 1 W.L.R. 119; B. Dale [1989] Conv. 63. On engaged couples, see N. Enonchong (2005) 121 L.Q.R. 567.

[102] For an example of actual undue influence being established, see *Desir v Alcide* [2015] UKPC 24.

[103] *Hewett v First Plus Financial Group Plc* [2010] 2 F.L.R. 177 (husband concealed affair when persuading wife to charge family home). Non-disclosure of material facts, as opposed to deliberate concealment, does not amount to undue influence; *Royal Bank of Scotland Plc v Chandra* [2011] EWCA Civ 192; [2011] 2 P. & C.R. DG 1; *Davies v AIB Group (UK) Plc* [2012] EWHC 2178 (Ch); [2012] 2 P. & C.R. 19.

the claimant would think of taking it.[104] For, as with many of the flexible remedies of equity, a defendant is not placed under an absolute bar by virtue of this equitable obligation, but has to adopt proper steps, in view of the obligation, if she wishes to proceed in certain ways. So a genuine insistence on independent legal advice from a fully informed adviser is a natural means of repudiating a charge of having exerted undue influence, even in a case where the possibility of influence was strong[105] and especially where there is a conflict of interest and duty.[106] But the presumption of undue influence is not rebuttable only by establishing insistence on independent legal advice (which, however, does not always suffice to rebut the presumption[107]); it may also be rebutted by showing that a gift was a "spontaneous and independent act".[108] In any event, the presumption will not operate unless the gift is so large or the transaction so improvident that it cannot reasonably be accounted for on grounds of friendship, relationship, charity or other motives.[109]

Most of the illustrations relate to situations of special relationship[110] existing between particular people, and often involve settlements of property. The principle is less often seen in operation in commercial matters, where it has had little impact in derogating from the more widely applicable principle that lies behind the maxim caveat emptor.[111] Mere inequality of bargaining power, which is a relative concept, does not justify interference with a commercial transaction. There is rarely absolute equality, and the court only interferes in exceptional

---

[104] *Baker v Monk* (1864) 4 De G.J. & S. 388; *Backhouse v Backhouse* [1978] 1 W.L.R. 243; *Cresswell v Potter* (1968); [1978] 1 W.L.R. 255n.

[105] See *Zamet v Hyman* [1961] 1 W.L.R. 1442 at 1445–1446; *Banco Exterior Internacional SA v Thomas* [1997] 1 W.L.R. 221.

[106] *Lloyds Bank Ltd v Bundy* [1975] Q.B. 326: the case also established that undue influence may be exercised by a corporation, although there may be no special personal relationship with any individual representative.

[107] *Credit Lyonnais Bank Nederland NV v Burch* [1997] 1 All E.R. 144 (because the influence may cause the advice to be disregarded); *Claughton v Price* (1998) 30 H.L.R. 396; *Niersmans v Pesticcio* [2004] W.T.L.R. 699; cf. *Banco Exterior Internacional SA v Thomas* [1997] 1 W.L.R. 221 at 230; *Smith v Cooper* [2010] 2 F.L.R. 1521. For the appropriate approach to be adopted by solicitors advising a party in such circumstances, see *Padden v Bevan Ashford Solicitors* [2011] EWCA Civ 1616; [2012] 1 W.L.R. 1759. *Re Brindley* [2018] EWHC 157 (Ch) (provision of legal advice had "an emancipating effect" on the testatrix's decision, at [114]).

[108] *Re Brocklehurst* [1978] Ch. 14. See also *Simpson v Simpson* [1992] 1 F.L.R. 601; *Goldsworthy v Brickell* [1987] Ch. 378.

[109] *Goldsworthy v Brickell* [1987] Ch. 378; (1987) 104 L.Q.R. 160; M. Furmston All E.R. Rev. 1987, p.311; *Turkey v Awadh* [2006] W.T.L.R. 553.

[110] For the view that the focus of the undue influence analysis is and should be on norms of the relationship between the parties, see M. Chen-Wishart (2013) 62 I.C.L.Q. 1

[111] "Extravagant liberality and immoderate folly do not provide a passport to equitable relief," per Evershed MR in *Tufton v Sperni* [1952] 2 T.L.R. 516 at 519; *The Libyan Investment Authority v Goldman Sachs International* [2016] EWHC 2530 (Ch) per Rose J at [427](b) "I find that there was no protected relationship of trust and confidence between the LIA and Goldman Sachs. Their relationship did not go beyond the normal cordial and mutually beneficial relationship that grows up between a bank and a client. Goldman Sachs did not become a trusted adviser or a 'man of affairs' for the LIA."

cases as a matter of common fairness.[112] The principles of undue influence have generally been discussed in the types of transaction which attracted equity's particular attention in the 19th century, such as the cases on bargains with expectant heirs, and the modern form of such cases. These include cases where a beneficiary under a trust, who, although past the age of majority, is still subject to parental influence, and is persuaded to use his fortune to support the family finances;[113] or where a secretary companion takes advantage of her dominance of a vulnerable old man;[114] or where an elderly farmer grants a tenancy on terms disadvantageous to himself to the manager upon whom he relies.[115] Bridge LJ summarised these cases as those in which there is a "duty on the donee to advise the donor, or a position of actual or potential dominance of the donee over the donor."[116] But there was no such position of dominance in *Re Brocklehurst*,[117] where an "autocratic and eccentric old gentleman" made a valuable gift of shooting rights to the defendant, a "subservient garage proprietor". The relationship was not one of confidence and trust such as to give rise to a presumption of undue influence.

29–010   The House of Lords reviewed the doctrine in *National Westminster Bank v Morgan*,[118] where it was held that the principle which justifies setting a transaction aside for undue influence is the victimisation of one party by the other. The party alleging undue influence must show, it was said, that the transaction was manifestly disadvantageous to him (which will, of course, be easier to establish in cases of gifts). While there are no precisely defined limits to the equitable jurisdiction to relieve against undue influence, the doctrine is sufficiently developed not to need the support of a principle of inequality of bargaining power. This decision, in rejecting the broad approach of inequality of bargaining power, restricted the scope of the doctrine of undue influence.

The requirement of manifest disadvantage proved troublesome, especially where a wife was seeking to set aside (on the basis of undue influence) a charge over the matrimonial home to secure a loan made to assist the husband's business. If the loan was the only way to keep the business afloat, the wife had difficulty in showing that it was to her manifest disadvantage even though the business ultimately failed.[119] "Manifest" means "clear and obvious", on an objective view as at the date of the transaction. It may be small, so long as it is more than de minimis. The House of Lords later held that manifest disadvantage need not be

---

[112] *Alec Lobb (Garages) Ltd v Total Oil GB Ltd* [1985] 1 W.L.R. 173; (1985) 101 L.Q.R. 306. The cases where a commercial transaction such as a mortgage may be set aside because the mortgagee has constructive notice of undue influence exerted by a third party are discussed below; paras 29–010—29–014.

[113] *Re Coomber* [1911] 1 Ch. 723 at 726, 727; *Bullock v Lloyds Bank Ltd* [1955] Ch. 317; *Re Pauling's ST* [1964] Ch. 303.

[114] *Re Craig* [1971] Ch. 95; *Hammond v Osborn* [2002] W.T.L.R. 1125 (large gifts by elderly man to his carer).

[115] *Goldsworthy v Brickell* [1987] Ch. 378. See also *Dalgleish Wright v Hodgkinson* [2005] W.T.L.R. 435.

[116] *Re Brocklehurst* [1978] Ch. 14 at 41.

[117] [1978] Ch. 14 (Lord Denning MR dissented).

[118] [1985] A.C. 686; N. Andrews (1985) 101 L.Q.R. 305 and (1985) 44 C.L.J. 192; D. Tiplady (1985) 48 M.L.R. 579.

[119] See *National Westminster Bank Plc v Leggatt* [2001] 1 F.L.R. 563.

shown in cases of actual, as opposed to presumed, undue influence.[120] It was considered that *National Westminster Bank v Morgan* did not intend to lay it down as a universal requirement, and that there was no logic in requiring it in a case of actual undue influence, which is a species of fraud. The requirement of manifest disadvantage remains in cases of presumed undue influence.[121] In *Royal Bank of Scotland Plc v Etridge (No.2)*, Lord Nicholls, however, said that the "manifest disadvantage" terminology should be discarded. The necessary element is that the transaction is not readily explicable by the relationship of the parties.[122] The Court of Appeal more recently confirmed that manifest disadvantage is relevant at the stage of considering whether the presumption of undue influence has arisen. It is not relevant at the second stage of considering whether the presumption has been rebutted: it is not sufficient at that stage to show that there was no manifest disadvantage.[123]

An important question which has arisen in the context of mortgages and guarantees is whether the creditor should be prejudiced by any misrepresentation or undue influence exercised by the debtor over a third party who executes the mortgage or guarantee in favour of the creditor, or agrees to give priority to the mortgagee. As a general rule, a creditor owes no duty to the debtor's surety or guarantor to ensure that the third party understands the transaction and has given a free and informed consent. The transaction will, however, be set aside if the creditor had actual or constructive notice at the time of the execution of the security that the third party's consent was procured by the undue influence or misrepresentation of the debtor. Likewise in the very rare case where the creditor has made the debtor its agent in procuring the execution of the security by the third party (agency not being established merely by reason that the creditor has left it to the debtor to procure the execution), and the debtor has been guilty of undue influence or misrepresentation.

29–011

These propositions were confirmed by the House of Lords in *Barclays Bank Plc v O'Brien*,[124] where the principles were fully reviewed.

> A wife (who was neither uneducated nor vulnerable) executed a charge securing her husband's unlimited guarantee of a company's liability to the bank. Owing to her husband's misrepresentation, she thought it was a temporary security for the sum of £60,000. The wife did not read the documents before signing. It was held that the bank could not enforce the charge because it had constructive notice of the wife's right to set aside the transaction. Such cases involved a consideration of two questions: was the creditor put on inquiry as to the existence of undue influence, misrepresentation or other legal wrong and, if so, had the creditor taken reasonable steps to ensure that the third party understood the transaction? If

---

[120] *CIBC Mortgages Plc v Pitt* [1994] 1 A.C. 200.
[121] See *Cheese v Thomas* [1994] 1 W.L.R. 129, below, para.29–018; *Mahoney v Purnell* [1996] 3 All E.R. 61; *Dunbar Bank Plc v Nadeem* [1998] 3 All E.R. 876; A. Chandler (1999) 115 L.Q.R. 213; *Vale v Armstrong* [2004] W.T.L.R. 1471; *Curtis v Pulbrook* [2011] W.T.L.R. 1503.
[122] *Royal Bank of Scotland Plc v Etridge (No.2)* [2002] 2 A.C. 773.
[123] *Smith v Cooper* [2010] 2 F.L.R. 1521.
[124] [1994] 1 A.C. 180. The bank had recovered £60,000, and the appeal did not deal with that. See generally F. Rose (ed.), *Restitution and Banking Law* (Oxford: Mansfield Press, 1998), Chs 3, 4; J. Cartwright [1999] R.L.R. 1; M. Draper [1999] Conv. 176; Fehlberg, *Sexually Transmitted Debt* (Oxford: Oxford University Press, 1997).

reasonable steps had not been taken, the creditor would have constructive notice[125] of the third party's right to set aside the transaction, which would be accordingly unenforceable by the creditor. Where a wife charged her property or stood surety for her husband's debt, the creditor would be put on inquiry by a combination of two factors: first, the transaction on its face was not to the wife's financial advantage; secondly, although there was no presumption of undue influence between husband and wife, there was a substantial risk that the husband had committed a legal or equitable wrong entitling the wife to set aside the transaction.[126] The principle was not confined to wives, but extended to cohabitants,[127] provided the creditor was aware of the cohabitation, and other relationships may be included.[128] It was emphasised, however, that the principle did not apply to a third party who merely misunderstood the transaction, without wrongdoing by the debtor.

Where the creditor is put on inquiry,[129] the next question, as mentioned above, is whether it can prove that it has taken reasonable steps to ensure that the third party understood the transaction. The guidelines given in *O'Brien* were that, unless the circumstances were exceptional, the creditor must warn the third party, at a meeting not attended by the debtor, of the potential liability and risks, and must advise the third party to take independent legal advice. Cases involving transactions entered into before the formulation of these guidelines are dealt with on their merits. As we shall see, the House of Lords later revised the guidelines.[130]

Some older authorities had treated the wife as having a "special equity" deserving of extra protection. Lord Browne-Wilkinson in *Barclays Bank Plc v O'Brien*, rejecting this theory,[131] considered the true basis to be the doctrine of notice, which "lies at the heart of equity".[132] Although his Lordship spoke in terms of earlier rights prevailing against later rights, it must be emphasised that it is not the traditional doctrine of notice which is at work here, because there is only one transaction, and not a contest between a prior interest and a later one. The concept is that a party to a contract may lose the benefit of his contract,

---

[125] For an example of the *O'Brien* approach to constructive notice in another context, see *Crédit Agricole Corp and Investment Bank v Papadimitriou* [2015] UKPC 13.
[126] An example is *Hewett v First Plus Financial Group Plc* [2010] 2 F.L.R. 177.
[127] [1994] 1 A.C. 180 at 198. See also *Massey v Midland Bank Plc* [1995] 1 All E.R. 929 (couple not cohabiting but longstanding relationship); *Allied Irish Bank Plc v Byrne* [1995] 2 F.L.R. 325 (divorced but partly reconciled). This reflects the Code of Banking Practice. *Barclays Bank Plc v Rivett* [1999] 1 F.L.R. 730 (wife intercepting mail to maintain husband's ignorance).
[128] The House of Lords approved *Avon Finance Ltd v Bridger* [1985] 2 All E.R. 281 (vulnerable elderly parents and adult son). See also *Credit Lyonnais Bank Nederland NV v Burch* [1997] 1 All E.R. 144 and *Steeples v Lea* (1998) 76 P. & C.R. 157 (employer and employee whose relationship gave rise to a presumption of undue influence); *National Westminster Bank Plc v Amin* [2002] 1 F.L.R. 735; M. Haley [2002] Conv. 499; J. Holland All E.R. Rev. 2002, p.342 (parents who secured son's debt spoke only Urdu).
[129] The burden of proving constructive notice is on the party seeking to set the transaction aside; *Barclays Bank v Boulter* [1999] 1 W.L.R. 1919; M. Thompson [2000] Conv. 43; K. Barker [2000] R.L.R. 114.
[130] Below, para.29–013.
[131] The "special equity" approach has been preferred in Australia; *Garcia v National Australia Bank Ltd* (1998) 194 C.L.R. 395; A.J. Duggan (1997) 19 Sydney L.R. 220; M. Bryan [1999] L.M.C.L.Q. 327; D. Capper (2010) 126 L.Q.R. 403. The principles in *O'Brien* are therefore of limited application in the general law of Australia: *Permanent Mortgages Pty Ltd v Vandenbergh* [2010] WASC 10 per Murphy J at [205]; *National Australia Bank Ltd v Wehbeh* [2014] VSC 431. See *Amtel Pty Ltd v Ah Chee* [2015] WASC 341 at [254], preferring the term "*Garcia* unconscionability".
[132] [1994] 1 A.C. 180 at 195.

entered into in good faith, if he ought to have known that the other's concurrence had been procured by the misconduct of a third party.[133] The doctrine of notice is applied in this extended sense, and for that reason is equally applicable to cases of registered title.[134]

Lord Browne-Wilkinson was concerned to hold a fair balance between the vulnerability of wives (and others) and the practical problems of lenders. This factor was particularly significant in the contemporaneous decision of the House of Lords in *CIBC Mortgages Plc v Pitt*,[135] where it was held that the bank was not put on inquiry because it was a joint loan and, in contrast with the surety cases, there was nothing to indicate that it was not for their joint benefit. To have decided otherwise would have had the detrimental result in practice of restricting the availability of joint mortgage loans for the purchase of homes.

29–012

The mere fact that the loan is joint will not, however, automatically disapply the principle of *Barclays Bank Plc v O'Brien*, if in substance the situation is one of suretyship,[136] or if the stated purpose is for the couple's joint benefit but the creditor knows that the money will be used for the husband's sole benefit,[137] or knows that the benefit to the wife is disproportionately small in comparison with her potential liability.[138] A loan to a company whose shares are held by the husband and wife is not to be treated as a joint loan.[139]

It was held by the Court of Appeal in *TSB Bank Plc v Camfield*[140] that where a third party has established the right to set aside a transaction against the creditor, the right is absolute. The court will not impose terms which make the security or guarantee partially enforceable. Thus where the husband misrepresented that the security was limited to £15,000, but in fact it was unlimited, the wife had no liability even as to the £15,000. Although the court recognised the "abstract justice" of partial enforcement, the position was the same as any other case where a person was affected by notice of another's rights. The right to rescind is that of the third party, who does not need to ask the court for equitable

---

[133] *Royal Bank of Scotland Plc v Etridge (No.2)* [2002] 2 A.C. 773.

[134] Above, para.1–048. See W. Swadling All E.R. Rev. 1993, 367; P. O'Hagan (1994) 144 N.L.J. 765; M. Dixon and C. Harpum [1994] Conv. 421; J. Mee (1995) 54 C.L.J. 536. For the position where the debtor was not a party to the transaction in question, see *Banco Exterior Internacional SA v Thomas* [1997] 1 W.L.R. 221.

[135] [1994] 1 A.C. 200; S. Cretney [1994] 2 R.L.R. 3. See also *Britannia Building Society v Pugh* [1997] 2 F.L.R. 7; *Scotlife Home Loans (No.2) Ltd v Hedworth* (1996) 28 H.L.R. 771 (not set aside where in fact used for joint benefit, contrary to stated purpose); *Chater v Mortgage Agency Services Number Two Ltd* (2004) 1 P. & C.R. 4.

[136] *Allied Irish Bank Plc v Byrne* [1995] 2 F.L.R. 325 (joint loan but bank aware that for benefit of husband). See also M. Thompson [1994] Conv. 140; M. Dixon (1994) 53 C.L.J. 21.

[137] *Halifax Mortgage Services Ltd v Stepsky* [1996] Ch. 207 (not set aside because knowledge of borrowers' solicitor acquired before instructed by lender not imputed to lender).

[138] *Goode Durrant Administration v Biddulph* (1994) 26 H.L.R. 625 (joint loan to spouses and company but wife entitled only to 2.5% shareholding); S. Cretney (1994) 24 Fam. Law 675.

[139] *Royal Bank of Scotland Plc v Etridge (No.2)* [2002] 2 A.C. 773. See also *Bank of Cyprus (London) Ltd v Markou* [1999] 2 All E.R. 707.

[140] [1995] 1 W.L.R. 430; A. Dunn [1995] Conv. 325; W. Swadling All E.R. Rev. 1995, 450; *Castle Phillips Finance v Piddington* (1995) 70 P. & C.R. 592; *De Molestina v Ponton* [2002] 1 Lloyd's Rep. 271. The point did not arise in *Barclays Bank Plc v O'Brien* [1994] 1 A.C. 180. *Camfield* has been rejected in Australia; *Vadasz v Pioneer Concrete (SA) Pty Ltd* (1995) 184 C.L.R. 102. See generally J. Poole and A. Keyser (2005) 121 L.Q.R. 273 supporting partial rescission.

relief, to which terms may be attached. In *Camfield*, however, the wife received no benefit from the transaction and thus had nothing to restore under the restitutio in integrum principle.[141] The Court of Appeal subsequently confirmed in *Dunbar Bank Plc v Nadeem*[142] that the restitutio principle applies in these cases where the wife has received a benefit, although on the facts it did not arise because the wife failed to set aside the mortgage. Where, however, a joint mortgage on the home is set aside by the wife, it may take effect as a charge on the husband's equitable interest, and in any event the creditor may bring about a sale of the home by making the husband bankrupt.[143] A wife who has recognised the validity of the charge in matrimonial proceedings is precluded from asserting its invalidity in possession proceedings.[144]

29-013   As stated above, the requirements laid down in *Barclays Bank Plc v O'Brien*, which a creditor with constructive notice must satisfy in order to establish that reasonable steps have been taken to ensure that the third party understood the transaction, apply in their full rigour only to post-*O'Brien* transactions. Subsequent decisions treated creditors somewhat leniently in this regard.[145]

The House of Lords reviewed the principles again in *Royal Bank of Scotland Plc v Etridge (No.2)*,[146] setting out clear and simple procedures to be operated by banks (and other lenders) in these cases. Where the circumstances are such that the bank has been put on enquiry, it must take reasonable steps to satisfy itself that the implications of the proposed transaction have been meaningfully explained to the wife. The bank should ask the wife who she wants to act for her, and should explain that it will require confirmation from the solicitor that he has advised her. It must always obtain such confirmation in writing. What must be confirmed is that the solicitor has explained the nature, effect and risks of the transaction, not that he has satisfied himself that there has been no undue influence or misrepresentation. If the bank does not itself wish to have a meeting with the wife, it must provide the relevant financial information to the solicitor. If the bank suspects wrongdoing, it must tell the solicitor. The solicitor who advises the wife may also be acting for the husband or the bank, but when advising the wife (at a meeting not attended by the husband), he will be concerned only with

---

[141] Below, para.29–018.

[142] [1998] 3 All E.R. 876 (loan for purpose of acquiring lease in joint names); criticised in P. Birks and W. Swadling All E.R. Rev. 1998, pp.407–8, where the result is said to be "barely intelligible". See also *Barclays Bank Plc v Caplan* (1999) 78 P. & C.R. 153 (a mortgage not vitiated by undue influence could be severed from later extensions of the liability which were so vitiated); *Yorkshire Bank Plc v Tinsley* [2004] 1 W.L.R. 2380 (remortgage with same lender after undue influence ended); M. Thompson [2004] Conv. 399.

[143] *Zandfarid v Bank of Credit and Commerce International SA (In Liquidation)* [1996] 1 W.L.R. 1420; *Alliance & Leceister Plc v Slayford* [2001] 1 All E.R. (Comm) 1; *Hewett v First Plus Financial Group Plc* [2010] 2 F.L.R. 177. See also *Albany Home Loans Ltd v Massey* [1997] 2 All E.R. 609 (possession proceedings against H to be adjourned where W has arguable *O'Brien* defence).

[144] *First National Bank Plc v Walker* [2001] 1 F.L.R. 505; M. Oldham (2001) 60 C.L.J. 250.

[145] S. Cretney (1994) 24 Fam. Law 563; A. Chandler (1995) 111 L.Q.R. 51; J. Mee [1995] Conv. 148; M. Oldham [1995] 7 C.F.L.Q. 104; P. Giliker (1995–96) 6 K.C.L.J. 108; B. Fehlberg (1996) 59 M.L.R. 675.

[146] [2002] 2 A.C. 773; M. Oldham (2002) 61 C.L.J. 29; R. Bigwood (2002) 65 M.L.R. 435; M. Thompson and G. Andrews [2002] Conv. 174 and 456 respectively; D. O'Sullivan (2002) 118 L.Q.R. 337; A. Phang and H. Tjio [2002] L.M.C.L.Q. 231; D. Capper [2002] 10 R.L.R. 100; K. Lewison [2011] 19 R.L.R. 1.

her interests. The bank is entitled to assume that the solicitor has done his job properly. If he has not, the wife's remedy is against him.

Thus the position which has developed is that a wife who has received independent legal advice will rarely succeed in setting aside the security. All the more so if the wife has ignored that lawyer's advice in signing an agreement.[147] On the other hand, the terms of the transaction may be so manifestly disadvantageous (as where a junior employee mortgaged her home to the bank to secure an unlimited guarantee of her employer's overdraft) that the creditor cannot be said to have taken reasonable steps even if it ensured that the third party took independent legal advice, if it must have known that no competent solicitor could have advised the third party to enter into the transaction.[148]

One significant feature of *Royal Bank of Scotland Plc v Etridge (No.2)* was the extension by Lord Nicholls of the principles discussed above to all "non-commercial" relationships. His Lordship considered that in future banks should regulate their affairs on the basis that they would be put on enquiry where the relationship between the surety and the debtor was non-commercial, and that this would impose only a modest burden on them.

It was held by the House of Lords in *Smith v Governor and Company of Bank of Scotland*[149] that these principles apply also in Scotland, although Lord Jauncey distinguished undue influence and misrepresentation, doubting whether it can be said in Scots law that one class of persons is more likely than any other to make a misrepresentation.[150] It was suggested that the doctrine rests on the principle of good faith rather than notice: good faith requires a creditor to give advice where it should reasonably suspect that the intimate relationship might undermine the validity of the transaction. Another view is that the courts are simply laying down a code of practice for a species of transaction which is regarded as unsafe to leave to the normal bargaining process.[151]

29–014

Some matters still remain uncertain in the light of the House of Lords case law,[152] in particular the relationship between cases of presumed undue influence, where "manifest disadvantage"[153] is still required, and cases of breach of fiduciary duty, where transactions can be set aside without proof of disadvantage. Likewise the distinction between cases of actual undue influence and "unconscionable bargains", discussed below, needs to be clarified.[154] In the

---

[147] *Hopkins v Hopkins* [2015] EWHC 812 (Fam) (in that case a post-nuptial settlement).

[148] *Credit Lyonnais Bank Nederland NV v Burch* [1997] 1 All E.R. 144; H. Tjio (1997) 113 L.Q.R. 10; A. Pugh-Thomas (1997) 147 N.L.J. 726, 767; J. Phillips (1997–98) 8 K.C.L.J. 139; *National Westminster Bank Plc v Breeds* [2001] Lloyd's Rep. Bank 98.

[149] [1997] 2 F.L.R. 862. This remains the general law in Scotland (see *Cooper v The Bank of Scotland* [2014] CSOH 16), although the point is not without complication: C. Anderson [2014] S.L.T. 185.

[150] [1997] 2 F.L.R. 862 at 866. See also C. Rickett (1998) 114 L.Q.R. 17; M. Kenny (2007) 70 M.L.R. 175. *Royal Bank of Scotland Plc v James O'Donnell* [2014] CSIH 84.

[151] P. Birks and W. Swadling All E.R. Rev. 1997, pp.390–397. See also J. Wadsley [2003] L.M.C.L.Q. 341.

[152] The Supreme Court has not directly considered the doctrine of undue influence since its inauguration in 2009.

[153] *Twinsectra Ltd v Sander*, unreported, 10 September 2016 (no manifest disadvantage on the facts as the defendant had at least received some proceeds of sale).

[154] J. Lehane (1994) 110 L.Q.R. 167, considering Lord Browne-Wilkinson's comments in *CIBC Mortgages Plc v Pitt* [1994] 1 A.C. 200; Sir Anthony Mason (1994) 110 L.Q.R. 238 at 249; cf. Sir

specific context of wills, the Law Commission has proposed the introduction of "a specific law of testamentary undue influence", based on either a structured or discretionary approach, in order to protect vulnerable testators from financial abuse.[155]

29–015   *(c) Unconscionable Bargains.*[156]   Equity intervenes to set aside unfair transactions made with "poor and ignorant" persons. The doctrine does not apply to gifts.[157] It is not enough to show that the transaction was hard and unreasonable,[158] or that the claimant had with hindsight acted foolishly in agreeing to the transaction.[159] Three elements must be established.[160] First, that one party was at a serious disadvantage to the other by reason of poverty, ignorance or otherwise,[161] so that circumstances existed of which unfair advantage could be taken[162]; secondly, that the transaction was at an undervalue; and thirdly, that there was a lack of independent legal advice.[163] A similar principle applies in the case of unconscionable bargains with reversioners or "expectant heirs".[164] The Court of Appeal has stated that the doctrine needs careful confinement if it is not itself to become an instrument of oppression.[165] It was held that a bank guarantee could not be set aside on the basis of illiteracy or unfamiliarity with English in the absence of substantial unfairness in the

---

Peter Millett (1995) 9 T.L.I. 35 at 37. See also D. Capper (1998) 114 L.Q.R. 479 and (2010) 126 L.Q.R. 403 and A. Phang and H. Tjio [2003] 11 R.L.R. 110, advocating merger of the two doctrines. N. Enonchong, *Duress, Undue Influence and Unconscionable Dealing* (2012).

[155] Law Com. CP No. 231, *Making a Will* (2017), Ch.7; see further P. Ridge, (2004) 120 L.Q.R. 61.

[156] D. Capper (2010) 126 L.Q.R. 403. A. Burrows, *A Restatement of the English Law of Unjust Enrichment* (2012), pp.79–82. M. Moore (2018) 134 L.Q.R. 257 (arguing that the relevant principle is "exploitation of constrained [decisional] autonomy").

[157] *Langton v Langton* [1995] 2 F.L.R. 890 (set aside only if undue influence or equitable fraud); S. Cretney (1996) 26 Fam. Law 87; D. Capper [1996] Conv. 308 and (1998) 114 L.Q.R. 479.

[158] *Alec Lobb (Garages) Ltd v Total Oil GB Ltd* [1985] 1 W.L.R. 173; *Boustany v Piggott* (1995) 69 P. & C.R. 298; J. Cartwright (1993) 109 L.Q.R. 530; M. Pawlowski [1996] Conv. 454; *Jones v Morgan* [2001] Lloyd's Rep. Bank 323; *Kalsep Ltd v X-Flow BV, The Times*, 3 May 2001; *Fineland Investments Ltd v Pritchard* [2011] 6 E.G. 102 (C.S.) ("undertones of constructive fraud" required).

[159] *Minder Music Ltd v Sharples* [2015] EWHC 1454 (IPEC); [2016] F.S.R. 2 (claimant had agreed to give up half her interest in an album version of a song for £2).

[160] *Fry v Lane* (1888) 40 Ch.D. 312. The list is not exhaustive; *Cresswell v Potter* [1978] 1 W.L.R. 255.

[161] See *Watkin v Watson-Smith, The Times*, 3 July 1986 (old age with diminution of capacity and judgment, together with a desire for a quick sale, satisfied the requirement). See also *Mountford v Scott* [1975] Ch. 258. The modern equivalent of "poor and ignorant" is a member of the lower income group or a "less highly educated" person; *Cresswell v Potter* [1978] 1 W.L.R. 255 at 257; *Credit Lyonnais Bank Nederland NV v Burch* [1997] 1 All E.R. 144. D. Capper (2010) 126 L.Q.R. 403. *Evans v Lloyd* [2013] EWHC 1725 (Ch).

[162] This requirement is not satisfied where, unknown to the purchaser, the vendor is of unsound mind; *Hart v O'Connor* [1985] A.C. 1000; A. Hudson [1986] Conv. 178. See further J. Devenney and A. Chandler [2007] J.B.L. 541. For the applicability of such principles to legal settlements, see *Dunhill v Burgin (Nos 1 and 2)* [2014] UKSC 18; [2014] 1 W.L.R. 933; P. Watts (2015) 74 C.L.J. 140.

[163] See *Butlin-Sanders v Butlin* (1985) 15 Fam. Law 126, where the claim was in any event barred by laches and acquiescence.

[164] Mere undervalue is not sufficient. See Law of Property Act 1925 s.174(1).

[165] *Barclays Bank Plc v Schwartz, The Times*, 2 August 1995. See also *Portman Building Society v Dusangh* [2001] W.T.L.R. 117; L. McMurtry [2000] Conv. 573; where a mortgage by an elderly, illiterate man for the benefit of his son was not set aside, as there was no unconscionable conduct by the son or the lender.

transaction itself, otherwise banks would not lend to those in a weak bargaining position. An example of substantial unfairness readily justifying the setting aside of a transaction was where a junior employee mortgaged her home to secure an unlimited guarantee of her employer's debts to a bank without receiving independent legal advice.[166] One view is that the unconscionable bargain cases should now be treated as cases where a presumption of undue influence arises from the facts[167]: However, the High Court of Australia has emphasised that although the doctrines of "undue influence and unconscionable conduct will overlap, they have distinct spheres of operation",[168] as conduct falling within one category may fall outside the other.

There are also other types of situation which call for relief. Oppressive hire purchase contracts and other credit arrangements are controlled by legislation,[169] and statutory protection is given in respect of unfair contractual terms, especially in the field of exemption clauses, by the Unfair Contract Terms Act 1977 and the Consumer Rights Act 2015.[170] Roth LJ has expressed doubt as to whether it remains "possible to align the equitable right to rescind for pre-contractual misrepresentation with the statutory scheme governing contractual rights" under the 2015 Act.[171]

Relief has long been given against oppressive provisions in mortgages,[172] and a similar general principle is evident in the protection of the weak against the strong in the context of relief against forfeiture, in the development of the principles of restraint of trade, and in certain other contexts.[173] The view of the House of Lords was that there is no need to erect a general principle of relief against inequality of bargaining power. Parliament has undertaken this essentially legislative task in specific areas, and the courts should not formulate further restrictions.[174]

---

[166] *Credit Lyonnais Bank Nederland NV v Burch* [1997] 1 All E.R. 144 (decided on the basis of undue influence, however).

[167] *Langton v Langton* [1995] 2 F.L.R. 890.

[168] *Thorne v Kennedy* [2017] HCA 49 at [40] (it must be conceded that the Australian doctrine of unconscionable conduct does not map directly onto the unconscionable bargains doctrine, but the basic point holds good for English law); see further Nettle J at [74]–[78].

[169] Consumer Credit Act 1974 (as amended by Consumer Credit Act 2006); S. Brown [2007] Conv. 316.

[170] Unfair Contract Terms Act 1977 ss.2 and 3; Consumer Rights Act 2015 ss.62 and 65.

[171] *Salt v Stratstone Specialist Ltd* [2015] EWCA Civ 745 at [49] (speaking specifically of the right to reject for breach under ss.20–24).

[172] See *Cityland and Property (Holdings) Ltd v Dabrah* [1968] Ch. 166; cf. *Multiservice Bookbinding Ltd v Marden* [1979] Ch. 84. That there are limits is shown by the latter case.

[173] e.g. salvage agreements; *The Port Caledonia and The Anna* [1903] P. 184.

[174] *National Westminster Bank Plc v Morgan* [1985] A.C. 686, disapproving wider statements in *Lloyds Bank Ltd v Bundy* [1975] Q.B. 326. *Bundy*'s status was accepted as current by Rose J in *The Libyan Investment Authority (incorporated under the laws of the State of Libya) v Goldman Sachs International* [2016] EWHC 2530 (Ch) at [141]–[145].

C. Loss of the Right to Rescind

29–016 Formerly a contract entered into in reliance upon an innocent misrepresentation could not be rescinded after execution of the contract by the transfer of property under it. This rule was abrogated by the Misrepresentation Act 1967 s.1. However, the court has a discretion under s.2(2) to award damages in lieu of rescission in any case of innocent misrepresentation if it would be equitable to do so.[175] This discretion is more likely to be exercised where the contract has been executed than where it remains executory.

More generally, the right to rescind may be lost in any of three ways.

29–017 **i. Affirmation.**[176] Where the party entitled to rescind affirms the contract, for example by taking a benefit under it, with knowledge of the facts giving rise to the right to rescind and of her legal rights,[177] she will be taken to have waived that right.[178] Affirmation may be shown by words or acts, or may be indicated by lapse of time, the remedy being subject to the doctrine of laches.[179]

29–018 **ii. Restitutio in Integrum not Possible.**[180] A contract will cease to be capable of rescission if the parties can no longer be restored to their original position.[181] Any money paid or other property transferred under the contract must be restored. But a precise restoration is not required, particularly in cases involving fraud or duress.[182] Equity is concerned to restore the parties, and especially the defendant, to their former positions so far as practically possible.[183] This might be achieved by, for example, ordering an account of profits and

---

[175] G. Treitel and P. Atiyah (1967) 30 M.L.R. 369; *Property Alliance Group Ltd v Royal Bank of Scotland Plc* [2016] EWHC 3342 (Ch).

[176] O'Sullivan, Elliott and Zakrzewski, *The Law of Rescission*, 2nd edn (2014), Ch.23.

[177] *Peyman v Lanjani* [1985] Ch. 457; L. Anderson [1985] Conv. 408; K. Handley (2006) 122 L.Q.R. 82; *Stevens & Cutting Ltd v Anderson* [1990] 1 E.G.L.R. 95; cf. *Goldsworthy v Brickell* [1987] Ch. 378.

[178] *Clough v London and North Western Rail Co* (1871–72) L.R. 7 Ex.Ch. 26. A. Sheppard [2007] J.B.L. 442. This principle does not of course apply where the party was misled as to its rights or the applicable circumstances by the other party: *TCG Pubs Ltd (In administration) v The Master and Wardens or Governors of the Art of Mystery of the Girdlers of London* [2017] EWHC 772 (Ch).

[179] *Life Association of Scotland v Siddal* (1861) 3 De G.F. & J. 58; *Alec Lobb (Garages) Ltd v Total Oil GB Ltd* [1985] 1 W.L.R. 173. In the case of company shares it seems that delay is viewed more strictly; *Re Scottish Petroleum Co* (1883) 23 Ch.D. 434. See also *Leaf v International Galleries* [1950] 2 K.B. 86 (doubted in *Salt v Stratstone Specialist Ltd* [2015] EWCA Civ 745 per Longmore LJ at [34]) and see more generally on lapse of time Roth LJ at [43]); P.S. Davies (2016) 75 C.L.J. 15. For the application of the Limitation Act 1980 s.32(1)(c), see *Peco Arts Inc v Hazlitt Gallery Ltd* [1983] 1 W.L.R. 1315.

[180] O'Sullivan, Elliott and Zakrzewski, *The Law of Rescission*, 2nd edn (2014), Ch.18; E. Bant [2007] 15 R.L.R. 13.

[181] *Thorpe v Fasey* [1949] Ch. 649; *Erlanger v New Sombrero Phosphate Co* (1873) 3 App.Cas. 1218.

[182] See *Halpern v Halpern (Nos 1 and 2)* [2008] Q.B. 195, discussing rescission for common law duress; L. Pearce [2008] 16 R.L.R. 124.

[183] *Spence v Crawford* [1939] 3 All E.R. 271; *Newbigging v Adam* (1886) 34 Ch.D. 582. See also *Logicrose Ltd v Southend United Football Club Ltd* [1988] 1 W.L.R. 1256.

making allowances for deterioration of the property,[184] or by ordering fair compensation in equity where it is not possible to restore the property nor (because its value has since been lost) to account for profits.[185]

> In *Cheese v Thomas*,[186] the claimant, aged 86, and the defendant, his great nephew, agreed to buy a house for £83,000 in the defendant's name, where the claimant would reside for life, after which it would belong to the defendant. The claimant contributed £43,000 and the defendant raised the balance of £40,000 on mortgage. When the mortgage payments fell into arrears, the claimant sought to set aside the transaction and to recover £43,000. The relationship of the parties was one of confidence, giving rise to a presumption of undue influence, but there was no evidence of impropriety. The lower court ordered a sale and division of the proceeds in the proportions of 43:40. Owing to a property slump, the sale realised only £55,000. The Court of Appeal confirmed that the claimant was entitled only to a proportionate share, and not £43,000. Justice required each party to be restored to his original position so far as possible; it would be harsh to make the defendant stand all the loss.

If the parties were cohabitants, unravelling the transactions is more difficult. The court should take a broad approach aimed at reversing the property transactions in substance, not rewriting the history of the relationship.[187]

The point will also apply where, though restitution would be possible, the party seeking rescission refuses to make restitution as a condition of the granting of the remedy:

In *Gamatronic (UK) Ltd v Hamilton*,[188] two companies brought claims against former directors for breach of fiduciary and contractual duties in secretly setting up a competing business. It was held that the defendants' non-disclosure potentially justified rescission of the SPA. However, that would have required the claimants to return shares to the defendants, which they refused to do because of the breakdown in relations between the parties: rescission was therefore refused.[189] The court is not concerned with the broader overall position of the parties in the light of other contracts made in consequence of the impugned transaction, such losses suffered under hedging contracts: the doctrine is "concerned with restoration of the position as regards the rights and obligations created by the contract in question, not some other contract(s)".[190]

---

[184] *Erlanger v New Sombrero Phosphate Co* (1873) 3 App.Cas. 1218. See also *O'Sullivan v Management Agency and Music Ltd* [1985] Q.B. 428 (contracts between manager and entertainer rescinded for undue influence; restitutio principle not applied with full rigour in cases of breach of fiduciary relationship; practical justice achieved by ordering account of profits, giving credit for defendant's labour and skill).

[185] *Mahoney v Purnell* [1996] 3 All E.R. 61 (sale of shares in company now in liquidation); J. Heydon (1997) 113 L.Q.R. 8; P. Birks [1997] 5 R.L.R. 72; T. Akkouh (2002) 16 T.L.I. 151.

[186] [1994] 1 W.L.R. 129; J. Martin (1994) 144 N.L.J. 264; M. Dixon (1994) 53 C.L.J. 232; M. Chen-Wishart (1994) 110 L.Q.R. 173, considering change of position a preferable basis. See also *Niersmans v Pesticcio* [2004] W.T.L.R. 699.

[187] *Smith v Cooper* [2010] 2 F.L.R. 1521.

[188] [2016] EWHC 2225 (QB); [2017] B.C.C. 670.

[189] [2016] EWHC 2225 (QB) at [224]. See also *Peak Hotels and Resorts v Tarek Investments* [2015] EWHC 1997 (Ch) per Barling J at [131]–[138] and *Al Nehayan v Ioannis Kent* [2018] EWHC 333 (Comm), in which the (counter-)claimant had at one stage sought to rescind only one element of the contractual relationship between the parties. *NGM Sustainable Developments Ltd v Wallis* [2015] EWHC 2089 (Ch) per Peter Smith J at [93].

[190] *UBS AG (London Branch) v Kommunale Wasserwerke Leipzig GmbH* [2017] EWCA Civ 1567; [2017] 2 Lloyd's Rep. 621 per Lord Briggs of Westbourne and Hamblen LJ at [223].

29–019   **iii. Third Party Acquiring Rights.**[191]   The right to rescind is lost if an innocent third party acquires an interest under the contract for value before the claimant seeks to set it aside,[192] although a remedy may be available against the other party to the original transaction.[193] There is no bar to rescission if the third party is a volunteer,[194] such as the defendant's trustee in bankruptcy.[195]

2. RECTIFICATION

A. Nature of the Remedy

29–020   Rectification[196] is a discretionary equitable remedy whereby an instrument[197] which does not accord with the intentions of the parties to it may be corrected. It operates as an exception to the "parol evidence rule", whereby oral evidence is not admissible to alter a written instrument. It must be emphasised that the court does not rectify a mistake in the contract itself, but only a mistake in the instrument recording the contract (or other transaction). It must be very clearly shown that the parties had come to a genuine agreement and that the instrument had failed to record it. Thus where both a written agreement to sell land and the ensuing conveyance incorrectly described the land which it had been agreed to sell, it was possible to obtain rectification on proof of the real oral agreement.[198] In *Pitt v Holt*, Lord Walker noted that "Rectification is a closely guarded remedy, strictly limited to some clearly-established disparity between the words of a legal document, and the intentions of the parties to it. It is not concerned with consequences."[199] We shall see that whether rectification has remained "closely guarded" since *Pitt* is open to question.[200]

It is no objection that one of the parties has since died.[201] It is also no objection that the rectification may have the effect of saving tax;[202] nor that the

---

[191] O'Sullivan, Elliott and Zakrzewski, *The Law of Rescission*, 2nd edn (2014), Part V.

[192] *Oakes v Turquand* (1867) L.R. 2 H.L. 325.

[193] See *Niersmans v Pesticcio* [2004] W.T.L.R. 699 (remedy against proceeds of sale of gifted house). See also B. Häcker [2006] 14 R.L.R. 21.

[194] For a study of the cases in the context of undue influence, see P. Ridge (2014) 130 L.Q.R. 112.

[195] *Re Eastgate* [1905] 1 K.B. 465.

[196] We are not here concerned with the provisions for "rectification" of the Land Register under Sch.4 of the Land Registration Act 2002, which is a distinct statutory scheme and is currently the matter of considerable controversy: see, e.g., *MacLeod v Gold Harp Properties Ltd* [2014] EWCA Civ 1084; [2015] 1 W.L.R. 1249; Dixon (2014) 131 L.Q.R. 207; E. Lees (2015) 78 M.L.R. 361 and *NRAM Ltd v Evans* [2017] EWCA Civ 1013; [2018] 1 W.L.R. 639;

[197] Distinguish cancellation of an instrument that is void or voidable on some ground, e.g. forgery: *Peake v Highfield* (1826) 1 Russ. 559. For the effect of an unexecuted alteration to a deed, see *Co-operative Bank Plc v Tipper* [1996] 4 All E.R. 366.

[198] *Craddock Bros v Hunt* [1923] 2 Ch. 136.

[199] [2013] UKSC 26; [2013] 2 A.C. 108 at [131].

[200] See e.g. S. Douglas (2018) 134 L.Q.R. 138 and P.S. Davies (2016) 75 C.L.J. 62 at 84–5.

[201] *Johnson v Bragge* [1901] 1 Ch. 28; *Allnutt v Wilding* [2007] W.T.L.R. 941 (action by settlor's executors failed on the facts).

[202] *Re Colebrook's Conveyance* [1972] 1 W.L.R. 1397; *Re Slocock's WT* [1979] 1 All E.R. 358; *Lake v Lake* [1989] S.T.C. 865; *Seymour v Seymour, The Times*, 16 February 1989; *Ashcroft v Barnsdale* [2010] W.T.L.R. 1675.

mistake arose through the negligence of the claimant or his legal advisers.[203] In *Lobler v HMRC*,[204] Proudman J allowed rectification of the terms of the claimant's withdrawals from an insurance policy where he had wrongly assumed (without taking advice) that there would no tax liabilities. It was held that he had not been careless, but in any case,

> "Even if this is wrong, the level of carelessness in not taking advice when he filled in the form was not to my mind such as would deprive him of the remedy of rectification ... One does not seek advice on everything, the legislation is not at all intuitive and no reasonable man would have expected the outcome."[205]

> In *Prowting 1968 Trustee One Ltd v Amos-Yeo*,[206] the intention was to qualify for capital gains tax entrepreneurs' relief, which depended (amongst other elements) upon a beneficiary in possession owning at least 5% of the total nominal value of the share capital in a company. The beneficiaries held 115,000 shares, which amounted to only 4.97% of the total value. Master Clark observed that "between ... clear cases, there is a continuum moving from a formulation of a general intent or objective to a specific understanding of how that objective is to be achieved in documentary form"[207] and on the instant facts granted rectification so that the defendants received the requisite number of shares to qualify for the tax relief.

The trend in these cases may however be criticised. It is arguable that rescission is better able to address appropriate cases of tax planning mistakes than rectification; in other cases, the proper remedy lies in a claim against the tax advisers or solicitors, where negligence can be demonstrated.[208] This view is consistent with the approach of Supreme Court of Canada in the twin decisions of *Jean Coutu Group (PJC) Inc v Canada (Attorney General)*[209] and *Canada (Attorney General) v Fairmont Hotels Inc.*[210] The appeals concerned transactions which had been entered into with the general intention that they would be tax neutral. By a majority, the Court denied rectification in each case:

> "when taxpayers agree to certain transactions and later claim that their advisors made mistakes by failing to properly advise them that the transactions they agreed to would produce unintended tax consequences, the appropriate avenue to recoup their ensuing losses is not through the retroactive amendment of their agreement. Rather, if the mistakes are of such a nature as to warrant it, taxpayers can bring a claim against their advisors, who generally have professional liability insurance, and try to prove that claim in the courts.[211]

---

[203] *Weeds v Blaney* (1977) 247 E.G. 211 (discussing also the position as to costs); *Central & Metropolitan Estates Ltd v Compusave* (1983) 266 E.G. 900 (rectification ordered on terms in such a case); *Boots The Chemist Ltd v Street* (1983) 268 E.G. 817.

[204] *Lobler v The Commissioners for Her Majesty's Revenue and Customs* [2015] UKUT 152 (TCC).

[205] [2015] UKUT 152 (TCC) at [73].

[206] [2015] EWHC 2480 (Ch).

[207] [2015] EWHC 2480 (Ch) at [32].

[208] S. Douglas (2018) 134 L.Q.R. 138 at 147: "The expansion of rectification has the potential to distort the settled distribution of risk, as it is effectively making the taxpayer an insurer against the solicitor's carelessness".

[209] 2016 SCC 55; [2016] 2 S.C.R. 670.

[210] 2016 SCC 56; [2016] 2 S.C.R. 720.

[211] 2016 SCC 55 per Wagner J at [43]. cf. Cote J dissenting at [90] "In advising their clients with respect to such acts, tax professionals are often called upon to resolve complex problems under significant time constraints. Mistakes happen. Depriving taxpayers of the ability to correct those mistakes undermines their right, long recognized in Canadian law, to organize their affairs so as to minimize tax liability".

"To be clear, a court may not modify an instrument merely because a party has discovered that its operation generates an adverse and unplanned tax liability."[212]

In tax cases, therefore, the better view is that rectification is only available where there was a specific view as to the mechanism of achieving the parties' objective.[213] The Law Commission has also recognised that "the doctrine of rectification should not be a means to protect testators from unwise estate planning decisions".[214] As with mistake,[215] we find here a concern that the more restrictive approach adopted to the rule in *Re Hastings-Bass*[216] is being off-set by a more liberal approach to other doctrines to achieve similar results.[217]

When rectification is ordered, a copy of the order may be indorsed on the instrument. There is no need to execute a new document.[218] Rectification is retrospective, and affects steps taken by the parties in the meantime.[219] But the instrument remains binding in its uncorrected form until rectification is actually ordered. The claimant may obtain rectification and specific performance in the same action.[220]

Rectification must be distinguished from the court's power to correct an obvious error as a matter of construction. If an instrument contains a manifest mistake in its drafting, neither common law nor equity is prevented from discerning the fact and substituting the words that were intended to be there. For example, in *HSBC Bank Plc v Alder*,[221] one clause of a trust deed provided that the settlor could be a discretionary beneficiary, but a further clause provided that the settlor was to be excluded from any benefit. The inclusion of the latter clause was held to be an obvious mistake, which should be corrected by a construction which omitted it. But this is a limited jurisdiction for it applies only when the mistake is obvious from the instrument itself and what should have been written is obvious too.[222] Extrinsic evidence is not admissible. This jurisdiction is one based on the duty of the court to construe documents correctly and is not a jurisdiction to rectify as such.

However, there is some reflexivity in the approach, for "there is a conceptual distinction between construction and rectification but that does not mean that there is not a close connection in their practical operation".[223] In *Marley v Rawlings*,[224] Lord Neuberger PSC noted that the difference between interpretation or rectification

---

[212] 2016 SCC 56 per Brown J at [3].

[213] D. Hodge, *Rectification: The Modern Law and Practice Governing Claims for Rectification for Mistake* (2nd edn, 2016), para.4–145. For an example of such specific intention being demonstrated, see *Vaughan-Jones v Vaughan-Jones* [2015] EWHC 1086 (Ch).

[214] Law Com. CP No. 231, *Making a Will* (2017), para.9.61

[215] Above, paras 29–002—29–003.

[216] Above, paras 18–046—18–048.

[217] S. Douglas (2018) 134 L.Q.R. 138.

[218] *White v White* (1872–73) L.R. 15 Eq. 247.

[219] *Malmesbury v Malmesbury* (1862) 31 Beav. 407.

[220] *Craddock Bros v Hunt* [1923] 2 Ch. 136.

[221] (2016) 19 I.T.E.L.R. 821 (Isle of Man).

[222] *Re Bacharach's WT* [1959] Ch. 245; *Re Doland* [1970] Ch. 267; *Schnieder v Mills* [1993] 3 All E.R. 377.

[223] *Simic v New South Wales Land and Housing Corp* [2016] HCA 47 per French CJ at [2].

[224] [2014] UKSC 2; [2015] A.C. 129; above, para.3–010; below, para.29–025.

"is by no means simply an academic issue of categorisation. If it is a question of interpretation, then the document in question has, and has always had, the meaning and effect as determined by the court, and that is the end of the matter. On the other hand, if it is a question of rectification, then the document, as rectified, has a different meaning from that which it appears to have on its face, and the court would have jurisdiction to refuse rectification or to grant it on terms (e.g. if there had been delay, change of position, or third party reliance)."[225]

B.   The Nature of the Mistake

i.   Common Mistake.[226]   The general rule is that rectification requires a mistake common to both parties, whereby the instrument records the agreement in a manner contrary to the intention of both.[227] It must be shown that there was some prior agreement, although not necessarily an enforceable contract, whereby the parties expressed a common intention regarding the provisions in question.[228] The question is what an objective observer would have thought their intentions to be.[229] It must also be shown that the common intention continued until the execution of the instrument. The general principle is that rectification is not possible where the instrument departs from the prior agreement because the parties had agreed to vary the terms.[230] Next, it must be established that the instrument is not in accordance with the true agreement of the parties, and that, if rectified in the manner claimed, it will represent the agreement. But only the actual agreement of the parties is relevant, not what they would have agreed if they had not been under a misapprehension. Thus in *Frederick E Rose (London) Ltd v William H Pim Jnr & Co Ltd*,[231] rectification was not possible where the parties agreed to buy and sell horsebeans, and the written contract referred to horsebeans, but the parties mistakenly believed that horsebeans were the same as feveroles. The mistake was made when entering into the contract in the first place. As Brown J put it in the *Fairmont Hotels* case[232]:

29–021

---

[225] [2014] UKSC 2; [2015] A.C. 129 at [40].

[226] On the distinction between common and unilateral mistakes in the context of rectification, see *Kowloon Development Finance Ltd v Pendex Industries Ltd* [2013] HKCFA 35; (2013) 16 H.K.C.F.A.R. 336.

[227] *Murray v Parker* (1854) 19 Beav. 305; *Fowler v Fowler* (1859) 4 De G. & J. 250; *Simic v New South Wales Land and Housing Corp* [2016] HCA 47 per Gageler, Nettle and Gordon JJ at [103].

[228] *Joscelyne v Nissen* [1970] 2 Q.B. 86. See also *Shipley UDC v Bradford Corp* [1936] Ch. 375; *Crane v Hegeman-Harris Co Inc* [1939] 1 All E.R. 662; [1971] 1 W.L.R. 1390; *CH Pearce & Sons v Storechester Ltd, The Times*, 17 November 1983.

[229] *Chartbrook Ltd v Persimmon Homes Ltd* [2009] 1 A.C. 1101; J. O'Sullivan (2009) 68 C.L.J. 510; R. Buxton (2010) 69 C.L.J. 253; D. McLauchlan (2010) 126 L.Q.R. 8; *LSREF III Wight Ltd v Millvalley Ltd* [2016] EWHC 466 (Comm). For the latest views on contractual interpretation, see *Arnold v Britton* [2015] UKSC 36; [2015] A.C. 1619 and *Wood v Capita Insurance Services Ltd* [2017] UKSC 24; [2017] A.C. 1173; D. McLauchlan [2015] L.M.C.L.Q. 406. See per Lord Hodge in *Wood* at 15 "The recent history of the common law of contractual interpretation is one of continuity rather than change. One of the attractions of English law as a legal system of choice in commercial matters is its stability and continuity, particularly in contractual interpretation."

[230] *Breadalbane v Chandos* (1837) 2 My. & Cr. 711.

[231] [1953] 2 Q.B. 450 (Denning LJ's dicta on rescission were disapproved in *Great Peace Shipping Ltd v Tsavliris Salvage (International) Ltd* [2003] Q.B. 679, above, para.29–004). See also *London Regional Transport v Wimpey Group Services Ltd* (1987) 53 P. & C.R. 356.

[232] [2016] 2 S.C.R. 720 at [19].

"rectification is available not to cure a party's error in judgment in entering into a particular agreement, but an error in the recording of that agreement in a legal instrument... rectification aligns the instrument with what the parties agreed to do, and not what, with the benefit of hindsight, they should have agreed to do"

In other words, the remedy exists to correct, but not to improve, an instrument. It is about "putting the record straight".[233]

The mistake is usually one of fact, but relief is also possible where the mistake is of law. In *Re Butlin's Settlement Trust*,[234] rectification was ordered where the settlor and his solicitor were mistaken as to the effect of a clause giving power to the trustees to decide by a majority. Similarly, rectification was granted in *Lee v Lee*,[235] where the parties had not appreciated the differences between a joint tenancy and a tenancy in common. Rectification has been granted where the parties used the then ineffective phrase "free of tax" to carry out their agreement to pay such sum as after deduction of tax would leave the sum in question.[236] It is no bar to rectification that the parties are in agreement and there is thus no dispute, but there must be an issue capable of being contested between the parties.[237] The remedy was accordingly refused in *Whiteside v Whiteside*[238] as the parties had already corrected the error by executing a supplemental deed.

A more liberal approach to rectification in a case of mutual mistake was taken by a majority of the Court of Appeal in *Daventry DC v Daventry & District Housing Ltd*.[239]

The claimant housing authority negotiated with the defendant social landlord for the defendant to purchase of the claimant's housing stock and housing staff. There was a dispute over which party should pay the staff pension deficit. The defendant's negotiator, Mr Roebuck, agreed with the claimant's negotiator, Mr Bruno, that the defendant should pay but then represented otherwise to the defendant's board. Both parties proceeded on the basis that the other was to pay the deficit. A draft version of the contract stated that the defendant would pay, but the final version of the contract stated that the claimant was to pay. The Court of Appeal allowed rectification, on the basis that the parties shared a mistaken belief that the contract gave effect to their previously agreed bargain,[240] and that the behaviour of the defendant's negotiator meant that it would not be unjust on the defendant to rectify the contract:

"although Mr Bruno was careless in approving the draft contract, Mr Roebuck could not reasonably in all the circumstances have supposed that Mr Bruno really intended at the eleventh hour that the agreement should be varied to DDC's considerable detriment for no intelligible commercial reason."[241]

---

[233] *Allnutt v Wilding* [2007] W.T.L.R. 941 at 944.

[234] [1976] Ch. 251.

[235] [2018] EWHC 149 (Ch).

[236] *Burroughes v Abbott* [1922] 1 Ch. 86.

[237] *Seymour v Seymour*, *The Times*, 16 February 1989; *Lake v Lake* [1989] S.T.C. 865; *Racal Group Services Ltd v Ashmore* [1995] S.T.C. 1151; *Ashcroft v Barnsdale* [2010] W.T.L.R. 1675.

[238] [1950] Ch. 65. The claimant's purpose in seeking the order was to improve his tax position. Such a motive is immaterial if the requirements of rectification are otherwise satisfied.

[239] [2011] EWCA Civ 1153; [2012] 1 W.L.R. 1333; D. McLauchlan (2014) 130 L.Q.R. 83; P.S. Davies (2012) 75 M.L.R. 387.

[240] [2011] EWCA Civ 1153 per Toulson LJ at [156]. Toulson LJ expressed some reservations about the breadth of Lord Hoffmann's dicta in *Chartbrook*: e.g. [2011] EWCA Civ 1153 at [176].

[241] [2011] EWCA Civ 1153 per Toulson LJ at [178]. For cases applying *Daventry*, see *Murray Holdings Ltd v Oscatello Investments Ltd* [2018] EWHC 162 (Ch) and *Persimmon Homes Ltd v Hillier* [2018] EWHC 221 (Ch).

Etherton LJ dissented, on the basis that it was the claimant's own oversight in failing to identify the change between the provisional and final versions of the contract.[242]

ii. Unilateral Mistake.   Where one party incorrectly records a term of the   **29–022**
agreement, but it is bona fide accepted as it is written by the other party, the mistake is unilateral and there is no ground for rectification. Thus, the rent may be incorrectly stated, or the lessor's obligations, or the land or buildings incorrectly described. The party making the mistake can only obtain rectification if he can show that the mistake is due to the fraud[243] of the other party, or that the other party was aware of the mistake.[244]

In *A Roberts and Co Ltd v Leicestershire CC*,[245] the claimant had undertaken to build a school for the defendants. The agreement provided that the school should be completed within 18 months, but the officers of the Council altered the period to 30 months in the draft contract, not drawing the company's attention to the alteration. The company signed the contract without noticing the change, and one of the defendant's officials was aware of the mistake. Rectification was ordered.

The Court of Appeal has held[246] that, in order for the *Roberts* doctrine to apply, it must be shown first that one party, A, erroneously believed[247] that the document sought to be rectified contained a particular provision; secondly, that the other party, B, was aware of the mistake and that it was due to an error on the part of A; thirdly, that B had omitted to draw the mistake to the notice of A; fourthly, that the mistake must be one calculated to benefit B.[248] Although it need not amount to sharp practice, the conduct of B must be such as to make it inequitable that he should be allowed to object to rectification. The graver the character of the conduct involved, the heavier the burden of proof, but the conduct must be such as to affect the conscience of the party who had suppressed the fact that he had recognised the presence of a mistake. Thus, rectification was ordered where a rent review clause in a lease failed to provide machinery for determining the rent in default of agreement. The landlord realised the omission only when the time for review arrived, whereas the tenant had been aware of the mistake at all times. An arbitration clause was ordered to be inserted into the lease, according to the original mutual intention of the parties. Similarly where the defendant "put up a smokescreen" during negotiations to divert the claimant

---

[242] [2011] EWCA Civ 1153 at [93].

[243] Constructive fraud suffices. See *Lovesy v Smith* (1880) 15 Ch.D. 655.

[244] *Yedina v Yedin* [2017] EWHC 3319 (Ch) (rectification denied as no evidence counterparty was aware of the mistake).

[245] [1961] Ch. 555. See D. McLauchlan (2008) 124 L.Q.R. 608, suggesting that the courts have been too restrictive in their requirements. cf. *Riverlate Properties Ltd v Paul* [1975] Ch. 133; *Agip SpA v Navigazione Alta Italia SpA* [1984] 1 Lloyd's Rep. 353; *HK Hua Tyan Development Ltd v Zurich Insurance Co Ltd* [2014] HKCFA 72; (2014) 17 H.K.C.F.A.R. 493.

[246] *Bates (Thomas) & Son Ltd v Wyndham's (Lingerie) Ltd* [1981] 1 W.L.R. 505; *Kemp v Neptune Concrete Ltd* (1989) 57 P. & C.R. 369. See, applying this approach, *Milton Keynes BC v Viridor (Community Recycling MK) Ltd* [2017] EWHC 239 (TCC).

[247] The belief need not have been induced by any misrepresentation by the other party; *Commission for the New Towns v Cooper (Great Britain) Ltd* [1995] Ch. 259.

[248] Or, per Eveleigh LJ, be detrimental to A: [1981] 1 W.L.R. 505 at 521.

from discovering its mistake.[249] In such a case it suffices that the defendant merely suspected the claimant's mistake, without proof of actual knowledge of it.

Where the *transaction* is unilateral, a unilateral mistake is sufficient. In *Lobler v HMRC*,[250] Proudman J held that "the unilateral mistake required for rectification of a voluntary disposition should be of similar seriousness to that required for rescission".[251]

C.   Proof of the Mistake

29–023   The burden of proof on the party seeking rectification is a heavy one. The claimant must establish the mistake with a "high degree of conviction",[252] or "convincing proof".[253] Oral evidence is admissible to prove the agreement, and there is no need to show anything in the nature of error on the face of the instrument. It is no objection that the transaction is one required by statute to be evidenced in writing; it suffices that the rectified instrument will comply with the statute.[254]

In the case of a settlement, the settlor's evidence alone,[255] or even a mere perusal of the document[256] may suffice to establish the mistake, but the traditional position has been that the court is slow to act without the support of other evidence such as any written instructions given by the settlor prior to the execution of the settlement. For example, in *Bullard v Bullard*,[257] the trust deed was rectified to exclude the operation of Trustee Act 1925 s.31, as the evidence was clear that the settlor had intended to create interests in possession for all the child beneficiaries. However, the Court of Appeal allowed rectification in the illustrative case of *Day v Day*.[258]

> The claimant and defendant's mother executed a general power of attorney in favour of her solicitor, who then executed a conveyance of her home on her behalf, declaring that it was to be held beneficially by herself and the defendant as joint tenants. Her will appointed both the claimants and the defendant as executor and provided that the property was to be sold, with the proceeds being divided equally between her six children. Since the defendant was beneficial joint tenant of the property, however, he became absolutely entitled to the property by survivorship on her death. The claimants sought rectification for the conveyance, on the basis that the mother's intention had been to enable the property to be used as security for funds raised by the defendant, not that he should be entitled to the property outright. The claimants

---

[249] *Commission for the New Towns v Cooper (Great Britain) Ltd* [1995] Ch. 259. See also *George Wimpey UK Ltd v VI Construction Ltd* [2005] EWCA Civ 77; [2005] B.L.R. 135; E. Palser [2006] L.M.C.L.Q. 139.

[250] *Lobler v The Commissioners for Her Majesty's Revenue and Customs* [2015] UKUT 152 (TCC).

[251] [2015] UKUT 152 (TCC) at [63].

[252] *Crane v Hegeman-Harris Co Inc* [1939] 4 All E.R. 68 at 71.

[253] *Joscelyne v Nissen* [1970] 2 Q.B. 86 at 98. See also *Bates (Thomas) and Son Ltd v Wyndham's (Lingerie) Ltd* [1981] 1 W.L.R. 505 at 514; *Racal Group Services Ltd v Ashmore* [1995] S.T.C. 1151.

[254] *Craddock Bros v Hunt* [1923] 2 Ch. 136.

[255] *Hanley v Pearson* (1870) 13 Ch.D. 545.

[256] *Banks v Ripley* [1940] Ch. 719.

[257] [2017] EWHC 3 (Ch); M. Roper (2017) 23 T. & T. 722.

[258] [2013] EWCA Civ 280; [2014] Ch. 114. F. Dawson (2014) 130 L.Q.R. 356; D. Rees [2014] P.C.B. 149 at 154–6; M. Yip (2014) 8 J. Eq. 46.

therefore argued that the conveyance should be rectified to state that the mother and defendant held the property on trust for the mother. The Court of Appeal allowed the rectification[259]:

> "the doctrine of rectification is concerned with intention, or rather the mistaken implementation of intention, rather than the power and authority to effect a particular transaction. ... In the case of a voluntary settlement, rectification hinges on whether the settlor executed the settlement in the mistaken belief that it implemented his or her intention."[260]

The focus in a voluntary settlement case is thus on the settlor's subjective intention.[261] It may be noted that, although there was an understandable desire to rectify here, it is unclear quite what evidence justified the court's conclusion on the facts, as it is not clear that Mrs Day has formed any view as to the form which the conveyance was to take.[262] Master Clark has noted that the combination of claims for either construction or rectification requires "mental gymnastics ... to ensure the evidence of subjective intent is disregarded when dealing with the issue of construction".[263]

In the case of a will (discussed below), extrinsic evidence of the testator's intentions is admissible but, although the standard of proof is the balance of probabilities, convincing proof is needed to rectify a formally executed will.[264]

D. Instruments which may be Rectified

i. General. The remedy is widely available, being applicable to leases and other conveyances of land,[265] insurance policies,[266] bills of exchange,[267] parental recognition and associated consent forms,[268] and many other instruments; but not the articles of a company.[269]   29–024

Rectification can also be obtained of a voluntary deed,[270] such as a deed of gift,[271] a unilateral notice of severance[272] or a settlement,[273] if the court is satisfied on the evidence that the donor's real intent at the time of entering into it

---

[259] It is noteworthy that again the defendant's conduct was questionable, although no reliance was place on his behaviour: [2013] EWCA Civ 280 per Sir Terence Etherton C at [19]–[20].

[260] [2013] EWCA Civ 280 per Sir Terence Etherton C at [25].

[261] [2013] EWCA Civ 280 per Lewison LJ at [50].

[262] F. Dawson (2014) 130 L.Q.R. 356 at 357–8.

[263] *A v D* [2017] EWHC 2222 (Ch) at [30].

[264] *Re Segelman* [1996] Ch. 171; E. Histed [1996] Conv. 379.

[265] *Bates (Thomas) and Son Ltd v Wyndhams (Lingerie) Ltd* [1981] 1 W.L.R. 505.

[266] *Collett v Morrison* (1851) 9 Hare 162; *Equity Syndicate Management Ltd v Glaxosmithkline Plc* [2015] EWHC 2163 (Comm).

[267] *Druiff v Lord Parker* (1867–68) L.R. 5 Eq. 131.

[268] *In re A and others (Legal Parenthood: Written Consents)* [2015] EWHC 2602 (Fam); [2016] 1 W.L.R. 1325 and *In re G (Human Fertilisation and Embryology Act 2008)* [2016] EWHC 729 (Fam); [2016] 4 W.L.R. 65.

[269] *Scott v Frank F Scott (London) Ltd* [1940] Ch. 794.

[270] Pensions deeds may be rectified, and it has been held that they are to be treated as voluntary settlements, even though they are neither conventional contracts nor voluntary settlements "in the classic sense": *Saga Group Ltd v Paul* [2016] EWHC 2344 (Ch). See also *The Girls' Day School Trust v GDST Pension Trustees Ltd* [2016] EWHC 1254 (Ch); [2016] Pens. L.R. 181 (wrong draft deed executed by mistake). cf. *Smithson v Hamilton* [2008] 1 W.L.R. 1453.

[271] *Glass v Segerman* [2008] W.T.L.R. 1615.

was not accurately reflected in the instrument.[274] It is not necessary to show that the intent of the trustees was inaccurately reflected.[275] Clearly the requirement of a common mistake has no application to unilateral transactions.[276] Rectification of a settlement may be ordered not only at the instance of the settlor but also at the instance of a volunteer beneficiary, although this will not be done during the settlor's lifetime without his agreement.[277] A unilateral document may not be rectified so as to make it into a document effecting something other than was intended at the time.[278] For example, a settlement creating a discretionary trust cannot be rectified so as to create a wholly different settlement with an interest in possession[279]; however, rectification was granted where the trustees sought to revoke the successive life interest of a family beneficiary's former spouse but by mistake "for no good reason revoked and reappointed" the trusts in relation to the family beneficiary as well.[280] If an omitted term invalidates the document, rectification requires clear and convincing evidence of the missing term.[281]

29–025   **ii. Wills**   Formerly it was not possible to rectify a will except in the case of fraud,[282] although the court could, as a matter of construction, correct a manifest error in drafting.[283] It is provided by s.20(1)[284] of the Administration of Justice Act 1982[285] that:

> If a court is satisfied that a will is so expressed that it fails to carry out the testator's intentions, in consequence—
> (a)   of a clerical error; or
> (b)   of a failure to understand his instructions,
> it may order that the will shall be rectified so as to carry out his intentions.

---

[272] *Lee v Lee* [2018] EWHC 149 (Ch) at [38] (although HHJ Matthews also took the view that since the notice was signed by both joint tenants, it "may properly be regarded as the result of an agreement between them").

[273] Similarly a unilateral deed of variation; *Martin v Nicholson* [2005] W.T.L.R. 175; or a deed of appointment executed by trustees; *Price v Williams-Wynn* [2006] W.T.L.R. 1633.

[274] *Lackersteen v Lackersteen* (1864) 30 L.J. Ch. 5; *Bonhote v Henderson* [1895] 1 Ch. 742; [1895] 2 Ch. 202 (where rectification was refused); *Tankel v Tankel* [1999] 1 F.L.R. 676; *Bartlam v Coutts & Co* [2006] W.T.L.R. 1165; *Stephenson v Stephenson* [2009] W.T.L.R. 1467 (settlor's right to capital); *Whalen v Kelsey* [2009] W.T.L.R. 1297.

[275] *Re Butlin's Settlement* [1976] Ch. 251 at 262.

[276] *Wright v Goff* (1856) 22 Beav. 207.

[277] *Thompson v Whitmore* (1860) 1 J. & H. 268; *Lister v Hodgson* (1867) L.R. 4 Eq. 30.

[278] *Collins v Jones* [2001] W.T.L.R. 1229 (ineffective nomination under pension scheme).

[279] *Allnutt v Wilding* [2007] W.T.L.R. 941 (settlor mistaken as to inheritance tax implications); distinguished in *Chisholm v Chisholm* [2011] W.T.L.R. 187.

[280] *RBC Trustees v Stubbs* [2017] EWHC 180 (Ch) at [33] (distinguishing *Allnutt v Wilding* [2007] W.T.L.R. 941).

[281] *Pappadakis v Pappadakis* [2000] W.T.L.R. 719 (no rectification of purported assignment of policy to unidentified trustees).

[282] *Collins v Elstone* [1893] P. 1.

[283] *Re Bacharach's WT* [1959] Ch. 245; *Re Doland* [1970] Ch. 267; above, para.29–020.

[284] See also s.21 on the interpretation of wills.

[285] For time limits and the position of the personal representatives, see s.20(2), (3). See generally A. Borkowski and K. Stanton (1983) 46 M.L.R. 191 at 201; R. Kerridge and A. Brierley (2003) 62 C.L.J. 750.

Examples of the application of s.20 include where a solicitor failed to delete a clause for which the testator had not given instructions and which restricted the class of beneficiaries intended by the testator,[286] and where the will purported to leave a gift to the non-existent and nonsensical "West Berkshire Ambulance Hospital" when the testatrix "clearly intended to benefit an air rescue or air ambulance service operating in, and serving, the West Berks[hire] area".[287]

The starting point, though, is that a document means what it says and so where formality requirements have been complied with,

> "the claimant has to overcome a presumption, and it is one of some weight, that the will as executed reflects the testator's intentions. Why else go to all the trouble of getting a solicitor to advise, draft and engross the will and then go through the process of execution, complete with witnesses and, in the instant case, sign each page of the document if the position were otherwise?"[288]

The Supreme Court considered rectification in the context of wills in the important case of *Marley v Rawlings*,[289] which considered for the first time at the highest level the scope of rectification under s.20 of the 1982 Act.[290]

> A solicitor prepared mirror wills for Mr and Mrs Rawlings which provided that their entire estate was to go to the surviving spouse, but if the other had already died or survived the deceased spouse for less than a month, their estate was to go to Terry Marley, whom they treated as their son (although they were not biologically related). The solicitor made an error when it came to presenting the wills to be signed, so that each spouse signed the other's will. Mrs Rawlings died in 2003, but the mistake was only noticed when Mr Rawlings died in 2006. The deceased couple's two biological sons challenged Mr Rawlings' will, as if it were invalid they would inherit as the next of kin. The Supreme Court held that the will could be rectified: indeed, Lord Neuberger PSC described the facts as giving rise to a "classic claim for rectification."[291]

Lord Neuberger of Abbotsbury PSC[292] offered a very broad interpretation of the jurisdiction to grant rectification, both in equity and under the Administration of

---

[286] *Re Segelman* [1996] Ch. 171. See further *Wordingham v Royal Exchange Trust Co Ltd* [1992] Ch. 412; *Goodman v Goodman* [2006] W.T.L.R. 1807; *Price v Craig* [2006] W.T.L.R. 1873; *Re Martin* [2007] W.T.L.R. 329; R. Kerridge and A. Brierley [2007] Conv. 558; *Pengelly v Pengelly* [2008] Ch. 375; *Sprackling v Sprackling* [2009] W.T.L.R. 897; *Re Ryan* [2011] W.T.L.R. 1029.

[287] *Re Harte* [2015] EWHC 2351 (Ch), HHJ Hodge QC at [18] ("The concept of an 'ambulance hospital' would suggest a hospital for ambulances.") See also *The Royal Society v Robinson* [2015] EWHC 3442 (Ch), where Nugee J dealt with the matter as one of construction but would also have ordered rectification to avoid the exclusion of assets in the Isle of Man and the Channel Islands, where the will referred only to property "situated... in the United Kingdom".

[288] *Fielden v Christie-Miller* [2015] EWHC 2940, per Sir William Blackburne at [39].

[289] [2014] UKSC 2; [2015] A.C. 129. B. Häcker (2014) 130 L.Q.R. 360; H. Cumber and C. Kynaston (2014) 25 K.L.J. 137; J. Seaman (2015) 21 T. & T. 438; M.D. Kelly (2017) 38 Statute L.R. 265. The Supreme Court gave a subsequent, complicated judgment on costs: *Marley v Rawlings (Costs)* [2014] UKSC 51; [2015] A.C. 157, described by Roohani and Teo (2015) 34 C.J.Q. 155 at 163 as "a useful (albeit unfortunate) reminder of the high costs of English litigation and how quickly they can become disproportionate to the amount in dispute"; G. Sarathy [2015] Conv. 273.

[290] B. Häcker (2014) 130 L.Q.R. 360 at 360.

[291] [2015] A.C. 129 at [53].

[292] Lord Hodge offered some complementary remarks on the position in Scots law, which relies upon the Law Reform (Miscellaneous Provisions) (Scotland) Act 1985, but by s.8(6) excludes from the statutory remedy's scope any "document of a testamentary nature". Lord Hodge considered the remedy of partial reduction and declarator as an alternative. Lord Neuberger opined (at [85]) that "the

Justice Act 1982. First, although exercising the statutory power under ss.20 and 21 and recognising cases which assumed the contrary,[293] Lord Neuberger said that he would have held "it was, as a matter of common law, open to a judge to rectify a will in the same way as any other document: no convincing reason for the absence of such a power has been advanced."[294]

It then was necessary to consider the applicability of the statutory provisions.[295] Lord Neuberger recognised a general proposition that "the greater the extent of the correction sought, the steeper the task for a claimant who is seeking rectification",[296] which must apply beyond the confines of the statutory context here. But that did not rule out the possibility of a wholesale correction in an appropriate case. Next, his Lordship considered that, notwithstanding what had gone "seriously wrong" with the preparation of the wills, the will that purported to be the will of Mr Rawlings was formally sufficient to satisfy s.9 of the Wills Act 1837: rectification and validity may be addressed together.[297]

The next issue was whether there a "clerical error" in the process. Such a major error as on the facts, which was nothing to do with drafting or a slip of the pen, might seem to fall outside the meaning of "clerical". But "clerical error" is to be given a wide meaning,[298] so as to ensure that s.20 offered a "rational and coherent basis for rectifying wills". In support of his point, Lord Neuberger gave the convincing parallel example of a solicitor drafting two wills who cuts and pastes the contents of someone else's will into the draft for his client: that would seem clearly to be clerical, and thus so must the error be in *Marley*. It is enough that the error "arose in connection with office work of a routine nature".[299] It was thus appropriate for the court to order that the will be rectified. *Marley*'s approach to "clerical error" has been described by the Inner House of the Court of Session as an

> "important extension... better suited to the reality of working in modern conditions, where the use of computers and electronic forms of communication permit the easy copying and pasting of material, and increase the range of situations in which an error in routine work may occur."[300]

However, Lord Neuberger indicated that "clerical error" did not extend to an "activity [that] involves some special expertise".[301] Thus, in *Reading v*

---

law north and south of the border each appear to have something to learn from the other, and to involve slightly different ways of arriving at the same outcome."

[293] *Harter v Harter* (1873) L.R. 3 P. & D. 11 (Sir James Hannen) and *Re Reynette-James, decd* [1976] 1 W.L.R. 161, per Templeman J.

[294] [2015] A.C. 129 at [28].

[295] The court rejected an argument that the cause could be resolved by deleting sections of the will refer to Mrs rather than Mr Rawlings, and convert the will into a will signed by Mr Rawlings: [2015] A.C. 129 at [47]–[49].

[296] [2015] A.C. 129 at [53].

[297] [2015] A.C. 129 at [63].

[298] [2015] A.C. 129 at [76]. Lord Neuberger also conceded that this "does nothing to discourage carelessness".

[299] [2015] A.C. 129 at [82]. See also *Slattery v Jagger* [2015] EWHC 3976 (Ch) (dictation error leading to failure to identify beneficiary of gift intended to be for testator's wife).

[300] *Perth & Kinross Council v Scottish Water* [2016] ScotCS CSIH 83 at [31].

[301] [2015] A.C. 129 at [75]. See *Jump v Lister* [2016] EWHC 2160 (Ch) at [63]–[66] (obiter).

Reading,[302] where a solicitor failed to appreciate that "issue" would not include the testator's stepchildren, Asplin J took the obiter view that it was not a "clerical error" but part of the activity of drafting the will[, which] related to his professional judgment and expertise in the choice of the necessary phrases to encapsulate the instructions given."[303]

It remains to be seen whether any courts take up the dicta in *Marley* that indicate for a wider still approach to rectification where s.20 cannot apply, but there is support for such a view in the literature.[304]

There is no rule that rectification must be sought before suing the solicitor for negligence.[305] The statutory power does not permit rectification where the testator himself has misunderstood the legal effect of the wording used.[306]

Overall, the newly expansive approach to rectification in *Marley* and other cases considered above seems to afford the courts greater flexibility.[307] However, there must be limits, and it has been emphasised that the courts should proceed in a manner that contributes to practical and commercial certainty:

> "Rectification is an equitable remedy, which means that its origins lie in conscience and fair dealing, but those origins cannot be invoked to justify an unprincipled approach: far from it. Particularly as rectification is normally invoked in a contractual context, it seems to me that its principles should reflect the approach of the law to contracts, in particular to the formation and interpretation of contracts. Similarly, as rectification most commonly arises in a commercial context, it is plainly right that the applicable principles should be as clear and predictable in their application as possible."[308]

E.   Defences

The remedy of rectification, which, like other equitable remedies, is discretionary, will not be granted where a bona fide purchaser for value without notice has acquired an interest under the instrument.[309] Laches or acquiescence will bar the claim[310]; similarly if the contract is no longer capable of performance,[311] or has

29–026

---

[302] [2015] EWHC 946 (Ch).

[303] [2015] EWHC 946 (Ch), per Asplin J at [51] and [53]. B. Häcker in B. Häcker and C. Mitchell (eds.), *Current Issues in Succession Law* (Oxford: Hart Publishing, 2016).

[304] B. Häcker (2014) 130 L.Q.R. 360 at 364–5 and D. Hodge [2017] Conv. 45.

[305] *Horsfall v Haywards (A Firm)* [1999] 1 F.L.R. 1182, distinguishing *Walker v GH Medlicott & Son (A Firm)* [1999] 1 W.L.R. 727; E O'Dell (2002) 65 M.L.R. 360.

[306] See *Collins v Elstone* [1893] P. 1.

[307] E. Drummond [2014] Conv. 357 at 360 (a "welcome result").

[308] *Daventry DC v Daventry and District Housing Ltd* [2011] EWCA Civ 1153; [2012] 1 W.L.R. 1333 per Lord Neuberger MR (as he then was) at [194]. See also P.S. Davies (2016) 75 C.L.J. 62 and R. Havelock (2016) 27 K.L.J. 188.

[309] *Smith v Jones* [1954] 1 W.L.R. 1089; *Lyme Valley Squash Club Ltd v Newcastle under Lyme BC* [1985] 2 All E.R. 405. In the case of registered land, the right to rectify may be asserted against the purchaser as an overriding interest under the provisions now found in s.11 and Sch.1 para.2 of the Land Registration Act 2002: *Blacklocks v JB Developments (Godalming) Ltd* [1982] Ch. 183; *Ramsden (DB) & Co Ltd v Nurdin & Peacock Plc, The Times*, 14 September 1998. The benefit of the right to rectify in cases concerning land will pass with the land; *Boots The Chemist Ltd v Street* (1983) 268 E.G. 817; Law of Property Act 1925 s.63.

[310] *Beale v Kyte* [1907] 1 Ch. 564; cf. *KPMG LLP v Network Rail Infrastructure Ltd* [2006] 2 P. & C.R. 7 (six-year delay no bar).

[311] *Borrowman v Rossell* (1864) 16 C.B.(N.S.) 58.

been fully performed under a judgment of the court.[312] In the case of a voluntary settlement, it has been held that the court may decline to rectify if a trustee, having taken office in ignorance of the mistake, has a reasonable objection to the rectification.[313]

---

[312] *Caird v Moss* (1886) 33 Ch.D. 22.
[313] *Re Butlin's ST* [1976] Ch. 251 (where rectification was granted).

CHAPTER 30

LICENCES AND ESTOPPEL

1.   GENERAL

A LICENCE is a permission. We are here concerned with licences to enter land.[1]   **30–001**
The licence makes lawful what would otherwise be a trespass.[2] The licence may
be express; or it may be implied; as in the case of a shopkeeper's invitation to
enter the premises to do business.

Express licences arise in a myriad of factual situations, as where the owner
invites guests to dinner; or to stay in a room in his hotel. Some of these situations
will be expected to give minimal rights to a licensee. She has no interest in the
land. The licence prevents her from being a trespasser, and no more. In other
situations there will be a contract which gives certain rights to the licensee; and
some situations create difficulties in determining whether a person is a
contractual licensee or a lessee.[3] Different situations create different types of
licences; and different levels of protection to the licensee.

---

[1] A licence, however, may be a permission to a neighbour to do on her own land something which
would otherwise be a wrong to the licensor; *Hopgood v Brown* [1955] 1 W.L.R. 213.
[2] *Millennium Productions Ltd v Winter Garden Theatre (London) Ltd* [1948] A.C. 173 at 193.
[3] *Street v Mountford* [1985] A.C. 809; P. Clark [2015] Conv. 474; *Stewart v Watts (Secretary of State
for Communities and Local Government intervening)* [2016] EWCA Civ 1247; [2017] 2 W.L.R. 1107
at [38]; *Gilpin v Legg* [2017] EWHC 3220 (Ch); [2018] L. & T.R. 6.

The main question for discussion in this chapter is the protection of the licensee; as where the licensor purports to revoke the licence. The common law cases prior to the Judicature Acts demonstrate what difficulties the common law met in dealing with this question; largely through the inadequacy of the remedies available at common law. If the licence was coupled with a proprietary interest, the licensor clearly could not revoke; but, as a licence was not a proprietary interest, it was difficult to see how the licensee could be protected. The common law judges found themselves saying that if a licence were granted by deed, it would not be revocable; which still leaves open the question of finding a proper remedy available to the licensee.

Equity provided the remedies. If the licensor could not lawfully revoke the licence, equity could grant an injunction to restrain him. The licence may be irrevocable for various reasons; most commonly because the terms of the contractual licence make it irrevocable; or because an estoppel has worked in favour of the licensee. Thus, the licensee would enjoy the licence for the period covered by the injunction.

The protection of the licensee against the licensor soon raised the question of whether the licensee should be protected against a third party; not being a bona fide purchaser of the legal estate for value without notice. Where the licensee is protected against third parties, the question arises whether the licence has, by this roundabout route, become an interest in land.

Another question is whether the licensee can only properly be satisfied by a permanent right, and not merely by an injunction. The doctrine known as "proprietary estoppel"[4] has developed, allowing the courts to exercise a wide range of remedies in favour of the licensee, including the award of a proprietary interest in the land, with or without monetary compensation; and intended to provide the solution which is the most just and proper in all the circumstances.

2.   THE SITUATION AT COMMON LAW

30–002   The common law never reached a satisfactory solution to the problem of the protection of the licensee. Essentially, this was because the inquiry was to see what it was that the licensor had *granted* to the licensee; and a licence *grants* nothing. The true issue is the extent of the protection which should be given against the licensor or against a third party; and, without the remedy of an injunction to restrain interference, the common law had no adequate means of protection. A number of propositions were, however, established prior to 1875.

---

[4] Below, para.30–022 and following. See B. McFarlane, *The Law of Proprietary Estoppel* (Oxford: Oxford University Press, 2014).

A.   Bare or Gratuitous Licence

A simple permission to enter the licensor's land gives no contractual or proprietary right to the licensee. The permission may be withdrawn at any time by the licensor. On revocation, the licensee becomes a trespasser, but is allowed a reasonable time to leave the land.[5]

30–003

B.   Licence Coupled with a Grant (or an Interest)

It has long been established that a licence coupled with a grant of a proprietary interest is irrevocable[6]; where for example an occupier sells some cut timber,[7] and expressly or by implication gives the purchaser permission to enter the land to collect it. Such a licence is irrevocable. Similarly where there is a grant of a right to take away part of the realty, as with a *profit à prendre*.[8] The grant carries with it an irrevocable licence to enter. We do not speak of a licence coupled with a grant where the proprietary interest is one which itself includes a presence on the land; with a lease or an easement, the grantee enters by force of the grant and not under any licence.

30–004

C.   Contractual Licences

Most of the difficulties which arose at common law were concerned with contractual licences. If the licensor (A) contracted to allow the licensee (B) to enter her land for a particular purpose or for a particular period of time, and A, in breach of contract, ordered B to leave, and perhaps forcibly ejected her, the common law held that B had become a trespasser and could be ejected.

30–005

> In *Wood v Leadbitter*,[9] the claimant purchased a ticket for the grandstand at Doncaster Racecourse. The defendant, on the orders of the steward, required him to leave. He refused to go, and was physically removed, no more force being used than was reasonably necessary. He sued for assault and false imprisonment, and failed. The Court of Exchequer distinguished between a mere licence, such as this, which was revocable; and a licence coupled with an interest, which was not.

In the circumstances, nothing had been *granted*. As Latham CJ said in *Cowell v Rosehill Racecourse Co*[10]: "50,000 people who pay to see a football match do not obtain 50,000 interests in the football ground." An action for breach of

---

[5] *Millennium Productions Ltd v Winter Garden Theatre (London) Ltd* [1948] A.C. 173 at 199. See J. Hill (2001) 60 C.L.J. 89.

[6] *Webb v Paternoster* (1619) Palm 71; *James Jones & Son Ltd v Tankerville* [1909] 2 Ch. 440.

[7] *James Jones & Son Ltd v Tankerville* [1909] 2 Ch. 440.

[8] Law Com. No. 327, *Making Land Work: Easements, Covenants and Proifits à Prendre* (2011).

[9] (1845) 13 M. & W. 838.

[10] (1937) 56 C.L.R. 605 at 616.

contract no doubt lay,[11] but that was not the issue. Whether or not the defendant had the *right*, under the terms of the contract, to eject the claimant, he had a *power* to do so.[12]

The conclusion must be that the common law provided no adequate doctrine nor any adequate remedies to deal with the problem of protection of licensees.

3. CONTRACTUAL LICENCES AFTER THE JUDICATURE ACTS

30–006 The treatment of contractual licences at common law was clearly unsatisfactory. This situation, and that of licences generally, was transformed by the application of equitable remedies, not available to common law courts; by the recognition of the part that estoppel had to play; and finally by the willingness of more modern courts to seek the most appropriate remedy for the particular situation. "It is for the court in each case to decide in what way the equity can be satisfied."[13]

A. Injunction to Restrain a Licensor from Breaking a Contractual Licence

30–007 The reasoning of the common law, established in *Wood v Leadbitter*,[14] was that a licence was revocable unless it validly granted a proprietary interest. In the absence of such a grant, it was said, even as late as 1944,[15] that, though the licensor had no *right* to revoke, he had a *power* to revoke, and could then turn the licensee into a trespasser. The opposite conclusion had been reached in 1915 in *Hurst v Picture Theatres Ltd*,[16] but on grounds that show that the courts still thought that it was the grant of a proprietary interest which made the licence irrevocable. In that case, the claimant paid to watch a cinema show in the defendants' theatre. The defendants mistakenly thought that he had entered without paying. On being requested to leave, he refused and was ejected. He sued for assault and false imprisonment and succeeded.

Buckley LJ gave two grounds for distinguishing the case from *Wood v Leadbitter*,[17] both based upon the availability of equitable doctrine, the first reason being, it is submitted, clearly wrong, and the second being the basis of the modern doctrine protecting contractual licensees. The first ground was that the claimant had a licence coupled with an interest—"the right to see"—and that the

---

[11] *Millennium Productions Ltd v Winter Garden Theatre (London) Ltd* [1948] A.C. 173 per Viscount Simon LC at 190.
[12] *Thompson v Park* [1944] K.B. 408 per Goddard LJ at 410; later disapproved in *Verrall v Great Yarmouth BC* [1981] Q.B. 202, considered above, para.27–015.
[13] *Ives (ER) Investments Ltd v High* [1967] 2 Q.B. 379 per Lord Denning MR at 395.
[14] (1845) 13 M. & W. 838.
[15] *Thompson v Park* [1944] K.B. 408 at 412.
[16] [1915] 1 K.B. 1.
[17] (1845) 13 M. & W. 838.

interest could now be granted in equity by a contract, whereas before 1875 a deed was required. The fallacy in this reasoning is that there was no identifiable proprietary interest to be granted.[18]

As a second ground for the decision, Buckley LJ treated the matter as one of construing the parties' rights under the contract. Here, "there was included in that contract a contract not to revoke the licence until the play had run to its termination".[19] This is the germ of the later development; and the significance of the Judicature Act in this context is that it made available the equitable remedy of an injunction to restrain the breach of contract by the licensor. This precludes the argument that he has no right to revoke, but has a power to do so; he has no power if an injunction is available to restrain him.

Millennium Productions Ltd v Winter Garden Theatre (London) Ltd[20] finally established that the rights of the parties must be determined upon the proper construction of the contract. In that case, as the licence was held to have been revoked in accordance with its terms, the problem in *Hurst's* case[21] did not arise. In the Court of Appeal, however, the contract had been construed as irrevocable by the licensor. In that situation, they held, the licensee would be protected by the issue of an injunction to restrain a breach of contract by the licensor. Lord Greene MR, in words referred to with approval in the House of Lords, explained that the revocation of the licence was a breach[22]:

> "The general rule is that, before equity will grant such an injunction, there must be, on the construction of the contract, a negative clause express or implied. In the present case it seems to me that the grant of an option which, if I am right, is an irrevocable option, must imply a negative undertaking by the licensor not to revoke it. That being so, in my opinion, such a contract could be enforced in equity by an injunction."

B.   The Licensee's Remedy for the Breach

i.   Damages.   The normal remedy for breach of contract is, of course, **30–008** damages; and there is little doubt that this was recognised even in the old common law cases which held that the licensee could be evicted. The question did not arise in *Wood v Leadbitter*,[23] because the form of action was for assault and not for breach of contract.

In *Tanner v Tanner*,[24] the defendant had a relationship with the claimant. She lived in a rent-controlled flat, which she left in 1970, when the claimant purchased a house for her and for their children. The relationship ended, and in 1973 the claimant offered her £4,000 to vacate. She refused, claiming that she could stay in the house until the children left school. The Court of Appeal would have permitted her to stay, but she had been rehoused by the local authority

---

[18] These matters are demonstrated by Phillimore LJ in his dissenting judgment in *Hurst* [1915] 1 K.B. 1 at 15–20; see *Hounslow LBC v Twickenham Garden Developments Ltd* [1971] Ch. 233 at 244; cf. *Cowell v Rosehill Racecourse* (1937) 56 C.L.R. 605.

[19] *Hurst v Picture Theatres Ltd* [1915] 1 K.B. 1 at 10; see also Kennedy LJ at 14.

[20] [1948] A.C. 173.

[21] [1915] 1 K.B. 1.

[22] [1946] 1 All E.R. 678 at 648.

[23] (1845) 13 M. & W. 838.

[24] [1975] 1 W.L.R. 1346.

before the appeal. The defendant's remedy was compensation for the loss of the licence, which was quantified at £2,000.

30–009 **ii. Injunction.** The normal way of protecting a contractual licensee against improper revocation is by issuing an injunction to restrain the breach by the licensor. A number of questions arise.

30–010 *(a) The Judge at your Elbow.* It was said in 1915,[25] in connection with *Hurst's* case, that an injunction would be a useless remedy unless a Chancery judge was sitting at your elbow, because the breach and ejection would take place before the injunction could issue. But the court will treat the licence as not revoked in circumstances in which an injunction would issue, and this will prevent the licensee from being a trespasser. As has been seen, monetary compensation was awarded in *Tanner v Tanner* where it was no longer practicable to issue an injunction. Moreover, a mandatory injunction may be obtained, in a suitable case, to enable the licensee to re-enter.[26]

30–011 *(b) Discretionary Nature of the Remedy.* As we have seen, an injunction, like all equitable remedies, is discretionary.[27] An injunction will not therefore be available to a licensee who is herself in breach of the terms of the licence. A licensee who herself misbehaves will not be protected.[28] Further, an injunction will not be granted where it will have the effect of compelling persons to live together in circumstances which are intolerable. If this situation arises in the case of a licence, an injunction may be refused, and the parties may be left to their rights at common law to sue for breach of contract.[29]

30–012 **iii. Specific Performance.** As we have seen,[30] the Court of Appeal had no hesitation in holding in *Verrall v Great Yarmouth BC*[31] that a contractual licence was enforceable by specific performance:

> The National Front entered into a contract in April 1979 with the Council to hire a hall for a conference. In May 1979, after local authority elections, the new Labour-controlled Council purported to revoke the licence; on the ground that the Front's extremist political stance would create unrest in the borough. Specific performance of the contract was granted. The old argument that a licence can be revoked by the licensor on payment of damages was firmly and finally disposed of. The Front was entitled to the benefits of the contractual licence.

---

[25] See Sir John Miles (1915) 31 L.Q.R. 217 at 221; and Lord Greene MR in *Millennium Productions Ltd v Winter Garden Theatre (London) Ltd* [1946] 1 All E.R. 678 at 685.

[26] As in *Luganda v Services Hotels Ltd* [1969] 2 Ch. 209.

[27] Above, para.28–008. Where damages are an adequate remedy, no injunction will be granted: *West End Commercial Ltd v London Trocadero (2015) LLP* [2017] EWHC 2175 (Ch); [2018] 1 P. & C.R. DG3.

[28] *Thompson v Park* [1944] K.B. 408. For a consideration of the question of the circumstances in which misbehaviour by a licensee by estoppel will allow a licence to be terminated, see *Williams v Staite* [1979] Ch. 291. A smaller degree of misconduct will prevent an estoppel licence arising, under the "clean hands" principle, than will cause it to terminate; *J Willis & Son v Willis* [1986] 1 E.G.L.R. 62.

[29] *Thompson v Park* [1944] K.B. 408 at 409.

[30] Considered above, para.27–015.

[31] [1981] Q.B. 202; A. Briggs [1981] Conv. 212.

The issue of an order for specific performance raised a number of questions of principle. It used to be said that specific performance would not issue in relation to a transient matter; because the issue may not come to the court in time.[32] That view was held to be out of date. Presumably, however, it would have been a defence if the date of the conference had passed before the issue was tried. Another possible difficulty might be the question of the continued supervision by the court, although, as we have seen,[33] inroads have already been made into the supervision principle. A further question is whether specific performance is available to enforce a contract which does not create a proprietary interest. The historical view was that the order would not be made in such a case.[34] But subsequent authorities indicate that specific performance is a remedy based on the inadequacy of damages rather than on the vindication of some proprietary interest.[35] This, it is submitted, is the current approach:

> "[I]t is the duty of the court to protect, where it is appropriate to do so, any interest, whether it be an estate in land or a licence, by injunction or specific performance as the case may be."[36]

Such an approach is consistent with the court's power to grant a prohibitory injunction to restrain the wrongful revocation of a contractual licence, or to grant a mandatory injunction to reinstate a licensee whose licence has been revoked in breach of contract.[37] That is not to say, however, that in any given case specific performance will or should be granted: it remains a matter within the discretion of the court according to the principles which we have already seen in Ch.27. Indeed, it has been suggested that *Verrall* represents an example of specific performance being granted "for a short period" and "in exceptional circumstances".[38]

C.   Express or Implied Contracts

The contract may be express or implied. In the older cases, which dealt mainly with commercial transactions, it was not difficult to recognise the existence of a contract, though its terms may have been difficult to construe.[39] Many of the recent cases concern arrangements within the family. These are situations in which the terms of an agreement are usually not spelled out; and a contract may in any case fail because of a lack of intention to create legal relations.

30–013

---

[32] Above, para.27–025.

[33] Above, para.27–020.

[34] *Booker v Palmer* [1942] 2 All E.R. 674 at 677, per Lord Greene MR This was the view that prevailed at the time of *Hurst's* case.

[35] *Beswick v Beswick* [1968] A.C. 58; *Tanner v Tanner* [1975] 1 W.L.R. 1346 at 1350; *Hutton v Watling* [1948] Ch. 26 at 36 (affirmed at 398); (1980) 96 L.Q.R. 483.

[36] [1981] Q.B. 202 at 220, per Roskill LJ.

[37] *Millennium Productions Ltd v Winter Garden Theatre (London) Ltd* [1948] A.C. 173 (prohibitory); *Luganda v Service Hotels Ltd* [1969] 2 Ch. 209 (mandatory).

[38] *Maloney v Filtons Ltd* [2012] EWHC 1395 (Ch) per Peter Smith J at [99].

[39] "[The] context here is a commercial contract entered into by two parties with the benefit of legal advice. It is not usually unfair to hold parties to the terms of the contract that they have agreed." *Dudley Muslim Association v Dudley MBC* [2015] EWCA Civ 1123 per Lewison LJ at [50].

In these circumstances, it is not surprising that it is difficult to distinguish clearly between cases in which a contract has been found and those where it has not. As has been seen, a contractual licence was implied in *Tanner v Tanner*.[40] That indeed was the only way to find an adequate remedy; and Lord Denning MR, conscious of the difficulty of finding a contract in the circumstances, went so far as to say that the court should "imply a contract by him—or if need be impose the equivalent of a contract by him."[41] In *Coombes v Smith*,[42] the court failed to find a contract in circumstances which were similar. There the defendant bought a house into which the claimant, his lover, moved. As she was pregnant, she gave up her job, the defendant assuring her that he would always provide for her. The defendant paid the outgoings, but the claimant did some decorating and gardening. When the couple separated 10 years later, the defendant offered her £10,000 to move out, but she claimed a contractual licence for life. Her claim failed, as she had provided no consideration, and it was impossible to infer a contract. *Tanner v Tanner* was distinguished as the claimant there had provided consideration in giving up her rent-controlled flat and was not claiming a licence for life. The defendant, however, conceded that the claimant could remain until the child was 17. It is indeed easier to see why there was not a contract in *Coombes*,[43] than it is to see how one could be implied in *Tanner v Tanner*.

In other cases, the occupier has received protection by the court's finding that there was a contractual licence which was irrevocable for a period of time.

> In *Hardwick v Johnson*,[44] a mother purchased a house, on her son's marriage, for occupation by him and his bride. The young couple were to pay £7 a week as rent to the mother. But this soon ceased to be paid, and the mother did not demand it because the couple had little money. The son left his bride, now pregnant, for another woman. The mother sued for possession. The wife claimed to be entitled to remain in possession on payment of £7 per week. The Court of Appeal found a contractual licence. The daughter-in-law was held entitled, subject to resuming the weekly payments, to protection by injunction for an indefinite period of time. Lord Denning MR thought, however, that no enforceable contract could arise in a family situation of this kind,[45] preferring to find a licence by estoppel.

On the face of it, it would seem to be unlikely that the parties would intend to bind themselves contractually in a situation of this type.

D. Contractual Licences and Third Parties

30–014   Protection of the licensee against the licensor inevitably gives rise to the question whether a licensee will be protected also against an assignee of the licensor. On the one hand, protection given to a licensee is in many cases of little use if the

---

[40] [1975] 1 W.L.R. 1346; J. Barton (1976) 92 L.Q.R. 168.

[41] [1975] 1 W.L.R. 1346 at 1350.

[42] [1986] 1 W.L.R. 808; D. Hayton (1986) 45 C.L.J. 394. See also *Horrocks v Forray* [1976] 1 W.L.R. 230; M. Richards (1976) 40 Conv.(N.S.) 362.

[43] More recently, Jeremy Cousins QC, sitting as a Deputy Judge of the Chancery Division, has analysed *Coombes* as the case not being made out on its facts rather than adopting a new legal test: *Murphy v Rayner* [2011] EWHC 1 (Ch) at [260].

[44] [1978] 1 W.L.R. 683. See also *Chandler v Kerley* [1978] 1 W.L.R. 693 ("mistress" entitled to remain for a period determinable upon 12 months' notice).

[45] [1978] 1 W.L.R. 683 at 688.

licensor can transfer the land and leave the licensee helpless. On the other hand, if a licensee is protected against third parties, the licence begins to look like some sort of proprietary interest.[46]

The extent to which a licence is binding on a third party will vary with the type of licence. Bare licences are obviously not binding. The question whether a contractual licence can bind a purchaser under a constructive trust is considered later[47]; likewise whether an estoppel licence can bind third parties.[48] First the position as to contractual licences outside these situations will be examined.

It is important to appreciate that there is no principle which requires that the availability of an injunction against one contracting party will make it available against third parties coming to the land. The jurisdiction to apply an injunction against a third party was demonstrated by the development of the law of restrictive covenants from *Tulk v Moxhay*.[49] The policy decision to refuse an injunction against third parties was shown by the unsuccessful attempts to make covenants run with chattels.[50]

As far as contractual obligations are concerned, the estate of a deceased party to the contract is not properly a third party. The devisee of the licensor is a third party, but takes as a volunteer. One of the landmark cases on the enforcement of licences against third parties, *Errington v Errington and Woods*,[51] is such a case; the report fails to say whether the licensor's widow, who was the devisee, was also his executrix; but both Lord Denning MR and Hodson LJ refer to her as successor in title. Such a person is in a different position from a purchaser.

The conclusion from the authorities is that contractual licences are not ordinarily binding on third parties.

> In *King v David Allen & Sons, Billposting Ltd*,[52] the licensor agreed that the licensees should have the exclusive right of affixing advertisements upon a building. Later the licensor leased the building to a cinema company, no provision being made to protect the rights of the licensees. The licensees sued the licensor for breach of contract. The licensor was liable if the lease to the company deprived the licensees of their contractual right. The House of Lords held that it did.

> In *Clore v Theatrical Properties Ltd*,[53] a deed which was drafted in the form of a lease purported to grant the lessee the "front of the house" rights in a theatre; that is, the right to use refreshment rooms, etc. to provide for the needs of patrons. The instrument provided that the terms "lessor" and "lessee" should include their executors, administrators and assigns. It was held to be a licence and not a lease. The "lessor" and "lessee" both assigned; and the question was whether the "lessee's" assignee could enforce the right under the agreement. He failed; because the licence was a personal contract and enforceable only between the parties to it.

---

[46] See, however, J. Dewar (1986) 49 M.L.R. 741, suggesting that it is wrong to attempt to fit licences into traditional academic land law.

[47] Below, para.30–016.

[48] Below, para.30–035.

[49] (1848) 2 Ph. 774.

[50] *Port Line v Ben Line Steamers* [1958] 2 Q.B. 146; *Lord Strathcona SS Co v Dominion Coal Co* [1926] A.C. 108; B. McFarlane (2004) 120 L.Q.R. 667.

[51] [1952] 1 K.B. 290.

[52] [1916] 2 A.C. 54.

[53] [1936] 3 All E.R. 483.

30–015   As has since been reaffirmed,[54] these cases lay down a correct doctrine relating to contractual licences. Licences were indeed treated as binding on third parties in a number of cases decided in the days when a deserted wife was treated as a licensee protected by injunction[55]; and these provided a very compelling case for applying the injunction also against the party to whom the deserting husband sold the house. But these cases were incorrect; because the House of Lords decided that a deserted wife was not a licensee of her husband, and had no interest capable of binding the land.[56] Legislation followed.[57] There are some cases in which a contractual arrangement, outside the context of a deserted wife, was held to bind a third party, but they are best explained as being decided on other grounds.

> In *Errington v Errington and Woods*[58] the father, A, of a young man who was about to be married purchased a house through a building society, made a down-payment and told the young couple the house would be theirs when they paid all the instalments due under the mortgage. They went into possession and paid all the instalments which fell due. Nothing was stated concerning the rights of the young couple during the currency of the mortgage payments. A died, leaving all his property to Mrs A. The son returned to his mother, who took steps to evict the daughter-in-law. She failed. The daughter-in-law was held to be a licensee who was entitled to protection not only against A in his lifetime, but also against Mrs A, taking as a volunteer.

There was clearly a flavour of contract in the licence, and the case is usually treated as one of contractual licence. But the wide views expressed in the case as to the enforceability of such licences were disapproved, obiter, by the House of Lords in *National Provincial Bank Ltd v Ainsworth*,[59] and have since been said by the Court of Appeal in *Ashburn Anstalt v Arnold*[60] to be neither practically necessary nor theoretically convincing. They could not be reconciled with *King* and *Clore*, but the decision was, however, correct on the facts. It could be justified on any of three grounds:

(i)   there was a contract to convey on completion of the payments, giving rise to an equitable interest in the form of an estate contract which would bind the widow as a volunteer;

(ii)   the daughter-in-law had changed her position in reliance upon a representation by the deceased, the estoppel binding the widow;

(iii) the payment of instalments gave rise to a direct proprietary interest by way of a constructive trust under the principle later formulated in *Gissing v Gissing*.[61]

---

[54] *Ashburn Anstalt v Arnold* [1989] Ch. 1; below, para.30–017.
[55] *Bendall v McWhirter* [1952] 2 Q.B. 466; *Lee v Lee* [1952] 2 Q.B. 489n; *Ferris v Weaven* [1952] 2 All E.R. 233.
[56] *National Provincial Bank Ltd v Ainsworth* [1965] A.C. 1175.
[57] Matrimonial Homes Act 1967; now Family Law Act 1996, Part IV; for the scope of Part IV, see for example *Derwent v Taylor* [2016] EWCA Civ 508; [2016] H.L.R. 25.
[58] [1952] 1 K.B. 290; *Duke of Beaufort v Patrick* (1853) 17 Beav. 60.
[59] [1965] A.C. 1175.
[60] [1989] Ch. 1.
[61] [1971] A.C. 886, above, para.13–014.

Thus the result could have been achieved without accepting Lord Denning's broad principles, which were unnecessary and per incuriam. The correct principle is that a contractual licence cannot bind a third party unless the circumstances are such that a constructive trust has arisen. Further examination of this principle will be deferred until the development of the constructive trust solution has been outlined.

4. CONSTRUCTIVE TRUSTS

Some cases in this field have been decided on the basis of a constructive trust. Lord Denning described a constructive trust as one:

30–016

> "[I]mposed by law whenever justice and good conscience require it. It is a liberal process, founded upon large principles of equity, to be applied in cases where the legal owner cannot conscientiously keep the property for himself alone, but ought to allow another to have the property or the benefit of it or a share of it."[62]

In those terms, the constructive trust solution is at once too vague and too far-reaching. Too vague in that such broad statements provide no way of determining when such a trust will be held to exist.[63] It may be unobjectionable in cases such as *DHN Food Distributors Ltd v Tower Hamlets LBC*,[64] where the issue was whether a contractual licensee could claim compensation for disturbance upon compulsory purchase. But it is not appropriate where title to land is at stake.

Lord Denning MR pioneered this solution in *Binions v Evans*.[65]

> Mrs Evans was the widow of an employee of the Tredegar Estate. The trustees made an agreement with her, under which she would be allowed to reside in a cottage, free of rent and rates, for life. She undertook to keep the cottage in repair. Two years later, the trustees sold the cottage to Mr and Mrs Binions, expressly subject to the agreement, the purchase price being reduced accordingly. The purchasers claimed possession of the cottage. Lord Denning MR held that the purchasers were bound by Mrs Evans' contractual licence and also by a constructive trust in her favour, whereas Megaw and Stephenson LJJ relied upon the agreement as creating a life interest.[66]

Clearly, the case is fact-specific and provides no support for the view that contractual licences generally are binding on third parties. Nevertheless, it was cited subsequently as authority for the proposition that a contractual licence is capable of binding a third party.[67]

---

[62] *Hussey v Palmer* [1972] 1 W.L.R. 1286, at 1290.

[63] R. Smith (1973) 32 C.L.J. 123 at 142.

[64] [1976] 1 W.L.R. 852; D. Hayton (1977) 36 C.L.J. 12. See also *Pennine Raceway Ltd v Kirklees MBC* [1983] Q.B. 382 (Licensee a "person interested in the land" within Town and Country Planning Act 1971 s.164).

[65] [1972] Ch. 359; PVB (1972) 88 L.Q.R. 336; J. Martin (1972) 36 Conv.(N.S.) 266; S. Bright [2000] Conv. 398.

[66] Applying *Bannister v Bannister* [1948] 2 All E.R. 133. See also *Costello v Costello* (1995) 70 P. & C.R. 297.

[67] See e.g. *Re Sharpe* [1980] 1 W.L.R. 219 (claim for possession by trustee in bankruptcy of nephew failed against his aunt who had lent money towards the purchase on the understanding that she could live there with him for the rest of her life); J. Martin [1980] Conv. 207.

30–017 The position was later clarified by the Court of Appeal in *Ashburn Anstalt v Arnold*,[68] which "put the *quietus* to the heresy that a mere licence creates an interest in land."[69] The claimant purchaser sought possession against the defendant, who was in occupation under an agreement with the purchaser's predecessor in title. The claimant had been aware of the agreement and had purchased expressly subject to its provisions "so far as the same are enforceable against the Vendor." In fact it was held that the defendant had a tenancy which was binding on the purchaser under the Land Registration Act 1925.[70] However, the Court of Appeal proceeded to consider the position if the defendant had been a contractual licensee. On the authority of *King v David Allen & Sons, Billposting Ltd*,[71] the correct principle was that a contractual licence could not normally bind a third party. However, the law must be free to develop, and the finding of a constructive trust was considered a beneficial adaptation of old rules to new situations in appropriate circumstances. But there could be no bare assertion that a licence gives rise to a constructive trust. It would arise only if the conscience of the third party was affected. Mere notice would not be sufficient,[72] nor the fact that the property was conveyed "subject to" the interest. Such a term does not mean that the grantee is necessarily intended to be under an obligation to give effect to the interest, but may be merely to protect the grantor against claims by the grantee (for example as in the case of an old restrictive covenant which may or may not be enforceable). The question is whether the grantee has acted in such a way that, as a matter of justice, a trust must be imposed on her. In the present case there would be no constructive trust because the transfer "subject to" the defendant's rights was done to protect the vendor, and the purchaser had not paid a reduced price. As far as the previous cases were concerned, *Binions v Evans* was a legitimate application of the constructive trust doctrine because the parties intended the purchaser to give effect to the interest and the price was reduced accordingly. Also approved was *Lyus v Prowsa Ltd*,[73] where the intention had been similar and the purchaser had given assurances. The doctrine was not, however, appropriate in *Re Sharpe*, where an aunt, who had lent money to her nephew, had not replied to his trustee in bankruptcy's enquiries as to her interest.

---

[68] [1989] Ch. 1; M. Thompson [1988] Conv. 201; A. P. Clarke All E.R. Rev. 1988 at 177; B. McFarlane (2004) 120 L.Q.R. 667.

[69] *IDC Group Ltd v Clarke* [1992] 1 E.G.L.R. 187 at 189, upheld (1993) 65 P. & C.R. 179 (where the issue was not discussed).

[70] On this point, the Court of Appeal was later overruled in *Prudential Assurance Co Ltd v London Residuary Body* [1992] 2 AC 386. The Supreme Court revisited the area in *Mexfield Housing Co-operative Ltd v Berrisford* [2011] UKSC 52; [2012] 1 A.C. 955. Baroness Hale described the legal position on certain terms as "curiouser and curiouser" (at [93]) and urged reform whether by the court or Parliament (at [96]). S. Bridge [2010] Conv. 492. On the application of *Berrisford*, see *Southward Housing Co-operative Ltd v Walker* [2015] EWHC 1615 (Ch); [2016] Ch. 443 (Hildyard J, adopting a contractual licence analysis); J. Roche [2016] Conv. 286; *Leeds City Council v Broadley* [2016] EWCA Civ 1213; [2017] 1 W.L.R. 738; and *Gilpin v Legg* [2017] EWHC 3220 (Ch); [2018] L. & T.R. 6.

[71] [1916] 2 A.C. 54, above, para.30–014.

[72] See *IDC Group Ltd v Clark* [1992] 1 E.G.L.R. 187 at 190 (in the High Court); *Chattey v Farndale Holdings Inc* (1998) 75 P. & C.R. 298; *Lloyd v Dugdale* (2002) 2 P. & C.R. 13; M. Dixon [2002] Conv. 584.

[73] [1982] 1 W.L.R. 1044; distinguished in *Chaudhary v Yavuz* [2011] EWCA Civ 1314; [2013] Ch. 249.

The Court of Appeal added that certainty was of prime importance as far as title to land was concerned, and it was not desirable to impose a constructive trust on slender materials.[74] As seen above,[75] the scope of the doctrine has been confined: Lloyd LJ has said that it will be only in exceptional circumstances that such a claim would and should succeed.[76] It should never be enough to establish such a trust "in any case where the third party right is only identified by way of general words in the contract", as the focus is on the purchaser's conscience being bound.[77]

One difficulty is that the imposition of a constructive trust, in the case of a fee simple, creates an equitable interest which is not registrable (in unregistered land).[78] If the interest protected by a constructive trust is for life only, problems once arose with the Settled Land Act, but settlements cannot now be created.[79] Similar points arise with the doctrine of proprietary estoppel, as discussed below.[80] In that context also the constructive trust has been invoked in order to achieve a just result.[81] But it may be doubted whether the constructive trust is the appropriate tool for achieving such justice, especially in the light of recent authorities on the general doctrine at the highest level.[82] Instead we must turn to the principles of estoppel.

5.   LICENCES BY ESTOPPEL

The doctrine of estoppel has played a significant part in the modern development of the law of licences.[83] A situation in which a licensee has acted to her detriment in reliance upon a representation or promise by the licensor presents a compelling case for the intervention of equity in order to protect the licensee; more compelling, in a sense, than the case of a contractual licence, because the licensee by estoppel has no alternative remedy in damages.[84] The doctrine of estoppel by encouragement or acquiescence has found a fruitful area of operation in the field of licences, under the name of proprietary estoppel; its success in this area has

30–018

---

[74] Reiterated in *IDC Group Ltd v Clark* [1992] 1 E.G.L.R. 187 (in the High Court).

[75] Above, para.12–020.

[76] *Chaudhary v Yavuz* [2011] EWCA Civ 1314; [2013] Ch. 249 at [64]; criticised by B. McFarlane [2013] Conv. 74. See also *Cosmichome Ltd v Southampton City Council* [2013] EWHC 1378 (Ch); [2013] 1 W.L.R. 2436 per Sir William Blackburne at [68]; *Groveholt v Hughes* [2012] EWHC 3351 (Ch) per David Richards J at [14]; and *Bryant Homes Southern Ltd v Stein Management Ltd* [2016] EWHC 2435 (Ch); [2017] 1 P. & C.R. 6.

[77] *Chaudhary v Yavuz* [2011] EWCA Civ 1314; [2013] Ch. 249 at [65]. In *Lyus v Prowsa Developments Ltd* [1982] 1 W.L.R. 1044, for example, the relevant third-party rights in question were specifically identified, and the claimants' right was not registrable.

[78] Formerly the interest of a beneficiary absolutely entitled under a constructive trust was not overreachable, but this has been changed by the Trusts of Land and Appointment of Trustees Act 1996; above, Ch.13, Part 3. Overreaching, however, requires two trustees.

[79] Life interests now give rise to the less complex trust of land under the 1996 Act, above.

[80] Below, para.30–034.

[81] *Re Basham* [1986] 1 W.L.R. 1498, below, para.30–032.

[82] Above, paras 12–028—12–030.

[83] It seems that a licence by estoppel was first so referred to judicially in *Inwards v Baker* [1965] 2 Q.B. 29 per Danckwerts LJ at 38; below, para.30–026.

[84] As to how far a contractual licence may also be a licence by estoppel, see M. Thompson and A. Briggs [1983] Conv. 50 and 285 respectively.

been largely due to the fact that, unlike estoppel by representation or promissory estoppel, it *can* found a cause of action and, in the licence context, enables the court to award a proprietary interest to the licensee. In the enthusiasm for the application of this doctrine, it has become confused with other estoppels, and has been credited with the solution to many cases in which it is quite clear that the judges reached their decision on other grounds. The utility of the doctrine stems from the fact that the court will "look at all the circumstances in each case to decide in what way the equity can be satisfied"[85]; and the most suitable solution is often an award to the licensee of a proprietary interest,[86] rather than merely an injunction. A sword and not a shield is sometimes required.[87]

A.   Types of Estoppel[88]

30–019   There are many different types of estoppel at law and in equity. We are concerned with three of these, each having a separate origin and history.[89] It has occasionally been asserted elsewhere in the Commonwealth that distinctions should not be drawn between the various categories of estoppel, nor between their common law or equitable origin.[90] The courts in this country have not reached this conclusion, although there have been dicta to the effect that it is

---

[85] *Plimmer v Wellington Corp* (1884) 9 App.Cas. 699 at 714; *Greasley v Cooke* [1980] 1 W.L.R. 1306 at 1312. It may be held that the claimant has already had sufficient satisfaction for her expenditure; *Sledmore v Dalby* (1996) 72 P. & C.R. 196.

[86] B. McFarlane, *The Law of Proprietary Estoppel* (2014).

[87] M. Barnes [2011] L.M.C.L.Q. 372. C. Knowles and M. Balen (2013) 24 K.L.J. 111.

[88] E. Bant and M. Bryan (2015) 35 O.J.L.S. 427.

[89] For estoppel by convention, i.e. by a course of dealing, see *Amalgamated Investment and Property Co (In Liquidation) v Texas Commerce International Bank Ltd* [1982] Q.B. 84; *Pacol Ltd v Trade Lines Ltd* [1982] 1 Lloyd's Rep. 456; P. Matthews (1982) 79 L.S.Gaz. 662; *Dixon v Blindley Heath Investments Ltd* [2015] EWCA Civ 1023; [2017] 3 W.L.R. 166 per Hildyard J at [73]ff. See generally Wilken and Ghaly, *The Law of Waiver, Variation and Estoppel*, 3rd edn (Oxford: Oxford University Press, 2012); Cooke, *The Modern Law of Estoppel* (Oxford: Oxford University Press, 2000). *HM Revenue & Customs v Benchdollar Ltd* [2009] EWHC 1310 (Ch) per Briggs J (describing at [44] the circumstances where it would be unconscionable to resile from a common assumption as "infinitely various"). The assumption must be shared: *Exsus Travel Ltd v Baker Tilly* [2016] EWHC 2818 (Ch) (no evidence that the defendants' solicitors shared the incorrect assumption of the claimants' solicitors, or otherwise took advantage); *Mears Ltd v Shoreline Housing Partnership Ltd* [2015] EWHC 1396 (TCC) per Akenhead J at [51]; and *Bristol Rovers (1883) Ltd v Sainsbury's Supermarkets Ltd* [2016] EWCA Civ 160. See also the recent Privy Council decision in *Prime Sight Ltd v Lavarello* [2013] UKPC 22; [2014] A.C. 436, which confirms the category of estoppel by deed as distinct from estoppel by representation or by convention (per Lord Toulson at [30]); A. Trukhtanov (2012) 130 L.Q.R. 3; K.R. Handley (2014) 130 L.Q.R. 370. K.C.F. Loi [2015] L.M.C.L.Q. 346; J. Braithwaite (2016) 132 L.Q.R. 120; *Chen v Ng* [2017] UKPC 27; [2018] 1 P. & C.R. DG2; M. Leeming (2018) 134 L.Q.R. 171.

[90] See *Commonwealth of Australia v Verwayen* (1990) 170 C.L.R. 394 at 410–413, per Mason CJ; M. Lunney [1992] Conv. 239. For the latest views of the High Court of Australia, see *Crown Melbourne Ltd v Cosmopolitan Hotel (Vic) Pty Ltd* [2016] HCA 26; (2016) 260 C.L.R. 1; J. Hudson (2016) 10 J.Eq. 137. Likewise in New Zealand: *Gillies v Keogh* [1989] 2 N.Z.L.R. 327 at 331 and *Wilson Parking New Zealand Ltd v Fanshawe 136 Ltd* [2014] 3 N.Z.L.R. 567. See Halliwell, *Equity and Good Conscience in a Contemporary Context* (London: Old Bailey Press, 1997) Ch.2; M. Bryan (2013) 7 J.Eq. 209. B. Hacker (2015) 131 L.Q.R. 424 at 449.

undesirable to distinguish between types of estoppel.[91] If this view prevails, the existing differences (such as whether the type of estoppel operates as a sword or a shield)[92] will have to be modified in order to achieve a coherent unified doctrine.[93] Later pronouncements, however, are against the idea of "an overarching principle" which would blur the distinctions.[94] Lord Scott in *Yeoman's Rowe Management Ltd v Cobbe*[95] expressed the view that proprietary estoppel was a sub-species of promissory estoppel, but this was a minority view at variance with the origin and development of the doctrines and was doubted by Lord Walker in *Thorner v Major*.[96] As the leading commentator Professor Ben McFarlane has argued, it is "a serious error to regard promissory estoppel and proprietary estoppel as simply examples of an overarching concept of equitable estoppel."[97] It remains the case in English law that one must distinguish between the species of estoppel.[98]

i. Estoppel by Representation. Estoppel by representation operates over a wide field of common law and equity. The basic principle is that a person who makes an unambiguous[99] representation, by words,[100] or conduct,[101] or by silence,[102] of an existing fact, and causes another party to act to her detriment[103] in reliance on the representation will not be permitted subsequently to act

30–020

---

[91] *Crabb v Arun DC* [1976] Ch. 179 at 193; *Amalgamated Investment and Property Co Ltd (In Liquidation) v Texas Commerce International Bank Ltd* [1982] Q.B. 84 at 103; cf. JMT (1981) 97 L.Q.R. 513; P. Evans [1988] Conv. 46; *JT Developments Ltd v Quinn* (1991) 62 P. & C.R. 33 at 45; *First National Bank Plc v Thompson* [1996] Ch. 231.

[92] It is always necessary to analyse whether such an estoppel is being used as a sword: *Mears Ltd v Shoreline Housing Partnership Ltd* [2015] EWHC 1396 (TCC) per Akenhead J at [51](e): "[while] a party cannot in terms found a cause of action on an estoppel, it may, as a result of being able to rely on an estoppel, succeed on a cause of action on which, without being able to rely on the estoppel, it would necessarily have failed."

[93] See M. Halliwell (1994) 14 L.S. 15, suggesting the remedying of unconscionable conduct as the unifying factor; J. Hudson (2016) 10 J.Eq. 137. See generally Pawlowski, *The Doctrine of Proprietary Estoppel* (London: Sweet & Maxwell, 1996).

[94] *Republic of India v India Steamship Co Ltd (No.2)* [1998] A.C. 878 at 914; R. Halson [1999] L.M.C.L.Q. 256; *National Westminster Bank Plc v Somer International (UK) Ltd* [2002] Q.B. 1286 at 1303.

[95] [2008] 1 W.L.R. 1752.

[96] [2009] 1 W.L.R. 776; below, para.30–023.

[97] B. McFarlane (2013) 66 C.L.P. 267, 304. See further B. McFarlane, *The Law of Proprietary Estoppel* (2014).

[98] See further *Prime Sight Ltd v Lavarello* [2013] UKPC 22; [2014] A.C. 436 per Lord Toulson at [30], endorsing the view of Lord Goff of Cheiveley in *Johnson v Gore Wood & Co* [2002] 2 A.C. 1 at 39–40.

[99] *Low v Bouverie* [1891] 3 Ch. 82.

[100] *Hunt v Carew* (1649) Nels. 46; or through an agent; *Moorgate Mercantile Ltd v Twitchings* [1977] A.C. 890.

[101] *Waldron v Sloper* (1852) 1 Drew. 193.

[102] *Fung Kai Sun v Chan Fui Hing* [1951] A.C. 489; *Pacol Ltd v Trade Lines Ltd* [1982] 1 Lloyd's Rep. 456; for the limits of *Pacol*, see *Costain Ltd v Tarmac Holdings Ltd* [2017] EWHC 319 (TCC) and *Woodward v Phoenix Healthcare Distribution Ltd* [2018] EWHC 334 (Ch).

[103] See *Kelly v Fraser (Jamaica)* [2012] UKPC 25 (Lord Sumption giving the judgment for the Board of the Privy Council); for doubt as to the differences as to the requirement of detriment as between estoppel by convention and estoppel by representation, see *Process Components Ltd v Kason Kek-Gardner Ltd* [2016] EWHC 2198 (Ch) per Proundman J at [117] and [135].

inconsistently with that representation. The doctrine was originally applied only where there was a representation of existing fact,[104] and not where the representation was one of law, but the better view is that it does now so extend.[105] The representor could not subsequently allege, in dealing with the representee, that the facts were different from those represented. Apart from a few long-established exceptions,[106] such an estoppel works negatively. It is not capable of creating a cause of action. It works like a rule of evidence, a rule which excludes a particular defence or line of argument.

This is not to say that estoppel is available only to a defendant. A claimant may take advantage of the doctrine if she has an independent cause of action, and can show that the defence is inconsistent with a representation of the defendant on which she relies.[107]

> A famous example is *Robertson v Minister of Pensions*,[108] where an officer claimed a pension, relying upon a statement by the War Office that his disability had been accepted as due to military service, and forbore to obtain an independent medical opinion. It was held that the Crown, through the Minister of Pensions, could not go back on the statement previously made. The officer was no longer in a position to supply the necessary evidence; but the Minister was estopped from denying that he qualified.

30–021 **ii. Promissory Estoppel.** The doctrine is expanded in equity, so as to include not only representations of fact, but also representations of intention; or promises. The doctrine came into prominence with the decision of Denning J in *Central London Property Trust Ltd v High Trees House Ltd* in 1947,[109] and became firmly established in later cases.[110]

Where, by words or conduct, a person makes an unambiguous[111] representation as to her future conduct, intending the representation to be relied on, and to

---

[104] *Jorden v Money* (1845) 5 H.L.C. 185; not followed in Australia; *Legione v Hateley* (1983) 152 C.L.R. 406; *Foran v Wight* (1989) 168 C.L.R. 385.

[105] See e.g. *Mears Ltd v Shoreline Housing Partnership Ltd* [2015] EWHC 1396 (TCC) per Akenhead J at [53].

[106] e.g. a tenancy by estoppel; see also *Ramsden v Dyson* (1866) L.R. 1 H.L. 129; below, para.30–030.

[107] Similarly with promissory estoppel; *Amalgamated Investment and Property Co (In Liquidation) v Texas Commerce International Bank Ltd* [1982] Q.B. 84; *Pacol Ltd v Trade Lines Ltd* [1982] 1 Lloyd's Rep. 456. See M. Barnes [2011] L.M.C.L.Q. 372.

[108] [1949] 1 K.B. 227; *Combe v Combe* [1951] 2 K.B. 215 at 219, per Denning LJ. See also *Western Fish Products Ltd v Penwith DC* [1981] 2 All E.R. 204.

[109] [1947] K.B. 130. *Collier v P & MJ Wright (Holdings) Ltd* [2008] 1 W.L.R. 643.

[110] *Combe v Combe* [1951] 2 K.B. 215; *Ajayi v RT Briscoe (Nigeria) Ltd* [1964] 1 W.L.R. 1326; *WJ Alan & Co Ltd v El Nasr Export and Import Co* [1972] 2 Q.B. 189.

[111] On the strictness of "unambiguity", see Patten LJ in *Kim v Chasewood Park Residents Ltd* [2013] EWCA Civ 239 at [23]. Keane J has reaffirmed the requirement of certainty in Australia: *Crown Melbourne Ltd v Cosmopolitan Hotel (Vic) Pty Ltd* [2016] HCA 26 at [143]: "It would tend to reduce the law to incoherence if a representation, too uncertain or ambiguous to give rise to a contract or a variation of contractual rights and liabilities, were held to be sufficient to found a promissory estoppel. Practical considerations such as the need of commerce for certainty, both as to the terms to which parties have agreed to be bound, and as to whether their bargaining process has concluded, also provide strong support for this approach."

affect the legal relations between the parties,[112] and the representee alters her position in reliance on it, the representor will be unable to act inconsistently with the representation if by so doing the representee would be prejudiced.[113]

The doctrine emerged in *Loffus v Maw*[114] and *Hughes v Metropolitan Railway Co*,[115] and developed through a line of cases which was little known until 1947. Denning J then applied it in *Central London Property Trust Ltd v High Trees House Ltd*.[116]

> The landlord company in 1937 leased to the defendant a block of flats for 99 years at a rent of £2,500 a year. Early in 1940, because of the war, the defendants were unable to find sub-tenants for the flats, and unable in consequence to pay the rent. The landlord agreed to reduce the rent to £1,250 from the beginning of the term. By the beginning of 1945 all the flats were let, and the landlord was held entitled to the full rent as from the middle of that year. Denning J, however, stated that the landlord would have been estopped from claiming the full rent for the period from 1940 to 1945, on the ground that though not technically bound because of the lack of consideration, the landlord had intended the defendants to rely on the promise and the defendants had acted on the faith of it.

Promissory estoppel contains a number of features which distinguish it from estoppel by representation of fact.[117] First, in that the representation may be one of intention and not one of fact; which raises the question whether it is inconsistent with the House of Lords decision in *Jorden v Money*,[118] but the doctrine is now well established. Secondly, the requirement of detriment to the representee is less stringent in the case of promissory estoppel. Financial loss or other detriment is of course sufficient; but it seems that it is not necessary to show more than that the representee committed herself to a particular course of action as a result of the representation.[119] Thirdly, the effect of the estoppel may not be permanent. The representor may escape from the burden of the equity if he can ensure that the representee will not be prejudiced[120]:

> "The generally accepted view is that promissory estoppel is usually only suspensory and that the representor may resile from his promise on reasonable notice unless it would be unconscionable for him to do so."[121]

---

[112] *Harvey v Dunbar Assets Plc* [2017] EWCA Civ 60 per Henderson LJ at [60] "The doctrine of promissory estoppel, normally at any rate, presupposes the existence of a legal relationship between the parties, in the context of which the promise or assurance which gives rise to the estoppel is made."

[113] See *Combe v Combe* [1951] 2 K.B. 215 at 220.

[114] (1862) 3 Giff. 592.

[115] (1877) 2 App.Cas. 439.

[116] [1947] K.B. 130.

[117] See generally G. Cheshire and C. Fifoot (1947) 63 L.Q.R. 283; J. Wilson (1951) 67 L.Q.R. 330; Denning LJ (1952) 15 M.L.R. 1; L. Sheridan (1952) 15 M.L.R. 325.

[118] (1854) 5 H.L.Cas. 185. See *Foran v Wight* (1989) 168 C.L.R. 385 at 411.

[119] *Central London Property Ltd v High Trees House Ltd* [1947] K.B. 130; *WJ Alan & Co Ltd v El Nasr Export and Import Co* [1972] 2 Q.B. 189; *Ajayi v RT Briscoe (Nigeria) Ltd* [1964] 1 W.L.R. 1326.

[120] *Tool Metal Manufacturing Co Ltd v Tungsten Electric Co Ltd* [1955] 1 W.L.R. 761.

[121] *Kim v Chasewood Park Residents Ltd* [2013] EWCA Civ 239, per Patten LJ at [41].

But, consistently with estoppel by representation, promissory estoppel does not create a cause of action. It is a shield and not a sword.[122]

iii. Proprietary Estoppel.

30-022   *(a)   General Principles.*   This doctrine is applicable where one party knowingly[123] encourages another to act, or acquiesces in the other's actions, to her detriment in the belief that she has or will have some property right against the first party.[124] The latter may be required to make good the expectation which she encouraged in the other party. Unlike other estoppels, therefore, this doctrine may, where appropriate, create a claim, and an entitlement to positive proprietary rights;[125] in others, it can operate negatively, or can produce a compromise situation suited to the particular circumstances. The doctrine "has developed rapidly" over the past half-century.[126]

The doctrine was restrictively interpreted by the House of Lords in *Yeoman's Row Management Ltd v Cobbe.*[127]

> The claimant, a property developer, made an oral "in principle agreement to buy the defendant's land. Section 2 of the Law of Property (Miscellaneous Provisions) Act 1989 requires contracts relating to land to be made in writing.[128] Although the claimant was aware that there was no binding contract, he spent time and money on obtaining planning permission in the expectation that the contract would be finalised, but it was not. His claim to an interest in the property under the doctrines of proprietary estoppel or constructive trust failed. (He was entitled to compensation under the quantum meruit principle for the value of his services.) Lord Scott explained that the doctrine could not normally arise in the "subject to contract"

---

[122] *Combe v Combe* [1951] 2 K.B. 215 at 224. See generally M. Thompson (1983) 42 C.L.J. 257; cf. *Waltons Stores (Interstate) Ltd v Maher* (1988) 164 C.L.R. 387. *Shoreline Housing Partnership Ltd v Mears Ltd* [2013] EWCA Civ 639.

[123] See further HHJ Paul Matthews in *Smyth-Tyrrell v Bowden* [2018] EWHC 106 (Ch), declining at [78] "to hold that an equity by way of proprietary estoppel can arise where a landowner ought to have realised, but did not realise, that the tenant believed that the landowner was promising an interest, and the landowner did nothing to encourage the tenant to act in the way that he did"; *Fielden v Christie-Miller* [2015] EWHC 87 (Ch); *Rawlings v Chapman* [2015] EWHC 3160 (Ch); and *AIB Group (UK) Plc v Turner* [2015] EWHC 3994 (Ch) (in all three cases no relevant promise was found to have been made).

[124] Law Com. CP No. 227, *Updating the Land Registration Act 2002: A Consultation Paper* (2016), xix and para.17.27, See I. Samet (2015) 78 M.L.R. 85, criticising the similarity of liability in estoppel in cases of acquiescence and active encouragement; cf. "A proprietary estoppel does not have to fit neatly into the pure acquiescence-based pigeon hole or the assurance one" *Hoyl Group Ltd v Cromer Town Council* [2015] EWCA Civ 782 per Floyd LJ at [72]. Our focus in this chapter is on land, but Birss J has recently indicated that a proprietary estoppel could arise in respect of a licence relating to intellectual property rights (although the claim failed on the facts): *Motivate Publishing FZ LLC v Hello Ltd* [2015] EWHC 1554 (Ch).

[125] *MWB Business Exchange Centres Ltd v Rock Advertising Ltd* [2016] EWCA Civ 553 per Kitchin LJ at [65] (distinguishing promissory and proprietary estoppel).

[126] B. McFarlane and Sir P. Sales (2015) 131 L.Q.R. 610 at 611.

[127] [2008] 1 W.L.R. 1752.

[128] The section provides, so far as relevant:

"2.—(1)   A contract for the sale or other disposition of an interest in land can only be made in writing and only by incorporating all the terms which the parties have expressly agreed in one document or, where contracts are exchanged, in each …

(5) … nothing in this section affects the creation or operation of resulting, implied or constructive trusts."

cases, as the claimant's expectation was always subject to a contingency controlled by the other party. The vendor had taken advantage of him, but he knew all along that there was no contract and took a commercial risk.[129]

"Proprietary estoppel requires, in my opinion, clarity as to what it is that the object of the estoppel is to be estopped from denying, or asserting, and clarity as to the interest in the property in question that that denial, or assertion, would otherwise defeat. If these requirements are not recognised, proprietary estoppel will lose contact with its roots and risk becoming unprincipled and therefore unpredictable, if it has not already become so."[130]

Section 2(5) of the 1989 Act provided an express exception for constructive trusts,[131] but not for estoppel, and it was considered that proprietary estoppel could not be prayed in aid to render enforceable an agreement that the statute has declared to be void. This view is open to question, although much may turn on the extent to which the agreement may be regarded as certain.[132] Lord Neuberger, writing extra-judicially, described s.2 of the 1989 Act as "that misconceived piece of legislation", and suggested that "section 2 offers no bar to a claim based in equity".[133] HHJ Paul Matthews has provisionally argued that s.2 does not apply to proprietary estoppel, as the doctrine is "not about enforcing a contract at all".[134] Kitchin LJ has taken a similar view,[135] and suggested that it is appropriate to consider whether the relevant claim would frustrate the policy of the Act.[136]

Cases of *promissory* estoppel, however, which do not fall within s.2(5), cannot operate to enable the claimant to do "what [they] could not do by informal contract".[137]

The approach of the House of Lords in *Yeoman's Row Management Ltd v Cobbe*, although not the result, attracted considerable academic criticism, and was viewed as a setback which had curtailed or even extinguished the doctrine.[138]   **30–023**

---

[129] See also *Attorney General of Hong Kong v Humphreys Estate (Queen's Gardens) Ltd* [1987] A.C. 114, where the claim failed on similar grounds; *Haq v Island Homes Housing Association* [2011] 2 P. & C.R. 17. *Reveille Independent Llc v Anotech International (UK) Ltd* [2016] EWCA Civ 443 per Cranston J at [42] (on certainty in respect of commercial negotiations).

[130] [2008] 1 W.L.R. 1752 at 1768.

[131] The exception may be relied on where estoppel gives rise to a constructive trust. See *Yaxley v Gotts* [2000] Ch. 162; *Kinane v Mackie-Conteh* [2005] W.T.L.R. 345; *S v S and M* [2007] 1 F.L.R. 1123. *Southern Pacific Mortgages Ltd v Scott* [2014] UKSC 52; [2015] A.C. 385; *Culliford v Thorpe* [2018] EWHC 426 (Ch). The view that s.2(5) does not apply to proprietary estoppel claims in themselves may lead to parties preferring to rely on a constructive trust instead: see eg *Matchmove v Dowling* [2016] EWCA Civ 1233 at [28]; above, para.12–010.

[132] *Herbert v Doyle* [2010] EWCA Civ 1095.

[133] (2009) 68 C.L.J. 536 at 546. See also G. Owen and O. Rees [2011] Conv. 495 and Patten LJ in *Kim v Chasewood Park Residents Ltd* [2013] EWCA Civ 239 at [46].

[134] See *Muhammad v ARY Properties Ltd* [2016] EWHC 1698 (Ch) at [46]–[50]. See also *Ghazaani v Rowshan* [2015] EWHC 1922 (Ch) (HHJ Behrens holding, at [192]–[195], that in exceptional circumstances it should be possible for a proprietary estoppel to operate notwithstanding s.2 of the 1989 Act).

[135] *Farrar v Miller* [2018] EWCA Civ 172 at [53]–[64].

[136] [2018] EWCA Civ 172 at [63].

[137] *Dudley Muslim Association v Dudley MBC* [2015] EWCA Civ 1123 per Lewison LJ at [33].

[138] B. McFarlane and A. Robertson [2008] L.M.C.L.Q. 449; A. Goymour (2009) 68 C.L.J. 37; J. Getzler (2009) 125 L.Q.R. 196; G. Griffiths [2009] Conv. 141.

However, those fears were allayed by the decision of the House of Lords in *Thorner v Major*,[139] where the doctrine was again reviewed in the context of an expectation of inheritance.

> Peter, a man of few words, owned a farm. His cousin's son, David, worked on the farm without pay for 29 years until Peter died. Peter never expressly promised to leave the farm to David, but that was the understanding between them. In 1990 Peter gave David some papers on his life policies worth £20,000, saying that David should use them to pay death duties. This was part of a pattern of conduct over many years indicating his intention to leave David the farm. In 1997 Peter made a will leaving David his estate apart from some pecuniary legacies. He later fell out with a pecuniary legatee and revoked the will, but he never made another and died intestate. The House of Lords, reversing the Court of Appeal, held that David was entitled to the farm.
>
> It was held that, in the appropriate context, "oblique assurances" could constitute a sufficiently clear and unequivocal representation. The representation had to be "clear enough", and that was hugely dependent on context. While the representations had to relate to identified property owned,[140] or perhaps about to be owned, by the defendant, changes in its character or extent over time did not exclude a remedy if it was still identifiable. Lord Scott considered that proprietary estoppel provided a remedy if assurances related to the acquisition of an immediate interest, but preferred to regard representations as to inheritance prospects as giving rise to a "remedial constructive trust."[141]

In *Thorner*, the approach of the House of Lords in *Yeoman's Rowe Management Ltd v Cobbe* was regarded as confined to the commercial context of a situation in which the parties were at arm's length and knew that neither was yet bound by any contract.[142] It was very different from a case concerning assurances of inheritance by one family member to another. Nevertheless, there are still restrictions based on the requirements of reasonable reliance on a clear representation, as Keane J has recently explained in the High Court of Australia[143]:

> "Observance of this limit on the operation of estoppel in equity ensures that it is not allowed to operate to underwrite unrealistic expectations or wishful thinking. Such an operation would be especially pernicious in a commercial context; but even in a non-commercial context estoppel should not be allowed to operate as an instrument of injustice."

Overall, *Thorner v Major* was generally welcomed for restoring the flexibility of the doctrine, but it has not resolved every issue, and the volume of litigation in

---

[139] [2009] 1 W.L.R. 776. See also *Suggitt v Suggitt* [2012] EWCA Civ 1140 and *Legg v Burton* [2017] EWHC 2088 (Ch); above, para.12–012.

[140] *Winkler v Shamoon* [2016] EWHC 217 (Ch).

[141] Since, as we have seen, above, paras 12–028—12–030, the remedial constructive trust is not established in this jurisdiction, his Lordship's analysis was surprising, and in any event a minority view.

[142] *Herbert v Doyle* [2010] EWCA Civ 1095 per Arden LJ at [56]; see also *Generator Developments Ltd v Lidl UK GmbH* [2018] EWCA Civ 396, considered above para.12–011. On coherence with the law of contract more generally, see *Crown Melbourne Ltd v Cosmopolitan Hotel (Vic) Pty Ltd* [2016] HCA 26 at [149]. In *Saunders v Al Himaly* [2017] EWHC 2219 (Ch), Henry Carr J distinguished *Yeoman's Row* on the basis (of assumed facts) that the relevant terms had been agreed and that (at [35]) in the House of Lords case "the parties were much more sophisticated and more experienced, than the Defendants in the present case and had legal advisors to advise them about the effects of agreement at a much earlier stage".

[143] *Crown Melbourne Ltd v Cosmopolitan Hotel (Vic) Pty Ltd* [2016] HCA 26 at [153].

this area is unlikely to diminish.[144] The relationship between the constructive trust and proprietary estoppel will remain "the subject of much discussion".[145]

As far as interests in the home are concerned, some dicta had suggested an attempt to assimilate proprietary estoppel and common intention constructive trusts, but there has been a lack of enthusiasm at the highest level for this approach.[146] It appears that, where the court is driven to impute an intention in order to quantify the shares for a common intention constructive trust, there will be some similarity with the approach seen in estoppel.[147] There may also be factual overlap between the doctrines,[148] which though distinct, have been said to "spring from the same source".[149]

One question which arises is whether the courts should award a remedy which fulfils the expectations of the claimant[150] or one which merely reverses the detriment or, to put it another way, is the minimum award to do justice. The latter is all that is required to avoid unjust enrichment, whereas the former might be said to give a promise unsupported by consideration the effect of a contract. The better view, which was favoured by the House of Lords,[151] is that the aim should be the reversal of detriment, as it would normally be inequitable to insist on a remedy which is disproportionate to the detriment.[152] There may, however, be special reasons for going further in some cases.[153] The Court of Appeal in

30–024

---

[144] B. McFarlane and A. Robertson (2009) 125 L.Q.R. 535; M. Dixon [2009] Conv. 260; B. Sloan (2009) 68 C.L.J. 518; Lord Neuberger (2009) 68 C.L.J. 536.

[145] *Southern Pacific Mortgages Ltd v Scott* [2014] UKSC 52; [2015] A.C. 385 at [28]. *Herbert v Doyle* [2010] EWCA Civ 1095.

[146] *Stack v Dowden* [2007] 2 A.C. 432 at 448; above, para.13–020; *Thorner v Major* [2009] 1 W.L.R. 776 (Lord Scott).

[147] *Aspden v Elvy* [2012] EWHC 1387 (Ch) (HHJ Behrens); J. Lee [2012] Conv. 421; above, para.13–013. See also *Ghazaani v Rowshan* [2015] EWHC 1922 (Ch) (also a decision of HHJ Behrens) at [193]: "This is an area where there is a considerable, but not a total overlap between the areas of constructive trust and proprietary estoppel."

[148] See e.g. *Wodzicki v Wodzicki* [2017] EWCA Civ 95 per David Richards LJ at [30] (defendant did not know of the promise made by her husband to the claimant); *Culliford v Thorpe* [2018] EWHC 426 (Ch) per HHJ Paul Matthews at [56]–[57].

[149] *Culliford v Thorpe* [2018] EWHC 426 (Ch), per HHJ Paul Matthews at [68], citing the speech of Lord Diplock in *Gissing v Gissing* [1971] A.C. 886, though conceding (at [69]) that in "recent times, it has become fashionable to seek to separate the two doctrines" (see also at [76]).

[150] *Pascoe v Turner* [1979] 1 W.L.R. 431, below, para.30–028; S. Moriarty (1984) 100 L.Q.R. 376; M. Thompson [1986] Conv. 406; *Re Basham* [1986] 1 W.L.R. 1498, below, para.30–032; *Wayling v Jones* (1995) 69 P. & C.R. 170; *Yaxley v Gotts* [2000] Ch. 162; *Kinane v Mackie-Conteh* [2005] W.T.L.R. 345 at 354. For the view that this approach is correct, see E. Cooke (1997) 17 L.S. 258; cf. A. Robertson (1998) 18 L.S. 360.

[151] *Stack v Dowden* [2007] 2 A.C. 432 at 448.

[152] cf. the position in Australia: see *Giumelli v Giumelli* (1999) 196 C.L.R. 101; *Delaforce v Simpson-Cook* (2010) 78 N.S.W.L.R. 483; *Sidhu v Van Dyke* (2014) 251 C.L.R. 505; M. Bryan (2012) 6 J.Eq. 131. See also *Crabb v Arun DC* [1976] Ch. 179 at 198; *Baker v Baker* [1993] 2 F.L.R. 247 (an unusual case where the detriment exceeded the value of the expected interest); *Sledmore v Dalby* (1996) 72 P. & C.R. 196; *Gillett v Holt* [2001] Ch. 210; *Evans v HSBC Trust Company (UK) Ltd* [2005] W.T.L.R. 1289. See generally A. Robertson [2008] Conv. 295.

[153] *Pascoe v Turner* [1979] 1 W.L.R. 431 (interest less than fee simple considered insecure against future purchasers); *Holman v Howes* [2007] W.T.L.R. 1539. See generally S. Gardner (1999) 115 L.Q.R. 438 and (2006) 122 L.Q.R. 492.

Jennings v Rice[154] reviewed the authorities and concluded that the claimant's expectation was no more than a starting point: the most essential requirement was proportionality between the expectation and the detriment. Other factors included any misconduct of either party, changes in the benefactor's circumstances, and the existence of other legal or moral claims against the benefactor. On this approach, £200,000 was awarded to the claimant who had acted as a carer in the expectation of inheriting a house worth £435,000. "Proportionality lies at the heart of the doctrine of proprietary estoppel and permeates its every application."[155] The range of remedies is further discussed below.[156]

However, it is appropriate to note some debate over the meaning of "proportionality" here, which may be interpreted in several ways. In *Suggitt v Suggitt*,[157] Arden LJ said (referring to Walker LJ in *Jennings v Rice*[158]):

> "this principle does not mean that there has to be a relationship of proportionality between the level of detriment and the relief awarded. What Walker LJ holds in this paragraph is that if the expectations are extravagant or 'out of all proportion to the detriment which the claimant has suffered', the court can and should recognise that the claimant's equity should be satisfied in another and generally more limited way. So the question is: was the relief that the judge granted 'out of all proportion to the detriment' suffered?"

Detrimental reliance need not involve the expenditure of money on the land.[159] As Arden LJ explained in *Suggitt*,

> "reliance is what a person does on the faith of some matter and detriment is usually the result: they are very closely connected. Clearly, the same factual matters may show both reliance and detriment."[160]

In *Greasley v Cooke*, Lord Denning MR appeared to suggest obiter that it was not necessary that the claimant should have acted to her detriment[161]:

> "[I]t is sufficient if the party, to whom the assurance is given, acts on the faith of it—in such circumstances that it would be unjust and inequitable for the party making the assurance to go back on it... There is no need for her to prove that she acted to her detriment or to her prejudice."[162]

---

[154] (2003) 1 P. & C.R. 8; M. Pawlowski (2002) 118 L.Q.R. 519; M. Thompson [2003] Conv. 225. See also *Campbell v Griffin* [2001] W.T.L.R. 981; M. Thompson [2003] Conv. 157; *Grundy v Ottey* [2003] W.T.L.R. 1253; M. Thompson [2004] Conv. 137.

[155] *Henry v Henry* [2010] 1 All E.R. 988 at 1002 (PC); see also *Davies v Davies (No.2)* [2016] EWCA Civ 463; [2017] 1 F.L.R. 1286 at [38].

[156] Below, para.30–025.

[157] [2012] EWCA Civ 1140 at [44].

[158] *Jennings v Rice* [2002] EWCA Civ 159 at [50].

[159] For the application of the doctrine to property other than land, see *Western Fish Products Ltd v Penwith DC* [1981] 2 All E.R. 204 at 218; *Moorgate Mercantile Co Ltd v Twitchings* [1976] Q.B. 225 at 242 (reversed by the House of Lords but not on this point; [1977] A.C. 890); P. Matthews (1981) 40 C.L.J. 340.

[160] [2012] EWCA Civ 1140 at [35]; see also *Gillett v Holt* [2001] Ch. 210 per Walker LJ at [225].

[161] Here in any event the claimant had foregone wages and perhaps lost job opportunities.

[162] [1980] 1 W.L.R. 1306 at 1311–1312. This resembles the requirements of promissory estoppel (above, para.30–021).

Subsequent cases, however, have made it clear that these comments related only to the burden of proving reliance. In *Coombes v Smith*[163] (the facts of which have already been given[164]), Lord Denning's statement was interpreted as meaning merely that where the claimant has adopted a detrimental course of conduct after the defendant's assurances, there is a rebuttable presumption that this was done in reliance upon the assurances. Here the claim based on proprietary estoppel failed. The claimant had no mistaken belief that she had a right to remain indefinitely, and in any event there was no detrimental act. Her acts in leaving her husband, becoming pregnant and looking after the house were not done in reliance on any expectation of an interest and were not detrimental.[165] The Court of Appeal recently declined to determine whether in principle a promise to marry could constitute sufficient detrimental reliance.[166]

Other decisions have shown more lenience on "reliance". In *Matharu v Matharu*,[167] a married couple had improved property owned by the husband's father, who had encouraged the wife to believe that it belonged to her husband. She was granted a licence to occupy for life even though some of the improvements were done after she discovered the truth. In *Wayling v Jones*,[168] the claimant helped the deceased, with whom he cohabited, to run a café merely for pocket money, and acted as his chauffeur and companion. The deceased promised to leave him a house and business, but all he received by will was a car and furniture. The café had been sold and at his death the deceased owned a hotel. The claimant was awarded the proceeds of sale of the hotel (over £72,000), even though his evidence was that he would have stayed with the deceased if no promise had been made. It was held that the promise did not need to be the sole inducement for the claimant's conduct. In *Culliford v Thorpe*,[169] the deceased promised to share his property with the defendant, his partner, and the defendant relied upon that promise in undertaking building work on the property. It was held that the promise should be given effect, but with the deceased having died, the appropriate order was that the property should be sold, with the defendant receiving half of the net proceeds, minus a one-half occupation rent.

---

[163] [1986] 1 W.L.R. 808; D. Hayton (1986) 45 C.L.J. 394; *Wayling v Jones* (1995) 69 P. & C.R. 170. See also *Stevens & Cutting Ltd v Anderson* [1990] 11 E.G.L.R. 95, suggesting that the headnote in *Greasley* is wrong: the decision was on the burden of proof of reliance, not of detriment.

[164] Above, para.30–013 (the contract claim).

[165] cf. *Grant v Edwards* [1986] Ch. 638. See also *Walsh v Singh* [2010] 1 F.L.R. 1658 (no estoppel where woman's contributions were in expectation of a long-term relationship, not a property interest).

[166] [2013] EWCA Civ 953 per Sales J at [62]. See also *Walsh v Singh* [2010] 1 F.L.R. 1658 (no claim where woman gave up Bar career and helped in man's business, expecting marriage); on detriment in the context of common intention constructive trusts, see *Curran v Collins* [2015] EWCA Civ 404 above, para.13–011.

[167] (1994) 68 P. & C.R. 93; J. Dewar (1994) 24 Fam. Law 625.

[168] (1995) 69 P. & C.R. 170; E. Cooke (1995) 111 L.Q.R. 389.

[169] [2018] EWHC 426 (Ch).

It should also be noted that the claimant's detrimental reliance is not only measured in terms of expenditure: "it is necessary to consider what alternative course or courses might have been open to" the claimant.[170] A good example of this case is *Davies v Davies (No.1)*[171]:

> The claimant claimed an interest in her parents' pedigree dairy farm. The daughter did extensive work on the farm, for minimal pay, forsaking more lucrative alternative employment elsewhere. She and her husband made improvements to the house. There had been some friction between the claimant and her parents over her marriage to a man of whom they disapproved. The first instance judge found that the claimant had acted to her substantial detriment in reliance on representations made by her parents and was entitled to an equity over the farm. The Court of Appeal affirmed the judge's decision.[172] We shall see below that the Court of Appeal has since had to consider the appropriate remedy to be awarded to the claimant.[173]

30–025 *(b) Remedies.* Once an estoppel has been established, it is then necessary for the court to consider how the equity should be satisfied, which involves the exercise of discretion at the remedial stage. Lewison LJ recently summarised the position in *Davies v Davies (No.2)*[174]:

> "There is a lively controversy about the essential aim of the exercise of this broad judgmental discretion. One line of authority takes the view that the essential aim of the discretion is to give effect to the claimant's expectation unless it would be disproportionate to do so. The other takes the view that essential aim of the discretion is to ensure that the claimant's reliance interest is protected, so that she is compensated for such detriment as she has suffered. The two approaches, in their starkest form, are fundamentally different... Much scholarly opinion favours the second approach... Others argue that the outcome will reflect both the expectation and the reliance interest and that it will normally be somewhere between the two."

Early illustrations of the doctrine dealt with the protection of a lessee; as where a life tenant granted a 30-year lease, to the knowledge of remainderman

---

[170] *Creasey v Sole* [2013] EWHC 1410 (Ch) at [111]. See further the point made in *Kelly v Fraser (Jamaica)* [2012] UKPC 25, a case of estoppel by representation, per Lord Sumption at [17]: "A common form of detriment, possibly the commonest of all, is that as a result of his reliance on the representation, the representee has lost an opportunity to protect his interests by taking some alternative course of action."

[171] [2014] EWCA Civ 568; [2014] Fam. Law 1252.

[172] Subject to a qualification that she was not entitled to an immediate beneficial interest, which was not challenged on appeal: [2014] EWCA Civ 568 at [26].

[173] *Davies v Davies (No.2)* [2016] EWCA Civ 463; [2017] 1 F.L.R. 1286 (the cases are not reported as "No 1" or "No 2", but we have adopted that labelling for ease of reference).

[174] *Davies v Davies (No.2)* [2016] EWCA Civ 463; [2017] 1 F.L.R. 1286 at [39] (references omitted), but the relevant academic literature is included below). His Lordship observed obiter that "Logically, there is much to be said for the second approach". See also *Culliford v Thorpe* [2018] EWHC 426 (Ch) at [74]–[76]. J. Mee [2013] Conv. 280. See generally S. Bright and B. McFarlane (2005) 64 C.L.J. 449; S. Gardner (2006) 122 L.Q.R. 492; A. Robertson [2008] 72 Conv. 295; J. Mee in M. Dixon (ed.), *Modern Studies in Property Law*, Volume 5 (Oxford: Hart Publishing, 2009); A. Robertson, in E. Bant and M. Harding (eds), *Exploring Private Law* (Cambridge: Cambridge University Press, 2010). B. McFarlane, *The Law of Proprietary Estoppel* (Oxford: Oxford University Press, 2014), Ch.9; B. McFarlane and Sir P. Sales (2015) 131 L.Q.R. 610; H. Biehler [2015] 54 Irish Jurist 7.

who "stood by and encouraged" the tenant to take the lease and incur expenditure. Lord Hardwick confirmed the tenant in the balance of his lease after the life tenant's death.[175]

Other cases deal with activities on a party's own land which require facilities from a neighbour; allowing that party to acquire a right in the nature of an easement; as where a mill owner erects a mill on the understanding, to the knowledge of a canal owner, that he could use canal water to generate steam[176]; or where the defendants constructed a sewer over a strip of the claimant's land, and the claimant failed to complain until the construction of the sewer was complete,[177] or where a landowner subdivides his land in reliance on a right of way being granted by a neighbour (the local authority) through a specified outlet[178]; or where one party with the knowledge and consent of his neighbour, builds so as to encroach on the neighbour's land[179]; or where a Council engaged a property owner to construct a private road and then sought to deny a right of way over it.[180]

The doctrine does not, however, apply where the claimant does acts on his own land which are not done in the expectation of acquiring rights over the land of another.[181]

The most extreme cases are those where a non-owner, in reliance upon a gratuitous promise of a gift of the land, has built on or improved the land. In *Republic Bank Ltd v Lochan*,[182] Lord Neuberger acknowledged that "building on another's land in the belief that it is one's land is a classic basis for a proprietary estoppel claim", where the owner "was, or ought to have been aware, of the relevant facts".[183] Clearly in such situations some remedy is required. In some cases the licensee has been protected from eviction without obtaining a proprietary interest in the land.

30–026

> In *Inwards v Baker*,[184] Mr Baker's son, Jack, decided to build a bungalow upon land which he hoped to purchase, but the project proved to be too expensive. Mr Baker suggested that Jack should put the bungalow on land already owned by him; that would save some expense, and

---

[175] *Huning v Ferrers* (1711) Gilb.Eq. 85; *Jackson v Cator* (1800) 5 Ves. 688 (tenant making alterations to landlord's knowledge).

[176] *Rochdale Canal Co v King* (1853) 16 Beav. 630.

[177] *Armstrong v Sheppard & Short Ltd* [1959] 2 Q.B. 384; *Gott v Lawrence* [2016] EWHC 68 (Ch).

[178] *Crabb v Arun DC* [1976] Ch. 179.

[179] *Hopgood v Brown* [1955] 1 W.L.R. 213; *Ives (ER) Investments Co v High* [1967] 2 Q.B. 379.

[180] *Joyce v Epsom and Ewell BC* [2012] EWCA Civ 1398. See also *Hoyl Group Ltd v Cromer Town Council* [2015] EWCA Civ 782.

[181] *Western Fish Products Ltd v Penwith DC* [1981] 2 All E.R. 204 (no estoppel where claimant spent money on own land relying on planning officer's assurance that planning permission would be granted; doctrine in any event not available against planning authority); *R. v East Sussex CC Ex p. Reprotech (Pebsham) Ltd* [2002] 4 All E.R. 58; *Lloyds Bank Plc v Carrick* [1996] 4 All E.R. 630; M. Thompson [1996] Conv. 295; P. Clarke All E.R. Rev. 1996 at 257; N. Hopkins (1998) 61 M.L.R. 486. cf. *Lim Teng Huan v Ang Swee Chuan* [1992] 1 W.L.R. 113 (co-owned land). *Baker v Craggs* [2016] EWHC 3250 (Ch); [2017] Ch. 295; G. Owen [2017] Conv. 230.

[182] *Republic Bank Ltd v Lochan (Trinidad and Tobago)* [2015] UKPC 26.

[183] [2015] UKPC 26 at [25]. No such awareness was found on the facts.

[184] [1965] 2 Q.B. 29; *Jones v Jones* [1977] 1 W.L.R. 438; *Matharu v Matharu* (1994) 68 P. & C.R. 93; *Thompson v Foy* [2010] 1 P.& C.R. 16.

Jack could build a bigger bungalow. This was done. Jack lived there some 40 years before the proceedings began in 1963. The father died in 1951, leaving a will dated 1922, under which the land was left to others.

The Court of Appeal held that the son should not be disturbed as long as he wished to stay, expressly referring to a licence "created by estoppel".[185] Negative protection only was considered, because "proprietary estoppel" had not yet been introduced into the licence cases.

30–027

The claim in *Suggitt v Suggitt*[186] arose out of a promise to a son by his father that someday the family farm would be his. The father died, leaving the entire estate to his daughter. The son claimed in proprietary estoppel on the basis that he had detrimentally relied upon the father's promise, by carrying out various pieces of work on the farmhouse and the farm, and attended farm college. The son had left for a period when he spent an inheritance from his aunt, before returning to the farm. He also received benefits from this father, staying on the farm and having his bills covered, amongst others.

The son succeeded at both first instance and on appeal, receiving a share valued at £3.3 million, leaving his sister with the remaining £700,000.

The difficulty with *Suggitt* is that the approach seems to be focused upon what the claimant expected, and not on the extent of his detrimental reliance. Mee commented that the amount awarded, in the light of the degree of detriment "seems grossly disproportionate",[187] and argued that the Court of Appeal should be more willing to scrutinise the awards of first instance judges for their proportionality. *Suggitt* was applied in the similar case of *Moore v Moore*, where the claimant's "whole-hearted commitment to the Farm and the business precluded him from pursuing any alternatives".[188] On the other hand, *Suggitt* was distinguished in *James v James*,[189] on the basis that the judge was not satisfied that the claimant would have done anything differently if alternative assurances had been made.[190]

On other occasions, the non-owner has been given a lien on the land for his expenditure[191]; or compensation for the value of the improvements[192]; or awarded the improved land on payment of a reasonable price for the site[193]; or a right to occupy until expenditure on improvements has been reimbursed[194]; or a non-assignable lease at a nominal rent, determinable on death.[195] A monetary award may be given where a right to occupy would be oppressive or

---

[185] [1965] 2 Q.B. 29 per Danckwerts LJ at 38.

[186] [2012] EWCA Civ 1140.

[187] J. Mee [2013] Conv. 280 at 286. See also *Bradbury v Taylor* [2012] EWCA Civ 1208.

[188] [2016] EWHC 2202 (Ch) per Mr S Monty QC (sitting as a Deputy Judge of the Chancery Division) at [148].

[189] [2018] EWHC 43 (Ch).

[190] [2018] EWHC 43 (Ch) at [43]–[44].

[191] *Unity Joint Stock Mutual Banking Association v King* (1858) 25 Beav. 72; *McGuane v Welch* [2009] W.T.L.R. 1201.

[192] *Raffaele v Raffaele* [1962] W.A.R. 29. See also *Plimmer v Wellington Corp* (1884) 9 App.Cas. 699.

[193] *Duke of Beaufort v Patrick* (1853) 17 Beav. 60; *Lim Teng Huan v Ang Swee Chuan* [1992] 1 W.L.R. 113 (house built on land co-owned by parties, but contract to build house void for uncertainty).

[194] *Dodsworth v Dodsworth* (1973) 228 E.G. 1115.

[195] *Griffiths v Williams* (1977) 248 E.G. 947.

unworkable,[196] or where the land in question has been sold.[197] In some cases, however, the minimum equity to do justice may have expired, so that it is no longer inequitable to enforce legal rights.[198] In other cases a conveyance of the freehold has been ordered.

> In *Dillwyn v Llewelyn*,[199] a father encouraged his son to build a house on the father's land, and signed a memorandum purporting to convey the land to the son; but it was not by deed. The father's will left all his land upon certain trusts in favour of others. The son spent some £14,000 in building a house on the land, with his father's knowledge and approval. On the father's death, it was held that the son was entitled to a conveyance of the land.

On its face, the decision is inconsistent with two basic rules, namely that a gratuitous promise is not enforceable, and that an incomplete gift will not be completed in favour of a volunteer.[200] Detrimental reliance is not consideration under English law. There was no compelling reason why the son should have a transfer of the land at the expense of the father's estate. However, the decision was referred to with apparent approval by the House of Lords in *Yeoman's Row v Cobbe*.[201]

Perhaps the most extreme of the cases on proprietary estoppel, resulting in a considerable windfall for the licensee, is *Pascoe v Turner*.[202]   **30–028**

> The claimant and defendant lived together in the claimant's home. Later the claimant purchased another house and the couple moved in. When the relationship ended he told the defendant that the house was hers and everything in it. In reliance on this gratuitous promise, she expended, to the claimant's knowledge, her own money on repairs, improvements and redecoration, and also on furniture. Later the claimant gave the defendant two months' notice to determine the licence. Even though the defendant never sought to establish that she had spent more money on the house than she would have done had she believed that she only had a licence to live there for her lifetime, the Court of Appeal felt that protection for her lifetime was insecure, and awarded a conveyance of the house.

Finally, the court will not make an order which would be unworkable in view of family discord. In such a case a clean break may be the best solution, involving an award of compensation rather than a proprietary interest.[203] Thus the equity may be satisfied in a different way from that which the parties intended when on good terms. The requirement of proportionality has already been discussed. An example of this approach is *Southwell v Blackburn*,[204] in which a couple had split up after years of living together. It was held that the fact that the claimant has received some benefits during the course of a relationship does not prevent a

---

[196] *Baker v Baker* [1993] 2 F.L.R. 247; *Campbell v Griffin* [2001] W.T.L.R. 981.
[197] *Wayling v Jones* (1995) 69 P. & C.R. 170. See further S. Bright and B. McFarlane [2005] Conv. 14.
[198] *Sledmore v Dalby* (1996) 72 P. & C.R. 196 (rent-free occupation for past 18 years sufficient recompense for improvements). See also *Clark v Clark* [2006] W.T.L.R. 823.
[199] (1862) 4 De G.F. & J. 517; *Chalmers v Pardoe* [1963] 1 W.L.R. 677; *Raffaele v Raffaele* [1962] W.A.R. 29; D. Allen (1963) 79 L.Q.R. 238.
[200] See S. Naresh (1980) 96 L.Q.R. 534 at 539–542.
[201] *Yeoman's Rowe Management Ltd v Cobbe* [2008] 1 W.L.R. 1752 at 1776.
[202] [1979] 1 W.L.R. 431; *Voyce v Voyce* (1991) 62 P. & C.R. 290.
[203] *Burrows v Sharp* (1991) 23 H.L.R. 82; J. Martin [1992] Conv. 54; *Baker v Baker* [1993] 2 F.L.R. 247; J. Martin (1994) 144 N.L.J. 264.
[204] [2014] EWCA Civ 1347; [2014] H.L.R. 47; A. Hayward (2015) 27 C.F.L.Q. 303.

finding of overall detriment: the "detriment must ... be assessed and evaluated over the course of the relationship".[205] The evaluation of detriment and benefit is neither "an exercise in financial accounting [nor] an arithmetical accounting exercise".[206]

30–029 In *Davies v Davies (No.2)*,[207] Lewison LJ recommended that the court should "deal with the whole chronological picture in an integrated way".[208] His Lordship described as a "useful working hypothesis"[209] counsel's suggestion that:

> "there might be a sliding scale by which the clearer the expectation, the greater the detriment and the longer the passage of time during which the expectation was reasonably held, the greater would be the weight that should be given to the expectation."[210]

However, the judge at first instance had "applied far too broad a brush and failed to analyse the facts that he found with sufficient rigour",[211] in awarding over £1 million. The volatile history of the parties' family relationship and the claimant's departures from the family farm[212] meant that the court was faced with "a series of different (and sometimes mutually incompatible) expectations, some of which were repudiated by [the claimant] herself, others of which were superseded by later expectations".[213] The claimant was found to have worked for long hours without full payment and that she could have worked shorter hours elsewhere in an environment that did involve the difficult family relationships.[214] It was held that a monetary award was the appropriate method of satisfying the claim, in the sum of £500,000.[215]

The judge at first instance rejected the claim for the the transfer of assets, but generally Lewison LJ recognised that "in some cases it may well be that the impossibility of evaluating the extent of imponderable and speculative non-financial detriment (for example life-changing choices) may lead the court to decide that relief in specie should be given."[216]

An application of the approach in *Davies* can be seen in *Habberfield v Habberfield*.[217]

> The case concerned a dispute over a family farm, Woodrow Farm. The claimant, Lucy, was the daughter of the defendant and her late husband. The couple had three other children. Lucy claimed that she had devoted her entire working life to the farm on the assurance that she

---

[205] *Southwell v Blackburn* [2014] EWCA Civ 1347 per Tomlinson LJ at [13].

[206] *Southwell v Blackburn* [2014] EWCA Civ 1347 per Tomlinson LJ at [17]. The discretion is a wide one: *Liden v Burton* [2016] EWCA Civ 275 at [35].

[207] [2016] EWCA Civ 463; [2017] 1 F.L.R. 1286; The facts were given at para.30–024 above.

[208] [2017] 1 F.L.R. 1286 at [3].

[209] [2017] 1 F.L.R. 1286 at [41].

[210] [2017] 1 F.L.R. 1286 at [41]. Viewed with some scepticism in *James v James* [2018] EWHC 43 (Ch) at 52: "either the promisor has created an expectation, on which the promisee has relied to his or her detriment, or not".

[211] [2017] 1 F.L.R. 1286 at [42]; *Moore v Moore* [2016] EWHC 2202 (Ch).

[212] Noted above, para.30–024.

[213] [2017] 1 F.L.R. 1286 at [48].

[214] [2017] 1 F.L.R. 1286 at [53].

[215] The parents had offered £350,000 at first instance.

[216] [2017] 1 F.L.R. 1286 at [66].

[217] [2018] EWHC 317 (Ch).

would take it over when he retired. There had been various family disagreements, including a fight in the milking parlour between the Lucy and her sister. Lucy had also refused an offer of involvement in the farm, balancing the interests of her siblings Birss J held that the assurances had been made that the claimant would receive a viable dairy farm[218] and that an estoppel arose in favour of Lucy. The case was different from *Davies*, because "a single promise was made albeit in different guises and reinforced over a single long period".[219]

> "In the intervening years, putting it in terms of a reciprocal arrangement, in effect Lucy has kept her side of the bargain. She did what was asked of her and in my judgment that means that to take an approach whose primary aim is only to compensate Lucy for her reliance losses would not be equitable."[220]

The judge therefore sought to give effect to Lucy's expectation. There were various practical and fiscal reasons for not ordering the division of the land, and so a monetary award was made of £1.17 million.

(c) Judicial Formulations.[221]   Two early judicial formulations of the doctrine   **30–030**
come from statements of Lord Kingsdown and Fry J. Lord Kingsdown, with the old cases of disappointed lessees in mind, explained the doctrine as follows in *Ramsden v Dyson*[222]:

> "If a man, under a verbal agreement with a landlord for a certain interest in land, or, what amounts to the same thing, under an expectation, created or encouraged by the landlord, that he shall have a certain interest, takes possession of such land, with the consent of the landlord, and upon the face of such promise or expectation, with the knowledge of the landlord, and without objection by him, laid out money on the land, a Court of Equity will compel the landlord to give effect to such promise or expectation."

Fry J in *Willmott v Barber*[223] laid down the principle in more specific detail, in what have been called the "five probanda" ("things to be proved"):

> "In the first place the [claimant] must have made a mistake as to his legal rights. Secondly, the [claimant] must have expended some money or must have done some act (not necessarily upon the defendant's land) on the faith of his mistaken belief. Thirdly, the defendant, the possessor of the legal right, must know of the existence of his own right which is inconsistent with the right claimed by the [claimant]. If he does not know of it he is in the same position as the [claimant], and the doctrine of acquiescence is founded upon conduct with a knowledge of your legal rights. Fourthly, the defendant, the possessor of the legal right, must know of the [claimant's] mistaken belief to his rights. If he does not, there is nothing which calls upon him to assert his own rights. Lastly, the defendant, the possessor of the legal right, must have

---

[218] It was held that a co-owner may be bound by representations made by another co-owner where they were made with the former's authority, relying on *Fielden v Christie-Miller* [2015] EWHC 87 (Ch).

[219] [2018] EWHC 317 (Ch) at [225].

[220] [2018] EWHC 317 (Ch) at [253].

[221] The Law Commission has considered that the Land Registration Division of the First-tier Tribunal (Property Chamber) should have an express statutory jurisdiction to determine the how an estoppel should be satisfied: Law Com. CP No. 227, *Updating the Land Registration Act 2002: A Consultation Paper* (2016), para.21.28.

[222] (1866) L.R. 1 H.L. 129 at 170. It would be otherwise if the expectation was not created nor encouraged by the landlord; at 171; *Gilpin v Legg* [2017] EWHC 3220 (Ch); [2018] L. & T.R. 6 at [98]. The House of Lords in *Yeoman's Row Management Ltd v Cobbe* [2008] 1 W.L.R. 1752 made it clear that the "verbal agreement" did not include an oral contract made void by statute.

[223] (1880) 15 Ch.D. 96 at 105–106.

encouraged the [claimant] in his expenditure of money or in the other acts which he has done, either directly or by abstaining from asserting his legal right."[224]

30–031   Modern judicial formulations of the doctrine have moved away from the inflexibility of the "five probanda",[225] in favour of "a more holistic approach",[226] for, as Floyd LJ has put it, "much water has flowed under this particular bridge"[227] since *Wilmott*. In *Taylors Fashions Ltd v Liverpool Victoria Trustees Co Ltd*,[228] Oliver J held that estoppel by acquiescence was not restricted to cases where the defendant knew his rights. There were many circumstances of estoppel, and it was not possible to lay down strict and inflexible rules. The application of the *Ramsden v Dyson*[229] principle:

> "[R]equires a very much broader approach which is directed to ascertaining whether, in particular individual circumstances, it would be unconscionable for a party to be permitted to deny that which, knowingly or unknowingly, he has allowed or encouraged another to assume to his detriment rather than to inquiring whether the circumstances can be fitted within the confines of some preconceived formula serving as a universal yardstick for every form of unconscionable behaviour…[230]
>
> "The inquiry which I have to make therefore… is simply whether, in all the circumstances of the case, it was unconscionable for the defendants to seek to take advantage of the mistake, which, at the material time, everybody shared… ."[231]

This broad approach was adopted in *Amalgamated Investment and Property Co Ltd (In Liquidation) v Texas Commerce International Bank Ltd*,[232] where Robert Goff J said that, "Of all doctrines, equitable estoppel is surely one of the most flexible… it cannot be right to restrict [it] to certain defined categories."[233] However, we saw that the House of Lords subsequently emphasised that the doctrine required more than unconscionable behaviour.[234] Proprietary estoppel:

---

[224] See *Brinnand v Ewens* (1987) 19 H.L.R. 415 (tenant had no claim for voluntary improvements where no reliance on any interest and no encouragement or acquiescence by landlord).

[225] For a different list of five factors see the distillation of authority by Jeremy Cousins QC, sitting as a Deputy Judge of the Chancery Division, in *Murphy v Rayner* [2011] EWHC 1 (Ch) at [274].

[226] *Hoyl Group Ltd v Cromer Town Council* [2015] EWCA Civ 782 per Floyd LJ at [37].

[227] [2015] EWCA Civ 782; [2015] H.L.R. 43 at [36].

[228] [1981] 2 W.L.R. 576; [1982] Q.B. 133n; P. Jackson [1982] Conv. 450. See also *Lester v Woodgate* [2010] 2 P. & C.R. 21.

[229] (1866) L.R. 1 H.L. 129. See generally K. Handley [2008] Conv. 382; H. Delaney and D. Ryan [2008] Conv. 401.

[230] [1981] 2 W.L.R. 576 at 593. See also *Ives (ER) Investments Co v High* [1967] 2 Q.B. 379; *Shaw v Applegate* [1977] 1 W.L.R. 970 at 977–978, 980; *Jones v Stones* [1999] 1 W.L.R. 1739 at 1743. See also M. Balen and C. Knowles [2011] Conv. 176, preferring "failure of basis" to unconscionability.

[231] [1981] 2 W.L.R. 576 at 596. It was suggested that the "five probanda" might be necessary in a case of "standing by", where the defendant has done no positive act. This was accepted by the House of Lords in *Yeoman's Row Management Ltd v Cobbe* [2008] 1 W.L.R. 1752. See generally K. Low (2012) 128 L.Q.R. 63.

[232] [1982] Q.B. 84; *Pacol Ltd v Trade Lines Ltd* [1982] 1 Lloyd's Rep. 456; *Lloyds Bank Plc v Carrick* [1996] 4 All E.R. 630.

[233] [1982] Q.B. 84 at 103. See also *Lim Teng Huan v Ang Swee Chuan* [1992] 1 W.L.R. 113 (where both parties wrongly assumed they had a contract); S. Goo [1993] Conv. 173; *John v George* (1996) 71 P. & C.R. 375.

[234] *Yeoman's Row Management Ltd v Cobbe* [2008] 1 W.L.R. 1752; above, para.30–022.

"[I]s not a sort of joker or wild card to be used whenever the Court disapproves of the conduct of a litigant who seems to have the law on his side. Flexible though it is, the doctrine must be formulated and applied in a disciplined and principled way. Certainty is important in property transactions."[235]

Yeoman's Row arose in a commercial context. Although the actual decision has not been questioned, we saw that, when the doctrine was again before the House of Lords a short time later, a more flexible approach was taken in the family context.[236] And unconscionability is "is not a watertight element in the estoppel but rather a feature which permeates all of its elements".[237]

It is clear that we have moved away from the basic rule that an estoppel is a shield and not a sword. If an injunction suffices as the remedy, the estoppel operates in the traditional way as a shield and not a sword. But if something more is justified, like the grant of a proprietary interest, then proprietary estoppel provides additional remedies. The constructive trust has also been called upon to fill in possible gaps in the estoppel doctrine.

30–032

In *Re Basham*,[238] the claimant's mother married her stepfather in 1936 when the claimant was aged 15. The claimant lived with them until her marriage in 1941, helping to run the business without pay on the understanding that she would inherit from her stepfather. He dissuaded her husband from taking a job with a tied cottage, saying he would help them to get a house. After the mother's death in 1976, the claimant and her husband helped her stepfather in his house and garden, prepared his meals, bought carpets for the house, and paid solicitors for advice over a boundary dispute. The stepfather constantly assured her that the house would be hers, but he died intestate. The claimant, who did not benefit under the intestacy, succeeded in her claim to the whole estate under the doctrine of proprietary estoppel. It was held that the doctrine was not confined to a case where the claimant's belief related to an existing right and to specific assets.[239] Where the belief related to a future right, a species of constructive trust arose. The doctrines of estoppel, mutual wills[240] and secret trusts[241] had a common theme, and thus reliance could be placed on cases such as *Re Cleaver*,[242] where an expectation of inheritance of non-specific assets gave rise to a constructive trust under the mutual wills doctrine. The proper remedy was an award of the entire estate, to satisfy the expectations encouraged by the deceased.

Clearly the claimant should have some remedy, however it is doubtful whether the introduction of the constructive trust is either necessary or desirable.[243] Under

---

[235] [2008] 1 W.L.R. 1752 at 1775 (Lord Walker).

[236] *Thorner v Major* [2009] 1 W.L.R. 776; above, para.30–022.

[237] *Southwell v Blackburn* [2014] EWCA Civ 1347 per Tomlinson LJ at [20]; *Hoyl Group Ltd v Cromer Town Council* [2015] EWCA Civ 782 per Floyd LJ at [44] and [55]; *Habberfield v Habberfield* [2018] EWHC 317 (Ch) at [52].

[238] [1986] 1 W.L.R. 1498; *Wayling v Jones* (1995) 69 P. & C.R. 170. The decision was discussed by the House of Lords in *Thorner v Major* [2009] 1 W.L.R. 776.

[239] cf. *Layton v Martin* (1986) 16 Fam. Law 212, where the deceased's assurances that he would provide for the claimant by will could not found a claim to proprietary estoppel, which arose only in connection with specific assets; C. Davis [1996] Conv. 193; *Lissimore v Downing* [2003] 2 F.L.R. 38 (estoppel may relate to whole estate but not to unascertainable property).

[240] Above, paras 12–012—12–018.

[241] Above, Ch.6, Part 4.

[242] [1981] 1 W.L.R. 939, above, para.12–012. If the analogy with the surviving testator in *Re Cleaver* is taken too far, a finding that the estopped party holds her estate on constructive trust seems to restrict the choice of discretionary remedies open to the court.

[243] See J. Martin [1987] Conv. 211; D. Hayton (1987) 46 C.L.J. 215; P. Clarke and C. Sherrin All E.R. Rev. 1987 at 156 and 263. See, however, *Sen v Headley* [1991] Ch. 425 at 440.

modern formulations of the doctrine of proprietary estoppel,[244] the claimant may succeed without a constructive trust. If that is not so, the claimant should not succeed under estoppel but should look to other remedies.[245]

30–033   Subsequently a restrictive approach was taken in relation to promises to leave property by will, on the basis that it is well known that a testator is free to change his testamentary intentions.[246]

> In *Taylor v Dickens*[247] the testatrix told her gardener that she planned to leave him her house by will, whereupon he said that he would no longer accept wages for his work. In her last will the testatrix left the property elsewhere but did not tell the gardener of her change of mind. His claim under the proprietary estoppel doctrine (and also in contract) failed on the ground that an unconscionable broken promise was insufficient. It was held that in the case of a promised legacy, it must be shown that the promisor created or encouraged a belief that he would not exercise his right to change his mind and that the promisee relied on that belief.

This was criticised as too rigid a view of proprietary estoppel.[248] The criticisms were held to be well founded by the Court of Appeal in *Gillett v Holt*.[249]

> There the defendant over many years had indicated that he would leave his farm to the claimant, who had worked there since the age of 16 in 1956, depriving himself of the opportunity of trying to better himself in other ways. In 1995 the friendship broke down and the defendant made a new will in favour of another. The proprietary estoppel claim against the defendant (who was still living) was upheld. In a case where assurances had been given over many years, the court should look at the matter in the round. If the assurances were intended to be relied on and had been relied on, it was not necessary to look for an *irrevocable* promise, as it was the other party's detrimental reliance which made it irrevocable. The inherent revocability of testamentary dispositions was irrelevant to an assurance that "all this will be yours."[250] The question of detriment should be approached as part of a broad inquiry as to whether repudiation of an assurance was unconscionable. A quantifiable financial detriment was not required, so long as the detriment was substantial. In this case the equity was satisfied by a transfer to the claimant of one of the three farms and £100,000 to compensate him for exclusion from the rest of the farming business.

We saw that the House of Lords in *Thorner v Major*[251] preferred a flexible approach in the context of assurances to leave property by will. An oblique assurance could be sufficiently unequivocal so long as it was "clear enough". Lord Scott considered *Gillett v Holt*[252] and *Re Basham*[253] to be constructive trust

---

[244] Above, para.30–030.

[245] For example, under the Inheritance (Provision for Family and Dependants) Act 1975.

[246] Though see the observations on testamentary freedom in practice of HHJ Paul Matthews in *Legg v Burton* [2017] EWHC 2088 (Ch).

[247] [1998] 1 F.L.R. 806, distinguishing *Re Basham*, and *Wayling v Jones* (1995) 69 P. & C.R. 170. An appeal in *Taylor* was settled.

[248] G. Douglas (1998) 28 Fam. Law 192; M. Thompson [1998] Conv. 210; M. Pawlowski (1998) 114 L.Q.R. 351.

[249] [2001] Ch. 210; M. Dixon (2000) 59 C.L.J. 453; R. Wells and M. Thompson [2001] Conv. 13 and 78. See also *Campbell v Griffin* [2001] W.T.L.R. 981; *Jennings v Rice* (2003) 1 P. & C.R. 8; *Jiggins v Brisley* [2003] W.T.L.R. 1141; *Uglow v Uglow* [2004] W.T.L.R. 1183; *Evans v HSBC Trust Company (UK) Ltd* [2005] W.T.L.R. 1289.

[250] cf. *Shirt v Shirt* [2012] EWCA Civ 1029, in which no sufficiently clear representation (in similar terms to the language in *Gillett*) was found to have been made.

[251] [2009] 1 W.L.R. 776. The facts were given above, para.30–022.

[252] [2001] Ch. 210.

[253] [1986] 1 W.L.R. 1498; above, para.30–032.

cases, but that was in the context of his view that representations relating to inheritance prospects gave rise to a remedial constructive trust. It must be borne in mind that Lord Scott's dicta in *Thorner* were not shared by the other members of the House of Lords. However, it was left open whether *Re Basham*[254] was correctly decided in so far as the claimant was awarded the whole estate. In *James v James*,[255] it was held that it remains possible for a

> "landowner to be able to express a present intention to leave property by will to another person but without making any promise to do so, such that he or she is not then bound so to leave the property even if that other, misunderstanding what the landowner has done, purports to rely to his or her detriment on a supposed promise".[256]

B. Conveyancing Problems Caused by Licences by Estoppel[257]

The question to be considered in this section is whether a licence by estoppel has the status of a proprietary interest prior to the litigation, and, if so, how it may be protected against successors in title of the estopped party.

30–034

i. Status Prior to Court Order. Clearly a recognised proprietary interest may be conferred by the court, such as the conveyance of the fee simple or the grant of a life interest. More difficult is the question whether the estoppel licensee has an interest capable of binding a third party prior to the order of the court. What would have happened, for example, if the legal owner in *Pascoe v Turner*[258] had conveyed the house to a purchaser before the matter came to court? Before the matter was clarified by legislation, one view was that the estoppel interest was too uncertain and unstable to qualify as a proprietary interest, even a "mere equity", before the court's decision. Another view was that the interest was a "mere equity" capable of binding third parties, at any rate volunteers and purchasers with actual notice. Another was that it could bind third parties under the ordinary rules of priorities, even though the interest was inchoate and did not "crystallise" until the court order.

30–035

The weight of authority supported the view that an estoppel interest had proprietary status before the court order, and this was confirmed by the Land Registration Act 2002. Section 116 provides as follows:

> "It is hereby declared for the avoidance of doubt that, in relation to registered land... an equity by estoppel... has effect from the time the equity arises as an interest capable of binding successors in title (subject to the rules about the effect of dispositions on priority)."

---

[254] [1986] 1 W.L.R. 1498. See further criticisms of *Re Basham* in *Macdonald v Frost* [2009] W.T.L.R. 1815.

[255] [2018] EWHC 43 (Ch).

[256] [2018] EWHC 43 (Ch) per HHJ Paul Matthews at [38], endorsed by Birss J in *Habberfield v Habberfield* [2018] EWHC 317 (Ch) at [49].

[257] See generally S. Moriarty (1984) 100 L.Q.R. 376; A. Briggs and P. Todd [1981] Conv. 212 and 347; M. Thompson and A. Briggs [1983] Conv. 50 and 285 respectively; J. Hill (1988) 51 M.L.R. 226; M. Pawlowski (2011) 41 Fam. Law 1251.

[258] [1979] 1 W.L.R. 431; above, para.30–028.

Although this provision applies only to registered land, it would be difficult to argue for a different position in unregistered land. In most cases the equity will be treated as having arisen when the other party acts to his detriment. At the latest, it will be when the circumstances make it unconscionable for the owner to go back on the expectation.

How the interest may be protected against a third party is discussed in the next paragraph. Section 116 does not operate to pre-empt the court's decision as to the appropriate remedy, which could still be a money payment rather than some right over the land.[259] There is nothing in s.116 to compel the conclusion that the estoppel right must give rise in all cases to a proprietary interest.[260]

30–036   **ii. Registered and Unregistered Land.**   As it is now clear that estoppel interests are capable of binding successors in title, the next point to consider is how they may be protected. In unregistered land such interests are not registrable under the Land Charges Act 1972[261] and, therefore, depend on the doctrine of notice. Occupation will normally give constructive notice. In registered land, estoppel interests would be overriding if coupled with occupation,[262] or could be protected by a notice.[263]

The Court of Appeal has stated that estoppel interests of a "family" nature are overreachable by a disposition by two trustees.[264] In cases where capital money is paid to a sole trustee, so that overreaching cannot occur, the interest will depend on the doctrine of notice in unregistered land or may be an overriding interest in registered land if coupled with occupation, as mentioned above. Estoppel interests of a commercial nature are not overreachable.[265] In *Mortgage Express v Lambert*,[266] the Court of Appeal held that the right to set aside an unconscionable bargain (in that case a mortgage) was a relevant equity for the purposes of s.116, albeit that on the facts that interested had been overreached and so the mortgagee was not bound by that interest.

iii. Other Problems Arising Under the Doctrine of Proprietary Estoppel.

30–037   *(a)   Necessity for Litigation.*   The problems here are the same as those met in the context of licences giving rise to a constructive trust. No one knows, without the court's decision, whether or not the licensee is entitled to have an interest in

---

[259] See B. McFarlane (2003) 62 C.L.J. 661, doubting whether, in such a case, the obligation to pay would be imposed on the purchaser. See also M. Dixon (2009) 125 L.Q.R. 401.

[260] See the HHJ Paul Matthews sitting in county court in *Shortland v Hill*, unreported, 2017.

[261] s.2 (easement, right or privilege, being merely equitable) has been narrowly construed; *Shiloh Spinners Ltd v Harding* [1973] A.C. 691.

[262] Land Registration Act 2002 s.29 and Sch.3 para.2. In the case of first registration of title, the overriding interests are set out in Sch.1, which includes the interest of an occupier (para.2).

[263] If the registered proprietor does not consent, a unilateral notice may be entered; Land Registration Act 2002 ss.34, 35.

[264] *Birmingham Midshires Mortgage Services Ltd v Sabherwal* (2000) 80 P. & C.R. 256; C. Harpum (2000) 116 L.Q.R. 341.

[265] (2000) 80 P. & C.R. 256. *Southern Pacific Mortgages Ltd v Scott* [2014] UKSC 52; [2015] A.C. 385

[266] [2016] EWCA Civ 555; [2017] Ch. 93.

the land transferred to her, nor what the interest will be. If the court orders the transfer of any interest, the documentation will be completed.

(b)   Effect of Life Interest.   Where the expectation of the licensee was to   **30–038** occupy the licensor's property for life, as is not uncommon in the family context, the award of a life interest to the licensee used to cause problems. The difficulty was that such a life interest brought the complex provisions of the Settled Land Act 1925 into play, under which the life tenant acquired the legal estate and extensive powers of sale and leasing. Thus, in *Ungurian v Lesnoff,*[267] a life interest under the Settled Land Act arose (either on the basis of estoppel or a common intention constructive trust[268]) in favour of the defendant, who had given up her flat, nationality and career to live with the claimant. He bought a house for them to live in, which the defendant improved, but they separated after four years. An irrevocable licence was considered inadequate, but an outright conveyance would have gone beyond what the parties intended.

Most cases, however, have avoided a solution involving the Settled Land Act. In *Dodsworth v Dodsworth,*[269] the defendants had spent over £700 on improvements in the belief that they would have a right to occupy for life. They were held entitled to occupy until the expenditure had been reimbursed. Similarly in *Griffiths v Williams,*[270] where a daughter looked after her mother and spent money on repairs and improvements to the house in the belief that she had a home there for life, but the house was left to another relative. In order to avoid the complications of the Settled Land Act, she was awarded a non-assignable lease at a nominal rent, determinable on death.

Since the Trusts of Land and Appointment of Trustees Act 1996 came into operation, it is no longer possible to create a settlement under the 1925 Act. The problem discussed above has diminished because the award of a life interest will now bring into play the less complex "trust of land", which was explained in Ch.13. A different remedy may, however, be preferred.[271]

---

[267] [1990] Ch. 206. The 1925 Act was also applied in *Costello v Costello* (1995) 70 P. & C.R. 297, where a deed provided that parents could occupy rent free for life.

[268] Above, para.13–005 and following.

[269] (1973) 228 E.G. 1115.

[270] (1977) 248 E.G. 947.

[271] *Campbell v Griffin* [2001] W.T.L.R. 981 (money award preferred to life interest under trust of land).

INDEX

LEGAL TAXONOMY
FROM SWEET & MAXWELL

This index has been prepared using Sweet and Maxwell's Legal Taxonomy. Main index entries conform to keywords provided by the Legal Taxonomy except where references to specific documents or non-standard terms (denoted by quotation marks) have been included. These keywords provide a means of identifying similar concepts in other Sweet and Maxwell publications and online services to which keywords from the Legal Taxonomy have been applied. Readers may find some minor differences between terms used in the text and those which appear in the index. Suggestions to *sweetandmaxwell.taxonomy@tr.com*.

All references are to paragraph number